DEDICATION

To those whom we love and who have made our lives very, very, happy and fun—Chris, Claire, Courtney, Eithne, Huon, Ivy, Jenn, Jennifer, Mason, Mikaela, Nat, Owen, Sarah, and Taylor.

And to some of the memorable teaching moments that now bring smiles to our faces and help us keep our work and lives in perspective—

A student came up after class and said, "I missed class yesterday and just wanted to ask if you did anything important." I was appalled because I thought that all the stuff I did in class was important or else why would I do it. I thought for a moment and said, "It was a day like the rest of the days." Naturally I expected the student to realize from my response that he had erred and to start the conversation again beginning with an apology. He said, "Good! I just thought I should ask in case there was something important that I should know about." Want to guess what the student's final grade was? Well, you don't have to because it wasn't very important for his graduation!

* * *

I was lecturing on validity one Monday morning. I was really into the topic (the class?—not so much). Anyway while I was lecturing, a woman on the front row all of a sudden projectile vomited. Shockingly, the long, white stream shot up toward the ceiling and was coming down at me! I spun on the heel of my shoe and contorted my body to get out of the way in time. While this was going on, the student got up from her desk, left her open notes, and proceeded out of the classroom to a water fountain just outside the classroom door. The remaining students had no immediate reaction other than being stunned. After drinking some water, she walked back into class as if nothing had happened, took her seat, grabbed her pen, and then raised her hand to speak. I was shocked to say the least. (If it were me, I would have dropped the class and hoped to never be seen again.) I called on her, and she said, "Would you mind repeating what you were saying about validity?" Now, that's what I call "a serious student." Nonetheless, I stayed on the side of the room for the rest of the class.

* * *

A student asked if it was really necessary to buy the book to take my selection class. Based on the incredulous expression on my face, he then went on to opine that since I was one of the authors, couldn't I just summarize all the important material that was going to be on the tests in my lectures? What really left me speechless was his concluding comment, "after all, this isn't rocket science. All you have to do is listen to your gut and you'll know who to hire." I don't think this story will embarrass the student who was involved because I am sure that he will not read it. Based on his subsequent grade, I am sure that this student didn't read the book for the course much less any other selection book.

BRIEF CONTENTS

Acknowledgments   *xv*

About the Authors   *xviii*

PART 1	**FOUNDATION FOR A SELECTION PROGRAM**	**1**

CHAPTER 1	An Introduction to Selection	3
CHAPTER 2	Job Performance Concepts and Measures	21
CHAPTER 3	Job Analysis in Human Resource Selection	47
CHAPTER 4	Legal Issues in Selection	105
CHAPTER 5	Recruitment of Applicants	151

PART 2	**MEASUREMENT IN SELECTION**	**201**

CHAPTER 6	Human Resource Measurement in Selection	203
CHAPTER 7	Reliability of Selection Measures	239
CHAPTER 8	Validity of Selection Procedures	279

PART 3	**SELECTION MEASURES**	**355**

CHAPTER 9	Application Forms and Biodata Assessments, Training and Experience Evaluations, and Reference Checks	359
CHAPTER 10	The Selection Interview	433
CHAPTER 11	Ability Tests for Selection	503
CHAPTER 12	Personality Assessment for Selection	535
CHAPTER 13	Simulation Tests	577
CHAPTER 14	Testing for Counterproductive Work Behaviors	613

PART 4	**USING SELECTION DATA**	**645**

| **CHAPTER 15** | Strategies for Selection Decision Making | 647 |

Author Index   *687*

Subject Index   *699*

CONTENTS

Acknowledgments xv

About the Authors xviii

PART 1   FOUNDATION FOR A SELECTION PROGRAM   1

CHAPTER 1
An Introduction to Selection   3

Definition of Selection   3
Collecting and Evaluating Information   3
Selection for Initial Job and Promotion   4
Constraints and Future Interests   6
Is There Evidence That Selection Is Important?   6

Selection and Other Human Resource Systems   7

Developing a Selection Program   8
Job Analysis Information   10
Identifying Relevant Job Performance Measures   10
Identification of Work-Related Characteristics   11
Development of Selection Measures   11
Validation Procedures   12

Constraints in Developing a Selection Program   13
Limited Information on Applicants   13
Applicant and Organization at Cross-Purposes   13
Measurement of Jobs, Individuals, and Work Performance   14
Other Factors Affecting Work Performance   15
Selection Research versus Selection Practice   15
So Why Should I Devote My Life to Selection? What Is Selection
    Doing That's Good for the World?   16

Plan of This Book   19

References   20

CHAPTER 2
Job Performance Concepts and Measures   21

Task Performance   24
Production Data   24
Judgmental Data   26

Organizational Citizenship Behaviors   29
What Prompts OCBs?   31
Relationship of OCBs with Other Performance Measures   32
Measurement of OCBs   33

Adaptive Performance *34*

Counterproductive Work Behavior *36*

Appropriate Characteristics of Job Performance Measures *39*
Individualization 39
Relevance 40
Measurability 40
Variance 40

Use of Criteria for Validation *41*
Single versus Multiple Criteria 41
When to Use Each 41
Forming the Single Measure 42

References *43*

CHAPTER 3
Job Analysis in Human Resource Selection 47

Job Analysis: A Definition and Role in HR Selection *47*
Growth in Job Analysis 50
Legal Issues in Job Analysis 50
Collecting Job Information 53

A Survey of Job Analysis Methods *53*

Job Analysis Interviews *55*
Description 55
Considerations on Applicability 56
An Example 57
Limitations of the Job Analysis Interview 59

Job Analysis Questionnaires *62*
Description 62
The Task Analysis Inventory 62

Critical Incident Technique *68*
Description 68
Application of Critical Incidents 69
Advantages and Disadvantages of Critical Incidents 70
Integrating a Task Analysis Inventory with Critical Incidents:
    A Suggestion 71
SME Workshops 73

Incorporating Job Analysis Results in Selection Procedures:
  A Cookbook *75*

Identifying Employee WRCs *75*
Determining Employee WRCs 77
An Operational Example 87
Determination of Selection Procedure Content 91
An Example Selection Plan for the Job of HR Selection Analyst 94

Employee Specifications for Jobs That Are About to Change or
  Yet to Be Created *97*

Conclusion *99*

References *99*

CHAPTER 4

Legal Issues in Selection   105

Federal Regulation of Business   106
EEO Laws and Executive Orders   106

Employment Discrimination   119
Discrimination Defined   119
Evidence Required   120
The Use of Statistics   122
Definition of Internet Applicant   127

The Uniform Guidelines on Employee Selection Procedures (1978)   129
Determination of Adverse Impact   129
Selection Methods   129
Defense of Selection Program   129
Selection Requirements   130
Recordkeeping   130
Comments about the *Uniform Guidelines*   131

Affirmative Action Programs   131
Federal Contractor   131
Court Order and Consent Decree   132
Voluntary AAP   133

Selection Court Cases   134
Griggs v. Duke Power (1971)   134
United States v. Georgia Power (1973)   136
Spurlock v. United Airlines (1972)   137
Watson v. Ft. Worth Bank & Trust (1988)   137
Rudder v. District of Columbia (1995)   139
Frank Ricci et al. v. John DeStefano et al. (2009)   140
OFCCP v. Ozark Air Lines (1986)   141
Jack Gross v. FBL Financial Services (2009)   141

EEO and Job Peformance Measurement   142
Performance Measurement and the *Uniform Guidelines*   143
Court Decisions Addressing Performance Measurement   143

EEO Summary   146
Basis of Discrimination   146
Evidence of Discrimination   146
Options of the Organization   147

References   147

CHAPTER 5

Recruitment of Applicants   151

A Model of the Recruitment Process   152
Stage 1: Attracting and Generating Interest   152
Stage 2: Maintaining Applicant Interest   171
Stage 3: Postoffer Closure   178

Summary Recommendations for Enhancing Recruitment   182

References   184

PART 2   MEASUREMENT IN SELECTION   201

CHAPTER 6
Human Resource Measurement in Selection   203

Fundamentals of Measurement: An Overview   203

The Role of Measurement in HR Selection   203
The Nature of Measurement   203
Scales of Measurement   207

Standardization of Selection Measurement   212
Measures Used in HR Selection   215
Standards for Evaluating Selection Measures   217
Finding and Constructing Selection Measures   219
Locating Existing Selection Measures   220
Constructing New Selection Measures   224

Interpreting Scores on Selection Measures   231
Using Norms   231
Using Percentiles   233
Using Standard Scores   234

References   237

CHAPTER 7
Reliability of Selection Measures   239

What is Reliability?   239
A Definition of Reliability   241
Errors of Measurement   241
Methods of Estimating Reliability   245

Interpreting Reliability Coefficients   261
What Does a Reliability Coefficient Mean?   261
How High Should a Reliability Coefficient Be?   264
Factors Influencing the Reliability of a Measure   266
Standard Error of Measurement   272
Evaluating Reliability Coefficients   274
Reliability: A Concluding Comment   275

References   276

CHAPTER 8
Validity of Selection Procedures   279

An Overview of Validity   279
Validity: A Definition   279
The Relation between Reliability and Validity   281
Types of Validation Strategies   282

Content Validation Strategy   282
Major Aspects of Content Validation   284
Some Examples of Content Validation   288
Appropriateness of Content Validation?   289

Criterion-Related Validation Strategies 294
Concurrent Validation 294
Predictive Validation 298
Concurrent versus Predictive Validation Strategies 300
Requirements for a Criterion-Related Validation Study 301
Criterion-Related Validation over Time 301
The Courts and Criterion-Related Validation 302
Content versus Criterion-Related Validation: Some Requirements 303

Construct Validation Strategy 303

*Empirical Considerations in Criterion-Related Validation
    Strategies 307*
Correlation 307
Prediction 312
Factors Affecting the Magnitude of Validity Coefficients 321
Utility Analysis 326

Broader Perspectives of Validity 332
Validity Generalization 332
Job Component Validity and Synthetic Validity 338

Validation Options for Small Sample Sizes 341

The Future of Validation Research 343

References 344

PART 3   SELECTION MEASURES   355

CHAPTER 9
Application Forms and Biodata Assessments, Training and Experience Evaluations, and Reference Checks 359

Application Forms and Biodata Assessments 359
Nature and Role of Application Forms in Selection 359

Evaluating Application Blanks as Predictors 363
Legal Implications of Application Forms 369
Composition of Application Forms 373
Selecting Application Form Content 374
Developing and Revising Application Forms 375
Resumes 384
Internet-Based Resume Screening 385
Using Application Forms in HR Selection 386

Training and Experience (T&E) Evaluations 387
Nature and Role of T&E Evaluations in Selection 387
Reliability and Validity of T&E Evaluations 392
Legal Implications 395
Recommendations for Using T&E Evaluations 395

Reference Checks 396
Nature and Role of Reference Checks in Selection 396
Types of Reference Data Collected 397
Usefulness of Reference Data 398
Legal Issues Affecting the Use of Reference Checks 401

Methods of Collecting Reference Data   406
Sources of Reference Data   411
Social Media   414
Recommended Steps for Using Reference Checks   414

Summary   416

References   417

CHAPTER 10
The Selection Interview   433

Brief History   435
Developing and Designing Effective Interviews   436
Making a Selection Decision   439
Conclusions about Designing the Interview   452

The Role of Technology and Global Trends   454

Evaluating Interviews as Predictors   455
Predictive Validity   455
Reliability   457

Discrimination and the Interview   458
Court Cases   458

Research Findings on Discrimination   462

A Model of Interviewer Decision Making   463
Expectations, Beliefs, Needs, and Intentions before the Interview   464

Recommendations for Using the Interview   471
Restrict the Scope of the Interview   472
Limit the Use of Preinterview Data   473

References   483

CHAPTER 11
Ability Tests for Selection   503

History of Ability Tests in Selection   503
Definition of Ability Tests   504

Cognitive Ability Tests   504
Development of Cognitive Ability Tests   505
What Is Measured   505
The Wonderlic Personnel Test   506
The Nature of Cognitive Ability Tests   507

The Validity of Cognitive Ability Tests   508
Project A   508
Validity Generalization Studies   508

Cognitive Ability Tests and Adverse Impact   514
So What?   517

Mental Ability Tests and the Internet   517

Effects of Practice and Coaching   520

Mechanical Ability Tests 521
The Bennett Mechanical Comprehension Test 522

Clerical Ability Tests 523
The Minnesota Clerical Test 523

Physical Ability Tests 524

Physical Abilities Analysis 524
Three Components of Physical Performance 525
Legal Issues in Testing Physical Abilities 526

Recommendations for the Use of Ability Tests in Selection 528
Review Reliability Data 529
Review Validity Data 530
Chapter Summary 531

References 532

CHAPTER 12
Personality Assessment for Selection 535

A Brief History 536

Definition and Use of Personality in Selection 536
Personality Traits 538
Other Personality Traits 542

Personality Measurement Methods 543
Inventories in Personality Measurement 543
Observer Ratings of Personality 546
The Interview in Personality Measurement 547
Ratings from Other Observers 549
Evaluating the Validity of Personality Tests as a Predictor 549
Legal Issues in the Use of Personality Tests 554
Role of Technology and Global Trends 558

Recommendations for the Use of Personality Data 559
Define Personality Traits in Terms of Job Behaviors 560
Define Work Effectiveness as Retaining Productive Employees 560
The Appropriateness of the Selection Instrument 563

Conclusions 565

References 565

CHAPTER 13
Simulation Tests 577

Consistency of Behavior 577
Limitations of Simulations 578

Work Samples 579
The Development of Work-Sample Tests 582
The Validity of Work-Sample Tests 586

Assessment Centers 588
The Beginning of Assessment Centers 588
What Is Measured and How 589

The Training of Assessors 592
The Validity of Assessment Centers 597

Situational Judgment Tests 602
Questions That We Know You Are Asking That We Can Answer 605

References 608

CHAPTER 14
Testing for Counterproductive Work Behaviors 613

Polygraph Testing 614

Integrity Testing 617
Paper-and-Pencil Integrity Tests 617
What We Know About Integrity Tests 619
Legal Issues in Integrity Testing 627

Drug Testing 628
Drug-Testing Methods 629
Accuracy of Chemical Tests 631
Legal Issues in Pre-Employment Drug Testing 631
Guidelines for Drug-Testing Programs with Job Applicants 633

Genetic Testing 634
What Is Genetic Testing? 635
Legal Concerns 635

What's Next? Neuroscience–Based Discrimination 638

References 639

PART 4   USING SELECTION DATA   645

CHAPTER 15
Strategies for Selection Decision Making 647

Modes for Collecting Predictor Information 649
Modes for Combining Predictor Information 651
Methods for Collecting and Combining Predictor Information 652
Which Method is Best? 653
Implications for Selection Decision Makers 655

Methods for Combining Predictor Scores 657
Method One: Multiple Regression 658
Method Two: Unit Weighting 660

Strategies for Making Employment Decisions 662
Strategy One: Top-Down Selection 662
Strategy Two: Cutoff Scores 663
Strategy Three: Multiple Cutoff Scores 668
Strategy Four: Multiple Hurdles 669
Strategy Five: Combination Method 671
Strategy Six: Banding 672

A Practical Approach to Making Selection Decisions 677

Auditing Selection Decisions: Learning from Your Successes and Failures   678

Recommendations for Enhancing Selection Decision Making   679

References   680

Author Index   687
Subject Index   699

ACKNOWLEDGMENTS

One of the nicest aspects of writing a book is that it presents a formal opportunity for the authors to thank individuals who have had positive influences on both them and this text.

Bob Gatewood. I thank my very smart and loving wife, Chris, for her advice on how to present some of the material in this book in an understandable way (rather than the way that I originally wrote it). Chris knows how to convey academic knowledge in clear and interesting ways to those who don't think like an academic but may have to use the information. Even more importantly, she put up with my complaining about having to work on "The Book." I am a terrible patient when I am sick, carrying on about how bad I feel and how others can help me. I am worse as a book writer. I thank each of my four children who have contributed to the various editions of this book in different ways. My oldest two, Jennifer and Nat, actually developed the topic and author indices for the first several editions. They have by now trained their children, my grandchildren, to ask what grandfather's book is about. Of course, I tell them in great detail. They seem very interested, even though I know they do not have the slightest idea of what I am saying. I guess in that way they are preparing for college. My younger two children, Mikaela and Mason, often ask "How is your book going, Dad?" They then congratulate me on any progress and tell me to hang in there because I am almost finished. They also ask what the book is about and have the same reaction as the grandchildren. Maybe this is because they all are about the same ages. At any rate, the interest and love of all of these people have been valuable and important to me. It is good to have personal and professional parts of one's life mix so well.

Hubert (I prefer "Junior") Feild. In writing a book, and for that matter, even a research article published in an academic journal, most authors are aware that their publication resulted, in part, because of other individuals who played key roles in their personal and professional development. I am one of those authors; there are so many to whom I am indebted.

I'm particularly grateful to Art Bedeian, who gave me the opportunity to work with Bob Gatewood, a wonderful friend and colleague, and Murray Barrick, a good man and one of the top names in our field, to explore some of the mysteries of human resource recruitment and selection. Without Art's encouragement, this book would not have been published, and I would have missed the opportunity to work with two great colleagues. My coauthors and I have been able to laugh together through eight editions of this book.

In learning about assessment, several former professors of mine were most instrumental—William Owens, Lyle Schoenfeldt, Bob Teare, and Jerry Bayley. My colleagues at Auburn have been particularly helpful in "keeping the buzzards off" and "keeping me vertical and on this side of the dirt." These include Achilles and Wilma Armenakis, Art Bedeian (now at LSU), Bill Giles, Stan Harris, Bill Holley, Brian Connelly, and Kevin Mossholder. My past doctoral students, namely Brett Becton, Katherine Buckner, Michael Cole, Robert Hirschfeld, Amy Livingston, and Jack Walker, have made me very proud; I learned and continue to learn so much from them. Thanks, folks! I (N4CLT) am also indebted to Bill Alsup (N6XMW) who has entertained and challenged me (physically and mentally) since age 5. (To hear some of our ham radio discussions, use a shortwave radio to tune into 14.190 MHz on Saturdays at 9:30 a.m. CST.)

In addition, I am indebted to my family. The first is Claire, my wife. She's listened to my many comments regarding chapter writes and rewrites, patiently put up with my idiosyncrasies and shenanigans (e.g., wearing t-shirts to work and other inappropriate places, installing a 50-foot-tall ham radio tower beside our house with a 25-foot horizontal beam antenna having five elements at the top), and yet has always loved, supported, never nagged, and encouraged me to be me. What more can one ask of a spouse or, for that matter, another person? Taylor (my Main Man) is a wonderful son, professional colleague, and close friend. He has provided guidance, counsel, support, and simply brought joy to me throughout my life in ways he could never imagine. My grandchildren, Huon (My Man) and Ivy (My Girl) are lights of my life. In the future, I look forward to watching Owen light my life as well. I simply did not know one could feel like I do about these kids. I also thank Bernice and Hubert Feild (my parents) and Carole and Ridley Parrish (my sister and brother-in-law) for their unwavering support throughout my 70 years. Finally, Catherine Helmuth is a hero of mine. She is a role model who reflects intelligence, grit, and humanness to all who encounter her. She demonstrates daily the plasticity and determination of people faced with challenges and that one can succeed (no matter how one defines success) and "keep on keeping on." Soon, she will make a fine faculty member for a most fortunate university.

Murray Barrick. I suspect I might be the luckiest person on Earth. While I did not know anything about selection when my wife and I started dating back in high school, I certainly made an excellent choice and have benefited from that good recruiting decision. In retrospect, I now realize this was a very lucky outcome indeed, given my applicant pool was not as plentiful as it should have been. Education has been the other fortunate opportunity for me, as I have had some outstanding teachers who were willing to invest in my path of lifelong learning. Although numerous people have directed and impacted my progress over the course of my life, a few mentors have been particularly influential including: Mrs. Anfinson, Mr. Herbst, David Whitsett, Ralph Alexander, Frank Schmidt, Mick Mount, John Hollenbeck, and most recently, Ricky Griffin and Mike Hitt. It is simply impossible to acknowledge the numerous ways my life was improved by being around you all. And every day, I have the unique opportunity to work with some of the smartest and most amusing academic colleagues (both faculty and Ph.D. students) in the entire field of HR. Thank you for converting the hours and hours I spend in the office into playtime rather than worktime.

Finally, I would like to acknowledge how fortunate I am to work with these two co-authors in revising this book. It has been a joy interacting with them as we hashed through the plethora of issues and concerns associated with selection and life.

No acknowledgment would be complete without recognizing the inestimable love, inspiration, and confidence my family has delivered. My wife Sarah and daughters Courtney and Jenn are the wellspring from which I draw motivation for everything I achieve. You three explain why I feel like the luckiest person around. Of course, this would not have been realized if not for the unflagging support, encouragement, and sacrifice provided by my parents Ray and Marietta Barrick and my in-laws, Jack and Bea Burt. You taught me to plan my work, then work my plan. I remain forever indebted to all of you.

Several people have been instrumental in reviewing this book. We especially thank the following reviewers for their time and comments, which improved the various editions:

Steven E. Abraham—*Oswego State University of New York*

Scott L. Boyar—*The University of Alabama at Birmingham*

James Breaugh—*University of Missouri at St. Louis*

Joy L. Bruno—*DeVry University*

Yongjun Choi—*Wright State University*

Cynthia F. Cohen—*University of South Florida*

Kristl Davison—*The University of Mississippi*

Fritz Drasgow—*University of Illinois, Champaign*

Debra S. Gatton—*Tiffin University*

Mary Gowan—*Elon University*

Jerald Greenberg—*The Ohio State University*

Hank Hennessey—*University of Hawaii, Hilo*

Jason L. Huang—*Wayne State University*

Susan Key—*University of Alabama, Birmingham*

Elliot D. Lasson—*SPHR, SHRM-SCP Lasson Talent Solutions, Executive Director of Joblink of Maryland, Inc., and University of Maryland Baltimore County*

Mark L. Legnick-Hall—*University of Texas, San Antonio*

Mary Lewis—*PPG Industries*

Julio Mosquera-Stanziola—*University of Louisville; Chief Operating Officer at Grupo Julmos*

Joel T. Nadler—*Southern Illinois University Edwardsville*

William Ross—*University of Wisconsin–La Crosse*

Joseph Rosse—*University of Colorado*

Robert S. Rubin—*DePaul University*

Deborah E. Rupp—*Purdue University*

Craig J. Russell—*University of Oklahoma*

Lyle F. Schoenfeldt—*Appalachian State University*

Kenneth S. Shultz—*California State University, San Bernardino*

Brian Steffy—*Franklin and Marshall College*

Cheryl K. Stenmark—*Angelo State University*

John Veres—*Auburn University, Montgomery*

Brian G. Whitaker—*Appalachian State University*

Patrick Wright—*University of South Carolina*

In closing, the people at Cengage were, of course, a main force behind this edition. We appreciate the hard work and dedication from our colleagues at Cengage who made this revision possible. A special thanks goes out to Mike Roche—Senior Product Manager, Jeffrey Hahn—Developmental Editor, and Rajachitra Suresh—Project Manager at Cenveo Publisher Services.

ABOUT THE AUTHORS

(Note: Each of the brief biographies has substantial contributions that are written by the other two coauthors. Therefore, they go a bit further than merely extolling each person's many achievements.)

ROBERT D. GATEWOOD had an uneven start to his career. Specifically, he attended three different universities for his undergrad degree. He started in one that his father picked for him because it offered a financially-needed scholarship. He accumulated many credits but didn't have much fun. So he dropped engineering as his major (much to his father's disgust), and transferred to an unnamed university in New Orleans. There, he became the embodiment of a very immature male in a sin-inducing city. Luckily, he was broke by Thanksgiving and saved his academic career by transferring to Washington University in St. Louis where he finished his degree after 3½ total years at college and losing 18 credits by transferring. Better yet he was a psychology major. He then went to Purdue University for grad school not only because of its excellence, but also it had good sports teams to watch and occupy his time.

Once in grad school, Bob learned that taking just three courses a semester actually consumed him. After completing his Ph.D. in industrial psychology, he worked as a consultant and then joined academia. His first position was as a member of the Department of Management at the Terry College of Business, University of Georgia. Thinking he may stay 5 years, Bob left 34 years later. During these years, Bob climbed the academic ranks from assistant to full professor and pursued an administrative career at Terry as a department chair and associate dean in the College of Business. Bob commented on several occasions, "I never saw an academic committee I didn't like." An indication of how well he did these jobs is contained on a plaque that he received when he retired that thanked him "… for his creative solutions to problems and unfailing sense of humor"—no mention, however, of how good these solutions were. Bob was also elected to five executive positions, including President, within the Human Resources Division of the Academy of Management. At the conclusion of his service, someone commented that the HR Division "… will never be the same." Debates still occur among the Academy as to precisely what that comment meant.

Since leaving the University of Georgia, Bob has lived in Fort Worth, Texas; Denver, Colorado; Lexington, Kentucky; and as of this writing was moving to Garden City, New York. On a personal level, Bob got lucky and has a very talented wife, who has built an exceptional career in academia both in research and in university leadership, serving as a Dean, a Provost, and University President. Bob celebrates her success and has enjoyed numerous good seats for events such as college football, hockey, lacrosse, Denver Bronco games, and NCAA basketball tournaments. It's like grad school was supposed to be. Over the years, Bob has been active with his four children by coaching his sons' various teams. Both sons are excellent soccer players—a sport he never helped them with. His sons think that is probably a key to their success. With his daughters, Bob has enjoyed keeping up with whatever bands are currently popular, the drama of middle and high school, but not with boyfriends. For his older daughter he called each one "Ralph" figuring why bother to learn the name of a short time visitor. For his younger daughter, he has dropped names and uses "The Boy." It is even easier to remember.

Bob really enjoys working on this selection book with his two coauthors every 3 or 4 years. He finds his interactions with Murray to be intellectually stimulating and complex. He finds his interactions with Jr. to be a much needed comic relief to the intense intellectual environment that he and Murray share.

HUBERT S. FEILD (I prefer "Junior") There are four things that you need to know about Feild to understand him completely. First, he has lived in the same house in Auburn, Alabama, for 42 years; second, in the year 2000 he threw out all clothing except for jeans, shorts, t-shirts, and tennis shoes because he never wore anything else; third, he refuses to go to professional meetings or to serve on academic journal review boards because these take too much of his time; fourth, when he was in college, a girl gave him a baseball signed by the 1927 New York Yankees team. He said "thank you" but did not ask why she gave it to him or how she got it. Even worse, he took it home, went back to college, and never saw it again. Never asked his parents what happened to it. Can you say "inquisitive"? Apparently Jr. can't. Would you say "individualistic" to describe Jr.? No, well try "eccentric"! He went to Mississippi State for undergrad school and played third base on great baseball teams. He was asked if he was interested in a contract for pro baseball from the Los Angeles Angels but said no because he had agreed to go to work with Humble Oil (now Exxon), which he quit after 5 months. Something about having regular hours and having to wear business dress.

Jr. received his Ph.D. in industrial psychology from the University of Georgia. While there he met Bob Gatewood, another author on this book. They have been good friends for over 40 years mainly because they have seen each other only four times during that time. They get along very well if it happens only once every 10 years. Murray Barrick has taken this fact to heart, which explains why he has not met Jr. First he would have had to travel to Auburn to do that, and second Gatewood has told him to wait 10 years for the first meeting. Then another 10 for the second.

Jr. has been both an impactful and influential faculty member during his time at Auburn. He has published consistently in the leading research journals in both management and psychology in a number of the major areas of human resource management; but especially in selection. In doing this he has been very successful as a mentor and friend of his many Ph.D. students who have gone on to be successful themselves. He has remained a true friend and a strong support network for all of these. Jr. is also an excellent teacher. Most of his classes are in selection or in other HR topics. His usual strategy is to develop in-class exercises to demonstrate principles in the text. He has shared these with his two coauthors of this book who have equally experienced success with these. Both of them attribute Jr.'s success to the fact that he thinks like 19- to 21-year-olds, especially immature ones. It is quite natural for him to come up with things to do that answer questions pertinent to this age group. It's adults that he has trouble dealing with.

Of his many fine attributes, perhaps Jr.'s strength is that once a friend, always a very good friend. This means that he is fun to be with, laughs at jokes about himself (which are numerous), does what he says he is going to do, and treats others with respect and emotional understanding. He could be the most popular person in the United States if he would ever leave Auburn and meet people. Of course the rest of the United States would have to have 10 years to get used to that thought.

MURRAY R. BARRICK is the thought leader of this book—partially because Feild does not think and Gatewood has known Feild too long to think. Murray proved how smart he was with this edition. He was the one who came up with the idea of making major changes to the conceptual framework of the book and then got Gatewood to write the chapters that were the most work because they explained the changes. As will become apparent, manipulating coauthors is an effective strategy for him. Murray attained his Ph.D. in industrial and organizational psychology (the same degree as the other two authors) from the University of Akron. His main reason for getting this degree is that he has always wanted to be like Gatewood since he was a small boy. If he would have known that Feild was an I/O psychologist, he probably would have gone into physics.

Murray has been quite successful. Currently, he is a University Distinguished Professor, the Robertson Chair at the Mays Business School at Texas A&M, and Director of the Center for Human Resource Management (all of which is very hard to get on one business card so he hands out flash drives instead). Following Gatewood's example again, he has spent time as Department Head of Management while at A&M. (It was a tossup as to who was happier about the end—Murray or his faculty.) He has also been a faculty member at the University of Iowa (twice, something to do with a bad penny) and Michigan State. Hence, he has frequently been involved in either trying to get a job or deciding whom to hire. And yes, he uses a structured interview and tries to assess each candidate's personality when visiting with them. Murray is famous because of his 50 published articles (all with coauthors) in research journals and numerous presentations (yep, coauthors) at professional meetings (Gatewood asked him to stream these presentations because he wants to sell the link to people who have trouble sleeping). Even more importantly to academics, is that these articles have been cited nearly 7,000 times. (This means that the article title has been printed in the reference section of other research articles. It doesn't necessarily mean that the article has been read.) His first publication as an Assistant Professor, published in 1991, has been cited over 2,000 times alone. The other two authors of this book, based on their own experiences, think all of this publication stuff is further proof that he is really good at selecting hard working coauthors and then manipulating them. Again mimicking Gatewood, Murray was elected as President of the HR Division of the Academy of Management and completed that 5-year term. His success can be measured by the question he was asked by a division member the year after concluding his term, "Barrick would you ever consider running for President of the HR Division?" When he is not maneuvering coauthors, Murray and his wife travel. They go anywhere that someone pays their way. So, he has served as a keynote speaker in South Africa and Australia, and has given a series of tutorial workshops in New Zealand, Switzerland, Israel, Saudi Arabia, and New Jersey (somehow he thought this was a distant country). When they stay in the United States, they head north and have been many places between Bar Harbor, Maine, and Puget Sound, Washington. This is the third edition of this book for which Murray has contributed his selection expertise. Given this, he now feels he has fully paid his dues and looks forward to the opportunity to actually meet one of his coauthors, Jr., before the next edition of the book. Gatewood thinks this is a mistake, like thinking that New Jersey was a distant country.

FOUNDATION FOR A SELECTION PROGRAM

In today's competitive business environment, managers in organizations are quite interested in increasing the performance of their employees. Their hope is that this increased performance will provide a competitive advantage over other firms. Many tactics and methods have been developed to enhance performance. Some, such as customer service and employee involvement programs, are organization-wide tactics. Others, such as the redesign of particular jobs and the improvement of communication between a manager and a work group, are specific to parts of the organization. In either case, almost all of these performance-enhancing tactics are based on the assumption that employees of the organization have the necessary capabilities to do the work. These tactics allow employees to use these capabilities more effectively.

Because having capable employees is so important for success, it is obvious (at least to us) that selection is the basis for employee performance. It identifies those individuals who have the characteristics to perform a job well. If employees do not have the appropriate talents for the jobs to which they are assigned, programs to improve performance will be unsuccessful. For example, changes such as increasing employees decision making or involving employees in customer satisfaction issues assume that employees can diagnose problems, evaluate alternative solutions, implement one of these alternatives, and communicate effectively with others. If, however, the employee does not have the necessary abilities to do these tasks, these changes may result in a decrease in job performance rather than an improvement.

We know that this description of selection brings an important question to mind: "Because selection is so important to the performance of employees, all organizations must have excellent selection programs—right?" Unfortunately, there is ample evidence that many selection programs in organizations do not function as well as they should. An appropriate match between worker talents and job demands frequently is not achieved. That is the downside. The upside, at least for us, is that selection programs often can be improved fairly easily, and that creates the need for this book. Selection programs can be useful if (a) proper steps are taken to develop selection instruments that collect job-related information from applicants and (b) this information is then used appropriately in making selection decisions. As you probably have guessed, the purpose of this book is to go into much (some say much too much) detail over how to accomplish these two objectives. Part 1, "Foundation for a Selection Program," explains the information that is necessary to gather and to understand before a selection program can be designed. (The word *foundation* in the part title also might have given a hint.) The five chapters in Part 1 should give you an understanding of these topics:

1. The steps to be taken in developing a selection program.

2. The various forms of job performance.

3. The steps necessary to identify worker characteristics that lead to job success.

4. The specific legal demands of selection. These demands take the form of laws, executive orders, court decisions, and guidelines for selection practices.

5. The composition of recruitment programs that will attract appropriate applicants.

An Introduction to Selection

DEFINITION OF SELECTION

In a time of increasing global competition, every organization is concerned about the level of work performance of its employees. This is because the performance of employees is a major determinant of how successful an organization is in reaching its strategic goals and developing a competitive advantage over rival firms. Therefore, influencing the work performance of employees is a major objective of organizations. Fortunately, there is agreement about how this can be accomplished. Organizational specialists have determined that an individual employee's work performance is made up of two factors: the ability of the individual and the effort that the individual puts forth.

Both of these factors can be influenced by the organization. Ability is a function of two organizational practices, selection, and training. An organization either finds individuals with the characteristics to do the work or it develops those characteristics in existing employees. Effort is a function of the organization's numerous practices for motivating employees. These practices include almost every topic found in an introductory management course, such as employee participation programs, compensation, goal setting, job design, and communication between managers and subordinates. All of these motivation practices, however, assume that the employee has the characteristics to perform the job. Motivation practices are intended to get the employee to use these characteristics in a concerted and continuous manner. Selection, in our unbiased but passionate viewpoint, is critical for an organization.

In this text we will use the following definition of human resource (HR) selection:

> Selection *is the process of collecting and evaluating information about an individual in order to extend an offer of employment. Such employment could be either a first position for a new employee or a different position for a current employee. The selection process is performed under legal and market constraints and addresses the future interests of the organization and of the individual.*

This is much too long to memorize. We will try to make it understandable so you can use it to meet people the next time you go out. (Like asking someone, "Hey what is your favorite selection text?") This works every time.

Collecting and Evaluating Information

The basic objective of selection is to separate from a pool of applicants those who have the appropriate characteristics to perform well on the job. We cannot assume that everyone who applies for a job is qualified to actually perform it well. Therefore, to separate the qualified applicants from those who are not qualified, the selection specialist must systematically collect information from the applicants about how much of the necessary characteristics each possesses. These characteristics are human attributes that can be demonstrated to be related to performance of the job of interest, and we will refer to these with the acronym *WRCs* (work related characteristics).[1] We also will discuss in great, great detail in later chapters the major types of WRCs, how they are determined, and how they can be measured. (These chapters will provide you with even more lines to use at parties!)

[**An Important Aside:** Those of you who have had experience in human resources (HR) or who have taken previous HR courses may be familiar with the term KSAs. This term is the traditional one that has been used to refer to human characteristics that are related to work. However, this term refers only to knowledge, skills, and abilities (hence, KSA). Selection specialists have long used other characteristics in selection, such as personality, which are not strictly KSAs. We use WRCs because we think it more accurately describes the range of human characteristics that are of interest to selection and HR.]

This systematic collection of information about characteristics of applicants can range from being fairly simple to very complex. For some jobs, a brief interview may provide all the data necessary to evaluate the applicant. For complex, managerial jobs, it may be necessary to use interviews, tests, job simulations, or other measures to properly assess candidates. A major purpose of this book is to discuss the various devices that are used to evaluate applicants.

Our use of the term *selection* does not include all offerings of employment that may occur within a firm. We make a distinction between selection and hiring. Selection, as we have just said, occurs when job-related information is collected from applicants and offers of employment are given to those who apparently possess the necessary levels of WRCs to do well on the job. Often, however, offers of employment are given with no evaluation of the applicant's job-related qualifications. We refer to this type of employment as *hiring*. One example of hiring occurs when family members, friends, or relatives of customers are given jobs. In these cases, employment is based primarily on one's relationship to a member of the organization, not on the possession of job-related qualifications. Such hiring is not necessarily inappropriate, nor does it always lead to employing incompetents. It is simply not selection as discussed in this text. Hiring also occurs when a company desperately needs individuals to fill unskilled or semiskilled positions within a very short period of time. As a result, the organization does little or no evaluation of the applicants' WRCs. Availability is the critical variable.

Selection for Initial Job and Promotion

You may think that selection refers only to choosing people for their first jobs with the organization, and not to the promotion or transfer of existing employees. We don't think that way. The basic objective is common in both selection situations. The company should be trying to collect job-related information from applicants for open positions so that it can identify individuals who have the best chance of performing well in the job activities and have a high level of productivity. There are, however, differences between selection for an initial job and selection for promotion.

Characteristics of Selection for an Initial Job

The following characteristics pertain to the selection of applicants:

1. Applicants are external to the organization. They are commonly students, people who have recently completed an education, those who are currently not employed, or those who are employed at other organizations.

2. Applicants are recruited through formal mechanisms such as media advertisement, Internet contact, employment agencies, and suggestions of present or former employees of the organization.

3. These recruitment mechanisms frequently produce a large number of applicants, especially when jobs are in short supply.

4. When there is a large number of applicants, the costs of selection become an important factor for an organization. Frequently, this number is reduced drastically by a brief selection instrument, such as an application form that collects only limited information. Only a small number of applicants complete additional selection instruments that gather more extensive information.

5. These remaining applicants go through a formalized program that has a series of steps such as interviews, ability tests, and job simulations.

6. Decisions about to whom to extend employment offers also are formalized. Either statistical analysis is used or multiple people meet to discuss the candidates and identify those who are offered positions.

Characteristics of Selection for Promotion

The following characteristics pertain to the selection of candidates for promotion:

1. Candidates are already internal to the organization—that is existing members of organization compete for a position.

2. A limited number of recruitment techniques are used, for example, postings of job vacancies either online or on bulletin boards, announcements by HR specialists or managers of the organization, and requests for nominations including self-nominations. Often no formal recruitment techniques are used. One or a small group of managers identify a small number of individuals who are thought to be able to do the job. Frequently these individuals do not even know they are being considered (are actual applicants) for the job.

3. Because the applicants are members of the organization, there is already a great deal of information about them, such as performance reviews, training records, work history, records of attendance, reprimands, awards, and so on. Few formal selection instruments are used.

4. Often the evaluation of applicants is not formalized—that is, the decision makers make the decision about whom to promote based on subjective decision making. As we will explain many times, we do not agree with such subjective selection decisions. Actually, we hate them.

Our view is that because internal and external applicant pools are so different, it is inevitable that selection of external applicants and promotion of internal ones seem to be very different. The fundamental task, however, is the same in both of these types of employment decisions and should be carried out as similarly as possible. There are more applicants than positions available. The decision maker must choose among applicants and identify the individuals who have the most developed WRCs. It is necessary to collect job-related information systematically for each applicant so direct comparisons of candidates can be made. Following these steps leads to better decisions being made more often. So, the truth and wisdom in this book is useful for both initial job selection and promotions. Matching the WRCs of individuals with the demands of the job is desirable and fair and should lead to a stronger economy. What more could you want out of life—or a textbook?

Constraints and Future Interests

From an organization's viewpoint, the selection decision is ideally made in circumstances in which the organization has a great deal of control over the number of applicants who seek the job, the information that can be gathered from these applicants, and the decision rules used by the organization in evaluating this information. The world, however, is not perfect for selection. For example, there are great fluctuations in the market of applicants, frequently the result of general economic or education conditions over which the organization has little control. Also, numerous federal and state laws and administrative rulings restrict both the information that can be gathered from applicants and the way this information can be evaluated. Equal Employment Opportunity laws and guidelines regarding discrimination in selection are good examples.

There is also a growing realization that the usefulness of the selection decision should be viewed in terms of its effects over time. The future interests of both parties must be considered in the selection process or the result will be less than optimal. Rapid and costly turnover, lower performance levels, and friction between an employee and the organization are among the results of a mismatch of interests.[2]

Now that you have a better understanding of what is meant by selection, our next task is to provide a clear overview of the various parts of this subject. To do this, the first chapter of a textbook frequently follows one of two paths: It either traces the history of the subject matter to the Greeks, Romans, and Egyptians, or it details how the subject relates to all that is important in the universe. We traced selection back to the Chinese, somewhere around 200 B.C. That reached only the Romans. Falling short of selection information for the Greeks and Egyptians, we adopted the second path for this chapter. The following sections, therefore, describe how selection is the foundation of all that is good. Specifically we will discuss how selection influences the performance of firms, how it relates to other human resource management (HRM) activities, and what HRM specialists must do to develop an effective selection program. We know you will be amazed. We hope you will gain a better understanding of the complexity of this field and the technical knowledge it requires. Our goal for the first chapter of the next edition of this book is to follow both paths—just to make the book longer—and, undoubtedly, more interesting. So please buy that edition, too. We think that Plato included his thoughts about selection when he wrote *The Republic*. That brings us back to the Greeks. Now if we can just find something about the Egyptians and selection!

Is There Evidence That Selection Is Important?

We summarize three studies that developed clear evidence that selection is significantly related to various types of performance of organizations. In one of these studies, Russell Crook and his colleagues focused on the importance of human capital, in our terms the WRCs, that were possessed by the members of organizations.[3] The resource-based theory of organizations holds that organizations can gain advantage over competitors by having and holding a valuable resource that is in short supply in the marketplace. If a resource is not in short supply, competitors of the firm could simply purchase the same resource and wipe out the competitive advantage of another firm. As the global economy becomes increasingly knowledge based, the acquisition and development of superior human capital is essential to a firm's success. The acquisition and development of human capital includes selecting and training employees. Analyzing the results of 66 different studies, the authors found that human capital, as measured by such variables as knowledge and skills, tenure, total years of experience, and education and training programs completed, was positively related to various operational measures of performance, such as customer satisfaction and innovation, that were direct products of human capital and also were related to financial performance of the firm. A second study looked at the effects of staffing and training on firm productivity and profit growth before, during, and after the Great Recession.[4] The years studied included 1999–2011 and 369 firms were included. The results indicated that selective staffing (selection) and internal training directly influence a company's profit because they influence labor productivity. The authors' concluded that high labor productivity helped buffer the negative effects of the recession and also aided recovery during the recession. Moreover, selection and training had different effects. Training was more important for prerecession profitability, and selection was more important for postrecession recovery. The results clearly indicated that firms that more effectively select and train employees outperformed competitors throughout pre- and postrecession periods even after controlling for how profitable the firms were before the recession occurred. The third study looked at the performance of 861 different units of the same fast-food restaurant chain.[5] Contrary to what many think, there are large differences between units of the same chain in terms of both selection and training. For this research, selection was scored on the basis of what percentage of new, entry-level workers had scored at or above a score that was recommended by the chain for employment on the combination of five selection tests. It was possible to employ applicants who scored below the recommended minimum if there were sufficient other reasons to employ. Similarly, training was scored on percentage of total employees that had completed a recommended two-week training course. Results were that selection and training were related to customer service performance and retention, which, in turn, were related to unit financial performance, such as profits. Data collection and analyses were completed at several different time periods so that causality could be identified more easily. The authors' concluded that selection and training applied to even low-skill jobs could yield returns in terms of customer service, retention of employees, and profits.

SELECTION AND OTHER HUMAN RESOURCE SYSTEMS

In addition to selection, other HR systems important for employee performance include recruitment, training, compensation, and job performance review. The relationships among these human resource systems are shown in Figure 1.1. To get the maximum benefits from the HR systems shown in this figure, firms must design all of the HR systems so they greatly enhance employees' work performance.[6] Therefore, selection should be coordinated with the activities the firm carries out under recruitment, training, compensation, and job performance review.

For example, training is designed to teach necessary job skills and abilities to those individuals who have accepted a job offer as a result of the selection process. The content, length, and nature of training are affected by the level of the skills and abilities of the individuals selected. If these skills and abilities are well developed for the job, then minimal training should suffice. If the new employees' job skills and abilities are low, then training should be more extensive. Compensation and selection interact; on the one hand, the specific qualifications possessed by the individual selected may affect the amount that he or she is paid. On the other hand, the salary offer that is determined through the organization's recruitment and selection activities affects the applicant's decision to accept the offer or not. As we will frequently point out, selection and work performance measurement also are linked. The purpose of selection is to identify those individuals who will perform well on the job. Work performance data are used to design the selection system and also measure its effectiveness. These topics are discussed in both Chapter 2, "Job Performance Concepts and Measures" and Chapter 8, "Validity of Selection Procedures."

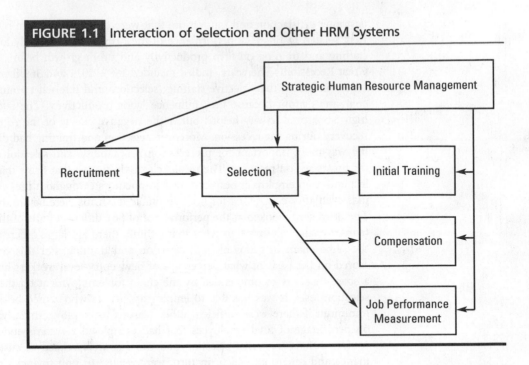

FIGURE 1.1 Interaction of Selection and Other HRM Systems

Selection is more closely related to recruitment than it is to the other HRM programs, because both recruitment and selection are concerned with placing individuals into jobs. Other HRM activities deal with individuals after they have begun working. We will define recruitment as those organizational activities (such as choosing recruiting sources, developing recruitment ads, and deciding how much money will be spent) that influence the number and types of individuals who apply for a position—and that also affect applicants' decisions about whether or not to accept a job offer.[7] We use this definition because it is important to think not only about attracting people but also about increasing the probability that those people will accept a position if it is offered. It is senseless to motivate people to apply and then turn them off when they do—but we all know this happens. Sara Rynes, in an extensive review of recruitment, points out the relationship between selection and recruitment.[8] At the very least, the WRCs of the job directly influence both the recruitment sources used and some of the specific information about the job that is included in the recruitment message. For example, an entry-level HR manager's position in a unionized manufacturing plant may require applicants to know about Equal Opportunity Employment laws, the interpretation of union contracts, and employee benefit plans. These requirements could limit recruitment sources to law schools, industrial relations programs, and HR programs. Also these knowledge requirements should be included in the recruitment message that is used. This information should help to reduce inappropriate applicants who may be interested in the position. We will go into much detail about recruitment in Chapter 5. See if you can control your curiosity and hunger to know about this topic until then.

DEVELOPING A SELECTION PROGRAM

We turn now to the way effective selection programs should be developed. HR specialists must complete a good deal of work before the selection process is applied to those who are being recruited. We contend that the adequacy of these developmental steps, illustrated in Figure 1.2, strongly determine the adequacy of the selection process. If little

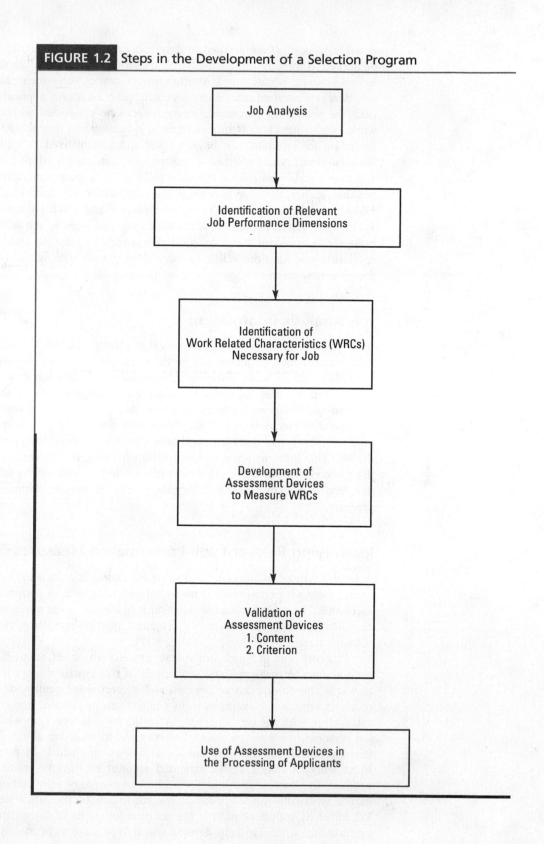

FIGURE 1.2 Steps in the Development of a Selection Program

Job Analysis

↓

Identification of Relevant
Job Performance Dimensions

↓

Identification of
Work Related Characteristics (WRCs)
Necessary for Job

↓

Development of
Assessment Devices
to Measure WRCs

↓

Validation of
Assessment Devices
1. Content
2. Criterion

↓

Use of Assessment Devices in
the Processing of Applicants

attention and effort are devoted to developing the selection program, its usefulness will be limited. If these developmental steps are seriously addressed, the usefulness of the selection program is maximized. Another way of viewing this issue is that what looks like a selection process itself can be implemented quite easily. An application form can quite easily be printed or purchased; interviews can be conducted without too much prior work; employment tests (with descriptions indicating that they should produce useful information for selection) can be purchased and administered to applicants. The crucial issue, however, is not whether an organization can collect information from applicants and then decide who among them are to be given employment offers. Obviously this is possible. Rather, the issue is whether the organization can collect information from applicants that is *closely* related to job performance and *effectively* use this information to identify the best applicants. It is the developmental steps of the selection program that make the information that is collected closely related to the job and useful in identifying applicants who have the WRCs to succeed on the job. The following paragraphs briefly describe these steps.

Job Analysis Information

If the purpose of the selection program is to identify the best individuals for a job, then information about the job should be the starting point in the development of this program. *Job analysis* is the gathering of information about a job in an organization. This information includes the tasks, outcomes produced (products or services), equipment, material used, and environment (working conditions, hazards, work schedule, and so on) that characterize the job. This information serves two main purposes. The first purpose is to convey to potential applicants information about the nature and demands of the job. This helps minimize inappropriate expectations. The second purpose is actually the more critical for the development of selection programs: The job analysis information provides a database for the other steps in the development of the selection program.

Identifying Relevant Job Performance Measures

A second type of information important for developing the selection program is determining how job performance is measured and what level of performance is regarded as successful. The main purpose of selection is to identify those applicants who will be successful on the job. To build such a program, selection specialists must know what constitutes success.

In many jobs in which individuals produce an object or meet customers, finding what should be measured and how much of this equals success is relatively straightforward. The objects can be counted and inspected for quality, or the customers who receive a service (for example, from a teller) can be counted and surveyed about their satisfaction with the service. There are other jobs, however, in which measurement of job performance is not as direct. For example, in team-based jobs, it is difficult to determine how much any one individual has accomplished. In research and development work, it may take an extended amount of time to translate an idea into a product. In situations such as these, the best source of information about job performance is usually the judgment of the supervisor or the other work team members. Whatever its source or nature, the information as to what constitutes successful job performance is used to help develop which WRCs are to be measured in the selection program.

Identification of Work-Related Characteristics

Using both job analysis information and job performance data, the HR specialist must identify the WRCs that a worker should possess to perform the job successfully. These WRCs become the basic pool of characteristics to be evaluated in applicants. This identification is difficult. As we discuss in Chapter 3, a few job analysis methods attempt to identify these WRCs directly. In most cases, however, HR specialists rely on their own judgments. *Work requirements, worker attributes, worker characteristics,* and *job requirements* are terms frequently used in the same context in which we use WRCs.

Development of Selection Measures

After the WRCs have been identified, it becomes necessary to either find or construct the appropriate selection measures or instruments. These measures can be classified into the following groups: application blanks, biographical data forms, and reference checks; the selection interview; mental and special abilities tests; personality assessment inventories; simulation and performance measures; and integrity measures There are two requirements for choosing selection devices to be used. The first is that the device must measure the WRCs the selection specialist has identified as needed for the job. "Duh!" you say. The problem is that many selection instruments that can be purchased or that have been developed by companies measure broad WRCS that are thought to be useful for work in general (like ambition) rather than the specific WRCs for a particular job. For example, application forms usually ask for brief information about previous job titles and job duties but do not collect enough detailed information to clearly determine whether the previous work experience matches the present job. In such cases, the person evaluating the application form must make some inferences (guesses) as to how closely the job title matches the job of interest. As you probably realize, making such inferences (guesses) reduces the accuracy of the selection decision of to whom to offer employment. Similarly, interviews frequently attempt to measure general skills, such as leadership, attitude, motivation, and personal interaction. These skills are difficult to measure and often are not closely related to the specific skills necessary for doing the job, such as the verbal ability to discuss computer hardware and software topics in a way that will be understandable to employees. Selection specialists use test construction principles, which we will discuss in later chapters, to determine the match of WRCs with the selection measure.

The second requirement of a selection measure is that it should be able to differentiate among applicants. The assumption in selection is that applicants possess *different amounts of the WRCs necessary for job performance.* The purpose of the selection instrument is to measure these differences by means of numerical scores. It is in this way that promising applicants can be distinguished from unpromising applicants. If nearly all applicants perform about the same on these selection instruments, selection decisions are difficult because the applicants appear to be equal. Choosing a few applicants from a large group of equals is guessing. The problem of lack of applicant differentiation often occurs when interviews use general questions about career goals (What is your ideal job?) or ask the interviewee for self-assessment of strengths and weaknesses (What are your weak points?). It also occurs when personality inventories are transparent in purpose—for example, scales measuring the amount of social interaction preferred (Do you prefer working with others or by yourself?) or attitudes toward stealing or dishonesty (Do you think that stealing should always be punished?). Training programs teach applicants how to respond to these questions. Knowing how tests are constructed will help the professional develop—or choose among—tests.

Let us briefly summarize the steps completed by an organization at this point in the selection program development process. Information has been collected describing important aspects of both job activities and outcomes. This information has been used to identify a set of WRCs a worker needs to succeed on the job. A set of selection measures has been identified that will measure the amount of the WRCs possessed by applicants. If these steps are performed with care, an organization should reasonably expect to obtain the information needed to choose the right applicants. Frequently, however, the developmental work of the selection program stops at this point. When this happens, very little direct evidence is available to verify the accuracy of these steps. Robert Guion has likened these first steps to the development of hypotheses.[9] That is, the HR specialist has formulated testable statements as to the worker characteristics that should be related to successful job performance. The last steps in the development of a selection program can be viewed as a testing of these hypotheses. Technically referred to as *validation,* these steps focus on the collection and evaluation of information to determine whether the worker characteristics thought to be important, in fact, are related to successful job performance. If they are related, then the selection program should be useful to the organization. If, on the other hand, it turns out that the identified worker characteristics are not related to job performance, it is better to learn this as early as possible so that the selection program can be changed.

Validation Procedures

There are several ways to validate the selection process. In *empirical validation,* for example, two types of data are collected: (a) the scores on the selection devices from a representative sample of individuals and (b) measures of how well each of these individuals is performing in important parts of the job. The purpose of validation is to provide evidence that data from the selection instruments are related to job performance. Statistical data analysis, usually correlational analysis (which measures how closely related two different sets of scores are), is the most straightforward manner of producing this evidence. Empirical validation involves calculating correlation coefficients between scores on the selection instruments and on the job performance measure.

In addition to empirical validation, *content* validation can be used. Content validation systematically takes the data produced by the judgments of workers and managers and uses them to determine the relationship between the selection test and job performance. We will discuss validation in more detail in Chapter 8. No matter which type is employed, it is really only after the validation phase has been completed that one has evidence that the information collected by the selection instrument is indicative of job performance and, therefore, useful for choosing among applicants. It is these steps from job analysis to validation that we are referring to when we say that much developmental work must precede the installation of the selection program. If all these steps are not completed, then, in Guion's terms, the organization is using a set of selection instruments believed to be useful for the identification of potentially successful workers but lacking the proper evidence to support this belief.

If the selection measures are not related to job performance, their use can be costly because a less-than-optimum group of workers is being selected for employment. Organizations, however, often choose not to fully carry out these steps in the development of their selection programs. Less time-consuming and less rigorous procedures are adopted. In such cases, long-term consequences and costs are downplayed or ignored. This is very, very bad and probably will lead to the end of the world.

CONSTRAINTS IN DEVELOPING A SELECTION PROGRAM

The essence of selection is *prediction* or forecasting. Specifically, we wish to use the information gathered from the selection devices to determine differences among applicants with regard to job-related WRCs and then choose those applicants who we predict will do well in the future in the job under consideration. In HR selection—as in medicine, stock market analysis, meteorology, and economics—prediction is an uncertain activity. Even with a well-developed selection program, not all of the decisions about future job performance will be correct. A number of factors greatly affect the accuracy of the selection process.

Limited Information on Applicants

The correctness of selection decisions depends in part on the accuracy and completeness of data gathered from the applicants. In general, the greater the amount of accurate data obtained, the higher the probability of making a correct selection decision. Especially early in the processing of applicants, however, the amount of the data collected often is limited severely by the cost of obtaining the data. The organization incurs costs for such things as materials and facilities, staff time, travel expenses for staff and applicants, and data storage and analysis. For example, a college campus interviewer frequently spends only 30 minutes with each applicant, and part of this time is devoted to presenting information about the organization. In other cases, application forms and résumés are used extensively as major screening devices. Campus interviewing and application and résumé forms, however, obtain only limited, basic information about applicants. When many people apply for only a few positions, the large majority of applicants will be dropped after this step. Because the information is limited and often superficial, mistakes will be made both with those who are selected and those who are rejected.

Applicant and Organization at Cross-Purposes

All applicants for a job are seeking to receive an offer of employment from the organization. The organization, on the other hand, usually is trying to not offer employment to the large majority of applicants but rather to offer employment only to one person or a few number of people. Therefore, the large majority of applicants and the organization are at cross-purposes. To improve the chances of being selected, an applicant tries to present him- or herself in the best manner possible. For example, it has been estimated that as many as 40 percent of applicants distort or falsify their applications, resumes, and interviews. Horrors! "Why would they do that?" you ask. (Which is better than you saying, "Wow, you've given me a good idea! I have finally gotten something useful out of this book.") You can guess the reasons. Applicants need jobs. They know that organizations usually are looking for employees who are friendly, honest, and hardworking, and who have experience in related jobs and have education related to the job. Without such background, and characteristics they probably will be rejected. So what have they got to lose? Probably the most that will happen is that even if the company discovers the distortion, they only will be eliminated from consideration. Most companies do not have the time, interest, or resources to try to punish the applicant in some way. If these applicants didn't distort the truth, they would be eliminated from consideration. So, in varying degrees ranging from slight exaggeration to cleverly planned deception, many applicants try to convince the people from the organization that they are the one or among the few that have the WRCs to do the job well. Applicants can even pay to go to training programs that will help them present themselves to their best advantage by teaching them how to write resumes, complete application forms, and respond to interview questions. Most of these programs "polish the delivery techniques" of the people who attend, but others outright fabricate company documents and degrees to form impressive files. The latter are bad, bad programs. At any rate, this distortion makes it more difficult to evaluate applicants because it adds a new issue into selection: the necessity to discern what is true and what may be false in the data collected from applicants. The chapters in this book that describe how to develop and use various selection measures are useful for addressing this problem. The general premise in these chapters is that the selection specialist should gather information that is related to job activities. This information should require an applicant to demonstrate that they know how to and can do job tasks as well as model the behaviors that are essential to working with others in these tasks.

Measurement of Jobs, Individuals, and Work Performance

A basic assumption of this book is that the development of a selection program requires the measurement of characteristics of jobs, individuals, and work performance. By *measurement* we mean quantitative description—that is, the use of numbers. Numbers are used to represent information such as the amount of time an applicant has spent in a job activity, or the level of mathematical knowledge an applicant needs to perform a task, or an applicant's score on a verbal skills test, or the quality of a worker's performance in preparing an advertisement. Numbers are necessary because they facilitate the comparison of people. They transmit information more succinctly than words, and they permit statistical manipulation (such as the adding of scores across selection tests to get a total score for each applicant), which provides even more information into the selection program. For example, assume that 12 people apply for an entry-level position in the loan department of a bank. All of the applicants are interviewed and all complete a brief test on financial terms and analysis. Quantifying the performance of each candidate on each of the two selection instruments is the most practical way to compare them. If scores are not developed, the selection specialist is placed in a complex situation; differences must be determined among the 12 using descriptive information, such as "He seemed able to express himself pretty well," or "She knew most of the financial terms but did not seem comfortable judging the risk of the loan." Obviously, when there are such statements about a number of individuals, the difficulty in identifying the most promising of the applicants is enormous.

The problem of measurement for the HR specialist, however, is to ensure that the numbers generated are accurate descriptions of the characteristics of the applicant, the job, or the job performance under study. We address specific measurement issues throughout this text, especially in Chapters 6 through 8. For now, we can say that the measurement of many WRCs is difficult and not as precise as we would wish.

A comment is necessary at this point to ensure that we do not give you a false impression. We have mentioned that it is important, when making selection decisions, to use selection instruments that generate scores about the characteristics of applicants. That is not to say, however, that selection decisions are always made by counting the scores and offering employment only to those who score the highest, even though some maintain that the best results occur when this is done. It is common that other factors also enter into the decisions—for example, a desire to balance the demographic composition of the workforce or an intuition about a specific applicant. In this type of situation, our position is that these additional factors should come into play only after the applicants have been measured on the selection devices and a group has been identified as being appropriate for the job. These other factors then can be considered when choosing individuals from this group. Very different, and much less desirable, results can occur if these other factors are used early in selection, before the applicant pool has been measured. In such situations, a great number of errors can be made before the selection instruments are even used.

Other Factors Affecting Work Performance

Another issue to keep in mind regarding selection programs is that many factors affect work performance. The primary purpose of selection is to enhance the probability of making correct employment decisions—extending offers to those persons who will perform well in the organization and not extending job offers to those who will not do well. Typically, any evaluation of the adequacy of the selection program is made in terms of job performance.

It is apparent, however, that the WRCs of those hired are not the sole determinants of job performance. Practitioners and researchers have identified numerous other factors in an organization that affect individual performance. Among these organizational factors are training programs for employees, appraisal and feedback methods, goal-setting procedures, financial compensation systems, work design strategies, supervisory methods, organizational structure, decision-making techniques, and work schedules.

The implication of these findings for the evaluation of selection programs is clear. A selection program focuses on a few of the many variables that influence performance. Often it is difficult to adequately assess its effectiveness. At times, a thoughtfully developed program might seem to have only a minimal measurable relationship to performance. It is possible in such cases that one or more of the other variables that we have mentioned may be affecting performance levels adversely and negating the contribution of the selection program. The conclusion is that it is advisable, in judging selection programs, to examine several other organizational systems when attempting to diagnose deficiencies in employee performance.

Selection Research versus Selection Practice

Both selection researchers and organizational employees who implement selection programs have realized during the past several years that the two groups differ in how they treat selection. Edward Lawler III, an academic researcher who works with organizations, has made this statement:

> A great deal that passes as "best practice" in HRM most likely is not. In some cases, there simply is no evidence to support what is thought to be best practice. In other cases, there is evidence to support that what are thought to be best practices are, in fact, inferior practices. In short, most organizations do not practice evidence-based human resource management. As a result, they often underperform with respect to their major stakeholders: employees, investors, and the community.[10]

This difference between what academic research has shown and what often is implemented in organizations is true of many fields in addition to HRM. *Evidence-based management* is a term that means managing by translating principles based on evidence into organizational practice. Through evidence-based management, practicing managers develop into organizational experts who make decisions informed by social science and organizational research. They move professional decisions away from personal preference and unsystematic experience toward those based on the best available scientific evidence.[11] Said another way, evidence-based management means that managers should become knowledgeable about research results in specific topics of management and how this research is translated into practice. Knowing this will help guide the decision making of managers so that more decisions are based on evidence and data rather than intuition and hunch.

Unfortunately, evidence-based management is not universal in organizations. Some organizations practice it, but many others do not. This divide between research findings and organizational practice occurs in many areas of management, not just in HRM. It is relatively common that practicing managers do not know about academic research and instead base decisions on their own experience, that of close associates, or common practices within their organizations. There are many reasons for this discrepancy. Most basic among them is that management is not an occupation like medicine, law, or teaching in which entrants to the field must pass some exam, provide a specific degree, or pass a specific test. As we know, managers come from all educational backgrounds. Some have little education, and some resist academic research findings as being too theoretical and impractical. Another reason for this discrepancy is that courses that make up a management major can vary greatly between colleges. Some majors require HRM courses; others do not even offer such courses. Related to this, some faculty members are quite good at translating HRM research into practice and others are unable to make this translation. Yet another reason is that practice managers usually do not have the research, statistical, and content knowledge to be able to read published academic research, understand the findings, and recognize the practice implications of these findings. This lack of understanding is to be expected; the knowledge of research and the specialized content of academic areas is what Ph.D. programs teach. Managers do not often attend Ph.D. programs. It is for this reason that some firms, including State Farm Insurance, recommend that some executives employ academic consultants who can discuss relevant research findings with them.

What this means is that this book makes recommendations about selection that you may not find implemented by a specific organization with which you are familiar. We know, however, that many organizations do practice the recommendations we make here. Think of the book as your basis for evidence-based selection (EBS). After you finish this course, send us a copy of your final grade and a blank, signed check; we will send you an official EBS button in the day-glow color of your choice. Wearing that button will add a nice touch when you interview for jobs.

So Why Should I Devote My Life to Selection? What Is Selection Doing That's Good for the World?

This section is based on John F. Kennedy's famous statement, "Ask not what selection can do for you but rather what you can do for selection." Here are three of the many important areas of selection that will be pertinent in the future.

Big Data

We are all familiar with the increased use of data and statistical analyses to assist and make decisions for sports teams, financial investments, health care diagnosis and delivery, and product marketing. In HR and especially selection this is becoming known as *people analytics.* Companies are in the early phases of collecting enormous amounts of electronic data about their employees' characteristics, their movements and actions at work, and their performance in a diverse set of work-based outcomes. Companies such as Google, HP, Intel, General Motors, and Proctor & Gamble have dedicated analytics teams in their HR departments.[12] Because selecting workers is so valuable and selection has used statistical analyses as a tool for many years, it is also at the forefront of this movement. One example of the analytics described in this book is Xerox's selection of employees for its call centers. Up through 2010, these positions had been filled using interviews and a few basic measures, such as a typing tests and previous work experience. In 2010, the company began to use an online series of tests of personality, cognitive skill, and multiple-choice questionnaires about how the applicant would handle specific situations. We will discuss each of these types of selection measures in depth in later chapters. Applicants' answers to these measures are entered into a statistical analysis, which results in a rating for each applicant of poor, middling, or superior in terms of selection for employment. Shortly after switching to this format, the rate of employees leaving the job fell by 20 percent and the promotion rate rose. Managers began using the scoring categories almost exclusively in employment decisions. We are familiar with this scenario in people analytics. The future of selection, however, could get more complex than the actions at Xerox. For example Knack, a small application-based video game operation, has developed games that have been designed by a team of neuroscientists, psychologists, and data analysis experts. Playing for as little as 20 minutes on these games generates large amounts of data about how information is used and how problems are solved. These data then are used to develop such scores as creativity, persistence, capacity to learn, and ability to prioritize. One such game was used by a department at Royal Dutch Shell with the purpose of identifying potentially disruptive business ideas and startups. Data collected from about 1,400 individuals who played this game were compared with their performance data collected over time by the company. Results were that the top 10 percent of idea generators as predicted by Knack's analyses were those who had done the best in company performance. Another example of what the future may hold is seen in an electronic badge developed in the Human Dynamics Laboratory of MIT. These badges transmit data about employee interactions throughout the workday, capturing information about such variables as formal and informal conversations; the tone of voice and gestures of people involved; how much people talk, listen, and interrupt; and the degree of various emotional and personality traits they demonstrate. The idea is to relate scores on these variables to many dimensions of job performance. People analytics will be a developing movement that could greatly increase the appropriate match between people and jobs and be a benefit for both workers and companies. On the other hand, it could be invasive of private lives, force compliance with arbitrary organizational rules or expectations, and make job and careers regimented. You, working in people analytics for selection, could help influence which alternative occurs.

The Magnitude of Demographic Group Differences and Their Effects

As we have mentioned many times already and will mention even more times in the following chapters, selection is best done when tests and assessments are used to measure the amounts of WRCs that applicants possess and numbers are used to represent those amounts. Using these numbers to make selection decisions has been done since the early 1900s so there are much data on scores of many individuals on many WRC tests. Selection researchers have used these data to find out more about what these tests measure and how the scores on these tests are related to various measures of work performance. One consistent finding in this examination about measures and scores on them is that there are consistent differences among demographic, ethnic, and racial groups in these scores. Some groups score consistently higher than do other groups. Because scores are used to make decisions on whom to select for employment, you can guess one of the effects of making such decisions—various groups are selected at different rates. Because employment is key to many aspects of life, these differences among various groups are of major concern and discussion. Some conclude that these differences are the result of tests that are culturally biased in item presentation, language, and content and, therefore, inherently unfair to use in making employment decisions. Others conclude that because test results are consistently related to various measures of job performance, they are not unfairly biased. Rather, they reflect actual differences among groups in abilities to perform jobs. We will present what has been found about subgroup differences in scores as we discuss each of the major types of selection measures. Selection researchers have looked at the types of items and specific WRCs that may be most frequently associated with these group differences. Others have examined the effects of training before selection testing or directly after selection to see whether differences in groups can be negated or minimized through training. Such investigation will continue in the future. Perhaps technology can be used to produce different types of selection tests that do not rely on language as a delivery method, such as the game-playing actions that we described earlier. The understanding of what constitutes work performance also may be relevant. Performance measures usually have been based on production items counted or supervisor judgment of how much work was done. We now think that other factors are more directly related to an individual's actions that are important to the final production of goods or services. These actions include behaviors such as helping coworkers, trying alternative work actions, finding customer problems, and improving customer satisfaction. It could be that using these types of measures of work performance are useful because they are both direct measures of an individual and they reduce the amount of measured differences in groups work performance. Want to take on a social-economic-psychometric problem?

The Use of Various Internet-Based Selection Measures

Like everything else in the world, selection is being transformed—from a testing-in-an-office to an electronic-based system. The advantages of this change are ease and financial savings. The traditional method required applicants to travel to a company facility to go through the selection program with the side effects of costing applicants time and money. For the company, the costs were mainly time of staff, maintenance of facilities, provision of testing supplies, and costs of scoring and report writing. Having applicants complete selection measures that can be presented, scored, and written up by programs is much less expensive and faster. There are, of course, different costs and issues. There are two general types of Internet selection testing. One is computer-based, supervised assessment. In this type, applicants come to a physical facility designated by the company and equipped with computers either in individualized spaces or in a large room that houses multiple computer stations. Such testing is very similar to traditional selection methods with the big difference being the computer versus paper-pencil or discussion-based testing. The second type is unproctored assessment. In this, the applicant can complete the selection measures at any location he chooses, at any time, and with any electronic device that can access the Web. Serious problems and limitations are common to both types. The main ones are as follows:

- **Computer literacy.** Can applicants easily and quickly operate equipment? We all know that there are large differences among individuals in their ability to operate electronic devices. The issue for selection is whether or not these differences are reflected in different scores among people. Selection is supposed to measure the differences in the WRC that is the subject of the test, not in the ability to operate equipment.

- **Graphic transmission.** For multiple reasons, it is not unusual for various electronic devices to present the same message differently. This can be a very serious especially when questions contain graphs that are essential to interpret. This issue is another example of a factor other than the content of the test being a cause of differences in selection test scores.

- **Technical failures.** This may never have happened to you, but we (especially the particularly inept coauthor) have experienced screens going blank and all work vanishing. Knowing what to do when this happens during electronic testing is serious, especially if the problem is one of transmission of the completed test, and the applicant does not even know that the transmission failed. Would you be happy about having to start from scratch?

- **Equivalence of electronic testing results to those from traditional testing.** Almost all we know about the test construction and validity of selection instruments is based on traditional testing, for example, paper-pencil, interactive discussions like interviews, and work simulations that closely replicate the actual materials used on the job. Can we use the same norms, correlations with other tests, and performance measures generated from traditional testing for electronic tests? Are differences among demographic groups less, the same, or more? Making the assumption that scores from electronic tests are the same as scores from traditional tests and that individuals will get the same score on both electronic and traditional tests seems a bit of a stretch.

Other problems are characteristic of unsupervised, online testing:

- **Cheating.** Applicants could get others (smarter others) to take their tests, use the Internet to get answers (it must be right if it is on the internet), or use books, notes, or friends sitting next to them.

- **Security of test items.** Groups of people could combine what they know and make copies of tests that have alternate questions (as happens on SAT tests) and develop a list of all questions that could be sold to others before they take the test.

- **Standardization of test environment.** One of the assumptions of test interpretation is that all respondents should complete the test in nearly identical situations. Such control reduces the chance of factors of noise, lights, temperature, and weather affecting scores differently. There can be no control in unsupervised, online testing (even telling people to stand in a closet would not do it). Therefore, we know that the chances of having test results differ somewhat because of factors other than differences in the WRC among applicants is probable.

These are the issues that selection will face in the future. Want to write an app to solve these issues?

PLAN OF THIS BOOK

The major purpose of this book is to discuss each of the steps necessary to develop selection programs within organizations. We will concentrate on the characteristics of the data that should be gathered and the types of decisions the HR specialist should make at each step. We incorporate research about selection and discuss its implications for the development of selection programs. There is no one blueprint for the development of selection programs, and we do not wish to give that impression. The steps we refer to are different stages in the accumulation and processing of information about jobs, individuals, and job performance. At each step, the HR specialist must make a number of decisions, not only about the kind of data needed, but also about the statistical analyses that should be done and about what decisions can be made based on that data. The particular selection needs of the organization will dictate the appropriate actions; we hope this book will provide the information necessary to evaluate options at each stage.

The book is divided into four parts. Part 1, "Foundation for a Selection Program," explains the data and information that must be gathered before a selection program is developed. It also includes a chapter on recruiting methods to attract applicants to enter the selection program. Part 2, "Measurement in Selection," provides the basic information necessary for assigning numbers to the characteristics of applicants, job, and job performance. These are the data used in selection decisions. Part 3, "Selection Measures," contains six chapters. Each one discusses a specific type of selection test. This discussion includes the content of the type of test, what WRCs are measured by the test, how the test may be best constructed, and how it can be used. Part 4, "Using Selection Data," explains how to use the data about WRCs to decide on which applicants to offer employment.

REFERENCES

1. The acronym *WRC* is adapted from the acronym *WoRC* that stands for work-related characteristics. That acronym was developed by the Personnel/Human Resources Research Group in their meeting in Atlanta, Georgia, in 2014. Their acronym was intended to replace the traditional acronyms *KSA* or *KSAO*.

2. Steven L. Premack and John P. Wanous, "A Meta-Analysis of Realistic Job Preview Experiments," *Journal of Applied Psychology* 70 (1986): 706–719.

3. Russell T. Cook, James G. Combs, Samuel Todd, David J. Woehr, and David J. Ketchen Jr., "Does Human Capital Matter? A Meta-Analysis of the Relationship Between Human Capital and Firm Performance," *Journal of Applied Psychology*, 96 (2011): 443–456.

4. Youngsang Kim and Robert E. Polyhart, "The Effects of Staffing and Training on Firm Productivity and Profit Growth Before, During, and After the Great Recession," *Journal of Applied Psychology* 99 (2014): 361–389.

5. Chad H. Van Iddekinge, Gerald R. Ferris, Pamela L. Perrewe, Alexa A. Perryman, Fred R. Blass, and Thomas D. Heetderks, "Effects of Selection and Training on Unit–Level Performance Over Time: A Latent Growth Modeling Approach," *Journal of Applied Psychology* 94 (2009): 829–843.

6. Christopher J. Collins and Kevin D. Clark, "Strategic Human Resource Practices, Top Management Team Social Networks, and Firm Performance: The Role of Human Resource Practices in Creating Organizational Competitive Advantage," *Academy of Management Journal* 46 (2003): 740–752.

7. Derek S. Chapman, Krista L. Uggerslev, Sarah A. Carroll, Kelly A. Piasentin, and David A. Jones, "Applicant Attraction to Organizations and Job Choice: A Meta-Analytic Review of the Correlates of Recruiting Outcomes," *Journal of Applied Psychology* 90 (2005): 928–944.

8. Sara L. Rynes, "Recruitment, Job Choice, and Post-Hire Consequences: A Call for New Research Directions," in *Handbook of Industrial and Organizational Psychology*, 2nd ed., vol. 2, ed. M. D. Dunnette and L. M. Hough (Palo Alto, CA: Consulting Psychologists Press, 1991).

9. Robert M. Guion, "Personnel Assessment, Selection, and Placement," in *Handbook of Industrial and Organizational Psychology*, 2nd ed., vol. 2, ed. M. D. Dunnette and L. M. Hough (Palo Alto, CA: Consulting Psychologists Press, 1991), 327–398.

10. Edward E. Lawler III, "Why HR Practices Are Not Evidence-Based," *Academy of Management Journal* 50 (2007): 1033–1044.

11. Denise M. Rosseau, "Is There Such a Thing as 'Evidence-Based Management"?' *Academy of Management Review* 31 (2006): 256–269.

12. Don Peck, "They're Watching You at Work," *The Atlantic*, December 2013, 72–84.

Job Performance Concepts and Measures

Now for a pop quiz! Complete the following multiple-choice question: In Chapter 1, we said that the objective of selection was the prediction of future _____.

a. batting averages in baseball
b. weather
c. JOB PERFORMANCE
d. stock market swings

Congratulations, you are right! The answer is job performance. (If you chose one of the other responses, you should probably find a different course or at least be more observant of chapter titles and capital letters.)

Specifically, those applicants who score high on selection tests are predicted to do well in their future job performance and are offered jobs. This is similar to what universities do when they admit freshmen. It is very common to use high school grades, ACT or SAT scores, and graded recommendations to predict future first-year GPA, the academic measure of student job performance. This emphasis on predicting job performance makes sense. But what is being predicted when we say *job performance*? What is the work equivalent of academic GPA? Traditionally, that is meaning for most of the past century or more, the answer has been task performance. That is, how well workers completed job activities (commonly referred to as job tasks) was how well they performed on their jobs. This thinking was born during the time when much of work was physical activities. A large portion of employed workers assembled various parts into complete products such as cars, clothing, toys, household furnishings, and so on. Many employees not working in manufacturing were in agriculture or small business. Both of these industries had physical tasks. In addition most workers operated individually with limited interaction with other workers. In the majority of jobs during this time, the results of these tasks could be seen and counted. The number of cars completed, animals milked, bushels of apples harvested, or dollars taken in sales could all be easily tallied. Moreover, these items were directly related to the success of the company, farm, or organization. The relationship between cars made, cows milked, apples harvested, and the resulting dollars earned by the firm was easy to understand. It was straightforward to think of job performance as the number of job activities completed because these activities were related to the number of items produced and sold. High performance from individual workers meant more money for the organization.

Selection at this time mainly involved gathering information from applicants that measured their knowledge of how to perform tasks, knowledge of topics necessary to perform tasks (e.g., how tools should be used, mathematical operations necessary for bookkeeping calculations, explaining product usage to customers), or actual performance on trial job tasks (e.g., cutting wood boards, repairing brakes on a car). Scoring of selection measures was also generally straightforward. Knowledge tests could be scored for right answers; mistakes in performing a task could be counted.

Over time, however, the nature of work changed and following that so did the concept of job performance and the nature of selection tests used to choose among applicants. Manufacturing jobs have decreased dramatically both because of less expensive labor in developing countries and the increased use of computerized assembly machines. With the decline of manufacturing jobs, the service industry has steadily increased. This was prompted by the growth of cities and the movement from farms and towns to urban centers to find employment. Urban dwellers had to purchase clothing, food, furniture, entertainment, and so on. This demand led to clothing stores, restaurants, furniture marts, entertainment venues, and so on that employed workers to interact with customers and deliver goods and services. As society and technology became more complex, the proportion of knowledge-based jobs grew dramatically. Specialized trades such as electricians, carpenters, heating specialists, teachers, physicians, and lawyers became major employment vehicles. Entertainment grew tremendously with the development of radio, television, sports, movies, and video games. Each of these fields was dominated by employees who had specialist training and education in somewhat narrow topics. The manner in which work was performed also changed drastically. Traditionally, manufacturing was usually done by individual workers. After the assembly line was developed, manufacturing was one person doing one or a few tasks and then passing the work on to another employee to add another step in the production process. With the rise of service and knowledge-based work, groups of employees interacting became common. Teams became more autonomous, with work groups frequently able to change work processes as they deemed appropriate. In addition, work such as health care, video production, computer engineering, and gaming became very complex and required collaboration among large numbers of experts in narrow fields. In addition, the observable part of job performance lessened. The most important parts of knowledge-based jobs really do not have easily observable actions. Incumbents think, plan, make observations, draw conclusions, interpret data, and so on.

With this change in work, the concept of job performance became more complex and more difficult to measure. For example in a restaurant, what should be counted? One could count the number of food items sold or their dollar value, but employees' interactions toward customers are also very important. Food may taste fine, but if it is uncomfortable or irritating to go to the restaurant, many customers will not return. How can these interactions be measured? What is a "good" interaction? The same situation exists with tellers at banks and health care professionals at clinics. One can count the number of interactions with customers or patients, but a high number of interactions can often negatively affect quality of interaction and, therefore, not be a useful performance measurement, especially if it is the only one collected. The reactions of customers or patients to interactions with employees are often important to know but are very difficult to collect systematically. The move to work teams has created similar problems with defining and measuring job performance. For example, teams are frequently used to install kitchen cabinets and appliances, with each team member having specific duties. When evaluating job performance of team members, what is counted? Do cabinet installers get a higher performance score than appliance installers because more cabinets than appliances are put in? Do all work team members get the same performance score because the same number of kitchens is completed for all members of the installation team?

These changes in the nature of work have led to major changes in how job performance is viewed, how it is measured, and the nature of selection measures that are or can be used to predict job performance for applicants. Let's discuss each of these changes briefly.

How Job Performance Is Viewed

Task performance is still the primary type or facet of job performance. That is, success in most jobs is based largely on how well an employee is carrying out the major activities that make up the job. Engineers are judged by the quality of their designs, marketing professionals on the change in sales resulting from marketing campaigns, managers on the amount and quality of products/services provided by their subordinates. However, selection researchers and practitioners realize that because work is knowledge-based and involves employees interacting with one another and customers, many complex facets of job performance are necessary before results such as engineering designs, marketing campaigns, and products and services can be produced. Evidence of the expansion of work behaviors necessary for performance is demonstrated on an online database called O*NET.[1] Sponsored by the U.S. Department of Labor/Employment and Training Administration through a grant to the North Carolina Department of Commerce, O*NET is, perhaps, the foremost source of occupational/job information. The O*NET database contains descriptive information about 277 work and worker characteristics for 974 occupations. These data are continually updated and the number of occupations described increases at each update. Work characteristics that are measured include numerous scales of social processes, culture, and work context. For our purposes, these characteristics require many work behaviors in addition to those that are strictly task behaviors. All of these behaviors are included in job performance.

Due to this expansion of the concept of job performance, we will discuss three facets of job performance in addition to task performance: organizational citizenship, adaptive performance, and counterproductive work behaviors. Organizational citizenship behaviors (OCBs) are most often helping behaviors that one employee directs to other employees such as assisting in finishing a task, sharing knowledge that is important to the job, and contributing to discussions about solutions to job problems. Adaptive performance (AP) is, as the name implies, how an employee responds to changes in the work environment, such as shorter time for project completion, change in work procedures, or change in managers or new work group members. The third category of work performance that has been of great interest in selection over the last several years is counterproductive work behaviors (CWBs). As you can guess, these are bad, bad behaviors such as stealing, embezzlement, fighting, fraud, and sabotage. As you can also guess, companies are trying to *not choose* those applicants who do these behaviors well. Rather they are trying to *avoid* selecting those applicants who have a higher probability of engaging in these behaviors.

How Job Performance Is Measured

As we mentioned, task performance was most frequently measured by counting the number of produced items or services rendered. As work changed, other methods of measuring performance were introduced. The most used method was asking supervisors to make judgments about how well employees were performing. That is, supervisors were asked to assign a number to a worker's adequacy in such job behaviors as deadlines met, quality of service, and generating new business. In doing this, supervisors evaluated the performance of subordinates by either rating (for example, on a 1 to 5 scale) or ranking (ordering from best to worst). The use of judgments has been expanded from being done only by supervisors to include fellow workers and customers. In this chapter, we will discuss the various ways that job performance is measured.

The Type of Selection Measures That Are Used to Predict Job Performance

As the nature of jobs changed and the concept of job performance expanded, selection specialists added to the types of selection measures used for prediction. Measuring WRCs with job-knowledge tests and having applicants perform parts of the job have continued to be used. However, many additional characteristics of applicants are also measured. O*NET identifies numerous WRCs by providing four general categories of characteristics: abilities, occupational interests, work values, and work styles. Among the most important selection instruments are various measures of cognitive ability, personality traits, integrity, and judgment of the best option to pursue in specific job situations. The traditional application blank that asked applicants for superficial information regarding education, work history, and previous personal behaviors has also been updated to provide information that is clearly job- and task-related. We have six chapters that discuss each of the major types of selection measures in very detailed detail! These are very exciting chapters—at least to us.

TASK PERFORMANCE

There are two forms of task performance measures that we have previously mentioned: production data and judgmental data. We will discuss each of these.

Production Data

Production data consist of the results of work. The data comprise things that can be counted, seen, and compared directly from one worker to another. Other terms that have been used to describe these data are *output, objective*, and *nonjudgmental performance measures*. Such measures are usually based on the specific nature of the job tasks; quite different measures have been used for the same job title. The variety of measures that can be used is actually so great that it is not possible to summarize them in any representative manner. Instead, Table 2.1 contains a list of job titles and some of the various production measures that have been used for each title. It is apparent from the table that data about both quantity and quality of production have been used. Quantity is usually expressed as the number of units produced within a specified time period. Quality is the goodness of the product; it may be indirectly measured by the number of defects, errors, or mistakes identified either per number of units or per unit of time (for example, one working day).

TABLE 2.1 Examples of Production Criteria Measures for Various Jobs

	PRODUCTION MEASURE	
Job Title	**Quantity**	**Quality**
University faculty member	Number of student credit hours taught	Rating by students as to amount learned in course
Skilled machine operator	Number of units produced per week	Number of defects
	Weight of output per week	Weight of scrap
Salesperson	Dollar volume of sales	Number of customer complaints
	Number of orders	Number of returns
Manager	Profit of unit	Number of unit returns to his or her department because of defects

Many consider the use of production data the most desirable type of measure for a number of reasons. First, such data are often easy to gather because they are collected routinely for business operations such as production planning and budgeting. The importance of such measures is thought to be obvious and easily understood. Production data are the direct result of job actions. They are the objectives of the work process. Finally, these data are thought to be unchallengeable and easily accepted by workers. Production output can be seen and counted; therefore, no argument can be made about its measurement. Our opinion is that such enthusiasm about production data serving as criteria measures is overstated. None of the measures of the four major categories of work is without limitation. Each is appropriate in some circumstances and inappropriate in others. To illustrate this point, we will discuss some of the limitations inherent in the use of production data.

Consider first the argument about the ease of gathering data through commonly used business operations. Frequently, such operations are concerned with the records of total work administrative units rather than of individuals. For example, the budgeting operation usually compares a departmental unit's actual production and cost to a prior projection of these variables. Production planning is frequently concerned with the optimum movement of goods through various departments in the manufacturing process. In neither of these cases is attention paid to the individual worker, especially if he or she frequently moves to different work stations. However, data on individuals are essential for selection. A validity coefficient correlates individual workers' selection test scores with the same individuals' performance scores. Therefore, if accurate *individual* worker data cannot be gathered, then validation is difficult to carry out and interpret.

The assumption that production data are countable, and, therefore, indisputable, is also tenuous. As Table 2.1 indicates, numerous measures are used for sales performance. All seem to be straightforward measures that would be acceptable to those concerned. However, the literature and the practice of sales management contradict such a notion. The consensus in sales work is that the most often used measure of sales performance, dollar sales volume, is closely related to the characteristics of the territory that is worked. Such items as population, store density, socioeconomic status of customers, number of competitors, and amount of advertising are all relevant characteristics.

Various modifications of dollar sales volume have been suggested to control for these differences in territory. One of the most popular is to calculate monthly sales as a percentage of a quota for the territory.[2] Quotas are usually set by the sales manager. However, this assumes that the judgment of the sales manager is accurate and acceptable to all. Another adjustment is to divide sales volume by years that the salesperson has been in the territory.[3] The rationale is that as a salesperson learns the territory, sales should increase rather than merely stay level. This simplified judgment can obviously be inaccurate.

Similar issues have been raised regarding the use of production data that relate to managers. That is, managers' performance can be measured by using the amount of production yielded by their work groups. Managers are the leaders of work units and are supposed to make critical decisions that affect the group's performance. However, many other factors (for example, staffing levels across units, ability levels of subordinates, quality of machines and technology) can have a strong limiting effect on a group's performance. Managers are better evaluated with data that reflect only their job duties.

In summary, production measures have frequently been used in selection and are desirable mainly because of their direct relationship to job activities. However, these measures are often limited and often must be corrected. Most correction factors require that a manager make a judgment about how to correct the raw data, and these judgments can vary considerably in their effects on performance measurement.

Therefore, production data must be reviewed carefully to determine its accuracy as a measure of employee work performance.

Judgmental Data

In this form of the measurement of task performance, an individual familiar with the work of another is required to judge this work. This measurement is usually obtained by using a rating scale with numerical values. In most cases, the individual doing the evaluation is the immediate supervisor of the worker being evaluated. However, it should be noted that these evaluations can be done by others. Subordinates, peers, or customers are used in some judgmental evaluations.

The use of judgmental data is unavoidable in modern organizations. Many jobs such as managerial, service, professional, and staff positions no longer produce tangible, easily counted products on a regular basis—for which the use of production data would be appropriate. Almost by default, judgmental data are increasingly being used for performance measurement. In addition to availability, there are other arguments for using this type of data. The information is supplied by individuals who should know firsthand the work and the work circumstances; after appropriate initial development, the use of the judgment scales should be relatively easy and quite accurate.

Types of Judgmental Instruments

Many different types of instruments have been used to collect judgmental data. We discuss three of the most commonly used ones. All three are various forms of rating scales.

Trait Rating Scales.   (This is a bad method! Read this section and then never use it.) This method requires the supervisor to evaluate subordinates on the extent to which each individual possesses personal characteristics thought to be necessary for good work performance. The evaluation uses rating scales that contain as few as 3 points or as many as 11. The scale points are usually designated with integers that may also have attached adjectives, for example, *unsatisfactory, average, superior*, and *excellent*. The personal characteristics that are most often used in this type of measure are personality traits such as dependability, ambition, positive attitude, initiative, determination, assertiveness, and loyalty. Frequently these traits are not defined on the rating scales that evaluators are asked to use. If they are defined, this is done in terms of general behaviors rather than specific work behaviors that demonstrate the trait. As a result, the rater is being asked to do a personality assessment of the person being evaluated without adequate definition of the trait.

Even though this type of judgmental data is commonly collected in organizations, it is regarded as inappropriate by selection specialists. Trait ratings are measures of personality characteristics that have no proven relationship to performance. Moreover, the accurate assessment of such traits by a supervisor is nearly impossible. John Bernardin and Richard Beatty have summarized the common viewpoint of these scales: "If the purpose of appraisal is to evaluate *past performance*, then an evaluation of simple personality traits … hardly fits the bill…. Trait ratings are notoriously error-prone and are usually not even measured reliably."[4] Instead of traits, therefore, acceptable judgmental measures require the evaluation of work behaviors. The following two types are examples.

Simple Behavioral Scale.   (This is a better method! This scale could be used.) This type of measure is based on information about tasks determined from job analysis. The supervisor is asked to rate each subordinate on major or critical tasks of the job. For example, a manager of information systems within an organization may be evaluated by her supervisor on the task of "Maintaining software packages to process compensation system data." The number of tasks used in the evaluation differs according to the complexity of the job, but commonly the range is between 4 and 10 tasks. A supervisor scores the subordinate using a rating scale similar to that described for use with trait rating scales, that is, usually 3-point to 7-point scales using integers and adjectives. The following is an example of such a scale.

	Unsatisfactory	Average			Superior
Reviews software packages that process compensation system data.	1	2	3	4	5

Scores can be added across all task scales to produce an overall measure of job performance, or an individual task scale can be used to obtain a measure of a specific aspect of job performance. The major limitation in using this type of measure is that supervisors of the same job often disagree on what level of performance on a task is required for a specific score (for example, a score of 3 or "average"). Training the supervisors in developing common interpretations of the performance associated with each scale point should be used to address this limitation.

BARS or BES. (This is an even better method!) *Behaviorally Anchored Rating Scales (BARS)* and *Behavioral Expectation Scales (BES)* are judgmental measures developed to define the scale's rating points by using job behaviors as examples.[5] Such definitions are intended to reduce the difficulty for supervisors of consistently interpreting the performance associated with various points on the scale. Figure 2.1 presents an example of one scale representative of this approach. This example has job behavior examples for four of seven points. Many scales have job behavior examples for all scale points.

These types of scales are systematically developed by obtaining information from workers and supervisors involved with a particular job. This development starts with gathering descriptions of important, specific job behaviors that make a difference between good and poor performance. Similar behaviors are grouped into dimensions and then assigned points depending on the extent to which the job behavior is indicative of good performance. These assigned points are then used to select behaviors that serve as the scale point for rating a worker's performance on each dimension.

The main difference between BARS and BES is in the wording of the incidents. BARS incidents are worded to reflect *actual* work behaviors, for example, "greets customer as he or she approaches." BES incidents are phrased as *expected* behavior, for example, "can be expected to greet a regular customer as he or she approaches."

FIGURE 2.1	An Example of a Behavioral Expectation Scale (BES) Rating Dimension for the Job of Bartender

Dimension: Interacting with Customers

7 Employee can be expected to smile, greet a regular customer by name as she approaches, and ask how specific family members are doing.

6

5 Employee can be expected to smile and ask to be of service to the customer.

4

3 Employee can be expected to greet customer by grunting or hissing.

2

1 Employee can be expected to remain silent until customer waves money or yells loudly.

The wording difference points out to supervisors that the employee does not need to demonstrate the actual behavior of the incident to be scored at that level. The incident is to be interpreted as representative of the performance of the employee. Scores can be obtained for each dimension or summed for a total score of job performance.

360-Degree Feedback.   Another form of using judgment data for measuring performance is 360-degree feedback. This is a useful technique that is designed for evaluating managers. This method is based upon the assumption that the nature of managerial work is so complex and includes so many interpersonal relationships that ratings from only a supervisor would provide very limited information. Gathering judgmental information from all the levels of people with whom the manager works would provide more useful and more complete information about the manager's job performance. Therefore, the 360-degree feedback technique gathers judgmental performance ratings from three groups: superiors, peers, and subordinates of the individual being reviewed. Ratings of the three groups are averaged separately, which provides three scores on each scale. The ratings are interpreted by a trained evaluator who then discusses the results of the surveys (hence the term *feedback*) with the manager. All raters are guaranteed anonymity. This is a necessary feature of this method because it provides some protection from retaliatory behaviors by the person being evaluated for those who provide low ratings or negative comments. Obviously, this protection is less probable with small work groups.

Listed below are the generally agreed-upon guidelines that should be used in developing a 360 assessment system:

1. The content of items should be about the individual's skill (proficiency at performing a task), knowledge (familiarity with content of subject necessary for job such as statistical analysis), or style (a pattern of behavior used in responding to others or environmental demands, such as speed of completion of task).

2. The items should be specific job behaviors (communication of what is needed to accomplish) not personal traits (for example, warmth, motivation).

3. The ratings should be worded as the demonstrated frequency of behavior, effectiveness of behavior, or importance of behavior.

4. The rating scale should have behavioral anchors (see BARS or BES that we discussed).

5. The number of raters per group should be 7 to 10.

6. The 360 questionnaire should be administered online rather than paper-and-pencil.

7. The person being evaluated should be asked to provide names of raters; the list should be approved by a superior.

8. The raters should be given instructions on why data are collected and how the data are used; how to use the rating scale; and information that should be utilized in writing of comments.

9. A trained evaluator should provide an interpretation of the survey results to the manager.

Issues with Judgmental Scales

Skepticism of judgmental measures centers on the problem of intentional and inadvertent bias by the individual making the judgment. Intentional bias is when the rater deliberately distorts the ratings to either be favorable or unfavorable. This bias is very difficult, if not impossible, to detect. The general thinking among selection specialists, however, is that it is not a widespread problem. In many situations there are multiple raters and an extreme deviation of one rater from others would be noted. In other situations, additional performance data are available, such as deadlines met, amount of sales, and complaints of customers. Large deviations from these data would also be noted.

Inadvertent bias in responses is a more frequently found problem. Commonly called *rater error*, this bias most frequently is described in one of the following four ways: halo, leniency, severity, and central tendency. We will describe these errors from the viewpoint of a manager making ratings of a group of subordinates. *Halo* is rating the subordinate equally on different performance items because of a rater's general impression of the worker. The rater does not pay specific attention to the wording of each individual scale but rather makes the rating on the basis of the general impression. *Leniency* or *severity* occurs when a disproportionate number of workers receive either high or low ratings respectively. This bias is commonly attributed to distortion in the supervisor's viewpoint of what constitutes acceptable behavior. *Central tendency* occurs when a large number of subordinates receive ratings in the middle of the scale. Neither very good nor very poor performance is rated as often as it actually occurs.

The best way to overcome rater bias is to train supervisors to avoid these errors. Various types of programs have proven to be very effective.[6]

Another issue in using judgmental data is the extent to which it is based upon production data. If it is largely based upon these data, then the judgment data are superfluous and unnecessary because they do not provide additional information. One way of examining the relationship between these two forms of task performance is to correlate production and judgmental measures for the same group of workers. One such study found a significant, but small, correlation of 0.39 between the two.[7] This means that judgmental and production measures are not interchangeable—they probably measure different aspects of job performance. Our idea is that production measures are usually very narrow. They focus on end products, not on the behaviors that are necessary to get to end products. Judgments, especially overall job performance ratings, logically take into account a variety of actions that are part of job performance such as communication with the supervisor, interaction with customers, and punctuality at meetings. Neither measure is right or wrong. Both measure job performance, but they measure different characteristics of it. A related topic is the similarity of ratings and objective production measures as criteria for validation. Calvin Hoffman, Barry Nathan, and Lisa Holden compared the validity correlations of two objective (production quantity and production quality) and two judgmental (supervisor and self-ratings) performance measures with a cognitive ability test used as the WRC for selection. Both supervisory ratings and production quantity resulted in significant validity coefficients.[8] We can conclude that judgment ratings are appropriate as a job performance measure. They are useful in validating selection instruments.

ORGANIZATIONAL CITIZENSHIP BEHAVIORS

The second form of job performance is Organizational Citizenship Behaviors (OCBs). These are behaviors individuals do at work that are not formally part of their job task behaviors but are done by the individual to assist other workers or the organization itself. OCBs are conceptually related to two other very similar concepts: prosocial behaviors and contextual performance.[9] Our discussion will concentrate on OCBs but will also include some comments that are applicable to the other two. That is an obtuse way of saying that for our purposes of discussing these types of behaviors we will not try to separate the three concepts.

OCBs became of great interest to researchers and managers in organizations after the nature of work changed from being individualized, task activities to service and team-based knowledge and technological activities. This interest most likely was prompted by the interpersonal interactions that were important for success in these types of work and the conceptual problems that inevitably accompany knowledge-based tasks. Google may be an extreme example, but the nature of teams interacting continuously, engaging in debates and arguments, and moving to different locations frequently is symbolic of an increasing amount of current work. The following are examples of specific OCBs that have positive effects on the interrelationships among team members and the team's productivity in terms of both task quantity and quality.

- *Teaching new workers*—New members to a work team usually need to develop additional technical knowledge, social knowledge of team interactions and norms, and organizational knowledge of what is expected within the organization and its important rules, policies, and procedures. The formal training of organizations is most often limited to technical knowledge and does not address the social or organizational knowledge. Fellow workers are most frequently the source of information about these types of knowledge.

- *Assisting other workers*—Individual differences in WRCs are the conceptual basis of selection. These differences exist even among those who are selected for employment. Some individuals work faster, pay more attention to details, or solve complex problems better than others. Usually the individual differences that are important for task performance are distributed across members of the work group, not concentrated in a few. Helping others in various ways becomes a reciprocal arrangement among high functioning teams.

- *Putting extra time and effort into work*—Demands and difficulties of work vary over time. When these increase it is useful if individual workers spend more hours at work. This behavior has become rather common in many professional occupations such as executives, investment managers, sales agents, teachers, and health care workers. Those workers who put in the extra effort contribute greatly to the success of the unit.

While behaviors such as these are beneficial and often times encouraged or somehow rewarded by the organization, they are not regularly included as statements in job analysis, which as we will explain in Chapter 3, is the process used by organizations to specify the activities that comprise each job. Task activities statements are the primary components of most job descriptions and are the actions that lead to task performance.

There are several models of the various dimensions of OCBs. We will use a model specified by Philip Podsakoff and his colleagues to present the dimensions of OCBs.[10] This work discusses the following dimensions:

1. Helping behavior—most frequently involves voluntarily helping others with, or preventing the occurrence of, work-related problems; also includes peacemaking, cheerleading, facilitation, and courtesy.

2. Sportsmanship—a willingness to tolerate the inevitable inconveniences and impositions of work without complaining, also maintaining a positive attitude even when things do not go one's way, not being offended when others do not follow

suggestions, willing to sacrifice personal interest for the good of the work group, and not taking the rejection of ideas personally.

3. Organizational loyalty—consists of speaking well of others, spreading goodwill, protecting the organization, and endorsing, supporting, and defending organizational objectives. Essentially, organizational loyalty entails promoting the organization to outsiders, protecting and defending it against external threats, and remaining committed to it even under adverse conditions.

4. Organizational compliance—internalization and acceptance of the organization's rules, regulations, and procedures, which results in unfailing adherence to them. The reason that this behavior is regarded as a form of citizenship behavior is that even though everyone is expected to obey company regulations, rules, and procedures at all times, many employees do not. Therefore, an employee who regularly obeys all rules and regulations, even when no one is watching, is regarded as a "good citizen."

5. Individual initiative—engaging in task-related behaviors at a level that is consistently above expected levels. Such behaviors include acts of creativity and innovation to improve one's job or the organization's performance, persisting with extra effort to accomplish one's job, volunteering to take on extra responsibilities, and encouraging others in the organization to do the same. All of these behaviors share the idea that the employee is going "above and beyond" the call of duty.

6. Civic virtue—commitment to the organization as a whole. This is shown by a willingness to participate actively in its governance (for example, attend meetings, engage in policy debates, express one's opinion about what strategy the organization ought to follow); to monitor its environment for threats and opportunities (for example, keep up with changes in the industry that might affect the organization); and to look out for its best interests (for example, reporting fire hazards or suspicious activities, locking doors), even at personal cost. These behaviors reflect a person's recognition of being part of a larger whole in the same way that citizens are members of a country and accept the responsibilities which that entails.

7. Self-development—improving one's knowledge, skills, and abilities on one's own. This includes seeking out and taking advantage of advanced training courses, keeping track of developments in one's field and area, and learning a new set of skills so as to expand the range of one's contributions to an organization.

Another common model of OCBs that we will mention later separates OCBs into the two categories of OCBI (individual) and OCBO (organizational). The first category would generally be helping behaviors, sportsmanship, individual initiative, and self-development. The second category includes organizational loyalty, organizational compliance, and civic virtue.

What Prompts OCBs?

This question is interesting to organizations because OCBs are not usually part of an employee's job duties and are, therefore, difficult to demand that employees do. However if we know what factors lead to OCBs, there may be ways of getting employees to do OCBs by manipulating or changing these factors (tricky, huh!). Research has focused on four major categories of probable causes of OCBs: employee characteristics, task characteristics, organizational characteristics, and leadership behaviors.

Several employee characteristics have consistently been found to be linked to OCBs. An early study found strong correlations with organizational commitment, perceptions of fairness, and perceptions of leader supportiveness.[11] Personality traits such as conscientiousness, self-definition, emotional maturity, and agreeableness also have positive relationships to OCBs. Indifference to rewards is negatively related to many OCBs—meaning that if one doesn't care about receiving rewards, he will not engage in many OCBs. Because of this and similar research, it is possible to identify traits as WRCs to be measured as predictors of OCBs in selection programs. Several other characteristics such as ability, experience, training, job knowledge, organizational tenure, and gender do not seem to be related to OCBs. That gender is not related is somewhat surprising as many thought that women exhibited this more often than did males.

Some task characteristics have consistent relationships with citizenship behaviors. Task feedback and intrinsically satisfying tasks are positively related to helping behavior, sportsmanship, and civic virtue.[12] On the other hand, routine tasks, role conflict, and role ambiguity are negatively related to OCBs. Therefore, there is evidence that jobs may be able to be specified in such a way as to encourage OCBs.

Studies of organizational characteristics found that group cohesiveness, organizational justice, goal setting, organizational climate, and organizational support were positively related to multiple OCBs whereas job stress was negatively related to OCBs.[13] These are also factors that organizations can change or design to encourage OCBs.

Research in the fourth category of interest, leadership behaviors, has found that articulating a vision, providing an appropriate role model, fostering the acceptance of group goals, high performance expectations, and intellectual stimulation have positive relationships with helping, sportsmanship, and civic virtue.[14]

Relationship of OCBs with Other Performance Measures

Evidence indicates that OCBs influence managers' judgments of individual workers' overall job performance. Podsakoff and his colleagues estimated that objective task performance accounted for 9.5 percent of the variance in judgmental performance evaluations, OCBs uniquely accounted for 42.9 percent, and the combination of OCBs and objective performance accounted for a total of 61.2 percent.[15] This suggests that OCBs account for substantially more variance in judgmental performance evaluations than does objective performance. A possible interpretation of this finding is that a leader's specified goals, rules, and policies may result in objective performance being relatively the same among workers. They all know how much they should produce. However, because OCBs are not usually included in goals and procedures, workers vary to a large extent in these behaviors. Because supervisors benefit from OCBs (generally OCBs reduce the supervisor's work load), they perceive that workers who demonstrate OCBs are better workers and contribute more to the productivity of the work group. Helping, sportsmanship, civic virtue, and individual initiative were the specific dimensions that accounted for the effects of OCBs in performance reviews.

Early research found that OCBs are positively related to measures of organizational effectiveness such as quantity of performance, quality of performance, financial efficiency (for example, operating efficiency), and customer service.[16] More recent research has indicated that the relationship between OCBs and organizational performance is complex. For example, one study found that OCBs were more strongly related to work unit performance in those units with decentralized, interactive decision making than in those that were more centralized.[17] In another example, the relationship between OCBIs and job performance was stronger in work units in which workers had discretion in carrying out their job tasks than in units in which that was not the case.[18]

Another indication of the complexity between OCBs and performance is that there is evidence that the use of OCBs may also have negative as well as positive outcomes to individuals. Diane Bergeron and her associates found that in organizations with outcome-based control systems (relying primarily on objective task performance to measure performance), time spent on OCBs had a cost. In such an organization, time spent on task performance was more important than OCBs in determining performance evaluation results, salary increases, career advancement speed, and promotions. Even when time spent on task performance was statistically controlled, employees who spent more time on OCBs had lower salary increases and advanced more slowly than employees who spent less time on OCBs.[19] Related to this research is a finding that there may be a curvilinear relationship between task performance and the amount of OCBs performed by an individual. That is, the two increased together until OCBs became very frequent and task performance then began to decrease. This was especially true when the OCBs were directed toward the organization (OCBO). These findings indicate that individuals can spend too much time on OCBs, thereby reducing the time available for task performance.[20]

Measurement of OCBs

Because OCBs are not job tasks, there are no measures that are usually gathered by organizations for measuring performance that would score individual workers on the frequency or quality of the OCBs that the person has performed. So, as you can guess, if there is nothing to count, the way of measuring OCBs is through judgmental scales. Early research about OCBs used self-report judgmental scales. In these scales, the worker responds to questions about how often she does the OCB action stated in the item. Table 2.2 contains examples of behaviors that make up OCB questionnaires. In other research, supervisors and/or other work group members made the ratings about OCBs for individual workers. There are arguments pro and con each source of ratings. The arguments concerning individual ratings are: because OCBs are not job tasks, they are usually not observed by many others so the individual may be the only one who actually knows how often he does these behaviors. However, because the questions used to measure OCBs are usually transparent as to what is good, a worker may deliberately rate herself very high on these behaviors. For example, for items such as, "How often have you helped others who have missed work time?" there would be a temptation (not for honest you, of course, but for others) to simply respond with the highest, most desirable response possible. Why look anything less than excellent? The arguments concerning supervisor or other-worker ratings are the

---

TABLE 2.2   Behaviors Commonly Used in OCB Scales*

1. Help others who have missed work
2. Give time to help others who have work-related problems
3. Adjust own work schedule to accommodate others' request for time off
4. Make new employees feel welcome
5. Express concern and courtesy toward coworkers even under trying times
6. Express loyalty to the organization
7. Defend organization when others criticize it
8. Offer ideas to improve the functioning of the organization
9. Attend functions that are not required but help the organization's image

*Based on Kibeom Lee and Natalie J. Allen, "Organizational Citizenship Behavior and Workplace Deviance: The Role of Affect and Cognitions," *Journal of Applied Psychology* 87 (2002): 131–142.

reverse of these points. The supervisor or other worker would usually have no reason to inflate the ratings of OCBs in others. However, they may also not have had adequate opportunities to observe these behaviors.

One study has addressed the question of differences between self-ratings and those made by others.[21] The findings were that there were not many differences between the two sources. First, the difference in means of OCB ratings is actually quite small between self- and other-raters. Second, analysis showed that self- and other-ratings are correlated and that self-ratings and supervisor ratings were also. Third, self-rated and other-rated OCB correlations with other variables indicated that while self-rated and other-rated OCBs have similar patterns of relationships with other variables, other-rated OCBs generally do not provide additional explanation of the relationship of OCBs with the variables. The researchers concluded that self-ratings may be the preferred source of ratings. Most, if not all, of the studies in this research were also research studies in which the performance ratings of OCBs did not affect the compensation or promotion possibilities of the workers. If OCBs are to be used for such decisions in the same manner as task performance data are, more study should be given to these patterns between self and other ratings of OCBs. Many think that workers who supply self-ratings may distort their ratings to gain advantage in salary and advancement.

ADAPTIVE PERFORMANCE

The third form of job performance is Adaptive Performance (AP). These behaviors are important for current organizations to remain competitive in an ever changing environment. We know quite a bit about AP including some WRCs that seem to be significantly related to them. However, there is only limited use of this form of performance being used in selection programs. Our best guess is that the inclusion of both OCBs and AP as parts of job performance should begin in the near future. You should view these two concepts as your opportunity to champion the "next best thing" and make yourself into a SELECTION HERO. We will obviously take credit for your success and want a large percentage of whatever riches being a SELECTION HERO may bring you.

Based upon the work of Elaine Pulakos and her colleagues, we define AP as a deliberate change in the thinking or behavior of an individual because of an anticipated or existing change in the work activities or work environment.[22] Change can include new individuals or groups of people, change in work activities or technology, organizational structure or systems change, or market place changes that affect the work of the individual. Almost all employees are aware that change will occur and that they will be required to change future job activities. However, just because almost all people are aware of change does not mean that all respond equally to it. Differences in WRCs can be used to predict differences in AP. The field of selection is at the stage that it has accepted that both OCBs and AP are facets of job performance and can be included in operational selection programs. However, we need to know more about how to most effectively measure these dimensions in HR performance review systems and which WRCs are significantly related to these dimensions. The field is currently in that work.

Perhaps the most complete taxonomy of the different types of AP is part of the work of Pulakos and her colleagues that is represented in Table 2.3.[23] This taxonomy was developed after extensive work with three large samples of workers from federal and state governments and the military. The first stage was collecting more than 9,000 critical work incidents from individuals who worked on 16 different jobs. The researchers reviewed these incidents taking out redundancies and choosing those that fit the definition of AP. This left more than 1,300 statements that were sorted into eight categories. In the second

TABLE 2.3	Dimensions of Adaptive Behavior*

Dimension	Definition
Handling emergencies or crisis situations	Reacting with appropriate and proper urgency in dangerous or emergency situations, quickly analyzing options for dealing with crises and their implications; making split-second decisions based on clear and focused thinking; maintaining emotional control and objectivity while keeping focused on the situation at hand.
Handling work stress	Remaining composed and cool when faced with difficult circumstances or a highly demanding workload or schedule: not overreacting to unexpected news or situations; managing frustration well by directing effort to constructive solutions rather than blaming others; demonstrating resilience and the highest levels of professionalism in stressful circumstances.
Solving problems creatively	Employing unique types of analyses and generating new, innovative ideas in complex areas; turning problems upside-down and inside-out to find fresh, new approaches; integrating seemingly unrelated information and developing creative solutions; entertaining wide-ranging possibilities others may miss; thinking outside the given parameters to see if there is a more effective approach.
Dealing with uncertain and unpredictable work situations	Taking effective action when necessary without having to know the total picture or have all the facts at hand: readily and easily changing gears in response to unpredictable or unexpected events and circumstances; effectively adjusting plans, goals, actions, or priorities to deal with changing situations; imposing structure for self and others that provides as much focus as possible in dynamic situations.
Learning work tasks, technologies, and procedures	Demonstrating enthusiasm for learning new approaches and technologies for conducting work; doing what is necessary to keep knowledge and skills current; quickly and proficiently learning new methods or how to perform previously unlearned tasks; adjusting to new work processes and procedures; anticipating changes in the work demands and searching for and participating in assignments or training that will prepare self for these changes.
Demonstrating interpersonal adaptability	Being flexible and open-minded when dealing with others; listening to and considering others' viewpoints and opinions and altering own opinion when it is appropriate to do so; being open and accepting of negative or developmental feedback regarding work; working well and developing effective relationships with highly diverse personalities; demonstrating keen insight of others' behavior.
Demonstrating cultural adaptability	Taking action to learn about and understand the climate, orientation, needs, and values of other groups, organizations, or cultures; integrating well into and being comfortable with different values, customs, and cultures; willingly adjusting behavior or appearance as necessary to comply with or show respect for others' values and customs; understanding the implications of one's actions.
Demonstrating physically oriented adaptability	Adjusting to challenging environmental states such as extreme heat, humidity, cold, or dirtiness; frequently pushing self physically to complete strenuous or demanding tasks; adjusting weight and muscular strength or becoming proficient in performing physical tasks as necessary for the job.

*Taken from Elaine D. Pulakos, Sharon Arad, Michelle A. Donovan, and Kevin E. Plamondon, "Adaptability in the Workplace: Development of A Taxonomy of Adaptive Performance," *Journal of Applied Psychology* 85 (2000): 612–624.

stage, the researchers used various survey construction techniques to determine 132 incidents that measured the eight dimensions with 15 to 18 incidents per dimension. This resulting survey was administered to another group of 175 respondents and further analyses were completed. The researchers then selected 68 items for the survey with each dimension having eight or nine items. This version of the survey was then given to 3,422 workers. Analyses of these responses resulted in the *Job Adaptability Inventory* (JAI), which is the most complete measuring instrument for AP at this time.

Most of the research work using AP in selection has concentrated on determining WRCs that would predict AP. Quite a few possible WRCs have been identified. One group is various types of cognitive abilities, examples of which are listed below.

- Cognitive complexity—to consider and integrate conflicting information.

- Frame changing—to alternate between multiple ways of attending to and interpreting problems and solution strategies.

- Resiliency—to persist and recover quickly.

- Problem solving—to persist and work through the details of a problem.

- Learning agility—to apply lessons learned from previous experience.

Another group of possible predictors is the Big 5 personality dimensions: conscientiousness, extraversion, openness to experience, stability, and agreeableness. A third group is interpersonal predictors such as cooperativeness, sociability, and social intelligence. A last group is physical abilities specifically for the dimension of physically oriented adaptability, such as stamina, strength, endurance, and agility. This research has provided evidence that each dimension of AP would most likely have a different combination of WRCs. Elaine Pulakos conducted a validation study of predicting AP using several of the predictors mentioned previously.[24] In this study, 789 respondents completed instruments to measure three types of WRCs. One set of these instruments was three questionnaires that measured respondents' previous adaptability experience. The first was 80 items that were similar to the JAI and asked respondents to rate the frequency of their experiences engaging in behaviors relevant to each of the eight AP dimensions of the JAI. The second measure provided an assessment of the respondents' interest in working in situations that demanded the types of adaptability represented in the eight dimensions. The last measure asked respondents to indicate their effectiveness in adapting in ways that are relevant to each of the eight dimensions. In addition, three personality measures were used: openness to experience, emotional stability, and achievement motivation. Finally a cognitive ability measure was added. The performance measures for this study were two questionnaires completed by supervisors that rated the demonstrated AP behaviors of the respondents in their jobs. Results indicated that the scales measuring both previous experience engaging in adaptability behaviors and interest in working in situations that demanded adaptability were significantly correlated to performance ratings. The cognitive ability scale as well as the personality measures of openness and achievement motivation were also significantly related to adaptability performance. The researchers concluded that all of these could be used as predictors of AP.

Other research has supported the contention that AP is linked to various other positive performance outcomes. One study found that AP was related to task performance for call center employees.[25] Another study found that adaptive skill uniquely contributed to overall performance of military leaders.[26] Other studies found a positive relationship between adaptive selling performance and sales performance.[27]

Taken together, this work means that there is a viable measure of AP that could be used by supervisors to rate the performance of subordinates. Also measures of past experience, interest, personality, and cognitive ability could be used as selection instruments.

COUNTERPRODUCTIVE WORK BEHAVIOR

The last type of performance that we will discuss is counterproductive work behavior (CWB). As the name implies, these are undesirable performance actions that harm the organization itself and often its employees and customers. A whole industry is devoted to developing, marketing, and selling selection tests, referred to as integrity tests, to organizations that will identify applicants that have a higher than normal probability of committing CWBs. Naturally, applicants identified will not be selected by the organization for employment. Chapter 14 is devoted to this topic so we will try to build intellectual tension for that chapter by teasing you with an overview of this type of performance. Don't spoil it by reading ahead!

Counterproductive work behavior is any intentional behavior by an organization member viewed by the organization as contrary to its legitimate interests. Behaviors such as stealing, punching a manager, and destroying property are the most commonly thought of as CWBs. CWBs often are linked to loss of property, money, reputation, customers, and suppliers and therefore are damaging and costly to the organization. There have been various estimates at how much cost organizations incur because of CWBs. Usually these estimates are billions of dollars. However as you can imagine, these estimates are based on many assumptions and incomplete data. For example, it is difficult to determine how much money is stolen from organizations by employees in a year. Employees are not going to volunteer such data. The employees who are caught stealing are simply one part of those stealing. Frequently estimates of stealing are based on company calculations of what volume of revenue was expected from a given amount of input such as customers or materials. Many companies do not make such estimates and others do not use a standard procedure for making the calculation. Despite these limitations, there is enough data to indicate that CWBs are indeed very costly. We just do not know exactly how many billions are lost. These losses have many effects on organizations. To make up for the losses, more revenue must be generated, which increases the work of employees. In addition, employees are terminated to reduce costs, cheaper materials are used as input, maintenance and safety corrections are postponed, and so on.

There are many proposed ways of grouping or classifying CWBs. Such grouping may lead to different ways of predicting, preventing, or counteracting various behaviors or groups of behaviors. Table 2.4 presents one such grouping.

You can see that the list could apply to some very common, fairly small behaviors such as making personal calls, excessive socializing with coworkers during the business

TABLE 2.4	**Counterproductive Work Behaviors**
Name	**Examples**
Theft	Taking cash or property, giving away goods or services, misuse of employee discount
Destruction of property	Defacing, damaging, or destroying property; sabotaging production
Misuse of information	Revealing confidential information; falsifying records
Misuse of time and resources	Wasting time, altering time card, conducting personal business during work time
Unsafe behavior	Failure to follow safety procedures, failure to learn safety procedures
Poor attendance	Unexcused absence or tardiness; misusing sick leave
Poor quality work	Intentionally slow or sloppy work
Alcohol use	Alcohol use on the job; coming to work under the influence of alcohol
Inappropriate verbal actions	Arguing with customers, verbally harassing coworkers
Inappropriate physical actions	Physically attacking coworkers, physical sexual advances toward coworker

Source: Paul R. Sackett, "The Structure of Counterproductive Work Behaviors: Dimensionality and Relationships with Facets of Job Performance," *International Journal of Selection and Assessment* 10 (2002): 5–11.

day, being late for work, or taking too much time for lunch. Companies vary considerably in their rules for such behavior. Often there are distinctions made between salaried and hourly workers in rules concerning these behaviors. Usually hourly employees have strict rules and could lose some part of their wages for violations whereas salaried employees are generally exempt from such rules. Having such a distinction could be a problem in itself and certainly limits any calculation as to how much time is lost and the cost of the lost time.

There have been many attempts to determine whether or not CWB can be classified into fewer groups or dimensions. The reason for this is if there are fewer, homogeneous groups of CWB, it may be easier to study and treat these deviant acts than if each group is regarded as a distinct type of behavior. That is, further grouping may be useful for the development of better theories of what prompts various types of CWB and how to prevent them. One such grouping is to divide CWBs into two groups: actions of deviance toward individuals (ID) and actions toward the organization (OD). For example, from the list in Table 2.4, ID items would include inappropriate verbal or physical action and usually alcohol and drug use and unsafe behavior. OD items are the majority of CWBs including such actions as theft; destruction of property; misuse of information, time, or resources; poor attendance; and poor quality work. Christopher Berry and his colleagues tried to determine if this two-group classification of CWB was correct. In doing so, they analyzed the results of 31 research studies that examined various kinds of CWB and variables related to the CWBs in the study. They concluded that while ID and OD scales were relatively highly correlated with each other and had similar relationships with many variables, they also had differential relationships with personality and other variables such as OCBs. Therefore the preponderance of evidence supports separate ID and OD dimensions.[28]

There has also been interest in examining the relationship between OCBs and CWBs. Some thought that these two forms of job performance were different ends of the same general behavior. Others thought the two were different behaviors. The question is important due to its implications for research about and the understanding of the two types of performance. If they were different ends of the same behavior, one theory of what prompts the behavior may explain both and lead to strategies for encouraging OCBs and discouraging CWBs. If they are different behaviors, at least two separate theories would be in order. Research has consistently found that OCBs and CWBs were moderately negatively correlated and had a number of different personality correlates. These findings lend support to OCB and CWB representing two distinct constructs rather than a single continuum.[29]

Related to the study of the relationship between OCBs and CWBs is research that examines the relationship of CWBs to individual and organizational characteristics. Knowledge of individual characteristics that are related can help develop selection programs and knowledge of organizational characteristics could assist in restructuring work activities, policies and rules, and interaction patterns that may eliminate causes of CWBs. One interesting study included 3,021 individuals applying for police officer jobs at 143 different agencies across several states in the United States. Various police agencies had preselected these individuals as promising applicants who were to undergo further psychological screening before receiving a job offer. The data used in this study were collected as part of this standardized psychological evaluation. Thus, all applicants underwent the same assessment procedure. Of the total applicants, 1,799 were hired and remained on the job long enough that CWB data could be obtained. These data were objectively measurable and quantifiable behaviors obtained from organizational records. For example, records on the number of citizen complaints formally filed against an officer or involvement in an at-fault car accident were in the files. These CWB data were grouped and correlated with cognitive ability scores that were part of the selection battery. The researchers found that the correlation between the two was significant and negative meaning that cognitive ability inversely predicted the extent to which individuals engaged in CWB. Additionally, the researchers classified the recorded CWBs into ID and OD categories and correlated these two scores. Results showed that while these two dimensions of CWB are clearly distinguishable using objective criterion data, individuals who engage in one kind of CWB also tend to engage in the other.[30]

Other studies have found relationships between CWBs and personality and job satisfaction[31] and also work stresses.[32] Self-control of emotions and actions has also been linked to CWBs.[33]

Two measurement methods are used to collect data about CWBs. One is the way that was described in the previous research using police force applicants, that is, written records are made by supervisors of behaviors that the employee has done. These records are then reviewed and a score is calculated depending on the number of CWBs that are written. This type of data is rare, as most organizations do not require supervisors to record such behaviors whenever they occur. Therefore as in collecting OCB data, the most commonly used method for collecting CWB data is judgmental surveys. Not surprisingly, the same issues apply to CWB surveys as we mentioned with OCB surveys. Employees usually do not want to implicate themselves by admitting that they have engaged in actions such as theft, wasting time, or confronting other employees. So supervisors and coworkers are asked to complete the surveys. Christopher Berry and others compared self-completed survey responses with those completed by supervisors and coworkers. They found that self- and other-ratings were moderately to strongly correlated with each other. Second, with some notable exceptions, self- and other-reports exhibited very similar patterns and magnitudes of relationships with a set of common variables such as personality, OCBs, and organizational justice measures. Third, self-raters reported engaging in more CWB than other-raters reported them engaging in it. Because others see only some of the behavior of those around them, other-ratings capture a narrower subset of CWBs. Although many have viewed self-reports of CWB with skepticism, the results of this meta-analysis support their use in most CWB research as a viable alternative to other-reports.[34] As we mentioned with OCBs, there is little evidence about how well self-report CWB data would work in performance evaluation measures that are frequently used for selection studies.

APPROPRIATE CHARACTERISTICS OF JOB PERFORMANCE MEASURES

We have discussed four types of job performance and some of the measures that have been used for each. In this section we will describe characteristics of performance measures that should be present to make the information collected with the measure useful— meaning that it yields data that accurately summarize an employee's performance. In many cases these characteristics are a function of the way that the measure is designed and implemented.

Individualization

The measure must collect data about performance that the individual controls. This seems logical but many work situations create job performance outputs that violate this principle. For example, team or group tasks are becoming increasingly popular. Even traditional manufacturing operations have formed groups of 10 to 12 workers who are assigned all operations necessary for completion of the product. Workers are interchangeable and move unsystematically from work station to work station. It would not be appropriate to use the number of items produced as a criterion measure for selection. Such a number would not measure the distinct performance of an individual and therefore is not appropriate for correlation with individual selection instrument scores. Another example is that it is common to evaluate branch managers' performance for financial service institutions partially on the basis of profits generated by the branch. Offhand this seems accurate, because profits are of central importance to financial institutions and branch managers are commonly assumed to be the chief executive of the unit and in charge of operations. But this assumption often does not hold. Interest rates for deposits are set by the highest level of management. Loans are often controlled by standard policy. Loans over a certain amount must be approved by others, and guidelines concerning loan evaluation are used for smaller loans. Other items, such as size and salary of staff are dictated by company headquarters. Many factors that greatly affect the profits of the branch are not determined by the branch manager.

Relevance

Selection is designed to contribute to the productivity of the organization. Individuals are employed primarily to perform well on the critical or important parts of a job. It is these parts, therefore, that should be included in job performance measures. Sometimes this principle is overlooked because other job performance measures are easy to obtain. For example, promptness and attendance usually are easily obtainable records. However, in many jobs such attendance is not a critical dimension of performance. This is commonly the case for managers and professionals in an organization in which little attention is paid to coming and going, or to the use of company time for doctor visits. Such events are irrelevant as long as "the work gets done." Our point is that this may also be true of other jobs for which attendance records are carefully kept. Therefore, these records are not appropriate criteria measures.

Measurability

It must be possible to generate a number that represents the amount or quality of the work performed. This can often be difficult. For example, a regional sales manager may be in charge of advertising for the region. Ultimately, the purpose of advertising is to increase sales. However, this end may not be achieved for a long period of time. This creates a problem. What should be measured in the meantime in place of sales that will measure the effectiveness of the advertising? In many cases, some associated measure is obtained. For example, a judgment is made about the quality of the advertising campaign based on its correspondence to accepted standards of advertising. This judgment becomes the job performance measure. Whatever is used must be logically and closely related to what is done on the job.

Variance

The scores that are generated must have differences among them. It is conceptually useless and statistically difficult to make sense out of numbers in which there is little, if any, difference in performance levels. If every worker performs at the same level, the differences in WRCs make no difference in performance levels. This lack of variance can be caused by two factors: (a) standardization in output due to work process, or (b) inappropriate use of the measurement device. Output for machine-paced manufacturing is an example of the former. If an assembly line is set to move continuously at a certain speed, all workers should produce the same output. The latter case is often demonstrated in supervisors' judgments of subordinates. At one time, the military experienced severe problems with its appraisal forms. Theoretically, 100 scale points were to be used for rating, with a score of 70 being designated as average performance. In practice, however, the great majority of personnel were rated between 90 and 100 to ensure their chances for promotion. The same problem has been repeated in other situations in which a supervisor thinks that all the subordinates are exceptionally good workers.

USE OF CRITERIA FOR VALIDATION

Single versus Multiple Criteria

One of the most perplexing issues for selection specialists involved in validation is how to decide on the number of measures of job performance to use. This issue is commonly referred to as the choice between single or multiple criteria. In validation, the use of a single measure of job performance translates into viewing it as overall or global performance. The argument for using a single performance measure in validation is partially based on the fact that validation procedures become more straightforward with one criterion. This makes both the interpretation of the findings and the judgment about the adequacy of the selection program relatively simple.

The argument for the use of multiple criteria measures is made on the basis of research findings and logic. Essentially, this argument starts with the fact that job analysis studies identify multiple tasks within jobs. Multiple tasks are indicative of the multiple aspects of job performance. Also, studies of job performance have concluded that a global measure of performance may not reflect all of the job activities even for simple entry-level jobs.[35] One example of this diversity of performance within jobs can be found in Project A, which identified multiple components of performance for 19 entry-level army jobs. John Campbell, Jeffrey McHenry, and Lauress Wise utilized multiple job analysis methods to yield more than 200 performance indicators, which were further reduced to 32 performance scores for each job.[36] The same argument can be made for other types of jobs, such as manufacturing operations, in which days present and lack of defective assembly items are, at the minimum, thought to be important. Even in typing and stenography jobs, the importance of both speed and accuracy serving as performance measures is obvious.

When to Use Each

Wayne Cascio has presented a straightforward solution to the dilemma, and the following discussion reflects his writings.[37] Cascio has made the distinction between using job performance measures to assist in managerial decision making and using them to serve research purposes. In most cases, a validity study is done to identify a set of selection devices that assist in managerial decision making. That is, the applicants' scores on the selection devices are used in making decisions about to whom to extend job offers. In these cases a composite criterion would generally be used. Managers are essentially interested in selecting individuals who, all things considered, perform well in an overall manner. The use of the composite criterion reflects this thinking.

When a validity study is done for research purposes, we may wish to study the relationship between specific mental abilities (mathematical reasoning, spatial visualization, and so on) and different parts of a research engineering job (development of research plans, preparation of technical reports, and so on). In such a case, the major emphasis is on linking a specific mental ability to each subpart of the job. Such information could later be used in selection, training, and career development work. It would therefore be appropriate to use multiple criteria and to validate the mental ability tests against each separate measure of job performance.

Forming the Single Measure

If a composite measure is desired, the immediate problem is how to combine the different measures into one. Essentially, three methods are used for doing this: dollar criterion, factor analysis, or expert judgment.

Dollar Criterion

The first method, which Cascio points out is the logical basis of combination, is to develop a composite that represents economic worth to the organization. This entails expressing the various job performance measures that we have discussed as a monetary amount that represents the value of worker performance to the organization. Put simply, the main purpose of selection is to improve the economic position of the firm through better workers, who are identified through a valid selection program. Expressing job performance in dollars would be a direct reflection of this thinking.

This line of reasoning was first expressed many years ago by Hubert Brogden and Erwin Taylor, who developed the dollar criterion.[38] In the years after this first work, refinements have been made in how to practically estimate the monetary worth of job performance. These refinements are part of the general topic of utility analysis. Without going through a detailed description of this topic, at least three major methods are used to determine this dollar value of job performance. One method requires that job experts estimate the monetary value of various levels of job performance.[39] A second method assumes that the dollar value of job performance is a direct function of yearly salary.[40] The third method also uses employee salary but partitions this among a job's activities, so that each activity is assigned a proportion of that salary in accord with the job analysis results.[41]

Factor Analysis

The second method of combining separate criteria measures into one composite relies on statistical correlational analysis. In this approach, all individual criteria measures are correlated with one another. The intercorrelation matrix is factor analyzed; this, statistically, combines these separate measures into clusters, or factors. Ideally, a majority of the separate measures would be combined into one factor that would then serve as the composite performance measure. The factor analysis procedure also provides weights that could be applied to each specific measure in forming the composite.

Expert Judgment

A third method uses judgments of job experts to form the composite. Essentially, the problem for these judges is to identify the relative weights of the specific performance aspects. For example, let us assume that the job of laboratory technician has five components we wish to combine. The role of the job experts is to specify the numerical value that each component should be multiplied by to derive the overall performance score. This weighting should reflect the importance of each of the five components with regard to overall performance. If all five components are regarded as equally important, then all five parts carry a weight of "1" and are directly added. If the five components are thought to be unequal in importance, there are, at that point, two different procedures that are often used to determine the appropriate weights. Under the first procedure, each judge is given 100 points and asked to divide them among the five parts. The weight for each part is the average number of points assigned to it by the judges. The second procedure asks each judge to assign a value of 1.0 to the most unimportant part. The number assigned to each of the other four is to represent how many times more important each part is to this least important one. The weight is again the average of these values. Both procedures assume reliability among the judges—in deciding the order of the five parts as well as in determining the relative importance among them. This means that if the judges do not closely agree on which components are unimportant and which are very important, the computed averages are conceptually meaningless and ought not to be used.

REFERENCES

1. http://www.onetonline.org/

2. William W. Ronan and Erich P. Prien, *Perspectives on the Measurement of Human Performance* (New York: Appleton-Century-Crofts, 1971), 73.

3. Ibid., 94.

4. H. John Bernardin and Richard W. Beatty, *Performance Appraisal: Assessing Human Behavior at Work* (Boston: West Publishing Co., 1984).

5. Gary P. Latham and Kenneth N. Wexley, *Increasing Productivity through Performance Appraisal* (Reading, MA: Addison-Wesley Publishing Co., 1982), 51–55.

6. Gary P. Latham, Kenneth N. Wexley, and Elliott Pursell, "Training Managers to Minimize Rating Errors in the Observation of Behavior," *Journal of Applied Psychology* 60 (1975): 550–555. See also Elaine Pulakos, "A Comparison of Rater Training Programs: Error Training and Accuracy Training," *Journal of Applied Psychology* 69 (1984): 581–588. See also Charles H. Fay and Gary P. Latham, "The Effects of Training and Rating Scales on Rating Errors," *Personnel Psychology* 35 (1982): 105–116.

7. William H. Bommer, Jonathan L. Johnson, Gregory A. Rich, Philip M. Podsakoff, and Scott B. Mackenzie, "On the Interchangeability of Objective and Subjective Measures of Employee Performance: A Meta-Analysis," *Personnel Psychology* 48 (1995): 587–605.

8. Calvin C. Hoffman, Barry R. Nathan, and Lisa M. Holden, "A Comparison of Validation Criteria: Objective versus Subjective Performance Measures and Self versus Supervisor Ratings," *Personnel Psychology* 44 (1991): 601–619.

9. Arthur P. Brief and Stephan J. Motowidlo, "Prosocial Organizational Behaviors," *Academy of Management Review* 11 (1986): 710–725; see also Walter C. Borman and Stephan J. Motowidlo, "Task Performance and Contextual Performance: The Meaning for Personnel Selection Research," *Human Performance* 10 (1997): 99–109.

10. Philip M. Podsakoff, Scott B. MacKenzie, Julie Beth Paine, and Daniel G. Bachrach, "Organizational Citizenship Behaviors: A Critical Review of the Theoretical and Empirical Literature and Suggestions for Future Research," *Journal of Management* 26 (2000): 513–563.

11. Dennis Organ and Katherine Ryan, "A Meta-Analytic Review of Attitudinal and Dispositional Predictors of Organizational Citizenship Behaviors," *Personnel Psychology* 48 (1995): 775–802.

12. Philip M. Podsakoff and Scott B. MacKenzie, "An Examination of Substitutes for Leadership Within a Levels-of-Analysis Framework," *Leadership Quarterly* 6 (1995): 289–328. Philip M. Podsakoff, Scott B. MacKenzie, and W. H. Bommer, "A Meta-Analysis of the Relationships Between Kerr and Jermier's Substitutes for Leadership and Employee Job Attitudes, Role Perceptions, and Performance," *Journal of Applied Psychology* 81 (1996): 380–399. Philip M. Podsakoff, Brian P. Niefoff, Scott B. MacKenzie, and M. Lawrence Williams, "Do Substitutes for Leadership Really Substitute for Leadership? An Empirical Examination of Kerr and Jermier's Situational Leadership Model," *Organizational Behavior and Human Decision Processes* 54 (1993): 1–44.

13. Lieven Brebels, David De Cremer, and Maius Van Dijke, "Using Self-Definition to Predict the Influence of Procedural Justice on Organizational-, Interpersonal-, and Job/Task Oriented Citizenship Behavior," *Journal of Management* 40 (2014): 731–763; see also Mark A. Kizilos, Chailin Cummings, and Thomas G. Cummings, "How High-Involvement Work Processes Increase Organizational Performance: The Role of Organizational Citizenship Behavior," *Journal of Applied Behavioral Science* 49 (2013): 413–436.

14. Min Z. Carter, Kevin W. Mossholder, Hubert S. Field, and Achilles A. Armenakis, "Transformational Leadership, Interactional Justice and Organizational Citizenship Behaviors: The Effects of Racial and Gender Dissimilarity Between Supervisors and Subordinates," *Group and Organizational Management* 39 (2014): 691–719. See also Podsakoff, MacKenzie, Paine, and Bachrach, "Organizational Citizenship Behaviors: A Critical Review of the Theoretical and Empirical Literature and Suggestions for Future Research," 513–561.

15. Podsakoff et al., *Journal of Management* 26 (2000): 513–563.

16. Philip. M. Podsakoff and Scott B. MacKenzie, "Organizational Citizenship Behaviors and Sales Unit Effectiveness," *Journal of Marketing Research* 3 (1994): 351–363. Philip M. Podsakoff, Michael Ahearne, and Scott B. MacKenzie, "Organizational Citizenship Behavior and the Quantity and Quality of Work Group Performance," *Journal of Applied Psychology* 82 (1997): 260–270; Sandra M. Walz and Brian P. Niehoff, "Organizational Citizenship Behaviors and Their Effect on Organizational Effectiveness in Limited-Menu Restaurants," in J. Bernard Keys and Lloyd N. Dosier (Eds.), *Academy of Management Best Papers Proceedings* (1996): 307–311.

17. Kizilos, Cummings, and Cummings, "How High-Involvement Work Processes Increase Organization Performance."

18. Muammer Ozer, "A Moderated Mediation Model of the Relationship Between Organizational Citizenship Behaviors and Job Performance," *Journal of Applied Psychology* 96 (2011): 1328–1336.

19. Diane M. Bergeron, Abbie J. Shipp, Benson Rosen, and Stacie A. Furst, "Organizational Citizenship Behavior and Career Outcomes: The Cost of Being a Good Citizen," *Journal of Management* 39 (2013): 958–984.

20. Robert S. Rubin, Erich C. Dierdorff, and Daniel G. Bachrach, "Boundaries of Citizenship Behavior: Curvilinearity and Context in the Citizenship and Task Performance Relationship," *Personnel Psychology* 66 (2013): 377–406.

21. Nichelle C. Carpenter, Christopher M. Berry, and Lawrence Houston, "A Meta-Analytic Comparison of Self-Reported and Other-Reported Organizational Citizenship Behavior," *Journal of Organizational Behavior* 35 (2014): 547–574.

22. Elaine D. Pulakos, Rose A. Mueller-Hanson, and Johnathon K. Nelson, "Adaptive Performance and Trainability As Criteria in Selection Research," *2012 Oxford Handbook of Personnel Assessment and Selection*, Ed. Neil Schmidt (New York: Oxford Press, 2012), 595–613.

23. Elaine D. Pulakos, Sharon Arad, Michelle A. Donovan, and Kevin E. Plamondon, "Adaptability in the Workplace: Development of A Taxonomy of Adaptive Performance," *Journal of Applied Psychology* 85 (2000): 612–624.

24. Elaine D. Pulakos, Neal Schmitt, David W. Dorsey, Sharon Arad, Jerry W. Hedge, and Walter C. Borman, "Predicting Adaptive Performance: Further Tests of A Model of Adaptability," *Human Performance* 15 (2002): 299–324.

25. Mindy K. Shos, L. A. Witt, and Dusya Vera, "When Does Adaptive Performance Lead to Higher Task Performance?" *Journal of Organizational Behavior* 33 (2012): 910–924.

26. Jennifer S. Tucker, Robert J. Pleban, and Katie M. Gunther, "The Mediating Effects of Adaptive Skill on Values-Performance Relationships," *Human Performance* 23 (2010): 81–99.

27. Ralph W. Giacobbe, Donald W. Jackson Jr., Lawrence A Crosby, and Claudia M. Bridges, "A Contingency Approach to Adaptive Selling Behavior and Sales Performance: Selling Situations and Salesperson Characteristics," *Journal of Personal Selling & Sales Management* 26 (2006): 115–142; see also Gilad Chen, Brian Thomas, and J. Craig Wallace, "A Multilevel Examination of the Relationships Among Training Outcomes, Mediating Regulatory Processes, and Adaptive Performance," *Journal of Applied Psychology*, vol. 90(5), (2005): 827–841.

28. Christopher M. Berry, Deniz S. Ones, and Paul R. Sackett, "Interpersonal Deviance, Organizational Deviance, and Their Common Correlates: A Review and Meta-Analysis," *Journal of Applied Psychology* 92 (2007): 410–424. See also Melissa L. Gruys and Paul R. Sackett, "Investigating the Dimensionality of Counterproductive Work Behavior," *International Journal of Selection and Assessment* 11 (2003): 30–42.

29. Paul R. Sackett, Christopher M. Berry, Shelly A. Wiemann, and Roxanne M. Laczo, "Citizenship and Counterproductive Behavior: Clarifying Relations Between the Two Domains," *Human Performance* 19 (2006): 441–463. See also Reeshad S. Dalal, "A Meta-Analysis of the Relationship Between Organizational Citizenship Behavior and Counterproductive Work Behavior," *Journal of Applied Psychology* 90 (2005): 1241–1255.

30. Stephan Dilchert, Deniz S. Ones, Robert D. Davis, and Cary D. Rostow, "Cognitive Ability Predicts Objectively Measured Counterproductive Work Behaviors," *Journal of Applied Psychology* 92 (2007): 616–627.

31. Michael Mount, Remus Ilies, and Erin Johnson, "Relationship of Personality Traits and Counterproductive Work Behaviors: The Mediating Effects of Job Satisfaction," *Personnel Psychology* 59 (2006): 591–622.

32. Zhiging E. Zhou, Laurenz L. Meier, and Paul E. Spector, "The Role of Personality and Job Stressors in Predicting Counterproductive Work Behavior: A Three-Way Interaction," *International Journal of Selection and Assessment* 22 (2014): 286–296. See also Laurenz L. Meier and Paul E. Spector, "Reciprocal Effects of Work Stressors and Counterproductive Work Behavior: A Five-wave Longitudinal Study," *Journal of Applied Psychology* 98 (2013): 529–539.

33. Bernd Marcus and Heinz Schuler, "Antecedents of Counterproductive Behavior at Work: A General Perspective," *Journal of Applied Psychology* 89 (2004): 647–660.

34. Christopher Berry, Nichelle C. Carpenter, and Clare L. Barratt, "Do Other-Reports of Counterproductive Work Behavior Provide an Incremental Contribution Over Self-Reports? A Meta-Analytic Comparison," *Journal of Applied Psychology* 97 (2012): 613–636.

35. Wayne F. Cascio, *Applied Psychology in Personnel Management*, 3rd ed. (Reston, VA: 1987), 116–118.

36. John P. Campbell, Jeffrey J. McHenry, and Lauress L. Wise, "Modeling Job Performance in a Population of Jobs," *Personnel Psychology* 43 (1990): 313–333.

37. Cascio, *Applied Psychology in Personnel Management*, 109.

38. Hubert E. Brogden and Erwin K. Taylor, "The Dollar Criterion—Applying the Cost Accounting Concept to Criterion Construction," *Personnel Psychology* 3 (1950): 133–154.

39. Frank L. Schmidt, John E. Hunter, Robert C. Mckenzie, and Tressie W. Muldrow, "Impact of Valid Selection Procedures on Workforce Productivity," *Journal of Applied Psychology* 64 (1979): 609–626.

40. Frank L. Schmidt, John E. Hunter, and Kenneth Pearlman, "Assessing the Economic Impact of Personnel Programs on Workforce Productivity," *Personnel Psychology* 35 (1982): 333–348.

41. Wayne F. Cascio, *Costing Human Resources: The Financial Impact of Behavior in Organizations* (Boston: Kent, 1982), 163.

Job Analysis in Human Resource Selection

When we come to this section of the book, we have become accustomed to hearing a common refrain from many students (and, for that matter, even from some academic colleagues). That refrain goes something like this: "*Job analysis*! *Ugh*! That is the most boring topic in human resource selection. Can't we do something that's more interesting, like watching paint dry or grass grow?" We have to admit that our discussion of job analysis may not be a life-changing event for you. **Warning:** If you think it might put you to sleep, do not read this chapter while lying down, before driving a car, or before operating heavy equipment. The chapter is a cure for insomnia, however. Seriously, trust us, job analysis plays a critical role in HR selection. We hope to persuade you of its importance in this chapter. So, hang in there; the fun is just beginning! Now, tighten your safety belt so you don't fall out of your chair, and let's get started.

JOB ANALYSIS: A DEFINITION AND ROLE IN HR SELECTION

There are probably as many definitions of job analysis as there are writings on the topic. For our purposes, though, when we refer to job analysis, we simply mean *a purposeful, systematic process for collecting information on the important work-related aspects of a job*. Some aspects of work-related information collected include the following:

1. Work activities, that is, what a worker does; how, why, and when these activities are conducted

2. Tools and equipment used in performing work activities

3. Context of the work environment, such as work schedule or physical working conditions

4. Requirements of personnel performing the job, such as knowledge, skills, abilities, personality characteristics, or other specifications (we refer to these various requirements as WRCs)[1]

Job analysis information serves a wide variety of purposes. For example, over 70 years ago Joseph Zerga identified more than 20 uses of job analysis data.[2] More recently, job analysis data have been used in such HR areas as compensation, training, and performance appraisal among others. Of particular interest to us is the application of job analysis data in HR selection.

Broadly speaking in the context of HR selection, job analysis data help to

1. Identify employee specifications or WRCs necessary for success on a job,

2. Select or develop selection procedures that assess these important applicant WRCs to forecast those job candidates who are likely to succeed on the job, and

3. Develop criteria or standards of job performance that represent employee job success.

By examining factors, such as the tasks performed on a job and the employee specifications needed to successfully perform these tasks, one can obtain an idea of what ought to be measured by predictors used in employment screening. As an example, consider the job of a bank teller. An analysis of bank tellers' jobs might identify a number of tasks critical to successful work performance. Examination of these tasks as well as the specifications needed to perform them might reveal some important findings. For instance, a job analysis may show that balancing receipts and disbursements of cash, performing arithmetic operations on numbers involving dollars and cents, and entering transaction information into a computer are critical teller tasks. Conversely, notarizing legal documents, opening savings accounts, and handling applications for customer loans are tasks that tellers typically do not perform. Further analysis of such job information may indicate that one of several important criteria of successful teller performance is the dollar balance of tellers' receipts and disbursements for a workday. That is, tellers should not take in more dollars (an "overage") or fewer dollars (a "shortage") than they have disbursed. An examination of the WRCs associated with tellers' balancing of receipts and disbursements might show that the ability to use an electronic calculator to add, subtract, multiply, and divide monetary numbers involving decimals is *one* important requirement. In searching for a predictor of teller success, one would consider using a selection procedure that provides information about tellers' ability to use a calculator to perform arithmetic operations on monetary values.

When predictors and criteria are identified from job analysis results, developing a selection system that is job-related is feasible. As we suggest in Chapter 4, by using a job-related selection system, we are in a much better position to predict who can and who cannot adequately perform a job. With a job-related selection system, we are far more likely to have an employment system viewed by job applicants as well as the courts as being "fair."

Figure 3.1 outlines a general framework for the application of a job analysis in the context of HR selection. Initially, numerous methods are available to make an analysis. Most often, two important pieces of information are obtained from the analysis. The first involves information on the critical job tasks, duties, or work behaviors performed on the job under study as well as the WRCs required to perform them. The second piece of job information gathered is that related to what represents successful work performance or success (criteria).

Identification of critical job tasks and information on what represents successful work performance help produce two important products that underpin a selection program. First, criteria measures (for example, performance evaluations, job tenure, and counterproductive work behaviors, such as absenteeism and tardiness) represent what we are interested in predicting about applicants' future work behavior if hired. Second, selection procedures or predictors (such as tests, application forms, and employment interviews) reflect the WRCs needed for job success and used in making predictions regarding future work performance (our criteria). Scores on predictors serve as employment decision-making tools.

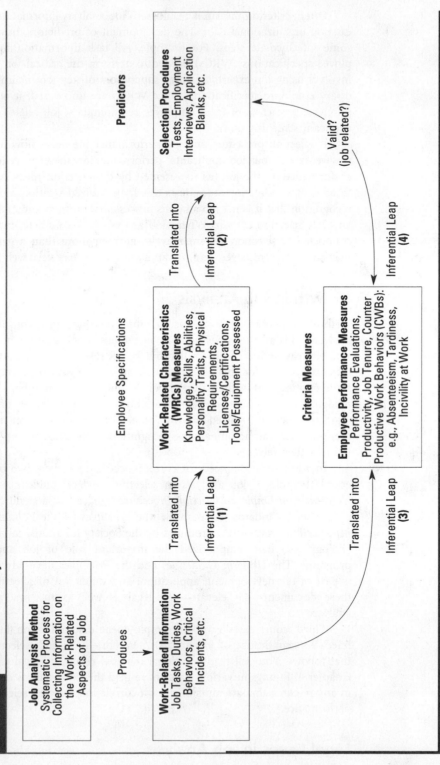

FIGURE 3.1   Role of Job Analysis in Human Resource Selection

Job Analysis Method
Systematic Process for
Collecting Information on
the Work-Related
Aspects of a Job

Produces

Work-Related Information
Job Tasks, Duties, Work
Behaviors, Critical
Incidents, etc.

Translated into
Inferential Leap
(1)

Employee Specifications

**Work-Related Characteristics
(WRCs) Measures**
Knowledge, Skills, Abilities,
Personality Traits, Physical
Requirements,
Licenses/Certifications,
Tools/Equipment Possessed

Translated into
Inferential Leap
(2)

Predictors

Selection Procedures
Tests, Employment
Interviews, Application
Blanks, etc.

Valid?
(job related?)

Inferential Leap
(4)

Criteria Measures

Translated into
Inferential Leap
(3)

Employee Performance Measures
Performance Evaluations,
Productivity, Job Tenure, Counter
Productive Work Behaviors (CWBs):
e.g., Absenteeism, Tardiness,
Incivility at Work

Often, criterion measures result from job analysis information or are identified from existing organizational data. The development of predictors, however, typically requires some intermediate steps. For example, job task information helps in identifying employee specifications (WRCs) needed to perform the critical job tasks. This step usually involves using job experts (such as supervisors or key job incumbents) to infer the necessary employee specifications. Once WRCs are uncovered, it is possible to develop or purchase predictors of these employee requirements; job-related predictors serve as job applicant screening tools.

If selection procedure and job performance measures flow from a sound job analysis, we expect that job applicants' performance on these procedures will relate to their performance on the job (as represented by the criterion measures). As we will learn in Chapter 8, a validation study tests this hypothesized relationship. Important here is the recognition that it is the job analysis process that is the foundation of the effectiveness of any HR selection system. Where job analysis is incomplete, inaccurate, or simply not conducted, a selection system may be nothing more than a game of chance—a game that employer, employee, and job applicants alike may very well lose.

Growth in Job Analysis

Within the past four decades or so, employers have give considerable attention to job analysis. This attention has focused on the use of job analysis not only in the basic personnel areas we mentioned earlier, but in HR selection as well. At least three interrelated reasons account for this renewed interest. First, many have realized that jobs are not static entities; that is, the nature of jobs change for any number of reasons, such as technological advancements, seasonal variations, or the initiatives of incumbents.[3] Thus, as managers have recognized the importance of job information in HR decision making, there has been an accompanying recognition of the need for up-to-date information on the jobs themselves.

In addition to the need for current, accurate job data, two other factors have influenced the role of job analysis in selection. Federal guidelines (namely, the *Uniform Guidelines on Employee Selection Procedures*[4]) have had a significant effect.[5] In addition, professional standards (for example, the *Principles for the Validation and Use of Personnel Selection Procedures*[6]) produced by the Society for Industrial and Organizational Psychology also have emphasized the important role of job analysis in HR selection programs. The *Uniform Guidelines* and the *Principles* have advocated that job analyses is part of the development, application, and validation of selection procedures. Each of these documents has elevated the legal as well as the practical importance of job analysis.

Third, court cases involving employment discrimination in selection have underlined the significance of job analysis.[7] We briefly discuss selected cases in the section that follows. You will read additional material related to legal cases and job analysis in Chapter 4. Rulings in various cases have held that job analysis *must* play an integral role in any research that attempts to show a correlation between selection procedures and job performance.

Legal Issues in Job Analysis

Job analysis has become a focal point in the legal context of HR selection. One major source for this development can be traced to the passage of Title VII of the 1964 Civil Rights Act. Title VII makes it illegal for an organization to refuse to select an individual or to discriminate against a person with respect to compensation, terms, conditions, or privileges of employment because of the person's race, sex, color, religion, or national origin. Because many Title VII cases have concerned the role of discrimination in selection for employment, job analysis has emerged as critical to the prosecution or defense of a discrimination case. Thus, job analysis and its associated methodologies have become intertwined with the law. Within this legal vein, two developments, in particular, amplified the importance of job analysis in selection research: (a) adoption of the *Uniform Guidelines on Employee Selection Procedures* by the federal government and (b) litigation involving discrimination in selection, arising under Title VII, the Fifth, and Fourteenth Amendments to the U.S. Constitution.

Key Court Cases Involving Job Analysis

Although a number of cases involving job analysis have been heard in the courts, two early Supreme Court cases are particularly important. Perhaps the seminal one with respect to job analysis is *Griggs v. Duke Power Co.*[8] Even though the term *job analysis* is not mentioned per se, *Griggs* gave the legal impetus to job analysis. The case implies that an important legal requirement in a selection procedure validation program is an analysis of the job for which the procedure is used.

In *Griggs*, Duke Power was employing a written test and a high school diploma as requirements for entry into a supervisory position. The Court noted that these selection standards were used "without meaningful study of their relationship to job-performance ability. Rather, a vice president of the company testified, the requirements were instituted on the company's judgment that they generally would improve the overall quality of the work force."[9] The Court ruled that "What Congress has commanded is that any test used must measure the person *for the job* and not the person in the abstract."[10] The ruling in *Griggs* implied that for employers to attempt to meet this job-relatedness standard, they must first examine the job. Examination of the job involves job analysis.

Albemarle Paper Co. v. Moody is equally important.[11] In *Albemarle*, the Court, for the first time, expressly criticized the lack of a job analysis in a validation study. The Court noted that "no attempt was made to analyze the jobs in terms of the particular skills they might require."[12] As with *Griggs*, the Court gave significant weight to the use of job analysis.

Albemarle is noteworthy for its support of job analysis. Like *Griggs*, its predecessor, *Albemarle* was a U.S. Supreme Court case. Plaintiffs and lower courts look for guidance from rulings of the Supreme Court. Thus, the Court's insistence on job analysis in selection cases encouraged other courts to look for the presence (or lack) of a job analysis.

This case is significant for a second reason. The Court supported the *Equal Employment Opportunity Commission (EEOC) Guidelines on Employee Selection Procedures,*[13] which required that a job analysis be performed in a validation study. As we see in the next section, the Court's endorsement of these guidelines, as well as the subsequently issued *Uniform Guidelines*, emphasized the role of job analysis in HR selection.

Numerous court cases could be cited in addition to *Griggs* and *Albemarle*. On the whole, decisions and remedies in these cases emphasize the importance of job analysis. An examination of these cases would be helpful in isolating the standards used by the courts in evaluating job analysis in validation research. In this light, Duane Thompson and Toni Thompson reviewed 26 selected federal court cases to determine the standards the courts apparently used in evaluating job analyses conducted in the development and validation of tests. Their review produced a set of job analysis characteristics, which they suggest are capable of withstanding legal scrutiny. Although these characteristics may vary depending on such issues as type of job analysis, type of validation strategy, and purpose of the analysis, the standards serve as a useful guide for understanding the judicial view. The legal standards identified by Thompson and Thompson involved the following:

1. Job analysis is mandatory and must be for the job for which selection procedures are used.

2. Analysis of the job should be in writing.

3. Job analysts should describe in detail the job analysis procedures used.

4. Knowledgeable job analysts should collect job data from a variety of current sources.

5. Sample size of individuals serving as subject matter experts (SMEs) should be large and representative of the jobs for which the selection procedures are used.

6. Tasks, duties, and activities should be included in the analysis.

7. The most important tasks should be represented in the selection procedures.

8. Competency levels of work performance for entry-level jobs should be specified.

9. WRCs including knowledge, skills, and abilities should be specified, particularly if a content validation strategy is used.[14]

Federal Guidelines on Employee Selection

From 1966 to 1978, the government issued various sets of federal regulations on employee selection.[15] The EEOC, the Office of Federal Contract Compliance (OFCC), the Civil Service Commission (currently the U.S. Office of Personnel Management), and the Department of Justice offered guidelines for employers to follow in their selection procedures. Although some employers treated these guidelines as nothing more than a guide, the *Albemarle* case enhanced their role. As noted earlier, the Court gave deference to the *EEOC Guidelines*, at least to the portion that discussed job analysis. The impact of the Court's opinion made it mandatory for HR selection practitioners to be intimately familiar with the *Guidelines'* content.

Current federal regulations note the *Uniform Guidelines* supersede previous regulations (a previous version referred to as the *Guidelines*) and represent a joint agreement among the EEOC, Department of Justice, Department of Labor, and Civil Service Commission. Given the substantial weight accorded to the *Uniform Guidelines* in legal cases, the courts likely will continue to emphasize the importance of job analysis in the near future.

Many of the legal issues surrounding job analysis concern the necessity for employing these methods when developing and implementing a selection program. Since the early 1980s, however, another set of legal questions has arisen concerning the actual application of job analysis procedures. Because most of these methods involve some degree of human judgment, cases have been appearing in the courts involving technical aspects of job analysis implementation. In many instances, the issue has been to determine whether the inferences made from job analysis data based largely on human judgments have a discriminatory impact on protected classes of job applicants. Returning to Figure 3.1, you will see four points at which judgment occurs using job analysis information. These judgments represent "inferential leaps." For instance, at inference point 1 in Figure 3.1, WRCs are inferred from the tasks performed on a job. Because humans are involved in the process of inferring human attributes from work-related information, there is the possibility of error. The greater the role of human judgment, the larger the inferential leap, and, therefore, the greater the opportunity for discriminatory impact. In particular, inference points 1 and 2 represent areas where much equal opportunity litigation has centered when job analysis issues are in question.

Of course, the extent of inferential leaps made in any job analysis application depends on the particular situation. Factors such as the validation strategy used (for example, content versus criterion), the type of job (for example, hourly versus managerial), the job analysis method used, and the WRCs assessed (for example, a physical skill versus a personality trait) affect the degree of inferential leaps made.

Although convenient, it is simply impossible to specify one clear, suitable, standard means for meeting *all* technical and legal considerations of a job analysis. Situations, problems, and technical issues are so varied that proper conduct of a job analysis is a complex, resource-consuming process. No one way is standard.

Collecting Job Information

Earlier we said that one principal role of job analysis in HR selection is to assess job content so that requisite WRCs are identified. We translate these WRCs into selection procedures' content, such as tests, interviews, and the like. Assuming our selection procedures are job related or valid, they, in turn, are usable for selection decision-making purposes. The process of developing job-related selection procedures that assess employee specifications requires judgments or inferences at several points. Figure 3.2 summarizes these inference points.

At the first inference point (**1**), data collected from a job analysis are used to infer relevant employee specifications. A second inference point (**2**) then is reached concerning the content of selection procedures that reflect these identified specifications. An important goal is to minimize the chance of error at each inference point. Our resulting specifications will be useful only to the extent that our inferences are accurate and complete. Frederick Morgeson and Michael Campion have noted a number of social and cognitive sources of inaccuracy can contaminate job analysis results (for example, loss of participant motivation, information overload among participants).[16] To the extent such sources of inaccuracy plague our inferences from job analysis data, the effectiveness of our selection measures for predicting successful work performance likely will fall.

Obviously, the entire process depends on the data derived initially from the job analysis. If these data are incomplete, inaccurate, or otherwise faulty, subsequent judgments based on these data will be incorrect. In the end, we likely will have inappropriate, invalid, perhaps illegal selection procedures. Thus, we must be careful in our choice and implementation of methods for collecting job information.

At this point, we should note that many of the methods we review and discuss tend to focus on the tasks performed by job incumbents. Other researchers in the field of HR selection do not necessarily agree with using these detailed job-task approaches for all HR selection applications. In particular, writers in the area of validity generalization have tended to support more holistic methods of job analysis.[17] Their argument is that task-oriented job analysis is not of much value for selection when measures of employee ability and aptitudes are concerned. On the other hand, when noncognitive attributes of applicants are being assessed or content validation strategies are being used with job knowledge or work sample tests, task-oriented job analysis is needed.[18]

A SURVEY OF JOB ANALYSIS METHODS

We divide our review of specific job analysis methods into two parts. The first part of the chapter reviews the following job analysis methods: (a) job analysis interviews, (b) job analysis questionnaires (including task analysis inventories), (c) Critical Incidents

FIGURE 3.2 Points of Inference in the Job Analysis → Employee Specifications → Selection Procedure Development Process

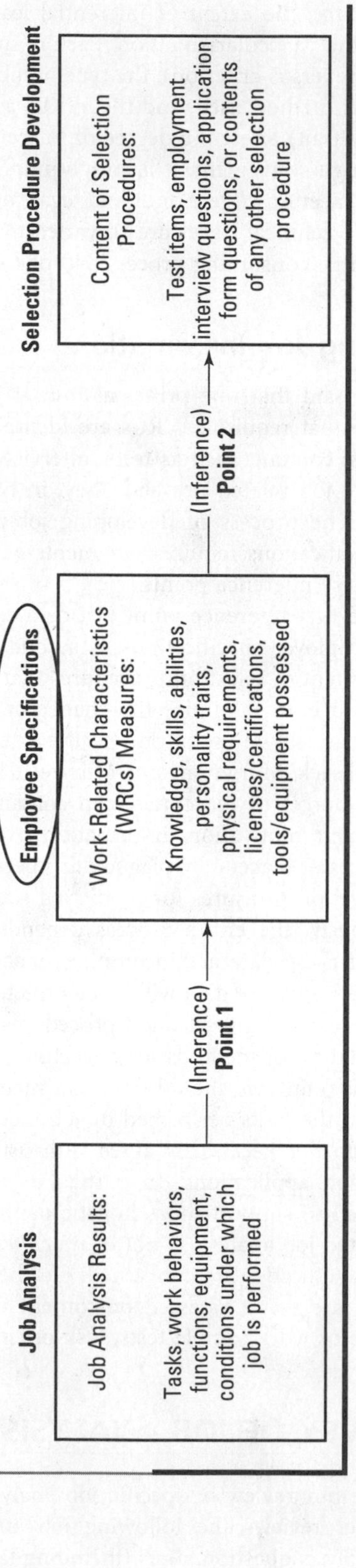

Job Analysis

Job Analysis Results:

Tasks, work behaviors, functions, equipment, conditions under which job is performed

(Inference)
Point 1

Employee Specifications

Work-Related Characteristics (WRCs) Measures:

Knowledge, skills, abilities, personality traits, physical requirements, licenses/certifications, tools/equipment possessed

(Inference)
Point 2

Selection Procedure Development

Content of Selection Procedures:

Test items, employment interview questions, application form questions, or contents of any other selection procedure

Technique, and (d) SME or job expert workshops. We describe each technique, its application, and its advantages and disadvantages. We do not advocate one particular method to the exclusion of others. Many methods are available to the user; do not view our omission of a specific method as a condemnation of it. This chapter concentrates on those methods that seem most popular in current HR selection practice. However, because all of the methods depend on interviews, questionnaires, or a combination of the two for collecting job information, we begin with and focus our discussion on these methods. Finally, in the last section of the chapter, we illustrate one method of using job analysis information for HR selection purposes.

JOB ANALYSIS INTERVIEWS

Description

The interview is one of the most frequently used methods of job analysis, capable of meeting a wide array of purposes. Essentially, a job analysis interview consists of a trained analyst asking questions about the duties and responsibilities, WRCs required, and conditions of employment for a job or class of jobs.

Job analysis data collected through interviews typically involve group or individual interviews with incumbents and supervisors. Because of their familiarity with job content, we often refer to such participants as SMEs (Subject Matter Experts). Large groups (15–20) of incumbents can participate when it is certain that all incumbents are performing the same major activities. In a separate meeting apart from employees, supervisors often verify incumbent information and provide information unavailable to employees in the job. In other cases, supervisors (versus incumbents) participate because they may feel less threatened in discussing incumbents' job activities with a stranger, or they may be better able to comment on the necessary WRCs required to perform job activities successfully.

With regard to job incumbents and supervisors as sources of job information, each of these sources may differentially experience psychological processes that affect the accuracy of job information they provide. Fred Morgeson and Michael Campion theorized that job incumbents are more vulnerable to social effects that affect their behavior in providing job information, such as social desirability or loss of motivation effects. On the other hand, supervisors are more likely to be predisposed to information-processing effects, such as information overload or having inadequate job-related information. For this reason, Morgeson and Campion[19] and other authors[20] have suggested combining both sources of information in a job analysis. Morgeson and Campion's recommendation applies not only to the job analysis interview but also to other job analysis methods.

A job analysis interview may be structured or unstructured. For selection purposes, a structured interview in which predetermined questions are asked, and means are available for recording answers to these questions (such as rating scales or interview answer forms) is essential. An unstructured interview consists of a job analyst collecting information about a job without a specific list of questions developed before the interview. Because of the technical and legal issues involved in job analysis, a structured interview is much more likely than an unstructured one to provide the job analysis data useful in selection applications. When we speak of a job analysis interview, we are referring to one that is structured.

In the context of HR selection, a job analysis interview typically is performed for one or more of the following reasons:

1. To collect job information—for example, information on job tasks—that will serve as a basis for developing other job analysis measures, such as a job analysis questionnaire

2. To clarify or verify information collected previously through other job analysis methods

3. To provide a method, preferably as one of several used, for collecting relevant job data for developing a selection system

Considerations on Applicability

The interview is applicable to a variety of jobs, from those composed of physical activities, such as a laborer's, to those with activities that are primarily mental, such as a manager's. When used with knowledgeable respondents, the interview makes it possible to identify activities that may go unobserved or occur over long periods.

An important step toward effective application of an interview is to plan the interview itself. Detailed plans are preferred. Plans should state the objectives of the interview (for example, identification and rating of job tasks); individuals to be interviewed (for example, incumbents representative of gender or racial groups; incumbents with six months or more of job experience); questions and means for recording answers (for example, an interview schedule listing the questions and forms for recording responses); and who will conduct the interviews (for example, consultants).

With regard to the interview questions themselves, numerous approaches can be taken in phrasing and posing questions. Figure 3.3 presents a sample job interview schedule for use with a single job incumbent. The schedule shown illustrates only some of the types of questions possible. Supplementary forms provide a means to systematically record job incumbents' responses to the questions.

FIGURE 3.3 An Example of a Job Analysis Interview Schedule for Use with a Job Incumbent

Name of Employee _____   Payroll Title _____

Job Analyst _____   Department _____

Date _____   Work Location _____

Important Job Tasks

1. Describe your job in terms of what you do.
2. How do you do your job? Do you use special tools, equipment, or other sources of aid? If so, list the names of the principal tools, equipment, or sources of aid you use.
3. Of the major tasks in your job, how much time does it take to do each one? How often do you perform each task in a day, week, or month?

Work-Related Characteristics Required

What does it take to perform each task in terms of the following:

1. Knowledge required

   a. What subject matter areas are covered by each task?
   b. What facts or principles must you have an acquaintance with or understand in these subject matter areas?
   c. Describe the level, degree, and breadth of knowledge required in these areas or subjects.

2. Skills required

   a. What activities must you perform with ease and precision?
   b. What are the manual skills that are required to operate machines, vehicles, and equipment, or to use tools?

(Continued)

FIGURE 3.3	(Continued)

3. Abilities required

   a. What is the nature and level of language ability, written or oral, required of you on the job? Are complex oral or written ideas involved in performing the task, or do you use simple instructional materials?
   b. What mathematical ability must you have?
   c. What reasoning or problem-solving ability must you have?
   d. What instructions must you follow? Are they simple, detailed, involved, abstract?
   e. What interpersonal abilities are required? What supervisory or managing abilities are required?
   f. What physical abilities such as strength, coordination, or visual acuity must you have?

Physical Activities

Describe the frequency and degree to which you are engaged in such activities as pulling, pushing, throwing, carrying, kneeling, sitting, running, crawling, reaching, climbing.

Environmental Conditions

Describe the frequency and degree to which you will encounter working conditions such as these: cramped quarters, moving objects, vibration, inadequate ventilation.

Typical Working Incidents

Describe the frequency and degree to which you do the following:

1. Work in situations involving interpretation of feelings, ideas, or facts in terms of personal viewpoint.

2. Influence people in their opinions, attitudes, or judgments about ideas or things.

3. Work with people beyond giving and receiving instructions.

4. Perform repetitive work, or continuously perform the same work.

5. Perform under stress when confronted with emergency, critical, unusual, or dangerous situations or situations in which work speed and sustained attention are make-or-break aspects of the job.

6. Perform a variety of duties, often changing from one task to another of a different nature, without loss of efficiency or composure.

7. Work under hazardous conditions that may result in violence, loss of body parts, burns, bruises, cuts, impairment of the senses, collapse, fractures, or electric shock.

Records and Reports

What records or reports do you prepare as part of your job?

Source of Job Information

What is the principal source for instructions you receive on how to do your job (for example, oral directions or written specifications)?

Supervisory Responsibilities

1. How many employees are directly under your supervision?

2. Do you have full authority to assign work; correct and discipline; and recommend pay increases, transfers, promotions, and discharge for these employees?

Other

Are there any additional elements about your job that would help me better understand what you do? If so, please describe them.

An Example

An approach adopted by the U.S. Office of Personnel Management is one possibility when a job analysis interview is used.[21] The key initial step in characterizing a job with this interview procedure is identification of critical job tasks. Once identified, each task is described in terms of factors, such as WRCs required for task performance and environmental conditions surrounding task performance. Because of the task's importance to the interview method, we will review how job tasks are analyzed and structured with this method. After all, WRCs ultimately are developed from the task statement.

Task statements are written so that each shows the following:

1. What the worker does, by using a specific action verb that introduces the task statement

2. To whom or what he or she does it, by stating the object of the verb

3. What is produced, by expressing the expected output of the action

4. What materials, tools, procedures, or equipment are used[22]

Using these task characteristics, let's see how they are applied in an actual interview context for the purpose of developing appropriate task statements.

Suppose, for example, an analyst is reviewing the job of welfare eligibility examiner in a state human services agency. Assume further that background and supplementary data have been obtained from a job incumbent. The interviewer asks each respondent to describe their job in terms of what is done—and how, for what purpose, and using what equipment or tools. The interviewee then describes the job as follows:

> *I interview applicants for food stamps—ask the applicants all the pertinent questions that will help to determine their eligibility. For example, are they working part time, receiving other assistance, and so on. To carry out the job, I have to interpret regulations, policies, and actually make decisions about eligibility. Some applicants are referred to other assistance units. Some applicants need detailed explanations of policies at a level they can understand, to avoid an unpleasant reaction over a decision. They also get advice about their appeal rights from me. I visit homes to evaluate a client's circumstances and make determinations. I verify what the client has said on the application: household composition, shelter arrangements, income, and so on. This helps me determine whether the food stamp costs have been determined correctly or incorrectly.*
>
> *At times, I work in outreach centers and homes of applicants to make determinations. I make personal appearances at high schools, colleges, and civic organizations to outline and explain the food stamp program.[23]*

Following these comments, the analyst uses the task statement criteria listed earlier to produce task statements representing important task activities. Table 3.1 summarizes the classification of content for one important task. Once classified, the content is rewritten to produce an easy-to-read, understandable statement. The goal of the rewriting

TABLE 3.1	Classification of Interview Content for the Purpose of Developing a Task Statement		
Performs What Action? (Verb)	**To Whom or What? (Object of Verb)**	**To Produce What? (Expected Output)**	**Using What Tools, Equipment, Work Aids, Processes?**
Asks questions, listens, records answers	To/of client on eligibility form	In order to determine eligibility	Eligibility form; eligibility criteria in manual; interviewing techniques

Source: U.S. Civil Service Commission, *Job Analysis: Developing and Documenting Data* (Washington, DC: U.S. Government Printing Office, 1973), p. 6.

process is to produce task statements that people unfamiliar with the job will understand. For example, the task content classified in Table 3.1 is rewritten as follows:

> 1. Asks client questions, listens, and records answers on standard eligibility form, using knowledge of interviewing techniques and eligibility criteria to gather information from which client's eligibility for food stamps can be determined.[24]

If the analyst follows through with the process just described, 10 to 20 important task statements typically are identified. From the interviewee description given earlier, additional tasks might include the following:

2. Determines eligibility of applicant (using regulatory policies as a guide) to complete client's application for food stamps.

3. Decides on and describes other agencies available to assist and refer client to appropriate community resources using worker's knowledge of resources available and knowledge of client's needs.

4. Explains policies and regulations appropriate to applicant's case to inform applicants of their status.

5. Evaluates information gained from home visit, interview, and observation to decide whether home conditions are consistent with original application, using original application and agency's housing standards as a guide.

6. Meets with, talks to, answers the questions of, and has discussions with members of high schools, colleges, and civic organizations to outline and explain food stamp program using knowledge and experience of food stamp program.[25]

After capturing the important job tasks, the analyst then characterizes each statement with regard to frequency of performance, WRCs required, physical activities required, environmental conditions, and other factors important to task performance.

Questions such as those in the sample interview schedule shown in Figure 3.3 help make these determinations for each task. An illustration may help clarify the task characterization process. For the moment, reexamine the second task identified in the study of welfare eligibility examiner. The task was stated as follows: "Determines eligibility of applicant (using regulatory policies as a guide) to complete client's application for food stamps." Figure 3.4 shows a description of the task using the interview schedule. In addition to those characteristics illustrated in Figure 3.4, additional task data, such as ratings of task importance or task frequency, also are obtained. Job incumbents make ratings, using rating scales, to further describe the job task. (We discuss such scales later in the chapter.) This same process proceeds for each task statement. In the end, we should have a clearer picture of the job's demands, activities, and conditions of employment.

The success of the interview as a job analysis technique depends, to a large extent, on the skill of the interviewer. A successful interviewer must possess several important skills—the ability to listen, put individuals at ease, probe and prompt for answers from reluctant interviewees, and control the direction of an interview—all vital to a successful job analysis.[26] With such skills, an interviewer can tease out job information that might go undetected by other forms of analysis. To enhance the likelihood of success in using the technique, certain guidelines need to be followed. Suggestions for improving the chance of success in using job analysis interviews are in Figure 3.5.

Limitations of the Job Analysis Interview

The job analysis interview is one option for collecting job data; however, it has its limitations. The interview often suffers from a lack of standardization and has limited

FIGURE 3.4	Example Characterization of a Selected Job Task: The Job of Welfare Eligibility Examiner

Task 2:

Determines eligibility of applicant (using regulatory policies as a guide) in order to complete client's application for food stamps

Task Characterization

Knowledge Required:

1. Knowledge of content and meaning of items on standard application form
2. Knowledge of Social-Health Services food stamp regulatory policies
3. Knowledge of statutes relating to Social-Health Services food stamp program

Skills Required:

None

Abilities Required:

1. Ability to read and understand complex instructions such as regulatory policies
2. Ability to read and understand a variety of procedural instructions, written and oral, and convert these to proper actions
3. Ability to use simple arithmetic—addition and subtraction
4. Ability to translate requirements into language appropriate to laypersons

Physical Activities:

Sedentary

Environmental Conditions:

None

Typical Working Incidents:

Working with people beyond giving and receiving instructions

Interest Areas:

1. Communication of data
2. Business contact with people
3. Working for the (presumed) good of people

Source: U.S. Civil Service Commission, *Job Analysis: Developing and Documenting Data* (Washington, DC: U.S. Government Printing Office, 1973), p. 13–14.

possibilities for covering large numbers of respondents, particularly if they are spread over a wide geographic area. If thorough documentation is missing as the interview is conducted, important legal requirements of job analysis information likely will go unmet. The skills and procedures used by the individual analyst principally determine the utility of the interview.

In addition, the job analysis interview has other limitations. Unless group interviews are possible, the technique requires a great deal of time and labor and is not cost efficient if many jobs need to be studied. Depending on the interviewee and the type of job reviewed, an interviewer may have to track through an entire job in specific detail. Such a process not only is expensive but also requires a highly skilled interviewer to build rapport, develop trust, and maintain respondents' motivation to identify the needed content.

FIGURE 3.5 Guidelines for Conducting a Job Analysis Interview

Opening the Interview

1. Put the worker at ease by learning his or her name in advance, introducing yourself, and discussing general and pleasant topics long enough to establish rapport. Be at ease.
2. Make the purpose of the interview clear by explaining why the interview was scheduled, what is expected to be accomplished, and how the worker's cooperation will help in the production of tools for use in personnel selection.
3. Encourage the worker to talk by always being courteous and showing a sincere interest in what he or she says.

Steering the Interview

1. Help the worker to think and talk according to the logical sequence of the duties performed. If duties are not performed in a regular order, ask the worker to describe the functional aspects of the duties by taking the most important activity first, the second-most important next, and so forth. Request the worker to describe the infrequent duties of his or her job—duties that are not part of the worker's regular activities, such as the occasional setup of a machine, occasional repairs, or infrequent reports.
2. Allow the worker sufficient time to answer each question and to formulate an answer.
3. Phrase questions carefully, so that the answers will be more than "yes" or "no."
4. Avoid the use of leading questions.
5. Conduct the interview in plain, easily understood language.
6. Control the interview with respect to the economic use of time and adherence to subject matter. For example, when the interviewee strays from the subject, a good technique for bringing him or her back to the point is to summarize the data collected up to that point.

Closing the Interview

1. Summarize the information obtained from the worker, indicating the major duties performed and the details concerning each of the duties.
2. Close the interview on a friendly note.

Miscellaneous Dos and Don'ts for Interviews

1. Do not take issue with the worker's statements.
2. Do not show any partiality to grievances or conflicts concerning the employer–employee relations.
3. Do not show any interest in the wage classification of the job.
4. Do not talk down to the worker.
5. Do not permit yourself to be influenced by your personal likes and dislikes.
6. Be impersonal. Do not be critical or attempt to suggest any changes or improvements in the organization or methods of work.
7. Talk to the worker only with permission of her or his supervisor.
8. Verify completed job analysis interview with an appropriate individual—such as a supervisor.

Source: U.S. Civil Service Commission, *Job Analysis: Developing and Documenting Data* (Washington, DC: U.S. Government Printing Office, 1973), p. 12--13.

Another major problem is that the technique may be plagued with a distortion of information. If interviewees believe conveying certain information is beneficial for them (for example, a perceived wage increase), they may exaggerate their activities and responsibilities to reflect a more complex job. Sometimes, it is difficult to identify distorted job information. Verification from a supervisor or other incumbents can serve as a check. Comparisons among subjective data, however, are difficult and expensive to make.

In our opinion, an individual job analysis interview should *not* be relied on as the *sole* method when the analysis is being conducted for selection purposes. When employed as a supplementary source, however, interview data are helpful. For example, interviews are useful in identifying content for other job analysis methods, such as the development of task analysis inventories or the clarification of responses to other methods.

JOB ANALYSIS QUESTIONNAIRES

Description

The job analysis questionnaire or survey is one way to handle some of the problems of the job analysis interview. This method consists of a questionnaire distributed to respondents through various means—in person, by a job analyst, by mail, or via an e-mail sent to participants, including a link to the questionnaire online. The questionnaire lists job information, such as activities or tasks, tools and equipment used to perform the job, working conditions in which the job is performed, and WRCs incumbents must possess to perform the job successfully. Participants make some form of judgment about job information presented on the questionnaire. Respondents often use a rating scale to indicate the degree to which various aspects of job information listed on the questionnaire apply to their jobs.

Numerous forms of job analysis questionnaires are available, but most fall into one of two classes: (a) *tailored* questionnaires developed for a specific purpose or a specific job, or (b) *prefabricated* or existing questionnaires. An organization (or its consultants) typically prepare tailored job analysis questionnaires for application to a *specific* job. Like prefabricated instruments, these questionnaires also include tasks or other aspects of jobs (for example, WRCs) about which respondents make judgments. Because the focus of tailored questionnaires is usually on one job, the aspects of the job listed on the questionnaire are more specific than job aspects given on an existing measure.

Prefabricated questionnaires are usually generic measures developed for use with a variety of jobs. These inventories usually consist of a preestablished set of items describing aspects of a job that respondents (incumbents, supervisors, observers) judge using rating scales. Frequently, the aspects of a job that respondents rate deal with job activities or functions performed. Because these questionnaires are already developed, knowledgeable users can take them "off-the-shelf" and apply them. Here are some examples of prefabricated job analysis questionnaires:

1. *Common Metric Questionnaire*[27] (www.cmqonline.com)

2. *Professional and Managerial Position Questionnaire*[28]

3. *Management Position Description Questionnaire*[29]

4. *Managerial and Professional Job Functions Inventory*[30] (www.creativeorgdesign .com)

5. *Position Analysis Questionnaire*[31] (www.paq.com)

6. *Threshold Traits Analysis System*[32] (www.flopez-associates.com)

7. *Occupation Analysis Inventory*[33]

8. *Personality-Related Position Requirements Form*[34]

We turn our attention now to one popular type of tailored job analysis questionnaire employed in HR selection, the task analysis inventory.

The Task Analysis Inventory

A task analysis inventory is a questionnaire or survey that includes a listing of tasks on which respondents make some form of judgment. Usually these judgments are ratings given by respondents using a task rating scale, such as frequency of task performance.

Because many different tasks exist in any job, this type of job analysis questionnaire usually concerns only one job or a class of very similar jobs. Most often, job incumbents complete a task analysis inventory. Supervisors can complete it—assuming they have current knowledge about the job studied.

Historically, the method has been widely used in military settings, in particular by the U.S. Air Force.[35] Although the origin of task inventories is traceable to the military, their use for selection purposes by both public and private employers has grown substantially. One reason for increasing use of these inventories is that many employers have adopted a content validation strategy for selection measures, for which task inventories are particularly helpful.

The Nature of Task Inventories

A task inventory often contains three major categories of information: (a) background information on respondents, (b) a listing of job tasks with associated rating scales, and (c) other or miscellaneous information. Information on respondents such as name, gender, ethnicity, tenure on the job rated, tenure with the employing organization, job location, and title of the job rated compose the task inventory. Identifying information is useful should the need arise to contact respondents (for example, for clarifying responses), and demographic information is valuable for performing analyses—such as a comparison of how different types of respondents view the job rated. In addition, respondent demographic information is important in dealing with any legal questions that arise about a job regarding who served as SMEs. With rater demographic information, it is possible to show that respondents to the task inventory are representative of minority or other protected groups or that the respondents have the necessary qualifications to serve as SMEs. The second part of a task analysis inventory includes the job tasks and their rating scales. Figure 3.6 presents a condensed example of this portion of a task analysis inventory.

The inventory shown analyzes various tasks associated with the job of personnel analyst. Because most inventories are similar to the one exhibited, we use it to point out two important characteristics: (a) *phrasing of tasks* rated and (b) using *rating scales* for judging the tasks.

First, we see that respondents make judgments regarding job tasks. If we compare the phrasing of the tasks shown in Figure 3.6 with those developed by the Office of Personnel Management interview procedure discussed earlier, we find that the two sets of tasks differ. From our comparison, we see that the task statements developed previously appear to be more complex. Tasks identified under the interview procedure described what the tasks consisted of, materials and equipment used in task performance, and the results of those tasks. In contrast, in our task inventory example, the tasks are not as fully developed. Most statements on a task analysis inventory are concerned with *what* gets done. Numerous tasks (more than 50 tasks is not unusual) listed on some inventories provide no information about the situation surrounding the activity. Tasks developed by other job analysis methods (for example, the Office of Personnel Management interview) usually provide information on what, how, and why and typically are fewer in number than tasks listed on a task analysis inventory.

Some task analysis inventories, however, incorporate on the survey the kinds of detailed task statements we saw with the Office of Personnel Management interview procedure. Because of the detail provided in these statements, inventories with detailed statements can be particularly helpful in selection applications. For instance, they are useful in planning and developing the actual content of specific selection procedures, such as in work sample tests or knowledge tests.

FIGURE 3.6	A Condensed Example of a Task Analysis Inventory for the Job of Personnel Analyst

Directions: We are interested in knowing more about your job. Below we have listed a number of tasks you might perform on your job. Using the rating scales given below, rate each task as to (a) how *frequently* you perform it and (b) how *important* it is for newly hired workers in a job like yours to be able to perform this task when they first begin work. Read each task and then place your rating in the two spaces to the right of each task.

Frequency of Performance	**Importance for Newly Hired Employees**
0 = Not performed at all	0 = Not important at all
1 = Seldom	1 = Somewhat important
2 = Occasionally	2 = Important
3 = Frequently	3 = Very important
4 = Almost all of the time	4 = Extremely important

Job Tasks	**Frequency of Performance**	**Importance for Newly Hired Employees**
1. Prepare job descriptions for secretarial jobs	☐	☐
2. Check file folders for disposition of medical and dental records	☐	☐
3. Initiate requests for identification cards from terminated personnel	☐	☐
4. Describe company policies to newly hired employees	☐	☐
5. Write computer programs using SPSS in order to analyze personnel absenteeism and turnover data	☐	☐
⋮	⋮	⋮
105. Plan and develop training programs for newly hired clerical personnel	☐	☐

Another important characteristic of any task inventory is the *rating scale* used by the respondent for judging the given tasks. A rating scale provides a continuum or range of options (most often consisting of five to seven steps) that respondents use to express their perceptions of a task. Numbers define various degrees of respondents' views. For example, *Relative Time Spent on Task Performance* is one example task rating scale[36] and looks as follows:

> **Relative to the time you spend in your job doing other tasks, how much time do you spend on this job task?**

0 = This task is not performed

1 = Much below average

2 = Below average

3 = Slightly below average

4 = About average

5 = Slightly above average

6 = Above average

7 = Much above average

This illustration is just one way of phrasing the rating scale for time spent on task performance. Other variations of the scale are possible. Regardless of the rating scale, the objective is to identify the *degree* to which a task is viewed as possessing a rated characteristic.

Quite often, respondents use more than one rating scale to assess job tasks. Most task analysis inventories use 3 to 5 rating scales. The scales chosen depend on any number of issues, such as the number of tasks rated, the time available, the capabilities of incumbents (for example, reading ability), the complexity of the job (the more complex, the more scales needed to assess the job adequately), and the purpose of the task analysis. For example, the following task-rating categories are important to consider when undertaking a content validation strategy:

1. Frequency of task performance

2. Task importance or criticality

3. Task difficulty

4. Whether the task can be learned on the job relatively quickly[37]

The third portion of the task inventory may focus on parts of the job, other than tasks, that also account for work performance. For instance, this last section sometimes assesses factors like the physical working conditions of the job (degree of heating and cooling; presence of dust or other allergens, amount of lifting, standing, sitting, walking, and so on; degree of job stress; or equipment and tools used for performing the job).

Development of Task Inventories

Because most task inventories involve a specific job, the user will likely have to develop the inventory. This process is time-consuming and often expensive. Access to previous inventories or analyses of the job in question—as well as use of technical experts in job analysis and questionnaire development—are important determinants of the cost and success of the method. For those organizations committed to the development and administration of a task inventory, a number of steps are needed.[38] Table 3.2 shows some of the major steps and guidelines for developing task inventories. Basically, task inventory development follows a sequential fashion such as that one outlined in the table. There is no one best way. However, suggestions like those noted increase the chances that the resulting questionnaire will meet its purposes and objectives.

Once developed, the inventory is ready for application. In using task analysis inventories, consider several issues. First, include respondents' names and other identifying information on the inventory. Using identifying information (a) helps ensure higher quality information, (b) is necessary if follow-up studies occur, and (c) is useful when combined with personnel file data (such as respondents' scores on performance measures and demographic characteristics). Second, distribute the inventory to a large number of incumbents, which generally improves generalizability and data reliability. Finally, when possible, use optical scanning sheets to minimize time, cost, and errors in coding and data entry. In some cases, it is possible to administer the inventories by accessing the Internet.

Application of Task Analysis in Selection

Results of a task analysis inventory define the most important tasks or activities that compose incumbents' jobs. This core group of job tasks is the basis for inferring employee characteristics needed to perform the job successfully. Because jobs we are interested in studying are quite likely complex, lists of task statements and accompanying rating scales are one of the principal means used for assessing job tasks. Once collected,

TABLE 3.2 Summary of Steps and Guidelines for Developing Task Analysis Inventories

Sequential Steps for Developing Content of Task Inventories

1. Technical manuals, previous job analyses, and other job-related reports are reviewed for possible task-item content.
2. Technical job experts (consultants, selected incumbents/supervisors) prepare lists of job tasks known to be performed.
3. Interviews are held with job incumbents and supervisors in order to identify additional tasks.
4. Tasks identified are reviewed for duplication, edited, and incorporated into an initial version of the inventory. Tasks are described according to task-writing guidelines.
5. First draft is prepared and submitted to a panel of experts (or incumbents and/or supervisors) for review.
6. Panel of reviewers adds, deletes, or modifies tasks for the development of another draft of the inventory.
7. Steps 5 and 6 are repeated, using the same or a similar panel, until an acceptable draft has been developed.
8. Task inventory is then pilot-tested on a sample of respondents to whom the final version will be given.
9. Appropriate modifications are made as needed.
10. Steps 8 and 9 are repeated until a final, acceptable version is developed.

Guidelines for Writing Task Statements

When task statements are identified, they should

1. Characterize activities, not skills or knowledge.
2. Have an identifiable beginning and ending.
3. Represent activities performed by an individual worker, not activities performed by different individuals.
4. Have an identifiable output or consequence.
5. Avoid extremes in the phrasing of activities; statements should not be too broad or too specific.
6. Be developed by full-time inventory writers (preferably); supervisors/incumbents should serve as technical advisers.

When task statements are written, they should

1. Mean the same thing to all respondents.
2. Be stated so that the rating scale to be used makes sense.
3. Be stated so that the incumbent is understood to be the subject of the statement. The pronoun "I" should be implied. For example "(I) number all card boxes."
4. Be stated so that an action verb is in the present tense.
5. Be stated so that the action verb has an object.
6. Use terms that are specific, familiar, and unambiguous.

Source: Based on Ernest J. McCormick, "Job Information: Its Development and Applications," *ASPA Handbook of Personnel and Industrial Relations*, ed. Dale Yoder and Herbert G. Heneman (Washington, DC: BNA, 1979), 4–66; and Joseph E. Morsh and Wayne B. Archer, *Procedural Guide for Conducting Occupational Surveys in the United States Air Force* (PRL-TR-67-11, AD-664 036) (Lackland Air Force Base, TX: Personnel Research Laboratory, Aerospace Medical Division, 1967), 8–11.

subsequent statistical analyses of the rating data help identify the most important or most critical aspects of the job.

To identify important job tasks, any of several statistical techniques are useful for rating data.[39] In many cases, these techniques involve calculating simple descriptive statistics (such as means, standard deviations, and percentages) and applying predetermined decision rules for defining critical job tasks. Let's look at a simple example: Assume for a moment that we have given a task analysis inventory to a large sample of bank clerks. Among other judgments, the clerks used a seven-point rating scale (1 = Of No Importance to 7 = Of Major Importance) to judge each task. Data analyses provided descriptive information on the ratings. We use two of the rated tasks to illustrate our point. Figure 3.7 shows the two example tasks and some associated descriptive statistics computed on the task ratings.

| FIGURE 3.7 | Example Task Statements and Associated Descriptive Statistics Used in Identifying Important Job Tasks |

Task Statement	Mean Importance[a]	Standard Deviation	% Employees Performing Task
9. Use basic arithmetic to add, subtract, divide, and multiply monetary amounts with decimals	6.74	0.68	99.2
•	•	•	•
•	•	•	•
•	•	•	•
67. Recommend to customers investment account options for investing savings	1.21	1.56	8.9

[a]The ratings of task importance were made using a rating scale ranging from 0 = Of No Importance to 7 = Of Major Importance.

In deciding which tasks are important to the job, we employed some *minimum* statistical criteria to define a critical job task. We set the following (in this example, arbitrary) cutoff points:

1. A task must receive a mean rating of 4.00 or higher (the higher the mean, the more important the task).

2. A task rating must have a standard deviation of 1.00 or lower (the lower the standard deviation, the higher the degree of agreement among employees in their task ratings).

3. Most employees (75 percent or more) must perform the task.

Using these standards, we choose Task 9 and omit Task 67 (see Figure 3.7). The task, "Use basic arithmetic to add, subtract, divide, and multiply monetary figures with decimals" is one among other tasks that pass our evaluation criteria. These are the most important tasks that compose the job. Inferences concerning the content of selection measures come from the pool of tasks derived from application of these criteria to the task ratings.

As we noted earlier, raters judging job tasks often employ several different rating scales. When multiple rating scales are used, some researchers simply sum all of the rating scores for each task.[40] As in our previous example, the results of these arithmetic procedures determine task importance. Others use the individual rating screens in a multiple-hurdle fashion. That is, a task must pass each sequential screen to be an important task.

Whatever the analyses used, the most important tasks are the basis on which inferences regarding the content of our selection procedures rest. The major idea behind the application of task analysis inventories is to define *important* job content. That determination serves as the source for WRCs used to develop or find selection procedures for choosing among job applicants. In addition, the defined job content serves as one basis for applying specific validation strategies such as content or criterion-related validity (see Chapter 8).

Advantages and Disadvantages of Task Analysis

Any job analysis technique will have unique assets and limitations; task analysis is no different. On the positive side, task inventories offer an efficient means for collecting data from large numbers of incumbents in geographically dispersed locations. Additionally, task inventories lend themselves to quantifying job analysis data. Quantitative data are most valuable in analyzing jobs and determining core job requirements.

Development of task inventories is time-consuming and somewhat expensive. Motivation problems often become significant when inventories are long or complex. Ambiguities and questions that arise during administration of the inventory may go unanswered; whereas, in a method such as the interview, problems can be resolved as they come up. As these difficulties multiply, one can expect respondents to become less cooperative, with a concomitant decline in the quality of data collected.[41]

With regard to data quality, a problem that can plague the use of task inventories, as well as other job analysis methods involving respondents who voluntarily participate, is respondent representativeness of the desired employee population. When actual respondents to a job analysis survey are not representative of the desired employee population (for example, in terms of gender, race, age), the results may not be generalizable. Potential for bias in job analysis studies can undermine job analysis results and content of selection procedures. Obviously, any source of bias can lead to legal as well as practical concerns regarding the validity of selection procedure content. Specific steps often are taken to encourage participation in job analysis surveys—for example, requiring names on surveys and conducting follow-up contacts with nonrespondents.[42]

CRITICAL INCIDENT TECHNIQUE

Description

The Critical Incident Technique involves the development of a series of behavioral statements developed by supervisors and other SMEs, such as job incumbents. The SMEs develop these behavioral statements based on direct observation or memory, describing incidents of good and poor work behaviors. These statements are important because they describe those behaviors that differentiate successful from unsuccessful work performance. Critical incidents provide valuable information about important components of the job. These components serve as a basis for developing descriptive information about a job.

The Critical Incident Technique was originally developed to gather information to determine training needs and develop performance appraisal forms.[43] Application of the technique generates a list of especially good and especially poor examples of performance (incidents) that job incumbents exhibit. The object of the Critical Incident Technique is to gather information regarding specific behaviors that actually have been observed, not judgmental or trait-oriented descriptions of performance. These behaviors then are grouped into job dimensions. The final list of job dimensions and respective critical incidents provides a great deal of qualitative information about a job and the behaviors associated with job success or failure. The basic elements of information collected are job behaviors rather than personal traits. Each critical incident consists of (a) a description of a situation, (b) the effective or ineffective behavior performed by a job incumbent, and (c) the consequences of that behavior. The result of the Critical Incident Technique is a list of events for which employees performed tasks poorly or exceptionally well. A representative sample of all job tasks may not be in the list, but the range of incidents provides information from which performance dimensions and worker specifications can be inferred.

Application of Critical Incidents

The Critical Incident Technique can serve a variety of selection purposes. Here, we examine the use of the technique to generate a list of job-related behaviors from which inferences are based regarding worker specifications. Job information collected from critical incidents is helpful in developing the content of task analysis surveys. In addition, critical incidents are particularly helpful in developing selection procedure content, such as situational interviews, behavioral description interviews, assessment center tasks, and situational judgment tests.[44] Information derived from critical incidents also facilitate the development of content comprising employee performance evaluations that often serve as criterion measures of job success. Implementing the method involves the following steps:

1. **Selecting the Method for Critical Incidents Collection**. Job analysts work with SMEs to facilitate the SMEs' generation of critical incidents (a) in a group setting, (b) in individual interviews, or (c) by completing a questionnaire. The most efficient method of gathering critical incidents is by working with a group of SMEs. The SMEs write as many critical incidents as they can. This approach entails less time for the participants, and upon discussion, participants can help jog each other's memories and subsequently generate a greater number of critical incidents.

   At times, it is not possible to gather the information in a group setting. For example, participants may not be skilled at writing. In this case, individual or group interviews are held, and incidents are recorded as the SMEs remember them. Individual interviews take place when the information is confidential, embarrassing, or not appropriate in a group setting. In addition, if the SMEs are managers or executives, it is often difficult to find a common time to meet as a group. The final incident-collection method, the questionnaire, is only applicable with individuals skilled at expressing themselves in writing and interested in participating in the process. Otherwise, the resulting critical incidents obtained may be insufficient in content and number.

2. **Selecting a Panel of Job Experts**. The Critical Incident Technique is applied by a job analyst working with SMEs. With this particular procedure, it is important to think carefully about the job experts chosen to participate in the process. Job incumbents, subordinates, and supervisors likely will provide different types of information. Individuals should include those who have had the opportunity to observe others' performance on the job. Normally, this would include supervisors and job incumbents who have been in the position for some time (four to five years).[45]

3. **Gathering Critical Incidents**. Use of a structured format for generating critical incident statements is best whether an interview or a questionnaire is being conducted. Job experts are asked to recall actions workers have taken while performing the job that illustrates unusually effective or ineffective performance. Then, job experts write statements describing effective and ineffective performance that meet the following four characteristics of a well-written critical incident:

   a. It is specific (a single behavior).
   b. It focuses on observable behaviors that have been, or could be, exhibited on the job.
   c. It briefly describes the context in which the behavior occurred.
   d. It indicates the consequences of the behavior.[46]

A resulting critical incident should be detailed enough to convey the same image of performance to at least two individuals who are knowledgeable about the job. The following is an example of a critical incident for a supervisory job:

A disposal company was picking up nontoxic waste. The order ticket was in error and read that the waste was toxic and to be disposed in a manner only suitable for nontoxic waste. The supervisor signed the disposal order without taking time to read it. As a consequence, the Environmental Protection Agency fined the company $5,000 for improper disposal of waste.

In this incident, only one critical behavior is exhibited by the supervisor: signing the disposal ticket without reading it. It is an observable behavior that could be exhibited on the job. It is also phrased in behavioral terms, not in reference to any personal traits of the supervisor (for example, careless, lacks attention to detail, hasty, trusting). There is enough detail for the reader to understand the situation, and the consequences of this behavior are clear.

4. **Rating and Classifying Critical Incidents into Job Dimensions.** Ratings of the developed incidents are typically made by SMEs. The goal of the ratings is to identify those behaviors most relevant in differentiating among behaviors leading to job success or failure. Those incidents passing various rating screens are sorted into job dimensions. Judges analyzing the content of the critical incidents and identifying common themes among the incidents determine the job dimensions. One way to do this is to write each critical incident on a separate card. A judge sorts these cards into piles representing common themes. The sorting continues until all incidents are in piles, and all piles are of a reasonable size. (Piles too big may be representative of more than one theme, and those with only one or two incidents may not really be a theme.) After sorting the incidents by theme, each theme is given a label that names the dimension. To help establish confidence in clustering incidents into dimensions, another group of job experts re-sorts the incidents into the dimensions. If there is not agreement about the dimension to which a critical incident belongs, it is prudent to drop that critical incident.

Advantages and Disadvantages of Critical Incidents

The Critical Incident Technique clearly results in a great deal of interesting, specific, job-related information. This information is behavioral in nature, not trait based. The described behaviors are "critical" incidents, so the information most likely represents important aspects of the job. On the other hand, it is not clear that the incidents reported represent the *full* scope of the job.[47] The process is labor intensive, and results often are situation specific. Considerable effort is required for each new endeavor, as it is doubtful that the information is transferrable from one setting to another. These disadvantages raise the question: Is the Critical Incident Technique really worth the time it requires and the limited focus on a job it may have? If one is interested in behavioral data, the incidents certainly provide such data. But, how can one expand the focus of the technique to, perhaps, uncover aspects of the job that might have been overlooked by a select sample of SMEs?

In the following section, we suggest an option to consider. We intermix two job analysis methods (the Task Analysis Inventory along with the Critical Incidents Technique) to leverage the assets of both methods while limiting, to a degree, some of the disadvantages of each.

Integrating a Task Analysis Inventory with Critical Incidents: A Suggestion

Figure 3.8 illustrates the results of a hybrid form of the Critical Incident Technique used to develop one job-related, selection interview question with an associated scoring key. Additional interview questions would be developed similarly. We will return to this example shortly.

As we have seen, use of the Critical Incident Technique is time and labor intensive. Moreover, because subject matter experts have free reign in incident development, there is a possibility that coverage of important aspects or dimensions of the job might be overlooked depending on the sample (for example, size, representativeness) of SMEs participating. However, critical incidents do translate into behavioral data, which are useful in developing selection procedures, such as an employment interview. In contrast, a task analysis inventory offers the possibility of wider coverage of the job domain. Importantly, once defined, the job domain facilitates identification of WRCs required for performance of the important job tasks. (In the next section of this chapter, we explain how important job tasks facilitate identification of essential WRCs.)

Our suggestion involves integrating the Task Analysis Inventory with the Critical Incidents Technique. We suggest our hybrid version of Critical Incidents might save time, obtain broader job task coverage, and, where appropriate, help translate our WRCs into behaviors that are measureable by selection procedures. For instance, this approach is particularly appropriate when developing behaviorally oriented selection interviews or situational judgment tests.

Below we summarize the basic steps involved. We present these steps in the context of the example shown in Figure 3.8. Before we walk you through the general process, it might be helpful to understand the organizational context we are using. In this example, a state public assistance agency has the responsibility of delivering prompt services to citizens eligible for and needing public assistance. The agency has been having problems with their clerical personnel who come into daily contact with these citizens in giving appropriate and timely service to deserving clients. The agency wants to add a behaviorally oriented selection interview to its battery of selection procedures to see whether they can improve on this personnel problem. Listed below are the steps involved in developing the interview:

1. **Identify Important Job Tasks**. Initially, employees and knowledgeable supervisors complete a task analysis inventory. As we explained earlier, participants rate the tasks on a series of rating scales. In turn, data from the ratings determine the critical job tasks. In Figure 3.8, we have listed one critical job task that resulted from the analysis.

2. **Identify Important WRCs**. In the next section of Figure 3.8, WRCs flow from critical job tasks. SMEs identify these WRCs and, like job tasks, they use rating scales to judge WRC importance. Analyses of these ratings help identify WRCs required for successfully performing the critical job tasks.

3. **Show Critical Job Task and WRC Information to SMEs**. At this point, SMEs review the identified critical tasks and essential WRCs. They use this information as stimuli for writing critical incidents using the guidelines we discussed earlier concerning the Critical Incident Technique. The one critical incident written in the present case is shown next in Figure 3.8.

4. **Rewrite the Critical Incident into a Selection Interview Question**. Then, using a bit of literary license (creative writing), the critical incident is rewritten in the

FIGURE 3.8	Use of a Critical Incident for Developing an Interview Question and Scoring Key for Selecting Public Assistance Clerks

---

Important Job Task

Meets with and assists agency clients through personal contacts in the completion of agency forms, determination of public assistance checks, and interpretation of agency eligibility requirements in order to facilitate distribution of public assistance funds from the state

Important Work-Related Characteristic (WRC) Tied to Important Job Task

Ability to interact with agency clients on a face-to-face basis with a customer-oriented service emphasis

Critical Incident

A client came into our agency and asked a public assistance clerk for help. The clerk told her that she would need to wait 20 minutes while the clerk went outside to take a cigarette break. The client had to wait for 20 minutes to explain her problem, which created a backlog of clients for the other agency clerks because this clerk did not attend to immediate need.

Selection Interview Question for Job Applicant

A client of your state agency walks up to your desk. She says she was told that a check she was due from the agency was sent 5 days ago. She claims she has not received the check. She says she has bills to pay, and no one will help her. She is very angry. How would you handle this situation?

Scoring Key for Rating Job Applicant Answer to Interview Question (a high score is better)

1—Tell her you will try and find the person with whom she talked, and you will have that person call her

2—

3—Apologize and tell her you will have to check into the problem and call her in a day or two

4—

5—Try to calm her and investigate the problem while she waits

---

form of an interview question. This is one strong point of critical incidents: They lend themselves to defining critical WRCs linked to critical job tasks in terms of behaviors. Perhaps, the most difficult part is writing the narrative of the interview question so that the desired response is not transparent.

5. **Develop a Key for Scoring Responses to the Interview Question.** SMEs use their expertise to develop a scale for rating applicant responses to the interview question. Initially, they generate a range of behaviors that are representative of the range of responses to the interview question. Once a response pool is identified, they independently rate these response behaviors on a rating scale where the poorest behavioral response = 1 and the best response = 5. Using means and standard deviations of the ratings, a behavioral response description is assigned to the points along the scoring key. Alternatively, supervisors serving as SMEs also might scale the behaviors in terms of those least to those most desired in a

public assistance clerk. Notice in Figure 3.8, we have blank spaces for scores 2 and 4. These spaces are for the interviewer to slot an applicant's answer that seems to fit in between the two defined response categories. Usually, a rating scale similar to the one shown in Figure 3.8 is sufficient. Notice that higher score points represent more desirable answers given by job applicants.

SME Workshops

The SME workshop, our final job analysis method, is not really a distinct job analysis method per se. Many different job analysis formats and methods, such as task analysis inventories and group interviews, lend themselves to SME workshops. Because of their use, particularly in content validation studies, we briefly outline how SME workshops produce job analysis data.

Description

SME workshops consist of groups or panels of 10 to 20 job incumbents per workshop session who work with a group leader to produce a job analysis. Because participants have current knowledge of their job, they are referred to as SMEs.

Although there is no one particular format for conducting the workshops, the following general steps seem to characterize most workshops: (a) selecting and preparing SMEs to participate, (b) identifying and rating job tasks, and (c) identifying and rating employee specifications (WRCs) associated with these job tasks. When a content validation strategy is undertaken, a fourth step is added. The fourth step requires that the SMEs judge the relevance of a selection measure's content (for example, items on an employment test, or selection interview questions) to the content of the job. In carrying out these steps, questionnaires and group interviews often are used to collect relevant job data. The steps are as follows:

1. **Selecting and Preparing SMEs.** SME workshop panelists should possess several important characteristics—a willingness to participate in the workshop, a minimum period of tenure in the job, a position representative of the employees on the job under study, reading, writing, and speaking skills, and so forth. From a legal perspective, particular care is necessary in choosing SMEs who are representative of legally protected groups. Lack of employee representativeness on SME panels can undermine any job analysis study. Once SMEs are chosen, the panelists are oriented and trained in the workshop's purpose and procedures.

   [**Technical Note:** SME panelists make importance ratings of both tasks and WRCs. Often, mean ratings (for example, SMEs' average ratings of the importance of a particular ability to performing a job) are calculated. Mean ratings, however, are subject to sampling error—that is, the error associated with data from a sample of individuals who are unrepresentative of the population. For example, assume for tasks and WRC ratings that the standard deviation equals roughly 1.0 ($SD = 1.0$). If 25 SMEs, using a 5-point rating scale gave a mean importance rating to a particular ability of 2.5, then the standard error of the mean rating is $1/(\sqrt{25}) = 0.20$. For 2 standard errors ($SD = 1.96$), the variation is approximately $2 \times 0.20. = 0.40$ around the estimated mean importance rating. Therefore, when possible, larger SME pools are preferable to reduce standard errors associated with SME judgments. In addition, standard errors should be considered when specifying minimum acceptable ratings for identifying critical job tasks and employee specifications or making job tasks and employee specifications' comparisons.[48] How large of a sample of SMEs is large enough? This

TABLE 3.3	Approximate Numbers of Participants Needed in a Job Analysis for Various Numbers of Employees in a Position Analyzed		
		Approximate Numbers of Participants Needed in a Job Analysis Study	
Number of Employees in Position Being Analyzed		**80% Confidence**	**90% Confidence**
20		15	17
50		22	32
100		30	50
200		35	65
300		38	75
500		40	80

Note: Because population standard deviations are unknown in each study being undertaken, the population proportion formula was used in estimating the numbers of participants needed (Dan Biddle, *Adverse Impact and Test Validation*, 52).

Source: Adapted from Dan Biddle, *Adverse Impact and Test Validation* (Burlington, VT: Gower Publishing Company, 2005), 32.

answer depends on the number of employees in the position for which selection procedures are being developed and the confidence level the user wants to have. Table 3.3 provides some general guidance. For instance, if there are, say, 300 individuals in the position of bank teller, for one to have roughly 90 percent confidence in the results, then a sample size of approximately 75 participants is needed. Note, however, that Table 3.3 is a general guide. The actual numbers will depend on such variables as the number of employees present on a given day, whether key employees are available on a given day, and other factors. Most important, ensure that SME panels are representative of the workforce in terms of characteristics such as protected group characteristics (demographics), work performance, shifts, and job experience.[49] If not representative, some groups will require oversampling.]

2. **Identifying and Rating Job Tasks**. Following training, the workshop leader serves as a group facilitator. The facilitator solicits from the group descriptions of the major job tasks performed. The group describes these major activities, and the facilitator records their comments on a projection screen or large sheets of paper so that the entire group can read the written tasks. The goal is to prepare task statements to accurately capture a consensus of the group's descriptions. Once prepared, the task statements are assembled into a survey whose format is like that of a task analysis inventory. Then, panelists and other SMEs use rating scales to make judgments about the task statements listed in the booklet.

3. **Identifying and Rating WRCs**. Following a group process similar to that used for generating task statements, SMEs next identify the employee specifications, which we refer to as WRCs necessary for successful work performance. Panelists judge these characteristics using rating scales. The purpose of these ratings is to identify the most essential WRCs required of those applying for the job.

4. **Judging Selection Measure—Job Content Relevance**. Whether or not to undertake this last step is determined by the purpose of the job analysis and the validation strategy being used. This step is essential in content validation. As we

describe in Chapter 8, SMEs judge the relevance of selection procedure content to the content domain of the job studied. These ratings help to establish content validity of selection procedures.

INCORPORATING JOB ANALYSIS RESULTS IN SELECTION PROCEDURES: A COOKBOOK

To this point, we have explored the actual application of job analysis in terms of collecting job information through several job analysis methods. By this time you may be wondering: "How do we actually use our collected information to develop or choose selection procedures?" Take another look at Figure 3.1. In that figure, we showed that job analysis results determine the relevant WRCs needed for effective performance. These WRCs, in turn, serve as the basis for *constructing* (for example, developing questions for an employment interview) or *choosing* (for example, purchasing a commercially available clerical ability test) needed selection procedures. Here, we study the last two elements of Figure 3.1: (a) identifying important WRCs from job analysis data and (b) incorporating these important WRCs in our selection procedures. These two elements are key steps in implementing job analysis results for HR selection purposes.

IDENTIFYING EMPLOYEE WRCs

Filip Lievens and Juan Sanchez have noted that in estimating employee specifications or WRCs, researchers use both *direct* and *indirect* methods.[50] *Indirect* methods involve using specific steps to break down large inferential leaps involved in deriving critical WRCs from job tasks. We described those inferential leaps in our earlier discussion of Figure 3.1. *Direct* methods of WRC identification require larger inferential leaps than indirect methods because SMEs simply rate the importance of WRCs listed on a survey for an entire job, not individual tasks. SMEs do not engage in the more manageable, step-by-step processes of indirect methods.

In Figure 3.1, we showed that inferences play an important role in identifying WRCs. The identified WRCs, however, are useful only if they are accurate and complete. If the inferences are wrong, our selection procedures will be useless for predicting work performance. We might as well flip a coin and say, "heads you're hired; tails you're not." Given current federal laws and executive orders, inappropriate selection procedures produce a situation ripe for charges of disparate impact against certain applicant groups, or one in which new employees are unqualified for the job. Both situations are unfair to employers and employees alike. Taking appropriate steps to ensure our inferences are accurate minimizes the probability of situations such as these arising. In this section, we address the inference problem by describing one approach to inferring WRCs to incorporate in our selection procedures.

The method we describe is an indirect procedure for WRC determination. The WRCs are (a) derived from task information and (b) make use of SMEs' judgments regarding important tasks and essential WRCs required for a job. Like most job analysis methods, specific steps are taken in collecting SMEs' opinions using surveys. The surveys, some composed of job tasks and others consisting of WRCs, are given to SMEs who judge these aspects of a job using rating scales. Figure 3.9 provides some example rating scales for judging tasks and WRCs that SMEs can use. Also, shown in Figure 3.9,

FIGURE 3.9   Examples of SME Rating Scales and Screens for Identifying Important Job Tasks and Essential WRCs

---

Job Tasks

Rating Scale: Do You Perform This Task?

    1 = No

    2 = Yes

Screen for Performance: At least 67 percent of SMEs must say "Yes," task is performed.

Rating Scale: How Important is it that You Perform This Task Successfully?

    0 = Not Important

    1 = Somewhat Important

    2 = Important

    3 = Essential

    4 = Critical

Screen for Importance: Task must have an average importance rating of at least 2.0 or higher.

Rating Scale: Should a New Employee, Upon Starting Your Job, be able to Perform This Task Successfully?

    1 = No

    2 = Yes

Screen for New Employee Importance: At least 67 percent of SMEs must say "Yes," new employee must be able to perform upon starting job.

Work-Related Characteristics (WRCs)

Rating Scale: How important is this WRC in performing your job effectively?

    0 = Not Important

    1 = Somewhat Important

    2 = Important

    3 = Essential

    4 = Critical

Screen for How Essential: WRC must have an average importance rating of at least 2.0 or higher.

Rating Scale: Should a newly hired employee possess this WRC on their first day of work in this job?

    1 = No

    2 = Yes

Screen for How Essential: At least 67 percent of SMEs must say "Yes," new employee must possess this WRC on their first day of work.

Linking Work-Related Characteristics (WRCs) to Job Tasks

Rating Scale: How important is this WRC in successfully performing this task on your job?

    0 = Not Important

    1 = Somewhat Important

    2 = Important

    3 = Essential

    4 = Critical

(Continued)

| FIGURE 3.9 | *(Continued)* |

> *Screen for Linkage: WRC must have an average linking rating of at least 2.0 or higher with one or more job tasks.*

Note: The **rating scale** information is used to determine if a job task or a work-related characteristic (WRC) is judged as important (task) to the job or essential (WRC) for a job incumbent to possess on the job.

The **screen** rating criterion is a *minimum* score on the rating scale that a task or WRC must receive to be considered as an important job task or essential WRC.

are "Screens for Importance." As explained later, these screens aid in identifying the most important job tasks and essential WRCs.

Group interviews of job incumbents in SME workshops are employed along with surveys to obtain task and WRC data. This method of WRC determination is specific to one job or family of jobs. Because it is job specific; the method is particularly appropriate for developing selection procedures, such as situational judgment tests or structured employment interviews. Implementation of the method's sequential steps facilitates identification of appropriate selection procedure content that representatively samples the content of the job. Before describing the development of WRCs, understand several caveats. First, numerous job analysis–WRC approaches exist other than ones we have mentioned. For example, Frank Landy[51] has illustrated how the tasks of a patrol police officer's job can be analyzed using Edwin Fleishman's taxonomy of human abilities.[52] The abilities required to perform the job tasks serve as the basis for choosing the type of selection predictor to use (for example, a written test or an interview) as well as the content of the measure (for example, test items requiring deductive reasoning).

Second, like all selection procedure development methods, the identification of WRCs we describe involves user judgment. Although judgment is involved, our approach involves a series of steps designed to lead *systematically* from (a) analyzing the job to (b) identifying WRCs to (c) determining selection procedure content. It is this methodical, step-by-step sequence that narrows the inferential leaps that SMEs have to make and enhances the validity of SMEs' WRC judgments.[53] Third, the sequence of steps taken helps a user comply with certain aspects of the *Uniform Guidelines on Employee Selection Procedures.*

Determining Employee WRCs

Initially, task or work activity data are collected, and these data, in conjunction with SMEs' judgments, help us ascertain the WRCs to compose selection procedure content. The following sequential steps are taken in specifying WRCs:

1. Identifying job tasks and work behaviors

2. Rating importance of job tasks and work behaviors

3. Specifying WRCs necessary for successful job performance

4. Rating importance of identified WRCs

5. Linking important WRCs to important job tasks and work behaviors

6. Developing content areas of selection procedures (that is, a *selection plan*)

The goals of this process are to (a) uncover job-related information that should compose the selection procedures content and (b) identify selection procedures that reflect these procedures' content. Before we see how we implement these steps, we need to clarify one point. As you read, you will see the terms "tasks" and "work behaviors" used. Understand that a *work behavior* is a broad description of the major activities of a job while a *task* is a more specific action associated with these work behaviors. Some strategies used in implementing a task analysis approach deal exclusively with job tasks while others focus on broader work behaviors. Nevertheless, many of the general procedures we discuss are similar, whether applied to tasks or work behaviors. Although we use the word *tasks* in our discussion, understand that our discussion applies to *work behaviors* as well.

1. Identifying and Rating Job Tasks and Work Behaviors.   The first step is specifying job tasks. This initial step is crucial. It serves as the foundation from which employee specifications evolve and selection procedures are produced. A number of different approaches are useful in uncovering task content. For example, observing and interviewing job incumbents and supervisors, and conducting brainstorming sessions with SMEs in workshops, are methods for deriving task content. Whatever the methods used, the goal is to produce a survey that SMEs can use to rate job tasks.

Because of the importance of task data, proper development of task statements is critical. Rules such as those we discussed earlier for developing task statements are important for generating the type of task information we need. In sum, task statements (a) begin with an action verb and (b) describe *what* the worker does, for *whom* or *what* the worker does it, *why* the worker does it, and *how* the worker does it. The following example portrays an incorrect and a corrected task statement:

Incorrect: *"Assists with inspection of construction projects."*

Comment: *First, the* **what** *is ambiguous and gives no real information as to the action. Second, neither the* **why** *nor the* **how** *questions have been answered.*

Corrected:

What?

"Inspects and construction operations (erosion control, Portland cement concrete paving, asphaltic concrete paving, painting, fencing, sign placement) …

Why?

to ensure compliance with construction specifications …

How?

by comparing visual observations with construction specifications and plans, and by following verbal instructions; while under daily review by the supervisor."[54]

Another example of task development is a procedure used by Katherine Jackson and her colleagues.[55] Job analysts work with SMEs to write work behavior statements (that is, broad descriptions of the major aspects of a job) and task statements (that is, narrow descriptions of the actions associated with these work behaviors) for a specific job. These actions lead to a precise description of the work activities involved on the

| FIGURE 3.10 | Example of a Work Behavior and of Associated Task Statements for the Job of Police Sergeant |

Work Behavior 3

Responds to life-threatening emergencies or critical incidents such as a plane crash, explosion, train wreck, tornado, flood, hazardous chemical spill, shooting, accident with injuries, hostage situation, bomb threat, and fire—using mobile data terminal (MDT), Fire and Rescue, robots, police vehicle, K-9, barricades, helicopter, radio, traffic vest, outside agencies, fire trucks, personal protective equipment, body armor, first aid kit, fire extinguisher, and firearms—following the Airport Aircraft Emergency Plan, County Police Department Critical Incident Response Plan, County Employee Manual, special orders, general orders, and HAZMAT guide in order to ensure the safety of property, self, and others during dangerous or hazardous situations. Stabilizes injured individuals until medical assistance arrives, and prevents the escape of an offender.

Associated Task Statements

1. Provides assistance to other agencies (e.g., State Police, local police department)
2. Extinguishes small fires (such as grass or vehicle fires) to prevent or minimize damage and prevent injury
3. Rescues people from dangerous situations such as burning buildings, damaged vehicles, and drowning
4. Administers first-aid to the injured at emergency scenes until medical help arrives
5. Evaluates an emergency or disaster scene to determine what assistance is required, whether evacuation is necessary, whether the ordinance disposal unit is necessary, whether the dispatching of emergency personnel is necessary, or if additional medical assistance is needed
6. Evacuates occupants of buildings and surrounding areas during emergencies or disasters
7. Maintains security in an emergency area and controls gathering crowds
8. Searches buildings and/or areas for bombs or other indications of criminal activity
9. Provides on-scene counseling to assist persons in dangerous situations or during emergencies, and reassures injured individuals that medical assistance is on the way
10. Determines if backup is necessary, and if so, requests backup assistance
11. Establishes a perimeter and if necessary diverts traffic and bystanders
12. Notifies the chain-of-command of the status of situations
13. Notifies Public Information Officer of the status of situations
14. Establishes a command post
15. Requests additional assistance from other personnel or agencies (HAZMAT, Fire Department, DOT, EPA, SWAT team)
16. Notifies hospitals

Source: Based on the Auburn University-Montgomery Center for Business and Economic Development, *Job Analysis and Content Validation Report: County Bureau of Police Services for the Rank of Sergeant* (Montgomery, AL: Auburn University-Montgomery Center for Business and Economic Development, 2004). Used by permission of Dr. Katherine Jackson.

job. For example, Figure 3.10 shows one work behavior and associated task statements identified for the job of police sergeant. As you can see, the level of detail is quite precise. For the sergeant's job, 24 work behaviors and an accompanying 497 task statements were developed. Although this information seems massive, it is this level of precision in the identified work behaviors and task statements that facilitate development of job-related selection procedure content. Therefore, job relevance of resulting selection procedures content is enhanced.

2. Rating Job Tasks and Work Behaviors.   Once we have task data for a specific job, the next step is to isolate the *important* tasks composing the job. Typically, we use job incumbents serving as SMEs to rate the tasks to make this determination using rating scales, such as frequency of task performance or task importance. We employ rating data to identify a job's most important activities. For instance, one possible strategy is to use statistical indices (for example, averages, percentages, or even more complex calculations) created from the rating scales. Then, we apply decision rules to these indices to define important tasks. We might require, for example, that important tasks receive a minimum average rating on one or more of our rating scales. We retain tasks whose ratings exceed our minimum rating requirements for further screening. For instance, we might specify that an important task composing a job is one for which (a) at least 67 percent of the SMEs perform the task and (b) the task receives an average rating of at least 2.0 (= Somewhat Important) on a 5-point rating scale, where 1 = Not Important and 5 = Critical. Any one or more of several criteria are available. The important point is that a common, objective standard is employed so that it is possible to objectively justify the identification of important job tasks.

On the basis of our earlier example of the police sergeant position (see Figure 3.9), Figure 3.11 illustrates the rating scales used to judge one work behavior and several associated task statements. Whatever the analyses used, the "most important" tasks are the basis on which inferences regarding selection instrument content rest (see Inference Point (2), Figure 3.1). The major idea behind using task analysis inventories is to define important job content. That determination serves as a guide for defining essential WRCs included in selection procedures.

It is important in constructing a job analysis survey to write the tasks and work activities and their rating scales as specific and concrete as possible. The more ambiguous, less observable the tasks and rating scales, the more likely raters will give inaccurate ratings. Inaccurate ratings distort the reliability and accuracy of a job analysis. Inaccuracy, in turn, affects determination of selection procedure content, which ultimately affects the quality of the human resource selection system.[56]

In addition to using specific, less ambiguous tasks and rating scales to counter respondent errors, another option is to remove respondents who provide inaccurate information. One means to identify inaccurate responders is by including several bogus tasks (that is, job tasks *known not* to be performed by the respondents) on the survey. If respondents indicate they perform the bogus tasks, then they are removed from the study.[57]

3. Specifying WRCs Necessary for Successful Job Performance.   Once critical job tasks have been identified, we are ready to specify the WRCs required for successful job performance. We cannot overemphasize the importance of producing accurate, complete WRC statements. As we will see, correct phrasing of the statements is *essential* to developing useful selection procedure content. Several steps are necessary for appropriately specifying these WRCs.

Selecting a WRC Rating Panel.   The first step is to select a panel of job experts (SMEs) who can identify important WRCs. Such a panel can consist of those who participated in a job's prior task analysis (see Steps 1 and 2), or formed from a new group of individuals. Listed here are several considerations in forming the WRC rating panel.[58]

- *A panel of SMEs (at least 10 to 20) is preferable over only one or two individuals.* Note, however, as we saw in Table 3.3, this guideline depends on the number of participants in the position being analyzed and the accuracy users want in their analyses. Do not give emphasis exclusively to *numbers* of experts; however, we are also interested in the *quality* of their job knowledge and participation. If their assessments and inferences regarding WRCs are incorrect, resulting selection procedures will necessarily suffer.

FIGURE 3.11 Example of Rating Scales Used to Rate a Work Behavior (Detailed in Figure 3.10) and Associated Job Tasks for the Job of Police Sergeant

Work Behavior:

Responds to life-threatening emergencies or critical incidents

If **No**, go to the next work behavior, if **Yes**, rate the following associated tasks:

DO YOU PERFORM THIS WORK BEHAVIOR?

Yes Ⓨ   No Ⓝ

Associated Task:	Perform		Frequency						DO YOU PERFORM THIS WORK BEHAVIOR? Importance					Necessary at Entry	
	Yes	No	Rarely	Seldom	Occasionally	Frequently	Continuously	Not	Somewhat	Important	Essential	Critical		Yes	No
1. Provides assistance to other agencies (e.g., State Police, local police department)	Ⓨ	Ⓝ	①	②	③	④	⑤	⓪	①	②	③	④		Ⓨ	Ⓝ
2. Extinguishes small fires (such as grass or vehicles to prevent or minimize damage and prevent injury)	Ⓨ	Ⓝ	①	②	③	④	⑤	⓪	①	②	③	④		Ⓨ	Ⓝ
• • • •															
15. Requests additional assistance from other personnel or agencies (HAZMAT, Fire Department, DOT, EPA, SWAT team)	Ⓨ	Ⓝ	①	②	③	④	⑤	⓪	①	②	③	④		Ⓨ	Ⓝ
16. Notifies hospitals	Ⓨ	Ⓝ	①	②	③	④	⑤	⓪	①	②	③	④		Ⓨ	Ⓝ

Note: **Perform** = Do you perform this job task? **Frequency** = How often do you perform this task in your current position? **Importance** = How important is it for you to perform this task successfully? **Necessary at Entry** = Should a new employee, upon starting the job of sergeant, be able to perform this task successfully?

Source: Based on the Auburn University-Montgomery Center for Business and Economic Development, *Job Analysis and Content Validation Report: County Bureau of Police Services for the Rank of Sergeant* (Montgomery, AL: Auburn University-Montgomery Center for Business and Economic Development, 2004). Used by permission of Dr. Katherine Jackson.

- *Focus on key characteristics in choosing the WRCs rating panel.* These characteristics include the following: (a) participation should be voluntary, (b) incumbents should have performed adequately on the job in question, (c) participants should have served on the job for a minimum period, and (d) importantly, members of protected groups should be represented on the panel.

Preparing WRC Panelists.   Whatever the data collection methodology, training WRC panelists is essential.[59] Panel members will likely require explanations as to what WRCs mean, why WRCs are important, and what are the SMEs' roles in identifying and rating WRCs.

Collection of WRC data can take several forms. Survey questionnaires completed by panelists is one form. Alternatively, group meetings of panel members can be convened, discussions held, and listings made of WRCs by panelists working within groups.

The development and specification of WRCs is not always as straightforward a task as we present it here. Just plan on problems arising. For example, if the panelists serving as SMEs are not trained properly, they tend to produce broad, undefined descriptions of WRCs that are relatively useless in developing a measure. Statements such as "ability to work under stress" are not helpful in understanding exactly the requirements needed for job success. Such WRCs likely will be developed when SMEs simply take a job task and add words to it such as "knowledge of," "ability to," or "skill at" in defining some WRCs. For instance, the task of handling customer complaints becomes "ability to handle customer complaints." Not only is the WRC undefined and of little use in developing a predictor, but this process assumes a unique WRC for each job task. Realistically, a WRC may underlie a number of job tasks. In sum, spend the time that it takes to prepare the SMEs for WRC development. It is an investment that ultimately will save time and yield operational WRCs that lend themselves to translating needed selection procedure content.

Soliciting WRCs from Panelists.   In actually specifying WRCs, SME panelists review tasks identified from the job analysis and ask themselves: "What WRCs should job incumbents have to perform each of these job tasks successfully?" In writing the WRCs, we recommend several guidelines. Again, appropriate phrasing of WRC statements facilitates making accurate inferences concerning employee job requirements.

Knowledge, skills, and abilities characteristics.   Among other characteristics, most all WRCs require some level of knowledge, skills, or abilities (KSAs). In writing KSA statements as well as other WRCs consider the following:

- **Panelists should have a clear understanding of what is meant by knowledge, skills, and abilities**. Definitions of these terms can vary, but for our use the following are helpful:
  Knowledge: A body of information, usually of a factual or procedural nature, about a particular domain (for example, information systems) that makes for successful performance of a task.[60]
  Skill: An individual's level of proficiency or competency in performing a specific task (for example, typing speed).[61] Level of competency is often expressed in numerical terms.
  Ability: A more general, enduring trait or capability an individual possesses when the person first begins to perform a task (for example, inductive reasoning).[62]
  Some analysts have difficulty distinguishing between skills and abilities.[63] For purposes of preparing WRC statements, it is not absolutely essential that a

statement be correctly classified as a skill or an ability. More important is the content and wording of the statement itself; the statement, not its classification, serves as the basis for inferring selection procedure content.

- **Statements should show the kind of knowledge, skill, or ability and the degree or level required for successful task performance.** For example, in describing "typing skill," it should be clear whether the typing skill requires typing tables of data and complex numbers within a specified time period, typing letters at a self-paced rate, or typing from handwritten manuscripts at the rate of 40 words per minute without error, and so forth.

- **Specific KSA statements are preferable to broad, general ones that lack clarity.** In preparing a statement, it is usually necessary that a facilitator probe the exact nature, degree, breadth, and precision of a stated KSA. If, for instance, there is a statement such as "knowledge of mathematics," it may be necessary to ask, "What kind?" "To what extent?" "To solve what types of problems?" and "Is use of special mathematical software required?" Use of probing questions should permit development of more useful statements of the job specifications.

- **Although it is possible to prepare a long list of KSAs for many jobs, emphasize those judged as essential to successful job performance.** That is, emphasize KSAs rated as most essential to job success by KSA-rating panelists. Sometimes, certain KSAs infrequently performed are critical when needed. Take, for example, the job of a fire investigator. The investigator is required to know how to investigate fires, their causes, probability of arson, the location of where the fire started initially, and so forth. However, the investigator might also need the physical ability to fight a fire in case one were to erupt on site putting other people at risk. In such a case, the task itself might rarely occur, but if it did, it is an essential physical ability for applicants applying for the fire investigator's job to have.

- **In preparing knowledge statements, avoid adjective modifiers relative to the degree or extent of knowledge required (for example, "thorough," "some").** Here are examples of appropriate knowledge statements: "Knowledge of the application of word processing procedures using Microsoft® Word, including setting margins, centering text, creating style sheets, and naming and storing files." "Knowledge of the use and interpretation of simple and multiple correlation statistical procedures, including knowing when to use a procedure, knowing the importance of statistical assumptions, and understanding the interpretation of results in the context of human resource selection."

Also, avoid vague adverbs implying some level of performance (for example, "*rapidly*" or "*effectively*") to modify the action of the statement. Ability statements should not confuse the action of the ability with the result of that action. For instance, look at this statement: "Ability to maintain accurate clerical accounting records." The result of the action, "Maintain accurate accounting records" is treated as the action itself. The statement would be better written as follows: "Ability to log accounting transactions using Microsoft Excel to maintain accurate and up-to-date accounting records."

After generating the WRCs, plan on editing the statements. When editing, the objective is to specify important content in as much detail as possible and give examples where appropriate. Again, the emphasis is on only the most critical WRCs, not every WRC mentioned. Figure 3.12 illustrates several knowledge, skills, and abilities developed in previous job analyses.

FIGURE 3.12 Examples of Knowledge, Skills, and Abilities (KSAs) Statements Developed in Previous Job Analyses

Knowledge:

"Knowledge of building materials including the uses, storage, and preparation of materials such as aluminum siding, Masonite®, concrete block, and gypsum board" (building materials company supervisor)

"Knowledge of the development, scoring, and application of employee performance appraisal techniques such as behaviorally anchored rating scales, 360-feedback, and graphic rating scales" (human resources consultant)

"Knowledge of basic and advanced first-aid procedures to include CPR techniques" (state police corporal)

"Knowledge of aircraft nomenclature (type, number of engines, manufacturer, jet/non-jet engine) and performance characteristics such as speed, climb/descent rates, turning radius, and weather and radio capabilities" (air traffic controller)

Skills:

"Skill in using a bank proof machine to process 50 checks per minute without error" (bank proof machine operator)

"Skill in typing business correspondence at 50 words per minute without error" (secretary)

"Skill in the use of handguns as needed to pass annual departmental qualifying standards" (state police corporal)

Abilities:

"Ability to give oral testimony in court as an expert witness in an employment discrimination suit regarding test validation issues" (human resources consultant)

"Ability to use basic arithmetic to calculate flow of current through an electrical circuit" (lighting company technician)

"Ability to obtain facts and information by using interviewing skills and techniques" (state police corporal)

Personality characteristics. In addition, many jobs require certain personality traits as essential WRCs, for example, extraversion for sales personnel. Personality traits such as "dependability," "extraversion," and "conscientiousness" are often-cited WRCs of successful employees. In Chapter 12, you will read about the empirical evidence regarding the relationships between such traits with work outcomes, such as job performance, absenteeism, and turnover, as well as other outcomes. Because the *Uniform Guidelines* does not permit content validation to be used with abstract personality characteristics such as those mentioned earlier, one strategy is to redefine the abstract characteristics into more observable, concrete outcomes of the traits.[64] For example, "dependability" might be characterized in terms of "is never late; always shows up for work on time" or "does not miss work without an excused absence." Conscientiousness might be described in terms, such as "works on an assignment until the completed project meets both predetermined quality standards and scheduled time lines." These traits and operational definitions obviously are not an exhaustive list; ones generated by SMEs will necessarily depend on the job itself.

Physical requirements characteristics. In addition to KSAs and personality traits, other worker characteristics are likely important. In the job analysis, a user should inquire about additional WRCs needed, such as physical requirements. Physical requirements are qualifications workers must possess to physically perform their jobs. These requirements can involve a number of physical abilities requiring specific levels of hearing, seeing, speaking, or lifting, to name a few. For example, the ability to lift, pull, or carry a specific amount of weight must be set for firefighters. Illustrations of such WRCs include the following: a firefighter must be "physically able to transport a 150-pound deadweight down a 75-foot ladder" or "physically hookup a truck-stored, fire hose to a hydrant within 1 minute; pull 100 feet of dry, fire hose to full extension within 3 minutes."

With regard to vision, minimum levels of corrected visual acuity are required in choosing certain nuclear plant workers, who must visually monitor dials and meters at a distance. In another case, "possessing the ability to see and distinguish among colors on a radar screen" is one physical requirement for a flight controller.

Operative or physically demanding jobs will require more physical abilities for adequate performance than will managerial positions. Thus, when setting employee specifications for operative positions, routinely consider physical ability qualifications. Be sure any specified physical abilities are *essential* to the job. Careful review of these abilities will help to ensure compliance with the Americans with Disabilities Act (ADA).

Where a listing and rating of physical abilities is concerned, the same methods described for generating and rating other WRCs are useful. That is, the goal centers on producing specific, observable, and measurable statements descriptive of physical job requirements. Additional examples of such statements include the following:

"Ability to read a voltmeter dial from a distance of 5 feet."

"Ability to drive a forklift, grab pallets holding four 55-gallon drums, and then transport the load, lift, and place on storage benches"

"Ability to hear and record equity purchase and sell orders in a loud (75–100 decibel level) commercial area"

Once listed, these characteristics are rated using scales like those used in judging other WRCs. Similarly, analyses are made of the ratings to determine those physical abilities most essential for a job. Development of selection procedures composed of essential physical abilities, such as work sample tests (see Chapter 13), then can proceed.

Ownership of tools and equipment characteristics.   Ownership of tools, equipment, or a car are sometimes specified as essential WRCs. With regard to tools, automotive shops and construction companies sometimes require that workers supply certain basic tools or safety equipment. Delivery personnel often are required to "have a current driver's license, own and drive a fully insured car, and have no moving vehicle violations within a prescribed time."

Possession of licensure and certification characteristics.   Teachers, health care workers, nurses, child care workers, and similar professionals are usually required to pass special certification examinations, pass licensing exams and hold a certificate of successful exam passage, and pass criminal background checks. WRCs such as these are certainly appropriate and often legally required not only of the applicant but also of the employer selecting employees.

Other WRCs.   More than likely, these "other" requirements are unique to a particular job; however, if "other" characteristics are critical to job success, they should be noted. Examples of these "other" characteristics might consist of such factors as "a willingness on the part of an applicant or incumbent to work under unusual conditions of employment, such as frequent relocation, frequent overtime, specific shifts, frequent travel, or under unusual working conditions (hot, cold, dusty, working alone, etc.).

4. Rating the Importance of WRCs.   Useful selection procedures should reflect the essential WRCs required for a specific job. That is, those WRCs most important for a job should account for more selection procedure content than less important ones. SMEs' ratings of WRCs usually determine WRC weighting of importance. Methods used in rating WRC importance are similar to those used in assessing job task importance. That is,

---

FIGURE 3.13 Examples of Typical Rating Scales Used in Rating Work-Related Characteristics (WRCs)

A. How important is this WRC in performing your job effectively?

0 = **Not important**—You can *definitely* perform your job effectively even if you do not possess this WRC. There is *no* problem if you do not possess this WRC.

1 = **Somewhat important**—You can *probably* perform your job effectively even if you do not possess this WRC. There is a *minor* problem if you do not possess this WRC.

2 = **Important**—It is *unlikely* that you can perform your job effectively unless you possess this WRC. There is a *problem* if you do not possess this WRC.

3 = **Essential**—You *cannot* perform your job effectively unless you possess this WRC. There is a *major problem* if you do not possess this WRC.

4 = **Critical**—You *cannot* perform your job effectively unless you possess this WRC. There is a *serious problem* if you do not possess this WRC.

B. Should a newly hired employee possess this WRC on their first day of work in this job?

Y = **Yes;** individuals on this job *should* possess this WRC on their first day of work.

N = **No;** individuals on this job do *not* need this WRC on their first day of work.

C. To what extent do individuals in this job who have *more* of this WRC do a better job than individuals in this job who have *less* of this WRC?

0 = **Not at all**—Having more of this WRC does *not* lead to better overall job performance.

1 = **Slightly**—Having more of this WRC leads to *slightly* better overall job performance.

2 = **Moderately**—Having more of this WRC leads to *moderately* better overall job performance.

3 = **Considerably**—Having more of this WRC leads to *considerably* better overall job performance.

---

respondents complete a questionnaire listing the identified WRCs. They use rating scales to judge WRC importance to job success. Actual questionnaire formats, including rating scales, can vary from one application to the next. However, most WRC rating scales employed resemble those shown in Figure 3.13.

5. Linking WRCs to Job Tasks and Work Behaviors.   It is critical to demonstrate the essential WRCs identified in Step 4 are required for performance of important job tasks.[65] For a WRC to be essential, *at least* one important task must require it. Demonstrating links between WRCs and important job tasks is important for several reasons. First, in the event of a discrimination charge, such linking information is necessary to defend a selection procedure. By showing a tie between important job tasks and essential WRCs, evidence demonstrates that these essential WRCs are required on a job. Second, limiting WRCs to only those that are most essential improves the efficiency and effectiveness of selection procedures. Basing selection procedure content on WRCs that are not job related is wasteful of resources. Most important, the selection procedures reflecting such WRCs will fail to identify qualified job applicants.

Methods of establishing WRC → job task and work behavior links.   There are several ways of showing WRC → job task and work behavior links. All involve using SMEs to review critical job tasks and then rating the extent to which a WRC is important for successful job task performance. We will describe one possible option; later, we will demonstrate it in an example.

At this point in the process, we have identified important job tasks and essential WRCs as judged by our SMEs. Next, we create a rating matrix (just imagine an Excel spreadsheet). Each important job task is a separate row and each essential WRC is a separate column. SMEs read each task. Then, they read across each column showing a WRC. They ask themselves: How important is this WRC in performing this job task? (Keep in mind, these linkage ratings are made *only* for those WRCs and tasks and work behaviors judged as important in our previous steps.) Then, SMEs use a rating scale such as the following to make their linkage ratings:

How important is this WRC in successfully performing this job task?

0 = **Not important**—You can *definitely* perform this task successfully even if you do not possess this WRC.

1 = **Somewhat important**—You can *probably* perform this task successfully even if you do not possess this WRC.

2 = **Important**—It is *unlikely* that you can perform this task successfully unless you possesses this WRC.

3 = **Essential;**—It is *very unlikely* that you can perform this task successfully unless you possess this WRC.

4 = **Critical**—You *cannot* perform this task successfully unless you have this WRC.

WRCs are considered "linked" to an important job task when the average SME rating equals or exceeds a predefined mean rating value, for example, ≥2.0 = **Important**.

The linking of WRCs to job tasks is a critical step. Do not take this linking step lightly. Linking data provide job- and task-specific cues as to the design and content of selection procedures that will have greatest physical and psychological fidelity with the job.

6. Developing Content Areas of Selection Procedures.   So far, in our exploration of the process of developing appropriate employee specifications, we have studied the tasks performed on a job, the WRCs needed for successful job performance, and the relationships between these characteristics and task performance. Our final step is to screen our task and WRC information to identify the content of our selection procedures. Once established, selection procedures are constructed or, where possible, chosen from existing procedures to match selection procedure specifications.

We are sure you are sitting there wondering, "If someone collects all this information, how do they possibly wade through it all to determine what a selection procedure ought to measure?" This is where our SME rating information comes into play. We use SMEs' ratings of tasks, WRCs, and the links between them to screen out those tasks and WRCs not essential to our selection procedures. To identify key tasks and procedures, we require important tasks and essential WRCs to pass multiple screens, such as those shown in Figure 3.9. These are examples of rating screens to consider for reducing important job tasks and essential WRCs to only those that are most essential. Whatever the ratings employed, use of standardized, objective screening procedures enhances our chances of producing selection procedures that reflect the important content of a job.

An Operational Example

To summarize and, hopefully, clarify our discussion, let's look at an example of the entire process. Suppose we are attempting to develop selection procedures for the job of HR selection analyst. HR selection analysts work in a state personnel department. They are generally responsible for helping to develop and implement selection procedures used by state agencies in employee selection.

FIGURE 3.14   SMEs' Average Ratings of Abbreviated Job Tasks for the Job of HR Selection Analyst

Abbreviated Job Tasks	Task Performed? (Yes)[a]	Task Frequency?[b]	Task Importance?[c]	Task Necessary at Job Entry? (Yes)[d]
1. **Computes adverse impact statistics for selection procedures**	70%	3.9	2.0	67%
2. **Constructs written tests for use in selection**	67%	4.1	3.0	88%
3. **Conducts job analyses on entry-level jobs**	75%	4.0	2.8	84%
4. **Develops affirmative action plans and programs and monitors impact**	69%	3.5	2.2	70%
5. Gives oral testimony in court regarding state selection procedures	10%	1.2	2.0	20%
6. Trains department managers in use of acceptable selection practices	27%	2.2	1.9	25%
• •				
15. **Maintains job applicant applications and selection test records**	71%	3.7	2.0	67%

Note: The task statements have been abbreviated to conserve space. Task statements shown in **bold** print are those passing the SME task rating screens.

[a]**Task Performed** ratings were made based on the following: **Do You Perform This Task? 1** = No, **2** = Yes.

[b]**Task Frequency** rating were made based on the following: **How Frequently Do You Perform This Task? 1** = Rarely, **2** = Seldom, **3** = Occasionally, **4** = Frequently, **5** = Continuously.

[c]**Task Importance** ratings were made using the following: **How Important is it that You Perform This Task Successfully?** **0** = Not Important, **1** = Somewhat Important, **2** = Important, **3** = Essential, **4** = Critical.

[d]**Necessary at Job Entry** ratings were made using the following: **Should a New Employee, Upon Starting Your Job, be able to Perform This Task Successfully? 1** = No, **2** = Yes.

Assume that a current job analysis of the HR selection analyst position identified 15 major job tasks. Figure 3.14 summarizes the ratings given by a large group of SMEs to a number of these tasks. (**Note:** To conserve space, we have shortened the actual task and WRC statements. Ideally, they would be complete statements and resemble the examples of job task and WRC wording, which we presented earlier.) For a task judged to be important to the job, SME ratings must meet the following rating specifications: (a) at least 67 percent of the SMEs must indicate they perform the task; (b) at least 67 percent of the SMEs must indicate successful performance of the task by a new employee is necessary at job entry; and (c) SMEs must give a task a mean importance rating of 2.0 or higher. An examination of the summarized ratings indicates that five tasks (Tasks 1, 2, 3, 4, and 15) meet the previous rating specifications. These tasks are important job tasks. The remaining tasks do not meet the specifications and are eliminated from the study.

Next, important job-related WRCs are identified. Figure 3.15 shows the mean importance ratings given to 6 of the 12 WRCs the SMEs previously identified. Like job tasks, WRCs must meet several rating criteria to represent the job content domain. These rating specifications are (a) SMEs must give a WRC a mean importance rating ≥ 2.0, (b) at least 67 percent of the SMEs must indicate that possession of the WRC is necessary for a new employee at job entry, and (c) SMEs must give a WRC mean relatedness to job performance rating ≥ 2.0. As seen in Figure 3.15, SMEs judged five of the six WRCs shown as essential in performing the job; "Knowledge of Record-Keeping

| FIGURE 3.15 | SMEs' Average Ratings of Abbreviated WRCs for the Job of HR Selection Analyst |

Abbreviated WRCs	WRC Importance?[a]	WRC Necessary at Job Entry? (Yes)[b]	WRC Relatedness to Job Performance[c]
1. Knowledge of recordkeeping procedures	2.0	50%	1.0
2. Knowledge of applied statistics	3.0	90%	3.0
3. Knowledge of test validation requirements	3.0	100%	3.0
4. Knowledge of development of task inventories	2.4	77%	2.0
5. Ability to read and understand technical written material	2.1	67%	2.1
•			
•			
12. Skill in using computerized data analysis packages (SPSS)	2.0	67%	1.8

Note: The WRC statements have been abbreviated to conserve space. WRC statements shown in **bold** print are those passing the SME WRC rating screens.

[a]**WRC Importance** ratings were made using the following: **How Important is this WRC in Performing Your Job?**
0 = Not Important, **1** = Somewhat Important, **2** = Important, **3** = Essential, **4** = Critical.

[b]**WRC Necessary at Job Entry** ratings were made using the following: **Should a Newly Hired Employee Possess this WRC on Their First Day of Work on This Job? 1** = No, **2** = Yes.

[c]**Relatedness to Job Performance** ratings were made using the following: **0** = Not at All, **1** = Slightly, **2** = Moderately, **3** = Considerably.

Procedures" was eliminated for failure to meet two of the rating criteria (other WRCs were judged as important but are not shown in Figure 3.15).

SMEs link the WRCs to the important job tasks by rating how important the screened WRCs are for each of the important tasks. Figure 3.16 illustrates the SMEs' mean ratings of WRC importance for performing the five job tasks. On the basis of the requirement that each WRC must receive a mean rating of ≥2.0 for at least one job task, Figure 3.16 shows that each of the five WRCs were tied to at least one important job task.

At this point, those WRCs that our selection procedures should contain are known. These WRCs serve as the basis for deriving selection procedure content. Comparing the WRC ratings summarized on our rating form with the preestablished rating criteria that we mentioned earlier helps us determine needed selection procedure content. Content areas of our selection procedures are defined by those WRCs that meet all of the prescribed rating criteria. That is, (a) if SMEs rate a WRC as important, (b) if at least two-thirds of SMEs believe that new employees should possess the WRC upon job entry, and (c) if SMEs link the WRC to performance of an important job task, then the WRC should compose selection measure content. Figure 3.17 summarizes the final tabulations of the WRCs evaluated.

In our HR selection analyst example and as shown in Figure 3.18, five WRCs meet all of the screening criteria (that is, Knowledge of Applied Statistics, Knowledge of Test Validation Requirements, Knowledge of Development of Task Inventories, Ability to Read and Understand Technical Written Material, and Skill in Using Computerized Data Analysis Packages [SPSS]). Therefore, these five WRCs should define the selection procedure content for the job of HR selection analyst. Next, we see how we might take these results and operationally translate them into a selection plan for the job.

FIGURE 3.16 Mean Ratings of WRC Importance Linked to Task Performance for the Job of HR Selection Analyst

Abbreviated Job Tasks	WORK-RELATED CHARACTERISTICS (WRCs)				
	Knowledge of Applied Statistics	Knowledge of Test Validation Requirements	Knowledge of Development of Task Inventories	Ability to Read and Understand Technical Written Material	Skill in Using Computerized Data Analysis Packages (SPSS)
1. Computes adverse impact statistics for selection procedures	3.7	2.0	0.9	0.0	3.8
2. Constructs written tests for use in HR selection	3.5	3.0	2.7	2.0	1.7
3. Conducts job analyses on entry-level jobs	2.9	3.7	3.9	0.0	2.1
4. Develops affirmative action plans and programs and monitors impact	0.7	1.2	0.8	1.0	1.3
• • •	• • •	• • •			• • •
15. Maintains job applicant applications and selection test records	0.5	0.3	0.0	0.0	0.0

Note: The task and WRC statements have been abbreviated to conserve space. **WRC ↔ Task Linkage** ratings were made using the following: **How Important is This WRC in Successfully Performing This Task on your Job?** 0 = Not Important, 1 = Somewhat Important, 2 = Important, 3 = Essential, 4 = Critical.

FIGURE 3.17	Summary of WRC Tabulations for Determining Content Areas of Selection Procedures for the Job of HR Selection Analyst

	WRC IMPORTANCE CRITERIA		
Work-Related Characteristics (WRCs)	Mean Importance of WRC[a]	Percentage Indicating a New Employee Should Possess This WRC[b]	Task Statements (Numbers) and Mean Ratings of Task Importance for Which a WRC is Necessary[c]
1. Knowledge of record-keeping procedures	2.0	50%	**2**(3.1), **3**(3.3), **4**(2.4), **15**(3.8)
2. **Knowledge of applied statistics**	2.0	90	**1**(3.7), **2**(3.5), **3**(2.9)
3. **Knowledge of test validation requirements**	3.0	100	**1**(2.0), **2**(3.0), **3**(3.7)
4. **Knowledge of development of task inventories**	2.4	77	**2**(2.7), **3**(3.9)
5. **Ability to read and understand technical written material**	2.1	67	**2**(2.0)
•	•	•	•
•	•	•	•
•	•	•	•
12. **Skill in using computerized data analysis packages (e.g., SPSS)**	2.0	67	**1**(3.8), **3**(2.1)

Note: The WRC statements have been abbreviated to conserve space. WRC statements shown in **bold** print are those selected for defining the content of selection procedures.

[a]Important WRCs are those receiving a rating of **2.0** or higher on the following scale:
0 = Not Important
1 = Somewhat Important
2 = Important
3 = Essential
4 = Critical

[b]WRCs that should be possessed by newly hired employees are those chosen by **67%** or more of the SMEs.

[c]Numbers *outside* of the parentheses are task statement numbers. Numbers *inside* the parentheses are average importance ratings of a WRC for that task's performance. The mean ratings are taken from Figure 3.16.

Determination of Selection Procedure Content

Now that we know what is required to perform a job, how do we translate these WRCs into selection procedures? The answer to this question is usually technical. The development of assessment methods requires the use of specially trained individuals, such as industrial psychologists. Yet job analysts and others working in HR can play an integral role in developing selection measures. The experience and information obtained during a job analysis is valuable for suggesting selection methods that reflect important WRCs.

Before building or choosing our selection procedures, we must decide on the relative importance of our WRCs as well as the type of procedure most appropriate for collecting this information. We refer to this process of specifying the relative WRC weights and choosing the appropriate procedures for measuring them as *developing a selection plan*. The preparation of a selection plan occurs in two phases:

1. Determining the relative importance of WRCs

2. Choosing the selection procedures to assess these WRCs

FIGURE 3.18	WRC Content Areas Identified for Measurement by Selection Procedures for the Job of HR Selection Analyst

Work-Related Characteristics (WRCs)	SELECTION PROCEDURE CONTENT AREA CRITERIA			
	Is This WRC an Important One?	Is This WRC Necessary for Newly Hired Employees to Possess?	Is This WRC Necessary for an Important Job Task?	Should This WRC Serve as a Selection Procedure Content Area?[a]
1. Knowledge of applied statistics	Yes	Yes	Yes	**Yes**
2. Knowledge of test validation requirements	Yes	Yes	Yes	**Yes**
3. Knowledge of development of task and inventories	Yes	Yes	Yes	**Yes**
4. Ability to read and understand technical written material	Yes	Yes	Yes	**Yes**
•	•	•	•	•
•	•	•	•	•
•	•	•	•	•
12. Skill in using computerized data analysis packages (e.g., SPSS)	Yes	Yes	Yes	**Yes**

Note: The WRC statements have been abbreviated in order to conserve space. WRC statements shown in **bold** print are those selected for defining selection procedure content.

[a]For a WRC to be chosen as a selection content area, each of the selection procedure content area criteria must show "Yes" as an answer.

Determining Relative Importance of WRCs. Previously in this chapter, we identified WRCs important to a job. For most jobs, it is unlikely that all WRCs will be equally critical to job success. Some WRCs are more important than others; these WRCs should play a more dominant role in determining selection procedure content and use. Before choosing selection procedures and their content, it is important to determine the relative importance of WRCs these measures should assess.

Several options are available for determining relative importance of employee specifications. For example, SMEs might complete a survey to make relative determinations of the WRCs' importance.[66] The questionnaire might consist of a listing of essential WRCs previously identified. Respondents assign a relative importance weight to each WRC from 0 to 100 percent, so that the sum of the weights totals 100 percent. The product of this process would be a relative weighting of the essential WRCs. Rather than administering a separate questionnaire that defines relative WRC importance, there is another option. Because we used a task analysis survey, we already have collected WRC and task importance information. We might assume that the WRCs rated by SMEs as being more important for several job tasks should represent greater selection measure content than the WRCs judged as being less important for fewer tasks. We can simply multiply our WRCs' *importance* ratings by the *task importance* ratings for those tasks requiring the WRC. This calculation will yield points for each WRC. Relative weights are determined by obtaining the proportion of each WRC's points for all total WRC points computed. The relative weight will indicate the extent of WRC coverage in the selection procedures. Using methods such as these, WRCs needed for a variety of important tasks will compose more selection measure content than WRCs used for only a few or less important tasks. Shortly, we will see the role these importance weights play in developing and choosing among predictors of job success.

Choosing Selection Procedures to Assess Employee WRCs.   A variety of procedures are available for assessing applicants. Many of the book chapters discuss the nature and application of these methods. Choosing ways to assess relevant WRCs requires consideration of a number of factors. Inferences and judgments play an important role in deciding which means are best for measuring which specifications. In considering possible alternatives, a personnel decision maker choosing a selection measure should ask the following types of questions:[67]

1. **Have job applicants demonstrated past behaviors or had experiences before taking the job that are associated with successful performance of the tasks of the job?** If so, consider evaluation of such past behaviors, such as through a structured interview or biographical data questionnaire.

2. **Can job applicants be observed performing the job or part of it? Is there a means for simulating the job in a test situation that is likely to require important behaviors as defined by the job? If so, is there a practical way of measuring simulated work performance?** When demonstration of successful performance is possible and measurable for a job applicant, a work sample or performance test is a possibility.

3. **Would a written test be best for examining worker requirements in terms of eliciting desired reactions and providing practical scoring?** If so, a paper-and-pencil or computer-administered test is often appropriate for assessing job knowledge.

4. **Would giving job applicants an opportunity to express themselves orally through an interview cover job requirements that might go unassessed using other means?** In this case, a structured selection interview is a sound option, depending on the number of job candidates who will interview for the position.

5. **Can the assessment method produce reliable and valid data for evaluating job applicants' possession of a WRC?** If not, drop the method from consideration and replace it with one for which there is prior evidence of reliability and validity for the desired inferences and applications.

6. **Is it practical and within our resources to use a particular method for measuring a WRC?** If not, consider another alternative.

John Campbell has illustrated how such a questioning approach might suggest alternative means for assessing the same WRC. For instance, suppose an ability, such as "ability to relate verbally with persons of varied socioeconomic levels," was important for the job of social worker. Campbell noted that in studying this ability, several selection methods are possible:

1. The applicant may have performed the same, or very similar, kinds of tasks in previous jobs. We then could try to find out how effective he or she was on that task in the past.

2. If previous experience does not exist, one might try to "simulate" the task in some fashion. For example, one might contrive a role-playing situation and include as many of the real-life dynamics as possible.

3. Several steps further removed from a direct sample of job behavior is the response of the applicant to open-ended questions when interviewed by members of the target group. The interview could pose hypothetical situations and focus on the content of the answers; minority group interviewers could play the role of a hostile minority group member to see how the applicant handled the hostility.

4. A paper-and-pencil predictor could be used that poses a number of hypothetical situations for the applicant (situational judgment test).

5. One could use a test such as Rokeach's Dogmatism Scale in the belief that it has something to do with how people relate to, for example, minority group members.[68]

Practical considerations will play a role in choosing the type of selection measure to use. For example, if an organization has hundreds of applicants applying for a position such as that of a bank teller in a large urban bank, the possibility of using a multiple-choice, paper-and-pencil, or computer-administered test will be given careful consideration because of its low cost and relative ease of administration to large groups of applicants.

An Example Selection Plan for the Job of HR Selection Analyst

Figure 3.19 shows an example selection plan for the HR selection analyst job. For illustration purposes, we are showing only five of several WRCs critical to the job. At the top of our plan, a variety of possible selection procedures is shown. You may be unfamiliar with some of these techniques (you will read about them in coming chapters); however, for our present purposes, complete understanding is not necessary. What is important is to understand is that we have chosen a variety of methods for illustration purposes. In practice, two or three methods would likely be used.

Let's study the example in more detail. With respect to the first two WRCs, "Knowledge of Applied Statistics" and "Knowledge of Test Validation Requirements," we are dealing with specific bodies of information and knowledge in two related technical fields. Because we are interested in the extent to which applicants possess knowledge of these technical areas, a written multiple-choice test is recommended. Test content could be based on actual problems encountered on the job. Because the two content areas are judged to be equally important, roughly half of the exam should concentrate on test validation issues and the remainder should focus on applied statistics.

With respect to "Knowledge of Test Validation Requirements," we want to know about applicants' knowledge and actual experiences with test validation matters. Three additional assessment methods are possible. The application form could ask applicants for a list of previous experiences in test validation research. We may contact previous employers through reference checks to verify certain stated test validation capabilities. A structured oral interview would let applicants describe in detail their experiences or, possibly, respond to technical questions or situations concerning their knowledge of test validation research. Our selection method weights show that greater emphasis is placed on the interview than on the application form or reference check in appraising this WRC.

"Knowledge of Development of Task Inventories" is assessed through a selection interview or, perhaps, a training and experience evaluation. In addition to questions about test validation, our selection interview also should incorporate questions involving applicants' knowledge about the development of task inventories. Training and experience

FIGURE 3.19   An Example Selection Plan for the Job of HR Selection Analyst

WRCs to be Used in Selection	WRC Weight	Selection Procedures					
		Application Form	Reference Check	Selection Interview	Work Sample (Performance) Test	Written Objective Test	Training and Experience Evaluation
1. Knowledge of applied statistics	15%					15%	15%
2. Knowledge of test validation requirements	15%	5%	5%	15%		15%	
3. Knowledge of development of task inventories	10%			5%			5%
4. Ability to read and understand technical written material	10%	5%				10%	
• • •				• • •			
12. Skill in using computerized data analysis packages (e.g., SPSS)	10%	5%			5%		
Total WRC Weight	100%	10%	5%	25%	5%	50%	5%

Note: The WRC percentage weights do not sum to 100% because other relevant WRCs and their weights are not shown.

evaluations could play a role in objectively judging applicants' experiences with task inventories.

Applicants' "Skill in Using Computerized Data Analysis Packages" also should be assessed. Relative to some WRCs, this skill plays a less critical role in accounting for selection analyst job success. An application form could ask for information on formal training, experience, or self-rated expertise with data analysis packages. Applicants also could be scored objectively on their skill by actually using a statistical or data analysis software package to solve a realistic problem. A work sample or performance test assesses this skill.

Besides suggesting alternative methods for appraising job-relevant WRCs, a selection plan has an additional value. That is, the weights assigned to a selection method for each WRC are useful in determining the relative emphasis placed on the content areas of the measures. For instance, think back to the job of HR selection analyst. Assume we plan to allocate 2 hours for assessing each HR selection analyst applicant. Some of our assessments will occur in groups (for example, a written test), whereas other assessments apply to individuals (for example, an interview). From examining our selection plan shown in Figure 3.19, we see that half of our time allocated for selection (50 percent of the WRC weights) should be assessed through a written, multiple-choice test. From previous experience, we know that roughly 50 multiple-choice items can be completed in an hour. Thus, we decide to use 50 items on our written test. How do we determine the proportion of these items that should be allocated to each WRC? Again, referring to our selection plan, we see that two WRCs are measured with our test; each has the same importance weight (15 percent). Therefore, 8 of the 50 multiple-choice items should be written to measure "Knowledge of Test Validation Requirements" and 8 should be written to measure "Knowledge of Applied Statistics." We would follow this same rationale in deciding how we want to allocate our remaining time to our other selection methods.

As you look at our proposed selection plan, you may notice an interesting result. Our job analysis appears to have produced a selection program whose contents seem to reflect the major contents of the job. Selection procedure and job content overlap is precisely what we want. The more we can ensure a match between the content of our selection methods and the demands of the job, the more confident we can be in the value of our selection program and its procedures. Of course, we would not stop with a job analysis as final evidence of selection method usefulness; job analysis is really the first step. Where feasible, we would plan validation research studies to examine how well our proposed measures predict successful job performance.

Some job analysis experts have questioned whether incumbents are capable of making the kind of inferences needed to identify the relevant worker attributes required to perform a job, particularly when attributes such as traits are abstract in nature.[69] Evidence suggests that job incumbents have greater difficulty in making reliable job analysis ratings than professional job analysts.[70] Recent research, however, has shed some light on the ability of incumbent SMEs to make accurate ratings of stimuli, such as WRCs. For example, Erich Dierdorff and Frederick Morgeson used a sample of more than 47,000 incumbents in more than 300 occupations to examine incumbents' ratings of tasks, responsibilities, knowledge, skills, and traits.[71] One of several conclusions they reached was that incumbents were capable of providing reliable and discriminating ratings of knowledge and skills. However, on less specific, less observable descriptors—namely, abstract traits—the raters could not make reliable ratings. Other research points to the important finding that certain forms of training, that is, frame-of-reference training, can enhance the quality of ratings given by job incumbents, even on abstract traits, such as personality traits.[72] Taken in total, when developing employee specifications, recent research seems to suggest that

1. A structured, systematic approach, such as the one we have described, should be used to reduce the size of inferential leaps made by job incumbents when rating their jobs.

2. Incumbents can reliably and validly rate the specifications for their position when the specifications deal with specific, more observable job descriptors, such as knowledge and skills.

3. Ratings of more abstract traits are improved when raters are properly trained using methods such as frame-of-reference training.

EMPLOYEE SPECIFICATIONS FOR JOBS THAT ARE ABOUT TO CHANGE OR YET TO BE CREATED

We have mentioned throughout our discussion that selection procedures must be based on a job analysis. We have discussed at length the use of methods to analyze jobs as they *currently* are being performed. But suppose a job does not yet exist or is about to undergo a drastic change—for example, through organizational restructuring. How do you develop employee specifications for a job about to change? How do you identify these specifications when a job that does not yet exist is being created? In these cases, selection procedures must be able to distinguish between individuals who can and who cannot perform the job as it *will* be performed in the future.

Conducting a job analysis of "future jobs" in our hypothetical situation is a problem. One option for handling current jobs that will change in the future is what Benjamin Schneider and Andrea Konz have referred to as "strategic job analysis."[73] The purpose of their approach is to define the tasks and WRCs thought to be needed for a job as it is predicted to exist in the future. In essence, the method consists of the following steps:

1. An analysis of the job is made to identify current tasks and WRCs.

2. Subject matter experts (for example, job incumbents, supervisors, managers) knowledgeable about the job are assembled in a workshop to discuss how future issues (for example, technological change) are likely to affect the job.

3. Information on expected future tasks and WRCs is collected from individuals knowledgeable about these expected job changes.

4. Differences between present and future judgments about the job are identified to isolate those tasks and WRCs for which the greatest change is anticipated. This task and WRC information serves as the basis for selecting incumbents in a job that does not currently exist.

Obviously, a key component of the entire process is the SME asked to predict future job change. If a current job is changed, incumbents, supervisors, managers, and other experts can forecast changes in job activities and WRCs.

If a new job is created, it will be necessary to use a more creative approach to selecting experts to make future job task and WRC predictions. Select individuals within the organization who can envision what the job will be like. Consider others outside the organization who have specific technical knowledge about the needed changes. For example, people in the organization who are familiar with corporate strategy and technological change might be helpful. Supervisors and incumbents of jobs who have tasks similar to those predicted for the new one also can participate. If the new job entails running a new piece of equipment, a technical representative of the manufacturer may provide useful information regarding the tasks and worker requirements necessary.

The process of strategic job analysis has many, yet-to-be-resolved issues. For example, what is the reliability and validity of experts' future job predictions? What experts are most helpful and accurate in forecasting change? What is the best way to conduct workshops and job analyses to collect the data needed? Will this approach be accepted if challenged in the courts? These are but a few of the unanswered questions that remain. Richard Arvey, Eduardo Salas, and Kathleen Gialluca have taken a different, empirical tack with regard to analyzing future jobs.[74] Rather than tasks, their concern is with statistically forecasting the future skills and abilities needed to perform job tasks. The need-to-know skills and abilities could occur, for instance, when the skills and abilities for operating new equipment in the future are unknown, when new plants with new jobs are being started, or when job redesign efforts involving reconfigurations of tasks into new jobs are occurring.

Using comprehensive task and ability inventories obtained from 619 skilled-trade incumbents, Arvey and his colleagues sought to determine whether it would be possible to predict required abilities from job tasks. Results from their analyses suggested that it was possible to forecast some needed abilities from task data. Other WRCs, however, were not particularly predictable. Nevertheless, results from their research were encouraging enough to suggest that when it is possible to build a comprehensive database of links between job tasks and abilities, forecasting future abilities from existing task information should be considered. All that is needed for future jobs is to estimate the key tasks that might be performed; required abilities could then be predicted. A major problem with such an approach is that collecting task and ability data on a large-scale basis is likely to be feasible only in large organizations.

Another approach to estimating the requirements of future jobs involves use of the Occupational Information Network or O*NET (www.onetonline.org) developed by the Department of Labor. O*NET is a comprehensive database of information that describes characteristics of workers and the work they do in jobs representative of the national labor force. Richard Jeanneret and Mark Strong conducted a study to determine whether it would be possible to identify selection instruments by using information on the occupations' generalized work activities stored in the O*NET database.[75] Generalized work activities are essentially groups of job behaviors used in performing major work functions (for example, identifying objects, actions, and events; teaching others; and thinking creatively). Results of their research showed that the generalized work activities were particularly helpful in choosing selection measures for occupations requiring intelligence and verbal and numerical aptitudes; they were less useful for occupations requiring manual dexterity. If it is possible to estimate generalized work activities required in an occupation, then knowledge of these activities might help in selecting appropriate selection instruments.

With regard to O*NET, we suspect that future research will draw on this database to examine the efficacy of using current O*NET data to infer required WRCs to use in selection. Current research using O*NET data has suggested the efficacy of these data in future research on employee specifications.[76] Use of O*NET to specify future work requirements is still being developed, and additional research is needed, but O*NET may hold particular promise for specifying selection procedures. Given the rapid technological change that many organizations are experiencing, the need to conduct some form of future-oriented job analysis is likely to become a necessity. At this point, the details of application have yet to be refined. Clearly, more research is needed on methods to identify employee specifications of future jobs and job tasks.

CONCLUSION

At this point in the chapter, we're guessing you must be thinking "C'mon, Man. You've taken me through a lot. Do you think this level of detail is really necessary?" The short answer is (you guessed it!), "Yes, we do." Now, that you are at the end of the chapter, keep the following quote in mind. Robert Guion, in commenting on the amount of detail and comprehensiveness of job analysis information required in HR selection research, said

> *The level of detail desired may also be determined by the likelihood of litigation. Prudent personnel researchers attend not only to the best wisdom of their profession but to the realities of the courtroom. In a specific situation, a detailed job analysis may not be necessary technically, but failure to have evidence of an "adequate" job analysis, in the view of the trial judge, may result in an adverse decision in court.*[77]

REFERENCES

1. Ernest J. McCormick, "Job and Task Analysis," in *Handbook of Industrial and Organizational Psychology*, ed. Marvin Dunnette (Chicago: Washington, DC: Rand McNally, 1976), 652–653.

2. Joseph E. Zerga, "Job Analysis, A Resume and Bibliography," *Journal of Applied Psychology* 27 (1943): 249–267.

3. Marvin D. Dunnette, *Personnel Selection and Placement* (Belmont, CA: Wadsworth, 1996).

4. Equal Employment Opportunity Commission, Civil Service Commission, Department of Labor, and Department of Justice, *Adoption of Four Agencies of Uniform Guidelines on Employee Selection Procedures*, 43 *Federal Register* 38,290–38,315 (August 25, 1978).

5. Paul Sparks, "Legal Basis for Job Analysis," in *The Job Analysis Handbook for Business, Industry, and Government*, ed. Sidney Gael (New York: John Wiley, 1988), 37–47.

6. Society for Industrial and Organizational Psychology, Inc., *Principles for the Validation and Use of Personnel Selection Procedures* (Bowling Green, OH: Society for Industrial and Organizational Psychology, Inc., 2003).

7. Duane E. Thompson and Toni A. Thompson, "Court Standards for Job Analysis in Test Validation," *Personnel Psychology* 35 (1982): 872–873.

8. *Griggs v. Duke Power Co.*, 401 U.S. 424, 436 (1971).

9. Ibid.

10. Ibid.

11. *Albemarle Paper Co. v. Moody*, 422 U.S. 405 (1975).

12. Ibid.

13. Equal Employment Opportunity Commission, *Guidelines on Employee Selection Procedures*, 35 *Federal Register* 12,333–12,336 (1970).

14. Thompson and Thompson, "Court Standards for Job Analysis in Test Validation," 872–873.

15. Equal Employment Opportunity Commission, Civil Service Commission, Department of Labor, and Department of Justice, *Adoption of Four Agencies of Uniform Guidelines on Employee Selection Procedures*, 43 *Federal Register* 38,290–38,315 (August 25, 1978), referred to in the text as the *Uniform Guidelines;* Equal Employment Opportunity Commission, Office of Personnel Management, and Department of Treasury, *Adoption of Questions and Answers*

to Clarify and Provide a Common Interpretation of the Uniform Guidelines on Employee Selection Procedures, 44 *Federal Register* 11,996–12,009 (1979); and Equal Employment Opportunity Commission, *Guidelines on Employee Selection Procedures*, 41 *Federal Register* 51,984–51,986 (1976).

16. Frederick P. Morgeson and Michael A. Campion, "A Framework of Potential Sources of Inaccuracy in Job Analysis," in *The Handbook of Work Analysis*, eds. Mark A. Wilson, Winston Bennett, Shanan Gwaltney Gibson, and George Alliger (New York: Routledge, 2012), 593–601.

17. See, for example, Frank L. Schmidt, John Hunter, and Kenneth Pearlman, "Test Differences as Moderators of Aptitude Test Validity in Selection: A Red Herring," *Journal of Applied Psychology* 66 (1981): 166–185.

18. Frank L. Schmidt, Deniz S. Ones, and John E. Hunter, "Personnel Selection," *Annual Review of Psychology* 43 (1992): 627–670.

19. Frederick P. Morgeson and Michael A. Campion, "Social and Cognitive Sources of Potential Inaccuracy in Job Analysis," *Journal of Applied Psychology* 82 (1997): 627–655.

20. Anna Koch, Anja Strobel, Robert Miller, Annegret Garrten, Christin Cimander, and Karl Westhoff, "Never Use One When Two Will Do: The Effects of a Multi-Perspective Approach on the Outcome of Job Analyses Using the Critical Incident Technique," *Journal of Personnel Psychology* 11 (2012): 95–102.

21. U.S. Civil Service Commission, *Job Analysis: Developing and Documenting Data* (Washington, DC: U.S. Civil Service Commission, Bureau of Intergovernmental Personnel Programs, 1973).

22. Ibid., 5.

23. Ibid., 11–12.

24. Ibid., 6.

25. Ibid., 12.

26. Sidney Gael, "Interviews, Questionnaires, and Checklists," in *The Job Analysis Handbook for Business, Industry, and Government*, ed. Sidney Gael (New York: Washington, DC: John Wiley, 1988), 394–402.

27. Robert J. Harvey, *CMQ, A Job Analysis System: Directions for Administering the CMQ* (San Antonio, TX: Washington, DC: The Psychological Corporation, 1992).

28. Ernest J. McCormick and P. Richard Jeanneret, "Position Analysis Questionnaire (PAQ)," in *The Job Analysis Handbook for Business, Industry, and Government*, ed. Sidney Gael (New York: John Wiley, 1988), 840.

29. Ronald C. Page, "Management Position Description Questionnaire," in *The Job Analysis Handbook for Business, Industry, and Government*, ed. Sidney Gael (New York: John Wiley, 1988), 860–879.

30. Melany E. Baehr, "The Managerial and Professional Job Functions Inventory (Formerly the Work Elements Inventory)," in *The Job Analysis Handbook for Business, Industry, and Government*, ed. Sidney Gael (New York: John Wiley, 1988), 1072–1085.

31. McCormick and Jeanneret, "Position Analysis Questionnaire (PAQ)," 825–842.

32. Felix M. Lopez, "Threshold Traits Analysis System," in *The Job Analysis Handbook for Business, Industry, and Government*, ed. Sidney Gael (New York: John Wiley, 1988), 880–901.

33. Joseph W. Cunningham, "Occupation Analysis Inventory," in *The Job Analysis Handbook for Business, Industry, and Government*, ed. Sidney Gael (New York: John Wiley, 1988), 975–990.

34. Patrick H. Raymark, Mark J. Schmit, and Robert M. Guion, "Identifying Potentially Useful Personality Constructs for Employee Selection," *Personnel Psychology* 50 (1997): 723–736.

35. Jimmy L. Mitchell, "History of Job Analysis in Military Organizations," in *The Job Analysis Handbook for Business, Industry, and Government*, ed. Sidney Gael (New York: John Wiley, 1988), 30–36.

36. This scale is typical of the relative scales that have been used in job analysis in the military.

37. Duane E. Thompson and Toni A. Thompson, "Court Standards for Job Analysis in Test Validation," *Personnel Psychology* 35 (1982): 872–873; and Edward L. Levine, James N. Thomas, and Frank Sistrunk, "Selecting a Job Analysis Approach," in *The Job Analysis Handbook for Business, Industry, and Government*, ed. Sidney Gael (New York: John Wiley, 1988), 345. Redundancy in task ratings can be an issue when considering which rating scales to use. See Lee Friedman, "Degree of Redundancy between Time, Importance, and Frequency Task Ratings," *Journal of Applied Psychology* 75 (1990): 748–752.

38. Ernest J. McCormick, "Job Information: Its Development and Applications," in *ASPA Handbook of Personnel and Industrial Relations*, ed. Dale Yoder and Herbert G. Heneman (Washington, DC: BNA, 1979) 4-66–4-67.

39. For a review of statistical techniques that can used in analyzing job analysis data, see Edwin T. Cornelius III, "Analyzing Job Analysis Data," in *The Job Analysis Handbook for Business, Industry, and Government*, ed. Sidney Gael (New York: John Wiley, 1988), 353–368.

40. Wayne Cascio and Robert Ramos, "Development and Application of a New Method for Assessing Work Performance in Behavioral/Economic Terms," *Journal of Applied Psychology* 71 (1986): 20–28. See also Patrick Manley and Paul Sackett, "Effects of Using High versus Low-Performing Job Incumbents as Sources of Job Analysis Information," *Journal of Applied Psychology* 72 (1987): 434–437, for an example of the application of empirical criteria for defining important job tasks.

41. Thomas A. Stetz, Mathew Beaubien, Michael J. Keeney, and Brian D. Lyons, "Nonrandom Response and Rater Variance in Job Analysis Surveys: A Cause for Concern?" *Public Personnel Management* 37 (2008): 223–239.

42. Ibid.

43. John C. Flanagan, "The Critical Incident Technique," *Psychological Bulletin* 51 (1954): 327–358.

44. Anna Koch, Anja Strobel, Guler Kici, and Karl Westoff, "Quality of the Critical Incident Technique in Practice: Interrater Reliability and Users' Acceptance Under Real Conditions," *Psychology Science Quarterly* 51 (2009): 3–15.

45. David A. Bownas and H. John Bernardin, "Critical Incident Technique," in *The Job Analysis Handbook for Business, Industry, and Government*, ed. Sidney Gael (New York: John Wiley, 1988), 1120–1137.

46. Ibid., 1121.

47. Ibid.

48. Philip Bobko, Philip L. Rother, and Maury Buster, "A Systematic Approach for Assessing the Currency ("Up-to-Dateness") of Job-Analytic Information," *Public Personnel Management* 37 (2008): 265–266.

49. Arthur Gutman and Eric M. Dunleavy, "Documenting Work Analysis Projects: A Review of Strategy and Legal Defensibility for Personnel Selection," in *The Handbook of Work Analysis*, eds. Mark A. Wilson, Winston Bennett, Shanan Gwaltney Gibson, and George Alliger (New York: Routledge, 2012), 139–167.

50. Filip Lievens and Juan Sanchez, "Can Training Improve the Quality of Inferences Made by Raters in Competency Modeling? A Quasi-Experiment," *Journal of Applied Psychology* 92 (2007): 812–813.

51. Frank J. Landy, "Selection Procedure Development and Usage," in *The Job Analysis Handbook for Business, Industry, and Government,* ed. Sidney Gael (New York: John Wiley, 1988), 271–287.

52. Edwin A. Fleishman and Marilyn K. Quaintance, *Taxonomies of Human Performance: The Description of Human Tasks* (Orlando: Academic Press, 1984).

53. Lievens and Sanchez, "Can Training Improve the Quality of Inferences Made by Raters in Competency Modeling? A Quasi-Experiment."

54. Iowa Merit Employment Department, *Job Analysis Guidelines* (Des Moines: Iowa Merit Employment Department, 1974), 10.

55. Center for Business and Economic Development, Auburn University—Montgomery, Montgomery, Alabama.

56. Ibid.

57. Thomas A. Stetz, Scott B. Button, and Joshua Quist, "Rethinking Carelessness on Job Analysis Surveys," *Journal of Personnel Psychology* 11 (2012): 103–106.

58. Samuel B. Green and Thomas Stutzman, "An Evaluation of Methods to Select Respondents to Structured Job-Analysis Questionnaires," *Personnel Psychology* 39 (1986): 543–564.

59. Lievens and Sanchez, "Can Training Improve the Quality of Inferences Made by Raters in Competency Modeling? A Quasi-Experiment."

60. Equal Employment Opportunity Commission, Civil Service Commission, Department of Labor, and Department of Justice, *Adoption of Four Agencies of Uniform Guidelines on Employee Selection Procedures,* 43 *Federal Register* 38,307–38,308 (August 25, 1978).

61. Ibid.

62. Ibid.

63. For an excellent discussion of the similarities and differences among knowledge, skills, abilities, and other employee characteristics, see Robert J. Harvey, "Job Analysis," in *Handbook of Industrial and Organizational Psychology,* ed. Marvin D. Dunnette (Palo Alto, CA: Consulting Psychologists Press, 1990), 75–79.

64. Dan Biddle, *Adverse Impact and Test Validation* (Burlington, VT: Gower Publishing Company, 2005), 35.

65. Equal Employment Opportunity Commission, Civil Service Commission, Department of Labor, and Department of Justice, *Adoption of Four Agencies of Uniform Guidelines on Employee Selection Procedures.* Section 14C4.

66. Stephan J. Mussio and Mary K. Smith, *Content Validity: A Procedural Manual* (Chicago: International Personnel Management Association, 1973), 24–27.

67. U.S. Civil Service Commission, *Job Analysis for Improved Job-Related Selection,* 10–11.

68. John P. Campbell, "Comments on Content Validity: A Procedural Manual" (unpublished report prepared for the Minneapolis Civil Service Commission), as cited in Stephan J. Mussio and Mary K. Smith, *Content Validity: A Special Report* (Chicago: International Personnel Management Association, 1973), 30–31.

69. Robert J. Harvey and Mark A. Wilson, "Yes Virginia, There is an Objective Reality in Job Analysis," *Journal of Organizational Behavior* 21 (2000): 829–854.

70. Erich C. Dierdorff and Mark A. Wilson, "A Meta-Analysis of Job Analysis Reliability," *Journal of Applied Psychology* 88 (2003): 635–646.

71. Erich C. Dierdorff and Frederick P. Morgeson, "Effects of Descriptor Specificity and Observability on Incumbent Work Analysis Ratings," *Personnel Psychology* 62 (2009): 601–628.

72. Herman Aguinis, Mark D. Mazurkiewica, and Eric D. Heggestad, "Using Web-Based Frame-of-Reference Training to Decrease Biases in Personality-Based Job Analysis: An Experimental Study," *Personnel Psychology* 62 (2009): 405–438; and Lievens and Sanchez, "Can Training Improve the Quality of Inferences Made by Raters in Competency Modeling? A Quasi-Experiment."

73. Benjamin Schneider and Andrea Konz, "Strategic Job Analysis," *Human Resource Management* 28 (1989): 51–63.

74. Richard Arvey, Eduardo Salas, and Kathleen Gialluca, "Using Task Inventories to Forecast Skills and Abilities," *Human Performance* 5 (1992): 171–190.

75. P. Richard Jeanneret and Mark H. Strong, "Linking O*NET Job Analysis Information to Job Requirement Predictors: An O*NET Application," *Personnel Psychology* 56 (2003): 465–492.

76. Erich C. Dierdorff, Robert S. Rubin, and Frederick P. Morgeson, "The Milieu of Managerial Work: An Integrative Framework Linking Work Context to Role Requirements," *Journal of Applied Psychology* 94 (2009): 972–988; Dierdorff and Morgeson, "Effects of Descriptor Specificity and Observability on Incumbent Work Analysis Ratings"; Christelle C. Lapolice, Gary W. Carter, and Jeff W. Johnson, "Linking O*NET Descriptors to Occupational Literacy Requirements Using Job Component Validation," *Personnel Psychology* 61 (2008): 405–441; Paul J. Taylor, Wen-Dong Li Kan Shi, and Walter C. Borman, "The Transportability of Job Information across Countries," *Personnel Psychology* 61 (2008): 69–111.

77. Robert M. Guion, "Personnel Assessment, Selection, and Placement," in *Handbook of Industrial and Organizational Psychology*, ed. Marvin D. Dunnette and Leatta M. Hough (Palo Alto, CA: Consulting Psychologists Press, 1992), 332.

Legal Issues in Selection

As discussed in Chapter 1, the development of a selection program is a formidable task even when we deal only with the technical issues, such as completing a job analysis, determining work-related characteristics (WRCs), gathering selection tests, and ensuring that the WRCs are valid. The task becomes even more complex when we add the legal policies that must be considered. These legal policies guide the records that must be kept on all employment decisions, the determination of fair treatment of all applicants, and the methods for identifying the job relatedness of selection devices.

If the organization does not attend to these legal policies in the development and use of selection programs, it will be vulnerable to charges of discrimination. A court judgment against the organization in such a case can be extremely costly. Courts can order organizations to make back-pay settlements to individuals they had not hired, to pay punitive damages, to change selection devices and decision rules, and to maintain specified percentages of women and minority group members in future employment patterns. It is imperative that human resource (HR) specialists have a thorough understanding of the legal guidelines for selection decisions. Actually, every selection program should have two objectives: (a) maximizing the probability of making accurate selection decisions about applicants and (b) ensuring that these selection decisions are carried out in such a manner as to minimize the chance of a judgment of discrimination being made against the organization. The two are not mutually exclusive objectives and overlap considerably in necessary procedures and data. It is also true, however, that there are examples of apparent conflict between these two objectives, which we will discuss in appropriate parts of the book. One example is affirmative action programs that, to many, seem to provide an advantage to minorities by specifying numerical goals for selecting among demographic groups. Another is the use of certain paper-and-pencil tests that almost always produce lower average scores for minority applicants than for nonminority applicants. Seemingly, these score differences provide advantage to nonminority applicants. This chapter will provide you with endless detail (and intellectual enjoyment!) about the following:

1. The basic principles of federal regulation of HR activities

2. An overview of the specific laws and executive orders appropriate to selection

3. The types of evidence used in deciding when discrimination has occurred

4. The types and characteristics of affirmative action programs

5. Major court cases in selection

6. The most important legal issues to consider in developing and implementing a selection program

FEDERAL REGULATION OF BUSINESS

Federal regulation of business activities can be traced back to the creation of the Interstate Commerce Commission (ICC) in 1887. In the years since, such regulation has occurred in almost all industries, such as finance, housing, health care, food and beverage, hotels and vacation destinations, and news media. Federal regulation in employment and selection in particular is known under the title of Equal Employment Opportunity (EEO).

EEO Laws and Executive Orders

EEO laws are federal laws whose purpose is the elimination of discrimination in HR management decisions. EEO executive orders are statements made by the executive branch of the government intended for the same purpose but aimed at organizations that do business directly with the government. The scope of EEO laws and executive orders affects other human resource management (HRM) decisions in addition to selection, although selection decisions have received a great deal of publicity, especially early in the history of the enforcement of EEO laws.

Table 4.1 lists nine employment laws and three executive orders and includes a brief summary of the major provisions of each.

Title VII Civil Rights Act of 1964

Under Title VII, private employers; unions; employment agencies; joint labor-management committees that direct apprenticeship and training programs; and federal, state, and local governments are prohibited from discriminating on the basis of *sex, race, color, religion*, or *national origin*. These are the only personal characteristics covered by Title VII. The law has been amended several times. In 1972, enforcement powers were strengthened and coverage was expanded to include government and education system employers as well as private employers with 15 or more employees. A 1978 amendment prohibited discrimination based on pregnancy, childbirth, or related conditions. The only employers not covered by Title VII are private clubs, religious organizations, places of employment connected with a Native American reservation, certain departments in the District of Columbia, and corporations wholly owned by the government of the United States.

The Equal Employment Opportunity Commission (EEOC) is the enforcement agency for Title VII. Basically, it acts in response to a charge of discrimination filed by one of the EEOC commissioners or initiated by an aggrieved person or someone acting on behalf of an aggrieved person. In most cases, the charge of discrimination must be filed within 180 days of the alleged act. After the EEOC has assumed jurisdiction, the first step is the no-fault settlement attempt, an invitation to the accused to settle the case without an admission of guilt. If this option is not accepted, the case is taken to the second step, that of investigation. During this period, the employer is prohibited from destroying any records related to the charge and is invited to submit a position paper regarding the charge, which becomes part of the investigatory data. At the completion of this phase, the district director of EEOC issues a statement of "probable cause" or "no probable cause." In the case of a probable-cause decision, an attempt is made at conciliation between the two parties. This usually involves some major concessions on the part of the employer regarding the employment practice under question. If the EEOC fails to obtain a conciliation agreement, it can either undertake litigation itself or issue a right-to-sue notice to the charging party, informing this party that it may bring its own action in federal court.

In one example of the enforcement of the Civil Rights Act of 1964, in March 2014 the EEOC and Ventura Corporation, a Puerto Rico–based wholesaler of makeup, beauty

TABLE 4.1	Major EEO Laws and Executive Orders Regarding Selection

Law	Demographic Characteristics	Employers Covered
Title VII Civil Rights Act of 1964	Race, color, religion, sex, or national origin	Private employers with at least 15 employees, governments, unions, employment agencies, employers receiving federal assistance
Civil Rights Act of 1991	Race, color, religion, sex, or national origin	Same as Title VII
Executive Order No. 11246	Race, color, religion, sex, or national origin	Federal contractors and subcontractors
Executive Order 11478	Race, color, religion, sex, national origin, handicap, or age	All civilians employed by the federal government
Executive Order 13087	Amends Exec Order 11478 to include sexual orientation	All civilians employed by the federal government
Executive Order No. 13672	Amends Exec Order 11478 to include gender identity	All civilians employed by the federal government
Age Discrimination in Employment Act of 1967	Age (older than 40 years)	Private employers, governments, unions, employment agencies
Americans with Disabilities Act of 1990	Physical and mental disability	Private employers, labor unions, employment agencies
ADA Amendments Act of 2008	Physical and mental disability	Private employers, labor unions, employment agencies
Immigration Reform and Control Act of 1986	Citizenship, national origin	Private employers with 4 or more employees, governments
U.S. Constitution 5th Amendment	All demographic characteristics	Federal government
U.S. Constitution 14th Amendment	All demographic characteristics	State and local governments
Civil Rights Act of 1866	Race, national, and ethnic origin	Private employers, unions, employment agencies
Civil Rights Act of 1871	All demographic characteristics	State and local governments

products, jewelry, and other personal care items to retail sellers, agreed to a $354,250 settlement for alleged sex discrimination in selection practices.[1] The EEOC charged in its suit that Ventura engaged in a pattern or practice of refusing to hire men as zone managers and support managers. The EEOC also alleged that Ventura promoted Erick Zayas into a zone manager position after he complained about its discriminatory practices, only to set him up for failure and termination in retaliation for his opposition to Ventura's sex-based hiring practices. According to the terms of the consent decree settling the suit, Ventura will pay $354,250, including a payment to Zayas of $150,000. The remaining settlement funds will be paid into an account that will be distributed to a class of qualified male job applicants who applied for zone or support manager jobs with Ventura from 2004 to 2014, but whom Ventura did not consider for hire. The agreement also requires Ventura to implement a detailed applicant tracking system, actively promote supervisory accountability for discrimination prevention, provide anti-discrimination training to all company employees and antidiscrimination training specific to those Ventura managers and employees who play a role in the hiring process, and provide bi-annual hiring reports to the EEOC for three years.

The EEOC said that the company was responsible for the loss or destruction of a great deal of critical evidence supporting the case. The disappeared evidence included job applications from qualified male applicants for the positions at issue and e-mails from key decision makers. The EEOC asked the court to award sanctions against the company based on the apparent destruction of evidence. The judge, agreeing with the EEOC's position, made a ruling that if the case were to proceed to a jury trial, he would instruct the jurors that they may draw an adverse inference from the vanished evidence and assume that this evidence would have supported the EEOC's case regarding the company's violations of discrimination law. A spokesperson for the EEOC stated that federal law protects both men and women from gender discrimination and that there is no protection in the law for reliance on outdated sex stereotypes.

Civil Rights Act of 1991

The Civil Rights Act of 1991 amends the Civil Rights Act of 1964. Its most important provisions address the extent of evidence that must be demonstrated in discrimination cases, the ceiling for damages for discrimination, the adjustment of scores on selection tests for different races, and the establishment of the Glass Ceiling Commission, which will recommend ways to remove barriers to women and minorities that limit advancement in organizations. Concerning the provision that treats the extent of evidence of discrimination, Congress passed the Civil Rights Act of 1991 to counter a series of Supreme Court rulings. These rulings—which increased plaintiffs' burdens of proof and reduced those of defendant organizations—were considered to have a limiting effect on those filing charges of discrimination. In essence, this act returned the burdens of proof to be similar to those that were used in early Supreme Court discrimination decisions. We will explain these burdens of proof later in this chapter.

Even though this act did return to early requirements for burdens of proof, it nevertheless had a large effect on the information that plaintiffs must include in any charge of discrimination: The 1991 Act required the complaining party to identify the particular selection practice in question and demonstrate the adverse impact caused by that practice. The only exception to this stipulation is when the plaintiff can demonstrate that the employer's selection decisions cannot be separated according to each selection instrument. In other words, the selection decision is based on information from all selection instruments. This requirement to present evidence in reference to a specific selection practice is in contrast to previous selection court cases. That is, plaintiffs usually had only to demonstrate that adverse impact occurred after the whole selection program was completed; they did not have to identify the specific part of the program that caused this adverse impact.

This act also allows victims of intentional discrimination, including sexual harassment, to sue for both compensatory and punitive damages. Compensatory damage is a monetary payment to the plaintiff to recover what he lost as a result of the discriminatory actions. Punitive monetary damages may be recovered if the complainant demonstrates that the respondent engaged in a discriminatory practice with malice or "reckless indifference." The act also allows for more extensive use of jury trials. Many legal experts think that the use of jury trials may increase the probability of the plaintiff being successful in discrimination lawsuits. This is because, historically, juries have been more sympathetic to plaintiffs than to defendants.

Another part of the act, makes it unlawful for an employer "in connection with the selection or referral of applicants or candidates for employment or promotion, to adjust the scores of, use different cutoff scores for, or otherwise alter the results of employment-related tests on the basis of race, color, religion, sex, or national origin."[2] This prohibits race norming: the practice of ranking test scores of minorities separately from nonminorities, and of choosing high scorers within each group to create or maintain a more diverse workforce. This practice originated within the U.S. Department of Labor in the early 1980s when the U.S. Employment Service decided to promote the use of its General Aptitude Test Battery (GATB) to individual state employment services.[3] The GATB is a general cognitive ability test composed of 12 subtests. The Employment Service found evidence that the use of the GATB inevitably led to significant between-group differences in average test scores. Blacks as a group typically scored well below the group of white applicants; Hispanics, on average, scored between these two groups.[4] Therefore, to promote federal equal employment opportunity and affirmative action goals, race norming of test scores was invented.[5]

Selection specialists have been mixed in their views of norming. Supporters point to the major benefit of helping employers hire a qualified but diverse workforce. Supporters' belief in this benefit is backed by the opinion that selection tests usually measure no more than 25 percent of how well people perform in jobs. Detractors have pointed out that minorities usually score lower than nonminorities on many valid selection tests, and any adjustment in the ranking of applicants can be expected to lower overall job performance.[6] The Glass Ceiling part of the act is based on Congress's findings that even though the number of women and minorities in the workforce had grown dramatically, they continued to be underrepresented in management and decision-making positions. The Glass Ceiling Effect refers to artificial barriers that impede their advancement to these higher positions. Under the act, a Glass Ceiling Commission was established to study (a) the manner in which business fills these higher positions, (b) the developmental and skill-enhancing practices used to foster necessary qualifications for advancement into these positions, and (c) the compensation programs and reward structures utilized in the workplace.

Executive Order 11246

Executive Order 11246 is directed toward contractors who do more than $10,000 per year in business with the federal government. Enacted in 1965, it prohibits the same discriminatory acts as Title VII. In addition, it requires contractors that have more than $50,000 in business with the government and more than 50 employees to develop *affirmative action plans*. These are formal, specific HR programs that are designed to increase the participation of protected groups. We discuss affirmative action plans later in the chapter. An affirmative action program is not a requirement of Title VII.

Enforcement of executive orders is the responsibility of the Department of Labor, specifically the Office of Federal Contract Compliance Programs (OFCCP). Investigations by the OFCCP do not depend on charges of discrimination being filed, but, instead, they are a product of the OFCCP's administrative review of contractors. The OFCCP can issue a statement of noncompliance that can adversely affect the contractor's participation in government business. When a statement of noncompliance is issued and the deficiencies are not corrected, an administrative hearing procedure before an administrative-law judge can be initiated. The whole procedure can take several years. During this time, the government can impose sanctions on the organization.

Executive Order 11478

Signed in 1969, this act extended EEO policy to all civilians employed by the federal government. Specifically it names the following characteristics: race, color, religion, sex, national origin, handicap, or age. It also seeks to promote the full realization of equal employment opportunity through a continuing affirmative action program in each executive department and agency. EEOC collects data and monitors compliance in all federal agencies.

Executive Order 13087

Signed in 1998, this order amends Executive Order 11478 to include sexual orientation.

Executive Order 13672

Signed in 2014, this order amends Executive Order 11478 and 11246 to include gender identity.

Age Discrimination in Employment Act of 1967 (ADEA)

The Age Discrimination in Employment Act of 1967 (ADEA), which has been amended several times, has the intention of promoting employment of older persons based on their ability and eliminating barriers to employment based on age. The underlying premise of the act is that there are large individual differences among workers of all ages; some older workers are superior to some young workers. Age, therefore, is not a valid indicator of ability to perform. The act prohibits discrimination against individuals who are 40 years old or older. This act applies to private industry, federal and state governments, employment agencies, and labor organizations.

Enforcement of the ADEA resides in the EEOC, and usually is initiated by the filing of a charge of discrimination. The EEOC also has the authority to review organizations when no charge has been filed. The act also provides for trial by jury. The following EEOC settlements are examples of the types of HR practices that have been found to be unacceptable.

Hawaii Healthcare Professionals, Inc.   Resolved in July 2012, the EEOC alleged that a then-54-year-old office coordinator was terminated based on age after the defendant's owner ordered a manager to fire the coordinator because she "looks old, sounds old on the telephone," and is "like a bag of bones." Case settled for $193,236 in monetary relief and injunctive relief.[7]

Kelley Drye & Warren.   Resolved in April 2012, the EEOC alleged that this law firm with more than 300 attorneys, had a system in which attorneys who practiced law after turning 70 years of age received dramatically reduced compensation compared with similarly productive younger attorneys solely because of their age.[8] The EEOC further charged that Defendant unlawfully retaliated against an attorney who had practiced law at the firm for more than 40 years, by further reducing his compensation after he complained about this discriminatory policy and filed a charge with the EEOC. (Kind of odd behavior for a law firm, isn't it?) The case settled for $574,000 for this attorney who continued to practice at the firm after he turned 70 years old and ended the policy requiring partners to give up equity in the firm once they reached 70 years of age.

Central Freight Lines.   Resolved in May 2012, the EEOC alleged that a class of employees was discriminated against based on age.[9] The defendant used a reduction-in-force as a ruse to fire eight dockworkers, some of whom had worked at the company for 20 or more years and were approximately 50 years old and older. Defendant subjected this class of workers to names like "grandpa," "old farts," and "old bastards." Eventually, the company replaced the class of workers with younger hires. The case settled for $400,000 in monetary relief and injunctive relief.

Americans with Disabilities Act of 1990

The Americans with Disabilities Act of 1990 (ADA) prohibits discrimination against qualified people with disabilities in all areas of employment. It is enforced by the EEOC and applies to employers with 15 or more workers.

Definition of Disability. An individual with a disability is someone who (a) has a physical or mental impairment that substantially limits one or more major life activities, (b) has a record of such an impairment, or (c) is regarded as having such an impairment. According to the ADA, a physical impairment is "any physiological disorder or condition, cosmetic disfigurement, or anatomical loss affecting one or more of the following body systems: neurological, musculoskeletal, special sense organs, respiratory (including speech organs), cardiovascular, reproductive, digestive, genito-urinary, hemic and lymphatic, skin, and endocrine."[10] The act also defines a mental impairment as "any mental or psychological disorder such as mental retardation, organic brain syndrome, emotional or mental illness, and specific learning disabilities."[11] It is worth noting that some groups are specifically excluded under ADA: homosexuals and bisexuals; transvestites, transsexuals, pedophiles, exhibitionists, voyeurists, and those with sexual behavior disorders; and compulsive gamblers, kleptomaniacs, pyromaniacs, and those currently using illegal drugs. Also active alcoholics who cannot perform their job duties or who present a threat to the safety or property of others are excluded. However, those individuals who have been rehabilitated and are no longer using drugs or alcohol are covered.

ADA's statement that the impairment must substantially limit one or more major life activities addresses walking, speaking, breathing, performing manual tasks, seeing, hearing, learning, caring for oneself, or working. The phrase also means that the impairment has significantly restricted an individual's ability to perform an entire class of jobs, or a broad range of jobs in various classes, as compared with the average person with similar training, skills, and abilities.

Another important statement of the ADA is that it pertains to "qualified individuals with a disability." This is an individual with a disability who meets the job-related requirements of a position and who, if reasonable accommodation is necessary, can perform the essential functions of the job. Reasonable accommodation generally means that the organization is required to make changes in the work process for an otherwise-qualified individual with a disability unless such accommodation would impose an "undue hardship" on the business. Common examples of reasonable accommodation are making facilities readily accessible (ramps, larger restrooms), restructuring jobs, altering work schedules or equipment, reassigning jobs, modifying examinations and training materials, and providing interpreters. Although no hard and fast rules exist concerning whether an accommodation would impose an undue hardship, generally the nature and cost of the accommodation as well as the size, type, and finances of the specific facility and those of the parent employer are considered. Accommodation is judged on a case-by-case basis and is related to both the job and the nature of a disability.

Because reasonable accommodation is not defined specifically in the ADA, the reasonableness of the accommodation is judged against imposition of an undue hardship. Elliot Shaller has offered his opinion of requirements, which is based on legislative history and on other state statutes.[12] First, an employer is not required to create a job for a disabled employee or maintain quotas. Second, reasonable accommodation does not require that preferences be awarded to people with disabilities. If, however, the choice is between a disabled individual who, without reasonable accommodation, cannot perform a task as fast or as well as a nondisabled person—but who, with accommodation, could perform better—the employer risks ADA liability if the nondisabled applicant is hired. Third, an employer is not required to hire a "shadow" employee, someone who actually performs the majority of essential functions of the disabled employee's position. Fourth, if an employee can be accommodated by a relatively simple and inexpensive redesign or piece of equipment, the employer likely will be required to make such accommodation.

Another important part of reasonable accommodation is the reference to "essential job activity." Job analysis, as used by selection specialists, does not define the term *essential*. Instead, job characteristics usually have been measured in terms of "importance" or "being necessary for job performance." Neither of these two terms, however, addresses the construct of *essential* as defined by the ADA. Following are several reasons why an activity could be considered essential to a job according to the ADA:

- The position exists to perform the activity.

- Only a limited number of other employees are available to perform the activity, or the activity can be distributed only among a limited number of employees.

- The activity is highly specialized, and the person in the position is hired for the special expertise or ability to perform it.

Furthermore, according to the ADA, a company may use various data to determine whether a job activity is essential. Among these data are the employer's judgment, supported by job analyses; a written job description; the amount of time spent performing the activity; and the consequences of not hiring a person to perform the activity.

Court decisions and EEOC settlements have more clearly defined the extent of reasonable accommodation. One example is the agreement between Finish Line, Inc., a nationwide athletic apparel retailer, and the EEOC.[13] The cause of the settlement was that Finish Line refused to grant Emma Armon, who has a physical impairment related to a right shoulder injury, a transfer to an available customer service representative position as a reasonable accommodation to her disability. Armon, who worked at Finish Line's Indianapolis store and warehouse, was qualified for the open position. The parties negotiated a consent decree that provides for $38,000 in monetary compensation to Armon, Armon's transfer to the customer service representative position, and injunctive relief in the form of antidiscrimination training for HR and management-level personnel. Finish Line further agreed to formal posting of antidiscrimination notices and an agreement not to discriminate further based on disabilities. In *PGA Tour v. Martin*, the issue was whether or not Casey Martin could ride a golf cart during PGA-sponsored tournaments.[14] He suffered from a physical ailment that prevented him from walking the course, a PGA rule, while playing in tournaments. The Court ruled that allowing Martin to use a golf cart was not a modification that would "fundamentally alter the nature" of PGA tournaments.

ADA's Impact on Selection.   The ADA prohibits the use of qualification standards, employment tests, or selection criteria that tend to screen out individuals with disabilities unless the standard is job-related and consistent with business necessity. Specifically, tests must be selected and administered to ensure that "test results accurately reflect the skills, aptitude, or whatever other factor ... that such test purports to measure, rather than reflecting the [impairment]."[15] This may require that the test administration be modified in accordance with the disability of the applicant.

An important part of the use of any modified selection test is that employers provide enough employment test information to applicants to help them decide whether they will require accommodations to take the test. This information should be exchanged early in the application process and should address what is required by the test, how information is presented, response format, and time limits. Test accommodation may be relatively simple and inexpensive, such as larger type required for those with impaired vision. Accommodation, however, may raise serious questions about the validity of the test and about how to compare the scores obtained on the "accommodated" test to those of the original test. For example, a written test that is usually self-administered might have to be read to a severely sight-impaired applicant. Such changes, however, raise the issue of whether the two tests measure the same WRCs. On the surface, they would seem to differ in terms of short-term memory, oral and written verbal ability, and the ability to make an immediate response. Similar arguments can be made when tests are administered through a language interpreter. In other words, key features of the test could be altered significantly because of an accommodation. If the employer determines that accommodation of the existing testing procedure is not reasonable, substitute methods for measuring WRCs should be explored.

The ADA also prohibits preemployment inquiries about a person's disability. If a disability is obvious to the employer, questions about the nature or severity of the disability can be asked only if they are about the performance of specific job-related tasks. Generally, the disabled person is responsible for informing the employer that accommodation is needed. Employers, however, may ask that individuals with disabilities request in advance any accommodations necessary for taking employment tests. Preemployment medical examinations are restricted to those that are job related and consistent with business necessity and should be undergone only after an employment offer has been made to the applicant. Furthermore, the employment offer may be contingent on the results of the examination *only* if the examination is required of all employees, regardless of disability, and if the information obtained is kept confidential and maintained in separate files. It is important to note that the ADA does not consider drug testing a medical examination.

ADA Amendments Act of 2008

ADA's 1990 broad definition of disability and its interpretation by EEOC was limited substantially in some notable Supreme Court decisions. In *Sutton v. United Air Lines*, Karen Sutton and Kimberly Hinton applied for employment as global airline pilots.[16] Both of them had severe myopic vision (uncorrected visual acuity of 20/200 or worse) that was correctable to 20/20 or better with eyeglasses or contact lenses. United Airlines required a minimum uncorrected visual acuity of 20/100 for global pilots. The two filed a complaint against the airline, claiming that its denial of employment violated the ADA. The Supreme Court did not support this claim, ruling that the two individuals did not adequately prove that they were disabled within the meaning of ADA. This was because their visual impairments could be fully corrected, and therefore they were not substantially limited in any major life activity. Furthermore, the court's opinion stated that the determination of whether an individual is disabled, under the ADA, should take into account measures that mitigate the individual's impairment (for example, eyeglasses). In fact, one judge expressed the view that the ADA does not apply to those people with correctable disabilities.

A similar judgment was made in *Murphy v. United Parcel Service* (UPS).[17] Murphy suffered from high blood pressure. When UPS erroneously hired him, his blood pressure was so high that he was not qualified for the Department of Transportation (DOT) health certification for drivers. The company requested that Murphy have his blood pressure retested and subsequently fired Murphy on the basis that his blood pressure exceeded the DOT's requirements for drivers of commercial motor vehicles. Murphy filed suit under the ADA, claiming that he was a disabled person and that he had been fired because UPS regarded him as disabled. The district court, appeals court, and Supreme Court disagreed. They held that to determine whether an individual is disabled under the ADA, the impairment should be evaluated in its medicated state. The courts then noted that when Murphy was medicated, he was inhibited only in lifting heavy objects but otherwise could function normally. In his medicated state, Murphy was not limited in life functions and should not be regarded as disabled. He was fired because he did not meet the legal standard for employment (blood pressure lower than the DOT requirement). Having high blood pressure, however, does not meet the ADA's definition of disabled.

Toyota Motor Mfg., Ky., Inc. v. Williams is a third case in which the Supreme Court restricted the definition of disability as applied to ADA 1990.[18] Ella Williams began working in a Toyota manufacturing plant in a position that required the use of pneumatic tools. Use of these tools eventually led to pain in her hands, wrists, and arms and she was diagnosed with bilateral carpal tunnel syndrome and bilateral tendonitis, which prevented her from doing tasks that required the movement of weighted objects. She worked for two years in a position that did not require such movement. When Toyota changed the tasks of her position to include such movement, Williams worked at the changed position until she again suffered from pain in her hands, wrists, and arms. After a period of discussion between Williams and Toyota, she was dismissed for poor attendance. Williams charged that Toyota had violated ADA. She argued that she was "disabled" under the ADA on the ground that her physical impairments substantially limited her in (a) manual tasks; (b) housework; (c) gardening; (d) playing with her children; (e) lifting; and (f) working, all of which, she argued, constituted major life activities under the act. She also argued that she was disabled under the ADA because she had a record of a substantially limiting impairment and because she was regarded as having such impairment. The Supreme Court ruled against this claim, indicating that to be substantially limited in performing manual tasks, an individual must have an impairment that prevents or severely restricts the individual from doing activities that are of central importance to most people's daily lives. The impairment's impact also must be permanent or long term. It is insufficient for individuals attempting to prove disability status to merely submit evidence of a medical diagnosis of impairment. Instead, the claimant must offer evidence that the extent of the limitation [caused by their impairment] in terms of their own experience is substantial.

These Supreme Court's judgments that limited the definition of disability caused a strong opposition among enough members of Congress to pass the ADA Amendments Act of 2008.[19] The express intent of this act was to reword the definitions of critical terms in the ADA of 1990 to explicitly counteract the decisions of the Supreme Court. The ADA Amendments Act contains the following statement of this disagreement with the Supreme Court's decisions:

> *Congress expected that the definition of disability under the ADA would be interpreted consistently with how courts had applied the definition of a handicapped individual under the Rehabilitation Act of 1973, but that expectation has not been fulfilled; the holdings of the Supreme Court in Sutton v. United Air Lines, Inc., and its companion cases have narrowed the broad scope of protection intended to be afforded by the ADA, thus eliminating protection for many individuals whom Congress intended to protect.[20]*

In the Act of 2008, the term *disability* was defined to mean (a) a physical or mental impairment that substantially limits one or more major life activities of an individual, (b) a record of such impairment, or (c) being regarded as having such impairment. In addition, the law states that the definition of disability shall be construed in favor of broad coverage of individuals under this act, to the maximum extent permitted.

The term *major life activities* was written to include, but not limited to, caring for oneself, performing manual tasks, seeing, hearing, eating, sleeping, walking, standing, lifting, bending, speaking, breathing, learning, reading, concentrating, thinking, communicating, and working. The term *major bodily functions* was written to include, but not limited to, functions of the immune system, normal cell growth, and digestive, bowel, bladder, neurological, brain, respiratory, circulatory, endocrine, and reproductive functions. An impairment that substantially limits one major life activity need not limit other major life activities to be considered a disability. An impairment that is episodic or in remission is considered a disability if it substantially limits a major life activity when active.

This act includes the following statements:

An impairment occurs when an individual meets the requirement of "being regarded as having such an impairment" if the individual establishes that he or she has been subjected to an action prohibited under this Act because of an actual or perceived physical or mental impairment whether or not the impairment limits or is perceived to limit a major life activity.

The determination of whether an impairment substantially limits a major life activity shall be made without regard to the corrective effects of measures such as medication, medical supplies, equipment, or appliances, low-vision devices (which do not include ordinary eyeglasses or contact lenses), prosthetics including limbs and devices, hearing aids and cochlear implants or other implantable hearing devices, mobility devices, or oxygen therapy equipment and supplies; The use of assistive technology; reasonable accommodations or auxiliary aids or services; or learned behavioral or adaptive neurological modifications.

These words may mean that a person should be considered disabled if he or she is diagnosed as having an impairment as defined by this act regardless of whether corrective devices can correct the disability.

Recent cases after the amendments have reflected their broader view of disability. For example, Creative Networks, LLC (which ironically provides services to disabled clients) agreed to pay $57,500 and furnish other relief to settle a disability discrimination lawsuit filed by the EEOC.[21] The EEOC objected to Creative Networks rigid policy of denying deaf and hearing-impaired applicants' requests for American Sign Language (ASL) interpreting services that cost more than $200. Rochelle Duran requested the services to complete the company's mandatory 24-hour preemployment orientation and training program. The company knew that this accommodation would greatly exceed its $200 limit and refused the request even though it admitted that it had sufficient resources to afford the interpretation services. When Duran was unable to attend the training because of this refusal, the company declined to hire her. The U.S. District Court for the District of Arizona held as a matter of law that Creative Networks failed to accommodate and failed to hire Duran because of her disability in violation of the ADA.

Pioneer Place, an assisted living and nursing home facility, agreed to pay $80,000 and apologize to a job applicant with epilepsy to resolve a disability discrimination lawsuit filed by the EEOC.[22] Pioneer Place refused to hire Pamila Bourasa for a cook position even though Bourasa had completed a positive interview and had discussed a start date. When informed that she needed to pass a drug test before beginning work, Bourasa mentioned that she had epilepsy and was taking a prescription medication that would show up on the drug test. Despite this information, Pioneer Place rejected her because of drug test results. Under the settlement, Pioneer Place paid Bourasa $80,000. It also was required to train all employees and managers on disability law, to implement antidiscrimination policies on interviewing and hiring, and to make annual reports to the EEOC for three years.

Immigration Reform and Control Act of 1986

Employers can face civil and criminal sanctions for knowingly employing any alien not authorized to work in the United States. Antidiscrimination provisions were added to address concerns that the employer sanctions might lead to discrimination against "foreign-looking" job applicants.

Regarding employment, the act states that it is unlawful for a person or other entity to hire or continue to employ an alien knowing that the alien is unauthorized. The company is required to verify authorization by attesting that it has examined any of the following documents produced by the individual being employed: a U.S. passport, a certificate of U.S. citizenship, a certificate of naturalization, an unexpired foreign passport with the proper endorsement of the attorney general, a resident alien card, or specified combinations of social security card, certificate of birth in the United States, documentation evidencing authorization of employment in the United States, driver's license, and documentation of personal identity.[23] A company has complied with these requirements "if the document submitted by the individual reasonably appears on its face to be genuine."[24]

Regarding discrimination, rules issued by the Department of Justice ban only those immigration-related employment practices in which an employer "knowingly and intentionally" discriminates. In terms explained later in this section, unintentional discrimination that creates adverse impact is not covered by this act. Also, it is not an unfair employment practice to prefer to select or recruit an individual who is a citizen or national of the United States instead of another individual who is a noncitizen, if the two individuals are equally qualified. The antidiscrimination provisions apply to any employer with four or more employees.

Complaints of discrimination are processed in the Justice Department by the Office of Special Counsel for Unfair Immigration-Related Employment Practice. Complaints must be filed within 180 days of discriminatory action, and the special counsel must investigate each charge within 120 days. All cases are heard by an administrative-law judge. An employer guilty of discrimination may be assessed back pay for up to two years, along with civil fines of up to $2,000 for subsequent violations.

One example of this type of discrimination was a settlement that the EEOC reached with Woodbine Health Care Center in 1999. Woodbine petitioned the Immigration and Naturalization Service (INS) to allow it to employ foreign registered nurses in its nursing home, claiming a shortage of registered nurses in the Kansas City area. Woodbine promised to employ a group of Filipino nurses and pay them the same wages it paid U.S. registered nurses. Contrary to its pledge, Woodbine paid the Filipino nurses about $6.00 an hour less than their U.S. counterparts. Moreover, rather than being employed as registered nurses, the Filipinos were assigned as nurses aides and technicians.

In 1996, two of the Filipino nurses filed discrimination charges with the EEOC. Woodbine rejected efforts to conciliate the matter, and one of the Filipino nurses, Aileen Villanueva, filed a private discrimination lawsuit. The EEOC intervened in the suit and Woodbine agreed to a settlement. Under the settlement, Woodbine agreed to pay $2.1 million to 65 Filipino nurses and their attorneys. The nurses shared compensatory damages of approximately $1.2 million and back pay and interest of approximately $470,000. The back pay was based on the average rate of pay that U.S. nurses earned while working for Woodbine.[25]

Constitutional Amendments and Civil Rights Acts of 1866 and 1871

In addition to these EEO statutes, discrimination complaints can be pursued on the basis of the Fifth and Fourteenth Amendments to the Constitution and the Civil Rights Acts of 1866 and 1871, which were part of reconstruction after the Civil War. Both constitutional amendments prohibit the deprivation of employment rights without due process. The Fifth Amendment covers the federal government and the Fourteenth Amendment addresses state and local governments. Unlike the EEO statutes, protection under these amendments applies to all citizens, not only to specific demographic groups. Therefore, discrimination charges can be filed for actions not covered by EEO statutes—for example, discrimination against homosexuals. Pursuit of a charge requires that the plaintiff establish discriminatory intent by the accused, not merely unequal effects of employment actions. This, of course, is often difficult to do.

The Civil Rights Act of 1866 states that "all persons … shall have the same right, to make and enforce contracts … as is enjoyed by white citizens."[26] Because of this wording, discrimination charges have been limited to racial and, to a lesser extent, ethnic and national background complaints. Sexual, religious, and other forms of discrimination are not considered to be appropriate. Charges can be filed against private employers, unions, and employment agencies. Whereas Title VII requires a minimum of 15 employees in an organization, no such limitation exists with this act. The Civil Rights Act of 1871 is similar to provisions of the Fourteenth Amendment. By its wording, it applies to state and local governments. It does not apply to purely private business or federal agencies unless there is state involvement in the questioned employment practices. Thus, this act has been applied to police and fire departments, public schools, colleges, hospitals, and state agencies. A broad range of bases for discrimination is applicable—for example, ethnicity, gender, sex, religion, age, sexual preference, citizenship, and physical attributes.

This brief review of the important EEO laws and executive orders highlights their major points. These laws are addressed to societal problems not business problems; they focus on safeguarding the fair treatment of demographic groups that frequently have had their access to the American dream of career success limited by non job-related factors. These laws created agencies designed to monitor the compliance of organizations with employment regulations and to represent the claims of individuals who think that they were treated unfairly. Such actions require both the evaluation of organizations' employment practices and also the methods of forcing organizations that do not comply with these regulations to provide restitution and employment to those damaged by this noncompliance.

This and That Stuff

Here is what we found out about three topics you may be interested in—not to imply, of course, that you are not interested in the other exciting material of this book.

Obesity.   Obesity is not a characteristic that is listed in any of the EEOC laws or regulations. In addition, EEOC indicates that not every physical characteristic constitutes an impairment that implicates potential ADA coverage. For example, normal deviations in height, weight, or strength are not impairments. Thus, it generally would not violate the ADA to exclude someone from a job who exceeds what an employer considers an acceptable weight. Morbid obesity (i.e., weight that is 100 percent or more over what is considered normal) is an impairment, however, and it will be considered a disability if the applicant or employee can show that the obesity substantially limits a major life activity, or substantially limited a major life activity in the past, or is regarded as substantially limiting. Although an individual with morbid obesity may experience limitations that make him or her unqualified for a particular job, it would violate the ADA to exclude someone with morbid obesity from a job for which he or she is qualified.

A court ruling also indicates that obesity can be considered a disability. In a 2012 suit settled between the EEOC and Resources for Human Development, Inc. (RHD), a treatment facility for chemically dependent women and their children, RHD paid $125,000 to settle a disability discrimination claim.[27] Lisa Harrison worked as a prevention and intervention specialist at RHD from 1999 until she was fired in September of 2007. In its suit, the EEOC charged that RHD violated the ADA when it fired Harrison because of her disability, severe obesity, even though she was able to perform the essential functions of her job. During the litigation, the issue was raised of whether severe obesity could be considered a disability only if it was caused by a physiological disorder rather than a lack of character or willpower. The court concluded that neither the EEOC nor the Fifth Circuit court have ever required a party with a disability to prove the underlying basis of an impairment. In addition to the money payout, the company agreed to provide annual training on federal disability law to all HR personnel and corporate directors of RHD nationwide. It also must report to the EEOC for three years on all complaints of disability discrimination and all denials of a request for reasonable accommodation of a disability. Finally, RHD also named a children's room at the Family House facility, and permanently installed a memorial plaque, in honor of Harrison, who taught at the facility for almost eight years and died before the settlement was reached.

Smoking.   Smoking in the workplace is primarily a state law issue as the federal EEO laws and executive orders do not list smokers as a protected class. State laws are variable in how they address smoking. Most states allow employers to ban smoking in their workplaces because employers have the right (some contend obligation) to control all employees' exposure to second-hand smoke and fire hazards. It is not discrimination to require that employees go outside to smoke or smoke only when off-duty. Some state laws, in fact, completely forbid smoking in any workplace. Regarding selection, in some states, employers can refuse to hire smokers. Applicants may be screened by being tested for nicotine. If the results are positive, the company can decline to offer the applicant a job. Once a person has been hired, however, most states forbid firing the person for being a smoker or taking up smoking. The American Civil Liberties Union has argued that refusing to hire a smoker is a form of discrimination, because employers are excluding applicants because of actions they take on their own time. Employers counter that they are not telling employees what to do when they are not working. They are just not hiring them, which is their right. Some states have enacted laws that protect smokers from workplace discrimination. In these jurisdictions, smokers have no right to light up while working, but they can do so after hours. Their employers cannot fire them or deny them jobs because of it. Of the remaining states, most have no legislation that addresses smokers' rights in the workplace. They're "silent," meaning they neither allow discrimination nor do anything to protect against it.

Ethnic Restaurants.   The selection issue is whether or not an ethnic restaurant (e.g., one that wishes to be Mexican, Greek, French, etc.) can select only those applicants who are in a specific demographic group to be "authentic." We could not find an EEOC settlement or court case that focused on this issue, but our opinion is that such selection would not be permissible. EEOC in a Web site devoted to national origin makes the following statements: (a) the law prohibits discrimination against anyone on basis of national origin and (b) customer preference is not a defense for violation of the use of national origin in selection. The site also uses the following examples of discrimination (a) a Chinese woman not being hired by a Greek restaurant would be contrary to national origin, and (b) a Bangladesh woman who wears a sari was told that she had been hired; however, when she showed up for the first day of work, she was told that she did not have a job. A Mexican woman who had about the same qualification was hired a week later. This would be discrimination because of national origin. In spite of these statements, we probably have all been in an ethnic restaurant in which all employees, especially wait staff, are of one nationality. Our thoughts on this are as follows: (a) the majority of all restaurants are small and exempt from EEO law because of size (this is especially true of those that are family owned and operated), and (b) wait staff are often not well paid and do not have time or resources to file discrimination suits. Thus, denied applicants are used to not getting a specific job and simply find another place of employment. Therefore, we believe that ethnic restaurants that are large enough are subject to national origin and ethnicity laws. Little if any legal history is available about this topic because of circumstances of the employment situation, including restaurant size, and lack of complaining applicants.

EMPLOYMENT DISCRIMINATION

The previously cited laws and orders clearly prohibit discrimination in selection and other HR actions. The difficulty for managers of organizations is to identify when discrimination is present. As we have said, laws state principles. Putting these principles into operation is another step. This step is based partially on court decisions in discrimination cases and partially on actions by regulatory agencies, such as the EEOC. The court decisions set legal precedent and yield specific comments about the treatment of evidence of alleged discrimination in specific situations. These legal precedents serve as benchmarks for subsequent legal interpretation. In addition, in 1978, the EEOC published the *Uniform Guidelines on Employee Selection Procedures*, which, while being neither law nor court decisions, are important because they represent the joint statement of the agencies empowered by law to enforce the EEO laws. The *Uniform Guidelines* describe what evidence will be considered in judging discrimination and how an employer may defend a selection program. In addition, the guidelines are given "great deference" by the courts when considering discrimination cases. We now discuss the definition and evidence of discrimination.

Discrimination Defined

It is important to understand the difference between two terms that frequently are used in reference to equal employment laws: adverse impact and discrimination. *Adverse impact* means that there are differences between demographically different individuals or groups with regard to the outcome of some selection procedure or process. For example, male applicants may score higher on a physical ability test than do female applicants. *Discrimination* means that these differences in scores on the selection test result in either a man (single case) or many more men being selected rather than a woman or many women, and there is not a valid, job-related explanation for the adverse impact. For example, more males are selected for a manual labor position after a test requiring applicants to lift a 100-pound sack of grass (lawn!) seed five times. The job itself, however, does not require lifting 100 pounds five times in a row. Therefore, the test that led to the disparity between men and women being selected is not job related and not defensible in terms of its negative effects on female applicants. A similar conclusion would be drawn if a personality test that measured emotional stability and extraversion resulted in many more women than men being hired for an entry-level management job, but these two personality traits could not be linked directly to job performance.

Disparate Treatment

The first form of discrimination is *disparate treatment*. This form of discrimination describes those situations in which different standards are applied to various groups or individuals even though there may not be an explicit statement of intentional prejudice. Examples include such practices as not hiring women with young children while hiring men with such children, or hiring minority group members to fill cleaning jobs in a restaurant while similarly qualified white people are made cashiers or waiters. The effect of such decisions, even though they may be prompted by the employer's idea of good business practice, is to subject a specific group to negative treatment because of a personal characteristic.

Disparate Impact

The second form of discrimination is that of *disparate impact*. In this form, organizational selection standards are applied uniformly to all groups of applicants, but the net result of these standards is to produce differences in the selection of various groups. The central issue is differences in the percentages of selected applicants from different demographic groups. Two classic examples of such discrimination are the requirement of a high school diploma, which has been used extensively for entry-level positions, and of height minimums, which have been used for police and some manual labor positions. Both standards are usually applied to applicants consistently and might not seem to be discriminatory.

The problem is that such standards have been demonstrated to have the effect of disqualifying from employment a much larger percentage of some demographic groups than others. High school diplomas are one example. Traditionally, the percentage of white people who have high school diplomas is higher than the percentage in minority groups. The requirement of a diploma would limit the percentage of minority applicants in comparison to white applicants. Similarly, a minimum height requirement usually limits the percentage of women, Asian American, and Latin American applicants. A number of other frequently used selection requirements have been the subject of disparate impact discrimination charges, including arrest records, type of military discharge, years of previous work experience, and financial history. The use of each of these has been linked to the disqualification of a high percentage of at least one demographic group of applicants.

Evidence Required

One major consequence of these two forms of employment discrimination is their differential effect on both plaintiffs and defendants when charges of discrimination are brought to court. That is to say that the legal burdens for plaintiffs and defendants are different depending on whether the case is heard as disparate treatment or disparate impact discrimination. In discussing this, we frame our points within Title VII litigation because that is the most prevalent.

In both types of cases, a logical sequence of events occurs. To start, the burden of proof is on the plaintiff to present arguments and facts that, if not rebutted, would convince the judge or jury hearing the case that the employer has engaged in practices in violation of one of the EEO laws. If this is done, the plaintiff is said to have established a *prima facie* case of discrimination. If this is not done, the case should be dismissed for lack of grounds. Once a prima facie case has been established, the burden of proof switches. The defendant must present arguments and facts that rebut the charges and provide a legally permissible explanation for the employment practices under question. If this is done, the burden shifts back to the plaintiff, who has a final opportunity to attack the defendant's evidence and otherwise challenge previous arguments.

Disparate Treatment Evidence

As indicated in Table 4.2, there are major differences in specific data, evidence, and arguments that must be made during this general trial process for the two types of discrimination cases. For disparate treatment cases, a guideline for establishing a prima facie case was specified in the *McDonnell Douglas v. Green* (1973) case, commonly

TABLE 4.2 Presentation of Evidence in Title VII Discrimination Cases

Sequence of Steps	Disparate Treatment	Disparate Impact
Plaintiff	Demonstrates that • He or she belongs to a protected class, • He or she applied and was qualified for the job, • He or she was rejected by the company, • The job remained open.	Demonstrates statistically that this management practice affects various groups differently in comparison to their distribution in the relevant labor market.
Defendant	Provides a clear and specific job-based explanation for actions.	Demonstrates at least one of the following: • business necessity • bona fide occupational qualification • validation data
Plaintiff	Proves that the defendant's argument is a pretext and the true reason for rejection was prejudice.	Proves that an alternative practice is available that has less adverse impact.

known as the McDonnell Douglas rule. This rule states that the plaintiff must show that the following conditions exist:

1. He or she belongs to a protected class (a demographic group included in an EEOC law).

2. He or she applied and was qualified for a job for which the company was seeking applicants.

3. Despite these qualifications, he or she was rejected.

4. After this rejection, the position remained open and the employer continued to seek applicants from people who had the complainant's qualifications.[28]

This rule reflects a basic premise of disparate treatment cases: The employer's *intention* to discriminate *must* be shown. The demonstration that a specific, qualified member of a demographic group was passed over and a member of a different demographic group with equal or fewer qualifications was selected suffices to prove intention if not rebutted.

When intent to discriminate is shown, the employer must provide a legitimate, nondiscriminatory reason for rejecting the plaintiff in order to rebut. This is relatively easy to do. For example, in the *McDonnell Douglas* case, the reason was that the plaintiff had participated in a protest by illegally stalling his car during a shift change at the McDonnell Douglas plant. In other cases, arguments have been made and accepted that the qualifications of the plaintiff were inferior to those of the individuals selected. In general, if the argument is clear and specific, the employer meets its burden of proof. The employer need not persuade the judge that it actually used this as the basis for rejecting the plaintiff. Rather, it is up to the plaintiff to prove that the employer did *not* use it. The employer's argument is usually more acceptable if it shows that the employer used numerical scores in making selection decisions. The argument is less acceptable, however, if the reasons are based on subjective judgments (opinion), especially if these are made without clear definition and procedures.

If the company is successful, the plaintiff must then refute these statements. In essence, this means that he must show that the company's defense is really a pretense, and that discrimination was being practiced. Examples of evidence that courts have accepted include sexual or racial slurs made by company managers, records that the company's treatment of the plaintiff was inconsistent with that of individuals of other demographic groups, and statistics showing the demographic group of the plaintiff was underrepresented in the company's workforce. If the data presented are not acceptable, the plaintiff is unsuccessful in countering the defense of the company.

Disparate Impact Evidence

In trials of this form of discrimination (see Table 4.2), the focus for establishing a prima facie case shifts from the intention of the employer to an evaluation of the results of an employment decision with regard to various demographic groups. That is, evidence mainly addresses whether various demographic groups have been affected in the same manner by employment decisions. For this reason, statistical data are a major part of these cases. Intention of the employer normally is not addressed, only the outcomes of decisions. Statistics, which we discuss in the following section, are used to analyze the pattern of selection decisions over a period of time. If these analyses, in fact, do indicate that a pattern of adverse impact has occurred, the prima facie case has been established. Once a prima facie case has been accepted, the company has the opportunity to present evidence showing that the results of the selection process in question are job related and, therefore, are not illegal discrimination. To do this, the company traditionally has three options: proving *business necessity*, *bona fide occupational qualifications* (BFOQ), or *validity*.

We discussed validation generally in Chapter 1 and go into detail about its procedures in Chapter 8. The requirements for the other two defenses are strict and apply only in limited cases. Business necessity has been viewed by the courts primarily in regard to safety of either workers or customers of the organization. It is necessary to present evidence that if the selection requirement were not used, the risk to members of these groups would be substantially raised. Ordinarily, the courts have not judged business necessity in terms of economic costs or profits. Therefore, demonstrating that not using the selection requirement would result in great cost or loss of business to the firm has not been acceptable.

A BFOQ defense means that the members of a specific demographic group are the only ones who could adequately or appropriately perform the job. This defense usually is used for sex or religious discrimination. For example, a company may have a requirement that only women can serve as attendants in women's restrooms. The company could use a BFOQ defense (no man could appropriately serve as such an attendant) if a male brought a discrimination charge against it. Similarly, a Presbyterian church could use a BFOQ defense to disqualify all applicants for a minister's position who were not practicing members of the Presbyterian faith. It is not possible to frame a BFOQ defense for race or color. For example, a school district with a predominately white student body could not use a BFOQ defense to disqualify all minority applicants for teaching positions.

If the company is successful in defending the adverse impact, the plaintiff has a chance to present another argument to refute this defense. The nature of this defense is to establish whether another selection procedure could be used that would have less adverse impact. This topic is not well developed, however, because courts seldom get to this stage in the weighing of evidence.

The Use of Statistics

As should be evident from the previous discussion, statistics are used in cases of both forms of discrimination. In disparate treatment cases, statistics are used mainly to assist the plaintiff in rebutting the defendant's explanation of the selection practice under question. In disparate impact cases, statistics are used most often by the plaintiff in demonstrating that a pattern of adverse effect has occurred. Two main types of statistics have been used: *stock* and *flow* statistics.

Stock Statistics

Statistics are used in discrimination cases mainly to compare proportions of various demographic groups with regard to the results of selection decisions. Stock statistics compare groups at one point in time. For example, the most common stock comparison is between the percentage of a specific demographic group in the organization and the percentage of that same demographic group in an appropriate external comparison group, such as total applicants or the relevant labor force. Here is the numerical model of the comparison:

$$\frac{\text{number of women managers in organization}}{\text{total number of managers in organization}} \quad \text{vs.} \quad \frac{\text{number of appropriately skilled women managers in labor force}}{\text{total number of appropriately skilled managers in labor force}}$$

If the percentage of women managers in the company's workforce is significantly smaller than the percentage in the comparison group, in this case the labor force, then evidence of discrimination in selection practices exists. For example, the company GFB Writers (guess what those initials stand for; the term writers is a hint) has 50 editors, 15 of which are women (30 percent), but the percentage of women editors in the labor force is 75 percent. What would you think about GFB? Yep, sexists pigs (although the alternate explanation that most women are smarter than to want to deal with these guys is also feasible).

The term applied to the comparison group is *relevant labor market* (RLM). To better understand the various statistical comparisons that are used in discrimination cases, it is important to know more about the concept of RLM.

EEO laws require employers to keep and update various records about the composition of the organization's workforce and the results of managerial decisions. One of these records is the Revised EEO-1 Form (see Figure 4.1), which must be filed by employers with 100 or more employees. In this form, data must be reported for 10 specific job categories as well as for the total organization. For each job category, the company must report the number of individuals in each demographic group listed on the Revised EEO-1 Form.

In stock analyses, the data from the Revised EEO-1 Form (or similar data) are compared with the RLM, and this result is used as evidence. It is in this context that the RLM becomes important. The RLM has two components: geographic location and skill level. The geographic location is that region from which applicants for the specific job category would likely come, absent any discrimination.[29] In general, determination of this region depends on the scope of the employer's recruiting efforts, the interest among prospective employees in working for the employer in question, and the availability of public transportation. Typically, the geographic region will be smallest for lower paying jobs and broadest, sometimes nationwide, for high-level executive positions.

Within a region, there is still the issue of who shall be counted. At this point, skill level becomes important. Skill level means the special qualifications needed to fill a specific job. Obviously, the number of individuals qualified to serve as electrical engineers is greatly different from that of the general population. The courts recognize that, in calculating stock statistics, it would not be relevant to compare the demographic composition of the company in each of the 10 EEO-1 job categories with that of the population as a whole. In general, as the skill level of the job category increases, the percentage of minorities and women in that job category decreases. Table 4.3 describes some of the relevant labor markets that have been used in selection discrimination cases.

FIGURE 4.1   Revised EEO-1 Form

Employment at this establishment—Report all permanent full- and part-time employees including apprentices and on-the-job trainees unless specifically excluded as set forth in the instructions. Enter the appropriate figures on all lines and in all columns. Blank spaces will be considered as zeros.

Job Categories	Number of Employees (Report employees in only one category)														
	Hispanic or Latino		Race/Ethnicity												Total Col A–N
			Not Hispanic or Latino												
			Male						Female						
	Male	Female	White	Black or African American	Native Hawaiian or Other Pacific Islander	Asian	American Indian or Alaskan Native	Two or more races	White	Black or African American	Native Hawaiian or Other Pacific Islander	Asian	American Indian or Alaskan Native	Two or more races	
	A	B	C	D	E	F	G	H	I	J	K	L	M	N	O
Executive/Senior-Level Officials and Managers	1.1														
First/Mid-Level Officials	1.2														
Professionals	2														
Technicians	3														
Sales Workers	4														
Administrative Support Workers	5														
Craft Workers	6														
Operatives	7														
Laborers and Helpers	8														
Service Workers	9														
Total	10														
Previous Year Total	11														

Source: Federal Register, November 28, 2005 (70 FR 712 94).

TABLE 4.3	Some Relevant Labor Markets Used for Statistical Comparisons

General population data

Labor force data (civilian, nonfarm, or total)

Qualified labor market data

Actual applicant flow data

Qualified actual applicant flow data

Employer's own workforce composition (promotion cases)

Employer's own qualified and interested workforce composition (promotion cases)

The labor market chosen for comparison frequently has been the subject of intensive debate between plaintiffs and defendants in court cases. This is because the percentage of various demographic groups can change depending on which combination of geographic region and skill level is used. For example, take a look at Table 4.4, which is based on EEOC 2012 data for the states of Washington and Florida for the EEO job class of First/Mid Level Officials and Managers. Scanning the percentages of each gender and the racial groups clearly indicates differences between the demographic workforces in the two states. In Washington, the percentages of males, whites, and Asians are substantially higher than in Florida while the percentages of women, blacks, and Hispanics are lower. Therefore, it would be possible to find companies in Washington with a large number of white, male mid-level managers that reflect the RLM of the state.

The difficulty in identifying a relevant labor market is the operational one of gathering the appropriate data. In most cases, existing data in the form of census, chamber of commerce, industry, and similar reports are used. In these reports, geographic units usually are reported in three forms: (a) the nation, (b) a state, or (c) the Standard Metropolitan Statistical Area (SMSA), which is the region surrounding a central city or town. Appropriate skill level is expressed in numbers reported as holding or qualified to hold specific jobs. In the U.S. census data, several different types of sales, technical, managerial, and other categories of jobs are reported. The selection of an RLM, in many cases, becomes a judgment as to the most appropriate geographic region and the most similar types of jobs available in existing data sources.

TABLE 4.4	Demographic Composition of First/Mid Level Officials and Managers in States of Washington and Florida[a]

	Washington	**Florida**
Men	64%	57%
Women	36%	43%
White	82%	72%
Black	3%	9%
Hispanic	4%	15%
Asian	9%	3%
American Indian	.7%	.3%
Hawaiian	.5%	.2%

[a]Based upon EEOC Demographic Employment Data, 2012.

Flow Statistics

The second type of statistic used is referred to as flow statistics. The term is used because this type of statistic compares proportions that occur at two points in time. A common flow statistic in selection is the following:

$$\frac{\text{number of minority applicants selected}}{\text{number of minority applicants}} \quad \text{vs.} \quad \frac{\text{number of nonminority applicants selected}}{\text{number of nonminority applicants}}$$

The comparison is made from numbers gathered at two different points in time— before and after selection has taken place. The purpose of the comparison is to determine how minority members fared in the selection process in comparison with nonminority members. For example say GFB Writers (the sexist pigs in the previous example) has selected 20 of 60 (33 percent) black applicants as editors. For white applicants, it has selected 40 of 60 applicants (66 percent). What do you think? Yep, they're racist pigs as well as sexist pigs! (Remember this is only a hypothetical example.) When the percentage for the minority group is significantly smaller than the percentage for the nonminority group, evidence of discrimination is present. Because the comparison is made between groups that are both being acted on by the company, the RLM usually is not an issue. The RLM, however, could be used before the calculation of the flow statistic to determine whether the recruitment process is adequate—meaning that the percentage of minorities recruited approximates the percentage of minorities in the RLM.

In making the comparison between the proportions previously discussed, the final step is for the court to decide whether any difference between the proportions is important enough to matter. This is the crux of deciding whether evidence of discrimination exists. If the proportions are close enough, insufficient evidence exists and the case should be dropped. If the proportions are different enough, sufficient evidence exists. To assist them in making this decision, the courts have used statistical tests. One of the most commonly used test is the *four-fifths rule*.[30] This test uses the basic flow statistic and adds that the ratio of any group must be at least 80 percent of the *ratio of the most favorably treated* group. For example, if 60 percent of white applicants are selected, then the selection proportion of any minority group should be at least 48 percent (0.80 × 0.60). Let us say that there are numerous entry-level retail clerk positions to be filled for a large department store. Through recruiting, 120 white applicants are processed and 72 (60 percent) are selected. Through the same recruiting process, 50 black people apply for the positions. If blacks were selected at the same rate as the whites, we would expect that 30 black applicants would be selected (50 × 0.60). According to this guideline, however, exact parity is not expected. The minimum number of black hires would be expected to be 24 (30 × 0.80), which is 80 percent of the 60 percent selection rate of whites. If the number is smaller, the *initial* conclusion is that adverse impact in selection has occurred.

A second statistical analysis that also has been used extensively for evaluating adverse impact in selection is the standard deviation rule. The general idea of a standard deviation test is to calculate the standard deviation of the variance in scores and compare that to the difference in mean scores between the two demographic groups. If the difference in means is greater than 1.96 standard deviations, this difference is considered to be significant between the two groups. Many selection specialists agree that both the four-fifths rule and the standard deviation rule have significant limitations in their use for measuring adverse impact in selection. Kevin Murphy and Rick Jacobs have pointed out the main problems with both of these tests.[31] The results of the standard deviation test are to a large extent dictated by the size of the samples used to do the analysis. Very large samples will almost always yield differences of more than 2 standard deviations in selection rates, even if these differences are very small (within a few percentage points of each other). This statistical limitation translates into practical significance in that large companies that employ large numbers of individuals in various job titles also will have samples of employees so large that there will be statistically significant differences in selection rates among at least *some* demographic groups when measured by the standard deviation rule. This makes these companies especially vulnerable to charges of discrimination because of the limitation of the statistical way adverse impact is measured. On the other hand, small companies have an advantage in that when the standard deviation rule is used with small samples of employees, it is mathematically difficult to obtain a result that would indicated statistical significance among demographic groups. Therefore, small and many medium-size companies are relatively safe in terms of demonstrating adverse impact because of the relatively small number of employees in any one job. Studies indicate that this problem exists even when samples number in the hundreds.

Research also indicates that the four-fifths rule has equivalent problems. The main reason is its differential sensitivity at different percentages of applicants selected for the job. If 10 percent of the applicant pool is selected, it only takes a few percentage points of difference between the sample of black applicants and the sample of white applicants to find adverse impact. For example, if 10.5 percent of white applicants are selected and 8.4 percent of black applicants are selected, the 80 percent rule is violated because the calculation would be that the minimum black selection rate should be 8.6 percent. On the other hand, if 90 percent of the applicant pool is selected and 95 percent of white applicants and 78 percent of black applicants are employed, the 80 percent rule is not violated (the minimum black selection rate is 76 percent). So when a low percentage of all applicants is selected, a small difference between the white and black selection percentages can indicated adverse impact. When many applicants are selected, however, much larger differences in the two selection percentages would not indicate adverse impact.

Murphy and Jacobs recommend two other statistics that would be better to use in determining adverse impact. One is the *d* statistic that actually describes the difference between groups in terms of standard *deviation* units. In the social and behavioral sciences, *d* values of 0.2, 0.5, 0.8, and 1.0, respectively, are widely used to describe small, medium, moderately large, and large effects, which allows for more interpretation of found differences. The value of *d* generally is not affected by the size of the samples used. Another useful statistic for defining adverse impact is one that is based on the proportion of total variance in scores explained by differences between the groups being compared. If, for example, differences between men and women explain less than 1 percent of the variance in selection decisions, that figure will have the same meaning and the same implications regardless of the sample size. Similarly, the finding that racial differences account for 10 percent of the variance in outcomes has the same meaning regardless of *N*. If, for example, the gender difference between men and women explain less than 1 percent of the variance in selection decisions, the evidence would indicated that gender was not the reason for any differences in selection. The finding that racial differences account for 20 percent of the variance in outcomes, however, may have a different interpretation. Other researchers have pointed out the advantages of using Fischer's Exact Test (FET) instead of the four-fifths or standard deviation rules, especially for use with small samples. This test may be used in combination with the Lancaster mid-P (LMP) test, which yields a better balance of Type I and Type II errors.[32] The LMP test has been accepted widely in the medical and statistics fields, and it is starting to receive attention in the equal employment opportunity literature.

Definition of Internet Applicant

We previously pointed out that statistics measuring the applicant selection rates for various demographic groups are important for the determination of adverse impact. That is, the selection rates for all demographic groups should be approximately equal. If the selection rates between two groups are very large, this difference can serve as evidence of adverse impact. One key component of examining selection rates is the definition of what is meant by an applicant. Should someone who briefly inquires about open jobs be considered an applicant? Should someone who fills out an application form but does not follow up with any other actions be considered an applicant?

The use of Internet recruitment and selection has made the definition of an applicant very important. By using the Internet, an individual can easily contact an organization and indicate some interest in employment or complete preliminary employment forms. Many of these individuals withdraw from the application process—but that may not matter if they are legally regarded as applicants and must be included in a calculation of selection rates.

To clarify who must be counted, the OFCCP has released a definition of who is considered to be an Internet applicant.[33] This definition includes the following points:

1. The person must submit an expression of interest in employment through the Internet or related electronic devices. The term "expression of interest" is not strictly defined, but examples include information about an individual that is gathered from e-mails, resume databases, job banks, electronic scanning devices, applicant tracking systems, and applicant screeners. Apparently, if any individual from these or related sources is considered an applicant, all individuals from these sources, who submit similar data, also should be considered applicants.

2. The organization is considering employing the individual for a particular position. This means that the employer evaluates any characteristic of the individual against any qualification needed for a particular position, even those considered to be basic requirements. Individuals may be excluded from consideration, however, if they do not use the organization's defined application procedure or if they do not apply for a specific position.

3. The individual's expression of interest indicates that the person possesses the basic qualifications for the position. Qualifications are those characteristics used to advertise the position or that the organization has predetermined who should be used in the selection of candidates. Qualifications also must be objective (not dependent on subjective judgment), noncomparative (not relative), and job related.

4. The individual must not remove herself from consideration for the position. The most obvious way to do this is to notify the company that she is withdrawing as an applicant. An organization may infer that an individual has removed herself if she does not respond to company inquiries, or if she has made statements in the application reflecting expectations that are incompatible with the employment conditions of the position (for example, salary, work location, or job duties). If the organization decides to remove individuals from the applicant roll for any of these reasons, the organization must be consistent in removing them. That is, all individuals who provide similar statements must be removed. Removal cannot be selective and limited to specific individuals.

5. Internet applicants are those who contact or are contacted through e-mail, resume databases, job banks, electronic scanning technology, applicant tracking systems or applicant service providers, and applicant screeners.

OFCCP's definition is very broad and possibly could impose on employers both the effort required for compliance and the cost of monitoring applicants who apply for employment electronically and must be recontacted to gather necessary demographic data.

THE UNIFORM GUIDELINES ON EMPLOYEE SELECTION PROCEDURES (1978)

The *Uniform Guidelines on Employee Selection Procedures* (1978) represent a joint statement of the EEOC, the Civil Service Commission, the Department of Labor, and the Department of Justice as to the characteristics of acceptable selection procedures.[34] As such, these guidelines are not themselves legally binding. However, because they represent the viewpoints of the federal agencies charged with the enforcement of EEO laws, the guidelines serve as a primary reference for court decisions and have been cited in various cases. The most important aspects of the *Uniform Guidelines* are summarized in this section.

Determination of Adverse Impact

The *Uniform Guidelines* are only addressed to selection systems that produce adverse impact. If adverse impact does not exist, there are no regulations (except recordkeeping) that concern selection systems. The guidelines clearly state that the decision rule in judging discrimination in selection is whether the use of a selection procedure leads to adverse impact as demonstrated by the statistical tests we have reviewed. It must be noted, however, that in certain cases the *Uniform Guidelines* provide exceptions to adverse impact. When large numbers of applicants are being selected, discrimination could be indicated even if comparison proportions of applicants are within the four-fifths rates. In such cases, enforcement agencies are quite concerned with differences in which large numbers of individuals are affected. Conversely, in cases in which very small numbers of applicants are processed, the four-fifths rule may not always be accepted as indicating discrimination. With small samples, differences in decisions about one or two applicants could greatly change the comparison ratios. This factor thus is taken into account, and in such cases, differences greater than the four-fifths ratio may not be viewed negatively.

Selection Methods

The *Uniform Guidelines* also state that *any* method of selection that results in an employment decision is covered. Many individuals have assumed incorrectly that only scored selection tests are addressed in the guidelines. This is clearly incorrect, as the following statement in the *Uniform Guidelines* indicates:

> *When an informal or unscored selection procedure that has an adverse impact is utilized, the user should eliminate the adverse impact or modify the procedure to one which is a formal, scored, or quantified measure.*[35]

Defense of Selection Program

For those selection programs that do have adverse impact, the options of the organization are specified. First, the organization may cease to use the selection devices under question and adopt other devices that do not result in adverse impact. If this is not acceptable, the organization may defend its practices by showing that its selection practices are valid. (We mentioned this term in Chapter 1 and will have way, way, way more discussion of it in Chapter 8.) If validation evidence is used, it specifically should address the use of the selection instrument with regard to all groups for whom the test is to be used. At a minimum, this means that statistical validation should include a representative number of women and minorities. In criterion validation, the steps should address the issue of "test fairness" or the comparative performance of various groups on the test. A large portion of the *Uniform Guidelines* is in fact devoted to the steps, data, and procedures of validation strategies. An added provision, however, is that the organization should demonstrate that no other alternative selection programs are both valid and have less adverse impact.

Selection Requirements

Several other aspects of selection programs are addressed specifically by the *Uniform Guidelines*. Skills and abilities easily learned during a brief training program are not acceptable as selection requirements. Requirements drawn from higher level jobs are permissible only if it can be documented that a majority of individuals move to the higher level job within a reasonable time. This time period is not defined precisely, but the *Uniform Guidelines* state that "a reasonable period of time will vary for different jobs and employment situations but will seldom be more than five years."[36] The various forms of selection cutoff scores also are discussed. The least stringent cutoff is a score above which all applicants are judged equally acceptable. A second form of cutoff scores is one in which similar scores are grouped together (for example, 81–90, 91–100). The first applicants considered for selection are those with scores in the highest group. Selection proceeds downward along score groups until all open positions are filled. This could result in selection being completed before some score groups are even considered. A third form of cutoff scores is to rank all applicants individually and proceed down this list of individuals. The *Uniform Guidelines* indicate when the second and third forms of cutoff scores are used and if adverse impact results, the organization must not only demonstrate the validity of the selection devices but also justify the assumption of these methods that scores above a minimum are indicative of higher job performance.

Recordkeeping

Another major requirement of the *Uniform Guidelines* is recordkeeping. All organizations are required to keep information about the demographic characteristics of applicants and those selected and to produce such information if requested. This requirement applies only to those groups that constitute at least 2 percent of the relevant labor market. Technically, all organizations are required to record such data; however, if adverse impact is not characteristic of the selection program, the probability of a request by an enforcement agency for this documentation is almost zero. Organizations with fewer than 100 employees should record by sex, race, and national origin the number of people selected, promoted, and terminated for each job level. Data indicating the number of applicants for both entry-level positions and promotion are also necessary. These data should be categorized by sex, race, and national origin. Finally, selection procedures should be described. Organizations with more than 100 employees must develop records indicating whether the total selection process for each job, or any part of that selection process, has had an adverse impact on any group that constitutes at least 2 percent of the relevant labor market. For cases in which the number of selections is insufficient to determine whether an adverse impact exists, the organization should continue to collect, maintain, and have available the information on individual components of the selection process until the information is sufficient to determine whether adverse impact has occurred, or until the job changes substantially. In the latter case, presumably a new round of recordkeeping would begin. The data in these records may be used on behalf of or against the company in a legal dispute about the selection program.

In summary, the *Uniform Guidelines on Employee Selection Procedures* direct HR specialists as to selection program components and records that must be kept. The determination of adverse impact as indicated by the four-fifths rule and other statistical analyses is of primary importance. When such impact is determined, the company must either cease the use of the selection procedure and adopt a nondiscriminatory one or produce evidence of the job relatedness of the selection procedure that produces the adverse impact.

Comments about the *Uniform Guidelines*

As mentioned, the *Uniform Guidelines* were published in 1978. Over time, they have been referred to in many selection court cases and have been given "great weight." This means that judges and juries have used the information in the *Guidelines* when making decisions. Selection researchers and managers, however, have advanced our knowledge of several issues that are incorporated into the *Guidelines*. For example, the *Guidelines* argue for performing a validation study in each selection site to ensure that all factors that may affect employees' performance are included in the validation effort. Research has clearly contradicted this argument and has demonstrated that validity can be generalized from several previous studies. As a matter of fact, the evidence is that a single validation study is not a very good indicator of validity and could err by either overestimating or underestimating the validity coefficient. We will discuss this issue in detail in Chapters 8 and 11. Similarly, researchers have shown that relying heavily on the four-fifths rule and other statistical measures as methods for identifying signs of adverse impact is more fruitful when these methods are combined with additional statistical tests. Using these measures alone could lead to incorrect conclusions about adverse impact. Clearly, the *Uniform Guidelines* should be revised to include such research findings.

AFFIRMATIVE ACTION PROGRAMS

Affirmative action programs (AAP) are another aspect of EEO laws and regulations that holds importance for companies. Generally, AAP applies to a set of specific actions taken by an organization to actively seek out and remove unintended barriers to fair treatment in order to achieve equal opportunity.[37] For example, an organization's AAP for the selection of women and minority college graduates might include identifying and visiting colleges with large proportions of women and minority students, staffing recruiting teams with women and minority members, developing internship programs, and training interviewers and other selection decision makers in appropriate techniques. An affirmative action plan is a written document produced by the company that explicitly states steps to be taken, information to be gathered, and the general baseline for decision making for each area of HRM. It serves as a guideline for actions to ensure that EEO principles are implemented within the organization. Such a plan is to be under the direction of a top-level manager and to be communicated to all within the organization.

Basically, a company would adopt an AAP in three situations: (a) the company is a federal contractor, (b) the company has lost a court discrimination case or has signed a consent decree, or (c) the company is voluntarily attempting to implement EEO principles. Let's discuss each of these.

Federal Contractor

Most of the EEO laws and executive orders dealing with federal contractors contain the requirement of affirmative action for those with contracts of at least $10,000. The OFCCP, a subdivision within the Department of Labor, usually is set up as the regulatory agency. It can review the employment practices of contractors and levy specified penalties if it finds a contractor to be out of compliance with AAP requirements. Three main activities must be carried out by a contractor in an AAP.[38] The first is a utilization analysis. Conceptually, this is similar to previously described stock statistical analyses, because it requires a comparison of the company's workforce to the relevant labor market. If there is a smaller percentage of a specific demographic group in the company's workforce than there is in the labor market, then that group is said to be underutilized. The complete determination of underutilization, however, also includes additional information such as the size of the minority unemployed group, the availability of promotable and transferable minorities within the company, the existence of appropriate training institutions, and the degree of training that the contractor may deliver.

The numerical results of a utilization analysis are important because they indicate the discrepancy between the workforce and the company's available labor force. This discrepancy then serves as the basis for the second activity, determining the "goals" that a company should strive to achieve in its employment practices. For example, if Hispanic skilled craft workers constitute 8 percent of the RLM and only 2 percent of the company's workforce, the company would be expected to set a specific numerical goal to achieve a balance between the two numbers, or, at least, to reduce the discrepancy substantially. In addition, a timetable should be developed that would indicate the dates at which the company expects to achieve milestones in reducing the discrepancy. As an example, the percentage in the company's workforce would be expected to increase by 2 percent for each of the next three years. There is a major debate on this topic concerning (a) the extent to which these goals should be considered to be desirable ends that are achievable within the specified timetable, and (b) the extent to which they should be considered to be "quotas" that must be achieved. This historically has been a source of conflict between contractors and OFCCP regulators. Theoretically, the contractor is to "put forth every good faith effort to make his overall affirmative action program work."[39] Obviously, the concept of "good faith effort" is open to interpretation and disagreement. It is a common opinion that to reduce underutilization, pressure often has been exerted on contractors to give preferential treatment to women and minorities.

The third major aspect of these AAPs is the actual steps that are required. Among these steps are publishing job openings through meetings with various minority organizations, taking ads in media with a high percentage of minorities as a target audience, and publicizing the company's affirmative action policy. Also included are conducting reviews of selection practices and instruments for adverse impact, and training organization members on the AAP's objectives and the procedures necessary for fulfilling its objectives.

Court Order and Consent Decree

When a company is acting under a court order and consent decree, it is legally required to engage in HRM actions that will directly, and in a specified period of time, lead to a balance between its workforce and the relevant labor market. The activities just discussed relative to AAPs for federal contractors become, in this situation, part of the AAP for companies. However, even less freedom of action exists for these companies. A primary requirement is that the company must meet specific numerical goals that have been stated and agreed to in the court order or consent decree. These numerical goals are considered to be mandatory, as opposed to desirable, achievements. Often, to reach these goals, a company must give preferential treatment to minority applicants in selection or in promotion (if the issue concerns internal movement within the company).

For example, part of the agreement signed by Ford Motor Company in its sexual discrimination case required the company to pay female employees $8 million in damages. Ford also agreed to train all of its employees in the prevention of job discrimination and to take appropriate measures to increase female representation in supervisory positions. The goal was to have women in 30 percent of the entry-level supervisory openings at the Chicago Stamping and Assembly Plants within a 3-year period. This meant that a number of women were moved into supervisory positions ahead of men.[40]

Voluntary AAP

The most controversial AAPs have been those initiated by an organization without the direct requirement of a court or government agency. The problem with these programs is the potential conflict between their results and the wording of Title VII of the Civil Rights Act of 1964. Part of this act expressly states that it is "an unlawful … practice … to fail or refuse to hire … any individual with respect to … race, color, religion, sex, or national origin."[41] Furthermore, it is written that "nothing contained in this title shall be interpreted to require any employer … to grant preferential treatment to any individual."

The potential difficulty with a voluntary AAP is that to increase the employment of minority groups, the company may bend over backward by discriminating against other groups and violate the parts of Title VII just cited. We have mentioned that in the two previous AAP situations, a company is in the direct review (some would say control) of a court or government agency and legitimately can grant preferential treatment to specific groups to meet goals or quotas. In voluntary AAPs, any preferential treatment given one group may be translated into disparate treatment against another group. Because white males are usually the group negatively affected in such instances, the term *reverse discrimination* has been used.

The resolution of such conflicts between voluntary AAPs and disparate treatment of other groups has been the subject of U.S. Supreme Court rulings. These rulings have determined that voluntary AAPs must have the following characteristics: be temporary, have no permanent adverse impact on white workers, and be designed to correct a demonstrable imbalance between minority and nonminority workers.

The importance of these characteristics was made clear in *Lilly v. City of Beckley.*[42] In 1975 the city of Beckley, West Virginia, undertook to remedy the lack of minority and women employees in city departments. In April 1976, a formal AAP was adopted to achieve this. This case arose over selection decisions made in the police department in January 1976, before the formal AAP was adopted. Lilly applied for a patrol officer position at that time and passed the essay test portion of the selection program but failed the interview. He was told that his chance of obtaining employment would be much greater if he were a minority member. He brought suit against the city. (Surprise, huh!) The city's argument in the case was that it was operating under an informal AAP pursuant to the formal adoption of the AAP in April 1976. The Fourth Circuit Court of Appeals compared the circumstances of this informal AAP with the Supreme Court's decisions and found for Lilly. In essence, the informal plan was rejected for lack of (a) specific goals and timetables, (b) evidence that it was used to remedy past discrimination, and (c) evidence that the informal AAP did not result in the hiring of unqualified applicants or unnecessarily trammel the interests of the white majority.

Another related Supreme Court decision, *Adarand Constructors, Inc. v. Pena*, addressed only federal-contract situations but can influence decisions in private industry. The basic issue of the case was that in 1989 the U.S. DOT awarded the prime contract for construction of a Colorado highway to Mountain Gravel and Construction Company. Mountain Gravel then solicited bids from subcontractors for the guardrail portion of the highway. Among the competing subcontractors were Gonzales Construction Company and Adarand Constructors, Inc. Adarand submitted the lowest bid. However, because of a clause in the contract from DOT that stated that "monetary compensation is offered for awarding subcontracts to small business concerns owned and controlled by socially and economically disadvantaged individuals,"[43] Mountain Gravel awarded the contract to Gonzales Construction.

The Court decided on behalf of Adarand Constructors and stated that affirmative action programs must be very narrowly tailored to achieve specific purposes. In the case of *Adarand v. Pena*, the government's purpose of encouraging contracts to be given to minority subcontractors and presuming that such an action was directed at socially and economically disadvantaged individuals was remanded back to the district court. In the various judges' opinions of the case, the view was expressed that the relationship between being socially and economically disadvantaged and being of a particular race or ethnic group is not clear. Such membership, therefore, is questionable as a basis for a federal affirmative action program.

SELECTION COURT CASES

This section reviews some of the major court decisions about selection practices. The cases presented in this section are not all of the major cases that deal with selection issues. Rather, they are a cross section chosen to represent demographic issues (age, ethnicity, gender, disability, and so on), measurement issues (job relatedness, test construction, principles, and so on), and different selection applications (entry level and promotion). This section will familiarize you with the manner in which courts review discrimination charges and present important decisions that affect selection practices in organizations.

The major points of each of these cases are summarized in Table 4.5. We can see that the result of the various court decisions is to identify selection practices that are either acceptable or unacceptable. Unfortunately for selection specialists, most decisions identify unacceptable actions. We, therefore, know more about what *not* to do than about what we can do. This is somewhat unsettling. It would be more convenient if the courts could assemble a description of acceptable selection practices. From all that has been said in this chapter, however, you should realize that such an action by the courts is not possible. Selection practices are too varied and too interrelated. As regards the regulatory model, the main responsibility of the courts and agencies is to stop organizations from perpetuating the societal problems that prompted the EEO laws. It is the responsibility of those who design selection programs to develop the various parts of their programs so they comply with the laws. Government regulation is a major reason why, as we said at the beginning of Chapter 1, selection has increasingly become such a complex activity.

Griggs v. Duke Power (1971)

The first landmark case decided by the Supreme Court under Title VII was *Griggs v. Duke Power*.[44] The case began in 1967 when 13 black employees filed a class-action suit against Duke Power, charging discriminatory employment practices. The suit centered on recently developed selection requirements for the company's operations units. The plaintiffs charged that the requirements were arbitrary and screened out a much

TABLE 4.5	Key Issues in Major Selection Court Cases

Court Case	Key Issues
Griggs v. Duke Power (1971)	1. Lack of discriminatory intent not sufficient defense 2. Selection test must be job related if adverse impact results 3. Employer bears burden of proof in face of apparent adverse impact
U.S. v. Georgia Power (1973)	1. Validation strategy must comply with EEOC guidelines 2. Validation must include affected groups 3. Validation must reflect selection decision practices 4. Testing must occur under standardized conditions
Spurlock v. United Airlines (1972)	1. College degree and experience requirements are shown to be job related 2. Company's burden of proof diminishes as human risks increase
Watson v. Ft. Worth Bank & Trust (1988)	1. Cases focusing on subjective selection devices, such as interviews and judgments, could be heard as disparate impact 2. Organization may need to validate interview in same manner as objective test
Rudder v. District of Columbia (1995)	1. Content validity is acceptable defense for adverse impact 2. Job analysis, ensuring adequate representation of minority groups in data collection, is essential 3. Clear links must be shown between job analysis information, test questions, and correct answers 4. Attention to test security and administration are important
Ricci v. DeStefano (2009)	1. Adverse impact present as blacks scored less well on tests than whites and Hispanics. 2. Discrimination directed toward whites and Hispanics 3. Threat of lawsuit is not defense for disregarding job-related selection tests 4. Adverse impact can be defended by job relatedness of selection tests
OFCCP v. Ozark Air Lines (1986)	1. In disability cases, organization must prove that individual cannot perform job 2. Reasonable accommodation must be given to disabled individual
Gross v. FBL Financial Services (2009)	1. Central question was how much evidence must plaintiff produce in age discrimination claim to force defendant to provide evidence that it did not use age in decision 2. Plaintiff must provide clear evidence that age was "but-for" reason for decision 3. Ruling significantly increases the amount of evidence that plaintiff must provide to obtain judgment that age discrimination occurred

higher proportion of blacks than whites. The requirements, which were implemented in 1965, included a high school diploma, passage of a mechanical aptitude test, and a general intelligence test. When the requirements were initiated, they were not retroactive and so did not apply to current employees in the company's operations units. The company made no attempt to determine the job relatedness of these requirements.

A lower district court found in favor of the company on the grounds that any former discriminatory practices had ended, and there was no evidence of discriminatory intent in the new requirements. An appellate court agreed with the finding of no discriminatory intent, and in the absence of such intent, the requirements were permissible. The Supreme Court, in a unanimous decision, reversed the previous decisions. The court ruled *that lack of discriminatory intent was not a sufficient defense against the use of employment devices that exclude on the basis of race.* In North Carolina at that time, 34 percent of white males had high school degrees, whereas only 12 percent of black males did. The court acknowledged that tests and other measuring devices could be used but held *that they must be related to job performance.* Duke Power had contended that its two test requirements were permissible because Title VII allowed the use of "professionally developed tests" as selection devices.

Because employees already were working in the operational units of the company who did not have a high school diploma or had not taken the tests and were performing their duties in a satisfactory manner, Duke Power had no evidence relating these requirements to job performance. The court stated that if "an employment practice that operates to exclude [blacks] cannot be shown to be related to job performance, it is prohibited."

Two important precedents were set by the *Griggs* case, both of which are related to burdens of proof. The first is that the applicant carries the burden of proving the adverse impact of a particular selection device. Once adverse impact has been determined, the burden shifts to the employer to prove the validity or job relatedness of the device. The second is that the court said that the 1970 *EEOC Guidelines* were entitled to "deference" when an organization tried to prove the validity of its selection program. Deference, in essence, means that the principles of the *Guidelines* are the standard against which to judge a company's defense.

United States v. Georgia Power (1973)

Because the Supreme Court held in the *Griggs* decision that employment tests must be job-related, attention in later cases was directed to the question of just what an employer must do to demonstrate job relatedness and the extent to which the *Guidelines* define that relatedness. For example, in February 1973, the Fifth Circuit Court of Appeals upheld the 1970 *EEOC Guidelines* in *United States v. Georgia Power.*[45]

In 1969 the attorney general brought suit against the Georgia Power Company for discrimination against black employees. Evidence was presented that at that time only 543 of the company's 7,515 employees were black (7.2 percent), despite the existence of a large pool of black applicants. Moreover, blacks were classified exclusively as janitors, porters, maids, and laborers; almost all white employees occupied higher positions. Beginning in 1960, to qualify for employment, all new employees were required to have a high school diploma or evidence of equivalent educational accomplishment. Then in 1963, all new employees also were required to pass a battery of tests developed by the Psychological Corporation. This requirement was instituted less than 1 month after the discontinuance of formal job segregation. In 1964 the company imposed the diploma requirement on all incumbent employees who wanted to transfer from the position of janitor, porter, or maid, but it did not add that requirement for transferring from elsewhere in the company's structure. No study of these tests to determine job relatedness had been conducted before the filing of the suit.

Recognizing its obligation under *Griggs* to provide proof of the job relatedness of its test battery, the company began a validation study after the initiation of the suit. An official of the company conducted a validity study using an all-white sample. The study collected supervisors' ratings on employees who had been hired earlier on the basis of the tests to be validated and then compared those ratings with the test scores. This sample was admittedly small and excluded the 50 percent of the applicants who failed the test. Nevertheless, statistical evidence produced by Georgia Power supported the relationship of its selection test scores to the job performance ratings of supervisors, thereby demonstrating job relatedness.

The court, however, held that the validation study did not meet the minimum standards recommended for a validation strategy by the EEOC Guidelines. One failure was the absence of blacks from the validation study. With an applicant population that was one-third black, the court concluded that such a study could at least have been attempted. The court also held that there were black employees in three of the company's job classifications in numbers as large as some of the all-white samples used by Georgia Power; therefore, the company could have attempted separate validation studies and, even though the studies would have been conducted on different job categories, some data could have been generated indicating whether the tests treated both races equally. The 1970 *EEOC Guidelines* also required that the sample of subjects be representative of the normal applicant group for the job or jobs in question. Because there was an absence of black people in the sample, the court ruled that this requirement had not been fulfilled. Also, according to the *Guidelines*, tests must be administered under controlled and standardized conditions. In this case, the court found that testing of new applicants was uniform, but that testing of incumbents was not.

Finally, in accordance with the *Griggs* decision, *the court struck down the company's use of diploma requirements on the grounds that there was no evidence relating the possession of a diploma to job performance.*

Spurlock v. United Airlines (1972)

The case of *Spurlock v. United Airlines* involved a demonstration of the job relatedness of selection instruments other than tests.[46] In this case, Spurlock filed suit against United Airlines after his application for the job of flight officer had been rejected. Spurlock charged the airline with discrimination against blacks and offered as evidence the fact that only 9 out of 5,900 flight officers were black. In the suit, Spurlock challenged two of the requirements for the job: a college degree and a minimum of 500 hours of flight time.

United contended that both these selection requirements were job related. Using statistics, United showed that applicants with a greater number of flight hours were more likely to succeed in the rigorous training program that flight officers must complete after being hired. Statistics also showed that 500 hours was a reasonable minimum requirement. In addition, United contended that, because of the high cost of the training program, it was important that those who begin the training program eventually become flight officers. United officials also testified that the possession of a college degree indicated that the applicant had the ability to function in a classroom atmosphere. This ability is important because of the initial training program, and because flight officers are required to attend intensive refresher courses every six months.

The 10th Circuit Court of Appeals accepted the evidence presented by United as proof of the job relatedness of the requirements. In a significant ruling, the court stated that when a job requires a small amount of skill and training and the consequences of hiring an unqualified applicant are insignificant, the courts should closely examine selection instruments that are discriminatory. On the other hand, *when the job requires a high degree of skill and the economic and human risks involved are great, the employer bears a lighter burden to show that selection instruments are job related.*

Watson v. Ft. Worth Bank & Trust (1988)

The case of *Watson v. Ft. Worth Bank & Trust* addressed the important question of whether discrimination cases focusing on the interview could be heard as disparate impact cases, even though traditionally these cases had been tried as disparate treatment.[47]

Clara Watson, a black woman, was hired by Ft. Worth Bank & Trust as a proof operator in August 1973, and she was promoted to teller in January 1976. In February 1980, she sought to become supervisor of the tellers in the main lobby; a white male, however, was selected for the job. Watson then sought a position as supervisor of the drive-in bank, but this position was given to a white female. In February 1981, after Watson had served for about a year as a commercial teller in the bank's main lobby and informally as assistant to the supervisor of tellers, the man holding that position was promoted. Watson applied for the vacancy, but the white female who was the supervisor of the drive-in bank was selected instead. Watson then applied for the vacancy created at the drive-in; a white male was selected for that job. The bank, which had about 80 employees, had not developed precise and formal criteria for evaluating candidates for the positions for which Watson unsuccessfully applied. It relied instead on the subjective judgment of supervisors who were acquainted with the candidates and with the nature of the jobs to be filled. All the supervisors involved in denying Watson the four promotions were white.

The U.S. District Court that heard the case addressed Watson's claims under the standards applied to disparate treatment cases. It concluded that Watson had established a prima facie case, but that the bank had met its rebuttal burden by presenting legitimate and nondiscriminatory reasons for each of the promotion decisions. Finally, Watson had failed to show that these reasons were pretexts, and her case was dismissed.

Watson appealed the decision on the basis that the district court had erred in failing to apply disparate impact analysis to her claim. From our previous discussion, we understand the significance of this argument. Under disparate treatment, the burden of proof required of the bank to defend its practices is lighter than under disparate impact processes. If the case were heard as disparate impact and Watson established a prima facie case, the bank most likely would have to provide validation evidence as a defense. Given its situation, with no defined criteria and no scored selection instruments, this would be difficult to do. The Fifth Circuit Court of Appeals, however, held that "a Title VII challenge to an allegedly discretionary promotion system is properly analyzed under the disparate treatment model rather than the disparate impact model." In so ruling, citations were given to various courts of appeals decisions that held that disparate treatment analysis was proper when subjective criteria (the interview) were of issue. In essence, this court said that disparate impact analysis should be applied only to objective selection devices (for example, tests), and disparate treatment to opinion or judgment devices. The implication for selection practices is obvious: The use of interviews and related instruments would be easier to defend in discrimination cases; therefore, they should be use extensively. Anything else would be far riskier.

The Supreme Court, however, took an opposing view and made several important statements. *One was that the ultimate legal issue in the two forms of discrimination cases is similar.* The ruling also stated the following:

> *We are persuaded that our decisions in* Griggs *and succeeding cases could largely be nullified if disparate impact analyses were applied only to standardized selection practices. However one might distinguish "subjective" from "objective" criteria, it is apparent that selection systems that combine both types would generally be considered subjective in nature. Thus, for example, if the employer in* Griggs *had consistently preferred applicants who had a high school diploma and who passed the company's general aptitude test, its selection system could nonetheless have been considered "subjective" if it also included brief interviews.... If we announced a rule that allowed employers so easily to insulate themselves from liability under* Griggs, *impact analysis might effectively be abolished.*[48]

Rudder v. District of Columbia (1995)

In the case of *Rudder v. District of Columbia*,[49] the most important part of this decision made by the U.S. District Court for the District of Columbia was the comments about appropriate procedures for demonstrating the content validity of selection measures. In content validity, the relationship between selection test performance and job performance is demonstrated through a number of judgments of experts. Other cases that we have summarized have discussed empirical validation, in which statistical evidence is used to link test performance to job performance.

The charge in this case was that the examinations for the positions of captain, lieutenant, and sergeant used by the District of Columbia Fire Department adversely affected black firefighters. There were three examinations for these positions. The Job Knowledge Test was a multiple-choice test of knowledge based on manuals, orders, and other material specified on a reading list that was made available to applicants. The Assessment Center was composed of exercises designed to test for behavioral characteristics essential to fire department officers. The Fire Scene Simulation presented two fire scenarios. Each scenario presented a drawing of a fire scene and its surroundings, and quotations from the dispatcher. The applicants responded to a series of questions about each scenario, writing down the decisions they would make and the orders they would give on the scene. To develop these examinations, extensive job analyses were conducted of the three different jobs. The job analyses began with interviews with a biracial group of approximately 20 fire department officers. These interviews resulted in a nine-page description of the tasks of fire sergeant, lieutenant, and captain. This document was distributed to a biracial sample of 54 officers for review and correction. On the basis of these steps, it was determined that the jobs of the three officers were essentially the same. They differed in level of authority at a fire scene, but did not differ in task activities. Therefore, the Job Knowledge Test and the Assessment Center exercises were the same for all three jobs. The Fire Scene Simulation did differ for each of the ranks. The Job Knowledge Test was developed in six phases:

1. Twenty officers reviewed the department's manuals and operating procedures and pinpointed those areas that were particularly relevant to their jobs.

2. Another sample of officers generated the same information, including managerial tasks performed at the firehouse.

3. A third sample of officers reviewed the information generated by the first two groups.

4. Multiple-choice items were written based on the information generated by the three groups of officers.

5. These items were carefully reviewed over a period of months by a consultant.

6. Another group of officers did a final review of items.

The Assessment Center exercises were developed using the following steps:

1. On the basis of the job analysis information, a consultant and groups of officers identified several behavioral dimensions that should be measured, including dealing with people, decisiveness, judgment, leadership, planning and organizing, verbal communication, and written communication.

2. The same individuals developed a number of simulations that were designed to measure these behavioral dimensions.

3. A racially balanced group of assessors (judges) were recruited from fire departments across the United States and Canada.

4. These assessors participated in a 2-day training program.

The following steps were used in developing the Fire Scene Simulation:

1. Information was collected during the job analysis, including the frequency of different types of fires, procedures used in responding to emergency calls, the types of equipment used, and communication procedures.

2. These data were used, in various combinations, to create each fire scene and its accompanying information. These combinations were reviewed by various groups of officers.

The three tests were administered under controlled, standardized conditions. The Job Knowledge Tests were graded by employees of the Metropolitan Police Department using a scoring key. The Fire Scene Simulations were graded by 34 battalion fire chiefs, who worked in pairs and were all present in the same classroom during grading. This grading used a double-blind procedure, so that test-takers could not be identified. Answers were based on published fire department materials. The Assessment Center was scored by the trained assessors. In its ruling, the district court explicitly stated that these procedures "*produced more than sufficient evidence that the ... examination was valid and job related.*"

Frank Ricci et al. v. John DeStefano et al. (2009)

The case of *Frank Ricci et al. v. John DeStefano et al.* was about the use of a written selection test and an interview that were used to identify candidates for promotion into the ranks of lieutenant and captain in the New Haven, Connecticut Fire Department.[50] Under its charter, the city of New Haven requires such examinations of candidates for promotion; then, after the examinations are scored, the department must draw up a list of candidates in the rank order of their scores. The top three candidates are considered for the next open position, and all other promotions within a specified time also use a group of three who have the highest scores on the selection exams.

These tests and interviews were developed for the fire department by a consulting firm that had extensive experience in developing promotion examinations for police and fire departments throughout the country. The consulting firm started the test development process by doing a job analysis to determine specific tasks of each position and also the knowledge, skills, or abilities required for each position. As part of this job analysis, the firm rode with experienced officers currently in the positions, interviewed many officers and firefighters, and developed written job analysis questionnaires that were distributed to officers within the department for completion. Minority officers were oversampled in each of these steps. When writing the test questions, which were all below the 10th-grade reading level, the firm gathered written policies, tactics, rules, and factual information to use as sources. After the items were written, all source materials were made available to those who wished to use it to prepare for the written test. The consulting firm also used similar procedures for the construction of the interview, which largely asked about behaviors to be taken in fire situations. The firm also chose and trained 30 individuals who would serve as interviewers. Twenty of the 30 interviewers were minority group members and each of the nine interview panels had two minority group members of the total three.

After the scores were computed, all 10 applicants of those immediately eligible for consideration for promotion to lieutenant were white. Of the nine immediately eligible for promotion to captain, seven were white and two were Hispanic. None of the black applicants were immediately eligible for promotion. Not surprisingly, these results caused much consternation among applicants, the legal counsel of the city, its director of human resources, and the Civil Service Board that was ultimately responsible for the usage of the testing. Black applicants threatened a lawsuit based on the adverse impact of the test results. After extensive consideration, the Civil Service Commission voided the exam and its results. Subsequently, a group of white and Hispanic applicants filed a suit against this decision, claiming that race and color were the deciding factors in the decision to void the exams.

The Supreme Court agreed with the white and Hispanic applicants, finding that the decision to void the exam scores violated Title VII of the Civil Rights Act of 1964. Specifically, the court commented that—

1. The threat of a lawsuit is not sufficient reason to void the results of the tests.

2. The adverse impact of test results can be defended by the job relatedness of tests.

3. There appears to be enough evidence in terms of the tests' construction to indicate that the tests in this case were job related.

4. There was no evidence that an alternative testing procedure would have less adverse impact than did the tests that were given.

5. Adjusting the test scores of black applicants would have violated Title VII.

The case was remanded to a lower court for reconsideration with the implicit understanding that the results of the test could be used to identify candidates for consideration for promotion.

OFCCP v. Ozark Air Lines (1986)

The case of *OFCCP v. Ozark Air Lines* concerns the Rehabilitation Act of 1973 and the refusal of the airline to employ a disabled person as an airline technician.[51] Gary Frey had a nonfunctioning left ear because of a childhood accident. His right ear was unimpaired. Ozark agreed that Frey had the necessary qualifications for the position, but they refused to hire him because of his hearing disability and his failure to prove that he could carry out the job duties without endangering himself and others. Because Ozark Airlines was regarded as a federal contractor, the case was decided by the OFCCP. Frey won the decision and was awarded back pay. In so doing, the OFCCP argued that *it was Ozark's burden to prove that Frey's employment would have endangered him and others*, not the burden of Frey and OFCCP to prove that he could do the work successfully. Second, it stated that *a disabled person is "qualified for employment if he [or she] is capable of performing a particular job with reasonable accommodation to his or her handicap."* The only evidence that Ozark submitted was the testimony of its personnel director who, responding to questioning as to whether he had given any thought to accommodating Frey or putting restrictions on his duties, stated that this was not possible because of limitations in the union contract. A related Ozark argument that the noise levels of the facility would endanger Frey's remaining hearing also was dismissed. Citing specific decibel levels, the OFCCP commented that Ozark failed to show that Frey's hearing could not be protected by wearing ear protectors.

Jack Gross v. FBL Financial Services (2009)

In *Jack Gross v. FBL Financial Services*, the central issue was about how much evidence a plaintiff must produce about age discrimination in an employment decision for the defendant (company in most cases) to be forced to provide evidence that it did not use age as a factor in making the employment decision in question.[52]

Jack Gross began working for FBL Financial Services in 1971 and by 2001 had become a claims administration director. In 2003, when he was 54 years old, Gross was reassigned as a claims project coordinator. Many of his previous job tasks were reassigned to a 43-year-old woman in a new claims administration manager position. Gross filed suit against the company, arguing that its action violated ADEA 1969 in that the decision to reassign him was at least partially due to his age. A suit in which age is one of several motives being used in an alleged illegal employment decision is referred to by the courts as a *mixed-motive* case. At the conclusion of the trial, the judge instructed the jury that it must return a judgment for Gross if it found that age was a motivating factor in FBL's decision to reassign him. *Motivating factor* meant that age played a role or was part of the reason that FBL made its decision regarding Gross. Following these instructions, the jury found on behalf of Gross.

The Supreme Court disagreed with the instructions given to the jury and reversed and remanded the decision. In explaining its decision, the Court stated that the burden of proof is different in cases filed under ADEA of 1967 than it is for Title VII of the Civil Rights Act of 1964. In ADEA cases, the plaintiff must provide clear evidence that age was the "but for" reason for the employment decision. That is, the employment decision would have been different (presumably more favorable to the plaintiff) but for the fact that age was used in the decision. In a mixed-motive case, this would mean that the plaintiff must offer evidence that age was the dominant or only motive for the negative decision. Furthermore, the burden of proof does not shift to the employer to provide an argument that a legitimate reason (in this case an organizational restructuring) was the reason for the decision if age is shown by the plaintiff to be part of or one factor in the decision. In explaining its ruling, the Supreme Court interpreted actions of Congress, previous case decisions, and the wording of ADEA 1967.

The obvious result of this decision is that it is much more difficult for a plaintiff to win a case of age discrimination under ADEA 1967. In essence, the plaintiff must offer direct evidence, for example, written documents or oral statements, that the decision against the plaintiff was made primarily because of age. Absent this kind of evidence, the plaintiff has not met his or her burden of proof—that is, has not produced sufficient evidence to make a claim that age discrimination occurred.

EEO AND JOB PEFORMANCE MEASUREMENT

The effect of EEO principles on job performance measurement is not as clear as it is for other areas of selection. Partially, this is because only a small part of the *Uniform Guidelines on Employee Selection Procedures* explicitly treats job performance measurement; it does not fully discuss the necessary features of such systems. Similarly, although a number of court cases have addressed job performance measurement, on only a few occasions has it been the major issue in the case. Moreover, the major proportion of even this sketchy treatment has focused on judgmental data, and not on the complete topic of job performance measurement. For these reasons, it is difficult to state specifically what actions HR specialists should take to minimize the chances of having a court disagree with a performance evaluation system.

To provide an understanding of what is known about this topic, this section indicates those parts of the *Uniform Guidelines* that pertain to job performance measurement, summarizes the results of relevant court decisions, reviews important research, and presents some recommendations regarding necessary features of job performance measurement systems. As other authors have put it, these recommendations ought to be treated as "a set of hypotheses regarding the legal ramifications" rather than a strict set of guidelines.[53]

Performance Measurement and the *Uniform Guidelines*

Three sections of the *Uniform Guidelines* contain the most direct statements about work measurement. Of these, section 2.B is cited most often. Its purpose is to make clear that any procedure that contributes to any employment decision is covered by the *Uniform Guidelines*. This is addressed by this statement: "These guidelines apply to tests and other selection procedures which are used as a basis for any employment decision."[54] Some experts interpret this section of the *Uniform Guidelines* to mean that all data collection instruments used in employment decisions are to be labeled as "tests" and subject to all the statements of the *Uniform Guidelines* directed at tests.

The second statement, section 14.B (3), mentions several important concepts. The first is that scores on selection tests are not to be treated as information that is used as input to measure job performance of individuals. This is to prevent the "halo" from selection test scores carrying over, whereby individuals scoring high on selection tests are assumed to also score high on performance measures. This is sensible based on research findings that indicate differences exist among racial and ethnic groups on selection test scores. Second, it is necessary that the performance measure represent important or critical job behaviors (we stressed this requirement in Chapter 2). Performance measures ought to apply to the most important parts of the job; however, as we have said, some measures such as trait ratings do not do this. Third, some performance measures can be used even without referring to job analysis information. Some of these measures are commonly accepted as basic for performance: tardiness, absenteeism, and length of service. Others are commonly accepted as direct measures of performance: production rate and error rate. Finally, comments are made about two other performance measures. A standardized rating of overall work performance may be used when a study of the job shows this to be appropriate. We also brought this up in Chapter 2 when we discussed judgment ratings and how these should be focused on job activities. Finally, performance in training programs that are required for jobs can be used as the criterion measure for selection test validation. These training programs must be demonstrably similar to the actual job. Such programs are frequently associated with technical jobs that change as frequently as the technology changes— for example, programing, installing computer systems, teaching old people (those over 28 years old) how to use new mobile phones. In these cases, training programs are used to determine whether the person can learn quickly because the job is largely made up of mastering changing technology or a changing knowledge base. A third section, 15.B (5), makes clear that the data that are used to identify and develop the job performance criterion measures must be made explicit: "The bases for the selection of the criterion measures should be provided." This includes the description of the criterion and how the measure was developed and collected.

Court Decisions Addressing Performance Measurement

Several reviews of court decisions have been completed regarding discrimination in performance measurement. These reviews examine whether the decision was in favor of the plaintiff or the defendant and which, if any, characteristics of the performance measurement system seem to be related to the decisions.[55] One of these reviews was done by Jon

Werner and Mark Bolino, who summarized 295 U.S. circuit court decisions that were rendered from 1980 to 1995.[56] Their analysis first examined whether contextual variables influenced court decisions. That is, they wanted to determine how issues regarding disparate treatment versus disparate impact, individual versus class action, the year of decision (before or after the 1991 Civil Rights Act), the circuit court district, the type of organization, the purpose of the appraisal, and the race and gender of the person who made the evaluation of job performance affected the outcome of the decision. Their findings determined that none of these variables was significantly related to the decisions, indicating that rulings apparently were made on the basis of the features of the appraisal systems rather than on features that were not directly relevant.

The features that were strongly related included the use of job analysis, the development and use of written instructions by the evaluators, and the employee's right to review the performance appraisal that the rater completed, as well as whether multiple raters were used in the performance appraisal. As you can probably guess, the court's decision usually was in favor of the organization if these characteristics were present. If they were not present, the plaintiff usually won. The authors found that it did not make a difference if the appraisal system used traits or behaviors. The effect of the raters' training on courts' rulings was unknown, because so few cases used this as an important factor in the decision. However, the authors noted that its absence was mentioned in several cases and that these cases usually were decided in favor of the plaintiff.

Werner and Bolino concluded from their findings that courts are primarily concerned with the fairness of the process of the appraisal system—that is, whether the procedures of the appraisal system indicate that it is based on job information, is carried out in a systematic manner, and is open to the individual being reviewed. The unimportance of the content of the items and scales similarly indicates that courts are more interested in the procedures of appraisal than the quality of the data that are collected and used. This is not unexpected. Issues of quality are very technical—often debated among practitioners—and are of less concern to many employees than the manner in which they are treated. The findings of this study provide excellent guidelines for the process of performance review in organizations.

Other research results complicate the issue of how to think about adverse impact in differences in scores among demographic groups on selection tests. This research looked at differences in the average job performance scores of black and white employees. One study explored differences across a large variety of performance measures: overall performance ratings, quality ratings, quantity ratings, objective measures of quantity, objective measures of quality, job knowledge scores, work samples, absenteeism, on-the-job training, and promotion.[57] Whites scored higher on all of these measures than did blacks. Specific findings were as follows:

- Whites and blacks differed by about one-third of a standard deviation unit ($d = 0.31$) across all measures of job performance.

- The average difference between the two groups was $d = 0.21$ for both quality and quantity performance ratings.

- The difference for all measures of job knowledge as performance criteria was $d = 0.48$.

- The difference for work sample tests as performance criteria was $d = 0.59$.

- The difference for absenteeism was $d = 0.19$.

- The differences for objective and judgmental measures of quality were equal, $d = 0.27$ and 0.26, respectively.

- The differences for objective and judgmental measures of quantity were 0.32 and 0.09, respectively. That is, the difference between the two groups was higher for objective measures of quantity than for judgmental measures.

- The differences between objective and judgmental measures of job knowledge were 0.55 and 0.15, respectively. Again, the difference between the groups was greater for objective measures of job knowledge than subjective measures.

- Differences occur at all levels of job complexity.

- Differences between white and Hispanic employees were smaller than those between white and black employees.

Some of the general conclusions were that (a) whites score higher on all measures of job performance, (b) the differences between blacks and whites are smaller for judgmental measures than for objective measures, and (c) differences on work samples and job knowledge criteria are larger than for other types of criteria. The reason these findings complicate the issue of adverse impact on selection test scores is that differences among demographic groups in job performance have the same pattern as differences among these groups in selection test scores. An indication of discrimination in selection testing would be differences among demographic groups in test scores but no differences among them on job performance measures. Some interpret the finding of similarity in differences on selection tests and job performance measures as meaning that the selection tests are doing what they are supposed to do—identify those applicants who will perform the highest regardless of demographic characteristics.

A second, larger meta-analysis study had similar findings.[58] These findings were as follows:

- There were differences between whites and blacks across all types of performance measures ($d = 0.27$).

- Differences in training proficiency criteria were $d = 0.46$.

- Differences are largest for performance criteria that are highly dependent on cognitive ability (work samples and job knowledge tests).

- Differences on performance measures that stress personal interaction or personality are much smaller than on other measures.

- Differences in work performance have decreased over the years that studies have been done.

These findings are interpreted by some as additional evidence that adverse impact on predictor scores is indicative (predictive) of differences in job performance. Therefore, adverse impact may occur but not be an indication of discrimination.

Other work is related to these findings of differences between whites and blacks in performance measures. In the mid-1990s various offices of the federal government released reports about the disparity between whites and blacks in performance ratings made by supervisors in the federal government. The explanation of these differences was that of racial bias in the perceptions of supervisors.[59] In an article, Gregory Baxter disagreed with this explanation and presented data both from the federal government and private industry that he interpreted as alternative reasons for the disparity in performance ratings. These data included findings that black workers exhibited worse absenteeism and other organizational delinquency behaviors and that they also scored lower than others on objective measures of job knowledge, work quantity, and work quality as well as on work-sample tests. Further examination of judgmental ratings did not support claims that white supervisors rated whites higher and black supervisors rated blacks higher. Generally, all raters rated whites higher and blacks lower, which partially could have been caused by the differences between the two groups in objective measures of job performance and differences in absenteeism and delinquency. Finally, the black–white measured performance gap is narrower when raters' subjective ratings are used than when objective performance measures are used.

EEO SUMMARY

This chapter has presented the major EEO principles and discussed their impact on HR selection programs. This last section summarizes the major legal concepts regarding discrimination that HR specialists must be aware of either in reviewing an existing selection program or developing a new one.

Basis of Discrimination

Charges of discrimination in selection practices must be linked to one of the personal characteristics specified in EEO law. The federal laws identify such characteristics as race, color, religion, sex, national origin, age (older than 40 years), and physical or mental handicaps. Executive orders for federal contractors also identify sexual orientation and sexual identity as protected classes. Although this is indeed a long list, it clearly means that, unless there is a state or local law, many charges of discrimination threatened against private organizations (for example, discrimination based on hair or clothing style or school affiliation) are not feasible according to EEO law unless the charge can be linked to one of the specified characteristics. The specification of these personal characteristics defines the groups HR specialists should consider when reviewing the vulnerability of a selection program to discrimination charges. An analysis of possible discrimination can be conducted on those groups with characteristics that are both specified in EEO law and that constitute at least 2 percent of the relevant labor market.

Evidence of Discrimination

A charge of discrimination can be brought against an organization with little substantiating evidence other than the fact that an individual was not selected for a position. In many cases, such a charge is a public embarrassment for the organization. Many organizations do not wish to bear the cost of legal action, especially if such action may be prolonged. The result is that the organization frequently will negotiate a settlement to the charge. Although this may be a pragmatic solution to a particular situation, it does little to resolve a potentially recurrent problem. It is important for HR specialists to realize that rulings about discrimination in selection practices generally have been based on patterns of selection decisions over a period of time rather than on an isolated instance. If sufficient evidence can be generated by a company against a charge of discrimination, the company's selection practice should be upheld by either EEOC or in a court. A particular selection decision means that one individual has (or a few individuals have) been hired from a pool of applicants. The other applicants have been denied employment. Perhaps several of these rejected applicants differ from the one who was selected on a personal characteristic specified in EEO law—for example, color, race, or religion. This difference and the denial of employment could serve as an *indicator* of discrimination in selection. Courts generally have recognized, however, that selection decisions are favorable to some applicants and unfavorable to others. The crucial information is the pattern that is evident when one views the overall result of a series of decisions. If such data indicate that one group—for example, white males—is selected in more cases than one would expect to find, given the relevant labor market's demographic characteristics, then there is evidence of adverse impact.

Options of the Organization

If, after reviewing selection patterns for specific jobs and applying the appropriate statistical analysis to the demographic groups specified in EEO law, the HR specialist notes large selection differences, the organization has two options for reducing its vulnerability. The first is to discontinue the current procedures and develop alternatives that would result in small differences in selection among the various demographic groups. At first this may seem a formidable task, but for many situations, such a change is actually fairly straightforward. We previously discussed the interaction between recruitment and selection. Some organizations have found that, especially for entry-level positions, a broadening of recruitment activities to systematically include women and minorities has provided a sufficiently qualified applicant pool to change selection patterns substantially. Other examples include the reevaluation of selection requirements, such as the number of years of experience and education degrees, to determine their necessity for job performance. Such requirements, especially if they are used stringently at an early stage of the processing of applicants, can have a large effect on the applicant pool. The second alternative, if large selection differences exist, is to conduct a validation study to support the organization's contention that the selection instruments are job related. As the *Uniform Guidelines* indicate, such studies must conform to professional standards for criterion or content validity. Chapter 8 presents the steps in these validation methods.

A final important point to keep in mind is that there is no legal requirement either to demonstrate the job relatedness of all selection devices if such instruments are not linked to adverse impact or to hire unqualified applicants to increase the "numbers" of specific groups. As has been pointed out, proof of job relatedness becomes necessary only if adverse impact is evidenced. If however, an organization goes through the process of building job relatedness into the data that are used for selection decisions, it is not obligated to ignore that process and hire an applicant only because he or she belongs to a certain demographic group. This point often is overlooked, and it frequently results in hiring decisions made primarily to increase the employment of certain groups. If these individuals are not qualified for the jobs into which they are hired, their selection is not a service to either themselves or the organization.

REFERENCES

1. *E.E.O.C. v. Ventura Corp, Ltd.*, 2013 WL 550550 (D.Puerto Rico Feb. 12, 2013).

2. Public Law 102–166 102d Congress—Nov. 21, 1991, 105 STAT. 1075.

3. Paul S. Greenlaw and Sanne S. Jensen, "Race-Norming and the Civil Rights Act of 1991," *Public Personnel Management* 25 (1996): 13–24.

4. J. A. Hartigan and A. K. Wigdor eds., *Fairness in Employment Testing: Validity Generalization, Minority Issues and the General Aptitude Test Battery* (Washington, DC: National Academy Press, 1989), 20.

5. Greenlaw and Jensen, "Race-Norming and the Civil Rights Act of 1991."

6. *APA Monitor* 23 (January 1992): 13.

7. *EEOC v. Hawaii Healthcare Professionals, Inc.* EEOC Press Release, July 19, 2012.

8. *EEOC v. Kelky, Drye, & Norman.* Bloomberg News, April 10, 2012.

9. *EEOC v. Central Freight Lines,* EEOC Press Release, May 10, 2012.

10. U.S. Equal Employment Opportunity Commission, *A Technical Assistance Manual on the Employment Provisions of the Americans with Disabilities Act* (U.S. Equal Employment Opportunity Commission, 1992).

11. Ibid.

12. Elliot H. Shaller, "'Reasonable Accommodation' under the Americans with Disabilities Act— What Does It Mean?" *Employee Relations Labor Journal* 16 (Spring 1991): 431–451.

13. *EEOC v. Finish Line, Inc.* EEOC Press Release, June 16. 2011.

14. *PGA Tour v. Martin*, 532 U.S. 661 (2001).

15. Act S102; 29 CFR S1630.11.

16. *Sutton v. United Airlines, Inc.* 119 Sup. Ct. 2139 (1999).

17. *Murphy v. United Parcel Service*, 527 U.S. 516 (1999).

18. *Toyota Motor Mfg., KY., Inc. v. Williams (00-1089)*, 534 U.S. 184 (2002).

19. ADA Amendments Act of 2008, PL 110-325 (S 3406).

20. Ibid.

21. *EEOC v. Creative Networks, LLC.* EEOC Press Release, September 23, 2013.

22. *EEOC v. Pioneer Place,* EEOC Press Release, May 24, 2012.

23. Immigration and Nationality Act, sec. 274B, 274C.

24. Ibid., 402.

25. U.S. Equal Employment Opportunity Commission, "EEOC Announces $2.1 Million Settlement of Wage Discrimination Suit for Class of Filipino Nurses," March 2, 1999, http://www.eeoc.gov/eeoc/newsroom/release/3-2-99.cfm.

26. Civil Rights Act of April 9, 1866, Chap. 31, 1, 14 Stat. 27.

27. *EEOC v. Resources for Human Development, Inc.* EEOC Press Release, April 10, 2012.

28. *McDonnell Douglas v. Green*, 411 U.S. 792 (1973).

29. Barbara Lindemann Schlei and Paul Grossman, *Employment Discrimination Law*, 2nd ed. (Washington, DC: Bureau of National Affairs, 1983), 1361.

30. Philip Bobko and Philip L. Roth, "An Analysis of Two Methods for Assessing and Indexing Adverse Impact: A Disconnect between the Academic Literature and Some Practice," in *Adverse Impact: Implications for Organizational Staffing and High Stakes Selection*, ed. James L. Outtz (New York: Routledge, Taylor and Francis Group, 2010).

31. Kevin Murphy and Rick R. Jacobs, "Using Effect Size Measures to Reform the Determination of Adverse Impact in Equal Employment Litigation," *Psychology, Public Policy, and Law* 18 (2012): 477–499.

32. Dan A. Biddle and Scott B. Morris, "Using Lancaster's Mid-Correction to the Fisher's Exact Test for Adverse Impact Analysis," *Journal of Applied Psychology* 96 (2011): 956–965.

33. Rules and Regulations, *Federal Register* 70, no. 194 (October 7, 2005).

34. U.S. Equal Employment Opportunity Commission, Civil Service Commission, Department of Labor, and Department of Justice, Adoption of Four Agencies of Uniform Guidelines on Employee Selection Procedures, 43 *Federal Register* 38, 290–38, 315 (August 25, 1978).

35. Ibid.

36. Ibid., 1607.5(1).

37. John P. Campbell, "Group Differences and Personnel Decisions: Validity, Fairness, and Affirmative Action," *Journal of Vocational Behavior* 49 (1996): 122–158.

38. James Ledvinka and Vida Scarpello, *Federal Regulation of Personnel and Human Resource Management*, 2nd ed. (Boston: PWS-Kent, 1991), 17.

39. Revised Order of No. 4, 41 Code of Federal Regulations, Part 60, at sec. 2. 10 (1979).

40. U.S. Equal Employment Opportunity Commission, "EEOC and Ford Motor Sign Multi-Million Dollar Settlement of Sexual Harassment Case," September 7, 1999, http://www.eeoc.gov/eeoc/newsroom/release/9 7 99.cfm.

41. The *Civil Rights Act of 1964*, Title VII, sec. 703(a).

42. *Lilly v. City of Beckley*, 797 F.2d 191, 41 FEP 772 (4th Cir. 1986).

43. *Adarand Constructors, Inc. v. Pena*, 115 Sup. Ct. 2097 (1995).

44. *Griggs v. Duke Power Co.*, 401 U.S. 424 (1971).

45. *United States v. Georgia Power*, 474 F. 2d 906 (1973).

46. *Spurlock v. United Airlines*, 475 F. 2d 216 (10th Cir. 1972).

47. *Watson v. Ft. Worth Bank & Trust*, 47 FEP Cases 102 (1988).

48. Ibid., 107.

49. *Rudder v. District of Columbia*, 890 F. Supp. 23 (1995).

50. *Ricci et al. v. DeSafano et al.* 557 U.S. ___ 2009, No. 07-1428 & No. 08-328.

51. *OFCCP v. Ozark Air Lines*, 40 FEP 1859 (U.S. Department of Labor, 1986).

52. *Jack Gross v. FBL Financial Services Inc.* 557 U.S. ___ 2009, No. 88-441.

53. H. John Bernardin and Richard W. Beatty, *Performance Appraisal: Assessing Human Behavior at Work* (Boston: West Publishing Co., 1984).

54. Adoption of Four Agencies of Uniform Guidelines on Employee Selection Procedures, 43 *Federal Register* 38, 290–38, 315 (August 25, 1978).

55. Hubert S. Feild and William H. Holley, "The Relationship of Performance Appraisal System Characteristics to Verdicts in Selected Employment Discrimination Cases," *Academy of Management Journal* 25 (1982): 392–406; see also Hubert S. Feild and Diane Thompson, "A Study of Court Decisions in Cases Involving Performance Appraisal Systems," *The Daily Labor Report*, December 26, 1992, E1–E5; and Glenn M. McEvoy and Caryn L. Beck-Dudley, "Legally Defensible Performance Appraisals: A Review of Federal Appeals Court Cases," paper presented at the Sixth Annual Conference of the Society for Industrial and Organizational Psychology, April 1991, St. Louis, Missouri.

56. Jon M. Werner and Mark C. Bolino, "Explaining U.S. Courts of Appeals Decisions Involving Performance Appraisal: Accuracy, Fairness, and Validation," *Personnel Psychology* 50 (1997): 1–25.

57. Philip L. Roth, Allen I. Huffcutt, and Philip Bobko, "Ethnic Group Differences in Measures of Job Performance: A New Meta-Analysis," *Journal of Applied Psychology* 88 (2003): 694–706.

58. Patrick F. McKay and Michael A. McDaniel, "A Reexamination of Black-White Mean Differences in Work Performance: More Data, More Moderators," *Journal of Applied Psychology* 91 (2006): 538–554.

59. Gregory Baxter. "Reconsidering the Black-White Disparity in Federal Performance Ratings," *Public Personnel Management* 41 (2012): 199–218.

Recruitment of Applicants

Recruitment is a distinctive process that is separate from, yet functions parallel to, the selection process. Nonetheless, the more successful the recruiting process is, the more the firm benefits from rigorous selection. By attracting more applicants and creating a large applicant pool, the firm can be "pickier" about who is hired; thereby enhancing the likelihood they will select candidates who are more likely to be high performers committed to the work. Furthermore, to the extent the recruiting process makes the organization more attractive to the candidate, the acceptance rate of highly sought-after candidates will increase. Thus, recruitment is critical to the organization because the success of a company is closely related to the quality of its workforce.

Attracting the attention of a job seeker, then generating and maintaining the candidate's interest throughout the selection process up to the job offer requires knowledge about the best recruiting methods, messages, and messengers (recruiters). Although prior research of recruitment has been less systematic and less informative than the complexity of the topic requires, in this chapter, we shine light on what is known. In addition, we also highlight what is understood about the use of new technologies (Internet and social media) that have radically transformed the speed and breadth of information disseminated to candidates.[1] To do so, we will discuss the key prehire applicant reactions and attitudes, including the candidate's perceptions of the organization's image or reputation, anticipatory fit to the job and the organization, and intention to pursue the job opportunity and accept a job, if an offer is extended.

This chapter primarily focuses on external recruiting, which requires generating interest when bringing a job opening to the attention of a potential applicant who does not currently work for the organization. Although internal recruitment from the organization's existing workforce also plays a role in selection, this chapter focuses on external recruiting for three reasons. First, there has been a sharp decline in the use of internal labor markets[2] and a concomitant increase in the use of external means driven by the Internet, like job boards and career Web sites, as well as the increased use of social media (Facebook, LinkedIn, Twitter, and so on). Second, there is very little research on internal approaches, like job posting and internal talent management.[3] Third, the ability to make the potential internal candidate aware of the opportunity and thus to *recruit* them is significantly different and easier. More important, because promotions are typically desired and valued by current employees, it is less challenging to manage the interest of internal applicants throughout the (truncated) selection process. In the next section, we discuss a model of the external recruitment process, followed by a detailed discussion of various recruiting strategies pursued over the entire selection process.

A MODEL OF THE RECRUITMENT PROCESS

As noted in Figure 5.1, the recruitment process proceeds through a few well-defined sequential stages, building on the pioneering work of Alison Barber, James Breaugh, and their colleagues.[4] The model also recognizes the shifting contextual factors and applicant perceptions of organizational activities across these stages.[5] The first stage involves attracting and capturing the interest of potential applicants. A few key steps are essential to realizing success in this stage of recruiting, including establishing recruiting objectives, delineating key targeting and messaging strategies to follow, and recognizing issues linked to social networking ties, as well as understanding the information-processing limitations that affect the efficacy of the message.

The second stage revolves around maintaining applicant interest sandwiched between the time the applicant has formally applied up through either receiving a job offer or no longer being under consideration for the position. Critical applicant perceptions are shaped by the recruiting and screening process, including its perceived fairness, the speed and informativeness of communications, and the quality of interactions with organizational agents (for example, recruiters, hiring manager).

The third and final stage follows the organization's decision to extend a job offer to the candidate and involves postoffer closure in terms of encouraging sought-after candidates to join the organization. These stages are delimited by two key applicant decisions: whether to apply to the organization and whether to accept or decline an opportunity to choose the job. The complexity of this process is magnified by the applicant's uncertainty as to whether the organization will extend a job offer to them. The remainder of this chapter focuses on organizational decisions and recruiting activities that can influence the applicants' choices, critical applicant reactions that are shaped by those activities, and the contextual and individual boundary conditions that frame the influence of the organizational activities and applicant reactions. To cover these topics, we break the recruiting process into three specific stages.

Stage 1: Attracting and Generating Interest

The first stage of the recruitment process involves a number of key organizational decisions that ultimately determine the potential value of the entire recruitment process.[6] First, the organization has to establish its recruitment objectives. These objectives include the number of minimally acceptable applicants for each position while keeping costs low, meeting the organization's legal and social obligations regarding the demographic composition of its workforce, and increasing the success rate of the selection process by reducing the proportion of applicants who are poorly qualified or are a poor fit to the organization.

Of course, the purpose of recruitment is to attract as many qualified people as possible with as little cost as possible. In part, this is because the more qualified candidates you have in your applicant pool, the better the selection decision will be.[7] As you'll find out in chapter 15, the larger the applicant pool, the lower (more selective) the selection ratio. When the selection ratio is near zero (lower), most of the applicants will not be hired. As long as the employer uses a valid predictor, being more selective means those few who are hired are even more likely to be the best performers. This is one critical way the recruiting process adds substantial value to the organization's selection activities.

This stage also includes a number of strategic decisions for reaching these objectives. These decisions include choosing which recruitment activities and message orientation the organization will use, when and how these activities will be done, whom to use as recruiters, what theme or message to convey, and even the timing of recruiting actions.

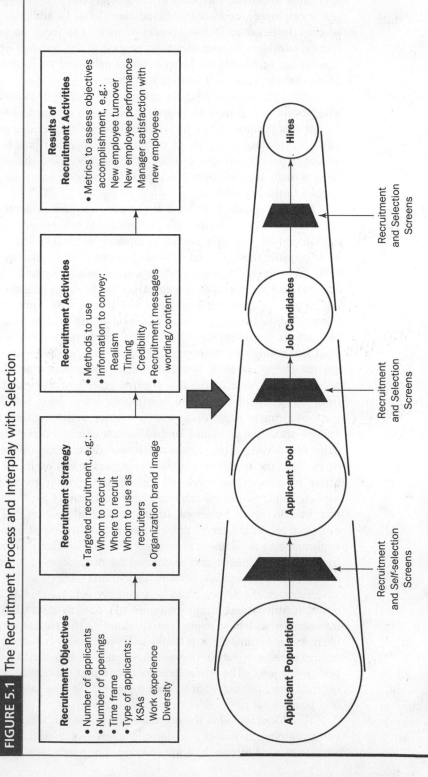

FIGURE 5.1 The Recruitment Process and Interplay with Selection

Recruitment Objectives
- Number of applicants
- Number of openings
- Time frame
- Type of applicants:
  KSAs
  Work experience
  Diversity

Recruitment Strategy
- Targeted recruitment, e.g.:
  Whom to recruit
  Where to recruit
  Whom to use as recruiters
- Organization brand image

Recruitment Activities
- Methods to use
- Information to convey:
  Realism
  Timing
  Credibility
- Recruitment messages wording/content

Results of Recruitment Activities
- Metrics to assess objectives accomplishment, e.g.:
  New employee turnover
  New employee performance
  Manager satisfaction with new employees

Applicant Population

Recruitment and Self-selection Screens

Applicant Pool

Recruitment and Selection Screens

Job Candidates

Recruitment and Selection Screens

Hires

Source: Top portion adapted from "Employee Recruitment: Current Knowledge and Important Areas for Future Research" by James Breaugh, *Human Resource Management Review* 18 (2008): 104.

Careful consideration must be given to these strategic decisions to achieve the previously defined recruitment objectives.

The first set of recruiting decisions involve targeting strategies about the type of applicants to pursue, including active job seekers, passive applicants (for example, currently employed), and nontraditional candidates. In addition, a decision must be made whether to target applicants broadly or instead to focus on person-to-person methods. Finally, considerable attention must be paid to the message orientation, use of diversity advertising, or reliance on Internet recruitment and social media versus other methods. These considerations will be discussed shortly.

Look again at Figure 5.1. By potential *applicant population*, we mean all individuals who possibly could have an interest in an open position and who might consider applying for this position. These individuals have not yet decided to apply for a position and might choose not to do so. In contrast, the *applicant pool* is a subset of the potential applicant population, and consists of those who have chosen to apply for a position. Even though they might not accept a job offer if one were made, they have at least applied to the organization.

At this stage, the key task is to generate a minimum level of attraction so the applicant considers the organization's job opening. Thus, research has focused on what information and how much is needed to catch an applicant's attention. Clearly, organizations must consider the types and sources of information applicants focus-on, including which Web sites, tweets, or blogs applicants are viewing.[8] By understanding what information the applicant has access to, the employer can begin to manage the content of the recruiting message, including the source of that information. One of the critical considerations in terms of the message's orientation involves the need to balance a desire to sell the job, product, or organization with the need to convey realism about doing the work. The need for "selling" the job opportunity is obvious, as the objective at this stage is to attract applicants. Nevertheless, to create realistic expectations and build trust, there is also a need to share some of the less positive aspects of the job. Doing so keeps new hires from being disappointed and quitting or even suing for fraudulent inducement or truth-in-hiring as might occur with "promises" regarding time to promotion or bonuses.[9] Talking about the good and the bad aspects of a job, however, does lead to some candidates withdrawing from consideration, and those often are the most sought-after candidates. Still, the conclusion is somewhat reassuring, as in the long run, it is (slightly) better to provide more relevant information during recruiting than not to do so.[10] In fact, failing to discuss some information (such as pay) can be interpreted negatively and lead to lower perceived attraction to the position.[11] The research that will be discussed in detail later in this chapter has shown that the quantity and quality of the applicant pool is significantly affected by both the source of the information (Web sites, friends, advertisements, and so on) and the orientation of the information (its specificity, realism, brand creation, credibility, and so on).

Although the advice could be succinctly summarized as "more information is better,"[12] recruiters and hiring managers still have to think through when to use realistic information and how strong the applicant's affective responses to the information is likely to be. Ultimately, it is useful to keep in mind that applicants stop considering an organization or opportunity when they conclude that they are a "misfit" to the organization or the job.[13] The challenge is to ensure that the "misfit" judgment is correct, as the organization does not want to miss the chance to hire talented candidates who will stay in a position.

To understand what the organization is trying to accomplish during the early stages of recruitment, it is useful to consider the effect these actions have on the applicant's attraction in or interest in a job opening. Ultimately, even though the labor market has an important influence on the total number of applicants that are searching, as more individuals are actively looking when the unemployment rate is higher, its effect on one organization is lost because it creates a uniform increase (or decrease) in interest across all organizations.[14] Instead, research has focused on those factors that are under an organization's control to influence interest in their job opening. The visibility, image of the brand or organization, familiarity, and reputation of the recruiting organization has emerged as the most significant predictors in attracting early interest in an organization's job openings.[15] Of these, organizational reputation is the most persuasive,[16] in large part because it represents an overall affective reaction or (dis)liking for the organization.

Key determinants of organizational reputation include organizational size and age, profitability, life cycle of the firm and industry, product awareness, location, organization-level social relationships, and what is called "celebrity effects."[17] For example, Dan Cable and Dan Turban found that job seekers recalled more information about familiar firms and anticipated increased pride from joining organizations with a favorable reputation.[18] Chris Collins and associates have shown how the brand image an organization builds over time clearly influences overall affective reactions toward an organization.[19] Because organizational reputation is viewed here as a more general, emotional reaction, the fact that image influences those emotional reactions underscores the central role organizational reputation plays in this process.[20]

The celebrity effect, which occurs when mass media dramatizes an event related to a firm, also can lead the general public to hold a more favorable view of that firm, regardless of actual merit.[21] For example, Glen Rollins, Orkin's chief executive officer, was reported to have stated during an earnings call that Web page traffic to the Orkin careers Web page jumped fivefold and actual job applications increased 70 percent the week following the chief operating officers appearance on CBS's "*Undercover Boss*."[22]

Of course, actually doing something of substance by adopting high-involvement work practices and being recognized in *Fortune* magazine's annual "100 Best Companies to Work For" is another way to create a favorable impression. For example, the first time Edward Jones was the number one–ranked company on this list, received applications are purported to have increased from 10,000 to 45,000 in one year.

Applicant attraction is also affected by the job seekers' desires, values, and self-image.[23] If the organization impresses others, is viewed as prestigious, or expresses values that are important to the candidate (for example, buy a pair of Tom's shoes and they will give a pair to needy children somewhere in the world), then attraction to the firm is greater.[24] As we will see, experienced workers or those currently employed react differently to recruiting tactics than undergraduate college students or the unemployed.[25] Similarly, those who thrive on competition will be more attracted to organizational cultures that encourage praise and recognition for individual accomplishments.

To understand how applicant perceptions to organizational reputation are formed[26] and to maximize the value of recruiting, James Breaugh[27] recently argued organizations should consider research on persuasion. Such research focuses on attributes often mentioned in recruiting research, including the importance of the source of the message (for example, credibility, expertise, willingness to disclose both good and bad, and so on), target of the message (whether or not the applicant currently has a job, personality and interests of the applicant, and so on), and the persuasiveness of the message itself (media richness, including multiple cues, specificity of feedback, and personal focus).[28]

Beyond attributes of the persuasive attempt, however, there is a need to understand the stages through which information is processed, initially leading to an attitude and, finally, to relevant behavior.[29] Early in the persuasion attempt, the critical issue is whether or not the target (the applicant) pays attention. Later, the focus shifts to comprehending the message, yielding to it, and retaining the message. Once the attitude has formed or changed, then and only then does it lead to relevant behavior change. As this suggests, the recruiting process requires an effective persuasion attempt to actually get the applicant to apply for the job.

In thinking about the process of persuasion, a couple of stages are particularly relevant to recruiting, as considerable research in the recruiting literature has emphasized the need for the target (applicant) to be motivated to attend to the recruiting message. This research tends to highlight the importance of the applicant's goals in determining whether they shift their attention to the message.[30] Direct experience with the object (organization, job) also plays a key role in whether one attends to a persuasive recruiting message.[31] Thus, having had an internship or friends and family work at the company, as well as the consistency of (especially when from a credible source) and increasing exposure to the message, have all been shown to influence attention to the message.[32] Furthermore, once an initial attitude has formed, it appears surprisingly difficult to change that attitude. Research suggests that the bias toward the status quo is the result of a number of heuristics that help reduce cognitive dissonance, including selective exposure and confirmation bias, which function because the person tends to be motivated to defend an attitude once formed. This leads them to avoid discrepant information and other information-processing biases that enable the person to focus on attributes that support the previously formed attitude, which leads them to recall information that confirms these attitudes in a biased way.[33] To illustrate this with recruiting, Derek Avery and Patrick McKay[34] reviewed several examples that suggested the lengths organizations had to go to overcome negative publicity regarding discriminatory practices using targeted recruitment activities. Another study showed that low involvement exposure to a positive message about an organization (containing no detailed information on the organization or job) did not change the negative reputation of a well-known organization,[35] again illustrating the difficulty in overcoming negative reputations. Such results are consistent with Tversky and Kahneman's well-known research, illustrating the power of the anchoring effect in the attitude–behavior relationship.[36] This research highlights the importance of positive early-stage recruiting information and explains why forming favorable organizational reputation judgments early can predict an applicant's interest in a company up through the job offer stage.[37]

Clearly, when developing a recruiting strategy, it will be important to focus on messages that can enhance the organization's reputation and image with potential job applicants. The position also matters, however, as the attractiveness of the position (high pay, prestige of the job),[38] whether the applicant believes he or she can get a job offer, and the number of other job opportunities or job offers available[39] can influence attraction to the organization.

Another important outcome for the organization to consider is the issue of person–environment (PE) fit. Although PE fit will become particularly important in latter stages of recruiting, when applicants perceive high fit with the organization and the job (the key environmental variables), they are more likely to apply for a position opening and ultimately to accept an offer.[40] Consequently, the applicant's perception of *anticipatory* PE fit is a critical outcome to keep in mind throughout the recruitment process, not just for attracting and generating interest initially. Moreover, research illustrates fit *on what* changes over this process. When one is considering whether to do more than just apply for a job (for example, to request letters of reference or do a phone interview) person–job (PJ) fit is the most influential fit measure, whereas later in the recruiting process (for example, when a job offer is being extended), person–organization (PO) fit becomes the key consideration.[41] As noted before, however, fit affects applicant interest most dramatically when a *lack* of fit or misfit is perceived. Apparently, applicants like to keep their options open by considering those with adequate fit, but once the applicant has formed an impression that they would not like to work at an organization, it is eliminated from further consideration.[42]

Fit is a challenging concept to understand, however. First, on what attributes is fit determined (matched on values, competencies, or even WRC needs)? Research suggests that the basis of fit is the match between the applicant and the job setting, where the match can be based on similarity between the two or that one makes the other "whole," and where the needs of the applicant are seen to be fulfilled by the organization (high pay, the opportunity to help others, and so on.). Second, for purposes of attracting an applicant, the person's overall perception of anticipatory fit is the critical assessment, as it is highly correlated to organizational attraction and willingness to apply for the job.[43] Although fit can consist of many different and unique judgments about the "match" on numerous characteristics (standing on personal values, goals, personality of both the individual and organization), ultimately, the overall judgment is the one that matters.[44] This perception is often affect-laden, which probably explains why firms often rely on highly favorable or positive information to influence these assessments.[45]

Slaughter and associates have developed a personality taxonomy for organizations that is also linked to organizational image.[46] In essence, they found organizations could be described using five personality types (and descriptive traits): the boy scout (honest, friendly, family oriented), dominant (busy, successful, popular), innovative (original, creative, unique), thrifty (simple, low budget, sloppy), and stylish (trendy, fashionable, hip). More important, organizations often were found to fit into one of these personality types, and when this happened, these organizations were seen to have more favorable reputations, seen as more attractive, and experienced higher job pursuit intentions when its personality type was seen to match or fit the applicant's preferences.[47]

At this stage of the recruiting process, the organization is interested in attracting the eye of the applicant, and they do so by building their reputation. Thus, in some sense, the overall recruiting objective at this point is to interest a large number of applicants to apply. Increasingly, however, in the twenty-first century, we see firms talking about an integrated strategic talent management approach, which shifts the focus from just any applicant to attracting only applicants who are viewed as high-quality targeted talent.[48] Consequently, the organization is likely to be interested in increasing the number of just those targeted applicants (for example, a competitor's employees, college graduates in electrical engineering). Three key considerations that should be addressed during this recruiting stage are reviewed next, including targeting strategies, recruiting message, and methods of recruiting.

Targeting Strategies

When considering who to recruit, a key consideration revolves around targeting specific types of individuals who are willing to apply to or accept a position if offered. Targeted recruiting is aimed at groups such as those defined by certain demographics (race, gender) or psychological characteristics (personality, mental ability).[49] Such a strategy can be used to enhance the diversity of a firm's applicant pool. Often, this strategy is used to address potential problems regarding disparate impact in selection, which can arise because of the use of certain selection procedures (for example, a mental ability test). Targeted recruiting designed to minimize disparate impact arising from the use of such selection procedures is generally legally defensible. For example, the *Uniform Guidelines on Employee Selection Procedures* focus mainly on *selection* procedures, and not as much on recruitment procedures. The *Uniform Guidelines*, however, recognize that targeted selection is often necessary.[50]

A second critical aspect of targeted strategies is how broadly to recruit, ranging from recruiting en mass by using messages with broad appeal that are not targeted to any one person, to attracting the interest of experienced hires and new graduates, or anything in between. At the other end of the spectrum is a recruiting approach that is targeted to specific, uniquely qualified types of individuals and that involves direct, one-to-one communication efforts.[51]

To determine whether or not to target specific applicants is a critical decision, as the next sections of this chapter are affected by that choice. Once one decides whom to target, the strategic issue shifts to how to reach or attract the interest of those targeted applicants. Although there is not enough research yet available on targeting individuals for recruiting, an important distinction is apparent between those who have work experience and new college graduates. More experienced applicants are viewed as holding greater technical skills and having a stronger work ethic, whereas students are seen as having a greater willingness to learn and to adapt to the "company's way" of doing things. One other important distinction, that may be reduced or even eliminated by college graduates with internship experience, is that experienced applicants have greater self-insight about their own talents and needs as well as hold more realistic expectations about the work itself.[52] Hence, again it is apparent that the targeting decision can have a significant effect on the size and quality of the applicant pool as well as the likelihood an applicant will accept a job offer.

Thus, where to recruit is a critical issue when developing the targeting strategy. Depending on other aspects of a firm's recruitment strategy, targeting a specific group can be very important. For example, to enhance racial diversity among technically trained job applicants, a company might target engineering programs at historically black colleges and universities or the National Society of Black Engineers. To attract conscientious and intelligent job applicants, a company can target specific groups of university students, such as those in Phi Beta Kappa or on the dean's or president's lists. To illustrate this practice, we next focus on the three groups of candidates that have received the most research attention.

First, organizations often are quite interested in targeting nontraditional candidates, including older workers, women, minorities, and disabled workers. Of course, it is difficult to know when one is recruiting disabled workers because the Americans with Disabilities Act (ADA) forbids organizations from inquiring about an applicant's disability status. The Equal Employment Opportunity Commission (EEOC), however, recently made an exception for federal contractors (with 50 or more full-time employees or $50,000 in federal contracts), who now have an "aspirational" target to hire at least 7 percent workers with disabilities.[53] Thus, for the first time up to 200,000 employers now have an incentive to actively recruit more disabled employees. The issues involved in such recruiting include the message as well as tactics for reaching nontraditional candidates.

Regarding recruiting messages, diversity initiatives have been found to be better received by applicants when merit is emphasized, diversity is included in advertisements (for example, via pictures), and the use of affirmative action is transparent.[54] Similarly, applicants react negatively to discriminatory questions during selection.[55] The use of diversity-related information in advertisements illustrates the challenges associated with attempts to attract a diverse pool of applicants. For example, research has found that including pictures or testimonials of black or Hispanic representatives can increase minority interest in a job opening, although the effect is greater if minorities are also portrayed in supervisory positions.[56] The actual effects on job offer acceptance are small, however, and if the recruiting efforts are seen as preferential treatment or a moral obligation instead of based on a business case justification, job seekers, particularly nonminorities, find it unappealing.[57]

Like all recruiting research reviewed in this initial stage of recruiting, the organization's reputation, in this case, reputation for diversity, is the best predictor of applicant intentions to apply.[58] Furthermore, conveying messages that relate to the needs and preferences of nontraditional candidates while signaling fairness and inclusion are also effective. For example, research shows older applicants are more likely to apply if the applicant anticipates being able to fulfill their own key needs. Thus, when the recruiting message suggests that the workforce includes both younger and older workers, that the position includes mentoring opportunities to transfer knowledge or conveys an entrepreneurial orientation, and that the job has flexible schedules, organizational attraction and application intentions are significantly higher.[59] Assertive tactics that have been successful for other nontraditional groups include employing minority recruiters, participating in diversity job fairs, targeting recruiting advertisements in minority-focused media or universities, and sponsoring minority events.[60] Again, we see evidence that the most successful recruiting approaches rely on multiple methods and messages.[61]

Second, college recruiting has been studied more than any other group, so in many ways, we know the most about this type of recruiting. Even here, however, research has been criticized by using college students who are freshmen and sophomores in psychology or business schools as participants. These may not be representative of science, technology, engineering, math students, for example, or even of graduating students. Nevertheless, the vast majority of recruiting research has involved college students. A series of studies by Chris Collins and his associates are particularly informative, as they found that college student attitudes were affected by sponsorship (the employer sponsors a department or scholarships), word-of-mouth endorsements from faculty or family, employee endorsements, and general and detailed recruitment ads, as the number and quality of applicants interested in and intending to apply increased to the extent these various recruitment variables were used.[62] These studies and those reviewed earlier suggest that to attract and generate interest, an organization needs to implement a variety of recruitment methods before recruiting on campus. Furthermore, because much of the prior conclusions reviewed here were based on college students, it is clear recruiters should try to use methods that will influence organizational reputation and image, although more recent research also suggests students are guided by career mobility prospects in the organization as well as its social responsibility and sustainability initiatives,[63] as these factors have been found to predict whether these applicants actually apply.

In the past few years, there has been considerable research on the third group of candidates, which involves recruiting passive job candidates. Passive candidates are currently employed and not actively searching for jobs, yet may be willing to consider another job opportunity. Sometimes called poaching, this targeting strategy is becoming more widespread.[64] For example, start-ups and growth companies often pursue this strategy to increase innovation or to avoid problems more established organizations already have experienced and in retaliation for prior poaching of their own employees.[65] Recent studies of executives as passive candidates found that executives were likely to consider alternative job opportunities when their stock options were underwater or had a market value below their exercise price, when they were unhappy in their current job, when they had board of director interlocks, and when they worked in smaller firms.[66] To lure current employees away, it also is argued that recruiting might emphasize how these jobs create opportunities to achieve a greater sense of meaning and purpose in one's life. For example, the message could emphasize that the individual will have the chance to participate in a big and exciting idea that is going to lead the industry forward or affect others' lives in significant ways.[67]

One theme that emerges from this research is that being currently employed has been shown to differentially influence the nature of the relationship for some of the recruiting outcomes reviewed earlier. For example, when job seekers are more experienced both in having previously worked as well as searched for a job, it appears that peripheral aspects related to such things as physical attractiveness of the people portrayed in the ad are less impactful on application intentions. Instead, these candidates tend to focus intently on job and organizational content.[68] Consequently, it would seem that recruiters should focus more on influencing employed candidates' PJ and PO fit perceptions and dispense with efforts to enhance attraction to the organization. Although such applicants are likely to be influenced by organizational reputation, the magnitude of that relationship will be attenuated relative to the effect on anticipatory fit perceptions. That is, these applicants want evidence that the job and organization will be better than their current work situation.

The Recruiting Message

The first critical question regarding the recruiting message concerns message orientation—whether to recruit by just emphasizing a positive message or to be realistic and allow job seekers to screen themselves out if they are a poor fit. The problem is that some desirable candidates will withdraw based on misperceptions about the realistic information presented, and losing those candidates can reduce the quality of the applicant pool.[69] Nevertheless, recruitment programs traditionally have been regarded as an opportunity to sell the organization as a favorable place to work, the message, therefore, tends to be universally positive. Pay excellence, the high quality of ones coworkers, physical facilities, advancement opportunities, benefits, even challenge in the job have been stressed. Because no work situation is without negative aspects, however, such traditional messages can instill false expectations in recruits that cannot be fulfilled in actual employment, and this may lead to higher turnover shortly after hire.

Realistic job previews, in which both good and bad (well, at least less positive and more realistic) information is conveyed, have been found to enhance applicant interest in a company.[70] However, it can adversely affect the attraction of the most sought-after candidates.[71] Of course, the overall effect of a realistic message on the quality and size of the applicant pool depends on the type of job, the industry, and even the nature of the information itself, as well as how experienced the applicant is and whether the applicant is currently employed.[72] Scott Highhouse and his colleagues have found that one negative or realistic piece of information can reduce the positive reaction from multiple positive messages.[73] Thus, as we will see throughout the selection process, negative information has a disproportionately large effect on selection decisions (and recruiting). Presumably, when one party is unsure about another (the applicant about the organization; later, the interviewer about the candidate when both are strangers), it is better to be safe than sorry.

Inflated expectations happen to some degree in most recruitment situations. Many now think that it is unproductive to create expectations in the applicant that cannot be fulfilled. Once employed, some individuals find the differences between their expectations and the actual job to be unpleasantly large. Thus, there is likely to be a quicker transition through the "honeymoon" period after hire and a more extreme "hangover" period.[74] Such discrepancies in expectations can cause both dissatisfaction with the organization and rapid job turnover. Obviously, in such cases, the whole cost of recruitment and selection must be repeated as other applicants are processed.

In place of such unrealistic recruitment messages, some recruitment researchers have recommended a "realistic job preview (RJP)."[75] During RJPs, applicants are given the negative aspects of the job as well as the positive. Recent research reveals negative or realistic information is seen as more credible and in some cases has not diminished attraction to the firm.[76] For example, studies have found recruiting messages for "dirty work" (for example, sanitation workers, pest exterminators) could be presented in a way that keeps undesirable jobs from being viewed as unattractive.[77] When such messages convey how valuable this work is to society or shows the satisfaction experienced by customers, applicants have not experienced negative reactions. The key is for organizations to identify those few attributes of the work that can lead to turnover and to clearly describe them in a way that applicants can make more accurate, informed decisions as to whether they are a poor fit, so that only those who are most likely to quit withdraw during recruiting.

Beyond message orientation, it is clear that the amount of information about the job and organization and the specificity of that information (for both, the rule is clear: more is better), influences how credibly and positively the messages are viewed.[78] Furthermore, the failure to provide information about key attributes (for example, pay, career development, even location) tends to lead to negative attributions and again can even lead to applicants withdrawing from consideration.[79] For example, in the past, location of the job may not have been quite as critical as pay or opportunities for career development because applicants only "heard" the recruiting message if they lived near where the job was (through local newspaper ads). With the vast reach possible through the Internet and social media, however, the importance of "willingness to relocate" is likely to increase as discovering the precise location of a job opportunity late in the recruiting process may reduce acceptance rates.[80] As noted here, considerable research evidence has demonstrated that applicants regard the amount and specificity of information to be a signal of the company's regard for employees. At the same time, when presented with inadequate information, applicants also use this as a signal to make negative inferences about the company. Consequently, the general principle is to provide more relevant information, and the more specific it is about the job and the organization, the better.[81]

One shortcoming of the principle that more information is better is that it ignores the attention span of the typical applicant early in the recruiting process.[82] TheLadders.com found that candidates spent an average of only 76.7 seconds reading online descriptions of the job in ads on their job board. Similarly, TheMuse.com allows only a two-sentence summary of a job description on its job board. Thus, to get ideal candidates to apply while discouraging unqualified candidates, the highlighted information is critical because it needs to be impactful, yet brief. Research clearly shows that job ads that reflect specific work experiences or even personality traits sought in applicants' leads to greater interest by those candidates with the necessary experience or matching personality traits.[83] A 2008 McKinsey summary of an internal study conducted by HP, however, found women were more likely to screen themselves out (not apply) if they did not meet all of the listed job requirements, whereas men in the same situation applied more frequently.[84] Consequently, companies are encouraged to avoid long-winded job descriptions, to minimize the use of jargon or clichés, and to focus on just a few critical WRCs or personality traits, while avoiding nonessential requirements that may lead applicants to screen themselves out when the firm actually would have wanted to hire them. Organizations are urged to convey a sense of the organization's culture or identity, especially those quirks or core beliefs that make the company different from other companies.[85]

One obvious way organizations can manage their image is by tailoring their recruitment strategies and methods to communicate the kind of image they wish to portray to applicants. Recruiting organizations should carefully consider the exact nature of their recruitment strategy as well as the design of recruitment media, such as Web sites, as such media can influence applicants' perceptions of an employer's organizational culture.[86] For example, organizations wishing to convey a culture of teamwork would use different images and messages than would organizations wishing to convey a culture of high achievement, high energy, and high individual rewards. As another example, job seekers viewing technically advanced recruitment Web sites tend to perceive such organizations as more technologically advanced than organizations without such sites.[87] As this suggests, the recruitment message has an important effect on recruits as it shapes perceptions of corporate reputation, which is a critical predictor as to whether an applicant applies initially for a job opening.

Finally, research by David Newman and Julie Lyon indicated that using certain adjectives to describe a job and the company successfully attracted applicants who had the "matching" job-related personality, ability, or demographic characteristic. From their results, they suggested that firms undertaking targeted recruiting should incorporate the following in their recruitment messages to attract candidates from a racial minority or recruits who are conscientious and high in cognitive ability:

- To target applicants with high cognitive ability, describe the job or work environment using terms such as *challenging* and *stimulating*; say that the job requires *quick thinking*, *intelligence*, and *knowledge*.

- To attract those high in conscientiousness, message content should incorporate terms such as these to describe a desirable recruit: *reliable*, *works hard*, *well organized*, *self-disciplined*, and *conscientious*.

- To attract racial minorities who are conscientious, message content should characterize companies as *innovative* and *progressive*.[88]

One caution, however, is that the recruitment message must accurately represent the true characteristics of the company and job. Otherwise, as noted earlier, low job performance and employee attrition is likely to ensue.

From an overall recruitment perspective, Newman and Lyon recommended that firms generally recruit applicants high in cognitive ability as well as racial minorities high in conscientiousness. They concluded that this particular strategy enhances average job performance among all hires as well as increases the percentage of hires from racial minority groups. Of course, recruitment message content alone would not be the only strategy that a firm should use to recruit those possessing the desired attributes. Other actions should be used to supplement recruitment message content.

Recruiting Methods

As we will see, organizations can use a number of different methods to bring a job opening to the attention of a possible candidate, and they differentially affect organizational reputation and attraction, which ultimately affects the quality and quantity of candidates in the applicant pool. Before we get into the gritty details, however, it is useful to recognize that the effectiveness of different methods revolves around three issues: media richness (multiple informational cues, with feedback, and a personal focus), media credibility (expertise and trustworthiness of the source), and degree of attention required during information processing (central processing routes involve higher attention; peripheral routes require less).[89] Furthermore, early in recruiting (stage 1: attracting applicant interest), organizational reputation and organizational attraction are the key outcomes that lead to applying for the position. However, as the applicant considers attending an employment interview later in recruiting (stage 2: maintaining interest), we notice an increase in the importance of the applicant's perceived PJ fit. Finally, as the candidate decides whether or not to accept a job offer, it appears that the applicant's perceived PO fit becomes critical.[90] Hence, to fully appreciate the usefulness of various recruiting methods, while it is essential to keep in mind the method's richness, credibility, and attention elicited, it is also vital to understand how the method is trying to influence the candidate: to get the person to think highly of the firm (reputation), to be able to imagine working in the job (PJ fit), or to perceive themselves holding the same values as the organization (PO fit). And when considering fit, keep in mind that the key issue is actually poor fit, not good fit—as applicant intentions to not apply or interview are influenced by a perceived belief that they will *not* fit well with the job or the organization rather than that they will fit well.[91]

As you evaluate the effectiveness of various recruiting methods, remember the following three considerations:[92] First, employee referrals and walk-ins tend to make better employees than other methods.[93] Second, use of more informal methods (employee referrals, walk-ins, interns, and rehired former employees) have the potential to create disparate impact, as research shows these methods can lead to a disproportionate increase in the number of whites and males in the applicant pool over more formal methods (employment agencies, job advertisements, job fairs, and Web sites).[94] Third, the magnitude of effects from different methods tends to be relatively small, particularly as the predictions shift from applying for a position to accepting an offer to being a better employee. Although there are consistent differences in the effectiveness of these methods, those effects are not large.

Some of the major methods of recruitment are presented in Table 5.1. These methods vary by a number of important characteristics that affect how organizations use them. One characteristic is *cost* of use. Generally speaking, employee referral methods and advertising, especially when only local media are used, are relatively inexpensive, meaning that cost per person contacted is usually low. Methods that require a good deal of travel and personnel time, such as college recruiting, are much more expensive. A second important characteristic, which is somewhat inversely related to the first, is the *speed* of the recruiting method. Among the slowest are college recruiting, technical and community college recruiting, and the use of search firms. Methods that rely on a personal touch, including employee referrals, professional conferences, and word-of-mouth endorsements are quite fast, as are Web pages, like company Web sites or job boards.

A third important characteristic is the *amount of information that can be presented* to potential applicants. The cost of television and newspapers is a direct function of the timing, geographic coverage, and length of the recruitment message. Most companies restrict the amount of information provided in these methods, even though they can effectively convey much more information. College recruitment is usually quite expensive—because of the recruiters' travel expenses and because each recruiter usually contacts only 8 to 12 applicants each day. Use of company recruitment Web sites, corporate links on social networking sites (such as Facebook, LinkedIn, Twitter), and current employees making referrals are often among the most cost-effective recruiting approaches.

A fourth factor is the *predictability of the number of applicants* recruited. It is commonly thought that advertising and employment agencies are less consistent in both the numbers and qualifications of applicants generated than are methods more directly under the control of the organization, such as school recruiting and employee referral. Variability in the numbers recruited can be caused by such factors as time of year, general economic and employment conditions, amount and intensity of competitors' recruiting efforts, applicants' perceptions about the specific media or agencies used, and the recruiting organization itself. A major part of the design of recruitment programs and the implementation of the recruitment strategy is deciding which combination of recruiting methods to use for specific jobs.

One obvious question about recruitment methods that we know you are thinking about is, "What are the differences in results among recruitment methods?" Much research has been done to investigate differences, and differences have been identified.[95] The results, however, have not been consistent across studies. In part, this lack of consistent findings occurred because firms often use more than one recruitment method and it

TABLE 5.1   Characteristics of Recruitment Sources

Recruitment Source	Cost	Amount of Information Given	Predictability Number of Applicants	Internal/ External Recruitment Source	Principally Used for Professional Positions	Principally Used for Non-professional Positions
Advertisements:						
Local newspapers	Moderate	Little	Low	External		✓
National newspapers	High	Little	Low	External	✓	
Trade publications/ magazines	Moderate	Little	Low	External	✓	
Television or radio	High	Little	Low	External		✓
Agencies and Organizations:						
Targeted minority recruiting	Moderate	Little	Low	External	✓	
Private employment agencies	Moderate	Little	Low	External		✓
State employment agencies	Low	Little	Low	External		✓
Temporary help agencies	Moderate	Little	Low	External		✓
Universities	Moderate	Moderate	Low	External	✓	
Community organization partnerships	Low	Little	Low	External		✓
Technical/community college	Low	Moderate	Low	External		✓
Search firms	High	Little	Low	External	✓	
Job fairs	Moderate	Little	Low	External	✓	✓
Professional Associations:						
Professional conferences	Moderate	Little	Low	External	✓	
Professional organizations	Low	Little	Low	External	✓	
Inside Organization Resources:						
Previous employees	Moderate	High	Low	Internal	✓	
Employee referrals	Low	Moderate	Moderate	Internal		✓
Job posting to current employees	Low	High	Moderate	Internal		✓
Company Web sites	Low	High	Moderate	External	✓	
Internships	Low	High	Moderate	Internal	✓	
Other Sources:						
Online job boards	Low	Moderate	Low	External	✓	
Walk-ins/unsolicited resumes	Low	Moderate	Low	External	✓	✓
Word-of-mouth	Low	Little	Low	External		✓
Retiree job bank	Low	Little	Low	External		✓

is not possible to isolate the effects of any single method. To illustrate, in a recent survey of 306 employers, organizations say they use university career centers (college recruiting), attend campus job fairs, contact student chapters of professional groups, serve on advisory boards at universities, meet and leverage contacts of key faculty, use social media (Intel has created a student lounge), and encourage employee referrals.[96] James Breaugh, however, identified three studies that used job applicants, collected data on specific recruiting methods, and involved only one employer.[97] In general, companies that obtained applicants from employee referrals and received unsolicited applications tended to yield more applicants and hires. Explanations for these differences include the realistic information hypothesis (some methods such as employee referrals provide more accurate information about a job) and the individual difference hypothesis (different recruitment methods deliver information about a job opening to different types of people who differ on key characteristics, and as a result, make different PJ or PO fit attributions).[98]

In terms of voluntary turnover among new hires, a recent study helped clarify why conflicting results have been found among some types of recruiting methods.[99] Ingo Weller and associates theorized that when applicants gather information about jobs, they tend to weigh information obtained from more personal recruitment methods (referrals from current employees, family, or friends; rehires) more heavily than information obtained from more formal methods (newspaper ads, employment agencies). Informal, more personal recruitment source information is valued by potential applicants because these personal methods are thought to provide more accurate and complete information about jobs and employers. Better information received by applicants leads them to perceive better personal outcomes if hired (better fit with the organization; higher quality of job held). Weller and colleagues reasoned that voluntary turnover should be lower for those individuals relying on personal recruitment methods than those relying on formal methods. They proposed, however, that these personal versus formal recruitment method differences in voluntary turnover rates were predicted to diminish over time. They reasoned that individuals new to an organization seek information in a deliberate manner when uncertainty is highest (that is, early in new employees' tenure). Better quality information obtained from personal methods gives individuals a better picture of what to expect from a new job. Over time, however, as individuals become more knowledgeable about their jobs, differences in turnover rates between personal recruitment methods and formal recruitment methods were expected to diminish.

To examine their expectations, they collected data on more than 2,700 individuals over a nine-year period to test for the effects of recruitment source differences on employee turnover. After studying turnover rates for two types of recruitment method (personal versus formal), they found roughly 25 percent less turnover among employees relying on personal recruitment methods for employment information versus those relying on more formal methods. This pattern was particularly evident during the first 24 months of employment, when voluntary turnover was particularly high. They concluded that use of personal recruitment methods is beneficial for those firms experiencing high turnover rates during the first 24 months of new hires' careers. For example, when Weller and colleagues computed the impact of personal recruitment methods (versus formal methods) on voluntary turnover in large national franchise operations such as in the fast-food industry (for example, Taco Bell, Burger King), they estimated a $20 million savings in turnover-related costs.[100]

The takeaway point regarding recruitment methods seems to be this: Use informal, personal recruitment methods in cases in which voluntary turnover is a problem during employees' first two years of employment.[101] There is a cautionary note, however. Although we are unaware of any recent research, past evidence has indicated that minorities, perhaps because of historic employment patterns in many industries, use formal recruitment methods more frequently than informal ones.[102] If this is the case, employers overemphasizing personal recruitment methods over formal ones might reduce the number of minority applicants in their applicant pools.

A related point about personal recruitment methods is that word-of-mouth information about jobs and employers also has been identified as an important source of recruits. Word-of-mouth recruitment involves personal communication about an employer, independent of the employer, which is viewed as more credible information by a potential job applicant. Research has demonstrated that potential applicants receiving positive word-of-mouth information about an employer early in the recruitment process tend to view that employer as more attractive and are more likely to submit an employment application.[103] Word-of-mouth recruitment information is particularly important when the recruit has close ties with the individual (a personal friend) providing positive employer information. For this reason, organizations might broaden their recruitment activities to include potential applicants' family and friends—sponsoring "refer-a-friend" programs for vacant positions on a recruitment Web site, ensuring that a company's employees have complete information about vacant positions, and rewarding employee referrals.[104] However, organizations must be careful that word-of-mouth recruiting does not lead to minority underrepresentation in applicant pools. Table 5.2 summarizes some general guidelines on how employers can avoid discrimination against protected groups in their recruitment activities.

Understanding how individuals process information from recruitment methods is as important as tracing the effectiveness of separate methods of recruitment. Christopher Collins and Cynthia Stevens found that recruitment methods interacted with one another[105] by affecting two perceptions of potential applicants: general company image and specific job attributes. These perceptions, in turn, were related to applicants' intention to apply for a job. In two other studies, a simulation was used to manipulate the presence of employee testimonials and their richness (pictures with text versus audio with video clips), the attractiveness of the individuals in the ads, and the proportion of racial minorities to nonminorities.[106] These attributes were found to influence

---

TABLE 5.2   How Can Employers Avoid Discrimination When Recruiting?

> **EEOC General Guideline:** It is illegal for an employer to recruit new employees in a way that discriminates against them because of their race, color, religion, sex (including pregnancy), national origin, age (40 or older), disability, or genetic information.

- **When Writing Job Advertisements:** Generally, employers should not express a preference for a protected group characteristic, for example, race, in job advertisements (including newspapers, Web sites, or other media). Employers can indicate that they are "equal opportunity employers."

- **When Using Employment Agencies:** Employment agencies may not honor employer requests to avoid referring applicants in a protected group. If they do so, both the employer and the employment agency that honored the request will be liable for discrimination.

- **When Using Word-of-Mouth Employee Referrals:** Word-of-mouth recruitment is the practice of using current employees to spread information concerning job vacancies to their family, friends, and acquaintances. Unless the workforce is racially and ethnically diverse, exclusive reliance on word-of-mouth should be avoided because it is likely to create a barrier to equal employment opportunity for certain protected groups that are not already represented in the employer's workforce. For example, an employer's reliance on word-of-mouth recruitment by its mostly Hispanic workforce may violate the law if the result is that almost all new hires are Hispanic.

- **When Using Homogeneous Recruitment Sources:** Employers should attempt to recruit from diverse sources to obtain a diverse applicant pool. For example, if the employer's primary recruitment source is a college that has few African American students, the employer should adopt other recruitment strategies, such as also recruiting at predominantly African American colleges, to ensure that its applicant pool reflects the diversity of the qualified labor force.

Sources: http://eeoc.gov/laws/practices/index.cfm and http://www.eeoc.gov/policy/docs/qanda_race_color.html

organizational attraction through media richness and media credibility; and perceptions differed based on minority status as well as among those with more work and job search experience. For example, minority applicants viewing testimonials from minority spokespersons rated the ads as having higher information credibility and organizational attraction than did the nonminority applicants. Similarly, participants with less work experience or job search experience rated the use of more attractive individuals for the testimonials as leading to greater attraction to the organization than did more experienced participants.

One conclusion that can be drawn is that recruitment methods will be more effective when they complement one another. For example, if a company wishes to emphasize in its recruitment process its goal of furthering the career development of employees, then its recruitment methods should emphasize this theme (using different examples and wording, as appropriate). Furthermore, greater use of rich media and enhanced credibility can significantly affect organizational attraction. These strategies help to incorporate some of the principles behind organizational branding and reputation that were discussed earlier.

Two key ways to differentiate these recruiting methods is to separate those types that rely heavily on social processes from those that focus on informational processes. As noted previously, word-of-mouth endorsements, especially from informal sources (friends and family), play a critical role in recruiting, particularly for inexperienced applicants.[107] For example, Martin Kilduff found that business administration students were far more likely to interview with the same companies as their close friends in the same program.[108] More broadly, research has long underscored that social networks affect recruiting by either making applicants aware of job openings or by shaping applicant decisions. A series of recent studies illustrated the influence of business network ties, particularly for companies in the start-up or growth phases, which were found to rely on strong, direct interfirm ties between organizations or executives through board interlocks in recruiting and hiring decisions.[109]

To illustrate the import of information on recruiting methods, we consider the transformational role that access to the Internet has played in recruiting, as it has become one of the most dominant recruiting methods in recent years.[110] A recent survey-based study found that the use of social media has grown from 34 percent of firms using it for recruiting in 2008 to 77 percent in 2013.[111] The most frequently endorsed social media Web site for recruiting purposes in that study was LinkedIn (used by 94 percent of firms using the Web). Between 2009 and 2014, LinkedIn's membership has exploded from less than 50 million to 313 million members. While the growth of the Web has enabled job seekers to have vast amounts of information at their fingertips, it is also purported to have led to a dramatic increase in the proportion of unqualified applicants applying for positions and those relatively unlikely to accept an offer, what Brian Dineen and colleagues have referred to as the "dark side" of online recruiting.[112]

Of course, the obvious benefits of the Web are that it is relatively inexpensive, allows for the presentation of large amounts of information, and can be accessed by individuals at any time and in almost any place. Some research has reported savings of up to 90 percent of the costs associated with traditional recruiting methods and 25 percent reductions in time in the hiring cycle.[113] As with previous recruiting research, we find that the effectiveness of a Web site depends on its media richness, the use of more credible sources, and good aesthetic features and ease of use.[114] We clearly need more research on how job seekers find relevant company Web sites, what Brian Dineen has called the "process of driving job seekers to their company Web site."[115] Again, we find that research demonstrates that those who perceive themselves as misfits are far more likely to withdraw from the applicant pool.[116] For example, Dineen and Noe[117] found that when the Web site had the capability to provide feedback on the applicant's fit with the organization's values and fit to ability levels needed to do the job, they reported better fitting applicant pools—that is, those who fit less well were significantly less likely to apply. Clearly, more research is needed on Web-based recruiting, but preliminary results suggest many of the features found to be influential with other recruiting methods also influence the success of the Web.

Companies can use the Web in a number of ways for recruiting. Some of the more popular ways include the following:

- Posting jobs on a company's home page

- Posting jobs on Web sites devoted to job announcements (www.Monster.com; www.CareerBuilder.com). Numerous job boards available, and they differ by being national (or local) and specialized by industry or profession (or general). It appears that applicants using specialized boards instead of general boards have better educational qualifications and higher skills, although substantially fewer applicants used these sites.[118]

- Posting links to a job advertisement on social networking Web sites (www. Twitter.com; www.Facebook.com; www.YouTube.com) or to a recruiting company's corporate Web sites (see, for example, Developmental Dimensions International [DDI®] corporate Web site at www.DDI.com).

- Screening for applicants using available search options on business social networks such as www.LinkedIn.com (approximately 313 million members have joined LinkedIn, with two-thirds of them living overseas). More and more, employers are searching for midlevel and professional candidates in materials posted on such Web sites (other companies' employee listings, member lists of associations, online news articles), rather than relying on recruitment agencies.[119]

Popular press writings about using the Web for recruiting discuss several actions leading to best results.[120] These actions include the following:

- **Use individuals who know your organization and the job to refer applicants.** All firms have both current employees and past employees who have left the firm but still hold positive feelings about it. These individuals can be sources for referrals of new employees. Keeping current with ex-employees' e-mail addresses is the biggest challenge for this activity.

- **Develop a recruiting Web site.** Most companies are trying to use their corporate Web sites for recruiting and have begun offering career opportunities or advice on their site. A recruiting Web site that is properly constructed (for example, making use of video clips and audio with employee testimonials, even employee blogs) and easy to access and navigate can provide many well-qualified applicants. Such a Web site should display much more than minimal information about open positions. Examples could include any of the following: a description of company culture or its sustainability policies, statements by existing workers at all levels about working in the company, success stories of individual workers or teams, a discussion of advancement or career development opportunities, a philosophy of employee rights and treatment, and a demographic summary of employees can all be used to present an inviting message to those that inquire.

- **Use employee testimonials.** Organizations using a recruiting Web site might specifically consider using employee testimonials on the Web site itself. Jack

Walker and his associates reported that video-with-audio employee testimonials (versus those presented with an employee picture and text versus no testimonials presented) included on an organization's Web site were particularly beneficial. Testimonials delivered via video and audio had higher organizational attractiveness and information credibility ratings among Web site viewers than those given via picture with text.[121] Finally, with regard to taking job applications via a corporate recruiting Web site, applicants' perceptions of the efficiency and user-friendliness of the Web site are important characteristics associated with applicant satisfaction.[122]

- **Find active candidates.** A multitude of active job boards are populated by innumerable job candidates actively seeking employment. These range from very large boards with several hundred thousand applicants at any one time to niche boards that specialize in particular industries, occupations, or jobs. Although time consuming, it is beneficial to learn about the various boards and the profiles and general skill levels of the typical applicants appearing on these boards. This knowledge can be used for targeting the search to those job boards that are the best matches for finding the desired employees. Examples of such boards include www.Monster.com, www.CareerBuilder.com, and www.Datafrenzy.com.

- **Find passive candidates.** Passive job candidates are not actively seeking another position, but often respond positively to being approached for new employment. This is the tactic that executive search firms or "headhunters" have traditionally used. Many search firms build listings of individuals in particular positions throughout the world and use these listings when the search firm is employed to find executives for open positions. In the twenty-first century, however, employers have found they can build their own lists of potential applicants (passive candidates) using information found on their own companies' Web sites, in news stories, on professional association membership rolls, and on meeting or convention registration and speaker lists, as well as by paying LinkedIn to search for likely job candidates and to e-mail them about job openings (called "talent solutions"). These listings have enabled more and more organizations to replace the "expensive" fees charged by executive-search firms (often a third of the first year salary, and often also includes an "administrative fee," even if a qualified candidate is not found) by conducting their own search for candidates.[123] One small anecdotal survey of 40 employers in the United Kingdom showed that more than 8 out of 10 employers used LinkedIn for recruitment purposes, and roughly 6 of 10 used Facebook. Less than half of the employers used any of the other social networking options (Twitter or blogs).[124]

- **Recruit passive job candidates.** The SHRM Staffing research study[125] found the top three reasons for using social networking approaches was to recruit passive job candidates (80 percent), to target candidates with specific skills (69 percent), and to increase the employer's brand and reputation (67 percent). The top three reasons companies gave for not using social media were legal risks of discrimination (52 percent), not enough HR staff time to respond effectively (48 percent), and questions about the veracity of information obtained (26 percent). Nevertheless, resistance to these social networks is dropping dramatically. In 2008, 45 percent of firms stated they would never use them, but by 2013, only 11 percent still stated they would never use them.

There is a legitimate concern for employers using social networks for screening decisions, although this is different than using those networks for recruiting (generating and maintaining applicant interest in a job opening). Lewis Maltby noted that 77 percent of employers recently reported using social networking sites to research job candidates and more than a third (35 percent) reported finding information that led them to not hire a candidate.[126] These searches were conducted during selection (not recruiting) and considered whether the candidate presented a professional image and would fit with the company culture, and also were used to learn about the candidate's qualifications, personality, creativity, or communication skills. One other study asked 86 college recruiters to rate the "suitability" of 416 Facebook profiles of college students who had applied for full-time work. Recruiter ratings of applicant suitability (based on the Facebook profiles) were found to be unrelated to later ratings of supervisory performance (ranging from 0.13 to −0.04) and actual turnover ($r = −0.01$ to 0.01). Furthermore, these ratings were found to lead to significant differences in hiring rates on the basis of sex and race (women and white applicants were favored over men, blacks, and Hispanics, average $d = 0.35$). Finally, when two recruiters rated the same Facebook page for "suitability," the raters had very low inter-rater reliability (0.23). This means recruiter ratings of Facebook pages are rather inconsistent across raters. Thus, the importance of the use of profane language, discussion of drug use, or complaints about previous employers, for example, was relatively unique for each rater. If searching for applicants online has "become a new job hurdle,"[127] this study suggests ratings will not predict retention nor job performance and may have a disparate impact.[128] Such results should not be surprising, given the ratings of Facebook profiles lack standardization about what is being measured or how to measure job-relevant constructs, the differential impact of negative information, and the incomplete information across candidates, making "apples to oranges" comparisons common.[129] The EEOC recently suggested it would hold hearings in Congress to explore concerns about discrimination against some candidates (on the basis of age, sex, religious affiliation, and so on). Although we believe the use of social networks has potential as a recruiting tool, at this time, it should not be used to make hiring decisions.

One study focused on recruiting developed a Web site for a fictitious company, including information about the company, the company's open positions, and company values. The Web site also provided feedback to applicants about their fit with the organization (one of the proposed advantages of online recruiting is the low cost of providing such information). Results of this study indicated that feedback information about applicants' potential fit with the organization generally influenced their attraction to the firm.[130] Another study using a Web site for a fictitious company manipulated the demographic diversity shown in various scenes on the site. White viewers were not affected by the diversity shown in the ad. In contrast, black viewers were attracted by ad diversity, but only when it included supervisory-level positions. Viewer reactions were also related to the viewers' openness to racial diversity.[131] We conclude that Web-recruiting can be a more effective and less costly recruiting source than almost all others.

It is important to consider several factors when determining which recruitment methods to use: (a) costs associated with various recruitment methods, (b) nature of the job being recruited, (c) image of the company in the external labor market, (d) attitudes of current employees, and (e) demographic mix of applicants being sought.

Recruitment costs are a key consideration. In general, Web-based recruitment methods tend to yield the greatest return on investment. Recruiting for complex jobs requires providing detailed information about the job, the company, and selection qualifications. This kind of detailed information can be given best by recruiters or a Web site. A strong, positive image of the organization is related to individuals' willingness to apply for employment. Image can be strengthened by written and graphic brochures and by television, newspaper, and Internet advertisements.

The fourth factor to consider is worker attitudes, which affect the extent to which an organization can rely on worker referrals. As noted, employee referrals can be an extremely effective recruitment source, but only if the employees are positive about their jobs and the company. All employee referrals are not equal. There is evidence to suggest that the performance level of individuals making a referral is associated with the quality of the people who are referred,[132] with higher performers recommending more talented recruits.

Fifth, various recruitment methods are better suited than others for reaching particular demographic groups that are sought by the organization. Some, such as the Hispanic Chamber of Commerce newsletters or electronic methods, such as www.Hirediversity.com and www.Minorityjobs.net, focus on specific minority groups. Usually these contact vehicles will provide information about job openings as well as information on minority job candidates.

Finally, a word about candidates who self-select out during recruitment, either because of perceptions of misfit or due to an attempt to realistically describe the job opportunity. During this stage of recruiting, some of the recruiting methods will serve as recruitment "self-selection screens" (for example, a video on a company recruitment Web site showing what activities a job incumbent performs; comments made by an employee about an employer; information about the culture of a firm conveyed on a company Web site) that help potential applicants decide whether to move into or out of the applicant pool. In that sense, self-selection screens, in contrast to selection procedures, play a dominant role early in the recruitment process. As you will see, recruitment screens can take a variety of forms; they play an important role in both the recruitment *and* selection processes, and they occur at different points in these processes. When meaningful recruitment screens are tied to requisite WRCs, worker competencies, or other job-related characteristics, the ratio of minimally qualified applicants to all applicants should be enhanced. These initial recruitment screens, along with others that occur during the recruitment process, help determine who is eventually hired (and, perhaps, even who stays or succeeds in the organization). Carefully considering issues such as the content, use, timing, type, and media for communicating these screens can reduce recruiting costs considerably as time and other resources will not be allocated to undesirable applicants who are unlikely to succeed with the firm. By ensuring, wherever possible, that all recruitment screens are indeed job related or have a justified business need, employers will be in a better position to (a) select from among high-quality candidates and (b) successfully defend themselves if an employment discrimination suit is filed.

How effectively an organization recruits influences its ability to retain productive employees. The first stage of recruiting is critical, because it involves attracting and generating initial interest in an organization's job openings. Thus, this phase requires a number of strategic decisions, including establishment of recruiting objectives, as well as planning a strategy for the type of talent to be targeted, the methods to be used to reach these sought-after individuals, and the message to attract and motivate them to apply for the job. Those organizations that can effectively manage the first stage of recruiting by attracting strategic talent are likely to experience more success in the two later stages of recruiting, which will be discussed next.

Stage 2: Maintaining Applicant Interest

The recruiting process transitions into the second phase (maintaining interest) after an applicant applies for a job but before the job offer is extended (or the applicant is no longer under consideration). This stage sometimes is not recognized as being relevant to the recruiting process as the focus for employers is on screening out unqualified applicants. Effective companies, however, recognize the typical candidate is anxious to receive ongoing information and thus, by managing this stage well, will keep applicants more interested in the job opportunity. What makes this somewhat challenging is that the organization will reject more candidates than they will extend job offers to. Nevertheless, as we will see, many of the applicant reactions to organizational treatment during this stage do influence applicant job choices. For example, if an applicant withdraws from consideration after the college campus interview because of the treatment they encountered, it shows that this stage of the recruiting process does matter. Ultimately, however, perceptions about the job, the career opportunity itself (for example, pay, promotion, learning opportunities, and so on), and the organization matter far more to the actual job acceptance decision.[133]

During this recruiting stage, the organization must manage three aspects of recruiting well. First, the recruiter has to be an effective administrator of this process. This includes being interpersonally skilled and treating the applicant in a professional manner. When the recruiter treats applicants well, is informative about the job and the remaining steps in the selection process, is professional in their behavior, and is timely and dependable, applicants are likely to react positively and view the job opportunity favorably.[134] Later, we will review the plethora of research that has focused on recruiter effects.

Second, during this stage, the recruiting process evolves into a two-way communication. Applicants are understandably anxious about the uncertainty associated with obtaining a job offer from the organization. Consequently, research demonstrates that there is considerable value in recruiters building rapport with the applicants and giving them a chance to interact by asking questions, even offering them a chance for input or to have a voice in the decision process.[135] Finally, organizations have to think strategically about the information conveyed during this time, especially about the job opportunity itself and the organization. At this stage, applicants begin to transition from focusing on organizational reputation and attraction, to considering the attractiveness or fit with the job and then, as they approach job acceptance, fit with the organization.[136] Clearly, organizations have to give consideration about what information is critical to share with the applicant at each recruiting stage to ensure accurate PJ and PO fit perceptions.

During this phase, applicants are particularly sensitive to information about the job as they try to form evaluations about PJ fit and the attractiveness of the opportunity. Applicants also respond favorably when they think they are likely to receive a job offer, if the job offer has a high probability of leading to an even better position (that is, career progression), and when more career development opportunities are provided. Consequently, organizations can significantly influence the applicant during this stage by shifting their focus from the recruiting message and building organizational reputation to paying attention to the individual applicant and the quality of the social exchange itself. This is reflected by noting that research begins to consider the applicant's self-esteem, impression management tactics, and even the self-fulfilling prophecies held by the applicant and employer on decisions and perceptions,[137] instead of focusing primarily on organizational practices that build its reputation and image.

The key applicant outcomes that matter during this recruitment stage deal with perceptions of anticipatory PJ fit, the attractiveness of the job, and intentions to accept an offer. Two recent meta-analyses summarized the literature by highlighting that anticipatory PJ fit is correlated with attraction to the organization ($\rho = 0.48$) and intentions to accept the job offer ($\rho = 0.45$).[138] These meta-analyses established the following as the most important antecedents to predicting attraction to the job and job pursuit intentions, including (a) perceived fit (ρ ranging from 0.45 to 0.55); (b) applicant reactions to the recruitment process (ρ from 0.27 to 0.42); (c) the favorability of job and organizational attributes ($\rho = 0.39$); (d) likelihood of generating a job offer ($\rho = 0.33$); (e) recruiter behaviors and characteristics (ρ ranging from 0.29 to 0.36); and (f) the existence of perceived alternatives ($\rho = 0.16$).[139]

Fit, however, has proven to be a difficult issue for both employers and researchers.[140] One reason for this is because fit perceptions can range beyond attributes of the job (for example, pay, type of work, and so on) to attributes of the supervisor (person–supervisor [PS] fit), the work group (person–work group [PG] fit), and the organization (PO fit). The complexity of fit judgments do not stop there, however, as fit also can be "matched" on a wide variety of attributes, including culture, climate, high-performance work practices, values, personality, and so forth. More important, and possibly due to the complexities just discussed, at present, the research has not clarified how fit perceptions are formed. PJ fit and PO fit, however, clearly have been found to predict applicant attraction to the job, which in turn has been linked to applicant job choices. Thus, there is substantial value to employers in trying to provide accurate information to applicants to manage their fit perceptions, and as noted previously, the most influential sort of fit assessment actually is due to perceptions of poor fit or even misfit. Ultimately, when an applicant believes they do not fit with the job or cannot see themselves working in that organization, they withdraw from further consideration.[141]

Nevertheless, it is important to recognize recruitment is not the only activity that affects an organization's ability to attract potential employees. Sara Rynes and Alison Barber have reminded us that recruiting effects are modest and have pointed out some other important factors.[142] Among these are the inducements offered by the firm (for example, salary, benefits, child care, flexible work schedules, and career paths), the firm's targeted applicant pools (for example, education level, experience level, and applicant demographics, such as age, gender, race, and ethnicity), external labor market conditions, and job and organizational characteristics. These authors clearly indicate that a firm's ability to attract candidates for employment depends on all of these factors rather than on recruitment practices alone. For example, a small business that pays minimum wage, has no benefits or child care arrangements, and does not offer training or a career path may have great difficulty attracting the candidates it desires. In the face of these other characteristics, changing only its recruitment practices may not alter the company's success in attracting and retaining desirable applicants.

Recent research also has highlighted the attractiveness to applicants of organizational reputation on ecological sustainability, work-life balance programs, and diversity initiatives.[143] Although the importance of each of these initiatives will be idiosyncratic to individual applicants based on their desires, the findings suggest these initiatives can have an even stronger influence on attractiveness than do pay or promotion opportunities.[144] These findings underscore the value of organizations systematically thinking about the factors that are likely to influence recruiting effectiveness.

Applicant Self-Selection

Although the employer is the one that has to decide to whom to offer a job, an applicant can decide to withdraw from further consideration during this stage—hence, the name of the recruiting stage: maintaining applicant interest. As noted, when applicants perceive a poorer fit, they are more likely to withdraw.[145] In part, this is a function of each applicant deciding fit based on what is important to them. Thus, a candidate who cannot relocate from Houston because of personal circumstances may withdraw from a job opportunity due to poor "fit" once it is clear the location of the job is in Minot, North Dakota, rather than the corporate office in Houston, where the candidate initially applied.

A recent study by Brian Swider and associates powerfully illustrated the influence of these fit assessments on recruiting effectiveness. This study repeatedly assessed the anticipatory fit of accounting students with each of the Big Four accounting firms during the semester they were recruited and correlated those fit judgments with later job choice (at the end of the semester).[146] At the start of recruiting, their results showed that anticipatory fit had a very low correlation with organizational attraction or intentions to take a job up to the on-campus interviews (average $r = 0.06$ over the first five assessments). However, immediately after the on-campus interview, applicant perceptions of fit became more predictive of job choice and steadily increased as the assessments grew closer to the job choice decision ($r = 0.22, 0.33$, and 0.48 over the last three assessments). Thus, this study illustrates the changing influence of fit perceptions throughout the recruiting process and underscores why PO fit may not be particularly influential in stage 1 (when generating interest), but it is important during this and later stages of recruiting. More important, these results emphasize that even though meta-analytic estimates across all available studies reveal only a modest relationship between anticipatory fit perceptions and job choice ($\rho = 0.18$),[147] the relationship is stronger the later the applicant is in the recruiting process (after the campus interview, ρ increases from 0.10 to almost 0.40 to nearly 0.60 before the acceptance decision is made). Consequently, employers would be well served to try to influence the applicant's view of their fit with the job and organization throughout the recruiting process, but particularly during the second and third stages.

The researchers also reported the lowest fit perception throughout the study (whenever it occurred) was the best predictor of job choice for that Big Four accounting firm. Hence, again, we see when an applicant concludes he or she does not fit well with the firm, it significantly predicts applicant withdrawal from that opportunity.

Research also has demonstrated that highly sought-after candidates are more likely to attach greater importance to negative information about companies, to withdraw quicker after employer delays, and in general, to view the recruiter as less effective.[148] In essence, it appears that higher quality applicants recognize that they are likely to have more job choices and consequently, are more willing to eliminate an organization if they perceive a high degree of misfit with the firm during the recruiting process. Because it is just such applicants (more talented, highly sought after) the employer ultimately wants to hire, the cost of incorrect misfit perceptions may be quite high. Consequently, it is critical that the organization work hard to present accurate fit information during the recruiting process, to ensure that applicants, especially highly sought-after candidates, make informed fit estimates.[149]

One other area of recent research interest in regards to applicant self-selection involves applicant reactions to the recruiting process. In this case, the outcome of interest focuses on the fairness of recruiting, not on whether the recruiting process is influencing organizational reputation, PJ fit, or PO fit, although applicant reactions obviously would influence the development of those outcomes too. Although much of this literature has focused on applicant reactions to specific selection procedures (for example, reactions to structured interviews versus unstructured interviews, and so on), here we focus on fairness reactions to the recruiting process itself. Three broad causes of perceptions of fairness include (a) procedural justice perceptions arising from the consistency of administration (moderate effects have been reported); (b) informational justice perceptions that occur because of the provision of timely feedback (or not) and the extent the communication is open, honest, and candid (strong effects have been shown, although research is limited); and (c) interpersonal perceptions of justice due to whether the recruiter treated the applicant with warmth and respect and the chance to have a two-way communication and social exchange (mixed support with moderate effects). Although the assumption has been that applicant perceptions of fairness would predict key recruiting outcomes, there is more evidence that these reactions predict prehire attitudes like organizational attraction (ρ ranges from 0.39 to 0.51)[150] than actually influence applicant decisions to join an organization. Nevertheless, these applicant reactions can be used to help inform an organization about any problems they may have with their recruiting processes, as it can explain whether the problem is due to fairness of the process itself (that is, a rejection letter containing a thorough explanation), the information presented during the on-site visit (not enough of a realistic preview), or the interpersonal interaction (the recruiter was rude and arrogant).[151]

The assumption made behind many of these studies is that when applicants stop pursuit of a job (that is, self-select out), it is bad for the organization. This is true to the extent that employers benefit from having a larger applicant pool or that these candidates are highly qualified. If the applicants that drop out of further consideration are more like those who ultimately are unsuccessful employees or are misfits, and hence are more likely to quit once hired, then self-selection actually may be better for the organization, as it avoids a poor selection decision. Surprisingly, there is very little research on those who withdraw from the selection process. The existing evidence, however, suggests those who withdraw from further consideration are more like unsuccessful employees than successful employees, at least in terms of attitudes held.[152] The challenge for organizations is to explore reasons for the self-selection decisions by applicants and to determine whether highly sought-after candidates are self-selecting out. Furthermore, organizations should explore the feasibility of providing accurate information about key job and organizational attributes that will permit applicants to correctly assess their PJ fit and PO fit.

Recruiter Characteristics

Logically, recruiters should have an important influence on the attitudes and behavior of applicants; recruiters are usually the first real people applicants encounter after they get through the Web site, brochures, media ads, and broadcasts. Much research has been conducted on the effects recruiters have and the strength of these effects. The general conclusion is that who the recruiter is does influence applicants, both positively and negatively, but that (surprise!) it is not crystal clear how this influence works.[153]

Research has examined the demographic characteristics, behaviors, personality, and training of recruiters to determine whether these characteristics affect the attitudes and behaviors of recruits (for example, their interest in the firm, whether they apply to the firm, or whether they accept job offers). The following is a brief summary of what has been concluded.[154]

- Recruiters usually influence the early opinions and behaviors of recruits. That is, recruiters affect applicants' decisions about whether to seek out more information or continue with recruitment. Recruiters have only a small effect on recruits' actual decisions about whether or not to accept the job. Nevertheless, by keeping sought-after applicants involved in the selection process long enough that they can learn about the merits of the job and the organization itself, the recruiter's characteristics and behavior matter.

- Recruiters who have race and gender in common with applicants may have some influence on those applicants, but such influence is neither clear nor consistent. "Demographic" effects encountered from the organization and community, not just the recruiter, as well as the quality of the interaction during those encounters, also affect applicant perceptions of organizational diversity climate and job pursuit intentions.

- Job and organization characteristics ultimately have a stronger influence on recruits than do recruiters.

- The training of recruiters in interviewing and in the management of the social interaction during recruitment interviews is important.

- Recruiters often are seen as less trustworthy and credible than members of the intended work group, perhaps because they have less knowledge about the work itself.

- Recruiters perceived as competent, informed, trustworthy, warm, personable, and concerned are generally regarded favorably.

- Recruiters can have a strong, negative influence on applicants. Unprofessional behavior or being untrustworthy are particularly problematic. This can cause applicants to discontinue pursuit of the firm.

- Recruiters vary in the way they mix the recruitment ("selling" of the firm) and selection (evaluation of the applicant) components of their applicant interviews. The best mix seems to be a combination. Heavy emphasis on recruitment is regarded negatively by applicants.

Derek Chapman and his fellow researchers have concluded that firms should select recruiters (not surprising in a selection textbook!) on the basis of personableness and other positive interpersonal behaviors and train them in interviewing and interpersonal conduct.[155] In the actual recruitment interview, recruiters will have to both describe the job and organization while also conducting a preliminary screening of the applicants' characteristics. In addition, they should explain the recruitment and selection process and address any questions or concerns the applicants have.

One limitation of much of the research on recruiter effects on applicants is that it is based on the initial impressions of college students interviewing for jobs at university placement centers. The generalizability of research based on well-educated, inexperienced college students to less-educated or more-experienced recruits in other recruitment contexts is unknown.[156] James Breaugh and his colleagues have suggested that the conclusion that certain recruiter characteristics (for example, recruiter experience) makes little difference to recruits might be premature.[157] There are several reasons why different types of recruiters might matter, particularly for more experienced job applicants, more than what has been reported in past studies. First, recruiters often differ in the job-related information they have and can share with job applicants. Second, recruiters are likely to differ more in the eyes of different types of job applicants. Third, because of these differences, they are likely to convey different things to different job candidates. Thus, future research should consider the ways in which both recruiters and applicants differ when studying recruiter effects.

The On-Site Visit Also Matters

The site visit has a significant influence on applicant intentions to accept an offer.[158] Visiting the actual work site and observing what people do provides a visceral feel about what it would be like to work with this group and organization. The visit communicates more useful comprehensive information about the job, the work group, and the organization than the corporate Web site or any other recruiting method for that matter (except possibly word-of-mouth information from a close, trusted other). Visiting the workplace provides a variety of multiple situational cues that can serve to verify information the candidate was told previously or had perceived, and this information can serve as a signal about other unknown or unobserved job and organizational attributes. Just as important, being invited on-site shows the organization is very interested in the applicant as a potential employee and, as noted, the higher the likelihood of being hired, the more attractive an employer becomes to a candidate.

Given the importance of the visit on actual offer acceptance, it is disconcerting that there has been so little research about its effectiveness and about which details of the site visit matters to the candidate. The likability of the employee hosting the visit, the opportunity to meet high-level executives and interact with the potential supervisor and co-workers, and even the visit arrangements—such as impressive hotel accommodations, a well-organized schedule, being able to bring a spouse, and having a high-quality interaction with others in the community—has been found to make for a significantly more effective site visit.[159] Yet some of these attributes will matter more, and it would be useful to know which matter the most when forming PJ fit and PO fit judgments.

Internal Selection

Organizations increasingly are taking a strategic talent management perspective by identifying pivotal jobs that are critical to realizing the firm's strategic goals and such approaches include striving to effectively identify and recruit current employees to promote into these pivotal jobs.[160] Another reason for the recent interest in internal recruiting is that multinational enterprises still rely on expatriates to fill top jobs in their overseas affiliates.[161] In one other trend, increasingly more companies are hiring interns, which begins with external recruiting but quickly shifts to internal selection. Sarah Doll, senior director of talent management at Enova International Inc.,[162] sees the internship as a "working interview." Similarly, Edwin Koc the National Association of Colleges and Employers' (NACE's) director of strategic and foundation research, has characterized the internship "as a direct recruiting device for a full-time employee ... the internship is essentially seen as a probationary period in which the student is evaluated as a potential full-time hire and is treated that way."[163] An NACE survey of 9,215 graduates this year found that nearly two-thirds of this year's college graduates reported having an internship during their undergraduate experience. The estimate from 306 employers responding to the same survey is that 38 percent of new college hires were from the employer's own interns,[164] a figure that compares to the one-third to one-half of masters of business administration students reportedly going to work after graduation for the organization for which they interned.[165]

Although the availability of research on internal recruitment lags the growing use of this approach, particularly growth in the use of internships, it makes sense that many of the same attributes that predict pursuit of job opportunities during external recruiting would generalize to internal recruiting. For example, one study found that current employees would be most willing to transfer if the opportunity involved an actual promotion (not just a lateral move) and was in the same location.[166] One advantage of promoting current employees is the much greater knowledge both the employer and the applicant have about each other. Consequently, perceptions of anticipatory PJ and PO fit are likely to be far more accurate. Nevertheless, there still may be some concern with unrealistic expectations, as two studies involving expatriate assignments illustrated the value of including RJPs to current managers.[167]

The internal recruitment approach will fundamentally differ if the purpose is to get candidates (current employees) to nominate themselves (for example, based on advertising a job opening on the company's intranet) or to have supervisors' nominate highly qualified employees. One issue in regards to supervisor nominations is whether they are more likely to nominate deserving candidates, and thus have a star employee transfer out, or whether instead, they fail to nominate the best candidates. A recent study contrasted agency theory with stewardship theory[168] and found that supervisors are just as likely to promote as fail to nominate valued employees to transfer internally. In essence, agency theory proposes supervisors will act out of self-interest and fail to nominate their best employees. In contrast, stewardship theory argues that managers will encourage more highly qualified employees to transfer internally to maximize both the organization's and employee's interests. Letting go of such valued talent inadvertently may benefit the manager, as doing so creates valuable social networking ties to other areas of the business, especially when those areas are tied to strategically critical positions within the organization.[169]

Finally, a hybrid form of internal recruiting would involve former employees who return to the organization. The "boomerang effect," typical at companies such as P&G,[170] is a growing recruiting approach, although some issues linked to loyalty may affect expected retention. Nevertheless, by having worked with the person before, the greater knowledge about the candidate's actual WRCs enhances the likelihood that the selection decision will result in a high-performing candidate.

Stage 3: Postoffer Closure

The last recruiting stage occurs when the organization selects the applicants who will receive job offers. Once offers are extended, the decision-making responsibilities shift to the applicant, who must now decide which job offer to accept. At this point in the recruiting cycle, applicant experiences and the information received throughout the recruiting and selection process should drive the applicant's perceptions of the desirability and fit with the organization. Some of the other factors that have been found to influence the applicant's decision include the job offer itself (for example, having a deadline or exploding offer, being required to sign a noncompete agreement, and so on), the timeliness of the offer, the location of the position, the organization's willingness to negotiate, the opportunity to do meaningful work or enhance one's own skills and capabilities, and the opportunities for a raise or promotion, as well as the social influence exerted by family and friends, the existence of alternative job offers, and the role of work–life balance on job choice.[171]

One particularly influential study longitudinally investigated how 14 job and organization factors influenced job acceptance decisions. Wendy Boswell and associates interviewed 96 undergraduates over all three recruitment phases. Early in recruiting, the students reported that compensation (71 percent mentioned), organizational culture (63 percent), the work itself (52 percent), and benefits (52 percent) would be important factors in their future job choice. After the offer was extended and the student had accepted, they reported that the work itself (38 percent), organizational culture (37 percent), location of the position (38 percent), advancement opportunities (26 percent), compensation (19 percent), and industry (14 percent) influenced offer acceptance. The students also commented on some other positive predictors, including treatment by the organization (83 percent); an opportunity to socially interact with current employees on the site visit (53 percent); the quality of the on-site visit (52 percent), including hotel accommodations, how well-organized the trip was, and being able to bring a spouse or significant other along; and timeliness of follow-up and feedback, including the offer itself (46 percent).

One other study attempted to establish the importance of various factors on job offer acceptance for new Ph.D. students, by using a policy capturing design to test whether fit perceptions (high versus low), financial support to the Ph.D. applicants (high versus low), prestige of the faculty and university (high versus low), or location (favorable versus unfavorable) had larger effects on the attractiveness of a job opportunity. The study showed that fit and funding became more important during the recruiting cycle and fit was particularly important to those who received more offers (that is, were higher quality applicants).

Taken together, these two studies illustrate that fit with the work itself and the organization are important to candidates making job choice decisions, although their actual importance was not as great as the students initially expected (early in recruiting, 63 percent and 52 percent expected them to be important, but only 38 percent and 37 percent reported they actually were). The importance of pay differs in these two studies, however, as it was not seen to be as important as the students expected in the first study (71 percent thought it would be important early in recruiting, whereas only 19 percent rated it so after the decision), but pay did grow in importance in the second study. These findings illustrate that the weight applicants place on various job and organizational factors changes throughout the job search process. Furthermore, although unexpected by the participants of the first study, a number of issues emerged over the recruiting process that were more important to the decision than initially anticipated, including location of the job and career advancement opportunities. Finally, the quality and timeliness of treatment during the recruiting process, as well as the on-site visit itself emerged as influential factors in the applicant's job choices as expected.

Recruiting success often is measured by the proportion of offerees that accepts the offer. Hence, job offer acceptances matter. Yet, as shown, little research has been done to show which factors affect that decision, even though the field has concluded that by the time of the actual job offer decision, recruiter effects, organizational reputation, and even PJ and PO fit are thought to be only modestly related to the decision. Instead, these outcomes are seen as influential primarily because they kept the candidate interested in pursuing the job during earlier recruiting stages. Consequently, organizations still have to evaluate which factors are critical to offer acceptances, particularly by high-quality applicants. This can be done by conducting "exit interviews" of those candidates who turn down job offers.

Administration of Recruitment

Recruiting is a complex process, involving decisions and activities initiated by both the organization and the applicant over time, beginning with the initial decision to apply up through job offer acceptance. An organization can significantly improve the quality of its workforce by more effectively administering this process. The small amount of research on recruitment administration indicates that the promptness of follow-up communication with the applicants between the various stages of recruitment is positively related to whether applicants stay in the recruitment pool.[172] Employers giving timely responses are linked to higher applicant perceptions of an employer's organizational attractiveness.[173] Prompt responses by the company seem to indicate to the applicant that the company is efficient and, therefore, a desirable place to work—or alternatively that it serves as a signal that the applicant has very favorably impressed the company and has a good chance of getting a job offer. Highly qualified applicants who have multiple job alternatives are most strongly affected by delays in communications. One study reported that when applicants to a police force were warned that it would take a month to make hiring decisions, the favorability of their perceptions of the organization did not change, whereas those who were not given the warning experienced decreased favorability perceptions.[174]

More empirical evidence between expenditures on recruiting (in the form of dinners, receptions, gifts, hotels, and so forth) and applicant response is needed.[175] Ignoring such a strategy when competing firms in the same industry are doing it (as large accounting and consulting firms do) would probably not be a wise decision. Applicants' visits to the physical site of the organization is an important predictor of job offer acceptance. Applicants note the importance of the people they meet, how they are treated, and the organization's professionalism.[176] Reactions to the job site visit have been found to be particularly impactful on PO fit perceptions and the applicants' ultimate job offer decision.[177]

Technology's Role in Recruiting

Internet recruiting continues to grow and even revolutionize identifying and connecting with both active and passive applicants[178] during the first two stages of recruitment.

Use of the Internet enables an organization to reach more potential applicants with more relevant information or feedback in less time and for less cost than many earlier recruiting methods.[179] Furthermore, it levels the playing field and enables small firms to engage in more of the same recruiting activities as larger firms.[180] It also provides a way an organization can be seen as "leading edge" through its innovative uses of technology.[181] To illustrate the breadth of impact the Internet has had on recruiting, consider McDonalds. In 2008, 24,000 of 3 million applicants submitted online applications. In contrast, by 2012, they received more than 2 million online applications and had more than 30 million visits.[182] Similarly, Macy's reported about 25 percent of applications now are submitted through their mobile application. Companies recruiting activities include providing workplace tours, simplified job application blanks, even the use of games and virtual worlds like "Second Life."[183]

Although there is the potential to realize unrivaled gains in the speed, efficiency, and effectiveness of recruiting activities in both generating greater interest initially and for maintaining applicant interest over time, there are a number of legal (for example, discrimination, invasion of privacy), practical (for example, sifting through the larger pool of applicants submitted due to ease of access), and scientific (for example, increase the number of highly quality applicants) issues that must be addressed to ensure the potential use of the Internet for recruiting is realized.[184] An article in the *Wall Street Journal* described a study that found 10 to 33 percent of U.S. firms searched social networks (for example Facebook) for applicants' information early in recruiting. If Facebook's public profile showed the applicant was of the Muslim faith, they were less likely to be called for interviews than Christian applicants, especially in conservative states (17 percent of the time Christian applicants got a call back, whereas Muslim applicants were called back 2 percent of the time). James McDonald, a partner at Fisher & Phillips LLP, who specializes in employment law said, "I advise employers that it's not a good idea to use social media as a screening tool ... You need to control the information you receive so you're only getting information that is legal for you to take into account."[185] Of course, discrimination may result through other means too, as evidence suggests women, older applicants, and members of several racial subgroups are more likely to have less computer access or skills to use the computer, thereby inadvertently reducing employment opportunities for various protected subgroups. Finally, although questions continue to be raised about the impact of privacy concerns on applicants' willingness to complete online forms,[186] there is very little empirical evidence of these effects. There is evidence, however, that organizations are receiving more online applications, and applicants apply even if they are not qualified to do the work.[187] Finally, because some applicants view technology as cold and inhuman, there will be a need to balance the speed and efficiency of the Internet with more high-touch experiences, particularly when maintaining the interest of the applicant during the second stage of recruitment.

To effectively utilize the Internet, organizations must present Web site content and use aesthetics in an interactive, easily usable, friendly, and engaging manner.[188] Furthermore, the use of customized messages targeted at specific talent pools, even making self-screening opportunities available (for e.g., assessing PJ and PO fit by describing abilities, personalities, and values linked to the job or organization),[189] can enhance the utility of Internet recruiting. At this point, little is known about specific ways to optimize the impact of the Internet on recruiting. The opportunity is great, however, for those researchers and employers who systematically study how to unleash its true potential.

Global Recruiting

Given the lack of research on recruiting in the United States, it probably will not surprise the reader to learn that even less research is available to guide the use of recruiting globally, even though there are likely to be large differences in organizational familiarity, image, and reputation around the world. Two critical issues that are likely to affect global recruiting success include the impact of cross-cultural differences and variations in socioeconomic conditions across regions.[190] For example, what constitutes warm and personable behavior for a recruiter may differ by region, because cultures differ in how appropriate assertive behavior by recruiters is in interviews.[191] Similarly, the use of referral programs is much higher in some countries than in the United States.[192] In Latin America, more than European and Asian Pacific countries, family and friends are a key way applicants find out about job openings. Which recruiting method is more frequently used also seems to meaningfully differ for blue-collar jobs versus white-collar jobs, and again, these practices can differ country to country. Socioeconomic differences also affect access to computers, as the "digital divide" varies by both economic and regional differences. And, of course, there are dramatic differences in the use of pay, promotion opportunities, job security, and even work–life balance concerns across different cultures and socioeconomic situations.[193]

Taken together, a number of unanswered questions require future study before understanding how to generate interest, maintain interest, and ensure job offer acceptance during recruitment across the globe. Until more research is conducted, organizations are trying a number of different approaches. For example, Envision has focused its recruiting for applicants with multinational experience by concentrating on areas with global pockets of excellence: to recruit engineers for alternative-energy skills in Denmark, software engineers in the United States, and managers with skills using lean manufacturing techniques from Japan.[194]

Recruiting Metrics

The last part of recruiting is to determine the results of recruiting: the number of people who applied, their skill levels, their diversity, the time it took to hire recruits, and how many actually became employed by the firm. Several metrics have been suggested for use in evaluating recruitment effectiveness. Among these are the following:[195]

- **New employee job performance.** Performance appraisal ratings for new employees 6–12 months after being hired.

- **New employee turnover.** Percentage of employees who voluntarily leave the organization after 6–12 months of employment.

- **New hire failure rate.** Percentage of employees who were fired or asked to leave during the first 6–12 months of employment.

- **Manager satisfaction with new employees.** Percentage of managers satisfied with new employees.

- **New employee training success.** New employees' performance on training measures, such as performance tests.

- **Cost per hire.** Costs associated with hiring new employees, which typically involves (a) internal costs such as employment/recruiting office salaries and benefits, staff members' travel, lodging, and entertainment; (b) external costs such as lodging, entertainment, and other recruiters' salaries; (c) company visit expenses such as candidate travel, lodging, meals, and interview expenses; and (d) direct fees such as advertising, Web site hosting, job fairs, agency search fees, and cash awards for employee referrals.

Usually, a series of recruitment metrics is necessary to get a more complete picture of recruitment effectiveness. These metrics can serve as a means for diagnosing and remedying problems in recruitment. For example, suppose a firm finds that it takes 94 days, on average, to hire for a position and that the average new employee stays 40 days. By enhancing recruitment materials and methods, improving application and other prescreening procedures, refining the interview and other applicant selection methods, streamlining new employee orientation and training procedures, and altering compensation packages, the firm reduces the time-to-hire period to an average of 35 days. New hires now stay an average of nine months. Such a needed change brought by an analysis of recruitment metrics can have a large financial impact on a firm. One recruitment metric by itself may have little value, but when viewed along with other metrics, they can serve an important diagnostic role, not only for recruitment but other HR functions as well. In sum, recruitment metrics can aid in determining whether a firm's recruitment strategy and execution are appropriate. If they are not, adjustments can be made in future recruiting efforts.

In addition to these metrics, employers should consider analyzing the recruitment Web site visitation patterns made by applicants—the time users spend on a Web site or an associated Web site link, the number of mouse clicks made during a visitation session, and visitors' associated navigation patterns. Results from these analytics can be used to improve Web site design. For example, if it were found that job applicants had to make too many mouse clicks to navigate through the recruitment Web site to submit an application, that information could be used to improve applicants' ease of navigating and using the Web site.

SUMMARY RECOMMENDATIONS FOR ENHANCING RECRUITMENT

Following is a summary of the major issues and suggestions we have discussed for attracting applicants to organizations. Although our list is not exhaustive and, in some cases, we depend on anecdotal evidence, we believe that carefully implementing these recommendations will facilitate recruitment program effectiveness. Our recommendations are as follows:

1. Carefully consider the sometimes-competing objectives of attracting versus selecting job seekers; the ratio of qualified applicants applying per position opening is one measure. Selection procedure norms (preferably, local norms—see Chapter 3) and performance evaluations are examples of measures used for monitoring changes in applicant quality.

2. Identify specific objectives of a recruitment program—the number of positions to be filled, WRCs required for those positions, and when positions should be filled.

3. Formulate a specific strategy for accomplishing recruitment program objectives.

4. Ensure that recruitment screens (including *self*-selection screens) reflect the desired job-related characteristics of job candidates. Change the focus of these recruitment screens as you progress through the recruitment stages. Early on,

when attracting and generating applicant interest, focus on organizational reputation. After applying, focus on maintaining applicant interest by providing information about PJ fit. As you approach the actual job offer, focus on PO fit.

5. Identify who represents the potential applicant population; the relevant labor market likely mirrors that population.

6. Use targeted recruitment to identify underrepresented protected groups in an organization. Search recruitment Web sites targeting such underrepresented groups and contact specific organizations representing such groups to find possible sources of applicants.

7. Develop a recruitment Web site that is attractive, easy to navigate, and easy to use for submitting application materials. Enhance the aesthetic quality of the recruitment Web site (including the use of video, podcasts, employee testimonials) on a recruitment Web site; all narrative content on the site should be well written in an engaging style. Be sure all materials (including photos or videos and themes presented) accurately reflect the true nature of the organization.

8. For organizations using recruitment Web sites and receiving large numbers of resumes, consider using resume screening and applicant tracking software to manage the number of resumes that must be individually reviewed and applicant contacts that must be made. As a form of prescreening, consider incorporating applicant assessments (team orientation; personal fit with the recruiting organization) as part of the recruitment program.

9. Evaluate an organization's image being communicated by recruitment and related media. Ensure that image is the desired organizational "brand."

10. Consider using recruitment Web sites for organizations searching for employees. If a recruitment Web site is used, establish links to it on popular social networking sites, particularly www.LinkedIn.com

11. Encourage referrals of potential applicants from employees; particularly valuable are those individuals recommended by high-performing employees.

12. Select recruiters who can play an important role in attracting initial interest in organizations on characteristics associated with dealing with people. They should be enthusiastic, personable, and extraverted. At a minimum, train them in interviewing and managing social interactions in recruitment and on knowledge of work operations for those jobs being recruited.

13. Use technology to aid in recruiting; however, use more personal means of communications (for example, making telephone calls) to contact applicants who are particularly desirable. Stay in touch with desired applicants throughout the recruitment process.

14. Use RJPs. Positive results are most likely to occur when (a) applicants have not formed an opinion of what a job is like, (b) applicants can predict how they will react to certain job characteristics presented in the RJP (for example, standing for an eight-hour day), and (c) applicants are aware of the WRCs they possess and their interests.

15. Use metrics and other measures to evaluate recruitment programs and associated activities to identify "what works."

REFERENCES

1. Robert E. Ployhart, "Staffing in the 21st Century: New Challenges and Strategic Opportunities," *Journal of Management* 32 (2006): 868–897.

2. Peter Cappelli, "Talent Management for the Twenty-First Century," *Harvard Business Review* 86, no. 3 (2008): 74–81; Peter Cappelli and J. R. Keller, "Talent Management: Conceptual Approaches and Practical Challenges," *Annual Review of Organizational Psychology and Organizational Behavior* (2014): 305–331.

3. James A. Breaugh, "Employee Recruitment: Current Knowledge and Suggestions for Future Research," *The Oxford Handbook of Personnel Assessment and Selection* (2012): 68–87.

4. Alison E. Barber, *Recruiting employees: Individual and Organizational Perspectives* (Sage Publications, 1998); James A. Breaugh and Mary Starke, "Research on Employee Recruitment: So Many Studies, So Many Remaining Questions," *Journal of Management* 26 (2000): 405–434; James A. Breaugh, Therese H. Macan, and Dana M. Grambow, "Employee Recruitment: Current Knowledge and Directions for Future Research," in *International Review of Industrial and Organizational Psychology*, ed. G. P. Hodgkinson and J. K. Ford (Hoboken, NJ: John Wiley & Sons, 2008), 45–82; Breaugh, "Employee Recruitment: Current Knowledge and Suggestions for Future Research."

5. Todd C. Darnold and Sara L. Rynes. "Recruitment and Job Choice Research: Same as It Ever Was?" in *Handbook of Psychology: Vol. 12, Industrial and Organizational Psychology*, ed. Irving B. Weiner, Neal W. Schmitt, and Scott Highhouse, 2nd ed. (Hoboken, NJ: John Wiley & Sons, 2013); Sara L. Rynes, and Daniel M. Cable, "Recruitment Research in the Twenty-First Century," in *Handbook of Psychology: Vol. 12, Industrial and Organizational Psychology*, ed. W. C. Borman, D. R. Ilgen, and R. J. Klimoski (Hoboken, NJ: Wiley & Sons, 2003), 55–76; Brian R. Dineen and Scott M. Soltis, "Recruitment: A Review of Research and Emerging Directions," in *APA Handbook of Industrial and Organizational Psychology*, ed. S. Zedeck (Washington, DC: American Psychological Association, 2011), 43–66.

6. Alison E. Barber, "*Recruiting Employees: Individual and Organizational Perspectives*" (Thousand Oaks, CA: Sage, 1998); Breaugh, "Employee Recruitment: Current Knowledge and Suggestions for Future Research."

7. Harold C Taylor and James Thomas Russell. "The Relationship of Validity Coefficients to the Practical Effectiveness of Tests In Selection: Discussion and Tables," *Journal of Applied Psychology* 23, no. 5 (1939): 565–578; Lee J. Cronbach and Goldine C. Gleser, "*Psychological Tests and Personnel Decisions*" (Hoboken, NJ: John Wiley & Sons, 1965).

8. Robert P. Vecchio, "The Impact of Referral Sources on Employee Attitudes: Evidence from a National Sample," *Journal of Management* 21 (1995): 953–965; Rynes and Cable, "Recruitment Research in the Twenty-First Century"; Ann Marie Ryan and Tanya Delany, "Attracting Job Candidates to Organizations," in *Handbook of Employee Selection*, ed. James L. Farr and Nancy T. Tippins (New York, NY: Routledge, 2010), 127–150.

9. F. Hansen, "Avoiding Truth-in-Hiring Lawsuits," *Workforce Management Online* (2007), December 13, 2007, http://www.workforce.com.

10. Alison E. Barber, Mark V. Roehling, "Job Postings and the Decision to Interview: A Verbal Protocol Analysis." *Journal of Applied Psychology* 78 (1993): 845–856; Jean M. Phillips, "Effects of Realistic Job Previews on Multiple Organizational Outcomes: A Meta-Analysis," *Academy of Management Journal* 41 (1998): 673–690; Payam Yuce and Scott Highhouse, "Effects of Attribute Set Size and Pay Ambiguity on Reactions to 'Help Wanted' Advertisements," *Journal of Organizational Behavior* 19 (1997): 337–352.

11. Scott Highhouse and Emily L. Hause, "Missing Information in Selection: An Application of the Einhorn-Hogarth Ambiguity Model," *Journal of Applied Psychology* 80 (1995): 86–93;

Steven D. Maurer, Vince Howe, and Thomas W. Lee, "Organizational Recruiting as Marketing Management: An Interdisciplinary Study of Engineering Graduates," *Personnel Psychology* 45 (1992): 807–833; Yuce and Highhouse, "Effects of Attribute Set Size and Pay Ambiguity on Reactions to 'Help Wanted' Advertisements."

12. Ryan and Delany, "Attracting Job Candidates to Organizations."

13. Darnold and Rynes, "Recruitment and Job Choice Research: Same as It Ever Was?"; Dineen and Soltis, "Recruitment: A Review of Research and Emerging Directions."

14. Jon Billsberry, *Experiencing Recruitment and Selection* (Hoboken, NJ: Wiley & Sons, 2007); Peter Cappelli, "Will There Really Be a Labor Shortage?" *Human Resource Management* 44 (2005): 143–149.

15. Daniel M. Cable and Daniel B. Turban "Establishing the Dimensions, Sources and Value of Job Seekers' Employer Knowledge during Recruitment," in *Research in Personnel and Human Resource Management*, Vol. 20, ed. G. Ferris (Greenwich, CT: JAI Press, 2001), 115–163; Derek S. Chapman, Krista L. Uggerslev, Sarah A. Carroll, Kelly A. Piasentin, and David A. Jones, "Applicant Attraction to Organizations and Job Choice: A Meta-Analytic Review of the Correlates of Recruiting Outcomes," *Journal of Applied Psychology* 90 (2005): 928–944; Christopher J. Collins and Cynthia Kay Stevens, "The Relationship between Early Recruitment-Related Activities and the Application Decisions of New Labor-Market Entrants: A Brand Equity Approach to Recruitment," *Journal of Applied Psychology* 87 (2002): 1121–1133; Daniel B. Turban, and Daniel M. Cable, "Firm Reputation and Applicant Pool Characteristics," *Journal of Organizational Behavior* 24 (2003): 733–751.

16. Darnold and Rynes, "Recruitment and Job Choice Research: Same as It Ever Was?"

17. Alison E. Barber, Michael J. Wesson, Quineita M. Roberson and M. Susan Taylor, "A Tale of Two Job Markets: Organizational Size and Its Effects on Hiring Practices and Job Search Behavior," *Personnel Psychology* 52 (1999): 841–868; Christopher J. Collins, "The Interactive Effects of Recruitment Practices and Product Awareness in Job Seekers' Employer Knowledge and Applicant Behaviors," *Journal of Applied Psychology* 92 (2007): 180–190; Christopher J. Collins and Jian Han, "Exploring Applicant Pool Quantity and Quality: The Effects of Early Recruitment Practices, Corporate Advertising, and Firm Reputation," *Personnel Psychology* 57 (2004): 685–717; Collins and Stevens, "The Relationship between Early Recruitment-Related Activities and the Application Decisions of New Labor-Market Entrants"; Aegean Leung, "Different Ties for Different Needs: Recruitment Practices of Entrepreneurial Firms at Different Developmental Phases," *Human Resource Management* 42 (2003): 303–320; Ian O. Williamson, and Daniel M. Cable, "Organizational Hiring Patterns, Interfirm Network Ties, and Interorganizational Imitation," *Academy of Management Journal* 46 (2003): 349–358.

18. Daniel M. Cable and Timothy A. Judge, "Managers' Upward Influence Tactic Strategies: The Role of Manager Personality and Supervisor Leadership Style," *Journal of Organizational Behavior* 24, no. 2 (2003): 197–214.

19. Collins, "The Interactive Effects of Recruitment Practices and Product Awareness in Job Seekers' Employer Knowledge and Applicant Behaviors"; Collins and Han, "Exploring Applicant Pool Quantity and Quality"; Collins and Stevens, "The Relationship between Early Recruitment-Related Activities and the Application Decisions of New Labor-Market Entrants."

20. Wei-Chi Tsai and Irene Wen-Fen Yang, "Does Image Matter to Different Job Applicants? The Influences of Corporate Image and Applicant Individual Differences on Organizational Attractiveness," *International Journal of Selection and Assessment* 18 (2010): 48–63.

21. Violina P. Rindova, Ian O. Williamson, Antoaneta P. Petkova, and Joy Marie Sever, "Being Good or Being Known: An Empirical Examination of the Dimensions, Antecedents, and Consequences of Organizational Reputation," *Academy of Management Journal* 48 (2005): 1033–1049.

22. *Wall Street Journal*, August 1, 2013, page C10, column 5.

23. Darnold and Rynes, "Recruitment and Job Choice Research: Same as It Ever Was?"; Ryan and Delany, "Attracting Job Candidates to Organizations."

24. Robert D. Bretz, Jr. and Timothy A. Judge, "Realistic Job Previews: A Test of the Adverse Self-Selection Hypothesis," *Journal of Applied Psychology* 83, no. 2 (1998): 330–343; Timothy A. Judge and Robert D. Bretz, "Effects of Work Values on Job Choice Decisions," *Journal of Applied Psychology* 77 (1992): 261–271; Scott Highhouse, Erin E. Thornbury, Ian S. Little, " Social-Identity Functions of Attraction to Organizations," *Organizational Behavior and Human Decision Processes* 103 (2007): 134–146.

25. Wendy R. Boswell, Mark V. Roehling, Marcie A. LePine, and Lisa M. Moynihan, "Individual Job-Choice Decisions and the Impact of Job Attributes and Recruitment Practices: A Longitudinal Field Study," *Human Resource Management* 42 (2003): 23–37; Connie R. Wanberg, Ruth Kanfer, and Maria Rotundo, "Unemployed Individuals: Motives, Job-Search Competencies, and Job-Search Constraints as Predictors of Job Seeking and Reemployment," *Journal of Applied Psychology* 84 (1999): 897–910.

26. Daniel M. Cable and Kang Yang Trevor Yu, "How Selection and Recruitment Practices Develop the Beliefs Used to Assess Fit," in *Perspectives on Organizational Fit*, ed. C. Ostroff and T. A. Judge (New York, NY: Lawrence Erlbaum, 2007): 155–182.

27. James Breaugh, "Employee Recruitment," *Annual Review of Psychology* 64 (2013): 389–416.

28. Gerd Bohner and Nina Dickel, "Attitudes and Attitude Change," *Annual Review Of Psychology* 62 (2011): 391–417; Breaugh, "Employee Recruitment"; Cable and Yu, "How Selection and Recruitment Practices Develop the Beliefs Used to Assess Fit"; Greg Maio and Geoffrey Haddock, "Attitude Change," in *Social Psychology: Handbook of Basic Principles*, ed. A. W. Kruglanski and E. T. Higgins (New York: Guilford, 2007): 565–586.

29. Bohner and Dickel, "Attitudes and Attitude Change"; Ap Dijksterhuis and Henk Aarts, "Goals, Attention, and (Un)consciousness," *Annual Review of Psychology* 61 (2010): 467–490; William J. McGuire, "Personality and Attitude Change: An Information-Processing Theory," in *Psychological Foundations of Attitudes*, ed. A. G. Greenwald, T. C. Brock, T. A. Ostrom (San Diego, CA: Academic, 1968): 171–196; Richard E. Petty and John T. Cacioppo, *Communication and Persuasion: Central and Peripheral Routes to Attitude Change* (New York: Springer-Verlag, 1986).

30. Bohner and Dickel, "Attitudes and Attitude Change"; Dijksterhuis and Aarts, "Goals, Attention, and (Un)consciousness."

31. Dolores Albarracin and Patrick Vargas, "Attitudes and Persuasion," in *Handbook of Social Psychology*, ed. S. T. Fiske, D. T. Gilbert, and G. Lindzey (Hoboken, NJ: Wiley, 2010): 394–427.

32. Albarracin and Vargas, "Attitudes and Persuasion"; Breaugh, "Employee Recruitment."

33. Bohner and Dickel, "Attitudes and Attitude Change"; Robert B. Cialdini, *Influence: Science and Practice* (Boston: Allyn & Bacon, 2008).

34. Derek R. Avery and Patrick F. McKay, "Target Practice: An Organizational Impression Management Approach to Attracting Minority and Female Job Applicants," *Personnel Psychology* 59 (2006): 157–187.

35. Collins and Han, "Exploring Applicant Pool Quantity and Quality."

36. Amos Tversky and Daniel Kahneman, "Judgement under Uncertainty: Heuristics and Biases," *Science* 185 (1974): 1124–1131.

37. James Breaugh, "Employee Recruitment"; Darnold and Rynes, "Recruitment and Job Choice Research: Same as It Ever Was?"; Alan M. Saks and Krista L. Uggerslev, "Sequential and

Combined Effects of Recruitment Information on Applicant Reactions," *Journal of Business Psychology* 25 (2010): 381–396.

38. Breaugh, "Employee Recruitment: Current Knowledge and Suggestions for Future Research"; Dineen and Soltis, "Recruitment: A Review of Research and Emerging Directions"; Filip Lievens and Scott Highhouse, "The Relation of Instrumental and Symbolic Attributes to a Company's Attractiveness as an Employer," *Personnel Psychology* 56 (2003): 75–102.

39. Breaugh, "Employee Recruitment: Current Knowledge and Suggestions for Future Research"; Chapman, Uggerslev, Carroll, Piasentin, and Jones, "Applicant Attraction to Organizations and Job Choice"; Rynes and Cable, "Recruitment Research in the Twenty-First Century."

40. Kristof-Brown and Guay, "Person-Environment Fit."

41. Aichia Chuang and Paul R. Sackett, "The Perceived Importance of Person-Job Fit and Person-Organization Fit between and within Interview Stages," *Social Behavior and Personality* 33 (2005): 209–226.

42. Darnold and Rynes, "Recruitment and Job Choice Research: Same as It Ever Was?"; Kristof-Brown and Guay, "Person-Environment Fit."

43. Chapman, Uggerslev, Carroll, Piasentin, and Jones, "Applicant Attraction to Organizations and Job Choice"; Amy L. Kristof-Brown, Ryan D. Zimmerman, and Erin C. Johnson, "Consequences of Individual's Fit at Work: A Meta-Analysis of Person-Job, Person-Organization, Person-Group, and Person-Supervisor Fit," *Personnel Psychology* 58 (2005): 281–342.

44. Cheri Ostroff and M. Schulte, "Multiple Perspectives of Fit in Organizations across Levels of Analysis," in *Perspectives on Organizational Fit*, ed. C. Ostroff and T. Judge (New York: Lawrence Erlbaum Associates, 2007): 3–69; Cheri Ostroff and Yujie Zhan, "Person-Environment Fit in the Selection Process," *The Oxford Handbook of Personnel Assessment and Selection* (2012): 252–273.

45. Breaugh, "Employee Recruitment: Current Knowledge and Suggestions for Future Research"; Kristof-Brown and Guay, "Person-Environment Fit"; Ostroff and Zhan, "Person-Environment Fit in the Selection Process."

46. Edgar E. Kausel and Jerel E. Slaughter, "Narrow Personality Traits and Organizational Attraction: Evidence for the Complementary Hypothesis," *Organizational Behavior and Human Decision Processes* 114 (2011): 3–14; Jerel E. Slaughter and Gary J. Greguras, "Initial Attraction to Organizations: The Influence of Trait Inferences," *International Journal of Selection and Assessment* 17 (2009): 1–18; Jerel E. Slaughter, Michael J. Zickar, Scott Highhouse, and David C. Mohr, "Personality Trait Inferences about Organizations: Development of a Measure and Assessment of Construct Validity," *Journal of Applied Psychology* 89 (2004): 85–103.

47. Slaughter, Zickar, Highhouse, and Mohr, "Personality Trait Inferences about Organizations: Development of a Measure and Assessment of Construct Validity"; H. Jack Walker, Hubert S. Feild, William F. Giles, Jeremy B. Bernerth, and Jeremy C. Short, "So What Do You Think of the Organization? A Contextual Priming Explanation for Recruitment Web Site Characteristics as Antecedents of Job Seekers' Organizational Image Perceptions," *Organizational Behavior and Human Decision Processes* 114 (2011): 165–178.

48. Darnold and Rynes, "Recruitment and Job Choice Research: Same as It Ever Was?"; Ryan and Delany, "Attracting Job Candidates to Organizations"; Rynes, and Cable, "Recruitment Research in the Twenty-First Century."

49. Daniel A. Newman and Julie Lyon, "Recruitment Efforts to Reduce Adverse Impact: Targeted Recruiting for Personality, Cognitive Ability, and Diversity," *Journal of Applied Psychology* 94 (2009): 299–312.

50. Ibid.

51. Alison E. Barber, *Recruiting Employees: Individual and Organizational Perspectives*, (Thousand Oaks, CA: Sage, 1998); Darnold and Rynes, "Recruitment and Job Choice Research: Same as It Ever Was?"; Sara L. Rynes, Marc O. Orlitzky, and Robert D. Bretz, "Experienced Hiring versus College Recruiting: Practices and Emerging Trends," *Personnel Psychology* 50 (1997): 487–521.

52. James A. Breaugh, Therese H. Macan, and Dana M. Grambow, "Employee recruitment: Current Knowledge and Directions for Future Research," in *International Review of Industrial and Organizational Psychology*, Vol. 23, ed. G. P. Hodgkinson & J. K. Ford (Hoboken, NJ: John Wiley & Sons Ltd, 2008): 45–82; Linda Brooks, Allen Cornelius, Ellen Greenfield, and Robin Joseph, "The Relation of Career-Related Work or Internship Experiences to the Development of College Seniors," *Journal of Vocational Behavior* 46 (1995): 332–349; Dineen and Soltis, "Recruitment: A Review of Research and Emerging Directions"; Sara L. Rynes and John W. Boudreau, "College Recruiting in Large Organizations: Practice, Evaluation, and Research Implications." *Personnel Psychology* 39 (1986): 729–757; Rynes, Orlitzky, and Bretz, "Experienced Hiring versus College Recruiting: Practices and Emerging Trends," *Personnel Psychology* 50 (1997): 487–521.

53. *Wall Street Journal*, March 19, 2014, B1, columns 1 to 3; B7.

54. Russell Cropanzano, Jerel E. Slaughter, and Peter D. Bachiochi, "Organizational Justice and Black Applicants' Reactions to Affirmative Action," *Journal of Applied Psychology* 90 (2005): 1168–1184; Madeline E. Heilman, William S. Battle, Chris E. Keller, and R. Andrew Lee, "Type of Affirmative Action Policy: A Determinant of Reactions to Sex-Based Preferential Selection?" *Journal of Applied Psychology* 83 (1998): 190–205; David A. Kravitz and Stephen L. Klineberg, "Reactions to Two Versions of Affirmative Action among Whites, Blacks, and Hispanics," *Journal of Applied Psychology* 85 (2000): 597–611; Barbara L. Rau and Gary A. Adams, "Attracting Retirees to Apply: Desired Organizational Characteristics of Bridge Employment," *Journal of Organizational Behavior* 26 (2005): 649–660; Donald M. Truxillo and Talya N. Bauer, "Applicant Reactions to Test Score Banding in Entry-Level and Promotional Contexts," *Journal of Applied Psychology* 84 (1999): 322–339.

55. Alan M. Saks, Joanne D. Leck, and David M. Saunders, "Effects of Application Blanks and Employment Equity on Applicant Reactions and Job Pursuit Intentions," *Journal of Organizational Behavior* 16 (1995): 415–430.

56. Derek R. Avery, Morela Hernandez, and Michelle R. Hebl, "Who's Watching the Race? Racial Salience in Recruitment Advertising," *Journal of Applied Social Psychology* 34 (2004): 146–161; Derek R. Avery, "Reactions to Diversity in Recruitment Advertising—Are Differences Black and White?" *Journal of Applied Psychology* 88 (2003): 672–679.

57. Sandra S. Kim and Michele J. Gelfand "The Influence of Ethnic Identity on Perceptions of Organizational Recruitment," *Journal of Vocational Behavior* 63 (2003): 396–416; Luis L. Martins and Charles K. Parsons, "Effects of Gender Diversity Management on Perceptions of Organizational Attractiveness: The Role of Individual Differences in Attitudes and Beliefs," *Journal of Applied Psychology* 92 (2007): 865–875; Jerel E. Slaughter, Carrie A. Bulger, and Peter D. Bachiochi, "Black Applicants' Reactions to Affirmative Action Plans: Influence of Perceived Procedural Fairness, Anticipated Stigmatization, and Anticipated Remediation of Previous Injustice," *Journal of Applied Social Psychology* 35 (2005): 2437–2476; Ian O. Williamson, Holly S. Slay, Debra L. Shapiro, and Sheryl L. Shivers-Blackwell, "The Effect of Explanations on Prospective Applicants' Reactions to Firm Diversity Practices," *Human Resource Management* 47 (2008): 311–330.

58. Avery and McKay, "Target Practice: An Organizational Impression Management Approach to Attracting Minority and Female Job Applicants"; James A. Breaugh, "Realistic Job Previews," in *Handbook of Improving Performance in the Workplace*, ed. R. Watkins,

D. Leigh (San Francisco: Pfeiffer, 2010), 203–220; Dineen and Soltis, "Recruitment: A Review of Research and Emerging Directions."

59. Gary A. Adams and Barbara L. Rau, "Job Seeking among Retirees Seeking Bridge Employment," *Personnel Psychology* 57 (2004): 719–744; Mark A. Davis, "Factors Related to Bridge Employment Participation among Private Sector Early Retirees," *Journal of Vocational Behavior* 63 (2003): 55–71; Derek R. Avery, Patrick F. McKay, and David C. Wilson, "Engaging the Aging Workforce: The Relationship between Perceived Age Similarity, Satisfaction with Coworkers, and Employee Engagement," *Journal of Applied Psychology* 92 (2007): 1542–1556.

60. Avery and McKay, "Target Practice: An Organizational Impression Management Approach to Attracting Minority and Female Job Applicants."

61. Breaugh, "Employee Recruitment: Current Knowledge and Suggestions for Future Research"; Dineen and Soltis, "Recruitment: A Review of Research and Emerging Directions."

62. Collins, "The Interactive Effects of Recruitment Practices and Product Awareness in Job Seekers' Employer Knowledge and Applicant Behaviors"; Collins and Han, "Exploring Applicant Pool Quantity and Quality"; Collins and Stevens, "The Relationship between Early Recruitment-Related Activities and the Application Decisions of New Labor-Market Entrants."

63. Dineen and Soltis, "Recruitment: A Review of Research and Emerging Directions."

64. Peter Cappelli, *The New Deal at Work: Managing the Market-Driven Workforce* (Boston: Harvard Business School Press, 1999).

65. Robert Rao and Hayagreeva Drazin, "Overcoming Resource Constraints on Product Innovation by Recruiting Talent from Rivals: A Study of the Mutual Fund Industry, 1986–94" *Academy of Management Journal* 45 (2002): 491–507; Cappelli, *The New Deal at Work*.

66. Benjamin B. Dunford, John W. Boudreau, and Wendy R. Boswell, "Out-of-the-Money: The Impact of Underwater Stock Options on Executive Job Search," *Personnel Psychology* 58 (2005): 67–101; Benjamin B. Dunford, Derek K. Oler, John W. Bourdreau, "Underwater Stock Options and Voluntary Executive Turnover: A Multidisciplinary Perspective Integrating Behavioral and Economic Theories," *Personnel Psychology* 61 (2008): 687–726; Timothy M. Gardner, "Interfirm Competition for Human Resources: Evidence from the Software Industry," *Academy of Management Journal* 48 (2005): 237–256; Ruth Kanfer, Connie R. Wanberg, and Tracy M. Kantrowitz, "Job Search and Employment: A Personality–Motivational Analysis and Meta-Analytic Review," *Journal of Applied Psychology* 86 (2001): 837–861; Ian O. Williamson and Daniel M. Cable, "Organizational Hiring Patterns, Interfirm Network Ties, and Interorganizational Imitation," *Academy of Management Journal* 46 (2003): 349–358.

67. Douglas A. Ready, Linda A. Hill, and Robert J. Thomas, "Building a Game-Changing Talent Strategy," *Harvard Business Review* Jan–Feb (2014): 62–68.

68. H. Jack Walker, Hubert S. Field, William F. Giles, and Jeremy B. Bernerth, "The Interactive Effects of Job Advertisement Characteristics and Applicant Experience on Reactions to Recruitment Messages," *Journal of Occupational Organization Psychology* 81 (2008): 619–638.

69. Robert D. Bretz and Timothy A. Judge, "Realistic Job Previews: A Test of the Adverse Self-Selection Hypothesis," *Journal of Applied Psychology* 83: (1998): 330–337; Dineen and Soltis, "Recruitment: A Review of Research and Emerging Directions."

70. Phillips, "Effects of Realistic Job Previews on Multiple Organizational Outcomes: A Meta-Analysis"; Steven L. Premack and John P. Wanous, "A Meta-Analysis of Realistic Job Preview Experiments," *Journal of Applied Psychology* 20 (1985): 706–719.

71. Bretz and Judge, "Realistic Job Previews: A Test of the Adverse Self-Selection Hypothesis"; Bruce M. Meglino, Angelo S. DeNisi, and Elizabeth C. Ravlin, "Effects of Previous Job Exposure and Subsequent Job Status on the Functioning of Realistic Job Preview," *Personnel Psychology* 46 (1993): 803–822; Todd J. Thorsteinson, Erin M. Palmer, Cynthia Wulff, and Alexee Anderson, "Too Good to Be True? Using Realism to Enhance Applicant Attraction," *Journal of Business and Psychology* 19 (2004): 125–137.

72. Dineen and Soltis, "Recruitment: A Review of Research and Emerging Directions"; Ryan and Delany, "Attracting Job Candidates to Organizations."

73. Scott Highhouse, Jeffrey M. Stanton, and Charlie L. Reeve, "Examining Reactions to Employer Information Using a Simulated Web-Based Job Fair," *Journal of Career Assessment* 12 (2004): 85–96; Charlie L. Reeve, Scott Highhouse, and Margaret E. Brooks. "A Closer Look at Reactions to Realistic Recruitment Messages," *International Journal of Selection and Assessment* 14, no. 1 (2006): 1–15.

74. Wendy R. Boswell, John W. Boudreau, and Jan Tichy. "The Relationship between Employee Job Change and Job Satisfaction: The Honeymoon-Hangover Effect," *Journal of Applied Psychology* 90 (2005): 882–891; Wendy R. Boswell, Abbie J. Shipp, Stephanie C. Payne, and Satoris S. Culbertson, "Changes in Newcomer Job Satisfaction over Time: Examining the Pattern of Honeymoons and Hangovers," *Journal of Applied Psychology* 94 2009): 844–858.

75. John P. Wanous, *Organizational Entry: Recruitment, Selection, and Socialization of Newcomers* (Reading, MA: Addison-Wesley, 1980), 34.

76. David G. Allen, James R. Van Scotter, and Robert F. Otondo, "Recruitment Communication Media: Impact on Prehire Outcomes," *Personality Psychology* 57 (2004):143–171; James A. Breaugh, "Employee Recruitment: Current Knowledge and Important Areas for Future Research," *Human Resource Management Review* (2008); Brian R. Dineen and Ian O. Williamson, "Effects of Environmental and Organizational Attributes on Recruitment Message Orientation," Presented at the annual meeting of the Society for Industrial/ Organizational Psychology, San Francisco, CA; M. Frase-Blunt, "Candidate Glut," *HR Magazine* August (2003): 89–93; Ian O. Williamson, David P. Lepak, and James King, "The Effect of Company Recruitment Web Site Orientation on Individuals' Perceptions of Organizational Attractiveness," *Journal of Vocational Behavior* 63 (2003): 242–263.

77. Blake E. Ashforth, Glen E. Kreiner, Mark A. Clark, and Mel Fugate, "Normalizing Dirty Work: Managerial Tactics for Countering Occupational Taint," *Academy of Management Journal* 50 (2007): 149–174; Maio and Haddock, "Attitude Change"; Greet Van Hoye and Filip Lievens, "Tapping the Grapevine: A Closer Look at Word-of-Mouth as a Recruiting Source," *Journal of Applied Psycholoigy* 94 (2009): 341–352.

78. Allen, Van Scotter, and Otondo, "Recruitment Communication Media: Impact on Prehire Outcomes"; David G. Allen, Raj V. Mahto, and Robert F. Otondo, "Web-Based Recruitment: Effects of Information, Organizational Brand, and Attitudes toward a Web Site on Applicant Attraction," *Journal of Applied Psychology* 92 (2007): 1696–1708; Breaugh, "Employee Recruitment: Current Knowledge and Suggestions for Future Research"; Scott Highhouse, David Beadle, Andrew Gallo, and Lynn Miller, "Get 'Em While They Last: Effects of Scarcity Information in Job Advertisements," *Journal of Applied Social Psychology* 28 (1998): 779–795; Ryan and Delany, "Attracting Job Candidates to Organizations."

79. Darnold and Rynes, "Recruitment and Job Choice Research: Same as It Ever Was?"; Ryan and Delany, "Attracting Job Candidates to Organizations"; Yuce and Highhouse, "Effects of Attribute Set Size and Pay Ambiguity on Reactions to 'Help Wanted' Advertisements."

80. William J. Becker, Terry Connolly, and Jerel E. Slaughter, "The Effect of Job Offer Timing on Offer Acceptance, Performance, and Turnover," *Personality Psychology* 63 (2010): 223–241; Breaugh, "Employee Recruitment: Current Knowledge and Suggestions for Future Research"; Peter Cappelli, "A Supply Chain Approach to Workforce Planning," *Organizational*

Dynamics 38 (2009): 8–15; Anat Rafaeli, Ori Hadomi, and Tal Simon, "Recruiting through Advertising or Employee Referrals: Costs, Yields, and the Effects of Geographic Focus," *European Journal of Work and Organizational Psychology* 14 (2005): 355–366.

81. Ryan and Delany, "Attracting Job Candidates to Organizations."

82. *Wall Street Journal*, October 2, 2013, B6.

83. Alison E. Barber and Mark V. Roehling "Job Postings and the Decision to Interview: A Verbal Protocol Analysis," *Journal of Applied Psychology* 78 (1993): 845–856; Nancy A. Mason and John A. Belt, "The Effectiveness of Specificity in Recruitment Advertising," *Journal of Management* 12 (1986): 425–432; Charles D. Stevens and Joseph G. Szmerekovsky, "Attraction to Employment Advertisements: Advertisement Wording and Personality Characteristics," *Journal of Management Issues* 22 (2010): 107–126.

84. *Wall Street Journal*, October 2, 2013, B6.

85. *Wall Street Journal*, October 2, 2013, B6.

86. Karen H. Ehrhart and Jonathan C. Ziegert, "Why Are Individuals Attracted to Organizations?" *Journal of Management* 31 (2005): 901–919.

87. Rynes and Cable. "Recruitment Research in the Twenty-First Century."

88. Newman and Lyon, "Recruitment Efforts to Reduce Adverse Impact: Targeted Recruiting for Personality, Cognitive Ability, and Diversity."

89. Cable and Turban, "Establishing the Dimensions, Sources and Value of Job Seekers' Employer Knowledge During Recruitment"; Cable and Yu, "How Selection and Recruitment Practices Develop the Beliefs Used to Assess Fit"; Collins and Han, "Exploring Applicant Pool Quantity and Quality"; Collins and Stevens, "The Relationship between Early Recruitment-Related Activities and the Application Decisions of New Labor-Market Entrants"; Petty and Cacioppo, "Communication and Persuasion: Central and Peripheral Routes to Attitude Change."

90. Aichia Chuang and Paul R. Sackett, "The Perceived Importance of Person-Job Fit and Person-Organization Fit between and within Interview Stages," *Social Behavior and Personality* 33, (2005): 209–226.

91. Breaugh, "Employee Recruitment: Current Knowledge and Suggestions for Future Research"; Kristof-Brown and Guay, "Person-Environment Fit"; Darnold and Rynes, "Recruitment and Job Choice Research: Same as It Ever Was?"

92. Breaugh, "Employee Recruitment: Current Knowledge and Suggestions for Future Research"; Darnold and Rynes, "Recruitment and Job Choice Research: Same as It Ever Was?"; Ryan and Delany, "Attracting Job Candidates to Organizations."

93. James A. Breaugh, Leslie A. Greising, James W. Taggart, and Helen Chen, "The Relationship of Recruiting Sources and Pre-Hire Outcomes: Examination of Yield Ratios and Applicant Quality," *Journal of Applied Social Psychology* 33 (2003): 2267–2287; Rafaeli, Hadomi, and Simon, "Recruiting through Advertising or Employee Referrals: Costs, Yields, and the Effects of Geographic Focus"; Valery Yakubovich and Daniela Lup, "Stages of the Recruitment Process and the Referrer's Performance Effect," *Organization Science* 17 (2006): 710–723.

94. Avery, "Reactions to Diversity in Recruitment Advertising—Are differences Black and White?"; Avery and McKay, "Target Practice: An Organizational Impression Management Approach to Attracting Minority and Female Job Applicants"; Patrick F. McKay and Derek R. Avery, "What Has Race Got To Do with It? Unraveling the Role of Racioethnicity in Job Seekers' Reactions to Site Visits," *Personnel Psychology* 59 (2006): 395–429.

95. Phillip W. Braddy, Adam W. Meade, J. Joan Michael, and John W. Fleenor, "Internet Recruiting: Effects of Website Content Features on Viewers' Perceptions of Organizational Culture," *International Journal of Selection and Assessment* 17 (2009): 19–34.

96. NACE survey, *HR Magazine*, November 2013, p. 26.

97. Breaugh, "Employee Recruitment: Current Knowledge and Important Areas for Future Research."

98. Ibid.

99. Ingo Weller, Brooks C. Holtom, Wenzel Matiaske, and Thomas Mellewigt, "Level and Time Effects of Recruitment Sources on Early Voluntary Turnover," *Journal of Applied Psychology* 94 (2009): 1146–1162.

100. Ibid., 1157.

101. Darnold and Rynes, "Recruitment and Job Choice Research: Same as It Ever Was?"; Weller, Holtom, Matiaske, and Mellewigt, "Level and Time Effects of Recruitment Sources on Early Voluntary Turnover."

102. Weller, Holtom, Matiaske, and Mellewigt, "Level and Time Effects of Recruitment Sources on Early Voluntary Turnover"; Jean P. Kirnan, John A. Farley, and Kurt F. Geisinger, "The Relationship between Recruiting Source, Applicant Quality, and Hire Performance: An Analysis by Sex, Ethnicity, and Age," *Personnel Psychology* 42 (1989): 293–308.

103. Van Hoye and Lievens, "Tapping the Grapevine: A Closer Look at Word-of-Mouth as a Recruitment Source."

104. Darnold and Rynes, "Recruitment and Job Choice Research: Same as It Ever Was?"; Dineen and Soltis, "Recruitment: A Review of Research and Emerging Directions"; Van Hoye and Lievens, "Tapping the Grapevine: A Closer Look at Word-of-Mouth as a Recruitment Source"; Ryan and Delany, "Attracting Job Candidates to Organizations."

105. Christopher J. Collins and Cynthia K. Stevens, "The Relationship between Early Recruitment-Related Activities and the Application Decisions of New Labor-Market Entrants: A Brand Equity Approach to Recruitment," *Journal of Applied Psychology* 87 (2002): 1121–1133.

106. Walker, Field, Giles and Bernerth, "The Interactive Effects of Job Advertisement Characteristics and Applicant Experience on Reactions to Recruitment Messages"; H. Jack Walker, Hubert S. Feild, William F. Giles, Achilles A. Armenakis, and Jeremy B. Bernerth, "Displaying Employee Testimonials on Recruitment Websites: Effects of Communication Media, Employee Race, and Job Seeker Race on Organizational Attraction and Information Credibility," *Journal of Applied Psychology* 94 (2009): 1354–1364.

107. Darnold and Rynes, "Recruitment and Job Choice Research: Same as It Ever Was?"; Dineen and Soltis, "Recruitment: A Review of Research and Emerging Directions"; Martin Kilduff, "The Interpersonal Structure of Decision Making: A Social Comparison Approach to Organizational Choice," *Organizational Behavior and Human Decision Processes* 47 (1990): 270–288; Russell N. Laczniak, Thomas E. DeCarlo, and Sridhar N. Ramaswami, "Consumers' Responses to Negative Word-of-Mouth Communication: An Attribution Theory Perspective," *Journal of Consumer Psychology* 11 (2001): 57–73; Van Hoye and Lievens, "Tapping the Grapevine: A Closer Look at Word-of-Mouth as a Recruiting Source."

108. Kilduff, "The Interpersonal Structure of Decision Making: A Social Comparison Approach to Organizational Choice."

109. Leung, "Different Ties for Different Needs: Recruitment Practices of Entrepreneurial Firms at Different Developmental Phases"; Deepak Somaya, Ian O. Williamson, and Natalia Lorinkova, "Gone but Not Lost: The Different Performance Impacts of Employee Mobility between Cooperators versus Competitors," *Academy of Management Journal* 51 (2008): 936–953; Williamson and Cable, "Organizational Hiring Patterns, Interfirm Network Ties, and Interorganizational Imitation."

110. Ployhart, "Staffing in the 21st Century: New Challenges and Strategic Opportunities."

111. SHRM Staffing Research Study, "To study the effectiveness of using social networking sites for recruitment and staffing" 2013, SHRM.org.

112. Brian R. Dineen, Juan Ling, Steven R. Ash, and Devon DelVecchio, "Aesthetic Properties and Message Customization: Navigating the Dark Side of Web Recruitment," *Journal of Applied Psychology* 92 (2007): 356–372; Frase-Blunt, "Candidate Glut."

113. Hella Sylva and Stefan T. Mol, "E-Recruitment: A Study into Applicant Perceptions of an Online Application System," *International Journal of Selection and Assessment* 17 (2009): 311–323.

114. Allen, Mahto, and Otondo, "Web-Based Recruitment: Effects of Information, Organizational Brand, and Attitudes toward a Web Site on Applicant Attraction"; Braddy, Meade, Michael, and Fleenor, "Internet Recruiting: Effects of Website Content Features on Viewers' Perceptions of Organizational Culture"; Richard T. Cober, Douglas J. Brown, Lisa M. Keeping, and Paul E. Levy, "Recruitment on the Net: How Do Organizational Web Site Characteristics Influence Applicant Attraction?" *Journal of Management* 30 (2004): 623–646; Collins, "The Interactive Effects of Recruitment Practices and Product Awareness in Job Seekers' Employer Knowledge and Applicant Behaviors"; Collins and Han, "Exploring Applicant Pool Quantity and Quality"; Dineen, Ling, Ash and DelVecchio, "Aesthetic Properties and Message Customization: Navigating the Dark Side of Web Recruitment"; David A. Jones, Jonas W. Shultz, and Derek S. Chapman, "Recruiting through Job Advertisements: The Effects of Cognitive Elaboration on Decision Making," *International Journal of Selection and Assessment* 11 (2006): 167–179; Walker, Feild, Giles, Armenakis, and Bernerth, "Displaying Employee Testimonials on Recruitment Websites: Effects of Communication Media, Employee Race, and Job Seeker Race on Organizational Attraction and Information Credibility"; Ian O. Williamson, James E. King, David Lepak, and Archana Sarma, "Firm Reputation, Recruitment Web Sites, and Attracting Applicants," *Human Resource Management* 49 (2010): 669–687.

115. Dineen and Soltis, "Recruitment: A Review of Research and Emerging Directions."

116. Brian R. Dineen and Raymond A. Noe, "Effects of Customization on Application Decisions and Applicant Pool Characteristics in a Web-Based Recruitment Context," *Journal of Applied Psychology 94* (2009): 224–234; Brian R. Dineen, Steven R. Ash, and Raymond A. Noe, " A Web of Applicant Attraction: Person-Organization Fit in the Context of Web-Based Recruitment," *Journal of Applied Psychology* 87 (2002): 723–734; Dineen, Ling, Ash, and DelVecchio, "Aesthetic Properties and Message Customization: Navigating the Dark Side of Web Recruitment."

117. Dineen and Noe, "Effects of Customization on Application Decisions and Applicant Pool Characteristics in a Web-Based Recruitment Context."

118. Dineen and Noe, "Effects of Customization on Application Decisions and Applicant Pool Characteristics in a Web-Based Recruitment Context"; Mia L. Jattuso and Evan F. Sinar, "Source Effects in Internet-Based Screening Procedures," *International Journal of Selection and Assessment* 11 (2003): 137–140.

119. *The Economist*, August 16, 2014, p. 51–52.

120. Michael Foster, *Recruiting on the Web: Smart Strategies for Finding the Perfect Candidate* (New York: McGraw-Hill, 2003).

121. Harvel J. Walker, Hubert S. Feild, William F. Giles, and Achilles A. Armenakis, "Displaying Employee Testimonials on Recruitment Web Sites: Effects of Communication Media, Employee Race, and Job Seeker Race on Organizational Attraction and Information Credibility," *Journal of Applied Psychology* 94 (2009): 1354–1364.

122. Sylva and Mol, "E-Recruitment: A Study into Applicant Perceptions of an Online Application System."

123. *The Economist*, August 24, 2013, p. 27.

124. Anonymous, "Recruiting and Marketing are Top Benefits of Social Media," *HRfocus* 87 (2010): S1–S4.

125. SHRM Staffing Research Study, 2013.

126. *Wall Street Journal*, May 12, 2014, R2.

127. Jennifer Preston, "Social Media History Becomes a New Job Hurdle," *StarNews*, July (2011), http://iw.newsbank.com.

128. Chad H. Van Iddekinge, Stephen E. Lanivich, Philip L. Roth, and Elliott Junco, "Social Media for Selection? Validity and Adverse Impact Potential of a Facebook-Based Assessment," *Journal of Management*, in press, 0149206313515524.

129. Philip L. Roth, Philip Bobko, and Chad H. Van Iddekinge, "Social Media in Employee Selection-Related Decisions: A Research Agenda for Uncharted Territory." *Journal of Management*, in press, 0149206313503018.

130. Dineen, Ash, and Noe, "A Web of Applicant Attraction: Person-Organization Fit in the Context of Web-Based Recruitment"; see also Derek S. Chapman and Janie Webster, "The Use of Technology in the Recruiting, Screening, and Selection Processes of Job Candidates," *International Journal of Selection and Assessment* 11 (2003): 113–120.

131. Avery, "Reactions to Diversity in Recruitment Advertising—Are Differences Black and White?"

132. Yakubovich and Lup, "Stages of the Recruitment Process and the Referrer's Performance Effect,"

133. Boswell, Shipp, Payne, and Culbertson, "Changes in Newcomer Job Satisfaction over Time: Examining the Pattern of Honeymoons and Hangovers"; Deidra J. Schleicher, Vijaya Venkataramani, Frederick P. Morgeson, and Michael A. Campion, "So You Didn't Get the Job ... Now What Do You Think? Examining Opportunity-to-Perform Fairness Perceptions," *Personnel Psychology* 59 (2006): 559–590.

134. Breaugh, "Employee Recruitment: Current Knowledge and Suggestions for Future Research"; Darnold and Rynes, "Recruitment and Job Choice Research: Same as It Ever Was?"; Dineen and Soltis, "Recruitment: A Review of Research and Emerging Directions"; Ryan and Delany, "Attracting Job Candidates to Organizations."

135. Breaugh, "Employee Recruitment: Current Knowledge and Suggestions for Future Research"; Dineen and Soltis, "Recruitment: A Review of Research and Emerging Directions"; Schleicher, Venkataramani, Morgeson, and Campion, "So You Didn't Get the Job ... Now What Do You Think? Examining Opportunity-to-Perform Fairness Perceptions."

136. Chuang and Sackett, "The Perceived Importance of Person-Job Fit and Person-Organization Fit between and within Interview Stages"; Kristof-Brown and Guay, "Person-Environment Fit"; Cheri Ostroff, "Person-Environment Fit in Organizations," in *Handbook of Organizational Psychology*, ed. S. W. J. Kozlowski (New York: Oxford University Press 2012); Ryan and Delany, "Attracting Job Candidates to Organizations."

137. Darnold and Rynes, "Recruitment and Job Choice Research: Same as It Ever Was?"; Cynthia K. Stevens, "Effects of Preinterview Beliefs on Applicants' Reactions to Campus Interviews," *Academy of Management Journal* 40 (1993): 947–966; Hao Zhao and Robert C. Liden, "Internship: A Recruitment and Selection Perspective," *Journal of Applied Psychology* 96 (2011): 221–229.

138. Chapman, Uggerslev, Carroll, Piasentin, and Jones, "Applicant Attraction to Organizations and Job Choice"; Kristof-Brown, Zimmerman, and Johnson, "Consequences of Individual's Fit at Work."

139. Chapman, Uggerslev, Carroll, Piasentin, and Jones, "Applicant Attraction to Organizations and Job Choice."

140. Darnold and Rynes, "Recruitment and Job Choice Research: Same as It Ever Was?"; Kristof-Brown and Guay, "Person-Environment Fit"; Ostroff and Zhan, "Person-Environment Fit in the Selection Process."

141. Breaugh, "Employee Recruitment: Current Knowledge and Suggestions for Future Research"; Darnold and Rynes, "Recruitment and Job Choice Research: Same as It Ever Was?"; Dineen and Soltis, "Recruitment: A Review of Research and Emerging Directions."

142. Sara L. Rynes and Alison E. Barber, "Applicant Attraction Strategies: An Organizational Perspective," *Academy of Management Review* 15 (1990): 286–310.

143. Lynda Aiman-Smith, Talya N. Bauer, and Daniel M. Cable, "Are You Attracted? Do You Intend to Pursue? A Recruiting Policy-Capturing Study," *Journal of Business and Psychology* 16 (2001): 219–237; Boswell, Shipp, Payne, and Culbertson, "Changes in Newcomer Job Satisfaction over Time: Examining the Pattern of Honeymoons and Hangovers"; Douglas J. Brown, Richard T. Cober, Lisa M. Keeping, and Paul E. Levy, "Racial Tolerance and Reactions to Diversity Information in Job Advertisements," *Journal of Applied Social Psychology* 36 (2006): 2048–2071; Sally A. Carless and Josephine Wintle, "Applicant Attraction: The Role of Recruiter Function, Work-Life Balance Policies and Career Salience," *International Journal of Selection and Assessment* 15 (2007): 394–404; Wendy J. Casper and Louis C. Buffardi, "Work-Life Benefits and Job Pursuit Intentions: The Role of Anticipated Organizational Support," *Journal of Vocational Behavior* 95 (204): 391–410.

144. Aiman-Smith, Bauer, and Cable, "Are You Attracted? Do You Intend to Pursue? A Recruiting Policy-Capturing Study."

145. Dineen and Noe, "Effects of Customization on Application Decisions and Applicant Pool Characteristics in a Web-Based Recruitment Context"; Dineen, Ling, Ash, and DelVecchio, "Aesthetic Properties and Message Customization: Navigating the Dark Side of Web Recruitment"; Kausel and Slaughter, "Narrow Personality Traits and Organizational Attraction: Evidence for the Complementary Hypothesis"; Slaughter and Greguras, "Initial Attraction to Organizations: The Influence of Trait Inferences."

146. Brian W. Swider, Ryan D. Zimmerman, and Murray R. Barrick, "Searching for the Right Fit: Development of Applicant Person-Organization Fit Perceptions during the Recruitment Process," *Journal of Applied Psychology*, in press, http://dx.doi.org/10.1037/a0038357.

147. Chapman, Uggerslev, Carroll, Piasentin, and Jones, "Applicant Attraction to Organizations and Job Choice."

148. Bretz and Judge, "Realistic Job Previews: A Test of the Adverse Self-Selection Hypothesis"; Mary L. Connerley and Sara L. Rynes, "The Influence of Recruiter Characteristics and Organizational Recruitment Support on Perceived Recruiter Effectiveness: Views from Applicants and Recruiters," *Human Relations* 50 (1997): 1563–1586; Sara L. Rynes, Robert D. Bretz Jr., and Barry Gerhart, "The Importance of Recruitment in Job Choice: A Different Way of Looking," *Personnel Psychology* 44 (1991): 487–521.

149. Breaugh, "Employee Recruitment: Current Knowledge and Suggestions for Future Research"; Dineen and Soltis, "Recruitment: A Review of Research and Emerging Directions."

150. Chapman, Uggerslev, Carroll, Piasentin, and Jones, "Applicant Attraction to Organizations and Job Choice"; John P. Hausknecht, David V. Day, and Scott C. Thomas, "Applicant Reactions to Selection Procedures: An Updated Model and Meta-Analysis," *Personnel Psychology* 57 (2004): 639–683; Donald M. Truxillo, Dirk D. Steiner, and Stephen W. Gilliland, "The Importance of Organizational Justice in Personnel Selection: Defining When Selection Fairness Really Matters," *International Journal of Selection and Assessment* 12 (2004): 39–53.

151. Stephen W. Gilliland and Dirk D. Steiner, "Applicant Reactions to Testing and Selection." *The Oxford Handbook of Personnel Assessment and Selection* (2012): 629–666; Ryan and Delany, "Attracting Job Candidates to Organizations."

152. Ryan, Sacco, McFarland and Kriska, "Applicant Self-Selection: Correlates of Withdrawal from a Multiple Hurdle Process."

153. Breaugh, "Employee Recruitment: Current Knowledge and Suggestions for Future Research"; Breaugh and Starke, "Research on Employee Recruitment: So Many Studies, So Many Remaining Questions." Darnold and Rynes, "Recruitment and Job Choice Research: Same as It Ever Was?"

154. Breaugh, "Employee Recruitment: Current Knowledge and Suggestions for Future Research"; Darnold and Rynes, "Recruitment and Job Choice Research: Same as It Ever Was?"; Dineen and Soltis, "Recruitment: A Review of Research and Emerging Directions"; Rynes and Cable, "Recruitment Research in the Twenty-First Century."

155. Chapman, Uggerslev, Carroll, Piasentin, and Jones, "Applicant Attraction to Organizations and Job Choice."

156. Breaugh, "Employee Recruitment: Current Knowledge and Important Areas for Future Research."

157. Breaugh, Macan, and Grambow, "Employee Recruitment: Current Knowledge and Directions for Future Research."

158. Avery and McKay, "Target Practice: An Organizational Impression Management Approach to Attracting Minority and Female Job Applicants"; McKay and Avery, "What Has Race Got To Do with It? Unraveling the Role of Racioethnicity in Job Seekers' Reactions to Site Visits"; Saks and Uggerslev, "Sequential and Combined Effects of Recruitment Information on Applicant Reactions"; Daniel B. Turban, James E. Campion, and Alison R. Eyring, "Factors Related to Job Acceptance Decisions of College Recruits," *Journal of Vocational Behavior* 47 (1995): 193–213.

159. Avery and McKay, "Target Practice: An Organizational Impression Management Approach to Attracting Minority and Female Job Applicants"; Boswell, Roehling, LePine, and Moynihan, "Individual Job-Choice Decisions and the Impact of Job Attributes and Recruitment Practices: A Longitudinal Field Study"; Breaugh and Starke, "Research on Employee Recruitment: So Many Studies, So Many Remaining Questions"; McKay and Avery, "What Has Race Got To Do with It? Unraveling the Role of Racioethnicity in Job Seekers' Reactions to Site Visits"; Ostroff and Zhan, "Person-Environment Fit in the Selection Process"; Saks and Uggerslev, "Sequential and Combined Effects of Recruitment Information on Applicant Reactions"; Turban, Campion, and Eyring, "Factors Related to Job Acceptance Decisions of College Recruits."

160. Billsberry, "Experiencing Recruitment and Selection"; Robert E. Lewis and Robert J. Heckman, "Talent Management: A Critical Review," *Human Resource Management Review* 16 (2006): 139–154; Ryan and Delany, "Attracting Job Candidates to Organizations."

161. *Wall Street Journal*, August 14, 2013, B6.

162. *Wall Street Journal*, June 6, 2013, B7.

163. *HR Magazine*, November 2013, p. 26.

164. Ibid.

165. *Wall Street Journal*, B7.

166. Cheri Ostroff and Mark A. Clark, "Maintaining an Internal Market: Antecedents of Willingness to Change Jobs," *Journal of Vocational Behavior* 59 (2001): 425–453.

167. Paula M. Caliguiri and Jean M. Phillips, "An Application of Self-Assessment Realistic Job Previews to Expatriate Assignments," *International Journal of Human Resource Management* 14 (2003): 1102–1116; Kaus J. Templer, Cheryl Tay, and N. Anand Chandrasekar, "Motivational Cultural Intelligence, Realistic Job Preview, Realistic Living Conditions Preview, and Cross-Cultural Adjustment," *Group and Organization Management* 31 (2006): 154–173.

168. Juan Ling and Brian R. Dineen, "Internal Transfers: A Tale of Human Capital, Social Capital, and the Manager as Agent or Steward," presented at the annual meeting of the Southern Management Association, Charleston, SC, 2005.

169. Somaya, Williamson, and Lorinkova, "Gone but Not Lost: The Different Performance Impacts of Employee Mobility between Cooperators versus Competitors."

170. Bruce Horovitz, "At P&G's Historic Reunion," *USA Today*, April 23, 2003, Section B, p. 1.

171. Ryan and Delany, "Attracting Job Candidates to Organizations."

172. Richard D. Arvey, Michael E. Gordon, Douglas P. Massengill, and Stephan J. Mussio, "Differential Dropout Rates of Minority and Majority Job Candidates Due to 'Time Lags' between Selection Procedures," *Personnel Psychology* 28 (1975): 175–180; Becker, Connolly, and Slaughter, "The Effect of Job Offer Timing on Offer Acceptance, Performance, and Turnover"; Rynes, Bretz Jr., and Gerhart, "The Importance of Recruitment in Job Choice: A Different Way of Looking"; Saks and Uggerslev, "Sequential and Combined Effects of Recruitment Information on Applicant Reactions"; Bert Schreurs, Eva Derous, Edwin A. J. Van Hooft, Karin Proost, and Karel De Witte, "Predicting Applicants' Job Pursuit Behavior from Their Selection Expectations: The Mediating Role of the Theory of Planned Behavior," *Journal of Organizational Behavior* 30 (2009): 761–783; Turban and Cable, "Firm Reputation and Applicant Pool Characteristics."

173. Boswell, Roehling, LePine, and Moynihan, "Individual Job-Choice Decisions and the Impact of Job Attributes and Recruitment Practices: A Longitudinal Field Study"; Chapman, Uggerslev, Carroll, Piasentin, and Jones, "Applicant Attraction to Organizations and Job Choice"; Saks and Uggerslev, "Sequential and Combined Effects of Recruitment Information on Applicant Reactions."

174. Donald M. Truxillo, Talya N. Bauer, Michael A. Campion, and Matthew E. Paronto "Selection Fairness Information and Applicant Reactions: A Longitudinal Field Study," *Journal of Applied Psychology* 87 (2002): 1020–1031.

175. M. Susan Taylor and Thomas J. Bergmann, "Organizational Recruitment Activities and Applicants' Reactions at Different Stages of the Recruitment Process," *Personnel Psychology* 40 (1987): 261–285.

176. Rynes, Bretz Jr., and Gerhart, "The Importance of Recruitment in Job Choice: A Different Way of Looking."

177. Boswell, Roehling, LePine, and Moynihan, "Individual Job-Choice Decisions and the Impact of Job Attributes and Recruitment Practices: A Longitudinal Field Study"; Swider, Zimmerman, and Barrick, "Searching for the Right Fit: Development of Applicant Person-Organization Fit Perceptions during the Recruitment Process."

178. Ann Marie Ryan and Robert E. Ployhart, "A Century of Selection," *Annual Review of Psychology* 65 (2014): 693–717; Ryan and Delany, "Attracting Job Candidates to Organizations."

179. Filip Lievens and Michael M. Harris, "Research on Internet Recruitment and Testing: Current Status and Future Directions," in *The International Review of Industrial and Organizational Psychology*, Vol. 18, ed. C. L. Cooper and I. T. Robertson (Chichester, England: John Wiley, 2003): 131–166; Ryan and Ployhart, "A Century of Selection."

180. Peter A. Hausdorf and Dale Duncan, "Firm Size and Internet Recruiting in Canada: A Preliminary Investigation," *Journal of Small Business Management* 42 (2004): 325–334.

181. Ryan and Delany, "Attracting Job Candidates to Organizations."

182. *Wall Street Journal*, November 21, 2013, B4.

183. Karl Flinders, "Harnessing Generation Y," *Computer Weekly* 142 (October 23, 2007).

184. Victoria R. Brown and E. Daly Vaughn, "The Writing on the (Facebook) Wall: The Use of Social Networking Sites in Hiring Decisions," *Journal of Business Psychology* 10 (2011): 11–21; H. Kristl Davison, Catherine Maraist, and Mark N. Bing, "Friend or Foe? The Promise and Pitfalls of Using Social Networking Sites for HR Activities," *Journal of Business Psychology* 26 (2011): 153–159; Steven D. Maurer and David P. Cook, "Using Company Web Sites to E-recruit Qualified Applicants: A Job Marketing Based Review of THEORY-BASED Research," *Computers in Human Behavior* 27 (2011): 106–117; Diana L. Stone and James H. Dulebohn, "Emerging Issues in Theory and Research on Electronic Human Resource Management (eHRM)," *Human Resource Management Review* 23, no. 1 (2013): 1–5; Diana L. Stone, Eugene F. Stone-Romero, and Kimberly Lukaszewski. "Factors Affecting the Acceptance and Effectiveness of Electronic Human Resource Systems," *Human Resource Management Review* 16 (2006): 229–244; Michael J. Zickar and Christopher J. Lake, "Practice Agenda: Innovative Uses of Technology-Enhanced Assessment," in *Technology-Enhanced Assessment of Talent*, ed. N. T. Tippins, S. Adler (San Francisco, CA: Jossey-Bass, 2011): 394–417.

185. *Wall Street Journal*, November 21, 2013, B4.

186. Talya N. Bauer, Donald M. Truxillo, Jennifer S. Tucker, Vaunne Weathers, Marilena Bertolino, Berrin Erdogan, and Michael A. Campion, "Selection in the Information Age: The Impact of Privacy Concerns and Computer Experience on Applicant Reactions," *Journal of Management* 32 (2006): 601–621; Filip Lievens and Michael M. Harris. "Research on Internet Recruiting and Testing: Current Status and Future Directions," *International Review of Industrial and Organizational Psychology* 18 (2003): 131–166; Donald H. Kluemper, Peter A. Rosen, and Kevin W. Mossholder, "Social Networking Websites, Personality Ratings, and the Organizational Context: More Than Meets the Eye?" *Journal of Applied Social Psychology* 42, no. 5 (2012): 1143–1172; Zickar and Lake, "Practice Agenda: Innovative Uses of Technology-Enhanced Assessment."

187. Derek S. Chapman and Jane Webster, "The Use of Technologies in the Recruiting, Screening, and Selection Processes for Job Candidates," *International Journal of Selection and Assessment* 11 (2003): 113–120; Dineen and Soltis, "Recruitment: A Review of Research and Emerging Directions."

188. Brown and Vaughn, "The Writing on the (Facebook) Wall"; Daniel M. Cable, Daniel M., and Kang Yang Trevor Yu, "Managing Job Seekers' Organizational Image Beliefs: The Role of Media Richness and Media Credibility," *Journal of Applied Psychology* 91, no. 4 (2006): 828; Richard T. Cober, Douglas J. Brown, and Paul E. Levy, "Form, Content, and Function: An Evaluative Methodology for Corporate Employment Web Sites," *Human Resource Management* 43 (2004): 201–218; Dineen, Ling, Ash, and DelVecchio, "Aesthetic Properties and Message Customization: Navigating the Dark Side of Web Recruitment"; Ryan and Ployhart, "A Century of Selection"; Stone, Stone-Romero, and Lukaszewski, "Factors Affecting the Acceptance and Effectiveness of Electronic Human Resource Systems"; Kang Yang Trevor Yu and Daniel M. Cable, "Exploring the Identity and Reputation of Departmental Groups: Whose Opinions Matter Most to Their Members?" *Human Resource Management Journal* 21, no. 2 (2011): 105–121.

189. Dineen, Ash, and Noe, "A Web of Applicant Attraction: Person-Organization Fit in the Context of Web-Based Recruitment"; Dineen, Ling, Ash, and DelVecchio, "Aesthetic Properties and Message Customization: Navigating the Dark Side of Web Recruitment."

190. Paula Caligiuri, Saba Colakoglu, Jean-Luc Cerdin, and Mee Sook Kim. "Examining Cross-Cultural and Individual Differences in Predicting Employer Reputation as a Driver of

Employer Attraction," *International Journal of Cross Cultural Management* 10, no. 2 (2010): 137–151; Ryan and Delany, "Attracting Job Candidates to Organizations."

191. Ryan and Delany, "Attracting Job Candidates to Organizations"; Charles Vance and Yongsun Paik, *Managing a Global Workforce: Challenges and Opportunities in International Human Resources Management* (London, England: M. E. Sharpe, 2006).

192. Ryan and Delany, "Attracting Job Candidates to Organizations."

193. Caligiuri, Colakoglu, Cerdin, and Kim, "Examining Cross-Cultural and Individual Differences in Predicting Employer Reputation as a Driver of Employer Attraction"; Ryan and Delany, "Attracting Job Candidates to Organizations."

194. Douglas A. Ready, Linda A. Hill, and Robert J. Thomas, "Building a Game-Changing Talent Strategy," 64.

195. Jean Phillips and Stanley M. Gully, *Strategic Staffing* (Upper Saddle River, NJ: Pearson Prentice Hall, 2009), 191.

MEASUREMENT IN SELECTION

Collecting information about job candidates through selection procedures and about employees through work performance measures is central to any human resource (HR) selection system. Information is the basis for all decisions concerning the selection of job applicants. Sometimes, however, HR selection decisions turn out to be wrong. Perhaps individuals predicted to be outstanding performers actually contribute very little to an organization. Others forecast to stay with an organization for a lengthy period leave after only a few weeks. Moreover, in cases that are not verifiable, people who were predicted to be a poor fit for a firm and not hired would have been valuable contributors had they been employed. In each of these situations, we would conclude that errors occurred in selection decision making. Yet, when we analyze the situation, we may find that the decisions themselves were not wrong; it may be that the data on which they were based were faulty. Thus, it is essential that managers have sound data on which to base selection decisions. What do we mean by "sound data"? The three chapters in Part 2 address this question. Specifically, the objectives of this section are to

1. Explore the role of HR *measurement* in selection decision making

2. Examine the concepts of *reliability* and *validity* of selection data as well as their role in choosing useful selection measures and making effective selection decisions.

Human Resource Measurement in Selection

FUNDAMENTALS OF MEASUREMENT: AN OVERVIEW

An important assumption in selection decision making is that information is available for making these decisions. But, what types of information can be used? Where does this information come from? What characteristics should this information have to be most useful for human resource (HR) selection purposes? This chapter addresses such questions. Specifically, we focus on the (a) basics of psychological measurement as they apply to HR selection; and (b) locating, developing, and interpreting measures commonly used in HR selection.

THE ROLE OF MEASUREMENT IN HR SELECTION

If you have watched competent carpenters build a house or a piece of furniture, you cannot help being impressed by how well the various pieces fit together. For example, when a door is hung in place, it has a snug fit with its frame. Or perhaps you made a trip to the clinic where you watched a veterinarian save Taco, your Toy Manchester dog, who was attacked by a neighbor's dog. What makes a skilled carpenter and your vet so skilled and successful? Although many things contribute to the success of a carpenter installing a door and a veterinarian dealing with a pet emergency, one factor common to the success of both is their ability to employ *measurement*. How could a door be made to fit if a carpenter could not determine the exact dimensions of the opening? How could your vet operate on Taco if she did not understand anatomy, physiology, and the depth needed for an incision? Neither could be done without measurement. As we will see, measurement is also essential to the successful implementation and administration of an HR selection program.

The Nature of Measurement

Imagine for a moment, you are in charge of employment for a large company. You have an opening for the position of sales representative. Because of current economic conditions and the nature of the job, many people are interested. Numerous candidates submit an application; complete a sales ability test; and interview for the job. After several days of assessing applicants, you draw at least one obvious conclusion (in fact, it is a basic law of HR selection): *People are different.* As you think about the applicants, you notice that some are talkative, some are shy, some are neat and professionally dressed, and others are sloppy and shabbily dressed. After interviewing them, you observe that some applicants seem intelligent and others dim-witted; some seem dependable and achievement-oriented, while others appear irresponsible and aimless. Although classifying individuals in these extreme categories may be useful for *describing* people in general, it may not be useful for choosing among applicants. In a personnel selection context, you find that few people fall into these extreme categories. For example, only a few of our applicants will be extremely bright, and only a few extremely dull. For the many others, you will need some way to make finer distinctions among them with regard to the various characteristics that are of interest to you (intelligence, extraversion, conscientiousness, and so on). You will need to use measurement to make these discriminations and to study in detail the relationship between applicant characteristics and employee performance on the job.

A Definition

But, what is measurement? Numerous writings have examined the topic; some emphasize the meaning of measurement, others address methods involved in applying measurement. From the perspective of human resource selection, we offer one definition. Simply put, *measurement* involves the systematic application of rules for assigning numbers to objects (usually, people) to represent the quantities of a person's attributes or traits.[1] Let's explore this definition. *Rules* suggest that the basis for assigning numbers is clearly specified and consistently applied. For any measures we might use in selection, for instance a test, it is important that different users who use the test administer it under the same conditions and score it in the same manner as all other users. Therefore, when job applicants take a test, differences among applicants' scores should be due to individual differences in test performance. Score differences should not be due to the way in which different users administered the test under different test-taking conditions or to how administers scored the test in a different manner. Rules for assigning numbers to our selection measures help to standardize the scoring of these measures. Use of scoring rules shows that measurement is not an end but a means in the process of assessing an individual's standing on a job-related characteristic.

A second point in our definition involves the concept of an *attribute*. In HR selection, when we measure a person, we usually do not measure the person per se; rather, we assess an attribute or trait of the person. Physical attributes, such as gender, usually can be assessed through direct observation. *Psychological* attributes or *constructs*, however, are not directly observable. Psychological constructs, such as conscientiousness and intelligence, must be inferred from a score (consisting of numbers or units of measurement) on a measure that represents an individual's standing on these unobserved psychological attributes.[2] A score on a mathematics test is a number that reflects a job applicant's mathematical ability, as defined by the content of that test. With our test, we are not measuring the applicant but the applicant's mathematical ability. Notice that in our description we have not talked about *how well* we measure an attribute. Obviously, if we want to measure mathematical ability, we want a score (from a test, for example) that is a good measure of this ability. Obtaining a good measure of these elusive but critical psychological attributes (such as various competencies, knowledge, skills, abilities, personality, and other relevant characteristics) is not always easy. Yet, most often, it is psychological rather than physical traits that are indicators of how job candidates will behave on a job.

When we use tests or interviews to obtain measurements of psychological attributes, we draw inferences from these measures. Because inferences are involved, however, we are on much shakier ground than when we can directly observe an attribute. Someone conducting a selection interview might infer that the extent of applicants' eye contact with the interviewer reflects applicants' interest in the company or that the firmness of a handshake reflects the interviewees' self-confidence. But, are these inferences warranted? It is important to answer such a question if we are to use numbers in a meaningful way to evaluate important psychological constructs and make accurate inferences when making selection decisions.

A third and final point in our definition of measurement is that *numbers* or units represent attributes. Numbers play a useful role in summarizing and communicating the degree, amount, or magnitude of an assessed attribute. For instance, if applicant A scores 40 out of 50 on an achievement test and applicant B scores a 30, we conclude that applicant A has more "achievement" than applicant B. Although these numbers suggest degrees of difference in achievement, one must remember that achievement itself is not measured directly; it is instead inferred from the test score. Nevertheless, this score is used as an indicator of the achievement construct. In this sense, numbers provide a convenient means for characterizing and differentiating among job applicants. For this reason, numbers play an important role in personnel selection.[3]

Criteria and Predictors in Selection Research

A fundamental challenge in personnel selection is choosing, from a large group of job applicants, a smaller group that is employable. The goal of personnel selection is to identify the individuals who should be offered a position. These individuals are chosen because the selection measures predict that they will best perform the job in question. When the term, *predict* is used, it is assumed that a selection decision maker has the information on which to base these predictions. Where does someone get this information? Basically, the information is derived from an analysis of work being done on a job. One purpose of a *job* or *work analysis* is to identify the work-related characteristics (WRCs) incumbents must possess to perform the job successfully. Once we know the attributes necessary for job success, we can measure applicants with respect to these attributes and make our predictions accordingly.

Measurement plays a vital role in helping selection managers make accurate predictions. In determining a measurement system for predicting who should be hired, identification of two types of variables is critical. The first of these is called the *criterion* (or *criteria* when more than one criterion is being considered). A criterion serves as a definition of what is meant by employee success on the job. Criteria are defined by thoroughly studying the jobs for which a selection system is being developed to determine how to measure job success. A wide array of variables might serve as criteria. Some criteria deal with such issues as absenteeism, turnover, or organizational citizenship behaviors. Other criteria represent work-related outcomes, including error rates, number of goods produced, dollar sales, amount of scrap produced in manufacturing tasks, and speed of performance. These are a sampling of criteria depicting employees' job success. The most frequently used performance criteria are supervisory ratings of work performance.

Numerous types of criteria can be predicted. Nevertheless, criteria should not be defined or chosen in a cavalier, unsystematic, or haphazard manner. They *must* be important to the job, and they *must* be appropriately measured. Because criteria are the basis for characterizing employee success, the utility of a selection system will depend to a significant degree on their relevance, definition, and measurement.

A second category of variables required in predicting applicants' job success comprises *predictor* variables. Predictors or selection procedures represent the measures of those employee attributes (WRCs) identified through a job or work analysis as being important for predicting job success. A predictor is used as a selection procedure if there is evidence to expect that the employee attributes or WRCs assessed by the predictor will predict one or more of the criteria that define job success. This book discusses a wide variety of predictors that have been found useful in predicting employee performance. Tests, interviews, biographical data questionnaires, application blanks, and assessment centers are just some of the types of selection procedures you will study. As with criteria, there are two important requirements for developing and using predictors: (a) they *must* be relevant to the job and (b) they *must* be appropriate ways to measure the employee WRCs identified as representing job success. (Notice that we use the terms "predictor" and "selection procedure" as synonyms.)

Measurement and Individual Differences

Earlier in this chapter, we noted a basic law of psychology applicable to HR selection: People fundamentally differ. Furthermore, we said that one goal of selection is to identify those individuals who should be hired for a job. Measuring individual differences with our selection procedures and criteria helps us to meet our goal. Suppose, for instance, you were charged with the responsibility for hiring workers who could produce high quantities of work output. The workers individually manufacture wire baskets. After looking at some recent production records, you plot graphically the quantity of output per worker for a large number of workers. Figure 6.1 shows the results of your plot. (**Note:** This is simply a hypothetical distribution of performance for our current purposes. We are illustrating a normal distribution, but recent research suggests that individual performance may not necessarily be normally distributed.[4,5,6])

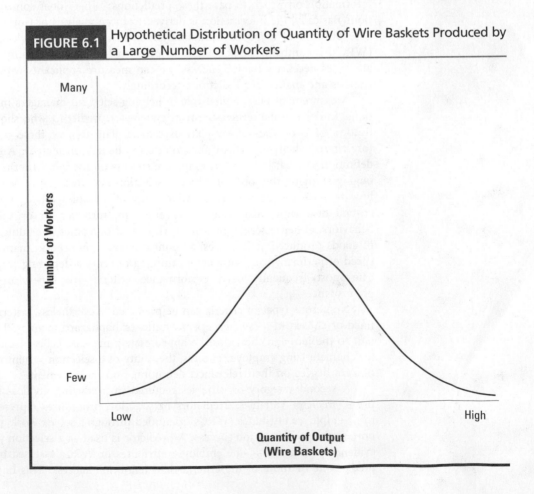

FIGURE 6.1 Hypothetical Distribution of Quantity of Wire Baskets Produced by a Large Number of Workers

Our plot suggests several things. First, because the productivity scores show a level of variability, individual employees differ in their levels of productivity. Second, relatively few produce a very large or very small number of baskets. Many employees, however, fall between these two extremes. If we can assume that quantity of production is a suitable criterion, our objective is to obtain a selection procedure that will predict the individual differences or variance in employees' productivity. If our predictor is useful, individuals' scores on the predictor will be associated with their productivity scores.

The preceding example highlights the important role of measurement in selection research. Numbers assigned to predictors and criteria enable us to make the necessary fine distinctions among individuals. Subsequent analyses of these numbers help us meet one of our goals: developing a system for predicting work performance successfully. Without measurement, we are left with our intuition and personal best guesses. Perhaps, for a very small number of us, these judgments will work. For most of us, however, deciding "by the seat of our pants" simply will not suffice.

Scales of Measurement

Use of selection procedures and criteria in selection research requires that these variables be measured, and measured rigorously. Because our ability to distinguish one person from another is determined by the *precision* with which we measure these variables, rigorous measurement is a prerequisite for performing any sound statistical analysis in a selection study. (By *precision*, we mean the number of distinct scores or gradations permitted by the selection procedure and criterion used.) The level of precision also will dictate what appropriate conclusions we can draw from these numbers obtained from measurement.

In the context of selection research, a *scale of measurement* is simply a means by which individuals can be distinguished from one another on a variable of interest, whether that variable is a predictor or a criterion. Because we use a variety of scales in selection research, the specific predictor or criterion variables chosen can differ rather dramatically in their precision. For example, suppose we were developing a selection program for bank management trainees. One criterion we want to predict is *trainability*, that is, trainee success in a management training program. We could measure trainability in several ways. On one hand, we could simply classify individuals according to who did and who did not graduate from the training program. (Graduation, for example, may be based on trainees' ability to pass a test on banking principles and regulations.) Our criterion would be a dichotomous category, that is, unsuccessful (fail) and successful (pass). We would search for a predictor variable that would enable us to distinguish between those applicants who could and those who could not successfully complete their training by passing the test.

On the other hand, we could evaluate trainability by the *degree* of trainee success as measured by training performance test scores (ranging, say, from 0 to 100). Our test might be used as an achievement test to reflect how much trainees know at the end of their training program. But, notice that in this case, our criterion is not categorical measurement (that is, success or failure) but rather a more precise way to describe the degree of trainee success.

Figure 6.2 shows the distributions of trainees' scores for the two methods of measuring trainability. As you can see, our simple "*classification* of success" criterion is not measured as precisely as our "*degree* of success" criterion. Greater individual differences in trainability are reflected by the latter criterion than for the former one. The variable *trainability* is the same in both examples. However, the two examples differ with respect to the level of measurement involved. Therefore, *it is the manner in which a variable*

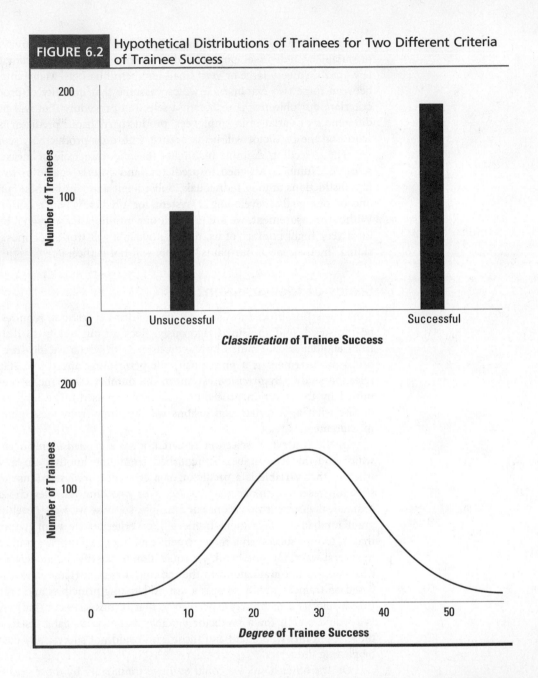

FIGURE 6.2   Hypothetical Distributions of Trainees for Two Different Criteria of Trainee Success

(predictor or criterion) is measured and not the variable itself that determines level of measurement. We can draw more precise conclusions with one trainability measure than we can with the other.

Four types of scales or levels of measurement exist: (a) nominal, (b) ordinal, (c) interval, and (d) ratio. The degree of precision with which we can measure differences among people increases as we move from nominal to ratio scales. Increased precision provides us with more detailed information about people with regard to the variables being studied—whether those variables are WRCs (such as mental ability and personality) or criteria (such as trainability, absenteeism, or job performance). With increased precision, we can draw conclusions that are more precise from our measurement and perform more meaningful statistical analyses on our data.

A *nominal scale* is one composed of two or more mutually exclusive categories. Numerical (1, 2, 3, etc.) values serve merely as "labels" for the category and do not imply any ordering of the attributes. For example, coding male applicants "1" and female applicants "2" does not signify females are twice whatever males are. These numbers, although meaningful and useful, carry no numerical rating. We could use other numbers as well (such as 0 and 1) to identify females and males. Both scoring schemes have the same meaning. The numerical codes themselves do not indicate how males and females differ. The only information we have from our numerical codes is an applicant's gender. Because we cannot state *how* members assigned to nominal scale categories differ, this type of scale is the simplest form of measurement.

Some statistical analyses can be performed with nominal scale data. For example, we can count and obtain percentages of members assigned to our scale categories. Other statistical procedures are possible, but we will not discuss them here because they are beyond the scope of our treatment. Examples of nominal scale measurement for the variables of applicant gender, applicant race, and job title include the following:

A. *Applicant Gender*
   1. Male
   2. Female

B. *Applicant Race*
   1. Black
   2. White
   3. Asian
   4. Other

C. *Job Title*
   1. Sales Manager
   2. Sales Clerk
   3. Sales Representative
   4. Salesperson
   5. Other

An *ordinal scale* is one that rank-orders objects, such as individuals, from "high" to "low" on some variable of interest. Numerical values indicate the relative order of individuals for the variable on which they are ranked. One example is shown in Figure 6.3, where supervisors have rank-ordered their subordinates' performance. Figure 6.3 shows that M. K. Mount, ranked 1, was ranked highest in quality of work completed. Furthermore, we know that each individual on the scale produces better quality work relative to the following individual (as judged by the individual doing the ranking). An ordinal scale, however, does not provide information on the *magnitude* of the differences among the ranks. Therefore, we do not know whether the distance between 1 and 2 is equivalent to the distance between 3 and 4. In our personnel-ranking example, M. K. Mount, the employee ranked 1, may be only marginally more productive in quality of work than A. DeNisi, who is ranked 2. A. DeNisi, however, may be considerably better than F. L. Schmidt, the employee ranked 3. Thus, differences among rankings indicate only that lower numbers (assuming that lower rank numbers indicate more of whatever attribute the scale is based on) represent *better* quality of work.

Another example of an ordinal scale often encountered in selection involves test scores. Percentiles sometimes are used to interpret the results of a test. A percentile represents the proportion of persons taking a test who make below a given score. If we know that a job applicant scored at the 76th percentile, we know that 76 percent of the individuals who took the test scored lower, and 24 percent scored higher. As in our previous example, we do not know how much better or worse the next individual performed in terms of a specific test score.

From our two examples, we can draw only "greater than" or "less than" conclusions with ordinal data; we do not know the amount of difference that separates individuals or objects being ranked. Our next two scales provide information relative to magnitude of differences.

FIGURE 6.3   Example of an Ordinal Scale of Measurement

Ranking of Employees

Below are listed the names of your 10 subordinates. Read the list and then rank the individuals on the quality of work completed in their jobs. By "quality of work completed," we mean the minimum amount of rework necessary to correct employee mistakes. Give the subordinate you believe is highest in quality of work performed a rank of "1," the employee next highest in quality of work a "2," the next a "3," and so on until you reach the employee who is lowest in quality of work completed, a "10."

> Note:
> 1 = Highest Quality
> •   •
> •   •
> •   •
> 10 = Lowest Quality

Employee	Rank on Quality of Work Completed
P. Bobko	4
A. DeNisi	2
M. K. Mount	1
R. G. Folger	7
F. Drasgow	9
W. C. Borman	5
F. L. Schmidt	3
P. R. Sackett	6
R. D. Pritchard	8
K. Murphy	10

With an *interval scale*, differences between numbers take on meaning. In addition to rank-order information, the scale uses constant units of measurement, affording a meaningful expression of differences with respect to a characteristic. For example, when we measure a group of job applicants with the mathematical ability test (points-correct scores range from 0 to 100), a *difference* between scores of 40 and 60 is equal to the *difference* between 60 and 80. The interval between scores can be interpreted. We cannot conclude, however, that an applicant with a score of 0 on the test does not have any mathematical ability. Such a conclusion would imply that our test covered *all* possible items of mathematical ability; in fact, our test is only a *sample* of these items. Obviously, we cannot make this statement because 0 refers only to the performance on our sample of test items, not 0 mathematics ability. Also, because of the absence of an absolute 0, we cannot state that an individual who scores 80 on our test has twice as much ability as one who scores 60.

Rating scales frequently are used as criterion measures in selection studies. For example, many work performance measures consist of performance appraisal or performance evaluation ratings. An example of a performance appraisal form is shown in Figure 6.4. When these ratings are treated as an interval scale, the magnitude of the difference between rating points is assumed to be the same. Raters using the form are

FIGURE 6.4 Example of an Interval Scale Used in Rating Employee Job Performance

Rating Factors

1. **Accuracy of Work:** the extent to which the employee correctly completes job assignments

1	2	3	4	5
Almost always makes errors, has very low accuracy	Quite often makes errors	Makes errors but equals job standards	Makes few errors, has high accuracy	Almost never makes errors, has very high accuracy

Comments: _____

2. **Quality of Work:** the extent to which the employee produces a volume of work consistent with established standards for the job

1	2	3	4	5
Almost never meets standards	Quite often does not meet standards	Volume of work is satisfactory, equals job standards	Quite often produces more than required	Almost always exceeds standards, exceptionally productive

Comments: _____

3. **Attendance/Punctuality:** the extent to which the employee adheres to the work schedule

1	2	3	4	5
Excessively absent or tardy	Frequently absent or tardy	Occasionally absent or tardy	Infrequently absent or tardy	Almost never absent or tardy

Comments: _____

4. **Coworker Assistance:** the frequency with which the employee assists coworkers in the completion of their job assignments

1	2	3	4	5
Almost never provides assistance to coworkers	Seldom provides assistance to coworkers	Sometimes provides assistance to coworkers	Often provides assistance to coworkers	Almost always provides assistance to coworkers

Comments: _____

5. **Timely Completion of Work Assignments:** the extent to which the employee uses time to accomplish job tasks effectively and efficiently

1	2	3	4	5
Almost never completes assignments on time	Seldom completes assignments on time	Sometimes completes assignments on time	Often completes assignments on time	Almost always completes assignments on time

Comments: _____

assumed to view the difference between points 1 and 2 on the scale in the same way as they view the difference between points 4 and 5.

Because many psychological constructs (for example, mental ability test scores) are assumed to be distributed normally, most of the predictors (and criteria) we use in HR selection are assumed to be measured with an interval scale. Predictors or criteria measured by interval scales tap the differences, order, and equality of the magnitude of the differences in the data. Interval scales offer more precision than nominal and ordinal scales; therefore, interval data can be analyzed by many of the statistical procedures important in personnel research. For example, researchers can employ means, standard deviations, and various inferential statistics, such as simple correlation. We discuss some of these procedures in later chapters. The critical point is that the precision of measurement determines the meaningfulness of the numbers or scores derived from our predictors and criteria. There is no substitute for using high-quality measures in selection, and because most predictors and criteria used in selection are treated as interval scales, the statistical analyses that can be conducted are useful in making selection decisions.

A *ratio scale* has an *absolute* zero point; as on the interval scale, differences between numerical values on a ratio scale have meaning. The presence of an absolute or true zero point permits us to make statements about the ratio of one individual's score to another based on the amount of the characteristic being measured. For instance, if one worker produces 100 wire baskets in an hour while another produces 50, we then can state that the second worker produces only half as much as the first.

Numerical operations that can be performed with the data suggest the origin of the name *ratio* scale. Numerical values on a ratio scale can be added, subtracted, multiplied, and divided. Ratios of scale numbers can be used, and the meaning of the scale will be preserved.

Most scales involving physical measurements (such as height, weight, eyesight, hearing, and physical strength) or counting (such as amount of pay, number of times absent from work, months of job tenure, number of promotions received, and dollar value of goods sold) are ratio scales. Ratio scales are not often encountered in the field of HR selection. As we discussed earlier, many of our measures are psychological rather than physical in nature; they do not lend themselves to ratio measurement because it is not meaningful to say, for example, that an applicant has "0" mathematical ability. Table 6.1 summarizes the general characteristics of the four types of scales of measurement.

From the preceding discussion, you can probably surmise that interval and ratio scales are most desirable for conducting sophisticated statistical analyses. Because of the precision of the scales and the statistical analyses they permit, results based on interval and ratio scales are capable of being interpreted rigorously and usefully. Our conclusions using the numbers or scores obtained from selection procedures or criteria depend on their measurement scale. Most measurement in personnel selection is indirect. That is, we cannot observe or directly assess an applicant's actual level of mental ability or achievement motivation or even attitude toward a proposed career. Instead, the person's standing on the unobservable trait (intelligence or work motivation) is inferred from their score on the predictor itself.

Quality measurement is critical in HR selection. The use of meaningless numbers will result in meaningless conclusions, no matter how complex the statistical analyses. Ultimately, there is no substitute for high-quality measurement methods. In selection, if the number signifies degrees of differences in units that reflect nearly equal interval units (that is, an interval scale), not just "more than" or "less than" (that is, an ordinal scale), then you have a *foundation* for a quality predictor or criterion.

STANDARDIZATION OF SELECTION MEASUREMENT

As we discuss in the next section, a variety of measurement methods are used in HR selection. When we refer to a *measurement method* in the context of selection, we mean the *systematic application of preestablished rules or standards for assigning scores to the attributes or traits of an individual*. A selection measure may provide information to be used as either a predictor (such as a test used as a selection procedure) or a criterion

TABLE 6.1 General Characteristics of Four Scales of Measurement

Type of Scale	Example	Example of Scale Use in Selection Research	Scale Characteristics			
			Classification	Order	Equality of Difference	Absolute Zero
Nominal	Men Women	*Classifying* applicants by their gender	Yes	No	No	No
Ordinal	1st 2nd 3rd	Supervisory *ranking* of subordinates	Yes	Yes	No	No
Interval	1 2 3 4 Very Dissatisfied Dissatisfied Satisfied Very Satisfied	Employee *rating* of job satisfaction	Yes	Yes	Yes	No
Ratio	(counting illustration)	*Counting* employee number of units produced	Yes	Yes	Yes	Yes

Source: Based in part on Uma Sekaran, *Research Methods for Managers* (New York: John Wiley, 1984), p. 134.

(such as a supervisor's performance appraisal rating used as a measure of job success). A particular measurement method can involve any one of our four scales of measurement that we just discussed.

An important characteristic of any predictor or criterion is its ability to detect *true* differences that exist among individuals with regard to the attribute being measured. For example, if *true* differences in knowledge of disease prevention exist among job candidates applying for a nurse practitioner's job, then a disease-prevention knowledge test must be able to detect these differences. If test score differences in disease prevention are found, these score differences should be due to differences in the candidates' knowledge and not due to extraneous factors, such as differences in the manner in which the test was given to the job candidates or the way in which it was scored.

Consider another example. Two job applicants (Shantel and Hildane) applied for the job of tax preparer with a tax-preparation firm. As part of their application, they took a preemployment math ability test. Shantel went to a branch office and took the paper-and-pencil test in the office's break-room. Every 10 minutes or so, a personnel assistant came by to look over Shantel's shoulder to see how she was doing. Hildane went to the main district office and took the same test as Shantel. The version she took, however, was on a computer. She worked alone and then submitted her test.

The two applicants' test scores (higher score indicates higher math ability) were

Hildane = 82

Shantel = 80

> **Question:** Is the difference in Hildane and Shantel's math ability test scores due to "true" differences in their math ability or, perhaps, is the score difference due to something else?

As you can tell, several factors are occurring that could contribute to the 2-point difference in test scores other than math ability. For one, if the personnel assistant frequently looked over Shantel's shoulder while she was taking the test, then that factor possibly affected Shantel's performance. If the break-room in which Shantel took her test was noisy or had people walking in and out, those factors could have had an effect on her scores. The two different modes of test administration—computer versus paper and pencil—also might have been a contributing factor. Those factors that affect test performance in undesired ways we frequently label as "error" because errors do not reflect the construct (in this case, math ability) we truly want to assess. Now, what can we do to help reduce this error?

To help control such factors, *standardized* measurement is needed in HR selection. A predictor or criterion measure is standardized if it possesses each of the following characteristics:

1. **Content.** All people assessed are measured by the same information or content. This includes the same format (for example, multiple-choice, essay) and medium (for example, paper and pencil, computer, video). When we say "same content," we do not necessarily mean that all questions asked are truly identical. For example, two versions of a test might be used. If that is the case, we should ensure that contents of the two versions are equivalent. For instance, on a math test, one form might ask: "What is 2 + 2 = ?" On the second version of the test, the question might ask: "What is 3 + 1 = ?" We all would probably agree that these two items measure the same construct, that is, the ability to add single digits, and that they are at the same level of difficulty.

2. **Administration.** Information is collected the same way in all locations and across all administrations each time the selection measure is applied. Equivalent administration also ensures that applicants are given the same directions, equal time to complete the test, and, ideally, matching physical test conditions.

3. **Scoring.** Rules for scoring are specified before administering the measure and are applied the same way with each scoring. For example, if scoring requires subjective judgment, steps should be taken such as having a pre-set answer key for scoring responses or giving raters training in how to make and record their ratings to ensure inter-rater agreement or reliability among raters.[7]

Have you ever taken a makeup exam because you missed the regularly scheduled exam due to an acceptable excuse? Think about the three characteristics of a standardized measure we listed above. Would your makeup exam have met the three conditions?

No matter how many times a measure is administered or to whom it is given, the same content, administration, and scoring is required before we can label it as a *standardized* measurement procedure. When viewed from the standpoint of professional practice, however, a measure that is truly standardized is more of an ideal than a reality. Standardization is a goal we strive for but do not always attain. Sometimes, it may even be necessary to alter the standardization of a selection procedure. For example, it may be necessary to modify the administration of a test to accommodate the special needs of a disabled job applicant.

Measures Used in HR Selection

One of the principal roles of any manager involved in HR selection decision making is deciding whether applicants should or should not be hired. Managers use predictors when making selection decisions. Predictors are selection procedures (such as a test or interview) that managers employ when deciding whether to accept or reject applicants for a specific job. Criteria (such as supervisory ratings of work performance) are employed as part of a research study designed to determine which selection procedures are related to job success and should be used in selection decision making. This type of research study is known as a *validation study*. We have more to say about validity and validation studies later in Chapter 8. For now, understand that criterion measures really help serve as a standard for evaluating how well predictors do the job they were intended to do. Predictors or selection procedures have a *direct* impact on the decisions reached by a manager involved in HR selection decisions. A manager actually reviews an applicant's scores on a selection procedure and uses this information in deciding whether to accept or reject the applicant. Criteria play an *indirect* role in that they determine which selection procedures actually should be used in making selection decisions.

We began this chapter by reviewing the impact of scales of measurement on the application and interpretation of data collected by predictors and criteria. The rest of the chapter discusses additional measurement principles that apply to the use of these two types of variables. These principles are important for understanding the application of the selection techniques and issues you will encounter in the remaining chapters. Before we continue our discussion in any meaningful way, it might be helpful to give you a brief overview of the various types of predictors and criteria employed in research involving HR selection. Later chapters will go into detail about specific measures. As you read, remember that when we talk about "selection measures," we mean *both* predictors (or selection procedures) and criteria. Now, let's look at some of the more common predictors and criteria in use.

Predictors or Selection Procedures

Numerous types of predictors or selection procedures have been used to forecast employee performance. In general, the major types tend to fall roughly into three broad categories. Keep in mind as you read these descriptions that our intention is not to give a complete account of each type of predictor. We simply want to acquaint you with the variety of predictors currently being used in selection. Subsequent chapters will provide a more detailed review of these measures. The predictor categories are as follows:

1. **Background information.** Application forms, training and experience evaluations, reference checks, and biographical data generally are used to collect information on job applicants and their backgrounds. *Application forms* typically ask job applicants to describe themselves, including contact information, educational background, relevant licenses, and the like. Training and experience often are assessed based on information on the application form. Prospective employers make *reference checks* by contacting individuals who can accurately comment on applicants' past work behaviors and associated characteristics as well as performance. These checks often are used to verify information stated on the application form as well as to provide additional data on the applicant. *Biographical data questionnaires* consist of questions about applicants' past life and work histories. Certain past life and work experiences are used based on the assumption that the best predictor of individuals' future behavior is their past behavior.

2. **Interviews.** Employment interviews are used to collect additional information about job applicants. The employment interview principally consists of questions asked by job interviewers. Responses often are used for assessing applicants' job suitability and their "fit" with an organization.

3. **Tests.** Literally hundreds of tests have been used for selection purposes. The types of tests available can be classified in many different ways; the descriptive labels indicated here will give you a feeling for the range of options available. *Aptitude*, or *ability*, tests, for example, measure how well individuals can perform a job or specific aspects of a job. Abilities measured by aptitude tests include intellectual, mechanical, spatial, perceptual, and motor. *Achievement* tests are employed to assess individuals' proficiency at the time of testing (for example, job proficiency or knowledge). (For the purposes of this book, you will see in Chapter 11 that we have combined aptitude and achievement tests into the general category "ability" tests.) *Personality* tests in the context of selection are used to identify those candidates who will work harder, cooperate with others, and cope better at work, which also should relate to their success on the job (discussed in Chapter 12).[8]

Most of the tests you encounter probably will fall into one of these categories. Keep in mind, though, that you will find some differences among tests within each of these categories. Some require test takers to respond with a paper and pencil or a computer; others require the manipulation of physical objects. Some will have a time limit; others will not. Some can be administered in a group setting, whereas others are given to only one applicant at a time.

Criteria or Measures of Job Success

As we saw in Chapter 3 on job and work analysis, criterion measures assess some form of behavior or performance related to the job (for example, organizational citizenship behaviors, sales, turnover, supervisory ratings of performance) that is important to the organization. They are called "criterion measures" because they help evaluate the selection procedures used in employment decision making. Thus, criteria represent what an organization means by "success on the job."

Although some of these measures focus on behavior—what the employee does or is perceived by a rater to have done—the behavior is a measure of a theoretical construct (for example, perceived work performance). Consequently, criterion measures are susceptible to the same measurement concerns as are written tests or employment interviews. As we have mentioned, however, criteria also are concerned with measuring things that can be used to assess the usefulness of the predictors (in Chapter 8, we discuss construct and criterion-related validity). And again, the criterion scale of measurement affects the quality of these inferences. Consequently, it is critical that the selection expert ensures that whenever possible, criterion measures approximate at least an interval scale. Numerous criteria are available to assess important aspects of work performance. One way to classify these criteria is by the measurement methods used to collect the data.[9] These categories include the following:

1. **Objective Production Data.** These data tend to be physical measures of work. Number of goods produced, amount of scrap left, and dollar sales are examples of objective production data.

2. **Personnel Data.** Personnel records and files frequently contain information on employees that can serve as important criterion measures. Absenteeism, tardiness, voluntary turnover, accident rates, salary history, promotions, and special awards are examples of such measures.

3. **Judgmental Data.** Performance appraisals or ratings frequently serve as criteria in selection research. They most often involve a supervisor's rating of subordinates on a series of behaviors or outcomes important to job success, including task performance, citizenship behaviors, and counterproductive work behaviors (CWBs). Supervisor or rater judgments play a predominant role in defining this type of criterion data.

4. **Job or Work Sample Data.** These data are obtained from a measure developed to resemble the job in miniature or sample of specific aspects of the work process or outcomes (for example, a typing test for a secretary). Measurements (for example, quantity and error rate) are taken on individual performance of these job tasks, and these measures serve as criteria. In practice, however, such measures are likely to be used as selection procedures rather than as criterion measures.

5. **Training Proficiency Data.** This type of criterion focuses on how quickly and how well employees learn during job training activities. Often, such criteria are labeled *trainability* measures. Error rates during a training period and scores on training performance tests administered during training sessions are examples of training proficiency data.

Standards for Evaluating Selection Measures

Now that we have provided an overview of some measures used in selection, assume you have already conducted a thorough analysis of the job in question to identify those WRCs thought to lead to job success. This step is critical because it enables us to identify the constructs or behavioral domains that the selection tests or predictors should assess. At this point, you are interested in choosing measures to be employed as predictors and criteria indicative of job success. One of several questions you are likely to ask is, "What characteristics should I look for in selecting a predictor or a criterion?"

You should consider a number of factors when choosing or developing a selection measure. Although it is not an exhaustive list, some of the factors that you should examine carefully are listed in question form in Table 6.2. Some are more important for predictors, some are more essential for criteria, and some are important for both types of measures. As you read these factors, think of them as a checklist for reviewing each measure you are considering. Unless you are sure that a measure meets these standards, you may not have the best measure you need for your selection research. In that case, you have at least two options: (a) determine whether you can adjust your data or the way you calculate the score itself so it will meet each measurement evaluation criterion (for example, ask the supervisor to rate each employee's performance on a 6-point rating scale instead of rank-ordering the employees); or (b) if this option is not viable, find or develop another, more suitable measure for the underlying job success construct.

The factors listed in Table 6.2 are not of equal importance. Issues concerning reliability, validity, and freedom from bias are more critical than administrative concerns, such as acceptability to management. Other factors will vary in importance depending on the specific selection situation. Regardless, the wise selection manager will give serious consideration to each one.

TABLE 6.2	Factors to Consider when Choosing or Developing Measures for Use in HR Selection Research

For Predictors:

1. **What does the predictor measure?** Is it likely to predict the criterion? A predictor is more likely to relate to the criterion if there is empirical research, a good theory, or a logical reason to expect a meaningful relationship between the predictor measure and the outcome of interest. A quality predictor will have a clear and concise definition of what underlying construct (for example, personality, mental ability) is measured.

2. **Is the predictor cost-effective?** The cost of purchasing or developing a predictor, as well as the cost of scoring and conducting validation studies, should be considered.

3. **Has the predictor been "standardized"?** If the predictor is distorted by extraneous, systematic variance (such as giving one group of applicants more time to complete a test than another group), then the meaning of differences in individual scores may be compromised. Consistent "standardized" administration, content, and scoring of a selection predictor across all locations and administrators is critical. There should be procedures for covering how to deal with any nonstandard administration of the predictor, including sessions that were disrupted (for example, computer malfunction, local emergency, illness of candidate) and other human errors (such as failure to track time accurately, non-matching test and answer sheets, and so on). Furthermore, employers should decide how to provide opportunities to reassess applicants or accommodate an applicant's known disability (if it is unrelated to the predictor construct being assessed). Standardization also extends to scoring. For example, if the selection procedure (such as an interview) requires subjective scores, the standardization of scoring becomes especially important.

4. **Is the predictor easy to use?** A predictor that can be administered and scored by persons who do not have high levels of training is less expensive than one that must be scored by those with higher training levels. Group predictors are more economical than individual predictors. Group predictors can be given to individuals, but many individual predictors cannot be given to groups. These are just a couple of factors that can affect how easy a predictor is to use.

5. **Is the predictor acceptable to the organization? To management? To the candidate?** An organization's past experiences with a selection procedure may mean it is unacceptable to—or is seen as controversial by—others (for example, investors, management, unions, and so on). Candidate reactions should also be considered. Content that is offensive or seen as an invasion of privacy may lead candidates to refuse to participate or to reject an employer's offer of employment.

For Criteria:

6. **Is the criterion relevant to the job for which it is chosen?** Important work-related activities, behaviors, or outcomes of the job should be relevant to the criterion. Trainability, for example, is a relevant criterion for an entry-level job.

7. **Is the criterion acceptable to management?** If management doesn't accept the criterion as worthwhile, managers will not support the system that may predict it. For example, if top executives value increasing revenues, actual sales will be more acceptable to management than will judgments of future trainability.

(Continued)

| TABLE 6.2 | *(Continued)* |

8. **Are work changes likely to alter the need for the criterion?** Jobs and situations change. Thus, measures of success today may be inappropriate a year later. Criteria should be periodically reviewed for their relevancy. When work changes are rapid or fluid, organization-wide criteria (such as turnover or effectively dealing with time deadlines) may be a better reflection of successful performance.

9. **Is the criterion uncontaminated and free of bias, so that meaningful comparisons among individuals can be made?** Unless jobs and work environments are identical, comparisons among individuals will be biased. Examples of contaminating variables include differences between sales territories, differences in tools and equipment, differences in work shifts, and differences in the physical conditions of the job. It is possible for the researcher to measure and account for possible sources of contamination. Systematic error that differentially affects the criterion performance of different subgroups (bias) must be minimized or eliminated insofar as possible. Group bias occurs when a group characteristic is assumed to relate to individual employee performance. Common examples of this kind of bias include age and job tenure, which are often assumed to be related to performance.

10. **Will the criterion detect differences among individuals if differences actually exist (discriminability)? Are meaningful differences among individuals actually scored with respect to the criterion?** A useful criterion will reflect the relative standing of employees with respect to work outcomes. If variance or individual differences in criterion scores cannot be obtained, then no predictor can be found to predict it. Hence, it is not possible to predict a criterion if all employees get the same performance rating (outstanding), when only 20% of the employees are actually outstanding performers.

For Predictors and Criteria:

11. **Does the measure unfairly discriminate against sex, race, age, or other protected groups?** Significant differences among protected groups on a measure do not necessarily mean discrimination. However, if predictor or criterion scores systematically differ across groups, one should carefully examine for predictive bias (that is, is the predictor equally predictive of performance for both men and women?).

12. **Does the measure lend itself to quantification?** For purposes of personnel selection, quantitative data are more desirable than qualitative data (for example, saying that the temperature is 105° F—rather than just saying that it is hot outside). Analysis and confirmation is more meaningful if the characteristic is systematically assessed using "assigned numbers." Numbers on an interval or ratio scale are preferred, because one can use more sophisticated statistical analyses.

13. **Is the measure scored consistently?** Specific rules and procedures should be available for scoring individuals on the measure. Different scores of an individual's performance should obtain the same score. All raters should receive the same training and have the same opportunities to observe and evaluate the applicant or employee.

14. **How reliable are the data provided by the measure?** A measure should provide dependable information. Individuals should consistently retain their relative position in the group across the predictor or criterion measures. Repeated application of a measure (if the context of measurement is the same with each application) should yield the same scores. Thus, if you get a 95 today on a mental ability test, you should get near 95 tomorrow if you retake the same test.

15. **How well does the device measure the construct for which it is intended (construct validity)?** The obtained scores on the predictor or criterion should assess what they are meant to (for example, intelligence or job performance).

Sources: Arne Evers, Neil Anderson, and Olga Voskuijl, *The Blackwell Handbook of Personnel Selection*, pp. 73–97 and 354–375. Copyright © 2005 by Blackwell publishers. Reprinted with permission; and Susana Urbina, *Essentials of Psychological Testing*, pp. 64–116. Copyright © 2004 by John Wiley & Sons, Inc. Reproduced with permission of John Wiley & Sons, Inc.

Finding and Constructing Selection Measures

The process of identifying selection measures to be used in an HR selection study should not be taken lightly. Identification of measures is not accomplished simply by familiarity with or personal whims about what measures are best in a specific situation. As we saw in Chapter 3, systematic work is conducted to identify what types of measures to use. Thorough analyses of jobs are made to identify the employee work-related characteristics necessary for successful work performance. Once we know the qualifications needed to successfully perform the job (our criteria), we are ready to begin the process of identifying and implementing our selection procedures. Obviously, the identification of selection procedures and criteria is important. Usually, a consultant—oftentimes an industrial–organizational psychologist—is needed. Choosing selection procedures requires an understanding of relevant empirical research and theory; a consultant should help provide a more informed professional judgment. Whether selection measures are identified by a consultant or by professional staff within large organizations, as an HR professional, you should be familiar with the basic approach. In identifying these measures, we have two choices: (a) we can locate and choose from existing selection measures, or (b) we can construct our own. In all likelihood, we might need to consider both options.

Locating Existing Selection Measures

There are several advantages to finding and using existing selection measures. These advantages include the following:

1. Use of existing measures is usually less expensive and less time-consuming than developing new ones.

2. If previous research was conducted on these measures, we will have some idea about the reliability, validity, and other characteristics of the measures.

3. Well-developed, existing measures are often superior to what could be developed in-house.

In searching for suitable selection measures, you will find that many types of measures are available. However, the vast majority of these, such as tests, are intended for use as selection procedures. A variety of selection procedures are commercially available—for example, intelligence, ability, interest, and personality inventories. Other predictors, such as application blanks, biographical data questionnaires, reference check forms, employment interviews, and work sample measures, might have to be developed. Criterion measures often are not commercially available and probably will have to be developed either from existing data or especially collected employee data.

Information Sources for Existing Measures

Sources in print and on the Internet (see Table 6.3) offer information on existing measures that can be used in personnel selection studies.[10] Although most of these sources will not present the measures themselves, they provide descriptive information on various options to consider. These sources are described here. Another way to choose preemployment tests is to review sources from major test publishers. Although a comprehensive list of all available tests is beyond one text, Table 6.4 indicates some of the larger test publishers.

Text and Reference Sources.   Several books provide excellent reviews of predictors and other measures that have been used in hiring for a variety of jobs. Some of the books are organized around the types of jobs in which various measures have been used. Others

TABLE 6.3   Internet Sources for Information on Existing Selection Procedures

Web Site	Source
http://www.unl.edu/buros	Buros Center for Testing
http://www.proedinc.com	Pro-Ed Inc.
http://www.ets.org	Educational Testing Service
http://eric.ed.gov	Education Resources Information Center
http://testpublishers.org	The Association of Test Publishers
http://www.apa.org	American Psychological Association
http://www.siop.org	Society of Industrial & Organizational Psychologists

TABLE 6.4	Selected List of Preemployment Test Publishers

Web Site	Publisher
https://www.cpp.com	Consulting Psychologists Press
http://www.hoganassessments.com	Hogan Assessment Systems, Inc
http://www.ipma-hr.org	International Personnel Management Association
http://www3.parinc.com	Psychological Assessment Resources
http://psychcorp.pearsonassessments.com	Pearson Assessments
http://corporate.psionline.com	Psychological Services, Inc
http://www.shl.com	Saville & Holdsworth, Inc.
http://www.valtera.com	Valtera Corporation
http://wonderlic.com	Wonderlic Personnel Test, Inc.

center on types of selection measures. Still others are organized around technical aspects of the HR selection process. Many relevant books on personnel selection are cited in this text.

In addition, users should consult the *Annual Review of Psychology* and *Research in Personnel and Human Resources Management*, both published annually. On occasion, reviews of current selection research are published. These reviews offer an excellent, up-to-date look at research on measures and other issues relevant to personnel selection.

Buros' Mental Measurements Yearbooks. The *Mental Measurements Yearbook* is the most important source for information on tests for personnel selection. It contains critical reviews by test experts and bibliographies of virtually every test printed in English. Oscar Buros was editor of the *Yearbook* for many years; following his death, the Buros' Institute of Mental Measurements moved to the University of Nebraska, where his work is being carried on. Historically, a new edition was published every six years; going forward, it is published roughly every two years. The most recent edition is the *Nineteenth Mental Measurements Yearbook* (in press).[11] Reviews of tests can be found on the Buros' Web site through *Test Reviews on Line* (www.unl.edu/buros) as well as on the *Mental Measurements Database* accessible through many university libraries. Unquestionably, Buros' publications present valuable information about existing tests that are used in personnel selection applications.

In addition, the Buros' Institute has published several supplementary books containing additional bibliographies and reviews. One of the most useful is *Tests in Print (TIP) I–VIII*, which serves as a comprehensive bibliography to all known commercially available tests currently in print. These reviews provide vital information to users, including test purpose, test publisher, in-print status, price, test acronym, intended test population, administration times, publication dates, and test authors. A Score Index is particularly valuable. The Score Index permits users to identify specific tests associated with constructs of most interest to the user. Thus, if users know specific construct(s) representative of WRCs, users then can read the reviews of tests associated with that construct(s) in the *Mental Measurements Yearbook* and ascertain whether the test(s) is suitable for the desired purpose. Similar searches also can be performed through the Buros' Web site.

Other Reference Sources

Pro-Ed, a testing corporation in Austin, Texas, offers a series of testing sources referencing a variety of psychological measures. The current source is *Tests: A Comprehensive Reference for Assessments in Psychology, Education, and Business* (6th edition). The book describes more than 2,000 assessment instruments categorized in 90 subcategories. This reference includes information on each test's purpose, scoring procedures, cost, and publisher. It does not critically review or evaluate tests as the Buros' publications do.

Educational Testing Service (ETS) of Princeton, New Jersey, has several reference sources available for identifying suitable selection measures. For instance, the *Test Collection* database (http://www.ets.org/test_link/about) has a library of more than 25,000 tests and other measurement devices, which can be searched online. The database includes information about tests used to assess abilities, aptitudes, interests, and personality as well as other variables related to various vocational and occupational fields. Use of the database is similar to that of the *Mental Measurements Yearbook Database* described earlier.

Another valuable source for test information is the Education Resources Information Center (ERIC), sponsored by the Institute of Education Sciences (IES) of the U.S. Department of Education. This Web site (http://web.calstatela.edu/library/dbs/~e6.htm) contains information on thousands of assessment instruments. Many of these instruments have been used in psychological and educational settings.

Journals.   Several journals are excellent sources for information about selection measures. In particular, the *Journal of Applied Psychology (JAP)* and *Personnel Psychology* are most relevant to many industrial applications. *JAP* has a long history as a major journal in the field of industrial psychology, focusing on empirical research in applied psychology. *JAP* includes articles about various predictors, criteria, and other issues related to personnel selection. Any search for information about measures used in personnel selection should definitely include *JAP* as a source to review. A second well-respected source is *Personnel Psychology*, which also has a long history of publishing articles concerned with personnel selection and related topics. Articles emphasize the practical application of research.

Other journals occasionally publish articles dealing with the application of selection measures. These include the *International Journal of Selection and Assessment, Journal of Personnel Psychology, Human Performance, Journal of Occupational and Organizational Psychology, The Industrial-Organizational Psychologist (TIP),* and *Applied Psychological Measurement.* At times, reviews of specific tests that may be relevant to industrial personnel selection also can be found in the *Journal of Educational Measurement, Journal of Vocational Behavior,* and the *Journal of Counseling Psychology.* As part of a thorough search, researchers should review these journals for possible ideas.

Online database resources available through many libraries also can help to identify potential selection measures. These databases include *Psychological Abstracts, Personnel Management Abstracts,* and computerized literature searches (for example, PsycARTICLES, PsycINFO, or Abstracted Business Information Database). Searching databases, such as PsycINFO, using a specific name of a test can provide bibliographic references and informative research articles regarding the usefulness of the test.

Test Publishers.   A number of organizations publish tests used in HR selection. Each publisher provides a catalog describing the various tests offered. A comprehensive list of test publishers and addresses is presented in *Buros' Mental Measurements Yearbook.* Many of these test publishers have Web sites that permit a search option to locate a particular test.

The Association of Test Publishers (ATP; http://www.testpublishers.org/), a nonprofit organization since 1992, represents a large number of test publishers and providers of assessment services. The Industrial/Organizational Division of the ATP focuses on the use of tests in selection, placement, development, and promotion and tries to uphold a high level of professionalism and business ethics related to the publishing of assessments.

These various sources present information on the most current tests available. Once a test that appears to meet a specific need is located, qualified users can order a test manual and specimen set. (Typical costs for specimen sets range from $25 to $75.) The test manual provides information on what the test measures and on the administration, scoring, and interpretation of results. In addition, reliability and validity data also are presented. These materials help users decide whether a test is appropriate before adopting it.

Just because a test is identified for use, however, does not mean that it is available for purchase. Some publishers use a framework for classifying their tests and for determining to whom tests can be sold. There are three levels of classification.

Level A. Level A consists of those tests that require little formal training to administer, score, and interpret. Most selection practitioners may purchase tests at this level. A clerical abilities test is representative of tests in this classification.

Level B. Tests classified in this category require some formal training and knowledge of psychological testing concepts to properly score and interpret. Ability tests designed to forecast an individual's performing potential are of this type. Individuals wishing to purchase level-B tests must be able to document their qualifications for correctly using such tests. These qualifications usually include evidence of formal education in tests and measurement as well as in psychological statistics.

Level C. Level-C tests require the most extensive preparation on the part of the test administrator. In general, personality inventories and projective techniques make up this category. A doctorate in psychology and documentation of training (such as courses taken on the use of a particular test) are required. Tests in this category tend to be used less frequently in selection contexts than tests in levels A and B.

Another approach to describing test selection practices, an approach more complex than the classification scheme just described, can be found in the *Standards for Educational and Psychological Testing*, published by the American Psychological Association (APA).[12] Although it is not a source of selection measures per se, APA's *Standards* provides an excellent treatment of the considerations in selecting and using tests.

Professional Associations. Various professional associations may be a source of selection measures. For example, the American Banking Association has supported research to develop selection measures for use in hiring for customer service, operations, and administrative jobs in banking. LIMRA, an association of insurance companies, has sponsored research to review the use of tests in the selection of life insurance sales management. The American Foundation for the Blind Web site (http://www.afb.org) contains a variety of information and even some selection measures for individuals with visual problems. Other trade and professional associations should be contacted as possible sources for selection measures or research on such measures.

Certain management associations may be able to provide guidance in locating selection measures for specific situations. The Society for Human Resource Management (SHRM) and the International Personnel Management Association (IPMA) are two potential sources of information. The Association of Test Publishers (ATP) has developed and published guidelines and standards. Finally, the Society of Industrial and Organizational Psychologists (SIOP), has published the *Principles for the Validation and Use of*

Personnel Selection Procedures (4th edition)[13] which is an excellent, authoritative source on sound personnel selection practices.

Following are the minimum recommendations for choosing an existing selection measure:

1. Be sure you clearly and completely understand the attribute or construct you want to measure. Decide on the best means for assessing the attribute, such as a paper-and-pencil test, a work sample test, and so on.

2. Search for and read critical reviews and evaluations of the measure. References mentioned earlier (such as Buros' *Mental Measurements Yearbook*) are excellent sources of such reviews. These sources should be able to provide background information on the test, including answers to relevant questions: What theory was the test based on? What research was used to develop the test? This is important because it provides information on the logic, care, and thoroughness with which the test was developed. It should allow you to assess how relevant this information is with regard to your organization's applicants or employees.

3. If a specimen set of the measure (including a technical manual) is available, order and study it. Ask yourself, "Is this measure appropriate for my intended purpose?" In answering this question, study carefully any information relative to the measure's reliability, validity, fairness, intended purpose, method of administration, time limits, scoring, appropriateness for specific groups, and norms. If such information is not available, that is a "red flag": buyers beware; consider other measures.

4. Once you have completed steps 1 through 3, ask yourself, "Based on the information I reviewed, are there compelling arguments for using this measure? Or, on the other hand, are there compelling arguments against using it?"

Constructing New Selection Measures

The advantages to using existing selection procedures are obvious; when suitable measures can be found, they certainly should be considered. Sometimes, however, selection researchers are not able to find the precise measure needed for their purposes. At this point, they have no choice but to develop their own measure. This section outlines the steps involved in developing a selection procedure.

Before proceeding, we must consider some important issues. HR professionals raise legitimate concerns about whether it is reasonable to expect practitioners to develop selection procedures, particularly in light of the technical and legal ramifications associated with them, and whether an organization has the resources, time, and expertise to develop such measures. In addition, we might ask, "Can't a little knowledge be dangerous? That is, won't some well-meaning practitioners be encouraged to attempt to develop and use measures that 'appear' to be 'good' but really are worthless?" Our intention is not to prepare you nor even encourage you to develop selection measures yourself, but rather to enable you to communicate and work productively with a selection specialist or expert. The development of such measures is a complex, resource-consuming process that usually requires expert advice. The risks associated with the process can be quite high. Most HR managers simply do not have the resources or skills available to engage in the development of selection measures. Consultants likely will be needed.[14] The material presented in this and related chapters is intended to serve as a means by which an organization can monitor and evaluate the work of a consultant as well as study and review the literature describing selection measures. Knowledge of the basic issues involved in selection measure development, validation, and application can help bridge any possible communications gap between the organization and the consultant.

Steps in Developing Selection Measures

Although the details can vary somewhat depending on the specific selection measure being developed, six major steps typically are required:

1. Analyzing the job for which a measure is being developed

2. Selecting the method of measurement to be used

3. Planning and developing the measure

4. Administering, analyzing, and revising the preliminary measure

5. Determining the reliability and validity of the revised measure for the jobs studied

6. Implementing and monitoring the measure in the human resource selection system

Let's examine each of these steps.

Analyzing the Job.   The first step in the instrument development process is perhaps the most crucial. After analyzing the work itself, one should be able to specify the knowledge, skills, abilities, competencies, and other characteristics the predictor(s) should assess. We have previously referred to these attributes as work-related characteristics or WRCs.

In addition, our job analysis should help identify the aspects of work performance or criteria that our predictors are designed to predict. These criteria represent our operational definition of what we mean by "job success or work performance." This initial step is a critical one; if carried out inappropriately, then all subsequent steps taken in selection procedure development likely will be flawed.

Historically, traditional job analysis methods were used to assess the demands specific jobs or job families make on employees. Today, some organizations often find that the nature of the work their employees perform is changing too rapidly to permit a traditional job analysis. Such changes include technological advances, the changing nature of the social setting at work (for example, greater interaction with customers, team members, or independent contract workers), organizational expectations regarding the work-related characteristics employees should possess and exhibit at work, and the external environment (for example, the outsourcing or offshoring of work and other changes in the competitive landscape). In such cases, a broader analysis of work activities common across a family of jobs or, perhaps, to the entire organization might be needed, rather than an emphasis on a specific job. In a recent review of job analyses, Paul Sackett and Roxanne Laczo[15] effectively summarize the status of work analysis by stating that today, there are no "one size fits all" job analysis procedures. Consequently, the role of a job or work analysis in the context of selection is to identify WRCs for various types of work activities using a broader analysis of work. Irrespective of the specific work analysis procedure adopted, an analysis of work must be performed as an initial step. This is true whether a measure is being developed or whether existing measures are being considered. From this analysis, the developer of a selection measure gains insights and forms hypotheses as to what types of measures are needed.

As we noted earlier, in addition to its role in developing and selecting selection measures, analysis of work also provides the foundation for developing or identifying criterion measures of work performance. We cannot do systematic research on the selection of personnel until we know which of our selected applicants have become successful employees. Intimate knowledge of the work gained through job–work analysis will help us to identify or develop measures of job success. Ultimately, through validation research, we will determine the extent to which our selection measures actually can predict these criteria.

A number of approaches to job analysis exist. There is no single job analytic method that is "correct" for every situation. Nevertheless, the more researchers know about a specific job and the work it entails, the more likely it is that their hypotheses and ideas about selection measures will have predictive utility for that job. Therefore, researchers must choose the method of analysis they believe will yield the most useful information about work in their employment setting.

Selecting the Measurement Method.   Once we have identified what to measure with regard to the WRCs for performing a job adequately, we are ready to consider the approach we will use in selection. A host of methods are available, including paper-and-pencil tests, job or work sample tests, ratings, interviews, and biographical data questionnaires, to name only a few. The specific nature of the job (such as tasks performed or level of responsibility); the skill of the individuals responsible for administering, scoring, and interpreting selection measures; the number and types of applicants making application (such as level of reading and writing skills or presence of physical or mental disabilities); the costs of testing; and the resources (such as time and dollars) available for test development are just some of the variables that will affect the selection of a measurement medium. If large numbers of applicants are applying for the job, paper-and-pencil measures will be carefully considered. If applicant social skills are critical, then some form of a behavioral exercise might be proposed. If finger dexterity skills appear to be critical to job success, then tests involving the manipulation of a physical apparatus may be necessary to measure applicants' motor responses. The method chosen ultimately depends on the identified WRCs and the organizational context in which the job is performed.

Figure 6.5 presents an example of a checklist used to match selection methods with job requirements for industrial electricians. The listing under "Job Requirements" consists of elements of the job, identified through a job analysis, that were found to be critical to the success of a company's industrial electricians. The requirements for this position are the WRCs that a newly hired electrician must possess upon entry into the job. The listing under "Selection Method" represents the possible means by which essential job requirements can be assessed. After studying the job and the organization, the selection researcher decided that certain methods would be suitable for assessing some requirements, whereas other measures would be appropriate for other job requirements. The methods judged suitable for specific job requirements are indicated by a check mark. For example, it was decided that a paper-and-pencil test was most suitable for determining applicants' "Knowledge of principles of electrical wiring," whereas a work sample test was chosen to determine applicants' "Ability to solder electrical connections." For the WRC, "Motivation to work hard, come to work, and continue in employment with the company," a personality inventory and biographical data form were chosen for use.

For our purposes in the following section, assume we want to construct a predictor for our industrial electrician's position. Briefly, we describe the steps that generally apply to most any selection procedure that we are developing. After reading through these steps, you will be motivated to look for quality, commercially available selection procedures whenever possible!

| FIGURE 6.5 | Checklist Used to Match Selection Procedure with Work-Related Characteristics for the Job of Industrial Electrician |

	Selection Procedure					
Work-Related Characteristics	Work Sample test	Paper-and-pencil test	Selection interview	Personality inventory	Biographical data form	Reference check
1. Knowledge of principles of electrical writing		√				
2. Ability to solder electrical connections	√					
3. Ability to trouble-shoot electrical wiring problems using a voltmeter	√					
4. Knowledge of maintenance and repair of electrical equipment		√				
5. Motivation to work hard, come to work, and continue in employment with the company				√	√	
⋮			⋮			⋮
N. Previous work experience in hazardous work environments			√		√	√

Planning and Developing the Selection Measure.   After a job has been analyzed and some tentative methods considered for assessing the important aspects of the work, the selection researcher probably has some vague mental picture of what each selection procedure might be like. In this step, the researcher attempts to clarify the nature and details of each selection procedure and prepares an initial version of each measure. The specifications required for the measure should include the following:

1. The stated purposes and uses the measure is intended to serve

2. The nature of the applicant population for which the measure is to be designed

3. The way each of the WRCs will be measured and scored
   For example, if a test (paper-and-pencil or computer administered) were going to be used, this step includes decisions about the method of administration, the format of test items and responses, and the scoring procedures to be used.[16]

   ▪ **Generating behavioral samples or items that reflect the job content domain.** Substantial work is involved in designing and selecting and refining the content (for example, test items) used to measure the WRC of interest. This work often involves having subject matter experts (SMEs) create the items or rewrite ones provided to them. In developing or rewriting these items, the SMEs should consider the appropriateness of item content and format for fulfilling its purpose, including characteristics of the applicant pool, clarity and grammatical correctness, and consideration of bias or offensive portrayals of a subgroup of the population.

- **Developing administration methods and scoring procedures.** It is important to take into consideration the various formats for eliciting responses from test takers. Broadly, there are two types of formats—the first uses objective or fixed-response items (multiple-choice, true-false); the second elicits open-ended, free-response formats (essay or fill-in-the-blank). The fixed-response format is the most popular; it makes efficient use of testing time, results in few (if any) scoring errors, and can easily and reliably be transformed into a numerical scale for scoring purposes. The primary advantage of the free-response format is that it can provide greater detail or richer samples of the candidates' behavior and may allow unique characteristics, such as creativity, to emerge. Primarily because of both the ease of administration and objectivity of scoring, fixed-response formats are most frequently utilized today, particularly if the test is administered in a group setting. Finally, explicit scoring of the measure is particularly critical. Well-developed hiring tools will provide an "optimal" response for each item that is uniformly applied.

- **Standardizing administration of the selection procedure, including the time limits for completion.** Consideration must be given to reasonable accommodations to administration based on the Americans with Disabilities Act. For example, allowing oral administration of a written inventory to blind applicants or helping an applicant having difficulty writing are just some of the accommodations that can be made. However, standardizing procedures during assessment is critical to ensure a more accurate, fairer assessment than if the procedure varies from one person to another. To the extent possible, steps must be taken to control the conditions and procedures of test administration and to keep them constant, even unvarying. The challenge is that standardization must be balanced with fairness to reasonably accommodate all candidates.

4. **The sampling design and statistical procedures used** in selecting and editing **items, questions, and other elements composing the measure.**[17] Selection procedures require a number of steps to ensure accurate measurement. Among the steps often taken are showing selection procedure content (for example, test items) to a panel of SMEs. These SMEs typically judge job-relevance of the selection procedure content and help screen out objectionable content that might produce bias against some respondents.

Development also may include pilot testing the selection procedure with an initial group comparable to the applicants with whom the device will be used. It may even involve a second, holdout sample to double-check findings. Robert Guion, among others, has noted that distorted results can be obtained when the usefulness of a selection device is evaluated for the *same* groups on whom the device was developed.[18]

Referring to the analysis the industrial electrician's job we mentioned earlier (see Figure 6.5), we can see how job content can be translated into selection measure content. Among other requirements, the job analysis identified two important types of knowledge essential to the job: "Knowledge of the principles of electrical wiring" and "Knowledge of maintenance and repair of electrical equipment." Because these two knowledge characteristics lend themselves to assessment with a paper-and-pencil test, assume we have decided to use such a multiple-choice test to measure what an industrial electrician must know to perform the job. In preparing the test, the first step is to develop a content outline. From discussions with incumbents and supervisors as well as additional job analysis information, we know that the two job knowledge components need to be broken down into more specific details. Figure 6.6 illustrates these details for one of the knowledge characteristics identified from the job analysis—that is, "Knowledge of the principles of electrical wiring."

In assessing these details, we determine that applicants must know the definitions of terms, safety principles, the correct steps to take in implementing electrical wiring procedures, and how to make specific computations involving electrical measurements (such as voltage, current, or amperage, Ohm's Law). Figure 6.7 helps us to specify the test item budget—that is, the specific number of items to be prepared for measuring the components of the job.

Be wary of commercially available tests or inventories that consist of a very limited number of items—for example, a 10-item test that purports to measure five different job

FIGURE 6.6 What an Industrial Electrician Needs to Know to Perform the Job

Knowledge of Principles of Electrical Wiring

- Reading schematic drawings
- Choosing appropriate gauges of wire for different electrical applications
- Installing circuit-breaker panels
- Selecting electrical fuses for different electrical applications
- Installing electrical grounds
- Checking voltages in electrical receptacles
- Computing voltage drops for various lengths and gauges of wiring
- Using copper and aluminum wiring

FIGURE 6.7 Form Used to Determine Item Budget for Knowledge Topics in the Industrial Electrician Test

	Knowledge Information				
Knowledge Topic	Definition of Terms	Safety Information	Procedural Applications	Computations	**Total Items**
Reading schematics	8				8
Choosing wire gauges			4		4
Installing circuit-breaker panels		4	4	3	11
Selecting electrical fuses		3		4	7
Installing electrical grounds		2	4		6
Checking electrical receptacle voltages		2	3	2	7
Computing voltage drops				3	3
Using copper and aluminum wiring			4		4
Total Items	8	11	19	12	50

Note: The knowledge topics listed in the chart were developed from the knowledge of principles of electrical wiring listed in Figure 6.6. Cells in the chart show the number of test items devoted to specific knowledge topics for various types of knowledge information.

applicant characteristics. Measuring an attribute or trait consistently and accurately typically requires more than just a couple of items. In the industrial electrician example, it was decided that 50 multiple-choice items would be used to assess "Knowledge of the principles of electrical wiring." Theoretically, multiple items could be developed for each cell in the chart shown in Figure 6.7. Our test, however, is only a *sampling* of the job domain; we cannot ask all possible questions covering all possible elements of information. By using the chart in collaboration with knowledgeable SMEs involved with the job, we can specify reasonable coverage of what an industrial electrician needs to know about wiring when they enter the job. We construct the test items in proportion to the number identified in the cells shown in Figure 6.7.

Administering, Analyzing, and Revising Content.   Following development, the initial version of the selection procedure should be pilot-tested. Ideally, the procedure should be given to a sample of people from the same population for which it is being developed. Choice of participants should take into account the demographics, motivation, ability, and experience of the applicant pool of interest. To provide data suitable for analyzing its contents, the developed procedure should be tried out on a sizable sample. For example, if a test is being developed for which item analyses (that is, information on how well the test items are working in the sample) are to be performed, a sample of at least a hundred, preferably several hundred, is needed.

On the basis of the data collected, item analyses are performed on the preliminary data. The objective is to revise the proposed measure by correcting any weakness and deficiencies noted. Item analyses are used to choose item content, permitting it to discriminate between those who know and those who do not know the information covered.

Item data analyses begin with summary statistics, including central tendency and variability (means and standard deviations), for the total group and for relevant subgroups (if large enough). A number of psychometric characteristics should be considered. These include evidence supporting the following:

1. **Reliability of Selection Procedure Content.** In part, reliability is based on the consistency and precision of the results of the measurement process and indicates whether items are free from measurement error. This point is discussed in more detail in Chapter 7.

2. **Validity of the Intended Inferences.** Do responses to an item differentiate among applicants with regard to the characteristics or traits that the measure is designed to assess? For example, if the test measures verbal ability, high-ability individuals will answer an item differently than those with low verbal ability. Often items that differentiate are those with moderate difficulty, where 50 percent of applicants answer the item correctly. This is true for measures of ability, which have either a correct or incorrect answer. Validity is discussed in Chapter 8.

3. **Item Fairness or Differences among Subgroups.** A fair selection procedure has scores that have the same meaning for members of different subgroups of the population. Such tests would have comparable levels of item difficulty for individuals from diverse demographic groups. Panels of demographically heterogeneous raters, who are qualified by their expertise or sensitivity to linguistic or cultural bias in the areas covered by the test, may be used to revise or discard offending items as warranted. An item sensitivity review is used to eliminate or revise any item that could be demeaning or offensive to members of a specific subgroup.

As our discussion suggests, a number of considerations must guide the item analysis and revision process. To successfully navigate this step, the developer of the selection procedure must possess extensive technical knowledge about test development, the discussion of which is beyond the scope of this book. In conclusion, the quality of the items used in the test has a significant impact on the overall quality of the measure. Consequently, this is a critical step in the development of a new measure.

Determining Reliability and Validity. At this point, we have a revised selection procedure that we hypothesize will predict certain aspects of job success. Now, we are ready to conduct reliability and validity studies to test our hypothesis. In the next two chapters, we examine how to conduct reliability and validation research. Essentially, we want to answer three questions: Are the scores on our selection measure dependable for selection decision-making purposes? Is the selection procedure predictive of job success? Does the selection procedure measure what we think it measures?

Implementing the Selection Measure. After we obtain the necessary reliability and validity evidence, we can then implement our measure. Cutoff or passing scores can be developed. Once the selection measure is implemented, we will continue to monitor its performance to ensure that it is performing the function for which it is intended. Ultimately, this evaluation should be guided by whether the current selection decision-making process has been improved by the addition of the test.

As you can see, a great deal of technical work is involved in developing a selection procedure. Shortcuts are seldom warranted; in fact, they are discouraged. This is a complicated process; it can take substantial resources to develop a successful test useful in operational situations. Do not approach the development of a new measure in a flippant way. The organizational ramifications, associated costs, and potential for legal action are three principal reasons why selection researchers use suitable, existing measures whenever possible rather than develop their own. Note, however, that just because a commercially available test is used, it does not mean that questions regarding issues such as reliability and validity do not have to be answered; they do. Use of existing measures does not shield a company from legal scrutiny.

INTERPRETING SCORES ON SELECTION MEASURES

Using Norms

If you took a test, had it scored, and then were told that you achieved a 68, how would you feel? Probably not very well. A moment after receiving your score, you probably would ask how this score compares to others. Your question illustrates one of the basic principles of interpreting the results of selection procedures. That is, to interpret the results of measurement intelligently, we need two pieces of information: (a) how others scored on the selection procedure and (b) validity of the selection procedure.[19]

Let's return to your test score of 68 for a moment. Suppose you were told that the top score was 73. You might suddenly feel a lot better than you did a few moments ago. Next, however, you are told that everyone else who took the test scored 73. Now how do you feel? Without relevant information on how others scored, an individual score is practically meaningless. To attach meaning to a score, we must compare it to the scores of others who are similar with regard to characteristics, such as level of education, type of job applied for, amount of work experience, and so on. Thus, a score may take on different meanings depending on how it stands relative to the scores of others in particular groups. Our interpretation will depend on the score's relative standing in these other groups.

Scores of relevant others in groups are called *norms*. Norms show how well an individual performs with respect to a specified comparison group. For example, standardized norms reported in test manuals rank-order examinees from high to low on the test characteristic assessed. The purpose is to determine how much of the measured characteristic a person has in relation to others for whom the same test information is available. This group of persons, for whom test score information is available and used for comparison purposes, is referred to as a *normative sample* or *standardization group*. The *Wonderlic Personnel Test*, for example, reports norms based on groups defined by the following variables: age of applicant, educational attainment, gender, position applied for, type of industry, and geographic region.

Normative data are useful in understanding and evaluating scores on selection procedures. Keep several points in mind when using norms to interpret scores. First, the norm group selected should be *relevant* for the purpose it is being used. Norms are meaningless or even misleading if they are not based on a group that is relevant (comparable) to those individuals being considered for employment. For example, suppose individuals applying for the job of an experienced electrician took the *Purdue Test for Electricians*. Assume that normative sample data are available for recent trade school graduates who had taken the test as well as for the employer's experienced electricians. If the company is trying to hire experienced electricians, the relevant norm group would be the experienced electricians rather than the norm group representing recent trade school graduates. Clearly, the former is more relevant to company needs for experienced personnel. If the norm group consisting of inexperienced personnel had been used, misleading results—perhaps some with serious consequences—could have occurred. Many different norm groups are reported in selection manuals. Exercise care to ensure the appropriate group is chosen when interpreting scores on measures.

Second, rather than using norms based on national data, an employer should accumulate and use *local* norms when appropriate. A local norm is one based on selection procedures administered to individuals applying for employment with a particular employer. Initially, when a test is implemented, appropriate norms published in a test manual may be used, but local norms can be developed as soon as 100 or more scores in a particular group have been accumulated. Rather than immediately destroying selection procedure scores of those rejected for employment, applicants' scores are useful for preparing local norms. Cutoff or passing scores then can be established on the basis of these local data rather than just taken from published manuals.[20]

A third point to consider is that norms are *transitory*. That is, they are specific to the point in time when they were collected. Norms can change over time. If the assessed applicant attribute is not likely to change, then older norms will continue to be more or less relevant. However, the more likely the attribute will change over time, the more current normative data should be. For example, individuals tend to score higher on general mental ability tests than test takers of 10 to 20 years ago.[21] Therefore, individuals' mental ability test scores would appear higher using older norms than if current norms were used.

There is no prescribed time period for publishers of selection measures to collect new normative data. Some collect such information every four or five years; others collect normative data every 10 years. Interpret norms that appear dated cautiously. Where feasible, normative data should be collected continuously by the user of selection measures; the time frame over which the normative results were established should be stated in a technical manual.

Norms are not always necessary in HR selection. For example, if five of the best performers on a test must be hired, or if persons with scores of 70 or better on the test are known to make suitable employees, then a norm is not necessary in employment decision making. One can simply use the individuals' test scores. On the other hand, if one finds applicants' median selection test scores are significantly below that of a norm group, then the firm's recruitment practices should be examined. The practices may not be attracting the best job applicants; normative data would help in analyzing this situation.

In using normative information, we rely on statistical methods to aid our interpretation of what a test score means. The two basic methods we use frequently for expressing and interpreting test scores with respect to norms are *percentiles* and *standard scores*.

Employers using norms in selection decision-making should avoid considering norms based on protected-group characteristics, such as race and gender. Before the 1991 Civil Rights Act, some federal agencies and private employers engaged in a practice called *race norming* when reviewing job applicants' test scores.[22] Race norming is the practice of adjusting scores on a selection test to account for job applicants' race or ethnicity. For instance, under race norming, Black, white, and Hispanic applicants who take a test are graded only against members of their same ethnic group. Percentile scores are then computed separately for each of these groups. It is possible, however, that minority candidates may obtain higher percentile scores than majority candidates who actually outperformed them based on raw test scores. The 1991 Civil Rights Act made this practice illegal. Employers making selection decisions would be wise not only to avoid using percentile test score norms based on race or ethnicity but also to avoid norms based on any group characteristic protected by law, for example, gender, age, or disability.

Although normative data are helpful in interpreting scores on selection measures, what we really want to know is how well a selection procedure predicts future work performance. Norms alone do not tell us what an applicant's score means in terms of on-the-job performance.

Using Percentiles

The statistic most frequently used in reporting normative data is the percentile. Because the purpose of a norm is to show relative standing in a group, percentile scores are derived to show *the percentage of persons in a norm group who fall below a given score on a measure*. If an individual makes a 75 on a test and this score corresponds to the 50th percentile, that individual will have scored better than 50 percent of the people in a particular group who took the test. A percentile score is not a percentage score. A percentage score is like a *raw* or *obtained* score. For instance, if 1 person out of 200 people taking a 100-item test correctly answered 50 questions, that person's score would be 50, or 50 percent correct. But, is this score high or low? By using percentiles, we can compare that score with the other 199 test takers' scores to make that determination. Thus, 50 percent correct may correspond to a percentile score ranging from 0 to 100, depending on how the 199 others performed on the test.

In general, the higher the percentile score, the better a person's performance relative to others in the normative sample. Scores above the 50th percentile indicate above-average performance; scores below this percentile represent below-average performance. Figure 6.8 illustrates how normative percentile data are reported in test manuals.

Percentile scores are useful in interpreting test scores; however, they are subject to misuse. Charles Lawshe and Michael Balma have pointed out the tendency for some users to interpret these percentile scores as if they were on a ratio scale.[23] For instance, if Susan Dustin, an applicant for a job, scores 5 percentile points higher on a selection test than Jack Fiorito, another job applicant, some may want to conclude that Susan is 5 percent better than Jack for the job. Percentile scores should not be used in this way—for at least two reasons.

FIGURE 6.8	Illustration of How Percentile Norms Are Reported in Test Manuals	
Test Raw Score	**z Score**	**Percentile**
50	3.0	99.9
45	2.0	97.7
40	1.0	84.1
35	0.0	50.0
30	−1.0	15.9
25	−2.0	2.3
20	−3.0	0.1

First, a difference of 5 percentile points may not indicate a real difference in people; the difference may be nothing but chance, resulting from unreliability of the test. (In the next chapter, you will see how the standard error of measurement can be used to make such a determination.) Second, percentile scores are on an *ordinal* scale of measurement, not a ratio scale. Recall from our earlier discussion, we can make greater-than or less-than statements in comparing scores, but we cannot say how much higher or how much lower one percentile score is from another. For instance, a percentile score of 60 is not twice as good as a percentile score of 30.

For a number of reasons, test scores frequently are expressed as *standard* scores. One example of standard scores is a *z* score, which represents the difference between an individual score and the mean, in units of the standard deviation (shown in Figure 6.8).

Given the cautions noted, norms can play an important role in evaluating an organization's recruitment practices. For example, if a company's norms consistently show most job applicants' scores falling, say, at the 35th percentile, then that company would seriously want to evaluate, among other organizational functions, its recruitment practices. Does the company need to change the media being used, recruitment appeals being made, recruiters' activities, where they recruit, or other recruitment strategies? Or, perhaps, the reputation of the firm may connote a negative image because of the company's pay and benefits offered or, perhaps, the opportunities available for growth at the firm. These are only several reasons as to why the company might not be attracting desired job applicants. Percentile norms can serve as a first alert to the quality of personnel that an organization is (or is not) attracting.

Using Standard Scores

Many different types of standard scores are reported in manuals accompanying commercially available tests used in selection. Some of the more common are *z*, *T*, and *stanine* scores. We will not go into all of the statistical details of these standard scores, but we want to comment about their role with regard to interpreting scores on selection measures.

In general, standard scores represent adjustments to raw scores, so it is possible to determine the proportion of individuals who fall at various standard score levels. These scales indicate, in common measurement units, how far above or below the mean score any raw score is. By *common measurement unit*, we mean these scores are on a scale that shows score differences having equal intervals; they can be added, subtracted, multiplied, and divided. Let's look at a few types of standard scores.

One of the most common standard scores is the z score. The formula is

$$z = \frac{(X - M)}{SD}$$

where

z = the standard score

X = an individual's raw or obtained score

M = the mean of the normative group's raw scores

SD = the standard deviation of the normative group's raw scores

Using this formula, z scores can be obtained for all individuals for whom test score data are available. The computations result in scores that range from −4.0 to +4.0; they can be directly interpreted regarding their distance from the normative group mean in standard deviation units. For example, a person with a z score of 1.0 is 1 standard deviation above the group mean; a person with a z score of −1.5 is 1½ standard deviations below the group mean.

To avoid negative numbers, T scores are often used. These scores are similar to z scores, but they are adjusted so that all T scores are positive. One common form of T scores has a mean of 50 and a standard deviation of 10. To compute such a T score, we simply compute the z score and then use the following formula: $T = 10z \pm 50$. For example, a person's z score of 1.0 is equivalent to a T score of 60.

Stanine scores are another form of standard score. In this case, a single number ranging from 1 to 9 is used to represent individuals' normative score performance. Stanines are computed by rank-ordering scores from lowest to highest. The 4 percent with the lowest scores get a stanine score of 1, the next 7 percent get a stanine of 2, and so on. The higher the stanine score, the better the performance on a selection procedure.

There is an interrelationship among percentiles and the other standard scores we have mentioned. Figure 6.9 depicts the relationships among these scores. The figure shows a normal distribution of scores made on a test. Under the normal curve are various standard scores expressed as percentiles, z scores, T scores, and stanines. As you can see, the mean score of this distribution corresponds to the 50th percentile, a z score of 0, a T score of 50, and a stanine of 5. An individual who scores 1 standard deviation above the mean would have a percentile score of 84, a z score of 1, and so forth. Many other comparisons are also possible using the concepts shown in Figure 6.9.

The biggest problem with the use of standard scores is that they are subject to misinterpretation. For this reason, percentiles are the most common score presented by test publishers. Although percentile scores show an individual test taker's relative position compared to a reference group, percentiles do not tell us what a score means in terms of success on the job.

We believe it important to reiterate what we said earlier in the chapter, that the quality of information used when making selection decisions is fundamental to an effective selection system. Rigorous measurement of our selection procedures and criteria, particularly regarding the role of precision in the level of measurement (for example, use of interval scales), has a substantial impact on the quality of our measures. However, to identify good measures and weed out the bad ones, we must consider other standard measurement criteria (that is, validity and reliability). Employers sometimes assume that a relationship exists between selection procedures and work performance criteria, but without reliability and validity evidence, we do not know whether this assumption is warranted. In the next two chapters, we review methods for determining the reliability and validity of selection procedures.

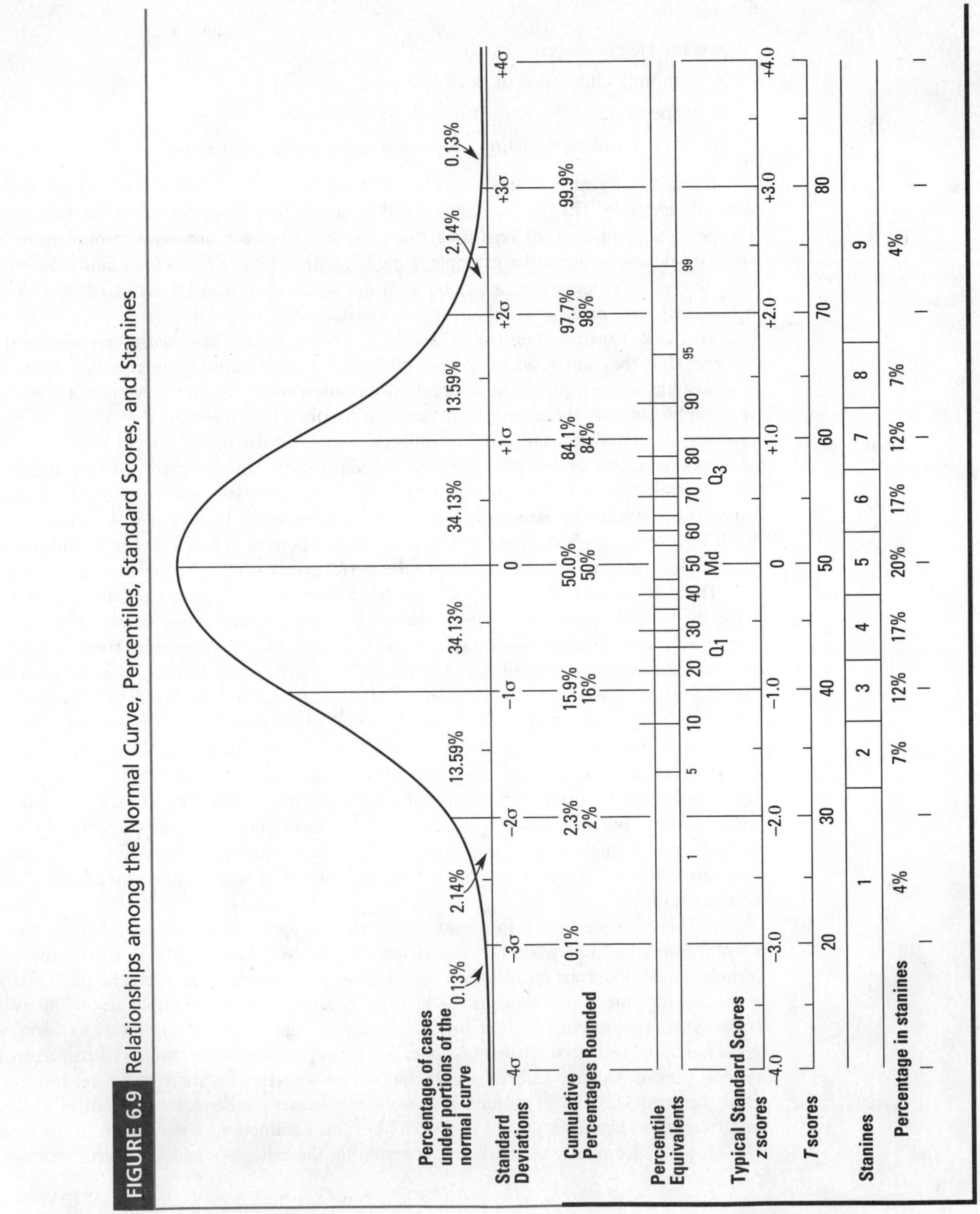

FIGURE 6.9   Relationships among the Normal Curve, Percentiles, Standard Scores, and Stanines

Percentage of cases under portions of the normal curve

| 0.13% | 2.14% | 13.59% | 34.13% | 34.13% | 13.59% | 2.14% | 0.13% |

Standard Deviations: −4σ   −3σ   −2σ   −1σ   0   +1σ   +2σ   +3σ   +4σ

Cumulative Percentages Rounded:
0.1%   2.3%   15.9%   50.0%   84.1%   97.7%   99.9%
         2%   16%   50%   84%   98%

Percentile Equivalents: 1   5   10   20 30 40 50 60 70 80   90   95   99
                                         Q₁   Md   Q₃

Typical Standard Scores
z scores: −4.0   −3.0   −2.0   −1.0   0   +1.0   +2.0   +3.0   +4.0

T scores: 20   30   40   50   60   70   80

Stanines: 1   2   3   4   5   6   7   8   9

Percentage in stanines: 4%   7%   12%   17%   20%   17%   12%   7%   4%

REFERENCES

1. Susana Urbina, *Essentials of Psychological Testing* (Hoboken, NJ: John Wiley, 2004), 64–116.

2. Elazur J. Pedhazur and Liora Pedhazur Schmelkin, *Measurement, Design, and Analysis: An Integrated Approach* (London: Lawrence Erlbaum Associates, 1991), 15–29.

3. Lewis R. Aiken, *Tests and Examinations* (New York: John Wiley, 1998), 30–52.

4. Ernest O'Boyle and Herman Aguinis, "The Best and the Rest: Revisiting the Norm of Normality of Individual Performance," *Personnel Psychology* 65 (2012): 79–119.

5. The *mean* is the average score of a group of scores on a variable such as a test. The *standard deviation* is a number that represents the spread of scores for a group of scores around the group's average score on a variable. As the standard deviation increases, the spread or differences among scores becomes larger. *Correlations* show the degree of relationship between variables. Chapter 6 gives a more thorough description of correlational procedures used in selection research.

6. Pedhazur and Schmelkin, *Measurement, Design, and Analysis: An Integrated Approach*; Hart Blanton and James Jaccard, "Arbitrary Metrics in Psychology," *American Psychologist* 61 (2006): 27–41; Susan E. Embretson, "The Continued Search for Nonarbitrary Metrics in Psychology," *American Psychologist* 61 (2006): 50–55; and Anthony G. Greenwald, Brian A. Nosek, and N. Sriram, "Consequential Validity of the Implicit Personality Test: Comment on Blanton and Jaccard (2006)," *American Psychologist* 61 (2006): 56–61.

7. Wayne F. Cascio and Herman Aquinis, *Applied Psychology in Human Resource Management*, 6th ed. (Upper Saddle River, NJ: Pearson Prentice Hall, 2005), 122–134; and Society for Industrial and Organizational Psychology, Inc., *Principles for the Validation and Use of Personnel Selection Procedures*, 4th ed. (Bowling Green, OH: Society of Industrial-Organizational Psychology, 2003), 8–18.

8. Murray R. Barrick and Michael K. Mount, "Select on Conscientiousness and Emotional Stability," in *Handbook of Principles of Organizational Behavior*, ed. E. A. Locke (Oxford: Blackwell Publishers, 2000), 15–28.

9. Robert M. Guion, *Assessment, Measurement, and Prediction for Personnel Decisions* (London: Lawrence Erlbaum Associates, 1998), 211–295; and *Principles for the Validation and Use of Personnel Selection Procedures*, 5–8.

10. Urbina, *Essentials of Psychological Testing*.

11. James C. Impara and Barbara S. Plake, *Thirteenth Mental Measurements Yearbook* (Lincoln: Buros Institute of Mental Measurements, University of Nebraska Press, 1998).

12. American Psychological Association, *Standards for Educational and Psychological Testing* (Washington, DC: American Psychological Association, 1999).

13. *Principles for the Validation and Use of Personnel Selection Procedures*, 42–43.

14. In several places throughout the book, we suggest that it may be necessary to hire a consultant to perform certain tasks or to accomplish specific selection objectives. Ideally, these tasks and objectives could be accomplished *within* the organization. However, access to needed organizational resources is not always possible. External consultants may be required. When should outside advice be sought? Ask yourself the following question: *Does the organization have the expertise, time, and other resources to adequately solve the selection problem?* If the answer is no, then a consultant is necessary.

Assuming a selection consultant is needed, we might ask, What qualities should we look for? *At a minimum*, a selection consultant should (a) hold a doctorate in industrial-organizational psychology or human resources management with training in psychological measurement, statistics, and selection-related content areas such as job analysis, test construction, and performance evaluation; (b) have experience conducting selection, test validation, and job analysis research projects in other organizations; and (c) provide references from client organizations for whom selection research projects have been completed. In addition to these criteria, a selection consultant likely will have published books or selection-oriented articles in the industrial–organizational or human resources management literature. Find additional resources for choosing a selection consultant on the SIOP Web page under the consultant locator link (http://www.siop.org/conloc/default.aspx).

15. Paul R. Sackett and Roxanne M. Laczo, "Job and Work Analysis," in *Handbook of Psychology: Industrial and Organizational Psychology*, vol. 12, ed. Walter C. Borman, Daniel R. Ilgen, and Richard Klimoski (Hoboken, NJ: John Wiley, 2003), 21–37.

16. Urbina, *Essentials of Psychological Testing*; Thomas M. Haladyna, *Developing and Validating Multiple-Choice Test Items*, 3rd ed. (Mahwah, NJ: Lawrence Erlbaum Associates, 2005), 82–111; and Arlene Fink, *How to Ask Survey Questions*, 2nd ed. (Thousand Oaks, CA: Sage Publications, 2002), 39–63.

17. Robert L. Thorndike, *Personnel Selection* (New York: John Wiley, 1949), 50.

18. Robert M. Guion, *Assessment, Measurement, and Prediction for Personnel Decisions* (London: Lawrence Erlbaum Associates, 1998), 211–295.

19. Cascio and Aquinis, *Applied Psychology in Human Resource Management*; and Guion, *Assessment, Measurement, and Prediction for Personnel Decisions*, 125–137.

20. Harold G. Seashore and James H. Ricks, *Norms Must Be Relevant* (Test Service Bulletin No. 3C) (New York: The Psychological Corporation, May 1950), 19.

21. William T. Dickens and James R. Flynn, "Heritability Estimates versus Large Environmental Effects: The IQ Paradox Resolved," *Psychological Bulletin* 108 (2001): 346–369.

22. "States Forbidden to Use Race-Norming in Job Test," *Atlanta Constitution*, December 14, 1991, A-8; and "Job Tests for Minorities Thrown a Curve," *Atlanta Constitution*, May 6, 1991, A-2.

23. Charles H. Lawshe and Michael J. Balma, *Principles of Personnel Testing* (New York: McGraw-Hill, 1966), 75.

Reliability of Selection Measures

WHAT IS RELIABILITY?

The use of physiological tests by physicians is a common practice in the United States; the most commonly performed test measures blood pressure. Elevated blood pressure is associated with a number of problems, including an increased risk of developing heart disease, kidney disease, hardening of the arteries, eye damage, and stroke.[1] Because hypertension affects one in four adults in the United States, Americans are routinely encouraged to have their blood pressure tested. Measuring blood pressure accurately, however, has proven difficult.[2] More importantly for our purposes, consideration of the difficulties of measuring blood pressure illustrates the importance of reliability.

Why is it so hard to reliably measure blood pressure? One reason is that patients often experience elevated blood pressure simply due to being subjected to the test in the doctor's office. This problem is so common it has been labeled "white coat" hypertension. It has been estimated that as many as 20 percent of diagnosed hypertensive patients (some estimates range up to 73 percent) have "white coat" hypertension— hypertension caused by anxiety about having their blood pressure checked.[3] Furthermore, blood pressure varies over the course of the day. A single blood pressure measurement is estimated to result in overdiagnosis of hypertension in 20–30 percent of cases, yet it misses one-third of those who truly have the disease.[4] Accurate blood pressure measurement also depends on correct handling by medical personnel. Noise or talking while assessing blood pressure can result in errors, as can using the wrong-sized cuff or releasing pressure too quickly during a manual assessment. In addition, inadequate equipment maintenance and calibration can result in inaccuracy. A recent study suggested that only 5 percent of these devices were properly maintained in one major teaching hospital, while another showed unacceptable measurement inaccuracy in up to 60 percent of devices evaluated.[5] The point is, there are a number of reasons why blood pressure tests are unreliable and can produce inaccurate and misleading information.

These data show that a test many view as essential produced results that, in many cases, were not dependable or reliable. Because of the unreliability of test results, people who underwent faulty blood pressure tests could have faced serious consequences. That is, persons who falsely tested normal could have forgone needed dietary and lifestyle changes or the use of blood pressure–reducing drugs prescribed by their physicians. Those testing falsely high could have suffered unnecessary anxiety and unpleasant side effects from prescribed drugs that were not needed, as well as the expense of unnecessary drug therapy.

The measures we use in HR selection do not have the same physiological implications as do tests used in medicine. However, as in our blood pressure testing example, we have similar concerns regarding the dependability of measures commonly used in selection decision making. That is, we want to be sure we have measures that will produce dependable, consistent, and accurate results when we use them. If we will be using data to make predictions concerning the selection of people, we must be sure that these decisions are based on data that are reliable and accurate. We do not want to use measures where the score obtained on one occasion differs from another due to some chance fluctuation rather than from some true difference in the underlying construct. Obviously, we need accurate data to identify the best people available. We also need accurate information for moral and legal reasons as well. Let's look at another example involving the dependability of information, but in this case, in the context of selection.

Robert Newmann, HR manager at Info Sources, Inc., had just finished scoring a computer programming aptitude test that was administered to 10 individuals applying for a job as a computer programmer. Because it was almost 5 p.m. and he had errands to run, he decided to carry the tests home and review them that night. While on his way home, Robert stopped by a store to pick up office supplies. Without thinking, he inadvertently left his briefcase containing the 10 tests on the front seat of his car. When he returned, the briefcase was missing. After filing a report with the police, Robert went home, wondering what he should do. The next day, Robert decided that all he could do was to locate the applicants and have them return for retesting. After a day of calling and explaining about the lost test scores, he arranged for the 10 applicants to come in and retake the programming aptitude test. But wouldn't you know it; the day after readministering the tests, Robert received a visit from the police. His briefcase was returned with contents intact. Robert removed the 10 original tests and set them beside the stack of 10 tests just taken. He muttered to himself, "What a waste of time." Out of curiosity, Robert scored the new exams, wondering how the applicants had done on the retest. He carefully recorded the two sets of scores. His recorded results are shown in Figure 7.1.

After reviewing the data, Robert thought, "What a confusing set of results!" The original test scores were dramatically different from the retest scores. Robert pondered the results for a moment. He had expected the applicants' test scores to be the same from one testing to the next. They were not. Each of the 10 applicants had different

FIGURE 7.1	Summary of Original Test and Retest Results for 10 Applicants Taking the Programming Aptitude Test	
Applicant	**First Test**	**Second Test**
T. R. Mitchell	35	47
G. L. Stewart	57	69
J. W. Johnson	39	49
H. M. Weiss	68	50
D. V. Day	74	69
M. Kilduff	68	65
J. Kevin Ford	54	38
A. M. Ryan	71	78
F. L. Oswald	41	54
L. M. Hough	44	59

scores for the two tests. "Now why did that happen? Which of the two sets of scores represents the applicants' actual programming aptitudes?" he asked himself.

The situation we've just described is similar to that represented by our blood pressure testing illustration. Robert, too, needs dependable, consistent data for selection decision making. Yet from our selection example we can see that his test scores are different for no apparent reason. Thus it appears he does not have the consistent, dependable data he needs. These characteristics of data we have mentioned—that is, consistency, dependability, and stability—all refer to the concept of reliability.

A Definition of Reliability

Reliability of scores from selection measures is a characteristic necessary for effective HR selection. In our earlier example, the computer programming aptitude test was apparently an unreliable measure; it is this unreliability in test scores that makes it difficult for Robert to know each applicant's actual level of programming aptitude.

The term *reliability* has a host of definitions. In our discussion, we will touch on several of these. But for now we want to consider a fundamental definition of the concept. In the context of HR selection, *reliability* simply means the degree of dependability, consistency, or stability of scores on a measure used in selection research (either predictors or criteria). In general, reliability of a measure is determined by the degree of consistency between two sets of scores on the same measure. In our earlier selection example, we would have expected the programming aptitude test to yield similar results from one testing period to the next if the test produced reliable data. Because the results were not similar, we would probably conclude that the test contained errors of measurement. Thus, attempts to establish the reliability of a "score" produced by a measurement procedure involves the careful study of the sources of error during measurement that cause variance in or inconsistency of scores over replications of that assessment. Reliability is trying to account for the expected degree of consistency in scores or "errors of measurement."

Errors of Measurement

It is important to keep in mind that reliability deals with errors of measurement. In this sense, a measure that is perfectly reliable is free of errors. None of our selection measures, whether predictor or criterion, will be free of measurement errors (although such errors tend to be less frequent with measures of physical attributes relative to measures of unobservable psychological characteristics). Selection measures designed to assess important job-related characteristics (such as knowledge, skills, and personality traits) may be prone to error due to the sample of items used, the test taker, the examiner, and the situation in which testing takes place. In general, the greater the amount of measurement error, the lower the reliability of a selection measure; the less error, the higher the reliability. Thus if errors of measurement can be assessed, a measure's reliability can be determined. What, then, are "errors of measurement"?

When we use selection devices such as tests, we obtain numerical scores on the measures. These scores serve as a basis for selection decision making. Because we are using scores as a basis for our decisions, we want to know the "true" scores of applicants for each characteristic being measured. For example, if we administer a mathematics ability test, we want to know the "true" math ability of each test taker. But unless our measure is perfectly reliable, we will encounter difficulties in knowing these true scores. In fact, we may get mathematics ability scores that are quite different from the individuals' true abilities. Let's see why.

The score obtained on a measure—that is, the *obtained* score—consists of two parts: a *true* component and an *error* component. The components of any obtained score (*X*) can be summarized by the following equation:

$$X_{\text{obtained}} = X_{\text{true}} + X_{\text{error}}$$

where

X_{obtained} = obtained score for a person on a measure

$\quad X_{\text{true}}$ = true score for a person on the measure; that is, the actual amount of the attribute measured that a person really possesses

$\quad X_{\text{error}}$ = error score for a person on the measure; that is, the amount that a person's score was influenced by factors present at the time of measurement that are unrelated to the attribute measured. These errors are assumed to represent random fluctuations or chance factors.

This notion of a score being composed of true and error parts is a basic axiom of measurement theory.[6]

True Score

The true score is really an ideal conception. It is the score individuals would obtain if external and internal conditions to a measure were perfect. For example, in our mathematics ability test, an ideal or true score would be one for which both of the following conditions existed:

1. Individuals answered correctly the same percentage of problems on the test that they would have if all possible problems had been given and the test were a construct valid measure of the underlying phenomenon of interest (see next chapter).

2. Individuals answered correctly the problems they actually knew without being affected by external factors such as lighting or temperature of the room in which the testing took place, their emotional state, or their physical health.

Another way of thinking about a true score is to imagine that an individual takes a test measuring a specific ability many different times. With each testing, his or her scores will differ somewhat; after a large number of testings, the scores will take the form of a normal distribution. The differences in scores are treated as if they are due to errors of measurement. The average of all test scores best approximates the test taker's true ability. Therefore, we might think of a true score as the mean or average score made by an individual on many different administrations of a measure.

This idealized situation does not exist. The notion of a true score, however, helps to define the idea that there is a specific score that would be obtained if measurement conditions were perfect. Because a true score can never be measured exactly, the obtained score is used to estimate the true score. Reliability answers this important question: How confident can we be that an individual's obtained score represents his or her true score?

Error Score

A second part of the obtained score is the error score. This score represents errors of measurement. Errors of measurement are those factors that affect obtained scores but are not related to the characteristic, trait, or attribute being measured.[7] These factors, present at the time of measurement, distort respondents' scores either over or under what they would have been on another measurement occasion. There are many reasons why individuals' scores differ from one measurement occasion to the next. Fatigue, anxiety, or noise during testing that distracts some text takers but not others are only a few of the factors that explain differences in individuals' scores over different measurement occasions.

Figure 7.2 shows the relationship between reliability and errors of measurement for three levels of reliability of a selection measure. Hypothetical obtained and true scores

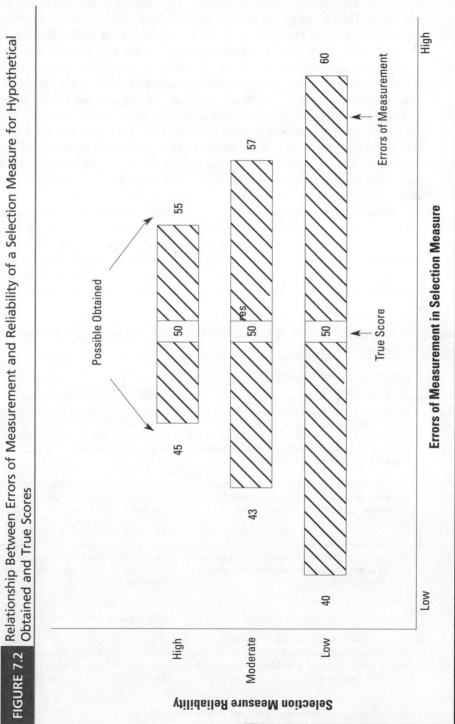

FIGURE 7.2   Relationship Between Errors of Measurement and Reliability of a Selection Measure for Hypothetical Obtained and True Scores

are given for each of the reliability levels. The shaded area of each bar shows errors of measurement. With decreasing errors of measurement, reliability of the measure increases. Notice that with increasing reliability, more precise estimates of an individual's true score on the measure can be made. Less random error is present. For example, suppose an individual's true score on the measure is 50. For a measure that has low reliability, a wide discrepancy is possible between the obtained scores (40 to 60) and the true score (50). That is, on one occasion a person might score as low as 40 and on another earn a score as high as 60. In contrast, in a measure with high reliability, the possible obtained scores (45 to 55) yield a closer estimate of the true score (50).

How much error exists in a score is an important attribute of the selection measure. If scores on a selection measure are due to chance or reflect an inconsistent or unpredictable error, we cannot have much confidence in the selection device. If we use a test that claims to measure general mental ability, but the reported reliability is so low that the test scores consist mostly of error, then our so-called "intelligence test" cannot possibly measure mental ability. With excessive error, a selection measure will not be useful. Only when there is relatively little error present can a measure be appropriate for selection. (The next chapter discusses other characteristics of a measure that make it effective.)

Where do these errors come from? Several different sources exist. The importance of any particular source will depend on factors such as the nature of the measure itself (for example, a paper-and-pencil measure, a behavior, the degree of standardization), what is being measured (an ability, a personality trait, an attitude), the test taker and test administrator, the situation in which the measure is being used, and the method of estimating reliability. Table 7.1 summarizes some of the more common sources of error that

---

TABLE 7.1   Examples of Sources of Errors of Measurement Contributing to Unreliability in Human Resource Selection Measures

Source of Error	Conditions Under Which an Error May Occur	Example of Error
Individual responding to a selection measure	Where an individual's physical and mental health, motivation, mood, level of stress, understanding of instructions, content of the items, and so on, affect how the individual responds to a selection measure	An applicant has an accident on the way to take a test. During the test, he is distracted by worries that his car insurance will not cover all of the expenses.
Individual administering a selection measure	Where the administrator of a selection measure affects the responses of the individual completing the measure	Two employment interviewers interview the same job applicants using the same interview questions. One interviewer frequently smiles and nods approvingly during the interview; the other does not.
Individual scoring a selection measure	Where judgment and subjectivity on the part of the scorer of a selection measure play a role in scoring	A supervisor does not attend a training session prior to using a new performance appraisal instrument. Thus when giving ratings, she completes the performance evaluation forms as soon as possible with no consistent or precise rules for evaluating each employee's actual job performance.
Physical conditions under which a selection measure is administered	Where heating, cooling, lighting, noise, and so on, affect how an individual responds to a selection measure	While taking a test, respondents are interrupted by a power failure that affects the cooling and lighting in the room.

Note: By use of the term *selection measure,* we mean both predictors and criteria.

contribute to the unreliability of selection measures.[8] As you examine the table, keep in mind that these errors can affect predictors (such as tests) as well as criteria (such as performance evaluations).

An important objective in developing and using selection measures is to reduce errors of measurement as much as possible. When these errors are reduced, individual differences in scores on selection measures will more likely be due to true differences rather than chance (or error) differences. The degree to which we are willing to trust differences among individuals' scores as being a real difference depends on the measure's reliability. Reliable measures that are useful in HR selection minimize the presence of these errors of measurement. Because errors are minimized, reliable measures give us more confidence in making decisions such as the suitability of one job applicant over another or the prediction of an applicant's future job performance. Selection decisions based on reliable measures are also fairer to the applicants involved.

Methods of Estimating Reliability

Reliability is generally determined by examining the relationship between two sets of measures measuring the same thing. Where the two sets of measures yield similar scores, reliability will be raised. If scores from the measures tend to be dissimilar, reliability will be lowered. Referring again to our earlier example involving Robert Newmann, HR manager of Info Sources, Inc., we saw that he had two sets of programming aptitude test scores. In Newmann's case, the two sets of test scores were different from each other, even though they were produced by the same programming aptitude test. The fact that the two sets of scores across occasions were different suggested that the stability of measurement of programming aptitude was low. Where scores are generally consistent for people across two sets of measures, reliability of a measure will be enhanced. For example, if a person's math ability score remains the same for two different administrations of a test, this fact will add to the reliability of the test. However, if factors such as fatigue or inconsistent administration procedures cause differential changes in people across sets of measures, the factors will contribute to unreliability. These factors are then considered sources of errors of measurement, because they are chance factors influencing responses to a measure.

Because reliability theory is only an idealized concept of what does or does not contribute to reliability, we cannot measure reliability per se. We can only estimate it. Thus we should not think of the reliability of a measure, but rather an estimate of reliability. We will see that alternative procedures can be used to provide different estimates of reliability. One of the principal ways in which these procedures differ is in how they treat the various factors (see Table 7.1) that may alter measurements of people. Some procedures will consider these factors to be error, whereas others will not. You might ask, "Which method should be used?" There is no one best method. The choice will depend on each specific situation for which a reliability estimate is desired.

Statistical procedures are commonly used to calculate what are called reliability coefficients. Oftentimes, techniques involving the Pearson product-moment correlation coefficient are utilized to derive reliability coefficients. We do not go into the statistical details of the correlation coefficient here (those are discussed in the next chapter), but we do describe briefly how the coefficient is obtained. The next section discusses the interpretation of the reliability coefficient.

A reliability coefficient is simply an index of relationship. It summarizes the relation between two sets of measures for which a reliability estimate is being made. The calculated index varies from 0.00 to 1.00. In calculating reliability estimates, the correlation coefficient obtained is regarded as a direct measure of the reliability estimate. The higher the coefficient, the less the measurement error and the higher the reliability estimate. Conversely, as the coefficient approaches 0.00, errors of measurement increase and reliability correspondingly decreases. Of course, we want to employ selection measures having high reliability coefficients. With high reliability, we can be more confident that a particular measure is giving a dependable picture of true scores for whatever attribute is being measured.

Many methods of estimating reliability exist. We discuss four principal methods most often employed in selection research studies: (a) test-retest, (b) parallel or equivalent forms, (c) internal consistency, and (d) interrater reliability estimates. As Milton Blum and James Naylor have pointed out, an important characteristic that differentiates among these procedures is what each method considers to be errors of measurement.[9] One method may treat a factor as error while another treats the same factor as meaningful information. The method chosen will be determined by what factors a researcher wants to treat as error and which of the following questions are to be addressed by reliability procedures.

1. How dependably can an individual be assessed with a measure at a given moment?

2. How dependably will data collected by a measure today be representative of the same individual at a future time?

3. How accurately will scores on a measure represent the true ability of an individual on the trait being sampled by a measure?

4. When individuals are being rated by more than one rater, to what degree do evaluations vary from one rater to another? Or, to what extent is an individual's score due to the rater rather than to the individual's behavior or other characteristics being rated?

As you examine these questions, you can see that each one considers reliability to be the degree of consistency between two or more measurements of the same thing.

Test-Retest Reliability Estimates

One obvious way to assess the reliability of scores obtained on a selection measure is to administer the measure twice and then correlate the two sets of scores using the Pearson product-moment correlation coefficient. This method is referred to as test-retest reliability. It is called test-retest reliability because the same measure is used to collect data from the same respondents at two different points in time. Because a correlation coefficient is calculated between the two sets of scores over time, the obtained reliability coefficient represents a coefficient of stability. The coefficient indicates the extent to which the test can be generalized from one time period to the next.

As an example of test-retest reliability estimation, suppose we wanted to determine the reliability of our mathematics ability test mentioned earlier. First, we administer the test to a representative group of individuals. After a period of time, say 8 weeks, we readminister and score the same test for the same individuals. To estimate test-retest reliability, we simply correlate the two sets of scores (test scores at Time 1 correlated with scores at Time 2) using the Pearson product-moment correlation.

Figure 7.3 illustrates the basic design for test-retest reliability determination. The figure also shows the effect on the reliability coefficient when the relative positions of individuals change from one testing to the next. (Of course, we would use many more than the five people listed in the figure for estimating reliability; we are showing their scores simply for illustration purposes.)

| FIGURE 7.3 | Illustration of the Design for Estimating Test-Retest Reliability |

	Test Scores Time 1 (t1)		Retest Scores Time 2 (t2)					
	Time 1	*Rank*	**Case A**		*Rank*	**Case B**		*Rank*
Job Applicant	**t1**	*t1*	**t2$_a$**	**t1 – t2$_a$**	*t2$_a$*	**t2$_b$**	**t1 – t2$_b$**	*t2$_b$*
J. R. Hollenbeck	96	1	90	–6	1	66	–30	2
M. A. Campion	87	2	89	2	2	52	–35	3
F. L. Morgeson	80	3	75	–5	3	51	–29	4
M. K. Burke	70	4	73	3	4	82	12	1
P. R. Sackett	56	5	66	10	5	50	–6	5

Note: Test-retest reliability for Time 1—Time 2 **(Case A) = 0.94**; test-retest reliability for Time 1—Time 2 **(Case B) = 0.07**.

Time 1 in the figure shows the five individuals' scores on the mathematics ability test for the initial administration of the test. At a later date, Time 2, the test is readministered to the same individuals. Figure 7.3 shows two possible outcomes (Case A and Case B) that could result from this retesting. (Only one retest is needed to compute reliability.) Case A presents one possible set of scores for the individuals. Notice two points in Case A. First, the scores have changed slightly from Time 1 to Time 2 testing. J. R. Hollenbeck's original test score of 96, for instance, fell to 90 upon retesting, a loss of 6 points. Some of the other applicants' scores also fell slightly, while others slightly increased. Second, the rank-ordering of the applicants' scores remained the same from one testing to the next. Hollenbeck's score (96) was the highest on the original test; and even though it fell upon retesting, his score (90) was still the best for the group. The others' rank-ordering of scores also remained the same across the two testings. Because of the relatively small changes in applicants' absolute test scores and no changes in the ranks of these scores over time, a high reliability coefficient would be expected. A test-retest reliability coefficient computed between the Time 1 scores and the Time 2 (Case A) scores is 0.94. This estimate confirms our expectation. It represents a high test-retest reliability coefficient with little error present. Reduced errors of measurement increase the generalizability of individuals' mathematics ability as measured by the initial testing.

Now look at Case B. When you compare this set of retest scores with those originally obtained at Time 1, you can see rather large differential rates of change among the individuals' scores. (Some individuals' scores changed more than others. Compare, for example, Campion's 35-point test score change with Sackett's 6-point change.) These differential rates of change have also altered the individuals' relative rank-orderings in the two sets of scores. Due to these differential test score and rank-order changes between Time 1 and Time 2 (Case B), the test-retest reliability is very low, only 0.07. This coefficient suggests a great deal of error in measurement. The obtained scores on the test represent very little of the mathematics ability of those taking the test.

The higher the test-retest reliability coefficient, the greater the true score and the less error present. If reliability were equal to 1.00, no error would exist in the scores; true scores would be perfectly represented by the obtained scores. A coefficient this high would imply that scores on the measure are not subject to changes in the respondents or the conditions of administration. If reliability were equal to 0.00, a test-retest reliability coefficient this low would suggest that obtained scores on the test are nothing more than error. Any factor that differentially affects individuals' responses during one measurement occasion and not on the other creates errors of measurement and lowers reliability. As we saw in Table 7.1, many sources of error change scores over time and, hence, lower test-retest reliability. Some of these errors will be associated with differences within individuals occurring from day to day (such as illness on one day of testing), whereas others will be associated with administration of a measure from one time to the next (such as distracting noises occurring during an administration). Further, two additional factors affect test-retest reliability: (a) memory and (b) learning.

Recall that earlier we said any factor that causes scores within a group to change differentially over time will decrease test-retest reliability. Similarly, any factor that causes scores to remain the same over time will increase the reliability estimate. If respondents on a selection measure remember their previous answers to an initial administration of a measure and then on retest respond according to memory, the reliability coefficient will increase. How much it increases will depend on how well they remember their previous answers.

The effect of memory, however, will be to make the reliability coefficient artificially high—an overestimate of the true reliability of scores obtained on the measure. Rather than reflecting stability of a measure's scores over time, a test-retest reliability coefficient may tend to reflect the consistency of respondents' memories. In general, when considering reliability we are not interested in measuring the stability of respondents' memories. Instead we are interested in evaluating the stability of scores produced by the measure. One way of lessening the impact of memory on test-retest reliability coefficients is to increase the time interval between the two administrations. As the length of time increases, respondents are less likely to recall their responses. Thus with increasing time intervals, test-retest reliability coefficients will generally decrease. How long a period should be used? There is no one best interval; from several weeks to several months is reasonable depending on the measure and the specific situation.

Although a lengthy interval between two administrations would appear to be a viable alternative for countering the effects of memory, too long a period opens up another source of error—learning. If respondents between the two time intervals of testing learn or change in such a way that their responses to a measure are different on the second administration than they were on the first, then test-retest reliability will be lowered. For instance, if respondents recall items asked on an initial administration of a test and then learn answers so their responses are different on the second administration, learning will have changed their scores. In another example, respondents may have been exposed to information (such as a training program) that causes them to alter their answers the second time a test is administered. Whatever the source, when individual differences in learning take place so that responses are differentially affected (that is, individuals learn at different rates), reliability will be lowered.

Notice that because of learning, our selection measure scores may appear to be unstable over time. Yet their unreliability is not really due to the errors of measurement we have been discussing. In fact, systematic but different rates of change among respondents through learning may account for what would appear to be unreliability but actually reflect changes in the true score. Nevertheless, the calculation of a test-retest reliability coefficient will treat such changes as error, thus contributing to unreliability. Therefore, with a long time interval between administrations of a measure, test-retest reliability may underestimate actual reliability because learning could have caused the actual score on the attribute to change.

In addition, the test-retest approach will not provide meaningful estimates of reliability if the trait or characteristic underlying the measure is unstable. For example, selection measures that involve attitudes or self-esteem or measures of self-concept are likely to be in a state of change. Here it may be inappropriate to use test-retest reliability because any changes found will be treated as error. Yet some of those changes reflect the instability of the trait itself (for example, the tendency of self-esteem to change over time). In contrast, reliability of measures involving characteristics that are relatively stable over time (such as mental ability) may be estimated with test-retest reliability.

Given some of the potential problems with test-retest reliability, when should it be used? There are no hard and fast rules, but some general guidelines can be offered. These guidelines include the following:

1. Test-retest reliability is appropriate when the length of time between the two administrations is long enough to offset the effects of memory or practice.[10]

2. When there is little reason to believe that memory will affect responses to a measure, test-retest reliability may be employed. Memory may have minimal effects in situations where (a) a large number of items appear on the measure, (b) the items are too complex to remember (for example, items involving detailed drawings, complex shapes, or detailed questions), and (c) retesting occurs after at least 8 weeks.[11]

3. When it can be confidently determined that nothing has occurred between the two testings that will affect responses (learning, for example), test-retest can be used.

4. When information is available on only a single item measure, test-retest reliability may be used.

If stability of measurement over time is of interest, test-retest reliability is a suitable method. If a measure has high test-retest reliability, we can conclude that the test is free of error associated with the passage of time. However, if the reliability coefficient is low, we will not know whether the low coefficient is because of low reliability or the lack of stability in the attribute being measured. If, on the other hand, our interest is in the dependability with which scores are provided by a measure at one point in time, then other reliability procedures (for example, internal consistency) are needed.

Parallel or Equivalent Forms Reliability Estimates

To control the effects of memory on test-retest reliability (which can produce an overestimate of reliability), one strategy is to avoid the reuse of a measure and to use equivalent versions of the measure instead. Each version of the measure has different items, but the questions assess the attribute being measured in just the same way. One form of the measure would be administered to respondents; the other form would be administered to the same respondents at a later time. Like our test-retest procedure, a Pearson correlation would be computed between the two sets of scores (Form A correlated with Form B scores) to develop a reliability estimate. Estimates computed in this manner are referred to as *parallel* or *equivalent forms* reliability estimates. The reliability coefficient itself is often called a coefficient of equivalence because it represents the consistency with which an attribute is measured from one version of a measure to another. As the coefficient approaches 1.00, the set of measures is viewed as equivalent or the same for the attribute measured. If equivalent forms are administered on different occasions, then this design also reflects the degree of temporal stability of the measure. In such cases, the reliability estimate is referred to as a *coefficient of equivalence and stability*. The use of equivalent forms administered over time accounts for the influence of random error to the test content (over equivalent forms) and transient error (across situations).

To achieve a parallel forms reliability estimate, at least two equal versions of a measure must exist. Looking again at the math ability test we referred to earlier, we can review the basic requirements of parallel forms of a measure. As shown in Figure 7.4, the

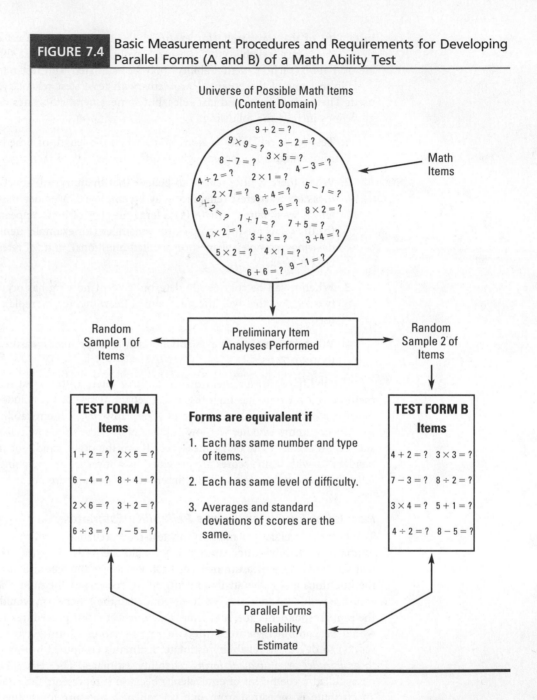

FIGURE 7.4 Basic Measurement Procedures and Requirements for Developing Parallel Forms (A and B) of a Math Ability Test

basic process of developing equivalent forms initially begins with the identification of a universe of possible math ability items. Items from this domain are administered to a large sample of individuals representative of those to whom the math ability test will be given. Individuals' responses are used to identify the difficulty of the items through item analyses and to ensure the items are measuring the same math ability construct (for example, the ability to add). Next, the items are rank-ordered according to their difficulty and randomly assigned in pairs to form two sets of items (Form A and Form B). If our defining and sampling of math ability item content has been correctly conducted, we should have two equivalent forms of our math ability test.

One form is administered after the other form has been given. The time interval between the two administrations can be brief (within a day or so) or long (for instance, 2 months). In this manner, we can obtain a reliability estimate rather quickly without being concerned about the effects of memory on responses.

In practice, equivalency of forms is not easy to achieve. Chance or the random effects of sample item selection can produce item differences in the forms. As a consequence, the forms will be different, thus curtailing reliability. For example, item differences on the two forms of our math ability test could result in one form being more difficult than the other. Form-to-form differences will cause changes in scores from one administration to the next, and reliability of test scores will be lowered. Because it is difficult to meet all of the criteria of equivalent forms, some writers use the term *alternate forms* to refer to forms that approximate but do not meet the criteria of parallel forms.[12]

For some selection measures (such as math, spelling, vocabulary, and others), it is possible to obtain reasonably equivalent forms. These and other ability measures are commercially available. They are often used to prevent individuals from improving their scores on a second testing simply due to memorization and to lessen the possibility that test content will be shared with others. The construction of equivalent forms that obtain the same true scores of a biographical data or personality inventory requires considerable effort, time, skills, and other resources.

Because genuine or true equivalent forms are nearly impossible to obtain, particularly when assessing noncognitive predictors, and because differences may exist from one administration occasion to another, reliability coefficients computed between parallel forms tend to be conservative estimates. Yet where equivalent forms can be obtained, this estimate of reliability is almost always preferable to test-retest reliability. This is particularly true when completion of the two forms is accomplished across time. If a high parallel forms reliability estimate is obtained over time, the coefficient suggests that individuals' scores on the measure would be as similar as if they had taken an equivalent test on a different occasion.

So far, we have discussed reliability in the context of two administrations of a measure. But what if we want to control the effects of memory on responses and do not have time to wait for memory to be diminished before administering a retest? Or what if an equivalent form of a selection measure does not exist? Or if the underlying trait is too unstable to measure over time (for example, day-to-day mood)? Or if it is not possible to get people to respond twice? Options are available to handle those situations where two administrations of the measures, either due to retests or equivalent forms, are not feasible.

Internal Consistency Reliability Estimates

One important characteristic of a reliable measure is that the various parts of the total measure are so interrelated that they can be interpreted as measuring the same thing. An index of a measure's similarity of content is an internal consistency reliability estimate. Basically, an internal consistency reliability estimate shows the extent to which all parts of a measure (such as items or questions) are similar in what they measure.[13] Thus a selection measure is internally consistent or homogeneous when individuals' responses on one part of the measure are related to their responses on other parts. For example, if we have five simple addition items on a test, individuals who can answer one of the items correctly (excluding guessing) can probably answer the remaining four also. Those who cannot answer one correctly will likely be unable to answer the others correctly. If this assumption is true, then our five-item test is internally consistent or homogeneous; individuals' performances on the test items are related. When a measure is created to assess a specific concept, such as mathematics ability, the items chosen to measure that concept represent only a portion of all possible items that could have been selected. If the sample of selected items truly assesses the same concept, then respondents should answer these items in the same way. What must be determined for the items chosen is whether respondents answer the sample of items similarly. Internal consistency reliability shows the extent to which the data are free from error due to the ways the items were phrased, interpreted by respondents, and so on.

To test the internal consistency hypothesis, we can examine the relationship between similar parts of a measure. The internal consistency hypothesis can be tested by simply correlating individuals' scores on these similar parts. A high estimate suggests that respondents' answers to one part are similar to their responses on other parts of the measure; hence, the measure is internally consistent. Like our other methods for estimating reliability, internal consistency reliability is applicable to many different types of selection measures, including predictors and criteria.

Internal consistency estimates tend to be among the most popular reliability procedures used. In general, the following three procedures are applied most often: (a) split-half reliability, (b) Kuder-Richardson reliability, and (c) Cronbach's coefficient alpha (α) reliability.

Split-Half Reliability Estimates. One of the internal consistency options is referred to as split-half or subdivided test reliability estimates. Split-half reliability involves a single administration of a selection measure. Then, for reliability calculation purposes, the measure is divided or split into two halves so that scores for each part can be obtained for each test taker. Because it is assumed that all items are measuring the same attribute, performance on one half of the test should be associated with performance on the other. To assess split-half reliability, the first problem we face is how to split the measure to obtain the most comparable halves. The most common method for creating these two halves of a measure is to score all even-numbered items as a "test" and all odd-numbered items as a "test." When split in this manner, the distribution of the items into the two test parts approximates a random assignment of items. Then, as in our previous estimates, the Pearson correlation is used to determine the extent of relation between the two test part scores. The resulting correlation coefficient is the reliability estimate.[14] A problem with split-half estimates is that there are many ways to split a measure into two halves; often, different "splits" do not yield the same reliability estimate. This probably explains why this procedure is not as common today. In fact, strictly speaking, a split-half reliability estimate is not a pure measure of internal consistency.[15] Like the parallel forms reliability coefficient, the obtained coefficient primarily represents a coefficient of equivalence. Thus the coefficient tends to show similarity of responses from one form to an equivalent one when administered at the same time.

Figure 7.5 illustrates how two parts of a measure may be developed and split-half reliability determined. However, this example is a bit different from some of our earlier illustrations. We employed predictors in previous examples, but in Figure 7.5 we are using a criterion measure. As we specified earlier in the chapter, reliability estimates are important for all variables being studied.

Let's assume that we wanted to know the reliability of an employee productivity measure that was serving as a criterion in a selection research study involving bicycle assemblers. Basically, the measure is the total number of bicycles assembled by each employee during a 28-day period. For purposes of brevity, Figure 7.5 shows the total number of bicycles assembled by employees during an abbreviated 28-day period.

Once we have complete data for our employees on each of the 28 days, we can subdivide our measure into two parts. The odd-numbered days (Days 1, 3, 5, ... , 25, 27) and

FIGURE 7.5	Representation of Odd-Even (Day) Split-Half Reliability Computed for a Job Performance Criterion Measure

Odd-Even Days	Empolyee Productivity (Bicycles Assembled)		
	P. Criss	R. Simms . . .	J. Veres
1	21	19	21
2	18	16	21
3	20	21 . . .	19
4	21	24	22
5	25	22	22
.	.	.	.
.	.	.	.
.	.	.	.
24	31	30	31
25	33	30	32
26	32	32 . . .	33
27	30	33	34
28	30	31	33
Total Bicycles	808	833 . . .	843

Part 1: **Odd** Days Productivity	
Employee	Total Bicycles
P. Criss	406
R. Simms	418
.	.
J. Veres	420

Part 2: **Even** Days Productivity	
Employee	Total Bicycles
P. Criss	402
R. Simms	415
.	.
J. Veres	423

Odd-Even Reliability Estimate

the associated production for each employee compose Part 1, and the even-numbered days (Days 2, 4, ... , 24, 26, 28) and their associated employee productivity data are assigned to Part 2, as is shown in Figure 7.5. We next obtain total scores or total productivity for each part by summing the respective daily production rates. Next, we compute a correlation between the employees' production rates (Part 1 correlated with Part 2) to obtain a reliability estimate of the employee productivity measure (total bicycles assembled). We could apply this same procedure to a predictor, such as a test, as well. Rather than using odd- and even-numbered days, we would use odd- and even-numbered items on the test. We would then apply identical procedures as outlined in Figure 7.5.

The obtained reliability coefficient developed on two halves of a measure is not a very precise estimate. In practice, we want to use the full measure, not half of it. What we want to know is the reliability of the whole measure.

Other things being equal, reliability increases with increasing length of a measure. Our split-half reliability estimate, however, is based on a correlation between scores on only half of the measure; it underestimates actual reliability. The length of the measure was reduced when we split it into two halves, odd-numbered and even-numbered parts. Therefore, a correction is needed to determine the reliability of the full or complete measure. A special formula, the Spearman-Brown prophecy formula, is used to make the correction.[16] Essentially, the formula shows what the reliability estimate would have been if the correlation had been based on the full rather than the part measures.

The Spearman-Brown formula used to correct a split-half reliability coefficient is as follows:

$$r_{ttc} = \frac{nr_{12}}{1 + (n-1)r_{12}}$$

where

r_{ttc} = the corrected split-half reliability coefficient for the total selection measure

n = number of times the test is increased in length

r_{12} = the correlation between Parts 1 and 2 of the selection measure.

For instance, let's examine the corrected split-half reliability of the criterion measure of bicycle assembler productivity. Part 1 of the productivity measure consisted of total bicycles assembled on all odd days of the month; Part 2 consisted of total bicycles assembled on all even days. Assume that the correlation between Parts 1 and 2 was 0.80. This correlation is the reliability coefficient for half the criterion measure (bicycles assembled). By applying the Spearman-Brown formula, the corrected reliability for the total criterion measure (bicycles assembled) is as follows:

$$r_{ttc} = \frac{2(0.80)}{1 + (2-1)0.80} = 0.89$$

With the corrected reliability estimate of 0.89, we have a more precise estimate of the reliability of the total criterion measure.

Because it is computed from a one-time-only administration of a measure, split-half reliability does not detect any of the errors of measurement that can occur over time (such as changes in individual respondents or changes in administration of a measure). Therefore, this procedure tends to result in a liberal or inflated estimate of reliability.

This method of reliability estimation is not appropriate for any measure that has a time limit associated with its completion. In many cases, for example, timed tests have rather easy questions; scores are a function of how many items are completed. If questions are very simple, then individuals are likely to correctly answer nearly all items that are attempted. As a result, individuals are likely to differ only in the number of questions they complete. Odd and even scores will be similar up until the point that time has expired, because most items will be answered correctly. Beyond that point, responses will also be similar because they were not answered. Consequently, a split-half reliability estimate computed on a test with a time limit will be spuriously high and meaningless.

Kuder-Richardson Reliability Estimates. Many methods other than an odd-even split are used to divide a measure to compute a split-half reliability estimate. Because the Kuder-Richardson reliability procedure takes the average of the reliability coefficients that would result from all possible ways of subdividing a measure, it helps solve the problem of how best to divide a measure for calculating reliability. (Kuder-Richardson formulas come in several different types. The most popular and the one on which this discussion is based is called K-R 20; it is the 20th formula in a series of reliability formulas discussed by George Kuder and Marion Richardson.[17]) It, too, involves the single administration of a measure. The procedure is used to determine the consistency of respondents' answers to any measure that has items scored in only two (dichotomous) categories, for example, questions on a verbal achievement test that are scored as either "right" ($= 1$) or "wrong" ($= 0$). Whereas the split-half method examines consistency of response between parts or halves of a measure, the Kuder-Richardson method assesses inter-item consistency of responses. The resulting coefficient estimates the average of the reliability coefficients that would result from all possible ways of subdividing a test.[18] Because it represents an average of all possible splits, Kuder-Richardson reliability estimates are usually lower than those obtained from split-half estimates.

In order to compute K-R 20, several pieces of information are needed on the test results for a group of individuals. As long as we can determine (a) how the group performed on each item of the test, as well as (b) each individual's total test score, the coefficient can be computed. Data such as those shown in Figure 7.6 are needed to compute K-R 20. The formula for computing K-R 20 is as follows:

$$r_{\text{tt}} = \frac{k}{k-1}\left(\frac{\Sigma p_i(1-p_i)}{\sigma_{y^2}}\right)$$

where

k = number of items on the test

p_i = proportion of examinees getting each item (i) correct

$1 - p_i$ = proportion of examiners getting each item (i) incorrect

σ_{y^2} = variance of examiners' total test scores.

FIGURE 7.6 An Example of Data Used in Computing K-R 20 Reliability Coefficient

Applicant Name	Test Items								Test Score
	1	**2**	**3**	**4**	**5**	**6**	**7**	**8**	
Neil Anderson	1	1	1	1	1	1	1	1	8
Tammy Allen	0	0	0	1	1	1	0	1	4
Gilad Chen	1	0	1	1	1	0	1	1	6
Richard DeShon	0	0	0	0	0	0	1	1	2
Sharon Parker	1	0	1	1	0	0	0	0	3
Robert Ployhart	1	0	0	1	1	1	1	0	5
Number Correctly Answering Item	4	1	3	5	4	3	4	4	

Note: 0 = incorrect response; 1 = correct response.

Cronbach's Coefficient Alpha (A) Reliability Estimates.   K-R 20 is a suitable approach for estimating internal consistency reliability when the items on a measure are scored with only two categories (for example, 0 = incorrect response; 1 = correct response). However, items or questions are often scored on a continuum or range of response options representing an interval scale. For example, suppose you have an employee performance appraisal rating form with five "items" or performance dimensions for which an overall job performance score can be obtained by summing the five items on the rating form. If we want to determine how well those items, when combined, reflect an overall picture of job performance, we need a method to estimate the internal consistency of these five combined items. Kuder-Richardson reliability would not be appropriate, because each item on the rating form involves more than two response categories on an interval scale. In those cases in which we are interested in knowing the internal consistency of responses to a measure but in which responses are based on an interval scale, we can employ Cronbach's coefficient alpha (α).[19] Alpha is a general version of K-R 20 reliability. K-R 20 reliability can be used only with dichotomously scored items (for example, correct or incorrect), whereas coefficient alpha can be used with any set of items regardless of the number of points on the response scale. Like K-R 20, it represents an average reliability coefficient computed from all possible split-half reliabilities.[20] Put another way, it represents the average correlation of each item with every other item on a measure. Coefficient alpha helps us answer questions such as these: "To what degree do items on the measure seem to be measuring the same attribute?" or "How well do items on a measure hang together?" When the items are measuring the same attribute, then we expect individuals' responses across these items to be highly consistent, that is, a high coefficient alpha. If coefficient alpha reliability is unacceptably low, then the items on the selection measure may be assessing more than one characteristic.

[*Technical Note:* We must make a few cautionary comments regarding the interpretation of coefficient alpha reliability.[21] First, alpha is a function of the number of items. With a sufficiently large number of items comprising a selection measure score (for example, 20 or more), alpha may be high even though the interrelatedness among these items is low (r = 0.30) and the score is multidimensional in nature. Second, although coefficient alpha reflects the interrelatedness among a set of items, it does not mean that the item set is necessarily unidimensional or homogeneous. If alpha for the set is low, the coefficient suggests that more than one dimension probably exists. However, if the coefficient is high (for example, in the 0.80s), then only one general dimension may be present, although it is also quite possible for several dimensions to underlie the set of items. Additional analyses are needed to make the determination.]

Let's consider in more detail another example of the use of coefficient alpha. Figure 7.7 shows the results of two sets (Case 1 and Case 2) of applicant scores on four items assessing conscientiousness. The purpose of the four items was to identify job applicants who had the "right" personality, that is, were likely to be conscientious and achievement oriented.

Case 1 illustrates the scores for one set of eight applicants, A through H. For each individual in Case 1, read down the columns and examine the scores obtained on the four items. For example, applicant A received scores of 4, 5, 5, and 4. Notice that although there were differences among the applicants on the scores received, the scores given to any one applicant were quite similar. That is, individuals in Case 1 who received high scores on one item tended to receive high scores on the other items. A similar pattern is found for those rated low on any one of the items.

FIGURE 7.7 An Example of Applicant Data in Computing Coefficient Alpha (α) Reliability

Items Used to Assess Applicant Conscientiousness—A Personality Trait	Case 1 Applicants								Case 2 Applicants							
	A	B	C	D	E	F	G	H	I	J	K	L	M	N	O	P
Item 1. Dependability	4	1	4	2	4	3	5	2	1	4	4	5	3	2	1	2
Item 2. Organized	5	1	4	2	4	4	5	2	2	3	1	4	3	3	1	5
Item 3. Hardworking	5	1	4	2	5	3	5	3	4	1	3	3	4	4	3	4
Item 4. Persistence	4	1	5	3	5	2	5	3	2	5	5	2	1	5	3	3
Total Score	18	4	17	9	18	12	20	10	9	13	13	14	11	14	8	14

Note: Applicants rate their behavior using the following rating scale: 1 = Strongly Disagree, 2 = Disagree, 3 = Neither Agree nor Disagree, 4 = Agree, and 5 = Strongly Agree. Case 1 coefficient alpha reliability = 0.83; Case 2 coefficient alpha reliability = 0.40.

Case 2 is different. As you read down the columns of data for applicants I through P, you can see that the scores show no apparent pattern. That is, an individual may obtain a high score on one item (such as applicant I on Item 3) yet be rated low on another (Item 1). This same, almost random pattern of ratings is true for the remaining applicants as well.

To check the internal consistency reliability of these scores, we must compute coefficient alpha reliability for both Cases 1 and 2. Because the item scores tend to go together in Case 1, there is the indication that whatever is being measured is being measured consistently. The computed coefficient alpha reliability of 0.83 confirms our conclusion that the item scores tend to hang together and measure the same construct—the underlying measure or trait. (We may not be sure just exactly what that construct is. That is a question to be answered by a validation study.) As you probably expected, coefficient alpha reliability of the scores in Case 2 is low, only 0.40. A coefficient this low suggests that the scores are unreliable and do not assess one common trait. Thus our total score does not reflect an overall assessment of an interviewee's conscientiousness. The data used in Case 2 must be improved (for example, by adding items assessing conscientiousness) prior to consideration of their use. The formula for computing coefficient alpha is conceptually similar to that of K-R 20. The only information needed is (a) individuals' total scores and (b) their responses to each item or question on the measure. The following formula summarizes the computation of coefficient alpha:

$$\alpha = \frac{k}{k-1}\left(1 - \frac{\Sigma\sigma_i^2}{\sigma_y^2}\right)$$

where

k = number of items on the selection measure

σ_i^2 = variance of respondents' scores on each item (i) on the measure

σ_y^2 = variance of respondents' total scores on the measure.

A more convenient computational formula for coefficient alpha is

$$\alpha = \frac{k}{k-1}\left(1 - \frac{n\Sigma i^2 - \Sigma T^2}{n\Sigma X^2 - (\Sigma X)^2}\right)$$

where

k = number of items

n = number of persons for whom data are available

Σi^2 = sum of the squared individual scores

ΣT^2 = sum of the squares of the k item total scores

ΣX^2 = sum of the squares of the n person total scores

ΣX = sum of the n person total scores.

Data such as those shown in Figure 7.7 can be used with this formula to compute coefficient alpha reliability.

K-R 20 and, in particular, coefficient alpha are two of the most commonly reported reliability procedures in the HR selection literature today. At a minimum, users and developers of selection measures should routinely compute and report these reliability estimates.

Interrater Reliability Estimates

In some measures employed in HR selection, scoring is based on the individual judgment of the examiner (the interviewer). In these situations, scoring depends not only on what is being rated, such as the behavior of a person, but also on the characteristics of the rater, such as the rater's biases and opinions. These two sources of scoring information contribute to errors of measurement. The rating of jobs by job analysts, the rating of subordinates' job performance by supervisors, the rating of candidates' performances in a selection interview by interviewers, and the judging of applicants' performances on a behavioral-based measure (such as answering a telephone in a simulated emergency call) are applications of measures that involve degrees of judgment in scoring. Subjective ratings of employee performance by raters pose a double problem for reliability. Unreliability of employee performance is being piled on top of the unreliability of ratings given by the rater.[22]

Conceptually, the way to estimate interrater reliability is to have at least two different ratings for the applicants or jobs being examined. If the trait or attribute is measured reliably, the two ratings should be similar or should at least roughly agree on the relative order of the applicants or jobs. However, as mentioned earlier, there are two sources of measurement error in ratings: randomness (error) in the judgments made by each judge due to the context, the candidate, and rating scales and idiosyncratic differences in rater perception (for example, halo).[23] If there is one thing we know, it is that perceptions of other people are replete with idiosyncratic biases arising from the rater's attitudes, motives, values, and the like. In fact, ratings seem to tell more about the raters than about the people they rate. *Halo error* occurs when the rater's general impressions about the candidate distort or bias ratings of distinct traits or attributes of the person. This is one of the most serious and pervasive sources of rating errors. The tendency to consistently rate others too high or too low is another. Because the idiosyncratic biases associated with each rater are not part of the trait or attribute being measured, this form of measurement error lowers reliability. When raters agree on the rank order of applicants, their judgment is reliable or consistent as far as agreement is concerned. The determination of consistency or agreement among raters has been termed *interrater reliability*.[24] Other terms used to describe interrater reliability are *interobserver* and *interjudge* reliability.

The purpose of calculating interrater reliability estimates is to determine whether multiple raters are consistent in their judgments. Determining the proper reliability estimate, however, is quite complex, in part because of the need to account for idiosyncratic errors across raters as well as random measurement error in their judgments. Complexity is further increased because interrater agreement is often used as a form of reliability, even though it is not. The conundrum is that rater agreement is important, too; two raters should agree in their ratings or categorizations. Nevertheless, although interobserver agreement about the degree to which a job requires teamwork may be quite high, interrater reliability may be low because the person being observed (e.g., interviewed) may respond differently, may draw upon a different experience to answer the same question, or even may show a different level of teamwork from one interview on campus to an onsite interview 3 months later. Although this shows that agreement is not an index of reliability, it's important to know the degree of reliability and agreement among raters performing judgmental ratings.

The computation of interrater reliability can involve any of a number of statistical procedures. Most of these procedures tend to fall into one of three categories: (a) interrater agreement, (b) interclass correlation, and (c) intraclass correlation. (A similar system of categorizing interrater reliability methods as applied to job analysis data has been developed by Edwin Cornelius.[25])

Interrater Agreement.   In some rating situations, a reliability coefficient for raters is not computed; rather, rater agreement is determined. For instance, two job analysts may be observing an employee performing her job. The analysts are asked to observe the individual's task activities and then indicate whether specific job behaviors are performed. Rater agreement indices are often used in such rating situations. Percentage of rater agreement, Kendall's coefficient of concordance (W), and Cohen's kappa (κ)[26] are three of the most popular indices for estimating interrater agreement. Unfortunately, as has already been pointed out, some of the interrater agreement indices are not good estimators of rating reliability. For example, when the behavior being examined occurs at a very high or very low frequency, indices such as percentage of rater agreement and the coefficient of concordance may produce a spuriously high indication of agreement between raters. This is because they fail to take into consideration the degree of rater agreement due to chance. In addition, interrater agreement indices are generally restricted to nominal or categorical data that reduce their application flexibility. Although interrater agreement indices have their limitations, they are still widely employed in selection research. Percentage of rater agreement is probably the most often reported estimate in this research.

Interclass Correlation. Interclass correlations are employed when two raters make judgments about a series of targets or objects being rated (such as interviewees, jobs, subordinates). Most often, these judgments are based on an interval rating scale. The Pearson product-moment correlation (r) and Cohen's weighted kappa (κ)[27] are the two procedures most commonly reported as an interclass correlation. Essentially, the interclass correlation shows the amount of error between two raters. Relatively low interclass correlations indicate that more specific operational criteria for making the ratings, or additional rater training in how to apply the rating criteria, may be needed to enhance interrater reliability.

Intraclass Correlation. When three or more raters have made ratings on one or more targets, intraclass correlations can be calculated. This procedure is usually viewed as the best way to determine whether multiple raters differ in their subjective scores or ratings on the trait or behavior being assessed. Intraclass correlation shows the average relationship among raters for all targets being rated. Figure 7.8 illustrates the basic research design of a study that computed an intraclass correlation. (If only two raters were involved, the figure would depict the typical design for an interclass correlation.) In this example, each of three employment interviewers interviewed a group of job applicants. After interviewing the applicants, each interviewer rated each applicant's performance in the interview. Intraclass correlation can be used to determine how much of the difference in

| **FIGURE 7.8** | Example of a Research Design for Computing Intraclass Correlation to Assess Interrater Reliability of Employment Interviewers |

Interviewee	Interviewer		
	1	2	3
A. J. Mitra	9	8	8
N. E. Harris	5	6	5
R. C. Davis	4	3	2
•	•	•	•
•	•	•	•
•	•	•	•
T. M. Zuckerman	7	6	7

Note: The numbers represent hypothetical ratings of interviewees given by each interviewer.

interviewees' ratings is due to true differences in interview performance and how much is due to errors of measurement. Intraclass correlation typically reveals two types of reliability information on the raters: (a) the average reliability for one rater, and (b) the average reliability for all raters making ratings. Benjamin Winer outlined the basic model and process for computing intraclass correlations. He also showed how the procedure could be used with ordinal as well as dichotomous rating data.[28]

The challenge with any indicator of interrater reliability is that the "unreliability" or disagreement can occur due to many different reasons, including (a) raters view the same behavior differently or at different times, (b) raters interpret the same behavior differently, (c) the role of idiosyncratic halo for each rater, such that general impressions bias ratings of specific behaviors, (d) the sample of behavior itself may be inappropriate or misleading, or (e) error in rating or recording each impression. Yet, the problem is that any measure of interrater reliability yields only a single index, which ignores the fact that there are many potential sources of errors in observational ratings. To compound this problem, there are many different ways to calculate interrater agreement or consistency and the results they produce may markedly differ for the same data or given use. Due to this, the reader must recognize that accurately estimating interrater agreement and reliability is particularly challenging; it may require more expertise than can be conveyed in a single chapter.

Table 7.2 provides a descriptive summary of the methods we have discussed for estimating the reliability of selection measures. In addition to the questions each method addresses, the table presents information on the assumptions as well as the procedural aspects of the methods.

INTERPRETING RELIABILITY COEFFICIENTS

The chief purpose behind the use of measures in HR selection research is to permit us to arrive at sound inferences or selection decisions concerning the people to whom these measures are applied. For these judgments to have any value, they must be based on dependable data. When data are not dependable, any decisions based on this information are of dubious worth. Thus one goal of selection managers is to utilize measures that will provide dependable information.

Reliability analyses help us to determine the dependability of data we will use in selection decision making. Through reliability we can estimate the amount of error included in scores on any measure we choose to study. Knowing reliability, we can estimate how precisely or loosely a score for a measure can be interpreted. But how do we go about interpreting a reliability coefficient? What exactly does a coefficient mean? How high or low must a coefficient be for a particular measure to be used? These are but a few of the questions that can be asked while interpreting a reliability coefficient. Next we examine some of the issues that bear on the interpretation of reliability.

What Does a Reliability Coefficient Mean?

Selection measures are not simply "reliable" or "not reliable." There are degrees of reliability. As we said earlier, calculation of reliability estimates results in an index or a coefficient ranging from 0.00 to 1.00. A variety of symbols are used to indicate reliability; typically, reliability is represented by an "r" followed by two identical subscripts. For example, the following would be the reliability symbols for the four measures of X, Y, 1, and 2: r_{xx}, r_{yy}, r_{11}, and r_{22}. (The symbol r followed by identical subscripts implies that a measure is correlated with itself.)

TABLE 7.2   Descriptive Summary of Major Methods for Estimating Reliability of Selection Measures

Reliability Method	Question Addressed	Number of Forms	Number of Administrations	Description	Assumptions	Sources of Error That Lower Reliability
Test-Retest	Are the scores on a measure consistent over time?	1	2	One version of a measure is given to the same respondents during two sessions with a time interval in between.	• Respondents do not let answers on first administration affect those on second administration. • Respondents do not "change" (for example, through learning) from one administration to the other.	• Any changes in respondents and differences in answers for test and retest due to changes occurring over time.
Parallel Forms (immediate administration)	Are the two forms of a measure equivalent?	2	1 or 2	Two versions of a measure are given to same respondents during one session.	• The two forms are parallel. • Respondents do not let completion of first version affect completion of second.	• Any differences in similarity of content between the two forms.
Parallel Forms (long-term administration)	Is the attribute assessed by a measure stable over time? Are the two forms of a measure equivalent?	2	2	Two versions of a measure are given to the same respondents during two sessions with a time interval in between.	• The two forms are parallel. • Respondents do not let completion of first version affect completion of second. • Respondents do not "change" (for example, through learning) from one administration to the other.	• Any differences in similarity of content between the two forms. • Any differences in learning with respect to topics covered by the test.

(Continued)

TABLE 7.2 (Continued)

Reliability Method	Question Addressed	Number of Forms	Number of Administrations	Description	Assumptions	Sources of Error That Lower Reliability
Split-Half (Odd-Even)	Are respondents' answers on one half (odd items) of a measure similar to answers given on the other half (even items)?	1	1	One version of a measure is given to respondents during one session.	• Splitting a measure into two halves produces two equivalent halves. • Measure is not speeded (answers are not based on a time limit).	• Any differences in similarity of item content in one half of the measure versus the other half.
Kuder-Richardson and Coefficient Alpha	To what degree do items on the measure seem to be measuring the same attribute? How well do items on a measure hang together?	1	1	One version of a measure is given to respondents during one session.	• Only one attribute is measured. • Measure is not speeded (answers are not based on a time limit). • K-R 20 is suitable for dichotomous items. Coefficient alpha is suitable for dichotomous items and items on a continuum.	• Any differences in similarity of item content. • More than one attribute, concept, or characteristic assessed by a measure.
Interrater (Interobserver/ Interjudge)	What is the correlation between any two raters rating a group of people?	1	1	One version of a measure is given to two or more raters during one session.	• Raters are equal or interchangeable. • Raters base their ratings on what is rated; extraneous factors do not influence ratings.	• Any biases of the raters that influence the ratings that are given. • Raters who are not knowledgeable of what to rate and how to make ratings.

After the symbol, a numerical coefficient is reported. Again, the values will range from 0.00, indicating no reliability (a measure composed entirely of error), to 1.00 or perfect reliability (no error present in the measure). Without going through too many of the technical details, let's see what the coefficient means. Harold Gulliksen showed that the reliability coefficient is equivalent to the squared correlation between true and obtained scores for a measure and can be directly interpreted as the coefficient of determination.[29] Or,

$$r_{xx} = r_{tx}^2$$

where

   r_{xx} = reliability coefficient

   r_{tx}^2 = squared correlation between true and obtained scores

   x = obtained scores

   t = true scores.

Therefore, the reliability coefficient can be interpreted as the extent (in percentage terms) to which individual differences in scores on a measure are due to "true" differences in the attribute measured and "remainder" (1 – reliability coefficient) depicts the extent to which they are due to chance errors. For example, if we have a test called "X," and the reliability of Test X equals 0.90 (that is, $r_{xx} = 0.90$), then 90 percent of the differences in test scores among individuals who took the test are due to true variance and only 10 percent due to error. The reliability coefficient provides an indication of the proportion (percent) of total differences in scores that is attributable to true differences rather than error.

The reliability coefficient summarizes the dependability of a measure for a group of individuals. It does not indicate which individuals within the group are or are not providing reliable data. When we examine a reliability coefficient, we should understand that the estimate refers to the scores of a group of individuals on a specific measuring device and not to a specific person. Thus it is quite possible to have a high reliability estimate for scores obtained from a reliable selection measure, but one or more people within the group may provide responses that contain considerable error. Unreliable performance by a respondent on a reliable measure is possible, but reliable performance on an unreliable measure is impossible.

In summary, when examining any particular reliability coefficient, consider that it is[30]

- specific to the reliability estimation method and group on which it was calculated,

- a necessary but not a sufficient condition for validity,

- based on responses from a group of individuals,

- expressed by degree, and

- determined ultimately by judgment.

How High Should a Reliability Coefficient Be?

This question has been asked many times. Different opinions exist. Unfortunately, there is no clear-cut, generally agreed upon value above which reliability is acceptable and below which it is unacceptable. Obviously, we want the coefficient to be as high as possible; however, how low a coefficient can be and still be used will depend on the purpose for which the measure is to be used. The following principle generally applies: The more critical the decision to be made, the greater the need for precision of the measure on which the decision will be based, and the higher the required reliability coefficient.[31]

In the practice of HR selection, employment decisions are based on predictors such as test scores. From the perspective of job applicants, highly reliable predictors are a necessity. In many selection situations, there are more applicants than job openings available. Competition can be keen for the available openings. Thus a difference of a few points in some applicants' scores can determine whether they do or do not get hired. Any measurement error in a predictor could seriously affect, in a negative and unfair way, some applicants' employment possibilities. You might be asking, "But isn't it possible this same measurement error could produce higher scores for some applicants than might be expected, thus helping them obtain employment?" Yes, it is possible for some scores to be inflated through error; yet here again, these scores could be unfair to the applicants "benefited" by errors of measurement. Due to misleading scores, organizations may be hiring these individuals and placing them in job situations they won't be able to handle. Job requirements may be too high relative to their true abilities. Although they may get the job, they may not be able to cope with it, leading to frustration and dissatisfaction for both employee and employer.

From the perspective of the organization attempting to hire executives or other key personnel (whose decisions may affect the success of the entire organization), reliable evidence of applicants' qualifications is also a necessity. The cost of being wrong in the assessment of key managerial personnel can be very high. Imprecise predictors can have long-term consequences for an organization. Dependable predictors are essential for accurately evaluating these key personnel.

But what about criteria? Isn't it just as important that criterion measures be reliable? Of course, criterion measures (such as employees' performance appraisal ratings) should be reliable. However, in the context of personnel selection decision making, their reliability need not be as high as that of predictors for them to be useful.[32] When predictors are used, they are generally employed to make individual decisions, for example, "How does one applicant's score compare with another?" or "Did the applicant make a passing score?" When scores are used for making decisions about individuals, it is critical that the measure used to produce these scores be highly reliable.

In contrast, selection researchers often employ criterion data to examine attributes that may be related to job performance. Employment decisions about individuals are not made with criteria; therefore, reliability coefficients need not be as high. However, as we see in the next chapter, it will not be possible to show empirical validity of a predictor if the criterion with which it is being correlated is not reliable.

Several writers have offered some rough guidelines regarding desirable magnitudes of reliability coefficients for selection measures.[33] Although these guidelines are based on astute logic, we do not believe it is prudent to propose a specific set of guidelines (for example, reliability must be 0.70 or higher) because they soon become self-propagating "crutches" applied without sufficient thought about the problems created by measurement error. A reliability estimate reflects the amount of error in a set of scores from a measure specific to the group on which it is calculated. It can be higher in one situation than another because of situational circumstances that may or may not affect the preciseness (reliability) of measurement. (For further information on this point, see the following sections on factors influencing the reliability of a measure and the standard error of measurement.) We believe test users must consider the specific circumstances surrounding their situations to determine how much measurement error they are willing to put up with. Stated another way, the user must use her best judgment to determine whether it is feasible or important to strive to reduce the influence of random error on her measures. A number of factors can influence the size of an observed reliability coefficient. By accounting for the impact of these factors, such as the range of talent in the respondent group, a specific test user should be able to determine whether a reliability coefficient is adequate for the purpose being considered. To clarify how these factors can influence reliability in a context involving selection measures, let's briefly examine several factors.

Factors Influencing the Reliability of a Measure

As we have discussed, a reliability coefficient is an estimate. Many factors can have an effect on the actual magnitude of a coefficient. Here, we mention nine important factors that can affect estimated reliability: (a) method of estimating reliability, (b) individual differences among respondents, (c) stability, (d) sample, (e) length of a measure, (f) test question difficulty, (g) homogeneity of a measure's content, (h) response format, and (i) administration and scoring of a measure.

Method of Estimating Reliability

We have seen that different procedures for reliability account for different errors of measurement. One result is that different reliability estimates will be obtained on a measure simply from the choice of procedure used to calculate the estimate. This makes sense because each procedure focuses on a different subset of errors that can occur. For example, test-retest examines consistency of results on retesting, while equivalent forms focuses on errors from form to form. Consequently, some methods will tend to give higher (upper-bound) estimates, whereas others will tend to be lower (lower-bound) in their estimates of the true reliability of a measure. Therefore, it is important for any individual evaluating a particular selection procedure to know which procedure was used and to know what methods tend to give higher and lower estimates, and why that is so.

Figure 7.9 presents a rough characterization of relative reliability in terms of whether methods tend to give upper- or lower-bound estimates of a measure's true reliability, other things being equal. We discuss a few of these "other things"—factors that can affect reliability—in this section. It is important to emphasize that the hierarchy in Figure 7.9 is based on general results reported for selected measures. In any one specific situation, it is possible that the rank order of methods may vary; a method characterized as usually providing lower-bound reliability may in fact give a higher estimate than one generally ranked above it.

Parallel forms reliability usually provides a lower estimate than other techniques because it may account for changes occurring over time as well as differences from one form or version of a measure to another. These changes contribute to errors of measurement. If a test is measuring more than one attribute, Kuder-Richardson or coefficient alpha reliability will underestimate true reliability; if a measure has a time limit, reliability will be overestimated by the procedure. Because of memory, test-retest reliability will likely be high, but as the time interval between administrations lengthens, memory will have less impact and estimated reliability will fall. The effect on reliability of lengthening the time interval between administrations will be similar for parallel forms reliability as well.

Individual Differences Among Respondents

Another factor influencing a reliability estimate is the range of individual differences or variability among respondents on the attribute measured. If the range of differences in scores on the attribute measured by a selection device is wide, the device can more reliably distinguish among people. Generally speaking, the greater the variability or standard deviation of scores on the characteristic measured, the higher the reliability of the measure of that characteristic.

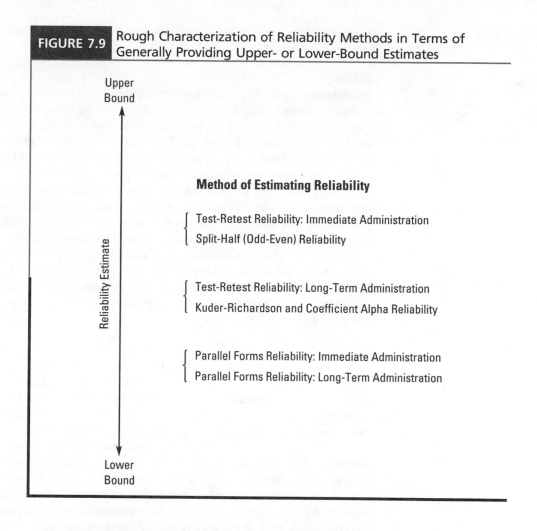

FIGURE 7.9 Rough Characterization of Reliability Methods in Terms of Generally Providing Upper- or Lower-Bound Estimates

In part, this finding is based on the conception of reliability and its calculation by means of a correlation coefficient. Change or variation within a person, such as changing a response from one administration to another, detracts from reliability; we have already discussed this issue as errors of measurement. On the other hand, differences among respondents are considered to be true differences. Such true variation contributes to reliability. Therefore, if variability or individual differences increase among respondents (true) while variation within individuals (error) remains the same, reliability will increase. Range of ability in the group of individuals being assessed is not something that can usually be controlled or manipulated. However, it should be kept in mind when reviewing reliability coefficients. For example, our criteria are often relatively homogeneous; low performers are fired or quit and high performers are transferred and promoted. In such settings, the total variance is likely to be smaller while the error variance is not reduced. Thus, the ratio of error to total variance increases, resulting in an underestimate of criterion reliability. Consequently, a reliability coefficient of 0.75 for a predictor might be acceptable in a very homogeneous group of people but unacceptable in a very heterogeneous group. Because individual differences can vary a great deal for some groups, such as those differences based on educational level or age, it is imperative that the user of selection measures review reliability data for relevant groups of respondents. Developers and publishers of commercially available predictors should report, at a minimum, separate reliability coefficients and predictor standard deviations for such respondent groups.

Stability

Reliability estimates that examine whether scores of a given test are consistent from time to time (test-retest) may be affected by the stability on the construct assessed by the test itself, as well as stability in measurement over time. That is, some of the characteristics and behaviors assessed through selection tests or job-relevant criteria may be subject to theoretically relevant change over time. For example, measures of anxiety or emotion are usually seen as less stable than constructs related to mechanical verbal abilities. Instability in scores on a test of mood over time would reflect "true" variance as well as measurement error. This underscores a point made earlier, that judgments about the reliability of test scores must be made in relation to what the predictor or criterion attempts to assess. To the extent scores of a given test assess relatively enduring characteristics or stable behaviors, fluctuations in scores from time to time are more likely to be due to measurement error. This is an important consideration, since the *Principles for the Validation and Use of Personnel Selection Procedures*[34] encourages employers to provide opportunities for reassessment of applicants, whenever technically and administratively feasible.

Sample

Results obtained from a sample should be "representative" of the population or situation in which the measure is to be used. Representativeness depends on both the choice of participants and the number of respondents. Individuals should be selected to be similar to the population with respect to sex, race, religion, and so forth, as well as ability, motivation, and prior experience with the measures. Of equal importance is precision of estimates. The precision of a reliability coefficient, like any other statistical parameter estimate (mean, standard deviation, and so on) is significantly affected by sample size. Larger sample sizes are important to ensure the influence of random errors is normally distributed, and therefore enables the sample estimate to better reflect the population parameter. As this suggests, the size and representativeness of the sample, not the size of the population itself, is the critical issue. A good sample estimate requires a sample size of at least 100 and preferably 200 participants.[35]

Length of a Measure

In general, as the length of a measure increases, its reliability also increases. One way of thinking about this relationship is to look out a window for a second or two and then try to describe in detail what you saw. As you increase the number of times you look out the window in one- to two-second intervals, you will probably find that the accuracy and details of your description increase. With increasing measurement, that is, observations, your description begins to approximate the true situation outside the window. A similar effect occurs when a selection measure is lengthened. Only a sample of possible items is used on a given measure. If all possible questions could be used, a person's score on the measure would closely approximate his or her true score. Therefore, as we add more and more relevant items to our measure, we get a more precise and reliable assessment of the individual's true score on the attribute measured. Figure 7.10 illustrates the link between selection measure length, probability of measuring the true score, and test reliability. Initially, we have a universe of all possible test items. As we select test items from the universe and double the test length from 5, 10, 20, … , 80 items, we see that the probability of measuring the true score increases. Using the Spearman-Brown prophecy formula we discussed earlier, we can see that reliability also increases, from 0.20 for a 5-item test to

| FIGURE 7.10 | Relation Among Test Length, Probability of Measuring the True Score, and Test Reliability |

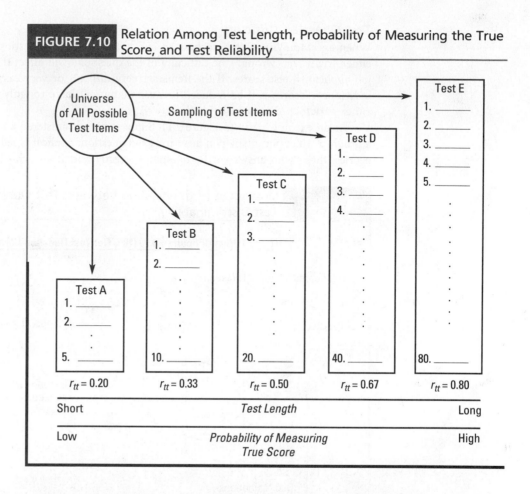

0.80 for an 80-item test. If we were to continue these calculations, we would see that the reliability of an unreliable short test increases rapidly as similar test items are added. However, after a point, these improvements in reliability begin to diminish with increasing test length.

A variation of the Spearman-Brown formula mentioned earlier and shown here can be used to determine how much a measure must be lengthened to obtain a desired reliability:

$$n = \frac{t_{ttd}(1 - r_{tt})}{r_{tt}(1 - r_{ttd})}$$

where

n = number of times a measure must be lengthened

r_{ttd} = desired level of reliability *after* the measure is lengthened

r_{tt} = reliability of the test *before* the measure is lengthened.

Suppose, for instance, the reliability of a 10-item test is 0.75. The selection researcher desires that the reliability should be 0.90. Substitution in the formula shows that to obtain the desired level of reliability, the test must be three times as long, or 30 items. It should be noted however, that gains in reliability due to test length are also influenced by the interrelations among the items. Thus, if one adds items that measure different things than those intended by the test, this will also affect reliability and it should. Other item characteristics that affect reliability estimates are discussed next.

Test Question Difficulty

When an employment test, such as an ability test, contains questions that are scored as either "right" or "wrong," the difficulty of the questions will affect the differences among job applicants' test scores. If the items are very difficult or very easy, differences among individuals' scores will be reduced because many will have roughly the same test score, either very low or very high.

As an example, refer to Figure 7.11. Suppose we administered a single test question to a group of 10 applicants. Upon answering the question, applicants fell into one of two categories: those who answered the question correctly and those who missed it. In Case 1,

---

FIGURE 7.11   Illustration of the Relation Between Test Question Difficulty and Test Discriminability

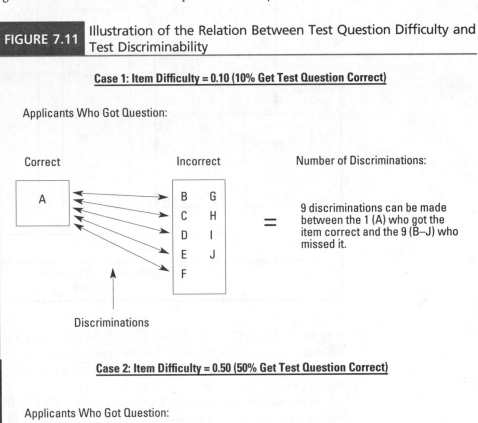

Case 1: Item Difficulty = 0.10 (10% Get Test Question Correct)

Applicants Who Got Question:

Correct — Incorrect

A → B G / C H / D I / E J / F

Discriminations

Number of Discriminations:

= 9 discriminations can be made between the 1 (A) who got the item correct and the 9 (B–J) who missed it.

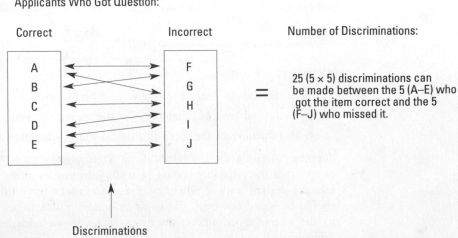

Case 2: Item Difficulty = 0.50 (50% Get Test Question Correct)

Applicants Who Got Question:

Correct — Incorrect

A B C D E — F G H I J

Discriminations

Number of Discriminations:

= 25 (5 × 5) discriminations can be made between the 5 (A–E) who got the item correct and the 5 (F–J) who missed it.

only 1 person (10 percent of the applicants) answers correctly. We can discriminate between that 1 individual and the 9 who missed it, a total of 9 comparisons or discriminations ($1 \times 9 = 9$ discriminations). We can also make the same number of discriminations if 9 answer correctly and only 1 misses the question ($9 \times 1 = 9$ discriminations).

If, as in Case 2, 5 applicants (50 percent) answer the question correctly and 5 miss it, we can make significantly more discriminations. In this case, we can make 25 discriminations (5×5 discriminations) between pairs of applicants from the two groups. We learned earlier that increasing variability in scores increases reliability. Therefore, because variability or variance in scores increases with greater numbers of discriminations, reliability of a selection test is enhanced.

Test questions of moderate difficulty (where roughly half or 50 percent of the test takers answer a question correctly) will spread out the test scores. Due to the greater range in individual scores, finer distinctions among test takers can be made. Test questions of moderate difficulty permit these finer distinctions, and tests that contain many items of moderate difficulty tend to be more reliable than those tests with many items that are either very difficult or very easy.

Homogeneity of a Measure's Content

In our discussion of Kuder-Richardson and coefficient alpha reliability, we noted that both of these internal consistency methods represent the average correlation among all items on a measure. To the extent that items on a measure do not relate to all other items on the same measure, internal consistency reliability will fall. Internal consistency reliability can be enhanced in several ways. First, new items can be added to a measure that are comparable in quality to and measure the same construct as the original items that compose the measure. Second, items on the measure that do not correlate with each other or with the total score on the measure can be eliminated. Either of these steps will enhance the homogeneity of a measure's content and, therefore, increase internal consistency reliability.

Response Format

Any factor that systematically contributes to differences among individuals' scores on a measure will enhance the reliability of the measure. One factor that will contribute to these differences is the response format for recording answers to a selection measure. As the number of response options or categories on a measure increases, reliability also increases. Suppose interviewers are using a 10-item rating form to judge the suitability of interviewees for a job. Answers to the 10 items are summed to obtain an overall employment suitability score for each interviewee. If each item has only two rating options (for example, 1 = unsuitable; 2 = suitable), then the only possible total scores range from 10 to 20. However, if five rating options are given for each of the 10 items, then possible scores can range from 10 to 50. Finer distinctions among interviewees can potentially be made with the latter scale. This scale can produce a greater spread in interviewees' employment suitability scores, thus enhancing reliability. Up to a point, increasing the number of possible scores possible for a selection measure can enhance reliability. For instance, research has shown that the reliability of rating scales can be improved by offering from five to nine rating categories.[36]

Administration and Scoring of a Measure

As we have noted, various factors we call errors of measurement can have a bearing on the reliability of a measure. For example, emotional and physical states of respondents, lack of rapport with the measure's administrator, unpleasant conditions (too noisy or too cold) during the measure's administration, respondents' inadequate knowledge of how to respond to the measure, and inconsistent scoring of responses can contribute to errors of measurement. Where errors of measurement are present, reliability is lowered. This underscores the importance of standardizing measure administration and scoring, as this helps reduce these errors.

Standard Error of Measurement

We have just seen that reliability coefficients are useful for describing the general stability or homogeneity of a measure. The coefficient gives us some degree of assurance of the dependability of most respondents' scores on a measure. However, the various methods of computing reliabilities that we have discussed do not give us an idea of the error to be expected in a particular individual's score on the measure. Reliability is a group-based statistic.

To obtain an estimate of the error for an individual, we can use another statistic called the *standard error of measurement*. The statistic is simply a number in the same measurement units as the measure for which it is being calculated. The higher the standard error, the more error present in the measure, and the lower its reliability. Thus the standard error of measurement is not another approach to estimating reliability; it is just another way of expressing it (using the test's standard deviation units). The formula for calculating the standard error is as follows:

$$\sigma_{meas} = \sigma_x \sqrt{1 - r_{xx}}$$

where

σ_{meas} = the standard error of measurement for measure X

σ_x = the standard deviation of obtained scores on measure X

r_{xx} = the reliability of measure X.

For example, let's assume that the mathematics ability test that we referred to earlier has a reliability of 0.90 and a standard deviation of 10. The standard error of measurement for a mathematics ability score on this test would be calculated as follows:

$$10\sqrt{1 - 0.90} = 10\sqrt{0.10} = 0.10(0.316) = 3.16$$

To illustrate how the standard error of measurement can be applied, let's look at an example. Suppose an applicant came into our employment office, took our math ability test, and made a score of 50. We could use the standard error to estimate the degree his or her test score would vary if he or she were retested another day. By adding and subtracting the standard error from the math test score (50 ± 3.16), we would obtain a range of math ability scores (46.84 to 53.16). One possible interpretation of this range might be that the chances are 2-to-1 that the applicant's true math ability lies somewhere between 46.8 and 53.2. Alternatively, we could say that if he or she were given the test 100 times, we would expect that roughly two-thirds (68 percent) of the time the math ability scores would fall within the range of 46.8 to 53.2.

The standard error of measurement possesses several useful application characteristics. First, the measure is useful in that it forces us to think of scores on a measure not as exact points but as approximations represented by a band or range of scores. Because selection measure scores contain error, an individual's score on a measure is only one of a variety of possible scores the individual could have obtained. We should think of every selection measure score as an approximation.

Second, the standard error of measurement can aid decision making in which only one individual is involved. For instance, suppose a passing or cutoff score on a test was set for a nuclear power facility operator's job. The job itself involves operations that could drastically affect the safety of both workers and citizens. If an individual applicant scores within 2 points of the passing score and the standard error of measurement for the test is 4 points, there is a very good chance that the employment decision will be in error. For this reason, the employer may consider only those applicants that score a minimum of one standard error of measurement above the passing score.

It's important to note that the standard error of measurement can also determine whether scores for individuals differ significantly from one another. For instance, imagine that two job applicants had taken our math ability test. Jacob Farrar scored 50; Alicia Tatum scored 47. Can we conclude that Jacob is the better applicant solely because of math ability as measured by the one test score? The standard error of measurement can help us decide. If our standard error is 3.16 and the difference between our two applicants' scores is 3, then it is entirely possible that the difference in scores is due to chance. On retesting, Alicia may score higher than Jacob.

This same principle also applies to a measure administered to a large group of individuals. If we administer and score a test for 50 job applicants, we can rank the applicants on the basis of their test scores from high to low. If the standard error of measurement is large relative to the differences among these scores (standard deviation), then our rank order is likely to change if the applicants are retested. In general, the higher the standard error, the more susceptible our rank order of test scores is subject to change upon retesting. As you can see, with a large standard error, it may simply be due to chance that one individual scored higher than a group of others. Without an error index, we may assume these differences are meaningful and make employment decisions on the basis of these differences. With this index, however, we are in a better position to determine who really scored significantly higher or lower on a measure.

With respect to interpreting differences in individuals' scores, Lewis Aiken has offered the following guidelines:

1. The difference between two individuals' scores should not be considered significant unless the difference is at least twice the standard error of measurement of the measure.

2. Before the difference between scores of the same individual on two different measures should be treated as significant, the difference should be greater than twice the standard error of measurement of either measure.[37]

The standard error of measurement is also used to establish how confident we may be in scores obtained from different groups of respondents. For example, suppose we had administered a test to 100 male and 100 female job applicants. For the male applicants, reliability for the test was 0.85 (standard deviation = 26); for the female applicants, it was 0.70 (standard deviation = 10). On the face of reliability information alone, we might have more confidence in individual scores obtained for men than in those for women. However, when we use the reliability data and standard deviation information to compute the standard error, we find that the standard error of measurement for men is 10.1, and for women it is 5.5. Therefore, we should have greater confidence in a female applicant's test score than we should in a male applicant's score. This example highlights an important conclusion: Without considering the variability of the group on the attribute measured (the standard deviation), reliability information alone will not permit us to compare relative confidence in scores for individuals in different groups. Because the standard error is not affected by group variability, the statistic can enable us to make this important comparison.

In using the standard error of measurement, we have implicitly made an important assumption: that is, a score on a measure is equally accurate for the complete range of scores. However, it is possible that a test may be more accurate for one range of scores than for another. For example, our math ability test may be a more accurate predictor for individuals scoring about average in math ability than for those scoring high. Yet, even where this assumption may be violated, the standard error of measurement offers many advantages as an overall estimate of error.[38]

The standard error of measurement is a statistic you will likely come across in reading and studying various commercially available predictors (in particular, tests) to be used in selection. It is one of the most popular measures used in reporting test results because it serves as a corrective for the tendency to place undue weight on one measurement. The measure has become so popular that the College Board includes information on the standard error of measurement and its interpretation when it sends results to people who take the college admissions Scholastic Aptitude Test (SAT).[39]

Because of its importance, the statistic should be routinely reported with each reliability coefficient computed for a measure. In practice, if you want to make a cursory comparison of the reliability of different measures, you can use the reliability coefficient. However, to obtain a complete picture of the dependability of information produced by a measure and to help interpret individual scores on the measure, the standard error of measurement is essential.

Evaluating Reliability Coefficients

From our discussion of reliability, you probably recognize that many issues must be considered in evaluating reliability coefficients. We have noted throughout our discussion that the estimation of the reliability of selection measures is one essential requirement in appropriately applying these measures. Some users may believe that commercially available measures will provide all requisite information, and the determination and assessment of reliability data will not be necessary. Past experience with some commercially available measures suggests otherwise. The Buros Institute of Mental Measurements reviewed more than 1,000 commercially available tests published in *The Eighth Mental Measurements Yearbook*. Its results on the availability of reliability information were not encouraging. For the tests listed, the Institute found that

- over 22 percent appeared without any reliability information,

- 7 percent showed neither reliability nor validity data,

- 9 percent showed no reliability data for certain subtests or forms, and

- 28 percent did not report any normative data.[40]

These facts suggest that one should not assume reliability information will be provided just because a user purchases a test from an apparently reputable test publisher. Any user should carefully search for and insist on reliability information about selection measures. Without such information, scores on tests are, essentially, uninterpretable.

Assuming such information can be found, the next step is to systematically evaluate the reported data. The key point to keep in mind is that one needs to know the extent to which a "score" is affected by error or the degree of inconsistency in scores over measurement procedures. To facilitate the evaluation of reliability data, we have summarized, in question form, some of the issues you should consider. These questions are listed in Table 7.3. All of the questions have been addressed in this chapter. When examining reliability coefficients of selection measures, this checklist can serve as a useful means for reviewing the major considerations involved in reliability interpretation.

TABLE 7.3	Questions to Consider in Evaluating Reliability Coefficients

Question	Comment
1. Does the coefficient reflect the precision of a measure by indicating how well items hang together in measuring an attribute?	If interest is in determining the degree to which items on a measure are assessing the same content, an internal consistency estimate is appropriate.
2. Does the coefficient reflect the stability of an attribute as assessed by a specific measure over time?	If stability of performance is of interest, some form of test-retest reliability should be reported.
a. Is the interval between test and retest so short that memory could influence scores?	Depending on the situation, the interval should not be shorter than several weeks.
b. Is the interval between test and retest so long that learning or other changes in respondents could have occurred?	Depending on the situation, the interval should not be longer than 6 months; a typical interval is 6 to 8 weeks.
c. Is the coefficient based on parallel forms of a measure administered over time?	If so, are data available to indicate that the forms are indeed parallel or roughly equivalent?
d. Is a test-retest coefficient computed for a measure that can be expected to change because of the nature of the attribute being measured?	Some measures can be expected to change over time because of their nature. Examples might include performance ratings and attitudinal measures.
3. Do scores on the measure for which the coefficient is computed depend on how quickly respondents can respond to the measure? Is a time limit involved?	If a time limit for completing a measure is involved, the coefficient should not be based on an internal consistency estimate.
4. Is the coefficient based on respondents like those for whom a measure is being considered?	A coefficient is more meaningful if it is based on a group like the one to which the measure will be administered. For example, if a measure is going to be given to job applicants, a coefficient should be available for similar job applicants.
5. Is the coefficient based on a large enough number of people that confidence can be placed on the magnitude of the coefficient?	The larger the sample size on which the coefficient is based, the more dependable the estimate of reliability. A sample size of at least 100, and preferably 200, is desired.
6. Is information provided on the range of ability for the attribute measured of the group on which the coefficient is based?	Standard deviations and ranges of scores should be given for each group on which a coefficient is reported.
7. Is a standard error of measurement provided for the reliability coefficient?	An index of the standard error of measurement should be given for each coefficient.
Once these questions have been addressed, then a user may ask:	
8. Is the coefficient high enough to warrant *use of the measure?*	The more important the selection decision (that will be based on a specific measure), the higher the required reliability coefficient.

Source: Questions 3, 4, 5, and 7 are based in part on Alexander G. Wesman, *Reliability and Confidence* (Test Service Bulletin No. 44) (New York: The Psychological Corporation, May 1952), p. 7.

Reliability: A Concluding Comment

In this chapter, we have discussed the concept of reliability of measurement and reviewed various approaches to its determination. What is surprising is how difficult it is to actually determine reliability, given how fundamental it is to effective selection. As we have seen, different approaches make different assumptions and even define error differently. However, to determine which method you should use we think it best to consider what you are trying to predict. For example, if the test is going to be used to predict an employee's performance over a long period of time, then test-retest stability is more important than simply showing internal consistency. If you will provide retesting opportunities to candidates, then reliability of equivalent forms will become more important. Conversely, if you want to ensure that each item of the test is helping to precisely measure the applicant's standing on a predictor, such as general mental ability or personality, then an alpha coefficient will provide a useful index of internal consistency. Finally, different raters seeing (or hearing it described in an interview) the same behavior should evaluate it consistently; hence interrater reliability will be the focus. Generally, we expect different methods of assessing reliability should agree fairly well. However, it is useful to keep in mind that even small differences in reliability can make large differences for individual applicants. For example, if retest scores have a reliability of 0.92 (which is very good), it still is true that 21 percent of those retaking the test will see their test score differ by more than one-half of a standard deviation.[41] In a competitive job environment, such differences can be the difference between being offered a job or not.

In summary, even though the assessment and interpretation of reliability can be complex, it nevertheless is a fundamental element to the proper use of HR selection measures. As we see in Chapter 8, the validity of a measure depends on its reliability; reliability of predictor scores and criterion scores is necessary, but not sufficient, for a score's validity or interpretation. The validity of a score or the appropriateness of the inferences based on that score cannot be made if the measure is not reliable. Knowledge of reliability information and other associated statistics (such as the standard error of measurement) is critical for making accurate assessments and decisions about individuals seeking employment.

REFERENCES

1. Ulrich Tholl, Klaus Forstner, and Manfred Anlauf, "Measuring Blood Pressure: Pitfalls and Recommendations," *Nephrology Dialysis Transplantation* 19, no. 4 (April 2004): 766–770.

2. Daniel W. Jones, Lawrence J. Appel, Sheldon G. Sheps, Edward J. Roccella, and Claude Lenfant, "Measuring Blood Pressure Accurately: New and Persistent Challenges," *Journal of the American Medical Association* 289, no. 8 (2003): 1027–1030; Anne Marie de Greef and Andrew Shennan, "Blood Pressure Measuring Devices: Ubiquitous, Essential, But Imprecise," *Expert Review of Medical Devices* 5, no. 5 (2008): 573–579.

3. Pater Cornel, "Beyond the Evidence of the New Hypertension Guidelines. Blood Pressure Measurement—Is It Good Enough for Accurate Diagnosis of Hypertension? Time Might Be In, for a Paradigm Shift (I)," *Current Controlled Trials in Cardiovascular Medicine* 6 (2005): 1.

4. Ibid.

5. Tholl, Forstner, and Anlauf, "Measuring Blood Pressure: Pitfalls and Recommendations."

6. Our treatment of reliability is based on a classical reliability theory. Other developments have offered alternative approaches to the study of reliability theory [see, for example, Lee J. Cronbach, Goldine C. Gleser, Harinder Nanda, and Nageswari Rajaratnam, *The Dependability of Behavioral Measurements: Theory of Generalizability for Scores and Profiles* (New York: John Wiley, 1972)]; however, for the beginning student, our approach will suffice. For a full treatment, see Kevin R. Murphy, "Models and Methods for Evaluating Reliability and Validity," in *Oxford Handbook of Personnel Psychology*, ed. Susan Cartwright and Gary L. Cooper (London: Oxford University Press, 2008), 263–290 or Dan J. Putka and Paul R. Sackett, "Reliability and Validity," in *Handbook of Employee Selection*, ed. James L. Farr and Nancy T. Tippins (New York: Routledge, 2010).

7. Our discussion of "errors of measurement" primarily assumes that these errors occur at random. Robert M. Guion, *Assessment, Measurement, and Prediction for Personnel Decisions* (London: Lawrence Erlbaum Associates, 1998), 221–226 distinguishes between random and constant or systematic errors. Constant errors appear consistently with repeated measurement, whereas random errors affect different measurements to different degrees.

8. Guion, *Assessment, Measurement, and Prediction for Personnel Decisions*.

9. Milton Blum and James Naylor, *Industrial Psychology: Its Social and Theoretical Foundations* (New York: Harper & Row, 1968), 41.

10. Susana Urbina, *Essentials of Psychological Testing* (Hoboken, NJ: John Wiley, 2004).

11. Gary Groth-Marnat, *Handbook of Psychological Assessment*, 4th ed. (New Jersey: John Wiley, 2003); Murphy, "Models and Methods for Evaluating Reliability and Validity."

12. John E. Hunter and Frank L. Schmidt, *Methods of Meta-Analysis: Correcting Error and Bias in Research Findings* (Newbury Park, CA: Sage Publications, 2004).

13. Groth-Marnat, *Handbook of Psychological Assessment*.

14. In practice, the coefficient must be "corrected" by use of the Spearman-Brown prophecy formula. The application of this formula is discussed later in this section.

15. Neal Schmitt and David Chan, *Personnel Selection: A Theoretical Approach* (Newbury Park, CA: Sage Publications, 1998).

16. Urbina, *Essentials of Psychological Testing*; Murphy, "Models and Methods for Evaluating Reliability and Validity."

17. George F. Kuder and Marion W. Richardson, "The Theory of the Estimation of Test Reliability," *Psychometrika* 2 (1937): 151–160.

18. Anne Anastasi and Susana Urbina, *Psychological Testing*, 7th ed. (Upper Saddle River, NJ: Prentice Hall, 1997).

19. Lee J. Cronbach, "Coefficient Alpha and the Internal Structure of Tests," *Psychometrika* 16 (1951): 297–334; M. C. Rodriquez and Y. Maeda, "Meta Analysis of Coefficient Alpha," *Psychological Methods* 11 (2006): 306–322.

20. Jose Cortina, "What Is Coefficient Alpha? An Examination of Theory and Applications," *Journal of Applied Psychology* 78 (1993): 98–104. Cortina notes that alpha is equal to the mean of all split-half reliabilities only if selection measure item standard deviations are equal. The greater the differences among item standard deviations, the smaller alpha reliability will be relative to the average of these split-half reliabilities.

21. This discussion is based on Cortina, "What Is Coefficient Alpha? An Examination of Theory and Applications."

22. Hunter and Schmidt, *Methods of Meta-Analysis: Correcting Error and Bias in Research Findings*; James M. LeBreton and Jenell L. Senter, "Answers to 20 Questions about Interrater Reliability and Interrater Agreement," *Organizational Research Methods* 11 (2008): 815–852.

23. Frank L. Schmidt, Chockalingam Viswesvaran, and Deniz S. Ones, "Reliability Is Not Validity and Validity Is Not Reliability," *Personnel Psychology* 53 (2000): 901–912.

24. For a discussion of interrater reliability issues in the context of collecting personnel selection data (such as job analysis data) through observation methods, see Mark J. Martinko, "Observing the Work," in *The Job Analysis Handbook for Business, Industry, and Government*, ed. Sidney Gael (New York: John Wiley, 1987), 419–431; and Sandra K. Mitchell, "Interobserver Agreement, Reliability, and Generalizability of Data Collected in Observational Studies," *Psychological Bulletin* 86 (1979): 376–390.

25. Edwin T. Cornelius, "Analyzing Job Analysis Data" in *The Job Analysis Handbook for Business, Industry, and Government*, ed. Sidney Gael (New York: John Wiley, 1987), 353–368.

26. Jacob Cohen, "A Coefficient of Agreement for Nominal Scales," *Educational and Psychological Measurement* 32 (1972): 37–46; Maurice G. Kendall and Alan Stuart, *The Advanced Theory of Statistics*, 4th ed. (London: Griffin, 1977).

27. Jacob Cohen, "Weighted Kappa: Nominal Scale Agreement with Provision for Scaled Disagreement or Partial Credit," *Psychological Bulletin* 70 (1968): 213–230.

28. Benjamin J. Winer, Donald R. Brown, and Kenneth M. Michels, *Statistical Principles in Experimental Design*, 3rd ed. (New York: McGraw-Hill, 1991).

29. Harold Gulliksen, *Theory of Mental Tests* (New York: John Wiley, 1950).

30. Guion, *Assessment, Measurement, and Prediction for Personnel Decisions*; Urbina, *Essentials of Psychological Testing*; and Murphy, "Models and Methods for Evaluating Reliabilty and Validity."

31. Elazur J. Pedhazur and Liora Pedhazur Schmelkin, *Measurement, Design, and Analysis: An Integrated Approach* (London: Lawrence Erlbaum Associates, 1991); and Alexander G. Wesman, *Reliability and Confidence*, Test Service Bulletin No. 44 (New York: The Psychological Corporation, May 1952), 3.

32. Groth-Marnat, *Handbook of Psychological Assessment*; Guion, *Assessment, Measurement, and Prediction for Personnel Decisions*; and Pedhazur and Schmelkin, *Measurement, Design, and Analysis: An Integrated Approach*.

33. Jum C. Nunnally and Ira Bernstein, *Psychometric Theory* (New York: McGraw-Hill, 1994); and Elliot A. Weiner and Barbara J. Stewart, *Assessing Individuals* (Boston: Little, Brown, and Company, 1984).

34. Society of Industrial-Organizational Psychology, Inc., *Principles for the Validation and Use of Personnel Selection Procedures*, 4th ed. (Bowling Green, OH: Society of Industrial-Organizational Psychology, 2003).

35. Wesman, *Reliability and Confidence*.

36. Paul E. Spector, *Summated Rating Scale Construction: An Introduction* (Newbury Park, CA: Sage Publications, 1992).

37. Lewis R. Aiken, *Psychological Testing and Assessment*, 2nd ed. (Boston: Allyn & Bacon, 1988).

38. Groth-Marnat, *Handbook of Psychological Assessment*; Guion, *Assessment, Measurement, and Prediction for Personnel Decisions*; and Urbina, *Essentials of Psychological Testing*.

39. Anne Anastasi, "Mental Measurement: Some Emerging Trends," in *The Ninth Mental Measurements Yearbook*, ed. James V. Mitchell (Lincoln, NE: Buros Institute of Mental Measurements, University of Nebraska, 1985), xxiii–xxix.

40. James V. Mitchell, "Testing and the Oscar Buros Lament: From Knowledge to Implementation to Use," in *Social and Technical Issues in Testing*, ed. Barbara S. Plake (Hillsdale, NJ: Lawrence Erlbaum Associates, 1984), 114–115.

41. Howard Wainer and David Thissen, "How is Reliability Related to the Quality of Test Scores? What is the Effect of Local Dependence on Reliability?" *Educational Measurement: Issues and Practice* 15 (1996): 22–29.

Validity of Selection Procedures

AN OVERVIEW OF VALIDITY

In the last chapter, we pointed out that *reliability* is one important characteristic we must have from data produced by any test, interview, or other selection procedure as well as criteria that we use. So far, we have examined in some detail various issues regarding the reliability of information from selection measures. Here, we focus on the topic of *validity*, its relation to reliability, and the principal analytic strategies available for determining the validity of selection procedure data. Validity represents the most important characteristic of data from measures used in human resource (HR) selection. Like reliability, the importance of validity applies to both selection procedures as well as criteria. It shows what is assessed by selection measures and determines the kinds of conclusions we can draw from data such measures produce.

Validity: A Definition

When we are concerned with the accuracy of judgments or inferences made from scores on selection measures, including predictors and criteria, we are interested in their *validity*. In this sense, validity refers to *the degree to which available evidence supports inferences made from scores on selection measures*. Often, when readers hear the word "validity" in a selection context, they think of only *selection procedure* validity. And, in many cases, practitioners and researchers are most interested in selection procedure validity. Keep in mind, however, that if our criteria are not supporting the kinds of inferences we would like to make about employees' job success, we might end up with predictors or selection procedures that do not predict as well or what we would like. Although we focus much of our discussion in this chapter on selection procedure validity, our discussion applies to criteria as well.

From the perspective of HR selection and selection procedure validity, we are most interested in evidence that concerns the hypotheses or inferences regarding a selection procedure's job relatedness. We want to evaluate our inferences. That is, we want to know how accurate are the hypothesized predictions we make (predictions based on data collected from a selection procedure, such as an employment interview or personality inventory) about employee work behaviors (such as absenteeism, turnover, dollar sales, service to customers, or other important aspects of work performance).[1]

One way to illustrate the process of inference making from a measure's scores is to consider a common measure that many of us often make—a simple handshake. Think of the last time you met someone for the first time and shook that person's hand. How did their hand feel? Cold? Clammy? Rough? Firm grip? Limp grip? Now, did you make any attributions about that person based on their grip? For example, if the person's hand was rough, did you conclude, "She must do physical labor"? If it was clammy and cold, did you think, "He must be anxious or nervous"? If you received a "limp" (or what some label, a "dead-fish") grip, did you deduce, "He must not be assertive"? If you had these or similar feelings, you drew inferences from a measure.

You might be wondering: Are job interviewees' handshakes associated with applicant personality characteristics such as extraversion? Are they related to how interviewers judge interviewees? Several studies have confirmed that firmness of handshakes is associated positively with interviewees' level of extraversion and interviewers' ratings of interviewees. Moreover, the relationship between handshake firmness and interviewers' ratings of women was particularly strong. (Thus, if you are meeting an interviewer for the first time, it is probably wise to make that first handshake a firm one![2]) Our next question is, What is the evidence to support the inferences we can draw from our selection procedures? We study validity to collect evidence about which inferences we can accurately make from these measures.

In the context of selection, we want to know how well a predictor (such as a test) is related to criteria important to us. If a predictor is correlated with work performance criteria, then we can draw inferences from scores on the predictor about individuals' future work performance in terms of these criteria. For example, if we have an ability test that is related to work performance, then scores on the ability test can be used to infer a job candidate's performance on the job in question. Because ability test scores are related to work performance, we can be assured that, on average, applicants who perform well on the test will do well on the job.

Historically, people have tended to talk in terms of the validity of a measurement *procedure*. Actually, it is not the procedure itself or the content of the measure (such as test items) that are valid; it is the validity of *inferences* that can be made from scores on the measure. There is not just one validity; there can be many. The number depends on the number of valid *inferences* to be made for the criteria available.

You may read or hear someone say, "This test is valid." However, understand that validity is not an inherent property of the test; rather, it depends on the inferences we can legitimately make from scores on the test. A legitimate inference is one in which the content or scores on the selection procedure are related to some aspect of job success or performance (for example, absenteeism, turnover, ratings of work performance). In some cases, the validity of inferences is expressed quantitatively; in other cases, judgmentally. Whatever the form, different validities may exist for data from any one predictor. These validities will simply depend on those criteria related to the selection procedure and on the inferences drawn from these relations. Therefore, with respect to a predictor, such as a test we are considering for use in employment decision making, we should always ask ourselves, *Valid for what?*

The research process we go through in discovering what and how well a selection procedure measures is called *validation*. In validation, we conduct research studies to accumulate information (that is, evidence) on the meaning and value of our inferences from a selection procedure.[3]

Results of the validation process represent evidence that informs us, which legitimate inferences can be made from selection procedure scores. For instance, let's use a simple example. Suppose a manager believes that an MBA degree is essential for satisfactory performance in a job involving technical sales. The manager is inferring that possession of the degree leads to adequate work performance and that lack of the degree results in unacceptable work performance. In examining the validity of the MBA educational credential as a selection standard, the manager attempts to verify the inference that the MBA is a useful predictor of work performance as measured by dollar sales and salesperson turnover. The manager is not validating the educational degree per se, but rather the inferences made regarding salespersons' holding the degree. For instance, from a validation study, she might find in her firm that for technical sales personnel having an MBA versus those who do not is unrelated to their sales performance. On the other hand, having the MBA is positively related to turnover within 12 months of employment. That is, employees who have an MBA degree tend to leave the firm within the 12-month employment period, whereas employees who do not possess the degree tend to stay. There can be few or many validities for a given predictor depending upon the different criteria investigated.[4] Thus, *validation* involves the research processes we go through in testing the appropriateness of our inferences from our selection procedures.

The Relation between Reliability and Validity

When we discussed the concept of reliability, we used terms such as *dependability, consistency*, and *precision* of measurement. Although these are important characteristics of any measurement device, it is possible to have a measure that is reliable yet does not assess what we want for selection. For example, imagine we have a device that will measure job applicants' eye color in a precise and dependable manner. In fact, our research shows the device has high test–retest reliability in assessing eye color. Now, suppose we use the device to predict applicants' work performance. After conducting our study, we find that color of applicants' eyes has no relation with how well people perform their jobs. (We are sure you are asking yourself: Why should eye color predict performance? If so, you are asking an important question.) This highly reliable eye-color measure is worthless for meeting our objective of predicting work performance. As we saw in our discussion of reliability, the dependability of information produced by a selection procedure is important. Knowledge regarding what is measured by this selection procedure and what it means for predicting work performance, however, makes validity information the most important standard for judging the value of a selection procedure.

Rather than existing as two distinct concepts, reliability and validity go hand in hand. With respect to our eye color measure, we have a highly reliable tool that has no validity in predicting work performance. In sum, high reliability is a necessary but not a sufficient condition for high validity.

Statisticians also have demonstrated the quantitative interrelationship between validity and reliability.[5] The *maximum possible* empirical validity of a predictor such as a test depends on its reliability as well as the reliability of the criterion with which it is correlated. Stated quantitatively, the relationship between validity and reliability is

$$r_{xy} = \sqrt{r_{xx}r_{yy}}$$

where

r_{xy} = *maximum possible* correlation between predictor X and criterion Y, the validity coefficient

r_{xx} = reliability coefficient of predictor X

r_{yy} = reliability coefficient of criterion Y

For example, if the reliability of a test (X) is 0.81 and the reliability of the criterion (Y) is 0.60, then *maximum possible* validity of the test is 0.70; that is,

$$r_{xy} = \sqrt{(0.81)(0.60)} = 0.70$$

Notice the formula is not saying what the actual or calculated validity of predictor X is. It is simply saying that actual calculated validity can be no higher than this maximum possible value because both our predictor and criterion scores contain random error. Because random errors are uncorrelated, the more random error present in scores from a predictor *or* a criterion (that is, the more that reliability falls), then maximum possible validity also will fall.

As you can tell from the formula, if reliability of *either* test *X* or criterion *Y* were lower, maximum possible validity would be lower as well. If either our test or criterion were completely unreliable (that is, reliability = 0.00), then the two variables would be unrelated; empirical validity would be zero. (We discuss the meaning of a validity coefficient later in this chapter.) Reliability or unreliability limits, or puts a ceiling on, possible empirical validity. Practically speaking, to enhance maximum possible validity, reliability should be as high as possible for our predictors *and* our criteria. Therefore, check the reliability of all predictors and criterion measures in a selection program.

Types of Validation Strategies

A *validation study* provides the evidence for determining the legitimate inferences that can be made from scores on a selection measure. Most often, such a study is carried out to determine the accuracy of judgments made from scores on a predictor about important job behaviors (for example, performance, withdrawal) as represented by a criterion. A number of different strategies are used to obtain this evidence to see whether these inferences are supported. For our purposes, we discuss several validation strategies in this chapter. We begin by describing three classical approaches used for validating measures in human resource selection: (a) *content validation*, (b) *criterion-related validation* (including both *concurrent* and *predictive* validation strategies), and (c) *construct validation*. Next, we explore some empirical issues involved in implementing the criterion-related strategies. Following our review of these classical approaches, we briefly examine additional strategies that take a broader perspective—that is, *validity generalization* as well as *job component validity* and *synthetic validity*.

From our overview of the chapter, you probably have the sense that each of the validation strategies represents a separate, distinct way of determining the validity of our selection procedures. We have organized our discussion around these validation strategy groupings because we think that for the student being introduced to validity, organizing our discussion this way will help clarify what the concept entails. It is important to recognize, however, that all of the strategies we discuss are interrelated and should not be logically separated. Ultimately, when the results of these strategies for any particular selection measure are taken together as a whole, they form the body of evidence for determining what is really being measured and what inferences from scores on this measure are warranted. Therefore, where possible, practitioners should rely on multiple validation strategies to support the use of a selection measure in employment decision making.

CONTENT VALIDATION STRATEGY

Content validation, sometimes called a "local" or "indirect" validation study is one strategy that has received much interest among practitioners involved in selection. There are several reasons for this interest. First, the strategy is amenable to employment situations in cases in which only small numbers of applicants actually are being hired to fill a position. Such a situation is characteristic of many small businesses. When adequate amounts of predictor or criterion data are not available, use of criterion-related validation strategies incorporating statistical procedures should be avoided.

Second, suitable measures of job success criteria may not be readily available. For some jobs, such as those involving the delivery of services to clients, customers, and so on, a feasible means for measuring employee success may be difficult and prohibitively expensive to obtain. In such a context, content validation is a viable option because it reduces the need for quantitative measures of employee performance.

Third, use of content validation can lead to selection procedures that will enhance applicants' favorable perceptions of an organization's selection system. As you will see, content validation examines the correspondence between content of a job and content of a selection procedure used for that job. Applicants' perceptions of correspondence between these two can improve applicants' views of an organization's selection methods. For some predictors, job candidates are more likely to view such procedures as fair and job related. (**Note**: Much of our discussion in this section focuses on selection procedures or predictors. However, the principles of content validation apply to criteria as well, such as in developing the content of a performance appraisal or evaluation form or in developing a criterion for assessing the value of predictors used in predicting the trainability or performance of trainees in a training program.)

Whatever the reasons, content validation continues to attract interest among selection consultants and researchers. Because of this interest, we spend some time reviewing this validation method.

Basically, a selection procedure (such as a test) or a criterion (such as a performance evaluation) has content validity when it is shown that its content (items, questions, behaviors, and so on) representatively samples the content or aspects of the job associated with successful performance.[6]

"Content of the job" is a collection of job behaviors (some physical, some psychological) and the associated knowledge, skills, abilities, and other characteristics (such as competencies, licenses, certifications, etc.) that are necessary for effective work performance. The behaviors and work-related characteristics (WRCs) that represent the content of the job to be assessed are referred to as the *job content domain*. For a selection measure, such as a predictor, to possess content validity, the measure's content must be representative of the requirements for successful performance in the job content domain as identified through a job analysis. The entire job domain does not have to be reflected in the selection procedures. Only those job behaviors, knowledge, skills, abilities, etc. deemed to be most essential to the job typically are assessed.

The more closely the content of a selection procedure is linked to actual job content, content validity is enhanced. For example, suppose a large trucking company employs drivers of large tractor-trailer rigs. One critical aspect of drivers' jobs involves backing a tractor-trailer rig into a warehouse space having only 2 feet of clearance on each side of the trailer. A driver must back the truck into the loading dock under heavy traffic conditions, taking no more than 3 minutes to complete the task. The truck must be backed up so that it does not hit the sides of the loading bay (each side of the bay has about 2 feet of clearance) but close enough to a loading dock so that freight can be loaded in a timely manner. Now suppose, as part of the selection program, applicants for the driver position are asked to back up a tractor-trailer rig to a loading dock like that actually encountered on the job. They must complete the task within 3 minutes (a requirement that is part of the actual job due to traffic buildup) and without damaging the trailer or loading bay. While undertaking the selection task, driver applicants experience simulated impatient automobile drivers who blow horns and make verbal comments, events that actually confront truck drivers on the job. For this type of selection situation, a content validation strategy is particularly appropriate.

Content validation differs from other validation strategies in an important way. The method emphasizes the role of expert judgment in determining the validity of a measure rather than relying on statistical methods. *Judgments* are used to describe the degree to which the content of a selection method reflects important aspects of what is meant by work performance. With its emphasis on *description*, content validation contrasts with concurrent and predictive validation strategies (which we discuss later), where emphasis is on *statistical prediction*.

Sometimes, *face* validity is confused with the concept of *content* validity. Whereas content validity deals with the representative sampling of the content domain of a job by a selection measure, face validity concerns the *appearance* of whether a measure is measuring what is intended. A selection test has face validity if it appears to job applicants taking the test that it is job related. However, just because a test appears to have face validity does not mean it has content or criterion-related validity—it may or may not. Hence, face validity is not a form of validity in a technical sense. Nevertheless, when technically feasible to incorporate in a selection system, face validity can be a positive attribute. In one study, for instance, participants in France and the United States were asked to rate the favorability of 10 selection procedures. Perceived face validity of the selection procedures was the strongest correlate of participants' beliefs regarding both the procedures' effectiveness in identifying qualified people and the procedures' fairness.[7]

If test takers perceive a test to be job related, then they likely will have a more positive attitude toward the organization and its selection procedures. Positive attitudes toward selection measures may yield positive benefits for an organization. For example, applicants who believe selection procedures are face-valid indicators of their ability to perform a job may be more motivated to perform their best on these procedures. Also, if rejected for a job, applicants may perceive the selection procedures to be less biased than if measures without face validity were used. In this situation, rejected applicants from protected groups may be less likely to file a discrimination charge against an organization that uses face-valid selection measures than an organization that does not. From this perspective, face validity may be thought of as a "comfort factor" for job candidates and some managers alike.

Major Aspects of Content Validation

There are a number of ways to examine the link between content of a job and content of a predictor. These include (a) showing that the predictor is a representative sample of important job content, (b) demonstrating that predictor content reflects the WRCs required for successful work performance, and (c) using subject matter experts (SMEs) to make judgments regarding the overlap between the WRCs required to perform well on a predictor and those WRCs needed for work performance.[8] Drawing on some earlier writings, Benjamin Schneider and Neal Schmitt described a number of these key elements for implementing a content validity strategy.[9] We summarize the major aspects of several of these strategies:

1. **Conducting a Comprehensive Job Analysis.** Job analysis is the heart of any validation study. In particular, job analysis is the essential ingredient in successfully conducting a content validation study. Results of a job analysis define the *job content domain*. The job content domain consists of the work activities and knowledge, skills, abilities, and any other WRCs needed to perform these work activities. The identified job content domain need not include all work activities and WRCs that compose the job. Only those work activities and WRCs deemed most critical to the job need to be considered. By matching the identified job content domain to the content of the selection procedure, content validity is established.

A number of court cases have affirmed the necessity for analyzing the content and nature of the job for which a selection procedure is used.[10] For example, the U.S. Supreme Court ruled in *Albemarle Paper Co. v. Moody* that job analysis must play an integral role in any validation study.[11] With respect to content validation studies per se, the *Uniform Guidelines on Employee Selection Procedures* specify that a job analysis should result in the following products:

A. Describing the tasks performed on the job

B. Measuring criticality and/or importance of the tasks

C. Specifying WRCs required to perform these critical tasks

D. Measuring the criticality and/or importance of WRCs, which include

   (1) an operational definition of each WRC

   (2) a description of the relationship between each WRC and each job task

   (3) a description of the complexity/difficulty of obtaining each WRC

   (4) a specification as to whether an employee is expected to possess each WRC before being placed on the job or being trained

   (5) an indication of whether each WRC is necessary for successful performance on the job[12]

E. Linking important job tasks to important WRCs.
Linking tasks to WRCs serves as a basis for determining the essential tasks to simulate in a behaviorally oriented selection measure, such as a work simulation, or for determining critical WRCs to tap in a paper-and-pencil measure, such as a multiple-choice test.

   Each important job task identified in the job analysis likely will require at least some degree of a WRC for successful task performance. Here, the WRCs required to perform these tasks are specified. Most often, these WRCs are identified by working with SMEs who have considerable knowledge of the job and the necessary WRCs needed to perform it. This step typically involves subjective judgment on the part of participants in identifying the important WRCs. Because inferences are involved, emphasis in this step is on defining specific WRCs for specific job tasks. By focusing on specific definitions of tasks and WRCs, judgments involved in determining what WRCs are needed to perform which tasks are less likely to be subject to human error.

2. **Selecting Experts Participating in a Content Validity Study.** As we have noted, the application of content validity requires the use of expert judgment. Usually, these judgments are obtained from job incumbents and supervisors serving as SMEs. SMEs are individuals who can provide accurate judgments about the tasks performed on the job, the WRCs necessary for performing these tasks, and any other information useful for developing selection measure content. Because of their importance, it is essential that these judges be carefully selected and trained. In using SMEs in a content validation study, it is important to report their qualifications and experience. Ideally, members of protected classes (for example, gender, race, or ethnicity) should be represented among the SMEs. Details also should be given regarding their training and the instructions they received while serving as SMEs. Finally, information on how SMEs made their judgments in the validation study—for example, as individuals or in a group consensus—should be provided.

3. **Specifying Selection Procedure Content.** Once the job tasks and WRCs have been appropriately identified, the items, questions, or other content that compose the selection procedure are specified. This phase of content validation often is called *domain sampling*. That is, the items, questions, or other content are chosen to constitute the selection measure so they represent the behaviors, WRCs, or other characteristics judged as important for work performance. The content included is in proportion to the relative importance of the WRCs and other characteristics identified as important for work performance. SMEs who are knowledgeable of the job in question review the contents of the selection procedure and judge their suitability for the job. Final determination of selection procedure content depends on these experts' judgments.

To aid the review of selection procedure content, such as items on a multiple-choice test or structured interview questions, Richard Barrett proposed the Content Validation Form II (CVFII).[13] Basically, the form consists of questions that serve as a guide for analyzing the appropriateness of selection measure content in a content validation study. Questions on the CVFII are organized into three test review areas. The CVFII review areas and sample questions from each are as follows:

A. Selection Procedure as a Whole

- Is an adequate portion of the job covered by the selection procedure?

- Does the selection procedure, combined with other procedures, measure the most important content of the job?

B. Item-by-Item Analysis

- How important is the ability to respond correctly to successful work performance?

- Are there serious consequences for safety or efficiency if the applicant does not have the WRCs needed to respond correctly?

C. Supplementary Indications of Content Validity

- Are the language, mathematics, and other demands of the test commensurate with those required by the job?

- Would applicants who are not test-wise be likely to do as well as they should?

Predictor Fidelity

In developing a predictor to be used in selection (for example, a selection interview, a work simulation, or a multiple-choice test), one key issue is the fidelity or comparability between the format and content of the predictor and the performance domain of the job for which the predictor will be used. Two types of predictor and work performance fidelity should be considered: (a) *physical* fidelity and (b) *psychological* fidelity. Physical fidelity concerns the match between how a worker actually behaves on the job and how an applicant for that job is asked to behave on the predictor used in selection. For example, a driving test for truck driver applicants that requires driving activities that an incumbent truck driver must actually perform has physical fidelity. A typing test requiring applicants to use certain word processing software to type actual business correspondence that is prepared by current employees using the same software and equipment used on the job also has physical fidelity. Depending on the nature of the WRCs being assessed, however, physical fidelity is not always easily feasible.

Psychological fidelity occurs when the same WRCs required to perform the job successfully are also required on the predictor. For example, a patrol police officer may have to deal with hostile and angry citizens. Asking police officer job applicants to write a statement describing how they would handle a hostile individual is not likely to have psychological fidelity. WRCs different from those required by this aspect of the job, such as the ability to express one's self in writing, may be called for by the written statement. On the other hand, psychological fidelity might be found in a role-playing simulation in which police patrol applicants interact with an actor playing the role of an angry citizen.[14]

One other point should be made with regard to selection procedures—that is, job fidelity. This issue concerns the extent to which a test measures WRCs that are *not* required by the job under study. This problem can be particularly troublesome with multiple-choice tests. Irwin Goldstein and his colleagues pointed out that often the real issue with multiple-choice tests is not so much whether they assess job-relevant WRCs but whether they measure WRCs that are *not* required for successful work performance. For example, candidates being assessed for promotion may be asked to memorize voluminous materials for a knowledge test, but on the job itself, incumbents are not required to retrieve the information from memory to perform the job. Necessary information for performing the job can be obtained from available manuals or other reference sources.[15]

Goldstein and Sheldon Zedeck described another situation in which WRCs covered on the selection procedure were different from those required to perform the job.[16] In this case, a job analysis for the position of lieutenant in a fire department showed that a lieutenant gives short orders orally regarding the placement of personnel and what equipment should be sent to a fire. If a paper-and-pencil selection procedure used with applicants for the position of lieutenant requires them to respond to a hypothetical fire scene by writing down what they would do in giving those orders, then there is a question as to whether writing an essay requires the same WRCs as those required for actual performance of the lieutenant's job. Then, too, if the written exam is scored for grammatical correctness and spelling, additional questions are raised about the job relevance of the selection test. These questions regarding content validity become particularly important when further examination of the job shows that lieutenants do not write out specific orders regarding a fire; they give oral commands. Thus, an option to the written test that was developed was to have applicants use a tape recorder and orally give their directions and orders.

In general, when physical and psychological fidelity of the selection predictor mirrors the performance domain of the job, content validity is enhanced. Such a measure is psychologically similar because applicants are asked to demonstrate the behaviors and WRCs required for successful incumbent performance.

4. **Assessing Selection Procedure and Job Content Relevance.** Another important element in content validation is determining the relevance of selection procedure content to job content.

    After a test or some other measure has been developed, an essential step in determining content validity is to have SMEs judge the degree to which WRCs identified from a job analysis are needed to answer the test questions. These incumbents actually take the test and then rate the extent of test content-to-WRC overlap. A rating instruction such as the following might be given:
    "To what extent are each of the following work-related characteristics needed to answer these questions (or perform these exercises)?"[17]

    1 = Not at all

    2 = To a slight extent

    3 = To a moderate extent

    4 = To a great extent

Charles Lawshe proposed a quantitative procedure called the *content validity ratio* (CVR) for making this determination.[18] Basically, the CVR is an index computed on ratings made by a panel of SMEs regarding the degree of overlap between the content of a selection measure and content of the job. Each panel member is presented with the contents of a selection measure and asked to make ratings of these contents. For example, the panel members are given cards with each individual item on a job knowledge test written on a separate card. SMEs who make up the rating panel independently judge each test item by indicating whether the WRC measured by the item reflects the work performance domain. A three-point rating scale is used (a) *essential*, (b) *useful but not essential*, or (c) *not necessary for work performance*. These ratings are used in the following formula to produce a CVR for each item on the test:

$$CVR = \frac{n_e - N/2}{N/2}$$

where n_e is the number of judges rating the test item as essential, and N is the total number of judges on the rating panel. The computed CVR can range from 1.00 (all judges rate an item essential) to 0.00 (half of the judges rate it essential) to −1.00 (none of the judges rate it essential). Because it is possible for an item CVR to occur by chance, it is tested for statistical significance.

[**Technical Note:** Lawshe presented a table for determining item CVR statistical significance. However, Robert Wilson and his associates identified some anomalies in Lawshe's original table. When the pool of SMEs is smaller than 10, they concluded that Lawshe's tables showing the CVRs used to determine whether an item should be included in a selection procedure, such as a test, had some mistakes. That is, for SME pools of less than 10, Lawshe's tables tended to exclude items that actually had statistically significant CVRs. Therefore, in testing CVR's for statistical significance, Wilson et al.'s table (on p. 206 of their article) showing critical values for CVRs should be consulted.[19]]

Statistically significant items suggest correspondence with the job. Nonsignificant items that most of the judges do not rate "essential" can be eliminated from the test. By averaging the CVR item indexes, a content validity index (CVI) for the test as a whole can be derived. The CVI indicates the extent to which panelists believe the overall ability to perform on the test overlaps with the ability to perform the job. Hence, the index represents overall selection procedure and job content domain overlap.

Some Examples of Content Validation

Because the content validation approach can have wide applicability in the selection of individuals for jobs, we examine some examples of content validation. Lyle Schoenfeldt and his colleagues sought to develop an industrial reading test for entry-level personnel of a large chemical corporation. There had been a major explosion at one of the plants, and lack of reading skills by employees indicated problems that contributed to the accident. They used job analysis to determine *what* materials entry-level personnel needed to be able to read upon job entry as well as the *importance* of these materials to work performance. Their analyses showed that entry-level employees read four types of materials: (a) safety (signs, work rules, safety manuals), (b) operating procedures (instruction bulletins, checklists), (c) day-to-day operations (logbooks, labels, schedules), and (d) other (memos, work agreements, application materials). The safety and operating procedures materials were judged to be most important because they accounted for roughly 80 percent of the materials read while performing the job. The test was then constructed so that approximately 80 percent of the test items reflected these two types of materials. The test itself was developed from the content of *actual* materials current employees had to read upon job entry.[20]

Silvia Moscoso and Jesus Salgado were faced with the problem of developing a job-related employment interview for hiring private security personnel. They used a content validation strategy in developing the interview questions and scoring procedures.[21] Following identification of behavioral incidents descriptive of critical aspects of the job, they developed seven interview questions to assess six work performance dimensions (for example, being a good observer, showing firmness, demonstrating initiative). They wrote interview questions to reflect the content of selected incidents identified from the job analysis. Subsequent analyses showed acceptable agreement among SMEs rating interviewees' responses to the questions. In addition, they established content validity for five of the seven interview questions.

In a hypothetical example, imagine we want to build content-valid measures to select typist-clerks in an office setting. Again, based on the job analysis procedures discussed previously, we know that incumbents need specific WRCs to perform specific tasks. From the example tasks and WRCs shown in Figure 8.1, we identify two specific work performance domains that we want to predict: (a) typing performance and (b) calculating performance. For our measures to have content validity, we build them in such a way that their content representatively samples the content of each of these domains. Where should the measures' contents come from? For the contents to be most representative, one strategy we could use is to derive test content from what incumbents actually do on the job. For example, we might develop a performance predictor that asks an applicant to format an actual business letter in a specific style and then type it within a prescribed period of time on a computer. Similarly, we might ask applicants to use a 10-key adding machine to compute and check some actual, reported business expenses. Furthermore, in computing scores, we might weight the measures so that each reflects its relative importance in performing the job. In our example, typing correspondence accounts for approximately 75 percent of the job, while 15 percent involves calculating expense claims. (The remaining 10 percent consists of other tasks.) Thus, our typing measure should be weighted 75 percent to reflect its relative importance to calculating. As you can tell from our example task statements, WRCs, and measures, we are attempting to develop selection measures whose content representatively maps the actual content of the job itself. To the extent we are successful, content validity of the measures is supported.

Job incumbents and supervisors serving as SMEs play an important role in establishing the content validity of our predictors. These experts identify the important tasks performed on the job and the relevant WRCs needed to perform these tasks successfully. Also, as we saw earlier through the computation of the CVR and content validity index, they also serve in judging the appropriateness of content for the selection procedures. These judgments taken in sum represent the foundation for determining the content validity of the selection procedures being developed for our typist-clerk position.

Appropriateness of Content Validation?

When the *Uniform Guidelines* was released in 1978, the guidelines specified what sort of psychological characteristics or constructs could not be supported using content validation. In Section C1 of the *Uniform Guidelines*, it was noted

| FIGURE 8.1 | Example Tasks, Work-Related Characteristics (WRCs), and Selection Procedures for Assessing WRCs of Typist-Clerks |

Example Job Tasks of Typist-Clerks

Example Work-Related Characteristics of Typist-Clerks	1. Types and proofreads business correspondence, reports, and proposals upon written instruction	•••	5. Checks and computes travel claims and expenses using a 10-key adding machine	Selection Procedures
1. Skill in typing reports and correspondence at a minimum of 50 words per minute	√			Speed typing test of business correspondence
2. Ability to read at 12th-grade reading level	√			Reading test involving reports, correspondence, and proposals at 12th-grade reading level
3. Knowledge of business letter styles used in typing business correspondence	√			Formatting and typing test of business correspondence
4. Knowledge of arithmetic at 10th-grade level including addition, subtraction, division, and multiplication			√	Arithmetic test requiring arithmetic calculations on business expense data using a 10-key adding machine
•	•	•	•	•
•	•	•	•	•
•	•	•	•	•
9. Ability to operate a 10-key adding machine			√	Arithmetic test requiring arithmetic calculations on business expense data using a 10-key adding machine
Percentage (%) of time performed	75%	•••	15%	

Note: A check mark (√) indicates that a WRC is required to perform a specific job task. Selection procedures are those developed to assess particular WRCs.

A selection procedure based upon inferences about mental processes cannot be supported solely or primarily on the basis of content validity. Thus, a content strategy is not appropriate demonstrating the validity of selection procedures which purport to measure traits or constructs, such as intelligence, aptitude, personality, commonsense, judgment, leadership, and spatial ability.[22]

At the time the *Uniform Guidelines* were released, it was interpreted that if content validity were going to be used with selection procedures, then those procedures should measure elements such as knowledge, skills, abilities, or observable behaviors shown to be job related. Recently, however, some industrial psychologists have taken a broader perspective with regard to the appropriateness of content validity for certain psychological constructs that the *Uniform Guidelines* seems to prohibit. For example, Frank Schmidt theoretically refuted arguments that content validity cannot be applied to general cognitive ability (GCA).[23] Three well-respected industrial psychologists[24] commented on Schmidt's rationale and generally agreed that "content validity is appropriate scientifically and professionally for use with tests of specific cognitive skills used in work performance."[25]

As we have seen, content validity provides evidence that a selection procedure representatively samples the universe of job content. As long as a selection measure assesses *observable*, important job behaviors (for example, a driving test used to measure a truck driver applicant's ability to drive a truck), the inferential leap in judging between what a selection device measures and the content of the job is likely rather small. However, the more abstract the work activities comprising a job and the WRCs necessary to perform the job (for example, the ability of a manager to provide leadership, the possession of emotional stability), the greater the inferential leap required in judging the link between the content of the job and content of a selection procedure. Therefore, it is likely more difficult to establish content validity for those jobs characterized by more abstract functions and WRCs than for jobs whose functions and WRCs can be seen. In cases in which these inferential leaps are large, some courts are less prone to accept a content validation strategy. For such situations, other validation strategies, such as criterion-related strategies are necessary.

Job Analysis and Content Validation

A central concept of content validity is that selection procedure content must appropriately sample the job content domain. When there is congruence between the WRCs necessary for effective work performance and those WRCs necessary for successful performance on the selection procedure, then it is possible to infer how performance on the selection procedure relates to job success. Without a clearly established link between these two sets of WRCs, such an inference is questionable. Whenever the specific content of the predictor and the WRCs required to perform the tasks of a job differ, then an inferential leap or judgment is necessary to determine whether the measure appropriately samples the job. How do we establish this job–WRC link with the selection procedure–WRC link in a content validity study? A carefully performed job analysis is the foundation for any content validity study. In a later chapter, we illustrate some of the steps necessary to perform a suitable job analysis for content validity purposes. For now, however, Figure 8.2 descriptively summarizes some major inference points that take place when using job analysis to help establish the content validity of a selection procedure.

The first inference point (**1**) in Figure 8.2 is from the job itself to the tasks identified as composing it. When careful and thorough job analysis techniques and knowledgeable SMEs are used, the judgments necessary for determining whether the tasks accurately represent the job probably will have minimal error. The next inference point (**2**) is from the tasks of the job to identified WRCs required for successful work performance. Here again, complete, thorough job analyses using capable SMEs can minimize possible error. The final inference point (**3**) is most critical. It is at this point that final judgments regarding content validity of the selection measure are made. Here, concerns can be raised regarding the physical and psychological fidelity between the selection procedure and the work performance domain. Specifically, to make the inferential leap supporting content validity, we must address three important issues that contribute to physical and psychological fidelity:

1. Does successful performance on the selection procedure require the same WRCs needed for successful work performance?

2. Is the mode used for assessing performance on WRCs the same as that required for job or task performance?

3. Are WRCs *not* required for the job present in the predictor?[26]

If we can deal with these issues successfully, our inferential leaps can be kept small. As long as the inferential leaps are acceptably small—that is, the selection measure is composed of content that clearly resembles important job tasks and WRCs—arguments

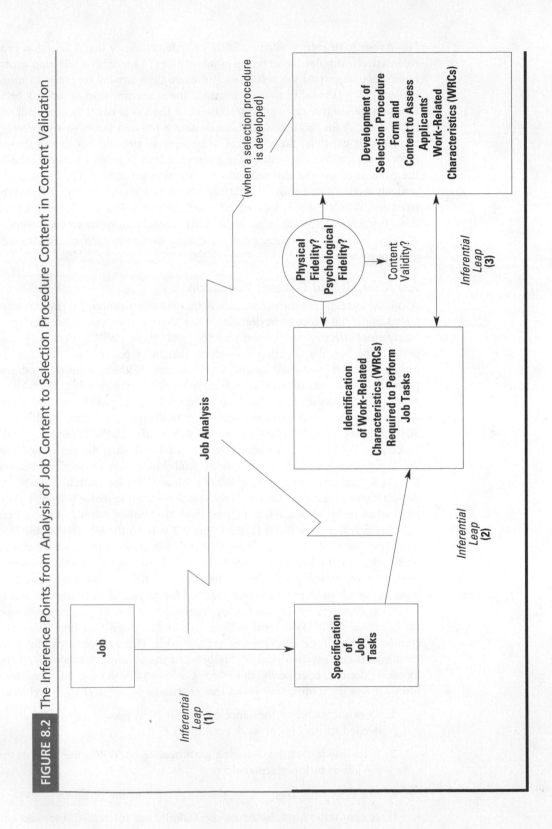

FIGURE 8.2   The Inference Points from Analysis of Job Content to Selection Procedure Content in Content Validation

for content validity inferences are plausible. For jobs involving activities and processes that are *directly observable* (such as for the job of a typist), only *small inferences* are required in judging the relation between what is done on the job, the WRCs necessary to do the job, and the WRCs assessed by the selection measure. For jobs whose activities and work processes are *less visible* and more abstract (such as those of an executive), greater inferences must be made between job activities, applicant requirements for successful performance, and selection measure content. In general, the greater the inferential leaps being made in a content validity study, the more difficult it is to establish content validity. At this point, other validation strategies are needed, such as criterion-related approaches (if possible).

The *Uniform Guidelines* recognize the limits of content validation and specify some situations in which content validation alone is *not* appropriate; in these situations, other validation methods must be used. These situations include the following:

1. When mental processes, psychological constructs, or personality traits (such as judgment, integrity, dependability, motivation) are not directly observable but inferred from the selection method.[27]

2. When the selection procedure involves WRCs, an employee is expected to learn on the job.[28]

3. When the content of the selection device does not resemble a work behavior, or when the setting and administration of the selection procedure does not resemble the work setting.[29]

We noted that some industrial psychologists have suggested that content validity can support certain cognitive abilities. You might be wondering if the *Uniform Guidelines* state that psychological constructs such as general cognitive abilities are not supported by content validation, how can it be said that content validity can be used to support such abilities? Although some judges at this point in time might differ, some writers have characterized the *Uniform Guidelines* as a "political–policy" document, while the more current *Standards for Educational and Psychological Testing*[30] (*Standards*) and *Principles for the Validation and Use of Personnel Selection Procedures*[31] (*Principles*) are based on scientific knowledge and professional practices. The *Uniform Guidelines* are more than 35 years old and simply have not kept up with new knowledge that has accumulated in personnel selection over that time. The *Standards* and the *Principles* pose no construct limitations on what can be validated.[32] At least among some industrial psychologists, there seems to be general agreement that content validity evidence (when properly identified through a job analytic foundation) can support some cognitive ability tests used in personnel selection.[33]

How Content Validation Differs from Criterion-Related Validation

As a validation method, content validation differs from criterion-related techniques in the following ways: (a) in content validity, the focus is on the selection procedure itself and its manifest relation with the job content domain, whereas in the others, the focus is on the relations of the selection procedure with an external criterion; (b) criterion-related validity is narrowly based on a specific set of data, whereas content validity is based on a broader base of data and inference; and (c) a statement of criterion-related validity is couched in terms of quantitative indices (*prediction* via statistical methods such as regression), whereas content validity is generally characterized using broader, more judgmental descriptors (*description*).[34]

In some situations (as we saw earlier), content validation is the only practical option available. For example, small sample sizes, which can occur in medium- and small-size businesses may necessitate a content validation approach. Criterion-related validation is simply not feasible. In addition, reliable criterion information may not be available because of existing lawsuits in an organization or union actions that prohibit the collection of work performance data.[35]

Logically, it might seem reasonable to conclude that inferences made from a content-related strategy will overlap those inferences made from criterion-related strategies. Michael Carrier and his associates tested the correspondence between criterion-related and content validation strategies for three structured interview guides used to select insurance agents.[36] They found significant relationships between the two strategies for agents with prior insurance sales experience, but not for those lacking experience. The study suggests that content validity does not automatically equate to criterion-related validity. In addition, Kevin Murphy and others concluded that for a set of cognitive predictors (such as psychomotor and performance tests, selection interviews, knowledge tests, work sample tests) that are positively correlated with one another as well as with a measure of job success, whether there is a match or a mismatch between content of the predictors and content of the job (that is, content validity) is unlikely to have a meaningful influence on *criterion-related* validity. For personality inventories, however, matching predictor and job content (that is, establishing content validity) might be an important determinant of criterion-related validity.[37] In sum, content validity reflects only the extent to which WRCs identified for the job domain are judged to be present in a selection procedure. Hence, as our database of inferences regarding validity is built, it is important that we examine other validity evidence whenever possible.

CRITERION-RELATED VALIDATION STRATEGIES

Inferences about performance on some criterion from scores on a predictor, such as an ability test, are best examined through the use of a criterion-related validation study. Two approaches typically are undertaken when conducting an empirical, criterion-related study: (a) a *concurrent* or (b) a *predictive* validation study. In some respects, these approaches are very similar. That is, information is collected on a predictor and a criterion, and statistical procedures are used to test for a relation between these two sources of data. Results from these procedures answer the question, Can valid inferences about job applicants' performance on the job be made based on how well they performed on our predictor? Although concurrent and predictive strategies share a number of similarities, we have chosen to discuss these strategies separately to highlight their unique characteristics.

Concurrent Validation

In a concurrent validation strategy, sometimes referred to as the "present employee method" or as a "local" or "direct" validation study, information is obtained on both a predictor and a criterion for a *current* group of employees. Because predictor and criterion data are collected roughly at the same time, this approach has been labeled "concurrent validation." Once the two sets of data (predictor and criterion information) have been collected, they are statistically correlated. The validity of the inference to be drawn from the measure is signified by a statistically significant ($p \leq .05$) relationship (usually determined by a correlation coefficient) found between the predictor and measure of job success or criterion.

An Example

As an example of a concurrent validation study, imagine we want to determine whether some ability tests might be valid predictors of successful work performance of industrial electricians working in a national firm employing a large number of industrial electricians. First, we make a thorough analysis of the industrial electrician's job. Drawing on job analysis methods, we attempt to uncover the critical tasks actually performed on the job as judged by knowledgeable job incumbents and supervisors. We refer to these individuals as subject matter experts or SMEs.

From these identified tasks, we then infer the WRCs required for successful work performance. The SMEs then rate WRCs' importance to task performance. Figure 8.3 summarizes four hypothetical, critical job tasks as well as several relevant WRCs judged as important in industrial electricians' jobs. (Remember, we are providing only some example job tasks and WRCs; there could be more or less depending on the nature of the job.) Four WRCs were thought as important in performing the job tasks: (a) knowledge of electrical equipment; (b) ability to design/modify mechanical equipment for new applications; (c) pays attention to work details; organized; team-oriented in implementing work plans; and (d) ability to follow oral directions.

The SMEs' average ratings of the link between each of the WRCs and critical job tasks are shown in the body of Figure 8.3. Based on these mean ratings, three of four

| FIGURE 8.3 | Selection of Experimental Selection Procedures to Predict Important Work-Related Characteristics (WRCs) for the Job of Industrial Electrician |

	Linking Work-Related Characteristics (WRCs) to Critical Job Tasks (1 = Not at All Important; 5 = Very Important)			
	WRCs			
Critical Job Tasks	**1. Knowledge of Electrical Equipment**	**2. Ability to Design/ Modify Mechanical Equipment for New Applications**	**3. Pays Attention to Work Details; Organized; Team-Oriented in Implementing Work Plans**	**4. Ability to Follow Oral Directions**
1. Maintains and repairs lighting circuits and electrical equipment such as motors, hand tools	4.8	3.4	2.1	1.3
2. Installs equipment following detailed written specifications and drawings	4.5	3.3	4.7	1.1
3. Works in a team on large electrical projects to meet project deadlines	3.8	3.6	4.8	1.8
4. Independently constructs basic electrical/ mechanical devices, e.g., servos	4.8	4.9	3.5	1.0
Chosen WRC Predictor	**Does Predictor Appear Suitable for Assessing This WRC?**			
A. Bennett Mechanical Comprehension Test (Form AA)	No	Yes	No	No
B. Purdue Test for Electricians	Yes	No	No	No
C. Purdue "Can Your Read A Working Drawing" Test	Yes	Yes	No	No
D. NEO Personality Inventory-Revised (NEO PI-R) Form S	No	No	Yes	No

Note: The numbers shown are mean ratings given by subject matter experts used in the analysis of the industrial electrician's job. High ratings indicate that particular WRC is relevant to the successful performance of a critical job task. "Yes" indicates that a predictor appears to be useful in assessing a particular WRC.

WRCs were chosen as important for performance of the listed tasks. The WRC: ability to follow oral directions was judged to be of less importance in successfully performing the job and was not used a basis for choosing a predictor.

After we have identified the requisite WRCs, the next step is to select or develop those methods that appear to measure the relevant attributes found necessary for job success. As shown in Figure 8.3, three commercially available tests and one commercially available personality inventory were selected as experimental predictors of electricians' job performance. The three tests were (a) *Bennett Mechanical Comprehension Test* (Form AA), (b) *Purdue Test for Electricians*, and (c) *Purdue "Can You Read a Working Drawing?" Test*. The personality inventory selected was the *NEO Personality Inventory-Revised* (*NEO PI-R*) *Form S*. How were these three tests and the personality inventory chosen? We chose these four predictors based (a) on our knowledge of which WRCs we identified for successful work performance and (b) our research on and knowledge of those existing tests and inventories we judged to capture our desired attributes. This process of inferring which devices might be used to measure the derived WRCs usually involves some form of subjective judgment. Expert advice can play an important role in choosing the most appropriate measures. For this reason, experienced selection consultants should play an important role in choosing or developing selection measures.

Next, our three tests and personality inventory are administered to industrial electricians currently working in numerous manufacturing and repair facilities operated by the company. They are told their participation is voluntary, the tests are being given for research purposes only, and their test scores will not affect how they are evaluated or their employment with the company. Convincing a large number of employees to take a test, and to try their best on the test, even though there is no personal, direct benefit to them is a challenging "sales job" for anyone conducting a direct validation study.

As part of our job analysis, we also identify measures of job success that serve as criteria. In this step, criterion information representing measures of electricians' work performance is collected. Performance appraisal ratings or more objective measures such as the number of errors in equipment repair or in electrical wiring projects might serve as criteria. Whatever the criteria, it is essential that the measures chosen be relevant indicators of performance as identified by the job analysis.

At this point, assume both predictor and criterion data have been collected (easy for us to say!). As depicted in Figure 8.4, the final step is to analyze the results using statistical procedures. A common practice is to statistically correlate (using the Pearson product–moment correlation coefficient) the sets of predictor and criterion data. Tests are considered as valid predictors of performance if statistically significant relationships with criteria exist. If one or more of our tryout tests is significantly correlated with a criterion, we will give serious consideration to incorporating the predictors in our selection program. Table 8.1 outlines the basic steps taken in a concurrent validation study.

Strengths and Weaknesses

If it can be assumed that the necessary requirements for conducting an empirical concurrent validation study are met, there is a positive argument for using this method. With a concurrent validation approach, an investigator has almost immediate information on the appropriateness of selection procedures as employment tools. However, several factors mitigate the usefulness of a concurrent validation study; these include (a) availability of a large sample of industrial electricians working in comparable settings who will voluntarily participate in the study, (b) differences in job tenure or length of employment of employees who participate in the study, (c) the representativeness (or unrepresentativeness) of present *employees* to job *applicants*, (d) certain employees failing to participate in the validation study, and (e) the motivation of employees to participate in the study or employee manipulation of answers to some selection predictors.

| FIGURE 8.4 | Representation of Relating Predictor Scores with Criterion Data to Test for Validity |

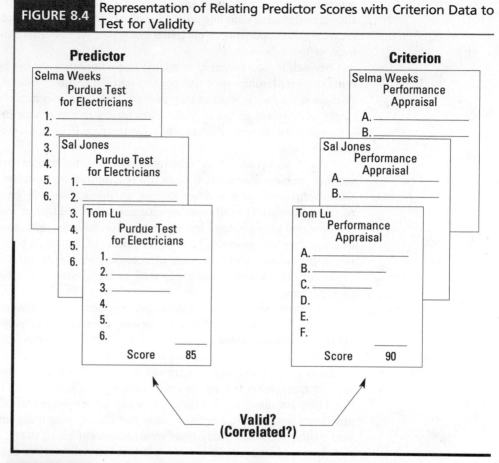

| TABLE 8.1 | Summary of Major Steps Undertaken in Conducting Concurrent and Predictive Validation Studies |

Concurrent Validation	Predictive Validation
1. Conduct analyses of the job	1. Conduct analyses of the job
2. Determine relevant WRCs required to perform the job successfully	2. Determine relevant WRCs required to perform the job successfully
3. Choose or develop the experimental predictors of these WRCs	3. Choose or develop the experimental predictors of these WRCs
4. Select or develop criteria of job success	4. Select or develop criteria of job success
5. Administer predictors to **current employees** and collect criterion data	5. Administer predictors to **job applicants** and file results
6. Analyze predictor and criterion data relationships	6. **After passage of a suitable period of time,** collect criterion data
	7. Analyze predictor and criterion data relationships

First, lack of access to a large number of employees working in comparable settings from whom both predictor and criterion information can be collected is one of the biggest problems in conducting any local validation study. Small size samples affect our ability to detect a statistical relationship between a predictor and criterion (assuming that one is actually present). In addition, any significant validity coefficient based on a small sample is subject to statistical sampling error. We will have more to say in a later section of the chapter regarding the importance of obtaining a large sample size before conducting any empirical form of test validation.

Second, if job experience is related to performance on the job, then any predictor–criterion relationship may be contaminated by an irrelevant variable—job tenure. Because most people learn as they perform their jobs, it is entirely feasible that job experience may indeed influence their scores on either a predictor or criterion measure. Job tenure can be controlled statistically by treating it as a control variable in statistical analyses.

Third, if a concurrent validation study is undertaken for a selection measure, another problem may arise. If there is a relationship between the predictor and criterion for current *employees* and we choose to use it, we will be predicting job success of job *applicants*. If applicants are characteristically different from job incumbents (for example, are younger, have less job experience, have less education, of a different gender or race), then the generalizability of the results of our study based on incumbents might not apply to applicants. Because of voluntary employee turnover or involuntary dismissal, our current employee group may be highly selective and not at all representative of applicants.

Fourth, a concurrent validation study excludes certain groups of individuals. For example, applicants who were rejected for employment and employees who left the organization or were promoted out of the job would not be available for the validation study. These factors can restrict the variability or range of scores on the criterion. Because of criterion range restriction, validity will be lowered. However, steps can be taken to correct for range restriction in the criterion.

Fifth, because we are basing our study on employees who have a job rather than applicants who do not, employee study participants may bring different levels of motivation to the validation study than would applicant participants. Employees simply may not want to participate in a study in which they do not see a direct benefit. They may give a poor, unrepresentative effort on the predictor, and this may affect the relationship with criteria representing work performance. Additionally, on some predictors—for example, a personality inventory—applicants may be more motivated than employees currently on the job to alter responses to create a favorable impression.

Predictive Validation

Rather than collecting predictor and criterion data at one point in time (like our concurrent validation approach), predictive validation (another local, direct validation strategy) involves the collection of data *over* time. In the context of HR selection, job *applicants* rather than job incumbents serve as the data source. For this reason, it is sometimes known as the "future-employee" or "follow-up" method. The basic steps are also summarized in Table 8.1.

An Example

To illustrate the predictive validation method, let's return to our industrial electrician example. The steps involving job analysis, choice of criteria, and the selection of predictors we want to try out are identical to those under the concurrent validation approach. The really significant difference between the two methods occurs at the *predictor administration step*. Here, our tests are administered to job *applicants* rather than current *employees*. Once administered, the trial predictor data are stored, and applicants are employed on the basis of other available selection data (such as tests, interviews, etc. currently used in selection). The predictors we are trying out are *not* used in selection decision making. Once applicants have been selected and trained, they are placed in jobs. These new employees are given enough time to learn their jobs adequately (perhaps as long as six months or more) so that performance differences are more likely due to actual performance rather than some other factor such as learning. After the learning acquisition period, criterion data representing job success are collected on these employees. Then, after criterion data have been assembled, the two sets of scores (scores on our trial predictors that we stored earlier and criteria) are statistically correlated and tested for possible relationships.

Strengths and Weaknesses

There are several important differences between predictive and concurrent validity. Under predictive validation, there is a time interval between the collection of data from predictors being tested and criterion data. Applicants rather than incumbents serve as the data source and, as such, may have a higher, more realistic level of motivation when they complete the predictor measure. Differences between these individuals and subsequent applicants with respect to job tenure are not a problem with the predictive approach, since the same level of job experience applies to both. Under the predictive validation method, the inference tested or question answered is, Can the predictors being tested predict future job success as measured by criterion data?

Because of the inference tested by predictive validation, the method is appropriate for measures used in HR selection. The method addresses itself to the basic selection issue as it normally occurs in the employment context—that is, how well job applicants will *be able* to perform on the job. One big weakness with the predictive validation model is the time interval required to determine the validity of the measure being examined. If an organization hires relatively few people a month, it may take many months to obtain a sufficient sample size to conduct a predictive validation study. Second, just like the concurrent validation strategy, it is very difficult to accumulate the large amount of data we need to conduct an appropriate statistical analysis. Large samples are, once again, needed. Moreover, it can be very difficult to explain to managers the importance of filing selection measure information *before* using the data for HR selection purposes. If we use our trial predictors in hiring, we will restrict the range of predictor scores; that is, we will eliminate those whose test scores fall below a cutoff or passing score, which reduces predictor score variance. Reduced variance will have a negative effect on the magnitude of any validity coefficient calculated for the predictor. Thus, it is necessary to avoid using trial predictors in selection decisions when conducting a predictive validation study. With regard to this last point, when conducting a predictive validation study for clerical positions in a large, regional bank, one of the authors of this text had the following discussion:

> The vice president of personnel commented on the predictive validation study that had been proposed, "Now, let me get this straight. You want to give tests to job applicants, but you are not going to use the tests to tell us who to hire?"

> "Yes," your author replied, "that's right."

> The vice president then asked, "Well, if these tests are any good, why in the heck don't you use them?"

> Sometimes, it is challenging to explain to managers why certain procedures are followed.

Our discussion of concurrent and predictive validation strategies suggests there is only one way to carry out each of these validity designs. In practice, however, several different ways for conducting concurrent and predictive validation studies are possible. Robert Guion and C. J. Cranny, for instance, summarized five variations in which a predictive study might be conducted.[38] These are illustrated in Figure 8.5. In a similar fashion, different versions of the concurrent validation strategy also exist. These different ways of conducting a criterion-related validation study show that, in practice, various approaches are possible.

At times, a particular criterion-related design might not fit neatly into our categories of predictive and concurrent validity. For instance, suppose an HR manager hypothesizes that college grade point average (GPA) is related to work performance of sales personnel. GPA was *not* used in making hiring decisions but is available only for *current employees.* To test her hypothesis, the manager correlates GPA with first-year sales and finds a relationship between the two variables. Because it was *not* really done with applicants, is this a predictive validity study? Is this a concurrent validity strategy if the criterion data were gathered over time? As you can see, our study design has elements of both predictive and concurrent validation strategies; it does not fall neatly into either category. Whatever the design employed, the critical issue is not so much the criterion-related validity category to which it belongs. As we have seen, some designs such as that of our college grades and sales performance example may be difficult to classify. Rather, the real question to be answered is, "What inferences will the design of a criterion-related validity study permit?"[39]

Concurrent versus Predictive Validation Strategies

It generally has been assumed that a predictive validation design is superior to a concurrent one because it more closely resembles an actual employment situation. Because of the problems we mentioned earlier in our discussion of the concurrent design, predictive designs have been thought to provide a better estimate of validity. There has been some older as well as newer work on comparing these designs. For example, as might be expected, a review of 99 published criterion-related validity studies showed a greater number of validation studies based on a concurrent validation design than on a predictive one.[40] Minimal

FIGURE 8.5 Examples of Different Predictive Validation Designs

Type of Predictive Validation Design	Description of Predictive Validation Procedure
1. Follow-up—Random Selection	Applicants are tested and selection is random; predictor scores are correlated with subsequently collected criterion data.
2. Follow-up—Present System	Applicants are tested and selection is based on whatever selection procedures are already in use; predictor scores are correlated with subsequently collected criterion data.
3. Select by Predictor	Applicants are tested and selected on the basis of their predictor scores; predictor scores are correlated with subsequently collected criterion data.
4. Hire and Then Test	Applicants are hired and placed on the payroll; they are subsequently tested (e.g., during a training period), and predictor scores are correlated with criteria collected at a later time.
5. Personnel File Research	Applicants are hired and their personnel records contain references to test scores or other information that might serve as predictors. At a later date, criterion data are collected. The records are searched for information that might have been used and validated had it occurred to anyone earlier to do so.

Source: Based on Robert M. Guion and C.J. Cranny, "A Note on Concurrent and Predictive Validity Designs: A Critical Reanalysis," *Journal of Applied Psychology 67* (1982), 240; and Frank J. Landy, *Psychology of Work Behavior* (Homewood IL: Dorsey Press, 1985), 65.

differences were found, however, in the validation results of the two types of designs. Another review of validity estimates of ability tests revealed no significant differences in validity estimates derived from the two designs.[41] For ability tests, results from these studies suggest that a concurrent validation approach is just as viable as a predictive one. On the other hand, this might not necessarily be true for other predictors. For instance, studies have reported different results for predictive versus concurrent validation designs for both personality and integrity measures.[42] In another review, Chris Van Iddekinge and Robert Ployhart concluded that predictive designs yield validity estimates roughly 0.05 to 0.10 lower than those obtained in concurrent designs for personality inventories, structured interviews, person–organization fit measures, and biographical data inventories.[43]

Requirements for a Criterion-Related Validation Study

Although a criterion-related validation study is desired, it does not mean that such a study can or even should be conducted. It must first be feasible, and to be feasible, certain minimum requirements must be met. In the case of a validation study, "a poor study is not better than none."[44] A poor validation study may cause an organization to reject selection procedures that would have been useful in selecting employees, or accept and use selection procedures that do not predict employee work performance.[45] An inadequate criterion-related validation study also may expose an organization to an unsuccessful defense against a charge of employment discrimination. At least four requirements are necessary before a criterion-related study should be considered.

1. The job should be reasonably stable and not in a period of change or transition. The results of a study based on a situation at one point in time might not apply to the new situation.

2. A relevant, reliable criterion that is free from contamination must be available or feasible to develop.

3. It must be possible to base the validation study on a sample of people and jobs that is representative of people and jobs to which the results will be generalized.

4. A large enough, and representative, sample of people on whom both predictor and criterion data have been collected must be available. Large samples are required to identify a predictor–criterion relationship if one really exists. With small samples, it may be mistakenly concluded that a predictor is not valid when in fact it is. The probability of finding that a predictor is significantly related to a criterion when it is truly valid is lower with small sample sizes than with larger ones. Therefore large sample sizes are *essential*.[46]

Criterion-Related Validation over Time

After spending time and money on a criterion-related validation study, one might ask, "How long will the validity of a predictor last?" A review by Charles Hulin and others indicated that the predictive validity of some measures rapidly decayed over time.[47] However, critics of the review noted that only one study reviewed incorporated an ability test to predict actual performance on the job.[48] Another study found that the predictive validity of mental ability tests actually increased over time, job experience validity decreased, and predictive validity remained about the same for dexterity tests.[49] For a weighted application blank scoring key, the utility of the key for predicting job success held up for a 38-year period.[50] Finally, the validity of mental ability tests for U.S. military occupational specialties remained stable for more than a five-year period.[51] These results suggest that at least for a properly developed mental ability test, the test's validity could be expected to hold up for at least a five-year period.

The Courts and Criterion-Related Validation

We may have given you the impression that, if taken to court, all an organization has to do is to trot out its significant validity coefficient and everything will be okay. Certainly, a statistically significant validity coefficient helps, but there is a lot more involved in the adjudication of employment discrimination cases. Even if proper actions have been taken in a criterion-related validation study, there is no guaranteed outcome of a legal case. Some outcomes hinge on elements of a case that go beyond the technical aspects of criterion-related validity—for example, a judge's personal biases. A review by Lawrence Kleiman and Robert Faley of 12 court cases involving criterion-related validity that were decided after publication of the 1978 *Uniform Guidelines* communicated some of the legal realities faced by employers and selection consultants.[52] Only 5 of 12 defendants won their case. Among their findings were the following:

1. Rather than considering empirical validity evidence, some courts preferred to judge validity on the basis of format or content of the selection instrument (for example, multiple-choice format, content of items).

2. Some courts were swayed by a test's legal history (for example, the Wonderlic Personnel Test that was contested in *Griggs v. Duke Power Co.*) even though existing evidence was available on the validity of the test; others were influenced by the type of test used (for example, general aptitude tests such as a vocabulary test).

3. Some judges had preferences for the use of a predictive validation strategy versus a concurrent validation strategy for demonstrating selection procedure validity.

4. A statistically significant validity coefficient alone did not guarantee a judgment for the defendant; some courts also considered the utility of the selection measure. However, they differed as to what evidence is needed to demonstrate utility.

5. Judges differed on their willingness to accept statistical corrections (for example, restriction of range corrections) to predictor scores or correction for unreliability of the criterion. Some judges apparently believed that corrections by the defendant were misleading and made validity coefficients higher than they really were.

Certainly, a predictor's validity coefficient that is statistically significant is essential for both practical and legal reasons. Other things being equal, a statistically significant validity coefficient is an important piece of evidence that helps assure users that their inferences regarding work performance from scores on a selection procedure are supported. As long as the validity coefficient is statistically significant, using the selection procedure to make employment decisions will be better than using a procedure unrelated to job success. Such a procedure is no better than flipping a coin and saying, "heads, you're hired; tails, you're not." But, how high should a validity coefficient be? And, in addition to statistical significance of validity coefficients, how do the courts, namely judges, look at the magnitudes of validity coefficients in judging an employment discrimination claim? As we will see, the higher the validity coefficient, the better for selection practice and the better for legal defense in the event a legal case is brought against an employer.

Daniel Biddle and Patrick Nooren cite a number of legal cases that adopted a value of 0.30 (assuming the coefficient was statistically significant) as a minimally acceptable threshold for a predictor's validity coefficient.[53] Biddle also reported that the Department of Labor's guidelines for interpreting correlations were as follows: (a) above 0.35 = very beneficial; 0.21 to 0.35 = likely to be useful; 0.11 to 0.20 = depends on circumstances; and (d) below 0.11 = unlikely to be useful.[54] (We will see in our discussion of *Utility Analysis*, appearing later in this chapter, that setting an arbitrary value of a validity coefficient for determining whether a selection procedure is useful is not a wise practice. In addition to the magnitude of the validity coefficient, other factors must be considered as well.) If employers used selection procedure scores to rank-order job candidates from high to low predictor scores; top-down hiring was based on these ranked scores; and if the degree of disparate impact associated with the procedure were large, this minimum validity threshold would be expected to be higher. Exactly how high a statistically significant validity coefficient would have to be to be seen by a judge as acceptable is unknown; it might well vary depending on the individual judge hearing a case. Thus, this conclusion would appear to be "especially true of judges who have less than adequate statistical training and are sometimes speculative about the statistical sciences (which is arguably most judges)."[55]

Recent research offers some promising guidance to users and even courts facing questions such as, "What are the anticipated consequences for adverse impact of various degrees of test validity and test bias?[56] Herman Aguinis and Marlene Smith have developed an online computer program to perform calculations to help with such questions.[57]

Content versus Criterion-Related Validation: Some Requirements

So far, we have discussed several approaches to validation. The choice of a validation strategy implies that certain requirements must first be evaluated and met. Each of the validation strategies discussed up to this point has a particular set of requirements. These requirements must be met for a specific strategy to be viable.

A review of these requirements provides a means for determining the feasibility of a particular validation methodology. We have prepared a summary of requirements in which HR selection issues are in question. Drawing principally from the *Uniform Guidelines*, the *Principles for the Validation and Use of Employee Selection Procedures*,[58] and other sources in the literature, the major feasibility requirements for conducting content and criterion-related (concurrent and predictive) validation methods are summarized in Table 8.2. The requirements shown are not meant to be exhaustive, only illustrations of major considerations when HR selection is involved. Also, the requirements serve as general guides for deciding the feasibility of a particular validation approach; they are not complete technical requirements.

CONSTRUCT VALIDATION STRATEGY

The next validation strategy we mention is construct validity. When psychologists use the term *construct*, they generally are referring to a theoretical psychological concept, attribute, characteristic, or quality. When a psychological measure such as a test is used in selection research, it is believed that the test assesses "something." That something is a construct.[59] Thus, terms such as *intelligence, sociability*, and *clerical ability* are all theoretical abstractions called constructs. Specific measures (such as a clerical ability test) are operational measures hypothesized to represent a specific construct. Construct validation helps us determine whether a measure does indeed reflect a specific construct.

TABLE 8.2	Considerations for Determining the Feasibility of Content and Criterion-Related Validation Strategies

Content Validation	**Criterion-Related Validation**[a]
1. Must be able to obtain a complete, documented analysis of each of the jobs for which the validation study is being conducted, which is used to identify the content domain of the job under study	1. Must be able to assume the job is reasonably stable and not undergoing change
2. Applicable when a selection device purports to measure existing job skills, knowledge, or behavior. Inference is that content of the selection device measures content of the job	2. Must be able to obtain a relevant, reliable, and uncontaminated measure of job performance (that is, a criterion)
3. Although not necessarily required, should be able to show that a criterion-related methodology is not feasible	3. Should be based as much as possible on a sample that is representative of the people and jobs to which the results are to be generalized
4. Inferential leap from content of the selection device to job content should be a small one	4. Should have adequate statistical power to identify a predictor-criterion relationship if one exists. To do so, must have a. adequate sample size b. variance or individual differences in scores on the selection procedure and criterion
5. Most likely to be viewed as suitable when skills and knowledge for doing a job are being measured	5. Must be able to obtain a complete analysis of each of the jobs for which the validation study is being conducted. Used to justify the predictors and criteria being studied
6. Not suitable when abstract mental processes, constructs, or traits are being measured or inferred	6. Must be able to infer that performance on the selection procedure can predict future job performance
7. *May* not provide sufficient validation evidence when applicants are being ranked	7. Must have ample resources in terms of time, staff, and money
8. A substantial amount of the critical job behaviors and WRCs should be represented in the selection measure	

Source: Based on Society of Industrial and Organizational Psychology, *Principles for the Validation and Use of Personnel Selection Procedures*, 4th ed. (Bowling Green, OH: Author, 2003); Equal Employment Opportunity Commission, Civil Service Commission, Department of Labor, and Department of Justice, *Adoption of Four Agencies of Uniform Guidelines on Employee Selection Procedures*; 43 Federal Register 38, 295, 300, 301, 303 (August 25, 1989); and Robert M. Guion, *Personnel Testing* (New York: McGraw-Hill, 1965).

[a]Criterion-related validation includes both concurrent and predictive validity.

For example, suppose we have a test called the General Mental Ability Test. The test is *thought* to assess general intelligence. As we review it, we may believe that the test is assessing the construct of intelligence. We look at the test's content and see items involving topics such as verbal analogies, mathematical problem solving, or scrambled sentences. But does this test really assess the construct of intelligence? We hypothesize that it does, but does it? Construct validation tests our hypothesis. In this sense, construct validation is a research process involving the collection of evidence used to test hypotheses about relationships between measures and their constructs.

Let's use a simple example to illustrate an approach to construct validation of a measure called the Teamwork Orientation Inventory (TOI). The TOI consists of items that ask respondents about their life experiences related to group activities, such as the extent they played or participated in team sports, or the extent to which they belonged to social organizations while growing up. The rationale behind the TOI is that to the extent people have successfully played or worked in teams in the past, the more likely it is that they will desire to work in teams in the future. Currently, many manufacturing and technology organizations maintain that the desire and ability of employees to work effectively as members of a work team is a critical requirement in manufacturing and technology-based jobs. Assume we have analyzed such a team-based job and found that the work performance dimension, *working as a team member* (a construct) is important to successful work performance. The *motivation to work with others* (another construct) is hypothesized to be an important attribute employees must possess to work successfully as a team member. As we look at our two constructs, we develop two operational measures to assess them. Peer ratings of team members' performance serve as a measure of the construct, *performing as a team member*, whereas the TOI is thought to assess the construct, *motivation to work with others*. Our particular interest is the construct validity of the TOI.

Figure 8.6 shows the hypothesized links between the constructs and their measures.[60] Construct validation is an accumulation of a variety of evidence or research that supports the links among the various measures and constructs. In our current example and from the perspective of personnel selection, we ultimately are interested in the link between the TOI measure and the *working as a team member* construct (**link 5**). Evidence of this link can come from several sources. One source might be a criterion-related validation study between individuals' TOI scores and peer ratings of these individuals performing as a team member (**link 1**). Content validation also studies might provide additional evidence (**links 2** and **3**). We can, however, also accumulate other forms of evidence to determine whether the TOI assesses the construct *motivation to work with others*.

For instance, literature reviews might suggest the characteristics of individuals who work effectively on teams. We might hypothesize, for instance, that such individuals would be extraverted; they also would have a high need for affiliation. We would administer measures of these variables, such as personality inventories, along with the TOI to current employees. If our hypothesized associations are found, we will have another piece of evidence regarding the construct validity of the TOI.

FIGURE 8.6 A Hypothetical Construct Validation Example of the Link between *Working as a Team Member* (Construct) and the Teamwork Orientation Inventory (*Predictor*)

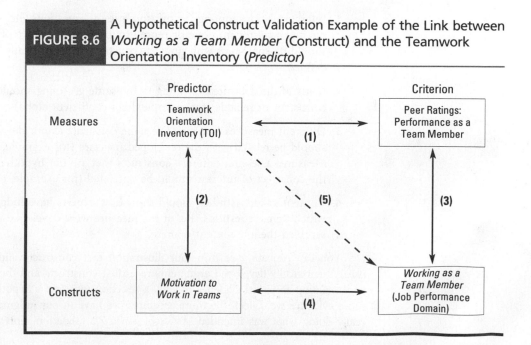

We might design another study in which the TOI and other selection measures are given to job applicants. Employees are hired without knowledge of TOI scores and placed in work teams. Six months or so later, we ask team members to rate how well individuals fit within their assigned team and collect absenteeism data. We hypothesized that individuals possessing high motivation to work on a team would show less absenteeism from the work group and be rated by their peers as being effective team members than individuals displaying little motivation to work in teams. If we find that employees who scored high on the TOI had less absenteeism and were rated more effective than individuals scoring low on the TOI, we have additional evidence to support our hypothesis regarding the TOI's construct validity.

In addition, studies investigating the relation between the TOI and professionally developed measures of our hypothesized teamwork construct could be conducted. We might hypothesize positive relationships between high team orientation as reflected in our TOI scores with other team-oriented measures. Experiments might be designed to determine whether individuals scoring high on the TOI behave in ways predictably different from those scoring low. If our anticipated results are found, we have even more evidence of TOI construct validity. As you can see, we use multiple studies to test our hypothesis that the TOI effectively reflects the *working as a team member* construct that characterizes the work performance domain. Our example highlights the major steps for implementing a construct validation study as follows:

1. The construct is carefully defined and theoretically developed; hypotheses are formed concerning the relationships between the construct and other variables.

2. A measure hypothesized to assess the construct is developed.

3. Studies testing the hypothesized relationships (formed in step 1) between the constructed measure and other, relevant variables are conducted.[61]

Because construct validation may be conducted when no available measure exists, the "attribute" or "construct" being studied requires a number of measurement operations. Results of studies such as the following are particularly warranted in construct validation research:

1. Intercorrelations among the measure's items, questions, etc. should show whether the items cluster into one or more groupings. The nature of these groupings should be consistent with how the construct is theoretically developed and defined.

2. Items of the measure belonging to the same grouping should be internally consistent or reliable (for example, high coefficient alpha).

3. Different measures assessing the same construct as our developed measure should be related with the developed measure (for example, convergent validity). Measures assessing different constructs that are not hypothesized to be related to the construct of interest should be unrelated (for example, discriminant validity).

4. Content validity studies should show how experts have judged the manner in which items, questions, etc. of the measure were developed and how these items sampled the job content domain.[62]

You can probably see from our illustration that construct validation is a process of using theoretically developed arguments regarding constructs and their measures and then accumulating empirical evidence of what a selection measure is hypothesized to reflect. The more evidence we collect, the more assurance we have in our judgments that a measure is really doing what was intended. As such, construct validation represents a much broader definition of validity than we might find in a single criterion-related or content validation study. Through accumulated evidence (that may come from other validation strategies, literature reviews, other research studies, controlled experiments, and so on), we can answer what and how well a selection measure assesses what it measures. Construct validation is still a developing issue.[63]

EMPIRICAL CONSIDERATIONS IN CRITERION-RELATED VALIDATION STRATEGIES

Even when we have conducted content validation studies on a selection procedure, if at all possible, we probably will want to answer two important questions:

1. Is there a relationship between applicants' or employees' responses to the selection procedure and their performance on the job?

2. If so, is the relationship strong enough to warrant the measure's use in employment decision making?

Questions such as these imply the need for statistical or empirical methods for determining validity, that is, criterion-related validity. Because of their importance, we review some of the empirical methods and issues most commonly encountered in conducting criterion-related validation research.

Correlation

Computing Validity Coefficients

One of the terms you often see in reading selection research studies and literature is *validity coefficient*. A validity coefficient is simply an index that summarizes the degree of relationship between a predictor and criterion. Where does the validity coefficient come from? What does it mean? To answer these questions, let's refer to an example. Consider for a moment that we are conducting a predictive validation study. We want to know whether a sales ability inventory is useful in predicting the work performance of sales personnel. During a one-week employment period, we administered the inventory to 50 job applicants. No employment decisions were based on the inventory scores. Six months later, we can identify 20 individuals who were hired and are still employed.[64] (**Note:** Because of space considerations, we have used a small sample to simply *illustrate* data in the accompanying tables and figures. In practice, we would want to have more than just 20 people in our validation study. We need a much larger sample size on whom both predictor and criterion data are available. Large sample sizes are *essential* in criterion-related validation research. We will say more about this issue in the coming pages.) As a measure of work performance, we use sales supervisors' ratings of employee performance after the employees have had six months of sales experience. Total scores on the performance appraisal forms are calculated, and they represent employee work performance. Thus, for each employee we have a pair of scores: (a) scores on the sales ability inventory (a predictor) and (b) six-month performance appraisal scores (a criterion). These example data are shown in Table 8.3.

We initially create a scattergram or scatterplot of the data, like those in Table 8.3, to visually inspect any possible relationships between predictor and criterion variables. Typically, the Y-axis of the plot represents criterion scores; the X-axis shows predictor scores. An example scattergram of the data is shown in Figure 8.7. Each point in the graph represents a plot of the *pair* of scores for a single salesperson. For instance,

TABLE 8.3	Hypothetical Sales Ability Inventory Score and Job Performance Rating Data Collected on 20 Salespeople	

Salesperson ID	Sales Ability Inventory Score (Predictor)	Salesperson Job Performance Rating (Criterion)
A	86	74
B	97	91
C	51	67
D	41	31
E	60	52
F	70	70
G	73	74
H	79	59
I	46	44
J	67	61
K	71	52
L	88	75
M	81	92
N	40	22
O	53	74
P	77	74
Q	79	91
R	84	83
S	91	91
T	90	72

Note: **Sales Ability Inventory Score (high scores)** = Greater sales ability. **Salesperson Job Performance Rating (high scores)** = Greater job performance of sales personnel as judged by sales supervisors.

employee **Q** has a sales ability inventory score of 79 and a performance rating of 91. Although a scattergram is useful for estimating the existence and direction of a relationship, it really does not help us specify the *degree* of relationship between our selection measure and work performance. For this purpose, a more precise approach is to calculate an index that will summarize the degree of any linear relationship that might exist. Most often, the Pearson product–moment or simple correlation coefficient (r) is used to provide that index. The correlation coefficient, or in the context of personnel selection the "validity coefficient," summarizes the relationship between our predictor and criterion. Often, the validity coefficient is represented as r_{xy}, where r represents the degree of relationship between X (the predictor) and Y (the criterion).

A validity coefficient has two important elements (a) its sign and (b) its magnitude. The sign (either + or −) indicates the *direction* of a relationship; its magnitude indicates the *strength* of association between a predictor and criterion. The coefficient itself can range from −1.00 to 0.00 to +1.00. As the coefficient approaches 1.00, there is *a positive* relationship between performance on a predictor and a criterion. That is, high predictor scores are associated with high criterion scores, and low predictor scores are related with low criterion scores. As the coefficient moves toward −1.00, however, a negative or inverse relation exists between scores on the predictor and criterion. As the index moves

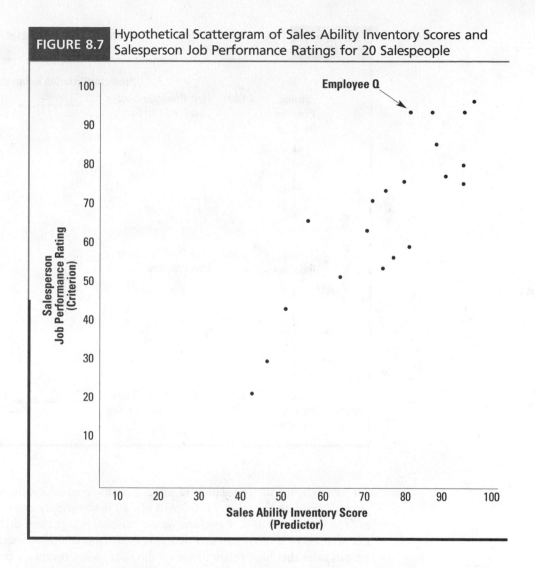

FIGURE 8.7 Hypothetical Scattergram of Sales Ability Inventory Scores and Salesperson Job Performance Ratings for 20 Salespeople

toward 0.00, any relationship between the two variables decreases. When the validity coefficient is not statistically significant or $r = 0.00$, then no relationship exists between a predictor and a criterion. Note that *if a validity coefficient is not statistically significant, then the selection measure is not a valid predictor of a criterion.* These predictor–criterion relations are summarized in Figure 8.8.

Using simple correlation, suppose we find that the validity coefficient for our example data in Figure 8.7 is 0.80. Next, after consulting the appropriate statistical table (usually found in psychological measurement or statistics books) or computerized results (that is, the statistical significance of the correlation coefficient as identified by statistical software used in calculating the simple correlation), we test the coefficient to see whether there is a statistically significant relationship between the sales ability inventory and work performance or whether the observed correlation is simply due to chance. A significance test helps determine the probability that the relationship identified for the sample of job applicants can be expected to be found only by chance in the *population* of job applicants from which the sample came. Usually, if the probability (p) is equal to or less than 0.05 (i.e., $p \leq 0.05$), we conclude that a statistically significant relationship exists between a predictor and criterion. That is, a relationship exists between the predictor

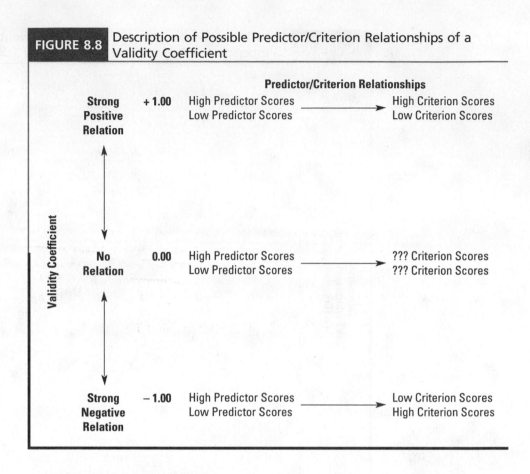

FIGURE 8.8 Description of Possible Predictor/Criterion Relationships of a Validity Coefficient

and criterion for the population of job applicants from which the sample came. In our example, assume the validity coefficient of 0.80 is statistically significant (usually written as "$r = 0.80$, $p \leq 0.05$"). Therefore, we are reasonably confident that the relationship did not arise because of chance and that a dependable relationship exists. We conclude that we can infer that high performance on the sales ability inventory is associated with high work performance. Thus, our sales ability inventory is valid for predicting future work performance.

Importance of Large Sample Sizes

The number of people on whom we have both predictor and criterion data for computing a validity coefficient is referred to as the *sample size* (or N) of a validation study. Following are the reasons why it is *absolutely essential* to have as large a sample size as possible in calculating a validity coefficient:

1. A validity coefficient computed on a small sample (say, for example, $N = 20$) must be higher in value to be considered statistically significant than a validity coefficient based on a larger sample (say, for example, $N = 320$).

2. A validity coefficient computed on a small sample is less reliable than one based on a large sample. That is, if we took independent samples of pairs of predictor and criterion scores and calculated the validity coefficient for each sample, there would be greater variability in the magnitudes of the validity coefficients for small samples than if the sample sizes were large.

3. The chances of *detecting* that a predictor is valid when the predictor is truly valid is lower for small sample sizes than for large ones. A predictor may be truly valid, but the correlational procedure may not detect it if the sample size on which the coefficient is based is small.[65] The term *statistical power* often is used when describing a validation study. One way of thinking about statistical power is the ability of a validation study to detect a correlation between a selection procedure and a criterion when such a relationship actually exists. Small sample sizes in a validation study have less statistical power than large samples. For example, if a criterion-related validation study had a sample size of 200, then there is about an 80 percent chance of identifying a validity coefficient of 0.20 or higher as being statistically significant ($p \leq 0.05$). For a sample size of 100, the chances are roughly 50 percent.

So, what is wrong with a small sample? The problem is this: As the sample size *decreases*, the probability of *not* finding a statistically significant relationship between predictor and criterion scores *increases*. Therefore, we would be more likely to conclude (and perhaps incorrectly so) that a predictor is not valid and is useless in selection. For this reason, we should use as large a sample size as possible in our criterion-related validation studies.

Research by Frank Schmidt has illustrated the effects of using small sample sizes on the variability of validity coefficients.[66] Clerical test validity data were available on a large sample ($N = 1,455$) of post office letter sorters. The clerical test validity coefficient for this large sample was 0.22. The large sample was divided randomly into 63 smaller groups of 68 individuals each. This sample size was chosen because previous research had shown that the average sample size used in test validation studies at that time was 68. Next, test validity coefficients were computed for each of the 63 smaller groups. The results showed that small sample sizes, even with an N of 68, can produce misleading outcomes. Test validity coefficients ranged from −0.03 to 0.48 among the 63 samples. Less than a third of the coefficients were statistically significant ($p < 0.05$) or valid. These results show that because of what is called "sampling error," which is pronounced when small sample sizes are used in validation research, the true validity of a predictor may go undetected.

Michael McDaniel et al. have characterized criterion-related sample sizes of 500 or less as being relatively small.[67] When such sizes are used (that is, $N < 500$), the calculated validity coefficient tends to be a rather imprecise estimate of the validity coefficient in the population. For example, a local validation study of a selection procedure, which yields a validity coefficient of 0.30 based on a sample size of 103 (the median sample size of criterion-related validation studies reported between 1983 and 1994 in three leading industrial psychology journals) has a 95 percent confidence interval of 0.11 to 0.47.[68] As you can see, the estimates of true validity of the test in the population vary widely. Thus, small sample sizes, which are common in local validation studies, lead to sampling error and affect the stability of calculated validity coefficients. Frank Schmidt has noted that even if N is less than 2,000, estimated validity still suffers from statistical sampling error.[69] In the present case, with our validity coefficient = 0.30 and $N = 2,000$, the 95 percent confidence interval is 0.26 to 0.34.

[**Technical Note**: The confidence interval was calculated using the confidence interval for population validity calculator at www.vassarstats.net/rho.]

Following is a portion of a recent e-mail sent by a former student to one of this text's authors. How would you reply to her based on your "new" knowledge regarding sample size in criterion-related validation research?

Hi Dr. Feild,

I don't know if you remember me, but I graduated in Human Resource Management from Auburn University. Since graduation, I have been working at ABC Bank in human resources for seven years. I have a question that I am hoping you might be able to help me regarding validation studies. We have 800 to 900 branch managers, and we have an outside firm helping us develop a selection program for these managers. The firm is suggesting that we include 200 (roughly 20–25 percent) of those branch managers in our sample group. In talking with an executive consultant, he indicated that he would not feel comfortable with validation data based on less than 50 percent of the sample group. Do you have any thoughts about the sample sizes or percentages of Branch Managers being proposed?

Interpreting Validity Coefficients

Once a statistically significant validity coefficient is found, we might well ask, "What does the validity coefficient mean?" We can take several approaches to answer this question.

One approach involves the use of the coefficient of determination. When we look at the distribution of our criterion scores shown in Table 8.3, one fact is evident. Some employees perform better than others; some do very well, others not so well. Of course, we expect such differences because people are different. If our predictor is useful, it should explain some of these differences or variance in employees' work performance. By squaring the validity coefficient (r_{xy}^2), we obtain an index that indicates our test's ability to account for these individual performance differences. This index, called the *coefficient of determination*, represents the percentage of variance in the criterion that can be explained by variance associated with the predictor. In our case, the coefficient of determination is 0.64 (0.80^2), indicating that 64 percent of the differences (or variance) in individuals' work performance can be explained by how they performed on the sales ability inventory.

In addition to the coefficient of determination, *expectancy tables* and *charts* are useful. Because expectancy tables are employed as an aid in interpreting validity coefficients, we save our discussion of them for the next section.

Finally, *utility analysis* can be used. Its computation is far more complex than the methods we just mentioned. Nevertheless, it offers, perhaps, the ultimate interpretation of a valid predictor and its impact in a selection program for managers in an organization. By translating the usefulness of a validity coefficient into dollars, utility analysis adds an economic interpretation to the meaning of a validity coefficient. Because of its importance in the field of HR selection, we devote a later section of this chapter to a discussion of utility analysis.

Prediction

A statistically significant validity coefficient is helpful in showing that for a *group* of persons a test is related to job success. However, the coefficient alone does not help us in predicting the job success of *individuals*. Yet, the prediction of a job candidate's likelihood of job success is what an employment manager wants. For individual prediction purposes, we can use linear regression and expectancy charts to aid us in selection decision making. These tools should be employed only for those predictors that have a statistically significant relationship with the criterion. In using these methods, a practitioner is simply taking predictor information, such as test scores, and forecasting the likelihood of an applicant's job success. For each method, one key assumption is that we are using information collected on employees (concurrent validation) or job applicants (predictive validation) and making predictions for a *future* group of employees.

Linear Regression

Linear regression involves the determination of how changes in criterion scores are related to changes in predictor scores. A regression equation is developed that mathematically describes the functional relationship between the predictor and criterion. If the validity coefficient is statistically significant, and the regression equation is known, criterion scores can be predicted from predictor information. In general, you are likely to come across two common types of linear regression: *simple* and *multiple* regression.

Simple Regression.   In simple regression, there is only one predictor and one criterion. To illustrate, let's refer to Figure 8.7. It depicts the relationship between sales ability inventory scores and work performance ratings for 20 salespeople. In Figure 8.9, we show the same scattergram fitted with a special line to the plotted scores. This line is called the *regression line*. It summarizes the relationship between the inventory scores and the work performance ratings. The line has been fitted statistically so that it is at a minimum distance from each of the data points in the figure. Thus, the regression line represents the line of "best fit."

FIGURE 8.9	Hypothetical Plot of the Regression Line for Sales Ability Inventory Scores and Job Performance Ratings for 20 Salespeople

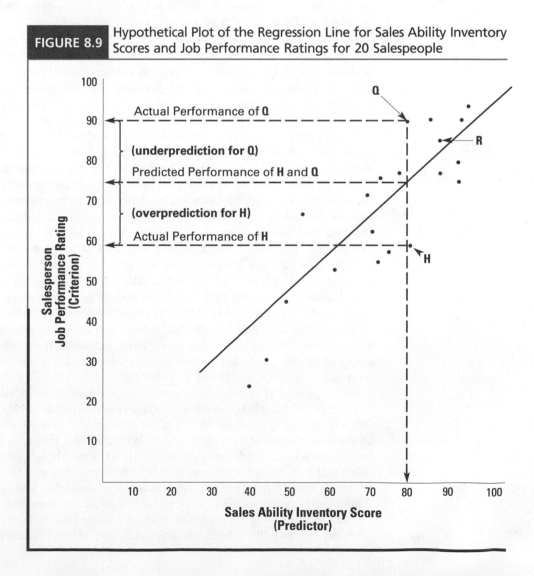

In addition to depicting the fit of the regression line graphically, we also can describe it mathematically in the form of an equation called the *regression* or *prediction equation*. This equation takes the form of the algebraic expression for a straight line, that is,

$$\hat{Y} = a + bX$$

where

$\hat{Y}$ = predicted score of the criterion variable

a = intercept value of the regression line

b = slope of the regression line or regression weight

X = score on the predictor variable.

The data points around the regression line and the validity coefficient are closely related. The validity coefficient represents how well the regression line fits the data. As the validity coefficient approaches +1.00 or −1.00, the data points move closer to the line. If a validity coefficient equals +1.00 or −1.00, then the data points will fall exactly on the regression line itself, and prediction will be perfect. As the coefficient moves away from +1.00 or −1.00 (toward 0.00), however, the points will be distributed farther from the regression line, and more error will exist in our predictions.

To illustrate the role of the regression line and regression equation in prediction, let's look further at our example. The regression line in Figure 8.9 is represented by the equation $\hat{Y} = 3.02 + 0.91(X)$, where $\hat{Y}$ is predicted work performance (our criterion), and X is a score on our sales ability inventory administered to applicants for the sales job. The intercept (3.02) is the value where the regression line crosses the Y-axis. It represents an applicant's predicted work performance if his or her sales ability inventory score were zero. Finally, 0.91 represents the slope of the line. The slope often is called a *regression weight* or *regression coefficient* because it is multiplied by the score on the predictor (our sales ability inventory). The slope or regression weight represents the amount of change in the criterion variable per one-unit change in the predictor. Thus, for every one-unit increase in an applicant's sales ability inventory score, we would expect a 0.91 increase in work performance. A positive validity coefficient indicates a positive slope of the regression line (see Figure 8.9) and, therefore, a positive regression weight. A negative validity coefficient means a negative slope and negative regression weight.

Once we have our regression line, we can use it to predict our criterion scores. For example, if an applicant applying for our sales job is given the sales ability inventory, we would locate the score on the X-axis, move upward to the regression line, and then move across to the Y-axis to find his or her predicted work performance score. As you can see in Figure 8.9, individual **R**, who has a test score of 84, is predicted to have a work performance rating of approximately 80. Since individual **R** actually has a performance rating of 83, our prediction is close. Because the correlation between the inventory and work performance scores is not a perfect 1.00, prediction will include some error. For instance, persons **H** and **Q** both scored 79 on the inventory, but notice our predictions have error. For person **H**, we would *overpredict* performance. With an inventory score of 79, performance is predicted to be 73, but it is actually only 59. Conversely, for person **Q**, performance would be *underpredicted*. With the same inventory score (79), predicted performance is 73, but actual performance is 91. Even though errors in prediction are made and even though some may appear rather large, they will be smaller for the *group* of people than if the predictor information and regression line is not used and only random guesses (for example, using an invalid predictor) are made.

Rather than using the regression line, we can use our regression equation to predict work performance. By substituting a person's sales ability inventory score for X in our regression equation, multiplying the score times the regression coefficient (0.91), and then adding it to the constant value (3.02), we can derive a predicted work performance score. Thus, for our inventory score of 86, we predict subsequent rated work performance to be equal to 81. Our calculation would be as follows:

$$\hat{Y} = 3.02 + 0.91(X)$$
$$\hat{Y} = 3.02 + 0.91(86)$$
$$\hat{Y} = 3.02 + 78.26$$
$$\hat{Y} = 81.28 \text{ or } 81$$

As we saw in our preceding example, because our sales ability inventory is not perfectly related to work performance, we have some error in our predictions. Only if all of our data points fall precisely on the regression line ($r_{xy} = \pm 1.00$) will error not be present. In making employment decisions, we must take this degree of error into account. The *standard error of estimate* is a useful index for summarizing the degree of error in prediction.[70] It is determined from the following equation:

$$sd_{y \cdot x} = sd_y \sqrt{1 - r_{xy}^2}$$

where

$sd_{y \cdot x}$ = standard error of estimate

sd_y = standard deviation of criterion scores Y

r_{xy} = validity coefficient for predictor X and criterion Y

The standard error of estimate represents the standard deviation of errors made in predicting criterion scores from predictor scores. On average, 68 percent of *actual* criterion scores will fall within ±1 standard error of *predicted* criterion scores, and 95 percent of actual criterion scores will fall within ±1.96 standard errors of *predicted* criterion scores. For example, assume the standard deviation of our work performance ratings is 7.5. Also, assume that the validity of our inventory designed to predict these ratings is 0.80. The standard error of estimate would be computed as follows:

$$sd_{y \cdot x} = 7.5\sqrt{1 - 0.80^2}$$
$$sd_{y \cdot x} = 7.5\sqrt{36}$$
$$sd_{y \cdot x} = 4.50$$

Now, assume that an applicant scores 86 on the inventory. Using the regression equation we discussed previously, we calculate that all persons scoring 86 on the inventory are predicted to have a work performance rating of 81. Notice that we have a *predicted* level of job success, but how confident can we be that the individuals' *actual* job success will approximate the predicted level? The standard error of estimate can help us. Basically, it enables us to establish a range of predicted criterion scores within which we would expect a percentage of actual criterion scores to fall. For applicants with a predicted performance rating of 81, we would expect, on average, 68 percent of them to have *actual* performance ratings between 77 and 86 (81 ± 4.50). For this same performance level, we also would expect 95 percent of applicants' actual work performance ratings to fall between 72 and 90 [81 ± (1.96 × 4.50)].

Multiple Regression. In addition to simple regression, *multiple* regression is also used to predict criterion scores for job applicants. Whereas simple regression assumes only *one* predictor, multiple regression assumes *two or more* predictors are used to predict a criterion. If the additional predictors explain more of the individual differences among job applicants' work performance than would have been explained by a single predictor alone, our ability to predict a criterion will be enhanced. As our ability to predict improves (that is, validity increases), we will make fewer errors in predicting applicants' subsequent work performance. The general model for multiple regression is as follows:

$$\hat{Y} = a + b_1X_1 + b_2X_2 + \cdots + b_nX_n$$

where

$$\hat{Y} = \text{predicted criterion scores}$$
$$a = \text{intercept value of the regression line}$$
$$b_1, b_2, b_n = \text{regression weights for predictors } X_1, X_2, \text{ and } X_n$$
$$X_1, X_2, \text{ and } X_n = \text{scores on predictors } X_1, X_2, \text{ and } X_n$$

If, for example, we had administered the sales ability inventory and a biographical data questionnaire, and if these two predictors were related to our work performance measure, we could derive a multiple regression equation just as we did with simple regression. In this case, however, our equation will have two regression weights rather than one. Suppose our multiple regression equation looked as follows:

$$\hat{Y} = 3.18 + 0.77X_1 + 0.53X_2$$

where

$$\hat{Y} = \text{predicted criterion scores (work performance measure)}$$
$$3.18 = \text{intercept value of the regression line } a$$
$$0.77 = \text{regression weight of the sales ability inventory}$$
$$0.53 = \text{regression weight of the biographical data questionnaire}$$
$$X_1 = \text{score on the sales ability inventory}$$
$$X_2 = \text{score on the biographical data questionnaire}$$

To obtain a predicted work performance score, we would simply substitute applicants' two predictor scores in the equation, multiply the two scores by their regression weights, sum the products, and add the intercept value to obtain predicted performance. For instance, suppose an applicant scored 84 on the sales ability inventory and 30 on the biographical data questionnaire. The predicted work performance score would be obtained as follows:

$$\hat{Y} = 3.18 + 0.77(84) + 0.53(30)$$
$$\hat{Y} = 3.18 + 64.68 + 15.90$$
$$\hat{Y} = 83.76 \text{ or } 84$$

The multiple regression approach has been called a compensatory model. It is called compensatory because different combinations of predictor scores can be combined to yield the same predicted criterion score. For instance, if an applicant were to do rather poorly on one measure, he or she could compensate for this low score by performing better on the other predictors. Examples of compensatory selection models include those used as a basis for making admission decisions in some professional graduate schools.

Cross-Validation

Whenever simple or multiple regression equations are used, they are developed to optimally predict the criterion for an existing group of people. But when the equations are applied to a new group, the predictive accuracy of the equations most always will fall. This "shrinkage" in predictive accuracy occurs because the new group is not identical to the one on which the equations were developed. Because of the possibility of error, it is important that the equations be tested for shrinkage *before* their implementation in selection decision making. This "checkout" process is called *cross-validation*. Two general methods of cross-validation are used: (a) *empirical* and (b) *formula* estimation. With empirical cross-validation, several approaches can be taken. In general, a regression equation developed on one sample of individuals is applied to another sample of persons. If the regression equation developed on one sample can predict scores in the other sample, then the regression equation is "cross-validated." One common procedure of empirical cross-validation ("split-sample" method) involves the following steps:

1. A large group of people on whom predictor and criterion data are available is *randomly* divided into two groups.

2. A regression equation is developed on one of the groups (called the "weighting group").

3. The equation developed on the weighting group is used to predict the criterion for the other group (called the "holdout group").

4. Predicted criterion scores are obtained for each person in the holdout group.

5. For people in the holdout group, *predicted* criterion scores are then correlated with their *actual* criterion scores. A statistically significant correlation coefficient indicates that the regression equation is useful for individuals other than those on whom the equation was developed.

Although the "split-sample" method of cross-validation has been used, Kevin Murphy has argued that the method can produce misleading results.[71] Rather than splitting a sample into two groups, he recommends collecting data on a second, *independent* sample. Of course, finding a second sample for data collection is not always easy.

As an alternative to empirical cross-validation, *formula* cross-validation can be used. Under this procedure, only one sample of people is employed. Special formulas are applied to predict the amount of shrinkage that would occur if a regression equation were applied to a similar sample of people. With the knowledge of (a) the number of predictors, (b) the original multiple correlation coefficient, and (c) the number of people on whom the original multiple correlation was based, the *predicted* multiple correlation coefficient can be derived. This predicted multiple correlation coefficient estimates the coefficient that would be obtained if all predictors were administered to a new but similar sample of people and the multiple correlation were statistically computed. The obvious advantage to these formulas is that a new sample of people does not have to be taken. Philippe Cattin summarized these formulas and the circumstances in which they are appropriate.[72] Kevin Murphy provided additional evidence on the accuracy of such formulas.[73] In general, he concluded that formula cross-validation is more efficient, simpler to use, and no less accurate than empirical cross-validation. More recently, researchers have found that cross-validation cannot be estimated accurately when small sample sizes are involved; ideally, the ratio of the number of people in the validation study relative to the number of predictors should be roughly 10:1.[74] With this 10:1 ratio, Burket's cross-validation formula is recommended.[75]

Whatever the approach, cross-validation is *essential*. It should be routinely implemented whenever regression equations are used in prediction. Without it, be skeptical of regression equation predictions.

Expectancy Tables and Charts

An expectancy table is simply a *table* of numbers that shows the probability that a job applicant with a particular predictor score will achieve a defined level of success. An expectancy *chart* presents essentially the same data except that it provides a visual summarization (for example, a bar chart) of the relationship between a predictor and criterion.[76] As we suggested earlier, expectancy tables and charts are useful for communicating the meaning of a validity coefficient. In addition, they are helpful as an aid in predicting the probability of success of job applicants. As outlined by Charles Lawshe and Michael Balma, the construction of expectancy tables and charts is a five-step process:

1. Individuals on whom criterion data are available are divided into two groups: (a) superior performers and (b) others. Roughly half of the individuals are in each group.

2. For each predictor score, frequencies of the number of employees in the superior performers' group and the others' group are determined.

3. The predictor score distribution is divided into fifths.

4. The number and percentage of individuals in the superior performers' group and the others' group are determined for each "fifth" of the predictor score distribution.

5. An expectancy chart that depicts these percentages is then prepared.[77]

To illustrate the development of an expectancy table and chart, let's go through a brief example. First, assume we have developed an employment interview to be used in hiring financial advisers who work with a large financial institution. Financial advisers are individuals who provide clients with financial services such as estate planning, personal investments, and retirement planning. In carrying out these activities, they also may sell investment products such as mutual funds to help clients meet their financial objectives.

In hiring financial advisers, we use a number of methods. These range from background and reference checks to administering financial knowledge exams. A most important measure that we also employ is a structured employment interview that takes about 1.5 hours to complete. In conducting the interview, we pose a series of specially developed questions designed to assess applicants' ability to provide sound financial advice to clients. We use other questions in the interview to assess applicants' ability to choose and sell appropriate financial products to clients. Once an applicant has completed the employment interview, the interviewer rates his or her performance on a series of rating scales. These quantitative ratings then are summed to obtain an overall interview performance score. The higher the applicants' scores on the interview, the better their interview performance.

Let's assume that we have scores from 65 financial adviser job applicants who completed the employment interview, were hired, and have worked as a financial adviser for 12 months. (Note that we are using a small sample for illustration purposes only. Remember our earlier points regarding sample size in validation studies.) Assume also that we have obtained the annual performance appraisal ratings given by their office managers at the end of their 12-month employment period. For our present purposes, we determine from discussions with these office managers that employees rated 9 or higher are considered to be "superior performers," whereas those with scores of 8 or less are classified as "other performers."

A simple correlation between the sets of interview scores and appraisal data for our 65 financial advisers indicates there is a statistically significant validity coefficient of 0.45 between the interview scores and performance ratings. Figure 8.10 shows the scattergram of the interview scores plotted against the performance ratings. (Note that in comparison to our earlier scattergrams, we have reversed the axes shown in Figure 8.10.) The horizontal lines represent roughly equal fifths of the distribution of predictor scores. Table 8.4 is the expectancy *table* developed from the plotted data. Basically, it shows the chances out of 100 of an individual's being rated superior on the job, given a range of employment interview scores. For example, people scoring between 30 and 34 have roughly an 85 percent chance of being rated superior, whereas those scoring between 1 and 6 have only a 33 percent chance. As shown in Figure 8.11, this information also can be formatted into a bar chart to form an *individual* expectancy *chart*.

Two types of expectancy charts can be prepared: (a) *individual* and (b) *institutional*. Figure 8.11 shows an individual expectancy chart. The *individual chart* shows the

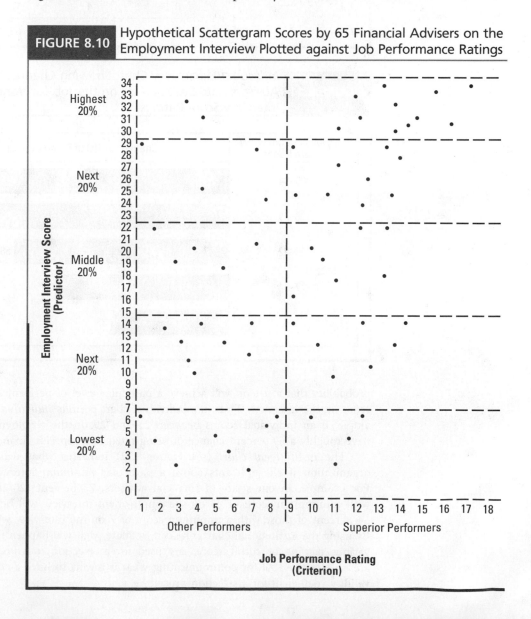

| FIGURE 8.10 | Hypothetical Scattergram Scores by 65 Financial Advisers on the Employment Interview Plotted against Job Performance Ratings |

TABLE 8.4	Percentage of Financial Advisers Rated as Superior on the Job for Various Employment Interview Score Ratings

Employment Interview Score Range	Other Performers	Superior Performers	Total	% Superior Performers
Top 20%: 30–34	2	11	13	85
Next 20%: 23–29	4	9	13	69
Middle 20%: 15–22	5	7	12	58
Next 20%: 7–14	8	7	15	47
Low 20%: 1–6	8	4	12	33
Total	27	38	65	

FIGURE 8.11	*Individual* Expectancy Chart Showing Chances in 100 of Financial Advisers Rated as Superior on the Job for Various Employment Interview Score Ratings

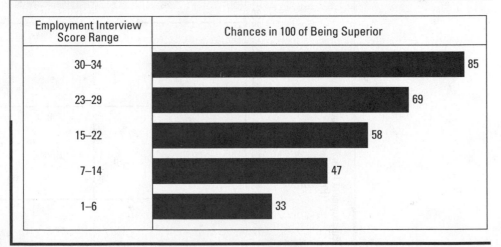

probability that a person will achieve a particular level of performance given his or her score on the interview. Thus, the individual chart permits *individual* prediction. For example, if an individual scores between 23 and 29 on the employment interview, they have roughly a 69 percent chance of being rated as a superior financial adviser.

The *institutional chart* (see Figure 8.12) indicates what will happen within an organization if all applicants above a particular *minimum* interview score are hired. For example, in our study of financial advisers, 77 percent (20/26) of the applicants with a minimum score of 23 on the employment interview will be rated superior, and 64 percent of those with a minimum score of 7 on the interview will be rated superior. By using the institutional chart, one can estimate what will happen in the organization if various passing or cutoff scores are used for a selection measure. Expectancy charts are an effective tool for communicating what it means to have a statistically significant validity coefficient for a selection procedure.

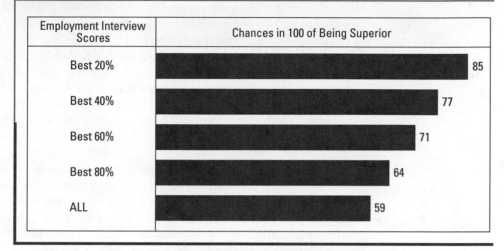

| FIGURE 8.12 | *Institutional* Expectancy Chart Showing Chances in 100 of Financial Advisers above Various Minimum Employment Interview Scores Expected to Be Judged Superior on the Job |

Employment Interview Scores	Chances in 100 of Being Superior
Best 20%	85
Best 40%	77
Best 60%	71
Best 80%	64
ALL	59

Factors Affecting the Magnitude of Validity Coefficients

Guion has pointed out that the size of a validity coefficient depends on a variety of factors.[78] Any number of factors may have an effect, but four seem to be predominant in determining the magnitude of a validity coefficient.

Reliability of Criterion and Predictor

Earlier we described the intimate interrelationship between reliability and validity. The point is that to the extent a predictor or criterion has error it will be unreliable. The more error present, the more unreliable and unpredictable these variables will be. *Any unreliability in either the criterion or predictor will lower the correlation or validity coefficient computed between the two.* If *both* predictor and criterion variables have measurement error, error is compounded, and the validity coefficient will be lowered even further. Because of the negative effect of lowered reliability on validity, we should strive for high reliability of *both* predictors and criteria to get an assessment of what maximum possible validity might be.

If the validity coefficient is restricted or attenuated by unreliability of the predictor or criterion (that is, measurement error), it is possible to make statistical adjustments to see what validity would be if the variables had perfect reliability. This adjustment is referred to as *correction for attenuation.* Although unreliability in predictor scores can be corrected, in HR selection situations we have to use predictor data as they normally exist. Selection decisions are made with the actual predictor information collected. Thus, correction for attenuation in predictor scores is not made typically. On the other hand, correction for unreliability in criterion data is made in selection using the following formula:

$$\hat{r}_{xy} = \frac{r_{xy}}{\sqrt{r_{yy}}}$$

where

$\hat{r}_{xy}$ = (corrected) validity coefficient of the predictor if the criterion were measured without error

r_{xy} = correlation between the predictor and criterion (that is, the validity coefficient)

r_{yy} = reliability coefficient of the criterion[79]

For example, assume the validity of a test is 0.35 and reliability of the criterion is 0.49. Substituting in the formula shows that with a perfectly reliable criterion, the correlation between the test and criterion would be 0.50, a respectable validity coefficient. The idea behind correction for unreliability in the criterion is that it is unfair to penalize the predictor because of lack of dependability of measurement with another variable, the criterion.

Correction for attenuation can be used to evaluate a predictor when we have a criterion that may be highly relevant for our use but having low reliability. In this situation, we will have a clearer picture of the true value of the predictor. Correction can suggest whether the search for another predictor may be worthwhile. For instance, if our original validity coefficient is very low, say 0.20, but correction for unreliability in the criterion shows the validity coefficient to be high, say 0.70 or higher, a search for better predictors of our criterion likely will be fruitless. Also, we may have avoided throwing out a valuable predictor.

In using the correction formula, accurate estimates of reliability are essential. From our discussion of reliability, we saw that many factors can affect the magnitude of reliability coefficients. If the correction formula is used with underestimates of true criterion reliability, misleading *over*estimates of corrected predictor validity will result. Performance ratings often are used as criteria in test validation research. Although many selection experts agree that ratings' criteria should be corrected for unreliability, there is currently no uniform agreement as to the best strategy for correcting ratings' criteria. With regard to correcting for unreliability in criterion measures, Chad Van Iddekinge and Robert Ployhart have made a number of recommendations.[80] Among these are the following:

1. Report validity coefficients corrected for inter-rater reliability. However, this step assumes that accurate rating information on participants can be collected from more than one supervisor.

2. If employees have only one supervisor (which is often the case), collect rating data from peers of those employees in the validation study.

3. If for some reason peer ratings cannot be obtained, other less-than-ideal solutions include (a) correcting validity coefficients based on meta-analytic estimates of inter-rater reliability (these are 0.52 for supervisor ratings and 0.42 for peer ratings) and (b) computing coefficient alpha for the ratings (which will tend to overestimate ratings' reliability and therefore yield a conservative estimate of corrected predictor validity).

Thus, it is important to use and interpret the results of reliability correction formulas with caution when accurate estimates of criterion reliability are unknown.

Restriction of Range

One of the important assumptions in calculating a validity coefficient is that there is variance among individuals' scores on the criterion and predictor. By *variance*, we simply mean that people have different scores on these measures, that is, individual differences. When we calculate a validity coefficient, we are asking, "Do these predictor and criterion score differences co-vary or move together?" That is, are systematic differences among people's scores on the criterion associated with their score differences on the predictor? If there is little variance in individuals' scores for one or both variables, then the magnitude of the validity coefficient will be lowered. Smaller differences on predictor or criterion scores mean that it will be more difficult for the predictor to identify differences among people as measured by the criterion. Thus, lowered validity will occur.

Restriction in range is the term used to describe situations in which variance in scores on selection measures has been reduced. In selection practice, range restriction can occur in a number of circumstances. For instance, in a predictive validation study, *direct* restriction occurs when an employer uses the test being validated as a basis for selection decision making. *Indirect* restriction happens when the test being validated is correlated with existing selection procedures currently used for selection. Later, when individuals' test scores are correlated with their criterion scores, the validity coefficient will be curtailed. Range restriction occurs because individuals scoring low on the test were not hired. Their test scores could not be used in computing the validity coefficient because criterion data were unavailable.

Criterion scores also may be restricted. Restriction of criterion scores may occur because turnover, transfer, or termination of employees has taken place before the collection of criterion data. Performance appraisal ratings also might be restricted because raters did not discriminate among ratees in judging their work performance and gave them very similar ratings.

From our examples, you can see that restriction of scores can happen for either predictor or criterion or for both variables. Any form of restriction will lower computed validity. What we need to know is what validity would be if restriction had not occurred. Fortunately, a number of formulas have been developed to make the necessary statistical corrections in selection practice; however, these formulas correct for restriction on the predictor, not the criteria.[81] To illustrate the application of one formula for estimating the true predictor validity when restriction of range has occurred on the predictor, the following example formula is provided:

$$\hat{r}_{xy} = \frac{r_{xy_r}\left(\frac{SD_\mu}{SD_r}\right)}{\sqrt{1 - (r_{xy_r}) + (r_{xy_r})^2 \left[\frac{(SD_\mu)^2}{(SD_r)^2}\right]}}$$

where

$\hat{r}_{xy}$ = estimated validity if restriction had not occurred

r_{xy_r} = validity coefficient computed on restricted scores

SD_u = standard deviation of predictor scores from unrestricted group

SD_r = standard deviation of predictor scores from restricted group

As an example, assume the standard deviation (a measure of individual differences) of applicants' scores on a test was 10. After making selection decisions using the test, the standard deviation of applicants' scores who were hired is 2. The validity coefficient computed for those hired is 0.20. Using the formula, we can estimate the test's validity if all individuals had been hired, and the range of test scores was not restricted. That is,

$$\hat{r}_{xy} = \frac{(0.20)\frac{10}{2}}{\sqrt{1 - (0.20)^2 + (0.20)^2[(10)^2 + (2)^2]}} = \frac{1.00}{1.40} = 0.71$$

The estimated validity of 0.71 is considerably higher than our original validity of 0.20. Thus, range restriction had considerable effect. Where range restriction is low (that is, standard deviation of unrestricted predictor scores approximates that of restricted scores), computed validity is very close to estimated validity. But where range restriction is high, estimated validity on unrestricted scores differs substantially from validity computed on restricted scores.

With regard to correction for restriction in range, several cautionary actions should be considered; these include the following:

1. Eleven types of range restriction can occur; applying the wrong formula in a specific situation can lead to an overestimate or an underestimate of true predictor validity. Articles by Paul Sackett and his colleagues and Schmidt and Hunter should be consulted for guidance on using the appropriate formula for a specific situation (see Van Iddekinge and Ployhart's article for these sources).

2. Concerns remain regarding the specific range restriction corrections that should be made. Initial use of sound validation designs and measurement procedures can help mitigate some of these concerns and should be implemented whenever possible.[82]

Correcting validity coefficients for both range restriction and criterion unreliability are steps that the Society for Industrial and Organizational Psychology has endorsed in its *Principles*.[83] We have given only one example of range restriction correction, that involving a single variable. Edwin Ghiselli, John Campbell, and Sheldon Zedeck provided formulas for correcting range restriction for one as well as for several variables.[84] In addition, Calvin Hoffman,[85] as well as Deniz Ones and Chockalingam Viswesvaran,[86] have shown how published test norms can be used to obtain unrestricted estimates of the predictor's standard deviations to be used when making corrections.

Criterion Contamination

If scores on a criterion are influenced by variables other than the predictor, then criterion scores may be contaminated. The effect of contamination is to alter the magnitude of the validity coefficient. For instance, one criterion frequently used in validation studies is a performance appraisal or evaluation rating. We may want to know whether performance on a predictor is associated with performance on the job. However, performance ratings are sometimes subject to contamination or biased by extraneous variables, such as gender and ethnicity of ratees or raters or by the job tenure of persons being rated. If criterion ratings are influenced by variables that have nothing to do with actual work performance, then our obtained validity coefficient will be affected. In some cases, the validity coefficient will be spuriously high; in others, it will be spuriously low. Moreover, it is not always possible to know in advance the direction of these effects. Consider another example. Some years ago, one of the authors was engaged in a validation study of a predictor for bank proof-machine operators (sometimes called "item processors"). Operators used a proof machine to encode magnetic numbers on the bottom of checks so a computer can process them. Individual operator records of the number of checks processed during specific time periods were available. It appeared that a sound behavioral measure of performance was available that could be used as a criterion in the validation study. Further analysis, however, showed that even though the machines looked the same externally, some of the machines had been refurbished and had upgraded internal components. These upgraded components permitted faster check processing. Our apparently "great" criterion measure was contaminated. Rather than solely measuring differences in operators' performance, the productivity measure also was tapping differences in equipment. Without proper adjustments, the measure would be useless as a criterion because of its contamination.

Another classic example of criterion contamination occurs when "total dollar sales" is used as a criterion in a validation study of tests designed to measure applicants' selling ability. Suppose there are differences in the types of geographic territories sales personnel must work. Some territories contain long-term customers, so that all a salesperson has to do is take an order. In other, less mature territories, sales are much more difficult to achieve. A salesperson must really work hard to make a sale. Without some adjustment in the total dollar sales measure, criterion contamination will be present. Sales performance differences, as measured by total dollar sales, will be due more to territory assignment than to selling ability. Without proper adjustments, the result will be a misleading validation study.

When contaminating effects are known, they should be controlled either by statistical procedures such as partial correlation, by the research design of the validation study itself (for example, including only those employees in a validation study that have the same length of employment), or by adjustments to criterion data such as the computation of ratios. Again, the reason for controlling contaminating variables is to obtain a more accurate reading of the true relationship between a predictor and a criterion.

Violation of Statistical Assumptions

Among others, one important assumption of a Pearson or simple correlation is that a linear or straight-line relationship exists between a predictor and a criterion. If the relationship is nonlinear, the validity coefficient will give an underestimate of the true relationship between the two variables. For example, Figure 8.13 shows two scattergrams summarizing various relations between a selection measure and criterion. Case 1 shows a linear or straight-line relationship. A simple correlation coefficient would be appropriate for representing this relationship. If, however, a simple correlation were calculated on the data in Case 2, the correlation would equal 0.00. Yet, we can see that there is a relationship. Low as well as high test performance is associated with high criterion scores. We know that a relation exists, but our simple correlation will not detect it; other analyses are needed. If we simply had computed the correlation without studying the scattergram, we could have drawn an incorrect conclusion. Before computing a validity coefficient, a scattergram *always* should be plotted and studied for the possibility of nonlinear association.

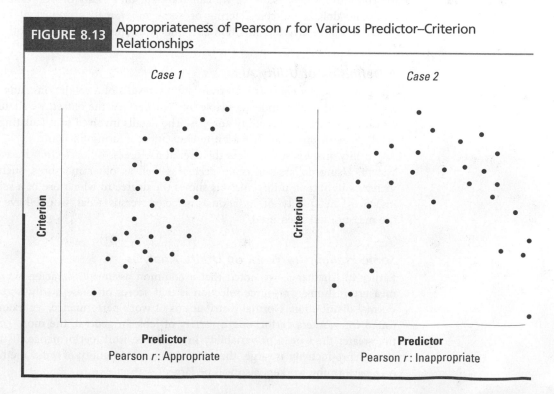

FIGURE 8.13 Appropriateness of Pearson *r* for Various Predictor–Criterion Relationships

Case 1

Case 2

Criterion

Predictor
Pearson *r*: Appropriate

Criterion

Predictor
Pearson *r*: Inappropriate

Utility Analysis

Picture yourself for a moment as an HR manager for a large computer manufacturing plant or as an HR consultant to the plant. Suppose you are looking at the results of a test validation study that shows a statistically significant validity coefficient of 0.50 for a test developed to predict the work performance of computer assembly workers in the plant. Obviously, you are excited about the results, because they suggest that the test can be used as an effective screening tool for computer assembly workers. Tomorrow you will be meeting with the executive staff of the plant; you have been asked to summarize the results and implications of the validation study. As you consider who will be at the meeting and what you will say, it becomes painfully obvious that the individuals in attendance (vice president of operations, vice president of accounting, and so on) are not likely to understand the meaning of a validity coefficient. You find yourself thinking, "What can I say so they will understand what this validity coefficient means?" "How can I get them to understand the value of the test and what we are doing in HR?"

The situation we just described is not unusual. Frequently, those of us working in the field of HR selection find ourselves in situations in which it is difficult to translate our research findings into practical terms that top management will understand and appreciate. This problem is compounded when validation studies are being conducted and communicated. Few top-level managers outside of HR understand what a validity coefficient is, much less what it means. Yet, as an HR manager, we must find a common terminology to communicate this meaning if we are going to compete with other departments in our organization for scarce resources. It is important that we find a means to translate our research findings into concepts and terms that management can understand and deal with if we hope to see the results of our work implemented.

As you think about a common terminology that most managers will understand, you probably will conclude that a dollars-and-cents' terminology is a practical option for communicating results. If we can translate the results of our validation work into economic dollars-and-cents' terms or some other metric important to managers, we probably will receive the attention and understanding we want from other managers.

A Definition of Utility Analysis

The goal of *utility analysis* is to translate the results of a validation study into terms that are important to and understandable by managers. At the outset, we should mention one caveat before discussing utility analysis. The details involved in calculating the utility of a valid selection procedure are a bit tedious and confusing for some.

Utility analysis summarizes the overall usefulness of a selection measure or selection system. Using dollars-and-cents' terms as well as other measures, such as percentage increases in output, utility analysis shows the degree to which use of a selection measure improves the quality of individuals selected versus what would have happened had the measure not been used.[87]

Some Preliminary Work on Utility Analysis

Earlier in Chapter 6, we noted that a common assumed characteristic of attributes we measure in human resource selection is that scores on these attributes tend to follow a normal distribution. Normal distributions of work performance, for example, have been found for workers performing a variety of jobs. In general, the more complex a job is, the greater the spread or variability in employee work performance. If the variability in worker productivity is large, then the usefulness or utility of valid methods to hire the best-performing workers also will be large.[88]

In examining productivity distributions, a common conclusion is that good workers produce roughly twice as much work as poor workers. This conclusion has naturally led to a series of logical questions, such as the following: "How much is a good worker worth?" and "If we identify and hire applicants who are good workers using a valid selection procedure, what will be the dollar return from using the procedure?" Utility analysis was developed to answer such questions.[89]

Although indices such as the validity coefficient, coefficient of determination, and index of forecasting efficiency have been used over the years, these procedures do not readily communicate to practitioners the utility of using valid selection procedures. None of these statistics relates to the economic value of a selection measure or recognizes that a measure's usefulness depends on the situation in which it is employed.[90] Early work by Hubert Brogden and H. C. Taylor and J. T. Russell often is recognized as laying the foundation for the development of utility analysis.[91] In sum, they suggested that the percentage of employees who will be identified as successful following the use of a valid selection procedure depends on three factors:

1. **Validity Coefficient.** The magnitude of the correlation of the selection procedure with a criterion.

2. **Selection Ratio.** The ratio of the number of people to be hired to the number of applicants available. (The smaller the ratio, the more favorable for the organization, because it can be more selective in who is hired.)

3. **Base Rate.** The percentage of employees currently successful on the job without use of the selection procedure. (A low base rate suggests that with the current selection system, there is difficulty in identifying satisfactory workers. Therefore, use of a valid selection procedure should improve identification of satisfactory employees.)

Taylor and Russell produced a series of tables showing that the utility of a test (that is, the increase in percentage of successful employees selected following use of a valid test) varied substantially depending on the test's validity, selection ratio, and the base rate. By means of the Taylor–Russell model, it was demonstrated that a test could be useful even when the validity coefficient was low.

Subsequent years led to additional, more complex utility models, such as those by James Naylor and Lester Shine,[92] Hubert Brogden,[93] and Lee Cronbach and Goldine Gleser.[94] These models refined the concept of utility and led to its translation into definable, measurable payoffs. In particular, the Brogden and Cronbach–Gleser models laid the foundation for most utility models in use today. They proposed that a valid test used in selection be evaluated based on specific (dollar) payoffs. That philosophy underlies much of utility analysis as currently applied in the field of personnel selection.

One of the biggest hurdles to translating the concept of utility analysis from a theoretical idea to a practical method has been in determining how to put a dollar value on differences in workers' productivity. This employee productivity dollar value has been referred to as SD_y or the standard deviation across individuals of the dollar value of employee productivity. SD_y represents how much differences in workers' productivity vary in dollar value to the employer. Or, to put it another way, SD_y shows in dollar terms the difference between good and poor workers' productivity. The tough question is how to estimate SD_y. Although a variety of approaches have been proposed to estimate SD_y, ranging from cost-accounting methods to Wayne Cascio's CREPID[95] procedure, debate persists as to which one is most appropriate in which situations. One common method that has been used is Frank Schmidt and John Hunter's rule: The value in the variability of employee work performance is estimated to be 40 percent of mean salary for the job. Without going through the technical details, the 40 percent rule is based on supervisors' estimates of the dollar value of productivity provided to the employer by good, average, and poor workers on a job. Basically, it says that SD_y for a job is roughly 40 percent of the average salary paid for the job. For example, if an average annual salary of $30,000 is being paid, and if performance on the job is normally distributed, then SD_y = at least $12,000. This means that workers' productivity at the 84th percentile, or +1 standard deviation above the mean, is worth at least $12,000 more per year than that of workers who are average. The difference between good workers at the 84th percentile and poor workers at the 16th percentile, or −1 standard deviation below the mean, is worth $24,000 per year. Notably, some have criticized the 40 percent rule's ability to estimate SD_y. Some research studies have supported the rule; others have not.

A number of equations have been proposed for examining selection method utility. One equation that has been used to calculate the utility of a selection program is the following:[96]

$$\text{Expected dollar gain from selection} = N_S\, r_{xy}\, SD_y\, Z_x - N_T(C)$$

where

Expected dollar gain from selection = the return in dollars to the organization for having a valid selection program

N_S = number of job applicants selected

r_{xy} = validity coefficient of the selection procedure

SD_y = standard deviation of work performance in dollars

Z_x = average score on the selection procedure of those hired expressed in z or standardized score form as compared to the applicant pool (an indication of the quality of the recruitment program)

N_T = number of applicants assessed with the selection procedure

C = cost of assessing each job applicant with the selection procedure

Applying Utility Analysis to Selection: Some Examples

To fully describe a complete application of utility analysis is too involved for our purposes here. However, we have prepared some examples that illustrate the use of utility analysis in determining the value of a valid selection method under various employment situations. The examples are based on the previous utility analysis equation.

Example 1: Costing the Value of a Selection Procedure. We have adapted a utility analysis outlined by Schmidt and his associates.[97] They applied a utility model to examine the gain in dollars obtained by using a valid test for selection as compared to using a predictor that was not valid. Figure 8.14 summarizes some hypothetical data for the utility analysis components or factors that we listed earlier. In Example 1, suppose that the validity of a general mental ability test we are using is 0.51. (This is the average validity of general mental ability tests in predicting work performance as reported by Schmidt and Hunter.[98]) Of every 100 applicants that apply for the job under study, 10 are hired; therefore, the selection ratio is 0.10 or 10 percent. Assuming that individuals are hired on the basis of their test scores, and the top 10 percent is hired, the average test score of the 10 hired—relative to our 100 in the applicant pool in standardized z-score

| FIGURE 8.14 | Examples of Utility Analysis Computed under Different Selection Conditions |

Utility Analysis Selection Factor	Example 1 Mental Ability Test	Example 2 Mental Ability Test	Example 3 Reference Check
Number of applicants selected (*N*)	10	10	10
Test validity (*r*)	0.51	0.51	0.26
Standard deviation of job performance ($) (*SD*)	$12,000	$12,000	$12,000
Average test score of those selected (*Z*)	1.00	1.25	1.00
Number of applicants tested (*N*)	100	100	100
Cost of testing each applicant (*C*)	$ 20	$ 20	$ 20
Expected payoff due to increased productivity per year for all employees hired	**$59,200**	**$74,500**	**$29,200**
Expected payoff per year for each employee hired	**$ 5,920**	**$ 7,450**	**$ 2,920**

form—is 1.00 (+1 *SD*), or at the 84th percentile. The standard deviation in dollars for work performance is estimated to be at least $12,000 per year (0.40 × $30,000 average annual salary). An individual who is 1 standard deviation above the mean on work performance is worth $12,000 more to the company than an individual with average work performance. Finally, suppose that the cost of purchasing, administering, scoring, interpreting, and filing the test is $20 per applicant. When these values are substituted in our utility analysis equation, the result is as follows:

$$\begin{aligned} \text{Expected dollar payoff due to increased} \\ \text{productivity per year for all} \\ \text{employees hired} &= 10(0.51)(\$12,000)(1.00) - 100(\$20) \\ &= \$59,200 \end{aligned}$$

Using the valid general mental ability test (versus using random selection or an invalid predictor) for one year to select workers would yield the company an expected net gain in productivity worth $59,200 for every 10 employees hired. Dollar gain each year per worker selected using the general mental ability test would be $5,920.

With the utility gain equation, it is possible to examine the effects of the equation's components on test utility. By systematically varying these components, impacts on expected gain can be seen. For example, increased testing costs, lowered validity, or an increased selection ratio (number of job applicants to be selected/total number of job applicants) will lower utility. Now, let's look at two more of these changes.

Example 2: Enhancing Recruitment. In this example, assume that all of the utility analysis components that we just described are the same, with one exception. Assume that the average test score in standardized *z*-score form is increased from 1.00 to 1.25. How might this occur? With an enhanced recruitment campaign that attracts better quality applicants, we will have higher quality applicants to choose from (that is, a lower selection ratio). Therefore, we can hire those who have test scores indicating higher general mental ability. Because the mental ability test is valid—that is, higher test scores are associated with higher work performance—we will have better performers on the job and enhanced productivity. As you can see from Example 2 in Figure 8.14, this change leads to an annual expected dollar payoff—in increased productivity for the 10 employees hired—of $74,500 or $7,450 per year per employee.

Example 3: Using a Method with Low Validity.   Now, assume that we use a scored reference check rather than the general mental ability test in making selection decisions. In this case, the validity coefficient of the reference check is 0.26, which is statistically significant. (This is the average validity of reference checks in predicting work performance as reported by Schmidt and Hunter.[99]) The average reference check score in standardized z-score form in this case is 1.00. Notice that even using a selection method with low validity, it is still useful in selection decision making. Use of the valid reference check produces an annual dollar payoff of $29,200 or $2,920 per employee per year. This example illustrates how a method with even low validity (as long as it is statistically significant) still can be useful. By manipulating the other components of our utility analysis, we can determine when the costs associated with the use of a measure would exceed its return on our investment in it.

In a published account of an actual utility analysis, Schmidt and his associates examined the dollar payoff of using a valid test (the Programmer Aptitude Test) to select computer programmers employed by the federal government.[100] Results of their analyses showed that under the most conservative selection conditions, an estimated productivity increase for one year's use of the test was $5.6 million. Other researchers also have translated selection procedure utility into dollar payoffs.[101]

Utility analysis is still a developing concept. For instance, some debate has centered on the size of economic returns found when estimating the utility of a valid selection procedure. In part, these estimates have been questioned when utility assumptions may not have been met and factors affecting the estimates have not been taken into account.

Utility analysis is based on several assumptions.[102] The first is that the relationship between a predictor and criterion is linear. Because the vast majority of ability and work performance relationships are linear, this assumption is not likely to be a troublesome one. A second assumption is that selection using the predictor is based on top-down hiring. That is, the top scorer is hired, followed by the rank-order hiring of other applicants until all positions are filled. Using methods other than a valid predictor in top-down hiring will result in a loss of utility. Third, when using top-down hiring, it is assumed that all applicants who are offered jobs accept their offers. When this result does not occur, lower scoring applicants on the predictor must be hired. Because of the first assumption (a linear relation exists between test performance and work performance), hiring lower scoring applicants with less ability (rather than higher scoring applicants) will result in lower work performance and lower selection procedure utility.

Finally, utility analysis assumes that individuals' work performance is distributed normally. Ernest O'Boyle and Herman Aguinis tested this assumption in five separate studies involving 198 samples, and 633,263 researchers, entertainers, politicians, and amateur and professional athletes.[103] The five studies' performance distributions were very similar and indicated that individual performance followed a Paretian distribution rather than a normal distribution. See Figure 8.15 for a visual comparison of normal and Paretian distributions. The figure shows the occurrence of extreme performers or "outliers" is more common in a Paretian distribution. Greater performance differences are identified between performers at the tail of the distribution versus those performing at the median than what has been assumed when using normal distributions. O'Boyle and Aguinis's results showed that, unlike a normal distribution, a small group of elite or star performers explained much of performance outcomes. With regard to utility analyses, they suggested that if work performance follows a Paretian distribution, future utility analyses should be made with that distribution in calculating SD_y. A valid selection procedure will show an even higher payoff than if a normal distribution were used to calculate SD_y.

Wayne Cascio has suggested that a truer picture of actual gains from a selection program will be obtained only by including additional factors in utility analysis equations.

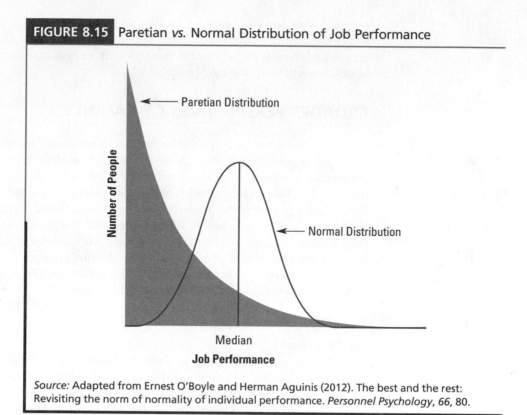

FIGURE 8.15 Paretian *vs.* Normal Distribution of Job Performance

Source: Adapted from Ernest O'Boyle and Herman Aguinis (2012). The best and the rest: Revisiting the norm of normality of individual performance. *Personnel Psychology, 66,* 80.

Factors affecting the economic payoffs of selection programs include job tenure of hires, recruitment costs, effects of taxes, and time lags in developing new-hire competence in performance, to name only a few.[104] Others, however, appear to have played down the significance of some of these factors regarding the usefulness of utility estimates.[105]

In addition, some debate has developed and research is continuing on the methods for deriving the suitable standard deviation of work performance measures (SD_y).[106] Some of these methods involve cost accounting approaches,[107] whereas others involve SMEs making ratings of performance.[108] These data are then used to compute standard deviations of performance.

Acceptance by Practitioners

As you recall, we began this discussion by noting that a means was needed to translate the value of a valid selection method into terms that could be understood by practicing managers. Utility analysis is one means for dealing with this need. Certainly, translating outcomes into economic gains would seem to be important to practicing managers. However, the method is not always seen positively. One survey of applied psychologists and human resource professionals reported that they found utility analysis difficult to understand and explain.[109] Another survey of 104 Swiss HR managers showed that only 9 percent reported having used the method.[110]

In two studies by Gary Latham and Glen Whyte, they concluded that the presentation to experienced managers of utility analysis results *decreased* managerial support for implementing a valid selection procedure.[111] Managers' lack of support might have been due to the managers' difficulties in understanding what the utility analysis' results meant.

Sole reliance on utility analysis' results alone does not appear to be a guarantee that practitioners will be persuaded to adopt a particular selection program. In addition to technical considerations, political, social, and institutional factors should be considered before implementing and communicating utility analysis results. For this reason, different methods have been proposed to modify utility analysis and simplify the presentation of utility results to managers.[112]

BROADER PERSPECTIVES OF VALIDITY

Content, concurrent, and predictive validity have been the strategies traditionally employed in validation studies involving predictors used in personnel selection. Other approaches, however, have been developed that take a broader view of selection procedure validity. Two such approaches are *validity generalization* and *job component validity*. Validity generalization relies on evidence accumulated from multiple validation studies that shows the extent to which a predictor that is valid in one setting is valid (that is, generalizable) to other similar settings. Job component validity is a process of inferring the validity of a predictor, based on existing evidence, for a particular dimension or component of work performance. This section will show how important these methods are to the future directions of validation research.

Validity Generalization

An Overview

For many years, selection specialists noted that validity coefficients for the same selection methods and criteria measures varied greatly for validation studies performed in different organizational settings. This was even true when the jobs for which the selection program had been designed were very similar. It was concluded that the idiosyncrasies of jobs, organizations, and other unknown factors contributed to the differences in validity results that were obtained. Therefore, it was assumed that the validity of a test is specific to the job or situation in which the validation study was completed. This assumption was based on what was called the *situational specificity hypothesis*. In the mid-1960s and early 1970s, Edwin Ghiselli published some classic studies involving hundreds of validation studies and validity coefficients classified by test and job types for two groups of criteria: job proficiency and training criteria.[113] Results from his work showed wide variations in the magnitudes of validity coefficients across validation studies, even when the same test had been used to predict the same criteria for practically identical jobs. Ghiselli's results as well as those of others appeared to confirm the situational specificity hypothesis— validity of a test is specific to the job situation on which the validity of the test has been determined. Supporters of the hypothesis believed that validity differences were due to dissimilarities in the nature of the specific employment situation or job in which a study was conducted—for example, the nature of the criteria used, the nature of the organization, or the inability of a job analysis to detect "real" job differences. This body of evidence led to the recommendation given by many that a separate validation study should be conducted for a selection procedure whenever a different employer uses that procedure in a different job situation.

In the late 1970s, the situational specificity hypothesis began to be challenged. Schmidt, Hunter, and their colleagues amassed and presented an impressive amount of evidence that cast considerable doubt regarding support of the situational hypothesis. Results from their analyses of validation studies involving cognitive ability tests as predictors led them to conclude that test validity does, in fact, generalize across situations. They argued that much of the differences found in a test's validity for similar jobs and criteria across different validation studies are not due to situational specificity but rather to methodological deficiencies in the validation studies themselves. Schmidt and Hunter hypothesized that these deficiencies accounted for differences among validity coefficients reported in validation studies. Differences among validity coefficients were due to the following factors:

1. The use of small sample sizes (which leads to sampling error and low statistical power)

2. Differences in predictor reliability

3. Differences in criterion reliability

4. Differences in the restriction of range of scores

5. The amount and kind of criterion contamination and deficiency

6. Computational and typographical errors

7. Slight differences among predictors thought to be measuring the same attributes or constructs[114]

Through a series of studies involving meta-analytic statistical techniques, Schmidt, Hunter, and others conducted a number of investigations called *validity generalization* studies. Their objective was to determine whether these hypothesized deficiencies explained differences found among validity coefficients computed for specific cognitive ability tests used as predictors in very similar jobs. If the deficiencies were found to explain a large portion of the differences among the validity coefficients, then the situational specificity hypothesis would be disconfirmed. Such a result would suggest that with appropriate evidence, the validity of a test is generalizable from one situation to another that is very similar (that is, similar in terms of the predictor and job on which the validity evidence had been accumulated). Conversely, if only a small portion of the differences in validity coefficients were explained by the deficiencies, it would indicate that test validity is situation specific. That is, rather than being generalizable from one situation to another, test validity information must be collected locally in each new setting in which a predictor is used.

Validity Generalization Methods

Validity generalization entails the statistical analyses of information accumulated from multiple validation studies involving a selection procedure whose results have been combined to determine the overall effectiveness of the procedure in new employment settings or locations. By combining data from multiple studies involving larger sample sizes than would be available in a single validation study, a population validity coefficient can be derived to yield a more accurate picture of the true validity of the predictor.

Several articles have outlined the details of the methodology used by Schmidt, Hunter, and their associates for testing the situational hypothesis and establishing validity generalization. Although their methodology basically corrects for the effects of the first four deficiencies just listed,[115] the remaining three deficiencies cannot be corrected with the available data. Their major steps are as follows:

1. Obtain a large number of published and unpublished validation studies for a selection procedure.

2. Compute the average validity coefficient for these studies.

3. Calculate the variance of differences among these validity coefficients reported in these studies.

4. Subtract, from the amount of these differences, the variance due to the effects of small sample size.

5. Correct the average validity coefficient and the variance for errors that are due to other methodological deficiencies (that is, differences in criterion reliability, predictor reliability, and restriction in the range of scores).

6. Compare the corrected variance to the average validity coefficient to determine the variation in study results.

7. If the differences among the corrected validity coefficients are very small, then validity coefficient differences are concluded to be due to methodological deficiencies and not to the nature of the situation. Therefore, validity is generalizable across situations.

Schmidt and Hunter's early validity generalization work focused on the generalizability of cognitive ability paper-and-pencil tests.[116] Additional work has suggested that validity generalization extends beyond mental ability testing. Validity generalizability has been reported for such predictors as biographical data,[117] personality inventories,[118] and assessment centers.[119] Current work continues with other predictors.[120]

Conclusions from Validity Generalization Studies

From a body of validity generalization investigations, Schmidt and Hunter rejected the "situational specificity hypothesis" regarding test validity in selection. They have used results of these analyses to draw some far-reaching conclusions. First, they concluded that it is not necessary to conduct validity studies within each organization for every job. If the job and selection procedure of interest for the selection program is one of those for which validity generalization data have been reported, then the selection procedure reported in the validity generalization study can be used in the organization for selection.[121] This is because there are no organization effects on validity; therefore, the same predictor can be used across all organizations for the relevant job or jobs. To set up the selection program, it is only necessary to show that the job with the organization is similar to the job in the validity generalization study. If job similarity can be shown, then the selection measure can be used; a separate validation study is not needed. Obviously, this reduces the time, effort, and cost of establishing a valid selection program. In addition, because larger samples are involved in validity generalization studies than local validation studies, a more accurate estimate of validity is possible.

Second, mental ability tests can be expected to predict work performance in most, if not all, employment situations.[122] Their usefulness as a predictor depends on the complexity of the job in question. Validity coefficients of these tests will be higher for jobs that are more complex than for less complex jobs. In other words, the more complex the job, the better mental ability tests will be able to predict work performance.

Criticisms of Validity Generalization

The findings of Schmidt, Hunter, and their colleagues have not gone unchallenged.[123] As we have mentioned, validity generalization studies apply correction formulas to the results of previous validity studies to correct the measurement deficiencies of these studies. Conclusions regarding the validity of the predictor and the generalizability of this validity estimate across organizations are based on the results of these correction formulas. Ideally, these corrections should be made to each study in the validity generalization analyses using data supplied by that study. The validity studies, however, usually do not report enough data to permit the corrections to be made in this manner. Instead, correction formulas use hypothetical values derived from other research work that are assumed appropriate for validity generalization analyses.

For the most part, criticisms of validity generalization studies have focused on the appropriateness of correction formulas. Many of these critical studies have used computer simulation as the method for examining appropriateness. In doing this, samples are generated from various populations of validation studies. For example, the population could be of studies in which the difference in validity coefficients among studies is actually zero; all differences are actually due to measurement errors. In other cases, the validity studies used for analyses are drawn from two populations that, in fact, differ in the magnitude of the validity coefficient. In this way, the researcher knows at the start of the study whether the validity coefficients are the same or different across situations (for example, organizations). The correction formulas then are applied to the data generated by the simulation model. This enables the researcher to determine whether the results of the correction formulas agree with what is already known about the validity coefficients being tested. If agreement exists, the formulas are thought to be appropriate; if disagreement exists, the formulas are thought to be in error.

In summary, it has been a common finding of these simulation studies that, under many conditions, validity generalization correction formulas overestimate the amount of variance attributable to study deficiencies. The result of overestimates may be the rejection of the proposition that organizational differences affect validity coefficients more often than would be appropriate. The authors of these simulation studies, therefore, generally have cautioned restraint in the interpretation of the results of validity generalization studies as well as careful consideration of the conclusions that have been drawn from them. We briefly summarize some of the points made in these critical studies. To obtain a more complete idea of the nature and extent of the criticism, it is necessary to read these studies directly.

Some studies have investigated the power of validity generalization analyses and the related concept of Type II error associated with these procedures. Power refers to the property of a statistical test for identifying differences when they exist. In the case of validity generalization, power refers to the rejection of generalizability and the determination of effects of organizational variables on the validity coefficients among the data. Type II error refers to the failure to determine situation specificity when it exists and, therefore, to finding no differences among the validity coefficients under study.

Two variables that seemingly affect the power of validity generalization analysis are the number of coefficients used in the analysis and the size of the samples on which these coefficients are calculated. Paul Sackett, Michael Harris, and John Orr concluded that "true population differences of 0.1 will not be consistently detected regardless of [sample size and number of correlations], and differences of 0.2 will not be consistently detected at small values [of these same two variables]."[124]

Other studies have questioned whether the conclusions drawn from the statistical formulas of the Schmidt–Hunter procedures are appropriate. For example, Lawrence James and his associates criticized several aspects of the Schmidt–Hunter procedures. Among these are that (a) the lines of evidence arguing for validity generalization are not nearly as strong as stated by Schmidt and Hunter; (b) the procedures call for double corrections for some measurement deficiencies; and (c) the use of sample validity coefficients in several formulas, as opposed to the Fischer z-transformations for these coefficients, is inappropriate. James et al. concluded "the prudent scientist/practitioner should be circumspect in interpreting results of [validity generalization] studies, especially those that support an inference of cross-situational consistency."[125]

In partial response to some of these criticisms, Larry Hedges developed an unbiased alternate correction for sampling error.[126] Central to this correction is the use of unbiased estimators of the population validity parameters that had been developed in previous research. Hedges demonstrated that while the correction formula for sampling error used in the Schmidt and Hunter technique is biased, the bias is usually quite small. Consequently, there is little reason to discount the results of existing validity generalization studies solely because of the bias in the correction of sampling error.

More recently, Neal Schmitt has acknowledged that the contributions of meta-analyses and validity generalization have transformed the field of HR selection. He has noted, however, that the corrections made for both direct and indirect range restriction in selection measures' scores appear overly optimistic and based on far too few actual studies. He also has argued that the assumption that organizations use top-down hiring in making employment decisions is simply not the case in most organizations. Thus, Schmitt has suggested that these assumptions regarding the level of range restriction and use of top-down hiring are simply untenable, and as a consequence, population validity estimates are very much inflated as compared with observed validity coefficients.[127]

Other criticisms have been aimed at validity generalization. A few of the major ones are summarized here:

1. **Lumping Together Good and Bad Studies.** Mark Cook reported that some critics have charged that validity generalization mixes together both good and bad studies when accumulating validity evidence. As Cook commented, however, a major problem in selection research is that no single study is perfect, particularly when it comes to sample size. Therefore, useful conclusions about validity may be reached only by pooling results of many investigations, as is done in validity generalization.[128]

2. **File Drawer Bias.** Another claim has been that journals are less likely to publish negative results—that is, results showing that a selection procedure is not valid. For this reason, some have alleged that many studies have been tucked away in file drawers, and their negative results are not known. Most validity generalization studies attempt to locate such studies for inclusion. Attempts have been made to derive a statistic for estimating the effect of file drawer bias on validity generalization results.[129]

3. **Criterion Unreliability.** The larger the estimate of criterion unreliability, the larger the increases in estimated true validity of the predictor. Another criticism of validity generalization has been that its advocates have used underestimates of criterion reliability in their studies. A common estimate used for supervisory ratings, the most frequently used criterion in empirical validation studies, has been 0.60.[130] In contrast, other studies have used 0.80 as the reliability estimate and, as might be expected, have found smaller increases in estimated true validity of ability tests. On the other hand, research appears to support the use of 0.60 as an estimate for supervisor rating criteria.[131]

Schmidt and his associates have concluded that such criticisms are concerned more with fine-tuning the method of validity generalization and do not detract significantly from its overall methodology and conclusions.[132] Some independent evidence seems to support their contention. The National Research Council Committee on the General Aptitude Test Battery of the U.S. Employment Service reviewed the statistical and measurement procedures of validity generalization and generally concluded that they were scientifically sound.[133]

Obviously, more research is necessary before the issues concerning assumptions and procedures of validity generalization studies can be completely agreed upon. Nonetheless, validity generalization studies have produced some of the most important findings regarding selection in recent years.

The work of Schmidt, Hunter, and their associates has important implications for the future of validation research in HR selection. The numerous validity generalization studies available suggest that the validity of a test is more generalizable across *similar situations* and *similar jobs* than previously has been thought. This conclusion should not be interpreted to mean that a test that is valid for one job will be valid for *any other* job. Sufficient validity information on one job, however, may be generalizable to other, very similar jobs. Ultimately, if validity generalization evidence for a test or some other predictor is available, a validation study might not be needed. Instead, it might be possible to use previous validation research to support the validity and use of the test for certain jobs.

Validity Generalization Requirements

In using validity generalization evidence to support a proposed selection procedure, a user would need to take a number of steps. Assuming that an appropriate validity generalization study does not exist, the first step is to gather all relevant validation studies, both published and unpublished, that investigate the relationship between the proposed selection procedure and the relevant criteria. Once these studies have been collected and proper meta-analytic methods have been applied to the studies, the *Principles* note the following conditions must be met:

1. The user must be able to show that the proposed selection procedure assesses the same WRCs or that it is a representative example of the measure used in the validity generalization study database.

2. The user must be able to show that the job in the new employment setting is similar (in job behaviors or knowledge, skills, and abilities) to the jobs or group of jobs included in the validity generalization study database.[134]

If these conditions can be met, then the new employment setting shows evidence of selection procedure validity. To meet these conditions, specific supporting information is needed. This information includes the following:

1. Validity generalization evidence consisting of studies summarizing a selection procedure's validity for similar jobs in other settings

2. Data showing the similarity between the jobs for which validity evidence is reported and the job in the new employment setting (an analysis of the job in the new employment setting is mandatory)

3. Data showing the similarity between the selection procedures in other studies that compose the validity evidence, and those procedures to be used in the new employment setting.[135]

So what is the future for validity generalization? At this point, it is another strategy that can be used to justify the use of a selection procedure.[136] Rather than conducting a local single validation study, this approach implies that one analyzes the accumulated validity evidence to develop generalized validity inferences. Professional judgment is needed to evaluate the results of meta-analytic research, which underlies validity generalization. As previously noted, the researcher must consider the meta-analytic methods used and the tenability of the underlying assumptions, particularly regarding the role of sampling error and other statistical artifacts. Further research on the validity generalization model, possible future versions of federal and professional guidelines on employee selection, future decisions in employment discrimination cases involving validity generalization as a validation strategy, and agreement among selection researchers on the technical details underpinning validity generalization will help resolve any remaining questions concerning this validation strategy.

An obvious advantage to using validity generalization—as compared with using traditional criterion-related validation research—is that resources saved in time and money could be considerable. Moreover, as we have noted, the cumulative predictor-criterion relationship evidence collected in a validity generalization study should be more accurate than any single validation study involving the same predictor.[137]

Although much of the controversy that characterized the application of validity generalization to personnel selection issues appears to have abated, and there is at least general acceptance of validity generalization methods among personnel selection scientists, important legal questions may remain. Schmidt and Hunter concluded that validity generalization has received generally favorable treatment by the courts.[138] In contrast, however, Frank Landy noted that a 1989 Sixth Circuit Court of Appeals conclusion that validity generalization was totally unacceptable under relevant case law and professional standards would have a chilling effect on the sole use of validity generalization as a legal defense for using a selection measure.[139]

Similarly, depending on validity generalization evidence alone to argue support for a predictor to a conservative court can produce some significant burdens for a defending organization. Daniel Biddle and Patrick Nooren theorize that conservative courts would rather see an *actual* validity coefficient that is derived at the defendant's specific locale than an *inferred* value derived from validity generalization procedures. They note that employers face an uphill climb in such courts because they must (a) show that factors specific to the applicant pool, the predictor itself, and the job itself do not limit the predictor from being valid in the employer's specific location; and (b) demonstrate that the validity generalization study and the predictor's inferred validity are large enough to be used for its intended purpose and will offset any disparate impact found with the selection procedure by the employer.[140]

After reading our previous discussion on validity generalization, you may ask, "If validity generalization can save time and resources in the undertaking of validation efforts—as well as produce more meaningful results than a single validation study could—why not just use a validity generalization strategy to study all of our selection procedures?" Certainly, this is a reasonable question, and some will agree with the sentiment implied. But, in addition to the political concerns we alluded to earlier, and some legal issues remaining to be addressed (for example, the level of detail required by the courts in a validity generalization job analysis), other factors may limit the implementation of validity generalization as a sole validation strategy. Calvin Hoffman and Morton McPhail have noted two of these factors.[141] First, existing validity generalization studies have not examined all of the jobs in the world of work. There are probably jobs in which few or no validity generalization results exist for use as validity-supporting arguments to implement selection procedures. Second, the amount of job analysis information collected in a typical validity generalization study may be too sparse to meet the requirements of the courts. Due to these concerns, Hoffman and McPhail concluded that "because the demands of practice sometimes necessitate more detail than required by the best wisdom of the profession ... sole reliance on VG evidence to support test use is probably premature."[142] Biddle would appear to concur with Hoffman and McPhail's conclusion; he has suggested that a validity generalization study be used to support a local validation study, assuming that the local study can show a statistically significant validity coefficient, practical significance, and relevant performance measures and that the scores are used appropriately given the level of adverse impact, for example, cutoff score or ranking of job applicants.[143]

Job Component Validity and Synthetic Validity

An Overview

There are a number of different approaches to what is job component validity or what some refer to as synthetic validity. Essentially, job component validity involves demonstrating that a correlation exists between a selection procedure and at least one specific aspect or component of a job.[144] Once established, it is assumed that the selection procedure is valid for predicting performance on that job component if it exists on other jobs. That is, validity for the selection procedure is generalizable to any job requiring that same job component.

Notice that selection procedure validity for a work component is inferred from existing validation research evidence rather than by directly measuring validity through the traditional methods we have discussed (for example, criterion-related or content-related strategies). Two important assumptions underlie this strategy: (a) when jobs have a work component in common, the work-related characteristics required for performing that component are the same across these jobs; and (b) a predictor's validity for work-related characteristics required for performing a work component is reasonably consistent across jobs.[145]

Conducting a Job Component Validity Study

Briefly, the major steps involved in one approach for conducting a job component validation study are as follows:

1. **Conduct an Analysis of the Job Using the Position Analysis Questionnaire (PAQ).** The PAQ is a commercially available, paper-and-pencil questionnaire that contains a comprehensive listing of general behaviors required at work. A respondent (for example, a job analyst) responds to the PAQ by indicating the extent to which these descriptions accurately reflect the work behaviors performed on a particular job.

2. **Identify the Major Components of Work Required on the Job.** Once the PAQ has been used to analyze a job, the most important work behaviors or components of the job are identified.

3. **Identify the Attributes Required to Perform the Major Components of the Job.** Using ratings from experts, the developers of the PAQ established links between 76 job attributes (including those related to mental ability, perceptual ability, psychomotor ability, interest, and temperament) and the work behaviors listed on the PAQ for approximately 2,200 job titles in the U.S. labor force.[146] This expert ratings' database serves as a basis for identifying which of the 76 attributes are needed to perform the most important work components of a new job being analyzed. For instance, when a new job is analyzed with the PAQ, results of the analysis show the importance of specific attributes, relative to the 2,200 jobs in the PAQ database, in performing the identified components of the job.

4. **Choose Tests That Measure the Most Important Attributes Identified from the PAQ.** Strictly speaking, actual validity coefficients are not computed in job component validity. Predicted validity coefficients and scores for selected general aptitude tests are estimated from an existing database of test scores and PAQ information. These coefficients estimate what the validity of a test would have been had an actual criterion-related validation study been performed. The results show which ability tests are likely to be most useful and valid for selecting among applicants for the job being analyzed.

Recall the two job component validity assumptions we mentioned earlier. These assumptions form the foundation for which test validity is argued under the job component validity approach. Most important, if a test has been found to predict performance for a job component across a wide array of jobs, it is assumed that the test should be valid for jobs in which that same component is most salient. The results of a job component validity analysis, using the PAQ, suggest tests to use for the job being analyzed and their predicted validity coefficients.

Accuracy of Job Component Validity Studies

Several studies have investigated the correspondence between predicted validity coefficients of tests using job component validity and actual computed validity coefficients. Studies by Morton McPhail[147] and L. M. Holden[148] reported that job component validity estimates were generally lower and more conservative than validity coefficients obtained in actual validation studies. Hoffman and McPhail compared predicted job component validity coefficients for 51 clerical jobs with actual validity coefficients computed for similar jobs in a prior validation study.[149] They concluded that the job component validity procedure produced predicted validity coefficients that were very similar to those that had been determined statistically. They reasoned that if the job component validity procedure was used to infer validity of tests for clerical jobs, the conclusions reached would be similar to those that had been drawn from actual validation studies.

We have seen how the PAQ can be used to conduct a job component validation study. Richard Jeanneret and Mark Strong have extended the job component validation concept by using the Department of Labor's O*NET database.[150] The O*NET database consists of job analysis information collected on a large array of occupations. Among the job data available is information on 42 generalized work activities that occupations may involve. A generalized work activity represents a work behavior used to perform major work functions, such as analyzing data or information. In their research, Jeanneret and Strong found that the O*NET's generalized work activity information was useful for identifying tests to be used in the selection for jobs that required specific types of aptitudes. Predictions were strongest for cognitive aptitudes and weakest for manual dexterity using O*NET's generalized work activities.[151]

At this point, use of the O*NET for job component validation is in its infancy. More developmental research is needed. Assuming this research is completed and supporting results are found, to analyze a job, all an employer might have to do is use the generalized work activities and, perhaps, other O*NET information. This information then would be used to obtain estimates of useful predictors for the job of interest. Again, assuming that the necessary developmental research takes place, O*NET may offer a promising option for those organizations, both large and small, that seek guidance in choosing selection procedures.

Criticisms of Job Component Validity Strategy

Among several specific criticisms, Kevin Mossholder and Richard Arvey have raised several general points concerning the job component validity approach.[152] Although there is limited evidence to the contrary, they have noted that the method has been less successful in predicting actual validity coefficients. Second, the strategy has been relatively less useful in predicting psychomotor test data. Finally, the strategy generally has reported test results from the General Aptitude Test Battery, which is available only to public employers. Results are available for only a relatively limited number of commercially available tests.

In spite of criticisms, the job component validity strategy offers another tool for examining the validity of predictors used in selection. A practitioner may use the method in several ways. A conservative use would be to apply the job component validity approach and then conduct a local validation of the tests identified. Another way the method could be used is to simply apply the job content validity approach and implement the recommended tests without a local validation study. Although this option apparently has not undergone a lot of legal scrutiny, there is at least one court case (*David Taylor v. James River Corporation*, 1989)[153] in which the method received a favorable review.

The method provides a unique approach for small organizations in which sample sizes for criterion-related validity are inadequate, or for those jobs yet to be created or undergoing significant change. Jeanneret described two cases illustrating the versatility of the strategy when implemented in a situation unsuited for use with conventional criterion-related approaches.[154] In the first case, a preemployment test battery was developed using the job component validity strategy for workforce selection in a state-of-the-art technology manufacturing facility under construction. In a second application, the strategy was implemented to design selection test specifications for space station personnel who would spend extended periods in an orbiting space station. These may seem to be unusual employment situations that are different from the typical employment context. Tests are being validated before the actual employment setting exists. Yet, situations such as these depict the future needs in many of today's technologically driven organizations; many do not lend themselves to study using traditional validation strategies. Such situations very likely may be the norm in coming years.

VALIDATION OPTIONS FOR SMALL SAMPLE SIZES

We have reviewed a number of strategies for validating selection measures, all of which are suitable for use in organizations. Some of these strategies, however, are practical only for large organizations that have large numbers of employees or applicants on whom validation data can be collected. What about situations in which only small numbers of people are available for data collection, for example, a small business? These situations can pose particular methodological challenges for those contemplating a validation study. But, these challenges do not mean selection procedure validation should be ignored. Selection measure validation is probably even more critical for a small business than it is for a large one. Small businesses often hire applicants who possess job-specific WRCs and work habits and who must immediately begin a job without completing an extensive training program. Large businesses generally have the resources to compensate for a hiring "mistake"; in small businesses, one or two bad hires could be financially devastating (for example, because of poor work performance, theft, a negligent hiring suit brought against the business, or even a discrimination lawsuit brought by an aggrieved applicant). Recall from our earlier reading that many equal employment opportunity laws cover organizations having 15 or more employees.[155] Given these issues, validation evidence is essential for small businesses. But what validation options are available?

We have several options among the strategies we have discussed. Content validity is one. We noted earlier that criterion problems—and the smaller numbers of people available to participate in a criterion-related validation study in many organizations—are two reasons for the increased use of content validity strategies. As Guion pointed out, when a small organization of 50 or so people is hiring only one or two people a year, ordinary empirical validation cannot be performed.[156]

A second option is validity generalization, assuming that it continues to mature as an acceptable means for validating predictors. To implement a validity generalization study, a small business has two main requirements (a) to show that the measure used in selection assesses the same constructs as a measure used in a previous validity generalization study, and (b) to show that the jobs for which the measure is used are similar to those jobs in the validity generalization study. If a suitable, existing validity generalization study cannot be found, then one would have to be conducted following the steps outlined earlier.

Finally, as discussed, job component validity or some other form of synthetic validity is a third option. *Synthetic validity* is a logical process of inferring test validity for components of jobs. Charles Scherbaum has discussed the major approaches to synthetic validity as well as the future trends and legal issues involving these methods.[157] Whatever the specific approach, all job component–synthetic validity approaches tend to involve the following steps: (a) analyzing jobs to identify their major components or dimensions of work; (b) determining the relationships of selection predictors with these job dimensions using content, construct, or criterion-related validity strategies; and (c) choosing predictors to use in selection based on their relationships with these important job dimensions.

To illustrate a form of synthetic validity that incorporates criterion-related validity, let's look at a simple example. Suppose an organization wanted to validate some tests for three different jobs—typist, clerk, and receptionist—using a criterion-related strategy. The problem is that the largest number of people in any one of the three jobs is 60 (typist); the smallest number of people is 40 (receptionist). In our discussion earlier in the chapter about computing empirical validity, recall that we said it was essential to use as large a sample size as possible in computing a validity coefficient. With small sample sizes, there is a greater likelihood of not finding that a test is valid than there is of finding it valid, even when the test is truly valid. Although the sample sizes are small, we will illustrate how synthetic validity might be accomplished.

Using a job analysis questionnaire, it is found that even though job titles are different, some of the jobs share some components of work. Figure 8.16 illustrates three jobs and work performance components that are common to each. The three jobs and the number of their incumbents are as follows: (a) typist ($N = 60$), (b) clerk ($N = 50$), and (c) receptionist ($N = 40$). Three work performance components characterizing these jobs include (a) *following directions*, (b) *typing*, and (cd) *Dealing with the public*. The Xs in the matrix represent the work performance components common to each job. For instance, *following directions* and *typing* characterize the job of typist, while *typing* and *dealing with the public* are most descriptive of the receptionist job.

The lower half of Figure 8.16 lists the measures that were developed or chosen from commercially available ones to assess each of the job components. For example, the Oral Directions Test was selected to determine whether it could predict the job component,

FIGURE 8.16   Illustration of Test Validation Using Synthetic Validity

Job	Number of Employees	Following Directions I	Typing II	Dealing with the Public III
		Job Performance Component		
Typist	60	X	X	
Clerk	50	X		X
Receptionist	40		X	X
Total number of employees in combined jobs		110	100	90

Selection Procedure	I	II	III
	Job Performance Component		
Oral Directions Test	√		
Typing Test		√	
Public Relations Test			√
Total number of employees available for test validation	110	100	90

Note: X represents job component characteristic of a job. Jobs sharing an X for the same component require the same job function. √ indicates the selection procedure chosen for predicting success on a particular job component.

following directions. Criterion measures (such as performance ratings) are developed for each job dimension. Jobs sharing a common work performance component are combined to validate the selection measure. For instance, for the job component *following directions*, the typist and clerk jobs are combined (combined sample size = 110); for the job component *typing*, the typist and receptionist jobs are grouped together (combined sample size = 100); and, finally, for the job component *dealing with the public*, the jobs of clerk and receptionist are combined (combined sample size = 90). Notice that by combining jobs that require the same work activity, we are able to increase our sample sizes substantially over those samples we would have had using only one job. We can collapse these jobs because we are studying a common work activity. In this sense, validity is "synthetic"; we are not creating validity per se, but rather we are creating a situation that will permit a better estimate of selection procedure validity. The major advantage of this is that selection measures are validated across several jobs in an organization that share common job dimensions, rather than for only one job.

Once the jobs have been combined on common work performance components, criterion measures (such as performance ratings) have been collected on each employee performing the job components, and selection measures have been administered, then test and criterion data are correlated. Statistically significant relationships indicate a valid selection measure. As you can see, rather than validating a measure for a whole job, we have broken down jobs into component work performance dimensions and validated our selection measures against these specific components. Because our sample sizes are larger than they would have been for any one job, we have a larger sample size to perform a criterion-related validation study. Our example illustrates only one approach to synthetic validation. Other synthetic validation options are available for small sample size situations.[158]

For the small firm with jobs in which there are a number of incumbents, synthetic validity may offer one solution to the thorny problem of small sample size in criterion-related validation studies. The principal assumption in employing a synthetic validity approach is that our analyses of jobs will identify job dimensions common to those jobs studied.

For the small organization, building a database sufficiently large to conduct an empirical validation study is a particularly difficult problem. Additional options include (a) combining similar jobs or components of jobs across different organizations such as in a cooperative validation study, (b) combining similar jobs or components of jobs within and across organizations, and (c) accumulating data over time.[159]

As compared with large organizations, the types of evidence available for showing job relatedness are often quite different in small organizations. Rational judgment is likely to play a far more important role in validity studies within small organizations than large ones. In such cases, the more evidence we can collect on job relatedness, even judgmental evidence, the better.

THE FUTURE OF VALIDATION RESEARCH

In 1983, a survey of 437 organizations by the Bureau of National Affairs revealed that only 16 percent of the firms had validated one or more of their selection techniques.[160] Ten years later, corporate use of validation strategies such as those we have discussed in this chapter had shown little change. A random sample survey of 1,000 companies listed in *Dun's Business Rankings* with 200 or more employees indicated that of the 201 firms responding, only 24 percent stated they had conducted validation studies of their selection measures.[161] Because of the importance of validation studies in defending legal challenges, one wonders whether the value of 24 percent might even be inflated. Unfortunately, we do not have current survey data showing the extent to which organizations are undertaking validation efforts. Nevertheless, if the older survey results still apply, they are surprising in light of both the current legal mandates to validate selection predictors and the productivity gains that can be reaped by organizations using valid predictors in selection.

This chapter has taken a classic approach to discussing validity and the strategies used for validity assessment. Much of our focus has assumed that predictor and criterion data are available on individuals, that data are available on sizable numbers of individuals,; and that jobs and the requirements for performing them remain relatively constant over time. A number of writers have noted, however, that yesterday's workplace is not today's, and it will not be tomorrow's.[162] Changes are occurring, and they likely will affect the assumptions we have made and the future of validation research. Such changes include the following:

1. Increasing numbers of small organizations without the resources (for example, time or money), technical requirements (for example, large sample sizes), and technical skills available to undertake traditional validation strategies

2. Increasing use of teams of workers rather than individuals[163]

3. Changes in the definitions of job success to include such criteria as organization and job commitment, teamwork, and quality of service delivered to customers

4. The changing nature of work—in that jobs and the requirements for performing them are becoming more fluid, requiring job analytic methods that focus on broader work capacities rather than on molecular task requirements

Because of changes such as these, nontraditional approaches to examining selection measure validity are being called for. For example, in the case of small organizations, Schmidt has argued that complex, expensive validation studies are not necessary.[164] He suggested that through validity generalization research, we already know what works. According to Schmidt, ability tests, assessment centers, interviews, and the like can be implemented in small organizations and can produce an immediate payoff in their selection systems. But will such strategies as validity generalization be widely adopted? As we suggested earlier, only time will tell. Before widespread adoption of these strategies, however, a balance must be struck among the competing issues, a balance involving (a) the technical requirements of validation research, (b) organizations' needs and the changing nature of work and work contexts, (c) societal demands, and (d) current laws and legal interpretations of the federal and professional guidelines and requirements that determine appropriate validation strategies. Until that balance is reached, we have chosen to provide you with a foundation of knowledge on the subject of those validation methods that have a proven record of usefulness. This foundation should help to prepare you for future needs, challenges, and developments that you may encounter with regard to the study of selection procedure validity.

REFERENCES

1. Society for Industrial and Organizational Psychology, *Principles for the Validation and Use of Personnel Selection Procedures*, 4th ed. (Bowling Green, OH: Author, 2003), 4.

2. Greg L. Stewart, Susan L. Dustin, Murray R. Barrick, and Todd C. Darnold, "Exploring the Handsake in Employment Interviews," *Journal of Applied Psychology* 93 (2008): 1139–1145; and William F. Chaplin Jeffrey B. Phillips, Jonathan D. Brown, Nancy R. Clanton, and Jennifer L. Stein, "Handshaking, Gender, Personality, and First Impressions," *Journal of Personality and Social Psychology: Personality Processes and Individual Differences* 79 (2000): 110–117.

3. Samuel Messick, "Validity," in *Educational Measurement*, ed. R. L. Linn (New York: American Council on Education and MacMillan Publishing Co., 1989), 13–104.

4. Charles H. Lawshe, "Inferences from Personnel Tests and Their Validity," *Journal of Applied Psychology* 70 (1985): 237–238.

5. Theresa J. B. Kline, *Psychological Testing: A Practical Approach to Design and Evaluation* (Thousand Oaks, CA: Sage, 2005), 212–213.

6. Lawrence S. Kleiman and Robert H. Faley, "The Implications of Professional and Legal Guidelines for Court Decisions Involving Criterion-Related Validity: A Review and Analysis," *Personnel Psychology* 38 (1985): 803–834.

7. Dirk D. Steiner and Stephen W. Gilliland, "Fairness Reactions to Personnel Selection Techniques in France and the United States," *Journal of Applied Psychology* 61 (1996): 134–141.

8. Kevin R. Murphy, Jessica L. Dzieweczynski, and Yang Zhang, "Positive Manifold Limits the Relevance of Content-Matching Strategies for Validating Selection Test Batteries," *Journal of Applied Psychology* 94 (2009): 1018.

9. Benjamin Schneider and Neal Schmitt, *Staffing Organizations* (Glenview, IL: Scott, Foresman, 1986).

10. Lawrence Kleiman and Robert Faley, "Assessing Content Validity: Standards Set by the Court," *Personnel Psychology* 31 (1978): 701–713.

11. *Albemarle Paper Company v. Moody*, 422 U.S. 405 (1975).

12. Equal Employment Opportunity Commission, Civil Service Commission, Department of Labor, and Department of Justice, *Adoption of Four Agencies of Uniform Guidelines on Employee Selection Procedures*, 43 *Federal Register* 38, 305 (August 25, 1978).

13. Richard S. Barrett, *Challenging the Myths of Fair Employment Practice* (Westport, CT: Quorum Books, 1998), 62–76.

14. Irwin L. Goldstein, Sheldon Zedeck, and Benjamin Schneider, "An Exploration of the Job Analysis–Content Validity Process," in *Personnel Selection in Organizations*, ed. Neal Schmitt and Walter C. Borman (San Francisco: Jossey-Bass, 1993), 7–10.

15. Ibid., 9.

16. Irwin Goldstein and Sheldon Zedeck, "Content Validation," in *Fair Employment Strategies in Human Resource Management*, ed. Richard S. Barrett (Westport, CT: Quorum Books, 1996), 29.

17. Goldstein, Zedeck, and Schneider, "An Exploration of the Job Analysis–Content Validity Process," 21.

18. Charles Lawshe, "A Quantitative Approach to Content Validity," *Personnel Psychology* 28 (1975): 563–575.

19. F. Robert Wilson, Wei Pan, and Donald A. Schumsky, "Recalculation of the Critical Values for Lawshe's Content Validity Ratio," *Measurement and Evaluation in Counseling and Development* 45 (2012): 197–210.

20. Lyle F. Schoenfeldt, Barbara B. Schoenfeldt, Stanley R. Acker, and Michael R. Perlson, "Content Validity Revisited: The Development of a Content-Oriented Test of Industrial Reading," *Journal of Applied Psychology* 61 (1976): 581–588.

21. Silvia Moscoso and Jesus Salgado, "Psychometric Properties of a Structured Behavioral Interview to Hire Private Security Personnel," *Journal of Business and Psychology* 16 (2001): 51–59.

22. Equal Employment Opportunity Commission, Civil Service Commission, Department Labor, and Department of Justice, "Uniform Guidelines on Employee Selection Procedures," *Federal Register* 43 (1978): 38290–39315.

23. Frank L. Schmidt, "Cognitive Tests Used in Selection Can Have Content Validity as Well as Criterion Validity: A Broader Research Review and Implications for Practice," *International Journal of Selection and Assessment* 20 (2012): 1–13.

24. Paul Sackett, "Cognitive Tests, Constructs, and Content Validity: A Commentary on Schmidt (2012)," *International Journal of Selection and Assessment* 20 (2012): 24–27; Robert E. Ployhart, "The Content Validity of Cognitively Oriented Tests: Commentary on Schmidt," *International Journal of Selection and Assessment* 20 (2012): 19–23; Jerard Kehoe, "What to Make of Content Validity Evidence for Cognitive Tests? Comments on Schmidt (2012)," *International Journal of Selection and Assessment* 20 (2012): 14–18.

25. Frank L. Schmidt, "Content Validity and Cognitive Tests: Response to Kehoe (2012), Ployhart (2012), and Sackett (2012)," *International Journal of Selection and Assessment* 20 (2012): 28–35.

26. Goldstein, Zedeck, and Schneider, "An Exploration of the Job Analysis–Content Validity Process."

27. Equal Employment Opportunity Commission et al., *Adoption of Four Agencies of Uniform Guidelines on Employee Selection Procedures*, 303.

28. Ibid., 302.

29. Ibid.

30. American Educational Research Association, American Psychological Association, and National Council on Measurement in Education, *Standards for Educational and Psychological Testing* (Washington, DC: American Educational Research Association, 1999).

31. Society for Industrial and Organizational Psychology, *Principles for the Validation and Use of Personnel Selection Procedures,* 4th ed. (Bowling Green, Ohio: Author, 2003).

32. Michael A. McDaniel, Sven Kepes, and George C. Banks, "The *Uniform Guidelines* are a Detriment to the Field of Personnel Selection," *Industrial and Organizational Psychology* 4 (2011): 508.

33. Sackett, "Cognitive Tests, Constructs, and Content Validity: A Commentary on Schmidt," 25.

34. Robert M. Guion, "Recruiting, Selection, and Job Placement," in *Handbook of Industrial and Organizational Psychology*, ed. Marvin D. Dunnette (Chicago: Rand McNally, 1974), 786.

35. Goldstein and Zedeck, "Content Validation," 36.

36. Michael R. Carrier, Anthony T. Dalessio, and Steven H. Brown, "Correspondence between Estimates of Content and Criterion-Related Validity Values," *Personnel Psychology* 43 (1990): 85–100.

37. Murphy, Dzieweczynski, and Zhang, "Positive Manifold Limits the Relevance of Content-Matching Strategies for Validating Selection Test Batteries," 1018, 1028.

38. Robert M. Guion and C. J. Cranny, "A Note on Concurrent and Predictive Validity Designs: A Critical Reanalysis," *Journal of Applied Psychology* 67 (1982): 239–244.

39. Frank J. Landy, *Psychology of Work Behavior* (Homewood, IL: Dorsey Press, 1985), 65.

40. Neal Schmitt, Richard Z. Gooding, Raymond A. Noe, and Michael Kirsch, "Metaanalyses of Validity Studies Published between 1964 and 1982 and the Investigation of Study Characteristics," *Personnel Psychology* 37 (1984): 407–422.

41. Gerald V. Barrett, James S. Phillips, and Ralph A. Alexander, "Concurrent and Predictive Validity Designs: A Critical Reanalysis," *Journal of Applied Psychology* 66 (1981): 1–6.

42. D. S. Ones, C. Viswesvaran, and F. L. Schmidt, "Comprehensive Meta-analysis of Integrity Test Validities: Findings and Implications for Personnel Selection and Theories of Work performance," *Journal of Applied Psychology* 78 (1993): 679–703; and R. P. Tett, N. Jackson, and H. M. Rothstein, "Personality Measures as Predictors of Work performance: A Meta-analytic Review," *Personnel Psychology* 44 (1991): 703–742.

43. Chad H. Van Iddekinge and Robert E. Ployhart, "Developments in the Criterion-Related Validation of Selection Procedures: A Critical Review and Recommendations for Practice," *Personnel Psychology* 61 (2008): 897.

44. Society for Industrial and Organizational Psychology, *Principles for the Validation and Use of Personnel Selection Procedures*, 3rd ed. (College Park, MD: Author, 1987), 7.

45. Society for Industrial and Organizational Psychology, *Principles for the Validation and Use of Personnel Selection Procedures* (2003), 10.

46. Society for Industrial and Organizational Psychology, *Principles for the Validation and Use of Personnel Selection Procedures* (1987).

47. Charles Hulin, R. A. Henry, and S. L. Noon, "Adding a Dimension: Time as a Factor in the Generalizability of Predictive Relationships," *Psychological Bulletin* 107 (1990): 328–340.

48. Gerald Barrett, Ralph Alexander, and D. Dorerspike, "The Implications for Personnel Selection of Apparent Declines in Predictive Validities Over Time: A Critique of Hulin, Henry, and Noon," *Personnel Psychology* 45 (1992): 601–617.

49. D. L. Deadrick and R. M. Madigan, "Dynamic Criteria Revisited: A Longitudinal Study of Performance Stability and Predictive Validity," *Personnel Psychology* 43 (1990): 717–744.

50. Steven H. Brown, "Long-Term Validity of a Personal History Item Scoring Procedure," *Journal of Applied Psychology* 63 (1978): 673–676.

51. Frank L. Schmidt, John E. Hunter, and A. N. Outerbridge, "Impact of Job Experience and Ability on Job Knowledge, Work Sample Performance, and Supervisory Ratings of Work performance," *Journal of Applied Psychology* 71 (1986): 432–439.

52. Lawrence S. Kleiman and Robert H. Faley, "The Implications of Professional and Legal Guidelines for Court Decisions Involving Criterion-Related Validity: A Review and Analysis," *Personnel Psychology* 38 (1985): 803–834.

53. Daniel A. Biddle and Patrick M. Nooren, "Validity Generalization vs. Title VII: Can Employers Successfully Defend Tests Without Conducting Local Validation Studies?" *Labor Law Journal* 57 (2006): 29.

54. Daniel A. Biddle, *Adverse Impact and Test Validation: A Practitioner's Guide to Valid and Defensible Employment Testing* (Burlington, VT: Gower, 2005), 50.

55. Biddle and Nooren, "Validity Generalization vs. Title VII: Can Employers Successfully Defend Tests Without Conducting Local Validation Studies?" 29.

56. Herman Aguinis and Marlene A. Smith, "Understanding the Impact of Test Validity and Bias on Selection Errors and Adverse Impact in Human Resource Selection," *Personnel Psychology* 60 (2007): 165.

57. Ibid., 165–199.

58. Society for Industrial and Organizational Psychology, *Principles for the Validation and Use of Selection Procedures* (2003).

59. Robert M. Guion, *Personnel Testing* (New York: McGraw-Hill, 1965), 128.

60. Based on John F. Binning and Gerald V. Barrett, "Validity of Personnel Decisions: A Conceptual Analysis of the Inferential and Evidential Bases," *Journal of Applied Psychology* 74 (1989): 478–494.

61. W. Bruce Walsh and Nancy E. Betz, *Tests and Assessment* (Englewood Cliffs, NJ: Prentice Hall, 1990), 67.

62. Edwin E. Ghiselli, John P. Campbell, and Sheldon Zedeck, *Measurement Theory for the Behavioral Sciences* (San Francisco: Freeman, 1981).

63. Paul R. Sackett and Richard D. Arvey, "Selection in Small *N* Settings," in *Personnel Selection in Organizations*, ed. Neal Schmitt and Walter C. Borman (San Francisco: Jossey-Bass, 1993), 431–432.

64. In some employment settings, an organization may not have as many applicants or employ as many people as given in our example. Thus, empirical validity may not be technically feasible. Under such circumstances, other approaches to validity—such as content validity, validity generalization, and synthetic validity—may need to be considered.

65. Richard D. Arvey and Robert H. Faley, *Fairness in Selecting Employees* (Reading, MA: Addison-Wesley, 1988), 164–165.

66. Frank L. Schmidt, Benjamin P. Ocasio, Joseph M. Hillery, and John E. Hunter, "Further Within—Setting Empirical Tests of the Situational Specificity Hypothesis in Personnel Selection," *Personnel Psychology* 38 (1985): 509–524.

67. McDaniel, Kepes, and Banks, "The Uniform Guidelines Are a Detriment to the Field of Personnel Selection," 497.

68. J. F. Salgado, " Sample Size in Validity Studies of Personnel Selection," *Journal of Occupational and Organizational Psychology* 71 (1998): 161–164.

69. Schmidt, "Cognitive Tests Used in Selection Can Have Content Validity as Well as Criterion Validity: A Broader Research Review and Implications for Practice," 5.

70. Ghiselli, Campbell, and Zedeck, *Measurement Theory for the Behavioral Sciences*, 145; also see Philip J. Bobko, *Correlation and Regression* (New York: McGraw-Hill, 1995), 142–143.

71. Kevin Murphy, "Fooling Yourself with Cross Validation: Single Sample Designs," *Personnel Psychology* 36 (1983): 111–118.

72. Philippe Cattin, "Estimation of the Predictive Power of a Regression Model," *Journal of Applied Psychology* 65 (1980): 407–414.

73. Kevin R. Murphy, "Cost-Benefit Considerations in Choosing among Cross-Validation Methods," *Personnel Psychology* 37 (1984): 15–22.

74. Van Iddekinge and Ployhart, "Developments in the Criterion-Related Validation of Selection Procedures: A Critical Review and Recommendations for Practice," 887.

75. Ibid., 889.

76. Charles H. Lawshe and Michael J. Balma, *Principles of Personnel Testing* (New York: McGraw-Hill, 1966), 301.

77. Ibid., 306–308.

78. Guion, *Personnel Testing*, 141–144.

79. J. P. Guilford, *Psychometric Methods* (New York: McGraw-Hill, 1954), 400–401.

80. Van Iddekinge and Ployhart, "Developments in the Criterion-Related Validation of Selection Procedures: A Critical Review and Recommendations for Practice," 883.

81. Robert L. Thorndike, *Applied Psychometrics* (Boston: Houghton Mifflin, 1982); and C. A. Olson and B. E. Becker, "A Proposed Technique for the Treatment of Restriction of Range in Selection Validation," *Psychological Bulletin* 93 (1983): 137–148.

82. Van Iddekinge and Ployhart, "Developments in the Criterion-Related Validation of Selection Procedures: A Critical Review and Recommendations for Practice," 884.

83. Society for Industrial and Organizational Psychology, *Principles for the Validation and Use of Personnel Selection Procedures* (2003).

84. Ghiselli, Campbell, and Zedeck, *Measurement Theory for the Behavioral Sciences;* see also Paul Muchinsky, "The Correction for Attenuation," *Educational and Psychological Measurement* 56 (1996): 63–75.

85. Calvin Hoffman, "Applying Range Restriction Corrections Using Published Norms: Three Case Studies," *Personnel Psychology* 48 (1995): 913–923.

86. Deniz S. Ones and Chockalingam Viswesvaran, "Job-Specific Applicant Pools and National Norms for Personality Scales: Implications for Range-Restriction Corrections in Validation Research," *Journal of Applied Psychology* 88 (2003): 570–577.

87. Milton L. Blum and James C. Naylor, *Industrial Psychology: Its Theoretical and Social Foundations* (New York: Harper & Row, 1968); and Wayne F. Cascio, *Costing Human Resources: Financial Impact of Behavior in Organizations* (Boston: Kent, 1982), 130.

88. Frank L. Schmidt and John E. Hunter, "The Validity and Utility of Selection Methods in Personnel Psychology: Practical and Theoretical Implications of 85 Years of Research Findings," *Psychological Bulletin* 124 (1998): 262–263; see also John E. Hunter, Frank L. Schmidt, and M. K. Judiesch, "Individual Differences in Output Variability as a Function of Job Complexity," *Journal of Applied Psychology* 75 (1990): 28–34.

89. Mark Cook, *Personnel Selection* (Chichester, NY: John Wiley, 1998), 277–286.

90. Schneider and Schmitt, *Staffing Organizations*, 264.

91. H. C. Taylor and J. T. Russell, "The Relationship of Validity Coefficients to the Practical Effectiveness of Tests in Selection," *Journal of Applied Psychology* 23 (1939): 565–578.

92. James C. Naylor and Lester C. Shine, "A Table for Determining the Increase in Mean Criterion Score Obtained by Using a Selection Device," *Journal of Industrial Psychology* 3 (1965): 33–42.

93. Hubert E. Brogden, "On the Interpretation of the Correlation Coefficient as a Measure of Predictive Efficiency," *Journal of Educational Psychology* 37 (1946): 64–76.

94. Lee J. Cronbach and Goldine C. Gleser, *Psychological Tests and Personnel Decisions* (Urbana: University of Illinois Press, 1965).

95. Wayne F. Cascio and R. A. Ramos, "Development and Application of a New Method for Assessing Work performance in Behavioral/Economic Terms," *Journal of Applied Psychology* 71 (1986): 20–28.

96. John E. Hunter and Frank L. Schmidt, "Fitting People to Jobs: The Impact of Personnel Selection on National Productivity," in *Human Performance and Productivity: Human Capability Assessment*, ed. Marvin D. Dunne He and Edwin A. Fleishman (Hillsdale, NJ: Lawrence Erlbaum Associates, 1982), 233–292.

97. Frank L. Schmidt, John E. Hunter, Robert C. McKenzie, and Tressie W. Muldrow, "Impact of Valid Selection Procedures on Work-Force Productivity," *Journal of Applied Psychology* 64 (1979): 609–626.

98. Ibid.

99. Frank Schmidt and John Hunter, "The Validity and Utility of Selection Methods in Personnel Psychology: Practical and Theoretical Implications of 85 Years of Research Findings," *Psychological Bulletin* 124 (1998): 265.

100. Ibid.

101. Schmidt, Hunter, McKenzie, and Muldrow, "Impact of Valid Selection Procedures on Work-Force Productivity."

102. Philip Roth, Philip Bobko, and Hunter Mabon, "Utility Analysis: A Review and Analysis at the Turn of the Century," in *Handbook of Industrial, Work, and Organizational Psychology, Volume 1: Personnel Psychology*, ed. Neil Anderson, Deniz S. Ones, Kepir Handan Sinangil, and Chockalingam Viswesvaran (Thousand Oaks, CA: Sage, 2002), 383–404.

103. Ernest O'Boyle and Herman Aguinis, "The Best and the Rest: Revisiting the Norm of Normality of Individual Performance," *Personnel Psychology* 65 (2012): 79–119. Also, see, Herman Aguinis and Ernest O'Boyle, "Star Performers in Twenty-First-Century Organizations," *Personnel Psychology* 66 (2013): 1–38.

104. Wayne Cascio, "Assessing the Utility of Selection Decisions," in *Personnel Selection in Organizations*, ed. Neal Schmitt and Walter C. Borman (San Francisco: Jossey-Bass, 1993), 318–320.

105. Frank L. Schmidt, "Personnel Psychology at the Cutting Edge," in *Personnel Selection in Organizations*, 509–510.

106. Michael J. Burke and James T. Frederick, "Two Modified Procedures for Estimating Standard Deviations in Utility Analysis," *Journal of Applied Psychology* 71 (1986): 334–339; and Jack E. Edwards, James T. Frederick, and Michael J. Burke, "Efficacy of Modified CREPID SDy's on the Basis of Archival Organizational Data," *Journal of Applied Psychology* 73 (1988): 529–535.

107. Olen L. Greer and Wayne Cascio, "Is Cost Accounting the Answer? Comparison of Two Behaviorally Based Methods for Estimating the Standard Deviation of Work Performance in Dollars with a Cost-Accounting Approach," *Journal of Applied Psychology* 72 (1987): 588–595.

108. Schmidt, Hunter, McKenzie, and Muldrow, "Impact of Valid Selection Procedures on Work-Force Productivity."

109. John T. Hazer and Scott Highhouse, "Factors Influencing Managers' Reactions to Utility Analysis: Effects of SD_y Method, Information Frame, and Focal Intervention," *Journal of Applied Psychology* 82 (1997): 104–112.

110. Cornelius J. Konig, Flurin Bosch, Amir Reshef, and Silvan Winkler, "Human Resource Managers' Attitudes Toward Utility Analysis," *Journal of Personnel Psychology* 12 (2013): 152–156.

111. Gary P. Latham and Glen Whyte, "The Futility of Utility Analysis," *Personnel Psychology* 47 (1994): 31–46; Glen Whyte and Gary Latham, "The Futility of Utility Analysis Revisited: When Even an Expert Fails," *Personnel Psychology* 50 (1997): 601–610; see also Steven F. Cronshaw, "Lo! The Stimulus Speaks: The Insider's View on Whyte and Latham's 'The Futility of Utility Analysis,'" *Personnel Psychology* 50 (1997): 611–615.

112. Silvan Winkler, Cornelius J. Konig, and Martin Kleinmann, "Single-Attribute Utility Analysis May Be Futile, But This Can't Be the End of the Story: Causal Chain Analysis as an Alternative," *Personnel Psychology* 63 (2010): 1041–1065.

113. Edwin E. Ghiselli, *The Validity of Occupational Aptitude Tests* (New York: John Wiley, 1966); and Edwin E. Ghiselli, "The Validity of Aptitude Tests in Personnel Selection," *Personnel Psychology* 26 (1973): 461–477.

114. Frank Schmidt and John Hunter, "History, Development, and Impact of Validity Generalization and Meta-analysis Methods," in *Validity Generalization: A Critical Review*, ed. Kevin R. Murphy (Mahwah, NJ: Lawrence Erlbaum Associates, 2003), 31–66.

115. Kevin R. Murphy, "The Logic of Validity Generalization," in *Validity Generalization: A Critical Review*, ed. Kevin R. Murphy (Mahwah, NJ: Lawrence Erlbaum Associates, 2003), 1–30.

116. Frank L. Schmidt and John E. Hunter, "The Future of Criterion-Related Validity," *Personnel Psychology* 33 (1980): 41–60.

117. Frank L. Schmidt and H. R. Rothstein, "Application of Validity Generalization Methods of Meta-Analysis to Biographical Data Scales Used in Employment Selection," in *Biodata Handbook: Theory, Research, and Use of Biographical Information in Selection and Performance Prediction*, ed. G. S. Stokes, M. D. Mumford, and W. A. Owens (Palo Alto, CA: CPP Books, 1994), 237–260.

118. Murray R. Barrick and Michael K. Mount, "Impact of Meta-Analysis Methods on Understanding Personality-Performance Relations," in *Validity Generalization: A Critical Review*, ed. Kevin R. Murphy (Mahwah, NJ: Lawrence Erlbaum Associates, 2003), 197–222.

119. Neal Schmitt, J. R. Schneider, and J. R. Cohen, "Factors Affecting Validity of a Regionally Administered Assessment Center," *Personnel Psychology* 43 (1991): 1–12.

120. Hannah R. Rothstein, "Progress is Our Most Important Product: Contributions of Validity Generalization and Meta-Analysis to the Development and Communication of Knowledge," in *Validity Generalization: A Critical Review*, ed. Kevin R. Murphy (Mahwah, NJ: Lawrence Erlbaum Associates, 2003), 115–154.

121. Schmidt and Hunter, "The Future of Criterion-Related Validity."

122. Schmidt and Hunter, "The Validity and Utility of Selection Methods in Personnel Psychology: Practical and Theoretical Implications of 85 Years of Research Findings."

123. Kevin R. Murphy, *Validity Generalization: A Critical Review*.

124. Paul R. Sackett, Michael M. Harris, and John M. Orr, "On Seeking Moderator Variables in the Meta-Analysis of Correlational Data: A Monte Carlo Investigation of Statistical Power and Resistance to Type 1 Error," *Journal of Applied Psychology* 71 (1986): 302–310.

125. Lawrence R. James, Robert G. Demaree, Stanley A. Mulaik, and Michael D. Mumford, "Validity Generalization: Rejoinder to Schmidt, Hunter, and Raju (1988)," *Journal of Applied Psychology* 73 (1988): 673–678.

126. Larry Hedges, "An Unbiased Correction for Sampling Error in Validity Generalization Studies," *Journal of Applied Psychology* 74 (1989): 469–477.

127. Neal Schmitt, "The Value of Personnel Selection: Reflections on Some Remarkable Claims," *Academy of Management Perspectives* 21 (2007): 19–23.

128. Cook, *Personnel Selection*, 119.

129. Ibid., 119–120.

130. Ibid.

131. Ibid., 121.

132. Frank L. Schmidt, Deniz S. Ones, and John E. Hunter, "Personnel Selection," in *Annual Review of Psychology* (Stanford: Annual Reviews, 1992), 631.

133. J. A. Hartigan and A. K. Wigdor, *Fairness in Employment Testing: Validity Generalization, Minority Issues, and the General Aptitude Test Battery* (Washington, DC: National Academy Press, 1989).

134. Society for Industrial and Organizational Psychology, *Principles for the Validation and Use of Selection Procedures* (2003), 28.

135. For a study illustrating the classification of jobs in the context of validity generalization, see Edwin I. Cornelius, Frank L. Schmidt, and Theodore J. Carron, "Job Classification Approaches and the Implementation of Validity Generalization Results," *Personnel Psychology* 37 (1984): 247–260.

136. Schmidt and Hunter, "History, Development, and Impact of Validity Generalization and Meta-Analysis Methods."

137. Ibid., 37.

138. Ibid.

139. Frank J. Landy, "Validity Generalization: Then and Now," in *Validity Generalization: A Critical Review*, ed. Kevin R. Murphy (Mahwah, NJ: Lawrence Erlbaum Associates, 2003), 155–196.

140. Biddle and Nooren, "Validity Generalization vs Title VII: Can Employers Successfully Defend Tests Without Conducting Local Validation Studies?" 230.

141. Calvin Hoffman and S. Morton McPhail, "Exploring Options for Supporting Test Use in Situations Precluding Local Validation," *Personnel Psychology* 51 (1998): 987–1003.

142. Ibid., 990.

143. Daniel A. Biddle, "Should Employers Rely on Local Validation Studies or Validity Generalization (VG) to Support the Use of Employment Tests in Title VII Situations?" *Public Personnel Management* 39 (2010): 323–324.

144. Society for Industrial and Organizational Psychology, *Principles for the Validation and Use of Selection Procedures* (2003), 27.

145. P. Richard Jeanneret, "Applications of Job Component/Synthetic Validity to Construct Validity," *Human Performance* 5 (1992): 83.

146. Ibid.

147. S. Morton McPhail, "Job Component Validity Predictions Compared to Empirical Studies," in *Current Innovations in PAQ-Based Research and Practice*, Annual Conference of the Society for Industrial and Organizational Psychology, Orlando, FL, May 1995.

148. L. M. Holden, "Job Analysis and Validity Study for the Distribution Planning Office Technical Progression," unpublished report (Los Angeles: Southern California Gas Company, 1992).

149. Hoffman and McPhail, "Exploring Options for Test Use in Situations Precluding Local Validation."

150. P. Richard Jeanneret and Mark H. Strong, "Linking O*NET Job Analysis Information to Job Requirement Predictors: An O*NET Application," *Personnel Psychology* 56 (2003): 465–492.

151. Ibid.

152. Kevin W. Mossholder and Richard D. Arvey, "Synthetic Validity: A Conceptual and Comparative Review," *Journal of Applied Psychology* 69 (1984): 328.

153. *Taylor v. James River Corporation*, CA 88-0818-T-C (TC) (S.D. AL, 1989).

154. Jeanneret, "Applications of Job Component/Synthetic Validity to Construct Validity," 91–93.

155. Mark N. Bing, H. Kristl Davison, and Richard Arvey, "Using a Repeated-measures Approach to Validating Personality Tests in Small Samples: A Feasibility Study with Implications for Small Businesses," *Journal of Managerial Issues* 21 (2009): 12.

156. Guion, *Personnel Testing*, 169.

157. Charles Scherbaum, "Synthetic Validity: Past, Present, and Future," *Personnel Psychology* 58 (2005): 481–515.

158. John R. Hollenbeck and Ellen M. Whitener, "Criterion-Related Validation for Small Sample Contexts: An Integrated Approach to Synthetic Validity," *Journal of Applied Psychology* 73 (1988): 536–544.

159. Sackett and Arvey, *Personnel Selection in Organizations*, 432–445.

160. Bureau of National Affairs, *Recruiting and Selection Procedures* (Personnel Policies Forum Survey No. 146) (Washington, DC: Bureau of National Affairs, 1983).

161. David E. Terpstra and Elizabeth J. Rezell, "The Relationship of Staffing Practice to Organizational Level Measures of Performance," *Personnel Psychology* 46 (1993): 27–48.

162. Lynn R. Offerman and Marilyn K. Gowing, "Personnel Selection in the Future: The Impact of Changing Demographics and the Nature of Work," in *Personnel Selection in Organizations*, ed. Neal Schmitt and Walter C. Borman (San Francisco: Jossey-Bass, 1993), 385–417.

163. José M. Prieto, "The Team Perspective in Selection and Assessment," in *Personnel Selection and Assessment: Individual and Organizational Perspectives*, ed. Heinz Schuller, James L. Farr, and Mike Smith (Hillsdale, NJ: Lawrence Erlbaum Associates, 1993).

164. Schmidt, "Personnel Psychology at the Cutting Edge," 501–502.

SELECTION MEASURES

Predicting future events is a common part of our lives. We have all tried to guess the winner of a sporting event, who might ask us out, or what the questions on our next test may be. Some people, such as fortune-tellers, meteorologists, stock brokers, and selection specialists, also make prediction a large part of their jobs. They use some limited amount of currently available information to make judgments about future events. Although all four of these types of practitioners could use our help in improving the accuracy of their own predictions, we predict that this section will be of more value to selection specialists than to the other three. Information the selection specialist uses to predict future job performance can be obtained from several different types of devices: application forms, interviews, tests, work simulations, and so on. Each of the chapters of this section treats a major selection approach in detail. Our viewpoint is that if selection measures are properly developed, administered, scored, and interpreted, the information about applicants that is obtained and used in predicting job performance improves. As this happens, the success rate of prediction should also get better.

Of course, successful prediction in selection is complex; hiring high performers depends on three factors described in Chapter 8 as part of our discussion about the utility of a predictor.[1] They are:

1. Validity coefficient—the correlation between the predictor scores and job performance or other criterion.

2. Selection ratio—the number of hires divided by number of applicants. The smaller the ratio of people hired from all applicants available, the greater the chance of choosing really top performers, because a company can "skim the cream" of the applicant pool.

3. Base rate of success—also a ratio, reflecting the proportion of employees who would be successful on the job if selection decisions were made by random choice among the applicants. In this case, the predictor is not referred to or used when making the hiring decision.

The effectiveness of predictions during selection varies with the size of the correlation, the selection ratio, and the base rate of success. Not surprisingly, the higher the correlation or validity coefficient of the predictor, the better the predictor will be at identifying applicants who will be high performers on the job. This relationship is straightforward; it simply means that prediction improves as validity rises. The other two factors' effect on prediction is not quite so obvious.

A smaller selection ratio means fewer applicants are hired. When the "best" available candidates are hired (top down selection), these few hires will be the highest scoring applicants on the test, interview, application blank, or other selection device. As long as these selection devices are valid predictors of job success, top scoring candidates have the best chance of being high performers if selected. Thus, the lower the selection ratio (0.05 versus 0.60), the more useful the test becomes. Although a smaller proportion of those in the applicant pool are hired when jobs are given to only the top 5 percent with the highest scores (versus the top 60 percent), more of those hired are higher performers, other things being equal. Because many of the rejected applicants could have succeeded if they had been hired, there is a cost to rejecting a larger proportion of the applicants. If only the top 5 percent are hired, you will not be surprised to hear that there are more who would also have been successful among the 95 percent who are rejected. Typically, the firm ignores the cost of rejecting these candidates because the gain is higher performance from those selected, which has obvious value to the firm. The cost is less visible to the firm and typically borne primarily by the applicant (who suffers through the rejection and loss of a job opportunity). Yet there is still a cost to the firm. Specifically, the firm loses the potential contributions of talented people who are not hired. If Apple failed to hire the person who developed the next innovative feature for the Apple cell phone, such a decision could be very costly. Nevertheless, the typical approach to selection is to assume that there is no cost to the firm for rejecting qualified applicants. Instead, to maximize prediction, we focus on selecting a greater proportion of qualified, successful applicants and downplay the cost of our "misses." Although it may seem heartless, we agree with this assumption in nearly all cases—except those rare instances when we have been turned down for a job. Then the science is less compelling.

Finally, the third factor, accounting for the effect of the base rate of success on selection decisions, is even less obvious than the effect for selection ratio just described. Base rate accounts for the "quality" of the applicant pool. That is, it recognizes the proportion of applicants in the pool who could do the job well if the predictor were not used to help make the selection decision. Predictors are most useful when 50 percent of the applicants are likely to be high performers and 50 percent likely to fail if hired. To understand this, think about the extremes. If 100 percent of the applicants would be successful if hired, there is no added information provided by the predictor; one would randomly pick from the pool of superstar candidates. Conversely, if every applicant in the selection pool would fail if hired, the predictor cannot help identify even one applicant who would be successful; none is available. Thus, when the base rate is either very high (most would be successful) or very low (few would be successful), using the predictor does not improve the quality of the decision as the additional information gained by the selection device does not improve our guess about future performance very much. There is only limited gain from using the predictor, less than we might expect. However, when the ratio of high performers to low performers is about 50/50, the predictor is able to improve the 50/50 ratio considerably if the test has high predictive validity and a small selection ratio. When making hiring decisions, we can be more accurate than a coin flip (a 50/50 chance) by making available additional information provided by the predictor (test, interview, and so on).

As this illustrates, it's not easy to predict which candidate has the most potential as an employee. Taylor and Russell tables are available that enable one to calculate the percentage of new hires who will be successful, given knowledge of these three factors.[2] Part of their tables are reported below in Table 9.1. The number embedded in the table represents the percentage of those hired who will be high performers or correctly hired candidates, given the base rate of success, the selection ratio, and validity coefficient. Take a moment to consider what proportion of candidates hired will be successful if the following is true: (a) current base rate of success is 0.20, (b) the firm is quite selective (selection ratio 0.05), and (c) the predictor has high validity ($r_{xy} = 0.65$). Then look what happens if the base rate goes up to 0.90 while everything else remains the same. What happens if the firm cannot be selective and must hire 95 percent of the applicants, all else being equal? Finally, what happens when the predictor is not very valid ($r_{xy} = 0.10$)? Are there situations when a predictor with relatively low validity is still useful?

This last question, at first blush, seems ridiculous. Why would you ever want to use a predictor with relatively low validity? (Such a good question!) To develop and use selection devices with high predictive validity typically requires considerable resources (time, money, or expert personnel) all of which can be in short supply. For instance, early in the selection process, when we have a very large number of applicants, it can

TABLE 9.1	Excerpts from the Taylor-Russell Tables[a]

A. Base Rate of Success 0.20

Validity (r_{xy})	Selection Ratio			
	0.05	0.30	0.60	0.95
0.10	26%	23%	22%	20%
0.25	37%	29%	24%	21%
0.45	54%	36%	28%	21%
0.65	73%	45%	31%	21%

B. Base Rate of Success 0.40

Validity (r_{xy})	Selection Ratio			
	0.05	0.30	0.60	0.95
0.10	48%	45%	42%	40%
0.25	61%	51%	46%	41%
0.45	94%	87%	81%	72%
0.65	99%	94%	86%	73%

C. Base Rate of Success 0.70

Validity (r_{xy})	Selection Ratio			
	0.05	0.30	0.60	0.95
0.10	77%	74%	72%	70%
0.25	86%	80%	76%	71%
0.45	94%	87%	81%	72%
0.65	99%	94%	86%	73%

D. Base Rate of Success 0.90

Validity (r_{xy})	Selection Ratio			
	0.05	0.30	0.60	0.95
0.10	93%	92%	91%	90%
0.25	97%	95%	93%	91%
0.45	99%	98%	95%	91%
0.65	100%	99%	98%	92%

Note: The percentage embedded in the table reflects the percent of applicants hired who are successful performers.
[a]From H. C. Taylor and J. T. Russell, "The Relationship of Validity Coefficients to the Practical Effectiveness of Tests in Selection," *Journal of Applied Psychology* 23 (1939): 565–578.

be quite daunting to figure out how to reduce the number of applicants to a manageable number of candidates. Consider the case where we want to hire 10 mid-level managers.

We certainly won't be able to administer our assessment center ($10,000 per applicant) to all 100 people who applied for our 10 new openings. More importantly, it's not necessary to have each applicant participate in the assessment center in order to make a good employment decision; we often can screen out a large proportion of the applicants simply by using a few basic characteristics or qualifications. Applicants who could be screened out relatively quickly include those who lack minimal experience or qualifications assessed in a resume or application blank, who get poor references from prior bosses, and who lack the "right" personality. These predictors (applications, letters of reference, personality tests) can be efficiently administered to large groups of applicants and, even though they do not predict job performance as well as the assessment center, they can still be extremely useful and valuable if the selection ratio is small and/or the base rate of success is near the ideal 50/50 ratio.

This explains why, early in selection, predictors with only modest validity can be quite effective (such as application blanks, reference checks, and personality tests). In contrast, by the time we get around to choosing the best finalist to hire from the remaining candidates, even a predictor with moderate validity (such as college grades) may not add useful information to the hiring decision. Our intent here is not to overwhelm you, but to simply underscore why selection is such a complex process—and why some predictors might be useful (the application blank or resume), even though they may not have a very high predictive validity coefficient. Given this, our purpose is to familiarize you with a variety of selection devices in the following chapters, and where appropriate, to discuss how these three factors (validity, selection ratio, and base rate) may affect their application.

Application Forms and Biodata Assessments, Training and Experience Evaluations, and Reference Checks

APPLICATION FORMS AND BIODATA ASSESSMENTS

Nature and Role of Application Forms in Selection

When candidates apply for a job in an organization, they are usually asked to complete an application form. Most organizations utilize employment applications as a means for collecting preemployment information to assess an applicant's likelihood of success. These forms are a way to begin to learn about the candidate's qualifications and job-relevant personal experiences.

An application form typically consists of a series of questions designed to provide information about the general suitability of applicants for jobs to which they are applying. Questions usually concern the applicant's educational background and previous job experiences and other areas that may be useful in judging a candidate's ability to perform a job. The form itself may be brief and general or long and detailed. Whatever its exact nature, its principal purpose is to serve as a preemployment screen regarding the future job success of job applicants. As such, it serves as a means for (a) deciding whether applicants meet the minimum requirements of a position and (b) assessing and comparing the relative strengths and weaknesses of individuals making application.

Taken at face value, an application form may appear to be innocuous; it may seem to offer no real threat to any particular group. However, when used as a basis for selecting among job applicants, these forms can provide information that unfairly discriminates against some individuals. For example, when application information unrelated to a person's ability to perform a job (such as gender, ethnicity, age) is collected, that application data can be used for discriminatory selection practices.

Because application forms have been used to discriminate unfairly against protected groups, federal and state laws (such as Title VII of the 1964 Civil Rights Act and Fair Employment Practice statutes) were passed to prevent discrimination by means of pre-employment inquiries. These legal restrictions will be discussed later.

Appropriately designed application forms can provide much useful information about job applicants. Even though this information might help managers make selection decisions, a key issue facing any application reviewer is in deciding *what* application data are most beneficial in choosing successful job applicants. Where clear guidelines are not provided, selection decisions focusing on application information may be based on the personal biases, prejudices, and whims of each application reviewer. For example, in considering applicants for first-line supervisory jobs, some managers believe only applicants possessing a high school diploma should be hired; others may not hold this view. Is a minimum level of education mandatory for successful performance as a supervisor? Unless relationships between application data and job success are known, this information may be of limited help to managers involved in selection decisions.

This creates a conundrum: most firms collect applicant personal history information on some type of application form. Yet surprisingly few firms systematically structure and standardize that information in order to exploit its full value to predict later employee performance and turnover.[3] In part, this is because practitioners are concerned about its practicality, its potential to create legal "issues," even its ability to validly predict job performance.[4] Although gathering information from some types of application forms does require large sample sizes and considerable expertise, that's not true in all cases. Furthermore, with forethought and care in selecting items focused on the demands of the work or outcomes of interest, it's possible to minimize or eliminate concerns about legal complications. For these reasons and others, which we'll talk about next, it is not clear what information is best obtained via the application form.

An application form is a tool for gathering self-report data. In nearly all cases, application forms include paper-and-pencil and Internet measures.[5] There is little agreement as to what constitutes relevant application information.[6] Some researchers argue the information should be restricted to prior work experience: time in prior positions, the number of jobs held and so forth.[7] Other researchers have taken a much broader perspective to personal history information and include personality, preferences, and interests; future expectations; values; and self-report skills.[8] Without a clear understanding of the meaning of application data, it will be difficult to conclude that this information does or does not predict later job performance or turnover.

To clarify matters, in the remainder of this book we refer to application information that is empirically developed and scored in a way to maximize prediction as *biodata*, to distinguish it from run-of-the-mill application form data. The core feature of biodata is that it is self-report data provided by the applicant. It reflects historical data that captures the applicant's past behaviors and experiences—in work contexts (for example, held 10 jobs in the past 5 years), in educational settings (high grades in math, graduated from college), as part of a family (mother worked outside the home), even in various community or extracurricular activities (coached 5-year-old children in soccer)—that predict outcomes at work. This definition excludes directly assessing personality traits, values, interests, skills, and abilities, though such attributes are likely to be related to applicants' personal history experiences.[9] For example, the applicant's interests and personality would influence what kinds of settings the person seeks out (for example, a highly extraverted, social person prefers working in a team to a job working alone). Certain experiences provide opportunities to develop specific knowledge and skills (leading the local United Way campaign develops leadership skills). By separating biodata from measures of personality, interests, and abilities, it is possible to better understand why and when biodata will be an effective predictor.

More than 50 years ago, organizations began to develop scoring keys that isolated specific individual items on the application form that distinguished between successful and unsuccessful employees.[10] Once identified, items related to employee job success are then weighted to reflect their degree of importance in differentiating good and poor performers. A total score could be determined by summing the collective weights for responses to the items, which can be used like any HR selection test to predict probable job success. The use of biodata has waned since the mid-1970s, primarily because many of these items resemble personality questions and their development requires considerable technical expertise and large sample sizes.[11] Nevertheless, biodata can be quite effective, particularly for a variety of lower-skilled jobs.

Biodata is based on the notion that a deeper study of applicants and their employment backgrounds and life experiences can be employed as an effective predictor.[12] Use of biodata is based on the cliché that the best predictor of future behavior is past behavior.[13] For example, if an applicant has held 15 different jobs over the past 5 years, it seems reasonable to anticipate that person wouldn't remain long at your firm either.[14] Similarly, if the applicant has prior experience with skills needed to successfully perform your job, it seems logical that using items to assess these skills will predict future job performance.[15]

Biodata approaches differ as to whether the items are empirically validated and optimally weighted statistically. Ideally, the items appearing on the application were developed from an analysis of the job, have validity evidence, and have been screened for possible discriminatory impact against protected groups.

There are at least two ways to categorize biodata: (a) based on the type of response options offered to a respondent (response-type), and (b) based on the specific behavioral content of the item itself (behavior-type). Response-type classification refers to the kind of scale a respondent is asked to use in answering biodata items.[16] Table 9.2 classifies

TABLE 9.2	**Classification of Exampler Application or Biographical Data Items by Response Type**

1. **Yes-No Response:**
   Are you satisfied with your life?
   a. Yes
   b. No

2. **Continuum, Single-Choice Response:**
   About how many fiction books have you read in the past year?
   a. None
   b. 1 or 2
   c. 3 or 4
   d. 5 or 6
   e. More than 6

3. **Noncontinuum, Single-Choice Response:**
   Which one of the following would you most prefer to do in your leisure time?
   a. Read a book
   b. Work crossword puzzles
   c. Attend a party
   d. Play golf, tennis, or softball
   e. Repair a broken appliance or make minor home repairs

4. **Noncontinuum, Multiple-Choice Response:**
   Check each of the following activities you had participated in by the time you were 18.
   a. Shot a rifle
   b. Driven a car
   c. Worked a full-time job
   d. Travelled alone more than 500 miles from home
   e. Repaired an electrical appliance

5. **Continuum, Plus Escape Option:**
   When you were a teenager, how often did your father help you with your schoolwork?
   a. Very often
   b. Often
   c. Sometimes
   d. Seldom
   e. Never
   f. Father was not at home

6. **Noncontinuum, Plus Escape Option:**
   In what branch of the military did you serve?
   a. Army
   b. Air Force
   c. Navy
   d. Marines
   e. Never served in the military

7. **Common Stem, Multiple Continuum:**
   In the last 5 years, how much have you enjoyed each of the following? (Use the rating scale of 1 to 4 shown below.)
   a. Reading books
   b. Watching TV
   c. Working at your job
   d. Traveling
   e. Outdoor recreation
   (1) Very Much
   (2) Some
   (3) Very little
   (4) Not at all

Source: Based on William A. Owens, "Background Data," In *Handbook of Industrial and Organizational Psychology*, ed. Marvin Dunnette (Chicago: Rand McNally, 1976), 613.

exampler items into seven categories of response type. The type of rating scale employed on a biodata questionnaire can significantly affect the subsequent scoring and analysis of items. Preferable (and the most common item format) is a biodata item having an underlying continuum and requiring a single choice (see Category 2 in Table 9.2). This item is the most amenable to various kinds of statistical analyses; the other item types require special steps for scoring and analysis. At times when constructing biodata, it is not possible to put all items in the continuum, single-choice format; it may make more sense to use something different. In these instances, other item formats should be considered (such as the others shown in Table 9.2). Scoring (through dummy variable coding and treating each item option as a separate variable) and statistical provisions can be made to handle these variations.

Table 9.3 presents another taxonomy of biodata items. This particular classification categorizes items according to behaviors to be judged by respondents.[17] With this system, biodata items can be classified along one or more of the following dimensions: (a) verifiable/unverifiable, (b) historical/futuristic, (c) actual behavior/hypothetical behavior, (d) memory/conjecture, (e) factual/interpretive, (f) specific/general, (g) response/response tendency, and (h) external event/internal event. Each of these dimensions represents a continuum. The categories are not mutually exclusive because it is possible for any single item to be characterized by more than one dimension. At any rate, the items listed provide some typical examples of those in a biodata questionnaire.

What makes a clear definition of biodata even more confusing is that it can be assessed by means other than an application blank, which makes it somewhat challenging

TABLE 9.3	Classification of Exampler Biodata Items Based on Behavioral Content

1. Verifiable: Did you graduate from college?	**Unverifiable:** How much did you enjoy high school?
2. Historical: How many jobs have you held in the past 5 years?	**Futuristic:** What job would you like to hold 5 years from now?
3. Actual Behavior: Have you ever repaired a broken radio?	**Hypothetical Behavior:** If you had your choice, what job would you like to hold now?
4. Memory: How would you describe your life at home while growing up?	**Conjecture:** If you were to go through college again, what would you choose as a major?
5. Factual: How many hours do you spend at work in a typical week?	**Interpretive:** If you could choose your supervisor, what characteristic would you want him or her to have?
6. Specific: While growing up, did you collect coins?	**General:** While growing up, what activities did you enjoy most?
7. Response: Which of the following hobbies do you enjoy?	**Response Tendency:** When you have a problem at work, to whom do you turn for assistance?
8. External Event: When you were a teenager, how much time did your father spend with you?	**Internal Event:** Which best describes the feelings you had when you last worked with a computer?

Source: Based on James J. Asher, "The Biographical Item: Can It Be Improved?" *Personnel Psychology*, 25 (1972): 252; and Wayne F. Cascio, *Applied Psychology in Personnel Management* (Englewood Cliffs, NJ: Prentice-Hall, 1991), 266.

to specify what exactly should be called biodata. Craig Russell, for example, used a system of structured interviews to gather biographical information on 66 candidates for general manager positions in a *Fortune 500* firm. Interview questions focused on three background areas of each applicant: (a) accomplishments and disappointments and what was learned from those experiences both in college and in positions held since entering the workforce; (b) accomplishments, disappointments, and situational experiences in the applicants' current position relative to nine performance dimensions that had been identified for the general manager's job; and (c) career aspirations, prior formal developmental activities, self-perceptions, and how others were believed to perceive the applicant.[18] In another biodata application, Russell coded biographical information from life history essays written by cadets at the U.S. Naval Academy. The biodata information was found to predict leadership and academic performance among cadets at the academy.[19] More commonly, biodata questions are presented in a self-report questionnaire. The questionnaire is usually in a standardized multiple-choice format that asks applicants to characterize themselves using past life experiences. What these methods have in common is that information is collected from the applicant about prior experiences. As we will soon see, there are legitimate concerns about the accuracy of this information when collected in a high-stakes employment context. Concerns about accuracy have important implications for reliability and validity.

Based on our earlier definition and description of biodata information, you are probably thinking at this point, "It seems to me that this information could measure a number of different attributes or constructs. Is that so?" The short answer to that question is yes. Although in this chapter we talk about personal history information as if it assesses a particular construct, in reality it can measure a host of attributes suitable for assessment by a predictor used in selection. What these forms measure simply depends on what constructs the biodata questionnaire was constructed to measure. It is preferable to think of application information more as a method than as a means for assessing one substantive construct, such as cognitive ability, which is assessed through a general mental ability test.[20] As we discuss various findings and compare various studies that use this information, it's important to keep in mind that different biodata forms may measure different constructs.

EVALUATING APPLICATION BLANKS AS PREDICTORS

There is value in evaluating past behavior to identify which applicant is likely to perform well if hired. One fundamental problem is identifying which information provides a useful assessment. This is illustrated by research that shows scored evaluations of personal life experiences using unweighted data are only moderate predictors of later job performance (average r_{xy} ranges from 0.10 to 0.20).[21] In contrast, when the application blank is systematically scored and weighted based on empirical evidence the resulting validity or prediction is compelling. For example, considerable meta-analytic evidence demonstrates average predictive validities for biodata questionnaires range between 0.30 and 0.40.[22] This shows that information obtained from application blanks can be useful, but to realize its potential, the form must either rely on an empirical analysis to identify items that predict the outcome of interest or begin with a job analysis to ensure that only job-related questions are posed. Besides focusing on attributes demanded by the work, it also requires consideration of the specific criterion to be predicted. Biodata can predict supervisory ratings of performance, productivity, promotion, tenure, turnover, and training success (see Table 9.4), but only when the criterion is taken into account when identifying which items to rely on.

TABLE 9.4	Summary of Biodata Validation Studies for a Variety of Criteria

Criterion	Investigator	Number of Validity Coefficients	Total Sample Size	Average Validity Coefficient
Performance	Dunnette[a]	115	N.A.	0.34
Rating	Hunter and Hunter[b]	12	4,429	0.37
	Reilly and Chao[c]	15	4,000	0.36
	Schmitt et al.[d]	29	3,998	0.32
Productivity	Schmitt et al.[d]	19	13,655	0.20
Promotion	Hunter and Hunter[b]	17	9,024	0.26
Tenure	Hunter and Hunter[b]	23	10,800	0.26
Turnover	Schmitt et al.[d]	28	28,862	0.21
Training Success	Hunter and Hunter[b]	11	6,139	0.30

Note: N.A. Data were not available.

[a]Marvin D. Dunnette, *Validity Study Results for Jobs Relevant to the Petroleum Refining Industry* (Washington, DC: American Petroleum Institute, 1972). The data reported in the table were taken from John E. Hunter and Ronda F. Hunter, "Validity and Utility of Alternative Predictors of Job Performance," *Psychological Bulletin* 96 (1984): 83.

[b]John E. Hunter and Ronda F. Hunter, "Validity and Utility of Alternative Predictors of Job Performance," *Psychological Bulletin* 96 (1984): 72–98.

[c]Richard R. Reilly and Georgia T. Chao, "Validity and Fairness of Some Alternative Employee Selection Procedures," *Personnel Psychology* 35 (1982): 1–62.

[d]Neal Schmitt, Richard Z. Gooding, Raymond A. Noe, and Michael Kirsch, "Metaanalyses of Validity Studies Published between 1964 and 1982 and the Investigations of Study Characteristics," *Personnel Psychology* 37 (1984): 407–422.

A validity generalization study by Hannah Rothstein and her colleagues showed that biodata instruments can be developed and validated so they lead to validity generalizability.[23] They selected and scored biographical items from the *Supervisory Profile Record* found to be related to the job performance of roughly 11,000 first-line supervisors in 79 different organizations. Mean estimated validities for the criteria of supervisory ability ratings and supervisory performance ratings were 0.33 and 0.32. These validities were judged to be stable over time and generalizable across groups based on age, gender, education, previous experience, tenure, and ethnicity.

Hannah Rothstein's work employed a biodata questionnaire developed for first-line supervisors employed in multiple organizations. Kevin Carlson and his coworkers sought to develop a biodata measure in one organization whose validity would be generalizable to managers above the first-line supervisor level in different organizations.[24] Following development, the biodata component of the *Manager Profile Record* was given to a sample of more than 7,300 managers working in 24 organizations. The biodata inventory was designed to predict managers' level of progression within their employing companies. Results showed that estimated true validity (following correction for range restriction on the predictor and criterion unreliability) was 0.53 and was generalizable across organizations. Like Rothstein's research, Carlson and coworkers concluded that when properly developed, biodata inventory validities are not restricted to a specific organization and are, in fact, generalizable to other organizations.

They posed the following guidelines for developing biodata inventories with generalizable validities:

- Are there sound reasons to expect that the validity of a biodata instrument should generalize to other populations and situations? No methods can make an instrument generalize more than is theoretically possible. Some predictive relationships would not be expected to generalize outside limited populations or situations.

- Has a valid criterion been selected and has a reliable measure of that criterion been constructed for scoring use in key development? The greater the validity of the criterion measure, the more accuracy is possible in identifying relationships between items and the criterion.

- Has the validity of each item been determined? Assuring that both empirical and conceptual justifications exist for each item's validity reduces the sample dependence of an instrument. Sample dependence is increased when strictly empirical analyses are performed.

- Does an adequate sample exist? The larger the sample, the more representative that sample is likely to be of the larger population and the more likely that validities in the development sample will generalize to the population.[25]

Results from both Rothstein's and Carlson's work show that with large samples available, it is possible to produce a biodata instrument that is predictive of performance across organizations and employee groups. These results should not be interpreted to apply to every biodata instrument, because specific methods of biodata construction and validation may differ from Rothstein's approach. Nevertheless, organizations without the resources for developing their own biodata questionnaires now have access to a generalizably valid procedure for using biodata in selection.

It's important to note that Rothstein's and Carlson's studies were based on *incumbent* supervisors and managers already on the job. Do their results generalize to job *applicant* groups? Common practice has been to develop biodata scoring keys on incumbents and assume they are generalizable to applicants. Some results suggest that this assumption may not be valid. Garnett Stokes and her coworkers compared the scoring keys of a biodata questionnaire for both applicant and incumbent groups.[26] They concluded there was little overlap in the scoring keys for the two groups. The implication is that biodata scoring procedures developed on job incumbents do not necessarily generalize to applicant groups.

The magnitude of this problem was effectively illustrated by Thomas Bliesener, who found that 135 of 165 biodata studies (82%) he reviewed collected biodata responses from current employees (concurrent validity design).[27] Thus, conclusions about the validity of biodata are primarily based on collecting responses from current employees, not applicants. The problem Bliesener found was that the average validity coefficient was 0.35 when involving current employees but only 0.29 or 0.21 when collecting information from applicants and either relying on, or better yet, not relying on, the information obtained from the application blank to make selection decisions (a predictive validity design). In a recent large-scale study, 20 biodata items were administered to 425 current call center employees and 410 applicants.[28] The predictive validity of those responses was significantly higher for current employees than it was for applicants ($r_{xy} = 0.27$ versus 0.17, respectively). If those validity coefficients are meaningfully higher with current employees, the experiences they gain while working on the job appear to contribute to gains in predicting job performance. Until further research has shown otherwise, it seems that scoring procedures of biodata forms should be based on job applicants rather than incumbents. Although a biodata predictor is likely to be effective, particularly when used to screen out unqualified applicants, the actual validity coefficients based on current employees may overestimate the validity of applying the procedure to select applicants.

Based on the data we have presented so far, we can conclude that biodata measures are valid predictors of job performance. But do these measures add to our ability to predict job performance over predictions made from measures such as mental ability tests? Frank Schmidt and John Hunter reported from their analyses that biodata measures did not significantly enhance the prediction of job performance over that attributed to general mental ability measures.[29] They reasoned that this was due, in part, to the substantial correlation (0.50) found between biodata and general mental ability measures. They imply that as far as the prediction of overall job performance is concerned, an employer would do about as well by simply using a readily available general mental ability test and avoiding a biodata inventory.

The prediction of job performance is important to most organizations. However, practitioners now recognize that the job performance domain includes broader aspects than specific performance of job tasks. These broader aspects include adaptive contextual performance factors, organizational citizenship behaviors, counterproductive behaviors, and even turnover (recall this from Chapter 2?). Measures such as biographical data inventories often predict these broader aspects of job performance better than mental ability measures.[30]

Overall, research results suggest that biodata is an effective predictor for a wide diversity of job success measures. In fact, for entry-level selection, biodata has been found to be one of the best predictors of job performance when compared to other types of predictors such as employment interviews, training and experience ratings, reference checks, personality inventories, and some ability tests.[31]

Given the positive results that recent research on biodata has produced, application blanks should at least be considered for adoption in selection programs, particularly as an early screen to help identify the viable candidates from which the finalists will be drawn. But as this section illustrates, there is considerable work to be done to obtain application form items that are as useful as the biodata results reported in Table 9.4.

One other problem associated with the use of personal life and work experiences is how to get information that is not embellished or otherwise distorted. When people are competing for a job, self-report application data are susceptible to distortion; applicants believe it is advantageous to "look good." Falsification of application data can range from inflation of college grades to outright lies involving types of jobs held, past salaries received, companies worked for, or educational degrees earned. Applicants may attempt to conceal gaps in their employment histories.

A common distortion seen by many HR managers involves reported college background. At some executive levels, applicants frequently misrepresent a specific degree such as the master of business administration (MBA). Research results suggest that applicants are most likely to distort those items believed to be related to whether a job offer will be made or whether a specific salary given; not surprisingly, an applicant's education can influence such outcomes.

How prevalent is the practice of giving fraudulent data on job applications? Few studies have explored the problem in detail, because applicants aren't very forthcoming about the lies they have told on the application itself (surprise, surprise). However, some limited investigations have addressed the issue. One conclusion from this research is that when people are directed to "fake good," they consistently skew their application responses toward what they believe an employer wants to hear.[32] Such distortion, however, is not a good indication of the *likelihood* of distortion or faking by real job applicants.

On this question, researchers are split; some find little evidence of faking in actual selection contexts, whereas others report substantial evidence of faking.[33] Although it is not possible to draw a definitive conclusion based on the research evidence, the popular press believes false information is more common than you might think. For example, ResumeDoctor.com[SM] reports that 42.7 percent of 1,000 resumes it vetted over 6 months contain major misstatements, while popular press articles suggest that about one-third to one-half of applicants list inaccurate dates of employment or exaggerate their accomplishments.[34]

When the stakes are high (a job opportunity exists), it appears that some applicants give distorted answers to questions—particularly when the correct, job-related answer is fairly obvious and burnishing one's credentials is seen as providing that last "nudge" to get the job offer. What is not known with certainty is how common such behavior is. However, a surprising amount of research on noncognitive predictors reveals that faking does not reduce predictive validity.[35] In fact, a study by Neal Schmitt and Fred Oswald concluded that even by removing 30 percent of those applicants who fake their responses, the mean gain in job performance would only be about 0.1 SD.[36] Consequently, it is unclear how distortion on application forms affects hiring decisions.

Several empirical studies have identified the specific application items where distortion is most prevalent as well as their frequency of occurrence. This research shows that when items are verifiable ("What was your cumulative grade point average in college?"), historical ("How many cars did you sell in the past year?"), and factual ("How many times were you late for work over the past 6 months?"), there is less faking by applicants (refer to Table 9.3).[37] The type of question asked and the likelihood of "getting caught" influence applicant responses.

A recent U.S. Supreme Court ruling (*McKenna v. Nashville Banner Publishing Co.*, 513 U.S. 352 [1995]) illustrates the risks an applicant assumes by distorting or exaggerating qualifications for a job. In this case, the Court concluded that evidence of application/resume fraud or misconduct—in cases where the individual would have been either terminated or not hired in the first place if the firm had known the truth— could limit the employer's liability on discrimination claims (that is, could limit the damages recovered by an employee). Such evidence, however, referred to as "after-acquired evidence," is not an absolute defense against discrimination, as the employee's wrongdoing may not bar the employee from winning a lawsuit. Nevertheless, an employer can fire the offending individual immediately for misrepresentation on the application or resume. Furthermore, if this wrong information was material to the selection decision, or the employer directly relied upon such information when making the selection decision, the employer may (as we have noted above) use these circumstances as a defense in a wrongful termination case.

Taking all of these factors into consideration, it is reasonable to conclude that some distortion of application form answers does take place. Most likely, distortion of these data is due to pressure on an applicant to obtain a desired job. However, it should not be concluded that employment applications are not useful. Even though distortion is a problem, application forms, with certain characteristics, can provide valid information for comparing and predicting the success of job applicants. This is particularly true for items that require verifiable, historical, and factual information. In the next section we show how the accuracy of application form data can be enhanced, even without such information.

Enhancing Application Form Accuracy.   As we have seen, accuracy of application form data can be a problem. Employers can take several steps to lessen the problems of applicant errors, distortion, and omission of data on the form. First, applicants should be told, preferably both verbally and in writing, that the information they give will affect their employability. Recent research demonstrates that the extent of faking can be reduced through instructions that include statements about the consequences of faking (invalidating a score or resulting in termination). For example, a statement such as this could be included: "Deliberate attempts to falsify information can be detected and may be grounds for either not hiring you or for terminating you after you begin work." Such instructions have been found to reduce attempts to fake responses by nearly half.[38] Second, applicants should be explicitly informed that the data they provide will be thoroughly checked.[39] For example, a statement such as the following should be included on the form:

All information you provide on this application will be checked. Driving, educational, employment, and any military records will be checked with appropriate individuals and groups such as local and state police, previous employers, or previous schools attended. Be sure to review your application to ensure that it is complete and that you did not omit any information.

The statement should be printed on the form so that it is easily seen and readable.

Applicants should be required to sign and date their application. They should be required to sign a statement certifying the accuracy of the information they provided on the form. Such a statement should warn applicants that misstatements or omission of relevant information are grounds for termination if uncovered after their employment. An example of such a statement is as follows:

By signing this application, I declare that the information provided by me is complete and true to the best of my knowledge. I understand that any misrepresentation or omission on this application may preclude an offer of employment, may result in a withdrawal of an employment offer, or may result in my discharge from employment if I am already employed at the time the misrepresentation or omission is discovered.[40]

Note, however, that if applicants are required to sign the application, some state labor codes require that a copy of a company's application be filed with a specific state department governing labor issues. A state labor code may also require that applicants be given a copy of their signed application if they request it. As we mentioned earlier, review all state labor codes, statutes, and fair employment practice regulations for state-specific information that may apply to the use of employment applications.

Finally, in states covered by an employment-at-will doctrine, an employer should be sure that no contract of permanent employment is implied in the employment application or any resulting job offer letter. Including a statement on the application informing applicants that the application does not create a binding obligation of employment for any specific period of time will help protect an employer. For example, the following statement that was included on an application helped an employer successfully defend against a subsequent wrongful discharge claim:

I, the undersigned, understand that I am being considered as a potential employee of Eastern Capital Corp. dba Fitness USA Health Spas (the "Company"), and hereby certify that:

1. I understand that if I am hired, such hiring will not be for any definite period of time. Even though, if hired, I will be paid my wages on a monthly, semi-monthly, or weekly basis, I understand that this does not mean I am being hired for a definite period of time.

2. *I understand that if hired, I will be an employee-at-will and I can be terminated at any time, with or without cause, with or without notice....*

3. *I understand that this agreement cannot be changed except in a written document signed by me and the Company President.*

4. *I have been given an opportunity to ask questions regarding Company rules and my potential status as an employee-at-will. No representative of Fitness USA Health Spas has made any promises or other statements to me that imply that I will be employed under any other terms than stated above.*

5. *I understand that if hired, this Statement is part of the employment arrangement between the Company and me, and will be binding on me.*[41]

Recent research suggests that one other approach to reducing score inflation is to require applicants to provide written support to the answers to biodata items. Two studies show that requiring elaboration to answers significantly reduces biodata scores.[42] Although this technique is a promising way to reduce embellishment, continued research is needed to establish whether predictive validity is also enhanced. These strategies underscore the importance of systematically approaching the planning, development, and use of application blank information in order to realize the substantial value that is possible when using biodata or personal history information as a predictor.

Legal Implications of Application Forms

Some employers think it desirable to obtain as much information as possible on the application form. With a lot of information available, it would seem easier to set up an initial screen for choosing among applicants. However, this "the more information, the better" mentality can create major problems for an employer. As we have said, federal and state laws affect the kinds of information that can be requested on the application blank. Under these laws, it is generally assumed that *all* questions asked on an application form are used in making hiring decisions. Under a charge of discrimination, the burden of proof may be on the employer to demonstrate that *all* application questions are indeed fair and not discriminatory. The law, according to EEOC preemployment guidelines, cautions against questions on the application form that (a) disproportionately screen out minority group members or members of one sex, (b) do not predict successful performance on the job, or (c) cannot be justified as a business necessity.[43] In judging the suitability of a potential item, an employer should thoroughly review each question. The rating criteria listed in Table 9.5 are useful for examining the appropriateness of application form questions.

An employer has the right to establish and use job-related information for identifying the individuals qualified for a job. With respect to an employment application, an organization is free to ask almost any question it regards as important in selecting among job applicants. However, as we discussed in Chapter 4, if a complainant can show adverse impact resulting from selection practices, then the burden of proof is on the employer to demonstrate that the information provided by the application questions is not used in a discriminatory manner prohibited by law. Most often a complainant will argue that application items result in (a) *adverse impact* or (b) *disparate treatment*. Under *adverse impact*, members of a protected minority group may respond differently to a question than members of a majority group (for example, "Do you own your home?"). Given census data indicate homeownership rates are substantially higher for whites versus blacks (71 percent versus 45 percent in 2010), white people may respond

TABLE 9.5	Questions to Be Asked in Examining Appropriateness of Application Form Questions

Yes	No	Question
[ ]	[ ]	1. Will answers to this question, if used in making a selection decision, have an adverse impact in screening out members of a protected group (that is, disqualify a significantly larger percentage of members of one particular group than of others)?
[ ]	[ ]	2. Is this information really needed to judge an applicant's competence or qualifications for the job in question?
[ ]	[ ]	3. Does the question conflict with EEOC guidelines, federal or state laws, or statutes?
[ ]	[ ]	4. Does the question constitute an invasion of privacy?
[ ]	[ ]	5. Is information available that could be used to show that responses to a question are associated with success or failure on a specific job?

Sources: Questions 1 and 2 are based on Equal Employment Opportunity Commission, *EEOC Guide to Pre-Employment Inquiries* (Washington, DC: Equal Employment Opportunity Commission, August 1981); questions 3 through 5 are based on Ernest C. Miller, "An EEO Examination of Employment Applications," *Personnel Administrator* 25 (March 1981): 68–69.

"yes" in greater proportion than black people. If persons responding "no" are screened out of employment consideration, then the question will have an adverse impact on minority applicants. When *disparate treatment* is involved, different questions may be posed for different groups. For instance, it is disparate treatment if only women are asked, "Do you have children under school age and, if so, what arrangements have you made concerning child care?" In response, an employer has two basic options to show that application form items do not unfairly discriminate among applicants. An employer can either demonstrate (usually with statistics) that (a) the questions being challenged are predictive of job success, or (b) the questions represent a bona fide occupational requirement. An item on an application form is justified as being a bona fide occupational requirement by showing "that it is necessary to the safe and efficient operation of the business, that it effectively carries out the purpose it is supposed to serve, and that there are no alternative policies or practices which would better or equally well serve the same purpose with less discriminatory impact."[44]

Because many of the laws that affect the content of application forms have existed for nearly 50 years, it might be assumed that most forms currently in use comply with the law. However, research consistently has shown that numerous public and private sector employers continue to request information that could be viewed as "inadvisable." (The term *inadvisable* does not mean that questions are illegal and cannot be asked. However, due to their phrasing, the courts would view the questions in such a light as to make a user vulnerable to charges of discrimination if an investigation of unfair discrimination were conducted. Then, it would be up to each employer to justify use of these questions.)

During the early 1980s, three research studies illustrated that many application forms reviewed had at least one inadvisable question; the average was 7.7 to 9.74 inadvisable questions per form.[45] In the first study of its kind, Ernest Miller reviewed the applications of 151 randomly sampled *Fortune 500* firms.[46] Only two used applications judged in an initial review to be completely fair. The applications used by almost 4 out of 10 firms (38 percent) had more than 10 inadvisable inquiries, and Miller reported an average of 9.74 inadvisable items per form. Following are two of the most frequently used inadvisable questions, and the percentage of firms in Miller's study that included these questions in application forms:

1. Have you ever been arrested for a misdemeanor or felony? Describe. (Used by 64.7 percent of firms surveyed; the EEOC has advised the answer might adversely impact minorities.)

2. During what dates did you attend grammar school? High school? (Used by 61.4 percent of firms surveyed; applicant age can be inferred from the answer and used in a discriminatory manner.)

At about the same time, two other published studies substantiated Miller's findings regarding the frequency of inadvisable questions on the application. Whether examining application forms from the state personnel office in each of the 50 states,[47] or from 50 large, well-known businesses,[48] nearly all (98 of 100 forms) contained at least one inadvisable item. On average, the states had 7.7 such inquiries per application. At that time, employers were just becoming aware that there could be problems with the content of application forms. Yet today the application form many organizations use still does not seem to comply with the law, as illustrated by research that continues to show there are a number of inadvisable items still being requested 50 years after these laws were passed.

In 2004, Craig Wallace and Stephen Vodanovich[49] reported that nearly all application forms they examined still contained at least one inadvisable question, with an average of 5.35 from 109 firms using customer service application forms and 2.99 inadvisable items, on average, from 191 *Fortune 500* Web application forms. Such results correspond to earlier findings, which reported similar results after examining 42 online state general employment applications in 2000,[50] 85 retail applications in 1992,[51] and 283 random application forms from American Society of Public Administration members in 1989.[52] Taken together, these studies reveal that today, although there are fewer inadvisable items than found in the early 1980s, a number of employers continue to ask questions the EEOC strongly advises against.

A recent study of more than 300 federal court cases involving the use of application forms powerfully demonstrates the relative frequency of employment discrimination litigation associated with various types of preemployment inquiries. This study found that questions associated with applicant sex and age were most likely to lead to litigation (53 percent of cases), and the plaintiff won over 40 percent of these cases. Furthermore, nearly 20 percent of the cases involved questions addressing educational requirements, convictions, height or weight requirements, and work history or experience requirements.[53] This evidence, when coupled with the finding that firms continue to ask inadvisable questions, underscores the severity of these concerns.

These research studies illustrate rather impressively that many organizations continue to use existing application forms that do not fully comply with current equal employment opportunity law. Resources must be directed toward reviewing and, where needed, revising these forms to ensure full compliance with the law while at the same time meeting an organization's selection needs. Although it is important to get as complete a picture of the candidate as possible, the information requested on the application form cannot be used in a discriminatory manner. As previously stated, the rating criteria listed in Table 9.5 are useful for examining the appropriateness of application form questions. Considering these criteria when screening biodata items should minimize concerns about adverse impact.[54]

The value of using empirical scoring, statistical analyses, and job analyses to isolate those specific application factors predictive of job success—that is using biodata items instead of formally scored application questions—becomes even more obvious when one considers legal issues involved in relying on information derived from the application blank. Once a case has been established against an employer (that is, a prima facie case of discrimination), users of information from application forms must provide evidence of validity and fairness of the item, total, or dimension score. Reliance on biodata-like procedures increases the likelihood the scores have validity, and thus, their use is more defensible because they predict future job success.

Because some biodata items involving topics such as education and socioeconomic background may very well be associated with applicant gender or ethnicity, caution is needed. If Title VII burden of proof requirements are carried out with regard to specific biodata items, such caution must include reviewing items to determine whether they show both logical *and* empirical evidence of appropriate biodata use. Thus reasonable care in selecting items would include undertaking an empirical review of item fairness. Validity and fairness should not be taken for granted. Job analysis and item review panels, as well as other steps, could be used to produce content-valid measures that may have less adverse impact on protected applicant groups.[55] Another legal issue that could arise with the use of biodata is that of invasion of privacy. Although many writers suggest that an application blank is an innocuous selection device, some questions appearing on some biodata forms could be considered offensive. For example, items that involve relationships with siblings and parents, socioeconomic status, or community activities (for example, politics or religious activities) could be viewed by some respondents as highly personal. Using rational item screening by subject matter experts to minimize objectionable biodata item bias is one way to handle this problem.[56] Another proposed strategy is simply to have applicants omit items that they consider personal or offensive. However, questions left blank by job applicants may produce negative perceptions on the part of prospective employers.[57]

Invasion of privacy and job applicant rights are issues likely to grow in importance in the future. Research must be directed toward invasion-of-privacy implications, particularly where biodata questionnaires composed of very personal items are being used as selection measures.

It is impossible to answer in the abstract and with complete certainty the question of whether biodata are discriminatory. Previous research on the matter is far from conclusive. Literature reviews of biodata often suggest that disparate impact across age, race, and sex groups is low.[58] On the other hand, the research on the use of inadvisable questions suggests that race and sex differences in biodata may exist.[59] At a minimum, given that cognitive ability often results in adverse impact and given evidence that biodata correlates with cognitive ability, there is cause for concern.[60] Furthermore, given evidence of the continued use of inadvisable questions, firms must examine each biodata item for fairness and discrimination.[61]

Little published literature exists regarding the relationship of protected group characteristics with biodata measures. There have been, however, at least two large validity generalization studies that reported the validity of a biodata measure for race and gender groups.[62] One of these investigations noted that the biodata measure's estimated true validities were higher for men than women and higher for white people than black people.[63] Both investigations concluded that the biodata measures' validity generalized across racial and gender groups. In other words, the measures were valid for both white and black people as well as for men and women. A recent study by Murray Barrick and Ryan Zimmerman supports this, as they reported minimal adverse impact with biodata.[64] This led Leatta Hough and colleagues to conclude that, compared to other selection devices, biodata can have low adverse impact against protected group members.[65]

Composition of Application Forms

Application forms can be valid and fair predictors, although job-relevant forms are typically called biodata rather than application blanks. Yet whether an application form is valid and fair or not, the composition of the form is relatively similar, although development of a biodata form requires the expenditure of a great deal of time, effort, and resources. As your mother used to say, "Do the work up front, you'll be thankful later." Our description of the composition of the application form below is based on the premise you are trying to develop a job-relevant and fair application form or biodata questionnaire; hence we will use the terms interchangeably. We realize this simplifies things too much, as there are many types of biodata forms. Nevertheless, we assume you will strive to enhance the predictive validity and fairness of your application form and there are some general steps involved in doing so. These are discussed next.

Most job applications consist of two major parts. The first part includes instructional information for completing and submitting the application. The second consists of questions whose answers are used in deciding applicant suitability for a position in the organization.

Instructions for Applicants

Instructions are important because they tell applicants how to complete the necessary forms. They should be clear and understandable. These instructions, however, serve another important purpose: They may help shield an employer from an unlawful employment charge. For instance, employers should consider stating in the instructions that an applicant giving unsolicited information on the application will be rejected. Extraneous information can be used by rejected applicants to argue that they were turned down for an unlawful reason. For instance, Timothy Bland and Sue Stalcup noted that some union organizers, when applying for a job, have written on the employment application that they are union organizers, even though such information was not requested.[66] Then when they were not employed, they sued, arguing that they were unlawfully denied employment because of their union activity.

The Americans with Disabilities Act (ADA) requires reasonable accommodation during the selection process. Employers should state in the instructions that disabled applicants can request reasonable accommodation in completing the application.

Recent research also illustrates that instructions may influence whether applicants react favorably or unfavorably to a firm's selection methods, which in turn determines whether they are willing to accept an offer and to work for that organization.[67] The most important factors that influence applicant reactions to selection procedures used by organizations include evidence that the selection procedure is useful, valid, and fair.[68] These results have implications for the instructions included on an application form, as applicant reactions should be accounted for whenever feasible. Consequently, there is merit in clearly stating that the application form has been reviewed to ensure it is job-related and fair, if such a review has indeed been conducted. Because many applicants are concerned about privacy issues, there is value in clearly stating who will see the information or how applicant responses will be used to arrive at a decision.[69]

As a selection *and* recruitment measure, the form should be reviewed for its attractiveness, fairness, and ease of use. In general, when applicants do not like application forms it is largely because they are seen to be less fair and less job-related than other selection methods (such as interviews and assessment centers).[70] Particularly during periods of low unemployment, employers must consider candidate reactions to the application form.

Employers covered by various federal and state requirements must collect and report demographic information (for example, gender, ethnicity, physical disability) on job applicants. Although it may appear efficient to simply collect the data on the application form, this strategy could lead to a discrimination charge. Collecting descriptive data separately from the application form or on a tear-off portion of the application form—together with a disclaimer that the information is voluntary and will be separated and stored anonymously—would be a more effective strategy.[71] Whether employers follow procedures established by state laws or develop procedures on their own, they would be wise to adopt policies for handling demographic data on job applicants.

Questions for Applicants

Requesting information, other than that necessary for initially judging applicants' qualifications to perform a job, opens an organization to the possibility of a discrimination charge. Organizations should ask job-related questions only and avoid those relating to personal information. It is in the interest of an organization to carefully review the necessity of information requested on the application form.[72]

Research has shown that including discriminatory questions on an application form influences applicants' perceptions of the employing organization. One study found that applicants who completed an application form having discriminatory questions viewed the company as less attractive, were less motivated to pursue employment with the organization, were less likely to accept an offer of employment, and were less likely to recommend the organization to friends than were individuals who completed a form without such questions.[73]

Selecting Application Form Content

What information is necessary? How does an organization decide whether the information is in fact essential? These are important questions. Answers depend on the job for which an application form will be used. Some essential data should be assessed in all forms, including (a) name, (b) current address, (c) telephone number, (d) work experience, (e) level of education and training received, (f) skills possessed, and (g) social security number.[74] What other data should be collected? In general, the lower the organizational level of a job or job class, the shorter, less detailed the content of the application. Using job analysis methods such as those discussed in Chapter 3, we can identify items that could be useful in screening applicants for a job. However, job analysis alone will not completely resolve the problem of which items should be included on an application form. Once we have identified the possible questions to appear on the form, it's important to review each one for its fairness and usefulness.

In reviewing application form items, employers should first research the fair employment practice laws that exist for their state. An employer conducting business in more than one state should review carefully each state's laws, regulations, and guidelines concerning the use of preemployment inquiries. State fair employment practice laws determine the legal status of preemployment inquiries, such as application form items, used by employers doing business within the state. One excellent source for review is *The Commerce Clearing House Employment Practice Guide*, State FEP Laws. A state-by-state review is important, because what is legal in one state may be illegal in another.[75] Furthermore, where state laws and regulations exist, the EEOC gives them more weight than federal standards, which are generally more permissive.

Employers might rightfully ask, "What do we do if it is permissible to ask a job application question in one state but not permissible in another state where we do business?" Employers in this situation might consider several options. Of course, the option chosen will depend on the specific situation (for example, the specific application question, the specific state in question). Some of these options are

1. Use a generic job application composed of items permissible in all relevant states.

2. Develop state-specific supplements that can be used with a generic job application.

3. Use an application instructing applicants from relevant states to ignore specific questions.

Using the rating criteria noted earlier in Table 9.5 and mandated by any state fair employment practice laws, employers should carefully review all items for their necessity and for their possible discriminatory impacts. For some questions under review (such as ethnicity), the answer is obvious. For others, discriminatory impact is not so evident yet discriminatory effects may be present. The way the questions themselves are used determines the legality of the application form. Of critical importance is the phrasing of the questions on the form. A miscast question can undermine the usefulness and legality of the form and leave an organization vulnerable to a lawsuit.

Using the research of a number of writers, we have summarized in Table 9.6 examples of some appropriate and inappropriate application form questions. In reviewing the table, keep several points in mind. First, phrase items to elicit information related to the specific job for which the application form is being used. Wallace and Vodanovich suggest that simple rephrasing using job-related language can eliminate some "inappropriate" items.[76] For example, a form could ask, "Are you at least 18 years old?" rather than, "What is your date of birth?" Second, an item that is acceptable in some situations might not be acceptable in others. For example, an item may be usable if it can be shown that it provides information useful for predicting the success of a new employee with regard to the job for which application is being made. Or, an item may provide information that represents a bona fide occupational requirement for a specific job. The example items listed are not an exhaustive treatment of what should and should not be asked on the application form. The items shown are meant to be illustrative of what can be used. Thus the examples serve as a guide to planning, developing, and using application forms.

Of course, whether an item is appropriate will also depend on laws enacted by the various states. For example, although federal law permits questions regarding criminal convictions, a few states limit the use of conviction records in the employment context. For example, in Ohio, applicants cannot be required to disclose convictions for minor misdemeanor violations (Ohio Rev. Code Ann. Tit. 29 § 2925.11). Employers must be aware of relevant state nondiscrimination laws as well as federal laws. Although the review in Table 9.6 is not an exhaustive treatment of items that could be included on an application form, it does provide some guidelines and comments to consider in preparing or revising a biodata questionnaire to be used in selection.

Developing and Revising Application Forms

Biodata, like application forms, consist of questions about the applicant's work and life experiences. As we have seen, the questions asked on a job application form determine its effectiveness in selecting the best, most appropriate job applicants. Some questions may result in a discrimination charge against the user or employer. It is imperative that employers study carefully the development or revision of their biodata forms.

TABLE 9.6	Examples of Appropriate and Inappropriate Questions Asked on Application Forms

Subject of Question	Appropriate Questions	Inappropriate Questions	Comments
Name	"What is your name?" "Have you worked for this company under another name?" "Have you used a name (such as an assumed name or nickname) the company would need to know to check your previous work and educational records? If so, please explain."	"What was your maiden name?" "Have you ever used another name?"	Questions about an applicant's name that may indicate marital status or national origin should be avoided.
Age	"Are you at least 18 years old?" "Upon employment, all employees must submit legal proof of age. Can you furnish proof of age?"	"What is your date of birth?" "What is your age?"	The Age Discrimination in Employment Act of 1967, amended in 1986, prohibits discrimination against individuals 40 years of age and older. A request for age-related data may discourage older workers from applying. Age data should be collected only when it can be shown to be a bona fide occupational requirement.
Race, Ethnicity and Physical Characteristics	"After employment, a photograph must be taken of all employees. If employed, can you furnish a photograph?" "Do you read, speak, or write Spanish [or other language required for the job]?"	"What is your race?" "Would you please submit a photograph with your application for identification purposes?" "What is the color of your hair? Your eyes?" "What language do you commonly use?" "How did you acquire your ability to read, write, or speak a foreign language?"	"Information relative to physical characteristics may be associated with sexual or racial group membership. Thus, unless such information can be shown to be related to job performance, the information may be treated as discriminatory.
Height and Weight	"After employment, all employees are required to submit a physical description (eye color, hair color, height, and weight)."	"What is your height and weight?"	Questions regarding height and weight should be asked only if an employer can demonstrate that minimum height/weight requirements are necessary for successful job performance.
Religion	The employer may state the days, hours, and shifts to be worked.	"What is your religious faith?" "Does your religion prevent you from working on weekends?"	Questions that determine an applicant's availability have an exclusionary effect because of some people's religious practices (e.g., whether an applicant can work on holidays or weekends). Questions should be used only if they can be shown not to have an exclusionary effect, if they are justified by business necessity, or where religion is a bona fide occupational qualification (BFOQ).

(Continued)

TABLE 9.6	(Continued)		

Subject of Question	Appropriate Questions	Inappropriate Questions	Comments
Gender, Marital Status, Children, Child Care	"If you are a minor, please list the name and address of a parent or guardian."	"What is your sex?" "Describe your current marital status." "List the number and ages of your children." "If you have children, please describe the provisions you have made for child care." "With whom do you reside?" "Do you prefer being referred to as Miss, Mrs., or Ms.?"	Direct or indirect questions about marital status, number and ages of children, pregnancy, and childbearing plans frequently discriminate against women and may be a violation of Title VII. Information on child care arrangements should not be asked solely of women. Questions about an applicant's gender should be avoided, unless gender is a BFOQ.
Physical or Mental Health	"Are you able to perform these job tasks (attach a list of specific tasks to the application) with or without an accommodation? If so, how would you perform the tasks, and with what accommodations"? "Can you meet the attendance requirements of this job?"	"Do you have any physical or mental disabilities, defects, or handicaps?" "How would you describe your general physical health?" "When was your last physical exam?" "Have you received workers' compensation or disability income payments?" "Have you any physical defects that could preclude you from performing certain jobs?"	The Americans with Disabilities Act prohibits any preemployment inquiries about physical or mental disability.
Citizenship[a] or National Origin	"If you are offered and accept a job, can you submit proof of your legal right to work in the United States?" "Do you have the legal right to live and work in the United States?"	"What is your country of citizenship?" "Please list your birthplace."	Consideration of an applicant's citizenship may constitute discrimination on the basis of national origin. The law protects citizens and noncitizens with legal authorization to work in the United States from discrimination on the basis of sex, race, color, religion, or national origin.
Military Service	"Please list any specific educational or job experiences you have acquired during military service that you believe would be useful on the job for which you are applying."	"Please list the dates and type of discharge you received from military service."	Minority service members have a higher percentage of undesirable military discharges. A policy of rejecting those with less than an honorable discharge may be discriminatory. This information may discourage minorities from applying for employment.

[a]The Immigration Reform and Control Act of 1986 contains specific language regarding the employment of citizens, impending citizens, and legal aliens. The act has a bearing on the questions that can be asked on the application form concerning citizenship and the use of citizenship information in selection. In addition, questions on the application that involve citizenship status must be worded carefully to avoid discrimination due to national origin covered by the Civil Rights Act of 1964.

(Continued)

TABLE 9.6   (*Continued*)

Subject of Question	Appropriate Questions	Inappropriate Questions	Comments
Arrest and Conviction Records	"Have you ever been convicted of a felony or, during the last two years, of a misdemeanor that resulted in imprisonment? If so, what was the felony or misdemeanor?" (A conviction will not necessarily disqualify you from the job for which you are applying. A conviction will be judged on its own merits with respect to time, circumstances, and seriousness.)	"Have you ever been arrested?" "Have you ever been convicted of a criminal offense?"	Arrest information is illegal. Federal courts have held that a conviction for a felony or misdemeanor should not automatically exclude an applicant from employment. An employer can consider the relationship between a conviction and suitability for a job. When questions are used, there should be a statement that factors such as age at time of offense, seriousness of violation, and rehabilitation will be considered, along with the factor of how the nature of the job relates to the conviction(s).
Hobbies, Clubs, and Organizations	"Do you have any hobbies that are related to the job for which you are making application?" "Please list any clubs or organizations in which you are a member that relate to the job for which you are applying." "While in school, did you participate in any activities or clubs that are related to the job for which you are applying?"	"Please list any hobbies you may have." "Please list all clubs or other organizations in which you are a member." "In what extracurricular activities or clubs did you participate while in school?"	Applicant information on membership in clubs and organizations can be discriminatory. If membership is associated with the age, sex, race, or religion of the applicant, the data may be viewed as discriminatory. If questions on club/organizational memberships are asked, a statement should be added that applicants may omit those organizations associated with age, race, sex, religion, or any other protected characteristic.
Education	"Did you graduate from high school? From college?"	"When did you attend high school? Elementary school?"	On average, minority members tend to have lower levels of education than nonminority group members. Where educational requirements disqualify minority group members at a higher rate than nonminority group members and it cannot be shown that the educational requirement is related to successful job performance, the courts have viewed educational requirements as discriminatory.
Credit Rating and Bonding	"Do you have the use of a reliable car?" (if car travel is required by the job)	"Do you own your own car?" "Do you own or rent your residence?" "Have you ever filed for bankruptcy?"	Use of credit rating questions tends to have an adverse impact on minority group applicants and women and has been found unlawful in some cases. Unless shown to be job-related, questions on car ownership, home ownership, length of residence, garnishment of wages, and so on, may violate Title VII.
		"Have you ever been refused an application for bonding or had your bonding cancelled?"	The federal Bankruptcy Code prohibits discrimination against job applicants who may have been bankrupt.

(*Continued*)

TABLE 9.6	(Continued)		

Subject of Question	Appropriate Questions	Inappropriate Questions	Comments
Off-the-Job Conduct	None	"Do you smoke?" "Do you drink alcoholic beverages?"	In general, employers cannot inquire into applicants' off-the-job conduct unless the conduct is associated with a BFOQ or conflicts with the employer's primary mission. However, a statement regarding an employer's policy for on-the-job behavior can be included; for example, "Our organization provides a smoke-free work environment for its employees."
Driver's License	"Do you have a current driver's license?"	"Do you have a driver's license?"	Employers should only ask this question if a driver's license is required for performance of the job.
Emergency Contact	"Please give a name and address of a person to be notified in case of an emergency."	"Please give a name and address of a relative to be notified in case of an emergency."	If this information is collected in order to have a contact in case of an emergency, request this after employment.

Sources: Based on Craig Wallace and Stephen J. Vodanovich, "Personnel Application Blanks: Persistence and Knowledge of Legally Inadvisable Application Blank Items," *Public Personnel Management* 33 (Fall 2004): 331–349; J. Craig Wallace, Mary G. Tye, and Stephen J. Vodanovich, "Applying for Jobs Online: Examining the Legality of Internet-Based Application Forms," *Public Personnel Management* 4 (Winter 2000): 497–504; Stephen J. Vodanovich and Rosemary H. Lowe, "They Ought to Know Better: The Incidence and Correlates of Inappropriate Application Blank Inquiries," *Public Personnel Management* 21 (1992): 363–370; Herbert G. Heneman and Timothy A. Judge, *Staffing Organizations*, 5th ed. (Mendota House, Middleton, WI, 2006); Bureau of National Affairs, *Equal Employment Opportunity Commission Guide to Pre-Employment Inquiries* (Washington, DC: Equal Employment Opportunity Commission—periodically updated), pp. 65–80; and Bureau of National Affairs, *BNA Handbook: Personnel Management* (Washington, DC: Bureau of National Affairs, 2003).

Similar to the development of any selection device, several steps are involved in the development of a biodata questionnaire. The steps include the following:

1. **Because There Are Many Types of Job, More Than One Application Form Will Probably Be Needed**. At the extreme, there could be one application form for each job. More realistically, however, one form will likely be used to cover a class or family of jobs, that is, jobs that require similar types of knowledge, skills, abilities, or tasks. For example, different versions of application forms may be used for job classes such as clerical/office personnel, sales personnel, operation workers, professional and technical personnel, executives, and managers.[77] Bryan Kethley and David Terpstra report that more than half of the lawsuits filed in federal court associated with application forms involved service (29 percent) or professional jobs (22 percent). Three other job categories were associated with legal challenges: executive/administrative/managerial (13 percent), operations/fabrication/laborers (13 percent), and administrative/ support/clerical (10 percent).[78] These findings underscore the need to tailor application forms to various jobs or classes of jobs.

2. **Job Analysis Data Should Serve as One Basis for Choosing Employment Application Questions**. Although job analysis data are commonly used in developing other selection devices such as tests, few users consider these data in

constructing their application forms. Not only should these analyses suggest useful items for the forms, but they should also serve as a basis for their legal justification. This suggests that while empirical data have traditionally been used to justify the validity of applicant information (for example, WAB), recent research has begun emphasizing whether items can be theoretically linked to job-relevant attributes and performance.[79] Thus, this approach relies on job analytic data to establish the content-validity of the inquiries used on application forms.

This step is crucial to developing highly valid biodata items. To know what antecedent behavior or life experiences to measure, it is important to identify the criterion or measure of job success or job performance we are interested in predicting. Many different types of criteria can be employed: (a) job tenure (or turnover), (b) absenteeism, (c) training program success, (d) rate of salary increase, (e) supervisory ratings, or (f) job performance. Criteria involving *behavioral* measures of performance such as job tenure, dollar sales, absenteeism, tardiness, compensation history, and job output are likely to provide more reliable data than subjective measures such as ratings. However, care should be taken to ensure that these behavioral measures provide reliable, uncontaminated, and meaningful assessments. In many cases, the most readily available criterion may not be the most useful. Biodata items may then be written or selected to reflect those attributes that can be used to predict our criterion or measure of success on the job.

3. **Develop a Pool of Biodata Items**. After hypothesizing life history experiences that may predict our identified criteria, we select or construct biodata items to reflect these experiences. Our hypotheses guide the development of specific life history items that will appear on the application form. As we have noted, the items can be selected from previous biodata research studies or be originally developed. Available publications can serve as sources of items. For example, James Glennon, Lewis Albright, and William Owens have prepared a compendium of life history items.[80] Their catalog consists of more than 500 biodata items classified into the following categories: (a) habits and attitudes, (b) health, (c) human relations, (d) money, (e) parental home, childhood, teenage years, (f) personal attributes, (g) present home, spouse, and children, (h) recreation, hobbies, and interests, (i) school and education, (j) self impressions, (k) values, opinions, and preferences, and (l) work. Items from the catalog can be selected if it appears that they may be useful in measuring the hypothesized life experiences thought to be predictive of success. Bibliographies of biographical data research can also be a valuable source of references with potentially useful items.[81]

Another approach to selecting biodata items relies on empirical analyses. In this approach, items statistically correlated with various criteria such as tenure, absenteeism, and job performance are retained. Example items include (a) size of hometown, (b) number of times moved in recent years, (c) length of residence at previous address, (d) years of education, (e) courses taken and preferred during high school, (f) types of previous jobs, (g) number of previous jobs, (h) tenure on previous jobs, (i) distance of residence from company, (j) source of reference to company, (k) reason for leaving last job, (l) length of time before being available for employment, and (m) whether current employer can be contacted. Many other item examples could be cited. Keep this in mind when items are being proposed. The simplest and most apparent form of an item on the application may not be the most useful. It may be possible to develop several potential items from one question appearing on an application. For instance, if a question asks about previous jobs within a specified period, we may be able to develop items on the *number* as well as the *type* of jobs held.

Michael Mumford, William Owens, Leatta Hough and colleagues have provided excellent reviews of research studies investigating various aspects of writing and formatting biodata items.[82] These investigations have important implications for the validity and reliability of biodata questionnaires. We do not review those studies per se, but we summarize some item-writing guides distilled from the research. These guidelines should be followed as biodata items are formatted into an application form:

1. Biodata items should principally deal with past behavior and experiences.

2. Items dealing with family relationships or other issues of a personal nature (for example, religion) are usually viewed as offensive.

3. Specificity and brevity of items and response options are desirable.

4. Numbers should be used to define a biodata item's options or alternatives.

5. All possible response options and an "escape" option (for example, "other") should be given; where possible, response options that form a continuum should be used.

6. Item options should carry a neutral or pleasant connotation.

7. Items dealing with past and present behaviors and with opinions, attitudes, and values are generally acceptable.[83]

8. Items should reflect historical events that are important in shaping a person's behavior and identity.[84]

9. To lessen the effect of individuals responding in ways considered to be socially desirable (that is, faking), biodata items should reflect external events (that is, prior behaviors occurring in real-life situations), be limited to firsthand recollections, be potentially verifiable, and measure unique, discrete events (such as age when first licensed to drive).

Prescreening and Pilot-Testing Biodata Items.   Like items appearing on other selection measures, biodata items can be objectionable and produce bias against some respondents. In this step, the biodata items developed are reviewed by a panel of judges and items that are objectionable or have potential bias against certain groups of respondents (for example, with regard to gender and ethnicity) are eliminated. Item content and response option review by a panel of subject matter experts has been found to be less objectionable and reduce bias while at the same time enhancing the clarity and job relevance of biodata items.[85]

Once a relevant group of items has been developed and its content prescreened, it should be tried out on an appropriate group of respondents. Ideally, this group should be large and representative of the applicant or employee population for which the biodata form will be used. Although biodata forms have been developed using sample sizes of 300 or so, more dependable, generalizable results are found with larger sample sizes (>500). In general, the larger the sample size, the better.

After administering the items to an appropriate sample, analyses are performed in order to choose those items that are most useful. For example, items are eliminated from the biodata inventory using one or more item specifications such as the following:

- Items exhibiting little response variance

- Items having skewed response distributions

- Items correlated with protected-group characteristics such as ethnicity
- Items having no correlation with other items thought to be measuring the same life history construct
- Items having no correlation with the criterion (that is, no item validity)

Those biodata items passing the prescreening and pilot-testing reviews are retained for inclusion in the final version of the application form.[86]

Scoring the Biodata Form.   After collecting responses to the biodata questionnaire from a large, representative sample, procedures for determining scores on the inventory are developed. The various options for scoring biodata measures tend to fall into two categories: (a) the calculation of a *single*, empirically keyed overall score that is predictive of employee success,[87] or (b) the development of multiple scores for dimensions or groups of related items appearing on a biodata inventory.[88] As we have noted before, there are many types of biodata. A fundamental distinction is whether the scores require the computation of a single score based on empirical keying. Several methods of empirical keying are available, including (a) vertical percentage,[89] (b) horizontal percentage,[90] (c) correlation,[91] (d) differential regression,[92] (e) deviant response,[93] and (f) rare response.[94] Of these, the vertical percentage method has been the most popular and useful. This method of scoring corresponds to what is also called weighted application blank (WAB). That is, each item on the biodata form is analyzed to determine its relation with some criterion of job success, such as job tenure or turnover. Items related to the criterion are identified, and weights are assigned to the item alternatives to reflect the strength of their relationship. Scores are obtained for individuals by summing the weights corresponding to their responses.

The other approach is to score clusters or groups of related or homogeneous items into dimensions or constructs reflecting a common life experience or behavior. Scores are derived for each of the biodata factors (usually 10 to 15 factors). A study by Robert Morrison and his associates illustrates how dimensions of biodata can be used to predict and understand aspects of employee job performance.[95] One of the purposes of their research was to examine how dimensions of life history were related to industrial research scientists' job performance. They factor analyzed 75 biodata items and three criteria (creativity ratings, overall job performance ratings, and number of patent disclosures) collected on 418 petroleum research scientists. The five biodata dimensions identified and brief descriptions of individuals with high scores on each dimension follow:

1. *Favorable Self-Perception*

   a. In the top 5 percent of performance in their occupation
   b. Could be a highly successful supervisor if given the chance
   c. Work at faster pace than most people
   d. Desire to work independently

2. *Inquisitive Professional Orientation*

   a. Completed Ph.D. degree
   b. Belong to one or more professional organizations
   c. Devote much time to reading with broad interests
   d. Have high salary aspirations

3. *Utilitarian Drive*

   a. Desire extrinsic rewards from business and society

   b. Prefer urban dwelling

   c. Feel free to express self and perceive self as influencing others

   d. Do not desire to work independently

4. *Tolerance for Ambiguity*

   a. Desire to have many work activities

   b. Are not single

   c. Have solicited funds for charity

   d. Have friends with various political views

5. *General Adjustment*

   a. Feel that school material was adequately presented

   b. Came from happy homes

   c. Express their opinions readily; feel effective in doing so

An examination of the association of the five dimensions or factors with the three criteria revealed some interesting findings. *Different* biodata factors were associated with *different* types of performance on the job. For example, scientists who received high ratings on overall job performance tended to be those with high scores on the biodata factors of *Favorable Self-Perception, Utilitarian Drive,* and *General Adjustment.* Scientists with many patent awards had an opposite life history profile. They scored high on *Inquisitive Professional Orientation* and *Tolerance for Ambiguity.* Among others, these results suggest that different types of life experiences (that is, biodata factors) might be used to predict different types and levels of job performance (criteria). By weighting some biodata factors more than others in selection decisions, we could affect subsequent performance in our organization. For instance, in the current example, if greater weight were given to hiring applicants high in *Inquisitive Professional Orientation* and *Tolerance for Ambiguity,* we would expect higher performance in number of patents awarded than if other factors such as *General Adjustment* were emphasized.

A recent study showed four empirically-keyed, cross-validated biodata dimensions that not only predicted unique criteria, further supporting the results described above, but also showed incremental validity above and beyond that accounted for by personality (using the five-factor model) and intelligence or general mental ability.[96] As this suggests, the approach popularized by William Owens and Lyle Schoenfeldt, to score biodata by identifying life history dimensions, appears to be the contemporary trend.[97]

Their research program supports the idea that prediction, as well as greater understanding of the relation between life history and employee job success, can be enhanced by scoring biodata in terms of dimensions. Whatever scoring option is taken, cross-validation of any scoring procedure is essential. In addition, validity and reliability information should be collected on any biodata measure.

The developmental approach just outlined can enhance the effectiveness of biodata as a predictor as well as our understanding of how and why biodata works. This method, or one similar to it, is also likely to enable you to develop a legally defensible approach for employing biodata in HR selection.

Resumes

The first impression many employers have of applicants often is from their resumes, as applicants typically submit a resume to a prospective employer before completing an application form. Although there has been some recent discussion about the use of video resumes or e-portfolios,[98] the primary format remains the written resume. Resumes are subject to the same kinds of distortions that plague many application forms. In one study, for example, 95 percent of college students surveyed said they were willing to tell at least one false statement to get a job; 41 percent had previously done so.[99] For this reason, resume reviewers are encouraged to carefully consider the following as indicators of possible "resume fraud":

- Inflated educational credentials (grades achieved, degrees attained)
- Omitted or inconsistent periods of employment or stretched employment dates
- Gaps in time periods listed (Where was the applicant? Prison?)
- Exaggerated claims of expertise and experience
- Claims of self-employment
- Claims of work as a consultant
- Claims of work with firms that are now out of business
- Evidence of a regressive work history (for example, moving down in levels of responsibility or compensation)
- Use of qualifiers such as "had exposure to," "assisted with," "attended a university"
- Use of vague details (such as indicating a state or city rather than the company's complete address)

In many of these cases, verification of the self-report information (through background checks of application and resume information) is likely warranted.

Little research has been done on the validity of inferences employers make in judging applicants' skills and abilities from their resumes. In one study, recruiters' perceptions of resume content were found to be predictive of the applicant's mental ability, as well as personality attributes such as conscientiousness and extraversion. These results are important; prior research has shown that these applicant traits, particularly mental ability and conscientiousness, are important predictors of job success. These findings show that recruiters can use resume information to screen applicants on characteristics that are likely to be predictive of job performance.[100] A second study focused on the attributes inferred from resume information. Barbara Brown and Michael Campion obtained ratings from 113 recruiters of the degree to which 20 resume items represented six job applicant abilities and skills—language ability, math ability, physical abilities, interpersonal skills, leadership ability, and motivation.[101] The resume items that were used by recruiters to infer job applicant attributes, regardless of the job under consideration, are shown in Table 9.7. Moderate interrater reliability (0.60s to 0.70s) was found among recruiters for the inferences made. In general, recruiters' inferred language and mathematics abilities from items related to educational achievement; physical abilities were judged from athletics or sports participation items; and leadership and interpersonal attributes were seen from items dealing with authority positions held and social activities participated in. Recruiters' inferences, such as those identified in these two studies, appear to have face validity; however, there is little evidence regarding the empirical validity of recruiters' inferences from resume information.

TABLE 9.7	Resume Items Used by Recruiters to Infer Job Applicant Abilities and Skills for Sales and Accounting Positions

	Inferred Job Applicant Attribute					
Resume Item	**Language Ability**	**Math Ability**	**Physical Abilities**	**Interpersonal Skills**	**Leadership Ability**	**Motivation**
Education Items:						
1. Pursuing job-related degree						✔
2. Grades obtained in major		✔				
3. Overall grades obtained						✔
4. Earned college expenses						✔
5. Has computer experience						✔
6. Has foreign language skills	✔					
Work Experience Items:						
7. Has full-time work experience						
8. Has supervised others				✔	✔	✔
9. Individual job achievements						✔
10. Held summer internship						✔
11. Worked while in college						✔
12. Served as dorm advisor				✔	✔	✔
Activities/Honors/Interests:						
13. Professional society member						✔
14. Held elected office				✔	✔	✔
15. Varsity athletics captain				✔	✔	✔
16. Participant in recreational sports			✔			
17. Participant in community activities				✔		✔
18. College clubs member				✔		✔
19. Social fraternity member				✔		
20. Has been on Dean's list						✔

Note: Definitions of job applicant abilities and skills: **Language ability**—capacity to read, write, and speak; **Math ability**—capacity to perform mathematical manipulations (addition, subtraction, statistics); **Physical abilities**—physical strength and fitness; **Interpersonal skills**—capacity to interact with and relate to others; **Leadership ability**—capacity to direct, control, and coordinate others; **Motivation**—drive and level of energy. A ✔ indicates that a resume item was used by recruiters to infer a particular job applicant attribute for *both* sales and accounting applicants. The results are based on ratings of 113 recruiters.

Source: Copyright © 1994 by the American Psychological Association. Based on Barbara K. Brown and Michael A. Campion, "Biodata Phenomenology: Recruiters' Perceptions and Use of Biographical Information in Resume Screening," *Journal of Applied Psychology* 79 (1994): 901–902. Reproduced with permission. No further reproduction or distribution is permitted without written permission from the American Psychological Association.

Internet-Based Resume Screening

The typical employer receives hundreds, if not thousands, of resumes. The rate of unsolicited resumes has exploded along with growth in Internet usage, which applicants and employers increasingly use as a way to search for job opportunities and qualified candidates. To indicate the scale of Internet usage, Monster.com, one of the largest Internet employment sites, reports over a million unique job postings each month and more than 30 million unique visitors. McDonald's alone reported receiving over 2 million applications from its mobile career site in 2012, up from just 24,000 in 2008. Given the surge in volume of resumes companies receive online today, the challenge is to quickly screen out applicants who are clearly unsuited for the job in a way that is fair and efficient and relies on job requirements. We will use the resume to discuss issues that arise from using online tools to facilitate searching (or screening) for jobs or applicants, and legal considerations that may emerge in this context.

Companies frequently automate scanning and scoring resumes using keyword searches to identify specific attributes that meet minimum qualifications or credentials—work experience, training or education, even whether the candidate currently resides near the job opportunity or is willing to relocate. Scores are generated based on measures such as the number of keyword matches between a resume and the job description or the number of community and extracurricular activities including leadership roles. As we noted previously, a problem with resumes is controllability; the applicant controls what information is reported. Although automating the process aids in extracting relevant information, verification of experience, education, and other qualifications is typically not feasible at this early stage; it is dealt with at a later step during the hiring process.[102] To ensure the information being collected is standardized (obtained from all applicants), more and more firms are requiring preformatted resume builders with preset fields and check boxes. The trade-off is convenience; applicants must spend more time cutting and pasting qualifications as prompted rather than simply submitting an existing resume. Such a requirement will reduce the number of applicants who submit a resume or application, but those who do respond are likely to be more motivated and committed to the opportunity. The firm will at least have the same information on each applicant.[103]

Two legal issues are particularly salient with online screening. First, to the extent qualified applicants from minority groups do not have equal access to the Internet, and consequently are overlooked during the screening process, there may be disparate impact. Employers using online screening techniques must make every effort to actively recruit minority members and use fair procedures during their assessment. The second concern relates to privacy. Sensitive data may be tracked by third-party vendors or the Web sites themselves without the knowledge of the applicant or employers.[104] J. M. Stanton reports that some legal cases (*Bohach v. City of Reno et al.*, 1996; *State v. Bonnell*, 1993) indicate selection related Web sites should provide "disclaimers that explicitly tell applicants what happens to their data, who has (and will have) access to their data, and the degree to which their data and their involvement in the hiring process are kept private and confidential."[105] Considerably more research is needed to establish the validity and usefulness of data obtained online. As it is, this is a new arena in a relatively uncontrolled environment. Consequently, many issues must be examined. At a minimum, an employer should utilize the same rigorous approach detailed above for successfully developing and administering an application form.

Using Application Forms in HR Selection

An employment application represents only one means for evaluating a job applicant's ability to perform a job. Certainly, other types of measures such as tests and interviews can be used in conjunction with the application form. For the moment, however, we are concerned with *how* the application might be used in selection. This is a critical issue, one that deserves more attention than it typically receives. Recent research shows that the application information managers say they rely on to make the initial screening decision often differs from what they actually use, as is reflected through a policy capturing analysis.[106] Some managers relied on gender, for example, rather than actual applicant qualifications for the job, when they evaluated candidates. How this information is assessed warrants careful consideration, because information from applications can be useful for predicting job performance.[107] As we have seen, the alternatives for utilizing application data can range from those that are objective in their treatment of information to those that are more or less subjective. These approaches can be general or detailed. Furthermore, even though various scoring options are available for handling application data, the methods that have been demonstrated to provide valid information tend to be either based on an empirical scoring key, resulting in an overall score, or they rely on multiple job-relevant constructs, as identified through job analysis, and each of these dimensions has a separate score.

Application forms can be used like a checklist. Because most checklists emphasize applicants' training, education, and experience, they are usually referred to as training and experience evaluations (or simply "T&E" evaluations). Because training and experience evaluations are important and used frequently, we treat T&E evaluations as another selection predictor.

TRAINING AND EXPERIENCE (T&E) EVALUATIONS

Nature and Role of T&E Evaluations in Selection

Training and experience (T&E) evaluations are a way to rationally assess previous experience, training, and education information given by job applicants. The information is reported by the applicant on the resume, on the application form itself, or on a separate questionnaire completed along with the application. Whatever the form, applicants provide job-related information in areas such as previous performance of specific tasks; work history; prior education and training received; credentials such as licenses; self-report ratings of the knowledge, skills, and abilities they possess; and past accomplishments at work. This information is then evaluated by a rater or HR selection specialist using a scoring plan. Scores from the evaluations can be used in a number of ways: (a) as the sole basis for deciding whether an individual is qualified, (b) as a means for rank-ordering individuals from high to low based on a T&E score, (c) as a basis for prescreening applicants prior to administering more expensive, time-consuming predictors (for example, an interview), and (d) in combination with other predictors used for making an employment decision. The objective of using the scores is to predict future job performance, and this information can be helpful in determining the minimum qualifications needed to perform a job.[108]

Examples of T&E Evaluations. To better understand T&E ratings, some examples may help. Our first example might be suitable when only a brief check is needed of relevant portions of a job application for minimal qualifications. The second example shows that a T&E evaluation may be appropriate when a more thorough review of minimum qualifications is being made.

Figure 9.1 illustrates an example of a brief check. It is a checklist to be completed by a company HR specialist for applications submitted for the job of clerk. The form is brief and simple, but it encourages the application reviewer to attend to those aspects of the application that are important for identifying a successful clerk. These aspects important to the job were identified in a previous job analysis. If an applicant meets each of the minimum qualifications listed, an employment decision may be made or additional

FIGURE 9.1	Brief Training and Experience Evaluation Used for Appraising Applications Submitted for the Job of Clerk

Name of Applicant: _____

Directions: Before completing this form, review the minimum qualifications for the job of Clerk that are listed below. Then, study each application form submitted for the job. After reviewing each application, indicate if the applicant possesses each minimum qualification. If an applicant meets the necessary requirements, check "Yes"; if not, then check "No." When there are job openings, applicants meeting all minimum qualifications will be invited in for additional consideration. After completing the checklist, please attach it to the application form and return the application to the personnel file.

Minimum Applicant Qualifications

Yes	No	
☐	☐	1. Maintained a filing system of letters, reports, documents, etc.
☐	☐	2. Used a personal computer and Microsoft Word® to type letters and reports.
☐	☐	3. Used a Dictaphone® or other digital recording device in transcribing correspondence.

Note: This form is completed by a selection specialist.

testing offered. For example, if a candidate possesses all basic qualifications for the job, the applicant might then be administered a filing or typing test or given an interview.

A T&E evaluation such as that in Figure 9.1 can be helpful in making a quick, cursory screening of job applicants. In particular, it is useful in initial screening for those jobs for which large numbers of people make application. When used in this context, the checklist can help to minimize unnecessary HR selection costs by ensuring that only suitable applicants receive further employment consideration. For example, if experience with Microsoft Word® is a necessary requirement for successfully performing the job of clerk, our checklist might include "Used a personal computer and Microsoft Word® to type letters and reports." An applicant must have at least this much relevant job experience, in addition to meeting other minimum qualifications, before being hired or asked to complete another selection measure such as a filing test. It is important to emphasize that the minimum qualifications listed on any preemployment checklist should meet the criteria for establishing employee specifications that we discussed earlier in Chapter 3.

Figure 9.2 presents an example of a separate T&E evaluation form for the job of personnel research analyst. This form is representative of those training and experience assessment methods that are based on job tasks. Using a previous job analysis, tasks critical to the job were identified. We have listed only a few. For each of the important job tasks, applicants are asked to indicate their specific work experiences and/or any training received. With regard to work experience, for example, applicants might be asked to list dates of employment, previous employers, previous job titles, and supervisory responsibilities. Applicants might also be asked to describe their educational background, specialized training, or specific skills acquired that might have prepared them to perform each of these tasks. In addition, applicants must provide names of persons who can be contacted to verify their self-reported information. Verification information helps to discourage applicants from inflating their training and job experiences.

One product of the job analysis is the determination of what experience, education, and training are relevant for successful task performance.[109] For instance, for the task "Computed and monitored applicant flow statistics for nonexempt job applicants using

FIGURE 9.2 An Example Training and Experience Evaluation Form for the Job of Personnel Research Analyst

---

Directions: Listed below are some important job tasks performed by a Personnel Research Analyst. Read each of the tasks. If you have had experience or training in performing a task, check the box marked "Yes." If you have not, then check the box marked "No." For the task(s) marked "Yes," please describe any experience and training you have had that you believe to be associated with each task. All of your responses are subject to review and verification.

Have you had experience or training with this task?

Yes   No
❑   ❑

Task

1. Computed and monitored applicant flow statistics for nonexempt job applicants using computerized statistical packages (for example, SPSS, SAS).

Describe Your Relevant Experience:

Employer: _____ Title: _____
Dates of employment: From _____ To _____
Describe your experience with this task: _____
_____
_____

Describe Your Relevant Training:

Formal coursework and location: _____
_____
Training programs attended and location: _____
_____
On the job training: _____

Name and address of person(s) who can verify this information: _____
_____
_____

Yes   No
❑   ❑

Task

2. Designed and conducted test validation studies for entry-level jobs.

•   •
•   •
•   •

Yes   No
❑   ❑

Task

3. Supervised research assistants in collecting data for human resource studies.

•   •
•   •
•   •

Yes   No
❑   ❑

Task

4. Trained personnel assistants in the use of personnel tests (for example, typing, basic math, and verbal tests) for entry-level jobs.

•   •
•   •
•   •

(Continued)

| FIGURE 9.2 | (*Continued*) |

Yes   No

☐   ☐

5. Made oral presentations to line and/or upper-level managers on the results of personnel research studies.

•
•
•

•
•
•

Describe Your Relevant Experience:

Employer: _____ Title: _____
Dates of employment: From _____ To _____
Describe your experience with this task: _____
_____
_____
_____

Describe Your Relevant Training:

Formal coursework and location: _____
_____

Training programs attended and location: _____

On the job training: _____
_____

Name and address of person(s) who can verify this information: _____
_____
_____

Note: This form is completed by the job applicant.

computerized statistical packages (for example, SPSS, SAS)," we may require knowledge of college-level introductory psychological statistics and training in the use of SPSS, SAS, or equivalent computerized statistical packages. The reviewer of the T&E would simply study the applicant's reported experience, education, and training descriptions to determine whether the applicant met minimum standards. Each task would be reviewed in a similar manner; that is, applicant descriptors would be compared with job task qualifications. These comparisons would be recorded using a summary form like that in Figure 9.3. Individuals who meet or exceed these minimum qualifications would be recommended for further consideration.

Evaluation of Work-Related Experience, Education, and Training. T&E calculations are based on ratings rather than using empirically keyed life history responses like those used in biodata. Thus, a critical question is *which* aspects of experience, education, and training are judged relevant by raters. Consider experience. It can be measured by the frequency or length of time on the task or job, (that is, quantity) or by the challenge, complexity, or quality of instruction/feedback given while doing the task or job (that is, quality). Prior research shows that quantity of experience is a useful predictor for up to 5 years for highly skilled work experience but only up to 3 years on routine jobs. In contrast, quality of experience that is based on challenging experiences may continue to increase competency and self-efficacy for years. Thus, measures of quality may predict beyond the 5-year limit of quantity measures. In addition to quantity and quality, relevancy is important; it may be the preferred approach to assessing aspects of work experience. In large part, relevancy is gauged in two ways: in terms of fit, based on similarity between prior job and the job the candidate is applying for, including size and kind of organization (large, private or public, small, family owned) and the level of supervisory responsibility, technical knowledge required, and complexity and criticality of those experiences.

Similar issues are associated with education and training. Both of these deal with learning, the former with general, non-job-specific learning and the latter with specific

| FIGURE 9.3 | An Example Rating Form for Use in Evaluating Training and Experience of Applicants for the Job of Personnel Research Analyst |

Directions: Read the minimum qualifications required to perform the job of Personnel Research Analyst. Then, compare these qualifications to the applicant's training and experience evaluations. If an applicant's qualifications meet or exceed the requirements for the job, check "Meets Requirements." If not, check "Does Not Meet Requirements."

Name of Applicant _____

Task	Minimum Qualifications	Applicant Rating
1. Computes and monitors applicant flow statistics for nonexempt job applicants using computerized statistical packages (for example, SPSS, SAS).	1. Has knowledge of college-level introductory psycho-logical statistics course; formal coursework training or on-the-job training in use of SPSS, SAS, or equivalent statistical packages.	❏ Meets Requirements ❏ Does Not Meet Requirements
2. Designs and conducts test validation studies for entry-level jobs.	2. Was responsible for conducting empirical vali-dation studies or selection tests. Is knowledgeable of the content of the *Uniform Guidelines*.	❏ Meets Requirements ❏ Does Not Meet Requirements
3. Supervises research assistants in collecting data for personnel selection studies.	3. Directed or was primarily responsible for the work of others involving the collection of empirical data.	❏ Meets Requirements ❏ Does Not Meet Requirements
4. Trains personnel assistants in the use of personnel tests (for example, typing, basic math, and verbal tests) for entry-level jobs.	4. Had college-level course or training in testing and test administration.	❏ Meets Requirements ❏ Does Not Meet Requirements
5. Makes oral presentations to line and/or upper-level managers on the results of personnel research studies.	5. Made formal oral presentations of 15 to 30 minutes duration involving the presentation of quantitative data and results to a non-technical audience.	❏ Meets Requirements ❏ Does Not Meet Requirements

Based on the information shown, the applicant

❏ Meets Requirements

❏ Does Not Meet Requirements for the job of Personnel Research Analyst

Notes: _____   Rater: _____
_____   Date: _____
_____
_____
_____

Note: This form is completed by a selection specialist.

---

job or task training. Brown and Campion found college recruiters differentiate facets by: job-related experiences including degree and grades in major; computer experience; foreign language; and more general experiences including overall grades, Dean's lists, scholarships, whether an applicant earned college expenses, varsity athletics, elected offices, college clubs, or social fraternities.[110]

Another way to categorize assessment experiences is to consider the inferences guiding these assessments. These evaluate the relationships between experience, education, and training and job knowledge and task proficiency.[111] These past ratings are, to a surprising degree, seen as assessing the candidates' motivation and work attitudes; along with skill and ability, these predict job performance and career development. As this shows, determining which measures to focus on requires some thought. Below, we show how useful this selection device can be, based on accumulated reliability and validity evidence.

Reliability and Validity of T&E Evaluations

Reliability.   As far as reliability is concerned, T&E evaluations tend to reflect rather high interrater reliability estimates. Ronald Ash and Edward Levine reported average interrater estimates in the 0.80s. The task-based method produced the highest reliability coefficient; the grouping method produced the lowest.[112] Frank Schmidt and his associates also reported interrater reliability estimates of T&E ratings in the 0.80s.[113]

Validity.   Although most organizations use prior training and work experience as a first cut in selecting applicants, surprisingly few studies examine the validity of these predictors. Given evidence this can lead to litigation,[114] there is a need for more research on the validity of these procedures. When such evidence is collected, it often shows that using evaluations of training and experience as a predictor of productivity can pay off.

In one of the most comprehensive reviews to date, Michael McDaniel, Frank Schmidt, and John Hunter conducted a meta-analysis of the validity of four methods for rating training and experience.[115] With overall job performance as the criterion, they examined a total of 132 validity coefficients based on more than 12,000 observations. They found that the validity of T&E ratings varied with the type of procedure used. The behavioral consistency method demonstrated the highest validity with a mean corrected validity coefficient of 0.45. Lower validities were found for the job element, point, and task methods with mean validities of 0.20, 0.15, and 0.11, respectively. Validity generalization was concluded to exist for the behavioral consistency and job element methods but not for the point-based and task-based approaches. However, Ronald Ash and associates have concluded that the point-based and task-based methods show useful validities for applicant groups having low levels of job experience (for example, 3 years or less).[116]

Other meta-analyses have been conducted of specific types of experience or training measures. One such predictor is work experience, which was found to have an overall correlation of 0.27 with job performance[117] and to correlate with salary (ρ 0.27)[118] in two separate, large-scale meta-analyses. The study by Miguel Quiñones and his associates is particularly informative.[119] They proposed that measurement of work experience is multidimensional. Different relationships between experience and job performance should be found depending on (a) how work experience is measured, that is, by amount, time, or type of experience; and (b) how specific the experience is to the task, job, or organization. An analysis of 22 studies examining work experience–job performance relationships showed the following:

1. Overall, the correlation between the two variables was 0.27, as previously stated.

2. Relationships varied among the studies depending on how work experience was measured and the level of experience received.

3. The amount of work experience had higher relationships with performance than those factors involving time or type of experience.

4. Task experience was more highly related with performance than job or organizational-level experience.

Practitioners and researchers developing systems to assess applicants' previous work experience should carefully consider exactly how they want to define and measure it. Based on research by Quiñones and his associates, this decision may impact the prediction of subsequent performance on the job.

Work experience has been operationalized using years of tenure. Two recent meta-analyses find the correlation between job tenure and job performance is 0.18[120] and 0.20 or 0.24 with salary and job performance,[121] depending on whether tenure is measured as organizational tenure or hours worked. As Paul Tesluk and Rick Jacobs have pointed out, there are a number of ways to operationalize tenure, including tenure in the job, organization, or occupation.[122] Here we find that two very different ways of measuring time on the job (organizational tenure and hours worked) result in similar predictive validities with salary.

Two meta-analyses that examine educational achievement illustrate that variation in how education is defined and measured differentially predicts work outcomes. Frank Schmidt and John Hunter[123] found that years of education was not a good predictor of future job performance ($\rho = 0.10$). Put another way, the validity coefficient of 0.10 suggests that the average job performance of those on a typical semi-skilled job with, say, 12 years of education will be only slightly higher than the performance of those on the same job having 9 or 10 years of education. However, if one were to measure educational achievement using grade point average (GPA), a recent meta-analysis demonstrates that this measure *is* correlated with job performance ($\rho = 0.32$).[124] Compounding this confusion, another meta-analysis finds educational level relates to later salary ($\rho = 0.29$); yet another finds education is unrelated to turnover ($\rho = 0.05$).[125] Thus, even if educational attainment doesn't predict job performance or turnover, it can predict how much a person makes during his or her career. These results suggest that the strength of the relationship to job performance depends on how educational achievement is measured. Furthermore, the usefulness of a measure is also influenced by the outcome being evaluated (for example, job performance, salary, or turnover).

Why do measures of experience and training provide useful information? Those applicants who are judged to be more experienced or to have more training relevant to the job have had more opportunities to learn in the past, which increases job performance even on the first day. Furthermore, greater experience and training enable applicants to acquire job knowledge faster, which in turn increases job performance. Consequently, applicants with more experience and training perform better on the job.[126] However, there is also evidence that these gains increase in a linear fashion up to a certain point; beyond this point the gains plateau. The meta-analysis by Michael McDaniel and his associates powerfully illustrates this; they show that the experience of newly hired employees (3 or fewer years of job experience) correlates highly with supervisory ratings of job performance ($\rho = 0.49$). This true-score correlation drops to 0.15 for incumbents with 12 or more years of experience.[127] That is, for the first few years of job experience there is a strong linear relationship with performance. However, at some point (generally thought to be at approximately 3 to 5 years of job experience, depending on the job's degree of complexity) the relationship begins to level off, showing that additional years of experience result in little increase in job performance. This nonlinear relationship between experience and performance has been supported by others[128] and suggests that beyond a certain point, more time and experience do not enhance learning or job performance. Thus experience and training is thought to predict future job experience only for the first few years of work.

These findings also illustrate why there is often concern about those candidates who are overqualified; the additional experience or training will not result in commensurate "one-to-one" gains in performance. A recent study published in the *Annals of Internal*

Medicine examined the relationship between years of experience in practice and the quality of care provided by medical doctors. The authors concluded that, "Our results suggest physicians with more experience paradoxically may be at risk for providing lower-quality care."[129] This conclusion is based on a review of 59 studies that examined the link between a physician's years of experience and patient care. They found that more than half of these studies (52 percent) found a decreasing quality of care associated with a doctor's increasing years in practice for all outcomes assessed; only 4 percent of the studies reported an increasing quality of care associated with a doctor's increasing experience for some or all outcomes. The authors argue these findings suggest that more experienced doctors possess less factual knowledge, are less likely to adhere to appropriate standards of care, and are less likely to adopt more proven therapies. These findings, which differ from those we just reviewed in the previous paragraphs about the experience–performance relationship, suggest that there is a decreasing performance—in other words, a concave relationship (where performance initially increases with experience, peaks, and than decreases)—associated with increasing experience, not just a "leveling off" of this relationship. This implies that hiring an overqualified person may be as harmful as hiring an underqualified applicant. These results contradict the findings from another meta-analysis, which concluded that "experience becomes more predictive of job performance in high complexity jobs" (medical doctor is a highly complex job).[130] Thus, we clearly need more research to fully understand the nature of the relationship between experience, age, and performance. Suffice it to say that this issue requires considerably more research before we fully understand implications of being "overqualified."

Taken together, these results reveal that measures of experience and training (a) consistently predict important work outcomes; (b) vary significantly in the strength of predictive validity found; and (c) are particularly valuable for the first 3 to 5 years on the job. To ensure that a company is effectively screening out the least-qualified applicants, and to be able to successfully refute a disparate impact claim of discrimination, practitioners must give careful consideration to the specific measures they utilize and assess the validity of those measures. As we have seen, empirical validity generally shows that these measures predict job performance, especially early in one's career.

One can illustrate validity without relying on empirical validity. This approach emphasizes content validity that relies on an understanding of the tasks and knowledge, skills, and abilities required by the job. The challenge is to identify the minimum, not preferred, qualifications an employee must possess at job entry in order to perform on the job at an adequate or barely adequate level. The problem, of course, is how to set and validate minimum qualifications. For example, in the grouping method, where years of experience may substitute for years of education and vice versa, how is it determined what combinations of education and experience are most relevant for a job? Two recent articles address this issue and detail the application of the content validity approach as a way to create procedures that ultimately were agreed to by the courts as part of a settlement from a lawsuit.[131] These studies highlight the importance of job analysis for identifying minimum qualifications in content-valid education and experience. Subject matter experts (SMEs) are relied upon to rate whether the personal attribute reflects that needed to perform at a barely acceptable level (that is, to exceed or match the level required of a barely acceptable employee). Obviously, it matters who the SMEs are; the group should include nonprobationary job incumbents and supervisors who vary by race and gender and who represent the various functional aspects of the job. Their performance on the job should also meet or exceed the level of "satisfactory" job performance. Although published research about content validity approaches are not common, these articles show that application of these approaches can result in the development of minimum qualifications for training and experience that withstand judicial scrutiny.

Legal Implications

Training and experience are often used as an initial screen focusing on the minimum qualifications needed for performing at a barely acceptable level on the first day of the job. Although it makes sense that the knowledge, skills, and prior work experience a candidate possesses should impact his or her level of productivity in the new job, evaluating training and experience is not as easy as one might expect. From a legal perspective, this information may be used to unfairly discriminate against certain individuals. For example, college GPA, which can be used as an indicator of educational achievement, was found in one recent large-scale study to result in fairly large differences in group means.[132] These results suggest that using GPA cut scores may produce disparate impact due to differences in mean GPA across minority groups, when compared to the majority (white) group. For example, if the average GPA for graduating accounting majors is 2.92 for whites and 2.52 for blacks and the accounting firm decides to interview only those students with GPAs greater than 3.0, significantly fewer blacks would be interviewed (only 11 percent of the blacks, but 34 percent of the whites). Bryan Kethley and David Terpstra examined the degree of federal litigation associated with the application form by studying more than 300 court cases between 1978 and 2004. A number of these cases dealt with information that would typically be considered representative of training and experience criteria. For example, education requirements (6 percent of total cases), experience requirements (7 percent of cases), and work history (3 percent of cases) were found to be common types of information involved in litigation. Further analyses revealed the plaintiff prevailed in nearly 30 percent of those cases.[133] Although it is not known whether these criteria were part of a training and experience evaluation, they could have been.

One conclusion that should be drawn from these studies is that as with application forms, organizations should ensure that the training and experience qualifications they rely on for initial selection decisions are fair and not discriminatory. The inference is that organizations should avoid collecting information that disproportionately screens out members of one sex or minority group, particularly when that information (a) does not predict successful performance on the job, (b) is not related to the requirements of the job, or (c) cannot be justified as a business necessity. To minimize legal exposure, these predictors should be based on a competent job analysis, have some validity evidence available, and be uniformly applied to all applicants. The maximum amount of minimum qualification should usually be limited to no more than 5 years and should exclude qualifications that are developed after a brief training period. Finally, to assure compliance with the Americans with Disabilities Act, consider oral administration for blind applicants and provide instructions that can be read and understood by applicants with suspect composition and reading skills.[134]

Recommendations for Using T&E Evaluations

Most formal applications of T&E evaluations have occurred in the public sector rather than the private sector. Previous studies suggest that T&E evaluations tap job performance dimensions not assessed by other predictors.[135] By tying minimum job requirements to essential job tasks and WRCs through a well-developed T&E evaluation, minimum qualifications predictive of job performance can be set.

To apply T&E evaluations effectively, the following guidelines are recommended:

1. Minimum amounts of training, experience, and education are among the most frequently used selection standards. **Use T&E evaluations to set specific**

minimum qualifications job candidates should hold, rather than using a selection standard such as a high school diploma (unless the diploma can be justified). These minimum qualifications may be expressed through job-relevant WRCs applicants possess, or by applicants' prior performance of job-relevant tasks. Consequently, the utility of any good T&E evaluation system will depend on a thorough job analysis.

2. **T&E evaluations are subject to the *Uniform Guidelines*.** Like all selection devices, validation studies should be conducted on their job relatedness. Studies by Edward Levine, Maury Buster, and their associates illustrate applications of content validity procedures that withstand court scrutiny.[136]

3. Although typical validity coefficients may be relatively low, the available evidence is reasonably clear that some T&E ratings are valid predictors of job performance. **Nevertheless, it has been recommended that these procedures be used only as rough screening procedures for positions where previous experience and training are necessary for job performance.** For those entry-level jobs where only minimal levels of previous experience or training are required, other predictors should be considered.[137]

4. **Forms and procedures for collecting and scoring T&E evaluations should be standardized as much as possible.**

5. **Because T&E evaluations involve self-report data, some form of data verification, particularly of data given by applicants who are going to be offered a job, should be made.**

6. **Where distortion of self-evaluation information is likely to be a problem, final hiring decisions based on other selection measures, such as ability, job knowledge, and performance tests, can minimize the inherent risks associated with T&E evaluations.**

REFERENCE CHECKS

Nature and Role of Reference Checks in Selection

Another technique that is nearly always used to select among job applicants is the checking of applicants' references or recommendations. This method requires the employer to collect information about prospective job applicants from people who have had contact with the applicants. Information collected is used for the following purposes: (a) to *verify* information given by job applicants on other selection measures (such as application forms, employment interviews, or T&E evaluations), (b) to serve as a basis for either predicting the job success of applicants or screening out unqualified applicants, and (c) to *uncover* background information (for example, a criminal record or unsafe driving record) about applicants that may not have been provided by applicants or identified by other selection procedures. The principle that underlies the use of reference checking is simple; the best way to find out about an applicant is to ask those who know him or her well.[138]

We saw in our earlier review of the accuracy of application form data that distortion can be a very real problem. Some job applicants give inaccurate information on prior employment, education, and acquired job skills in order to enhance their employability. Therefore, one principal purpose of a reference check is to verify what applicants have stated on the application form. The method is useful only when it fails to confirm previous selection measure information given by applicants. Thus *reference checking serves more as a basis for screening out selection decisions—that is, detection of the unqualified—rather than identification of the qualified.*

The second purpose of the reference check is to serve as a predictor of job success. Like application form data, a reference check used in this way assumes that past performance is a good predictor of future performance. While an application form may summarize what applicants say they did, a reference check is meant to assess how well *others* say the applicants did. It is presumed that information provided by others can be used to forecast how applicants will perform on the job in question.

Some applicants distort application information; others omit background information such as a criminal record. Applicants often fail to report background information when they believe it will affect their chances for employment. However, because unreported background information affects job performance or perhaps endangers the mental or physical well-being of coworkers, clients, or customers, a prospective employer may use reference checks for a third purpose—to identify applicants' job-relevant, but unreported, background histories. Uncovering potential problems is one way a firm can defend itself against negligent-hiring lawsuits.[139]

Reference checking is a common practice of many employers. It is one of the most popular preemployment procedures for screening job candidates. Several surveys have documented that over 95 percent of the firms they sampled said they engaged in checking references.[140] When reference information is collected, a significant number of organizations state they use the data for prediction rather than just for verification purposes. For example, a survey of 345 public and private organizations showed that more than half found the reference-checking method always (19 percent) or sometimes (51 percent) useful for obtaining additional information about the applicant's previous job performance or overall employability. This compares to those organizations reporting that reference checks always (68 percent) or sometimes (30 percent) provided adequate verification information, such as dates of employment. This method helps the employer get a more complete picture of the candidate, as indicated by the fact that more than half of the 345 firms using reference checks found the method very (18 percent) or somewhat (55 percent) effective in identifying poor performers.[141]

Types of Reference Data Collected

Generally speaking, four types of information are solicited through reference checks: (a) employment and educational background data, (b) appraisal of an applicant's character and personality, (c) estimates of an applicant's job performance capabilities, and (d) willingness of the reference to rehire an applicant.[142] With the passage of the Illegal Immigration Reform and Immigrant Responsibilities Act of 1996, ensuring that applicants are legally eligible to be employed in the United States became the most common kind of information verified by employers.

Table 9.8 illustrates the usefulness of employment and personal background information collected through reference checks. The data are based on a nationwide survey of HR professionals from 345 organizations conducted by the Society for Human Resource Management (SHRM).[143] Nearly all (96 percent) conducted reference checks; the most frequent types of information sought and received were dates of employment (98 percent at least sometimes) and whether an ex-employee was eligible for rehire (83 percent at least sometimes). Most of the employers said that information they received on personality traits (47 percent) and violent or "bizarre" behavior was inadequate

| TABLE 9.8 | Getting Adequate Employment Information on Job Applicants |

Employment Information	Always	Sometimes	Rarely or Never
Dates of employment	68%	30%	2%
Eligibility for rehire	23%	60%	17%
Prospective hire's qualifications for a specific job	16%	54%	30%
Overall impression of employability	19%	51%	30%
Salary history	13%	48%	39%
Reason candidate left previous employer	12%	55%	33%
Candidate's work ethic (absences, tardiness, etc.)	14%	54%	33%
Interpersonal skills	17%	47%	36%
Personality traits	9%	45%	47%
Malpractice, professional disciplinary action, etc.	9%	26%	65%
Violent or bizarre behavior	6%	25%	69%

Source: Data are based on a survey—*report for Reference and Background checks*—conducted by the Society for Human Resource Management, January 2005.

(69 percent). Nevertheless, almost three out of four respondents said that reference checking was very or somewhat effective and only 2 percent said it was not at all effective. Even though employers want this information, more than half of the organizations contacted (53 percent) refused to provide the information for fear of legal action; 25 percent had a policy prohibiting them from supplying any information beyond employment verification.[144] These findings probably account for some of the results presented in Table 9.8. As you can see from the table, the types of information HR professionals receive drops off rather dramatically after "dates of employment." This is likely due to reference givers' unwillingness to comment on applicants' personal backgrounds for fear of being held legally accountable.

With regard to types of reference data requested, we should make one comment concerning legal guidelines established by the Americans with Disabilities Act (ADA) and reference checking on disabled applicants. Employers are prohibited from asking any questions of references that they may not request of applicants. (For example, see our earlier discussion on employment applications.) Employers may not inquire about applicants' disabilities, illnesses, or compensation histories. Employers may make inquiries concerning previous job tasks performed, job performance, attendance records, and other job-related issues not associated with applicants' disabilities.[145]

Usefulness of Reference Data

We have studied several aspects of the reference check, including the reference check's role in selection, approaches to collecting reference data, and sources of reference data. The next question is, how valuable are these data in predicting the success of job applicants? Although not many empirical studies have examined the effectiveness of the method, we present some of the limited results that are available on the reliability and validity of reference data.

Reliability and Validity of Reference Data. Despite the widespread use of reference checks, there is surprisingly little research evidence available regarding their reliability and effectiveness in predicting applicants' subsequent job performance. Studies of reference data reliability have been rare. When reliability data have been reported, they have typically involved interrater (for example, among supervisors, acquaintances, and coworkers) reliability estimates of 0.40 or less.[146] Although these estimates are low, they are not all that surprising. We might anticipate that different groups of raters focus on different aspects of candidates and judge them from different perspectives. These differences will contribute to different ratings and, thus, lower reliability. Furthermore, the lack of agreement between two reference givers for the same person restricts the predictive validity of the reference check.

Michael Aamodt and Felice Williams conducted a meta-analysis of 30 studies reporting validity data between references or letters of recommendation and performance and reported a mean sample-weighted correlation of 0.18, with a corrected true score correlation of 0.29.[147] This result is comparable to the meta-analytic results reported in two influential studies conducted in the early 1980s. John and Ronda Hunter's meta-analysis showed a true-score correlation of 0.26 for supervisor ratings of performance,[148] which is remarkably similar to the 0.29 estimate reported by Aamodt and Williams more than 30 years later. Furthermore, the mean sample-weighted correlation of 0.18 found by Aamodt and Williams matches that reported by Richard Reilly and Georgia Chao's meta-analysis (conducted in 1982) of the validity of reference checks.[149] Taken together, these findings show that the relationships between reference ratings and measures of employee success (performance ratings and turnover) are low to moderate at best. Other predictors such as biographical data and cognitive ability tests generally fare better than reference checks in predicting job success. Nevertheless, reference checks provide information that is related to work performance and can provide evidence of fraud or of other information not disclosed by the applicant (for example, the reason the candidate left a firm), which can be used to screen out undesirable applicants.

You may wonder why reference checks do not perform better than they do in predicting an applicant's subsequent performance. There are several possible explanations. First, the criteria or success measures with which reference checks have been statistically correlated have generally suffered from low reliability. As we saw in Chapters 7 and 8, when a criterion is characterized by unreliable information, we should not expect reference data to predict it statistically. Many of the criteria utilized in reference data validity studies have had poor reliability. Supervisory ratings have frequently served as criteria, and these are notorious for their subjectivity and, sometimes, low reliability.

Another explanation for the apparent low validity of reference data is that applicants preselect who will evaluate them.[150] Because applicants recognize that references may have a bearing on their employability, they are most likely to choose those who will have something positive to say about them. As we have noted, leniency is the rule rather than the exception. The result is a narrow or restricted range of scores characteristic of many reference reports. Scores tend to be high with little negative information being given on an applicant. If all applicants generally receive the same high reference scores, then it is unreasonable to expect a reference check to predict how applicants will perform on a subsequent job. If we used only positive information, we would predict that all applicants would succeed. Yet we know that differences in job success will exist.

Other factors we have already listed also contribute to the low value of reference measures. Reference givers may not have had sufficient opportunity to observe the applicant on a job; they may not be competent; they may distort their ratings to help the applicant; and they may not be able to adequately communicate their evaluations. One factor emphasized by recent research that appears to have a significant bearing on the utility of references for predicting job success involves the level of structure, with greater structure being found to increase validity. As noted previously, Julie McCarthy and Richard Goffin reported a multiple correlation of 0.42 when using a standardized questionnaire, one that required reference givers to rate the candidate's standing on a number of job-relevant attributes using a standardized scale. This scale ranged from 0 to 100, with a score of 50 representing the performance of an average peer.[151] Similarly, Paul Taylor and his associates found that a structured telephone reference check predicted supervisory ratings of job performance (uncorrected r 0.25; a true-score correlation 0.36).[152] These validities are larger than the mean uncorrected correlations reported in prior meta-analyses. Moreover, the fact that higher predictive validities are obtained using structured rather than unstructured interviews (something you will learn in Chapter 10) suggests the potential value of structuring reference checks.

Researchers have recently begun to consider the construct validity of the measures that can be assessed in a letter of reference.[153] As mentioned above, Paul Taylor and associates not only relied on more highly structured reference checks, but also assessed three job-related personality/interpersonal dimensions (conscientiousness, agreeableness, and customer focus).[154] This resulted in considerably higher validities than typically are found. Similarly, Ryan Zimmerman, Maria Triana, and Murray Barrick reported five separate constructs that predicted academic and occupational success.[155] These results suggest the inherent value in measuring structured, standardized constructs in references.[156] Providing frame-of-reference training for assessors has been found to be one way to encourage construct validity.[157] Just as with the interview, there is evidence that physical attractiveness and gender can bias the assessment of reference check constructs.[158] Considering what construct is being measured and the rigor involved in assessing it is likely to matter to reference ratings, though there is still a need for continued research to establish predictive validity.[159]

Yet another factor that has the potential to increase the predictive validity of reference information is systematic assessment ratings from others familiar with the candidates' performance in previous work situations (supervisors, customers, coworkers, and subordinates). More and more organizations are using multi-source performance ratings or 360-degree feedback that relies on ratings from diverse organizational perspectives. Results from meta-analyses examining the usefulness of information from raters from different organizational levels illustrates that these raters observe different facets of a ratee's job performance.[160] Systematically incorporating information from these different organizational perspectives should increase the predictive validity of references by adding unique variance. Michael Mount, Murray Barrick, and Judy Perkins Strauss found that observer ratings (supervisor, coworker, and customer) that were based on a questionnaire assessing job-relevant personality traits predicted performance as well as (and perhaps better than) self ratings.[161] Even though these ratings were not collected during reference checking, these results suggest that the use of multiple raters from different organizational perspectives could provide more valid reference information than raters from just one organizational perspective. Nevertheless, it should be noted that researchers are concerned about the reliability or interrater agreement derived from such ratings.[162] Fortunately there is evidence that the underlying applicant characteristics being measured tend to be the same across different sources (that is, tend to have measurement equivalence).[163] Taken together, these findings underscore the need to obtain ratings from multiple observers across organizational levels. Aggregating across multiple raters will provide a more reliable and valid reference measure.

Finally, Frank Schmidt and John Hunter have noted that past validity estimates of reference checks may no longer be accurate.[164] Because of lawsuits by former employees (see our discussion in the next section), many past employers have restricted information given to prospective employers simply to dates of employment and job titles held. However, recent as well as future changes in the legal climate may significantly impact the quantity and quality of information given by past employers. Currently, 40 of 50 states have provided immunity from legal liability for employers giving reference information in good faith, and other states are considering such laws.[165] In the future, these changes may enhance the validity of reference checks in predicting job performance.

Applicant Acceptability.   Applicant reactions to references are likely to vary, depending upon how intrusive the information being requested is (for example, credit check versus verifying employment dates). However, a recent meta-analysis examines the perceived favorability of 10 different selection tools, including references. Results show that references are viewed more favorably by applicants than cognitive ability evaluations, personality tests, biodata, and integrity tests, but not as favorably as employment interviews, work samples, and resumes. These reactions suggest applicants view references as a reasonable tool to rely on for making hiring decisions because the information assessed bears a close relationship to how successfully the candidate would perform actual job duties.[166]

Legal Issues Affecting the Use of Reference Checks

As with any HR selection measure, there are important legal concerns an employer should consider when using reference checks for selection or providing reference data to another employer. Two broad categories of legal issues are particularly critical. The first of these comprises two matters: (a) the discriminatory impact reference checks may have on a job applicant and (b) the defamation of a job applicant's character through libel or slander.

The second category is one that is somewhat unique to reference checks. That issue involves complaints filed against employers for "negligent hiring" of employees. As we see in the following sections, the possibility of libel or slander suits *discourages* employers from providing reference information; the possibility of negligent hiring charges *encourages* prospective employers to use reference checks.

Discriminatory Impact and Defamation of Character.   A few cases have appeared in the courts dealing with claims of discriminatory impact through reference checks. For example, in *Equal Employment Opportunity Commission v. National Academy of Sciences* (1976), a job applicant was refused employment on the basis of a poor reference by her previous supervisor. It was argued by the plaintiff that the reference check excluded a disproportionate number of black people and was not related to performance on the job. Evidence presented by the defense led the court to conclude that there was no adverse impact, and that the reference check (verified with a validation study) was job related.[167]

Defamation is another problem that can occur in reference checking, but it concerns the former employer giving reference information, not the one using the information for selection decision making. Although defamation is beyond the present scope of this book, it is an important problem for employers giving reference data and it deserves a few comments.

Defamation in this context involves a written (libel) or oral (slander) false statement made by an employer about a previous employee that damages the individual's reputation.[168] For instance, in *Rutherford v. American Bank of Commerce* (1976), an individual brought a charge against her former employer, who mentioned in a letter of recommendation that she had brought a sexual discrimination charge against the firm. She was able to demonstrate that she could not obtain later employment because of the letter of recommendation. The court ruled on her behalf, saying that the employer illegally retaliated against her because she exercised her rights under Title VII.[169]

For defamation to occur, several elements must be present:

1. A written or oral defamatory statement must have been given.

2. There must be a false statement of fact. To be considered not false, the employer must prove that the statement was made in good faith and was believed to be true.

3. Injury must have occurred to the referee, such as the inability of the referee to get another job because of the previous employer's statement.

4. The employer does *not* have absolute or qualified privilege. (Under *absolute* privilege, an employer has immunity from defamation, such as in a legal proceeding. Under *qualified* privilege, an employer will not be held liable unless the information is knowingly false or malicious.) Information that is judged to be truthful, based on facts, limited to the appropriate business purpose (that is, reference information), made on the proper occasion, and given to appropriate parties is likely to be judged as qualified privilege and, therefore, appropriate.[170]

Two additional cases help to illustrate further the impact of libel or slander in reference checking. *True v. Ladner* (1986) is a case in which True, a public high school teacher, brought suit for libel and slander against Ladner, the school superintendent, based on Ladner's statements given during an inquiry by a prospective employer. Ladner characterized True as being a poor mathematics teacher, more concerned with living up to his contract than going the extra mile as a teacher, and unable to "turn students on" as a teacher. Although Ladner argued that these were his personal opinions and protected by his First Amendment rights, the jury found from the evidence presented that Ladner's reference statements were given with "reckless disregard of their truth or falsity" and, therefore, libel and slander were committed against True. Under appeal, the jury's verdict was upheld by the Maine Supreme Judicial Court.[171] In *Hall v. Buck* (1984), Buck, an insurance salesman, was fired by Hall & Co., Inc. Although he had a history of high success in insurance sales, Buck was unable to find employment with several other insurance firms. Buck hired an investigator to find out the real reasons he was fired from Hall, Inc. Several employees of the firm made derogatory statements to the investigator about Buck. Testimony by one of Buck's prospective employers indicated that he did not make a job offer because a reference giver at Hall, Inc. said, among other comments, that he would not rehire Buck. Evidence presented at the trial showed that the reference givers at Hall, Inc. made their statements based on secondhand information, and that the statements made were not substantially true. Thus it was concluded that Hall, Inc. had committed slander and libel against Buck.[172]

The cases cited illustrate some legal ramifications for reference givers. However, a California case illustrates a situation where former employers provided positive references for a problem employee. In this case, a school district obtained letters of reference from four school districts who collectively extolled the candidate's ability and concern for students and recommended him for employment. In each case, the school districts were allegedly aware that the former teacher had engaged in sexual misconduct with female students. The court found all four school districts liable for negligent misrepresentation, noting that although the school was under no duty to provide this information, once the reference givers offered opinions about the teacher's personal qualities ("genuine concern for students" and "high standards") they should also have discussed the alleged inappropriate incidents.[173]

The point in this case is that some reference givers tend to go beyond necessity in describing people. Potential employers would be wise to recognize the signals of defamation and discount such reference data. Because of the *Uniform Guidelines*, Fair Credit Reporting Act (1971), Family Educational Rights and Privacy Act (1974), and some statutes included under state labor codes, there is a growing concern among employers about the legal implications of using reference checks in selection. Libel, slander, and defamation of an applicant's character are becoming significant issues for some employers. As a consequence, some may believe that it is not permissible under the law to check references. *However, it is legal and even the duty of employers to check references.* They have the right to seek job-related reference information, to use such information in an appropriate manner in selection decision making, and to share appropriate information with individuals who have a legitimate need to know.[174]

To limit the civil liability of employers, a number of states have passed laws to offer protection to employers that provide good-faith job references for former employees. As we mentioned earlier, 40 states have passed such legislation. However, from a legal perspective, laws limiting a former employer's liability could increase a hiring employer's responsibility for checking references.[175] Although the details in each law differ state to state, they often require the employer to show the reference to the employee and allow him or her to correct it or provide another version of events.

Negligent Hiring. A charge of negligent hiring occurs when a third party such as a coworker, client, or customer of an organization files suit against an employer for injuries caused by an employee.[176] For example, suppose an exterminator for a pest control company who has come to inspect an apartment physically assaults a resident. The victim in this incident might bring a negligent hiring suit against the pest control company. The focus of the plaintiff's charges in such a suit is that the employer knew or should have known that the employee causing the injuries was unfit for the job and that the employer's negligence in hiring the individual produced the plaintiff's injuries.

For an employer to be held liable in negligent hiring, five points must be covered:

1. Injury to a third party must be shown to be caused by an individual employed by a firm.

2. The employee must be shown to be unfit for the job he or she holds. To address whether the candidate was fit to perform the job duties and responsibilities extends beyond assessing only the employee's technical skills; it includes ascertaining whether the individual is trustworthy, honest, and free from any violent, criminal, or improper tendencies that should have disqualified the candidate for the position.

3. It must be shown that the employer knew or should have known that the employee was unfit for the job, and that had the employer conducted a background check or criminal check, the firm would have discovered the candidate's lack of fitness for the job (for example, a propensity for assaulting coworkers or a third party.

4. The injury received by the third party must have been a foreseeable outcome resulting from the hiring of the unfit employee. This will depend on the type of job in question. Those jobs involving safety or protection of property or those jobs that expose coworkers or customers to unsupervised contact with the employee are particularly likely to lead to a negligent hiring lawsuit.

5. It must be shown that the injury is a reasonable and probable outcome of what the employer did or did not do in hiring the individual.[177]

Suits involving negligent hiring typically encompass the following types of issues: (a) those in which there was intentional employee misconduct, such as a theft committed by an employee with a history of dishonesty; (b) those in which physical harm occurred, such as a physical attack or sexual assault by an employee with a violent past or previously exhibited sexually deviant behavior; or (c) those in which an employee does not possess the skill or ability to perform a job task (for example, an inexperienced truck driver) and an individual is injured as a result.[178] In judging employer negligence, the courts consider the steps an employer has taken to identify whether an employee is unfit, given the nature of the tasks performed by the employee. Reference checks and background investigations are two types of preemployment screens that many courts view as suitable for identifying potential problems. Both of these screens are particularly appropriate for jobs that involve (a) access to others' residences, (b) little supervision, (c) public safety (for example, transportation industry) or substantial personal contact with the general public, and (d) work with individuals receiving personal care (for example, health care industry). For many jobs, documented reference checks alone can serve as important evidence in defending a negligent hiring suit.

As you read and think about reference checks, you may be wondering, "Can't a company find itself in a catch-22 situation? That is, on the one hand, to avoid a negligent hiring lawsuit, it may be important to obtain reference information prior to hiring; on the other hand, many employers do not provide such information for fear of libel or slander suits by past employees. What then?" Certainly, employers are concerned about the type of information released on past employees. For example, the following recommendations are frequently proposed for releasing reference information: (a) do not give out reference information over the telephone, (b) document all information that is released, (c) provide only specific, objective information, (d) obtain written consent from the employee prior to releasing reference information, and (e) do not answer a question involving an opinion as to whether a previous employee would be rehired.[179]

Obviously, if many organizations follow these guidelines, it will be difficult for prospective employers to obtain much more than dates of employment and the last position held in the organization. The results from a survey of 335 public and private organizations support this concern, as they found that a majority of firms (54 percent) have a policy not to provide references or information about current or former employees. Furthermore, 53 percent of the organizations surveyed had at least one manager or HR professional who refused to provide reference information for fear of legal action, while 25 percent had a policy not to provide any information beyond employment verification.[180] A recent examination of federal court cases revealed there were more lawsuits involving reference checks and background investigations than lawsuits involving medical exams, drug tests, or polygraph tests. Furthermore, the results indicated organizations were more likely to lose reference-check lawsuits.[181]

These results indicate that employer fears of legal liability are certainly not unfounded, particularly since a lawsuit can be expensive in terms of monetary damages and legal fees. Yet, the same survey of 335 employers found that the percentage of organizations that reported a legal issue in the past 3 years regarding references and background checks was quite small; less than 5 percent reported claims due to defamation (2 percent), negligent hiring (3 percent), or failing to provide adequate warning about the threat posed by a former employer (1 percent). Based on this, it appears that employer concerns may be exaggerated. One way to address these concerns is to have the candidate sign a waiver relieving former employers of liability. The survey found that 66 percent of HR professionals believe that signed waivers by their former employees would increase the odds that they would provide references.[182]

In encouraging former employers to supply information on a past employee, the following strategies have been recommended:

- Submit a written request for information on specific questions that are relevant to making an employment decision, and use the same questions with every applicant (such as "Was the person ever disciplined or discharged for fighting?").

- Include a release form signed by the applicant stating that (a) the applicant has read and approves the information requested, and (b) the applicant requests that the information be given.

If the previous employer refuses to provide such information, then do the following:

- Call the person in charge of human resources and ask why the request was not honored.

- Ask how a request should be made so it will be honored.

If the previous employer still refuses to give the information, then do the following:

- Inform the individual that failure to cooperate is being documented with date, time, and name of the person refusing the request.

- At a minimum, verify the candidate's statements about the position held, the number of years spent in that position, and the final salary.

- If the missing information is so relevant that the applicant will not be hired without it, tell the individual that the applicant will be told that the previous employer's refusal was the reason for the lack of an offer.[183]

Refusing to give information on a past employee does not necessarily shield an employer from a lawsuit. Employers have responsibility to provide relevant information on a past employee who is under consideration for employment by another employer. In fact, refusal to do so may legally jeopardize an employer. Legal jeopardy for such firms may be a particular problem in states that have laws protecting employers giving references. Hiring employers should also be vigilant about noticing abbreviated periods of employment, frequent changes in residences, or gaps in employment. Whenever such "suspicious" employment gaps are revealed, the hiring employer should inquire further into the candidate's background and consider conducting a criminal record search.

Bill Leonard has described a legal case involving reference giving in Florida, a state with a law protecting employers from civil liability when they give reference information.[184] The case, against Allstate Insurance Co., involved a workplace shooting in which two employees of Fireman's Fund Insurance Co. were killed by a coworker who had been fired.

The accused assailant had worked for Allstate but was fired for carrying a pistol in his briefcase. As part of his severance package, Allstate gave him a letter of reference stating that he had not been terminated due to his job performance. Fireman's Fund hired him but fired him 2 years later. He returned to the company and killed two employees and himself. Families of the slain workers sued Allstate, alleging that Allstate violated its responsibility to fully and truthfully disclose information on the assailant concerning his character and propensity toward violence. The case was settled out of court.

From the perspective of negligent hiring suits, a key element is that written documentation must show that the employer *attempted* to collect background data on prospective employees. Even though necessary reference information was not given by a past employer, a firm using reference checks should carefully document what questions were asked and what information was obtained. From a legal point of view, the important question is this: *Did the employer take reasonable steps and precautions to identify a problem employee, given the risks inherent in the job tasks the employee would be required to perform?* Depending on the nature of these tasks, steps other than reference checks (such as providing comprehensive training, giving close supervision, and conducting an extensive background investigation) may be required. However, for many jobs, verifying and checking references is considered an appropriate degree of care for identifying potential problem employees.

Methods of Collecting Reference Data

Reference information is collected in a number of ways, including (a) by telephone, (b) from the Internet, (c) by e-mail, (d) by fax or mail, or (e) in person. A recent survey of HR professionals from 345 organizations revealed that the telephone is the most frequently used method of conducting a reference check (98 percent either always or sometimes use it); just over 50 percent always or sometimes use either fax or mail. The Internet is being used more and more (36 percent either always or sometimes use it; 43 percent never use it); e-mail and in-person methods are the least frequently used (less than 5 percent always use either method; 62 percent and 92 percent rarely or never use it, respectively).[185] Organizations can use a number of criteria to decide which reference-checking method to use; three critical factors include the speed with which information can be collected, the type of information being gathered, and the cost associated with collecting the information. Although the weight of each factor will vary depending on the employment position being filled, the telephone appears to be the best way to satisfy these criteria.

Telephone Checks.   Telephone checks are relatively fast, result in a relatively high reference return rate, allow the reference checker to ask follow-up questions or clarify what type of information is needed, and are inexpensive to conduct. In addition, the personal nature of the telephone check contributes to greater responsiveness from the reference giver; the way that oral comments are given (voice inflections, pauses) may be useful for revealing what a person really thinks. This should lead to greater disclosure—because information is sometimes given orally that would not be given in writing. Finally, on the telephone it is easier to ensure that reference comments are being given by the person named rather than by a clerk or secretary. The sheer number of advantages attributed to the telephone method probably accounts for its disproportionate use.[186]

It's wise to use prepared questions while conducting the telephone reference check interview. In fact, telephone reference checks should be treated as an "informal" interview. Consequently, you will want to utilize the same principles and techniques that make an interview effective. More will be said about this in Chapter 10, but let us say now that enhanced structure is an important element of successful interviews.[187] If an unstructured approach is used over the telephone, the utility of the data collected will be highly dependent on the skill and training of the telephone interviewer. Table 9.9 lists some questions frequently asked during a telephone reference check; these are not necessarily recommended questions.

Internet and E-mail Reference Checks.   These methods are also fast and relatively inexpensive, though not as interactive. It is not as easy to ask follow-up questions or clarify ambiguous requests for information. Furthermore, e-mail reference-checking methods are likely to be seen as less desirable due to their lack of privacy and informality.

TABLE 9.9	**Some Example Questions Frequently Asked in a Telephone Reference Check**

1. The candidate states that he or she was employed with your firm in the position of (position) from _____ to _____, and that his or her final salary was $_____ per annum. Is this correct?
2. Would you rehire the job candidate? Is the candidate eligible for reemployment?
3. Why did the candidate leave your firm?
4. How would you rate the candidate's overall job performance—on a scale of 1 to 10 (10 being high)—compared to the performance of others with similar responsibilities?
5. On average, how many times did the candidate miss work? Come in late? Did he or she fail to meet commitments?
6. Does the candidate work well with others (coworkers, superiors, subordinates, customers)? Is he or she a team player?
7. What were the candidate's responsibilities in order of importance? Describe the candidate's general duties: [Or you could ask] Let me read you what the candidate says his or her duties were at your organization. [After reading them ask] Is this accurate?
8. What were the candidate's principal strengths, outstanding successes, and significant failures in his or her job activities?
9. Describe the candidate's last job performance evaluation: What were his or her strengths? What recommended improvement areas were noted?
10. How would you describe the applicant's success in training, developing, and motivating subordinates?
11. What does the candidate need to do for continued professional growth and development? What is the biggest change you have observed in him or her?
12. Were there any vehicle or personal injury accidents while the candidate was employed by you?
13. Do you know of anything else that would indicate whether the applicant is unfit or dangerous for a position such as _____?
14. Is there anything else you would like to tell me about the candidate?

Note: The questions here are those that have frequently been used to collect information on job applicants. These questions are *not* being recommended. In general, any question may be asked, but the user should be sure that the information collected is related to the job for which the applicant is being considered—before using the information in selection decision making.

Source: Questions are based on H. C. Pryon, "The Use and Misuse of Previous Employer References in Hiring," *Management of Personnel Quarterly* 9 (1970): 15–22; Peter A. Rabinowitz, "Reference Auditing: An Essential Management Tool," *Personnel Administrator* 24 (1979): 37; Edward C. Andler and Dara Herbst, *The Complete Reference Checking Handbook*, 2nd ed. (New York, NY: AMACOM, 2004); and *Human Resources Guide*, ed. Robert J. Nobile, Sandra King, Steven C. Kahn, and David Rosen (Boston: West Group, A Thomson Company, 2000).

However, these methods may be necessary when searching public records. As organizations continue to integrate their HR management technologies with these new technologies, Internet and e-mail methods could significantly affect how organizations go about conducting reference checks. One relatively simple way to demonstrate this is to use Internet search engines to "Google" the applicant. This approach can yield relevant information about companies the applicant was affiliated with; it may provide news reports, press releases, or even personal "blogs" that disclose connections and personal characteristics that make the applicant an undesirable candidate. Finally, recent federal legislation makes references submitted electronically as legally binding as if the employer used the U.S. mail, a factor likely to increase the use of electronic reference checking.[188]

Mail Checks.   Reference checks requested through the mail use a written questionnaire or letter. To increase the likely response rate, the company should have the candidate sign a release form that gives the candidate's former employers permission to release information without liability for doing so. This form is sent with the written questionnaire or letter. With a questionnaire, reference givers are usually asked to rate an applicant on a variety of traits or characteristics. When used in this manner, reference checks resemble traditional employee job-performance ratings. Raters provide judgments of individual characteristics using some form of graduated rating scale. Space may also be provided for comments as well. Figure 9.4 presents one example of a typical reference questionnaire.

Reference checks collected through the mail can be a systematic, efficient means for collecting reference data. However, one of the biggest problems associated with mail questionnaires is their low return rate. This can present a significant problem for employers if some applicants have relevant reference information from letters while others do not. This problem is exacerbated if unfavorable and favorable reference responses have different rates of return. In such a case, the resulting information would necessarily be biased. There may be fewer unfavorable references returned because many employers are concerned that they are more likely to be sued over written information, especially if that information is negative.[189] The other concern with mail is that it tends to be a relatively slow way to get information; it can take weeks to get a reply.

Letters of Recommendation.   Another form that traditionally was mailed, but more and more is sent through e-mail is the letter of recommendation. In this case, references write a letter evaluating a job applicant. Reference givers may be asked to address specific questions about an applicant or simply told to express any comments of their choice. Although there do not appear to be comparative data on their frequency of use, letters of recommendation are probably restricted to high-skill or professional jobs. When properly completed by a knowledgeable reference, letters may provide greater depth of information on an applicant than that obtained on a rating scale. However, since letters of recommendation usually come from writers suggested by a job applicant, negative comments are seldom given.

Letters of recommendation are becoming increasingly positive. For example, a two-part national survey found that though writers of letters of recommendation claimed they would provide relevant negative information about candidates applying as interns to psychology programs, negative characteristics were found to be rarely disclosed.[190] A recent study found that less than 1 percent of references rate applicants as "below average" or "poor."[191] Rodney Miller and George Van Rybroek humorously asked, "Where are the other 90 percent?"[192] This leniency bias occurs for a number of reasons, including fear of diminished rapport with former colleagues and subordinates, retaliation or even violence, and legal repercussions. Evidence for the latter is shown by the finding that when letters of recommendation are kept confidential (that is, applicants waive their right to see the letter), the letter was rated less positive than those not kept confidential.[193]

There are few empirical studies about the predictive validity of the letter of recommendation method, even though they are commonly used. Julie McCarthy and Richard Goffin uncovered nine studies assessing the predictive validity of this method. They concluded that although the findings from early research (pre-1980) suggested that letters of recommendation have low predictive validity, more recent research reveals that when a more structured, rigorous evaluation approach is used, the validity results are higher.[194] For example, two studies involving graduate students and instructors in an academic setting found that specific traits (for example, mental ability, vigor, dependability, and so on) obtained from letters of recommendation could be reliably classified into general trait categories (for example, intelligence) and that adjectives dealing with these categories were predictive of student and instructor performance.[195] This approach reveals that a seemingly positive letter of recommendation may actually be "damning with faint praise." For example, if your former supervisor says you were "well intentioned" or "an average performer," it probably will not advance your candidacy. Other research suggests

FIGURE 9.4	Example of a Mail Questionnaire Reference Check

Sales Applicant Reference Check

We are in the process of considering *James Ridley Parrish* (SS Number: 123-45-6789) for a sales position in our firm. In considering him/her, it would be helpful if we could review your appraisal of his/her previous work with you. For your information, we have enclosed a statement signed by him/her authorizing us to contact you for information on his/her previous work experience with you. We would certainly appreciate it if you would provide us with your candid opinions of his/her employment. If you have any questions or comments you would care to make, please feel free to contact us at the number listed in the attached cover letter. At any rate, thank you for your consideration of our requests for the information requested below. As you answer the questions, please keep in mind that they should be answered in terms of your knowledge of his/her previous work with you.

1. When was he/she employed with your firm? From _____ to _____. Final Salary: _____.
2. Was he/she under your direct supervision? ❑ Yes ❑ No
3. If not, what was your working relationship with him/her? _____
   _____
4. How long have you had an opportunity to observe his/her job performance? _____
   _____
5. What was his/her last job title with your firm? _____
6. Did he/she supervise any employees? ❑ Yes ❑ No If so, how many? _____
7. Why did he/she leave your company? _____

Below is a series of questions that deal with how he/she might perform at the job for which we are considering him/her. Read the question and then use the rating scale to indicate how you think he/she would perform based on your previous knowledge of his/her work.

8. For him/her to perform best, how closely should he/she be supervised?
   ❑ Needs no supervision
   ❑ Needs infrequent supervision
   ❑ Needs close, frequent supervision
9. How well does he/she react to working with details?
   ❑ Gets easily frustrated
   ❑ Can handle work that involves some details but works better without them
   ❑ Details in a job pose no problem at all
10. How well do you think he/she can handle complaints from customers?
   ❑ Would generally refuse to help resolve a customer complaint
   ❑ Would help resolve a complaint only if a customer insisted
   ❑ Would feel the customer is right and do everything possible to resolve a complaint
11. In what type of sales job do you think he/she would be best?
   ❑ Handling sales of walk-in customers
   ❑ Traveling to customer locations out-of-town to make sales
12. With respect to his/her work habits, check *all* of the characteristics below that describe his/her *best* work situation:
   ❑ Works best on a regular schedule
   ❑ Works best under pressure
   ❑ Works best only when in the mood
   ❑ Works best when there is a regular series of steps to follow for solving a problem
13. Do you know of anything that would indicate that he/she would be an unfit or dangerous choice (for example, for working with customers or coworkers or driving an automobile) for a position with our organization?
   ❑ Yes ❑ No

   If "yes," please explain.
   _____

(Continued)

FIGURE 9.4 (*Continued*)

---

14. Would you rehire her/him?   ❑ Yes   ❑ No

15. If you have any additional comments, please make them on the back of this form.

Your Name: _____   Your Signature: _____

Your Title: _____

Address: _____

_____

City	State	ZIP

Company: _____

Telephone: _____   E-mail: _____

Thank you for your cooperation and prompt response to this inquiry. The information you provided will be very useful as we review all application materials.

Note: This form is completed by the reference giver.

---

that the length of the letter of recommendation was a better indicator of a reference giver's attitude toward the person written about than the content itself. This body of research shows that a long letter is more indicative of a positive attitude than a short letter. For example, one recent study found that the acceptance of candidates by letter of recommendation reviewers was related not only to the lack of negative information in the letter, but to its length as well.[196] These studies suggest that even if only positive comments are given, it may still be possible to obtain some indication of the writer's true feelings, and this information can be used to predict performance in the new job.

In part, an applicant's evaluation from a letter of recommendation depends on the individual reading the letter. George Tommasi and his colleagues found that although information indicative of the quality of an applicant influenced human resource managers' evaluations of applicants, some managers were influenced by job-irrelevant information such as the gender of the applicant and the gender and status of the letter writer.[197] They concluded that letters of recommendation could be improved by imposing a more structured format on the letter writer. In essence, they seem to be suggesting that employers should use a more structured format, such as one incorporating rating scales that the reference giver would then use to evaluate applicants on job-relevant dimensions. McCarthy and Goffin followed just such an approach and found that when referents compared candidates on a scale from 0 to 100 to the candidates' peers doing similar work, they found that ratings derived from 31 job-relevant attributes were significantly predictive of subsequent supervisory ratings of performance (multiple $r = 0.42$).[198]

One recent finding that is particularly troubling is that letters of recommendation may tell us more about the letter writers than about the candidates themselves. In one study, Tim Judge and Chad Higgins demonstrated that letter writers who possess a "positive" personality were more likely to write favorable letters than would reference writers who tended to be more critical or negative.[199] Two other studies found that letters written by the same letter writer about two separate candidates were actually found to be more consistent in content than two different authors describing the same candidate.[200] These results make it difficult to trust letters of recommendation as an accurate evaluation tool.

Consequently, even though there may be some positive aspects to letters of recommendation, some important disadvantages are associated with them. Some of these disadvantages include the following:

1. Writers have the difficult task of organizing the letter and deciding what to include. Thus, the job relevance of the information will vary across letter writers.

2. Letter quality will depend on the effort expended by the writers and their ability to express their thoughts.

3. Writers tend to be quite positive in their evaluations and often lack specificity and accuracy in letter writing.

4. The same job-relevant information will not be obtained on each applicant, which makes it hard to compare candidates.

5. Information relevant to areas or issues important to the hiring organization may be omitted in the letter.

6. The scoring of the letter is subjective and based on the reader's interpretation.[201]

Despite these disadvantages, the small possibility that letters of recommendation will produce important negative information about an applicant—and the fact that such information can have serious implications for a hiring organization—justify for most users the continued use of letters of recommendation as a reference-checking method.

In-Person Checks.   In-person checks involve face-to-face personal contact with a reference giver. This allows high levels of interaction, which may lead to more useful information being exchanged. Most often, these contacts are part of background investigations and concern jobs in which an incumbent is a potential security or financial risk. Although in-person contact may uncover information not captured by written methods, it is expensive, time-consuming, and often impractical. In-person checks are not frequently used in most selection programs.

Sources of Reference Data

Many different types of individuals, including friends, relatives, college professors, teachers, immediate supervisors, coworkers, subordinates, and HR managers, can serve as reference sources. For these data to be useful, reference givers must meet four conditions: (a) they must have had a chance to observe the candidate in relevant situations, (b) they must have knowledge of the candidate, (c) they must be competent to make the evaluations requested and be able to express themselves so their comments are understood as intended, and (d) they must want to give frank and honest assessments. Simply reviewing those whom the candidate has listed as references may provide the employer with useful information. For example, a candidate who lists all former bosses is often most forthright. In the following section, we report typical characteristics of the different sources of reference information that should be considered when conducting a reference check.

Former Employers.   As we have noted, former employers are an important source for verifying previous employment records and for evaluating an applicant's previous work habits and performance. If available, data from former employers will more than likely be released through a personnel office. Information from previous supervisors is particularly valuable, because the supervisor is able to evaluate the candidate's performance in light of the organization's overall objectives and in comparison to others who are similarly situated. A supervisor who has had direct experience with, or firsthand knowledge of, the applicant at work is often the best person to provide the reference. References from employers will be more useful and accurate as the reference givers' experience with and knowledge of the applicant increases.

Personal References.   Personal references supplied by the applicant are another source of information. As might be expected, most applicants choose those individuals they believe they will give a positive evaluation. If personal references are requested, they should be contacted. Through careful questioning, it may be possible to obtain useful information about the applicant. Personal references can provide information about the applicant's prior employment and detailed descriptions of the candidate's qualities and behavior characteristics. It is important to ask how long and in what capacity the reference has known the applicant.

Investigative Agencies.   At a cost of several hundred dollars per applicant, investigative agencies will conduct background checks on applicants. Background checks focus on resume and application information, educational accomplishments, credit ratings, police and driving records, personal reputation, lifestyle, and other information. These investigative agencies often obtain more detailed information about a candidate than other sources can; this may be helpful for making the hiring decision and for building a defense against a claim of negligent hiring (discussed earlier in this chapter). However, investigative agencies are expensive and require more time for obtaining results. Many of these checks take the form of consumer reports, of which two basic types exist:[202]

1. *Consumer reports*—Any written or oral communication collected by an agency concerning an individual's credit standing, character, general reputation, or personal characteristics used to establish an individual's eligibility for employment. The Fair Credit Reporting Act (15 U.S.C. 1681), as amended by the Consumer Credit Reporting Reform Act of 1996 (CCRRA) and further amended by the Consumer Reporting Employment Clarification Act of 1998 (CRECA), reveals that inquiries about the candidate's financial status and credit rating should be obtained only where there is a legitimate business necessity for the information. Although this is a sensitive area, employment generally qualifies as a legitimate business necessity.[203]

2. *Investigative consumer reports*—A consumer report or part of a consumer report concerning an applicant that is based on personal interviews with an applicant's friends, neighbors, or acquaintances. Federal and state laws impose certain requirements that employers must meet *before* and *when* taking adverse action against a candidate based on information contained in the consumer report. For example, use of a credit check requires that the employer must obtain the candidate's written authorization and provide the candidate with a clear and conspicuous disclosure of how and whether the credit information will be used for employment purposes. Furthermore, if a job offer is not made to an applicant because of information included in a consumer report, the individual must be so informed. The employer must indicate the name, address, and telephone number of the consumer reporting agency making the report and provide information about how to check and correct (if necessary) the agency's report.[204]

Public Records.   In addition to the sources just listed, public records also include useful information. As with any application information, an employer should use caution when accessing public records. *The employer should be sure that the information solicited does not discriminate against a protected group and that it can be justified by the nature of the job for which applicant screening is being undertaken.* With this caution in mind, public records can be searched rather easily. These records include the following:[205]

1. *Criminal records*—Before using these records, an employer should check to see whether such use is likely to discriminate against a protected group and whether there is actual business necessity for using criminal record information. Furthermore, employers must be aware of state and local laws regarding criminal conviction inquiries.[206] A search of criminal records is often required for jobs that involve high degrees of public contact, have limited supervision, involve working at private residences or other businesses, involve personal care of others (such as children), or have direct access to others' personal belongings, valuables, or merchandise. Assuming that such information is needed and can be used, there are two ways to collect criminal record data. First, if allowed by law, the employer can access the state's central criminal record repository. Each state has such a repository. Second, criminal record data are available from counties where the candidate has lived or worked. State police records are also sources of information. Whatever the source used, there are several points to keep in mind. Criminal record data may be inaccurate or incomplete. If employment is not offered to an applicant because of his or her criminal record, employers covered by the Fair Credit Reporting Act must disclose to the applicant the name, address, and telephone number of the agency reporting the criminal record. The applicant must be given an opportunity to check the records. Criminal convictions cannot serve as an absolute bar to employment. Users of criminal record data should consider factors such as the nature and seriousness of the offense, the relation of the offense to the nature of the job sought, the individual's attempts at rehabilitation, and the length of time between the conviction and the employment decision.

2. *Motor vehicle department records*—Driving record information can be obtained from the state department of motor vehicles. Driving records should be obtained only when driving is an essential function of the job. Information is available about traffic violations, license suspension or revocation, and other offenses such as driving under the influence of alcohol or drugs. In addition, these records can be used to check the name, birthdate, address, and physical description of an applicant. This is useful for identifying falsified information given on the application form and for confirming that applicants are who they claim to be.

3. *Workers' compensation records*—These records are usually available from a state agency, although the organization and completeness of the records can vary from one state to the next. They show the types and number of claims that have been filed by an individual. The Americans with Disabilities Act (ADA) prohibits an employer from asking about a worker's compensation claims during selection. However, a job offer can be contingent upon the candidate passing a medical examination, which could include information about the candidate's workers' compensation history.

4. *Federal court records*—Civil and criminal federal court case information is available through federal court records. If the employer knows where an applicant has lived or worked, it's possible to search federal court records to identify civil, criminal, or bankruptcy cases in which an individual has been involved. Information about violations of federal law can be obtained through the National Criminal Information Center (NCIC) and the National Instant Check System

(NICS). A person's name and social security number can be run through both systems to search multiple databases that hold the names of millions of people. At present it is illegal for any employers but the government to use these systems for employment purposes.

5. *Educational records*—We have pointed out the importance of checking educational records. Many universities and colleges will verify an individual's dates of attendance and degrees held. Surveys have shown that a large percentage of colleges will provide the information over the telephone; many will send an applicant's actual transcript when the proper requesting procedures are followed. For example, schools may require a signed authorization from the candidate before releasing educational records to a prospective employer. Employers should obtain written consent on the application or on a separate release form.

Social Media

Many employers apparently are using social media (e.g., Facebook, LinkedIn, Twitter) to conduct their own informal "reference checks," as hiring managers report viewing these sites to evaluate whether the job candidate is presenting him or herself professionally, or to learn more about the candidate's qualifications, personality, even evidence of communication skills and creativity.[207] In this same article, it was suggested that this information is used as often to screen out a candidate as to lead them to hire the candidate. The caution emphasized earlier about the use of public records seems germane to the use of social media too: *The employer should be sure that the information solicited does not discriminate against a protected group and that it can be justified by the nature of the job for which applicant screening is being undertaken.*

Employers sometimes contract with outside firms to run background checks on applicants. A typical check will cost from $50 to $200 and require 1 to 5 days to complete. If a background investigation firm is used, employers should understand that the firm is serving as the employer's agent; the employer may be held liable for the agent's actions. It is important to evaluate carefully any firm hired to undertake background investigations. *The Sourcebook to Public Record Information*, available from BRB Publications at http://BRBPub.com, is a comprehensive reference book that many employers find useful for accessing information contained on public records.

Recommended Steps for Using Reference Checks

From legal and practical perspectives, employers wanting to use reference checks should undertake several steps.

1. **Reference data are most properly used when the data involve job-related concerns**. Requested data should address WRCs of the applicant that are necessary for successful job performance. Emphasis should be given to those characteristics that distinguish effective from ineffective performance. How do we identify which WRCs are critical? As we discussed in earlier chapters, we make the determination based on an analysis of the job for which we are selecting employees. If questions or ratings are restricted to those that can be demonstrated as related to the job, then there should be no difficulties.

2. **Because we are tailoring the content of our reference check to the content of a specific job, we will likely need more than one general form for all positions**

in an organization. At the very least, we will need a reference form for each cluster or family of jobs that require similar WRCs. Multiple forms obviously add multiple costs and additional work. But if we are going to obtain useful, legal selection data, and if we choose to use reference checks, multiple forms will probably be necessary.

3. **Reference checks are subject to the *Uniform Guidelines*.** As for any selection measure, it's important to monitor the fairness and validity of the reference check. If our reference checking system unfairly discriminates against protected groups or is not related to job success, we should change or eliminate our system. To do otherwise is not only legally foolish but jeopardizes our ability to choose competent employees.

4. **A more structured reference checking system (for example, a system that focuses on factual or behavioral data related to the applicant), rather than an unstructured system (such as one focusing on general overall evaluative judgments), is less likely to be open to charges of discrimination**. Methods that rely on greater structure are more amenable to the development of scoring procedures, reliability, and validity analyses. Such methods consist of those that focus on behaviors and have a specific scoring system. Structured approaches also help to ensure that the same information is obtained systematically on all applicants, and that the information is used in a consistent manner. Information that qualifies or disqualifies one applicant must qualify or disqualify all. Written recommendations (such as a letter of reference) followed by a brief review often lead to subjective impressions and hunches that may not be valid. If we use these measures in our selection program, we should be aware that unstructured ratings are woefully inadequate.

5. **Applicants should be asked to give written permission to contact their references**, including educational institutions, former employers, past and present landlords, credit bureaus, and other sources the employer relies on. When prospective employers actually contact references, the employer should also collect information on how long that reference giver has known an applicant and the position the reference giver holds. This information can be useful for verifying responses or, if necessary, legally proving that the person contacted is in a position to provide the assessments being requested.

6. **Reference takers collecting information by telephone or in person should be trained in how to interview reference givers**. Reference takers must be prepared to formulate questions and record responses systematically. Here again, a structured approach to information collection will improve the quality of the data ultimately collected.

7. **All reference check information should be recorded in writing**. If a legal suit is brought against an employer, reference data may serve as important evidence in defending against the suit. Documentation in writing is essential for the defense.

8. **If a job applicant provides references but reference information cannot be obtained, ask the applicant for additional references**. Consider *not* hiring an applicant if complete reference information is not available. Hiring an applicant without such information can be risky.

9. **Check all application form and resume information**. In particular, focus on educational background (for example, schools attended, degrees earned, academic

performance) and previous employment records (for example, dates of employment, job titles, duties performed). Gaps in information reported are red flags that signal a need for special attention. For instance, an individual may have recently spent time in jail for a crime directly related to the position to which he or she is applying.

10. A caveat on the use of negative information: Negative information received during a reference check frequently serves as a basis for rejecting an applicant. Caution is advised in using *any* negative data as a basis for excluding applicants. **Before negative information is employed, prospective employers should (a) verify its accuracy with other sources, (b) be sure that disqualification on the basis of the information will distinguish between those who will fail and those who will succeed on the job, and (c) use the same information consistently for all applicants.**

As you read the literature on reference data, note an apparent pattern. Practitioner-oriented journals tend to view reference checks as playing an important role in HR selection. Apparently, the belief is that reference checks provide information not given by other measures. In contrast, articles in research-oriented journals generally regard reference checks as a relatively minor selection tool. Research studies investigating the utility of selection devices have typically concluded that references are not especially useful. Although reference reports may not be as useful as other measures in predicting employee job success, they may be the *only* basis for detecting some information that would indicate unsatisfactory job performance. In this role, reference data will serve as a basis for identifying a relatively small number of applicants who should not be considered further for a job. However, it may not be efficient to incorporate reference checks in the selection of applicants for every job in an organization. The decision about whether to employ reference checks will vary across organizations and jobs. But we suggest that the higher the responsibility level associated with a particular position—or the greater the risk posed by the position to customers, clients, and coworkers—the greater the need for a reference check.

SUMMARY

Earlier in the chapter, we examined application blanks, training and experience (T&E) ratings, and reference checks as measures that can be used in employee selection. Application forms, resumes, reference checks, and ratings of training, education, and experience are relatively inexpensive and easy to collect. The data can provide useful information for predicting which applicants are likely to be high performers, although these selection devices do not have high predictive validities. Applicants expect to provide this information and see it as having high face validity. Collecting basic background information enables one to ensure the applicant has the minimal skills and qualifications to do the job. Practically, at this point, there are a large number of applicants to consider; one must screen out scores of applicants to reduce the pool to a manageable set of candidates who are suited for the job. At this stage we have a small selection ratio; it is not unusual to eliminate 70 percent to 90 percent of all applicants during the first cut. After these initial cuts, we proceed to more expensive, time-consuming selection devices such as the interview, tests, even an assessment center. Even if the predictive validity for the selection tool (for example, a semi-structured application blank) is only modest, it can still have very high value due to the small selection ratio. In conclusion, we strongly encourage those making hiring decisions to carefully consider each piece of information that is requested in the early stages of selection; there is considerable utility to be gained by rigorously measuring minimum qualifications and applicant ability and motivation at this stage.

REFERENCES

1. H. C. Taylor and J. T. Russell, "The Relationship of Validity Coefficients to the Practical Effectiveness of Tests in Selection," *Journal of Applied Psychology* 23 (1939): 565–578.

2. Ibid.

3. James A. Breaugh, "The Use of Biodata for Employee Selection: Past Research and Future Directions," *Human Resource Management Review* 19 (2009): 219–231.

4. Adrian Furnham, "HR Professionals' Beliefs about and Knowledge of Assessment Techniques and Psychometric Tests," *International Journal of Selection and Assessment* 16 (2008): 300–305.

5. Robert E. Ployhart, Jeff A. Weekley, Brian C. Holtz, and C. Kemp, "Web-based and Paper-and-pencil Testing of Applicants in a Proctored Setting: Are Personality, Biodata, and Situational Judgment Tests Comparable?" *Personnel Psychology* 56 (2003): 733–752; and Chad H. Van Iddekinge, Carl E. Eidson, Jeffrey D. Kudisch, and Andrew M. Goldblatt, "A Biodata Inventory Administered via Interactive Voice Technology (IVR) Technology: Predictive Validity, Utility, and Subgroup Differences," *Journal of Business and Psychology* 18 (2003): 145–156.

6. James A. Breaugh, "The Use of Biodata for Employee Selection: Past Research and Future Directions," *Human Resource Management Review* 19 (2009): 219–231; and Fred A. Mael, "A Conceptual Rationale for the Domain and Attributes of Biodata Items," *Personnel Psychology* 44 (1991): 763–792.

7. B. J. Nickels, "The Nature of Biodata," In *Biodata Handbook,* eds. Garret A. Stokes, Michael D. Mumford, and William A. Owens (Palo Alto, CA: Consulting Psychologists Press, 1994): 1–16; and Matthew S. O'Connell, Keith Hattrup, Dennis Doverspike, and Alana Cober, "The Validity of 'Mini' Simulations for Mexican Salespeople," *Journal of Business and Psychology* 16 (October, 2004): 593–599.

8. Joel Lefkowitz, Melissa I. Gebbia, Tamar Balsam, and Linda Dunn, "Dimensions of Biodata Items and Their Relationship to Item Validity," *Journal of Occupational and Organizational Psychology* 72 (1999): 331–350; Michael K. Mount, L. A. Witt, and Murray R. Barrick, "Incremental Validity of Empirically Keyed Biodata Scales Over GMA and the Five Factor Personality Constructs," *Personnel Psychology* 53 (2000): 299–323; M. A. Oviedo-Garcia, "Internal Validation of a Biodata Extraversion Scale," *Social Behavior and Personality* 35 (2007): 675–692; Howard Sisco and Richard R. Reilly, "Development and Validation of a Biodata Inventory as an Alternative Method to Measurement of the Five Factor Model of Personality," *The Social Science Journal* 44 (2007): 383–389; and Chad H. Van Iddekinge, Carl E. Eidson, Jeffrey D. Kudisch, and Andrew M. Goldblatt, "A Biodata Inventory Administered via Interactive Voice Technology (IVR) Technology: Predictive Validity, Utility, and Subgroup Differences," *Journal of Business and Psychology* 18 (2003): 145–156.

9. James A. Breaugh, "The Use of Biodata for Employee Selection: Past Research and Future Directions," *Human Resource Management Review* 19 (2009): 219–231; Fred A. Mael, "A Conceptual Rationale for the Domain and Attributes of Biodata Items," *Personnel Psychology* 44 (1991): 763–792; and Neal Schmitt, Danielle Jennings, and Rebecca Toney, "Can We Develop Measures of Hypothetical Constructs?" *Human Resource Management Review* 9 (1999): 169–183.

10. George W. England, *Development and Use of Weighted Application Blanks* (Minneapolis: Industrial Relations Center, University of Minnesota, 1971), 60–65.

11. George W. England, *Development and Use of Weighted Application Blanks* (Minneapolis: Industrial Relations Center, University of Minnesota, 1971), 60–65; Raymond Lee and Jerome M. Booth, "A Utility Analysis of a Weighted Application Blank Designed to Predict Turnover for Clerical Employees," *Journal of Applied Psychology* 59 (1974): 516–518; and Ann Marie Ryan and Robert E. Ployhart, "A Century of Selection," *Annual Review of Psychology* 65 (2014): 1–25.

12. Fred A. Mael, "A Conceptual Rationale for the Domain and Attributes of Biodata Items," *Personnel Psychology* 44 (1991): 763–792.

13. Paul F. Wernimont and John P. Campbell, "Signs, Samples, and Criteria," *Journal of Applied Psychology* 52 (October 1968): 372–376; and William A. Owens, "Background Data," in *Handbook of Industrial and Organizational Psychology*, ed. Marvin Dunnette (Chicago: Rand-McNally, 1976), 252–293.

14. Murray R. Barrick and Ryan D. Zimmerman, "Reducing Voluntary, Avoidable Turnover through Selection," *Journal of Applied Psychology* 90 (2005): 159–166.

15. Leatta Hough and Cheryl Paullin, "Construct-oriented Scale Construction," in *Biodata Handbooks*, eds. Garnett Stokes, Michael D. Mumford, and William A. Owens (Palo Alto, CA: Consulting Psychologists Press, 1994), 109–145; and Neal Schmitt, Danielle Jennings, and Rebecca Toney, "Can We Develop Measures of Hypothetical Constructs?" *Human Resource Management Review* 9 (1999): 169–183.

16. William A. Owens, "Background Data," in *Handbook of Industrial and Organizational Psychology*, ed. Marvin Dunnette (Chicago: Rand-McNally, 1976), 252–293.

17. James J. Asher, "The Biographical Item: Can It Be Improved?" *Personnel Psychology* 25 (1979): 759.

18. Craig J. Russell, "Selecting Top Corporate Leaders: An Example of Biographical Information," *Journal of Management* 6 (1990): 73–86.

19. J. Russell Craig, Joyce Mattson, Steven E. Devlin, and David Atwater, "Predictive Validity of Biodata Items Generated from Retrospective Life Experience Essays," *Journal of Applied Psychology* 75 (1990): 569–580.

20. Philip Bobko, Philip L. Roth, and Denise Potosky, "Derivation and Implications of a Meta-Analytic Matrix Incorporating Cognitive Ability, Alternative Predictors, and Job Performance," *Personnel Psychology* 52 (1999): 573.

21. John E. Hunter and Rhonda F. Hunter, "Validity and Utility of Alternative Predictors of Job Performance," *Psychological Bulletin* 96 (1984): 72–98; and Neal Schmitt, Richard Z. Gooding, Raymond A. Noe, and Michael Kirsch, "Metaanalysis of Validity Studies Published between 1964 and 1982 and the Investigation of Study Characteristics," *Personnel Psychology* 37 (1984): 407–422.

22. Thomas Bliesener, "Methodological Moderators in Validating Biographical Data in Personnel Selection," *Journal of Occupational and Organizational Psychology* 69 (1996): 107–120; Kevin D. Carlson, Steven E. Scullen, Frank L. Schmidt, Hannah Rothstein, and Frank Erwin, "Generalizable Biographical Data Validity Can Be Achieved Without Multi-Organizational Development and Keying," *Personnel Psychology* 5 (1999): 731–755; John Hunter and Ronda Hunter, "The Validity and Utility of Alternative Predictors of Job Performance," *Psychological Bulletin* 96 (1984): 72–98; Frank L. Schmidt and John E. Hunter, "The Validity and Utility of Selection Methods in Personnel Psychology: Practical and Theoretical Implications of 85 Years of Research Findings," *Psychological Bulletin* 124 (1998): 262–274; Neal Schmitt, Richard Z. Gooding, Raymond A. Noe, and Michael Kirsch, "Metaanalysis of Validity Studies Published between 1964 and 1982 and the Investigation of Study Characteristics," *Personnel*

Psychology 37 (1984): 407–422; and Andrew J. Vinchur, Jeffrey S. Shippmann, Fred S. Switzer, and Phillip L. Roth, "A Meta-Analytic Review of Predictors of Job Performance for Salespeople," *Journal of Applied Psychology* 83 (1998): 586–597.

23. Hannah R. Rothstein, Frank L. Schmidt, Frank W. Erwin, William A. Owens, and C. Paul Sparks, "Biographical Data in Employment Selection: Can Validities Be Made Generalizable?" *Journal of Applied Psychology* 75 (1990): 175–184.

24. Kevin D. Carlson, Steven E. Scullen, Frank L. Schmidt, Hannah Rothstein, and Frank Erwin, "Generalizable Biographical Data Validity Can Be Achieved Without Multi-Organizational Development and Keying," *Personnel Psychology* 52 (1999): 731–755.

25. Ibid., 745.

26. Garnett S. Stokes, James B. Hogan, and Andrea F. Snell, "Comparability of Incumbent and Applicant Samples for the Development of Biodata Keys: The Influence of Social Desirability," *Personnel Psychology* 46 (1993): 739–762.

27. Thomas Bliesener, "Methodological Moderators in Validating Biographical Data in Personnel Selection," *Journal of Occupational and Organizational Psychology* 69 (1996): 107–120.

28. Crystal M. Harold, Lynn A. McFarland, and Jeff A. Weekley, "The Validity of Verifiable and Non-Verifiable Biodata Items: An Examination Across Applicants and Incumbents," *International Journal of Selection and Assessment* 14 (2006): 336–346.

29. Schmidt and Hunter, "The Validity and Utility of Selection Methods in Personnel Psychology: Practical and Theoretical Implications of 85 Years of Research Findings," 269.

30. Bobko, Roth, and Potosky, "Derivation and Implications of a Meta-Analytic Matrix Incorporating Cognitive Ability, Alternative Predictors, and Job Performance," 562, and Michael D. Mumford, Jamie D. Barrett, and Kimberly S. Hester, "Background Data: Use of Experiential Knowledge in Personnel Selection," *Oxford Handbook of Personnel Assessment and Selection* (2012): 353–383.

31. Hunter and Hunter, "Validity and Utility of Alternative Predictors of Job Performance."

32. Gary J. Lautenschlager, "Accuracy and Faking of Background Data," in *Biodata Handbook*, ed. Garnett S. Stokes, Michael D. Mumford, and William A. Owens (Palo Alto, CA: Consulting Psychologists Press, 1994), 391–419; Lynn A. McFarland and Ann Marie Ryan, "Variance in Faking Across Noncognitive Measures," *Journal of Applied Psychology* 85 (2000): 812–821; Thomas E. Becker and Alan L. Colquitt, "Potential versus Actual Faking of a Biodata Form: An Analysis Along Several Dimensions of Item Type," *Personnel Psychology* 45 (1992): 389–406; Stephen A. Dwight and John J. Donovan, "Do Warnings Not to Fake Reduce Faking?" *Human Performance* 16 (2003): 1–23; and John J. Donovan, Stephen A. Dwight, and Gregory M. Hurtz, "An Assessment of the Prevalence, Severity, and Verifiability of Entry-Level Applicant Faking Using the Randomized Response Technique," *Human Performance* 16 (2003): 81–106.

33. Lautenschlager, "Accuracy and Faking of Background Data"; and Fred Morgeson, Michael Campion, Robert L. Dipboye, John R. Hollenbeck, Kevin Murphy, and Neal Schmitt, "Reconsidering the Use of Personality Tests in Personnel Selection Contexts," *Personnel Psychology* 60 (2007): 683–729.

34. Barbara Kate Repa, "Resume Inflation: Two Wrongs May Mean No Rights," *Nolo.com* (August 8, 2001); Edward C. Andler and Dara Herbst, *The Complete Reference Checking Handbook*, 2nd ed. (New York, NY: AMACOM, 2004); Lisa Teuchi Cullen, "Getting Wise to Lies," *Time* (May 1, 2006): 59; and Steven D. Levitt and Stephen J. Dubner, *Freakonomics: A Rogue Economist Explores the Hidden Side of Everything,* New York, NY: Harper Collins, 2006.

35. Neal Schmitt and Frederick L. Oswald, "The Impact of Corrections for Faking on the Validity of Noncognitive Measures in Selection Settings," *Journal of Applied Psychology* 91 (2006): 613–621; Margaret A. McManus and Jaci Jarrett Masztal, "The Impact of Biodata Item Attributes on Validity and Socially Desirable Responding," *Journal of Business and Psychology* 12, no. 3 (1999): 437–446; Murray R. Barrick and Michael K. Mount, "Effects of Impression Management and Self-Deception on the Predictive Validity of Personality Constructs," *Journal of Applied Psychology* 81 (1996): 261–272; and Becker and Colquitt, "Potential versus Actual Faking of a Biodata Form: An Analysis Along Several Dimensions of Item Type."

36. Schmitt and Oswald, "The Impact of Corrections for Faking on the Validity of Noncognitive Measures in Selection Settings."

37. Becker and Colquitt, "Potential versus Actual Faking of a Biodata Form: An Analysis Along Several Dimensions of Item Type"; Garnett S. Stokes, James B. Hogan, and Andrea F. Snell, "Comparability of Incumbent and Applicant Samples for the Development of Biodata Keys: The Influence of Social Desirability," *Personnel Psychology* 46 (1993): 739–762; Lautenschlager, "Accuracy and Faking of Background Data"; and Kenneth E. Graham, Michael A. McDaniel, Elizabeth F. Douglas, and Andrea F. Snell, "Biodata Validity Decay and Score Inflation with Faking: Do Item Attributes Explain Variance across Items?" *Journal of Business and Psychology* 16 (2002): 573–592.

38. Neal Schmitt and C. Kunce, "The Effects of Required Elaboration of Answers to Biodata Measures," *Personnel Psychology* 55 (2002): 569–588; Neal Schmitt, Fred L. Oswald, Brian H. Kim, Michael A. Gillespie, Lauren J. Ramsay, and Tae-Yong Yoo, "Impact of Elaboration on Socially Desirable Responding and the Validity of Biodata Measures," *Journal of Applied Psychology* 88 (2003): 979–988; Dwight and Donovan, "Do Warnings Not to Fake Reduce Faking?"; and Donovan, Dwight, and Hurtz, "An Assessment of the Prevalence, Severity, and Verifiability of Entry-Level Applicant Faking Using the Randomized Response Technique."

39. Dwight and Donovan, "Do Warnings Not to Fake Reduce Faking?"; and Donovan, Dwight, and Hurtz, "An Assessment of the Prevalence, Severity, and Verifiability of Entry-Level Applicant Faking Using the Randomized Response Technique."

40. Timothy S. Bland and Sue S. Stalcup, "Build a Legal Employment Application," *HR Magazine* 44 (1999): 129–133.

41. *Jenkins v. Eastern Capital Corp.*, 846 F. Supp. 864 (N.D. Cal 1994).

42. Neal Schmitt and Charles Kunce, "The Effects of Required Elaboration of Answers to Biodata Questions," *Personnel Psychology* 55 (2002): 569–587; Neal Schmitt, Fred L. Oswald, Brian H. Kim, Michael A. Gillespie, Lauren J Ramsay, and Tae-Yong Yoo, "Impact of Elaboration on Socially Desirable Responding and the Validity of Biodata Measures," *Journal of Applied Psychology* 88 (2005): 979–988.

43. "Equal Employment Opportunity Commission," *Guide to Pre-Employment Inquiries* (Washington, DC: Equal Employment Opportunity Commission, August 1981), 1.

44. Ibid.

45. Ernest C. Miller, "An EEO Examination of Employment Applications," *Personnel Administrator* 25 (March 1981): 63–70; Debra D. Burrington, "A Review of State Government Employment Application Forms for Suspect Inquiries," *Public Personnel Management* 11 (1982): 55–60; and Richard S. Lowell and Jay A. Deloach, "Equal Employment Opportunity: Are You Overlooking the Application Form?" *Personnel* 59 (1982): 49–55.

46. Miller, "An EEO Examination of Employment Applications."

47. Burrington, "A Review of State Government Employment Application Forms for Suspect Inquiries."

48. Lowell and Deloach, "Equal Employment Opportunity: Are You Overlooking the Application Form?"

49. J. Craig Wallace and Stephen J. Vodanovich, "Personnel Application Blanks: Persistence and Knowledge of Legally Inadvisable Application Blank Items," *Public Personnel Management* 33 (Fall 2004): 331–349.

50. J. Craig Wallace, Mary G. Tye, and Stephen J. Vodanovich, "Applying for Jobs Online: Examining the Legality of Internet-Based Application Forms," *Public Personnel Management* 4 (Winter 2000): 497–504.

51. Stephen J. Vodanovich and Rosemary H. Lowe, "They Ought to Know Better: The Incidence and Correlates of Inappropriate Application Blank Inquiries," *Public Personnel Management* 21 (1992): 363–370.

52. James P. Jolly and James G. Frierson, "Playing It Safe," *Personnel Administrator* 25 (1989): 63–81.

53. R. Bryan Kethley and David E. Terpstra, "An Analysis of Litigation Associated with the Use of the Application Form in the Selection Process," *Public Personnel Management* 34 (2005): 357–373.

54. Garnett S. Stokes, "Introduction to Special Issue: The Next One Hundred Years of Biodata," *Human Resource Management Review* 9 (1999): 111–116.

55. James C. Sharf, "The Impact of Legal and Equal Employment Opportunity Issues on Personal History Inquiries," in *Biodata Handbook*, ed. Garnett S. Stokes, Michael D. Mumford, and William A. Owens (Palo Alto, CA: CPP Books, 1994): 370.

56. Mumford, Cooper, and Schemmer, *Development of a Content Valid Set of Background Data Measures.*

57. Dianna L. Stone and Eugene F. Stone, "Effects of Missing Application Blank Information on Personnel Selection Decisions: Do Privacy Protection Strategies Bias the Outcome?" *Journal of Applied Psychology* 72 (1987): 452–456.

58. Mumford, Barrett, and Hester, "Background Data: Use of Experiential Knowledge in Personnel Selection," and Owens, "Background Data."

59. Reilly and Chao, "Validity and Fairness of Some Alternative Employee Selection Procedures," 1–62; Vodanovich and Lowe, "They Ought to Know Better: The Incidence and Correlates of Inappropriate Application Blank Inquiries"; and Wallace and Vodanovich, "Personnel Application Blanks: Persistence and Knowledge of Legally Inadvisable Application Blank Items."

60. Bobko, Roth, and Potosky, "Derivation and Implications of a Meta-Analytic Matrix Incorporating Cognitive Ability, Alternative Predictors, and Job Performance"; and Schmidt and Hunter, "The Validity and Utility of Selection Methods in Personnel Psychology: Practical and Theoretical Implications of 85 Years of Research Findings," 269.

61. J. Craig Wallace and Stephen J. Vodanovich, "Personnel Application Blanks: Persistence and Knowledge of Legally Inadvisable Application Blank Items," *Public Personnel Management* 33 (Fall 2004): 331–349; J. Craig Wallace, Mary G. Tye, and Stephen J. Vodanovich, "Applying for Jobs Online: Examining the Legality of Internet-Based Application Forms," *Public Personnel Management* 4 (Winter 2000): 497–504; Stephen J. Vodanovich and Rosemary H. Lowe, "They Ought to Know Better: The Incidence and Correlates of Inappropriate Application Blank Inquiries," *Public Personnel Management* 21 (1992): 363–370; James P. Jolly and James G. Frierson, "Playing It Safe," *Personnel Administrator* 25 (1989): 63–81; and R. Bryan Kethley and David E. Terpstra, "An Analysis of Litigation Associated with the Use of the Application Form in the Selection Process," *Public Personnel Management* 34 (2005): 357–373.

62. Rothstein et al., "Biographical Data in Selection: Can Validities Be Made Generalizable?"; and Carlson et al., "Generalizable Biographical Data Can Be Achieved without Multi-Organizational Development and Keying."

63. Carlson et al., "Generalizable Biographical Data Can Be Achieved without Multi-Organizational Development and Keying."

64. Murray R. Barrick and Ryan D. Zimmerman, "Reducing Voluntary, Avoidable Turnover through Selection," *Journal of Applied Psychology* 90 (1999): 159–166.

65. Leaetta M. Hough, Fred L. Oswald, and Rob E. Ployhart, "Determinants, Detection and Amelioration of Adverse Impact in Personnel Selection Procedures: Issues, Evidence, and Lessons Learned," *International Journal of Selection and Assessment* 9 (2001): 152–194.

66. Timothy S. Bland and Sue S. Stalcup, "Build a Legal Employment Application," *HR Magazine* 44 (1999): 129–133.

67. John P. Hausknecht, David V. Day, and Scott C. Thomas, "Applicant Reactions to Selection Procedures: An Updated Model and Meta-Analysis," *Personnel Psychology* 57 (2004): 639–683.

68. Brad S. Bell, Ann Marie Ryan, and Darrin Weichmann, "Justice Expectations and Applicant Perceptions," *International Journal of Selection and Assessment* 12 (2004): 24–38; Ann Marie Ryan and Robert E. Ployhart, "Applicants' Perceptions of Selection Procedures and Decisions: A Critical Review and Agenda for the Future," *Journal of Management* 26 (2000): 565–606; Sara L. Rynes and Mary L. Connerley, "Applicant Reactions to Alternative Selection Procedures," *Journal of Business and Psychology* 7 (1993): 261–277; Donald M. Truxillo, Talya N. Bauer, Michael A. Campion, and M. E. Paronto, "Selection Fairness Information and Applicant Reactions: A Longitudinal Field Study," *Journal of Applied Psychology* 87 (2002): 1020–1031; and Donald M. Truxillo, Dirk D. Steiner, and Stephen W. Gilliland, "The Importance of Organizational Justice in Personnel Selection: Defining When Selection Fairness Really Matters," *International Journal of Selection and Assessment* 12, no. 1 (2004): 39–53.

69. Truxillo, Steiner, and Gilliland, "The Importance of Organizational Justice in Personnel Selection: Defining When Selection Fairness Really Matters."

70. Ryan and Ployhart, "Applicants' Perceptions of Selection Procedures and Decisions: A Critical Review and Agenda for the Future"; Hausknecht, Day, and Thomas, "Applicant Reactions to Selection Procedures: An Updated Model and Meta-Analysis"; and Alan M. Saks, Joanne D. Leck, and David M. Saunders, "Effects of Application Blanks and Employment Equity on Applicant Reactions and Job Pursuit Interactions," *Journal of Organizational Behavior* 16 (1995): 415–430.

71. Wallace, Tye, and Vodanovich, "Applying for Jobs Online: Examining the Legality of Internet-Based Application Forms"; and Department of Fair Employment and Housing, "State of California," *Pre-Employment Inquiry Guidelines* (Sacramento, CA: Department of Fair Employment and Housing, May 1982).

72. Wallace and Vodanovich, "Personnel Application Blanks: Persistence and Knowledge of Legally Inadvisable Application Blank Items"; Wallace, Tye, and Vodanovich, "Applying for Jobs Online: Examining the Legality of Internet-based Application Forms"; and Ernest C. Miller, "An EEO Examination of Employment Applications."

73. Alan M. Saks, Joanne D. Leck, and David M. Saunders, "Effects of Application Blanks and Employment Equity on Applicant Reactions and Job Pursuit Interactions," *Journal of Organizational Behavior* 16 (1995): 415–430.

74. *Human Resources Guide;* and Ernest C. Miller, "An EEO Examination of Employment Applications."

75. Andler and Herbst, *The Complete Reference Checking Handbook*, 2nd ed. Sandra King, Steven C. Kahn, and David Rosen, *Human Resources Guide*, ed. Robert J. Nobile (Boston: West Group, A Thomson Company, 2000); and Philip Ash, "Law and Regulation of Preemployment Inquiries," *Journal of Business and Psychology* 5 (1991): 291–308.

76. Wallace and Vodanovich, "Personnel Application Blanks: Persistence and Knowledge of Legally Inadvisable Application Blank Items."

77. Richard R. Reilly and Georgia T. Chao, "Validity and Fairness of Some Alternative Employee Selection Procedures," *Personnel Psychology* 35 (1982): 1–63.

78. Kethley and Terpstra, "An Analysis of Litigation Associated with the Use of the Application Form in the Selection Process."

79. Garnett Stokes and L. A. Cooper, "Content/Construct Approaches in Life History Form Development for Selection," *International Journal of Selection and Assessment* 9 (2001): 138–151; Erich P. Prien and Garry L. Hughes, "A Content-Oriented Approach to Setting Minimum Qualifications," *Public Personnel Management* 33, no. 1 (2004): 89–104; and Elizabeth Allworth and Beryl Hesketh, "Job Requirements Biodata as a Predictor of Performance in Customer Service Roles," *International Journal of Selection and Assessment* 8 (2000): 137–147.

80. James R. Glennon, Lewis E. Albright, and William A. Owens, *A Catalog of Life History Items* (Greensboro, NC: The Richardson Foundation, 1966); Owens and Henry, *Biographical Data in Industrial Psychology*.

81. W. M. Brodie, Lillian A. Owens, and M. F. Britt, *Annotated Biography on Biographical Data* (Greensboro, NC: The Richardson Foundation, 1968); Owens and Henry, *Biographical Data in Industrial Psychology*.

82. Michael D. Mumford and William A. Owens, "Methodology Review: Principles, Procedures, and Findings in the Application of Background Data Measures," 6–8; Leaetta M. Hough, "Development and Evaluation of the 'Accomplishment Record' Method of Selecting and Promoting Professionals," *Journal of Applied Psychology* 69 (1984): 135–146; and Leaetta M. Hough, Margaret A. Keyes, and Marvin D. Dunnette, "An Evaluation of Three 'Alternative' Selection Procedures," *Personnel Psychology* 36 (1983): 261–276.

83. Mael, "A Conceptual Rationale for the Domain and Attributes of Biodata Items."

84. Lawrence S. Kleiman and Robert Faley, "A Comparative Analysis of the Empirical Validity of Past and Present-Oriented Biographical Items," *Journal of Business and Psychology* 4 (1990): 431–437.

85. Williams, "Life History Antecedents of Volunteers versus Nonvolunteers for an AFROTC Program," 8.

86. William A. Owens and Lyle F. Schoenfeldt, "Toward a Classification of Persons," *Journal of Applied Psychology Monograph* 64 (1979): 569–607.

87. See, for example, Sam C. Webb, "The Comparative Validity of Two Biographical Inventory Keys," *Journal of Applied Psychology* 44 (1960): 177–183; Raymond E. Christal and Robert A. Bottenberg, *Procedure for Keying Self-Report Test Items* (Lackland Air Force Base, TX: Personnel Research Laboratory, 1964); and William H. Clark and Bruce L. Margolis, "A Revised Procedure for the Analysis of Biographical Information," *Educational and Psychological Measurement* 31 (1971): 461–464.

88. Owens and Schoenfeldt, "Toward a Classification of Persons," 569–607; Michael T. Matteson, "An Alternative Approach to Using Biographical Data for Predicting Job Success," *Journal of Occupational Psychology* 51 (1978): 155–162; Michael T. Matteson, "A FORTRAN Program Series for Generating Relatively Independent and Homogeneous Keys for Scoring Biographical Inventories," *Educational and Psychological Measurement* 30 (1970): 137–139;

and Terry W. Mitchell and Richard J. Klimoski, "Is It Rational to Be Empirical? A Test of Methods for Scoring Biographical Data," *Journal of Applied Psychology* 67, no. 4 (1982): 411–418.

89. England, *Development and Use of Weighted Application Blanks*.

90. William H. Stead and Carol L. Shartle, *Occupational Counseling Techniques* (New York: American Book, 1940).

91. William B. Lecznar and John T. Dailey, "Keying Biographical Inventories in Classification Test Batteries," *American Psychologist* 5 (1950): 279.

92. Michael P. Malone, *Predictive Efficiency and Discriminatory Impact of Verifiable Biographical Data as a Function of Data Analysis Procedure* (Minneapolis: Doctoral Dissertation, University of Minnesota, 1978).

93. Webb, "The Comparative Validity of Two Biographical Inventory Keys."

94. Paul A. Telenson, Ralph A. Alexander, and Gerald V. Barrett, "Scoring the Biographical Information Blank: A Comparison of Three Weighting Techniques," *Applied Psychological Measurement* 7 (1983): 73–80.

95. Robert F. Morrison, William A. Owens, J. R. Glennon, and Lewis E. Albright, "Factored Life History Antecedents of Industrial Research Performance," *Journal of Applied Psychology* 46 (1962): 281–284.

96. Michael K. Mount, L. Alan Witt, and Murray R. Barrick, "Incremental Validity of Empirically Keyed Biodata Scales Over GMA and the Five Factor Personality Constructs," *Personnel Psychology* 53 (2000): 299–323.

97. William A. Owens and Lyle F. Schoenfeldt, "Toward a Classification of Persons," *Journal of Applied Psychology Monograph* 64 (1979): 569–607.

98. Susan Eisner, "E-employment? College Grad Career Building in a Changing and Electronic Age," *American Journal of Business Education (AJBE)* 3, no. 7 (2010), 25–40; Abdou Ndoye, Albert Dieter Ritzhaupt, and Michele A. Parker, "Use of ePortfolios in K-12 Teacher Hiring in North Carolina: Perspectives of School Principals," *International Journal of Education Policy and Leadership* 7, no. 4 (2012): 1–10; and Ryan and Robert E. Ployhart, "A Century of Selection."

99. Jane H. Philbrick, Barbara D. Bart, and Marcia E. Hass, "Pre-employment Screening: A Decade of Change," *American Business Review* 17 (1999): 77.

100. Michael S. Cole, Hubert S. Feild, and William F. Giles, "Using Recruiter Assessments of Applicants' Résumé Content to Predict Applicant Mental Ability and Big Five Personality Dimensions," *International Journal of Selection and Assessment* 11, no. 1 (2003): 78–88.

101. Barbara K. Brown and Michael A. Campion, "Biodata Phenomenology: Recruiters' Perceptions and Use of Biographical Information in Resume Screening," *Journal of Applied Psychology* 79 (1994): 897–908.

102. Edward L. Levine, Ronald A. Ash, and Jonathan D. Levine, "Judgmental Assessment of Job-Related Experience, Training and Education for Use in Human Resource Staffing," *Comprehensive Handbook of Psychological Assessment* 16 (2004): 269–293.

103. Ibid.

104. J. M. Stanton, "Validity and Related Issues in Web-Based Hiring," *The Industrial-Organizational Psychologist* 36 (January 1999): 69–77.

105. L. I. Machwirth, H. Schuler, and K. Moser, "Entscheidungsprozesse bei der Analyse von Bewerbungsunterlagen," *Diagnostica* 42, no. 3 (1996): 220–241; and George W. Tommasi, Karen B. Williams, and Cynthia R. Nordstrom, "Letters of Recommendation: What

Information Captures HR Professionals' Attention?" *Journal of Business and Psychology* 13, no. 1 (1998): 5–18.

106. Kevin D. Carlson, Steven E. Scullen, Frank L. Schmidt, Hannah Rothstein, and Frank Erwin, "Generalizable Biographical Data Validity Can Be Achieved Without Multi-Organizational Development and Keying," *Personnel Psychology* 5 (1999): 731–755.

107. Paul E. Tesluk and Rick R. Jacobs, "Toward an Integrated Model of Work Experience," *Personnel Psychology* 51 (1998): 321–355.

108. Erick P. Prien and Garry L. Hughes, "A Content-Oriented Approach to Setting Minimum Qualifications," *Public Personnel Management* 33 (2004): 89–98; and Beryl Hesketh and Elizabeth Allworth, "Job Requirements Biodata as a Predictor of Performance in Customer Service Roles," *International Journal of Selection and Assessment* 8 (September 2000): 137.

109. W. R. Porter, Edward L. Levine, and A. Flory III, *Training and Experience Evaluation: A Practical Handbook for Evaluating Job Applicants, Resumes, and Other Applicant Data* (Tempe, AZ: Personnel Services Orientation, 1976); and Miguel A. Quinones, J. Kevin Ford, and Mark S. Teachout, "The Relationship between Work Experience and Job Performance: A Conceptual and Meta-Analytic Review," *Personnel Psychology* 48 (1995): 887–910.

110. Barbara K. Brown and Michael A. Campion, "Biodata Phenomenology: Recruiters' Perceptions and Use of Biographical Information in Resume Screening," *Journal of Applied Psychology* 79 (1994): 897–908.

111. Walter C. Borman, Mary Ann Hanson, Scott H. Oppler, Elaine D. Pulakos, and Leonard A. White, "Role of Early Supervisory Experience in Supervisor Performance," *Journal of Applied Psychology* 78 (1993): 443–449; and Frank L. Schmidt, John E. Hunter, and Alice N. Outerbridge, "Impact of Job Experience and Ability on Job Knowledge, Work Sample Performance, and Supervisory Ratings of Job Performance," *Journal of Applied Psychology* 71 (1986): 432–439.

112. Ronald A. Ash and Edward L. Levine, "Job Applicant Training and Work Experience Evaluation: An Empirical Comparison of Four Methods," *Journal of Applied Psychology* 70, no. 3 (1985): 572–376.

113. Schmidt et al., *The Behavioral Consistency Method of Unassembled Examining.*

114. Kethley and Terpstra, "An Analysis of Litigation Associated with the Use of the Application Form in the Selection Process."

115. Michael A. McDaniel, Frank L. Schmidt, and John E. Hunter, "A Meta-Analysis of the Validity of Methods for Rating Training and Experience in Personnel Selection," *Personnel Psychology* 41 (1988): 283–314.

116. Ronald Ash, James Johnson, Edward Levine, and Michael McDaniel, "Job Applicant Training and Work Experience Evaluation in Personnel Selection," in *Research in Personnel and Human Resource Management*, ed. Kenneth Rowland and Gerald Ferris (Greenwich, CT: JAI Press, 1989), 187–190.

117. Miguel A. Quinoñes, J. Kevin Ford, and Mark S. Teachout, "The Relationship between Work Experience and Job Performance: A Conceptual and Meta-Analytic Review," *Personnel Psychology* 48 (1995): 887–910.

118. Thomas W. H. Ng, Lillian T. Eby, Kerry L. Sorensen, and Daniel C. Feldman, "Predictors of Objective and Subjective Career Success: A Meta-Analysis," *Personnel Psychology* 58 (2005): 367–408.

119. Miguel A. Quinoñes, J. Kevin Ford, and Mark S. Teachout, "The Relationship between Work Experience and Job Performance: A Conceptual and Meta-Analytic Review," *Personnel Psychology* 48 (1995): 887–910.

120. John Hunter and Ronda Hunter, "The Validity and Utility of Alternative Predictors of Job Performance," *Psychological Bulletin* 96 (1984): 72–98.

121. Thomas W. H. Ng, Lillian T. Eby, Kelly L. Sorensen, and Daniel C. Feldman, "Predictors of Objective and Subjective Career Success: A Meta-Analysis," *Personnel Psychology* 58 (2005): 367–408.

122. Tesluk and Jacobs, "Toward an Integrated Model of Work Experience."

123. Frank L. Schmidt and John E. Hunter, "The Validity and Utility of Selection Methods in Personnel Psychology: Practical and Theoretical Implications of 85 Years of Research Findings," *Psychological Bulletin* 124 (1998): 262–274.

124. Philip L. Roth, C. A. Bevier, F. S. Switzer, and J. S. Schippmann, "Meta-Analyzing the Relationship between Grades and Job Performance," *Journal of Applied Psychology* 81 (1996): 548–556.

125. Thomas W. H. Ng, Lillian T. Eby, Kerry L. Sorensen, and Daniel C. Feldman, "Predictors of Objective and Subjective Career Success: A Meta-Analysis," *Personnel Psychology* 58 (2005): 367–408; and Rodger W. Griffeth, Peter W. Hom, and Stefan Gaertner, "A Meta-Analysis of Antecedents and Correlates of Employee Turnover: Update, Moderator Tests, and Research Implications for the Next Millennium," *Journal of Management* 26 (2000): 463–488.

126. Frank L. Schmidt and John E. Hunter, "General Mental Ability in the World of Work: Occupational Attainment and Job Performance," *Journal of Personality and Social Psychology* 86 (2004): 162–173; Malcolm J. Ree, Thomas R. Carretta, and Mark S. Teachout, "Role of Ability and Prior Job Knowledge in Complex Training Performance," *Journal of Applied Psychology* 80 (1995): 721–730; Charles E. Lance and Winston R. Bennett, "Replication and Extension of Models of Supervisory Job Performance Ratings," *Human Performance* 13 (2000): 139–158; and Charles A. Scherbaum, Karen L. Scherbaum, and Paula M. Popovich, "Predicting Job-Related Expectancies and Affective Reactions to Employees with Disabilities from Previous Work Experience," *Journal of Applied Social Psychology* 35 (2005): 889–904.

127. Michael A. McDaniel, Frank L. Schmidt, and John E. Hunter, "A Meta-Analysis of the Validity of Methods for Rating Training and Experience in Personnel Selection," *Personnel Psychology* 41 (2006): 283–309.

128. Bruce J. Avolio, David A. Waldschmidt, and Michael A. McDaniel, "Age and Work Performance in Nonmanagerial Jobs: The Effects of Experience and Occupational Type," *Academy of Management Journal* 33 (1990): 407–422; Rick Jacobs, David A. Hofmann, and S. D. Kriska, "Performance and Seniority," *Human Performance* 3 (1990): 107–121; Frank L. Schmidt, John E. Hunter, and Alice E. Outerbridge, "Impact of Job Experience and Ability on Job Knowledge, Work Sample Performance, and Supervisory Ratings of Job Performance," *Journal of Applied Psychology* 71 (1986): 431–439; and Michael C. Sturman, "Searching for the Inverted U-Shaped Relationship between Time and Performance: Meta-Analyses of the Experience/Performance, Tenure/Performance, and Age/Performance Relationships," *Journal of Management* 29, no. 5 (2003): 609–640.

129. Niteesh K. Choudry, Robert H. Fletcher, and Stephen B. Soumerai, "Systematic Review: The Relationship between Clinical Experience and Quality of Health Care," *Annals of Internal Medicine* 142 (2005): 260–273.

130. Michael C. Sturman, "Searching for the Inverted U-Shaped Relationship between Time and Performance: Meta-Analyses of the Experience/Performance, Tenure/Performance, and Age/ Performance Relationships," *Journal of Management* 29, no. 5 (2003): 609–640.

131. Edward L. Levine, Doris M. Maye, Ronald A. Ulm, and Thomas R. Gordon, "A Methodology for Developing and Validating Minimum Qualifications (MQs)," *Personnel Psychology* 50 (2004): 1009–1023; and Maury A. Buster, Philip L. Roth, and Philip Bobko, "A Process for Content Validation of Education and Experienced-Based Minimum Qualifications: An

Approach Resulting in Federal Court Approval," *Personnel Psychology* 58 (August 2005): 771–799.

132. Philip Bobko and Philip L. Roth, "College Grade Point Average as a Personnel Selection Device: Ethnic Group Differences and Potential Adverse Impact," *Journal of Applied Psychology* 85 (2000): 399–406.

133. R. Bryan Kethley and David E. Terpstra, "An Analysis of Litigation Associated with the Use of the Application Form in the Selection Process," *Public Personnel Management* 34 (2005): 357–376.

134. Richard D. Arvey and R. H. Faley, *Fairness in Selecting Employees*, 2nd ed. (Reading, MA: Addison-Wesley, 1988); Edward L. Levine, Doris M. Maye, Ronald A. Ulm, and Thomas R. Gordon, "A Methodology for Developing and Validating Minimum Qualifications (MQs)," *Personnel Psychology* 50 (1997), 1009–1023.

135. Miguel A. Quinoñes, J. Kevin Ford, and Mark S. Teachout, "The Relationship between Work Experience and Job Performance: A Conceptual and Meta-Analytic Review," *Personnel Psychology* 48 (1995): 887–910; and Tesluk and Jacobs, "Toward an Integrated Model of Work Experience."

136. Edward L. Levine, Doris M. Maye, Ronald A. Ulm, and Thomas R. Gordon, "A Methodology for Developing and Validating Minimum Qualifications (MQs)," *Personnel Psychology* 50 (1997): 1009–1023; and Maury A. Buster, Philip L. Roth, and Philip Bobko, "A Process for Content Validation of Education and Experienced-Based Minimum Qualifications: An Approach Resulting in Federal Court Approval," *Personnel Psychology* 58 (August 2005): 771–799.

137. Schmidt and Hunter, "General Mental Ability in the World of Work: Occupational Attainment and Job Performance"; Quinoñes, Ford, and Teachout, "The Relationship between Work Experience and Job Performance: A Conceptual and Meta-Analytic Review"; and Tesluk and Jacobs, "Toward an Integrated Model of Work Experience."

138. David E. Terpstra, R. Bryan Kethley, Richard T. Foley, and Wanthanee Lee Limpaphayom, "The Nature of Litigation Surrounding Five Screening Devices," *Public Personnel Management* 29, no. 1 (2000): 43–53; and Andler and Herbst, *The Complete Reference Checking Handbook*.

139. Andler and Herbst, *The Complete Reference Checking Handbook*.

140. Stephanie L. Wilk and Peter Cappelli, "Understanding the Determinants of Employer Use of Selection Methods," *Personnel Psychology* 56 (2003): 103–124; Ann Marie Ryan, Lynn McFarland, Helen Baron, and Ron Page, "International Look at Selection Practices: Nation and Culture as Explanations for Variability in Practice," *Personnel Psychology* 52 (1999): 359–392; *Reference and Background Checking Survey Report*, Society of Human Resources Research (January 2005): 1–27; and Sara L. Rynes, Marc O. Orlitzky, and Robert D. Bretz, "Experienced Hiring Versus College Recruiting: Practices and Emerging Trends," *Personnel Psychology* 50 (1997): 309–339.

141. *Reference and Background Checking Survey Report*.

142. Wayne F. Cascio and Herman Aguinis, *Applied Psychology in Human Resource Management*, 6th ed. (Upper Saddle River, NJ: Prentice Hall, 2005); and Jose M. Cortina and Joseph N. Luchman, "Personnel Selection and Employee Performance," *Handbook of Psychology: Industrial and Organizational Psychology* 12 (2012): 525–559.

143. *Reference and Background Checking Survey Report*.

144. Ibid.

145. Equal Employment Opportunity Commission, *Disability Discrimination* (Washington, DC: Equal Employment Opportunity Commission, Technical Assistance Program, April 1996), V15–V16.

146. George W. Tommasi, Karen B. Williams, and Cynthia R. Nordstrom, "Letters of Recommendation: What Information Captures HR Professionals' Attention?," *Journal of Business Psychology* 13 (2004): 5–18; Michael G. Aamodt and Felice Williams, "Reliability, Validity, and Adverse Impact of References and Letters of Recommendation," *Society for Industrial and Organizational Psychology* (Los Angeles: April 2005); and K. Moser and D. Rhyssen, "Reference Checks as a Personnel Selection Method," *Zeitschrift Fur Arbeits-Und Organisationspsychologie* 45 (2001): 40–46.

147. Michael G. Aamodt and Felice Williams, "Reliability, Validity, and Adverse Impact of References and Letters of Recommendation."

148. John E. Hunter and Ronda F. Hunter, "The Validity and Utility of Alternative Predictors of Job Performance," *Psychological Bulletin* 96 (1984): 72–98.

149. Richard R. Reilly and Georgia T. Chao, "Validity and Fairness of Some Alternative Employee Selection Procedures," *Personnel Psychology* 35 (1982): 1–62.

150. Michael G. Aamodt, *Industrial/Organizational Psychology—An Applied Approach*, 5th ed. (Belmont, CA: Thomson/Wadsworth, 2007).

151. Julie M. McCarthy and Richard D. Goffin, "Improving the Validity of Letters of Recommendation: An Investigation of Three Standardized Reference Forms," *Military Psychology* 13 (2001): 199–222.

152. Paul J. Taylor, Karl Pajo, Gordon W. Cheung, and Paul Stringfield, "Dimensionality and Validity of a Structured Telephone Reference Check Procedure," *Personnel Psychology* 57 (September 2004): 754–772.

153. Jeffrey D. Facteau and Craig B. Bartholomew, "Are Performance Appraisal Ratings from Different Rating Sources Comparable?" *Journal of Applied Psychology* 86 (2001): 215–227; Todd J. Maurer, Nambury S. Raju, and William C. Collins, "Peer and Subordinate Performance Appraisal Measurement Equivalence," *Journal of Applied Psychology* 83 (1998): 693–702; and David J. Woehr, M. Kathleen Sheehan, and Winston Bennett Jr., "Assessing Measurement Equivalence Across Rating Sources: a Multitrait-Multirater Approach," *Journal of Applied Psychology* 90 (2005): 592–600.

154. Paul Taylor, Karl Pajo, Gordon W. Cheung, and Paul Stringfield, "Dimensionality and Validity of a Structured Telephone Reference Check Procedure," *Personnel Psychology* 57 (September 2004): 754–772.

155. Ryan D. Zimmerman, Mary Triana, and Murray R. Barrick, "Predictive Criterion-Related Validity of Observer-Ratings of Personality and Job-Related Competencies Using Multiple Raters and Multiple Performance Criteria," *Human Performance* 22 (in press).

156. Paul R. Sackett and Filip Lievens, "Personnel Selection," *Annual Review of Psychology* 59 (2008): 1–32.

157. Filip Lievens, "Assessor Training Strategies and Their Effects on Accuracy, Interrater Reliability, and Discriminant Validity," *Journal of Applied Psychology* 86 (2001): 255–264; and Deidra J. Schleicher, David V. Day, Bronston T. Mayes, and Ronald R. Riggio, "A New Frame for Frame-of-Reference Training: Enhancing the Construct Validity of Assessment Centers," *Journal of Applied Psychology* 87 (2001): 735–746.

158. Jessica A. Nicklin and Sylvia G. Roch, "Biases Influencing Recommendation Letter Contents: Physical Attractiveness and Gender," *Journal of Applied Social Psychology* 38 (2008): 3053–3074.

159. Paul R. Sackett and Filip Lievens, "Personnel Selection," *Annual Review of Psychology* 59 (2008): 1–32.

160. Dennis P. Bozeman, "Interrater Agreement in Multi-Source Performance Appraisal: A Commentary," *Journal of Organizational Behavior* 18 (1997): 313–316; and James M. Conway, Kristie Lombardo, and Kelley C. Sanders, "A Meta-Analysis of Incremental Validity and Nomological Networks for Subordinate and Peer Rating," *Human Performance* 14 (October 2001): 267–303.

161. Michael K. Mount, Murray R. Barrick, and Judy Perkins Strauss, "Validity of Observer Ratings of the Big Five Personality Factors," *Journal of Applied Psychology* 79 (1994): 272–280.

162. Dennis P. Bozeman, "Interrater Agreement in Multi-Source Performance Appraisal: A Commentary," *Journal of Organizational Behavior* 18 (1997): 313–316; and James M. Conway, Kristie Lombardo, and Kelley C. Sanders, "A Meta-Analysis of Incremental Validity and Nomological Networks for Subordinate and Peer Rating," *Human Performance* 14 (October 2001): 267–303.

163. Jeffrey D. Facteau and Craig B. Bartholomew, "Are Performance Appraisal Ratings from Different Rating Sources Comparable?" *Journal of Applied Psychology* 86 (2001): 215–227; Todd J. Maurer, Nambury S. Raju, and William C. Collins, "Peer and Subordinate Performance Appraisal Measurement Equivalence," *Journal of Applied Psychology* 83 (1998): 693–702; and David J. Woehr, M. Kathleen Sheehan, and Winston Bennett Jr., "Assessing Measurement Equivalence Across Rating Sources: A Multitrait-Multirater Approach," *Journal of Applied Psychology* 90 (2005): 592–600.

164. Schmidt and Hunter, "The Validity and Utility of Selection Methods in Personnel Psychology: Practical and Theoretical Implications of 85 Years of Research Findings."

165. Donald L. Zink and Arthur Gutman, "Legal Issues in Providing and Asking for References and Letters of Recommendation," *The Society for Industrial and Organizational Psychology Paper* (Los Angeles: April 2005).

166. John P. Hausknecht, David V. Day, and Scott C. Thomas, "Applicant Reactions to Selection Procedures: An Updated Model and Meta-Analysis," *Personnel Psychology* 57 (2004): 639–683.

167. *Equal Employment Opportunity Commission v. National Academy of Sciences*, 12 FEP 1690 (1976).

168. Ralph L. Quinoñes and Arthur Gross Schaefer, "The Legal, Ethical, and Managerial Implications of the Neutral Employment Reference Policy," *Employee Responsibilities and Rights Journal* 10, no. 2 (1997): 173–189; and Beverly L. Little and Daphne Sipes, "Betwixt and Between: The Dilemma of Employee References," *Employee Responsibilities and Rights Journal* 12, no. 1 (2000): 1–8.

169. *Rutherford v. American Bank of Commerce*, 12 FEP 1184 (1976).

170. D. L. Zink and A. Gutman, "Legal Issues in Providing and Asking for References and Letters of Recommendation," *The Society for Industrial and Organizational Psychology Paper* (Los Angeles: April 2005); and Ann Marie Ryan and Maria Lasek, "Negligent Hiring and Defamation: Areas of Liability Related to Pre-Employment Inquiries," *Personnel Psychology* 44 (1991): 307–313.

171. *True v. Ladner*, 513 A. 2d 257 (1986).

172. *Frank B. Hall & Co., Inc. v. Buck*, 678 S.W. 2d 612 (1984).

173. *Randi W. v. Livingston Union School District*, 49 Cal. Rptr. 2d 471 (Cal. Ct. App. 1996).

174. Aamodt, *Industrial/Organizational Psychology—An Applied Approach;* and Cascio and Aguinis, *Applied Psychology in Human Resource Management.*

175. D. L. Zink and A. Gutman, "Legal Issues in Providing and Asking for References and Letters of Recommendation"; and *Human Resources Guide.*

176. Ibid.

177. Ralph L. Quinoñes and Arthur Gross Schaefer, "The Legal, Ethical, and Managerial Implications of the Neutral Employment Reference Policy," *Employees Responsibilities and Rights Journal* (November 2004): 173–189; Beverly L. Little and Daphne Sipes, "Betwixt and Between: The Dilemma of Employee References," *Employees Responsibilities and Rights Journal* (October 2004): 1–8; Charles R. McConnell, "Employment References: Walking Scared between the Minefield of Defamation and the Specter of Negligent Hiring," *Health Care Management* 19, no. 2 (2000): 78–90; and Charlotte Hughes Scholes, "Potential Pitfalls in Providing a Job Reference," *Legal Information Management* 6 (2006): 58–60.

178. *Human Resources Guide.*

179. *Human Resources Guide;* and Andler and Herbst, *The Complete Reference Checking Handbook.*

180. *Reference and Background Checking Survey Report.*

181. David E. Terpstra, R. Bryan Kethley, Richard T. Foley, and Wanthanee (Lee) Limpaphayom, "The Nature of Litigation Surrounding Five Screening Devices," *Public Personnel Management* 29, no. 1 (2000): 43–53.

182. *Reference and Background Checking Survey Report.*

183. *Human Resources Guide;* and Andler and Herbst, *The Complete Reference Checking Handbook.*

184. Bill Leonard, "Reference Checking Laws: Now What?" *HR Magazine* 40 (1995): 57–60.

185. *Reference and Background Checking Survey Report.*

186. Andler and Herbst, *The Complete Reference Checking Handbook.*

187. Paul J. Taylor, Karl Pajo, Gordon W. Cheung, and Paul Stringfield, "Dimensionality and Validity of a Structured Telephone Reference Check Procedure," *Personnel Psychology* 57 (2004): 745–772; and Tommasi, Williams, and Nordstrom, "Letters of Recommendation: What Information Captures HR Professionals' Attention?"

188. Nancy J. King, "Is Paperless Hiring in Your Future? E-Recruiting Gets Less Risky," *Employee Relations Law Journal* 26, no. 3 (2000): 87.

189. Michael G. Aamodt, *Industrial/Organizational Psychology—An Applied Approach*, 5th ed. (Belmont, CA: Thomson/Wadsworth, 2007); and Andler and Herbst, *The Complete Reference Checking Handbook.*

190. Christopher L. Grote, William N. Robiner, and Allyson Haut, "Disclosure of Negative Information in Letters of Recommendation: Writers' Intentions and Readers' Experiences," *Professional Psychology: Research and Practice* 32 (2001): 655–661.

191. Michael G. Aamodt and Felice Williams, "Reliability, Validity, and Adverse Impact of References and Letters of Recommendation."

192. Rodney K. Miller and George J. Van Rybroek, "Internship Letters of Reference: Where Are the Other 90 Percent?" *Professional Psychology: Research and Practice* 19 (1988): 115–117.

193. Stephen J. Ceci and Douglas Peters, "Letters of Reference: A Naturalistic Study of the Effects of Confidentiality," *American Psychologist* 39 (1984): 29–31.

194. Julie M. McCarthy and Richard D. Goffin, "Improving the Validity of Letters of Recommendation: An Investigation of Three Standardized Reference Forms," *Military Psychology* 13, no. 4 (2001): 199–222; and Michael G. Aamodt, Devon A. Bryan, and Alan J. Whitcomb, "Predicting Performance with Letters of Recommendation," *Public Personnel Management* 22 (1993): 81–90.

195. Ryan D. Zimmerman, Mary Triana, and Murray R. Barrick, "Predictive Criterion-Related Validity of Observer-Ratings of Personality and Job-Related Competencies Using Multiple Raters and Multiple Performance Criteria," *Human Performance* 22 (in press).

196. Brian T. Loher, John T. Hazer, Amy Tsai, Kendel Tilton, and J. James, "Letters of Reference: A Process Approach," *Journal of Business and Psychology* 13 (1998): 5–18.

197. George W. Tommasi, Karen B. Williams, and Cynthia R. Nordstrom, "Letters of Recommendation: What Information Captures HR Professionals' Attention?" *Journal of Business and Psychology* 13, no. 1 (1998): 5–18.

198. Julie M. McCarthy and Richard D. Goffin, "Improving the Validity of Letters of Recommendation: An Investigation of Three Standardized Reference Forms," *Military Psychology* 13 (2001): 199–222.

199. Timothy A. Judge and Chad A. Higgins, "Affective Disposition and the Letter of Reference," *Organizational Behavior and Human Decision Processes* 75 (1998): 207–221.

200. Michael G. Aamodt, Mark S. Nagy, and Naceema Thompson, "Employment References: Who Are We Talking About?" *Paper presented at the annual meeting of the International Personnel Management Association Assessment Council* (Chicago: June 22, 1998).

201. Christopher L. Grote, William N. Robiner, and Allyson Haut, "Disclosure of Negative Information in Letters of Recommendation: Writers' Intentions and Readers' Experiences," *Professional Psychology: Research and Practice* 32 (2001): 655–661; Aamodt, *Industrial/ Organizational Psychology—An Applied Approach*; and Stephen B. Knouse, "Letter of Recommendation: Specificity and Favorability of Information," *Personnel Psychology* 36 (1983): 331–342.

202. Andler and Herbst, *The Complete Reference Checking Handbook.*

203. Ibid.

204. Ibid.

205. Ibid.

206. Ibid.

207. *Wall Street Journal*, "Should companies monitor their employees' social media?" May 12, 2014, page R2.

The Selection Interview

As a selection tool, the employment interview is distinctive, in large part because it is an agenda-driven social exchange between strangers. In fact, it may even be the first and only opportunity for the employer to meet and directly interact with the candidate. Often it provides the only chance to witness an applicant's social "competence."[1] The demands that arise from this social exchange, however, does create a number of "challenges." These challenges include the fact there are competing interests infused throughout the interview. For example, the candidate wants to get a job offer, yet the interviewer wants to get accurate information about the candidate's suitability to do the job. Furthermore, the candidate almost always is a "stranger" to the interviewer, yet the candidate is dependent on the interviewer to recommend he or she be extended a job offer. Such demands generally lead people to try to maximize their own interests. This means candidates actively manage the image they portray in the interview.[2] At times, this leads candidates to intentionally misrepresent past accomplishments, even to the point of making them up.[3] And therein lies the "two-handed challenge" with using the interview: on one hand, it provides an efficient means of meeting and evaluating applicants; on the other hand, interviewer judgments—too often misled by common biases and errors—are sometimes intentionally misrepresented by the applicant.

Recognizing these challenges, the selection interview can still be "one of the most powerful selection tools available,"[4] if the hiring manager applies a few "rules" when developing and using it. The alternative approach simply ignores those rules and encourages the hiring manager to conduct the interview as he or she thinks best. Given this, do you think most hiring managers would choose option A (which applies the few rules) or option B (conduct the interview as the hiring manager thinks best)? Before you answer, you should know that the interview is likely the most frequently used selection tool. Furthermore, if the manager conducts the interview as he or she thinks best (that is, choose option B), it appears the interview is "almost entirely useless."[5] Clearly, you would choose option A and use what is referred to as a structured interview by applying a few "rules." Even today, after nearly 25 years of unambiguous empirical evidence that a structured interview (option A) results in better hiring decisions than an unstructured interview (option B), a majority of hiring managers still continue to choose option B and rely on an unstructured interview.[6]

How unambiguous is the evidence that a structured interview is better than an unstructured interview? To make as good a selection decision as that generated from one structured interview, evidence suggests the applicant must participate in 3.56 unstructured interviews.[7] If you prefer evidence that relies on validity coefficients, numerous meta-analytic analyses have revealed that over hundreds of studies that use option A (a well-designed structured interview), the predictive validities range from 0.44 to 0.62 when predicting job performance. In contrast, these same meta-analyses suggest when studies rely on option B (an unstructured interview), they have a predictive validity that ranges from only 0.20 to 0.33.[8]

What are the "few rules" that if applied can turn an unstructured interview (option B) into a structured interview (option A)? Stated another way, is having to follow these rules so onerous that it explains why interviewers choose not to rigorously follow option A (a structured interview)? At least 15 different rules are linked to option A, and each will be discussed in greater detail later in this chapter; however, if adopted, a few key rules make the interview highly valid and reliable. The guiding principle underlying these "rules" for selection purposes is to treat the interview as a test. To do so, the first "rule" is the interview questions asked should be demonstrably job related or based on critical job requirements. This requires that the hiring manager examine the job's analytic results (quick go back and read chapter 3) to identify those work-related characteristics (WRCs) that are best measured in the interview. The second "rule" is to ask all applicants the same precise questions that can differentiate candidates on those WRCs to deliver a standardized "test." Third, to ensure rigorous evaluation of these answers, the answer to each question should be rated using anchored rating scales that define good, average, and poor answers (or G-A-P answers) to enhance reliability of the judgments themselves. Fourth, use multiple interviewers each independently evaluating the candidate's answers. Finally, providing training to the interviewers (not surprisingly) also enhances their ability to apply the interview "test" consistently and reliably.[9] Following those few rules does not seem overly onerous. Although it may take longer and cost more to develop a structured interview than to use an unstructured interview, the substantial gains in performance attained by using the interview "like a test" will far exceed this small incremental increase in cost.

Yet, why do unstructured interviews remain so popular, if "structured interviews have been declared so clearly superior to unstructured interviews that researchers should no longer even bother with the latter" (unstructured interviews)?[10] The most compelling answer seems to be because an unstructured interview is flexible, which both applicants and interviewers like.[11] Candidates like unstructured interviews because they have more discretion in answering these questions, which enables the applicant to better convey their own skills and abilities. At the same time, through the greater give-and-take that is a hallmark of this flexibility, the applicant has the chance to learn more about the job opportunity itself, including what the job, the work group and manager, and even the organization are like.[12] This enables the applicant to put a shine on their own talents while at the same time answering a key concern, "is this a good fit for me?" Interviewers like this format because it allows them flexibility to just have a conversation to get to "know the person" rather than follow a scripted "test." It also provides an opportunity to win the applicant over and portray the best side of their job, products or services, and the organization itself. Furthermore, some indication suggests that interviewers are able to generate more accurate ratings of applicant personality using unstructured interviews.[13] Perhaps more important, it also turns out that interviewers are quite confident in their own ability to make a good hiring decision,[14] even when using an unstructured interview. Although these reasons seem reasonable and suggest an unstructured interview may be more effective for recruiting,[15] the problem is that for selection purposes, the evidence is stark—unstructured interviews do not predict future job performance very well, which is why they are viewed as "almost entirely useless."[16]

In fact, the previous discussion highlights the opportunities and costs of the employment interview. It is a widely used selection tool and, more important, it can be one of the, if not the, most effective selection tool used. Interviewers certainly believe they can personally do a better job of predicting a candidate's success than they could by using a test score or by relying on a candidate's education achievements or work experience.[17] A reasonable case can be made that because the interview is given the most weight in many selection decisions, it is the most important selection tool. Yet, in far too many cases, the interviewer prefers the *least* effective interview method possible[18] and conducts an "unstructured interview" (option B). Thus, instead of treating the interview as a test, the interviewer asks his or her favorite question, like "What color best represents your personality?" "If you could be any superhero, who would it be?" or "What animal are you?"—questions purported by job candidates to have been asked at such organizations as Johnson & Johnson, AT&T, and Bank of America.[19] Such questions are thought to be effective at helping the interviewer get to know the applicant or to see how they handle uncertainty or can think on the "spot." Unfortunately, as noted by our selection experts, such unstructured interviews make the interview "almost entirely useless."[20] This result occurs because unstructured interviews fail to systematically assess WRCs (assessing which animal you are instead of your interpersonal skills), rely on informally constructed subjective scales instead of G-A-P scales (red is better than blue), and tend to form an overall impression of the candidate (who doesn't like Wonderwoman or Wolverine), rather than provide a more precise score for each candidate. Although more spur-of-the-moment conversations about the job and the organization occur during unstructured interviews, which are "liked" by both the interviewer and applicant, much less time is spent trying to assess the candidate's capabilities and talents, which minimizes its value for selection.

This chapter describes the background of the selection interview and summarizes what currently is known about the selection interview by stressing the results of empirical research studies. We also discuss procedures that have been demonstrated through this research to improve the interview. We hope to provide sufficient information so that you will be able to effectively design and implement this important selection tool.

BRIEF HISTORY

Partially because of its widespread use and cost, selection scholars have conducted a great deal of research on the interview over the past century.[21] Until recently, their studies generally produced negative conclusions regarding the interview's reliability, validity, and usefulness in selection.[22] These early studies were based on what came to be known as unstructured interviews and were shown to suffer from both low reliability and low validity due to a combination of both the use of inappropriate questions and extraneous factors that affected an interviewer's evaluation of an applicant.[23] A quarter of a century ago,[24] however, a number of researchers began to establish that when employment interviews were treated as rigorous, standardized tests (that is, a structured interview) "conducted to determine the qualifications of a given individual for a particular open position,"[25] the criterion-related validities across all levels of the organization were substantially higher.[26] In fact, validity generalization studies (quick, go back and read the validity generalization section in Chapter 8!) have produced strong evidence of the predictive validity of structured interviews. This research prompted other work, which led to a detailed understanding of the ways the interview could be improved.

These improvements all revolve around structuring the interview as a test—hence the name, structured interview. As noted, a few key rules or principles have developed that when followed, lead to a more structured interview. Although there at least 15 different "rules"[27] we'll discuss later, using these improvements in the design of the selection interview will improve reliability and validity. As a result, it is accurate to conclude that *when designed appropriately and used correctly, the structured interview is good.* Frank Schmidt and John Hunter conducted a comprehensive review of cumulative empirical findings from research over the past 85 years. They concluded that the corrected validity coefficient for the structured interview ($\rho = 0.51$) is comparable to similar coefficients produced for cognitive ability tests ($\rho = 0.51$)—and higher than one determined for assessment centers ($\rho = 0.37$).[28] In fact, when it is combined in a standardized regression equation with cognitive ability, they found a 24 percent increase in job performance produced by a selection procedure relying solely on cognitive ability. This clearly shows the utility of the (correctly conducted) interview and reveals that using the interview can result in substantially better hiring decisions.

In recent years, there has been an active focus on understanding which WRCs are assessed in the structured interview[29] and which ones may be best measured with an interview instead of a paper-and-pencil test, including creativity, personality (agreeableness, extraversion, emotional stability, and conscientiousness), interpersonal skills, leadership, and even organizational fit or job fit.[30] In addition, there has been substantial interest in the utility structured interviews provide, as they consistently have been found to add incremental validity over other predictors, including personality tests and cognitive ability tests.[31] The role of technology also has been studied, from the use of phone interviews[32] to videoconferencing.[33] Finally, there is greater recognition that interviews involve a social exchange, often between strangers, and hence, there has been considerable research interest in examining the role of impression management, or more broadly, managing one's self-presentation tactics during the interview. This includes examining the impact that rapport building, even the handshake right at the start of the interview, has on an interviewer's ratings.[34]

Although many issues still need more research, one particularly important need is to determine what changes can be made to structured interviews without sacrificing the predictive validity that would lead our hiring managers mentioned in the opening paragraph of this chapter to stop choosing option B and instead choose option A. Obviously, unstructured interviews continue to be used so frequently for some reasons. The challenge is to determine whether we can design the structured interview in a way that retains its higher predictive validity and reliability, and at the same time, gets at whatever information or reactions the hiring manager believes they are learning from the unstructured interview. For example, it is informative that interviewers prefer focusing on job-relevant information and report consistently asking those questions.[35] Yet, at the same time, interviewers do not like using anchored ratings scales and want to use the interview to get to know the applicant and will allow, even encourage, applicants to ask questions.[36] The critical issue appears to be that interviewers dislike the structured interview to the extent it makes it difficult to use the interview for recruiting purposes or to establish rapport and hold a friendly conversation with the applicant, complete with introductions and casual chit-chat to make the applicant comfortable.[37] As we will see, research suggests the unstructured interviews may be particularly effective at recruiting,[38] even if they are not very effective for selection. And therein lies the "two-handed challenge" of using the interview: On one hand, it provides an efficient means of meeting and evaluating candidates; on the other hand, interviewer judgments are too often misled by common biases and errors. Taken together, all of this suggests the interview is a complex selection tool, and it is challenging to use it effectively. We now look at the steps one can take to maximize the utility of the employment interview.

Developing and Designing Effective Interviews

The employment interview is a flexible tool that affects many key staffing outcomes. For example, when properly conducted, interviews provide a wealth of information that can be used by both the interviewer and interviewee for making quality decisions. Thus, a first step in understanding the appropriate use of the interview is a discussion of the range of outcomes possible when using the interview. Generally, these outcomes fall into five main categories: the interview (a) provides an opportunity to select the best set of candidates from the applicant pool; (b) is an opportunity for the organization to recruit highly qualified candidates and to sell them on the organization, the product, or the service, as well as the job; (c) simultaneously enables the applicant to assess their fit with the organization and the job, as well as ask about procedural aspects linked to the job decision; (d) is an efficient and practical method for measuring a number of applicant WRCs; and (e) can be used to make either an early decision about an applicant's acceptability (that is, screening out an applicant) or a later one (that is, selecting in an applicant). We discuss each of these outcomes in the next sections. Our general conclusion is that to fully gain the advantages from the interview, organizations must correctly develop and design the interview. If improperly managed, it will detract from the usefulness of the selection interview.

Recruiting the Applicant to the Organization: Providing Job Information

At least some of the time spent in selection interviews is used by the interviewer to describe the job and the organization together with selling the job and organization to the applicant. Although the interview can be used for these purposes, some limiting factors should be noted. Both personal anecdotes and communication research studies provide examples of oral discussions between two individuals being recalled differently by each person. Thus, we have good reason to give a written job description to applicants that supplements much of the information usually transmitted during the interview. This could save some of the time allocated for recruiting during the interview—time that could be used to obtain more job-relevant information.

Alison Barber and her colleagues reported important research regarding the mixing of recruitment and selection purposes in the interview.[39] Using a sample of undergraduates and a campus job, they manipulated the focus of the interview. One applicant group experienced a recruitment-only interview; the other group received an interview that combined recruitment and selection. The researchers found that applicants clearly retained more information about the position from the recruitment-only interview than from the mixed-focus interview. This effect was especially pronounced for those applicants who were high in anxiety and low in self-monitoring abilities. Apparently, being anxious and not monitoring how others see them reduces candidates' ability to collect and remember information about the job. Moreover, there was a strong relationship between the amount of information acquired in the interview and the amount of information retained two weeks later, which indicated a continuing effect of the recruitment interview. These results are supported by more recent research showing intentions to accept a job offer are higher when the interview consists of a mix of recruiting and selection, rather than just recruiting or just selection.[40] One explanation for this is that the interviewer's behavior changes depending on the degree to which recruitment is emphasized over selection in the interview. As the recruitment function increases, evidence indicates that the interviewer places relatively more emphasis on job characteristics than on applicant characteristics, describes vacant positions in more favorable terms, and asks questions that are less likely to lead to applicant disqualification.[41] Logically, increasing the recruiting emphasis at the expense of selection has costs in terms of the amount and quality of pertinent information that is gathered for selection decisions. Similarly, emphasizing only selection during the interview also incurs costs, in this case, decreasing the likelihood the applicant will say yes if the firm decides to make an offer.

Our recommendation is to design the employment interview using a mix of selection and recruiting, as this not only increases the applicant's willingness to later accept an offer if extended, but also allows the employer to assess the candidate's qualifications. Procedurally, the first part of the interview could focus on selection assessment and the latter part could address recruiting information and addressing candidate questions. Future research may actually illustrate that taking this "Goldilocks approach" (not too much recruiting, nor too little selection, but just the right balance) also increases the likelihood the hiring manager will decide to follow the structured interview rather than take an unstructured approach, which would further enhance the practical value of the interview itself.

Effect on Attracting Applicants: Recruiting Outcomes

One of the earliest outcomes critical to continued participation in the selection procedure is how the applicant views the organization's reputation or image.[42] It commonly is assumed that the interview has value as a public relations device. That is, the personal contact between organizational member and applicant positively affects the attitudes of the applicant. This is not always the case. Clearly the interview is only part of the information that applicants use to form impressions about the organization and to make job search and job acceptance decisions. That is, applicants use information from multiple sources (friends, Web sites, social media, class materials, advertisements, product/service usage, recruitment brochures, site visits, and employer location information, as well as recruiters) to make these decisions.[43] The problem for applicants is that they often have to make a decision with inadequate information about the firm. For example, early in the process, individuals must decide in which companies they will invest the time, effort, and money to continue as an applicant. It is simply not possible to continue with all possible companies. In making the decision to continue or not, the applicant uses whatever information is available to infer an organization's characteristics. For example, research demonstrates when the applicant perceives poor fit, they tend to withdraw from the process.[44]

Recruiter characteristics and behaviors are only part of this information, although reactions to the recruiter seem to serve as a "signal" about the organization's reputation.[45] Furthermore, a recent meta-analysis by Derek Chapman and his associates[46] has revealed that recruiters with the "right" qualities (who are personable and skilled in listening and conveying information) who were trained to consistently and fairly provide correct information about the company and job had a significant impact on the candidate's attitudes toward a job. These "right" qualities, to a lesser extent, also influenced whether the applicant actually accepted the job offer. In contrast, the findings reveal that the "demographic characteristics" of the individual interviewer (organizational function, sex, race) did not affect the candidate's perception of the job or organization or alter intentions to pursue or accept a job. Nevertheless, after controlling for actual job and organizational characteristics, the effect of recruiter behavior on candidate attitudes or intentions to accept an offer becomes a relatively modest effect, albeit one that remains statistically significant.[47]

One reason the effect of the recruiter may be relatively modest is because it seems to be a function of the personal characteristics of the candidate as well. For example, one study found that recruiters had only a minimal effect on individuals with previous work experience.[48] Other studies found that recruiters had a stronger effect on female candidates[49] and black candidates,[50] who often have less work experience. Although demographic similarity of interviewers and candidates has been found to have small and inconsistent effects on candidate evaluations, attitudinal similarity does appear to increase the candidate's attraction to the job;[51] at the same time, however, it does not appear to reduce the predictive validity of interviewer ratings of the candidate's likely job performance. These results illustrate the complexity of studying recruiter effects.

Nevertheless, taken as a whole, this information is important to the applicant and influences whether he or she continues in the selection process, and even accepts an offer.

Making a Selection Decision

Theoretically, one advantage of the interview over other selection instruments is that the data gatherer, interpreter, and decision maker is a human being who understands the job and organization. Ratings by an interviewer, however, can reflect the method of measurement (subjective ratings) as much as or more than the construct the rating is thought to be measuring. One common stereotype held by many raters is the "what-is-beautiful-is-good stereotype."[52] If an interviewer's rating of job knowledge is artificially inflated by a particularly attractive candidate *and* the supervisor's later rating of employee performance on the job is also artificially inflated by the employee's attractiveness, then the relatively high validity coefficient reported between the interviewer's rating of candidate job knowledge and supervisor's performance evaluation actually is not based on greater job knowledge. Instead, it is based on attractiveness of the individual. This underscores the complexity of establishing validity—in this case, we see a correlation is not definitive evidence of validity. To establish the validity of a job knowledge question on the interview, we would want to see that higher scorers not only lead to more successful performance on the job but also lead to coworkers actually having more job knowledge and being able to solve more work-related problems.

Concern about method of measurement bias in the interview is legitimate.[53] A recent meta-analysis shows an interviewer's rating of candidate suitability is significantly affected by physical attractiveness and professional demeanor ($\rho = 0.42$), use of impression management behavior ($\rho = 0.44$), and verbal and nonverbal behavior of the candidate ($\rho = 0.40$).[54] Given that physical attractiveness and impression management also have been found to affect supervisory ratings of performance,[55] it is important that we try to ensure interviewer ratings are focused on job-relevant WRCs, and not on non-job-relevant attributes, such as attractiveness" (I would emphasize this point even if I had not just glanced in a mirror).

Restricting bad or biased decision making to just these causes, however, understates the potential problem. A vast research literature has developed in cognitive psychology that demonstrates a number of biases or heuristics can affect the accuracy of one's judgments. These are thoroughly described in Daniel Kahneman's (2011) book, *Thinking, Fast, and Slow*.[56] Although not a comprehensive list, those biases most relevant to the interview include the following:

- **Anchoring.** Locking onto salient information too early, while failing to adjust the rating to reflect conflicting or new information.

- **Confirmation bias.** The tendency to look for confirming evidence rather than look for evidence to refute an early judgment, even if the disconfirming evidence is more persuasive or definitive.

- **Illusory correlations.** Perceiving associations where none exist (for example, the what-is-beautiful-is-good stereotype).

- **Overconfidence bias.** The tendency to act on incomplete information or hunches; to be more confident than is warranted by the evidence available.

Although decision makers often believe they are highly rational in arriving at their own judgments, there is considerable evidence people can be impressively unreliable, even irrational. Fortunately, the accuracy of the decision-making processes of interviewers has been studied extensively. Evidence clearly illustrates that when the interview is appropriately designed, the interviewer, in fact, can minimize the influence of these biases and errors, and consequently make more valid predictions about job performance.[57] The results of the meta-analytic studies that concerned the increased reliability and validity of interview data (we referred to these studies at the beginning of this chapter) show that decision-making quality is highly dependent on a structured format. Research conducted in the decision-making literature clarifies this further, as evidence indicates that there is less bias and more diagnostic information collected when the rater is charged with making a judgment rather than an overall decision.[58] This may explain why rating each interview question separately (using a behaviorally anchored rating scale) results in more predictive, less biased judgments than when making overall evaluations about a candidate.[59]

A few recent studies have suggested that some interviewers make better judges than others, as there is substantial variation in the reliability and validity of interviewer judgments.[60] Although more research is needed, it appears that interviewers who are smarter, more extraverted, and more experienced, and who are motivated to provide more accurate ratings, make better judges.[61] Not surprisingly (for a book about selection), care should be taken to select the best interviewers possible.

Screening versus Selection Interview

Frequently the interview is used at two different stages of the selection program. At the first stage, the interview is used to assess applicants on general characteristics. A first-stage interview might be done by a campus recruiter, for example, and frequently is referred to as a *screening* interview. At the second stage, the interview is used to assess more specific job-related WRCs. This is a *selection* interview, for which specific job-related questions—such as those developed in a structured interview—would be appropriate. One recent meta-analysis examined the constructs assessed in two different interviews: conventional interviews and behavioral interviews, which correspond to what we are calling (respectively) screening interviews and selection interviews. The conventional or screening interview focuses on the checking of credentials and licensure requirements and the evaluation of an applicant's minimum work requirements and experiences needed for the job. Selection or behavior interviews are composed of questions concerning job-related knowledge, interpersonal skills, problem-solving skills, and other work-related experiences and behaviors.[62]

The meta-analytic results showed that interviewer recommendations from the screening interviews were highly correlated with the applicant's social skills ($\rho = 0.46$), general mental ability ($\rho = 0.41$), and personality traits (on emotional stability, extraversion, openness to experience, agreeableness, and conscientiousness, ρ ranges from 0.26 to 0.38). These results show that these characteristics have a significant impact on interviewer evaluations of the candidate during the screening interview. In the interview, successful candidates had higher scores on specific work-related experiences ($\rho = 0.71$), social skills ($\rho = 0.65$), job knowledge ($\rho = 0.53$), and skills assessed by situational judgment tests ($\rho = 0.46$).[63] On the basis of these findings, the researchers concluded that screening and selection interviews focus on different constructs. The biggest difference is that screening interviews were designed to measure general traits (such as personality and intelligence), whereas selection interviews assess more specific job-related skills and habitual behaviors (such as work-related experiences, job knowledge, problem-solving skills, and so on).

Surprisingly little research has been conducted as to how to develop questions for the screening interview that predict job performance. This is unfortunate; such interviews are often the first step in the selection program, and their results determine which members of the applicant pool will complete the other selection instruments. On the basis of the small amount of relevant research, and even more upon careful thought, we recommend the following options to develop questions for a screening interview:

1. Use job analysis information to identify general or fundamental WRCs that an applicant must possess and for which the organization does not provide training. Examples include the verbal ability to explain instructions, the ability to respond to points made in conversation by others, the ability to work on multiple projects simultaneously, and the ability to analyze problem situations similar to what would occur on the job. In addition, several interpersonal behaviors may be important, especially if work teams are a primary vehicle for work processes. These may include giving a friendly first impression, playing multiple roles in group projects, assisting others in the work group, and changing tasks easily and often.

2. Use "job experts" to identify the most important of these characteristics. That is, job incumbents and supervisors can be asked to rate these characteristics on such scales as *importance for team interaction, importance for job performance*, or *importance for initial training*. On the basis of these responses, identify a set of two to three WRCs for use in the screening interview.

3. Use a modified critical-incidents technique to identify questions. That is, job incumbents and supervisors can be asked to supply examples only in reference to the WRCs identified in the previous step. Examples could be obtained about good and poor behaviors related to giving instructions, coordinating one's efforts on multiple projects, and taking action during slack work demands. Questions and scoring systems that reflect typical highly structured interviews could be developed. The following are examples of possible questions:

"Please give me instructions about how to assemble some piece of equipment or how to do some activity that is part of one of your hobbies."

"When you worked with other students on a group class assignment, what would you do when you finished your part of the project?"

"You started a work assignment yesterday, but today you are not sure you are doing it correctly. What would you do at this point?"

Our view is that the screening and selection interviews serve the same purpose—they both measure WRCs relative to the employee requirements of a job. The two differ, however, in the type and specificity of behaviors and knowledge assessed. The screening interview evaluates *general* work and interaction behaviors and knowledge. The selection interview is focused on more narrowly defined WRCs that are critical for doing the job, such as specific job knowledge, work-related experiences, and social skills required to perform the job.

Measuring Applicant WRCs

More Is Not Better.   This issue addresses the number and type of applicant characteristics that interviewers often attempt to measure. During the early 1970s, there was a decrease in the use of scored ability and performance selection tests and an increase in the use of unscored interviews. In part this was due to the courts' reviews of selection programs. Early selection discrimination cases revolved around the use of written mental and special ability tests. Courts stated that these tests must be validated before they could be used for selection. Only recently has it become expressly clear that the selection interview is viewed as a selection test and also must be validated before use. In the interim, however, the interview was used to assess a wide variety of applicant characteristics without rigorous scoring associated with specific dimensions. The use of the interview in this way often results in superficial data of limited value. Also, by substituting the interview for other assessment devices, which may be better suited to measure particular applicant characteristics (for example, a test to assess intelligence), a human resource (HR) specialist may be collecting less accurate, more expensive data than are necessary.

Most major studies that have reviewed the use of the interview have agreed in their conclusions. For example, Lynn Ulrich and Don Trumbo have stated that "the interviewer is all too frequently asked to do the impossible because of limitations on the time, information, or both, available to him. When the interviewer's task was limited to rating a single trait, acceptable validity was achieved."[64] They further pointed out that even when the interviewer concentrates on only a few characteristics, some of these are not addressed profitably. For example, they have contended that all too often a conclusion about the applicant's mental ability, arrived at during a 30-minute interview, may be less efficient and accurate than one based on the administration of a 10-minute test, the use of which would leave the interviewer time to assess those areas in which his or her judgment was more effective. The key point is to focus on only a few key WRCs and assess those thoroughly.

Appropriate WRCs for the Interview.   Which specific characteristics, then, are best assessed in the interview? Allen Huffcutt and colleagues recently conducted a meta-analysis on 47 interview studies and found the interview is designed to evaluate seven major dimensions. Table 10.1 provides a list and brief definition of these dimensions and reports the frequency of use for each. This meta-analysis reveals that the interview frequently is used to assess personality (for example, conscientiousness, extraversion), applied social skills (for example, oral communication and interpersonal skills, leadership, persuasiveness), mental ability (for example, general intelligence and applied mental skills such as judgment and decision making), and knowledge and skills (for example, job knowledge and skills, experience, and general work history).[65] Less than 5 percent of interviews assessed either interests and preferences, physical attributes, or organizational fit. Interestingly, interviewer ratings of organizational fit—or the match between the candidate and demands of the job—had one of the highest mean validities for predicting later job performance ($\rho = 0.49$). They also found that interviewer ratings of personality—particularly agreeableness and emotional stability ($\rho = 0.51$ and 0.47, respectively) and, to a lesser extent, conscientiousness and extraversion (both $\rho = 0.33$)—also predicted later job performance. These predictive validities are substantially higher than those typically found using personality tests (ρs in the low 0.20s to high 0.10s).[66] Other constructs evaluated in the employment interview were found to significantly predict later performance evaluation, including the assessment of specific job knowledge and skills ($\rho = 0.42$ for job knowledge and skills and 0.49 for experience and general work history) and applied social skills ($\rho = 0.49$ for leadership, 0.39 for interpersonal skills, and 0.26 for oral communication skills).

To further illustrate the value of the interview, the researchers concluded that these predictors were not highly correlated with the single-best predictor of performance—that is, measures of general mental ability.[67] A meta-analytic study found only a 0.40 correlation between the interview and cognitive ability tests, indicating that the two overlap by only 16 percent of their variance.[68] Moreover, the correlation between the two instruments decreases as the level of structure of the interview increases. Stated another way, the interview has been shown to add incremental validity after accounting for cognitive ability or personality or even after the assessment center.[69] Thus, asking the same job-related questions of all candidates and systematically scoring the answers will decrease

TABLE 10.1 Behavioral Dimensions Frequently Measured in the Structured Interview

Dimension	Frequency of Use	Definition
General Intelligence	16%	Ability to learn and evaluate information quickly; ability to effectively plan and organize work; application of mental ability for solving problems.
Job Knowledge and Skills	10%	Declarative information (i.e., terms, values, names, and dates) and procedural knowledge (i.e., actions, skills, and operations) specific to the job; technical knowledge.
Personality	35%	Long-term disposition to act in certain ways; reflection of habitual behavior with regard to five dimensions: conscientiousness, extraversion, agreeableness, openness to experience, emotional stability.
Applied Social Skills	28%	Ability to function effectively in social situations; includes interpersonal skills, oral communication skills, leadership, and persuasiveness.
Interests and Preferences	4%	Tendency toward certain activities; preference for certain work environments or a particular type of work or profession; interest in certain topics or subjects.
Organizational Fit	3%	Match between candidate and the organization's values, goals, norms, and attitudes; fit with unique organizational culture or climate.
Physical Attributes	4%	Evaluation of stamina and agility; and general characteristics, like an evaluation of physical appearance.

Note: Frequency of Use = the relative frequency with which these constructs are evaluated in the interview.

Source: From Allen I. Huffcutt, James M. Conway, Philip L. Roth, and Nancy J. Stone, "Identification and Meta-Analytic Assessment of Psychological Constructs Measured Employment Interviews," *Journal of Applied Psychology,* 86 (2001): 897–913.

the correlation with measures of general mental ability, personality tests, and assessment centers. Consequently, interviews are likely to add significantly to the quality of selection decisions, particularly with structured interviews. Robert Dipboye, however, has cautioned that researchers should not forget that predictive validity will be achieved only if the specific traits assessed in the interview are job related.[70] Consequently, although creativity had the highest mean validity ($\rho = 0.58$) in the meta-analysis conducted by Huffcutt and associates, it will not be useful to assess this construct if creativity is irrelevant to the job.[71]

Employment interviews are flexible and can be used to assess a number of different constructs. Careful inspection of Table 10.1—and consideration of the predictive validity of these dimensions—reveals that the interview, because of its interactive nature, may be uniquely suited for measuring applied social skills (such as interpersonal and communication skills), personality or habitual behaviors (such as conscientiousness, emotional stability, and extraversion), and fit with the job and organization. Applied social skills reflect those characteristics important for successful personal interaction, oral communication, and specific characteristics, such as leadership and negotiation. The interview, by its very nature, is an example of such a situation; it should be an accurate indicator of skills in these areas. Personality characteristics often are evaluated as a way to assess work habits, tasks completed in a previous job, and the candidate's typical approach or habitual ways of doing things at work. Interviewer ratings on these attributes strive to assess the candidate's long-term dispositional behavior in specific work environments. Recent research has shown interviewer ratings of personality can predict later job performance.[72] Although it may be somewhat surprising that a stranger can assess personality, we have found that these ratings collected in the interview do predict job performance for candidates who are hired. Finally, the interview is likely to be a particularly effective way to assess whether the candidate's values, norms, goals, and attitudes "fit" or correspond to those of the organization. Such discussions usually require the clarification or elaboration of statements made by the respondent on the application form, cover letter, or resume—or require clarification of statements made by others in letters of reference. The interview, because of its interactive nature, provides a suitable means for such probing by the interviewer.

The characteristic *job knowledge* has been evaluated successfully in interviews. There are some guidelines as to when an interview would be useful for assessing this characteristic. If assessment includes many job knowledge questions, and especially if the answers are fairly short and routine, a written test is preferable to an interview. Such a test is usually less expensive to administer and score, provides a permanent record, and is often a more familiar format for the applicant. If interview questions ask about complex job behaviors, such as diagnosing product defects, operating equipment, and manipulating data or information, job simulation instruments are usually more appropriate. One situation that certainly would argue for the use of job knowledge questions in the interview occurs when the applicant has serious reading or writing deficiencies that would impede selection evaluation but not job performance. The interviewer would be able to determine whether the applicant understands the question and could clarify unclear or poorly worded responses. Another situation that would be appropriate for job knowledge questions occurs when selecting for jobs that require the verbalization of technical information and work procedures, such as advisory or consulting jobs in which most of the requests for service are oral. In such situations, the interview approximates a job simulation selection device.

One set of constructs that are not explicitly included in Table 10.1 and warrant consideration for assessment through the interview includes emotional intelligence and social intelligence. Applied skills and social skills have certainly been assessed frequently in the interview, particularly the structured interview, as shown in Table 10.1. Emotional intelligence is defined as the ability to monitor one's own and others' emotions and thereby more effectively cope with environmental demands and constraints.[73] Although such a set of attributes would seem critical to success in a variety of jobs—after all, who doesn't want to be seen as "emotionally smart"—the predictive validities have only been found to be modest, with low incremental validity over other common predictors.[74] Part of the explanation for this is that emotional intelligence is highly correlated with personality, as 65 percent of the descriptors of the construct could be sorted into the one of the five "Big Five" personality traits, with most either from agreeableness or emotional stability.[75] Until research clears up what emotional intelligence and social intelligence are and how to best assess them, it is not likely to add much to a hiring decision. Nevertheless, the intuitive appeal of these measures and their relevance to assessment through the "social interaction" that lies at the heart of the interview implies these notions bear watching for future inclusion.

One important issue to consider with regard to the behavioral dimensions mentioned in Table 10.1 (as well as emotional intelligence) is how to measure them. Unfortunately, the research does not provide many examples of specific questions that have been used to assess these behaviors or characteristics. We think, however, that these characteristics should be measured with questions that are intended expressly for these WRCs. We will discuss specific techniques that can be used to develop such questions later in the chapter. For now, we will provide a general example.

Sociability and verbal fluency, in some form, are demonstrated in every interview. For the purposes of selection, these WRCs should be defined to reflect specific behaviors of the job of interest. For example, sociability for a retail clerk may be demonstrated in brief interactions with customers. Thus, these characteristics may be assessed using only the general comments and remarks that start most interviews. If the behaviors are of interactions that include technical content, however, then specific questions should be formed. For example, medical sales personnel must meet and interact with the physicians and nurses who order their products. Usually, even initial conversations and interactions include discussion of the technical qualities of the products. Physicians and nurses simply do not have a lot of free time in their schedules. For such a job, questions that require the interviewee to explain some technical topic would be appropriate. In predicting future job performance, it is more appropriate that applicants demonstrate that they can quickly and easily discuss technical information than that they can initiate and continue a general discussion about the weather, the local baseball team, or a hit movie.

When interviews are viewed as a selection tool, the importance of which constructs to focus on becomes particularly salient. This is a chance to ask questions and assess the interpersonal competence of the candidate. As emphasized earlier, however, a single interview will be most effective if it limits the number of attributes to be assessed. Based on this finding, we strongly encourage that only two or three characteristics be evaluated during an interview. Those characteristics selected should be constructs that are critical to doing the work, cannot be assessed in other ways, and are particularly suited to assessment during the interview.

Types of Structured Interviews

Structured versus Unstructured Interviews.   Using an unstructured get-acquainted interview results in subjective, global evaluations that are not very useful, even though interviewers will have great confidence in their ability to select the best candidate. Thus, the interviewer can become his or her own worst enemy when using an unstructured interview. This occurs because the interviewer's decisions are being influenced by extraneous factors, such as physical attractiveness or the strength of a handshake, factors that may have little to do with later job success.[76] We are, after all, prewired to quickly form overall impressions of strangers; these ratings, which at best are influenced haphazardly by job-relevant attributes, not surprisingly, are only moderately valid.

To combat the potential weaknesses of casual conversation that leads to subjective global evaluations or reactions, current evidence stresses the use of structured interactions. Structured interviews rely on a disciplined method for collecting job-relevant information, including the use of a job analysis that identifies questions aimed at attitudes, behaviors, knowledge, and skills that differentiate high performers for a particular job. Interviewers are trained to take notes and record ratings to reduce the interviewers' memory distortions and to evaluate candidate responses to each question systematically. In essence, structured interviews rely on more objective evaluation procedures (asking only job-related questions, providing training on interviewing skills, and rating on established scoring formats). This standardization in the gathering, recording, and evaluating of information improves the quality of selection decisions. As you can probably guess, structured interviews make use of standardization and unstructured interviews do not. In reality, structured interviews vary in the use of these evaluation procedures, especially the use of predetermined questions. It is not accurate to refer to interviews as being either highly structured or not. For our purposes, however, we follow the common practice of distinguishing between structured and unstructured types of interviews and encourage the reader to remember that these vary on a continuum from highly structured to highly unstructured.

Recent research has centered on explaining what is meant by the concept of a structured interview. Derek Chapman and David Zweig identified a four-factor model of interview structure consisting of the following: (a) evaluation standardization, which includes scoring each item, relying on anchored rating scales, and summing scores across multiple dimensions; (b) question sophistication focusing on job-related behaviors, including the use of follow-up probes; (c) question consistency, which is based on asking all applicants the same questions derived from a job analysis, using the same interviewers; and (d) rapport building, which involves getting to know each other through casual conversation at the beginning of the interview.[77] By including rapport building, this factor structure implicitly recognizes the importance of another purpose of the interview—recruitment. Effective rapport building at the start of the interview may help to attract the best candidates or increases the likelihood they will accept a later offer. At the same time, higher levels of rapport building may be seen as a characteristic of less structured interviews. Consequently, future research must examine whether greater rapport enhances predictive validity. To the extent that more rapport elicits greater disclosure (due to the candidate being more comfortable with the interview), such rapport may increase validity. Recent research in a forensics context suggests that rapport-building tactics, like using a gentler tone with a more relaxed posture, acting friendlier, and using the person's name, do lead the interviewee to talk more and produce significantly more accurate information, which suggests the potential value of effectively building rapport.[78] More research is needed, however, to establish what constitutes "effective" rapport and whether it provides more relevant information than potential bias. At present, the position of many scholars is that greater rapport results in the inclusion of more contaminated, non-job-relevant information.[79] Hence, building rapport is likely to bias hiring decisions.

How big of an impact does the rapport-building "stage" have on later hiring recommendations? Although very little research is available on the effect of candidate first impressions during the initial stage of the interview, conventional wisdom holds that interviewers make their minds up about the hirability of a candidate within 4 minutes of starting the interview. This belief is based on a study conducted in 1958, which showed that, on average, the interviewer took 4 minutes to tic a checkmark on the answer sheet indicating whether or not she would recommend hiring an applicant.[80] This conclusion is not surprising, given findings in social psychology that individuals form reactions almost instantaneously and effortlessly—and that they do this based on minimal information received upon meeting a person for the first time.[81] Murray Barrick, Brian Swider, Greg Stewart, and colleagues recently conducted a series of studies that shows the impact of first impressions formed at the start of the interview.[82] In one study, they found the "quality" of the candidate's handshake (firmness, completeness of grip, vigor in shaking, and eye contact) influenced the end of interview suitability rating from the interviewer.[83] In other studies, they found that interviewer evaluations collected after the brief introduction and rapport-building stage of the interview—but before the asking of any substantive, job-related "structured" questions—were highly correlated with hiring recommendations made after the interview and even affected the proportion of invitations to a second interview as well as actual job offers received.

The results from four separate samples reveal that first impressions formed early in the interview have a substantial effect on whether the interviewer recommended extending a job offer.[84] In these studies, these evaluations were made in the absence of prior information about the candidate. We mention this, because in practice, many practitioners report looking at preinterview information, including applications, resumes, and letters of recommendation, and perhaps more disturbingly, even looking at such sources as Facebook or Linkedin.[85] Scholars view such information as a source of contamination that biases the ratings obtained in the interview.[86] Findings from these studies show interviewers do form early impressions of the candidate, and these early impressions appear to establish an anchor for the interviewer that filters all subsequent evaluations of the candidate. Surveys suggesting that 78 percent of interviewers preview information even before the interview underscores the likelihood that initial impressions are formed before the structured interview begins.[87]

Taken together, these results illustrate that the information collected during the rapport-building stage (or even before the interview begins) can have a significant impact on hiring recommendations at the end of the interview. The use of preinterview information and rapport building is one crucial reason interviewers prefer using unstructured interviews rather than structured interviews, which would severely limit access to any preinterview information and even may eliminate the handshake or formal introductions before the structured part of the interview.[88] The big question is whether or not these impressions are job related. For example, if a casino employee has only brief interactions with customers, but those interactions significantly influence customer relations, could a rigorously scored "first impression" at the conclusion of the rapport-building stage be a useful predictor of actual job success? To date, the only evidence addressing this question is indirect, but it suggests these impressions may be somewhat job related,[89] although we await more direct evidence establishing whether these reactions are primarily biased or job relevant.

The other three interview structure factors emphasize the importance of standardized interview content, centered on the kinds of questions asked during the structured interview (that is, question sophistication and question consistency) and use of standardized evaluation scoring. Michael Campion and his colleagues have identified and discussed 18 separate characteristics of interviews that have been used to determine whether an interview is a structured interview[90] (reported in Table 10.2). Their 1997 findings (based on the first 15 characteristics) influenced the work of Chapman and Zweig (mentioned earlier) and show that the most frequently used characteristics of a structured interview include using job analysis as a basis for questions, asking the same

| TABLE 10.2 | Dimensions of a Structured Interview |

1. **Standardized content of interview questions:**
   - (0.71)   a) basing questions on a job analysis
   - (0.74)   b) asking the same questions of each applicant
   - (0.27)   c) limiting prompting, follow-up, and elaboration on questions
   - (0.78)   d) using better types of questions (situational or behavioral questions)
   - (0.19)   e) using longer interviews by asking more questions
   - (0.17)   f) controlling preinterview (ancillary) information
   - (0.06)   g) not allowing questions from applicant until after the structured interview

2. **Standardized evaluation of candidate responses:**
   - (0.71)   a) rating each answer
   - (0.66)   b) using anchored rating scales
   - (0.19)   c) taking notes
   - (0.45)   d) using multiple interviewers, each independently rating
   - (0.13)   e) using the same interviewers across all applicants
   - (0.04)   f) not discussing applicants or answers between interviews
   - (0.52)   g) providing interviewer training
   - (0.11)   h) using statistical aggregation of ratings, not just an overall judgment of "hirability"

3. **New dimensions of structured interviews to consider:**
   - (0.05)   a) limiting or standardizing rapport building
   - (0.30)   b) recording interviews (to ensure structured interview)
   - (0.05)   c) informing applicants about WRCs to be assessed (enhancing transparency)

Note: Usage score (in parentheses): This score indicates the percent of studies of structured interviews reviewed in the meta-analysis included each dimension in its "structured interview." If all studies included this dimension, the usage score would be 1.0; if it was absent in all studies, the score would be 0.00. No dimension was included in all (1.0) or none (0.0) of the studies reviewed, and 74 percent of the studies did "ask the same question of each applicant."

Source: Adapted from Julia Levashina, Chris J. Hartwell, Fred P. Morgeson, and Michael A. Campion, "The Structured Employment Interview: Narrative and Quantitative Review of the Research Literature," *Personnel Psychology* 67, no. 1 (2014): 241–293.

questions of all applicants, posing better (using situational or behavioral) questions, scoring each answer, having anchored WRC scoring scales that use behavioral examples to illustrate scale points, using multiple interviewers (in the field), and training interviewers. Three new dimensions were added in the 2014 review by Julie Levashina, Michael Campion, and colleagues. These dimensions have been used infrequently, and more important, the evidence is not clear about how these dimensions will influence the structured interview,[91] and hence, more research is needed.

Table 10.2 also shows those components of the structured interviews that interviewers do not use very often, including failing to control for ancillary information (preinterview information, as previously discussed) or limiting the use of follow-up prompts (which can "give away" the answer that is being sought), allowing questions from applicants during the structured interview and discussions between interviews about candidates, and failing to take notes or even rate individual answers (instead, making overall evaluations). Careful examination of this table suggests some of the reasons why unstructured interviews have proven to be more popular with practitioners.[92] These infrequently used requirements in combination with the desire to use rapport building to put the candidate at ease may explain why unstructured interviews are consistently preferred by both the interviewers and the applicants.[93] Conversely, this preference may be the result of interviewers being overconfident in their ability to accurately assess the candidate even when using an unstructured interview coupled with the perceived effectiveness for providing recruitment information. More research is critical to identify how interviews can be designed so that they can retain nearly all the value of a structured interview, while contributing to recruitment and resulting in equally positive reactions from candidates as provided by unstructured interviews.

Of course, applicant reactions to the interview also influences whether the interviewer prefers to use unstructured interviews. Unstructured interviews allow the applicant to ask more questions, which aids in forming perceptions about fit to the organization and job. Furthermore, unstructured questions provide an opportunity for applicants to answer questions as they prefer. Applicants perceive these interviews favorably because they have high face validity, give each applicant a fair shot at succeeding at the task (that is, gives the opportunity to perform), is not seen as invading the person's privacy, and is a common (even expected) selection procedure.[94]

Ultimately, the main advantage of a structured interview is that information regarding major job-related WRCs is rigorously collected from all applicants, which makes the comparison across applicants easier and minimizes the influence of non-job-related impressions and guesses. Obviously, the more time that is spent in the interview asking construct-valid questions and evaluating answers that differentiates qualified from unqualified candidates, the more likely it will be that the interviewer will select the best candidate. Nevertheless, we must do a better job of helping interviewers realize their goal of attracting the best candidates to the organization, as well as recognizing what the applicants want from the interview, including being able to generate a job offer and simultaneously ascertaining whether they are a misfit for the job opportunity.[95] Acknowledging that all of these objectives reside in one single interview and striving to design an interview that can fulfill these competing objectives will enable firms to obtain applicant evaluations using more effective structured interviews that interviewers actually follow.

Developing Appropriate Interview Questions

The interviewer's evaluation of candidates should be more accurate if more information is obtained about the candidate's job qualifications. The relevant question becomes, "How does an interviewer develop specific job-related questions?" We answer this question using the two types of structured interviews: situational and behavior description.

The Situational Interview.   The situational interview method was developed by Gary Latham, Lise Saari, Elliot Pursell, and Michael Campion.[96] Its basic intent is first to identify specific activities representative of the job and then to use this information to form questions that ask applicants how they would behave in the situation. The first step is to do a job analysis of the position using the *critical-incidents technique*. (Go back to Chapter 3 to refresh your memory about this technique. Aren't you impressed with how tightly interwoven this book is?) Critical incidents are descriptions of work behaviors that actually have occurred and are examples of particularly good or particularly poor job performance. A well-written incident is a description of the action, not an evaluation. It describes the circumstances leading up to the incident, what actually happened, and the result. These incidents are gathered from job incumbents as well as from supervisors. They can be gathered either through personal interviews or questionnaires. Both methods require that the term *critical incident* be defined and that examples be provided to focus the respondents' thinking.

Typically, several hundred incidents are obtained for a single job. These incidents are then sorted into groups of similar behaviors, referred to as *behavioral dimensions*, by a small group of judges. Only those behaviors that are reliably sorted are retained. These behavioral dimensions then are named according to the content of the similar behaviors—for example, technical skills, the diagnosing of defects, customer service, and so on.

The next step is to review the incidents for each behavioral dimension, select a small number of the most appropriate incidents, and use these to write interview questions. There appears to be no one best way of selecting the small number of appropriate incidents. The judgments used frequently are provided by supervisors who are experienced in interviewing for the job. The exact number of incidents that are chosen depends on the planned time of the interview and the number of dimensions to be addressed. At least two incidents per dimension is common.

These incidents are then rephrased as interview questions appropriate for job applicants. Table 10.3 contains examples of such questions. This rephrasing is fairly straightforward; it usually includes a brief description of the circumstances of the incident and the question, "What would you do?" Here's an example: "You are to start your shift as convenience store manager at 5 A.M. When you attempt to start your car at 4:45 A.M., you realize that a family member left the gas tank nearly empty. What would you do?"

Scoring of applicants' responses to these questions is simplified by the development of scales for each question. Usually, these are five-point scales on which examples of low, average, and high responses are written. Table 10.3 contains examples of such a scale for each question. Developing the examples for each scale also makes use of the judgment of supervisors of the job of interest. Either the supervisors are asked to note actual behaviors they have observed, or they are asked to write down applicant responses they have heard in an interview. Again, only those examples showing agreement between low, average, and high behaviors are used on the scale. This scale is not revealed to the applicant but is used only by the interviewer. In scoring the interview, the interviewer places a check on the scale using the example responses as a frame of reference. If the

---

TABLE 10.3	**Examples of Situational Interview Questions and Scoring Scales**

1. Your spouse and two teenage children are sick in bed with colds. There are no relatives or friends available to look in on them. Your shift starts in 3 hours. What would you do in this situation?

   1 (low)   I'd stay home—my family comes first.

   3 (average) I'd phone my supervisor and explain my situation.

   5 (high)   Since they only have colds, I'd come to work.[a]

2. A customer comes into the store to pick up a watch he had left for repair. The repair was supposed to have been completed a week ago, but the watch is not back yet from the repair shop. The customer is very angry. How would you handle the situation?

   1 (low)   Tell the customer the watch is not back yet and ask him or her to check back with you later.

   3 (average) Apologize, tell the customer that you will check into the problem, and call him or her back later.

   5 (high)   Put the customer at ease and call the repair shop while the customer waits.[b]

3. For the past week you have been consistently getting the jobs that are the most time consuming (e.g., poor handwriting, complex statistical work). You know it's nobody's fault because you have been taking the jobs in priority order. You have just picked your fourth job of the day and it's another "loser." What would you do?

   1 (low)   Thumb through the pile and take another job.

   3 (average) Complain to the coordinator, but do the job.

   5 (high)   Take the job without complaining and do it.[c]

[a]Gary P. Latham, Lise M. Saari, Elliot D. Pursell, and Michael A. Campion, "The Situational Interview," *Journal of Applied Psychology* 4 (1980): 422–427.

[b]Jeff A. Weekley and Joseph A. Gier, "Reliability and Validity of the Situational Interview for a Sales Position," *Journal of Applied Psychology* 3 (1987): 484–487.

[c]Gary P. Latham and Lise M. Saari, "Do People Do What They Say? Further Studies on the Situational Interview," *Journal of Applied Psychology* 4 (1984): 569–573.

example responses have been carefully prepared, it is common for the applicants' responses to be similar to the examples. A total score for the interview can be obtained by summing the ratings across all scales. Alternatively, a series of separate scores can be generated by treating each scale score independently.

The Behavior Description Interview.   This method, first described by Tom Janz, is similar to the situational interview and uses many of the same steps.[97] It starts by generating critical incidents and identifying behavioral dimensions in the same manner as was described for the situational interview. Unlike the situational interview, however, the behavior description interview calls for a review of these behavioral dimensions as well as the identification of each dimension as essentially describing either maximum or typical performance of the individual. The difference between these two types is described as follows:

> *If how much the applicant* knows *or* can do *is critical to job performance, the dimension tends toward maximum performance. If what the applicant* typically will do *relates more closely to job performance, the dimension tends toward typical performance.*[98]

Maximum performance dimensions usually deal with technical skills and knowledge. Typical performance dimensions deal with getting along with others, working hard versus wasting time, and being organized, courteous, or punctual. The importance of this distinction is that, for the *behavior description interview*, it is recommended that maximum performance dimensions be omitted from the interview and almost complete emphasis be placed on typical performance dimensions.

The development of questions is essentially the same as discussed previously for a situational interview. Two aspects, however, are different from the situational interview. First, each question is formed with appropriate probes (follow-up questions). The main question serves to locate a particular instance from the applicant's past and focus the applicant on that type of event. Probes seek out exactly how the applicant behaved and what the consequences were of that behavior. Second, a distinction is made between questions appropriate for applicants who have work experience related to the job of interest and applicants who don't have such experience. The latter type of question should focus on the same behavior as the former, except the type of event or situation is more general and need not be part of a job at all. For example, a question asked of an experienced salesperson might be, "Tell me about the most difficult new client contact you made in the last six months." An equivalent question for an applicant with no sales experience might be, "We have all tried to convince someone we did not know well of the merits of a product or idea we were promoting. I would like you to tell me of a time when this was especially tough for you." Table 10.4 contains examples of the basic and accompanying probe questions using behavior description interviewing.

Scoring is done *separately* for each of the behavioral dimensions. When the interview is completed, the interviewer should review his or her notes (or the tape recording if one has been used). Based on the judged quality of their responses, applicants are placed in one of five rank-order groups for each dimension (see Table 10.4). Each group on the scale represents 20 percent of all applicants—that is, a score of "1" indicates that the applicant ranks in the bottom 20 percent; a score of "5" means that he or she ranks in the top 20 percent of all applicants. Each dimension is assigned a weight derived from judgments made by the interviewers, judgments that reflect its importance to overall job performance. Dimensions should not be weighted differentially unless some dimensions are at least two to three times more important than other dimensions. If this is not the case, equal weights are recommended. The dimension score described previously is multiplied by this dimension weight to obtain the total score for the dimension. Total score for the interview is obtained by summing all the dimension total scores.

TABLE 10.4	Examples of Behavioral Description Interviewing Questions and Scoring

1. It is often necessary to work together in a group to accomplish a task. Can you tell me about the most recent experience you had working as part of a group?

   (The following are probe questions.)

   a. What was the task?
   b. How many people were in the group?
   c. What difficulties arose as a result of working as a group?
   d. What role did you play in resolving these difficulties?
   e. How successful was the group in completing its task?
   f. How often do you work as part of a group?

2. Tell me about a time when you aided an employee in understanding a difficult policy.

   (The following are probe questions.)

   a. What was the policy?
   b. How did you know that the employee was having trouble understanding?
   c. What did you do or say that helped?
   d. How did you know that you had been successful?
   e. What steps did you take to change the policy?

Applicant Assessment Form for Scoring Behavioral Description Interview

	1	2	3	4	5
Dimension	Bottom 20%	Next 20%	Middle 20%	Next 20%	Top 20%
1. Working with group					×
2. Understanding policy					
•					
•					
•					
10.		×			

Dimension	Dimension Score		Weight (optional)		Cumulative Total
1.	5	×	25	=	125
•	•		•		
•	•		•		
•	•		•		
10.	3	×	10	=	325

Source: Janz, *Behavior and Descriptive Interviewing*, 1st Edition, © 1986, pg. 113, 117, 138, 181. Reprinted by permission of Pearson Education, Inc., Upper Saddle River, NJ.

Use of either approach (situational or behavior description interviews) should result in content-valid interview questions, which should be predictive of performance in the job. Taken together, considerable research conducted over the past 15 years documents the predictive validity of structured interviews. If the primary purpose of the employment interview is to select the best candidates in the applicant pool, one would be well advised to utilize a structured interview.

Conclusions about Designing the Interview

It seems to us that some often-found deficiencies in the interview can be directly attributed to misperceptions about its use in selection. Our examination indicates that it is not appropriate to use a significant portion of the selection interview for attracting applicants, providing detailed employment information, and developing the company's image. We do not intend this to mean that these activities are unimportant. We are simply saying that spending a significant portion of a 30-minute to 40-minute interview on these activities limits the effectiveness of this device in its primary purpose—evaluating the suitability of the applicant's attributes. Alternate vehicles that are designed primarily to provide information about the company and to promote a positive company image, we contend, would be more effective.

It is also clear that the validity of the interview is improved when a limited number of specific applicant characteristics are measured. In reality, this means designing the interview in the same manner as other selection devices. It generally is held that application blanks, tests, and work samples can measure some applicant characteristics. Selection programs are designed to take this into account. For some reason, however, the selection interview is often viewed as a general measuring device. This likely occurs because interviewers are overly confident that they can make accurate judgments about a variety of applicant characteristics. The social-perception literature tells us that these intuitive judgments automatically occur when first meeting a person.[99] This research, however, also tells us that such judgments usually are made with very little data and often are inaccurate. Consequently, to overcome these biases and to obtain higher predictive validity and construct validity, the interview should assess fewer dimensions, following the principles likened to the structured interview discussed in Table 10.5.[100]

So, where does this leave us? We believe a selection interview should try to accommodate some of the other interview objectives, although its number one purpose must remain on accurately assessing a few construct valid WRCs. Thus, we suggest the following:

1. Train interviewers about rapport building. Discuss ways to greet and put the candidate at ease. Furthermore, because we are naturally predisposed to forming a first impression about the candidate, we would consider highlighting job-relevant information the interviewer could focus on during this interaction, such as professional appearance and demeanor, maybe even "customer friendliness" during a meet-and-greet interaction.

2. Just before transitioning into the structured interview, we would train the interviewer on a script that tells the applicant what to expect during the remainder of the interview. An example script is provided below:

   "I (the interviewer) will be taking some notes during the structured interview (describe what it is and your purpose), which may contain some pauses while I complete my notes or prepare to ask my next question. At the end of the structured interview, which is likely to last about _____ minutes (for example, 25 minutes), there will be time (about _____ minutes, for example, 10 minutes) for you to ask questions any you may have and for me to talk about the organization and the job. At the end of this time, I will summarize the next steps of our selection process and the timing of our decisions as we go forward."

3. If this is acceptable to the applicant, begin the structured interview. Because this is a selection interview, this should be the heart of the interview and should involve the most time. Besides training the interviewer on taking notes, at the end of each answer, the interviewer should record a rating for that answer; this must be completed before proceeding to ask the next question. The point is that the interviewer has to be comfortable with some pauses, as these ratings are completed. At the completion of the structured interview, it will be possible to obtain an overall score by summing all of these ratings.

4. Once the interviewer has finished asking all questions and all answers have been rated, then the structured interview ends and the notes are put away. To ensure that these evaluations are not biased by the non-job-relevant discussion that follows, training should emphasize that these are the final ratings. The remainder of the time is dedicated to answering questions the applicant may have (and the applicant is encouraged to take the lead in this process) and by providing information on the position and organization. We believe that to offset the rigor of the structured interview, which required substantial disclosure by the applicant (about their capabilities), we believe it should be made clear to interviewers that they should view the applicant as a partner and help them determine whether there is good or poor fit. This may require more transparency about the position and organization than typically occurs and may mean that the information shared is not all high on favorability.

In summary, employment interviews can be used to achieve multiple goals or purposes, including recruiting, initial screening, and final selection, as well as otherwise exchanging information so that decision makers are more comfortable with the hiring decision. These diverse goals can be in conflict, however, which makes the interview a difficult technique to utilize effectively. For example, using the interview to make a selection decision, whether for initial screening or final selection, will require (because of the money and time needed to interview each applicant) reducing the number of candidates—thereby counteracting the objective of recruiting, which is to increase the number of candidates in the applicant pool.[101] As we have discussed, the structured interview is the best format to use for identifying the best candidate; however, some evidence suggests that these interviews are not useful for recruiting, probably because they are seen as impersonal and do not allow candidates to control how they express themselves.[102] Consequently, organizations should recognize that the usefulness of an interview is likely to depend on the importance of pursuing selection or recruitment goals; the format of the interview may need to reflect the most important goal to ensure that both organizations and candidates get the most out of the interview.

THE ROLE OF TECHNOLOGY AND GLOBAL TRENDS

Technology is beginning to change the way we conduct interviews. Historically, the interview was "a face-to-face interaction conducted to determine the qualifications of a given individual for a particular open position."[103] With the spread of Skype and videoconferencing, interviews increasingly are occurring at a distance.[104] Although this area will see more research, preliminary evidence suggests comparable predictive validities[105] to more traditional face-to-face interviews. For example, in one large scale meta-analysis, it was discovered that when the interview was conducted by telephone and scored based on a taped transcript, the overall predictive validity was .40, which is comparable to that reported earlier for traditional interviews.[106] And similar to other interviews, the predictive validity was larger when used in skilled and semiskilled positions (less complex jobs), but it was less predictive when used in higher complexity jobs (for example, managerial jobs). Evidence based on two studies also indicates that applicants react more negatively in videoconference interviews and computerized interviews than in traditional face-to-face interviews.[107] Although applicants typically perceive interviews positively, it may be that technology may interfere with the social interaction, thus leading to more negative reactions.

Future research likely will explore whether the impact of impression management behaviors, such as the loss of nonverbal behavior, changes the amount or quality of information gleaned from an interview. Furthermore, it is possible that as the quality of language software improves, the direct assessment of the interaction transcript may provide an alternative means of evaluating the candidate's qualifications. This certainly bears watching. Nevertheless, at this point, the evidence to date suggests that more "nontraditional" interviews likely will have comparable predictive validities, in large part because the types of WRCs assessed have so far remained the same.[108]

Turning to the growing influence of global labor markets, again very little research is available about the utility of interviews across different countries, although there is reason to believe that culture and national identity may influence the administration and design, if not the validity, of the interview.[109] Although nearly all of the research about the popularity of the interview has been done in the United States, evidence from a number of European countries, including Belgium, France, Germany, Greece, Italy, and the United Kingdom, indicates that the employment interview remains one of the most frequently used, if not the most frequently used, selection tool.[110]

Although only limited empirical and theoretical evidence currently is available about cross-cultural differences, what is available suggests reactions to structured interviews may differ, and possibly might even be illegal in different countries. On the basis of Geerdt Hofstedt's (1980) cultural dimensions,[111] high uncertainty avoidance is one dimension that may differ, as Ann Marie Ryan and Nancy Tippins have shown that applicants from such cultures prefer tests with objective answers over structured interviews with subjective answers.[112] Similarly, Ma and Allen have speculated that high-power distance also may influence interview outcomes. Ryan and colleagues have shown that in such countries, one is unlikely to rely on peers as interviewers, for example.[113] Beyond these cultural differences, there are differences in acceptable questions. For example, in other countries, it appears that interviewers often ask about private or personal behavior (in India) or about family, age, and annual income (in China) that would be off limits or even illegal in the United States.[114]

One other important area in which we need more research is whether cultural differences influence the rate and interpretation of impression management behaviors in the interview. As noted previously, most such research has been conducted in America or Europe. However, there may be meaningful differences in the use of self-promotion, assertiveness, and ingratiation.[115] For example, emphasizing one's accomplishments instead of the group's efforts may be perceived as bragging, while a weak handshake and poor eye-contact may be expected in China.[116] We are sure that future research will address these issues. Until then, if you are conducting interviews in other countries, you would be well served by considering the influence of cultural differences on your employment practices. Nevertheless, the interview does have the potential to be an effective predictor given that the critical "global WRCs" have been identified as adaptability, cultural agility, global mind-set, and relationship management.[117] These are the sorts of WRCs that the interview can help measure.

EVALUATING INTERVIEWS AS PREDICTORS

Predictive Validity

As we mentioned in the beginning of this chapter, we now have considerable evidence about techniques that enable the employment interview to yield more reliable and valid information for selection decisions. This is due to the concerted effort of a number of researchers over the past 25 years or so, researchers who have enhanced our understanding about what makes the interview an effective selection tool. Knowing that you are probably hungering for more details, we will share with you what we know. The single most important finding is that structured interviews are more valid than unstructured interviews. As least 12 meta-analytic studies supported this conclusion, with corrected validity coefficients ranging from the 0.40s to the low 0.60s for structured interviews and 0.20s to mid-0.30s for unstructured interviews.[118]

One meta-analysis directly examined the influence the level of interview structure has on predictive validity for entry-level jobs: Huffcutt and Winfred Arthur assigned prior interview studies to one of four levels of structure, thereby capturing the fact that structure exists on a continuum from highly structured to highly unstructured. At one extreme, Level I reflected unstructured interviews with no standardized scoring and no constraints on what questions to ask. The other extreme, Level IV, relied on a highly standardized or structured interview complete with a preestablished scoring "key" and a requirement to ask the same question to every candidate with no follow-up questions allowed. The mean observed predictive validity (uncorrected for measurement error) was 0.20 for unstructured interviews (Level I) and increased to 0.35 for Level II, 0.56 for Level III, and 0.57 for highly structured (Level IV) interviews.[119] These results reveal that the substantial gains in predictive validity for structured interviews is the result of standardizing the process of gathering, recording, and interpreting applicant suitability. The use of a standardized "instrument," similar to a test, appears to be an effective way to overcome the weaknesses inherent in the unstructured interview.

As noted previously, however, it is misleading to talk about structured interviews as if they were one "type" of interview. For example, one way these interviews fundamentally differ is with regard to the questions asked. Behavior description interviews are past-oriented questions involving prior work experiences. The questions ask the applicant "Can you tell me a time when you did…?" In contrast, situational interviews are future-oriented questions that ask applicants to imagine a work situation. Such questions ask, "What would you do if…?" Two recent meta-analyses have examined the validity coefficients of both the situational and the behavior description interview. Both types of interviews have produced good results, with corrected correlations in the 0.40s for situational interviews and 0.50s for behavior description interviews.[120]

To try to explain the difference in these predictive validities, a number of recent studies have directly compared the two types of interviews. One surprising finding was that even when designed to assess the same construct, the two types of interviews seemed to reflect different measures. Specifically, when answering questions about what one might do (that is, situational questions), answers were highly correlated with job knowledge and cognitive ability, whereas when answering questions about past behaviors and experiences (that is, behavioral questions), answers were related to more accumulated work experience and personality.[121] More important, this research suggests that when assessing professional jobs higher in complexity (for example, managers, sales, and so on), behavioral interviews have somewhat higher predictive validities than do situational interviews. Much of the validity evidence of the situational interview has been produced from studies involving entry-level, clerical, and hourly jobs; jobs for which many applicants have no prior work experience. When it comes to more complex jobs, however, perhaps using hypothetical questions (in situational interviews) may not be as appropriate as using questions about what the candidate has done in actual situations (as in behavioral description interviews).[122] Nevertheless, it recently has been suggested that instead of using just behavioral questions, interviews should include both situational and behavioral interview questions.[123] Given the different constructs such answers draw from (cognitive ability versus personality), it may be the case a combination of these questions will predict better than either alone. At any rate, with entry-level jobs or moderately complex jobs, it appears that structured interviews using either type of question result in comparably (high) predictive validities.

Finally, when evaluating the predictive validity of the employment interview, it is important to consider how correlated this predictor is with other predictors. To the extent the interview assesses WRCs that differ from other predictors, it will increase the amount of variance explained in the outcomes we hope to achieve by hiring the candidate. And although it is difficult to say precisely which WRCs are being measured in the interview (as each interview is unique), typically the interview adds value to a prediction, including cognitive ability, personality, and even scores based on an assessment center.[124] Thus, not only is the interview a valid predictor of critical criteria like job performance and turnover, but also their scores incrementally improve the quality of the prediction possible when using other common selection predictors.

This review of the validity of the interview has focused on criterion-related or predictive validity. A content validity strategy is also a relevant approach, particularly for structured interviews that rely on questions that are related specifically to the job. The courts have accepted the job-relatedness of structured interviews, and this has proven to be an effective defense against discrimination lawsuits.[125] A recent study illustrates the content validation approach, in which expert ratings were converted to a content validity ratio using Charles Lawshe's method.[126] Results showed considerable content validity at both the question and overall evaluation level, with a content validity index (CVI) of 0.89 (a value of 0.59 is necessary to reach a significant level when 11 experts are involved). This implies a high degree of overlap between performance during the interview and the capability to effectively do the job on the defined dimension of job performance.[127]

Reliability

One explanation of why structured interviews work better than unstructured interviews relates to differences in reliability. The notion is that by improving the structure or standardization of the interview, one increases reliability and—all else being equal—higher reliability leads to higher validity (refer to Chapters 7 and 8 to examine the role of reliability on validity, if this does not sound familiar). A recent meta-analysis provides evidence that structured interviews are more reliable than are unstructured interviews, which may explain why structured interviews have higher predictive validity. In this study, individual interviews using unstandardized questions were found to have a mean reliability of 0.37, which was significantly lower than the mean reliability of 0.66 and 0.59 for the top two highest levels of structure (level 5 and 6).[128] The researchers concluded that reliability creates an upper limit on predictive validity of 0.67 for highly structured interviews and 0.34 for unstructured interviews. Frank Schmidt and Ryan Zimmerman showed that much of the difference in criterion-related validity between structured and unstructured interviews could be reduced by increasing the reliability of the unstructured interview.[129] Because the level of standardization, by definition, cannot be increased for unstructured interviews, the only way to increase reliability is to increase the number of interviews given to each job candidate. The use of multiple independent raters increases the reliability of the interview simply by aggregating overall available ratings. This increases the amount of available information on which a hiring recommendation can be based and should correct for the idiosyncratic biases of individual interviewers. They found that averaging the ratings of three or four independent interviewers who conducted unstructured interviews resulted in the same level of predictive validity obtained from a structured interview conducted by a single interviewer. These results underscore the importance of reliability, which can be enhanced by standardizing the interview or by relying on multiple interviewers arriving at independent evaluations for each candidate.

One potentially important finding about situational interviews is that coaching of interviewees can significantly improve their performance in the interview (as measured by interviewers' ratings).[130] This coaching, given to applicants for four different police and fire jobs, consisted of descriptions of the interview process, logistics of the interview, advantages of structured interviews, the WRC list measured in the interview, participation in and observation of interview role plays, and tips on how to prepare for the interview. Further research illustrated that interviewee coaching appears to work by teaching candidates to be more organized, to pause and think before answering, and even to take notes before answering. This form of coaching is given by many colleges and universities to its students and by many private organizations to its customers. Coaching effects may be greatest for situational interviews, because these interviews request answers to hypothetical questions rather than asking questions about prior experiences as behavioral description interviews do.

DISCRIMINATION AND THE INTERVIEW

Our viewpoint of the legal issues relative to the interview is similar to our viewpoint about its validity—the interviewer (and organization) could be in big trouble if specific features that closely tie the interview to job activities are not incorporated into the interview. As described in Chapter 4, an organization would be in a vulnerable position with regard to discrimination if two conditions occurred: (a) decisions of the selection interview led, or assisted in leading, to disparate treatment or a pattern of disparate impact; and (b) the interview could not be defended regarding job relatedness.

As noted in the chapter dealing with application forms (Chapter 9), employers should avoid asking questions relating to race, color, religion, sex, national origin, marital status (including family responsibilities), sexual orientation, age, handicap or disability, and status as a Vietnam-era or disabled veteran.[131] In Chapter 9, Table 9.2 lists questions that have been deemed appropriate or inappropriate on an application form or during an employment interview. We encourage the reader to review those questions again. Using non-job-related questions to elicit these answers during the interview, even innocently, may provide the basis for an employment discrimination lawsuit. As this suggests, the twenty-first-century employment interview should be viewed as a source of potential liability for employers. The best way to protect the employer from discrimination claims is to ask questions that provide information about the candidate's ability to meet the requirements of the job.

Court Cases

As we discussed in Chapter 4, the *Watson v. Ft. Worth Bank & Trust* case has had a major impact on how the selection interview is treated by courts and companies in discrimination cases.[132] Because unscored interviews were considered to be subjective selection devices, previous to this decision interview, cases most often were heard as disparate treatment issues. Disparate impact cases usually were associated with formally scored objective devices, such as tests. As we have noted, defending a disparate treatment charge does not require as precise a score as defending a disparate impact charge. Therefore, it was in the best interest of companies, for legal defense reasons, to keep the interview as a less precisely scored selection instrument. Because of this, a conflict existed between the most effective use of the interview (scoring applicants) and the ease of defending a discrimination charge (not precisely scoring applicants).

The *Watson v. Ft. Worth Bank & Trust* decision changed this by stating that a case in which the selection interview is central to the charge of discrimination could be heard as a disparate impact case if the appropriate data were presented. Because validation is the most common defense of disparate impact, and because such a defense commonly requires statistical data, many companies now use a scored interview.

Although the *Watson v. Ft. Worth Bank & Trust* case addresses an important legal procedural issue, other cases have focused on the specific practices used by companies to conduct the selection interview. We discuss some of the more important findings of these cases in the next paragraphs. Table 10.5 is a summary of these cases.

TABLE 10.5 Selected Court Cases Treating the Selection Interview

Cases in Which Discrimination Was Found	Court Comments
Stamps v. Detroit Edison (1973)	All interviewers were white Interviewers made subjective judgments about applicant's personality No structured or written interview format No objective criteria for employment decisions
Weiner v. County of Oakland (1976)	All interviewers were male Interview questions suggested bias against females Selection decision rule not clearly specified
King v. TWA (1984)	Female applicant did not receive same questions as males History of interviewer's gender bias
Robbins v. White-Wilson Medical Clinic (1981)	No guidelines for conducting or scoring interview Interviewer's evaluation seemed racially biased based on own comments
Gilbert v. City of Little Rock, Ark. (1986)	Content validity inappropriate defense for measurement of mental processes Failure to operationally define WRCs Dissimilarity between exam questions and actual work situations
Bailey et al. v. Southeastern Area Joint Apprenticeship (1983)	Content of questions discriminatory toward women Defense did not conform with EEOC *Uniform Guidelines* Unclear instructions for rating applicant performance
Jones v. Mississippi Dept. of Corrections (1985)	Little evidence of specific questions used No scoring standards No cutoff score for selection

Cases in Which Discrimination Was Not Found	Court Comments
Harless v. Duck (1977)	Structured questionnaire Questions based on job analysis Relationship between interview performance and training
Maine Human Rights Commission v. Dept. of Corrections (1984)	Measurement of personality-related variables permitted WRCs listed Formal scoring system used
Minneapolis Comm. on Civil Rights v. Minnesota Chemical Dependency Assoc. (1981)	Permissible to use subjective measures of certain applicant characteristics that cannot be fully measured with objective tests Additional questions asked only of this applicant were appropriate Qualifications for job were posted A set of formal questions was asked of all applicants
Allesberry v. Commonwealth of Penn. (1981)	Nonscored questions used Written qualifications available to interviewer Posted notice of required qualifications Permissible to use subjective measures of administrative ability that cannot be fully measured with objective tests

Discrimination Found

In *Stamps v. Detroit Edison Co.*, the court noted that disparate impact had occurred and that the interview was a subjective process that unnecessarily contributed to this impact.[133] The interviewers had not been given specific job-related questions to follow, nor had they been instructed in either the proper weights to apply to specific pieces of information or the decision rules for evaluating the applicant as acceptable or unacceptable. In addition, all interviewers were white; a high percentage of the people in the applicant pool were black. In *Weiner v. County of Oakland*, the organization partially addressed the issues of the preceding case in that the interview was scored in a systematic fashion.[134] The court, however, specifically reviewed the questions asked in the interview. The court ruled that questions such as whether Mrs. Weiner could work with aggressive young men, whether her husband approved of her working, and whether her family would be burdened if she altered her normal household chores were not sufficiently job-related to warrant their use in the interview.

King v. TWA dealt with disparate treatment regarding the questions asked of males and females for a job of kitchen helper.[135] A black woman was asked about her recent pregnancy, her marital status, and her relationship with another TWA employee, who previously had filed an Equal Employment Opportunity Commission (EEOC) complaint against the company. The interviewer also inquired about her future childbearing plans and arrangements for child care. The company claimed other reasons for her rejection, but the court did not agree for two reasons: (a) the questions at issue were not asked of anyone else, and (b) a previous TWA HR specialist testified that the interviewer in this case had a history of discriminating against women because he felt child-care problems created a high rate of absenteeism.

Robbins v. White-Wilson Medical Clinic was a case of racial discrimination in an unscored interview that was intended to measure a pleasant personality and the ability to work with others.[136] The court tentatively accepted the requirement of personality as legitimate, but it found the rejection of the plaintiff to be on racial grounds. There were two crucial pieces of evidence: (a) a written comment in the margin of the application blank ("has a bad attitude—has called and asked many questions. She is a black girl. Could cause trouble") and (b) a response given by the interviewer in cross-examination about a black woman who was employed by the clinic that "she's more white than she is black."

There also have been cases in which discrimination was found despite the use of structured or scored interviews. In *Gilbert v. City of Little Rock*, a formal oral interview was scored, weighted, and combined with scores on other promotion devices.[137] The court ruled that the interview resulted in adverse impact against black officers in promotion evaluations. The police department attempted to justify the interview by content validity, showing that it measured attributes important to the position of sergeant. The court rejected this by pointing out that content validity is normally appropriate to justify specific tasks called for on the job. This interview required inferences to be made about mental processes and failed to define operationally the WRCs it purportedly measured.

A formally scored interview was also the focus of *Bailey v. Southeastern Area Joint Apprenticeship*.[138] In this case, formally scored questions were asked of each applicant. These questions dealt with education, military service, work history, interests, and personal activities and attitudes. Interviewers summarized responses and assigned points to applicants based on these responses. The court held that sex discrimination had occurred, despite these formal procedures. Questions involving military service, prior vocational training, shop classes, and prior work experience in boiler-making caused adverse impact. The defendant did not show the business necessity of these questions. Also, interviewers were inexperienced and used ambivalent instructions in rating applicant performance.

Another related case was *Jones v. Mississippi Department of Corrections*.[139] A scored oral interview was given by members of a promotion interview panel. Applicants were asked about job duties and prison rules and regulations. Each interviewee was rated on a 5-point scale for each of the following characteristics: attendance and punctuality, self-improvement efforts, prior performance of duties, current job knowledge, knowledge of new grade responsibilities, command presence and leadership qualities, personal appearance, overall manner, and education level. This interview was ruled to be racially discriminating because the department could not prove it to be job related. Furthermore, insufficient data were available concerning the actual questions used to measure these characteristics or standards used in scoring responses.

Discrimination Not Found

The interview also has been upheld in a number of court cases. In *Harless v. Duck*, the police department used an interview board to gather responses to approximately 30 questions asked of applicants. These questions tapped such WRCs as the applicant's communication skills, decision-making and problem-solving skills, and reactions to stress situations.[140] The court accepted the defendant's arguments that the interview was valid because the questions were based on dimensions identified through job analysis and that interview performance was related to performance in training at the police academy.

Maine Human Rights Commission v. Department of Corrections involved an interview designed to measure general appearance, self-expression, alertness, personality, interest in work, public relations ability, and leadership ability.[141] This interview was used in selection for the position of juvenile court intake worker. Multiple interviewers used a Department of Personnel Form that included a numerical grade for each of seven characteristics. The court regarded personality and the other variables to be acceptable in selection for this position. A major portion of the department's defense of its procedures was a job description for the position that listed necessary entry-level WRCs, such as the ability to maintain composure in stressful situations, the ability to exercise judgment in interpersonal situations, the ability to relate to a variety of people, and the ability to listen and act appropriately in counseling relationships. As this shows, although we would question the wisdom of assessing seven attributes in one interview, the court accepted the interview as a legally defensible selection procedure.

In *Minneapolis Commission on Civil Rights v. Minnesota Chemical Dependency Association*, the plaintiff, who had a history of gay rights activism, was asked additional questions that were not asked of other applicants.[142] Included among these was the comment, "The one thing that bothers me [the interviewer] about it is this, that in this position,… it seems to be that although you have special interests or anyone that took this position would have some special interests, that this job requires someone else to carry the ball of those special interests." While acknowledging that the plaintiff was asked additional questions, the court found that the previous history of extensive involvement in outside activities was a legitimate concern and this justified the additional questions. The fact that the plaintiff indicated that, in his opinion, neutrality might unfairly suppress his interests and that he would resign if the agency's decisions were insensitive to these interests was held to support the use of the additional questions and to properly serve as a basis of rejection.

In *Allesberry v. Commonwealth of Pennsylvania*, an unscored interview was one of several complaints referred to by the black plaintiff, who was not hired when two white applicants were.[143] The court did not find discrimination, judging that the two white applicants were better qualified and citing educational degrees and previous work history in support of this position. In addressing the interview specifically, the court said that "decisions about hiring in supervisory jobs and managerial jobs cannot realistically be made using objective standards alone." Subjective measures, therefore, were acceptable. In this case, the interviewer had access to a posted notice of the WRCs required for the position. Included in this notice were such statements as "ability to plan, organize, and direct specialized programs" and "ability to establish and maintain effective working relationships."

Laura Gollub Williamson and her colleagues have analyzed 130 federal court discrimination cases.[144] They have found links between interview structure and the way that judges explained their verdicts. Several specific interview characteristics were shown to be important: behavior-based versus trait-based criteria, specific versus general criteria, the use of multiple interviewers, interviewer training, the interviewer's familiarity with WRC requirements, validation evidence, guides for conducting interviews, minimal interviewer discretion in decision making, standardized questions, and the review of the interviewer's decisions. These results are supported in a recent analysis of 75 cases involving charges of discrimination in Canada. These findings show that tribunals give great weight to whether or not the employer used structured interviews.[145]

RESEARCH FINDINGS ON DISCRIMINATION

Legal restrictions against using race, ethnicity, sex, age, and disability in employment decisions should minimize or eliminate the influence of these characteristics when making hiring decisions. Several studies have examined the influence these demographic variables have on interview outcomes, and recent reviews of the literature have concluded that direct (main) effects resulting from candidate race, sex, age, and other demographic characteristics on interviewer ratings generally are small and inconsistent, particularly in the case of structured interviews.[146] A second stream of research has focused on the effects of similarity between the candidate and the interviewer. The basic premise is that interviewers who are of the same race as the candidate will tend to rate the candidate more favorably. Again, research reveals small and inconsistent effects on interviewer evaluations, based on whether the candidate and interviewer share demographic characteristics. This finding is similar to findings in the performance appraisal literature, which show that demographic similarity between employee and interviewer results in mixed or small effects on supervisor performance ratings.[147]

It is possible that the small effects these demographic variables have on interviewer ratings is due to the positive influence of EEOC legal restrictions. To support this contention, a few studies show that demographic variables tend to have larger effects on interviewer thoughts and beliefs than on actual hiring decisions.[148] It may well be that if there are causal effects resulting from these demographic variables, they are due to reasons other than discrimination. Such effects may simply reflect more complex underlying factors, such as the tendency of an interviewer to make inferences about candidate attitudes and values, and that therefore these demographic variables are one way interviewers draw such inferences.

The area of physical and mental disabilities is an area in which research does demonstrate some influence of demographic variables on interview outcomes. Since the passage of the Americans with Disabilities Act of 1990, a number of studies have been conducted on this topic. Although the results are not uniform, findings suggest that applicant disclosure of nonobvious disabilities—as well as early discussion during the interview about obvious applicant disabilities—tends to increase the likelihood of a hiring recommendation.[149] Although employers are barred from asking candidates questions about their disabilities before making a job offer, these results suggest that candidates will receive a favorable response to such disclosures, particularly if the applicants are not seen as threatening (likely to pursue litigation).

Research on demographic characteristics has suggested two ways to further reduce any effects due to age, race, sex, and other demographic variables: using highly structured interviews and relying on more experienced interviewers who have more training. The use of structured interviews appears to reduce the influence of biases due to discrimination.[150] For example, Jennifer DeNicolis Bragger, Eugene Kutcher, and their associates found that the use of structured interviews reduced interviewer biases against overweight candidates when hiring decisions were made. This study found that by focusing on job-related factors, the bias against overweight job candidates was reduced.[151] Although the effects are less clear, there is also evidence that the more skilled interviewers are in experience and training, for example, the less likely they are to be biased by the candidate's demographic characteristics.[152]

Does this mean there is not likely to be disparate impact on race, sex, and so forth in employment interviews? A recent meta-analysis of 31 studies conducted by Huffcutt and Philip Roth showed that black and Hispanic candidates received candidate evaluations that, on average, were about one-quarter of a standard deviation lower than those for white candidates.[153] Thus, employment interviews show some evidence of disparate impact on the basis of candidate race. Nevertheless, those differences are substantially smaller than the group differences often found when cognitive ability tests are used. Recent research, however, illustrates that the magnitude of the mean standardized difference between the candidate evaluations of white and black or Hispanic candidates is likely to be larger if one accounts for the impact of only interviewing the top 30 percent of applicants (range restriction).[154]

One other finding is particularly important to this discussion—that is, that structured interviews result in smaller subgroup differences ($d = 0.23$ and 0.17, respectively, for black and Hispanic candidates) than structured interviews ($d = 0.32$ and 0.71, respectively).[155] This supports the point made in prior paragraphs. One way to reduce discrimination is to use a structured interview. A recent study examining 158 U.S. federal court cases revealed that unstructured interviews were involved in charges of hiring discrimination in 57 percent of these cases, whereas structured interviews were involved in only 6 percent of cases.[156] Furthermore, although the unstructured interview was ruled to be the cause of discrimination in 41 percent of these cases, the structured interview was never found to be discriminatory (0.00 percent). Not surprisingly, reliance on job-related questions increases the odds of an organization winning a lawsuit. The utility of structured interviews will be discussed more extensively later in this chapter. For now, it is important to recognize that using structured interviews will reduce the likelihood of a disparate impact lawsuit and will provide a job-related basis for defending the selection decision.

A MODEL OF INTERVIEWER DECISION MAKING

Recent research on the interview illustrates that a number of important factors influence interviewer decision making, including social and cognitive factors, individual differences between the applicant and the interviewer, and the interview context itself.[157] As we mentioned previously, early research on the interview pointed out deficiencies in its reliability and validity. Consequently, research over the past 15 to 20 years has attempted to identify which characteristics of the interviewer, the candidate, or the interview process were related to low reliability and validity. Although such research produced some interesting and useful results, in general, it was disorganized. Many interview factors were studied unsystematically, often because they were easy to measure rather than because they were theoretically important. Consequently, results of studies were often inconsistent. We know that structured interviews generally are superior to unstructured interviews, but we still need a comprehensive model to explain why this is so.

Models that focus on factors that affect decision making during the interview provide a way to organize the conduct of research and the interpretation of results. Basically such models assume that the interviewer and candidate are gathering and processing information about each other as well as the organization and job. Research in cognitive and social psychology becomes the basis for many of the propositions of such decision-making models. Dipboye's model (shown in Figure 10.1) briefly summarizes the existing large body of research that identifies critical factors affecting the decision-making process over the different phases of the interview (before, during, and after the interview).[158] We hope that familiarizing yourself with this model will help elucidate the recommendations we make at the end of the chapter.

Expectations, Beliefs, Needs, and Intentions before the Interview

Interviewers and candidates bring to the interview their own expectations, beliefs, needs, and intentions with regard to the job, the interview, the organization, and each other. These are a product of the previous knowledge, training, education, and experience of the interviewer and the candidate. These expectations, beliefs, needs, and intentions influence all three stages of the interview (see Figure 10.1). In the preinterview phase, these factors have been shown to have a significant impact on impressions held by the interviewer and candidate, which in turn have been found to influence interviewer evaluations of those candidates.[159] Research also shows that interviewers seek out and recall (even distort) information that supports or confirms their preinterview impressions of the candidate,[160] thereby creating a self-fulfilling prophecy. Interview outcomes have been shown to be influenced by interviewer preconceptions about what the ideal candidate or group of applicants should be.[161]

One of the requirements of a highly structured interview is that the interviewer's evaluation of the candidate should not be influenced (or biased) by examining applicant information before the interview. Not surprisingly, if an interviewer finds out Candidate A scored at the 99th percentile on an intelligence test, whereas Candidate B was at the 70th percentile, at the end of the interview, they are likely to view "A" as a brainiac and "B" as just smart.[162] Access to the Internet has compounded this problem as previewing applicant Facebook pages has been shown to influence the interviewer's intentions to recommend hiring a candidate.[163] Two surveys indicate the extent of this problem as 77 percent of executive recruiters and 78 percent of Canadian practitioners reported using such information when making screening decisions.[164] The Jones survey was particularly informative, as it reported candidates were eliminated for bad-mouthing a former employer (19 percent), behavior linked to alcohol or drug use (19 percent), and sexually inappropriate pictures or the use of profanity (11 percent). This finding was supported by a lab experiment that found hypothetical job candidates posting negative work-related activity or alcohol abuse and drug use or sexually inappropriate pictures or the use of profanity (11 percent) were significantly less likely to

FIGURE 10.1 A Model of the Selection Interview

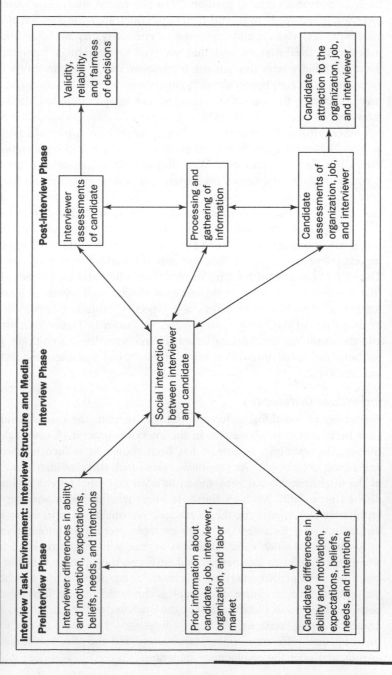

Interview Task Environment: Interview Structure and Media

Preinterview Phase — Interview Phase — Post-Interview Phase

Interviewer differences in ability and motivation, expectations, beliefs, needs, and intentions

Prior information about candidate, job, interviewer, organization, and labor market

Candidate differences in ability and motivation, expectations, beliefs, needs, and intentions

Social interaction between interviewer and candidate

Interviewer assessments of candidate

Processing and gathering of information

Candidate assessments of organization, job, and interviewer

Validity, reliability, and fairness of decisions

Candidate attraction to the organization, job, and interviewer

Source: Robert L. Dipboye, "The Selection/Recruitment Interview: Core Processes and Contexts," in *The Blackwell Handbook of Personnel Selection*, ed. Arne Evers, Neil Anderson, and Olga Voskuijil (Oxford, UK: Blackwell Publishers, 2004), 121–142.

be recommended by the recruiter.[165] Even more problematic, women were rated significantly lower than men for the use of profanity or sexually explicit activities. To ensure the interview generates independent evaluations of the candidate, it is recommended that access to preinterview applicant information be restricted, a practice routinely ignored by recruiters.[166]

In contrast, little research has been done on the influence of the candidate's preinterview expectations, beliefs, needs, and intentions. For example, the interview process is likely to be significantly different for those candidates who approach the interview with an expectation that they will receive and accept a job offer than for those who are less likely to pursue an offered position.[167] In one recent study, candidates who thought the interviewer was likely to extend them a job offer after the first few minutes of the interview were less vigilant and motivated to effectively manage their image during the remainder of the interview and thus received lower ratings from the interviewer than those candidates who thought the interviewer had a less favorable reaction.[168] In this case, the candidate's beliefs about the interviewer's initial reaction was found to influence how effectively the candidate managed the image projected during the rest of the interview.

Access to the Internet also has had an impact on applicant's preinterview behavior, as it facilitates their search for information on the job and organization. Research shows candidates view organizational Web sites to infer organizational personality or culture, diversity, friendliness, and to gain a sense of person–organization fit, all of which influences the organization's reputation as well as shapes how motivated the applicant is to participate in the selection process and the intent to further pursue employment.[169]

Of course, to the extent this leads the applicant to prepare for the interview, by setting goals, thinking about how to present themselves, and improving on prior interviewing experiences, the higher their job search self-efficacy and success at interviewing.[170] The lack of research with regard to candidate beliefs and expectations is surprising, given that the cost incurred by an organization can be high when, as a result of negative or unrealistic expectations or beliefs, a prospective candidate fails to apply for a position or drops out of the hiring process early. As shown in Figure 10.1, what the interviewer and the candidate are thinking before the interview has a significant and dynamic effect on both the social interaction that occurs during the interview and on postinterview outcomes.

Individual Differences

A number of individual difference variables of both the candidate and the interviewer have been shown to play a role in the interview process. A candidate's physical attractiveness, for example, repeatedly has been shown to influence interviewer evaluations and hiring decisions.[171] As previously mentioned, the candidate's handshake at the start of the interview also has been shown to affect the interviewer's evaluations.[172] The candidate's personality has been shown to affect whether he or she prepares rigorously for an interview. Furthermore, the candidate's personality is expected to have a direct effect during and after the interview.[173] For example, gregarious, outgoing candidates are likely to experience a much different interview than will shy, introverted candidates. Finally, whether a candidate has participated in a coaching program before the interview has been found to predict interview outcomes.[174] As discussed in this book's legal section, the influence of candidate demographic characteristics on interviewer evaluations has been investigated. Results reveal that these attributes have small and inconsistent effects on actual hiring decisions.[175] These findings show that more research should be done on the individual differences among candidates—and the effects of these differences before, during, and after the employment interview.

Individual interviewer differences also have a significant effect on the interview. Surprisingly, there appear to be relatively large differences across interviewers about which of these differences are ideal attributes for person–job fit.[176] If recruiters hold idiosyncratic beliefs about what makes for good person–job fit or person–organization fit, it will be tough to get agreement on which are the best applicants. This suggests the importance of interviewer training. Fortunately, a number of studies have assessed the utility of providing interviewer training. Unfortunately, these studies show only modest effects on interviewer evaluations. This is surprising, given the cost borne by organizations to provide such training.[177] Relatively little research has been done about the value of interviewer experience, although increasing experience should positively affect interviewer evaluations. One explanation for the relative dearth of studies about interviewer experience is that the conditions needed for learning (training and feedback) are not present in the typical interviewer's job. Dipboye and Susan Jackson found a positive relationship between interviewer experience and interviewer decisions when the experience was associated with higher levels of cognitive complexity (that is, the ability to deal with complex social situations).[178] This finding, however, may be due to the influence of differences among interviewers' general mental abilities rather than interviewer experience. Further research should examine the effect interviewer intelligence has on decision making. In fact, better understanding is needed about how the interviewer's personality, cognitive complexity, emotional intelligence, self-esteem, or interviewer self-efficacy affect the validity and accuracy of interviewer judgments. The finding that some interviewers are able to render more valid judgments than other interviewers underscores the need to study how these individual differences between interviewers affect evaluations.[179]

Social Interaction during the Interview

The interview is fundamentally a social interaction between the candidate and interviewer. Because these interactants are almost always strangers and because the candidate is dependent on the interviewer to get a job offer, there is considerable incentive to manage one's image. Consequently, there has been considerable research about factors that influence the quality of this relationship. Two related factors that have been studied extensively involve the similarities between the interviewer and the candidate and candidate's fit with the job or organization. Similarity with regard to demographic characteristics (race, sex) and attitudes is expected to increase attraction. This should lead to liking and positive impressions, which lead the interviewer to rate the candidate more favorably.[180] As noted previously, however, research on demographic similarity has led to small and inconsistent effects on the ratings of candidates.[181] In contrast, the findings for attitudinal similarity (similarity in work attitudes and personal values) seems to affect interviewer evaluations of candidates positively, particularly evaluations relating to perception of the candidate's competence. Furthermore, the effect due to similarity does not seem to reduce the predictive validity of interviewer ratings.[182] Applicant and interviewer perceptions of attitudinal similarity, however, take time to manifest; consequently, attitudinal similarity is harder to assess during an interview than similarities that are based on demographic factors. This likely explains why attitudinal similarity effects are not even larger in the interview. In general, research on similarity (both attitudinal and demographic) has shown that effects are much less pronounced when the interview is structured and job requirements are clear.[183]

In addition to similarity, another area that has garnered considerable study is the fit between the candidate and the job or organization. In this case, the research focuses on the impact of congruence between the candidate and characteristics of the position or organization rather than characteristics of the interviewer. A recent meta-analysis of person–environment fit conducted by Amy Kristof-Brown, Ryan Zimmerman, and

Erin Johnson demonstrated the value of attaining a good fit of the candidate to the position or firm, as the candidate's attraction to the organization is significantly influenced—whether due to person–job fit ($\rho = 0.48$) or person–organization fit ($\rho = 0.46$). Results also showed that the employer's intention to hire the candidate ($\rho = 0.67$ and 0.61, respectively, for person–job fit and person–organization fit) increased when the employer thought the candidate was the "right type."[184] Although the meta-analysis by Huffcutt and associates found organizational fit was only rarely measured during the interview (in 3 percent of interviews), it had a relatively high mean validity for predicting performance ($\rho = 0.49$).[185] Furthermore, "fit" is one of those constructs that is relevant to all jobs, whether for an entry-level position or a senior manager job.

Another recent meta-analysis illustrates that what the recruiter does during the interview has a significant effect on candidate attitudes. For example, interviewers who are more personable, competent, and informative increased the candidate's attraction to the job or organization ($\rho = 0.29$–0.42).[186] Recruiter behaviors also influenced whether the candidate chose to actually join the organization, although this effect was smaller. This study also found that demographic characteristics of the interviewer did not influence candidate attitudes or job choices ($\rho < 0.10$). These results show that it does not matter whether the recruiter is from a specific functional area (already does the job being interviewed for) or is of a particular gender or race. Thus, who the interviewer is does not matter as much as how the interview is conducted. Research also shows that interviewer ratings of the candidate tend to be higher when the interview itself is longer and the interviewer talks more during the interview.[187] Taken together, these findings suggest that candidates use the behavior of the recruiter to make inferences about the organization, the job, and even the likelihood of receiving a job offer, which in turn affects candidate attitudes about the attractiveness of the position.

Studies examining the influence of the candidate's behavior during the interview have centered on the self-presentation tactics the candidate relies on to influence the interviewer's evaluation. Tactics include the candidate's professional demeanor and physical attractiveness, use of impression management behaviors, and verbal and nonverbal behavior.[188] For example, two recent meta-analyses found that attractive candidates were more likely to be hired than less-attractive individuals, even when decision makers have job-relevant information available about the candidate.[189] Stephen Motowidlo and his associates have studied both verbal and nonverbal behaviors in videotapes of actual interviews. They found that interviewer ratings had greater accuracy when the interviewers had both a high level of verbal cues (voice pitch, pitch variability, speech rate) and moderate to high levels of nonverbal cues (attractiveness, eye contact, head movements, smiling, hand gestures, and so on) from candidates.[190] It appears that interviewer evaluations of candidates are significantly affected by what and how the candidate communicates, verbally and nonverbally.[191] Some evidence indicates that these behaviors also may predict performance on the job.[192] That is, the same visual and vocal cues that positively influenced interviewers were also positively related to a candidate's future job performance ratings. The authors explain that these cues affect interviewers; they cause liking and trust, which affects job performance by facilitating interpersonal relationships that are important for success in many jobs.

Does this mean that the candidate can manipulate the outcome of the interview through such behaviors as smiling, posture, and hand movements? Such manipulation is part of what is termed "impression management," and a number of studies have shown that these behaviors do, indeed, influence hiring decisions.[193] Studies show that candidates frequently engage in assertive influence tactics (self-promotion or ingratiation tactics) during employment interviews.[194] The effects of impression management tactics, however, are not always consistent. One study found that such tactics affect different interviewers in different ways and, under certain conditions, can create negative images of the applicant.[195] Another recent study showed that applicants who reported higher rates of faking behavior received lower ratings from interviewers,[196] which is somewhat reassuring. And yet, research suggests it is hard to detect lying.[197] Thus, this is an area for which more research is needed. After all, organizations do not want to hire those who tell blatant lies.

Two recent meta-analyses of the impression management literature shows that both ingratiation (tactics that focus on the interviewer by flattering or agreeing with the target, and which includes nonverbal behavior, such as smiling, head nodding, and so on) and self-promotion (describing one's past experience and accomplishments in a positive manner to generate a perception of competence) positively affect interviewers' evaluations of job candidates.[198] In fact, these studies found that when ingratiation and self-promotion were studied in the context of employment interviews, the effect sizes were roughly equal. Interestingly, the use of ingratiation was found to positively relate to supervisory ratings of job performance ($\rho = 0.26$), suggesting that these tactics also may be related to success on the job. In contrast, although self-promotion tactics were useful in the interview, these tactics were negatively related to supervisor assessments of performance ($\rho = -0.25$).[199] This may be because a candidate is expected to "brag" about him or herself during the interview, but continuing to do so as an employee leads others to evaluate the person in a less positive way or even negatively. These findings bring into question whether impression management tactics create bias or instead enable the candidate to convey job-related qualifications. This is an important question future research must examine. It should be noted that research shows that the influence of impression management tactics is reduced when structured interviews are used.[200]

One final area that we know is critical to the reliability and validity of the employment interview relates to the nature of the questions asked. If the questions are not related to the job, we should not expect validity to be high. If interviewers ask different questions, we should not expect the interviewers to be reliable in their evaluations of candidates, because each interviewer in fact has collected different information about the applicants. When research has examined interviewers' questions, Susan Taylor and Janet Sniezek found that interviewers often disagreed among themselves about which topics should be covered in an interview.[201] These differences seemed to relate more to individual preferences than to the perceived importance of job requirements. Interviewers consistently failed to cover topics that they believed to be important; applicants report that the most frequently covered topics are the relatively unimportant ones of university life and extracurricular activities, not topics related to the demands of the job. Even today, many interviewers continue to resist using the structured interview format even though research shows that it is more useful for predicting later job success.[202] It is reasonable to assume that questions tend not to be consistently asked of all candidates if the interview is unstructured.

Information Processing and Decision-Making Factors

The interview ultimately requires that interviewers and candidates make decisions. Considerable research has been conducted on the decision-making process of managers; across multiple theories, we find that decision makers use a two-stage decision process.[203] Dipboye applied this finding to explain how decisions are made during the interview.[204] In the first stage, the decision maker is trying to reduce choices by screening out unsuitable candidates, often using relatively simple decision rules. Dipboye has argued that interviewers *categorize* applicants in a relatively unthinking way during this initial screening process. At the second stage, interviewers evaluate choices more rigorously in an attempt to choose the "best" candidate. This stage results in a process called *characterization.* During the *characterization* process, traits are inferred based on a candidate's behavior and answers to interview questions.[205] The model posits that if the interviewer gains information that contradicts his initial categorization, he may engage in a process of *correction* and change his initial impression to incorporate this new information. Researchers have found that a number of factors influence decision making within this two-stage evaluation process. The most important of these factors is reviewed next.

Interviewers appear to use *heuristics,* or simple rules of thumb, when making decisions. The tendency to use prior estimations as an anchor around which future judgments revolve is one well-known psychological heuristic commonly used by decision makers. Two other commonly used heuristics, representativeness and availability, also are expected to influence interviewers.[206] Both of these heuristics would lead the interviewer to overestimate the likelihood a candidate possesses a "rare" characteristic because it is similar to another more common attribute (representativeness) or has high emotional impact (availability). Gary Latham and associates found that interviewers were affected by anchoring and adjustment heuristics, just like other decision makers. In this study, interviewers were given either a high or low anchor score (prior estimation) about the candidate's hirability. Those candidates with a high anchor score led to more favorable interviewer evaluations than did candidates with a low anchor score. It should be noted, however, that the effect from the anchoring heuristic was significantly reduced when the interview was structured, again underscoring the importance of using a structured interview.[207]

Order or contrast effects have been found to influence interviewer judgments. A number of studies have found that interviewers compare or contrast candidates. The contrast effect occurs when an "average" candidate is rated "above average" when contrasted with other candidates who were "below average." However, if the same "average" candidate instead had been contrasted against other "above-average" candidates, the interviewer would have rated the candidate below average. Consequently, the rating obtained for a candidate is partly determined by others against whom the candidate is being compared.[208]

There is evidence of a strong primacy effect—that initial information carries considerable weight in the interview.[209] One stream of research, which was discussed earlier, illustrates the effect of first impressions formed about candidates during the initial stage of the interview.[210] Findings in social psychology show that individuals form reactions to strangers rather quickly—and this research suggests we are "prewired" to evaluate strangers based on minimal information.[211] The first impression appears to establish an anchor for the interviewer that filters all subsequent evaluations of the candidate.[212] As previously noted, the primacy effect emerges from preinterview perceptions of candidate competency, based on information from application forms, resumes, and other tests administered before the interview. Therese Macan and Dipboye found that preinterview beliefs and impressions interviewers bring to the session—beliefs based on knowledge of an applicant's coursework and job experience—were strongly related to postinterview ratings of the candidate. Nevertheless, they also found that performance during the interview significantly affected interviewer evaluations, even after accounting for this preinterview impression.[213]

The other type of applicant information that is given a disproportionate weight by interviewers is negative information. Somewhat surprisingly, it has been found that even experienced interviewers give more weight to negative information than to positive information in decision making.[214] For example, in one study, unfavorable ratings on only one of several characteristics resulted in the rejection of the applicant in more than 90 percent of the cases.[215] In some cases, the source of these negative judgments is not clear. There is evidence that impressions formed during the interview—rather than the facts gathered—are related to these judgments. Such decision making would clearly be at odds with the stated purpose of the interview—but consistent with the evidence that physical attractiveness, liking, and nonverbal cues affect the decision.[216] We can explain this emphasis on negative information by thinking about the costs of the various outcomes of an interview. The greatest cost to the interviewer comes from making the mistake of selecting a candidate who fails on the job. Professional reputation and company expenditures suffer. On the other hand, rejecting an applicant who in fact would be a successful performer if selected has no real costs. Who would know? Therefore, cost is lowered when an interviewer rejects all candidates who appear to be marginal or doubtful, even if they would have been successful in the job.

Another reason ratings are not accurate is due to the amount of information an interviewer can recall after an interview. In one study, managers watched a 20-minute video of an interview. Immediately after the video, they were asked 20 factual questions. The average manager missed 10 of the 20 facts mentioned during the interview. Managers who had taken notes during the interview were much more accurate (some missed none), whereas those managers without notes missed as many as 15 out of 20 questions. Those managers with notes rated the candidate more critically and demonstrated more variance in their ratings across dimensions. In contrast, managers without notes assumed that the overall applicant evaluation was more favorable and provided comparable ratings across all dimensions. Thus, those interviewers who knew the facts were more accurate and recognized that the candidate could differ from dimension to dimension.[217] Other research shows, however, that to get the most benefit from note taking, interviewers must be trained on how to take notes.[218]

One conclusion that can be drawn from research on information processing and decision making is that many factors that only marginally relate to job activities often influence an interviewer's evaluation, even when the interviewer is experienced. Does this all mean that the interview is worthless? Of course not; as we have shown, studies clearly have revealed the validity of this device. These studies, however, have been conducted on interviews that were designed to counteract many of the problems just discussed. The last section of this chapter develops recommendations for the design of an interview.

RECOMMENDATIONS FOR USING THE INTERVIEW

We have discussed a lot of information about the selection interview. Let's put this information to use by discussing specific recommendations for how to build a better interview. These recommendations are summarized in Table 10.6.

TABLE 10.6   Recommendations for Interview Use

1. Restrict the scope of the interview to selection (not recruiting) and focus on the most job-relevant WRCs, preferably just two or three WRCs.
2. Limit the use of preinterview data about applicants.
3. Adopt a structured format by predetermining major questions to be asked.
4. Use job-related questions.
5. Use multiple questions for each WRC.
6. Rely on multiple independent interviewers.
7. Apply formal scoring that allows for the evaluation of each WRC separately.
8. Train interviewers in the process of the selection interview.

Restrict the Scope of the Interview

We believe that one of the major weaknesses of the interview is that it often is used to accomplish too many purposes. As we have discussed, the interview is frequently and simultaneously used as a public relations vehicle to project an image of the organization, as a recruitment vehicle to convey job description and organization information to potential applicants, and as a selection vehicle to evaluate the job-related WRCs of the applicants. Although recruitment, selection, and projecting a good public image all must be dealt with when hiring, we ought not confuse time similarity with function similarity. Just because these three functions are compressed into a short period at the beginning of the HR management cycle, it does not mean they should be addressed at the same time.

We think that recruitment and selection should be separated systematically separated. If it is decided that the interview, as a process, should be used in either one of these functions, then each separate interview process ought to be planned according to the models for effective use that have been developed for that function. In this way, the selection interview becomes focused and each purpose is dealt with separately. This should substantially increase its usefulness.

There is a second way in which the interview suffers from a multiple-purpose use. Earlier in this chapter, we noted that several writers have concluded that often too many WRCs are evaluated in the interview. It has been recommended that the scope of the interview be limited to a much narrower band of applicant characteristics: *job knowledge, applied social and interpersonal skills,* and *personality and habitual behaviors* (work habits, conscientiousness, emotional stability, agreeableness, and so on).

Let us use the information presented in Table 10.6 to demonstrate the appropriate use of the interview in a selection program. Using the procedures previously described in Chapter 3, we have completed a job analysis for the job of maintenance supervisor. The WRCs listed in Table 10.7 have been derived from this job analysis. The remainder of the table illustrates the appropriate way to use various selection instruments to measure the WRCs; the table shows the percentage of the selection program that should be devoted to each of the selection instruments.

Our judgment is that only three of the eight WRCs are appropriate for assessment in the interview and that, because of the importance of these WRCs, the interview should account for 45 percent of the selection program. "Ability to give verbal work instructions to laborers regarding construction and repair" is best demonstrated through a verbal exchange process such as the interview. Measurement of "ability to schedule work crews for specific tasks" frequently would entail the exchange of information about specific characteristics of tasks and also an explanation of the reasoning used in making specific assignments. Such an exchange is more appropriate for an interview than for a written test. The "ability to direct multiple work crews and work projects simultaneously" is, perhaps, the most difficult of the WRCs to measure accurately. Ideally, we would use a simulation that creates several situations and evaluates the applicant's responses. To be accurate, however, the simulation should be carried out for an extended period of time. This would not usually be feasible. Our approach, therefore, would be to view this ability as a work habit and to use the interview to determine information about the applicant's behavior in similar, previous situations.

We thus conclude that of the eight WRCs being measured in this selection program, only these three should be assessed by the interview. As Table 10.7 indicates, three other WRCs are tapped by a combination of the application form and ability tests. The remaining two WRCs are best measured by performance tests.

TABLE 10.7	Selection Plan for the Job of Maintenance Supervisor

	Selection Instruments				
Job: Maintenance Supervisor	**WRC Importance**	**Application Form**	**Interview**	**Performance Test**	**Ability Test**
WRC					
Knowledge of construction principles of small buildings	15%	3%			12%
Knowledge of building systems: heating, electrical, plumbing	15%	3%			12%
Knowledge of inventory control methods	10%	3%			7%
Skill in performing basic carpentry, plumbing, electrical wiring operations	5%			5%	
Ability to diagnose defects in building and building systems	10%			10%	
Ability to give verbal work instructions to laborers regarding construction and repair	20%		20%		
Ability to schedule work crews for specific tasks	10%		10%		
Ability to direct multiple work crews and work projects simultaneously	15%		15%		
	100%	9%	45%	15%	31%

Limit the Use of Preinterview Data

Perhaps the most common sequence of steps in selection programs is that the applicant first completes an application form or provides a resume and then participates in a screening interview. In most cases, the interviewer has access to this information and uses it, at least initially, to formulate questions and direct conversation during the interview.

There is some question as to whether this preinterview information is of real benefit to the interviewer. Many argue that preinterview information is essential to good interviewing. It provides basic information about previous work and education experience that can be developed in the interview. Some interview guides even recommend that interviewers develop hypotheses about the type of WRCs possessed by a specific applicant based on application information, and then use the interview to test these hypotheses. Recent research, however, that has closely studied this issue has not supported these proposed advantages of using preinterview data—and, in fact, has found detrimental effects. We have presented the model developed by Dipboye, which emphasizes that preinterview information is used to develop assessments of applicants before the interview is conducted. Furthermore, with the widespread accessibility of social media (Facebook, LinkedIn), the availability of this information also has become an issue. Preinterview information affects the interview process and can serve as sources of error in the evaluation of applicants. The meta-analysis by Mike McDaniel and his associates found higher predictive validities when interviewers do not have access to test scores or other background information.[219] These results indicate the direct effect that preinterview impressions can have on the interviewer. As noted earlier, interviewers typically have preinterview ancillary information available before the interview (test scores, letters of reference), which demonstrates the magnitude of the problem. Given this finding, our recommendation about the use of preinterview data is based on a combination of research and common sense.

Assuming that the interview focuses on a small number of WRCs, our recommendation is to limit interviewers to two types of preinterview information. The first type is *complete data about any of the WRCs to be covered in the interview*. This information could save time or allow for more detailed questioning. The second type is the *incomplete or contradictory statements presented on the application blank or other similar instruments*: employment gaps, overlapping full-time positions, a nonregular career movement pattern, and so on. This kind of irregularity could be clarified in the interview.

There is enough evidence to indicate that access to data not directly relevant to the purposes of the interview only contributes to deficiencies in interviewers' decisions. Therefore, data such as ability test scores, letters of reference, and brief reactions of others should be withheld until after the interview is completed. Furthermore, before the interview, recruiters should be actively discouraged from examining any social media. Providing access to some (relevant) preinterview information coupled with a "formal" rapport-building phase during the meet-and-greet phase of the interview may be sufficient to overcome the desire to "know" the applicant before they meet them.

Adopt a Structured Format

One of the most consistent recommendations made by those who have written about ways to improve the use of the interview in selection has been to impose structure on the verbal exchange between the parties. This can be achieved by providing the interviewer with a set of questions that must be asked of all interviewees.

In this format, *a set of questions should be formulated for each WRC* identified as appropriate for the interview. Referring to the previous example of the maintenance supervisor job, this would mean a set of questions concerning each of the three WRCs: "ability to give verbal instructions," "ability to schedule work crews," and "ability to direct multiple work crews simultaneously." These questions must be asked of each applicant. The interviewers, however, are permitted to go beyond these questions as they feel necessary, either to clarify a given response, to seek other important details, or to pursue a closely related area. The logic behind imposing this structure is to build consistency in the interview regarding the appropriate WRCs from each applicant. The major benefit of this consistency in questioning is that it makes comparisons among applicants much easier. If done properly, *this method would provide* the HR specialist with information from each applicant on the same WRCs. This would facilitate the identification of those applicants most suitable for the job.

Use Job-Related Questions

Having a structured format for the interview is of limited value if the predetermined set of questions provides information that is only marginally related to job performance. Therefore, another concern in the interview is to ensure that the questions used are job related—that is, information gathered must be useful in measuring the appropriate knowledge, skills, abilities, and other characteristics required in the job.

We have discussed the two primary techniques that have been used to develop job-related questions: the *situational interview* and the *behavior description interview*. In the following paragraphs, we discuss questions that are useful for each of the three types of

WRCs we think are appropriately measured in an interview. The two techniques (situational and behavior description interviews) described previously can be used in developing specific questions for each type of WRC.

Questions of Job Knowledge.   This is the most straightforward WRC, both for measuring and for developing interview questions. Basically, the interviewer is trying to find out whether the applicant knows some specific information. Appropriate questions could include the following:

- What steps would you take to perform an empirical validation study?

- How do you string a 220-volt electric cable in a laboratory building that is under construction?

- What are the current tax laws regarding borrowing from an IRA?

There are a number of important points to remember when asking this type of question. The first is that the knowledge being discussed should be important to the overall performance of the job. It should not be information that is difficult but only peripheral to the job. Asking an applicant for a production supervisor's job about the principles of just-in-time management is appropriate. Asking about the programming features of Microsoft Outlook® software, which might be used in scheduling, usually would not be appropriate. The second is that the question should not ask about material easily learned on the job or material taught as part of a training program for the job. Third, it is not useful to ask questions about a series of specific facts or operations. A written test would be more appropriate to gather this type of information.

Commonly, interviewers phrase would-be job knowledge questions something like this:

- Have you ever directed a construction crew?

- Do you know how to do a performance appraisal?

- Have you taken any courses in accounting?

Questions of this type are not very useful for measuring job knowledge, because they require the interviewer to make inferences to evaluate the answer. For example, if the applicant responds that he or she taken two accounting courses, the interviewer normally would ask what the courses were, what grades were received, and so on. Even at this point, however, there is no direct evidence that the applicant knows specific information necessary for the job. All accounting courses with the same name do not cover the same material. All grades of "B" do not indicate the same mastery of material. The interviewer must infer the applicant's knowledge from this circumstantial data. A better method is to ask questions about material that is important for the job and then judge whether the answer given is correct. Little inference is necessary; the applicant indicates directly whether he or she has the knowledge. In practice, the use of job knowledge questions requires the selection specialist to work with technical specialists in various parts of the organization. This is because the selection specialist usually does not have enough technical knowledge of accounting, engineering, maintenance, and so on to properly formulate and evaluate answers to this type of question. Therefore, it is necessary to involve those people who are working in the functional area to develop and score interview questions.

Questions of Social Interaction.   Measuring WRCs related to applied social skills seems to be especially dependent on how the questions are stated. For example, an office receptionist position usually requires short-term, nonrecurring interaction with individuals. The WRCs necessary for such behavior would be evaluated appropriately in an interview. If these WRCs are specified by general characteristics, such as "poise," "friendliness," "pleasantness," or "professional bearing," assessment becomes more difficult because of the ambiguity of these terms.

A better tactic would be to try to phrase the WRCs as abilities and skills. For example, the receptionist's position may require "the ability to provide preliminary information to angry customers about the resolution of product defects" or "the ability to query customers regarding the exact nature of complaints to route them to appropriate personnel." Phrased in this manner, it is easier to develop questions that require the demonstration of these skills and abilities. *Situational interview questions* would be appropriate.

Questions of Personality or Habitual Behaviors.   The group of WRCs encompassing these traits is, perhaps, the most difficult to assess accurately in applicants. This group includes work habits, such as persistence in completing assignments, ability to work on multiple tasks simultaneously, and ability to plan future actions. The very general term *motivation* frequently is used to refer to these WRCs. Other attributes included in this category are "helping coworkers with job-related problems, accepting orders without a fuss, tolerating temporary impositions without complaint, and making timely and constructive statements about the work unit."[220] Research suggests that personality can effectively be assessed during the interview, but to do so, the interview must directly assess these traits by using specific structured questions.[221]

One method frequently used to measure these attributes is asking the applicant in various ways whether he or she has worked or is willing to work in circumstances requiring these habits or personality traits. The limitation of this type of question is that the information is virtually unverifiable and subject to distortion by the respondent, who wishes to portray favorable characteristics. Most job applicants, especially experienced ones, know that almost all organizations desire employees who cooperate with other workers, plan ahead, accept orders, and tolerate impositions. It is in the self-interest of applicants to portray themselves as having demonstrated, or being willing to demonstrate, these characteristics. A strategy that is increasingly being used, at least partially, to avoid such self-enhancement is to question the applicant in detail about participation in activities that are similar to those that are part of the job under consideration. David Grove has described such an interview that was used by the Procter & Gamble Company for entry-level selection.[222] This interview is aimed at forming judgments of the applicant based on five factors that are important for effectiveness at P&G: stamina and agility, willingness to work hard, working well with others, learning the work, and initiative. The applicant is asked to write answers to "experience items" on a special form. These experience items ask the applicant to describe several relevant experiences that may have occurred in either a work or nonwork setting for each of the five factors. For example, one experience item for assessing the factor "working well with others" may be "Describe a situation in which you had to work closely with a small group to complete a project." Responses to these experience items are then probed in each of two separate interviews. The interviews are conducted separately by a member of the plant employment group and a line manager, and each independently rates the applicant on a 7-point scale for each of the five factors.

We have developed a list of questions that could be used in a selection interview for the job of maintenance supervisor. These questions, presented in Table 10.8, are intended to gather information about the three WRCs that were identified in Table 10.7

TABLE 10.8	Selection Interview Questions for the Job of Maintenance Supervisor

WRC 1: Ability to give verbal work instructions to laborers regarding construction and repair

1. What instructions would you give a work crew that was about to string a 220-volt electric cable in a laboratory building under construction?

2. Two laborers, with limited experience, ask about the procedures for tuckpointing and restoring a damaged brick wall. What instructions would you give them regarding what equipment they should use and how they should operate it?

3. You assign a group of four to inspect the flat tar-and-gravel roofs on four buildings. They are also to make minor repairs and describe to you the major repairs that will need to be made in the future. What instructions do you give them? (Assume that each worker knows how to operate any necessary equipment.)

4. You will use eight summer employees to do the repainting of the third floor hall, ten private offices, and two public restrooms. What instructions do you give them about both general work and specific painting procedures?

WRC 2: Ability to schedule work crews for specific tasks

1. You need to send a work crew to the far part of the industrial park to inspect and (if necessary) repair a 40′ × 10′ brick wall and to prepare a 40′ × 60′ flower bed. It is Monday morning. Rain is expected Tuesday afternoon. How many people do you assign to which tasks? How long should each task take?

2. You are in charge of a work crew of twelve. Included in this are four experienced carpenters and two electricians. These six are also permitted to do other jobs. You are to finish a 100′ × 200′ area that will have five separate offices and a general meeting room. Tell me the first five tasks that you would assign your crew and how many people you would put on each task. How long should each task take?

WRC 3: Ability to direct multiple work crews and work projects simultaneously

1. Go back to the situation in the previous question. Tell me which tasks you would try to complete in the first two days. Which sequence of tasks would you schedule? How would your work crews know when to start a new task?

2. Describe a specific experience in the past few years in which you had at least five people reporting to you who were performing different parts of a bigger project. This could either be in work, school, community activities, or the military.

3. Describe a specific experience in the past few years in which you and a group of others were working under a tight deadline on a project that had several parts. This could either be in work, school, community activities, or the military.

as appropriate for being measured with an interview. The number of questions used for each WRC was determined from the importance assigned to each WRC in Table 10.7.

Finally, as stated previously, recent research shows that the usefulness of the "type" of question asked—whether those questions are focused on past behavior (behavior description interview) or on hypothetical, future-oriented situations (situational interview)—differs as the complexity of the job increases. Although this conclusion has not been supported universally,[223] research does suggest that the predictive validity of situational interview questions may be lower than that of behavioral description questions in complex jobs, such as management. One possible explanation is that prior experience may be needed to successfully answer questions related to such jobs. For example, the best candidates for a management position may be those with prior supervisory experience. Nevertheless, in less complex or moderately complex jobs, predictive validity is comparable for both situational interviews and behavior description interviews. In fact, the situational interview actually should be "easier" for those applicants with little or no prior work experience. Although more research is needed, practitioners would do well to keep these findings in mind as they design their employment interview questions.

Use Multiple Questions for Each WRC.   As discussed in Chapter 6, a basic psychological measurement principle specifies that for the assessment device to be a useful instrument, *the device should contain several items or parts that gather answers about the same variable.* To a certain extent, both reliability and validity of measurement generally are related to the number of items on the measuring device. In selection, all else being equal, the means the more items an assessment device possesses that measure the same WRC, the greater its reliability and validity.

Returning once more to our example of the maintenance supervisor in Table 10.8, the use of this principle of multiple questions means that applicants would be asked to respond to four questions to provide examples of instructions given to work crews, to two questions to measure ability to schedule work crews for specific tasks, and to three questions to measure the ability to direct multiple work crews and work projects simultaneously. There is no rule for the exact number of questions to be asked. This is primarily a function of two factors: (a) the information developed from the job analysis and (b) the time available for each applicant. Concerning the information developed from the job analysis, it is necessary to consider first the relative importance of the WRCs being measured in the interview. In our previous example in Table 10.7, "Ability to give verbal work instructions" had the highest weight (20), followed by "ability to coordinate and direct multiple work crews" (15), and "ability to schedule work crews" (10). The number of questions listed in Table 10.8 for each of these WRCs generally reflects these weights. The second consideration is the diversity of the tasks that relates to each WRC being assessed in the interview. If the maintenance supervisor must give instructions about many different types of tasks, it may take more questions to have a representative sample than if these tasks are very similar. Nevertheless, the broader point is the more "items" or questions asked to assess a construct during the interview, the more useful the score for that construct when predicting later job performance.

The total amount of time available for the interview, in some cases, is beyond the control of the interviewer—for example, on-campus interviews or many job fair situations. In these cases, an estimate should be made before the interview of the number of questions possible based on the total time allocated for the interview and the estimated length of time required for answering each question.

Rely on Multiple Independent Interviewers.   Another basic psychological measurement principle discussed in Chapter 6 is that the use of multiple interviewers will enhance reliability, as long as their ratings are independent of the influence of other interviewers (or managers). This conclusion was supported by the findings of Frank Schmidt and Ryan Zimmerman,[224] who found that the predictive validity of an unstructured interview could be raised to that of a single structured interview by aggregating the hiring recommendations of three to four interviewers who utilized an unstructured interview.

As noted, however, meta-analyses have found predictive validities for panel interviews that are comparable to or somewhat lower than the correlations reported for single interviewers. At least two studies that have been reviewed found that individual interviewers, using structured interviews ($\rho = 0.63$ or 0.46), had the same or higher validity coefficients than did panel interviews ($\rho = 0.60$ and 0.38).[225] These findings suggest a lack of support for the commonly held opinion that a panel interview (two or more interviewers asking at once) is superior to an individual interview. This counterintuitive finding likely has emerged because these meta-analyses have not distinguished those studies in which groups of interviewers make independent decisions based on different interviews from those in which the group arrives at an overall consensus decision based on one interview. Pooling or averaging interviewer judgments can only increase reliability in those cases in which multiple interviewers have made judgments independently. Pooling or averaging judgments reduces the influence of measurement error, particularly if these judgments are from different interviews of the same candidate. As we know, because reliability limits validity, increasing inter-rater reliability will enhance the predictive validity of the hiring recommendation. But again, the critical element necessary for successfully using multiple interviewers is that interviewers provide independent ratings based on more than one interview (rather than a group of interviewers who give one interview).

Recent research also illustrates that the same interviewers should be used across all candidates. Huffcutt and David Woehr compared the results from 23 studies in which the same interviewers interviewed all of the candidates with the results from 100 studies in which different interviewers interviewed different candidates. They found that using the same interviewers to rate across all candidates substantially increased the validity of the interview.[226] How frequently does this occur? The survey of the actual practices of HR managers revealed that 80 percent of interviews use two or three interviewers (and 18 percent use only one), and that 73 percent used the same interviewers across all candidates.[227] These results show that many companies are following "best practices," at least with regard to using multiple interviewers, and that the same interviewers are conducting all interviews.

Apply a Formal Scoring Format.   The study of the interview has consistently concluded that an interview format that provides a formal, defined scoring system is superior in many ways to a format that does not. This is in terms of legal defensibility as well as the reliability and validity of interviewer judgments. We have made the point that measurement is the essence of a selection program. Without measurement of the WRCs of applicants, any comparison of these applicants becomes too complex to be done accurately. It simply is not possible for a selection specialist to retain all relevant information, weigh it appropriately, and use it to compare a number of individuals—at least in a consistent and effective manner. The issue, therefore, becomes not whether to score the interview but rather how best to score it.

The most commonly used systems require the interviewer to rate the interviewee on a series of interval measurement scales. The number of rating points on such scales varies, but it usually consists of between four and seven scale points. These scale points have a number at each point that is used to reflect various degrees of the applicant characteristics being judged. These scale points usually have either a set of adjectives describing differences among them (for example, not acceptable, marginal, minimal, good, superior) or a brief behavioral definition for each scale point (for example, instructions given were not understandable, instructions given were understandable but mainly incorrect, instructions were understandable and generally correct). Behavior-based rating scales are preferable—in part because they are based on critical behavioral incidents representative of the performance dimensions in question. A meta-analysis by Paul Taylor and Bruce Small illustrated the value of using behaviorally anchored rating scales; they found that—if they used such rating scales—the predictive validity of behavior description interviews increases ($\rho = 0.63$) in comparison with those interviews without behaviorally anchored rating scales ($\rho = 0.47$).[228] These findings show that there is value in anchoring the scoring format to job-relevant behaviors.

A second aspect of scoring concerns the dimensions to be scored. Table 10.9 contains an example of a scoring form that can be used in interviews for the position of maintenance supervisor. It seems best to rate the applicant directly on the WRCs for which the interview was intended and for which the questions were designed. It is not necessary to score each question, just the WRCs that are measured by multiple questions.

The rating form should provide space for comments about the applicant's performance on the WRC being rated. These comments are usually summary examples of the responses provided by the applicant to the questions designed to assess the WRC. The purpose of the comments is to provide not only documentation to support the rating, if

| TABLE 10.9 | An Example of Interview Rating Scales of WRCs | | | | | |

Job Analysis WRCs	Unsatisfactory	Minimal	Average	Good	Superior
1. Ability to give verbal instructions.	1	2	3	④	5
Comments: Accurate instructions generally given. However, instructions lacked specificity as to worker assignment and standard of performance.					
2. Ability to schedule work crews	1	2	3	4	⑤
Comments: Responses correctly estimated appropriate crew size and length of time needed for completing project.					
3. Ability to direct multiple crews and projects	1	②	3	4	5
Comments: Previous situations indicate difficulty in setting priorities among tasks. Also, little evaluation of adequacy of completed tasks was done by the individual.					
4. Overall rating	1	2	3	④	5
Comments: Candidate demonstrates strong performance with regard to two of three abilities measured by this interview. Individual can learn third ability with moderate amount of training.					

it is questioned in the future, but also more information that can be used to compare a series of applicants. Not surprisingly, a recent study shows that note taking significantly improved the predictive validity of the employment interview.[229] Another analysis demonstrates that note taking results in better interviewer recall of what happened in the interview, but it did not significantly improve the decisions made by the interviewer.[230] Consequently, interviewers should be trained on how to most effectively take notes to enhance their accuracy when scoring the interview.

Finally, if an overall score is sought, this rating should simply be a summation of the interviewer's ratings on each of the candidate's responses to the job-related questions rather than an overall judgment.[231] That is, the interviewer should add the separate ratings together, not simply score the candidate on the basis of his judgment as a whole across all factors of the interview. Evidence consistently shows that statistical aggregation of ratings invariably yields more valid and reliable ratings than does the use of global judgments.[232]

Train the Interviewer.   Another point important to reiterate is the value of training the interviewer. Huffcutt and Woehr compared the results of 52 studies that included interviewer training with results of 71 studies that did not. They found that training should be provided to interviewers; this was true regardless of whether the interview was structured or unstructured.[233] It is commonly agreed that the focal skills of an interviewer are the abilities to (a) accurately receive information, (b) critically evaluate the information received, and (c) regulate his or her own behavior in the delivery of questions.[234] Most training programs focus on at least one of these areas; many address all three. Although it is not within the scope of this book to present the specific features of such training programs, the following characteristics frequently have been included in successful programs.

Receiving Information.   In training interviewers to receive information accurately, instruction has concentrated on factors that influence (a) hearing what the respondent has said, (b) observing the applicant's behavior, and (c) remembering the information received. In accomplishing this, programs frequently address such topics as learning listening skills, taking notes, reducing the anxiety of the interviewee, establishing rapport with the interviewee, taking measures to reduce the fatigue and loss of interest of the interviewee, and minimizing the effect that interviewer expectations have on perceptions about what the applicant says.

One purpose of this training is to create an interview situation in which the candidate feels relaxed and comfortable. Logically, this should make it easier for the candidate to think of difficult-to-remember information and to provide complete answers about the topics asked. Another purpose of this training is to minimize what may be called *administrative errors* that can occur in the interview. These are errors such as misunderstanding what was said, not correctly remembering information provided by the applicant, tipping off the applicant as to the "best" answers to questions, and being able to deliver questions consistently so as to cover all topics. The general purpose of such training is to increase the amount of information obtained in the interview and to ensure its accuracy.

Evaluating Information.   Training interviewers in the critical evaluation of information obtained from the interviewee usually focuses on improving the decision-making process of the interviewer by pointing out common decision errors and providing methods to overcome these errors. Common errors include the halo effect (ratings across all performance dimensions influenced by the rating on one "important" dimension), distributional rating errors (including central tendency and leniency error—rating everyone in the middle or high end of the distribution), the similar-to-me effect, the contrast effect, and the first-impressions error. Training programs often rely on videotapes or simulated interviews. The trainees evaluate candidates through these means, then follow this with a group discussion about the reasons for each trainee's ratings. Such programs frequently focus on the effect of candidate appearance and mannerisms and interviewer stereotypes and biases that cause inappropriate weighting. The major point of such training is that learning the nature of typical errors will minimize the distortion caused by these errors in actual interviews. Another type of training program emphasizes how an interviewer weighs various pieces of information about the applicant. In one study, interviewers were trained on the optimal weights for different WRC dimensions based on a multiple regression model. The training significantly improved their predictive validities, often with correlations of 0.40 or higher.[235]

A final theme advocates systematic scoring of the interview. It is almost universally recognized that the intuitive evaluation of a candidate by an interviewer, still very common in interviewing, is to be avoided. Formal evaluation forms usually contain a number of defined candidate characteristics that are related to job performance, a separate rating scale for each characteristic, and a rating of the overall acceptability of the candidate. Research shows that mechanically combining the scores for each characteristic into an overall rating will maximize predictive validity.

Interviewing Behavior. The third area often addressed by interviewer training is how interviewer behavior influences the conduct of the interviewer–applicant interaction. Training sessions often address such topics as techniques for questioning the candidate and the role of interview structure on this interaction. For example, if the interviewer talks excessively, it limits the amount of job-related information obtained from interviewees. More important, if the interviewer perceives himself or herself to be similar to the candidate, he or she is likely to interact differently with the candidate. The point is that the interview is fundamentally a social and interpersonal process. Consequently, the behavior of the interviewer can affect the candidate's responses. These training programs focus on improving the interviewer's skill at maintaining control throughout the interview and on enhancing awareness of how the interviewer's behavior is influencing the interaction.

Results of Training. How much improvement have these changes brought about in the way that interviews are carried out? The results of training generally have been encouraging, but not all problems have been corrected. For the most part, the various training programs have reduced some of the more common rater errors: contrast, halo, leniency, and central tendency. Furthermore, training has been found to enhance the reliability of interviewer judgments.[236] Other studies, however, have demonstrated modest effects of training on interviewer behavior, especially when shorter training programs, which are less comprehensive, are examined.[237] This finding corresponds to that reported in the training literature, which shows modest incremental gains in actual behavioral change.[238] Another explanation is that the length of interviewer training is simply too short to be effective. This is a viable alternative explanation for these mixed effects, as there is evidence that the median time for an interview training program is only 6 hours long.[239] Nevertheless, many popular interview training programs focus on using structured interview questions and systematic scoring; this has been shown to improve the reliability and validity of evaluations among sets of interviewers. Evidence clearly shows that during evaluation, trained interviewers are found to be more standardized and formalized; they consistently use more sophisticated questioning strategies.[240] Thus, training enables the interviewer to more fully realize the benefits of a highly structured interview, which supports the use of training.

It seems obvious that organizations would provide training to interviewers—particularly given the importance of this selection technique on hiring decisions. Yet, two recent studies suggest that this may not be the case, as only about a third of interviewers report receiving formal interviewer training.[241] This underscores a need to emphasize the value of training.

To summarize, it seems that the critical components of training consist of identifying the specific behavioral objectives to be addressed in the training program, providing the trainees with opportunities to demonstrate and review their skills, and having a method to evaluate a trainee's demonstrated behavior and to offer suggestions for change. Raymond Gordon has observed that although practice and analysis can quickly improve interviewer skills, these skills deteriorate over time through disuse or lack of critical self-analysis.[242] This implies that interviewers should attend training sessions on a regular basis to maintain necessary skills.

Account for Social Dynamics and Multiple Purposes. The interview is a complex challenging task in part because it is based on a social exchange between two people who have conflicting objectives. The organization should explicitly address the multiple purposes it has to deal with in a systematic way. For example, the employer should clarify the trade-off between selection and recruiting or public relations. This may mean using the interview only for selection purposes, as many scholars suggest.[243] To increase the usage of structured interviews, however, we have suggested that the interview instead be broken into distinct phases, beginning with a "meet-and-greet" rapport-building period. To facilitate transparency, at the end of this period, the interviewer would explicitly describe the remaining steps of the interview and explain why this is done. This would be followed by a lengthy structured interview, which after all evaluations are made, could be followed by an open exchange between the candidate and interviewer that would conclude after all the applicant's questions have been addressed. In doing so, the interview would shift from being viewed as an "interrogation" (that is not followed by the interviewer), to a conversation to establish fit with the organization and the job. Such an interview, complete with a structured interview, has a great chance of actually being followed by the interviewer.

As this suggests, the interview is more challenging than it appears. For a number of reasons, however, the interview that is typically conducted—an unstructured interview— is simply not very useful. Yet, if systematically designed and conducted, it can provide some of the most valuable predictor information about the candidate, while also being viewed favorably by the applicant.[244] Consequently, we encourage organizations to work hard to effectively implement the interview to realize its full potential.

REFERENCES

1. Richard A. Posthuma, Frederick P. Morgeson, and Michael A. Campion, "Beyond Employment Interview Validity: A Comprehensive Narrative Review of Recent Research and Trends over Time," *Personnel Psychology* 55 (2002): 1–82.

2. Murray R. Barrick, Brian Swider, and Greg L. Stewart, "Initial Evaluations in the Interview: Relationships with Subsequent Interviewer Evaluations and Employment Offers." *Journal of Applied Psychology* 95 (2010): 1037–1046. Murray R. Barrick, Jonathan A. Shaffer, and Sandra W. DeGrassi, "What You See May Not Be What You Get: A Meta-Analysis of the Relationship between Self-Presentation Tactics and Ratings of Interview and Job Performance," *Journal of Applied Psychology* 94 (2009): 1394–1411; Brian Swider, Murray R. Barrick, Brad L. Harris, and Adam Stoverink, "Managing and Creating an Image in the Interview: The Role of Interviewee Initial Impressions," *Journal of Applied Psychology* 96 (2011): 1275–1288.

3. Julia Levishina and Michael A. Campion, "Measuring Faking in the Employment Interview: Development and Validation of an Interview Faking Behavior Scale," *Journal of Applied Psychology* 92 (2007): 1638–1656; Julia Levashina, Chris J. Hartwell, Fred P. Morgeson, and Michael A. Campion, "The Structured Employment Interview: Narrative and Quantitative Review of the Research Literature," *Personnel Psychology* 67, no. 1 (2014): 241–293.

4. Jose Cortina and Joseph Luchman, "Personnel Selection and Employee Performance," *Handbook of Psychology* 12 (2012): 143–183.

5. Ibid.

6. Derek S. Chapman and David I. Zweig, "Developing a Nomological Network for Interview Structure: Antecedents and Consequences of the Structured Selection Interview," *Personnel Psychology* 58 (2005): 673–702.

7. Frank L. Schmidt and Ryan D. Zimmerman, "A Counterintuitive Hypothesis about Employment Interview Validity and Some Supporting Evidence," *Journal of Applied Psychology* 89 (2005): 553–561.

8. Willi H. Wiesner and Steven F. Cronshaw, "A Meta-Analytic Investigation of the Impact of Interview Format and Degree of Structure on the Validity of the Employment Interview," *Journal of Occupational Psychology* 61 (1988): 275–290; Michael A. McDaniel, Deborah L. Whetzel, Frank L. Schmidt, and Steven D. Maurer, "The Validity of Employment Interviews: A Comprehensive Review and Meta-Analysis," *Journal of Applied Psychology* 79 (1994): 599–616; and Allen I. Huffcutt and Winfred W. Arthur Jr., "Hunter and Hunter (1984) Revisited: Interview Validity for Entry-Level Jobs," *Journal of Applied Psychology* 79 (1994): 184–190.

9. Michael A. Campion, David K. Palmer, and James E. Campion, "A Review of Structure in the Selection Interview," *Personal Psychology* 50 (1997): 655–702; Huffcutt and Arthur Jr., "Hunter and Hunter (1984) Revisited: Interview Validity for Entry-Level Jobs"; Levashina, Hartwell, Morgeson, and Campion, "The Structured Employment Interview"; and McDaniel, Whetzel, Schmidt, and Maurer, "The Validity of Employment Interviews: A Comprehensive Review and Meta-Analysis."

10. Robert L. Dipboye, Therese Macan, and Comila Shahani-Denning, "The Selection Interview from the Interviewer and Applicant Perspectives: Can't Have One Without the Other," in *The Oxford Handbook of Personnel Assessment and Selection*, ed. Neil Schmitt (Oxford Publishing, 2012), 335.

11. Melinda C. Blackman, and David C. Funder, "Effective Interview Practices for Accurately Assessing Counterproductive Traits." *International Journal of Selection and Assessment* 10 (2002): 109–116; John P. Hausknecht, David V. Day, and Scott Thomas, "Applicant Reactions to Selection Procedures: An Updated Model and Meta-Analysis," *Personnel Psychology* 57 (2004): 639–683.

12. Robert L. Dipboye, "Structured Selection Interview Publications: Why Do They Work? Why Are They Underutilized?" In *International Handbook of Selection and Assessment*, eds. N. Anderson and P. Herriot (Chichester: John Wiley and Sons, 1997): 455–473; Lynnette Harris, "Procedural Justice and Perceptions of Fairness in Selection Practice," *International Journal of Selection and Assessment* 8 (2000): 148–156.

13. Melinda C. Blackman, "Personality Judgment and the Utility of the Unstructured Employment Interview," *Basic and Applied Social Psychology* 24 (2002): 241–250; William Ickes, Mark Snyder, and Stella Garcia, "Personality Influences on the Choice of Situations," in *Handbook of Personality Psychology*, ed. R. Hogan, J. A. Johnson, and S. R. Briggs (San Diego, CA: Academic Press, 1997), 165–195.

14. Chapman and Zweig, "Developing a Nomological Network for Interview Structure."

15. Karen I. Van der Zee, Arnold B. Bakker, and Paulien Bakker, "Why Are Structured Interviews Used So Rarely in Personnel Selection?" *Journal of Applied Psychology* 87 (2002): 176–184.

16. Cortina and Luchman, "Personnel Selection and Employee Performance."

17. Angelo J. Kinicki, Chris A. Lockwood, Peter W. Hom, and Rodger W. Griffeth, "Interviewer Predictions of Applicant Qualifications and Interviewer Validity: Aggregate and Individual Analyses," *Journal of Applied Psychology* 75 (1990): 477–486; Posthuma, Morgeson, and Campion, "Beyond Employment Interview Validity"; and Steffanie L. Wilk and Peter Cappelli, "Understanding the Determinants of Employer Use of Selection Methods," *Personnel Psychology* 56 (2003): 103–124.

18. Sheldene K. Simola, Simon Taggar, and Geoffrey W. Smith. "The Employment Selection Interview: Disparity among Research-Based Recommendations, Current Practices and What Matters to Human Rights Tribunals," *Canadian Journal of Administrative Sciences* 24 (2007): 30–44; Van der Zee, Bakker, and Bakker, "Why Are Structured Interviews Used So Rarely in Personnel Selection?"

19. Cortina and Luchman, "Personnel Selection and Employee Performance."

20. Ibid.

21. Dipboye, Macan, and Shahani-Denning, "The Selection Interview from the Interviewer and Applicant Perspectives."

22. Neal Schmit, "Social and Situational Determinants of Interview Decisions: Implications for the Employment Interview," *Personnel Psychology* 29, no. 1 (1976): 79–101; Lynn Ulrich and Don Trumbo, "The Selection Interview since 1949," *Psychological Bulletin* 63 (1965): 100–116; Ralph Wagner, "The Employment Interview: A Critical Summary," *Personnel Psychology* 2 (1949): 17–46.

23. Robert L. Dipboye, "The Selection/Recruitment Interview: Core Processes and Contexts," in *The Blackwell Handbook of Personnel Selection*, ed. Arne Evers, Neil Anderson, and Olga Voskuijil (Oxford, England: Blackwell Publishers, 2004), 121–142; and Posthuma, Morgeson, and Campion, "Beyond Employment Interview Validity."

24. Wiesner and Cronshaw, "A Meta-Analytic Investigation of the Impact of Interview Format and Degree of Structure on the Validity of the Employment Interview"; Michael A. McDaniel, Deborah L. Whetzel, Frank L. Schmidt, and Steven D. Maurer, "The Validity of Employment Interviews: A Comprehensive Review and Meta-Analysis"; and Huffcutt and Arthur Jr., "Hunter and Hunter (1984) Revisited: Interview Validity for Entry-Level Jobs."

25. Allen I. Huffcutt and Satoris S. Youngcourt, "Employment interviews." In *Applied Measurement: Industrial Psychology in Human Resource Management*, eds. D. L. Whetzel and G. R. Wheaton (London: Psychology Press, 2007), 181–199.

26. James M. Conway, Robert A. Jako, and Deborah Goodman, "A Meta-Analysis of Interrater and Internal Consistency Reliability of Selection Interviews," *Journal of Applied Psychology* 80 (1995): 565–579; Allen I. Huffcutt, James M. Conway, Philip L. Roth, and Nancy J. Stone, "Identification and Meta-Analytic Assessment of Psychological Constructs Measured in Employment Interviews," *Journal of Applied Psychology* 86 (2001): 897–913; John E. Hunter, and Rhonda F. Hunter, "Validity and Utility of Alternative Predictors of Job Performance," *Psychological Bulletin* 96 (1984): 72–98; Marc C. Marchese and Paul M. Muchinsky, "The Validity of the Employment Interview: A Meta-Analysis," *International Journal of Selection and Assessment* 1 (1993): 18–26; Wiesner and Cronshaw, "A Meta-Analytic Investigation of the Impact of Interview Format and Degree of Structure on the Validity of the Employment Interview."

27. Campion, Palmer, and Campion, "A Review of Structure in the Selection Interview."

28. Frank L. Schmidt and John E. Hunter, "The Validity and Utility of Selection Methods in Personnel Psychology: Practical and Theoretical Implications of 85 Years of Research Findings," *Psychological Bulletin* 124 (1998): 262–274.

29. Huffcutt, Conway, Roth, and Stone, "Identification and Meta-Analytic Assessment of Psychological Constructs Measured in Employment Interviews," *Journal of Applied Psychology* 86 (2001): 897–913; Allen I. Huffcutt, "An Empirical Review of the Employment Interview Construct Literature," *International Journal of Selection and Assessment* 19 (2011): 62–81.

30. Huffcutt, Conway, Roth, and Stone, "Identification and Meta-Analytic Assessment of Psychological Constructs Measured in Employment Interviews"; Huffcutt, "An Empirical Review of the Employment Interview Construct Literature."

31. Chris M. Berry, Paul R. Sackett, and Ron N. Landers, "Revisiting Interview-Cognitive Ability Relationships: Attending to Specific Range Restriction Mechanisms in Meta-Analysis," *Personnel Psychology* 60 (2007): 837–874; Jose M. Cortina, Nancy B. Goldstein, Stephanie C. Payne, H. Kristl Davison, and Steven W. Gilliland, "The Incremental Validity of Interview Scores over and above G and Conscientiousness Scores," *Personnel Psychology* 53 (2000)

325–351; Allen I. Huffcutt, Philip L. Roth, and Michael A. McDaniel, "A Meta-Analytic Investigation of Cognitive Ability in Employment Interview Evaluations: Moderating Characteristics and Implications for Incremental Validity," *Journal of Applied Psychology* 81 (1996): 459–473; Jesus F. Salgado and Silvia Moscoso, "Comprehensive Meta-Analysis of the Construct Validity of the Employment Interview," *European Journal of Work and Organizational Psychology* 11 (2002): 299–324.

32. Frank L. Schmidt and Mark Rader, "Exploring the Boundary Conditions for Interview Validity: Meta-Analytic Validity Findings for a New Interview Type," *Personnel Psychology* 52 (2006): 445–464.

33. Erica Baker and Julius Demps, "Videoconferencing as a Tool for Recruiting and Interviewing," *Journal of Business and Economics Research* 7, no. 10 (2011): 9–14.

34. Barrick, Shaffer, and DeGrassi, "What You See May Not Be What You Get"; Chapman and Zweig, "Developing a Nomological Network for Interview Structure"; Martin Kleinmann and Ute-Christian Klehe, "Selling Oneself: Construct and Criterion-Related Validity of Impression Management in Structured Interviews," *Human Performance* 24 (2011): 29–46; Murray R. Barrick, Brian Swider, and Greg L. Stewart, "Initial Evaluations in the Interview: Relationships with Subsequent Interviewer Evaluations and Employment Offers," *Journal of Applied Psychology* 95 (2010): 1037–1046; Swider, Barrick, Harris, and Stoverink, "Managing and Creating an Image in the Interview: The Role of Interviewee Initial Impressions"; Greg L. Stewart, Susan D. Dustin, Murray R. Barrick, and Todd C. Darnold, "Exploring the Handshake in Employment Interviews," *Journal of Applied Psychology* 93 (2008): 1139–1146.

35. Chapman and Zweig, "Developing a Nomological Network for Interview Structure."

36. Chapman and Zweig, "Developing a Nomological Network for Interview Structure";" Eva Derous, "Investigating Personnel Selection from a Counseling Perspective: Do Applicants' and Recruiters' Perceptions Correspond?" *Journal of Employment Counseling* 44, no. 2 (2007): 60–72.

37. Dipboye, Macan, and Shahani-Denning, "The Selection Interview from the Interviewer and Applicant Perspectives";" Chapman and Zweig, "Developing a Nomological Network for Interview Structure"; Van der Zee, Bakker, and Bakker, "Why Are Structured Interviews Used So Rarely in Personnel Selection?"

38. Van der Zee, Bakker, and Bakker, "Why Are Structured Interviews Used So Rarely in Personnel Selection?"

39. Alison E. Barber, John R. Hollenbeck, Spencer L. Tower, and Jean M. Phillips, "The Effects of Interview Focus on Recruitment Effectiveness: A Field Experiment," *Journal of Applied Psychology* 79 (1994): 886–896.

40. Cortina and Luchman, "Personnel Selection and Employee Performance"; Cynthia Kay Stevens. "Antecedents of Interview Interactions, Interviews' Ratings, and Applicants' Reactions," *Personnel Psychology* 51 (1998): 55–85.

41. Aichia Chuang and Paul R. Sackett. "The Perceived Importance of Person-Job Fit and Person-Organization Fit between and within Interview Stages," *Social Behavior and Personality: An International Journal* 33, no. 3 (2005): 209–226.

42. Brian R. Dineen and Scott M. Soltis, "Recruitment: A Review of Research and Emerging Directions," in *APA Handbook of Industrial and Organizational Psychology*, vol. 2, ed. S Zedeck (Washington, DC: American Psychological Association, 2011), 43–66; Todd C. Darnold and Sara L. Rynes, "Recruitment and Job Choice Research: Same as It Ever Was?" *Handbook of Psychology* 12 (2012): 104–142; Wei-Chi Tsai and Irene Wen-Fen Yang, "Does Image Matter to Different Job Applicants? The Influences of Corporate Image and Applicant Individual Differences on Organizational Attractiveness," *International Journal of Selection and Assessment* 18 (2010): 48–63.

43. Dineen and Soltis, "Recruitment: A Review of Research and Emerging Directions"; Daniel Turban, James E. Campion, and Alison R. Eyring, "Factors Related to Job Acceptance Decisions of College Recruits," *Journal of Vocational Behavior* 47 (1995): 193–213; Brian R. Dineen, Steven R. Ash, and Ray A. Noe, "A Web of Applicant Attraction: Person-Organization Fit in the Context of Web-Based Recruitment," *Journal of Applied Psychology* 87 (2002): 723–734.

44. Darnold and Rynes, "Recruitment and Job Choice Research: Same as It Ever Was?"

45. Darnold and Rynes, "Recruitment and Job Choice Research: Same as It Ever Was?"; Amy Kristof-Brown, and Russell P. Guay. "Person–Environment Fit," in *APA Handbook of Industrial and Organizational Psychology*, vol. 3, ed. S. Zedeck, (Washington, DC: American Psychological Association, 2011), 3–50.

46. Derek S. Chapman, Krista L. Uggerslev, Sarah A. Carroll, Kelly A. Piasentin, and David A. Jones, "Applicant Attraction to Organizations and Job Choice: A Meta-Analytic Review of the Correlates of Recruiting Outcomes," *Journal of Applied Psychology* 90 (2005): 928–944.

47. Posthuma, Morgeson, and Campion, "Beyond Employment Interview Validity."

48. Michael M. Harris and Laurence S. Fink, "A Field Study of Applicant Reactions to Employment Opportunities: Does the Recruiter Make a Difference?" *Personnel Psychology* 40 (1987): 765–784.

49. Sara L. Rynes, Robert D. Bretz Jr., and Barry Gerhart, "The Importance of Recruitment in Job Choice: A Different Way of Looking," *Personnel Psychology* 44 (1991): 24.

50. Robert C. Liden and Charles K. Parsons, "A Field Study of Job Applicant Interview Perceptions, Alternative Opportunities, and Demographic Characteristics," *Personnel Psychology* 39 (1986): 109–122.

51. Posthuma, Morgeson, and Campion, "Beyond Employment Interview Validity"; and Jack L. Howard and Gerald R. Ferris, "The Employment Interview Context: Social and Situational Influences on Interviewer Decisions," *Journal of Applied Social Psychology* 26 (1996): 112–136.

52. Barrick, Shaffer, and DeGrassi, "What You See May Not Be What You Get"; Megumi Hosoda, Eugene F. Stone-Romera, and Gwen Coats, "The Effects of Physical Attractiveness on Job-Related Outcomes: A Meta-Analysis of Experimental Studies," *Personnel Psychology* 56 (2003): 431–462.

53. Winfred Arthur Jr. and Anton J. Villado, "The Importance of Distinguishing between Constructs and Methods When Comparing Predictors in Personnel Selection Research and Practice," *Journal of Applied Psychology* 93 (2008): 435–442; Paul R. Sackett and Filip Lievens, "Personnel Selection," *Annual Review of Psychology* 59 (2008): 419–450.

54. Barrick, Shaffer, and DeGrassi, "What You See May Not Be What You Get."

55. Hosoda, Stone-Romera, and Coats, "The Effects of Physical Attractiveness on Job-Related Outcomes: A Meta-Analysis of Experimental Studies"; and Chad A. Higgins, Timothy A. Judge, and Gerald R. Ferris, "Influence Tactics and Work Outcomes: A Meta-Analysis," *Journal of Organizational Behavior* 24 (2003): 89–106.

56. Daniel Kahneman, *"Thinking, Fast and Slow"* (New York: Macmillan, 2011).

57. Neal Schmitt, Elaine D. Pulakos, Earl Nason, and David J. Whitney, "Likability and Similarity as Potential Sources of Predictor-Related Criterion Bias in Validation Research," *Organizational Behavior and Human Decision Processes* 68 (1996): 272–286.

58. Eva Jonas, Stefen Schulz-Hardt, and Deter Frey, "Giving Advice or Making Decisions in Someone Else's Place: The Influence of Impression, Defense, and Accuracy Motivation on the Search for New Information," *Personality and Social Psychology Bulletin* 31 (2005): 977–990.

59. Dipboye, Macan, and Shahani-Denning, "The Selection Interview from the Interviewer and Applicant Perspectives"; Amy C. Lewis, and Steven J. Sherman, "Hiring You Makes Me Look Bad: Social-Identity Reversals of the Ingroup Favoritism Effect," *Organizational Behavior and Human Decision Processes* 90 (2003): 262–276.

60. Robert L. Dipboye, Barbara B. Gaugler, Theodore L. Hayes, and Debra Parker, "The Validity of Unstructured Panel Interviews: More Than Meets the Eye?" *Journal of Business and psychology* 16, no. 1 (2001): 35–49; Chad H. Van Iddekinge, Chris E. Sager, Jennifer L. Burnfield, and Tonia S. Heffner, "The Variability of Criterion-Related Validity Estimates among Interviewers and Interview Panels," *International Journal of Selection and Assessment* 14 (2006): 193–205; Shelly Zedeck, Amos Tziner, and Stephen E. Middlestadt, "Interviewer Validity and Reliability: An Individual Analysis Approach," *Personnel Psychology* 36 (1983): 355–370.

61. Blackman and Funder, "Effective Interview Practices for Accurately Assessing Counterproductive Traits," *International Journal of Selection and Assessment* 10 (2002): 109–116; Neal Christiansen, Shaina Wolcott-Burnam, Jay E. Janovics, Gary N. Burns, and Stuart W. Quirk, "The Good Judge Revisited: Individual Differences in the Accuracy of Personality Judgments," *Human Performance* 18, no. 2 (2005): 123–149; Allen I. Huffcutt and Sartoris S. Culbertson, "Interview," in *APA Handbook of Industrial and Organizational Psychology*, vol. 2, ed. S Zedeck (Washington, DC: American Psychological Association, 2011), 43–66.

62. Salgado and Moscoso, "Comprehensive Meta-Analysis of the Construct Validity of the Employment Interview."

63. Ibid.

64. Lynn Ulrich and Don Trumbo, "The Selection Interview since 1949," *Psychological Bulletin* 63 (1965): 100–116.

65. Huffcutt, Conway, Roth, and Stone, "Identification and Meta-Analytic Assessment of Psychological Constructs Measured in Employment Interviews."

66. Murray R. Barrick, Michael K. Mount, and Timothy A. Judge, "The FFM Personality Dimensions and Job Performance: Meta-Analysis of Meta-Analyses," *International Journal of Selection and Assessment* 9 (2001): 9–30; and Huffcutt, Conway, Roth, and Stone, "Identification and Meta-Analytic Assessment of Psychological Constructs Measured in Employment Interviews."

67. Huffcutt, Conway, Roth, and Stone, "Identification and Meta-Analytic Assessment of Psychological Constructs Measured in Employment Interviews."

68. Huffcutt, Roth, and McDaniel, "A Meta-Analytic Investigation of Cognitive Ability in Employment Interview Evaluations."

69. Berry, Sackett, and Landers, "Revisiting Interview–Cognitive Ability Relationships"; Cortina, Goldstein, Payne, Davison, and Gilliland, "The Incremental Validity of Interview Scores over and above G and Conscientiousness Scores"; Richard D. Goffin, Mitchell G. Rothstein, and Norman G. Johnston, "Personality Testing and the Assessment Center: Incremental Validity for Managerial Selection," *Journal of Applied Psychology* 81 (1996): 746–756.

70. Dipboye, "The Selection/Recruitment Interview: Core Processes and Contexts."

71. Gary P. Latham and Daniel P. Skarlicki, "Criterion-Related Validity of the Situational and Patterned Behavior Description Interviews with Organizational Citizenship Behavior," *Human Performance* 8 (1995): 67–80; and Posthuma, Morgeson, and Campion, "Beyond Employment Interview Validity: A Comprehensive Narrative Review of Recent Research and Trends over Time."

72. Brian S. Connely and Deniz S. Ones, "An Other Perspective on Personality: Meta-Analytic Integration of Observers' Accuracy and Predictive Validity," *Psychological Bulletin* (2010):1092–1122.

73. Richard E. Boyatzis and Fabio Sala, "The Emotional Competence Inventory (ECI)." ed., R. E. Boyatzis, F. Sala, and Glenn Gehrig, Measuring emotional intelligence: Common ground and controversy, (Hauppauge, NY, US: Nova Science Publishers, 2004): 147–180; Dana L. Joseph and David A. Newman, "Emotional Intelligence: An Integrative Meta-Analysis and Cascading Model," *Journal of Applied Psychology* 95, no. 1 (2010): 54–78; John D. Mayer, John D., Peter Salovey, and David R. Caruso, "Emotional Intelligence: Theory, Findings, and Implications," *Psychological Inquiry* 15, no. 3 (2004): 197–215.

74. Neal D. Christiansen, Jay E. Janovics, and Brian P. Siers, "Emotional Intelligence in Selection Contexts: Measurement Method, Criterion-Related Validity, and Vulnerability to Response Distortion," *International Journal of Selection and Assessment* 18 (2010): 87–101; Peter D. Harms and Markus Crede, "Remaining Issues in Emotional Intelligence Research: Construct Overlap, Method Artifacts and Lack of Incremental Validity," *Industrial and Organizational Psychology-Perspectives on Science and Practice* 3 (2010): 154–58; Dragos Iliescu, Alexandra Ilie, Dan Ispas, and Andrei Ion, "Emotional Intelligence in Personnel Selection: Applicant Reactions, Criterion, and Incremental Validity," *International Journal of Selection and Assessment* 20, no. 3 (2012): 347–358; Dana L. Joseph and Daniel A. Newman, "Emotional Intelligence: An Integrative Meta-Analysis and Cascading Model," *Journal of Applied Psychology* 95, no. 1 (2010): 54–78; Kenneth S. Law, Chi-Sum Wong, and Lynda J. Song, "The Construct and Criterion Validity of Emotional Intelligence and Its Potential Utility for Management Studies," *Journal of Applied Psychology* 89 (2004): 483–496; Robert P. Tett, Kevin E. Fox, and Alvin Wang, "Development and Validation of a Self-Report Measure of Emotional Intelligence as a Multidimensional Trait Domain," *Personality and Social Psychology Bulletin* 31, no. 7 (2005): 859–888; David L. Van Rooy, Chockalingam Viswesvaran, and Paul Pluta, "An Evaluation of Construct Validity: What Is This Thing Called Emotional Intelligence?" *Human Performance* 18, no. 4 (2005): 445–462.

75. Boele De Raad, "The Trait-Coverage of Emotional Intelligence," *Personality and Individual Differences* 38, no. 3 (2005): 673–687; W. Lee Grubb III and Michael A. McDaniel, "The Fakeability of Bar-On's Emotional Quotient Inventory Short Form: Catch Me If You Can," *Human Performance* 20, no. 1 (2007): 43–59; Joseph and Newman, "Emotional Intelligence: An Integrative Meta-Analysis and Cascading Model."

76. Barrick, Shaffer, and DeGrassi, "What You See May Not Be What You Get"; and Stewart, Darnold, Barrick, and Dustin, "Exploring the Handshake in Employment Interviews."

77. Chapman and Zweig, "Developing a Nomological Network for Interview Structure."

78. Roger Collins, Robyn Lincoln, and Mark G. Frank. "The Effect of Rapport in Forensic Interviewing," *Psychiatry, Psychology and Law* 9 (2002): 69–78; Dipboye, Macan, and Shahani-Denning, "The Selection Interview from the Interviewer and Applicant Perspectives."

79. Levashina, Hartwell, Morgeson, and Campion, "The Structured Employment Interview"; Julie M. McCarthy, Chad H. Van Iddekinge, and Michael A. Campion. "Are Highly Structured Job Interviews Resistant to Demographic Similarity Effects?" *Personnel Psychology* 63 (2010): 325–359.

80. B. M. Springbett, "Factors Affecting the Final Decision in the Employment Interview," *Canadian Journal of Psychology* 12 (1958): 13–22.

81. Soloman E. Asch, "Forming Impressions of Personality," *Journal of Abnormal and Social Psychology* 41 (1946): 258–290; Robert B. Zajonc, "Feeling and Thinking: References Need No Inferences," *American Psychologist* 35 (1980): 151–175; Robert B. Zajonc, "On the Primacy of Affect," *American Psychologist* 39 (1984): 117–123; and Peter Borkenau and Anette Liebler, "Convergence of Stranger Ratings of Personality and Intelligence with Self-Ratings, Partner

Ratings, and Measured Intelligence," *Journal of Personality and Social Psychology* 65, no. 3 (1993): 546–553.

82. Murray R. Barrick, Brian Swider, and Greg L. Stewart, "Initial Evaluations in the Interview: Relationships with Subsequent Interviewer Evaluations and Employment Offers," *Journal of Applied Psychology* 95 (2010): 1037–1046; Swider, Barrick, Harris, and Stoverink, "Managing and Creating an Image in the Interview: The Role of Interviewee Initial Impressions."

83. Stewart, Darnold, Barrick, and Dustin, "Exploring the Handshake in Employment Interviews."

84. Barrick, Sweider, and Stewart, "The Impact of First Impressions on Interviewer Judgments"; and Dustin, Barrick, Parks, Stewart, Zimmerman, and Darnold, "The Impact of First Impressions on Interviewer Judgments."

85. K. C. Jones, "'Digital Dirt' Derailing Job Seekers" (2006), retrieved November 30, 2007, from http://www.informationweek.com/story/showArticle.jhtml?articleID=190302836; Simola, Taggar, and Smith, "The Employment Selection Interview"; S. Sullivan, "One-in-Four Hiring Managers Have Used Internet Search Engines to Screen Job Candidates; One-in-Ten Have Used Social Networking Sites," *CareerBuilder.com Survey Finds* (2006), retrieved November 30, 2007, from http://www.careerbuilder.com/share/aboutus/pressreleasesdetail.aspz?id=pr331anded=12%2F31%2F2006andsd=10%2F26%2F2006andcbREcursionCnt=1andcbsid=a5015667d80f4b599c46d2b08f406b67-241548812-RI-4andns_siteid=ns_us_g_One%2din%2dFour_Hirin_.

86. Levashina, Hartwell, Morgeson, and Campion. "The Structured Employment Interview."

87. Simola, Taggar, and Smith, "The Employment Selection Interview."

88. Levashina, Hartwell, Morgeson, and Campion, "The Structured Employment Interview"; McCarthy, Van Iddekinge, and Campion, "Are Highly Structured Job Interviews Resistant to Demographic Similarity Effects?"

89. Barrick, Shaffer, and DeGrassi, "What You See May Not Be What You Get"; Kleinmann and Klehe, "Selling Oneself"; Swider, Barrick, Harris, and Stoverink, "Managing and Creating an Image in the Interview: The Role of Interviewee Initial Impressions."

90. Campion, Palmer, and Campion, "A Review of Structure in the Selection Interview"; Levashina, Hartwell, Morgeson, and Campion, "The Structured Employment Interview."

91. Levashina, Hartwell, Morgeson, and Campion. "The Structured Employment Interview."

92. Chapman and Zweig, "Developing a Nomological Network for Interview Structure."

93. Cornelius J. Konig, Ute-Christine Klehe, Matthias Berchtold, and Martin Kleinmann, "Reasons for Being Selective When Choosing Personnel Selection Procedures," *International Journal of Selection and Assessment* 18 (2010): 17–27; Van der Zee, Bakker, and Bakker. "Why Are Structured Interviews So Rarely Used in Personnel Selection?"

94. Neil Anderson, Jesus F. Salgado, and Ute R. Hülsheger, "Applicant Reactions in Selection: Comprehensive Meta-Analysis into Reaction Generalization versus Situational Specificity," *International Journal of Selection and Assessment* 18 (2010): 291–304; Stephen W. Gilliland and Dirk D. Steiner, "Applicant Reactions to Testing and Selection," in *The Oxford Handbook of Personnel Assessment and Selection*, ed. Neil Schmitt (Oxford Publishing, 2012), 629–666; Hausknecht, Day, and Thomas, "Applicant Reactions to Selection Procedures."

95. Dipboye, Macan, and Shahani-Denning, "The Selection Interview from the Interviewer and Applicant Perspectives."

96. Gary P. Latham, Lise M. Saari, Elliott D. Pursell, and Michael A. Campion, "The Situational Interview," *Journal of Applied Psychology* 65 (1980): 422–427.

97. Tom Janz, "Initial Comparisons of Patterned Behavior Description Interviews versus Unstructured Interviews," *Journal of Applied Psychology* 67 (1982): 577–580.

98. Tom Janz, Lowell Hellervik, and David C. Gilmore, *Behavior Description Interviewing* (Boston: Allyn and Bacon, 1986), 62.

99. Kahneman, 2011.

100. Paul R. Sackett and Filip Lievens, "Personnel Selection," *Annual Review of Psychology* 59 (2008): 419–450.

101. Posthuma, Morgeson, and Campion, "Beyond Employment Interview Validity."

102. Laura Kohn and Robert L. Dipboye, "The Effects of Interview Structure on Recruiting Outcomes," *Journal of Applied Social Psychology* 28 (1998): 821–843; and Silvia Moscoso, "A Review of Validity Evidence, Adverse Impact and Applicant Reactions," *International Journal of Selection and Assessment* 8 (2000): 237–247.

103. Huffcutt and Youngcourt. "Employment interviews," in *Applied Measurement: Industrial Psychology in Human Resource Management*, ed. D. L. Whetzel, and G. R. Wheaton (London: Psychology Press, 2007), 181–199.

104. Erica Baker and Julius Demps II, "Videoconferencing as a Tool for Recruiting and Interviewing," *Journal of Business and Economics Research* 7, no. 10 (2009): 9–14; Derek S. Chapman and Patricia M. Rowe, "The Impact of Videoconference Technology, Interview Structure, and Interviewer Gender on Interviewer Evaluations in the Employment Interview: A Field Experiment," *Journal of Occupational and Organizational Psychology* 74 (2001): 279–298; Gary C. Oliphant, Katharine Hansen, and Becky J. Oliphant, "A Review of a Telephone-Administered Behavior-Based Interview Technique," *Business Communication Quarterly* 71, no. 3 (2008): 383–386.

105. Chapman and Rowe, "The Impact of Videoconference Technology, Interview Structure, and Interviewer Gender on Interviewer Evaluations in the Employment Interview"; Frank L. Schmidt, and Mark Rader, "Exploring the Boundary Conditions for Interview Validity."

106. Schmidt and Rader, "Exploring the Boundary Conditions for Interview Validity."

107. Susan G. Straus, Jeffrey A. Miles, and Laurie L. Levesque, "The Effects of Videoconference, Telephone and Face-to-Face Media on Interviewer and Applicant Judgments in Employment Interviews," *Journal of Management* 27 (2001): 363–381; Christopher L. Martin and Dennis H. Nagao. "Some Effects of Computerized Interviewing on Job Applicant Responses," *Journal of Applied Psychology* 74, no. 1 (1989): 72.

108. Levashina, Hartwell, Morgeson, and Campion, "The Structured Employment Interview."

109. Paula Caligiuri, I. Tarique, and Rick Jacobs, "Selection for International Assignments," *Human Resource Management Review* 19 (2009): 251–262; Paula Caligiuri, "Developing Global Leaders," *Human Resource Management Review* 16, no. 2 (2006): 219–228; Dipboye, Macan, and Shahani-Denning, "The Selection Interview from the Interviewer and Applicant Perspectives."

110. Neal Anderson and Carlijn Witvliet, "Fairness Reactions to Personnel Selection Methods: An International Comparison between the Netherlands, the United States, Franc, Spain, Portugal, and Singapore," *International Journal of Selection and Assessment* 16 (2008): 1–13; Alexandra Eleftherious, and Ivan Robertson, "A Survey of Management Selection Practices in Greece," *International Journal of Selection and Assessment* 7 (1999): 203–208; Dan Ispas, Alexandra Ilie, Dragos Iliescu, Russell E. Johnson, and Michael M. Harris, "Fairness Reactions to Selection Methods: A Romanian Study," *International Journal of Selection and assessment* 18 (2010): 102–110; Konig, Klehe, Berchtold, and Kleinmann, "Reasons for Being Selective When Choosing Personnel Selection Procedures," *International Journal of Selection and Assessment* 18 (2010): 17–27; Silvia Moscoso and Jesus F. Salgado, "Fairness Reactions to

Personnel Selection Techniques in Spain and Portugal," *International Journal of Selection and Assessment* 12 (2004): 187–196; Ioannis Nikolaou and Timothy A. Judge, "Fairness Reactions to Personnel Selection Techniques in Greece: The Role of Core Self-Evaluations," *International Journal of Selection and Assessment* 15 (2007): 206–219; Viv Shackleton and Sue Newell, "European Management Selection Methods: A Comparison of Five Countries," *International Journal of Selection and Assessment* 2 (1994): 91–102; Dirk D. Steiner and Stephen W. Gilliland, "Fairness Reactions to Personnel Selection Techniques in France and the United States," *Journal of Applied Psychology* 81 (1996): 134–141; Dirk D. Steiner and Stephen W. Gilliland, "Procedural Justice in Personnel Selection: International and Cross-Cultural Perspectives," *Journal of Applied Psychology* 9 (2001): 124–137.

111. Geert Hofstede, "Motivation, Leadership, and Organization: Do American Theories Apply Abroad?" *Organizational Dynamics* 9 (1980): 42–63.

112. Ann Marie Ryan, Lynn McFarland, Helen Baron, and R. Page, "An International Look at Selection Practices: Nation and Culture as Explanations for Variability in Practice," *Personnel Psychology* 52 (1999): 359–392; Ann Marie Ryan and Nancy T. Tippins, *Designing and Implementing Global Staffing Systems* (West Sussex, England: Wiley-Blackwell, 2009).

113. Rong Ma and David G. Allen, "Recruiting across Cultures: A Value-Based Model of Recruitment," *Human Resource Management Review* 19 (2009): 334–346; Ryan, McFarland, Baron, and Page, "An International Look at Selection Practices."

114. Choon-Hwa Lim, Richard Winter, and Christopher CA Chan, "Cross-Cultural Interviewing in the Hiring Process: Challenges and Strategies," *Career Development Quarterly* 54 (2006): 265–268; Ann Marie Ryan, Darin Wiechmann, and Monica Hemingway, "Designing and Implementing Global Staffing Systems: Part II—Best Practices," *Human Resource Management* 42 (2003): 85–94.

115. Andrew Molinsky, "Language Fluency and the Evaluation of Cultural Faux Pas: Russians Interviewing for Jobs in the United States," *Social Psychology Quarterly* 68 (2005): 103–120; Ryan and Tippins, *Designing and Implementing Global Staffing Systems.*

116. Dipboye, Macan, and Shahani-Denning, "The Selection Interview from the Interviewer and Applicant Perspectives."

117. Wayne F. Cascio and Herman Aguinis, "Research in Industrial and Organizational Psychology from 1963 to 2007: Changes, Choices, and Trends," *Journal of Applied Psychology* 93, no. 5 (2008): 1062–1081.

118. James M. Conway, Robert A. Jako, and Deborah Goodman, "A Meta-Analysis of Interrater and Internal Consistency Reliability of Selection Interviews," *Journal of Applied Psychology* 80 (1995): 565–579; Huffcutt and Arthur Jr., "Hunter and Hunter (1984) Revisited: Interview Validity for Entry-Level Jobs"; Allen I. Huffcutt, James M. Conway, Philip L. Roth, and Ute-Christian Klehe, "The Impact of Job Complexity and Study Design on Situational and Behavior Description Interview Validity," *International Journal of Selection and Assessment* 12 (2004): 262–273; John E. Hunter, and Ronda F. Hunter, "Validity and Utility of Alternative Predictors of Job Performance," *Psychological Bulletin* 96 (1984): 72–98; Marc C. Marchese and Paul M. Muchinsky, "The Validity of the Employment Interview: A Meta-Analysis," *International Journal of Selection and Assessment* 1 (1993): 18–26; Gary P. Latham and Christina Sue-Chan, "A Meta-Analysis of the Situational Interview: An Enumerative Review of Reasons for Its Validity," *Canadian Psychology* 40 (1999): 56–67; McDaniel, Whetzel, Schmidt, and Maurer, "The Validity of Employment Interviews: A Comprehensive Review and Meta-Analysis"; Richard R. Reilly, and Georgia T. Chao, "Validity and Fairness of Some Alternative Selection Procedures," *Personnel Psychology* 35 (1982): 1–62; Schmidt and Rader, "Exploring the Boundary Conditions for Interview Validity"; Schmidt and Zimmerman, "A Counterintuitive Hypothesis about Employment Interview Validity and Some Supporting Evidence"; Wiesner and Cronshaw, "A Meta-Analytic Investigation of the

Impact of Interview Format and Degree of Structure on the Validity of the Employment Interview."

119. Huffcutt and Arthur Jr., "Hunter and Hunter (1984) Revisited: Interview Validity for Entry-Level Jobs."

120. Paul J. Taylor and Bruce Small, "Asking Applicants What They Would Do versus What They Did Do: A Meta-Analytic Comparison of Situational and Past Behaviour Employment Interview Questions," *Journal of Occupational and Organizational Psychology* 75 (2002): 272–294; and Huffcutt, Conway, Roth, and Klehe, "The Impact of Job Complexity and Study Design on Situational and Behavior Description Interview Validity."

121. Levashina, Hartwell, Morgeson, and Campion, "The Structured Employment Interview."

122. Huffcutt, Conway, Roth, and Klehe, "The Impact of Job Complexity and Study Design on Situational and Behavior Description Interview Validity"; Levashina, Hartwell, Morgeson, and Campion, "The Structured Employment Interview"; Paul J. Taylor and Bruce Small, "Asking Applicants What They Would Do versus What They Did Do: A Meta-Analytic Comparison of Situational and Past Behavior Employment Interview Questions," *Journal of Occupational and Organizational Psychology* 75 (2002): 277–294.

123. Levashina, Hartwell, Morgeson, and Campion. "The Structured Employment Interview."

124. Berry, Sackett and Landers, "Revisiting Interview–Cognitive Ability Relationships"; Cortina, Goldstein, Payne, Davison, and Gilliland, "The Incremental Validity of Interview Scores over and above G and Conscientiousness Scores"; Huffcutt, Roth, and McDaniel, "A Meta-Analytic Investigation of Cognitive Ability in Employment Interview Evaluations"; Salgado and Moscoso, "Comprehensive Meta-Analysis of the Construct Validity of the Employment Interview."

125. David E. Terpstra, A. Amin Mohamed, and R. Bryan Kethley, "An Analysis of Federal Court Cases Involving Nine Selection Devices," *International Journal of Selection and Assessment* 7 (1999): 26–34.

126. Charles H. Lawshe has shown that a form of quantitative analysis may be applied in content validity; see Charles H. Lawshe, "A Quantitative Approach to Content Validity," *Personnel Psychology* 28 (1975): 563–575.

127. Silvia Moscoso and Jesus F. Salgado, "Psychometric Properties of a Structured Behavioral Interview to Hire Private Security Personnel," *Journal of Business and Psychology* 16 (2001): 51–59.

128. James M. Conway, Robert A. Jako, and Deborah Goodman, "A Meta-Analysis of Interrater and Internal Consistency Reliability of Selection Interviews," *Journal of Applied Psychology* 80 (1995): 565–579.

129. Schmidt and Zimmerman, "A Counterintuitive Hypothesis about Employment Interview Validity and Some Supporting Evidence," *Journal of Applied Psychology* 89 (2005): 553–561.

130. Todd J. Maurer, Jerry M. Solamon, and Deborah D. Troxtel, "Relationship of Coaching with Performance in Situational Employment Interviews," *Journal of Applied Psychology* 83 (1998): 128–136.

131. *Human Resources Guide*, eds. Robert J. Nobile, Sandra King, Steven C. Kahn, and David Rosen (Cincinnati, OH: West Group, A Thomson Company, 2000), 2-70–2-84; Fred P. Morgeson, Matthew H. Reider, Michael A. Campion, and Rebecca A. Bull, "Review of Research on Age Discrimination in the Employment Interview," *Journal of Business Psychology* 22 (2008): 223–232.

132. *Watson v. Ft. Worth Bank and Trust*, 47 FEP Cases 102 (1988).

133. *Stamps v. Detroit Edison Co.*, 6 FEP 612 (1973).

134. *Weiner v. County of Oakland*, 14 FEP 380 (1976).

135. *King v. TWA*, 35 EPD 34, 588 (1984).

136. *Robbins v. White-Wilson Medical Clinic*, 660 F.2d 1210 (1981).

137. *Gilbert v. City of Little Rock, Ark.*, 799 F.2d 1210 (1986).

138. *Bailey v. Southeastern Joint Apprenticeship*, 561 F. Supp. 895 (1983).

139. *Jones v. Mississippi Department of Corrections*, 615 F. Supp. 456 (1985).

140. *Harless v. Duck*, 14 FEP 1,616 (1977).

141. *Maine Human Rights Commission v. Department of Corrections*, 474, A.2d 860 (1984).

142. *Minneapolis Commission on Civil Rights v. Minnesota Chemical Dependency Association*, 310 N.W.2d 497 (1981).

143. *Allesberry v. Commonwealth of Pennsylvania*, 30 FEP 1634 (1981).

144. Laura Gollub Williamson, James E. Campion, Stanley B. Malos, Mark V. Roehling, and Michael A. Campion, "Employment Interview on Trial: Linking Interview Structure with Litigation Outcomes," *Journal of Applied Psychology* 82 (1997): 900–912.

145. Rick D. Hackett, Laurent M. Lampierre, and Helen P. Gardiner, "A Review of Canadian Human Rights Cases Involving the Employment Interview," *Canadian Journal of Administrative Sciences* 21 (2004): 215–228.

146. Ellyn Brecher, Jennifer Bragger, and Eugene Kutcher, "The Structured Interview: Reducing Biases toward Job Applicants with Physical Disabilities," *Employee Responsibilities Rights Journal* 18 (2006): 155–170; Michael M. Harris, "Reconsidering the Employment Interview: A Review of Recent Literature and Suggestions for Future Research," *Personnel Psychology* 42 (1989): 691–726; Levashina, Hartwell, Morgeson, and Campion, "The Structured Employment Interview"; and Posthuma, Morgeson, and Campion, "Beyond Employment Interview Validity."

147. Levashina, Hartwell, Morgeson, and Campion, "The Structured Employment Interview"; Paul R. Sackett and Cathy L. DuBois, "Rater-Ratee Race Effects on Performance Evaluation: Challenging Meta-Analytic Conclusions," *Journal of Applied Psychology* 76 (1991): 873–877.

148. Dipboye, "The Selection/Recruitment Interview: Core Processes and Contexts"; Dipboye, Macan, and Shahani-Denning, "The Selection Interview from the Interviewer and Applicant Perspectives"; Ricardo A. Frazer and Uco J. Wiersma, "Prejudice versus Discrimination in the Employment Interview: We May Hire Equally, but Our Memories Harbour Prejudice," *Human Relations* 54 (2001): 173–191; Benoit Monin and Dale T. Miller, "Moral Credentials and the Expression of Prejudice," *Journal of Personality and Social Psychology* 81 (2001): 33–43; and Posthuma, Morgeson, and Campion, "Beyond Employment Interview Validity."

149. Dipboye, Macan, and Shahani-Denning, "The Selection Interview from the Interviewer and Applicant Perspectives"; Posthuma, Morgeson, and Campion, "Beyond Employment Interview Validity."

150. Jennifer DeNicolis Bragger, Eugene Kutcher, John Morgan, and Patricia Firth, "The Effects of the Structured Interview on Reducing Biases against Pregnant Job Applicants," *Sex Roles* 46, nos. 7/8 (2002): 215–226; Allen I. Huffcutt and Philip L. Roth, "Racial Group Differences in Employment Interview Evaluations," *Journal of Applied Psychology* 83 (1998): 179–189; and Joshua M. Sacco, Christine R. Scheu, Ann Marie Ryan, and Neal Schmitt, "An Investigation of Race and Sex Similarity Effects in Interviews: A Multilevel Approach to Relational Demography," *Journal of Applied Psychology* 88 (2003): 852–865.

151. Bragger, Kutcher, Morgan, and Firth, "The Effects of the Structured Interview on Reducing Biases against Pregnant Job Applicants"; Ellyn Brecher, Jennifer Bragger, and Eugene

Kutcher, "The Structured Interview: Reducing Biases toward Job Applicants with Physical Disabilities," *Employee Responsibilities Rights Journal* 18 (2006): 155–170.

152. Dipboye, "The Selection/Recruitment Interview: Core Processes and Contexts."

153. Huffcutt and Roth, "Racial Group Differences in Employment Interview Evaluations"; Levashina, Hartwell, Morgeson, and Campion, "The Structured Employment Interview."

154. Philip L. Roth, Chad H. Van Iddekinge, Allen I. Huffcutt, Carl E. Eidson Jr., and Philip Bobko, "Corrections for Range Restriction in Structured Interview Ethnic Group Differences: The Values May Be Larger Than Researchers Thought," *Journal of Applied Psychology* 87 (2002): 369–376.

155. Huffcutt and Roth, "Racial Group Differences in Employment Interview Evaluations"; Levashina, Hartwell, Morgeson, and Campion, "The Structured Employment Interview."

156. Terpstra, Mohamed, and Kethley, "An Analysis of Federal Court Cases Involving Nine Selection Devices."

157. Cynthia K. Stevens, "Structure Interviews to Hire the Best People," in *Handbook of Principles of Organizational Behavior*, ed. Edwin A. Loeke (Oxford, England: Blackwell Publishers, 2009), 45–68; Posthuma, Morgeson, and Campion, "Beyond Employment Interview Validity"; and Dipboye, "The Selection/Recruitment Interview: Core Processes and Contexts."

158. Dipboye, "The Selection/Recruitment Interview: Core Processes and Contexts."

159. Therese H. Macan and Robert L. Dipboye, "The Relationship of Interviewers' Preinterview Impressions to Selection and Recruitment Outcomes," *Personnel Psychology* 43 (1990): 745–768; Therese H. Macan and Robert L. Dipboye, "The Effects of the Application on Processing of Information from the Employment Interview," *Journal of Applied Social Psychology* 24 (1994): 1291–1314; and Daniel M. Cable and T. Gilovich, "Looked Over or Overlooked? Prescreening Decisions and Postinterview Evaluations," *Journal of Applied Psychology* 83 (1998): 501–508.

160. Thomas W. Dougherty, Daniel B. Turban, and John C. Callender, "Confirming First Impressions in the Employment Interview: A Field Study of Interviewer Behavior," *Journal of Applied Psychology* 79 (1994): 659–665; and Anthony T. Dalessio and Todd A. Silverhart, "Combining Biodata Test and Interview Information: Predicting Decisions and Performance Criteria," *Personnel Psychology* 47 (1994): 303–315.

161. Micki K. Kacmar, Sandy J. Wayne, and Shannon H. Ratcliffe, "An Examination of Automatic versus Controlled Information Processing in the Employment Interview: The Case of Minority Applicants," *Sex Roles* 30 (1994): 809–828; Neil C. Anderson and Vivian J. Shackleton, "Decision Making in the Graduate Selection Interview: A Field Study," *Journal of Occupational Psychology* 63 (1990): 63–76; Cheryl L. Adkins, Craig J. Russell, and James D. Werbel, "Judgments of Fit in the Selection Process: The Role of Work Value Congruence," *Personnel Psychology* 47 (1994): 605–623.

162. Barbara K. Brown and Michael A. Campion, "Biodata Phenomenology: Recruiters' Perceptions and Use of Biographical Information in Resume Screening," *Journal of Applied Psychology* 79 (1994): 897–908; Macan, and Dipboye, "The Relationship of Interviewers' Preinterview Impressions to Selection and Recruitment Outcomes."

163. K. Hanley, A. Farabee, and T. Macan, "Generation Y Hide Your Secrets? The Impression and Interview Ratings," Poster presented at The Society for Industrial and Organizational Psychology, Atlanta, GA, 2010.

164. Jones, "'Digital Dirt' Derailing Job Seekers" (2006), retrieved November 30, 2007, from http://www.informationweek.com/story/showArticle.jhtml?articleID=190302836; Simola, Taggar, and Smith, "The Employment Selection Interview."

165. Katherine Karl, and Joy Peluchette, *Facebook Follies. Who Suffers the Most?* (Kansas City, MO: Midwest Academy of Management, 2007).

166. Chapman and Zweig, "Developing a Nomological Network for Interview Structure"; Dipboye, Macan, and Shahani-Denning, "The Selection Interview from the Interviewer and Applicant Perspectives."

167. Dipboye, "The Selection/Recruitment Interview: Core Processes and Contexts."

168. Swider, Barrick, Harris, and Stoverink, "Managing and Creating an Image in the Interview: The Role of Interviewee Initial Impressions."

169. David G. Allen, Raj V. Mahto, and Robert F. Otondo, "Web-Based Recruitment: Effects of Information, Organizational Brand, and Attitudes toward a Web Site on Applicant Attraction," *Journal of Applied Psychology* 92 (2007): 1696–1708; Derek R. Avery, "Reactions to Diversity in Recruitment Advertising—Are Differences Black and White?" *Journal of Applied Psychology* 88 (2003): 672–679; Derek R. Avery, Morela Hernandez, and Michelle R. Hebl, "Who's Watching the Race? Racial Salience in Recruitment Advertising," *Journal of Applied Social Psychology* 34 (2004): 146–161; Phillip W. Braddy, Adam W. Meade, Joan J. Michael, and John W. Fleenor, "Internet Recruiting: Effects of Website Content Features on Viewers' Perceptions of Organizational Culture," *International Journal of Selection and Assessment* 17 (2009): 19–34; Darnold and Rynes, "Recruitment and Job Choice Research: Same as It Ever Was?"; Dineen, Ash, and Noe, "A Web of Applicant Attraction: Person-Organization Fit in the Context of Web-Based Recruitment"; Jerel E. Slaughter and Gary J. Greguras, "Initial Attraction to Organizations: The Influence of Trait Inferences," *International Journal of Selection and Assessment* 17 (2009): 1–18; Wei-Chi Tsai and Irene Wen-Fen Yang, "Does Image Matter to Different Job Applicants?"; Jack H. Walker, Hubert S. Feild, William F. Giles, Achilles A. Armenakis, and Jeremy B. Bernerth, "Displaying Employee Testimonials on Recruitment Web Sites: Effects of Communication Media, Employee Race, and Job Seeker Race on Organizational Attraction and Information Credibility," *Journal of Applied Psychology* 94 (2009): 1354–1364.

170. Alan M. Saks, "Multiple Predictors and Criteria of Job Search Success," *Journal of Vocational Behavior* 68 (2006): 400–415; Daniel B. Turban, Cynthia K. Stevens, and Felissa K. Lee, "Effects of Conscientiousness and Extraversion on New Labor Market Entrants' Job Search: The Mediating Role of Metacognitive Activities and Positive Emotions," *Personnel Psychology* 62 (2009): 553–573.

171. Hosoda, Stone-Romera, and Coats, "The Effects of Physical Attractiveness on Job-Related Outcomes: A Meta-Analysis of Experimental Studies," *Personnel Psychology* 56 (2003): 431–462; and Barrick, Shaffer, and DeGrassi, "What You See May Not Be What You Get."

172. Stewart, Darnold, Barrick, and Dustin, "Exploring the Handshake in Employment Interviews."

173. David F. Caldwell and Jerry M. Burger, "Personality Characteristics of Job Applicants and Success in Screening Interviews," *Personnel Psychology* 51 (1998): 119–136.

174. Todd J. Maurer, Jerry M. Solamon, Kimberly D. Andrews, and Deborah D. Troxtel, "Interviewee Coaching, Preparation Strategies, and Response Strategies in Relation to Performance in Situational Employment Interviews: An Extension of Maurer, Solamon, and Troxel (1998)," *Journal of Applied Psychology* 86 (2001): 709–717; and Maurer, Solamon, and Troxel, "Relationship of Coaching with Performance in Situational Employment Interviews."

175. Levashina, Hartwell, Morgeson, and Campion, "The Structured Employment Interview"; Posthuma, Morgeson, and Campion, "Beyond Employment Interview Validity."

176. Amy L. Kristof-Brown, "Perceived Applicant Fit: Distinguishing between Recruiters' Perceptions of Person-Job and Person-Organization Fit," *Personnel Psychology* 53 (2000): 643–671; Amy Kristof-Brown and Russell P. Guay. "Person–Environment Fit," in *APA*

Handbook of Industrial and Organizational Psychology, vol. 3, ed. S. Zedeck (Washington, DC: American Psychological Association, 2011), 3–50; K. Van Dam, "Trait Perception in the Employment Interview: A Five-Factor Model Perspective," International Journal of Selection and Assessment 11 (2003): 43–55.

177. Levashina, Hartwell, Morgeson, and Campion, "The Structured Employment Interview"; Posthuma, Morgeson, and Campion, "Beyond Employment Interview Validity."

178. Robert L. Dipboye and Susan J. Jackson, "Interviewer Experience and Expertise Effects," in The Employment Interviewer Handbook, ed. Robert W. Eder and Michael M. Harris (Thousand Oaks, CA: Sage Publications, 1999), 259–278.

179. Cascio and Aguinis, Applied Psychology in Human Resource Management; Laura M. Graves and Ronald J. Karren, "Are Some Interviewers Better Than Others?" in The Employment Interviewer Handbook, ed. Robert W. Eder and Michael M. Harris (Thousand Oaks, CA: Sage Publications, 1999); and Harris, "Reconsidering the Employment Interview: A Review of Recent Literature and Suggestions for Future Research."

180. Neal Schmitt, Elaine D. Pulakos, Earl Nason, and David J. Whitney, "Likability and Similarity as Potential Sources of Predictor-Related Criterion Bias in Validation Research," Organizational Behavior and Human Decision Processes 68 (1996): 272–286.

181. McCarthy, Van Iddekinge, and Campion, "Are Highly Structured Job Interviews Resistant to Demographic Similarity Effects?"; Posthuma, Morgeson, and Campion, "Beyond Employment Interview Validity."

182. Posthuma, Morgeson, and Campion, "Beyond Employment Interview Validity."

183. Wayne F. Cascio and Herman Aguinis, Applied Psychology in Human Resource Management, 7th ed. (Upper Saddle Brook, NJ: Pearson Prentice Hall, 2010); Levashina, Hartwell, Morgeson, and Campion, "The Structured Employment Interview."

184. Amy L. Kristof-Brown, Ryan D. Zimmerman, and Erin C. Johnson, "Consequences of Individuals' Fit at Work: A Meta-Analysis of Person–Job, Person–Organization, Person–Group, and Person–Supervisor Fit," Personnel Psychology 58 (2005): 281–342.

185. Huffcutt, Conway, Roth, and Stone, "Identification and Meta-Analytic Assessment of Psychological Constructs Measured in Employment Interviews."

186. Darnold and Rynes, "Recruitment and Job Choice Research: Same as It Ever Was?"; Uggerslev, Carroll, Piasentin, and Jones, "Applicant Attraction to Organizations and Job Choice: A Meta-Analytic Review of the Correlates of Recruiting Outcomes."

187. Cascio and Aguinis, Applied Psychology in Human Resource Management.

188. Barrick, Shaffer and DeGrassi, "What You See May Not Be What You Get"; and Kleinmann and Klehe "Selling Oneself."

189. Barrick, Shaffer and DeGrassi, "What You See May Not Be What You Get"; and Hosoda, Stone-Romera, and Coats, "The Effects of Physical Attractiveness on Job-Related Outcomes: A Meta-Analysis of Experimental Studies."

190. Jennifer R. Burnett and Stephen J. Motowidlo, "Relations between Different Sources of Information in the Structured Selection Interview," Personnel Psychology 51 (1998): 963–983; and Timothy DeGroot and Stephen J. Motowidlo, "Why Visual and Vocal Interview Cues Can Affect Interviewers' Judgments and Predict Job Performance," Journal of Applied Psychology 84 (1999): 986–993; Eva Krumhuber, Antony S. R. Manstead, Darren Cosker, Dave Marshall, and Paul L. Rosin, "Effects of Dynamic Attributes of Smiles in Human and Synthetic Faces: A Simulated Job Interview Setting," Journal of Nonverbal Behavior 33 (2009): 1–15.

191. Barrick, Shaffer and DeGrassi, "What You See May Not Be What You Get."

192. DeGroot and Motowidlo, "Why Visual and Vocal Interview Cues Can Affect Interviewers' Judgments and Predict Job Performance."

193. Aleksander P. J. Ellis, Bradley J. West, Ann Marie Ryan, and Richard P. DeShon, "The Use of Impression Management Tactics in Structured Interviews: A Function of Question Type?" *Journal of Applied Psychology* 87, no. 6 (2002): 1200–1208; Higgins, Judge, and Ferris, "Influence Tactics and Work Outcomes: A Meta-Analysis"; and Cynthia K. Stevens and Amy L. Kristof, "Making the Right Impression: A Field Study of Applicant Impression Management During Job Interviews," *Journal of Applied Psychology* 80, no. 5 (1995): 587–606; Barrick, Shaffer and DeGrassi, "What You See May Not Be What You Get."

194. Ellis, West, Ryan, and DeShon, "The Use of Impression Management Tactics in Structured Interviews: A Function of Question Type?"; and Stevens and Kristof, "Making the Right Impression: A Field Study of Applicant Impression Management during Job Interviews."

195. Michael J. Crant, "Doing More Harm than Good: When Is Impression Management Likely to Evoke a Negative Impression?" *Journal of Applied Social Psychology* 26 (1996): 1454–1471.

196. Swider, Barrick, Harris, and Stoverink, "Managing and Creating an Image in the Interview: The Role of Interviewee Initial Impressions."

197. Levishina and Campion, "Measuring Faking in the Employment Interview: Development and Validation of an Interview Faking Behavior Scale"; Brent Weiss, and Robert S. Feldman, "Looking Good and Lying To Do It: Deception as an Impression Management Strategy in Job Interviews," *Journal of Applied Social Psychology* 36 (2006): 1070–1086.

198. Higgins, Judge, and Ferris, "Influence Tactics and Work Outcomes: A Meta-Analysis"; Barrick, Shaffer, and DeGrassi, "What You See May Not Be What You Get."

199. Higgins, Judge, and Ferris, "Influence Tactics and Work Outcomes: A Meta-Analysis."

200. Barrick, Shaffer, and DeGrassi, "What You See May Not Be What You Get"; Levashina, Hartwell, Morgeson, and Campion, "The Structured Employment Interview"; and Wei-Chi Tsai, Chien-Cheng Chen, and Su-Fen Chiu, "Exploring Boundaries of the Effects of Applicant Impression Management Tactics in Job Interviews," *Journal of Management* 31 (2005): 108–125.

201. M. Susan Taylor and Janet A. Sniezek, "The College Recruitment Interview: Topical Content and Applicant Reactions," *Journal of Occupational Psychology* 57 (1984): 157–168.

202. Filip Lievens and Ananeleen De Paepe, "An Empirical Investigation of Interviewer-Related Factors That Discourage the Use of High-Structure Interviews," *Journal of Organizational Behavior* 25 (2004): 29–46; and Van der Zee, Bakker, and Bakker, "Why Are Structured Interviews Used So Rarely in Personnel Selection?"

203. Stevens, "Structure Interviews to Hire the Best People"; Jonathan Evans and Keith E. Stanovich, "Dual-Process Theories of Higher Cognition Advancing the Debate," *Perspectives on Psychological Science* 8, no. 3 (2013): 223–241.

204. Dipboye, "The Selection/Recruitment Interview: Core Processes and Contexts"; T. Macan and S. Merritt, "Actions Speak Too: Uncovering Possible Implicit and Explicit Discrimination in the Employment Interview Process," in *International Review of Industrial and Organizational Psychology*, vol. 26, 2011: 293–337.

205. Ibid.

206. Posthuma, Morgeson, and Campion, "Beyond Employment Interview Validity"; and Amos Tversky and Daniel Kahneman, "Judgment under Uncertainty: Heuristics and Biases," *Science* 185 (1974): 1124–1130.

207. Heloneida C. Kataoka, Gary P. Latham, and Glen Whyte, "The Relative Resistance of the Situational, Patterned Behavior, and Conventional Structured Interviews to Anchoring Effects," *Human Performance* 10 (1997): 47–63.

208. Herbert G. Heneman III, Donald P. Schwab, D. L. Huett, and John J. Ford, "Interviewer Validity as a Function of Interview Structure, Biographical Data, and Interviewee Order," *Journal of Applied Psychology* 60 (1975): 748–753; and Gary P. Latham, Kenneth N. Wexley, and Elliott D. Pursell, "Training Managers to Minimize Rating Errors in the Observation of Behavior," *Journal of Applied Psychology* 60 (1975): 550–555.

209. Posthuma, Morgeson, and Campion, "Beyond Employment Interview Validity."

210. Springbett, "Factors Affecting the Final Decision in the Employment Interview."

211. Asch, "Forming Impressions of Personality"; Zajonc, "Feeling and Thinking: References Need No Inferences"; Zajonc, "On the Primacy of Affect"; and Borkenau and Liebler, "Convergence of Stranger Ratings of Personality and Intelligence with Self-Ratings, Partner Ratings, and Measured Intelligence."

212. Dustin, Barrick, Parks, Stewart, Zimmerman, and Darnold, "The Impact of First Impressions on Interviewer Judgments."

213. Macan and Dipboye, "The Relationship of Interviewers' Preinterview Impressions to Selection and Recruitment Outcomes"; Macan and Dipboye, "The Effects of the Application on Processing of Information from the Employment Interview."

214. Patricia Rowe, "Individual Differences in Selection Decisions," *Journal of Applied Psychology* 47 (1963): 305–307.

215. B. Bolster and B. Springbett, "The Reaction of Interviewers' to Favorable and Unfavorable Information," *Journal of Applied Psychology* 45 (1961): 97–103.

216. Barrick, Shaffer, and DeGrassi, "What You See May Not Be What You Get."

217. Robert E. Carlson, Paul W. Thayer, Eugene C. Mayfield, and Donald A. Peterson, "Improvements in the Selection Interview," *Personnel Journal* 50 (1971): 268–275.

218. Jeremy C. Biesanz, Steven L. Neuberg, T. Nichole Judice, and Dylan M. Smith, "When Interviewers' Desire Accurate Impressions: The Effect of Note Taking on the Influence of Expectations," *Journal of Applied Social Psychology* 29 (1999): 2529–2549; Jennifer R. Burnett, Chenche Fan, Stephen J. Motowidlo, and Timothy DeGroot, "Interview Notes and Validity," *Personnel Psychology* 51 (1998): 375–396; and Catherine H. Middendorf and Therese H. Macan, "Note Taking in the Employment Interview: Effects on Recall and Judgment," *Journal of Applied Psychology* 87 (2002): 293–303.

219. McDaniel, Whetzel, Schmidt, and Maurer, "The Validity of Employment Interviews: A Comprehensive Review and Meta-Analysis."

220. Thomas S. Bateman and Dennis W. Organ, "Job Satisfaction and the Good Soldier: The Relationship between Affect and Employee 'Citizenship,'" *Academy of Management Journal* 26 (1983): 587–595.

221. Levashina, Hartwell, Morgeson, and Campion, "The Structured Employment Interview."

222. David Grove, "A Behavioral Consistency Approach to Decision Making in Employment Selection," *Personnel Psychology* 34 (1981): 55–64.

223. Taylor and Small, "Asking Applicants What They Would Do versus What They Did Do: A Meta-Analytic Comparison of Situational and Past Behaviour Employment Interview Questions"; and Conway, Roth, and Klehe, "The Impact of Job Complexity and Study Design on Situational and Behavior Description Interview Validity."

224. Schmidt and Zimmerman, "A Counterintuitive Hypothesis about Employment Interview Validity and Some Supporting Evidence."

225. Two other meta-analyses show the same results; see Marc C. Marchese and Paul M. Muchinsky, "The Validity of the Employment Interview: A Meta-Analysis," *International Journal of Selection and Assessment* 1 (1993): 18–26; Wiesner and Cronshaw, "A Meta-Analytic Investigation of the Impact of Interview Format and Degree of Structure on the Validity of the Employment Interview"; and Whetgel, Schemidt, and Manrer "The Validity of Employment Interviews: A Comprehensive Review and Meta-Analysis."

226. Allen I. Huffcutt and David J. Woehr, "Further Analysis of Employment Interview Validity: A Quantitative Evaluation of Interviewer-Related Structuring Methods," *Journal of Organizational Behavior* 20 (1999): 549–560.

227. van der Zee, Bakker, and Bakker, "Why Are Structured Interviews Used So Rarely in Personnel Selection?"

228. Taylor and Small, "Asking Applicants What They Would Do versus What They Did Do: A Meta-Analytic Comparison of Situational and Past Behaviour Employment Interview Questions."

229. Huffcutt and Woehr, "Further Analysis of Employment Interview Validity: A Quantitative Evaluation of Interviewer-Related Structuring Methods."

230. Middendorf and Macan, "Note Taking in the Employment Interview: Effects on Recall and Judgment."

231. Dipboye, "The Selection/Recruitment Interview: Core Processes and Contexts"; and Posthuma, Morgeson, and Campion, "Beyond Employment Interview Validity."

232. Ibid.

233. Huffcutt and Woehr, "Further Analysis of Employment Interview Validity: A Quantitative Evaluation of Interviewer-Related Structuring Methods."

234. Raymond L. Gordon, *Interviewing: Strategy, Techniques, and Tactics*, 3rd ed. (Homewood, IL: Dorsey Press, 1980), 480.

235. Thomas W. Dougherty, Ronald J. Ebert, and John C. Callender, "Policy Capturing in the Employment Interview," *Journal of Applied Psychology* 71 (1986): 9–15.

236. Conway, Jako, and Goodman, "A Meta-Analysis of Interrater and Internal Consistency Reliability of Selection Interviews."

237. Steven D. Maurer and Charles Fay, "Effect of Situational Interviews, Conventional Structured Interviews, and Training on Interview Rating Agreement: An Experimental Analysis," *Personnel Psychology* 41 (1988): 329–344. See also Michael A. Campion and James E. Campion, "Evaluation of an Interviewee Skills Training Program in a Natural Field Experiment," *Personnel Psychology* 40 (1987): 675–691.

238. George M. Alliger, Scott I. Tannenbaum, Winston Bennett Jr., Holly Traver, and Allison Shotland, "A Meta-Analysis of the Relations among Training Criteria," *Personnel Psychology* 50 (1997): 341–358.

239. The Bureau of National Affairs, Inc., *PPF Survey No. 146—Recruiting and Selection Procedures* (Washington, DC: Bureau of National Affairs, Inc., May 1988). 240–163; Chapman and Zweig, "Developing a Nomological Network for Interview Structure."

240. Chapman and Zweig, "Developing a Nomological Network for Interview Structure."

241. Chapman and Zweig, "Developing a Nomological Network for Interview Structure"; and van der Zee, Bakker, and Bakker, "Why Are Structured Interviews Used So Rarely in Personnel Selection?"

242. Gordon, *Interviewing: Strategy, Techniques, and Tactics*, 486.

243. Levashina, Hartwell, Morgeson, and Campion, "The Structured Employment Interview."

244. Levashina, Hartwell, Morgeson, and Campion, "The Structured Employment Interview"; Klaus G. Melchers, Nadja Lienhardt, Miriam Von Aarburg, and Martin Kleinmann, "Is More Structure Really Better? A Comparison of Frame-of-Reference Training and Descriptively Anchored Rating Scales to Improve Interviewers' Rating Quality," *Personnel Psychology* 64 (2011): 53–87.

Ability Tests for Selection

HISTORY OF ABILITY TESTS IN SELECTION

The history of the use of ability tests in selection is almost as old as the fields of industrial psychology and HR management. In 1908, Par Lahy described his work in developing tests for use in the selection of street car operators for the Paris Transportation Society.[1] Among the abilities he measured in applicants were reaction time, ability to estimate speed and distance, and ability to choose correct driving behavior in reaction to street incidents. These tests were administered to individual applicants using specially designed equipment in a laboratory. The following nine years saw other ability and performance tests used in selection for jobs such as telegraph and telephone operators, chauffeurs, typists, and stenographers.

World War I, with its need for rapid mobilization of military human resources, became a major impetus in the development of other tests used in selection. In 1917, a five-man Psychology Committee of the National Research Council was formed and chaired by Robert Yerkes. The group decided that the development and use of tests was the greatest contribution that psychology could offer to military efficiency. The immediate objective of this committee was to quickly develop paper-and-pencil tests that could be administered to large groups of military recruits and that would provide scores to be used as a basis for rejecting recruits thought to be unfit for military service.

The first test developed by this group was a mental ability or intelligence test. The committee required that this test correlate with existing individually administered tests of intelligence. It would have objective scoring methods, a format that could be rapidly scored, alternate forms to discourage coaching, responses that required a minimum of writing, and a structure that permitted an economical use of time.[2] These same requirements have characterized industrial ability tests ever since. The result of the committee's work was the famous Army Alpha (famous, at least, among test specialists). Five forms were developed, each containing 212 items and taking about 28 minutes to administer. Approximately 1.25 million men were tested in 35 examining units located across the United States.

The conspicuous use of this test generated interest in the development of other ability tests for use in vocational counseling and industrial selection. The next two decades saw the development of mechanical, motor, clerical, and spatial relations ability tests, among others. World War II provided another boost to test development: All three U.S. military organizations had extensive psychological testing programs. One emphasis was the development of specialized tests to assist in placing recruits in the most appropriate jobs. By this time the military had tremendously increased both the technical complexity and the diversity of its jobs. Similar tests were used extensively by industrial organizations after the war, partially because many jobs in these organizations closely resembled military jobs and also because a large number of war veterans suddenly became available as applicants; efficient selection devices were needed. The growing use of some ability tests halted abruptly in the late 1960s and 1970s, mainly because of EEO laws and early Supreme Court decisions that specifically addressed a few of the most popular of these tests (especially mental ability tests). Recently, the use of ability tests in selection has increased substantially.

In this chapter, we discuss the major types of ability tests that have been used in selection and describe a few representative tests in some detail to show what these tests actually measure. We also discuss their usefulness in present-day selection. Overwhelmingly, evidence indicates that these tests, when used appropriately, are valid selection measures, can be nondiscriminatory in their effects, and can cut costs significantly when used in employment decision making.

Definition of Ability Tests

As a first step, we will discuss briefly what we mean when we use the term *ability test*. Except for physical ability tests, generally these tests measure some form of knowledge. In this chapter, we discuss devices that measure mental, mechanical, clerical, and physical abilities. Although these are the tests most often used, other ability tests—for example, musical and artistic tests—have been included in selection programs. Space does not permit us to discuss them all. Except for physical ability, ability tests are almost always paper-and-pencil tests administered to applicants in a standardized manner. They have been developed to be given to several applicants at the same time. Tests of physical abilities, as the name implies, measure muscular strength, cardiovascular endurance, movement coordination, and other physical characteristics. Usually special equipment is required for these measurements.

The devices we call ability tests have often been referred to as *aptitude* or *achievement* tests. These two terms have been employed to connote slight differences in the uses of the two types of tests. Several years ago, ability tests were thought to measure the effects of formal learning experiences such as courses in English grammar or computer programming. Scores were interpreted to be an indication of how much an individual knew as a result of the learning experience. Aptitude tests, on the other hand, were thought to indicate how much knowledge or skill the individual had acquired "naturally" or without formal training. Therefore, aptitude scores were to be indicative of inherent (maybe genetic) levels of WRCs.

In reality, distinctions between achievement and aptitude tests are arbitrary. *All tests measure what a person has learned up to the time he or she takes the test.* A distinction between formal and informal learning is meaningless. A test respondent necessarily must have learned what to write, say, or do before being able to respond to a test question. There must be previous information or acquired actions to draw on. Psychologists agree that test behaviors reflect a large degree of previous learning. Tests cannot be measures of "innate" or unlearned potential.[3]

For these reasons, terms such as *aptitude* and *achievement* have been replaced by the term *ability*. We now take a look at some types of ability tests that have been used in selection.

COGNITIVE ABILITY TESTS

Cognitive or mental ability tests were at the center of many of the early Supreme Court decisions regarding the discriminatory effects of the use of tests in selection. As we mentioned previously, after these decisions, the use of cognitive ability tests in selection dropped significantly. HR managers were reluctant to use tests that had been implicated in disparate impact situations. However, much work in selection indicates that for almost all jobs, cognitive ability tests are related to job performance. Because of their wide use in selection and the fact that many of the principles governing the appropriate use of ability tests have been developed for cognitive ability tests, we spend more time discussing these ability tests than we do other types.

Development of Cognitive Ability Tests

To fully understand the use of cognitive ability tests in selection, it is important to know something of the history of their development. What is generally thought to be the first work on mental ability or intelligence tests was done by the French psychologists Alfred Binet and Theodore Simon from 1905 to 1911. They attempted to develop tests that would identify mentally retarded children in the French school system who should be assigned to special education classes. Most of the items that made up the tests were written through consultation with teachers in the school system. Binet and Simon sought to develop an age scale for each year between age 3 years and adulthood. An age scale contained a sample of curriculum questions that were appropriate for instruction at each academic grade level. For example, if the average age for children in grade 1 was 6 years, then the 6-year age scale would be composed of items learned in grade 1.

A child's mental age was based on correct answers to the various grade-level scales. For example, if a child correctly answered the items for the first grade and incorrectly answered the items on the second-grade scale, the child's mental age was estimated at 6 years (average age of first-grade students). Mentally retarded students were identified as those whose calculated mental age was substantially below their chronological age. Mentally superior students (gifted or genius) were those who could correctly answer questions at grade levels above their chronological ages.[4]

Binet and Simon's test items involved a variety of activities: including omissions in a drawing, copying written sentences, drawing figures from memory, repeating a series of numbers, composing a sentence containing three given words, naming differences between pairs of abstract terms, and interpreting given facts.[5] This mental ability test was designed to be administered by a trained professional to one individual at a time. In 1916, this test was modified for use in the United States and published as the *Stanford-Binet Intelligence Scale*. It is modified periodically and still used extensively today. The first group-administered mental ability test to have widespread use in the industry was the *Otis Self-Administering Test of Mental Ability*. This test took approximately 30 minutes to complete and consisted of written multiple-choice questions that measured such abilities as numerical fluency, verbal comprehension, general reasoning, and spatial orientation. The *Otis* served as the model for several other mental ability tests that have been used in HR selection.[6]

What Is Measured

Three points about the early cognitive ability tests are important for understanding this type of test. The first is the close association between the content of these tests and academic achievement.[7] As we just mentioned, the first mental ability test was developed using formal educational materials. Many later tests have closely followed the same strategy. Moreover, mental ability tests have commonly been validated using educational achievement as a criterion measure. Early studies correlated scores on a mental ability

TABLE 11.1	Abilities Measured by Various Mental Ability Tests
Memory Span	Figural Classification
Numerical Fluency	Spatial Orientation
Verbal Comprehension	Visualization
Conceptual Classification	Intuitive Reasoning
Semantic Relations	Ordering
General Reasoning	Figural Identification
Conceptual Foresight	Logical Evaluation

test with such measures as amount of education completed, degrees obtained, or, occasionally, grade point average. The rationale was that mental ability should be related to success in school. Robert Guion has commented that it seems acceptable to equate this type of test with scholastic aptitude, meaning that an adequate definition of what is measured by these tests is the ability to learn in formal education and training situations.[8]

The second point is that cognitive ability tests actually measure several distinct abilities (see Table 11.1 for a list). As we can see, the main abilities included are some form of verbal, mathematical, memory, and reasoning abilities. This clearly indicates that cognitive ability tests can actually differ among themselves in what is measured. All of the topics in Table 11.1 are mental abilities. However, they obviously are not the same ability. What this means is that *mental ability tests are not interchangeable*. They could differ in the abilities that are measured because the items of the tests differ in content.

Third, a variety of scores can be obtained from tests called cognitive ability tests. General cognitive ability tests measure several different mental abilities and report scores on all items as one total score. This total score, theoretically, indicates overall cognitive ability. Other tests provide separate scores on each of the tested abilities and then add these scores together to report a general ability total score. A third type of test measures each of several separate abilities and does not combine scores into a general ability measure. Instead, each of the cognitive abilities that are measured are reported individually. We now discuss one of the more famous and widely used cognitive ability tests in order to illustrate the concepts we have mentioned.

The Wonderlic Personnel Test

The *Wonderlic Personnel Test* was developed in 1938 and is still widely used. It is the mental ability test that was used by the Duke Power Company and questioned by Griggs in the landmark EEO selection case. (Yes, you're right—Chapter 4!) The *Wonderlic* is a multiple-choice test that consists of 50 items. The items cover vocabulary, "common-sense" reasoning, formal syllogisms, arithmetic reasoning and computation, analogies, perceptual skill, spatial relations, number series, scrambled sentences, and knowledge of proverbs. Table 11.2 contains items similar to those used in the *Wonderlic*. They are not part of the test itself. Statistical analysis has found that the primary factor measured by the test is verbal comprehension; deduction and numerical fluency are the next two factors in order of importance.[9]

There are two forms of the *Wonderlic*. The Quicktest (WPT-Q) is an abbreviated, unproctored version that can be given through the Internet. Its purpose is to do a preliminary assessment of the mental ability of applicants so that obviously unqualified applicants can be dropped from further testing and a company can save the related time

| TABLE 11.2 | Example Items Similar to Items on the Wonderlic Personnel Test |

1. Which of the following months has 30 days?

   (a) February   *(b) June   (c) August   (d) December

2. Alone is the opposite of:

   (a) happy   *(b) together   (c) single   (d) joyful

3. Which is the next number in this series: 1, 4, 16, 4, 16, 64, 16, 64, 256,

   (a) 4   (b) 16   *(c) 64   (d) 1024

4. Twilight is to dawn as autumn is to:

   (a) winter   *(b) spring   (c) hot   (d) cold

5. If Bob can outrun Murray by 2 feet in every 5 yards of a race, how much ahead will Bob be at 45 yards? [Bob, you wish.—Murray]

   (a) 5 yards   *(b) 6 yards   (c) 10 feet   (d) 90 feet

6. Bob is to Jr. as

   (a) knowledge is to   (b) light is to dark   *(c) both of these
       blank mind

Note: An asterisk (*) indicates the correct response.

and cost. The Wonderlic Personnel Test (WPT-R) is 50 items that are arranged in order of ascending difficulty. With items ranging from quite easy to fairly difficult, this test takes 12 minutes to complete. It has several forms, must be proctored, and is available in English and Spanish.

One very appealing feature of the test is the extensive set of norm scores that has been developed through its long history. The test publisher provides tables indicating the distribution of scores by education level of applicants, position applied for, region of the country, gender, age, and ethnicity. Parallel form reliability among the forms is given, ranging from 0.73 to 0.95; test-retest reliability is 0.82 to 0.94. During the many years of its use, selection programs that use the *Wonderlic* as a predictor device have been described in various academic journals. Data within these journal articles have become part of validity generalization studies, which we discuss later in the chapter. These studies have been used to examine some critical selection issues.

An interesting point for you sports enthusiasts: The *Wonderlic* is given to all players at the NFL Scouting Combine; scores are reported to NFL teams before the annual draft. The link footballiqscore.com provides a Quick Quiz (15 questions, 3 minutes) and a Full Quiz (50 questions, 12 minutes) for you to take and compare your score to those of "famous football players."

The Nature of Cognitive Ability Tests

As is obvious from the preceding sections, cognitive ability tests and those that have been called intelligence, or I.Q., tests are the same type of tests. We think that because of widespread misconceptions about the terms *intelligence* and *I.Q.*, selection specialists can more appropriately conceptualize these tests as cognitive ability. The term *cognitive ability* makes explicit that these tests measure various mental abilities. These cognitive abilities are most directly identified by the general factors that compose the test or, in some cases, from the content of the items themselves. That is, these are measures of an individual's ability to mentally manipulate words, figures, numbers, symbols, and impose logical order to solve problems.

Following from this, it is fairly easy to understand the strong relationship between mental ability test scores and academic performance. Formal education heavily stresses cognitive exercises and memorization of facts, and these are the components that make up a large part of most mental ability tests. Many mental ability tests have been validated against educational achievement, because it is sensible to think that, in general, those with the greatest mental ability will progress farther and do better in school situations than those with lesser ability. For these reasons it has been said that these tests measure academic ability. This, however, does not mean that mental ability is useful only for academic selection. Almost all jobs in organizations, including managerial, technical, and some clerical jobs, demand the use of mental abilities. We develop this topic next.

THE VALIDITY OF COGNITIVE ABILITY TESTS

The extensive use of cognitive ability tests has prompted studies of their validity. These studies have uniformly concluded that mental ability tests are among the most valid of all selection instruments. In this section, we summarize that research.

Project A

Project A was a multiple-year effort to develop a selection system appropriate for all entry-level positions in the U.S. Army. John P. Campbell and his associates describe some of the findings of Project A that are important for our discussion of the validity of mental ability tests.[10]

One of the major tasks of this project was the development of 65 predictor tests that could be used as selection instruments. Statistical analyses were applied to the scores on these tests of 4,039 incumbents of entry-level army jobs. These analyses resulted in six categories of predictor instruments: general cognitive ability, spatial ability, perceptual psychomotor ability, temperament/personality, vocational interest, and job reward preference. Another major task was the development of categories of work performance across entry-level jobs. Five categories were determined: core technical task proficiency; general soldiering proficiency; peer support and leadership, effort, and self-development; maintaining personal discipline; and physical fitness and military bearing.[11]

You can probably guess what a group of selection specialists would do if they found themselves with six predictors and five measures of job performance for 4,000 people. Yep, they conducted a giant validity study. Table 11.3 presents only a small part of the results. The validity coefficients are corrected for range restriction and adjusted for shrinkage. The general cognitive ability predictor category of tests correlated 0.63 and 0.65 with the two factors that most directly measured job task performance. Spatial ability, an ability that sometimes has been included in measures of general cognitive ability, also had high validity coefficients. It is important to remember that these data were calculated across all entry-level jobs in the army. Our conclusion is that these data indicate that general mental ability tests are valid selection instruments across a large variety of military jobs.

Validity Generalization Studies

We discussed validity generalization in Chapter 8. (On the off chance that you don't remember that discussion, you should go back and look it over. It will make the following

| TABLE 11.3 | Project A: Validity Coefficients |

Job Performance Factor	Predictor					
	General Cognitive Ability	Spatial Ability	Perceptual Psychomotor Ability	Temperament/ Personality	Vocational Interest	Job Reward Preference
Core technical proficiency	0.63	0.56	0.53	0.26	0.35	0.29
General soldiering proficiency	0.65	0.63	0.57	0.25	0.34	0.30

Source: Jeffrey J. McHenry, Leaetta M. Hough, Jody L. Toquam, Mary A. Hanson, and Steven Ashworth, "Project A Validity Results: The Relationship between Predictor and Criterion Domains," *Personnel Psychology* 43 (1990): 335–354.

easier to understand!) For many years, selection specialists had noted that validity coefficients for the same combination of cognitive ability tests and job performance measures differed greatly for studies in different organizations. This was true even when the jobs for which the selection program was designed were very similar. Selection specialists explained these differences in validity coefficients as caused by undetermined organizational factors that affected the correlation between selection instruments and criteria. They concluded that a validation study is necessary for each selection program being developed.

Importance in Selection

The conclusions that have been drawn from meta-analytic studies of cognitive ability tests and job performance are very different from those we just mentioned. Frank Schmidt, John Hunter, and their colleagues conducted many of these early studies and concluded that the differences in validity coefficients among studies that have used mental ability tests for similar jobs are not a function of unknown organizational factors. Rather, these differences are due to methodological deficiencies in the validation studies themselves. When these methodological deficiencies are corrected, the differences among these validity coefficients are close to zero. Validity generalization studies have applied these corrections to validation works conducted previously. These studies corrected for differences in sample size, reliability of criterion measures, reliability of predictor measures, and restriction in range.

Validity Generalization for the Same Job

One approach of validity generalization studies has been to analyze data from validity studies conducted for the same job—for example, computer programmers—that all used the same type of test as a predictor. Table 11.4 summarizes the corrected mean validity coefficients of some of these studies. The most prominent finding of these studies is that, as Schmidt and Hunter hypothesized, there is evidence that after statistical corrections are made the differences among studies in terms of validity coefficients are greatly reduced. In some instances, all differences have been eliminated. This interpretation means that the validity coefficients for cognitive ability and other types of tests are stable across organizations.

A second finding of these studies has been that the statistical corrections to the validity coefficients raised the magnitude of these coefficients. This is the same concept we discussed in Chapter 8 regarding the factors that may artificially reduce a validity coefficient. Many validity coefficients from single studies are understatements of the true

TABLE 11.4	Selected Validity Generalization Results for Various Jobs

Job	Test Type	Estimated Average Validity Coefficient	
		Performance Criteria	Training Criteria
Computer programmer[a]	Figure analogies	0.46	—
	Arithmetic reasoning	0.57	—
	Total score all tests	0.73	0.91
First-line supervisor[b]	General mental ability	0.64	—
	Mechanical comprehension	0.48	—
	Spatial ability	0.43	—
Computing and account-recording clerks[b]	General mental ability	0.49	0.66
	Verbal ability	0.41	0.62
	Quantitative ability	0.52	0.66
	Reasoning ability	0.63	—
	Perceptual speed	0.50	0.38
	Memory	0.42	—
Police and detectives[c]	Memory	—	0.41
	Quantitative ability	0.26	0.63
	Reasoning	0.17	0.61
	Spatial/mechanical ability	0.17	0.50
	Verbal ability	—	0.64

Note: Data for missing cells are not reported.

[a]Frank Schmidt, Ilene Gast-Rosenbery, and John Hunter, "Validity Generalization for Computer Programmers," *Journal of Applied Psychology* 65 (1980): 643–661.

[b]Kenneth Pearlman, Frank Schmidt, and John Hunter, "Validity Generalization Results for Tests Used to Predict Job Proficiency and Training Success in Clerical Occupations," *Journal of Applied Psychology* 65 (1980): 373–406.

[c]Hannah Rothstein Hirsh, Lois Northrup, and Frank Schmidt, "Validity Generalization Results for Law Enforcement Occupations," *Personnel Psychology* 39 (1986): 399–420.

relationships between predictors and criteria, because they are affected by factors that are corrected in validity generalization studies. As Table 11.4 indicates, some of these corrected coefficients for mental ability tests are relatively high, in the 0.50s and 0.60s. Such coefficients demonstrate a much stronger relationship between mental ability and performance than was previously thought.

A third finding is that selection instruments predict training results very well. The coefficients for training criteria in Table 11.4 are, as a whole, higher than those for job performance, sometimes reaching 0.70 to 0.90.

Validity across Jobs

A second focus of validity generalization studies has been to examine differences in validity coefficients for the same set of predictor-criterion measures across different jobs.

This can be regarded as a logical extension of the previously described studies. If situation specificity between organizations is false, perhaps specificity between jobs is also false. As you might guess from our previous comments, the conclusion of these validity generalization studies has been that mental ability tests are valid across a large variety of jobs and can serve as useful selection instruments.[12] Table 11.5 presents some results obtained by John Hunter that are representative of these studies.

The upper part of Table 11.5 presents the results of the validity correction formulas applied to studies within each of nine occupations. The argument for the validity of mental ability tests is strongly made, because the average coefficient presented in the table is significant for each occupation. One conclusion is that mental ability tests are valid for each of these occupations, although there are differences in the magnitude of the coefficients among the occupations.

The lower part of Table 11.5 extends these conclusions. This part is based on 515 validation studies conducted by the U.S. Employment Service on the validity of the General Aptitude Test Battery (GATB), a cognitive ability test battery. Data on jobs were reported using six different job analysis systems. All systems had one dimension that measured complexity. Jobs in these 515 validation studies were grouped into low, medium, and high complexity based on their scores on this dimension. A second method of grouping jobs on complexity level was used for jobs in industrial families. Using the "things" scale of the *Dictionary of Occupational Titles*, published by the Department of

TABLE 11.5 Selected Validity Generalization Results for Mental Ability Tests Across Jobs

Occupations	Performance Criteria	Training Criteria
Manager	0.53	0.51
Clerical	0.54	0.71
Salesperson	0.61	—
Sales clerk	0.27	—
Protective professions	0.42	0.87
Service workers	0.48	0.66
Vehicle operators	0.28	0.37
Trades and crafts	0.46	0.65
Industrial	0.37	0.61
Job Families	**Performance Criteria**	**Training Criteria**
General job families		
high complexity	0.58	0.50
medium complexity	0.51	0.57
low complexity	0.40	0.54
Industrial families		
setup work	0.56	0.65
feeding/offbearing	0.23	—

Note: Data for empty cells are not reported.

Source: John Hunter, "Cognitive Ability, Cognitive Aptitudes, Job Knowledge, and Job Performance," *Journal of Vocational Behavior* 29 (1986): 340–362.

Labor, these jobs were grouped into setup work (more complex) and feeding/offbearing work (less complex).

Validity generalization analyses were applied to the studies within each complexity level. This meant that many different jobs were grouped together within each of these five complexity categories. As Table 11.5 shows, the GATB was valid for each category with both performance and training criterion measures.

However, there are differences among the performance validity coefficients, with those for more complex jobs being higher than those for less complex jobs. Coefficients for training criteria are uniformly high. These results are interpreted to show that mental ability tests are valid for a great many jobs and increase in the predictability of job performance as the job becomes more complex. For training success, mental ability tests are consistently very high in validity.

The meta-analytic studies that we have summarized all examine the relationship of cognitive ability scores and measures of task performance. In addition to this relationship, there is limited evidence that cognitive ability is also related to other forms of performance that we have discussed. One research study was based upon a theoretical connection between cognitive ability and voluntary turnover. Voluntary turnover is often regarded as a withdraw behavior and grouped with counterproductive work behaviors (CWBs). Integrating data from three different sources, the researchers found that the relationship between cognitive ability and voluntary turnover is, in general, curvilinear. That is, high ability and low ability workers will leave more readily than medium ability workers. This is due to high ability workers feeling bored with medium or low demanding jobs and low ability workers being pressured by the organization to leave. Complexity of the job can also modify this general relationship between cognitive ability and voluntary turnover. For example, with regard to jobs with low complexity, there is a negative linear relationship between cognitive ability and voluntary turnover, such that higher cognitive ability employees are less likely to leave voluntarily. This is due to the premise that high ability workers have more opportunities when they choose a job. Therefore high ability individuals who choose low complexity jobs probably do so for other benefits, for example, time for child care or leisure activities, that continue to hold them to the job.[13] Another study was a meta-analysis to measure the correlation of GMA with CWBs and organizational citizenship behaviors (OCB). Overall, the results show that the correlation between GMA and CWB is essentially 0 (−0.02). The correlation between GMA and OCB is positive but modest in magnitude (0.23). The second purpose of this study was to determine the relative importance of GMA and the five-factor model of personality traits in predicting OCB, CWB, and task performance. Results were that the personality traits are substantially more important for CWB than cognitive ability, that the personality traits are roughly equal in importance to cognitive ability for OCB, and that cognitive ability is substantially more important for task and overall job performance than the personality traits are.[14]

Comparison of Cognitive Ability and Other Selection Tests

In yet another meta-analysis study, Schmidt and Hunter compared the validity of mental ability tests to that of 18 other selection procedures.[15] This study had two purposes. The first was to estimate the validity of each type of selection test. The second was to examine how much increase in validity could be gained by adding these other instruments to a cognitive ability test in a selection battery. Schmidt and Hunter's findings for some of the types of selection instruments that we discuss in this book are presented in Table 11.6.

TABLE 11.6	Validity of Mental Ability and Other Selection Tests		
Selection Test	**Validity**	**Validity of Both Tests**	**Gain in Validity**
Mental ability	0.51		
Work sample	0.54	0.63	0.12
Integrity	0.41	0.65	0.14
Personality (conscientiousness)	0.31	0.60	0.09
T&E application form	0.45	0.58	0.07
Biographical data	0.35	0.52	0.01
Assessment Center	0.37	0.53	0.02

Source: Frank L. Schmidt and John E. Hunter, "The Validity and Utility of Selection Methods in Personnel Psychology: Practical and Theoretical Implications of 85 Years of Research Findings," *Psychological Bulletin* 124 (1998): 262–274.

The "validity" column of Table 11.6 states the corrected validity that Schmidt and Hunter determined for each of the selection devices listed. Only one of these devices, the work sample test, has a higher validity than does the mental ability test. However, each of these other selection devices can improve the validity of the selection program when it is added to a cognitive ability test. The second column of numbers in the table presents the combined validity of a cognitive ability test and the other selection measure. For example, the combined validity for a cognitive ability test and a work sample test is 0.63. The third column of numbers presents the increase in validity over the cognitive ability test obtained by using the second test. In the case of work sample, this gain is 0.12. According to the two authors, these findings clearly indicate that mental ability tests should be regarded as a primary selection device; other selection tests can be added also to form a higher validity test battery.

Implications for Selection

The studies we have summarized resulted in some far-reaching conclusions. The first is that it is no longer necessary to conduct validity studies within each organization. If the job of interest for the selection program is one of those for which validity generalization data have been reported, then the selection instruments reported in the validity generalization study can be used for selection. There are no organizational effects on validity; therefore, the same predictor can be used across all organizations. To set up the selection program, it should be necessary only to demonstrate through job analysis that the job within the organization is similar to the job in the validity generalization study. Obviously, this reduces the time, effort, and cost of establishing a valid selection program.

A second conclusion is that cognitive ability tests are valid predictors for a wide variety of jobs. However, the magnitude of the validity correlation between cognitive ability and task performance varies from job to job. The variable that moderates the magnitude of the validity correlations is most likely the differing information-processing and problem-solving demands of jobs, not task differences themselves. That is, cognitive ability has "more predictability" for jobs with greater information-processing and problem-solving demands than for those jobs with fewer demands.

One explanation for this is that cognitive ability is highly correlated with job knowledge, and job knowledge is highly correlated with job performance.

Moreover, cognitive ability is related to job performance itself, not just to job knowledge. Hunter writes:

> *This may be because high ability workers are faster at cognitive operations on the job, are better able to prioritize between conflicting rules, are better able to adapt old procedures to altered situations, are better able to innovate to meet unexpected problems, and are better able to learn new procedures quickly as the job changes over time.*[16]

A third conclusion is that scores obtained from a general cognitive ability test are as good a predictor of job performance as are scores from a composite test of specific abilities seemingly related to the job. In support of this, Hunter analyzed data obtained from military validity studies. He grouped jobs into four categories: mechanical, electronic, skilled services, and clerical. Five tests were examined: general mental ability and four separate composite tests tailored to each job group (mechanical composite, electrical composite, skilled service composite, and clerical composite). Results indicated very little difference between the magnitude of the validity coefficient of the general mental ability test and the appropriate composite test for each of the four job groups. In fact, the coefficient for the general mental ability test was higher than the validity for the composite in three of the four job categories.

A fourth conclusion that can be drawn from this series of meta-analyses is that parts of the *Uniform Guidelines on Employee Selection Procedures* (discussed in Chapter 4) are not appropriate at this point in time. The *Uniform Guidelines* are based upon the premise of situational specificity of validity. That is, they assume that the validity of a selection test is partially dependent upon the characteristics of the organization. The *Uniform Guidelines* require that in order to demonstrate empirical validity, a company must conduct a validity study, using its own applicants or employees and performance measures. As we stated previously, these meta-analyses clearly point out that situational specificity is not correct. Following from that, the requirement of conducting a validity study within a specific organization is not appropriate. In fact, meta-analysis demonstrates that single organization validity studies are usually flawed due to small sample size and other methodological limitations. Because of these limitations, the resulting validity coefficient cannot be regarded as an accurate indicator of the validity of the selection test in question. We are therefore in a quizzical legal arena in which the precedent of court cases and the *Uniform Guidelines*, which should be given "great weight" in legal decisions of discrimination, both argue for a validation strategy that has been discredited by empirical research conducted subsequent to the early court cases and the publication of the *Uniform Guidelines*. Clearly the *Uniform Guidelines* must be updated to include validity generalization as an appropriate validation strategy for the explanation of adverse impact in selection decisions.

COGNITIVE ABILITY TESTS AND ADVERSE IMPACT

A downside of using cognitive ability tests in selection is the adverse impact that results. That is, large differences exist in mean scores between white and black respondents and between white and Hispanic respondents. Using these tests in making selection decisions usually results in a higher percentage of whites being selected than are members of the other two groups. These differences are the definition of adverse impact.

Phil Roth and his colleagues completed a thorough meta-analysis of these differences and the following is a brief summary of what was found. The important statistic in measuring differences between demographic groups is the *d-statistic*. This is defined as the difference in means (for example, white mean vs. black mean) divided by the sample-weighted average of the standard deviations. "Of course it is!" you say. This is complex, but it is a way of determining differences among groups as a function of differences within the groups. Large between-group differences are more significant if there are very small differences within each of the groups. Between-group differences are less significant if there are very large differences within each of the groups. At any rate, Roth and his associates examined several different samples because they used data from military, education, and industrial settings; different job complexity levels; and incumbent and applicant status. Across all samples they found d = 1.10 for the black–white differences (white higher) and 0.72 for the Hispanic–white differences (white higher). However there was variability in the d scores across various comparison samples. For instance, across job complexity levels the black–white d values were 0.86 (low cx), 0.73 (medium cx), and 0.63 (high cx). In industrial samples for the same groups, the d value for applicants was 0.74 and 0.54 for incumbents.[17]

Another study by Denise Potosky and the two prolific Phils (Bobko and Roth) investigated how adding applicants' scores on other types of selection tests to their scores on a cognitive ability test would affect measured adverse impact.[18] This follows from a common assumption that developing selection programs including selection instruments thought to produce less adverse impact than cognitive ability tests would inevitably produce a final selection score that would "soften" the demographic differences in scores using the cognitive ability test alone. The hoped-for result would be significantly less, or perhaps no, adverse impact among demographic groups. In three separate analyses, the authors added measures of conscientiousness, biodata, and a structured interview to the cognitive ability score. Their main conclusion was that the validity of the composite battery does not always go up in comparison to the cognitive ability score by itself and the addition of noncognitive predictors had little if any effect on the occurrence of adverse impact. That is, even when adverse impact was lessened, it still usually resulted in significant adverse impact as measured by the four-fifths rule we discussed in Chapter 4. The authors, in fact, raised the question of whether or not it is possible for organizations to avoid adverse impact if a cognitive ability test is used as part of the selection program.

These consistent differences in scores among demographic groups on cognitive ability tests coupled with their high validity and low cost, prompted attempts to try to determine explanations of these differences and how they may be minimized in selection. Many organizations desire to select both a high performing and a diverse workforce. Cognitive ability tests can help produce the first but apparently not the second.

One of the early explanations was that the content of mental ability tests is based on white middle-class culture and, therefore, the wording of test items does not mean the same thing to other groups as it does to whites. Nonwhite respondents use different words and terms and this difference reduces their scores on the test. These test scores will not have the same distribution for whites and nonwhites, nor will the pattern of validity coefficients with other measures—such as job performance—be the same for the two groups. *Differential validity* is the term that is used to describe the hypothesis that employment tests are less valid for black and Hispanic group members than for whites. The situation is one in which the validities for the same selection test in the two groups are statistically significant but unequal. For example, the test may be significantly more valid for white than for black applicants. Differential validity implies that selection managers should develop separate but equivalent selection programs for each applicant group for each job. This would be necessary in order to control the differences in terms and symbols of selection tests among the various cultures.

To examine the problem more closely, researchers have done meta-analyses (what else?) on data collected from selection programs. These studies consistently conclude that *differential validity does not exist*. Those few selection programs in which differential validity has been observed have been characterized by methodological limitations that seem to account for the observed differences. For example, one investigation examined 31 studies in which 583 validity coefficients were reported.[19] These studies were also scored on methodological characteristics such as sample size, use of criteria measures that were identified as being for research purposes only, and use of a predictor chosen for its theoretical relationship to the criterion measures. For the most part, differential validity was observed only in those studies with several methodological limitations. For the methodologically sound studies, no differences in validity coefficients between black and white groups were observed.

Another study used 781 pairs of validity coefficients. The pairs were made up of the correlation between the same predictor variable (commonly a cognitive ability test) and criterion variable for both a white and a black group of workers.[20] These correlations ranged from approximately 0.37 to 0.55. The validity correlations for white and blacks were graphed separately and the plots of the graphs compared. The two plots looked almost identical. This was interpreted to mean that these tests acted in the same manner for both black and white people. The conclusion of the study was that differential validity was not demonstrated and that tests that ordered white people successfully with respect to some given job criterion *also* ordered black people with equal success.

Other research, however, has found support for the existence of differential validity between whites and blacks or Hispanics.[21] This study pointed out that military and educational selection studies have consistently found differences in the magnitude of validity coefficients using cognitive ability as a predictor and various performance criteria. The reason that differential validity has not been found in civilian samples is mainly due to differences in sample sizes (civilian samples are smaller) and the statistical method of comparing validity coefficients between white and minority. Samples of civilian, military, and educational selection were combined for the analyses and results indicated a consistent difference in the magnitude of validity coefficients between white samples and those of blacks and Hispanics. This consistent difference was interpreted to be evidence of differential validity. However, another study found that the level of differences between validity coefficients of black and white groups may be caused by range restriction (which limits the magnitude of the validity coefficient) rather than by differential validity.[22] The idea of this research was that when a score on a cognitive ability test is used as a cutoff, the large differences in mean scores between white and black groups results in the range of scores of accepted black applicants being much smaller than it is for the white groups. This restricted range of scores lowers the *estimated sample* validity coefficient for the black group so that it may appear to be differential validity when it is instead only a statistical artifact. The researchers concluded that previously estimated differential validity between the two groups is likely caused by this range restriction rather than actual differential validity.

Another way of addressing the issue of adverse impact caused by cognitive ability tests in selection is a statistical procedure adjustment. As we discussed in Chapter 8, multiple regression is a statistical formula used to predict job performance when there are multiple selection tests. The formula develops a weight that is applied to scores of applicants for each selection test in the selection battery. Each test in the selection program usually has a different weight. After all weights are applied and individuals' scores are determined, it is possible to arrange the applicants in order of their total predicted performance scores. Those with the highest predicted scores are usually the ones offered employment. Multiple regression predicts the outcome of main interest to the company and most often this is task performance. In an oversimplified explanation, pareto analysis is a procedure that allows for two different types of performance to be identified and have the resulting weights for the selection tests reflect how to maximize both performance dimensions simultaneously. In this case, the two dimensions can be task performance and some level of diversity.[23] In one example of the use of pareto analysis, Serena

Wee and colleagues developed a strategy for differentially weighting cognitive subtests (that is, specific cognitive abilities rather than overall cognitive ability) to predict both job performance and to increase diversity in the applicant pool. Using data from two large validation studies that included a total of 15 job families, they demonstrated that this pareto analysis led to improvement in diversity hiring (for example, doubling the number of job offers extended to minority applicants) without significantly reducing the criterion-related validity.[24]

So What?

One of the most difficult problems facing many selection specialists is the adverse impact caused by one of the most valid and least expensive selection measures, cognitive ability tests. In addition, ample research evidence supports the use of cognitive ability tests in legal cases when these tests are a central part of a discrimination charge. For these reasons, many think that cognitive ability tests should be used often because they provide a means to predict a very productive labor force. Others, however, also value diversity as a major goal pointing out broader business reasons for its value. For these, the ways to increase diversity have been to emphasize recruitment of minorities so there are larger applicant pools and to increase the training of minorities who are employed so that there is a rapid development of skills that are important for job success. Both of these are difficult to execute well and also expensive. The pareto analyses that we discussed are interesting because this procedure may provide another alternative to achieving both high performance and increased diversity.

It must be clearly noted that the studies summarized above only present the cognitive score differences among demographic groups. They do not attempt to explain the causes of or possible reasons for such differences. It is not appropriate for anyone to use these studies to argue for genetic, educational, or cultural factors as the sole cause of differences.

MENTAL ABILITY TESTS AND THE INTERNET

In the interest of reducing the costs of selection, many organizations use electronic delivery systems for gathering data about job candidates. For example, application blanks and resumes are often submitted online. Telephone or video interviews are frequently conducted at initial stages of applicant screening. Mental ability tests and other knowledge-based tests are increasingly used in selection in online forms. This is because they consist of multiple-choice questions and do not require interaction between the test administrator and the applicant taking the test. This combination makes them suitable for remote administration. Despite the growing use of online testing, there are two issues that are of much concern. One is the equivalence of the electronic and traditional forms of the tests and the other is cheating. We will discuss both.

Equivalence of Paper-and-Pencil and Electronic Tests

There is much research that has used two different groups of people as test subjects for examining the equivalency of tests and surveys. One group completes the paper version of the test and the other group does the computer version. Several types of tests have been used in this research with widely different content: Big 5 personality, depression, attention deficit/hyperactivity, obsessive compulsiveness, high school end-of-the-year tests in English and algebra, and transformational leadership behaviors are examples.

Almost unanimously these studies have reached the conclusion that the two forms are equivalent. The evidence for this conclusion has been statistical measurement data: comparable factor structure of the two forms, scale score correlations with contextual variables, and items statistics.

A study by Denise Potosky and Philip Bobko used a different research protocol. They used two cognitively based tests, one timed and the other untimed.[25] Adult subjects from a variety of jobs took both paper-and-pencil and computer versions of each of the two tests. The computer tests were identical to the paper-and-pencil versions in terms of the wording of instructions and items, and the same person was the administrator for all testing situations. One test was the *Test of Learning Ability* (TLA), a 12-minute timed general mental ability test. Many cognitive ability tests are timed tests when given in their paper form. The other was an untimed Situational Judgment Test that presented 10 situations and required the subject to choose one of four multiple-choice answers as the best action to take in the situation described. Potosky and Bobko's main conclusions are presented in Table 11.7. The correlation between scores on the two versions of the timed TLA was 0.60. The difference in the rank order of scores of individuals on the two versions of this test was great enough that the same individuals would not have been selected on the two tests. Also there was a significant difference in the mean scores of the two timed tests with the paper version being significantly higher than the computer version. In contrast, the correlation between the two versions on the untimed SJT was 0.84, which was the same as the reliability of the test. In addition the means of the two versions were not significantly different. Therefore the two versions of that test were thought to be equivalent. In terms of the subjects' preference for a version, the computer test was strongly favored in both tests. The clear implication is that timed tests are much more problematic to translate into an electronic version than are untimed tests and probably do not result in equivalent forms. The mixing of scores on a paper timed test and the scores of an online timed test would be uninterpretable. The two authors provide some guidelines for developing computer versions of timed tests:

- Internet time and actual time are not equivalent. The time allowed for Internet test taking must be adjusted for the "load time" of screens—and there must be a way of meaningfully presenting that time to test takers.

TABLE 11.7	Considerations Regarding the Use of Internet Tests	
Timed Tests	**Test-Taking Behaviors**	**Design Considerations**
• Virtual time is not equal to actual time. • Time needed to load Web pages varies within tests and between users. • Timer should be used in Internet tests as a signal to test-takers. • Time must be appropriate for items and format. • Load time may affect test performance.	• Respondents often answer items in order. • Distinction between items and instructions can be blurred. • Respondents attend to instructions differently than do respondents using paper-and-pencil tests. • Role of test proctor differs for paper-and-pencil and Internet tests. • Respondents may differ with regard to preference for using mouse clicks versus keystrokes.	• Internet tests usually have fewer items per page and more pages than paper-and-pencil versions. • Color and graphics may be necessary. • User expectations are important for design.

Source: Adapted from Denise Potosky and Philip Bobko, "Selection Testing via the Internet: Practical Considerations and Exploratory Empirical Findings," *Personnel Psychology* 57 (2004): 1003–1034.

- Test takers frequently do not respond the same way to the test instructions and ancillary information presented online as they would in a paper-and-pencil testing situation. Emphasis on the presentation of test titles and instructions should be increased to orient individuals to the test. This may be addressed by having a proctor read instructions or by including audio files with the electronic test.

- The design of screens for electronic testing is important; graphics and color are useful.

- There also seemed to be differences between the two versions with regard to test-taking behavior. In electronic testing, subjects more often answered test items in order because it was difficult to move to items on different screens. Note taking or marking among alternative answers is not feasible on electronic tests.

- Respondents' beliefs about their computer and Internet abilities had little effect on test scores. However, age did have an effect; older subjects did not perform as well as young subjects.

Unproctored Internet Testing

Many selection specialists in organizations favor Internet testing because it allows applicants to answer a selection instrument at any time in any place. This allows the processing of applicants to be completed and applicants to be selected more quickly. However, providing applicants with such flexibility usually means that the applicants are taking unproctored tests. That is, the applicant is taking the test without the presence of an organizational representative who monitors the testing behaviors of the applicant. Such a testing situation means that decisions about applicants are made using test scores of unproctored tests. These scores can be affected by several sources of error: someone other than the applicant completing the test, the use of books or Internet material, and aid from accomplices. In addition, differences among the various computers used by applicants in terms of speed and software functioning may artificially affect scores.

Several writers have addressed issues in unproctored Internet testing.[26] The main issues are the type of test (mental ability versus other kinds of tests), whether the test is used for selection or development, the importance of the test score to the test taker, the effects of cheating on the test's validity, and the cost and feasibility of measures to reduce cheating. Although writers do not completely agree on most of these issues, there seems to be consensus that brief biodata tests, situational judgment tests, and personality tests are the most appropriate for Internet testing. These are tests for which identifying the correct response is more difficult; they are, therefore, less susceptible to cheating.[27] Knowledge and cognitive ability tests are more problematic to use. Some argue that the optimum system for selection is to use unproctored tests as an initial screening followed by a proctored test for those who pass; at that point, applicants' identities can be confirmed.

The few studies that investigated the occurrence of cheating by comparing results of unproctored and proctored test taking found little differences between scores of the two types of test administration and, therefore, little evidence of cheating. The main types of tests studied in this research were personality[28] and cognitive ability.[29] One of these studies computed validity coefficients for the test scores of each type of test administration. The predictors were measures of biodata, conscientiousness, and sales potential. The task performance data were supervisors' judgments and various objective measures of performance such as sales data. The validity coefficients for all three predictors and the task performance measures were not statistically different for the proctored and unproctored tests.[30] These findings are significant because validity equivalence is one of the most important criteria to meet before launching unproctored, online selection testing.

Even though there is little evidence of rampant cheating occurring with unproctored Internet testing, there is a large literature that discusses cheating and ways of identifying and preventing it. Much of this literature presents various statistical analyses that can be used to detect cheating. Most of these analyses are based on the intercorrelation patterns of individual test items. Another method is to have applicants complete a brief unproctored test online, then administer a second longer test in supervised conditions to those who passed the online test, and finally analyze responses to comparable items of the two tests. A third way is to use computer adaptive testing (CAT). This type of testing is based on having a very large test item pool. In CAT there is neither a predetermined series of questions that form a test nor one version of the test. Instead, CAT uses sophisticated item response theory to choose a next item based upon the respondent's answers to previous items. The result is a test that is formed for each candidate. The unique testing experience for each candidate greatly increases the security of the assessment and almost eliminates cheating due to pre-knowledge of the test questions. An additional way of reducing cheating is by using webcams at remote testing locations to continually record the actions of all respondents. This method, of course, has limited applications because it requires a specific location for applicants to visit in order to take a preliminary selection test. To an extent this reduces some of the benefits of online testing that are linked to reducing the cost of testing sites and increasing the applicant flow by allowing an applicant to complete the test at his convenience in a location of his choice.

EFFECTS OF PRACTICE AND COACHING

Several organizations, especially public organizations, allow applicants to repeat the application and testing process multiple times. For example, many fire and police departments permit those who failed a test to retake it after some period of time. As a result, many applicants take a mental ability test two or more times. It is useful to know how practice affects test scores. Similarly, coaching of applicants who take mental ability tests is a growing industry. You are most familiar with those organizations that teach applicants how to take a standardized test for college admission (the Scholastic Aptitude Test—SAT or the Graduate Management Aptitude Test—GMAT). The success of such organizations has given rise to others that prepare applicants for taking mental ability tests for employment. Advocates of minority groups argue that individuals should be coached on how to respond to mental ability tests in order to overcome what some regard as the cultural bias of these tests.

Studies of the effects of coaching have found that such training has a minimal effect on test scores.[31] For example, coaching has been found to change scores 0.15 to 0.20 standard deviation units on the SAT. If, for example, the standard deviation of a standardized test is 80 points, coaching would change scores on the average of only 12 to 16 points. If the standard deviation is 40 points, the average change would be 6 to 8 points. Another study of students preparing for a standardized undergraduate medical admission test found that coaching had no effect on performance on two of three parts of the test. Scores on the third section were significantly higher for coached students, but this was the case only for high ability students. Coaching had a slight negative effect for lower ability students.[32]

The effects of practice (that is, reapplying and taking the same test two or more times), have been studied using data collected from 4,726 individuals who applied multiple times for law enforcement positions.[33] Scores on mental ability tests were found to increase between the first and second test completions and also between the second and third completions. Such a change could improve the applicant's chances of being selected. There are three possible explanations for this improvement in scores. Applicants could develop a better understanding of the test format and methods of responding (this understanding is what many coaching programs emphasize). Second, applicants could reduce test anxiety before taking subsequent tests. Third, applicants could learn the specific skills tested (such as vocabulary or mathematical operations). Although the study could not determine which one of these explanations was appropriate for the test score increase, it did find related information. The validity coefficient between the mental ability test and job training performance was higher for those individuals who were hired after one test completion than it was for those with two or more test completions. The researchers speculated that those who took the test multiple times improved on specific skills such as vocabulary—but not on general ability that was related to training performance. The logical conclusion from this study is that practice can improve an applicant's score on a mental ability test—but that improvement does not necessarily translate into improved job performance, which is the ultimate goal of the organization and the selection process. Of course, this is only one study; more replication is needed before we can accept these findings as proven fact.

There is some evidence that coaching and test preparation can lessen the gap between white and black test takers on a job knowledge test that was necessary for promotion. The three-hour written test consisted of between 97 and 117 multiple-choice items (depending on the job) and was part of the information used for promotion into officer positions for fire and police departments. The content of the tests was based on a list of materials that were provided to applicants and that tapped various knowledge clusters required for the job in question. Coaching and practice materials were optional tutorials and written documents that provided job knowledge information. Individuals who participated in a tutorial scored higher on the promotion test than those who did not participate in the tutorial. The same pattern was found for the self-report measure of usage of the written materials. Black candidates used the written materials more frequently than did white candidates and the difference between the two groups on the promotion test was less than that found in other research. The authors concluded that engaging in test preparation activities reduced the white–black gap in testing and should be of interest to organizations looking for methods to reduce adverse impact.[34]

MECHANICAL ABILITY TESTS

There is no strict definition for the construct of mechanical ability, even though the term has long been used by testing specialists. For the most part, mechanical ability refers to characteristics that tend to make for success in work with machines and equipment.[35] One of the earliest tests of this type was the *Stenquist Mechanical Assembly Test*, developed in 1923 by John Stenquist. It consisted of a long, narrow box with ten compartments. Each compartment had a simple mechanical apparatus (mousetrap, push button) that the test taker had to assemble. Stenquist also developed two picture tests designed to measure the same abilities. The Stenquist thus demonstrated the two testing methods that have been generally used in mechanical ability tests: manual performance and written problems. Early tests like the Stenquist and the Minnesota Mechanical Assembly Test (1930) emphasized actual mechanical assembly or manipulation. However, the cost and time involved in administering and scoring such tests for large numbers of individuals can quickly become prohibitive. Therefore, group-administered paper-and-pencil tests that attempted to present problems of mechanical work through pictures and statements were developed. The use of paper-and-pencil tests has greatly exceeded the use of performance tests.

Attempts have been made to more precisely determine the abilities measured by mechanical ability tests. As with mental ability tests, these abilities vary from test to test; in general, the main factors are spatial visualization, perceptual speed and accuracy, and mechanical information.[36] Mechanical ability tests can measure either general or specific abilities. We will discuss one of the most frequently used general mechanical ability tests, the Bennett Mechanical Comprehension Test. This test has been utilized for a large number of different jobs. Specific mechanical ability tests have been developed and used for jobs such as carpenter, engine lathe operator, welder, electrician, and other skilled crafts.

The Bennett Mechanical Comprehension Test

The Bennett Mechanical Comprehension Test has been the most widely used mechanical ability test for more than 50 years. There are two 68-item, 30-minute parallel forms of this test, *S* and *T*. These are paper-pencil tests in English or Spanish that require proctored testing situations. There is also a 55-item, 25-minute online version that is only in English. The Bennett is most appropriately used for jobs in industries such as manufacturing, production, energy, and utilities and in occupations such as automotive mechanic, engineer, installation, maintenance, repair, skilled trade, technical sales, transportation trade, and equipment operator.

The items of the Bennett contain objects that are generally familiar in American culture: airplanes, carts, steps, pulleys, seesaws, and gears. The questions measure the respondent's ability to perceive and understand the relationship of physical forces and mechanical elements in practical situations. Although they require some familiarity with common tools and objects, the questions purportedly assume no more technical knowledge than can be acquired through everyday experience in an industrial society such as ours. Partially supporting this assumption is evidence that formal training in physics only slightly increases test scores. Items are pictures with a brief accompanying question. For example, one item is a picture of two men carrying a weighted object hanging down from a plank; it asks, "Which man carries more weight?" Each figure has a letter below its base. Because the object is closer to one man than to the other, the correct answer is the letter that identifies the closer man. Another item has two pictures of the same room of a house. In one picture the room contains several pieces of furniture, carpeting, and objects on the wall. In the other picture the room contains only a few objects and no carpeting. The question is, "Which room has an echo?" Given some basic knowledge or experience, the question can be answered by logical analysis of the problem rather than the mastery of detailed and specific facts. The Bennett is used so frequently that there are online links to practice tests with similar questions as the Bennett and others that provide methods of how to determine correct answers for the main subjects on the Bennett, for example pulleys and gears.

A score is the number of items answered correctly. The manuals for the different forms provide percentile norms for various groups including industrial applicants, employees, and students. Reported reliabilities range from 0.81 to 0.93. The test purportedly focuses on spatial perception and tool knowledge rather than manual dexterity. It is best used for assessing job candidates for positions that require a grasp of the principles underlying the operation and repair of complex devices. It is also intended to measure an individual's learning ability regarding mechanical skills. Studies have correlated scores on the Bennett with scores on other ability tests in order to further understand the abilities being measured. Results indicate a moderate correlation with both verbal and mathematical mental ability tests and tests of spatial visualization. The relationship to verbal ability and spatial visualization can partially be explained by the fact that it is a written test with pictures as items. As one indication of the validity of this test, Paul Muchinsky found that in a study of 193 employees who produced electromechanical components, the Bennett had the highest correlation with supervisors' performance ratings among three mechanical tests (the Flanagan Aptitude Classification Test—Mechanics, the Thurstone Test of Mental Alertness—Form A, and the Bennett).[37] Finally, we found no studies that reported differences between racial or ethnic groups on the Bennett.

CLERICAL ABILITY TESTS

Traditionally, clerical jobs have been thought of as any job that required extensive checking or copying of words and numbers and the movement and placement of objects such as office equipment, files, and reports. Clerical ability tests have predominantly measured perceptual speed and accuracy in processing verbal and numerical data. These tests have traditionally been used in selection for office clerical and staff positions.

The Minnesota Clerical Test

Developed in 1933, the Minnesota Clerical Test is generally regarded as the prototype of clerical ability tests and has been the most widely used of these tests for much of its existence. The test is brief, easily administered, and easily scored. It has one form consisting of two separately timed and scored subtests: number checking and name checking.

Each subtest contains 200 items. Each item consists of a pair of numbers or names. The respondent is asked to compare the two names or numbers and place a check on a line between them if they are identical. If the two entries are different, no mark is placed on the line. The entries in the numbers subtest range from 3 through 12 digits; the entries in the names subtest range from 7 through 16 letters. The tests are timed separately at eight minutes for numbers and seven minutes for names. The score is the number right minus the number wrong; scores are determined for each subtest separately as well as for the total score. Table 11.8 contains items similar to those used in these subtests.

TABLE 11.8	Example Items Similar to Items on the Minnesota Clerical Test

Name Comparison

Neal Schmitt	_____	Frank Schmidt
Hubert field	_____	Herbert Field
Chris Riordan	_____	Kris Reardan
Tim Judge	_____	Jim Fudge
Murray Barrick	_____	Mick Mount

Number Comparison

84644	_____	84464
179854	_____	176845
123457	_____	12457
987342	_____	987342
8877665994	_____	8876659954

Although the two subtests are related, they do measure separate abilities. The names subtest has been found to be correlated with speed of reading, spelling, and group measures of intelligence. The numbers subtest has been related to the verification of arithmetic computations.[38] Scores on the subtests are only slightly related to either education level or experience in clerical positions. Reliability has been estimated as 0.90 for parallel forms and 0.85 for test-retest. Norm-group scores are provided for various job groups for each gender. Adverse impact has not been reported for scores of this test.

PHYSICAL ABILITY TESTS

Another area of importance for selection specialists is the testing of physical abilities of applicants for placement into manual labor and physically demanding jobs. As Michael Campion has pointed out, there are three reasons for this type of testing.[39] First, EEO legislation has prompted an increase in women applicants for traditionally male-dominated physical labor jobs. Although women, as a group, score lower than men on many physical ability tests, applicants must be evaluated as individuals, not as members of a group. Individual evaluation is best done by testing all applicants on the specific physical demands that are related to the job. Second, the use of appropriate selection devices for physically demanding jobs can reduce the incidence of work-related injuries. The insurance, compensation, and therapy costs associated with back, knee, and shoulder injuries continue to rise dramatically. Physical ability tests should improve the selection of individuals who are better suited to job demands. Third, because the Americans with Disabilities Act prohibits pre-employment medical examinations, the most feasible way to collect data about the physical status of applicants is through the use of specific physical ability tests that measure the worker characteristics required by the job.

One example of the use of physical ability and cognitive ability is that of the selection of fire fighters. Job analysis of these positions indicated that in large city fire service jobs, there are many technical training demands and on-the-job fire/rescue decision making requirements, that require mastery of a breadth of knowledge and understanding of engineering, science, and medical principles. In addition, there are numerous physical tasks that require strength, endurance, agility, and dexterity among other physical abilities. The selection battery, therefore, included a cognitive ability test and two timed tests that had various physical activities such as dragging a hose, carrying a ladder, climbing five flights of stairs in full gear, and so on. Job performance measures were gathered systematically over 21 years for the validation study. These were the results of physical tests at various times over the period and annual ratings by supervisors. Both the cognitive ability test and the physical timed tests had high validity coefficients ranging from 0.72 to 0.86, both after training and during the 21-year period.[40]

Most physical ability tests require demonstrations of strength, oxygen intake, and coordination. In the next sections we summarize the work of two experts, Edwin Fleishman and Joyce Hogan, who have developed test batteries that measure these characteristics.

PHYSICAL ABILITIES ANALYSIS

Edwin Fleishman and his colleagues have developed a taxonomy of 52 different abilities, both physical and nonphysical, that are necessary for performing work activities.[41] We will discuss only the measurement of the nine physical abilities.

Fleishman has identified these physical abilities, all of which have been extensively used to select employees for physically demanding jobs:[42]

1. *Static strength*—maximum force that can be exerted against external objects. Tested by lifting weights.

2. *Dynamic strength*—muscular endurance in exerting force continuously. Tested by pull-ups.

3. *Explosive strength*—ability to mobilize energy effectively for bursts of muscular effort. Tested by sprints or jumps.

4. *Trunk strength*—limited dynamic strength specific to trunk muscles. Tested by leg lifts or sit-ups.

5. *Extent flexibility*—ability to flex or stretch trunk and back muscles. Tested by twist-and-touch test.

6. *Dynamic flexibility*—ability to make repeated rapid, flexing trunk movements. Tested by rapid, repeated bending over and touching floor.

7. *Gross body coordination*—ability to coordinate action of several parts of body while body is in motion. Tested by cable-jump test.

8. *Gross body equilibrium*—ability to maintain balance with nonvisual cues. Tested by rail-walk test.

9. *Stamina*—capacity to sustain maximum effort requiring cardiovascular exertion. Tested by 600-yard run-walk.

The following validity coefficients for specific jobs are among the results reported by Fleishman for the use of these abilities in selection: pipeline workers (0.63), correctional officers (0.64), warehouse workers (0.39), electrical workers (0.53), and enlisted army men (0.87).[43] All coefficients represent the correlation of a battery of two to four physical abilities with job performance.

Three Components of Physical Performance

The extensive work of Joyce Hogan has produced the three components of physical performance described in Table 11.9. She combined two lines of research in the development of this taxonomy. The first was data about physical requirements derived from job analysis. The second was data based on physical ability tests already developed for selection. Her idea was that by examining these two sources of information about physical work performance, a comprehensive model of physical abilities could be developed.

Factor analyses were performed on several sets of data. Results consistently identified three factors, or components, of physical abilities.[44] The first, *muscular strength*, is the ability to apply or resist force through muscular contraction. Within this component are three more specific subelements: muscular tension, muscular power, and muscular endurance. The second component is *cardiovascular endurance*, which refers to the capacity to sustain gross (as contrasted with localized) muscular activity over prolonged periods. It is aerobic capacity and general systemic fitness involving the large muscles. The third component, *movement quality*, concerns characteristics that contribute to skilled performance. This component also has three subelements: flexibility, balance, and muscular integration. Hogan concluded that this three-component model describes the true structure of physical abilities necessary for work activities. As such, the model

TABLE 11.9	Three Components of Physical Performance

Component	Sub element	Sample Work Activities	Sample Tests
Muscular strength	Muscular tension	Activities of pushing, pulling, lifting, lowering, or carrying a heavy object	Handgrip strength, dynamometer (scored in pounds/kilos)
	Muscular power	Use of hand tools, raising a section of a ladder with a halyard	Ergometer, medicine ball put (scored in pounds)
	Muscular endurance	Repetitions of tool use, loading materials onto pallets	Push-ups, arm ergometer (scored in number of repetitions)
Cardiovascular endurance	None	Search and rescue, climbing stairs, wearing protective equipment	Step-up time, distance run (scored in amount of time taken)
Movement quality	Flexibility	Mining operations, installing light fixtures	Sit and reach, twist and touch (scored in distance of limb displacement, repetitions)
	Balance	Pole climbing, ladder usage, elevated construction	Static rail balance (scored in time or distance)
	Neuromuscular integration	Accessing an offshore platform, intercepting an object	Minnesota rate manipulation (scored in lapsed time or target error)

Source: Based on Joyce C. Hogan, "Physical Abilities," in *Handbook of Industrial & Organizational Psychology*, 2nd ed., Vol. 2, edited by Marvin Dunnette and Leaetta Hough (Palo Alto, CA: Consulting Psychologists Press, 1991).

could be used as the basis for selection. The major issue in developing a selection program would be to determine which subset of abilities correlates with job performance for the job under study.

The importance of Hogan's work was demonstrated in the development of a selection program for seven jobs in various industries, with a total sample of 1,364 individuals. These jobs were law enforcement officer, firefighter, customer gas service, pipeline construction and maintenance, pipefitter, utility worker, and utility line repair and installation. Job analyses indicated that for each of these jobs muscular strength, one of the three components of Hogan's model, was a major factor necessary for performing several important tasks. A series of tests were developed. Results indicated that these tests were significantly correlated with both supervisors' ratings of physical performance and work simulations of critical job tasks.[45]

Legal Issues in Testing Physical Abilities

Selection specialists working with physically demanding jobs must be especially concerned with three groups of applicants: females, disabled workers, and older workers. Adverse impact for scores on physical ability tests is a common occurrence for each group. Because physical ability tests emphasize strength, aerobic power, and coordination, frequently males will score higher than females, the nondisabled higher than the disabled, and younger workers higher than older. A major study examined these differences and presented meta-analytic estimates of sex differences in physical abilities and the effects of selection system design, specificity of measurement, and training in possibly reducing sex differences on physical ability test scores.[46] There were a number of important findings:

- Males score substantially better on muscular strength and cardiovascular endurance tests but there are no meaningful sex differences on quality of physical movement tests.

- Sex differences are similar across selection systems that emphasize basic ability tests versus job simulations. This suggests that developing a selection system that emphasizes basic ability tests over a job simulation (or vice versa) does not reduce sex differences.

- Sex differences are smaller for finer rather than broader dimensions of muscular strength, and there is substantial variance in the sex differences in muscular strength across different body regions. For example, while sex differences were greatest for muscular tension, they decreased substantially for muscular endurance and muscular power. Sex differences decreased even further when muscular strength tests were specifically geared toward measuring strength in the core area of the body (that is, lumbar spine and abdominal areas). However, differences increased dramatically with tests that focused on total body strength.

- Training was advantageous to women in the sense that women showed higher improvement scores than men on muscular strength and cardiovascular endurance tests. However, post-training d values on muscular strength decreased only slightly.

One essential issue in using physical ability in selection is that the tests must clearly be linked to critical job tasks that *require* physical abilities in their completion. However, this statement is complicated by the question of whether the tasks can be modified to reduce or eliminate these physical demands. Such modification can occur either through the use of additional equipment or personnel. If such modifications can be made, the use of the physical ability test appropriate for the original tasks may be unwarranted. We now briefly discuss some of the main legal issues that have been raised in court cases in which physical tests have been used in selection.

Two selection requirements that have been treated in court cases are height/weight standards and state laws prohibiting women from lifting items that exceed certain weight. In *Weeks v. Southern Bell*, the court ruled that even though the state of Georgia had protective legislation prohibiting women from lifting 30 pounds, "Title VII of the 1964 Civil Rights Act rejects just this type of romantic paternalism as unduly Victorian and instead vests individual women with the power to decide whether or not to take on unromantic tasks."[47] Similarly, height and weight standards have been equally hard to defend. Usually the argument has been that height and weight are surrogate measures of strength necessary for many jobs. Courts have consistently held that if measuring strength is the objective, then selection requirements should assess that directly rather than using secondary indicators such as height or weight. As the previously summarized research indicates, physical ability tests differ in the amount of adverse impact they produce in the testing of women. For that reason, cutoff scores must be well documented.

Joyce Hogan has demonstrated another way of lessening the adverse impact of physical ability tests by allowing applicants to prepare for these types of tests in various ways (such as callisthenic training, total body workouts including the use of weights, and applicant tryouts of the actual physical ability tests used in a selection program for several jobs). She found that women significantly increased their physical performance as a result of these methods of preparation. Also, the differences between men and women on the physical ability tests used in the selection program significantly decreased. For example, for the position of firefighter, more than one-half of 53 female applicants passed the physical ability portion of the selection program. Prior to this study, no woman had successfully completed this part of the selection battery. It should be noted, however, that it is unrealistic, and perhaps undesirable, to develop a selection program for physical abilities that eliminates all test score differences between men and women. The general evidence is that although women score lower than men on strength and endurance tests, they also demonstrate lower performance on jobs that require these abilities. In such cases, the adverse impact may be inherent in the job activities, not in the content of the test. To reduce male–female differences, the appropriate strategy would be to alter the job tasks rather than the tests used for selection.

As discussed in Chapter 4, the Americans with Disabilities Act of 1990 prohibits discrimination on the basis of disability and requires employers to consider "reasonable accommodation" of the disabled worker in the work processes and physical setting of the job. This has generally been interpreted to mean that adjustments should be made for the known physical and mental limitations of an otherwise qualified disabled applicant or employee unless the organization can demonstrate that the accommodation would cause undue hardship to the firm. Both financial and safety costs are weighed in this consideration of undue hardship.

An employer is not justified in presuming that a disabled worker is unable to perform a job. It is necessary that a thorough job analysis be conducted and physical ability tests be identified for important corresponding job tasks. Even if this is done, the job tasks may still be subject to the reasonable accommodation directive. In general, courts have placed a more stringent demand for reasonable accommodation on employers when the disabled individuals are employees returning to work after illness or injury than when they are new workers. Of direct importance for physical ability testing is the ruling in *E. E. Black, Ltd. v. Marshall.*[48] In this case the plaintiff was rejected for the job of apprentice carpenter, which required a good deal of lifting and carrying, because of a back condition detected in the medical screening for the job. The court ruled, based on other evidence including the examination of an orthopedist, that even though the plaintiff should be considered disabled (the back condition), he still could perform the job. The court expressly disagreed with the company's position that the plaintiff should be denied employment because he constituted a future risk for injury. In this case, an employment decision made on the basis of a valid physical ability test rather than a medical screening test may have avoided the confrontation.

No general presumptions can be made about the physical abilities of older applicants, either. That is, an organization cannot assume that an applicant over the age of 40 years (threshold age in the Age Discrimination in Employment Act of 1967) is incapable of any physical demands of a job. However, the use of physical ability tests that correspond to job requirements should be an acceptable basis for selection decisions.

RECOMMENDATIONS FOR THE USE OF ABILITY TESTS IN SELECTION

In this chapter we presented brief descriptions of a few tests that are representative of ability tests. These tests were included because of their extensive use in selection over several years. However, we have not described a large number of other ability tests that are available to HR specialists. For example, the Buros Institute of Mental Measurements provides online reviews of over 4,000 tests; its 2014 volume of *The Nineteenth Mental Measurements Yearbook* contains information on more than 200 tests. The sheer number of these tests creates a difficult situation for HR specialists. What is needed is a way to evaluate an ability test in order to assess its potential usefulness. Obviously, the best method of doing this would be to become familiar with the principles of psychological test construction and measurement. We have already presented some—but not nearly all—of these principles in Chapters 6 through 8, which were devoted to the role of measurement in selection. We now apply these concepts to the problem of assessing the potential usefulness of available ability tests.

Review Reliability Data

Our primary assumption is that a useful ability test should have development information available to users. One part of such information should consist of work done to estimate the reliability of the test. As we discussed previously, reliability is a necessary characteristic of a selection test. High reliability is an indication that the test can be expected to yield consistent scores for applicants and that uncontrolled factors that might affect the score of applicants are minimized. Therefore, information about the method of estimating reliability, the size and nature of the sample used to collect these data, and the magnitude of the reliability estimate should all be fully presented to users.

As we know, each of the major ways of estimating reliability is appropriate for specific circumstances and inappropriate for others. For example, test-retest reliability calculated with a very short intervening period of time (such as a few hours or even a few days) may be an inflated estimate due to the effect of memory factors. It is necessary for the test user to determine whether the appropriate method of estimating reliability was employed, and whether this method was carried out correctly. It is clear that using larger samples (500+) yields better estimates of reliability than using smaller samples. Occasionally, samples of 30 to 100 respondents have been used in reliability studies. This size is generally agreed to be too small for calculating a meaningful estimate of reliability.

It is desirable that the sample of respondents used in reliability studies be similar to the individuals for whom the HR specialist intends to use the test. Perhaps the most common way to judge similarity is on the basis of demographic characteristics such as ethnicity, gender, average age, average education level, and occupational background. One can argue that these are not the most accurate indicants of similarity, because similarity between two groups actually means that the test is interpreted and answered in the same fashion by the two groups. However, collecting such data would require work far beyond that normally done in test development. Information about demographic characteristics allows the user to at least note major differences and form hypotheses about the meaning of such differences. For example, if the reliability of a test of English grammar and writing has been estimated using a sample of college students, and the applicant pool in the selection situation is mainly high school students, the reliability may not be the same for the two groups. If the test is of moderate difficulty for the college students, it may be very difficult for high school students. Difficult tests often have low reliability because respondents frequently guess in making their responses, and such guesses are sources of error of measurement. Therefore, the stated reliability of the test may not be accurate for the applicant pool. The same argument can be applied to many craft or mechanical ability tests that have used experienced workers rather than inexperienced ones in reliability estimates.

A minimum reliability estimate of 0.85 to 0.90 is commonly thought to be necessary for selection use. This is because selection involves making a decision for each applicant about whether to extend a job offer. This decision is based on the scores of the selection tests used. If the test is not highly reliable, the large standard error of measurement accompanying a test score would make choosing among applicants very uncertain. For example, using the standard error of measurement information contained in Chapter 7, we would estimate that the range of true scores for a test with an estimated reliability of 0.60 and a standard deviation of 15 is 9.5 points with a 68 percent confidence level. If an applicant scores an 80 on this test, the true score realistically could be anywhere between 70 and 90. With such a large range, identifying meaningful differences among applicants is very difficult. However, if the same test has a reliability of 0.90, then the standard error becomes 4.7 points with the same confidence level. The range of probable true scores becomes much smaller, and the test results are more precise and easier for the selection specialist to use.

Review Validity Data

The second major kind of information that should be made available to test users is validity data accumulated during test development and use. Two kinds of validity data are desirable. One kind indicates that the ability test measures what it is said to measure. Frequently this information is reported in terms of statistical analyses of the scores. Two of the most common types of analyses are (a) correlational analyses of the scores of the test with other psychological measures and (b) factor analyses of the items of the test or of the test with other tests. We mentioned examples of such correlational analyses when we discussed mental ability tests. To know that scores on mental ability tests are correlated with various measures of educational achievement greatly improves our understanding of what these tests measure. In some cases, correlations with other tests are conducted. For example, we noted that the Bennett Mechanical Comprehension Test was correlated with verbal ability and spatial visualization tests. This indicates that the test may measure more than mechanical concepts.

Factor analysis is a technique for analyzing the interrelationships among several tests or a set of test items. For example, if 20 test items have been given to 400 individuals, the first step is to correlate each item with every other item. Further statistical manipulations attempt to identify small groups of items that are highly correlated with one another and minimally correlated with other groups of items. Each group of items is called a *factor* and named by the common psychological characteristic measured. For example, on this 20-item test, one group of 10 basic arithmetic problems might be identified as one factor and 10 vocabulary questions might be identified as a second factor. This test can then be said to measure arithmetic ability and vocabulary. The ability that is measured is identified from the common content of the items that make up the factor. The importance of this type of information is that the HR specialist can examine the correspondence between the factors that are identified and the WRCs that are to be tested in the selection program. It is necessary that the test, in fact, match the WRCs identified from the job analysis.

The second type of validity information that can be provided is the correlation of the test scores with some measure of training or job performance. This is the criterion-related validity to which we have frequently referred. Demonstration of validity for a measure of training or job performance similar to the one of interest to the test specialist is, obviously, the most desirable data.

Our opinion is that this information about reliability and validity of the ability test, at minimum, must be available to the user. Other test construction data (such as norm group scores, difficulty levels of items, and whether the test measures one or multiple topics) can also be useful. However, such data are usually of secondary importance compared to basic reliability and validity information. If reliability and validity data are not provided or are inappropriately calculated, the HR specialist should be wary of using the ability test. It is not a difficult task physically to construct a purported ability test. Most intelligent individuals, with a few friends and a long weekend, could write 50 multiple-choice test items that were intended to measure any of several abilities (for example, mathematics, English, logical reasoning or, given enough reference books, technical areas such as computer programming, football analysis, and carpentry). The trick is to make sure that the test is what it is intended to be. The only way an HR specialist who is considering using an ability test can tell this is by examining the reliability and validity information. *No amount of verbal assurance provided by the test seller can substitute for such information.* After all, the test seller has a vested interest in describing the test in favorable terms in order to sell more tests.

Chapter Summary

We could tell you much more about ability tests, but you should move on to the remaining chapters so you can become a well-rounded selection expert. We will leave you with the following thoughts to dwell on at your leisure. You can also use this list as a basis for asking your instructor a series of endless questions about ability tests. That would surely affect your grade!

Ability tests are:

1. Useful—they are valid predictors for all forms of job performance.

2. Cheap—most can be purchased for a reasonable price from a test publisher.

3. Fast—most take an applicant 30 minutes or less to complete.

4. Easy—they can be administered individually or in group settings.

5. Versatile—many come in several languages.

6. Scorable—publishers usually provide a scoring key that can be used by an organization member.

7. Understandable—many ability tests reflect knowledge that is job based, especially mechanical, skilled crafts, and clerical ability tests. Both applicants and organization members who review scores can usually understand what the test is measuring.

8. Sometimes falsely marketed—because ability tests have worked so well and are familiar to many applicants, sometimes unscrupulous and nefarious individuals make up their own tests. They write items that seem to measure important knowledge or abilities, describe the test in glowing terms, develop elaborate brochures or Web sites, and aggressively sell these tests to the unwary. Do not be among the unwary (or unwashed, but that is a different story). Look at the test development data! Ask about the reliability and validity studies! Be suspicious! Be wary!

REFERENCES

1. Par Lahy, "La selection psycho-physiologique des machinistes de la société des transports en commun de la région Parisienne," *L'Année Pschologique* 25 (1924): 106–172.

2. Philip DuBois, *A History of Psychological Testing* (Boston: Allyn & Bacon, 1970).

3. Anne Anastasi, *Psychological Testing*, 5th ed. (London: Macmillan, 1982), 393.

4. Lewis Aiken, *Psychological Testing and Assessment*, 2nd ed. (Boston: Allyn & Bacon, 1988), 107.

5. Ibid., 108–109.

6. Anastasi, *Psychological Testing*, 387.

7. Christopher M. Berry, Melissa L. Guys, and Paul R. Sackett, "Educational Attainment as a Proxy for Cognitive Ability in Selection: Effects on Levels of Cognitive Ability and Adverse Impact," *Journal of Applied Psychology* 91 (2006): 696–705.

8. Robert Guion, *Personnel Testing* (New York: McGraw-Hill, 1965), 234.

9. Ibid., 221.

10. John Campbell, "An Overview of the Army Selection and Classification Project (Project A)," *Personnel Psychology* 43 (1990): 243–257.

11. Jeffrey J. McHenry, Leaetta M. Hough, Jody L. Toquam, Mary Ann Hanson, and Steven Ashworth, "Project A Validity Results: The Relationship between Predictor and Criterion Domains," *Personnel Psychology* 43 (1990): 335–354.

12. John E. Hunter, "Cognitive Ability, Cognitive Attitudes, Job Knowledge, and Job Performance," *Journal of Vocational Behavior* 29 (1986): 340–362; see also Gwen E. Jones and Malcolm James Ree, "Aptitude Test Score Validity: No Moderating Effect Due to Job Ability Requirement Differences," *Educational and Psychological Measurement* 58 (1998): 284–294.

13. Mark A. Maltarich, Greg Reilly, and Anthony J. Nyberg, "A Conceptual and Empirical Analysis of the Cognitive Ability-Voluntary Turnover Relationship," *Journal of Applied Psychology* 95 (2010): 1058–1070.

14. Erik Gonzalez-Mule, Michael K. Mount, and Oh In-Sue, "A Meta-Analysis of the Relationship Between General Mental Ability and Nontask Performance," *Journal of Applied Psychology* 99 (2014): 1222–1243.

15. Frank L. Schmidt and John E. Hunter, "The Validity and Utility of Selection Methods in Personnel Psychology: Practical and Theoretical Implications of 85 Years of Research Findings," *Psychological Bulletin* 124 (1998): 262–274.

16. Hunter, "Cognitive Ability, Cognitive Attitudes, Job Knowledge, and Job Performance," 354.

17. Philip L. Roth, Craig A. Bevier, Philip Bobko, Fred S. Switzer III, and Peggy Tyler, "Ethnic Group Differences in Cognitive Ability in Employment and Educational Settings: A Meta-Analysis," *Personnel Psychology* 54 (2001): 297–330.

18. Denise Potosky, Philip Bobko, and Philip Roth, "Forming Composites of Cognitive Ability and Alternative Measures to Predict Job Performance and Reduce Adverse Impact: Corrected Estimates and Realistic Expectations," *International Journal of Selection and Assessment* (2005): 304–315.

19. Virginia Boehm, "Different Validity: A Methodological Artifact," *Journal of Applied Psychology* 62 (1977): 146–154.

20. John Hunter, Frank Schmidt, and Ronda Hunter, "Differential Validity of Employment Tests by Race: A Comprehensive Review and Analysis," *Psychological Bulletin* 85 (1979): 721–735.

21. Christopher M. Berry, Malissa A. Clark, and Tara K. McClure, "Racial/Ethnic Differences in the Criterion-Related Validity of Cognitive Ability Tests: A Qualitative and Quantitative Review," *Journal of Applied Psychology* 96 (2011): 881–906.

22. Philip L. Roth, Oh In-Sue, Maury A. Buster, Le Huy, Chad H. Van Iddekinge, Steve B. Robbins, and Michael A. Campion, "Differential Validity for Cognitive Ability Tests in Employment and Educational Settings: Not Much More Than Range Restriction?" *Journal of Applied Psychology* 99 (2013): 1–20.

23. Wilfried DeCorte, Filip Lievens, and Paul R. Sackett, "Combining Predictors to Achieve Optimal Trade-offs Between Selection Quality and Adverse Impact," *Journal of Applied Psychology* 92 (2007):1380–1393; see also Paul R. Sackett, Wilfried De Corte, and Filip Lievens, "Pareto-optimal Predictor Composite Formation: A Complementary Approach to Alleviating the Selection Quality/Adverse Impact Dilemma," *International Journal of Selection and Assessment* 16 (2008): 206–209.

24. Serena Wee, Daniel A. Newmann, and Dana L. Joseph, "More Than g: Selection Quality and Adverse Impact Implications of Considering Second-Stratum Cognitive Abilities," *Journal of Applied Psychology* 99 (2014): 547–563.

25. Denise Potosky and Philip Bobko, "Selection Testing via the Internet: Practical Considerations and Exploratory Empirical Findings," *Personnel Psychology* 57 (2004): 1003–1034.

26. Nancy T. Tippins, James Beaty, Fritz Drasgow, Wade M. Gibson, Kenneth Pearlman, Daniel O. Segall, and William Shepherd, "Unproctored Internet Testing in Employment Settings," *Personnel Psychology* 59 (2006): 189–225.

27. William Shepherd, B. R. Do, and Fritz L. Drasgow, "Assessing Equivalence of Online Non-Cognitive Measures: Where Research Meets Practice," *paper presented at the Annual Conference of the Society for Industrial and Organizational Psychologists*, 2003, Orlando, Florida.

28. Winfred Arthur Jr., Ryan M. Glaze, Anton J. Villado, and Jason E. Taylor, "The Magnitude and Extent of Cheating and Response Distortion Effects on Unproctored Internet-based Tests of Cognitive Ability and Personality," *International Journal of Selection and Assessment* 18 (2010): 1–16; see also James C. Beaty, Christopher D. Nye, Mathew J. Borneman, Tracy M. Kantrowitz, Fritz Drasgow, and Eyal Grauer, "Proctored Versus Unproctored Internet Tests: Are Unproctored Noncognitive Tests as Predictive of Job Performance?" *International Journal of Selection and Assessment* 19 (2011): 1–10.

29. Filip Lievens and Eugene Burke, "Dealing with the Threats Inherent in Unproctored Internet Testing of Cognitive Ability: Results from a Large-Scale Operational Test Program," *Journal of Occupational and Organizational Psychology* 84 (2011): 817–824; see also Tracy M. Kantrowitz and Amanda M. Dainis, "How Secure are Unproctored Pre-Employment Tests? Analysis of Inconsistent Test Scores," *Journal of Business and Psychology* 29 (2014): 605–616.

30. Kantrowitz and Dainis, *Journal of Business and Psychology* 29 (2014): 605–616.

31. J. A. Kulik, R. L. Bangert-Downs, and C. C. Kulik, "Effectiveness of Coaching for Aptitude Tests," *Psychological Bulletin* 95 (1984): 435–447.

32. Barbara Griffin, Sally Carless, and Ian Wilson, "The Effect of Commercial Coaching on Selection Test Performance," *Medical Teacher* 35 (2013): 295–300.

33. John P. Hausknecht, Charlie O. Trevor, and James L. Farr, "Retaking Ability Tests in a Selection Setting: Implications for Practice Effects, Training Performance, and Turnover," *Journal of Applied Psychology* 87 (2002): 243–254.

34. Beth G. Chung-Herrera, Karen Holcombe Ehrhart, Mark G. Ehrhart, Jerry Solamon, and Britta Kilian, "Can Test Preparation Help to Reduce the Black–White Test Performance Gap?" *Journal of Management* 35 (2009): 1207–1227.

35. Donald E. Super and John O. Crites, *Appraising Vocational Fitness*, revised edition (New York: Harper & Row, 1962): 219.

36. Ibid., 220–221.

37. Paul M. Muchinsky, "Validation of Intelligence and Mechanical Aptitude Tests in Selecting Employees for Manufacturing Jobs," Special Issue: Test Validity Yearbook: IL, *Journal of Business and Psychology* 7 (1993): 373–382.

38. R. B. Selover, "Review of the Minnesota Clerical Test," *The Third Mental Measurements Yearbook*, ed. Oscar K. Buros (New Brunswick, NJ: Rutgers University Press, 1949), 635–636.

39. Michael A. Campion, "Personnel Selection for Physically Demanding Jobs: Review and Recommendations," *Personnel Psychology* 36 (1983): 527–550.

40. Norman D. Henderson, "Predicting Long-Term Firefighter Performance from Cognitive and Physical Ability Measures," *Personnel Psychology* 63 (2010): 999–1039.

41. Edwin A. Fleishman and Michael D. Mumford, "Ability Requirement Scales," in *Job Analysis Handbook for Business, Industry, and Government*, Vol. 2, ed. Sidney Gael (New York: John Wiley, 1988).

42. Edwin A. Fleishman, *Physical Abilities Analysis Manual*, rev. ed. (Palo Alto, CA: Consulting Psychologists Press, 1992).

43. Fleishman and Mumford, "Ability Requirement Scales."

44. Joyce Hogan, "Structure of Physical Performance in Occupational Tasks," *Journal of Applied Psychology* 76 (1991): 495–507; see also Joyce Hogan, "Physical Abilities," in *Handbook of Industrial Psychology*, 2nd ed., vol. 2, ed. Marvin D. Dunnette and Leaetta M. Hough (Palo Alto, CA: Consulting Psychologists Press).

45. Barry R. Blakley, Miguel A. Quinones, Marnie Swerdlin Crawford, and Ann I. Jago, "The Validity of Isometric Strength Tests," *Personnel Psychology* 47 (1994): 247–274.

46. Stephen H. Courtright, Brian W. McCormick, Bennet E. Postlethwaite, Cody J. Reeves, and Michael K. Mount, "A Meta-Analysis of Sex Differences in Physical Ability: Revised Estimates and Strategies for Reducing Differences in Selection Contexts," *Journal of Applied Psychology* 98 (2013): 623–641.

47. *Weeks v. Southern Bell Telephone & Telegraph Co.*, 408 F.2d 228, 1 Empl. Prac. Dec. (CCH) 9970 (5th Cir. 1969).

48. *E. E. Black, Ltd. v. Marshall*, 24 Empl. Prac. Dec. (CCH) 31260 (D. Haw. 1980).

Personality Assessment for Selection

Now that you are well on your way to becoming an expert in selection (which must be true because there are only four chapters left, including this one, and we know what kind of student you are), you will be fascinated to learn about the use of personality measures in selection, one of the most complex and rapidly changing topics in the field. Personality, in addition to cognitive ability (see Chapter 10), reflect two key individual differences that affect success at work. Personality, however, does so by enhancing social engagement and work motivation more than through learning and the acquisition of job knowledge, although personality does affect those processes as well. Thus, personality, which is unique to each person, determines how a person copes with uncertainty, adjusts to setbacks, gets along with others, exerts extra effort in striving for accomplishments at work, and in other ways determines behavior at work. It encompasses a person's relatively stable way of thinking, feeling, and acting in a variety of situations. Because personality in adulthood only changes over long time periods, managers can realize tremendous value by selecting individuals with personality traits that are compatible to the demands of the work environment. For example, outgoing, talkative, assertive people who enjoy socializing (that is, extraverted) tend to be effective in sales jobs. Conversely, those who are curious, creative, and open to new experiences are prone to be bored or impatient with routine work. Although these relationships seem obvious to the casual reader, as we will see, there has been considerable controversy over the usefulness of personality.

Selection researchers have found that personality data, when gathered appropriately, can provide valid information for making selection decisions.[1] As a result, the use of personality tests to screen job applicants is rapidly increasing, up from 30 to 40 percent just over five years ago to 60 to 70 percent today.[2] Larger organizations apparently are more likely than smaller ones to use these instruments; as many Fortune 100 companies use them to hire at least some job applicants, ranging from entry level positions to chief executive officers.[3] Furthermore, a recent study of staffing practices in 20 countries found personality tests are used more frequently in other countries than they are in the United States, although the United States may be "catching up." In fact, up to 80 percent of firms use these tests in New Zealand, South Africa, Spain, and Sweden.[4] This chapter summarizes the major issues with regard to the use of personality data, along with the relevant research. We conclude that personality data can make an independent contribution to selection decisions. Moreover, there is no evidence that only people with so-called great personalities succeed. That gives me great hope.

A BRIEF HISTORY

In the late 1960s, the utility of personality was questioned in the field of psychology by Walter Mischel (1968) and in the work setting by Robert Guion and Richard Gottier (1966).[5] Both critiques concluded that personality traits have little to no predictive relationship to actual behavior. Consequently, there was a nearly two-decade break in the use of and research into personality at work. In the late 1980s, a confluence of research merged to revive interest in the usefulness of personality in selection settings. First, the U.S. Army began a large-scale personnel selection research project (Project A) that revealed some personality traits were systematically related to specific work-related outcomes and that those traits added incremental predictive validity beyond that attributed to cognitive ability.[6] Second, personality was found to predict a number of major life outcomes, including divorce, drug use, health behaviors and illness, and even mortality (a rather significant outcome).[7] Third, a series of highly influential meta-analyses of personality research at work were published at about the same time, taking a construct-oriented approach building on the Five-Factor taxonomic model of personality and found that specific personality traits were significantly related to critical performance and withdrawal outcomes, with some traits being relevant in all or nearly all jobs and others being predictive only for certain jobs or certain work-related outcomes.[8] When these positive findings were supported in research based on data from the European community in the late 1990s, a wave of research followed.[9] Nearly two decades later, we review what was learned and which concerns you must consider if you adopt personality testing as part of your selection approach.

DEFINITION AND USE OF PERSONALITY IN SELECTION

In popular usage, personality often is equated with social skill. It is thought of as the ability to elicit positive reactions from others in one's typical dealings with them. Work psychologists who study personality professionally view this differently as they typically focus on traits linked to motivational work habits. Although there is not a single standard definition of the term *personality*, most formal definitions agree that personality refers to the unique set of characteristics that define an individual and determine that person's pattern of interaction or engagement with the work environment. The term *characteristics* usually is interpreted to include what people habitually think, feel, and act. The environment includes both human and nonhuman elements (organizational demands, managerial practices, motivational characteristics of the job and social environment, and so on). We can see, then, that personality involves much more than social skill; in fact, many believe that no other area of psychology represents as broad a topic as personality.[10]

Personality, therefore, would seem to be critically important in selection. After all, everyone has a personality, each person has a unique personality profile that results in a distinctive compilation of traits, and more important, that personality influences performance at work. When we review job analysis information, we find the employee's personality characteristics are essential for job performance. Two broad personality traits, conscientiousness and emotional stability, are likely to be valid for all or nearly all jobs. These traits relate to how hardworking, persistent, and achievement oriented one is, and they predict the candidate's ability to cope with the stress of hazardous conditions or emotionally demanding work. What manager, after all, sets out to hire a lazy, irresponsible worker who is always stressed out and unable to cope at work? One other trait, agreeableness, recently has emerged as an important predictor for all or nearly all jobs. The importance given to agreeableness, however, is the result of it being a powerful predictor of withdrawal behavior at work (for example, counterproductive behavior, absenteeism, even voluntary turnover) and citizenship behavior,[11] because it only predicts task performance in jobs that emphasize interaction with other people, such as a customer service representative, secretary, or even team member. The two remaining personality traits, extraversion and openness to experience, are valid for some but not all jobs or activities. For example, extraversion relates to how active, ambitious, and even narcissistic a person is, which has been found to be important in jobs that require influencing, negotiating, and leading other people, such as sales or management jobs.[12]

Given these findings, we should expect to find evidence that personality data are valid for selection. Until recently, however, this has not proved to be the case. As noted earlier, in the mid-1960s, several individuals reviewed the use of personality data in selection. The following comments by Robert Guion and Richard Gottier are typical of the conclusions of this work:

> *It cannot be said that any of the conventional personality measures have demonstrated really general usefulness as selection tools in employment practice.... The number of tests resulting in acceptable statements of validity is greater than might be expected by pure chance—but not much. The best that can be said is that in some situations, for some purposes, some personality measures can offer helpful predictions.*[13]

Some researchers still generally agree with these earlier conclusions. In fact, Kevin Murphy, Fred Morgeson, and other colleagues would still assert that the problems cited in the mid-1960s have not yet been resolved.[14] Predictive validities of specific personality traits when predicting a single work criterion are still quite low, rarely exceeding 0.20. Furthermore, our theoretical understanding of why specific personality traits are useful in specific jobs is still inadequate. But other work has offered evidence supporting the use of personality data in selection decisions. Murray Barrick, Michael Mount, Deniz Ones, and colleagues summarized this evidence.[15]

First, agreement is growing among researchers that personality characteristics can be grouped into five broad dimensions, referred to as the Five-Factor Model. These five traits are conscientiousness, emotional stability, agreeableness, extraversion, and openness to experience. We will discuss these traits extensively in the next few pages, but suffice it to say that the emergence of a consensus—and believe me, psychologists rarely agree on anything—enables researchers to develop better theories, addressing the criticisms raised by Morgeson, Murphy, and others.

Second, managers intuitively believe personality traits matter at work. Not surprisingly, research shows managers' view relevant personality traits (which depend on the context or demands of the job) as being nearly as important to the candidate as general mental ability.[16]

Third, and perhaps most important, recent meta-analytic data show these traits can be relevant predictors of the broad criteria of work effectiveness, retaining productive employees.[17] In fact, the multiple R using all five traits to predict the broad work performance factor is in the low 0.30s, consisting of task performance, citizenship behavior, and adaptive performance, but multiple R is in the 0.60s when predicting the broad retention criterion containing (avoiding) absenteeism, counterproductive work behavior, and turnover. This will be discussed later, but again, although these traits do not predict job performance as well as some other selection tools (for example, general mental ability or work samples), they are useful predictors of overall work performance and even more so when predicting retention. Consequently, we now realize personality has been found to be a significant predictor of a number of important outcomes managers care about, including exhibiting more teamwork and leadership, providing more effective customer service, contributing more citizenship behavior, avoiding counterproductive behavior, influencing job satisfaction and commitment to the firm, reducing turnover and absenteeism, and enhancing safety. Furthermore, because more than one trait is simultaneously used to predict these work performance and withdrawal behaviors, we must recognize the multiple correlation instead of just talking about the predictive validity of one personality trait. The importance of using the multiple correlation, which jointly considers all relevant personality traits, is that it yields higher predictive validities because we know that personality traits are not highly intercorrelated (do not extensively overlap) with each other.[18]

Fourth, because personality is not highly correlated to other useful selection tools (general mental ability, biodata, and so on) either, personality traits contribute incremental validity to the prediction of success at work—above and beyond what is added by these other predictors.[19] Fifth, there is little or no adverse impact, as mean scores are comparable across racial and ethnic groups and differences between men and women tend to be smaller at the Five-Factor level then at the facet level of each Five-Factor Model trait.[20] And, of course, the threat of a discrimination lawsuit is an important consideration for any hiring manager. Sixth, even if the effect for a personality trait is small to modest, the employer obtains this benefit every single day the employee shows up for work. Research reveals that personality assessed in high school could predict career success 50 or more years later. This study showed that the multiple correlation or composite validity of the Five-Factor Model traits was more than 0.60 when predicting occupational success (status and income) 30 to 50 years after personality was assessed.[21] Finally, research reveals personality tends to change in a consistent trajectory during adulthood, with conscientiousness, emotional stability, and agreeableness—the three most important traits that predict *retaining productive* employees across nearly all types of jobs—having been found to increase about one-third to one-half standard deviation from the late 20s to the early 50s years of age.[22] The fact that these modest effects compound throughout one's entire career and are continuously on an upward trajectory underscores why scholars now accept as true that personality traits matter. We will discuss each of these points in more detail. As a start, we present background information derived from writings in personality theory.

Personality Traits

The use of personality data in selection requires classifying and measuring individuals according to some set of personality characteristics referred to as traits. A *trait* is a continuous dimension on which individual differences may be measured by the amount of the characteristic the individual exhibits.[23] *Sociability, independence,* and *need for achievement* are examples of traits. Each individual has a unique profile across the full set of personality traits that distinguishes each of us from other people. Furthermore, across different people, there tend to be relatively large differences in the degree to which they demonstrate each of these traits. The compilation of traits that is characteristic for each of us is fairly stable over time, changing as little as 2 percent a year in adulthood.[24]

The concept of traits begins with the common observation that individuals may differ sharply in their reactions to the same situation. For example, one individual enjoys a routine job working with data, whereas another is quite unhappy about the same task features. Similarly, one person is verbal and actively engaged in negotiating with others in a committee meeting, while another is reticent. The concept of trait is used to explain these different reactions to the same situation. In these cases, individuals are thought to have different amounts of traits that could be referred to as openness to new experiences and dominance, a facet of extraversion. Traits are used to explain the consistency of an individual's behavior over a variety of situations. It has been observed that an individual who strives for dominance in a committee meeting frequently acts similarly in other group interactions. From this brief description, we can understand that some psychologists and many non-psychologists frequently regard traits as the cause of a person's reactions to situations. The essence of traits has been conceptualized in many ways. The one element common to these different perspectives is that traits are viewed as the dispositional or relatively stable and enduring ways people tend to think, feel, and act.[25]

The use of personality data in selection requires, first, the specification of job tasks and, second, the identification of traits that are linked to these tasks. Table 12.1, which is derived from several studies, provides examples of personality traits that have been used in selection based on these steps. In previous chapters, we discussed the difficulties associated with the specification of employee knowledge, skills, and abilities (or work-related characteristics [WRCs]) in general. The first problem with specifying employee personality traits in particular is determining which personality traits to use.

It is in this regard that the recent work in the Five-Factor Model, which we referred to previously, is important. Generally, personality psychologists now agree there are five general factors of personality that can serve as a meaningful taxonomy for describing traits. In other words, these five factors can be thought of as the five core traits that influence behavior.[26]

Typically, the research that led to the development of the Five-Factor Model involved collecting vast amounts of data. A large sample of subjects completed several personality questionnaires, each of which was designed to measure multiple personality traits. Statistical analyses, such as factor analyses, then was used to determine whether all of these measured personality traits can be reduced to a smaller number. Such analyses have consistently identified five traits, each of which is composed of several related traits measured by the various personality questionnaires. The same five traits have been identified using different instruments, in different cultures, and using data obtained from different sources.[27]

TABLE 12.1	Personality Traits for a Sample of Jobs Studied in Selection
Job	**Personality Trait**
Executive	Conscientiousness, emotional stability, extraversion, ambition (especially)
Supervisor	Persistence, endurance, emotional stability, nurturance
Salesperson	Conscientiousness, achievement (especially), ambition, extraversion
Secretary	Conscientiousness, dependability (especially), emotional stability, agreeableness
Computer Programmer	Conscientiousness, original thinking, openness to new experiences
Insurance Agent	Conscientiousness, extraversion, original thinking
Newspaper Writer	Conscientiousness, emotional stability, openness to new experiences
Carpenter	Conscientiousness, dependability (especially), emotional stability

Extraversion is the first dimension. Traits frequently associated in forming this dimension include (from the positive pole) sociability, gregariousness, assertiveness, optimism, ambition, and activity. Some personality specialists have interpreted this dimension to represent two basic components: ambition and sociability.[28] The second dimension is called *emotional stability* or neuroticism, if viewed from the negative pole. Traits usually associated with this trait are calmness, security, confidence, resistance to upset, and lack of emotion. The third dimension, usually interpreted as *agreeableness*, is made up of courtesy, flexibility, trust, good-naturedness, supportiveness, generosity, cooperativeness, forgiveness, and tolerance. The fourth dimension is labeled *conscientiousness*, characterized by responsibility, organization, dependability, decisiveness, hard work, achievement orientation, and perseverance. The fifth dimension is labeled *openness to experience;* it also has been referred to as *intellect* or *culture*.[29] This dimension includes imagination, culture, curiosity, intelligence, artistic sensitivity, originality, and broad mindedness.

The Five-Factor Model depicts personality at its broadest level of abstraction, as nearly all of a person's characteristics are described using just these five traits. In turn, each of these personality traits are thought to be composed of a number of more narrowly defined specific traits, often called facets. These more refined facets are homogeneous in nature and are able to differentiate the multiple aspects of which a broad Five-Factor Model trait is composed. For example, achievement, planfulness, decisiveness, and dependability would be four separate facets of conscientiousness. In fact, a widely used Five-Factor personality test has differentiated the five broad factors into 30 more specific facets, with each factor consisting of six distinctive facets. These facets are listed in Table 12.2, along with a less refined 10-facet taxonomy of the Five-Factor Model. Tim Judge and colleagues have shown that when predicting more specific criteria, the use of refined personality facets will predict better.[30] In contrast, Ning Li and his associates also have shown rather compellingly that if one is interested in predicting very broad, aggregated criteria like retaining productive employees, the Five-Factor level predicts such broad overall work effectiveness criteria much better.[31]

How to resolve this conundrum? In essence, you might consider using narrower facets when you want to predict specific criteria better. For example, if you are extremely interested in one's ability to sell door to door, you might focus on ambition, narcissism, gregariousness, and stress tolerance. Doing so would likely predict selling performance better than extraversion and emotional stability. If, however, you're also interested in whether a person will show up every day, not claim false business expenses, and speak highly of your company or coworkers to others, as well as stay with the firm longer, then you might get better overall prediction using the broad personality traits. The multiple R when predicting a broad criterion like overall work effectiveness is likely to be lower than the multiple R for a specific criterion like door-to-door selling behavior. This makes sense because a correspondingly broader set of antecedents likely can explain the broader work performance criterion. Thus, the more modest prediction when trying to predict a diverse set of behaviors, all of which may be important to a manager, underscores the complexity of making a selection decision.[32]

To further compound the difficulty of this decision (whether to use broad or specific predictors), there is a relatively high level of agreement across researchers about the composition of the Five-Factor taxonomy (that is, what each factor depicts), but very little agreement across personality scholars about the taxonomic model at the facet level of personality. There isn't even consensus on the number of facets that are necessary to comprehensively describe the components of the Five-Factor Model, much less other personality traits. Consider impulsiveness, which has been characterized as arising from neuroticism (the low side of emotional stability): although some authors have argued it is

TABLE 12.2 A Hierarchical Representation of the 30 NEO Personality Sub-facets Mapped onto 10 Facets by DeYoung, Quilty, and Peterson (2007) onto the Five Factor Model

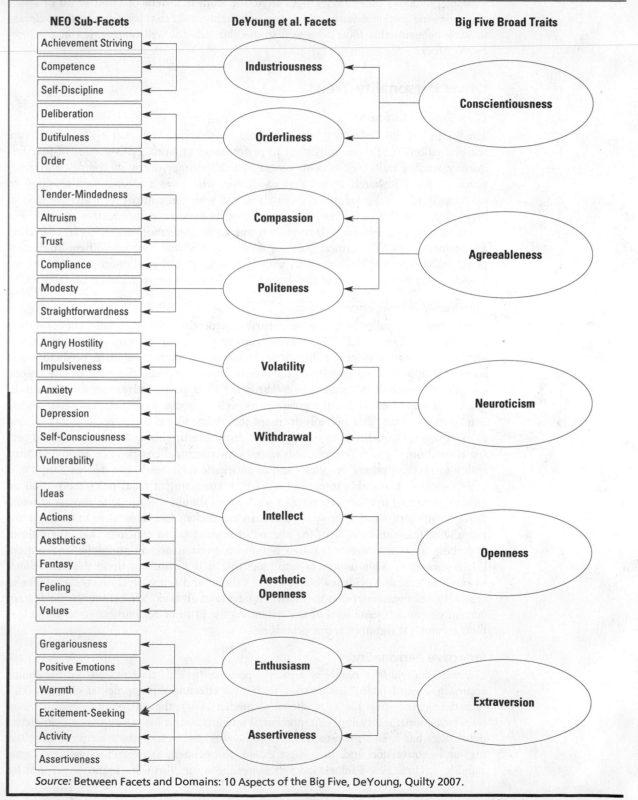

Source: Between Facets and Domains: 10 Aspects of the Big Five, DeYoung, Quilty 2007.

part of conscientiousness, other authors have suggested it is a blend of extraversion, conscientiousness, and neuroticism.[33] Besides this, the sheer number of facets proposed as relevant predictors potentially ranges anywhere from hundreds of facets to 10 or less.[34] The following section discusses a few key personality traits that have emerged as relevant to work behavior that have been well studied but are not well represented in the Five-Factor Model.

Other Personality Traits

Core Self Evaluation

Tim Judge and his colleagues have presented considerable empirical evidence that core self-evaluations (CSEs) are important to performance at work. CSEs consist of four frequently studied traits: self-esteem, generalized self-efficacy, locus of control, and emotional stability. Research shows that candidates who have a strong predisposition to confidence, who feel good about themselves, and who can control their anxiety tend to be happier, see their work as more interesting, and are more productive at work. For example, a recent meta-analysis revealed a true-score correlation of 0.30 when predicting job performance.[35] The critical question is whether CSE meaningfully differs from emotional stability; it certainly overlaps with it. Consequently, like emotional stability, we would expect this trait to be a useful predictor of success across many, if not all jobs.

Emotional Intelligence

The second personality trait that has elicited considerable interest in selection contexts is emotional intelligence (EI). EI is a broad construct, one that appears to be composed of attributes beyond just personality. It includes nearly all noncognitive predictors and some that appear to be cognitive measures. In many respects, this may be the biggest question EI research is focused on: What is EI? EI is purported to measure the candidate's self-awareness and self-regulation, as well as social awareness and relationship management. Thus, this measure includes the ability to recognize one's emotions and to exert control over them, to manage one's disruptive impulses, and to pursue and persist toward one's goals. The trait also assesses interpersonal competence, including one's ability to perceive others' emotions and to anticipate their needs and desires.[36]

Obviously, being able to control one's own emotions, to focus one's motivation on critical goals, and to effectively interact with others should contribute to success at work. Research in work settings, however, has been insufficient to enable us to fully realize the promise of this construct. This led one set of researchers to conclude that "the ratio of hyperbole to hard evidence is rather high, with overreliance on anecdotes and unpublished surveys."[37] This underscores the fact that it is incumbent upon the practitioner to carefully examine evidence of predictive validity and other psychometric evidence to ensure the EI measure relates to important outcomes at work. We believe the field is not currently at an adequate level of understanding for EI to be recommended as a selection tool, although it certainly seems promising.

Proactive Personality

The third individual measure is proactive personality. This trait reflects a dispositional approach toward taking initiative at work and effecting environmental changes. This "action-oriented" trait has been shown to predict salary, the rate of promotions, use of transformational leadership, entrepreneurial intentions, and job performance.[38] Proactive personality has been shown to relate to conscientiousness (especially achievement striving) and extraversion and, to a lesser extent, to openness to experience and emotional stability.[39] These Five-Factor Model measures, however, also were found to account for only about 25 percent of the variance in proactive personality. Consequently, proactive personality reflects something more than just the Five-Factor Model. Because employers are increasingly demanding their employees to take responsibility for their own career development and be more self-directed at work, we anticipate this construct will continue to garner interest from both researchers and practitioners.

PERSONALITY MEASUREMENT METHODS

We stated in Chapters 1 and 6 that the accurate measurement of many human characteristics is difficult because we are trying to quantify intangible constructs through the use of inferred data. This is especially true in the measurement of personality. To fully understand the use of personality in selection, it is necessary to understand the nature and characteristics of these measurement methods. The three most commonly used methods in selection are self-report inventories, the judgment of interviewers, and the judgment of other observers, especially former coworkers or supervisors.

Without a doubt, the most frequently used technique to assess personality is to ask for self-reports. Reliance on self-report questionnaires, however, may limit the validities of these personality traits, and this is not the result of the biasing effects of intentional distortion. Rather, self-ratings of personality are influenced by a broad "frame of reference" that includes non-job-relevant behaviors as well as behaviors at work. In contrast, when we obtain personality ratings from others who observe us at work, their ratings reflect our reputation at work. Self-reports may introduce irrelevant effects that reduce the correlation between trait scores and measures of job performance. In contrast, ratings of supervisors, coworkers, and customers are limited to job behaviors, which are particularly relevant. The authors of one study gathered self-report ratings of the Five-Factor Model from 105 sales representatives, as well as ratings from at least one supervisor, coworker, and customer. Results showed that self-ratings produced either insignificant or lower validity coefficients than those produced from ratings of the other three sources for all traits except conscientiousness.[40] The tentative explanation for this finding is that the frame of reference for self-ratings differed from that of the other ratings, which accounted for the differences in validity coefficients. A second study using personality ratings from high school (ratings were provided by a psychologist) found that the Five-Factor dimensions, especially conscientiousness and emotional stability (the universal predictors), were related to career success 50 or more years later.[41] Again, these predictive validities were larger than those typically resulting from self-reports. Taken together, these results underscore the value of considering alternative ways of assessing personality. On the following pages, we review some of these approaches.

Inventories in Personality Measurement

Inventories use the written responses of an individual as the information for determining personality. There are literally hundreds of such measures, all differing substantially in their characteristics. Many can be found in the test sources mentioned in Chapter 6—for example, the Buros Institute's *Mental Measurements Yearbook*. Some of these inventories are designed to measure abnormal personality traits; others measure normal traits. Some devices measure several personality dimensions, and others measure only one. It would be impossible to discuss each one of these devices here. Instead, we discuss only two major types of inventories—self-report inventories or questionnaires and projective techniques—to illustrate their principal characteristics.

There is one issue to note regarding using inventories to predict performance at work. Research shows that "contextualized personality items" predict job performance better than general-purpose personality items.[42] In other words, if the items in the personality inventory put the respondent in the same frame-of-reference as when doing the job ("at work"), the items will predict performance better. Specifically, evidence demonstrates that an item that states, "At work, I tend to be outgoing and talkative" is more predictive than "I am the life of the party." On the basis of this finding, when selecting a personality test to use during selection, there would be value in ensuring that the test is developed to predict success in work settings.

Self-Report Questionnaires

These instruments usually consist of a series of brief items asking respondents to use a multiple-choice answer format to indicate personal information about thoughts, emotions, and past experiences. Typical items begin with such statements as "I am happy" or "I enjoy going to small parties" or "I think good things happen to those who work hard." Respondents are frequently given only three response categories: agree, undecided, or disagree. These questionnaires assume that a correspondence exists between what people say about themselves and what is actually true. They also assume that individuals are aware of their thoughts and emotions and are willing to share them openly. For illustrative purposes, we will discuss one often-used self-report inventory. In addition, we will discuss three other measures that have been found to predict work behavior. Each of these measures focuses on a single personality trait. But first, we review the Five-Factor Personality Model.

The Five-Factor Model

We discussed the Five-Factor Model earlier. Actually, there are several different measuring devices of the five core personality dimensions. The two most often used in selection are the *NEO-Personality Inventory*, developed by Paul Costa and Robert McCrae, and the *Personality Characteristics Inventory (PCI)*, developed by Murray Barrick and Michael Mount. We will discuss the PCI in detail, as at least one of the authors of this book is somewhat familiar with this test (Murray Barrick is a coauthor).

The PCI has 150 multiple-choice items derived from empirical research using several Five-Factor Model inventories. Each item has three possible responses: "agree," "undecided," and "disagree." Typically it takes 30 to 45 minutes to complete the PCI. The five personality dimensions measured, together with examples of typical (not actual) items, are presented in Table 12.3. Each of the five factors can best be understood in

TABLE 12.3	Scales and Representative Items of Five-Factor Personality Dimensions
Personality Scale*	**Typical Item**
Extraversion	I tend not to say what I think about things.
Agreeableness	I tend to trust other people.
Conscientiousness	I approach most of my work steadily and persistently.
Stability	Whenever I'm by myself, I feel vulnerable.
Openness to Experience	I enjoy eating in new restaurants I know nothing about.

*Based on the revised *Personality Characteristics Inventory* by Murray P. Barrick and Michael K. Mount, published by Wonderlic, Inc., Libertyville, Illinois, 2009.

terms of more specific related traits that characterize the broad trait.[43] Think of each of these traits as bipolar: Opposite extreme scores on each dimension represent opposite behaviors of the trait measured.

Other Self-Report Personality Inventories

A number of different personality inventories using self-report methodologies are available to the practitioner; we have described the PCI as one example. Not all of these measure the Five-Factor Model. For example, the 16 Personality Factor Test (the 16 PF) contains more than 5 factors—16 "primary" factors, to be precise. These factors correspond to the notion of facets discussed previously. Although research has shown that these 16 personality factors can be subsumed into the Five-Factor measures, effective prediction also can be obtained using non–Five Factor measures. Later in the chapter, for example, we introduce three such measures. Some frequently used self-report personality inventories and the names of the original authors are reported in Table 12.4.

Forced-Choice Inventories

As the name implies, forced-choice measures of personality require test-takers to choose the most liked item of two to four equally desirable items. The primary advantage of this is that faking or response distortion tends to be reduced; "faking good" is difficult when the items are equally "desirable." For example, when applying for an engineering job, you are asked to endorse either "I like football" or "I like bowling." In this case, applicants don't know the right answer; because they happen to live in Texas, they are comfortable answering "I like football." In reality, based on criterion keying, the correct answer is actually whichever answer high-performing engineers consistently select.

The U.S. Navy and Army recently developed forced-choice computer adaptive personality tests creatively called the Navy Computer Adaptive Personality System (NCAPS) and the Army's Assessment of Individual Motivation (AIM). Answering these types of tests invokes deeper processing and is cognitively more demanding, but the tests do reduce acquiescent responding and other response biases (as well as faking). One trade-off is that because the tests rely on computer-adapted assessment, the number of items answered is shorter. Testing is more efficient because it more accurately measures personality traits; each question asked depends on the desired level of the trait measured in the previously answered question (estimated using item response theory).[44]

Forced-choice inventories are psychometrically challenging in a number of ways—including negative intercorrelations as a product of the dependencies between item

TABLE 12.4	Examples of Personality Inventories and Authors
16 Personality Factor Test (16 PF)	Raymond Cattell
California Psychological Inventory (CPI)	Harrison Gough
Myers-Briggs Type Indicator (MBTI)	Katherine Cook Briggs and Isabel Briggs Meyers
Conditional Reasoning Test (of Aggression)	Lawrence James and Michael McIntyre
NEO-Personality Inventory (NEO-PI)	Paul T. Costa, Jr. and Robert R. McCrae
Hogan Personality Inventory (HPI)	Robert and Joyce Hogan
Global Personality Inventory (GPI)	PDI, Inc.
Gordon Personal Profile (GPP)	Leonard Gordon
Jackson Personality Inventory (JPI)	Doug Jackson
Guilford-Zimmerman Temperament Survey (GZTS)	J. P. Guilford and Wayne Zimmerman

responses and the fact each applicant responds to a unique set of items.[45] Nevertheless, a few studies yield predictive validities that are as good as or better than more traditional Likert-scale self-report personality scales.[46] Although there are issues to be resolved with forced-choice inventories, they do warrant consideration as another way to assess personality.

Projective Techniques

Projective techniques are similar to self-report questionnaires in that they require verbal responses that are scored to obtain measures of personality characteristics. These devices, however, differ noticeably on several other important aspects. In contrast to the structure of both the questions and the answers of self-report questionnaires, projective techniques are intentionally ambiguous. For example, the respondent is presented with a series of inkblots or pictures and asked to make up a story about each one. Instructions are usually kept brief and vague. Another frequently used technique is to present the respondent with a series of sentence stems, such as "My father …" or "My favorite …" Respondents are asked to complete each sentence. In both types of tests, respondents are encouraged to say whatever they wish. The inkblots, pictures, or sentence stems are purposefully chosen to be open to a wide variety of reasonable answers. The assumption underlying projective techniques is that they allow respondents to expose central ways of "organizing experience and structuring life" because meanings are imposed on a stimulus having "relatively little structure and cultural patterning."[47] In this sense, these devices might be classified as "weak testing situations" in which individual differences in personality mainly account for the differences in responses among people. These techniques are called "projective" because, given the ambiguity of the items, the respondent must project interpretation on them. This interpretation is held to be an extension of the personality of the individual. The proposed advantage of these devices for obtaining data on personality is that the respondent is not supposed to realize the possible interpretation of the information provided. This encourages the respondent to make public certain information that otherwise might not be provided. For example, a subject might interpret a picture of two interacting people as a violent argument that will lead to one individual physically assaulting the other. According to the theory of projective techniques, the aggression expressed in this story is more a function of the aggressive impulses of the individual than the context of the picture, which was deliberately chosen to be ambiguous. It then would be hypothesized, given additional data, that the respondent is an angry person with a predisposition to experience the world as peopled by hostile individuals.[48]

Observer Ratings of Personality

Observers can rate an applicant's personality, even after brief conversations. This finding corresponds to those reported in social psychology, in which even strangers can rate a target person's personality with modestly high agreement with others who know the target person well.[49] Because we routinely make decisions in everyday life based on our observations of people, it makes sense to consider alternative sources when assessing personality. To a large degree these decisions, based on our observations, have a substantial impact in determining how successfully we interact with others. This leads to the notion that we might enhance our understanding and better predict behavior on the job if we also account for observer ratings of the applicant's personality. The results from recent research, to be reviewed shortly, underscores this notion.

In some respects, observer ratings of personality "get at" a person's public self or social reputation; they reflect the way we are perceived by others. In contrast, self-reports of personality likely reflect perceptions of ourselves over many situations. They incorporate less observable information about the dynamics and processes inside us and include our motives, intentions, feelings, and past behaviors. In many respects, self-reports depict our "identity." We believe ratings of personality, based on reputation, will be a second way to predict the employee's success at work.[50]

Two recent meta-analyses suggest that observer ratings of personality enhance predictions of job performance, with magnitudes often twice as large as the predictive validities for self-report responses.[51] This suggests that personality traits based on observer ratings are psychologically meaningful ways to organize information about people, information that has real implications for understanding and predicting work performance. Does this mean that an individual does not know himself better than his coworkers? Although we would not say this, we do believe the research evidence shows coworkers who know us well do know something about how we tend to think, feel, and act, which in turn predicts behavior at work. The information captured in other-reports of personality ratings has been shown to add incremental validity to self-report ratings of personality.

The Interview in Personality Measurement

We discussed the selection interview in Chapter 10 as a device used to predict performance through the assessment of applicant characteristics. We will not repeat that information here, so this section is brief. It is known, however, that the interview serves as a primary device for estimating personality characteristics of applicants.

An interview frequently is used as a convenient way to determine how an applicant would typically act on the job. One thorough review found that traits are the most frequently assessed constructs in the employment interview.[52] In fact, conscientiousness is the single most frequently measured WRC in the interview; it is assessed as often as all other personality traits combined. Because this trait is a universal predictor reflecting proclivity to be motivated at work, we are not surprised that hiring managers want to measure it. Although there are not a large number of studies showing the predictive validity of these measures, the available evidence suggests that interviewer ratings of applicant personality are moderately related to job performance, with true score predictive validities of 0.33 for extraversion and conscientiousness. The predictive validity for the trait of agreeableness was 0.51, although this measure was assessed in less than 10 percent of the studies examining personality in this meta-analysis.[53] We believe these findings highlight the importance of specifying whether a personality trait is likely to be relevant in a specific situation. At least for agreeableness, the predictive validity is quite high when the measure is deemed to be relevant in a specific work setting. Furthermore, these estimates are based on only relationships with job performance. If we use these estimates to also predict the other criteria linked to retaining productive workers, we expect the multiple R would further underscore the utility of assessing personality during the employment interview.

Psychologists and human resource (HR) managers have examined predictive validity when assessing personality through observer ratings and have come up with several important findings that likely affect the accuracy and validity of interviewer ratings of personality. First, interviewers need to be aware of the natural tendency to attribute others' behavior to personality rather than to situational causes. Such attributions contrast with the way we analyze our own behavior, in which we believe that the conditions of a situation are more often the determinants of our own actions than are personality traits.[54] To compound this belief, raters often interpret even small amounts of behavior as signs of underlying traits and motives.[55] This may explain why interviewer ratings of personality often do not correlate very highly with self-reported measures of personality.[56]

Accurate assessment of a job candidate's personality may actually increase when using an unstructured interview rather than a structured interview. The notion is that an unstructured interview relies on questions that are often open-ended and can be answered with a wide variety of responses. Because there are no obvious right or wrong answers to these questions, the responses given are expected to be influenced by the candidate's own personality. Because the interview is less structured, it is likely to be a weaker situation, which also allows the applicant's personality to emerge more. These reasons may allow unstructured interviews to result in more accurate assessment of the candidate's personality. Some recent research supports this notion.[57]

Does this mean that we are encouraging you to use unstructured interviews? As discussed in Chapter 10, structured interviews have higher predictive validity. Furthermore, a recent meta-analysis examining the constructs that are assessed in the employment interview also supported the utility of the structured interview when assessing personality. The researchers found that the predictive validities for personality constructs reported for highly structured interviews were higher than those reported for interviews with less structure (extraversion, $\rho = 0.40$ versus 0.22; conscientiousness, $\rho = 0.37$ versus 0.24). Although interviewer assessments of personality may be more accurate in an unstructured interview, these data reveal that whatever is influencing interviewer ratings in structured interviews also contains valid job-related information.[58] Future research is needed to examine what information is being used to form impressions of candidate personality during the interview and whether that information is more easily assessed using structured or unstructured interviews. Our hunch is that the "personality infused" information that is most useful for predicting later job performance will be obtained best by using structured interviews that focus on job-relevant WRCs.

The Appropriate Use of the Interview

Having said all this, what statements can we make about the use of the interview in personality assessment? Recall from Chapter 10 that we concluded the interview is an appropriate way to assess interpersonal skills and work habits, both of which are influenced by personality traits. Our first recommendation with regard to such assessments is that the scope of the interview be limited. Instead of attempting to assess all aspects of the applicant's personality, it would be more feasible to measure social interaction patterns and work patterns (such as attention to detail, meeting difficult objectives, and so on) identified through job analysis information. This would limit the number of personality traits that must be judged and identify more carefully the ones that are to be assessed. For example, attention to detail may be an important personal characteristic for clerical or computer system jobs within organizations. The interviewer should, therefore, attempt to find information about this trait rather than attempting a more complete personality description that would include such traits as *ambition, aggressiveness,* and *sociability*. These may seem desirable, but they are not directly related to job activities.

The problem, however, is how to successfully accomplish this. One way to assess personality is to concentrate on previous behaviors that seem to depend on the same personality trait. In this case, interview questions and discussion could be addressed to previous instances in which the interviewee demonstrated behaviors requiring attention to detail. The *behavior description interview* discussed in Chapter 10 is appropriate here. It is hoped that information could be obtained about the nature of the behavior or activity, length of time involved, relevance to the demands of the job or work context, and whether one or multiple instances of the behavior can be cited. In interviews, the interviewer is the measuring device. It is hoped that by limiting the scope of decisions that the interviewer must make, and by maximizing the correspondence between the information gathered and the type of assessment that must be made, personality assessment accuracy will be increased.

The foregoing discussion implies that observers (for example, interviewers) have a difficult time assessing the personality of others. This may not be the case, as the study of evolution implies people are naturally predisposed to evaluate the personalities of strangers. A recent study by Michael Cole, Hubert Feild, and William Giles showed that recruiters are able to assess candidate personality just from the applicants' resumes. Similarly, Samuel Gosling and colleagues have found that people can rate another person's degree of conscientiousness and openness to experience just based on looking in their office or bedroom. Still other researchers use publicly available Facebook information to assess the personality of individuals. These results suggest it may not be as difficult to form valid judgments about candidate qualifications or "personality" as one might expect.[59]

Ratings from Other Observers

The quality of prediction using ratings of personality will improve the better the rater knows the subject. Consequently, it would be particularly useful to obtain "reputation-infused" ratings from supervisors or coworkers. When making a hiring decision (unless it is a promotion), one generally does not have access to the candidate's coworkers or the prior supervisor. In fact, it seems to us that this is one way that headhunter's are able to add value during the selection process. To the extent a headhunter is able to visit with people who worked with and know the candidate well, they may be able to learn about the candidate's reputation and ultimately use that to infer knowledge about their personality. Similarly, it is possible that a letter of reference could also serve as a way to assess the candidate's personality. Ryan Zimmerman, Mary Triana, and Murray Barrick found a structured letter of reference, relying on ratings on a number of personality items, predicted later job performance better than typical self-report responses.[60] This, coupled with the meta-analysis data reviewed earlier, illustrates the potential of obtaining coworker ratings of the applicant's personality.

Evaluating the Validity of Personality Tests as a Predictor

Substantial research has been conducted over the past 25 years to illustrate the predictive validity of personality. Nearly all of these studies have assumed the nature of the relationship between personality and performance, like other predictors reviewed in this book, is linear—that more of the trait is better for work performance. A few recent studies, however, have questioned this assumption. In essence, these researchers have argued that it is possible that one can have too much of a good thing. Consider entrepreneurship: To be successful, an entrepreneur must have passion and believe in their ideas and business model. However, it may be possible to have too much passion, as it can blind founders to pitfalls in their business plan and even lead them to be overconfident in the desirability of the product. Similarly, a few personality studies have begun to suggest that personality traits may have an inverted U–curvilinear relationship with work performance, in which case too high a standing on a trait may hinder performance in some situations. For example, in clerical positions, both speed and accuracy are necessary for higher performance. It is possible that as long as the employee has "enough" conscientiousness to be careful and thorough, it enhances performance; too much conscientiousness, however, leads to slower performance as the person stops work to double- and triple-check accuracy.[61] Taken together, these recent findings suggest that predictive validity may be highest in the middle range of personality scores and that extreme scores may predict less highly in some cases. Future research will examine this issue more thoroughly and clarify if and when predictive validity is not linearly related to work effectiveness (that is, more is better), as currently assumed. The next section reviews the findings regarding the predictive validity of personality.

The Validity of Self-Report Inventories

Many recent studies have examined the validity of several different self-report inventories. A large number of these studies have focused on inventories that measure the Five-Factor Model. A recent study conducted by Murray Barrick, Michael Mount, and Tim Judge, which relied on a second-order meta-analysis of prior meta-analyses, will be reviewed here because it provides a thorough review of the predictive validity of these Five-Factor personality traits.[62] This study quantitatively summarized the findings from 15 prior meta-analyses of the Five-Factor Model's predictive validity across five occupational groups and four specific work criteria, along with an overall measure of work performance. The study, however, did not focus on the broader retaining productive criteria that we now know can be predicted at hire, as it primarily focused on predicting job performance. Using sample sizes that at times exceeded 80,000, the authors concluded the following:

1. Conscientiousness and emotional stability were valid predictors of overall work performance over all studies examined (the estimated true correlation at the construct level, $\rho = 0.24$ and 0.17, respectively). This led them to conclude that these two predictors were universal predictors across all jobs. Nevertheless, even though conscientiousness was a valid predictor across all occupations and over all specific criteria, emotional stability was consistently related only to some of the specific criteria.

2. Extraversion was a valid predictor for some occupational groups, such as managers ($\rho = 0.21$), and specific criteria, such as training performance ($\rho = 0.28$).

3. Agreeableness and openness to experience demonstrated modest validity overall. However, each trait was related to a specific criterion. Agreeableness was related to teamwork ($\rho = 0.27$), whereas openness was associated with training performance ($\rho = 0.33$).

Whereas two of these traits are universal or generalizable predictors (conscientiousness and emotional stability), the other three traits (extraversion, agreeableness, and openness) were found to be contingent predictors, predicting performance in only a few jobs or jobs with specific criteria (for example, training or teamwork). Thus, the authors labeled these "niche" predictors.

Joyce Hogan and Brent Holland extended these findings by illustrating the value of matching specific personality traits to relevant work criteria using a theoretically driven rationale for expecting significant relationships between personality and performance.[63] Given this, the previous estimates likely underestimate the true predictive validity of the traits, because they include all correlations, even when there isn't a theoretical rationale as well as theoretically based estimates. In the Hogan and Holland meta-analysis, the criterion measured getting along with others or getting ahead of others. Getting along was defined as those behaviors that relate to gaining the approval of others, cooperating more, or building and maintaining relationships. On the other hand, getting ahead related to behavior that involves negotiating, striving to be recognized, and leading others, which enables the person to advance in the job, team, or organization.

On the basis of this theory, the authors expected emotional stability, conscientiousness, and agreeableness to be important predictors of the getting along with others criterion, and the results supported this (true score correlation, ρ = 0.34, 0.31, and 0.23). Theoretically, they expected ambition (a facet of extraversion), emotional stability, and openness (labeled intellect) to predict getting ahead of others. In general, the results corresponded to the hypotheses (ρ = 0.26, 0.22, 0.12, respectively), although conscientiousness had a stronger relationship (ρ = 0.20) with getting ahead than did openness to experience (ρ = 0.12).[64] The latter finding is not surprising to us, as we would expect conscientiousness (and emotional stability) to predict both criteria, because it is a "universal" predictor. In this case, however, it should be noted that the specific measure of conscientiousness used in this study actually reflected a narrow measure, as it only assessed prudence or dependability, but not striving for achievement. The latter component is likely to be particularly important for the getting ahead criterion; hence, the estimate reported here should be viewed as an underestimate of the validity for a broader measure representing all aspects of conscientiousness. The finding that agreeableness matters for one criterion, whereas extraversion matters for the other, shows that "niche" predictors work best when they are carefully matched to relevant criteria or situations. These results also reveal that predictive validities do "improve" when theory is used to identify which personality traits to include in the selection battery. Consequently, selection experts should ensure that the personality test they are using assesses those personality traits that are relevant for the specific demands of the job and that only these traits are used to make the hiring decision.

A number of other meta-analyses recently have been conducted that examine unique criteria (such as leadership, expatriate success, and so on). To enhance your understanding of when specific traits may be particularly useful, we next summarize the results from these studies:

1. When selecting effective leaders from ineffective ones, results reveal that those candidates high in extraversion, openness to experience, and emotional stability experience the greatest success on the job (ρ = 0.24, 0.24, 0.22, respectively). Conscientiousness and agreeableness are also related to effective leadership (both ρ = 0.16). If one is interested in identifying those candidates who will most likely *emerge* as leaders, conscientiousness and extraversion were the most important personality traits (both ρ = 0.33).[65] Taken together, these results show that great leaders inspire and influence others around them (are extraverted), can manage their own anxiety (are emotionally stable), are able to adapt as needed (open to new experiences), and have an "inner fire" as they strive for achievement (are conscientious).

2. Teamwork is another important criterion. A recent meta-analysis showed that conscientiousness, emotional stability, and agreeableness were useful predictors of teamwork and performance in jobs involving interpersonal interactions (ρ = 0.26, 0.27, and 0.33).[66] Not surprisingly, these results correspond to those reported by Hogan and Holland with regard to "getting along" criteria. Nevertheless, they powerfully illustrate that agreeableness is likely to be a meaningful predictor in jobs requiring teamwork or extensive interpersonal interaction, such as customer service.[67]

3. Two other meta-analyses show how these personality traits relate to expatriate job performance as well as entrepreneurial status. Although expatriates are managers working in a country and culture other than that of their upbringing or legal residence, entrepreneurs are owners or managers who undertake and operate a new business venture. In both cases, all Five-Factor Model traits except openness to experience meaningfully predicted success—either as an expatriate or an entrepreneur. Extraversion is a particularly important predictor. This is not

surprising, given the "risky" nature of both undertakings. Again, being hardworking and persistent (that is, conscientious) as well as emotionally stable and confident contributes to an individual's degree of success.[68]

4. Two other recent studies examine deviant behavior and turnover. Candidates with higher conscientiousness and agreeableness scores were less likely to exhibit deviant behavior ($\rho = -0.26$ and -0.20).[69] These same two traits, plus emotional stability and extraversion, were found to also predict those who were more likely to stay with the firm ($\rho = 0.31, 0.22, 0.35$, and 0.20, respectively).[70] These results show that organizations can avoid bad "outcomes" (counterproductive behavior or turnover) as well as obtain desirable "outcomes" (for example, higher performance) when selecting for these core personality traits.

5. The final set of meta-analyses we will discuss investigates the process through which personality affects job performance. Although these results are not directly relevant to selection, understanding the way personality influences performance will help you develop more useful theories regarding which traits should be particularly relevant in a specific job. Taken together, these studies show that the primary means through which personality operates is motivation and interpersonal competence, as these traits influence what makes you happy, what keeps you working at the activity, and how well you get along or influence and lead others. Tim Judge, Daniel Heller, and Michael Mount found the estimated true score correlation with regard to job satisfaction is meaningful for at least three traits: 0.29 for emotional stability, 0.25 for extraversion, and 0.26 for conscientiousness.[71] Thus, although most researchers focus on ways to change the job to enhance job satisfaction, these results show that one can also select people who are more likely to be satisfied and committed to their work. The second study found conscientiousness and emotional stability were related to three different measures of performance motivation. These two universal predictors influence whether the person has the confidence to accomplish the task ($\rho = 0.22$ and 0.35), is more likely to set and pursue goals ($\rho = 0.28$ and 0.29), and possesses high expectations about being able to complete the work ($\rho = 0.23$ and 0.29).[72] It is not surprising that these two traits are universal predictors of success at work, as they determine how motivated the person is while doing the job and influence how happy about and committed they are to doing the work.

In some ways, studying individual personality traits may not be the best way to determine the usefulness of the candidate's "entire" personality, at least for selection. Because these personality traits are relatively independent, simultaneously accounting for their effects should add extra predictive power. For example, Tim Judge and his colleagues have reported that the Five-Factor Model had a multiple correlation of 0.48 with leadership, 0.41 with job satisfaction, and an average multiple correlation of 0.49 with performance motivation criteria.[73] Hao Zhao and Scott Seibert found a multiple correlation of 0.37 with entrepreneurial status.[74] These results, which are substantially larger than the trait-by-trait validities reported previously, powerfully illustrate the utility of personality as a useful selection tool.

Also, as discussed, when people who know you well at work rate your personality, the evidence is clear—these observer-based ratings add incremental validity to predictions solely based on self-reports of personality.[75] In fact, the predictive validities when peers or supervisor's rate your personality are nearly twice as large. However, the ratings these results are based on were collected on employees, not applicants; the reason for obtaining the ratings was to help employees grow and develop. The point is, these raters had every incentive to tell the whole, unvarnished truth about the personality of the employees they were rating. What we do not know is how accurate such ratings would be if they were collected as part of a letter of reference or other selection tool.[76] Hence, there still are a few unknowns about relying on coworker ratings in selection contacts. Nevertheless, the results suggest these ratings may be useful as part of a selection battery.

Finally, one other important issue regarding the validity of personality inventories is whether they provide any prediction of job performance over that provided by other selection instruments. Recent studies have yielded evidence that personality data do so when used with cognitive ability measures, biodata, situational judgment tests, and employment interviews.[77] Rather than review each of these studies, the upshot is that adding a personality test is likely to add incremental validity or enhance the accuracy of the selection decision.

Critics have asked, "why does personality matter?" We contend the question should be "who wouldn't care about the candidate's personality?" Hiring managers care about it. Empirical studies show we should care about it if we want to enhance performance and motivation at work. This is particularly evident if we consider the multiple correlation from all relevant personality traits (simultaneously), as they likely add incremental validity to the other predictors one uses when making a quality hiring decision. Finally, personality predicts many outcomes organizations care about—not just overall job performance, but also whether an employee is less likely to steal, quit, or alienate the customer and whether an employee is more likely to be a leader, a team player, and a good citizen while also being happier and more motivated to work every day. In essence, personality aids us in hiring employees who are likely to remain committed and stay with the firm as well as those who are likely to be more productive in doing their work, which has been referred to as retaining the productive employee *at hire*. Because these traits are habitual or dispositional predictors that change only slowly over time, the organization obtains these benefits every single day throughout the individual's career. Thus, personality matters at work. By accounting for personality, we will likely enhance the quality of a selection decision.

Validity of Projective Techniques

On the surface, it would seem that projective techniques could provide more beneficial information than self-report questionnaires in assessing personality. After all, it is not clear what the correct answer is when an applicant is asked to describe what he or she sees in an ambiguous inkblot or photograph. One would expect that socially appropriate answers would not be as evident as they would be in the responses to personality self-report questionnaires and that responses would be reflective of the respondent's personality characteristics. This is, in fact, the basic assumption of projective techniques. Various issues have arisen concerning the scoring and use of the information obtained from projective instruments that have questioned their general usefulness in selection. The following points address these issues.

The first issue is the reliability of an individual's responses at two different times. In all other selection devices, it is assumed that the characteristic demonstrated by the respondent is consistently measured. The scores derived from projective tests, however, often have low reliabilities.[78] There is a question about the proper measurement of reliability and whether, in fact, this is a useful concept for these techniques. It has been thought that observed changes in test responses over time reflect real changes in the individual, because many of the characteristics measured, like emotion and mood, change over time. The problem this causes for HR selection decisions is significant. Usually, the applicant completes a projective test only once. The information obtained then is generalized to descriptions of the applicant. Even if changes in response patterns are indicative of real changes in the individual, the selection specialist can have little confidence in the usefulness of such personality data in predicting long-term job performance.

The second issue in the use of projective techniques is the impact on an individual's score due to the total number of responses given. This is not a major issue for most assessment devices, as they limit responses to a relatively constant number for all subjects. For those instruments that encourage free response, however, there is evidence that the scores of personality characteristics are related to the volume of information given.[79] The problem here is that the number of responses given may not be a function of personality but rather of specific verbal or test-taking skills. If this is the case, the accuracy of the personality data would be reduced, as would be its usefulness in selection.

A third major concern is the scoring of the information provided, for which the proposed benefit of projective instruments becomes a liability. The quantity and complexity of the responses make scoring, even using a designated scoring manual, very difficult. This is a greater problem for those instruments that encourage free response and less of a problem for those that limit response. The result is that, at times, the same answers have not been scored and interpreted identically by different scorers.[80] Such findings cloud the usefulness of the resulting personality scores for selection, because it would appear that the scoring of the information is indicative of the examiner's particular scoring system and judgment as well as of the individual's responses. This adds error to the scores as far as HR specialists are concerned; it is necessary that the scores reflect the applicant only, particularly as the selection decision is to be made about this individual.

A fourth and related concern is that few HR specialists are trained in administering, scoring, and interpreting data from projective tests. This means that consultants must be hired to administer and score them. At times, such consultants are not familiar with the job under consideration, and they evaluate the candidate in comparison to a general profile of a good worker. In many cases, this profile is based only on the opinion of the consultant. Given the complexity of projective test data and the unfamiliarity of the HR specialist with scoring, it is difficult to find an alternative route. As a result, the personality description is often accepted by the specialist but actually is of little value. These criticisms show that this technique is often based on poorly developed instruments or scoring "keys" and on poorly conducted validity studies. There are, however, psychometrically sound instruments, detailed scoring guides, and well-done studies. For example, the Miner Sentence Completion (MSC) Test is one of these instruments, and it warrants consideration for use in selecting managers. The MSC Test was developed by John Miner specifically to assess the motives that are characteristically manifested at work and in the managerial role. The respondent is presented with 40 items or sentences and asked to complete each one. Answers are evaluated based on a complete scoring guide. Work with the MSC generally has focused on describing managerial motivation and success within large, bureaucratic organizations. Test–retest correlations indicate acceptable levels of reliability (about 0.80). Furthermore, evidence of both construct and criterion-related validation has been reported. For example, one meta-analytic study found that the MSC demonstrated a predicted pattern of correlations with other personality measures, was positively related to various measures of managerial effectiveness, and was predictive of those individuals who opt for a career in management.[81]

Legal Issues in the Use of Personality Tests

Two large-scale meta-analyses demonstrate mean differences between most subgroup comparisons on personality measured during personnel selection that are relatively small or virtually the same when compared to the "majority" group (for example, whites or males).[82] Blacks, Hispanics, and Asians were found to have nearly the same mean score as whites on extraversion, emotional stability, agreeableness, and conscientiousness. The only issue that might make a practical difference was that black applicants had lower average scores on openness to experience measures than white applicants in one meta-analysis ($d = -0.20$), but in the other meta-analysis, the difference was small ($d = -0.10$). Also, there were small gender differences, favoring women for agreeableness and favoring men for emotional stability. In general, personality tests have no or negligible adverse impact when using the Five-Factor Model. This is notable as some preliminary evidence suggests somewhat more adverse impact or larger subgroup mean differences at the facet level of the Five-Factor Model.[83]

Although personality tests have not been found to produce an adverse impact on any given demographic group (race, ethnicity, or gender), two major legal issues accompany the use of personality tests in selection. The first has to do with the Americans with Disabilities Act (ADA). As you might recall from Chapter 4, this act prohibits preemployment medical examinations. It is not clear whether a personality test should or should not be included in such an examination. All tests are reviewed on a case-by-case basis, which includes such questions as (a) Is the test administered by a health care professional? (b) Are the results interpreted by a health care professional? and (c) Is the test designed to reveal an impairment of physical or mental health? Because psychiatrists and clinical psychologists can use personality tests to diagnose mental health deficiencies, such tests could be viewed as medical examinations and therefore deemed inappropriate for use before a job offer has been made.

In the past, however, the Equal Employment Opportunity Commission (EEOC) has taken the position that personality tests are more likely to be classified as medical examinations to the extent that they include personality scales with clinical designations of psychiatric disorders, such as depression, schizophrenia, and paranoia. The EEOC continues to investigate whether a personality test might be construed as discriminating against people with disabilities.[84] If the test focuses on general traits, such as positive commitment toward work, responsiveness to supervision, honesty, and loyalty, it has not been considered a medical examination.[85] Clearly if the test does focus on these general traits, it should not make disability-related inquiries such as (a) whether an individual has sought mental health services, (b) the extent of prior legal or illegal drug use, and (c) the extent of prior or current alcohol use.

In a recent lawsuit (*Karraker v. Rent-A-Center*, 2005), the Seventh Circuit Federal Court ruled that the company used a personality test, the Minnesota Multi-Phasic Personality Inventory (MMPI), which asked questions that could reveal a mental disability. On the basis of this finding, the test was held to be a "medical examination" under the ADA; its use was deemed illegal as a preemployment test. The court went on to note that psychological tests that measure personal traits, such as honesty, integrity, preferences, and habits, do not qualify as medical examinations.[86] Under this ruling, the types of tests discussed in this chapter, such as the Five-Factor questionnaires, would not constitute a medical examination and therefore would not violate the ADA. As noted, however, the EEOC has been investigating this issue; hence, it will be important to stay current on any new decisions. Clearly, HR professionals should ensure that when using a personality test, it does not include items that may assess depression (for example, often feel sad), anxiety (for example, often panic easily), or other diagnostic outcomes. Such items should be replaced with work-related items.[87]

A second issue is the privacy rights of individuals. Although a right to privacy is not explicitly set forth in the U.S. Constitution, individuals are protected from unreasonable government intrusions and surveillance. Therefore, the selection of employees for public institutions may be affected by the use of personality tests, which by their nature, reveal an individual's inner thoughts and feelings. In addition, several states have constitutional privacy protection acts or recognize a statutory right to privacy; these acts affect both private and public employment.[88] To date, litigation about privacy has occurred in reference to questions that dealt with an applicant's sexual inclinations or religious views. In *Soroka v. Dayton Hudson*, the California Court of Appeals stopped Dayton Hudson's Target stores from requiring applicants for store security positions to take a personality test that contained questions about such topics.[89] The court also stated that employers must restrict psychological testing to job-related questions. The ruling was later dismissed as the parties reached a court-approved settlement. Under terms of the settlement, Dayton Hudson agreed to stop using the personality test and established a $1.3 million fund to be divided among the estimated 2,500 members of the plaintiff class who had taken the test.

Faking in Personality Inventories

One important issue that may affect the validity of personality inventories is the faking of responses by applicants. These personality inventories are self-reports of how the candidate tends to think, feel, and act. To optimally predict, it is assumed that people respond as they actually are. Applicant answers can be intentionally distorted or faked, and because they are not objectively verifiable, it will be difficult to prove they were faked. Moreover, when people really want a job, they have a strong incentive to distort their answers or to guess which answer the company wants based on the requirements of the job.

Do candidates intentionally alter their responses to increase the likelihood of receiving a job offer? Although it seems plausible that candidates would change their responses to increase their chances of being hired, empirical evidence is contradictory. In some studies, but not in others, mean scores for applicants are higher than those for current employees. For example, Jeff Weekley, Rob Ployhart, and Crystal Harold found applicants ($N = 7,259$) scored on average 0.64 standard deviation (SD) higher than current employees ($N = 2,989$) on three personality measures from the Five-Factor Model. This is quite similar to the 0.69 SD higher average for applicants over current employees ($N = 270$) reported by Joe Rossé and colleagues, also using Five-Factor Model scales.[90] In contrast, Leatta Hough found no significant mean score differences for applicants and current employees across three large samples of applicants ($N = 40,500$) and current employees ($N = 1,700$).[91] This finding was supported in a second large study that was based on a within-subject design in which people completed the personality test as an applicant and completed another for developmental purposes.[92] Researchers have examined indirect evidence that applicants are distorting scores by investigating whether the factor structure of the measures changes when using applicant responses. In one study, the dominant factor in applicant personality responses reflects an "ideal applicant" factor. The explanation for this factor was that the job applicant responds as he thinks he should to appear to be a competent or ideal employee, not as he actually sees himself on various personality traits. These responses vary from the self-image that the respondent reports in a nonemployment setting. Other studies show no evidence that the factor structure of a Five-Factor inventory is different for applicants than it is for respondents in a nonemployment situation.[93]

One explanation for these contradictory findings is that the studies differ in one crucial way: Those showing differences for applicants rely on research designs that tell or direct subjects to fake their answers or instruct them to answer in a way to get hired. In contrast, in cases in which subjects are allowed to naturally express themselves, even in settings in which they have an incentive to distort (that is, in a selection setting in which one tries to obtain a job), the evidence that applicants fake is less compelling and suggests that applicants are not faking.[94] Even though research does not clearly show applicants intentionally distort responses, it may be best to approach personality testing as if applicants do fake. A recent study of applicant practices suggests at least some applicants attempt to intentionally distort perceptions of their characteristics and traits. This study found approximately 30 percent of entry-level applicants report faking on selection tests, which presumably would include personality inventories.[95] Thus, it appears that at least some applicants do fake, with estimates ranging from 0 to 50 percent.[96] One implication of this is that if an HR practitioner is considering adopting a personality test, if the use of the test is validated with current employees (a concurrent research design), it would be a very good idea to compare the mean scores from the current employee sample to later mean scores under applicant conditions. To the extent the two means significantly differ, there would be evidence that applicants are exaggerating when answering the personality test.

What are the implications if candidates do fake? A number of studies in organizational settings have found little evidence that such faking affects the predictive validity of personality inventories.[97] Instead, these researchers have concluded that distortion does not significantly alter validity coefficients and, in fact, may relate to real personality differences among individuals that, in turn, may predict retention and performance. A recent study illustrates that even when all those who are faking are removed, mean performance will increase by only about 0.1 SD.[98] Thus, instead of worrying about faking, these results imply that a selection expert should focus on selecting the test with the highest predictive validity.

Faking may make decisions about *individual* applicants incorrect, however, as applicants who do distort may be hired at the expense of those who do not fake. There is evidence that some (honest) applicants are harmed by those who fake and that this effect is greatest when only a small proportion of applicants are selected (for example, when less than one applicant out of five is hired).[99]

These findings have encouraged researchers to consider ways to reduce the effects of faking. Research suggests that instructions should include a warning that faking may be detected or technology may be harnessed by using computer-based administrations to monitor response latencies (fakers take longer to answer) and eye-tracking technology to monitor eye movement (fakers are "shifty") or to identify and warn those who appear to be faking early on during the testing period.[100] A recent review of the literature found that warnings not to fake can reduce faking by 0.23 SD.[101] While not having a large impact, warning instructions can reduce applicant scores, particularly if the warning includes a description of the potential consequences of intentionally distorting one's answers. Because this is an inexpensive solution, it is recommended that selection experts include instructions warning test-takers about the consequences of faking.

Statistical techniques have been developed to correct for distortion in responses. In one approach, regression is used to account for the effect of response distortion in personality responses. The "corrected" score is assumed to be free of contamination from faking. The second approach is to eliminate applicants who have extremely high scores on scales that are constructed to detect lying. People with scores in the top 2.5 or 5 percent on these lie scales are eliminated from the pool, based on the assumption that if they are lying on these items, they also will lie on the other questions. Research shows these corrections do not affect the predictive validity of the instrument. It has been found that even though a correction for distortion may not affect validity coefficients, it may result in different individuals being selected than those who would have been selected on the basis of uncorrected scores. This is because validity coefficients refer to the whole sample of applicants. Correction formulas or the elimination of candidates with high scores on the lie scale change individual scores, but they do not change all scores by the same amount. In fact, applying correction formulas fails to produce a corrected score that accurately reflects the score achieved by the individual who is not instructed to fake responses.[102] It seems quite clear that statistical correction techniques do not affect the estimated validity of an instrument. However, they do adjust individual scores. Because an applicant's score after correction is not more strongly related to performance, it is not advisable to base selection decisions on these corrected scores.

It is obvious that one important concern with using personality tests is that employers do not want to hire applicants who lie. Of course, one person's "white lie" might be another's attempt to make a positive impression on others. And furthermore, the tendency to actively manage how others regard us is natural. After all, people do like strangers to think well of them. As noted previously, the evidence that personality scores are changed so dramatically that the firm hires more dishonest candidates is mixed and, on average, suggests they do not. To compound this challenge, however, concerns about dissimulation are not limited solely to personality tests, as faking is also an issue for biographical data measures and job application blanks (see Chapter 9), employment interviews (see Chapter 10), situational judgment tests and assessment centers (see Chapter 13), and integrity tests (see Chapter 14).[103] An effective selection approach should include multiple selection methods, some that are susceptible to faking and some that are not.

Finally, self-reports may be less accurate than we anticipate for reasons other than faking. For example, people actually may give "aspirational" answers to the personality items. When asked whether the candidate likes to lead and influence others, the person may answer, "yes, I always have the intention of being leaderlike," even if their actual level of leadership behavior is only modest. Relatedly, there is also value in examining the extent to which individuals can accurately assess or even have accurate insight about their own personality. It is possible that some of what appears to be intentional faking is just inadvertent overestimation of one's standing on these personality traits. After all, people tend to be wildly overoptimistic about their own standing on most positive traits; sometimes called the Lake Wobegon effect, "Lake Wobegon, where all the children are above average."[104]

Role of Technology and Global Trends

Rapid changes in computer technology and Web-based assessments continue to provide greater efficiency in testing; offer access to a larger, more diverse applicant pool; and even provide more precise measurement of constructs, through application of item-response theory.[105] Research has shown that Web-based personality tests result in high levels of internal consistency, as evidence shows the scores are equivalent to paper-and-pencil personality scores and have similar correlations between items. This is important because the degree of standardization (or control) over the administration of the exam often is lower when using a Web-based test. Evidence of test equivalence is critical because it suggests the same predictive relationships found for paper-based tests with work-related criteria will exist for computer-based tests.[106] Furthermore, there is even some evidence of equivalence between proctored and unproctored administrations.[107] This finding is noteworthy because of the enhanced possibility of response distortion (faking) if not outright cheating on unproctored personality tests. A relatively common approach to dealing with this problem is to use the unproctored exam results as an early screen and to warn respondents that scores will be verified later by having a smaller group of examinees retake the exam in a proctored setting.[108] Nevertheless, unproctored tests, because they fail to maintain standardization of testing conditions, likely violate common professional testing standards, although this issue is hotly debated currently in the literature.[109] Consequently, we recommend at present that Web-based personality assessments be supervised and proctored to maximize the standardization of assessment procedures (for example, instructions, length of time allowed, retesting opportunities, and so on). Finally, the selection decision should not be based solely on Web-based test results. Instead, it is probably best suited as an initial screen.

Clearly, the impact of technology on personality testing, like all testing, will see future innovations in the application of testing that will create many opportunities and challenges for employers. HR professionals must closely monitor those innovations and adapt testing procedures in ways that will ensure a core set of measurement principles so that employers can continue to infer that the test scores accurately reflect the candidate's actual personality profile. Practitioners must also monitor EEOC implications, to ensure that Internet access is equally accessible and the quality of that access is comparable across different EEO groups to avoid inadvertent disparate impact.

The use of personality has been on the increase globally, as well as in the United States. A review of prior surveys of the use of this practice in various countries indicates increased usage, particularly in Norway, Spain, Belgium, South Africa, New Zealand, and the United Kingdom.[110] Responses to personality tests do seem to be influenced by cultural norms, as there are differences in scores across cultural groups resulting from different response tendencies, such as acquiescence, avoidance of or preference for extreme scores, and modesty or self-enhancing response biases, even real differences due to construct nonequivalence across cultures.[111] What this means is that to interpret test scores (is the score high or low?), be sure to compare the score to norms based on a cluster of countries that are culturally similar and confirm that intercorrelations among traits and other constructs are comparable across different testing methods for these cultural clusters of countries. Additionally, at least two personality tests have been used extensively in cross-cultural contexts: (a) the Occupational Personal Questionnaire, which has 32 facets that can be organized into the Five-Factor Model; and (b) the Global Personality Inventory, with 30 facets that can be mapped onto the Five-Factor Model.[112] We are not suggesting there is a global personality, even though the Five-Factor Model has been captured in all countries and cultures tested. Instead, note that personality tests are used across the globe, some have even been developed using multiple cross-cultural samples, and that with attention to local culture-based norms, scores from those tests can be effectively used to predict retaining productive workers.

RECOMMENDATIONS FOR THE USE OF PERSONALITY DATA

We started this chapter with a discussion about the apparent disagreement about the utility of using personality data in selection programs. Ample evidence indicates that personality should be a worker characteristic related to performance in many jobs. This type of data conceivably should be as useful in selection decisions as data about the applicants' skills and abilities that have been stressed in other chapters. The magnitude of the predictive validities with job performance when using personality data, however, is not as high as we would like. A possible explanation of this is that the methods or traits focused on during personality assessment in selection are inadequate. The major focus of the chapter, therefore, has been on the definition and measurement methods of personality assessment. Because personality psychologists have studied these topics in much more depth than HR specialists have, much of the information in this chapter has been drawn from psychology. Thus, it is possible to draw some conclusions that should be useful to selection specialists.

Define Personality Traits in Terms of Job Behaviors

Of fundamental importance is the definition of which personality characteristic should be used in a selection program. We are reminded of the saying, "If you don't know where you are going, any way will take you there." As mentioned, the definition of important worker attributes is necessary for all selection measures; however, the lack of a definition seems to be more common with personality measurement than with other types of worker attributes.

This lack of definition usually takes one of two forms. In the first, a personality instrument is used without much attention being paid to the specific traits being measured. The instrument is used because someone vouches for its effectiveness, or even because it has been used in previous selection work. Such reasons are not proper justification for use. As we have said, it is necessary to have a job-related basis for whatever WRCs are measured in selection. Personality characteristics should be thought of as another type of WRC.

The second form this lack of definition takes is the use of generalized statements to describe personality traits—for example, "a manager that fits in well with our staff" or a "salesperson who has a good personality." Given this impreciseness, it is unlikely that different selection specialists would agree about which particular personality traits should be evaluated. Even if only one specialist is involved, there is little assurance that the personality traits evaluated are, in fact, the appropriate ones.

Job analysis information could supply information to generate adequate definitions in two way. The first is through the task approach described in Chapter 3. If this approach is carried out completely, it should yield information about job tasks, interaction patterns between the incumbent and others, working conditions, equipment used, and work patterns. From these data, an HR specialist should be able to infer personality traits in much the same way that other WRCs are inferred. That is, for example, traits such as "control of stress caused by steady demands of users for quick answers to programming difficulties" and "diligence in review of details of complex programs" could be identified for a computer programmer's job. The second is by means of those job analysis methods that directly produce worker attributes, some of which are personality dimensions. One such method is the Position Analysis Questionnaire, which measures "attributes of an interest or temperament nature," that we presented in Chapter 3. Included in these attributes were *working alone, pressure of time, empathy, influencing people*, and so on. Another method is the Personality-Related Position Requirements Form (PPRF) that has been developed to directly identify the personality dimensions necessary for job performance.[113] The PPRF consists of 136 items that measure 12 personality dimensions. These dimensions, in turn, can be grouped into the Five-Factor Model traits. Job incumbents complete the questionnaire; analyses of their responses produce scores on these 12 dimensions. These scores indicate how much of each of the 12 personality dimensions—or of the broader Five-Factor Model traits—is associated with job performance.

Define Work Effectiveness as Retaining Productive Employees

To decide which personality traits to assess, the HR manager must first understand what is meant by effective employee performance. As we noted in Chapter 2, task-related performance historically was *the* key and often the only consideration during selection. Over the past decade, there has been a recognition that work effectiveness is composed of more than just task-related performance.[114] As a result, we now recognize organizations want employees who also can be good citizens, are proactive and willing to change, and avoid counterproductive work behaviors, including workplace aggression, theft, and voluntarily quitting.

The answer to the question, "What am I predicting" is critical because it shapes which personality traits should be measured during selection. As discussed in Chapter 2, we now appreciate it is possible to identify and predict a broad overall work effectiveness criterion *at hire*, but only if we simultaneously consider those WRCs that predict retaining employees who are also highly productive. To do this, we have argued that our predictors need to be comparably broad to the overall work effectiveness measure and each personality trait should be psychologically meaningful yet capture the general factor common to the many diverse facets of that trait. Furthermore, to maximize the contribution of each personality trait assessed vis-à-vis all the other WRCs we are trying to assess (the applicant's cognitive ability, job related knowledge and experience, interpersonal skills, and so on), we generally need to focus on a small set of predictors to ensure significant gains in incremental validity.[115]

Our recommendation is to focus on the Five-Factor Model to comprehensively measure an applicant's personality, thereby ensuring adequate incremental predictive validity when selecting those who are most likely to be productive and to remain committed to both the job and firm. Other researchers accurately note that instead of using the broad Five-Factor Model traits, an advantage of using facets is one can more reliably assess a more specific well-defined aspect of personality (for example, dependability rather than conscientiousness). In turn, these more precise traits are better predictors of more specific performance measures, such as who is able to do the task well or is likely to exhibit good citizenship or even practice more safety behavior at work (but not all three simultaneously). As noted earlier, Tim Judge and colleagues have compellingly demonstrated that 10 facets predicted task performance better than the five factors and that 30 facets predicted it even better.[116] Given this finding, if the HR manager wants to make a selection decision on just one specific criterion, even one as important as task performance, these results convincingly illustrate one should use facets of personality rather than the Five-Factor Model. However, to predict an aggregate measure of all the critical work effectiveness criteria simultaneously, including task and adaptive performance, and good citizenship, with a reduction in absenteeism, counterproductive behavior, and turnover, Ning Li and associates revealed the need to rely, instead, on an equally broad and comprehensive measure of personality—that is, the Five-Factor Model.[117]

Relevance of the Work Context

Behavior is the result of a person's personality and the situation.[118] Neither personality nor the situation will determine behavior in all cases; rather, each exerts an influence on behavior and their relative influence differs depending on the circumstances. Thus, extraverted people talk more than shy people. However, even highly extraverted people can be quiet when the situation demands, such as at a funeral. This example shows that personality traits interact with the situation to predict behavior. This is a critical concept; it clarifies that whether specific personality traits matter in selection depends on the relevance of the work context. In other words, when the behaviors linked to specific traits are relevant to the situation or are required for high performance, those personality traits matter. Extending the previous example to a work setting, extraverts enjoy interacting with people and—not surprisingly—tend to be more effective in sales. In this case, the trait of extraversion enables the sales representative to exhibit behaviors, such as more frequently engaging and talking to strangers, which result in higher sales performance. This same trait would not be as important, though, in jobs for which these behaviors are not linked to success. Consequently, personality traits are most relevant in those specific situations that reward the behavior that matches the personality trait.

Robert Tett and Dawn Burnett have developed a model that seeks to explain, by explicitly accounting for the person–situation interaction, when personality effects on work behaviors are most likely to occur.[119] This model proposes that specific personality traits are "activated" in response to specific trait-relevant situational cues. These cues are a function of task, social, and organizational demands in the work setting. To illustrate how the work context cues specific traits, consider the influence of the organizational reward system. Greg Stewart found that whether highly extraverted sales representatives emphasized customer service behavior that was related to adding new members or retaining current customers depended on the pay system. Specifically, he found that when the firm rewarded sales representatives for identifying and adding new members, extraverted sales representatives achieved higher performance related to new sales but not for customer retention. In contrast, when the firm rewarded representatives for contacting and renewing existing members, extraverted sales representatives had higher performance related to customer retention with no change in new sales.[120] In both cases, the "nonrewarded" behavior, whether it was adding new clients or retaining current customers, did not increase; this suggests that extraverted people are quite sensitive to situational cues. These results reveal that personality traits have the greatest influence on performance when traits lead to or are aligned with the specific behaviors associated with high performance and when those behaviors are elicited by the situational cues or demands of the work environment.

Research suggests that personality may be less important for technical jobs and more important for nontechnical jobs.[121] Similarly, jobs that are routine in terms of work behaviors would seem to be less related to personality than those jobs that are unstructured and involve more discretionary behavior.[122] This is just another way of saying that for some jobs, it appears that the application of knowledge and predetermined ways of doing things is critical for successful job performance. For these jobs, cognitively based WRCs would seem to be more important for selection than personality traits. Yet, even for these jobs, who wouldn't want to hire a hardworking, dependable candidate who will show up for work every day (be conscientious), approach work with confidence, and possess a general sense of well-being, which enables them to manage anxiety and stress effectively (be able to demonstrate emotional stability or core self-evaluation)? Because personality is a dispositional predictor of motivation, personality matters at work, even in technical or highly structured jobs.

Other jobs rely less on specific knowledge or predetermined procedures and have a number of acceptable ways for producing desired performance. It is for these jobs that personality is even more clearly related to job performance. Thus, more traits than just the two universal predictors (conscientiousness and emotional stability) will be relevant for success, depending on the specific work context. For example, if the job requires considerable teamwork or customer service, agreeableness or possibly even emotional intelligence will be more important. Conversely, if the job requires negotiating or influencing others, extraversion will be more relevant. If, on the other hand, the job requires creativity and involves considerable uncertainty, we expect that openness to new experiences or proactive personality also would predict task performance. Such results underscore the importance of considering the nature of the job under consideration when making a decision about whether to use personality measures in the selection program.

Over the past two decades, work has been dramatically changing, whether due to changes in information technology or to offshoring or outsourcing work. This has important implications for the use of personality in selection. One implication is that jobs will change more rapidly and become less structured—implying that personality will increasingly predict work behaviors since it influences work motivation and willingness to change. Another implication is that work will continue to become even more knowledge based or information intensive. This not only enhances the importance of cognitive ability but also relates to personality; specific traits (for example, extraversion and openness to experience) can predict employee success in (continuous) training and identify those applicants who will be more motivated and more committed (that is, conscientious and emotionally stable) to the organization. Third, as organizations continue to eliminate layers of management, they increasingly rely on the use of teams to coordinate work efforts. In general, personality predicts success even better in team settings, and a few traits emerge as particularly important: agreeableness, extraversion (in some settings), and emotional intelligence. Thus, the changing nature of work is likely to increase the importance of personality as a predictor of performance in most selection decisions.

The Appropriateness of the Selection Instrument

The instruments discussed or listed in Table 12.4 are only part of a very large number of self-report personality inventories used in selection. Many of them, such as *Edward's Personal Preference Schedule*, the *California F Scale*, and the *Thurstone Temperament Schedule*, are products of extensive pretesting and developmental work.

From our previous discussion, it should be clear that two important characteristics of the personality selection measure should be considered. The first, as just discussed, is the breadth of the personality trait being measured. Our conclusion is that it seems to be more effective in selection to use traits that affect a wide set of behaviors simultaneously rather than a narrow set. That is, hire the "whole person" to do the "whole job."

Our recommendation is to only use those tests with enough developmental information available to show that the instrument actually measures those personality traits it is said to assess. This, of course, means that data should be provided regarding the reliability, item statistics, and construct-oriented evidence for each of the scales measuring a personality dimension. Given the extreme difficulty in constructing personality instruments, it would be foolhardy to use any personality device in selection that does not have supporting information. Without supporting data, an instrument really can be considered only a theory of the writer. The value of such an instrument therefore would be unknown and undocumented. We stress this point because numerous instruments of this type are being sold to organizations for managerial and executive selection. Often these instruments are quite costly but useless.

The second important characteristic of a personality instrument in selection is whether respondents can learn "correct" responses to the instrument. This topic was part of our discussion about ambiguous measuring devices. It is our opinion that instruments for which appropriate responses are not apparent are preferable to those for which answers are apparent. We mentioned such limitations with regard to the interview (as it is commonly used) and with regard to many self-report personality inventories. We see this with the emergence of forced-choice personality inventories, which force applicants to choose between two to four equally attractive alternatives (option a: "I am open to new experiences"; option b: "I am friendly towards others"; option c: "I am highly extraverted"), where only one of the choices are relevant to success in the job (option a for architects; option b for customer relations).

As this discussion highlights, there are a number of methodological challenges to measuring personality in a high-stakes selection setting. Although these are complex issues, we will try to summarize the key measurement findings in the next section.

Source of Measurement

Observer ratings of personality have been shown to predict performance better than self-reports. Consequently, there is considerable value to considering ways to assess personality in either the interview, through letters of reference, possibly even through headhunters, who talk to former associates.

Incremental Validity over Other Selection Measures

Low correlations among various predictors reduce the extent of overlap or redundant information on WRCs being assessed and thus result in incremental gains in predictive validity when combining multiple predictors. Personality has been shown to have low correlations with cognitive ability, interviews, biodata scores, and assessment centers. Therefore, superior prediction results when personality is combined with these other predictors during selection.

Trade-offs between Validity and Disparate Impact

Personality, particularly when assessed at the Five-Factor level, has few consistently large differences in mean scores across subgroups by race, color, national origin, religion, age, or sex, although there are a few consistent, modest differences for the last two groups. For example, women tend to be 0.20 SD higher on conscientiousness, but 0.20 SD lower on emotional stability; similarly, we tend to get nicer, more conscientious, and emotionally stable with age. Because of the reduced likelihood of finding disparate impact when using personality tests, Gerald Barrett has indicated that the U.S. Department of Justice and plaintiffs' lawyers often advocate these tests should be used instead of tests of cognitive ability, which may have higher disparate impact.[123] As so often happens with selection, however, it is not necessarily the case that combining a predictor with lower disparate impact to a predictor with higher disparate impact will actually lower disparate impact overall. Statistically, it is even possible disparate impact would increase. For these reasons, practitioners should continue to examine mean score differences between different subgroups of applicants to ensure disparate impact is, in fact, reduced.

Faking "Good" during Selection

Organizations do not want to hire applicants who would not have been hired if not for "faking good" on the personality test. Yet, people routinely put their "best foot forward," whether it is on a first date, having dinner with the chief executive, or even during an employment interview. Obviously, this is going to occur when responding to a personality test too. The question researchers continue to hotly debate is whether some applicants intentionally distort their answers so much that it leads to hiring dishonest candidates. We cannot resolve this here. What we do know is that "faking good" does not substantially alter predictive validity. Some argue that it actually may provide a way to identify more socially competent candidates, as those who can figure out how to present themselves more favorably on the personality test are also able to figure out what to do on the job. Using this argument, a candidate who fakes good on the personality test also may be able to figure out how to overcome a customer's objections to buying the product. We do know that including warnings in the instructions that faking on the personality test can be detected, and may require retesting, tends to discourage faking. Warnings work.

Cheating during Selection

The Internet has created a revolution in testing procedures, as it provides for more efficient testing more cheaply. We recommend such tests be proctored to enhance standardization of the testing procedures as well as to ensure test security.

Using "At-Work" Personality Tests

Contextualizing personality items so that they encourage the test-taker to think about their behavior "at work" has been found to lead to superior predictive validity. Linking responses through at-work items is a simple modification that leads to significant gains in predictive validity.

Realizing Prediction Gains over Time

The stability of personality through adulthood, especially from 30 to 55 years of age, underscores that careful selection can realize significant gains in work effectiveness for years. One study showed that those individuals with higher scores on conscientiousness, emotional stability, openness to experience, and agreeableness in high school were significantly correlated with higher performance from that person year after year up to 50 years later. The finding that hiring candidates based on their personality "as is," due to the stability of personality, can lead to substantial long-term gains for both the individual and the organization powerfully reveals the value of using personality to ensure effective selection.

CONCLUSIONS

We have introduced much information from the field of personality psychology and have drawn implications from this work for the use of personality in organizations. We have done this because simply administering personality instruments to applicants and attempting to relate the scores on these to job performance is not a worthwhile strategy. Instead, the appropriate use of personality data calls for understanding three important findings in personality research. First is the observation that traits vary greatly in the extent to which they influence behavior. A seemingly small number of core traits have a strong influence on behavior when aggregated over many instances of that behavior. A larger number of narrower facets of these traits will achieve higher predictive validity, but only for relatively limited or more precise (albeit critical) outcomes (for example, just task performance rather than retaining productive employees). The second major observation is that the situation also has an important influence on an individual's behavior. Although two of the Five-Factor Model's personality traits, conscientiousness and emotional stability, are relevant to work performance in nearly all jobs, other personality traits predict valued behaviors at work only in relevant situations or for specific criteria. The third observation is that measuring personality is challenging. Steps must be taken to reduce "faking good" or cheating on Web-based assessments. These observations offer a partial explanation for the lack of uniform positive findings in the use of personality data for selection. Yet, the payoff can be higher predictive validity, particularly when observer ratings are used, with significant incremental gains in validity and reduced disparate impact when combined with other predictors.[124]

REFERENCES

1. Murray R. Barrick, Michael K. Mount, and Timothy A. Judge, "The FFM Personality Dimensions and Job Performance: Meta-Analysis of Meta-Analyses," *International Journal of Selection and Assessment* 9 (2001): 9–30.

2. SHRM Practitioner Survey of Selection practices, 2005; *Wall Street Journal*, page A1 and page A12. September 30, 2014.

3. Matthew Heller, "Court Ruling That Employer's Integrity Test Violated ADA Could Open Door to Litigation," *Workforce Management* 84, no. 9 (2005): 74–77; Paul B. Erickson, "Employer Hiring Tests Grow Sophisticated in Quest for Insight about Applicants," *Knight Ridder Tribune Business News* (May 16, 2004): 1.

4. Ann Marie Ryan, Lynn McFarland, Helen Baron, and Ron Page, "An International Look at Selection Practices: Nation and Culture as Explanations for Variability in Practice," *Personnel Psychology* 52 (1999): 359–401.

5. Robert M. Guion and Richard F. Gottier, "Validity of personality measures in personnel selection." *Personnel Psychology* 18, no. 2 (1965): 135–164; Walter Mischel, *Personality and Assessment* (New York: Wiley, 1968).

6. John P. Campbell, "An Overview of the Army Selection and Classification Project (Project A)," *Personnel Psychology* 43, no. 2 (1990): 231–239.

7. Brent W. Roberts, Nathan R. Kuncel, Rebecca Shiner, Avshalom Caspi, and Lewis R. Goldberg, "The Power of Personality: The Comparative Validity of Personality Traits, Socioeconomic Status, and Cognitive Ability for Predicting Important Life Outcomes," *Perspectives on Psychological Science* 2 (2007): 313–345.

8. Murray R. Barrick and Michael K. Mount. "The Big Five Personality Dimensions and Job Performance: A Meta-Analysis," *Personnel Psychology* 44, no. 1 (1991): 1–26.; Leatta M. Hough, Newell K. Eaton, Marvin D. Dunnette, John D. Kamp, and Rodney A. McCloy, "Criterion-Related Validities of Personality Constructs and the Effect of Response Distortion on Those Validities," *Journal of Applied Psychology* 75, no. 5 (1990): 581–595; Robert P. Tett, Douglas N. Jackson, and Mitchell Rothstein, "Personality Measures as Predictors of Job Performance: A Meta-Analytic Review." *Personnel Psychology* 44, no. 4 (1991): 703–742.

9. Jesus F. Salgado, "The Five Factor Model of Personality and Job Performance in the European Community," *Journal of Applied psychology* 82, no. 1 (1997): 30; Tett, Jackson, and Rothstein, "Personality Measures as Predictors of Job Performance."

10. Walter Mischel, *Introduction to Personality*, 3rd ed. (New York: CBS College Publishing, 1981), 2.

11. Ning Li, Murray R. Barrick, Ryan D. Zimmerman, and Dan S. Chiaburu, "Retaining the Productive Employee: The Role of Personality," *The Academy of Management Annals* 8 (2014): 347–395.

12. Murray R. Barrick and Michael K. Mount, "Yes, Personality Matters: Moving on to More Important Matters," *Human Performance* 18 (2005): 359–372; Barrick, Mount, and Judge, "The FFM Personality Dimensions and Job Performance: Meta-Analysis of Meta-Analyses"; M. K. Mount, M. R. Barrick, & G. L. Stewart, "Personality Predictors of Performance in Jobs Involving Interaction with Others," *Human Performance* 11 (1998): 145–166.

13. Robert M. Guion and Richard F. Gottier, "Validity of Personality Measures in Personnel Selection," *Personnel Psychology* 18 (1966): 135–164.

14. Frederick P. Morgeson, Michael A. Campion, Robert L. Dipboye, John R. Hollenbeck, Kevin Murphy, and Neal Schmitt, "Reconsidering the Use of Personality Tests in Personnel Selection Contexts," *Personnel Psychology* 60 (2007): 683–729; Kevin R. Murphy and Jessica L. Dzieweczynski, "Why Don't Measures of Broad Dimensions of Personality Perform Better as Predictors of Job Performance?" *Human Performance* 18 (2005): 343–357.

15. Barrick and Mount, "Yes, Personality Matters: Moving on to More Important Matters"; Deniz S. Ones, Stephan Dilchert, Chockalingam Viswesvaran, and Timothy A. Judge, "In Support of Personality Assessment in Organizational Settings," *Personnel Psychology* 60 (2007): 995–1027.

16. Wendy Dunn, Michael K. Mount, Murray R. Barrick, and Deniz S. Ones, "The Five Factor Personality Dimensions, General Mental Ability, and Perceptions of Employment Suitability," *Journal of Applied Psychology* 80 (1995): 500–509.

17. Barrick, Mount, and Judge, "The FFM Personality Dimensions and Job Performance: Meta-Analysis of Meta-Analyses."

18. Li, Barrick, Zimmerman, and Chiaburu, "Retaining the Productive Employee: The Role of Personality"; Fred L. Oswald and Leatta Hough, "Personality and Its Assessment: Measurement, Validity, and Modeling," in *APA Handbook of Industrial and Psychology*, vol. 2, chapter 5 (in press); Deniz S. Ones, S. Dilchert, C. Vishwesvaran, and T. A. Judge, "In Support of Personality Assessment in Organizational Settings," *Personnel Psychology* 60 (2007): 995–1027.

19. Oswald and Hough, "Personality and Its Assessment: Measurement, Validity, and Modeling"; Paul R. Sackett and Filip Lievens, "Personnel Selection," *Annual Review of Psychology* 59 (2008): 1–16.

20. Oswald and Hough, "Personality and Its Assessment: Measurement, Validity, and Modeling."

21. Timothy A. Judge, Chad A. Higgins, Carl J. Thoresen, and Murray R. Barrick, "The Five Factor Personality Traits, General Mental Ability, and Career Success across the Life Span," *Personnel Psychology* 52 (1999): 621–652.

22. Oliver Lüdtke, Brent W. Roberts, Ulrich Trautwein, and Gabriel Nagy, "A Random Walk Down University Avenue: Life Paths, Life Events, and Personality Trait Change at the Transition to University Life," *Journal of Personality and Social Psychology* 101 (2011): 620–633; Brent W. Roberts, Dustin Wood, and Avshalom Caspi, "The Development of Personality Traits in Adulthood," in *Handbook of Personality: Theory and Research*, vol. 3 (2008), 375–398; Brent W. Roberts, Kate E. Walton, and Wolfgang Viechtbauer, "Patterns of Mean-Level Change in Personality Traits across the Life Course: A Meta-Analysis of Longitudinal Studies," *Psychological Bulletin* 132 (2006): 1.

23. Mischel, *Introduction to Personality*, 18.

24. James J. Conley, "The Hierarchy of Consistency: A Review and Model of Longitudinal Findings on Adult Individual Differences in Intelligence, Personality, and Self-Opinion," *Personality Individual Differences* 5 (1984): 11–25; Roberts, Wood, and Caspi, "The Development of Personality Traits in Adulthood."

25. Robert Hogan, "In Defense of Personality Measurement: New Wine for Old Whiners," *Human Performance* 18 (2005): 331–342; Mischel, *Introduction to Personality*, 18.

26. John M. Digman and Jillian Inouye, "Further Specification of the Five Robust Factors of Personality," *Journal of Personality and Social Psychology* 50 (1986): 116–123; Barrick, Mount, and Judge, "The FFM Personality Dimensions and Job Performance: Meta-Analysis of Meta-Analyses."

27. Gerard Saucier and Lewis Goldberg, "The Structure of Personality Attributes," in *Personality and Work: Reconsidering the Role of Personality in Organizations*, ed. Murray R. Barrick and Ann Marie Ryan (San Francisco: Jossey-Bass, 2003), 1–29; Murray R. Barrick, Terrence R. Mitchell, and Greg L. Stewart, "Situational and Motivational Influences on Trait-Behavior Relationships," in *Personality and Work: Reconsidering the Role of Personality in Organizations*, ed. Murray R. Barrick and Ann Marie Ryan (San Francisco: Jossey-Bass, 2003), 60–82.

28. Saucier and Goldberg, "The Structure of Personality Attributes."

29. R. R. McCrae and P. T. Costa Jr., "Updating Norman's 'Adequate Taxonomy': Intelligence and Personality Dimensions in Natural Language and in Questionnaires," *Journal of Personality and Social Psychology* 49 (1985): 710–721. See also W. T. Norman, "Toward an Adequate Taxonomy of Personality Attributes: Replicated Factor Structure in Peer Nomination Personality Ratings," *Journal of Abnormal and Social Psychology* 66 (1963): 574–583; Saucier and Goldberg, "The Structure of Personality Attributes."

30. Timothy A. Judge, Jessica B. Rodell, Ryan L. Klinger, Lauren S. Simon, and Eean R. Crawford, "Hierarchical Representations of the Five-Factor Model of Personality in

Predicting Job Performance: Integrating Three Organizing Frameworks with Two Theoretical Perspectives," *Journal of Applied Psychology* 98 (2013): 875–925.

31. Li, Barrick, Zimmerman, and Chiaburu, "Retaining the Productive Employee: The Role of Personality."

32. Barrick, Mount, and Judge, "The FFM Personality Dimensions and Job Performance: Meta-Analysis of Meta-Analyses."

33. Paul T. Costa and Robert R. McCrae, "Neo PI-R Professional Manual" (1992); William Revelle, "Extraversion and Impulsivity: The Lost Dimension?" *The scientific Study of Human Nature: Tribute to Hans J. Eysenck at Eighty* (1997): 189–212; Roberts, Wood, and Caspi, "The Development of Personality Traits in Adulthood."

34. Barrick, Mitchell, and Stewart, "Situational and Motivational Influences on Trait-Behavior Relationships"; Li, Barrick, Zimmerman, and Chiaburu. "Retaining the Productive Employee: The Role of Personality."

35. Timothy A. Judge, Annelies E. M. van Vianen, and Irebe E. de Pater, "Emotional Stability, Core Self-Evaluations, and Job Outcomes: A Review of the Evidence and an Agenda for the Future Research," *Human Performance* 17 (2004): 325–346; Timothy A. Judge and Joyce E. Bono, "Relationship of Core Self-Evaluation Traits—Self-Esteem, Generalized Self-Efficacy, Locus of Control, and Emotional Stability—with Job Satisfaction and Job Performance: A Meta-Analysis," *Journal of Applied Psychology* 86 (2001): 80–92; Timothy A. Judge, Edwin A. Locke, Cathy C. Durham, and Avraham N. Kluger, "Dispositional Effects on Job and Life Satisfaction: The Role of Core Evaluations," *Journal of Applied Psychology* 83 (1998): 17–34.

36. Kenneth S. Law, Chi-Sum Wong, and Lynda J. Song, "Construct and Criterion Validity of Emotional Intelligence and Its Potential Utility for Management Studies," *Journal of Applied Psychology* 89 (2004): 483–496; Dana L. Joseph and Daniel A. Newman. "Emotional Intelligence: An Integrative Meta-Analysis and Cascading Model," *Journal of Applied Psychology* 95 (2010): 54–78; David L. van Roy and Chockalingham Viswesvaran, "Emotional Intelligence: A Meta-Analytic Investigation of Predictive Validity and Nomological Net," *Journal of Vocational Behavior* 65 (2004): 71–95.

37. Gerald Matthew, Moshe Zeidner, and Richard D. Roberts, *Emotional Intelligence: Science and Myth* (Cambridge, MA: MIT Press, 2002), 542.

38. Scott E. Seibert, Michael J. Crant, and Maria L. Kramer, "Proactive Personality and Career Success," *Journal of Applied Psychology* 84 (1999): 416–427; Scott E. Seibert, Maria L. Kramer, and Michael J. Crant, "What Do Proactive People Do? A Longitudinal Model Linking Proactive Personality and Career Success," *Personnel Psychology* 54 (2001): 845–874; Michael J. Crant and Thomas S. Bateman, "Charismatic Leadership Viewed from Above: The Impact of Proactive Personality," *Journal of Organizational Behavior* 21 (2000): 63–75; Michael J. Crant, "The Proactive Personality Scale as a Predictor of Entrepreneurial Intentions," *Journal of Small Business Management* 34 (1996): 42–49; Jeffrey A. Thompson, "Proactive Personality and Job Performance: A Social Capital Perspective," *Journal of Applied Psychology* 90 (2005): 1011–1017; Michael J. Crant, "The Proactive Personality Scale and Objective Job Performance among Real Estate Agents," *Journal of Applied Psychology* 80 (1995): 532–537.

39. Thomas S. Bateman and Michael J. Crant, "The Proactive Component of Organizational Behavior: A Measure and Correlates," *Journal of Organizational Behavior* 14 (1993): 103–118; Crant, "The Proactive Personality Scale and Objective Job Performance among Real Estate Agents"; Crant and Bateman, "Charismatic Leadership Viewed from Above: The Impact of Proactive Personality."

40. Michael K. Mount, Murray R. Barrick, and J. Perkins Strauss, "Validity of Observer Ratings of the Five Factor Personality Factors," *Journal of Applied Psychology* 79 (1994): 272–280.

41. Judge, Higgins, Thoreson, and Barrick, "The Five Factor Personality Traits, General Mental Ability, and Career Success across the Life Span."

42. Jonathan A. Shaffer and Bennett E. Postlethwaite, "A Matter of Context: A Meta-Analytic Investigation of the Relative Validity of Contextualized and Noncontextualized Personality Measures," *Personnel Psychology* 65 (2012): 445–494.

43. Barrick, Mount, and Judge, "The FFM Personality Dimensions and Job Performance: Meta-Analysis of Meta-Analyses."

44. Janis S. Houston, Walter C. Borman, William F. Farmer, and Ronald M. Bearden, "Development of the Navy Computer Adaptive Personality Scales" (NCAPS) (NPRST-TR-06-2) (Millington, TN: Navy Personnel, Research, Studies, and Technology, 2006); Deirde J. Knapp, Eric D. Heggestad, and Mark C. Young, "Understanding and Improving the Assessment of Individual Motivation (AIM) in the Army's GED Plus Program (ARI Study note 2004-03) (Alexandria, VA: U.S. Army Research Institute for the Behavioral and Social Sciences, 2004); Houston, Borman, Farmer, and Bearden, "Development of the Navy Computer Adaptive Personality Scales"; Oleksandr S. Chernyshenko, Stephen Stark, Matthew S. Prewett, Ashley A. Gray, Frederick R. Stilson, and Matthew D. Tuttle, "Normative Scoring of Multidimensional Pairwise Preference Personality Scales Using IRT: Empirical Comparison with Other Formats," *Human Performance* 22 (2009): 105–127.

45. Oswald and Hough, "Personality and Its Assessment: Measurement, Validity, and Modeling."

46. H. Baron, "Strengths and Limitations of Ipsative Measurement," *Journal of Occupational and Organizational Psychology* 69 (1996): 49–56.

47. Mark Sherman, *Personality: Inquiry and Application* (New York: Pergamon Press, 1979), 205; Scott O. Lilienfeld, Jim Wood, and Howard N. Garb, *The Scientific Status of Projective Techniques* (Oxford, England: Blackwell Publishers, 2000).

48. Sherman, *Personality: Inquiry and Application*, 206.

49. David Watson and Lee A. Clark, "Self- versus Peer Ratings of Specific Emotional Traits: Evidence of Convergent and Discriminant Validity," *Journal of Personality and Social Psychology* 60 (1991): 927–940; David C. Funder, "On the Accuracy of Personality Judgement: A Realistic Approach," *Psychological Review* 102 (1995): 652–670.

50. David C. Funder and Stephen G. West, "Consensus, Self-Other Agreement, and Accuracy in Personality Judgment: An Introduction," *Journal of Personality* 61 (1993): 457–476; Robert J. Hogan and David Shelton, "A Socioanalytic Perspective on Job Performance," *Human Performance* 11 (1998): 129–144.

51. Brian S. Connelly and Deniz S. Ones, "An Other Perspective on Personality: Meta-Analytic Integration of Observers' Accuracy and Predictive Validity," *Psychological Bulletin* 136 (2010): 1092–1122; In Sue Oh, Gang Wang, and Michael K. Mount, "Validity of Observer Ratings of the Five-Factor Model of Personality Traits: A Meta-Analysis," *Journal of Applied Psychology* 96 (2011): 762–773.

52. Allen I. Huffcutt, James M. Conway, Philip L. Roth, and Nancy J. Stone, "Identification and Meta-Analytic Assessment of Psychological Constructs Measured in Employment Interviews," *Journal of Applied Psychology* 86 (2001): 897–913.

53. Ibid.

54. Mischel, *Introduction to Personality*, 490.

55. Ibid.

56. Philip L. Roth, Chad H. van Iddekinge, Allen I. Huffcutt, Carl E. Eidson Jr., and Mark J. Schmit, "Personality Saturation in Structured Interviews," *International Journal of Selection and Assessment* 13 (2005): 261–285; Murray R. Barrick, Gregory K. Patton, and

Shanna N. Haugland, "Accuracy of Interviewer Judgments of Job Applicant Personality Traits," *Personnel Psychology* 53 (2000): 925–954.

57. Melinda C. Blackman, "Personality Judgement and Utility of the Unstructured Employment Interview," *Basic and Applied Social Psychology* 24 (2002): 241–250; Melinda C. Blackman and David C. Funder, "Effective Interview Practices for Accurately Assessing Counterproductive Traits," *International Journal of Selection and Assessment* 10 (2002): 109–116; Chad H. van Iddekinge, Patrick H. Raymark, and Phillip L. Roth, "Assessing Personality with a Structured Employment Interview: Construct-Related Validity and Susceptibility to Response Inflation," *Journal of Applied Psychology* 90 (2005): 536–552.

58. Huffcutt, Conway, Roth, and Stone, "Identification and Meta-Analytic Assessment of Psychological Constructs Measured in Employment Interviews."

59. Michael S. Cole, Hubert S. Feild, and William F. Giles, "Using Recruiter Assessments of Applicants' Resume Content to Predict Applicant Mental Ability and Five Factor Personality Dimensions," *International Journal of Selection and Assessment* 11 (2003): 78–92; Jennifer Golbeck, Cristina Robles, and Karen Turner, "Predicting Personality with Social Media," in *CHI'11 Extended Abstracts on Human Factors in Computing Systems* (ACM, 2011), 253–262; Samuel D. Gosling, Sei Jin Ko, Thomas Mannarelli, and Margaret E. Morris, "A Room with a Cue: Personality Judgments Based on Offices and Bedrooms," *Journal of Personality and Social Psychology* 82 (2002): 379.

60. Ryan D. Zimmerman, María del Carmen Triana, and Murray R. Barrick, "Predictive Criterion-Related Validity of Observer-Ratings of Personality and Job-Related Competencies Using Multiple Raters and Multiple Performance Criteria," *Human Performance* 22 (2010): 361–378.

61. Michael J. Benson and John P. Campbell, "To be, or Not to Be, Linear: An Expanded Representation of Personality and Its Relationship to Leadership Performance," *International Journal of Selection and Assessment* 15, no. 2 (2007): 232–249; Adam M. Grant and Barry Schwartz, "Too Much of a Good Thing The Challenge and Opportunity of the Inverted U," *Perspectives on Psychological Science* 6 (2011): 61–76; David M. LaHuis, Nicholas R. Martin, and John M. Avis, "Investigating Nonlinear Conscientiousness-Job Performance Relations for Clerical Employees," *Human Performance* 18, no. 3 (2005): 199–212; Huy Le, In-Sue Oh, Steven B. Robbins, Remus Ilies, Ed Holland, and Paul Westrick, "Too Much of a Good Thing: Curvilinear Relationships between Personality Traits and Job Performance," *Journal of Applied Psychology* 96 (2011): 113–133; "How an Entrepreneur's Passion Can Destroy a Startup," *Wall Street Journal*, August 25, 2014, R1, R2.

62. Barrick, Mount, and Judge, "The FFM Personality Dimensions and Job Performance: Meta-Analysis of Meta-Analyses."

63. Joyce Hogan and Brent Holland, "Using Theory to Evaluate Personality and Job-Performance Relations: A Socioanalytic Perspective," *Journal of Applied Psychology* 88 (2003): 100–112.

64. Ibid.

65. Timothy A. Judge, Joyce E. Bono, Remus Ilies, and Megan W. Gerhardt, "Personality and Leadership: A Qualitative and Quantitative Review," *Journal of Applied Psychology* 87 (2002): 765–780.

66. Michael K. Mount, Murray R. Barrick, and Greg L. Stewart, "Personality Predictors of Performance in Jobs Involving Interaction with Others," *Human Performance* 11 (1998): 145–166.

67. Murray R. Barrick, Greg L. Stewart, Mitch Neubert, and Michael K. Mount, "Relating Member Ability and Personality to Work Team Processes and Team Effectiveness," *Journal of Applied Psychology* 83 (1998): 377–391.

68. Stefen T. Mol, Marise P. Born, Madde E. Willemsen, and Henk T. van der Molen, "Predicting Expatriate Job Performance for Selection Purposes," *Journal of Cross-Cultural Psychology* 36 (2005): 590–620; Margaret A. Shaffer, David A. Harrison, Hal Gregersen, J. Stewart Black, and Lori A. Ferzandi, "You Can Take It with You: Individual Differences and Expatriate Effectiveness," *Journal of Applied Psychology* 91 (2006): 109–125; Hao Zhao and Scott E. Seibert, "The Five Factor Personality Dimensions and Entrepreneurial Status: A Meta-Analytical Review," *Journal of Applied Psychology* 91 (2006): 259–271.

69. Jesus F. Salgado, "The Five Factor Personality Dimensions and Counterproductive Behaviors," *Journal of Selection and Assessment* 10 (2002): 117–125.

70. Salgado, "The Five Factor Personality Dimensions and Counterproductive Behaviors"; Ryan D. Zimmerman, "Understanding the Impact of Personality Traits on Individual Turnover Decisions: A Meta-Analytic Path Model," *Personnel Psychology* 61 (2008): 309–348.

71. Timothy A. Judge, Daniel Heller, and Michael K. Mount, "Five-Factor Model of Personality and Job Satisfaction: A Meta-Analysis," *Journal of Applied Psychology* 87 (2002): 530–541.

72. Timothy A. Judge and Remus Ilies, "Relationship of Personality to Performance Motivation: A Meta-Analytic Review," *Journal of Applied Psychology* 87 (2002): 797–807.

73. Judge, Bono, Ilies, and Gerhardt, "Personality and Leadership: A Qualitative and Quantitative Review"; Judge, Heller, and Mount, "Five-Factor Model of Personality and Job Satisfaction: A Meta-Analysis"; Judge and Ilies, "Relationship of Personality to Performance Motivation: A Meta-Analytic Review"; Oswald and Hough, "Personality and Its Assessment: Measurement, Validity, and Modeling."

74. Zhao and Seibert, "The Five Factor Personality Dimensions and Entrepreneurial Status: A Meta-Analytical Review."

75. Connelly and Ones, "An Other Perspective on Personality: Meta-Analytic Integration of Observers' Accuracy and Predictive Validity"; In Sue Oh, Wang, and Mount, "Validity of Observer Ratings of the Five-Factor Model of Personality: A Meta-analysis."

76. Zimmerman, Triana, and Barrick, "Predictive Criterion-Related Validity of Observer-Ratings of Personality and Job-Related Competencies Using Multiple Raters and Multiple Performance Criteria."

77. Jeff J. McHenry, Leatta M. Hough, Jody L. Toquam, Mary Ann Hanson, and Steven Ashworth, "Project A Validity Results—The Relationship between Predictor and Criterion Domains," *Personnel Psychology* 43 (1990): 335–354; Margaret A. McManus and Mary L. Kelly, "Personality Measures and Biodata: Evidence Regarding Their Incremental Value in the Life Insurance Industry," *Personnel Psychology* 52 (1999): 137–148; Michael K. Mount, Alan Witt, and Murray R. Barrick, "Incremental Validity of Empirically-Keyed Biographical Scales over GMA and the Five Factor Personality Constructs," *Personnel Psychology* 53 (2000): 299–323; Frederick L. Oswald, Neal Schmitt, Brian H. King, Lauren J. Ramsay, and Michael A. Gillespie, "Developing a Biodata Measure and Situational Judgment Inventory as Predictors of College Student Performance," *Journal of Applied Psychology* 89 (2004): 187–207; Jesus F. Salgado and Filip de Fruyt, "Personality in Personnel Selection," in *The Blackwell Handbook of Personnel Selection*, ed. Arne Evers, Neil Anderson, and Olga Voskuijil (Oxford, England: Blackwell Publishers, 2004), 174–198; Frank L. Schmidt and John E. Hunter, "The Validity and Utility of Selection Methods in Personnel Psychology: Practical and Theoretical Implications of 85 Years of Research Findings," *Psychological Bulletin* 124 (1998): 262–274; Jeff Weekley and Robert E. Ployhart, "Situational Judgment: Antecedents and Relationships with Performance," *Human Performance* 18 (2005): 81–104.

78. Richard L. Lanyon and Leonard D. Goodstein, *Personality Assessment*, 2nd ed. (New York: John Wiley, 1982), 144.

79. Ibid., 145.

80. Sherman, *Personality: Inquiry and Application*, 213.

81. John B. Miner, *Motivation to Manage: A Ten-Year Update on the Studies in "Management Education" Research* (Atlanta, GA: Organizational Measurement Systems Press, 1977), 6; Kenneth P. Carson and Debora J. Gilliard, "Construct Validity of the Miner Sentence Completion Scale," Journal of Occupational and Organizational Psychology 66 (1993): 171–175.

82. Hannah J. Foldes, Emily E. Duehr, and Deniz S. Ones, "Group Differences in Personality: Meta-Analyses Comparing Five U.S. Racial Groups," *Personnel Psychology* 61 (2008): 579–616; Leatta Hough, Robert E. Ployhart, and Frederick L. Oswald, "Determinants, Detection and Amelioration of Adverse Impact in Personnel Selection Procedures: Issues, Evidence and Lessons Learned," *International Journal of Selection & Assessment* 9 (2001): 152–170.

83. Foldes, Duehr, and Ones, "Group Differences in Personality"; Hough, Ployhart, and Oswald, "Determinants, Detection and Amelioration of Adverse Impact in Personnel Selection Procedures"; Oswald and Hough, "Personality and Its Assessment: Measurement, Validity, and Modeling."

84. Matthew Heller, "Court Ruling That Employer's Integrity Test Violated ADA Could Open Door to Litigation," *Workforce Management* 84, no. 9 (2005): 74–77; *Wall Street Journal*, September 30, 2014, A1–A12.

85. Jonathan R. Mook, "Personality Testing in Today's Workplace: Avoiding the Legal Pitfalls," *Employee Relations* 22 (1996): 65–88.

86. *Karraker v. Rent-A-Center, Inc.*, 411 F.3d 831 (7th Cir. 2005), Case No. 04-2881.

87. John W. Jones and David W. Arnold, "Protecting the Legal and Appropriate Use of Personality Testing: A Practitioner Perspective," *Industrial and Organizational Psychology* 1, (2008): 296–298.

88. *Karraker v. Rent-A-Center*; Oswald and Hough, "Personality and Its Assessment: Measurement, Validity, and Modeling."

89. *Soroka v. Dayton Hudson*, 18 Cal. App. 4th 1200, 1 Cal. Rptr. 2nd 77 (Cal. App. 1991).

90. Jeff A. Weekley, Robert E. Ployhart, and Crystal M. Harold, "Personality and Situational Judgment Tests across Applicant and Incumbent Settings: An Examination of Validity, Measurement, and Subgroup Differences," *Human Performance* 17 (2004): 433–461; Joseph G. Rosse, Mary D. Stecher, Janice L. Miller, and Robert A. Levin, "The Impact of Response Distortion of Preemployment Personality Testing and Hiring Decisions," *Journal of Applied Psychology* 83 (1998): 634–644.

91. Leatta M. Hough, "Effects of Intentional Distortion in Personality Measurement and Evaluation of Suggested Palliatives," *Human Performance* 11 (1998): 209–244.

92. Jill E. Ellingson, Paul R. Sackett, and Brian S. Connelly, "Personality Assessment Across Selection and Development Contexts: Insights into Response Distortion," *Journal of Applied Psychology* 92 (2007): 386–395; Sackett and Lievens, "Personnel Selection."

93. Judith M. Collins and David H. Gleaves, "Race, Job Applicants, and the Five-Factor Model of Personality: Implications for Black Psychology, Industrial/Organizational Psychology, and the Five-Factor Theory," *Journal of Applied Psychology* 83 (1998): 531–544; Jill E. Ellingson, Paul R. Sackett, and Leatta M. Hough, "Social Desirability Corrections in Personality Measurement: Issues of Applicant Comparison and Construct Validity," *Journal of Applied Psychology* 84 (1999): 155–166; Deniz S. Ones and Chockalingham Vishwesvaran, "Job-Specific Applicant Pools and National Norms for Personality Scales: Implications for Range Restriction Corrections in Validation Research," *Human Performance* 11 (1998): 245–269.

94. Leaetta M. Hough and Frederick L. Oswald, "Personnel Selection: Looking toward the Future—Remembering the Past," *Annual Review of Psychology* 51 (2000): 631–664; Leaetta M. Hough, "Emerging Trends and Needs in Personality Research and Practice: Beyond Main Effects," in *Personality and Work: Reconsidering the Role of Personality in Organizations*, ed. Murray R. Barrick and Ann Marie Ryan (San Francisco: Jossey-Bass, 2003), 289–325.

95. John J. Donovan and Stephen A. Dwight, "Do Warnings Not to Fake Reduce Faking?" *Human Performance* 16 (2003): 1–23; John J. Donovan, Stephen A. Dwight, and Gregory M. Hurtz, "An Assessment of the Prevalence, Severity, and Verifiability of Entry-Level Applicant Faking Using the Randomized Response Technique," *Human Performance* 16 (2003): 81–106.

96. Ellingson, Sackett, and Hough, "Social Desirability Corrections in Personality Measurement: Issues of Applicant Comparison and Construct Validity"; Neal Schmitt and Frederick L. Oswald, "The Impact of Corrections for Faking on the Validity of Noncognitive Measures in Selection Settings," *Journal of Applied Psychology* 91 (2006): 613–621.

97. Murray R. Barrick and Michael K. Mount, "Effects of Impression Management and Self-Deception on the Predictive Validity of Personality Constructs," *Journal of Applied Psychology* 83 (1996): 261–272; Neal D. Christiansen, Richard D. Goffin, Norman G. Johnston, and Mitchell G. Rothstein, "Correcting the 16PF for Faking: Effects on Criterion-Related Validity and Individual Hiring Decisions," *Personnel Psychology* 47 (1994): 847–860; Leatta M. Hough, Newell K. Eaton, Marvin D. Dunnette, John D. Kamp, and Rodney A. McCloy, "Criterion-Related Validities of Personality Constructs and the Effect of Response Distortion on Those Validities [Monograph]," *Journal of Applied Psychology* 75 (1990): 581–595; Deniz S. Ones, Chockalingham Viswesvaran, and Angela D. Reiss, "Role of Social Desirability in Personality Testing for Personnel Selection: The Red Herring," *Journal of Applied Psychology* 81 (1996): 660–679.

98. Schmitt and Oswald, "The Impact of Corrections for Faking on the Validity of Noncognitive Measures in Selection Settings."

99. Patrick D. Converse, Fred L. Oswald, Anna Imus, Cynthia Hendricks, Radha Roy, and Hilary Butera, "Comparing Personality Test Formats and Warnings: Effects on Criterion-Related Validity and Test-taker Reactions," *International Journal of Selection & Assessment* 16 (2008): 155–169; Christiansen, Goffin, Johnston, and Rothstein, "Correcting the 16PF for Faking: Effects on Criterion-Related Validity and Individual Hiring Decisions"; Ellingson, Sackett, and Hough, "Social Desirability Corrections in Personality Measurement: Issues of Applicant Comparison and Construct Validity"; Rose Mueller-Hanson, Eric D. Heggestad, and George C. Thornton III, "Faking and Selection: Considering the Use of Personality from Select-In and Select-Out Perspectives," *Journal of Applied Psychology* 88 (2003): 348–355; Rossé, Stecher, Miller, and Levin, "The Impact of Response Distortion of Preemployment Personality Testing and Hiring Decisions."

100. Jinyan Fan, Dingguo Gao, Sarah A. Carroll, Felix J. Lopez, T. Siva Tian, and Hui Meng. "Testing the Efficacy of a New Procedure for Reducing Faking on Personality Tests within Selection Contexts," *Journal of Applied Psychology* 97 (2012): 866–878; Edwin A.J. van Hooft and Marise Ph Born, "Intentional Response Distortion on Personality Tests: Using Eye-Tracking to Understand Response Processes When Faking," *Journal of Applied Psychology* 97, (2012): 301–316.

101. Dwight and Donovan, "Do Warnings Not to Fake Reduce Faking?"

102. Christiansen, Goffin, Johnston, and Rothstein, "Correcting the 16PF for Faking: Effects on Criterion-Related Validity and Individual Hiring Decisions"; Ellingson, Sackett, and Hough, "Social Desirability Corrections in Personality Measurement: Issues of Applicant Comparison and Construct Validity"; Mueller-Hanson, Heggestad, and Thornton III, "Faking and Selection: Considering the Use of Personality from Select-In and Select-Out Perspectives"; Rossé, Stecher, Miller, and Levin, "The Impact of Response Distortion of Preemployment Personality Testing and Hiring Decisions"; Sackett and Lievens, "Personnel Selection";

Schmitt and Oswald, "The Impact of Corrections for Faking on the Validity of Noncognitive Measures in Selection Settings."

103. Michael J. Cullen, Paul R. Sackett, and Filip Lievens, "Threats to the Operational Use of Situational Judgment Tests in the College Admission Process," *International Journal of Selection and Assessment* 14 (2006): 142–155; Helga Peeters and Filip Lievens, "Situational Judgment Tests and Their Predictiveness of College Students' Success: The Influence of Faking," *Educational and Psychological Measurement* 65 (2005): 70–89; Julia Levashina and Michael A. Campion, "Measuring Faking in the Employment Interview: Development and Validation of an Interview Faking Behavior Scale," *Journal of Applied Psychology* 92, (2007): 1638; Lynn McFarland, Janet Gunna Yun, Crystal M. Harold, Luciano Viera, and Lorie G. Moore, "An Examination of Impression Management Use and Effectiveness across Assessment Center Exercises: The Role of Competency Demands," *Personnel Psychology* 58 (2005): 949–980; Neal Schmitt, Fred L. Oswald, Brian H. Kim, Michael A. Gillespie, Lauren J. Ramsay, and Tae-Yong Yoo, "Impact of Elaboration on Socially Desirable Responding and the Validity of Biodata Measures," *Journal of Applied Psychology* 88 (2003): 979–988; Jennifer L. Wood, James M. Schmidtke, and Diane L. Decker, "Lying on Job Applications: The Effects of Job Relevance, Commission, and Human Resource Management Experience," *Journal of Business and Psychology* 22 (2007): 1–9.

104. David Dunning, Chip Heath, and Jerry M. Suls, "Flawed Self-Assessment Implications for Health, Education, and the Workplace," *Psychological Science in the Public Interest* 5 (2004): 69–106; Garrison Keillor, "In Search of Lake Wobegon" *National Geographic*, December 2000.

105. John C. Scott and Daniel V. Lezotte, "Web-Based Assessments," in *The Oxford Handbook of Personnel Assessment and Selection*, ed. Neil Schmitt (New York, NY: Oxford Publishing, 2012): 485–513.

106. Dave Bartram and Anna Brown, "Online Testing: Mode of Administration and the Stability of OPQ 32i Scores," *International Journal of Selection and Assessment* 12 (2004): 278–284; Jesús F. Salgado and Silvia Moscoso, "Internet-Based Personality Testing: Equivalence of Measures and Assesses' Perceptions and Reactions," *International Journal of Selection and Assessment* 11 (2003): 194–205; John C. Scott and Alan D. Mead. "Foundations for Measurement." *Technology-Enhanced Assessment of Talent* (2011): 21–65.

107. Bartram and Brown, "Online Testing: Mode of Administration and the Stability of OPQ 32i Scores"; J.C.C.D. Beaty, Nye, M. J. Borneman, T. M. Kantrowitz, F. Drasgow, and E. Grauer, "Proctored vs. Unproctored Internet Tests: Are Unproctored tests as Predictive of Job Performance?" *International Journal of Selection and Assessment* (2010): 1468–1481.

108. John A. Weiner and John D. Morrison, "Unproctored Online Testing: Environmental Conditions and Validity," *Industrial and Organizational Psychology* 2 (2009): 27–30; Neal Schmitt, "Personality and Cognitive Ability as Predictors of Effective Performance at Work," *Annual Review of Organizational Psychology and Organizational Behavior* 1 (2014): 45–65.

109. American Psychological Association, "Ethical Principles of Psychologists and Code of Conduct," (Washington, DC: APA, 1999); Douglas H. Reynolds and Deborah E. Rupp, "Advances in Technology-Facilitated Assessment," in *Handbook of Workplace Assessment: Evidence-Based Practices for Selecting and Developing Organizational Talent* (San Francisco, CA: Jossey-Bass, 2010), 609–641.

110. Dirk D. Steiner, "Personnel Selection across the Globe," *The Oxford Handbook of Personnel Assessment and Selection*, ed. Neil Schmitt (New York, NY: Oxford Publishing, 2012): 740–767.

111. Dave Bartram, "Global Norms: Towards Some Guidelines for Aggregating Personality Norms across Countries," *International Journal of Testing* 8 (2008): 315–333; Rob E. Ployhart and Jeff A. Weekley, "Strategy, Selection, and Sustained Competitive Advantage," *Handbook of*

Employee Selection (2010): 195–212; *Designing and Implementing Global Selection Systems*, eds. Ann M. Ryan and Nancy T. Tippins, vol. 20 (West Sussex, England; John Wiley & Sons, 2009).

112. Dave Bartram, "Global Norms: Towards Some Guidelines for Aggregating Personality Norms across Countries"; Dave Bartram, Ilke Inceoglu, Helen Fung, and Moyang Yang, "Equivalence of the OPQ32 Constructs across China, South Africa and the UK," in Division of Occupational Psychology Annual Conference, Stratford-upon-Avon, England, England, 2010; Anuradha Ramesh, Joy F. Hazucha, and Jurgen Bank, "Using Personality Data to Make Decisions about Global Managers," *International Journal of Testing* 8 (2008): 346–366; Mark J. Schmit, Jenifer A. Kihm, and Chet Robie, "Development of a Global Measure of Personality." *Personnel Psychology* 53 (2000): 153–193.

113. Patrick H. Raymark, Mark J. Schmit, and Robert M. Guion, "Identifying Potentially Useful Personality Constructs for Employee Selection," *Personnel Psychology* 50 (1997): 723–736.

114. Dan S. Chiaburu, In-Sue Oh, Christopher M. Berry, Ning Li, and Richard G. Gardner, "The Five-Factor Model of Personality Traits and Organizational Citizenship Behaviors: A Meta-Analysis," *Journal of Applied Psychology* 96 (2011): 1140–1166; Li, Barrick, Zimmerman, and Chiaburu, "Retaining the Productive Employee: The Role of Personality."

115. Barrick, Mount, and Judge, "The FFM Personality Dimensions and Job Performance: Meta-Analysis of Meta-Analyses"; Jose Cortina and Joseph Luchman, "Personnel Selection and Employee Performance," *Handbook of Psychology* 12 (2012): 143–183; Greg L. Stewart, "Let Us Not Become Too Narrow," *Industrial and Organizational Psychology* 1 (2008): 317–319.

116. Judge, Rodell, Klinger, Simon, and Crawford, "Hierarchical Representations of the Five-Factor Model of Personality in Predicting Job Performance: Integrating Three Organizing Frameworks with Two Theoretical Perspectives."

117. Li, Barrick, Zimmerman, and Chiaburu, "Retaining the Productive Employee: The Role of Personality."

118. Hugh Hartshorne and Mark May, *Studies in the Nature of Character* (New York: Macmillan, 1928), 384.

119. Robert P. Tett and Dawn D. Burnett, "A Personality Trait-Based Interactionist Model of Job Performance," *Journal of Applied Psychology* 88 (2003): 500–517.

120. Greg L. Stewart, "Reward Structure as a Moderator of the Relationship between Extraversion and Sales Performance," *Journal of Applied Psychology* 81 (1996): 619–627.

121. Barrick, Mount, and Judge, "The FFM Personality Dimensions and Job Performance: Meta-Analysis of Meta-Analyses."

122. Murray R. Barrick and Michael K. Mount, "Autonomy as a Moderator of the Relationships between the Five Factor Personality Dimensions and Job Performance," *Journal of Applied Psychology* 78 (1993): 111–118; Barrick, Mitchell, and Stewart, "Situational and Motivational Influences on Trait-Behavior Relationships."

123. Gerald V. Barrett, "Practitioner's View of Personality Testing and Industrial–Organizational Psychology: Practical and Legal Issues." *Industrial and Organizational Psychology* 1, no. 3 (2008): 299–302.

124. Barrick and Mount, "Select on Conscientiousness and Emotional Stability."

Simulation Tests

This chapter describes selection devices that assess applicants by means of testing situations that resemble actual parts of the job being considered. We refer to this type of device as a *simulation test*, although the term *performance test* is also frequently used. Examples of simulation tests are requiring applicants to write a simple computer program to solve a common work problem, to fix a plumbing leak in a house, or to work together to design a marketing strategy for a new product.

CONSISTENCY OF BEHAVIOR

Paul Wernimont and John Campbell made the most direct statement of the principles of simulation tests as selection devices.[1] Their major thesis is that selection decisions are most accurate when "behavioral consistency" is the major characteristic of the selection program. To clarify their point, Wernimont and Campbell have categorized all selection devices as either signs or samples.

Signs are selection tests used as secondary indicators of an individual's behavior in job activities. To the extent that these signs differ from the job behaviors being predicted, their ability to predict future job performance is limited. Examples of signs are common application forms that ask for degrees, former job titles, and years of work experience. Another example of a sign is an unstructured interview that asks such questions as, "Who do you most admire and why?", "If you could do anything, what is your ideal job?", or "What color, animal, or planet (yes, believe it!) is most like you?". The main deficiency in signs is that many (often illogical) inferences have to be made about the meaning of the applicant's responses and how the questions and responses relate to actual job performance.

Samples, on the other hand, are selection tests that gather information about behaviors consistent with the job behaviors being predicted. To the extent these samples are similar to the job behaviors, their ability to predict job behavior is increased. Two major types of selection instruments are regarded as samples. One type consists of instruments that gather information about an applicant's work experience and educational history in terms of actions that the applicant has performed that are related to specific, important job behaviors. Rating methods are used to score the frequency of these actions, the applicant's success in performing them, and the similarity of these actions to the actual job behaviors addressed in the selection program. These data are, in turn, used for rating the probability that the applicant will demonstrate good work performance. These ideas were part of our previous discussions of the appropriate design of training and experience evaluations, biodata forms, structured interviews, and the gathering of behavioral descriptions in personality assessment. In each of these instruments, we emphasized gathering several descriptions of behavior closely related to job activities.

The second type of sample selection instrument discussed by Wernimont and Campbell is simulation exercises that require the applicant to complete a set of actions that replicate job behaviors. These instruments provide direct evidence about the extent to which the job applicant successfully completed the job behavior. Using this evidence, a straightforward decision can be made about how well the applicant can perform the job of interest.

Wernimont and Campbell's work obviously emphasizes the match between the selection test and the job task as being the cause of the validity of the sample test. More recent work has added another dimension to this explanation. Anne Jansen and her co-authors found evidence that individuals' abilities to assess the demands of a selection test and also the demands of the job to which it relates also explain the validity of sample tests.[2] People high in situational assessment ability use cognitive processes to find out which criteria are being used to judge their performance in evaluative situations. That is, they scan the situation to pick up cues, distinguish between relevant and irrelevant cues, see relationships among multiple cues, validate prior cues with newer ones, and use this information to infer the key situational demands. Individuals can do this in both testing and work situations. In one part of their research, the authors found a significant correlation between scores on the selection test and job performance. However, when scores of the individuals' situational assessment ability were statistically controlled, this correlation was no longer significant. The authors concluded that individuals who do well on both the sample type selection test and job performance have higher ability to determine the situational demands of both the test and the job and use that information to increase their performance on both.

Limitations of Simulations

After our persuasive arguments about the wonderfulness of simulation tests, you are probably asking yourself, "If simulation tests are so sensible and efficient, shouldn't they be used in all selection situations?" Good question! In fact, such instruments are used widely. They first were common in the selection of clerical and skilled manual labor positions. Recently, simulation tests have also been used extensively in the form of *assessment centers* for managerial and professional selection. However, a number of factors can limit their use in selection programs. For one, much care must be taken in the construction of simulation tests to ensure that they are representative of job activities. For many complex and multiple-demand jobs, this is difficult. We are all familiar with selection devices that may be intended as simulations but really are not. One example is the attempt by an interviewer to create a stressful situation during the interview by asking questions rapidly, not allowing time for the applicant's response, or acting in a cold, aloof manner. Even if the job of interest is one of high work demands that produce stress, the situation staged in the interview is not representative of those demands. Few, if any, jobs create stress by way of semi-hostile individuals rapidly questioning the job holder. The behavior of the applicant in such an artificial interview situation is not readily generalizable to the job; the interview should not be viewed as a simulation test.

A second limitation is that simulations are usually developed on the assumption that the applicants already have the knowledge, ability, and skill to complete the job behavior required in the test. This assumption is most appropriate for jobs with tasks that are similar to jobs in other organizations, or tasks that can be taught in formal education programs. In other words, the most appropriate tasks for performance tests are those that do not depend on specialized knowledge, abilities, or skills regarding company products, personnel, materials, or customers. When the performance test does require specialized knowledge, the selection specialist must include training in that specialized knowledge before the test begins. That inclusion, obviously, makes the test longer and more difficult to administer.

A third factor limiting the use of simulation tests is the cost. Usually, simulations are much more expensive than other selection devices. Such costs include equipment and materials used only for selection; the time and facilities needed for individual or small-group administration of the selection instruments; the staff time spent in identifying representative tasks during job analysis; and the development of test instructions, testing situations, and scoring procedures.

Types of Simulation Tests

Simulation tests can be described in two ways. One is by the content of the test. They are labeled as either *motor* or *verbal* depending on the problems posed to applicants.[3] *Motor* (behavioral) tests require the physical manipulation of things or equipment or the physical movement of the applicant—for example, operating a machine, installing a piece of equipment, or making a repair. *Verbal* tests describe primarily language- or people-oriented exercises—for example, simulating an interrogation, editing a manuscript for grammatical errors, or demonstrating how to train subordinates. A second descriptive term is fidelity. *Fidelity* refers to the degree to which the simulation matches or replicates the physical and/or psychological demands and activities of the job for which it is designed. High-fidelity simulations duplicate part of the job. For example, an applicant for an instructor position at a college is brought into an introductory management class and gives a presentation to a class of students on leadership principles and techniques. After the presentation, both the students and other instructors who observe the presentation grade the applicant on specific teaching behaviors. Low-fidelity simulations present the essential components of a job activity in some fashion but do not include all of the people, equipment, or surroundings that occur when the job activity is performed. Commonly, in low-fidelity simulations, the job activity is described to the applicant either in a written document or verbally by a person or electronic equipment. For example, the same instructor applicant in the previous example is told through an electronic simulation that the class is made up of high-quality, verbally aggressive, intellectually curious students who enjoy enacting the most important points of leadership principles during the class session. (On the other hand, the class could be made up of students like everybody else in your class but you—students who are only slightly motivated and spend most of class playing with their phones.) The applicant then either describes what he would do to conduct the leadership principles class or even delivers a few minutes of such a class session either to the laptop or an existing instructor. The students of the class are not present. In case you are wondering, there is not a clear rule that marks the difference between a job-knowledge test and a low-fidelity simulation. So don't ask your instructor. She may give you a sensible difference and we will be embarrassed.

The rest of the chapter will discuss three major types of simulation tests: work samples, assessment centers, and situational judgment tests. Most simulations are slotted into one of these three groups.

WORK SAMPLES

Arguably the earliest form of simulations, work-sample simulations were used in the early 1900s to select clerical staff (tests of typing and editing a business letter) and skilled tradespeople (automobile repair, carpenters, and masons). As the name implies, these simulations are actual samples of job tasks that applicants are asked to perform, and their performances are scored. Therefore, work-sample simulations are considered high-fidelity simulations; they can be either motor (tests of typing, skilled craft tasks) or verbal (editing a business letter).[4]

Table 13.1 presents examples of various work-sample tests and the jobs for which they have been used. As is evident from the table, a wide variety of tests have been used, even for the same job.

| TABLE 13.1 | Examples of Work-Sample Tests Used in Selection |

Test	Job
Motor	
Lathe	Machine operator
Drill press	
Tool dexterity	
Screw board test	
Packaging	
Shorthand	Clerical worker
Stenographic	
Typing	
Blueprint reading	Mechanic
Tool identification	
Installing belts	
Repair of gearbox	
Installing a motor	
Vehicle repair	
Tracing trouble in a complex circuit	Electronics technician
Inspection of electronic defects	
Electronics test	
Verbal	
Report of recommendations for problem solution	Manager or supervisor
Small business manufacturing game	
Judgment and decision-making test	
Supervisory judgment about training, safety, performance, evaluation	
Processing of mathematical data and evaluating hypotheses	Engineer or scientist
Describing laboratory tests	
Mathematical formulation and scientific judgment	
Oral fact finding	Customer service representative
Role playing of customer contacts	
Writing business letters	
Giving oral directions	

James Campion described one example of a motor work-sample test used in the selection of maintenance mechanics:[5]

Motor Performance Test for Maintenance Mechanics—The development of this test begin with extensive job analysis that resulted in a list of task statements. Those statements were job-related and could be performed by a large number of applicants. Thus tasks were part of the job and within the repertoire of job applicants. Experts identified two major work activities that differentiated good and poor job performance: use of tools and accuracy of work. Included in the test were tasks such as installing pulleys and belts, disassembling and repairing a gearbox, installing and aligning a motor, pressing a bushing into a sprocket, and reaiming the bushing to fit a shaft. A distinct feature of the scoring system was that experts tried to identify all possible task behaviors an applicant might demonstrate in the test. Each possible behavior was evaluated and weighted and placed on the list. The rater, therefore, had only to observe the applicant's behaviors and check them off the list. Adding weights assigned to the checked behavior determined the applicant's overall score.

David Robinson outlined a verbal work-sample test used to select a construction superintendent:[6]

Scrambled Subcontractor Test—In the construction business, interruption of the critical construction path can be costly. The most important factor in staying on the critical path is that subcontractors appear in the right order to do their work. Knowledge of the proper order of subcontractor appearance is a prerequisite to staying on this path. In order to test this knowledge, applicants were given a list of 30 subcontractors (for example, roofing, framing, plumbing, fencing) and were asked to list them according to order of appearance on the job site. The order of appearance given by the applicant was compared with the order of appearance agreed upon by the company managers. The applicants were given the opportunity to discuss their rationale for particular orders. Minor deviations from the managers' solution were accepted.

Trainability tests are another variation of work-sample tests. This type of test is most often used in selection for two kinds of jobs: (1) jobs that do not presently exist but are anticipated in the near future and for which extensive training is necessary, and (2) jobs that do exist but are so specialized or technical that applicants could not be expected to possess the knowledge or skill to complete appropriate ability tests.

Richard Reilly and Edmond Israelski described AT&T's development and use of trainability tests, which were known in the company as minicourses.[7] The major purpose of the minicourse is to place the applicant in a test situation that closely resembles the training setting. In this way, an assessment can be made of the applicant's ability to learn critical material and complete the necessary, extensive training program. The strategy is clearly one of selection for performance in training. The applicant is required first to read and study a standardized sample of programmed training material, the minicourse. A typical minicourse had a 6-hour time limit; the range was between 2 hours and 3 days. After completing the minicourse, the applicant answered test questions designed to measure how well he or she learned the material. A passing score qualified the applicant to be admitted into the training program. He or she must then successfully complete this training to be offered employment.

Two types of minicourses can be developed. The first type consists of highly specific material that matches training content closely. An example would be a course containing material relevant to learning to use a particular piece of equipment. The second type of minicourse consists of more general material; it is used for jobs that are expected to change frequently because of technological advancement. In this case, the purpose of the minicourse is to present basic information that is appropriate despite the specific technology currently being used on the job. For example, a minicourse was developed about understanding binary, octal, hexadecimal, and decimal numbering systems. This was considered basic information appropriate for a variety of software programs and statistical analyses.

The Development of Work-Sample Tests

Even though work-sample tests vary considerably in the jobs for which they are used and the problem situations they present to applicants, similar steps are taken to develop these tests. The steps listed in Table 13.2 are essential to the construction of work-sample tests that are both legally defensible and valid for selecting applicants.[8] This section presents the details of these steps.

Step 1: Perform Job Analysis. The information presented in Chapter 3 on the methods and procedures of job analysis is relevant in developing a work-sample test. Job tasks must be described in detail in order to identify job-related equipment and material (important for motor simulation tests) and pinpoint the kinds of personal interaction required for the job (important for verbal simulation tests). To maximize the likelihood that the statement of the job tasks is accurate, one should obtain information from several job incumbents and supervisors. Consider the proficiency level of the workers and supervisors involved. It is necessary to rely heavily on information supplied by individuals who perform the job well. If the information in the job analysis is to be used to design and score the work-sample test, accurate information about the correct method of working is necessary.

Step 2: Identify Important Job Tasks to Be Tested. Judging job tasks according to frequency, importance, time required, level of difficulty, and/or consequence of error is important. The results of such evaluation should contribute significantly to the identification of the content of a work-sample test. The test should address those tasks that have a strong bearing on job performance. Usually task ratings provide such information. Pay special attention to tasks that are seasonal or sporadic. Such tasks may be critical and may have major consequences if not performed correctly. For this reason, ratings of task importance should be obtained from several individuals.

Step 3: Develop Testing Procedures. Once the tasks that will serve as the basis for the work-sample test have been identified, another important judgment must be made as to whether an applicant can realistically be expected to perform the task. As we mentioned previously, in most work-sample tests it is assumed that the applicant can do the task. In other cases in which the job task has some idiosyncratic features and cannot be done except by experienced workers, modifications must be made in the test situation. One modification is to provide the applicant with instructions about the operation of

TABLE 13.2 Steps in the Development of Work-Sample Tests

1. Perform job analysis
2. Identify important job tasks to be tested
3. Develop testing procedures
4. Develop scoring procedures
5. Train judges

equipment, features of special materials used, or background information about company policy before the test is given. Obviously, this modification will work only in those cases in which the amount of information necessary to perform the job task is relatively simple and easy to learn. In those cases in which this preliminary information is complex or difficult, the work-sample test is modified to measure the applicant's ability to develop the skill to perform the task. Our previous description of trainability tests is an example of this type of a modification.

Select Tasks. After the most appropriate job tasks have been identified, they must be further studied to make the most efficient use of testing time. The most important considerations in this study are the following:

1. The total time required to perform the task must be reasonable. It is expensive to administer work-sample tests, and the cost increases as the length of the task to be completed increases.

2. Tasks that can be done by either many applicants or few applicants provide little help in discriminating among good and poor applicants.

3. If there is a choice between two approximately equal tasks in the work-sample test and one of the two uses less expensive materials, equipment, or facilities, usually this task is chosen.

4. Tasks should be judged on the content of the material that would be scored in a test. All else being equal, tasks that have standardized operations or products or easily defined verbal or interaction components are more appropriate in work-sample tests than tasks not so characterized. It is usually far easier and less expensive to both develop and score the test for these types of tasks.

Specify Testing Procedures. As with other selection tests, it is important that the work-sample test be consistently administered to all applicants and graded consistently by all scorers. Standardization of testing conditions requires that a set of instructions be developed to inform the applicant of the nature of the task, what is expected, and the materials and equipment to be used. The same or identical conditions for testing should be provided to each applicant. Information about what actions, products, or outcomes will be scored should be provided. For grading, rules must be developed to specify what constitutes a "correct" response and how many points should be deducted for various deficiencies. All scorers should be thoroughly trained in the interpretation of these rules.

Establish Independent Test Sections. In developing the task problem used in the work-sample test, another important consideration is the independence of various parts of the test. All else being equal, it is preferable that the applicant's performance on one part of the test not be closely tied to a previous part of the test. If all errors are independent of one another, it is possible to obtain a large sample of the applicant's behavior. If, on the other hand, the test is developed so that the identification of one or two errors would disclose other errors, there is a strong probability of obtaining a distorted measurement of the applicant's performance. Applicants who do not recognize the one or two central errors have no opportunity to identify the remaining errors correctly; if they do identify the central errors, then the rest become apparent. This actually makes the test only a one- or two-item test for applicants.

Lack of independence is most likely when the work-sample test is a sequence of steps in a job process such as sewing a garment or constructing a small piece of apparatus. In either case, an error in measuring the materials to be used would adversely affect the remaining steps. To avoid this problem, some tests have been designed to provide a new set of acceptable materials for each phase of the job process. For example, if the first phase of a work-sample test is measuring and cutting the necessary pieces, the applicant stops after this phase. The pieces are taken to be scored by the judges, and the applicant is provided with a set of acceptable pieces to use in the next phase of the construction task.

Eliminate Contaminating Factors. In developing a work-sample test, it is important to ensure that apparatus, jargon, or other testing elements that have only a minor influence on job performance do not interfere with or limit the test performance of applicants who are not familiar with these elements. For example, in a work-sample test for an HR specialist, some numerical data may be provided from a company's attitude survey. The applicant is asked to make preliminary data analyses and use these results to answer a few specific management questions about the employees' attitudes about company procedures. The data analyses are to be performed on a personal computer. A serious problem could occur if an applicant did not know how to operate the computer provided for the work-sample test. In cases such as this, it is appropriate to provide a variety of computers, to train the applicant in the use of the computer before the work-sample test begins, or to provide an operator for the computer. Modifications such as these are not necessary when the operation of a particular apparatus is essential to the job task and not easily learned after one starts on the job. In such a case, the apparatus becomes an essential part of the work-sample test.

Select the Number of Test Problems. The final point we address in test construction is the number of times an applicant will be asked to perform a job activity during a work-sample test. A trade-off usually exists between the time required and the cost of testing and the increased reliability that results from having the applicant demonstrate the task more than once. The general guideline is to have the applicant repeat the task several times within cost limitations. For example, many skilled craft positions, such as typing, sewing, maintenance, or machine operation, have short-cycle tasks. An applicant can provide several products within a relatively brief time period by repeating the cycle of tasks. Obviously, if the task of the work-sample test is long or costly to stage, a limited number of trials should be scheduled.

Step 4: Develop Scoring Procedures. The criteria for scoring work-sample tests must be clearly defined, because the decisions facing the scorer are often difficult. In many cases a judgment must be made about the acceptability of task performance when multiple factors are present. Scoring generally is a function of comparing the applicant's test task performance to a standard defined by the organization to be satisfactory. Table 13.3 provides examples of several factors that have been used primarily in scoring *motor* work samples. In this type of test, the *task process* or the *task product* is scored. The task process is the actions or observable behaviors the applicant demonstrates when performing the task. The task product is the result of the task process. In motor work samples, products are often physical objects such as a typed document, a piece of sewn clothing, or a set of joined pieces of wood or other building materials. In general, a process is scored when there are clearly a small number of ways to do the job, and these ways invariably lead to an acceptable product. The operation of machinery in a continuous job process is one example. A product is scored in those situations in which a large number of different behaviors can lead to an acceptable product.

TABLE 13.3	Criteria Used in Scoring Motor Work-Sample Tests	

Standard	Process Criteria	Product Criteria
Quality	Accuracy	Conformance to specifications
	Error rate	Dimensions or other measures
	Choice of tools and/or materials	Spacing
	Efficiency of steps taken	Position
		Strength
		Suitability for use
		General appearance
Quantity	Time to complete	Quantity of output
Learning time	Number of steps for which guidance is needed	Improvement in meeting quantity standards
		Improvement in meeting quality standards
Cost	Amount of material used	Number of rejects
Safety	Handling of tools	Safety of completed product
	Accident rate	

Source: Lynnette B. Plumlee, *A Short Guide to the Development of Performance Tests* (Washington, DC: Personnel Research and Development Center, U.S. Civil Service Commission, Professional Series 75–1, January 1975).

Standards.   As Table 13.3 indicates, a number of separate standards can be scored for both process and product categories. Quality is vital, of course, to almost all jobs. Quantity is important for those performance tests in which the amount produced within a given time period is under the control of the worker. One example is the number of sales orders prepared for shipping. Cost becomes important as a scorable standard when there are a variety of options possible to the worker and the options vary in cost. An example would be tasks such as the repair of a research apparatus in which several options are available that vary greatly in expense.

The remaining two standards—learning time and safety—are used much less frequently than the other standards. Learning time is a logical standard for tasks that are characterized by the variety of novel demands they place on the incumbent; the technical repair of a variety of sophisticated electronic equipment is one example. In many cases, the task of repair requires the worker to constantly learn and use new methods of diagnosis. The length of time that an employee takes to learn these new methods translates directly into costs for the organization. Scoring the dimension of safety is obviously important if physical injury can be caused by an incorrect process or product.

More than one of these standards can be used in scoring; for example, quantity and quality are often used together. Also, process and product can both be scored in the same performance test. Process dimensions used in scoring can be identified by observing performance of the job. The selection specialist can use both demonstration and descriptions of task steps given by these workers. Most organizations have defined the physical dimensions or properties of satisfactory products. This information is often used in scoring the product dimensions of motor work samples. For example, the diameter of rolled wire, the strength of welds, and the location of buttons sewn on a blouse are all such standards.

Rules for Scoring.   In scoring the motor work-sample test, the assignment of numbers to the applicant's test performance must be performed according to defined rules. Most often, especially if the test has several repetitions or separately scored parts, a simple "0, 1 rule" is used. Performance that meets the standard is scored "1" and performance that does not is scored "0." The total score for the test is obtained by summing across all parts of the test. Another scoring option is to use scales, for example 1 to 5. The highest number on the scale is assigned when the performance meets the desired level; other numbers are assigned to less acceptable performance in descending order of acceptability. It is necessary to determine how much of a deviation from the desired level each number on the scale represents. Finally, if many different standards are scored in the performance test—for example, quality of the products, quantity produced, and cost of the work process—a rule must be stated to allow these separate scores to be combined into one total score.

Scoring verbal work-sample tests is different from scoring motor performance tests. The general principle is essentially the same—the verbal performance of the applicant is compared against a standard that the organization has deemed satisfactory. The use of words and concepts, however, and the interaction among individuals cannot be as precisely defined as standards of motor tests. In many cases the scoring of verbal performance tests depends on the extensive training of judges. We examine such scoring methods later in our discussion of assessment centers, which have a large component of verbal performance tests.

Step 5: Train Judges.   For motor work samples, training raters in how to judge applicants' performance is relatively straightforward if scoring standards and rules have been well defined. Videotapes of applicant task behaviors have been used to train raters to make judgments about process dimensions.[9] When videotapes or live demonstrations are used in training, the rater is given an explanation and a description of appropriate job process behaviors, including the sequence of the behaviors. Emphasis is then placed on demonstrations of appropriate and inappropriate behavior. Videotapes seemingly have an advantage in this phase because they can be used frequently, stopped at critical moments, and replayed to demonstrate specific points. Logically, it is important to present numerous inappropriate behaviors during this training to familiarize the rater with errors before actual testing begins.

Reliability of measurement must be maximized in developing a scoring system and training raters to use it. By using some measure of interrater reliability (discussed in Chapter 6), high agreement among raters in measurement and scoring should be demonstrated. If raters do not demonstrate reliability in their judgments after training, either more training is necessary, the scoring system must be changed, or the raters are replaced. If you have by now become a strong advocate of work-sample tests and hunger for more information, Neal Schmitt and Cheri Ostroff have described the development of a work-sample test that was used for selecting emergency telephone operators for a police department.[10] Reading this should satisfy your hunger.

The Validity of Work-Sample Tests

Studies that examine the validity of work-sample tests in selection have been consistently positive. Many of these were single-sample studies. A meta-analysis reported by Philip Roth, Philip Bobko, and Lynn McFarland found a 0.33 validity coefficient for performance tests, after appropriate methodological corrections.[11] The authors also determined only a small difference in validity when objective (usually a measured outcome of the task) or subjective (usually a supervisor's judgment) job performance criteria measures were used. Objective criteria were associated with a 0.30 validity coefficient and subjective criteria with a 0.34 coefficient. Finally, they found that performance tests added to the prediction of job performance when cognitive ability was also used as a predictor.

A common view of selection specialists is that work-sample tests demonstrate much smaller differences between groups of black applicants and white applicants than do many written tests, especially cognitive ability tests. However, many of the studies underlying this view were single-sample studies, studies that used job incumbents rather than job applicants, or studies with various methodological limitations. A meta-analytic study conducted by Philip Roth, Philip Bobko, Lynn McFarland, and Maury Buster addressed many of these limitations as it examined the validity of work-sample tests.[12]

These researchers found that differences in test performance between blacks and whites were greater than usually thought. The studies that they used for their meta-analysis met a strict definition of work sample (the same definition that we have used) so as to rule out studies that included lower-fidelity simulations. Studies also had to have compared similar samples, that is, applicants to applicants and/or incumbents to incumbents. The issue is that mixing the two types of samples hinders interpretation of results because of the factor of job learning while doing the job. Such learning would lower any differences in comparison between groups. Finally only studies were included that used samples of black job applicants or incumbents rather than samples of various minority groups combined together. Several important analyses were conducted. One of these compared differences between black and white groups in studies that used military personnel versus studies that used samples in other types of organizations. Job incumbents were the subjects in this comparison. Results found almost no differences between scores of blacks and whites in the military ($d = 0.03$) but a much larger difference between the two groups in nonmilitary samples ($d = 0.53$, whites higher). Second, as suspected, the differences between white and black job applicants in nonmilitary samples were quite large. (That is, $d = 0.73$ or 0.67 when one outlier sample was omitted; whites scored higher.) This difference was much greater than the previous estimate of 0.35. This difference clearly indicated that work-sample tests could yield differences between the two groups that could be indicators of adverse impact. In addition, the difference between the two groups on the work-sample tests was only slightly lower than the difference between the two groups on cognitive ability tests. Because the cost of the development and implementation of work-sample tests is very high, these findings give pause to attempts to use work-sample tests mainly for the reason of having a valid selection test with low adverse impact. A third finding was that the differences in scores between white and black groups varied according to the type of work sample used. Work-sample tests that featured written documents had larger differences between the two groups (whites higher) than did tests that were essentially verbal communication.

Other Results of Using Work-Sample Tests.   In addition to being valid, work-sample tests provide other benefits when used in selection. One study reported that during the first 17 months that these tests were used, no complaints were lodged about their appropriateness. This was in contrast to the previous applicant complaint rate of 10 to 20 percent that occurred when other types of tests were used.[13]

Work-sample tests can also serve as a way of displaying the actual job to applicants. An example of such a benefit concerns the selection of sewer pumping station operators. During an initial 1-hour instruction period, a sewer mechanic explained and demonstrated (as if he were the applicant's supervisor) procedures for the general maintenance of sewer pipes and equipment, for example, how to clean filters, grease fittings, and read a pressure chart. The test was given during the second hour, when each applicant was required to repeat the demonstration as if on the job. Follow-up interviews revealed that those who qualified for and accepted the job had an accurate idea of the job demands. Before the performance test was used, the job turnover rate was approximately 40 percent. During the 9 to 26 months after performance testing was started, this rate dropped to less than 3 percent.[14]

ASSESSMENT CENTERS

When simulation tests are used for the selection of managers, professionals, and executives, they are commonly referred to as *assessment centers* (ACs).

An AC is a procedure for measuring WRCs in groups of individuals (usually 6 to 12 people) using a series of devices, many of which are verbal simulation tests.

ACs have been used for both selection and career development. In selection, the emphasis is on identifying those participants who demonstrate behaviors thought necessary for performing the position being considered. When used for career development, the emphasis is on determining those behaviors each participant does well and those in which each needs improvement. Participants who need improvement are then sent to appropriate training programs. For our purposes, we will concentrate on the ACs used for selection. ACs are generally considered to be verbal simulations. The fidelity of simulations in an AC can vary from high to fairly low depending on the specific makeup of the AC. Some ACs use only simulations designed for a particular job, others use general simulations appropriate for a group of jobs, and some include traditional tests. Because of this variation in fidelity among AC tests, we think about ACs as having moderate fidelity.

The Beginning of Assessment Centers

The Management Progress Study of AT&T marked the beginning of the use of the AC for industrial organizations.[15] This program was begun in 1956 to study the career development of men (remember, it was the 1950s) hired for managerial positions. One major focus of the study was to identify the WRCs thought to be related to the successful career progress of managers. Twenty-five of these were identified from research literature, opinions of industrial psychologists specializing in management career patterns, and opinions of senior executives at AT&T. The study measured these characteristics in 274 new managers periodically over several years and related the data to these employees' progress through the levels of management. During this time, none of the data were made available to anyone but the researchers.

One big challenge for the researchers was developing measuring devices for the 25 characteristics. To do this, a three-and-a half-day assessment center was devised. Managers were brought together in groups of 12, and several ways were tried to measure personal characteristics. These included traditional measures of general mental ability, personality and attitude questionnaires, projective tests of personality, and interviews. Newly developed simulations of individual and group problem solving, and an individual administrative exercise were added. The reports from this study consistently found that the data obtained from these measures were related to subsequent movement through managerial levels. This, of course, prompted much interest in the use of ACs for managerial selection. The use of multiple-day, multiple-exercise testing programs quickly grew. Although there were variations among these programs, they used similar types of assessment devices, which usually paralleled those used in the AT&T study. In the next section we discuss some of these types of exercises.

What Is Measured and How

Dimensions. The development of an AC starts with a job analysis to identify clusters of job activities that are the important parts of the job of interest. Each cluster should be specific and observable, comprising job tasks that are related in some way. These job clusters, referred to as *dimensions*, are measured by the assessment center devices. You should think about dimensions as the WRCs measured in ACs. Table 13.4 provides brief definitions of nine dimensions commonly used in ACs. It is important to note that these dimensions are defined based on actual job activities. As you can see, the definitions in Table 13.4 illustrate such activities. In ACs the definitions are more detailed. For example, the dimension of *tolerance for stress* is often defined by describing the actions taken to meet specific multiple demands (from subordinates, superiors, outside pressure groups, and so on) and the specific multiple roles (negotiator, public relations specialist, performance evaluator, and so on) that characterize the job under study. The behaviors for each dimension serve as the basis for the development of the simulations thought to measure the dimension. It is easy to understand why ACs have relied heavily on simulations as a primary measurement device; it is usually a straightforward process to translate these job activities into test activities.

Traditional Assessment Devices. As we mentioned, the AT&T ACs often used various types of traditional tests and interviews. The tests include mental ability, projective personality, and paper-and-pencil personality tests. Because of the expense of using and

TABLE 13.4	Behavioral Dimensions Frequently Measured in Assessment Centers
Dimension	**Definition**
Oral communication	Effectively expressing oneself in individual or group situations (includes gestures and nonverbal communications)
Planning and organizing	Establishing a course of action for self or others in order to accomplish a specific goal; planning proper assignments of personnel and appropriate allocation of resources
Delegation	Utilizing subordinates effectively; allocating decision making and other responsibilities to the appropriate subordinates
Control	Establishing procedures for monitoring or regulating the processes, tasks, or activities of subordinates; monitoring and regulating job activities and responsibilities; taking action to monitor the results of delegated assignments or projects
Decisiveness	Expressing a readiness to make decisions, render judgments, take action, or commit oneself
Initiative	Actively attempting to influence events to achieve goals; showing self-starting actions rather than passive acceptance. Taking action to achieve goals beyond those called for; originating action
Tolerance for stress	Maintaining a stable performance under pressure or opposition
Adaptability	Maintaining effectiveness in varying environments, with various tasks, responsibilities, or people
Tenacity	Staying with a position or plan of action until the desired objective is achieved or is no longer reasonably attainable

Source: George C. Thornton III, *Assessment Centers in Human Resource Management* (Reading, MA: Addison-Wesley Publishing Co., 1992).

interpreting such tests (e.g., many of these tests required that specially trained psychologists do the interpretation), these types of tests are no longer used very often. However ACs do commonly use an in-depth interview that is similar to the selection interview we recommended using in Chapter 10. Commonly referred to as the *background interview*, the emphasis of the AC interview is to gather information from the candidate about job activities that represent the behavioral dimensions being evaluated in the AC. The interviewer's objective is to gather as much information as possible about these dimensions. Many of the recommendations made in Chapter 10 for the use of the interview are used in the AC background interview: Each interview is structured and focuses on previous job behaviors; relatively few behavioral dimensions are utilized; multiple questions are prepared to tap each dimension; interviewers are trained to record relevant job actions for each behavioral dimension; and a formal scoring system is used to evaluate each candidate on each behavioral dimension. When combined with the information generated from other AC devices, the background interview has been shown to be effective at arriving at a final evaluation of a candidate.

Simulation Tests.   The use of simulation tests distinguishes ACs from other selection programs. The most frequently used simulation test devices are In-Basket tests, leaderless group discussion, and case analysis. Each is discussed below.

In-basket.   The *in-basket test* is a paper-and-pencil test designed to replicate administrative tasks of the job under consideration. The name of the test is taken from the "in" and "out" baskets on some managers' desks used to hold organizational memos coming to and going from the managers.

The content of the administrative issues included in the set of memos that make up the in-basket test should be obtained from job analysis information and should be representative of the actual administrative tasks of the position. Examples of typical in-basket items are presented in Table 13.5. The in-basket test is completed individually; it usually takes 2 to 3 hours. The candidate sits in a private area at a desk on which is found the written material of the test. Usually no oral directions are given by the AC staff, nor is there any interaction between the AC staff and the candidate while the test is being taken. Recently, ACs have been developed as electronic simulations that contain electronic forms of all of the written materials necessary for the simulation. Electronic simulations are much less expensive than are traditional ACs.

The in-basket test includes an introductory document that describes the hypothetical situation. This situation is a variation of this theme: The candidate has recently been placed in a position because of the resignation, injury, vacation, or death of the previous incumbent. A number of memos, describing a variety of problems, have accumulated and must be addressed. The candidate is given organization charts, mission statements, and company policy statements that provide background information about the unit he or she is now managing. The candidate is informed that, unfortunately, previous plans require that he or she be away from the office for the next several days. Before departing, the candidate must indicate what action should be taken concerning the problem issues by leaving written memos in the out-basket. No other office members can be contacted.

The memos themselves are presented on different types and sizes of paper and are both typed and handwritten to add realism. The candidate is to read the memos and write a recommendation as to what action should be taken and which personnel should be involved. Each candidate is given a standard time period in which to complete the test. After the candidate has finished, he or she is usually interviewed by one of the AC staff and asked to explain the overall philosophy used in addressing the memos, as well as the reasoning behind the specific recommendations made for each administrative

TABLE 13.5	Examples of In-Basket Memos

To: Robert Gatewood

From: Philip Bobko and Philip Roth (authorship order is alphabetical and does not indicate contribution level)

Re: Using Our Discoveries

We are both aware that you have frequently used our published research over the last few editions of your book. In fact, in the seventh edition we counted, and you used 11 of our articles (which was good because we only published 7 but are not telling you which ones were wrongly attributed to us). Your discussion of these articles took up 21 paragraphs, 108 sentences, 242 lines, and 2107 words (unless one counts meta-analysis as two words). It is clear to the both of us that you owe us a lot for our great contributions to your book. In fact, you need to give both of us authorship on the book. However, we will not go for alphabetical authorship because one of us (unnamed) would be last author. We would prefer first and second authorship or second and third at the very least. What we are really after is a cut of the royalties for the book because journals do not pay anything. We are both getting old and need to save for our retirements. Let us know about the authorship and amount of royalties we can expect as soon as you can.

To: Robert Gatewood

From: Jeffrey Hahn, editor

Re: Junior Feild is driving me crazy!

Can you distract Junior so I can get your book edited? The guy is occupying most of my time. First he wants me to set up an office for him in Australia that has to be high on a hill to improve his HAM RADIO transmissions. Something about working while he is visiting his family and making new friends in the southern hemisphere. Second, he won't stop giving me his thoughts for the cover. He wants his car (if that is what it is loosely called) on it with each chapter featuring a picture of him with an individual part. I would like it if you could reduce the book to five chapters! He has even sent me selfies of him with each part. Third, he wants a crew to video each of his lectures for his selection class, package all those on a disc, and send one to each faculty member who orders the book so that faculty could just show the videos. According to Junior his classes are perfect and everyone else is simply not providing the right education to students. Thing is I have watched three of these videos and there are problems. First is Junior standing in front of the classroom with a big smile, shorts, t-shirt, and running shoes. Even accountants look more engaging. Then the video occasionally pans to the class, which is worse, if possible. Most seats are vacant, about half of those present have their heads down on their desks moaning, others are staring vacantly at the ceiling, and one is simply watching the timer tick down on his phone and announces the minutes left in the class as each minute changes. Help me! Help me!

To: Robert Gatewood

From: Studnts Agaist Big Boks

Re: Your and the other guys bok

We are righing because of your bok. It be two big and longg. We hav to red it becase it is in the bokstoore. We r in HR becase we like peeple not becase we like to red. Is their a comic bok of this or mayb a t-shirt with the impurtunt stuff? We all have straght A in skool. We not want to mess up width a big bok for a clas.

Piece, World Fredum, and Beer

Studnts Agaist Big Boks

problem. The AC staff member uses the written and oral information to evaluate dimensions measured in the in-basket.

Leaderless Group Discussion (LGD).   The LGD is designed to represent those managerial activities that require the interaction of small groups of individuals in order to solve a problem successfully. In the LGD, participants are tested in groups of six. These six are seated around a conference table usually placed in the middle of a room. AC assessors are seated along the walls of the room to observe and record the behavior of the LGD participants.

The LGD is so named because no one member is designated as the official leader or supervisor of the group. The meeting is one of equals addressing a common problem. This problem could emphasize either cooperation or competition among the six participants. One example of cooperation is a situation in which the company must issue a public statement in response to a racial discrimination charge made by some of its employees. Competitive problems are usually characterized by a small amount of some organizational resource (e.g., money for raises or new equipment, a one-time fund for capital investment) that is not large enough to satisfy the wishes of all LGD members. In both types of problem, the group members are provided with a written description of the issue and relevant supporting material—for example, individual work-performance records, maintenance costs, equipment capacity charts, and so on. The group is then usually charged with producing a written report that specifies the action to be taken by the company. In most cases, 90 minutes to 2 hours is the maximum time allotted.

In addition to being classified as cooperative or competitive, the LGD problem can have either defined or undefined roles. With defined roles, each group member is given specific information, unknown to the others, that both describes his or her position in the company and provides additional information about the department or the individuals that the LGD participant is supposed to be representing. The participant may use this information as he or she sees fit to influence the actions of the group. Unassigned roles are obviously those for which such information is not provided to each participant. Assigned roles are most commonly used in competitive LGD problems. Each member's role information is used to argue that the scarce resource should be allocated for that participant's purposes. Table 13.6 contains examples of a general problem and two as-signed roles that could be used in such LGD situations.

Case Analysis.   In case analysis exercises, each participant is provided with a long de-scription of an organizational problem that changes according to the job being consid-ered in the AC. Some of your classes may use this same type of simulation and require you to discuss your opinions about specific topics. For a higher-level position, the case frequently describes the history of certain events in a company, with relevant financial data, marketing strategy, and organizational structure. Frequently, industry data concern-ing new products, consumer trends, and technology are introduced. The case focuses on a dilemma that the participant is asked to resolve. In resolving it, the candidate must give specific recommendations, present supporting data presented, and detail any changes in company strategy.

The content of the case is varied to make it appropriate for the position being con-sidered. For middle-management jobs, the major issue frequently concerns the design and implementation of operational plans or systems—for example, management infor-mation systems or job process systems. For first-level management, the focus often is on either the resolution of subordinate conflicts, subordinate nonconformity with poli-cies, or the reevaluation of specific work methods. After the candidate has been given time to read and analyze the case, he or she may be asked to prepare a written report, make an oral presentation to AC staff members, or discuss the case with other participants.

The Training of Assessors

As we discussed previously, scoring the verbal simulation tests that characterize ACs is usually more difficult than scoring motor simulation tests. If an AC is to be useful as a selection device, it is crucial that *assessors* (staff members who have the responsibility of observing and evaluating the behaviors of the participants) have the necessary training. As we pointed out, ACs focus on the behavioral dimensions. The exercises require the participants to provide behaviors relative to these dimensions. Each dimension must be measured by more than one exercise and each exercise usually measures multiple dimen-sions. The major duty of an assessor is to record the behavior of a participant in an

TABLE 13.6	Example of Leaderless Group Discussion Problem

Problem: The three of you are authors of a textbook *Human Resource Selection* and it is time to work with your editor in developing an idea for the cover of the book.

Assigned Role #1 Hubert S. Feild

You remember the cover of the most recent scientific journal that you have read, the 1968 March edition of *Psychology Today*. It had a whole bunch of pictures of nuts and bolts, plugs and adapters, screws and screwdrivers, hammers and nails all fitting together. You immediately fell in love with that cover and want something very much like it for this book. So you are going to try to talk the two other authors and the editor into this idea. This is what you have worked out so far as your opening argument for such a cover.

"I like the idea of squares, rectangles, circles, etc. trying to fit comparable holes in an organization cube. You know, a three-dimensional block. However, when I see a book that I like I often wonder what the author looks like. That's why I spend so much time in chatrooms trying to get people to send me their pictures. I think we ought to have a cover that has both of these things that I like. For example, the cover could be a three-dimensional cube with each of us getting one dimension and choosing the shapes that we want on our dimension. I want a trapezium, an irregular heptagon, and an irregular decagon. I love those shapes and have decorated my whole office in those. Then we can put our picture on each of the shapes in our dimension. The cover would have it all!"

Assigned Role #2 Robert Gatewood

The one thing that you have learned about books for college courses is that it makes no difference what the students like—about either the cover or the content. Faculty members choose the book for their courses and assign that book to the students. So you think that in order to increase sales your cover ought to have something that draws the faculty into wanting the book. You have two ideas to do this. First is to put the picture of each faculty member on the cover who selected your book for a class over the past 5 years. This should not be hard because only 15 faculty members have chosen the book in that time. Each of you three authors could contact five of these faculty and ask for a photo. Then use Photoshop to put all 15 into one group picture. If you cannot sell that idea to the others then go to your second idea. Have the cover of each book be blank but have a Velcro strip on each side of what will be the cover. Then you could attach a picture of the instructor who ordered the book on each cover of the books that he/she ordered for a class. The instructors would love this and as word spread you know that sales would increase.

Assigned Role #3 Murray Barrick

You think that the book cover should attract attention but be fairly sophisticated because it is a professional book and influences what others think of the authors. You also know that such a line of reasoning has little influence on the other two authors. Feild never leaves Auburn so no one has any thoughts about him, which is probably the most upside reaction that he could ever get from other people. Gatewood is a little more reasonable than Feild, which is not a high bar, and may be won over to your idea by manipulation. For faculty members, sophistication means citations of their work. So you want to divide the book cover into thirds; one-third for each author. On that third, each author can list all of his citations. You have over 9000 citations and Gatewood has about 3 so you figure that you can win him over to your view by giving him a couple thousand of yours. Just change the name of the last author of a bunch of your articles to his. Then he gets the citations. Besides it is the only way all 9000+ of yours will get on. Even then they will have to be printed very small with abbreviations. Winning Feild may be easier. He thinks a citation means that a person read an article. That's why he brags about his citation on the cover of a 1968 *Psychology Today* issue. So you could just tell him that he could list all the Ham Radio Manuals that he has read. He will love that.

exercise and use the data to rate the participant on each behavioral dimension appropriate for the exercise. These ratings are referred to as post-exercise dimension ratings (PEDRs). For example, if the LGD is designed to measure the dimensions of oral communication, adaptability, and persuasiveness, the assessor must use his or her observations of the actions of a participant in the LGD problem to rate the participant on these dimensions. Usually, the rating is done on a 5-point scale.

In most cases, there are half as many assessors in an AC as there are participants. These assessors are usually managers within the organization in positions one level above the position of interest for the AC. In this way the assessors are assumed to be familiar with the job and the behaviors required in the job. After recording and judging the participants' behavior in the AC, and after all exercises have been completed, the assessors come together to discuss their observations. The ratings and data gathered by each assessor are used to develop group or final scores of each participant on each behavioral dimension. We will refer to these ratings as dimension ratings (DRs). These ratings are then used to develop a single, Overall Assessment Rating (OAR) of the acceptability of each candidate for the position of interest. In summary (which means you should know this for later in the chapter), assessors make three different ratings. The first is a rating on each dimension in each exercise (PEDRs). These are used to form a dimension rating across exercises that contain that rating (DRs). These are then used to form one rating (OAR) of the overall performance of the individual on the complete assessment center.

The major difficulty in having managers within the organization perform these activities is that, even though they are knowledgeable about the job behaviors, they are usually unskilled in systematically observing behaviors representative of each dimension and then using the behaviors to develop ratings. The purpose of assessor training programs is to develop those skills. If assessors are not adequately trained in these observation and rating methods, the value of the AC evaluation is lessened.

William Byham has written an excellent detailed description of the training of assessors.[16] Much of the material in the following paragraphs is drawn from his ideas. Essentially, this training is meant to develop the six key abilities listed in Table 13.7. We describe some steps for doing this.

Understanding the Behavioral Dimensions.   As we mentioned, one fundamental part of an AC is the determination of which behavioral dimensions of the job are to be evaluated. These should be dimensions that are representative of and important to the job. The first step in training assessors, therefore, is to thoroughly familiarize them with the dimensions. Often this is done by providing assessors with a clear and detailed definition of each dimension, and then spending time discussing them. The major goal is to ensure that all assessors have a common understanding of the dimensions. Dimensions such as adaptability, decisiveness, and tolerance for stress may have different meanings for different individuals. The following is an example of a definition that could be used for an AC dimension focused on first-line supervisors:

Tolerance for stress: Stability of performance under pressure and/or opposition. A first-line supervisor finds himself in a stressful situation because of three main factors: (a) multiple demands on the work unit that must be completed at approximately the same deadline, (b) the joint roles he must play as both a representative of management to nonmanagement employees and a representative of nonmanagement employees to management, and (c) confrontation by employees who are angry or hostile because of a work situation.

TABLE 13.7   Types of Abilities to Be Developed in Training Assessors

- Understanding the behavioral dimensions
- Observing the behavior of participants
- Categorizing participant behavior as to appropriate behavioral dimensions
- Judging the quality of participant behavior
- Determining the rating of participants on each behavioral dimension across the exercises
- Determining the overall evaluation of participants across all behavioral dimensions

Observing the Behavior of Participants.   After the assessors have become familiar with the dimensions to be used in the AC, the next step is to train them to observe and record behavior. The initial tendency of most managers when they first become assessors is immediately to make evaluative judgments about the performance of participants in the AC exercises. For example, when observing an LGD problem, a common reaction is to make the judgment that a participant can or cannot handle stress. However, such immediate judgments are dysfunctional with regard to the purpose of the AC. An AC, you will remember, is to provide *multiple* exercises or opportunities for participants to demonstrate behaviors that *exemplify* the dimensions under study.

This step in training, therefore, is designed to overcome the tendency of assessors to form immediate judgments and instead to focus on recording the behavior of the participant. Commonly, this step has two parts. One part explains to the assessors in detail the differences between recording behavior and making judgments; to clarify this difference, examples of each are provided. Often a list of statements is prepared about each of the dimensions, and the assessor is asked to indicate whether the statement reflects behavior or judgment. The following is an example:

Dimension: Tolerance for Stress

Indicate whether each of the following is a statement of a participant's behavior or a statement of an assessor's judgment.

Participant Behavior	Assessor Judgment	
	✓	*Resolved the conflict quietly*
✓		*Listened to the explanations of both parties as to how the conflict started*
✓		*Offered some tentative suggestions as to changes that could be made*
	✓	*Broke down when the argument heated up*

After assessors understand the meaning of the term *behavior*, the second part of training presents examples of participant behavior in the exercises; this allows assessors to practice recording behaviors. These examples can be taken from either live or videotaped exercises. The advantage of a videotaped exercise is that it can be stopped at specific points, or parts can be replayed for discussion.

Categorizing Participant Behavior.   The next step of training teaches the assessor to record the behavior of the participant under the proper dimension. This ensures that assessors are consistent in recording participant behaviors that are examples of the dimensions. This consistency is also essential to the reliability and validity of the ratings.

For the most part, training in this phase centers on both descriptions and discussions of the behavior representative of each dimension and also demonstrations of these behaviors. For descriptions, assessors are provided with material that briefly defines each dimension and presents a list of behaviors that are representative of both high and low levels of the dimension. Such a list may take the following form:

Tolerance for stress: Stability of performance under pressure or opposition.

Examples:

When engaging the two arguing parties, participant soon began screaming at them.

Suggested that the two arguing parties walk with her to an unoccupied conference room. Asked the individuals observing the arguing parties to return to work stations.

Physically grabbed the nearest arguing party and pulled him from the area.

A list of the representative behaviors is prepared for each dimension and is reviewed in group discussion among the assessors. Other example behaviors are frequently generated during this time. In some cases, the assessors are then provided with a list of recorded behaviors that have been drawn from previous ACs; they are asked to indicate which dimension is identified by the described behavior. The correct answers are reviewed by the group and differences of opinion discussed. During the last part of training for this step, the assessors observe either a live set of exercises or a videotaped set and record the behaviors that demonstrate each dimension. A group discussion of the records that the members of group generate is then carried out.

Determining the Rating of Participant Behavior. This portion of training attempts to develop consistency among assessors in the use of rating scales to evaluate the behavior of participants on the dimensions. In most ACs, each dimension is rated using the following 6-point scale:

5 A great deal of the dimension was shown (excellent).

4 Quite a lot of the dimension was shown.

3 A moderate amount of the dimension was shown (average).

2 Only a small amount of the dimension was shown.

1 Very little of the dimension was shown, or this dimension was not shown at all (poor).

0 No opportunity existed for this dimension to be shown.

The major objective in using a scale such as this is to develop a common frame of reference among assessors, so that each will assign the same scale point to the same observed behaviors. Developing a common frame of reference across different raters is a problem in other HR activities (performance appraisal, scoring interviews, assessing training needs, and so on). AC training revolves around providing examples of behaviors that are representative of scale points for each dimension. Frequently, these example behaviors are drawn from other ACs.

This part of training often focuses on each exercise separately and can be thought of as training to make PEDRs. In training, the group of assessors is presented with either written descriptions or videotapes of examples of behaviors for one exercise and asked to rate the behaviors on all appropriate dimensions. After each assessor has completed the ratings, a discussion follows that brings out any differences in ratings. This discussion is intended to identify common definitions of each scale point. When practicing managers are used as assessors, this phase of the training is usually completed quite easily. Often such managers have a common viewpoint about what constitutes extremely good or extremely poor behaviors on the dimension. For example, most assessors agree that physically grabbing a person is an unsatisfactory demonstration of tolerance for stress. More difficulty arises in arriving at a consensus for the middle scale points. Even in this case, however, a common understanding is reached fairly quickly, owing greatly to the common work experiences of the assessors.

Determining Dimension and Overall Evaluation Ratings. The training in these steps is similar in that it involves the use of rating scales and draws heavily on the training previously discussed.

After a participant's behaviors for any one AC exercise are described appropriately on the dimensions, the next task is to combine the data on the same dimension across two or more exercises. This part of training focuses on using PEDRs to develop DRs. For example, say that data about tolerance for stress are gathered on three different exercises. Assessors must learn to combine these data into one overall dimension rating for each individual participant. Again, training is primarily based both on group discussions that form a common frame of reference and several examples that serve as trials. Differences in ratings are fully discussed. Important in forming overall dimension ratings are such factors as the relative importance of that dimension across the exercises, how good each exercise is at bringing out a variety of behaviors, and the strength and duration of behaviors.

The last training step concerns how to use the DRs to form the OAR of the participant's ability in the complete AC. Job analysis information is critical for this. From the job analysis, it can be determined which dimensions are the most critical or the most frequently used in the job. These dimensions are then weighted more heavily than other dimensions in producing the overall rating. As a means of training for these last two steps, assessor groups are often required to complete a mock assessment of a small group of candidates under the observation of experienced assessors.

The Validity of Assessment Centers

Assessment Centers began to be used in the 1950s. That is a long, long time ago. They are almost as old as two of the authors of this book and have aged much better than the authors. If ACs have been in use for that long, you can probably guess that they have proven to be valid. You would be correct but understanding why they are valid has been a big question. Obviously knowing why ACs work is important for designing them properly and using their results for selection and individual development. The research on the validity of ACs can be viewed as having three different phases.

Phase 1: We Love Assessment Centers!

As we mentioned earlier, AT&T did a number of studies that examined the validity of ACs throughout the 30+ years of their subjects' careers. All of these provided evidence that ACs ratings were predictive of movement into middle-level management within 10 years of AC assessment and continued career progress over subsequent years. In addition OAR ratings were also significantly correlated with supervisory ratings of job performance. The first meta-analysis of 50 different studies containing 107 validity coefficients found a 0.36 correlation between OAR ratings and job performance and 0.36 correlation between ratings and career advancement.[17] Another study measured the validity of AC ratings and career salary growth in a longitudinal study and estimated the validity coefficient at 0.35.[18] All of these validity studies used the final OAR measure as the predictor. In addition to job performance and salary growth, other studies showed the benefits of AC experience on managers who were used as assessors (improved interviewing skills, job communication, and reduced error in performance reviews).[19] Even assessees benefited from the experience, as it was found that those who participated in ACs showed a significant increase in their self-rated skills of organizing and planning, analyzing, decision making, influencing others, and flexibility.[20]

In addition to these positive outcomes, various actions indicated that ACs reduced or eliminated both racial and gender differences. For example, in the much-publicized sex-discrimination case against AT&T, ACs were identified as a method to use in changing AT&T's promotion policies.[21] The essence of the discrimination charge was the adverse impact against women in promotion through management ranks. Under the agreement between AT&T and the EEOC, ACs were to be used extensively to identify those women who were most likely to be successful in higher management positions.

Similarly, in *Berry v. City of Omaha*, ACs were used in selection for the position of deputy police chief. The main issue was whether the three different assessor groups that evaluated candidates used different standards.[22] After reviewing descriptions of the development of the AC and data analysis with regard to reliability among assessors, the court upheld the use of the AC.

However there is some evidence that ACs could, in fact, produce adverse impact. One study that compared paper-and-pencil tests to AC-type simulations found that simulations did, in fact, produce score differences between black and white respondents, even though these differences were smaller than differences between the groups on written tests.[23] This pattern of differences was also found in a meta-analytic study that compared various racial and gender groups' differences on AC scores.[24] The d-scores for white–black applicants was estimated as 0.56 (whites higher), the white–Hispanic d-score was 0.28 (whites higher), and the male–female d-score was −0.19 (females higher). A point of reference when evaluating d-scores of various selection instruments is the commonly accepted d-score on cognitive ability tests of 0.73. The d-score of 0.56 found in this last study indicates that while the score difference between the two groups is slightly lower for ACs than cognitive-ability tests it is much greater than what was commonly thought. ACs clearly do not result in equivalent mean scores between the two groups and ACs may not be the way to minimize adverse impact between whites and blacks.

In summary, for about 25 years after AC development at AT&T, selection specialists were in love with ACs. They contained replications of job activities, were validly related to a number of work-performance measures, seemed to reduce adverse impact in testing (until more recent research indicated otherwise), and had benefits for both assessors and assessees. There were minor criticisms such as their very great cost in development and implementation and some evidence that traditional selection tests such as cognitive ability, bio data, and personality inventories produced measures that significantly correlated with AC measures. But like many love affairs, the relationship between selection specialists and ACs grew stormy. (By the way, when was the last time one of your textbooks made the analogy between love and the text subject matter? Not many times, we guess!)

Phase 2: This Is Not Working and It's Your Fault, Not Mine!

In 1982 Paul Sackett and George Dreher published a major research study that focused on the failure of ACs to demonstrate the pattern of correlations among dimension ratings that they were predicted to produce.[25] As we mentioned previously, ACs supposedly measure the behavioral dimensions across several exercises. Based upon measurement theory of that time, the ratings given for the same dimension in various exercises should be highly correlated. After all, the same characteristic is being measured. For example, if the dimension of planning and organizing is to be measured with the in-basket test, the interview, and a case analysis, then the correlations of the ratings for participants for this dimension among these three devices should be quite high. This is commonly referred to as *convergent* validity.

The evidence was quite clear, however, that the correlations among such dimension ratings were very low, often ranging from 0.05 to 0.15. This is puzzling because a lack of convergent validity indicates that behavior on each dimension is either very specific to a testing situation, is not reliably judged by assessors, or both. In any case, the validity of the overall rating of the dimension is questionable. Even more disturbing is the finding that the correlations among dimensions that are measured within the same exercise are very high.[26] This is referred to as a **lack** of *discriminant validity*; it should not occur. Discriminant validity exists when relatively low correlations are found among dimensions—such as problem solving, leadership, and verbal communication—within a single exercise. The dimensions are regarded as separate characteristics of the participants. For example, an in-basket may be intended to measure five separate dimensions of the participants. The design of an AC assumes that these dimensions are independent. If this is so, the correlations among dimensions should be low to moderate.

In addition, other evidence suggests that assessors' ratings do not act as they should. For example, the ratings by the same assessor of the same participants in two similar LGD problems do not correlate very highly.[27] A related study explored how contrast effects influence assessor ratings of candidates.[28] Specifically, a low-performing candidate was rated significantly lower than she actually performed when evaluated in a group consisting of two similar low performers.

There are several possible explanations for both this lack of convergent validity within dimensions and discriminant validity across dimensions. One is that cognitive ability and personality traits underlie participants' performance in ACs. Assessors' ratings merely reflect the amount of these traits that the individuals going through the AC possess. In support of this explanation, one study found that measures of cognitive ability, extraversion, emotional stability, openness, and agreeableness had a multiple correlation of 0.84 with OAR scores that assessors assigned to participants.[29]

A second explanation is that AC exercises intended to measure the same dimensions are too dissimilar to actually do so. That is, exercises such as in-baskets, LGDs, and role plays present situations to participants that differ in terms of psychological demands. The exercises cannot be considered to be parallel measures of the same dimensions.[30] Some research has supported this explanation by demonstrating that assessors' ratings of dimensions across similar exercises are higher than those across dissimilar exercises.[31] However, even in these studies the correlations for the same dimension across similar exercises have not been as high as one would anticipate from the intended design of ACs.

A third explanation is that ACs are frequently not designed as well as they should be and among other problems they contain too many dimensions for assessors to successfully distinguish. That is, the information-processing demands of ACs are too high for assessors to be able to separate behaviors and map them onto each of the multiple dimensions that are contained in ACs. Partial support of this explanation was found in a meta-analysis that determined that assessor ratings on four dimensions had a higher correlation with job performance than did correlations based upon more dimensions.[32] Following from this explanation, AC designers have reduced the number of dimensions that assessors are asked to evaluate, or provided assessors with checklists of behaviors to use in scoring.[33] They have also provided more training,[34] used only psychologists and experienced managers as assessors,[35] and reduced the number of participants that each assessor has to judge.[36] However, these changes have only marginally improved the convergent and divergent validity issues.

A fourth explanation is that exercises—not dimensions—are important components of ACs. Exercises are specific work-related situations related to work behaviors and performance. The high correlations among dimensions within an exercise are not error but rather represent consistent behavior in a specific testing/work situation. One study found that assessors' ratings could be separated into both exercise and dimension factors.[37] The exercise factors correlated with the OARs as well as with measures of cognitive ability, job knowledge, and job performance. The authors concluded that (a) assessors apparently rate overall exercise behavior rather than dimension behavior; (b) assessors may view exercise ratings as evaluations of work samples—in which case they provide global ratings of how well participants perform important job activities; or (c) assessors view exercises as demonstrations of trait behaviors. That is, the assessors may primarily see the LGD as an exercise that measures persuasiveness or leadership and therefore evaluate that trait in participants. This explanation fits with the study (described previously) that found that personality characteristics and cognitive ability correlated very highly with OARs. Based upon these findings, ACs could be designed such that exercises become the focus. These exercises should be developed on the basis of content validity of work samples demonstrated through job analysis.[38]

Related work has described a model for developing Task-Based Assessment Centers.[39] Exercises should be developed after a detailed job analysis and designed such that they capture the most important job tasks or activities. The essential idea is that the correlations among measures of what are thought to be separate dimensions within an exercise are not error but actually the accurate measure of how well the participant is performing an important job activity. Viewing an exercise this way allows for feedback and training about how that activity should be performed correctly.

Phase 3: Well I Might Have Made A Mistake And We May Be Okay After All.

This phase of thinking and research on ACs started in the early 2000s. Its major theme is that the measurement model that expected PEDRs to correlate for the same dimension across exercises and not to correlate among different dimensions within an exercise is an incorrect way of thinking about ACs. Even though the expected pattern of correlations was consistently shown to not occur, AC OAR scores were found to be correlated consistently with various measures of work performance. These patterns were confusing. If ACs did not function the way they were supposed to, how could they be valid? The work in this phase has taken several different approaches but most of them are based upon the idea that PEDRs are not the appropriate measure to emphasize. Rather the focus should be on the DRs, the ratings formed for each dimension after all exercises have been completed by the participants. As we have previously said, the DR is based upon the various PEDRs for each exercise that have been used to measure that dimension. We will summarize a representative sample of the research in this phase.

Andrew Speer and his colleagues studied the effect of situational bandwidth across exercises measuring the same dimension.[40] Bandwidth refers to how much the circumstances of the exercises that measure a dimension (e.g., communication) vary across exercises. One exercise may require the participant to join in a group discussion (LGD), another may require a verbal presentation by only the participant (case study), and the third may require written notes (in-basket). Traditional thinking about ACs would argue that these three exercises all measure communication so the correlations among the three PEDRs should be high. However, Speer and his co-researchers have a different idea: Because communication is a complex concept, the three exercises measure different aspects of the concept. They may not be correlated very highly because of their differences, but their combined DR score may be a valid measure of communication because the three different exercises do a good job of replicating the various work situations that require communication. Thought of another way, ACs are very expensive. What good does it do to replicate the same aspect of communication in three exercises that all require the same communication behavior? The PEDRs' correlations for these exercises may be high but they may not adequately measure all the aspects of communication and therefore would not make a good predictor. A test of simple mathematical knowledge does not ask 30 questions about the multiplication of one-digit numerals. It will ask 30 different questions about different types of mathematical calculations. As a result it will be a more valid measure than will be a test that asks the same calculation 30 times.

The findings of their research supported their ideas. They developed a method of scoring the bandwidth of exercises measuring the same dimension and then compared correlations among PEDRs with various levels of bandwidth. When exercises were different (high bandwidth), correlations among PEDRS were low. When exercises were similar (low bandwidth), correlations among PEDRs were higher. This indicated that the low correlations across exercises measuring the same dimension may be caused by dissimilarity of the exercises. They also found that DRs from exercises with high bandwidths were more predictive of job performance than exercises with low bandwidths. This supported their contention that dimensions that used varied exercises to measure the dimension would be better predictors than would be dimensions with very similar exercises. One conclusion of these findings is that low correlations among PEDRs for the same dimension may be irrelevant. The DR derived from these PEDRs may be quite valid. This is, of course, quite contradictory to the Phase 2 thoughts about PEDRs. However, research in that phase did not examine the validity of the resultant DRs either.

Other research has examined dimension scores in a different way—broadening the dimensions that are measured and correlating those broad DRs with work-performance measures. Winfred Arthur and his colleagues examined the results of studies of AC validity and identified 712 correlations from 168 different dimensions.[41] Yes that is a lot of dimensions; many of these seemed to be the same concept but with different specific names. Remember that when ACs became popular there was not a fixed list of dimensions to be measured. In various ways, the researchers combined the 168 dimensions into a set of six dimensions to be studied. These dimensions and their corresponding estimated validity coefficients with work performance were: problem solving (0.39), influencing others (0.38), organizing and planning (0.37), communication (0.33), drive (0.31), and consideration/awareness of others (0.25). The estimated validity coefficients for the first three dimensions were higher than those of earlier meta-analysis studies that estimated the validity of OAR measures. The researchers also correlated all six dimensions with the criteria measures and calculated a multiple correlation of 0.45. Related work by John Meriac and others also examined the validity of these six dimensions plus a seventh of stress tolerance.[42] The multiple correlation of these seven dimension scores with measures of work performance was 0.40. In addition, the researchers found that the seven dimensions were significantly related to job performance over the amount of job performance explained by measures of cognitive ability and Big Five Personality dimensions.

Other studies have used various statistical analyses to carefully examine the correlations among the various measures of ACS, that is PEDRs, DRs, and OARs. Nathan Kuncel and Paul Sackett found that as dimension scores are aggregated across multiple exercises, the variance associated with dimension scores definitely exceeds the variance associated with exercise scores.[43] That is, the specific exercise effects that were previously identified were not as prevalent as when PEDRs were used. However, the research found that one large general dimension did exist. That is, differences among assessees in AC ratings were accounted for both by differences in dimension scores (which is what ACs try to measure) and also by individual differences in performance across all exercises. Kuncel and Sackett could not explain the nature of this general dimension factor but postulated three possibilities. First, performance on AC exercises could be affected by a common set of individual differences such as general mental ability or personality. Second, it could be differences in assessees' ability to consistently figure out the construct that the exercise is designed around and to perform better because of this insight. Either of these two explanations could be useful in the prediction of job performance. The third possible explanation is that individuals differ in terms of "test wiseness" of simulations, which would probably not be correlated with job performance.

Brian Hoffman and his colleagues also examined the construct validity of ACs by comparing models containing factors of exercises, dimensions, and general performance.[44] They tested various models to explain the pattern of correlations among ratings found in four different ACs. Their generalized findings across the four ACs were that the correlations among ratings in an AC are most appropriately explained by a model that consists of broad dimension factors, exercise factors, and a general performance factor across exercises. To form broad dimension factors, the researchers combined ratings from similar dimensions in much the same fashion that we have previously described. The various dimensions that were derived were communication, interpersonal, leadership, and conceptual/administrative. Not all four ACs contained all of these exercise factors nor were the four ACs similar in amount of variance that the four dimensions explained. It is reasonable to believe that the broad dimensions of an AC depend on the nature of the job for which the AC was developed and the content of the exercises chosen for inclusion. In the ACs for which criteria data were available, broad dimension ratings were significant predictors. Exercise factors were found to be true measures, not errors, as they were also statistically related to criteria measures. The general performance factor that was identified was similar in concept to the work of Kuncel and Sackett summarized earlier. However, in this research, the general performance factor was not related to work performance, as were dimension and exercise factors. In a related study, Hoffman and his colleagues determined that the general performance factor was actually composed of three separate factors. In the AC that they examined these were interpersonal facilitation and communication, technical activities and mechanics of management, and leadership and supervision.[45] The main practical advantage of knowing the specific performance factors rather than assuming that one general factor exists is for providing feedback to participants. For example, a participant could be told that she performed well in terms of facilitation and communication in group discussion (LGD) but not as well in written format (in-basket).

YOU, the Reader: Okay, summarize this so I have something to remember.

Us, the Writers: Sure, you can remember these points but learn more words to explain them.

1. ACs are valid.

2. PEDRs should be thought of as building blocks to form DRs not as complete measures by themselves.

3. DRs contain more specific information than OARS.

4. DRs can be usefully combined into broad dimension scores.

5. Broad DRs can predict work performance—maybe even better than OARs can.

6. Broad DRs can be more useful than OARs in providing feedback to participants.

7. Exercise factors exist in ACs and can also predict job performance.

SITUATIONAL JUDGMENT TESTS

Partially because of the cost and the feared lack of convergent and discriminant validity of ACs, selection specialists turned their attention to other types of simulation devices. One of these is situational judgment tests (SJTs). SJTs are verbal simulations and regarded as low-fidelity because they are almost exclusively descriptions of work situations or behaviors (rather than actual replications), presented in either paper-and-pencil or electronic formats. They ask the respondent to choose among multiple-choice alternatives that are various behaviors that may be taken to address the work situation described in the question. (Yes, an SJT is like a multiple-choice exam in college! It just doesn't have a corresponding chapter in a textbook that contains the answers.)

Michael McDaniel and Nhung Nguyen have described the steps traditionally taken to develop SJTs.[46] We summarize their work in the following list and add some of our thoughts:

1. Collect stories from incumbent or supervisory subject matter experts (SMEs) about situations encountered on the job that are important for successful performance. For example, for a customer service job, these experts might be asked to write critical incidents concerning understanding customers' needs, promoting the product to customers, and seeking a balance between the needs of the customers and the company's interests.

2. Review the situations that are described. The goal is to identify a series of situations that will serve as item stems for the SJT. This involves grouping the situations according to similarity of content, selecting representative situations, eliminating redundant situations, and ensuring that the situations vary in terms of difficulty or complexity.

3. Edit the situations into item stems. That is, rephrase situations in a simple form that can be used in the item posed as a question on the SJT. It is desirable that all stems be approximately the same length and represent all important aspects of the job. Table 13.8 contains examples of item stems and possible responses that may be contained in an SJT.

4. Drop inappropriate situations or those that may raise legal concerns. For example, situations including activities that cannot be performed by disabled applicants. Other situations may be excluded because they are too job-specific and would be unknown to applicants or because they represent undesirable behaviors (for example, robbery or violence).

5. Perform a job analysis including gathering ratings of the importance of and time spent on specific tasks. Compare these ratings with the written situations in order to determine that the situations address the most important and time-consuming tasks.

TABLE 13.8	Examples of Items of a Situational Judgment Test for Entry-Level Management in Financial Institutions

Item Stem #1. It is Friday afternoon and your immediate manager has just told you to stay until the office is finished compiling its weekly reports—until about 8:30 p.m. However, you have tickets for you and your date for an 8 p.m. concert. What would you do?

 a. Tell your manager that you cannot stay because of the concert (−1 point).
 b. Explain the situation to your manager's manager (−2 points).
 c. Tell your manager that you will stay and explain the situation to your date (+2 points).
 d. Try to find someone else at your level to do this, but stay if you cannot find someone else (+1 point).

Item Stem #2. A customer with a relatively small asset base complains to you that the institution does not provide enough appropriate information about financial markets for him to be able to develop his own investment strategy. What would you do?

 a. Listen and tell him that you will speak with your manager about this (−2 points).
 b. Take notes and tell him that you will look into this (−1 points).
 c. Take notes and briefly discuss the situation with the market-knowledge manager to determine what can be done (+1 point).
 d. Take notes, speak with the market-knowledge manager, and spend time thinking of possible actions (+2 points).

6. Assemble the chosen items into a survey. The survey should be formatted, laid out in survey form, and reviewed for grammar and spelling.

7. Administer the survey to a sample of SMEs. The purpose of this step is to collect information that can be used to write alternative responses to each item. Respondents for this step could either be job incumbents or supervisors of the job of interest. The SJT developer asks respondents to identify one or more responses to each situation listed as an item stem. The specific instruction is usually either "Describe what you would do in this situation" or "Describe what you should do (or is the best action to take) in this situation." Sometimes respondents are given both instructions and complete two versions of responses. Research has indicated that asking what one "would do" leads to better test development than asking what one "should do." That is, the criterion-related validities of items were substantially higher when the "would do" instructions were used.[47]

8. The test developer reviews all the offered responses to each situation and prepares an edited list of potential responses to each situation. He or she edits the responses to remove duplicates and improve the understandability of the response and may also omit responses that are too obviously socially desirable, long, complex, or clearly inappropriate for the situation described. Typically, the developer wants to have multiple responses to each situation and responses that span a range of effective reactions to the situation.

9. The list of situations and alternative responses is circulated to the same people who provided alternative responses to the item or an equivalent group. The question for this round of review is essentially "How appropriate is each of these responses to the situation described in the item stem?" Respondents frequently rate each alternative on a 1-to-5 scale. The test developer selects for inclusion in the survey those responses that: (a) have a high level of agreement among the raters in terms of scaled scores to the item-question, and (b) have different average scale scores, which indicates that the alternatives are different in terms of their appropriateness.

10. The next step is to choose a response format that those who take the SJT must use to answer the questions of the test. There are three common formats.[48] The first of these formats is to ask the respondent to rate each alternative of every question on the SJT on a scale according to how well that alternative addresses the situation presented in the item. Most often these are 5-point scales in which a response of 5 means that the respondent thinks the alternative is an excellent response for the situation presented in the item. The second format asks the respondent to rank-order the alternatives for each question as to how well they address the question. The third format requires the respondent to identify both the best alternative and the worst alternative in terms of responding to each question.

11. The final step is to develop a scoring system in order to grade the answers given by the respondent. Of course each of the three response formats just described differ in terms of scoring procedures because they collect different types of data. All of them, however, use information provided by the SME ratings of response alternatives described in Step 9 as the basis for their scoring systems. In the format of rating all alternatives, 1 point can be given for each alternative that is rated the same (or approximately the same) as that alternative is rated by the SMEs. For the ranking format, 1 point can be given for each alternative that

matches the ranking of that alternative given by the SMEs. (Ranking of the alternatives for each item can be obtained by ranking the rating-scale scores provided by SMEs.) There are different ways of scoring the responses of best and worst alternatives. One way is to award 1 point if the best SME alternative is the one chosen as best by the respondent. Similarly 1 point is given if the alternative that the respondent identifies as the worst is the one identified by the SMEs as worst. A +2 is the highest score per item. However a score of −1 can be given if the alternative chosen as the best one by the respondent is the worst one according to the SMEs. Not surprisingly, a −1 score is also given if the alternative chosen as the worst one by the respondent is the best one according to the SMEs. In other words, if the respondent is badly wrong, he loses points. It doesn't pay to be a dummy! No points are given if the alternatives that the respondent identifies as best and worst simply do not match the best and worst responses of the SMEs. Just being wrong doesn't hurt so much. If you follow this scoring, you realize that the range of scores for each item is −2 to +2. As this list indirectly points out, the SJT is a method of test development rather than a content type of test. That is, the content base for SJT questions is not a narrowly defined subject area as is true with cognitive ability or personality tests. We should think about an SJT as analogous to a structured interview. (We know you remember Chapter 10 vividly and will not go into details!) The interviewer asks predetermined questions and the SJT asks predetermined questions. The content of the questions can include a variety of topics.

Questions That We Know You Are Asking That We Can Answer

Q1. *Are SJTs Valid or Just Good Looking?*

Well, SJTs are pretty faces (meaning face validity because of their similarity with job activities—pretty clever, huh?). However many research studies have consistently found that SJTs are significantly related to various measures of work performance. One group of studies has examined SJTs composed of a collection of heterogeneous content areas rather than SJTs that focus on one content area such as interpersonal skill. These studies have correlated SJT scores with overall supervisory performance ratings and produced significant correlations in the range of 0.20 to 0.36.[49] Another group of studies has examined specific content topics of SJTs. This is useful research because it helps answer an important question, "Is it better to write SJTs as work sample instruments (heterogeneous SJTs using job incidents) or as instruments that measure WRCs (single content SJTS)?" One study related to this question found significant correlations between medical program applicants' scores on an interpersonal skills content SJT (e.g., social sensitivity, relationship building, working with others, listening, communication) and supervisory doctors' ratings of performance in both internships (7 years later) and job performance (9 years later).[50] These findings point to testing WRCs of interpersonal skills as being important for success as a doctor. In addition, a meta-analyses study classified SJTs into the following content categories: leadership skills, interpersonal skills, personality dimensions, teamwork, job knowledge, and heterogeneous.[51] Results of the research were that both content and heterogeneous SJT scores were related to three different measures of work performance: task (mainly supervisors' ratings of general performance), contextual performance (mainly OCB helping behaviors), and managerial performance (leadership and related behaviors). Specifically content SJTs that measured teamwork and personality were more strongly related to task performance than were heterogeneous SJTs. SJTs concentrated on interpersonal skills and leadership were related about the same as heterogeneous SJTs and those of job knowledge were lower. SJTs on teamwork and leadership had higher correlations with contextual performance than did heterogeneous SJTs while interpersonal skills SJTs were about equal. Both SJTs of teamwork and leadership had higher correlations with managerial performance than did heterogeneous SJTs. These results indicate that content SJTs are consistently related to various work performance measures and that SJTs of leadership and various interaction skills may be more strongly related to these performance measures than are heterogeneous SJTs. Perhaps this is indicative of how important interaction with other individuals is for many jobs.

Another interesting part of this research was that the researchers compared the validity of video SJTs (test situations were presented by video enactment of a work situation and paused at a point at which the respondent had to choose among a set number of alternative behaviors) and written SJTs. The content of the SJTs studied were interpersonal skills, leadership, and heterogeneous. In each of the three, the video SJT had a higher validity coefficient than did the written version. Another single study also found video presentation superior to written presentation of SJT situations.[52] This superiority of the video presentation may be because video can more effectively present the complex human interactions in work situations than can written items. Filip Lievens and Fiona Patterson studied another critical question of how the validity of low-cost, low-fidelity SJTs compares to the validity of both high-cost, higher-fidelity ACs and low-cost job-knowledge tests.[53] The SJT and AC both measured the same five predictors and the job-knowledge test was the application of medical knowledge to specific patient situations. Scores on each of the three types of testing were correlated with supervisory ratings of doctors' performance. Each of the three (SJTs, ACs, and job-knowledge tests) was significantly related to job performance. In addition, both SJTs and ACs added incremental validity over the job-knowledge test and there were no validity differences between the SJT and the AC. So in this case, the low-cost, low-fidelity SJT simulation was as effective as the AC.

Q2. *It is good that SJTs are valid but do they have adverse impact?*

Ah, good question. It shows you are thinking like a selection specialist, which we know is one of your life goals. Research has generally found differences between white–black groups (whites scoring higher) on SJTs. These differences are larger on SJTs whose content was classified as cognitive ability or job knowledge but are smaller on SJTs with content consisting mainly of interpersonal skills. Only small differences in SJT scores were found between males and females, regardless of content.[54] Another research study specifically addressed SJT score differences among demographic groups of applicants only.[55] Other studies usually used job incumbents as subjects or even formed samples of incumbents and job applicants. As we mentioned previously, the difficulty with such samples is that job experience is a confounding variable in measuring differences. It is usually thought that job experience lessens any differences because of the learning that exists while doing the job. This study by Phil Roth, Phil Bobko, and Maury Buster examined differences between job applicants only on SJTs for four different jobs. For each job, the SJT was the first of three tests that were given at different testing sessions. The applicants with low scores were dropped after each test so all applicants completed the SJT. Their findings had the same pattern as the previous research we discussed. There were differences between white and black applicants on both SJTs that were mainly cognitive ability/job knowledge and also those that were mainly interpersonal skills. For the SJTs of interpersonal skills, the d-score was small (d = 0.21, whites higher), which was in the same general range of other studies. However, the difference between the groups on SJTs of cognitive ability/job knowledge was much larger (d = 0.63, whites higher). While this d-score was still lower than d-scores on cognitive ability tests (d = 0.73), the authors commented that SJTs should not be thought of as a testing method that can be used to greatly reduce mean score differences (adverse impact) between white and black applicants.

Q3. *Anything Else to Know About SJTs?*

Well, we are a bit disappointed because this question is not as focused as the first two of your questions! But it does give us a lot of room to answer. One topic that has been examined is respondents faking responses on SJTs. One study looked at faking on both knowledge-based and behavior-based SJTs.[56] The researchers found that faking occurred with the use of behavior-based SJTs but not with knowledge-based SJTs. This makes sense because knowledge-based SJTs require technical knowledge to select the correct alternative. It is difficult to fake technical knowledge if you don't have it. Behaviors are often more obvious. This finding about faking behavior-based SJTs complements another study that found that samples of undergraduates students who had no job-specific knowledge could produce responses to a behavioral SJT that were significantly correlated with responses of SMEs to the same items.[57] Moreover when the undergraduates' responses were used in the development of a scoring key, which was then used to grade job incumbents' responses to the SJT items, the resulting scores were significantly correlated to the job incumbents' supervisors' ratings of job performance. The reason for this validity of the responses of undergraduates with no specific job knowledge is that the undergraduates did possess some general knowledge about appropriate responses to the SJT situations. Specifically, undergraduates knew that agreeableness and conscientiousness were appropriate in many job situations and used this knowledge when responding to specific situations of the SJT. One might guess that faking measured in the first study may not be faking in a traditional sense but could actually be the use of general knowledge of how to act in answering the behavior-based items.

Another topic is the interrelated issues of coaching, response instructions, faking, and scoring of SJTs. The effect of coaching is estimated to be 0.5 sd, which is a significant score increase in most circumstances, especially those in which relatively few applicants are selected.[58] Another study compared responses to two of the most often used response instructions: "What is the best alternative?" and "What would you do in this situation?" It was generally assumed that these two instructions would lead to two different responses. The first asks the applicant to demonstrate knowledge of what is the correct response. The second asks the applicant for his/her most likely behavior without regard to correct answer. However, it was found that the responses given by two randomly assigned groups to these two instructions were not statistically different.[59] The conclusion was that it is best to ask the respondent to indicate what is the correct answer. One way to think about this conclusion is that in selection situations, the respondent is going to try to pick the correct answer even if that is not what he or she would do. The applicant usually tries to make the best impression possible. The authors of another study looked at the effects of three scoring formats: rating, ranking, and choosing most/least acceptable alternatives that we described previously.[60] The authors thought that the rating format was generally the most acceptable. It had higher reliability, lower overlap with general mental ability scores, took less time, and had smaller score differences between blacks and whites than the ranking and choose the best-worst alternatives. Another interesting point was that the content to the SJT in this research was counterproductive behaviors, indicating the importance of this performance variable to many organizations. Another major work examining scoring of SJTs found that two adjustments in scoring can improve individual item validity, reduce white–black mean score differences, and lessen the effect of coaching on scores.[61] The first of these two adjustments applies to scoring systems using ratings and reduces the elevation (the mean item response for a respondent) and also scatter (the magnitude of the respondent's standard deviation from her own mean). These two variables are frequently thought of as response-pattern errors, not components of true scores. The second adjustment was to eliminate items with midrange scores on the scoring key (not the best or the worst answers).

Q4. *Could you summarize what you just wrote about instructions and scoring?*
Sure we can! At this point in our understanding of how to use SJTs, it is optimal to write the items to measure a single construct (such as teamwork, or ethical practices), ask respondents to rate the adequacy of each alternative to each item (using a 5-point rating scale), use those alternatives that have been rated either highly or lowly by SMEs while omitting those alternatives with midrange ratings, and make statistical corrections for individual respondents' elevation and scatter among responses. Doing these will reduce faking, coaching effects, demographic group differences, and increase validity with measures of performance. Can you think of any better goals in your life?

REFERENCES

1. Paul Wernimont and John Campbell, "Sign, Samples, and Criteria," *Journal of Applied Psychology* 52 (1968): 372–376.

2. Anne Jansen, Klaus Melchers, Filip Lievens, Martin Kleinmann, Michael Brandli, Laura Fraefel, and Cornelius J. Konig, "Situation Assessment as an Ignored Factor in the Behavioral Consistency Paradigm Underlying the Validity of Personnel Selection Procedures," *Journal of Applied Psychology* 98 (2013): 326–341.

3. James Asher and James Sciarrino, "Realistic Work Sample Tests: A Review," *Personal Psychology* 27 (1974): 519–533.

4. Robert M. Guion, *Assessment, Measurement, and Prediction for Personnel Decisions,* (Mahwah, NJ: Erlbaum, 1998).

5. James E. Campion, "Work Sampling for Personnel Selection," *Journal of Applied Psychology* 56 (1972): 40–44.

6. David Robinson, "Content-Oriented Personnel Selection in a Small Business Setting," *Personnel Psychology* 34 (1981): 77–87.

7. Richard R. Reilly and Edmond W. Israelski, "Development and Validation of Minicourses in the Telecommunication Industry," *Journal of Applied Psychology* 73 (1988): 721–726.

8. Lynnette B. Plumlee, *A Short Guide to the Development of Performance Tests* (Washington, DC: Personnel Research and Development Center, U.S. Civil Service Commission, Professional Series 75–1, January 1975).

9. Joseph L. Boyd and Benjamin Shimberg, *Handbook of Performance Testing* (Princeton, NJ: Educational Testing Service, 1971), 24.

10. Neal Schmitt and Cheri Ostroff, "Operationalizing the 'Behavioral Consistency' Approach: Selection Test Development Based on a Content-Oriented Strategy," *Personnel Psychology* 39 (1986): 91–108.

11. Philip L. Roth, Philip Bobko, and Lynn A. McFarland, "A Meta-Analysis of Work Sample Test Validity: Updating and Integrating Some Classic Literature," *Personnel Psychology* 58 (2005): 1009–1037.

12. Philip Roth, Philip Bobko, Lynn McFarland, and Maury Buster, "Work Sample Tests in Personnel Selection: A Meta-Analysis of Black-White Differences in Overall and Exercise Scores," *Personnel Psychology* 61 (2008): 637–662.

13. Wayne Cascio and Niel Phillips, "Performance Testing: A Rose among Thorns?" *Personnel Psychology* 32 (1979): 751–766.

14. Cascio and Phillips, "Performance Testing: A Rose among Thorns?"

15. Douglas W. Bray, Richard J. Campbell, and Donald L. Grant, *Formative Years in Business: A Long-Term AT&T Study of Managerial Lives* (Huntington, NY: R. E. Krieger Publishing Co., 1979).

16. William C. Byham, "Assessor Selection and Training," in *Applying the Assessment Center Method*, ed. J. L. Moses and W. C. Byham (New York: Pergamon Press, 1977), 89–126.

17. Barbara B. Gaugler, Douglas B. Rosenthal, George C. Thornton III, and Cynthia Bentson, " Meta-Analysis of Assessment Center Validity," *Journal of Applied Psychology* 72 (1987): 493–511.

18. Paul G. Jansen and Claartje J. Vinkenburg, "Predicting Managerial Career Success for Assessment Center Data: A Longitudinal Study," *Journal of Vocational Behavior* 68 (2006): 253–266.

19. Robert V. Lorenzo, "Effects of Assessorship on Managers' Proficiency in Acquiring, Evaluating, and Communicating Information about People," *Personnel Psychology* 37 (1984): 617–634.

20. Neal Schmitt, Kevin J. Ford, and Daniel M. Stults, "Changes in Self-Perceived Ability as a Function of Performance in an Assessment Centre," *Journal of Occupational Psychology* 74 (1986): 327–335.

21. "Landmark AT&T–EEOC Consent Agreement Increases Assessment Center Usage," *Assessment & Development* 1 (1973): 1–2.

22. *Berry v. City of Omaha*, 14 FEP 391 (1977).

23. Neal Schmitt and Amy E. Mills, "Traditional Tests and Job Simulations: Minority and Majority Performance and Test Validities," *Journal of Applied Psychology* 86 (2001): 451–458.

24. Michelle A. Dean, Philip L. Roth, and Philip Bobko, "Ethnic and Gender Subgroup Differences in Assessment Center Ratings: A Meta-Analysis," *Journal of Applied Psychology* 93 (2008): 685–691.

25. Paul R. Sackett and George F. Dreher, "Constructs and Assessment Center Dimensions: Some Troubling Empirical Findings," *Journal of Applied Psychology* 67 (1982): 401–410.

26. Peter Bycio, Kenneth M. Alvares, and June Hahn, "Situational Specificity in Assessment Center Ratings: A Confirmatory Factor Analysis," *Journal of Applied Psychology* 72 (1987): 463–474. See also Ivan Robertson, Lynda Gratton, and David Sharpley, "The Psychometric Properties and Design of Managerial Assessment Centres: Dimensions into Exercises Won't Go," *Journal of Occupational Psychology* 60 (1987): 187–195; and David Chan, "Criterion and Construct Validation of an Assessment Centre," *Journal of Occupational and Organizational Psychology* 69 (1996): 167–181.

27. Robert D. Gatewood, George Thornton III, and Harry W. Hennessey Jr., "Reliability of Exercise Ratings in the Leaderless Group Discussion," *Journal of Occupational Psychology* 63 (1990): 331–342.

28. Barbara B. Gaugler and Amy S. Rudolph, "The Influence of Assessee Performance Variation on Assessors' Judgments," *Personnel Psychology* 45 (1992): 77–98.

29. J. M. Collins, F. L. Schmidt, M. Sanchez-Ku, L. Thomas, M. A. McDaniel, and H. Le, "Can Basic Individual Differences Shed Light on the Construct Meaning of Assessment Center Evaluations?" *International Journal of Selection and Assessment* 11 (2003): 17–29.

30. Filip Lievens, Christopher S. Chasteen, Eric A. Day, and Neil D. Christiansen, "Large-Scale Investigation of the Role of Trait Activation Theory for Understanding Assessment Center Convergent and Discriminant Validity," *Journal of Applied Psychology* 91 (2006): 247–258. See also Filip Lievens and James M. Conway, "Dimension and Exercise Variance in Assessment Center Scores: A Large Scale Evaluation of Multitrait-Multimethod Studies," *Journal of Applied Psychology* 86 (2001): 1202–1222.

31. Stephanie Haaland and Neil D. Christiansen, "Implications of Trait-Activation Theory for Evaluating the Construct Validity of Assessment Center Ratings," *Personnel Psychology* 55 (2002): 137–163.

32. Winfred Arthur Jr., Eric Anthony Day, Theresa L. McNelly, and Pamela S. Edens, "A Meta-Analysis of the Criterion-Related Validity of Assessment Center Dimensions," *Personnel Psychology* 56 (2003): 125–154.

33. Barbara B. Gaugler and George C. Thornton III, "Number of Assessment Center Dimensions as a Determinant of Assessor Accuracy," *Journal of Applied Psychology* 74 (1989): 611–618. See also Richard R. Reilly, Sarah Henry, and James W. Smither, "An Examination of the Effects of Using Behavior Checklists on the Construct Validity of Assessment Center Dimensions," *Personnel Psychology* 43 (1990): 71–84; A. Jones, Peter Herriot, B. Long, and R. Drakely, "Attempting to Improve the Validity of a Well-Established Assessment Centre," *Journal of Occupational Psychology* 64 (1991): 1–21; and Ted H. Shore, George C. Thornton III, and Lynn McFarlane Shore, "Construct Validity of Two Categories of Assessment Center Dimension Ratings," *Personnel Psychology* 43 (1990): 101–115.

34. Beverly Dugan, "Effects of Assessor Training on Information Use," *Journal of Applied Psychology* 73 (1988): 743–748. See also Deidra J. Schleicher, David V. Day, Bronston T. Mayes, and Ronald E. Riggio, "A New Frame for Frame-of-Reference Training: Enhancing the Construct Validity of Assessment Centers," *Journal of Applied Psychology* 87 (2002): 735–746; and Filip Lievens, "Assessor Training Strategies and Their Effects on Accuracy, Interrater Reliability, and Discriminant Validity," *Journal of Applied Psychology* 86 (2001): 255–264.

35. Filip Lievens, "Trying to Understand the Different Pieces of the Construct Validity Puzzle of Assessment Centers: An Examination of Assessor and Assessee Effects," *Journal of Applied Psychology* 87 (2002): 675–686.

36. Klaus G. Melchers, Martin Kleinmann, Marion A. Prinz, "Do Assessors Have Too Much On Their Plates? The Effects of Simultaneously Rating Multiple Assessment Center Candidates on Rating Quality," *International Journal of Selection and Assessment* 18 (2010): 329–341.

37. Charles E. Lance, Robert D. Gatewood, William H. Newbolt, Mark S. Foster, Nita R. French, and David E. Smith, "Assessment Center Exercises Factors Represent Cross-Situational Specificity, Not Method Bias," *Human Performance* 13 (2000): 323–353.

38. Charles E. Lance, Mark R. Foster, William A. Gentry, and Joseph D. Thoresen, "Assessor Cognitive Processes in an Operational Assessment Center," *Journal of Applied Psychology* 89 (2004): 22–35. See also J. D. Thoresen, "Do We Need Dimensions? Dimensions Limited or Unlimited," paper presented at the meeting of the International Congress of Assessment Center Methods, Pittsburgh, Pennsylvania, 2002.

39. Duncan Jackson, Jennifer A Stillman, and Paul Englert, "Task-Based Assessment Centers: Empirical Support for a Systems Model," *International Journal of Selection and Assessment* 18 (2010): 141–154. See also Charles E. Lance, "Why Assessment Centers Do Not Work the Way They Are Supposed To," *Industrial and Organizational Psychology* 1 (2008): 84–89.

40. Andrew B. Speer, Neil D. Christiansen, Richard D. Goffin, and Maynard Goff, "Situational Bandwidth and the Criterion-Related Validity of Assessment Center Ratings: Is Cross-Exercise Convergence Always Desirable?" *Journal of Applied Psychology* 99 (2014): 282–295.

41. Winfred Arthur Jr., Eric A. Day, Theresa L. McNelly, and Pamela S. Edens, "A Meta-Analysis of the Criterion-Related Validity of Assessment Center Dimensions," *Personnel Psychology* 56 (2003): 125–154.

42. John P. Meriac, Brian J. Hoffman, David J. Woehr, and Matthew S. Fleisher, "Further Evidence for the Validity of Assessment Center Dimensions: A Meta-Analysis of the Incremental Criterion-Related Validity of Dimension Ratings," *Journal of Applied Psychology* 93 (2008): 1042–1052.

43. Nathan R. Kuncel and Paul R. Sackett, "Resolving the Assessment Center Construct Validity Problem (As We Know It)," *Journal of Applied Psychology* 99 (2014): 38–47.

44. Brian J. Hoffman, Klaus G. Melches, Carrie A. Blair, Martin Kleinmann, and Robert T. Ladd, "Exercises and Dimensions Are the Currency of Assessment Centers," *Personnel Psychology* 64 (2011): 351–395.

45. Brian J. Hoffman and Adam Meade, "Alternate Approaches to Understanding the Psychometric Properties of Assessment Centers: An Analysis of the Structure and Equivalence of Exercise Ratings," *International Journal of Selection and Assessment* 20 (2012): 82–97.

46. Michael A. McDaniel and Nhung T. Nguyen, "Situational Judgment Tests: A Review of Practice and Constructs Assessed," *Journal of International Selection and Assessment* 9 (2001): 103–113.

47. Robert E. Ployhart and Mark G. Ehrhart, "Be Careful What You Ask For: Effects of Response Instructions on the Construct Validity and Reliability of Situational Judgment Tests," *International Journal of Selection and Assessment* 11 (2003): 1–16.

48. Winfred Arthur, Jr., Ryan M. Glaze, Stephen M. Jarrett, Craig D. White, Ira Schurig, and Jason E. Taylor, "Comparative Evaluation of Three Situational Judgment Test Response Formats in Terms of Construct Related Validity, Subgroup Differences, and Susceptibility to Response Distortion," *Journal of Applied Psychology* 99 (2014): 535–545.

49. David Chan and Neal Schmitt, "Situational Judgment and Job Performance," *Human Performance* 18 (2002): 233–254. See also Stephen J. Motowidlo and Margaret E. Beier, "Differentiating Specific Job Knowledge from Implicit Trait Policies in Procedural Knowledge Measured by a Situational Judgment Test," *Journal of Applied Psychology* 95 (2010): 321–333, and Michael A. McDaniel, Nathan S. Hartman, Deborah L. Whetzel, and W. Lee Grub III, "Situational Judgment Tests, Response Instructions, and Validity: A Meta-Analysis," *Personnel Psychology*, 60 (2007): 63–91.

50. Filip Lievens and Paul Sackett, "The Validity of Interpersonal Skills Assessment Via Situational Judgment Tests for Predicting Academic Success and Job Performance," *Journal of Applied Psychology* 97 (2012): 460–468.

51. Michael S. Christian, Bryan D. Edwards, and Jill C. Bradley, "Situational Judgment Tests: Constructs Assessed and a Meta-Analysis of Their Criterion-Related Validities," *Personnel Psychology* 63 (2010): 83–117.

52. Janneke K. Oostrom, Marise Born, Alec Serlie, and Henk T. Van der Molen, "A Multimedia Situational Test with a Constructed-Response Format: Its Relationship with Personality, Cognitive Ability, Job Experience, and Academic Performance," *Journal of Personnel Psychology* 10 (2011): 78–88.

53. Filip Lievens and Fiona Patterson, "The Validity and Incremental Validity of Knowledge Tests, Low-Fidelity Simulations, and High-Fidelity Simulations for Predicting Job Performance in Advanced-level High-stakes Selection," *Journal of Applied Psychology* 96 (2011): 927–940.

54. Deborah L. Whetzel, Michael A. McDaniel, and Nhung T. Nguyen, "Subgroup Differences in Situational Judgment Test Performance: A Meta-Analysis," *Human Performance* 21 (2008): 291–309; Matthew S. O'Connell, Nathan S. Hartman, Michael A. McDonald, and Walter Lee Grubb, "Incremental Validity of Situational Judgment Tests for Task and Contextual Job Performance," *International Journal of Selection & Assessment* 15 (2007): 19–29.

55. Philip Roth, Philip Bobko, and Maury A. Buster, "Situational Judgment Tests: The Influence and Importance of Applicant Status and Targeted Constructs on Estimates of Black-White Subgroup Differences," *Journal of Occupational and Organizational* Psychology 86 (2013): 394–409.

56. Nhung T. Nguyen, Michael D. Biderman, and Michael A. McDaniel, "Effects of Response Instructions on Faking a Situational Judgment Test," *International Journal of Selection & Assessment* 13 (2005): 250–260.

57. Stephan J. Motiwidlo and Margaret E. Beier, "Differentiating Specific Job Knowledge from Implicit Trait Policies in Procedural Knowledge Measured by a Situational Judgment Test," *Journal of Applied Psychology* 95 (2010): 321–333.

58. Filip Lievens, Tine Buyse, Paul R. Sackett, and Brian S. Connelly, "The Effects of Coaching on Situational Judgment Tests in High-Stakes Selection," *International Journal of Selection and Assessment* 20 (2012): 272–282.

59. Filip Lievens, Paul R. Sackett, and Tine Buyse, "The Effects of Response Instructions on Situational Judgment Test Performance and Validity in a High-Stakes Context," *Journal of Applied Psychology* 94 (2009): 1095–1101.

60. Winfred Arthur, Jr., et al. *Journal of Applied Psychology,* 2014.

61. Michael A. McDaniel, Joseph Psotka, Peter J. Legree, Amy Powell Yost, and Jeff A. Weekly, "Toward an Understanding of Situational Judgment Item Validity and Group Differences," *Journal of Applied Psychology* 96 (2011): 327–336.

Testing for Counterproductive Work Behaviors

The previous chapters focused on selection procedures that measure the WRCs that are important for job performance. In this chapter, we take a different tack—we primarily concentrate on testing for characteristics that applicants should *not* have. Yep, here, we are exposing the dark side of selection. The first part of the chapter deals with the legal and illegal use of the polygraph for determining if certain applicants are lying when asked questions about their past "undesirable" behaviors, such as stealing property or money or use of illegal drugs. The next section presents information about integrity testing—that is, how to tell which applicants have a higher probability of doing bad stuff (such as stealing, sabotage, or punching out supervisors) and even worse stuff (such as being late, quitting, and not ratting on bad guys to management).

Integrity testing has been found to be useful in testing for certain undesirable work behaviors; here, we present evidence on the validity of integrity tests. Currently, there is some disagreement regarding the strength of the relationships between integrity test scores and certain undesirable employee behaviors. We examine the evidence underpinning this validity controversy as well. We then follow this section with a discussion about physically testing for illegal drugs and the controversial topic of genetic testing. (Yes, the drug-abuse legacy of the 1960s lives on and presents a growing problem to employers.) Finally, we briefly explore the use of neural imaging of the brain for detecting lying and, possibly, predicting other characteristics of job applicants.

"Bad behaviors" that some applicants engage in once employed are generally categorized as *counterproductive work behaviors*, or CWBs. CWBs represent a wide array of illegal or unethical forms of purposeful employee conduct that harms organizations or people. Examples include theft of money, equipment, or other organizational resources; illicit drug use; violence; cursing at other employees or customers; sabotaging company equipment; and purposely doing work incorrectly.[1] One particular CWB that has exhibited a growing cost to American business and, therefore, has attracted a comparable growing concern among business leaders is employee theft. Obviously, estimates of the amount of theft are difficult to verify, but a common opinion is that 2 to 5 percent of each sales dollar is a premium charged to customers to offset losses resulting from internal crime. A survey of 451 companies indicated that more than one-half believed their employees would steal from them in the next 12 months.[2]

The average loss per each retail employee is estimated to be over \$1,900.[3] An international survey involving 4,200 retailers in 41 countries revealed an estimated *annual* \$50.5 billion loss due to employee theft from retail inventory.[4] With regard to the theft rate per employee, one study used sophisticated survey methods that guaranteed participant anonymity and found a theft rate of 58 percent.[5]

Given the pressure from international competition, often with lower labor costs, and the critical need to reduce production costs to maintain competitive positions, the interest of American firms in controlling employee theft is acute. The theft data we have presented here clearly point to the need to identify those job applicants most prone to engage in CWBs, such as theft. We begin this chapter by mentioning procedures that have been used to combat the CWB problem: polygraphs and paper-and-pencil integrity tests. In the following discussion, we describe the nature of both of these forms and present opinions about their use.

POLYGRAPH TESTING

A polygraph, or lie detector, is a machine that measures the physiological responses of examinees that accompany examinees' verbal responses to the direct questions of a polygraph operator. These data, in conjunction with the opinion of the polygraph operator, are used to evaluate the truthfulness of examinees' responses to questions regarding their present or past behaviors. Although once a mainstay for hiring retail personnel in large, "big-box" stores, for all practical purposes, the use of polygraphs for selection is now illegal. A federal law, the Employee Polygraph Protection Act of 1988 restricts the use of the polygraph for personnel selection to a very narrow set of circumstances.[6] Most of these legal applications involve organizations engaged in police work or domestic security.

The most common field polygraph examination uses readings of three types of physiological data. One set of readings, the electrodermal channel, displays changes in palmar skin resistance or galvanic skin response. The second set, the "cardio" channel, records changes in upper-arm volume associated with the cardiac cycle. From this channel, it is possible to determine heart rate and some changes in pulse volume. The third channel, connected pneumatically or electrically to an expandable belt placed around the respondent's chest, records respiration. The purpose of these sets of data is to provide the polygraph examiner with information about the examinee's physiological reactions during questioning. The assumption is that the examiner can detect lying by observing changes in respondents' physiological response patterns due to their reactions to questions posed by the examiner.

Procedures

In most polygraph examinations, the examiner conducts a pretest discussion with the examinee that covers all questions used in the test. The purpose is to make sure the examinee understands the wording and meaning of the questions and can answer them with a simple yes or no. After this discussion, the polygraph is attached to the examinee, and the actual interview is conducted. The list of questions is usually repeated once or twice to obtain more reliable data from the examinee. The examination typically entails three types of questions. One type is the irrelevant, nonemotional question, such as, "Are you six feet tall?" A second type is the emotional control question. Such questions are designed to elicit an emotional reaction, preferably of guilt. Questions such as, "Did you ever lie to escape punishment?" are frequently asked. The third type is specifically about the behavior of interest. In employment selection, this type usually concerns issues, such as prior thefts of organizational resources (for example, merchandise, equipment, money).

To detect lying, the polygraph operator looks for evidence of autonomic disturbance associated with the answers to the last type of question.[7] When the examinee is lying, there should be a disturbance that is more intense and persistent than that associated with the other two types of questions. Most polygraph examiners make an overall judgment of lying based on the polygraph information and other data, such as the demeanor of the examinee, the examiner's knowledge of the evidence, the respondent's prior history, and so on.[8]

Limitations

One of the difficulties with polygraph testing, however, is that other reactions besides guilt can trigger an emotional response in an examinee. Specifically, responses can be affected by an examinee's *lability*—the autonomic arousal threshold that differs from individual to individual. Examinees with high lability are more likely to display physiological reactions that might be interpreted as lying behavior than are respondents with low lability.

Another difficulty is the variety of countermeasures that examinees can use to avoid detection. Any physical activity that affects physiological responses is a potential problem for interpretation of polygraph readings. Such movements as tensing muscles, biting the tongue, flexing the toes, and shifting one's position can affect physiological responses. Similarly, mental countermeasures such as mental relaxation or attempts to concentrate on exciting memories during the presentation of the emotional control questions can be effective.[9] In general, polygraph examiners try to monitor these attempts. The use of drugs to obscure physiological reaction differences is more difficult to detect unless a urinalysis is conducted before the exam. Examinees' experience with polygraphs and biofeedback training also affect polygraph results.

The major drawback to using the polygraph in employment testing is the frequency of false-positive results. *False positives* are test results indicating individuals are lying when, in fact, they are not. The frequency of false positives depends on both the validity of the test and the base rate of the lying behavior in the population. To illustrate the possible magnitude of false-positive identification, assume the following: (a) the polygraph is 90 percent accurate (commonly regarded as a high estimate; some suggest 60 percent accuracy), and (b) the rate of stealing is 5 percent of the working population. (This estimate has been regarded as accurate for many years. However, as we discussed previously, some evidence suggests that the dishonesty rate among employees is much higher.) If 1,000 polygraph tests are conducted, we would expect that 50 ($0.05 \times 1,000$) of the examinees would be lying, and that 45 (0.90×50) of them would be detected. The serious problem concerns the remaining 950 examinees. Assuming a 90 percent accuracy rate, 95 of these (950×0.10) would be inaccurately identified as lying about their actions. Therefore, 140 individuals would be identified as lying, 68 percent of whom would be false positives. The consequence of such examinations is that those singled out for lying are denied employment or, if they were current employees, terminated from employment. This example shows that unless a polygraph test has perfect validity, a large number of false-positive identifications can occur when the device is used to test for a behavior that has a low incidence rate in the general population. Given the limitations in the accuracy of the polygraph, it is reasonable to conclude that the actual frequency of false positives is much greater than this example indicates.

Another group, *false negatives*, has also received attention. *False negatives* occur when test results are judged as truthful when, in fact, they are not. Individuals in this group are, understandably, of much interest to organizations; it is thought that these employees are most likely to be the source of undesired future behaviors, such as theft or drug abuse. In fact, in many ways, false negatives are of more immediate concern to organizations than are false positives.

We have mentioned several times in this text that incorrect judgments about applicants occur with the use of all selection procedures. That is, some applicants who do not achieve scores high enough to be selected would have performed well on the job had they been selected. In addition, there are applicants who do score high enough to be selected but, subsequently, do not perform well on the job.

The problem with misjudgments using the polygraph is the public statement that is made about individuals who incorrectly fail these tests, the false positives. These individuals could be negatively labeled by an incorrect judgment about a behavior, for example, honesty, which is highly valued in our society. It is obviously much more damaging to reject applicants because they failed a polygraph test than it is to reject them because the applicants' knowledge and ability do not meet the demands of a job. For this reason, public outcry about false positives grew as the use of polygraphs, and the number of individuals falsely labeled, increased. Other reasons given for the rejection of polygraph use in personnel selection included a lack of scientific research showing that applicants' polygraph scores predicted theft at work; that examinees' scores depended to a large degree on the individual examiner; and that use of the polygraph created a stressful, unpleasant experience for job applicants. These reasons only deepened public complaints.[10] Consequently, the Employee Polygraph Protection Act of 1988 essentially ended polygraph use in human resource selection and greatly restricted its use in other employment situations. The following is a summary of the major parts of this Act, under which it is unlawful for most private employers (some exceptions follow) to take any of the following actions:

1. Directly or indirectly require, request, suggest, or cause any employee to take or submit to any lie detector test, for example, a polygraph, deceptograph, voice-stress analyzer, psychological-stress evaluator, and any similar mechanical or electrical device used to render a diagnostic opinion about the honesty of an individual

2. Use, accept, refer to, or inquire about the results of any lie detector test of any job applicant or current employee

3. Discharge, discipline, discriminate against, or deny employment or promotion to (or threaten to take such adverse action against) any prospective or current employee who refuses, declines, or fails to take or submit to a lie detector test.

However, the following employers are exempted from these prohibitions on pre-employment polygraph testing of job applicants:

1. Private employers whose primary business purpose is to provide security services. Prospective employees may be tested if the positions for which they are applying involve the protection of nuclear power facilities, public water supply facilities, shipments or storage of radioactive or other toxic waste materials, public transportation, currency, negotiable securities, precious commodities, or proprietary information.

2. Employers involved in the manufacture, distribution, or dispensing of controlled substances. Employers can administer polygraph tests to applicants for positions that provide direct access to the manufacture, storage, distribution, or sale of a controlled substance.

3. Federal, state, and local government employers. The federal government can test private consultants or experts under contract to the Defense Department, the Energy Department, the National Security Agency, the Defense Intelligence Agency, the Central Intelligence Agency, and the Federal Bureau of Investigation.

Testing of current *employees* is also permitted if the following conditions are met:

1. The polygraph test is given only in connection with an investigation into a workplace theft or other incident that has resulted in an economic loss to the company.

2. The employee has had access to the property that is the subject of the investigation.

3. The employer must have a "reasonable suspicion" that the employee was involved in the incident.

4. Before testing, the employee must have been given specific written information about the incident being investigated and reasons for the testing.

One may conclude that the Act was intended to restrict pre-employment polygraph testing of job applicants to those situations that have a large, significant public interest, and the testing of current employees to those situations in which there is enough evidence to reasonably implicate an individual of a specific illegal act.

INTEGRITY TESTING

Paper-and-Pencil Integrity Tests

Before the Employee Polygraph Protection Act of 1988 was passed, more than 30 states had enacted legislation to prohibit, or severely limit, the use of polygraphs in employment decisions. Similar to the federal Act, most of these state laws were worded to address only mechanical or electronic devices. Therefore, paper-and-pencil integrity tests were adopted to provide a legal means to predict CWBs.

Originally labeled as "honesty" tests, integrity tests have been available for selection purposes for roughly 65 years. However, a few states passed laws that either prohibit or restrict the use of paper-and-pencil integrity tests. These laws were passed for the same reasons as those prohibiting the use of polygraph testing. For most states, however, integrity tests are legal when properly used. Because of the need to identify job applicants who are likely to engage in CWBs, the market for such tests has grown rapidly. There are more than 50 integrity tests available from a minimum of 30 test publishers.[11]

Integrity tests are typically aimed toward identifying job applicants predisposed to participate in or exhibit counterproductive behaviors, such as violence, theft, or illicit drug use. Two forms of these tests have been developed: (a) *overt integrity tests* directly ask for information about attitudes toward theft and other types of counterproductive behaviors; and (b) *personality-oriented measures*, which do not ask about theft behaviors directly. Instead, they are personality inventories, measuring traits linked to certain employee behaviors detrimental to an organization. Theft is only one of these behaviors.

Overt Integrity Tests

Examples of overt integrity tests are the *Personnel Selection Inventory*, the *Reid Report*, and the *Stanton Survey*. The rationale underlying this type of test is to measure job applicants' attitudes and cognitions toward theft that might predispose them to steal at work, especially when both the need and the opportunity to steal are present. William Terris and John Jones have explained this testing approach in the following way. Past research has shown that the "typical" employee-thief (a) is more tempted to steal; (b) engages in many common rationalizations for theft; (c) would punish thieves less; (d) often thinks about theft-related activities; (e) attributes more theft to others; (f) shows more inter-thief loyalty; and (g) is more vulnerable to peer pressure to steal than is an honest employee.[12]

Items on this type of test follow directly from these points. Some example items are the following:[13]

- Most people who have had jobs where they handled money or had expense accounts have probably taken some money without their employer's permission. This includes directly taking cash, borrowing money that is not returned, or padding expense accounts. Estimate how much you have taken from all employers in the past 5 years.

- Did you ever think about doing something that, if you had done it, would have been a crime?

- In any of your other jobs, did you find out a way a dishonest person could take money if a dishonest person had your job?

- Do you believe that making personal phone calls from your employer's place of business without an OK is stealing?

- Have you ever overcharged someone for your personal gain?

- Is it true that to be human is to be dishonest?

Another type of question poses a situation that focuses on dishonest behavior. Here is an example: "A store manager with 15 years of good work performance has an 8-year-old son who is dying of cancer. The manager takes $25 per week from the store for 3 months to buy toys and games for the child. Another employee sees this behavior and tells the district manager." A number of questions follow that ask respondents' opinions about the theft, the action of the employee who informed the district manager, and respondents' choices of alternative actions that can be taken by the district manager.

Personality-Oriented Measures

A second type of integrity test takes the form of a general personality inventory. The central idea for this approach is that employee theft is just one element in a larger syndrome of antisocial behavior or organizational delinquency. Such delinquency includes dishonesty, theft, drug and alcohol abuse, vandalism, sabotage, assault actions, insubordination, absenteeism, excessive grievances, bogus workers' compensation claims, and violence. The assumption is that there is a common personality pattern underlying organizational delinquency, and it is feasible to identify individuals who have this personality pattern by using personality inventories applicable to the public. Frequently, these personality measures will contain a subset of items that are identified as an integrity scale. These items are part of the personality inventory and the only items scored to measure test takers' integrity, honesty, and likelihood of engaging in counterproductive behaviors. Having a set of items within a personality inventory that assesses integrity and CWB tendencies has two advantages. First, in comparison with an overt integrity test, the items on a personality integrity test are not as transparent in their intention to measure theft and related transgressions. Lack of item transparency reduces the probability of respondents' attempting to fake their responses. Second, applicants who are not selected because of the personality test need not be rejected due to failing an integrity test. Rather, they are rejected for a mismatch between their personality profile and that of successful employees.

The Hogan Personality Inventory (HPI) is one such personality-based integrity measure.[14] It is a 206-item, Big-Five type of personality survey that has been developed for use in employment situations. It contains seven primary scales and six occupational scales, which are shown in Table 14.1. The publisher provides normative data from more than 30,000 working adults across a wide variety of industries. The primary scales are personality dimensions measured by the 206 items. The occupational scales are composed of various combinations of the 206 items of the primary scales and were developed to provide information about specific employment topics.

One of these occupational scales is the Reliability scale, composed of 18 items that measure honesty, integrity, and organizational citizenship (for example, assisting others, engaging in nonmeasured performance). High scores are good; low scores are bad.

| TABLE 14.1 | Scales of the Hogan Personality Inventory |

Primary Scales

Adjustment—Self-confidence, self-esteem, and composure under pressure
Ambition—Initiative, competitiveness, and the desire for leadership roles
Sociability—Extraversion, gregariousness, and a need for social interaction
Interpersonal Sensitivity—Warmth, charm, and the ability to maintain relationships
Prudence—Self-discipline, responsibility, and conscientiousness
Inquisitiveness—Imagination, curiosity, vision, and creative potential
Learning Approach—Enjoying learning, staying current on business and technical matters

Occupational Scales

Service Orientation—Being attentive, pleasant, and courteous to customers
Stress Tolerance—Being able to handle stress, being even-tempered and calm under fire
Reliability—Honesty, integrity, and positive organizational citizenship
Clerical Potential—Following directions, attending to detail, and communicating clearly
Sales Potential—Energy, social skills, and the ability to solve customers' problems
Managerial Potential—Leadership ability, planning, and decision-making skills

Source: © 2014 Hogan Assessment Systems, http://www.hoganassessments.com/?q=content/hogan-personality-inventory-hpi

The authors reported test-retest reliability as high as 0.90 for the Reliability scale. Concurrent validity studies have been conducted with various groups of workers in a variety of jobs. Table 14.2 contains a list of the various criteria used in these studies. The diversity of the measures indicates two points: (a) the index predicts employee performance as well as organizational delinquency, and (b) there is a wide scope of employee behaviors included in organizational delinquency. Other research has also supported the validity of the Reliability scale and the HPI.[15]

What We Know About Integrity Tests

Perhaps because integrity tests offer so much potential value to American industry, there has been much research about these instruments. For example, Paul Sackett and his colleagues have published five extensive reviews of integrity tests since 1979, each of which has addressed several important topics. The following discussion draws from these reviews, especially the review that Sackett did with Christopher Berry and Shelly Wiemann.[16] It also relies heavily on a comprehensive meta-analysis as well as a series of studies done by Deniz Ones, Chockalingam Viswesvaran, and Frank Schmidt.[17] We also draw upon Chad Van Iddekinge and his colleagues' most recent meta-analysis of the criterion-related validity of integrity tests[18] as well as other research studies not included in these reviews.

Constructs Measured. As mentioned previously, integrity tests were first used to detect employee theft because that is such a large and expensive issue for businesses. Recent research has indicated that it is more appropriate to think of integrity tests as measuring three of the Big-Five factors, that is conscientiousness, agreeableness, and emotional stability.[19]

CWBs include a number of actions such as theft, sabotage, restriction of performance, confrontation, and others. It seems appropriate to think of CWBs as a hierarchical model

TABLE 14.2   Criteria Measures Correlated with Employee Reliability Index

Job	Negative Behaviors Correlated with Reliability Index	Positive Behaviors Correlated with Reliability Index
Truck driver	Discharges from work Grievances filed Claims for equipment failure	Commendations
Psychiatric counselor		Supervisor's ratings of performance
Hospital service worker	Times counseled for aberrant behavior	
Rehabilitation therapist	Injuries sustained Incidents reported to insurance fund State dollars spent for treatment	
Nuclear power plant worker		Supervisor's ratings of attitude, accuracy, punctuality
Service operations dispatchers	Absences	
Navy electronics students		Course time completion
Customer service representatives		Supervisor's ratings of quality, teamwork, performance
Telemarketers		Sales performance Sales lead generation

Source: Based on Joyce Hogan and Robert Hogan, "How to Measure Employee Reliability," in *Employee Testing: The Complete Resource Guide* (Washington, DC: Bureau of National Affairs, Inc., 1988).

with a general factor at the top, mid-range factors (such as interpersonal and organizational deviance) below the general factor, and specific factors such as theft below the mid-range factors.[20] Integrity tests can measure CWBs at all three levels of this model. Therefore, integrity tests should be thought of as multifaceted, and the constructs they are measuring may be hierarchical in nature[21] with conscientiousness, agreeableness, and emotional stability representing the general factor.

Variables Related to Integrity Tests.   Several meta-analytic studies have examined the relationships among integrity tests and the Big-Five personality measures. Both overt and personality-oriented honesty tests correlated with a variety of these personality dimensions.[22] In all cases, personality-oriented tests correlated more highly with several of the Big-Five dimensions than did overt tests. With both types of tests, however, the correlations were substantial with the three dimensions of conscientiousness, agreeableness, and emotional stability.

Recent work in personality measurement has postulated the addition of a sixth personality dimension to the Big Five. The HEXACO model of personality adds the Honesty-Humility dimension that measures fairness, sincerity, lack of conceit, and lack of greed.[23] One study tested the relationship of the six-factor HEXACO model versus the Five-Factor Model of personality with workplace delinquency in three countries: the Netherlands, Canada, and Australia. Results indicated that the HEXACO model outperformed the Five-Factor Model in predicting both workplace delinquency and scores on overt honesty tests.

Integrity test scores have also been correlated with cognitive test scores. Initial findings were that overall or general integrity test scores are not correlated with cognitive ability test scores. Therefore, they can provide additional predictive validity over cognitive ability tests.[24] However, other work investigated the relationships between cognitive ability and 23 integrity sub-factors rather than overall scores.[25] Several sub-factors were positively correlated with cognitive ability while others negatively related to cognitive ability. Thus, the near-zero correlation reported using overall integrity scores might result from combining positively and negatively related integrity sub-factors with cognitive ability. The relationship between integrity measures and cognitive ability may depend on which factors of integrity are measured by a test.

Relationship Between Overt and Personality-Oriented Tests. Research has also examined how similar overt integrity tests are to personality-based integrity tests. That is, do the two forms of integrity tests measure the same constructs? One study addressing this question used 798 test items (remember that no matter what the developer says the test measures, it measures what the items ask about and how respondents interpret and respond to them!) from three overt and four personality-oriented integrity tests.[26] These items were sorted into 23 distinct, interpretable themes, such as theft thoughts/ temptations, self/impulse control, risk taking/thrill seeking, and perception of dishonesty norms. These themes were then analyzed to form four factors or dimensions: antisocial behavior, socialization, positive outlook, and orderliness/diligence. The authors then used data from 1,428 individuals to derive correlations among the 23 behavioral themes, the four dimensions, the seven integrity tests, and two Big-Five personality inventories. The purpose was to determine (a) how closely correlated integrity tests were to each other, and (b) how closely they were correlated with personality measures. The following were some of the authors' conclusions:

1. There were positive correlations among all seven integrity tests across five themes—theft thoughts/temptations, perception of dishonesty norms, social conformity, association with delinquents, and theft admissions. Therefore, the integrity tests studied showed a great deal of similarity in what they measured.

2. There were some differences among overt and personality-based tests. Overt tests correlated more highly with honesty and supervision attitudes. Personality tests correlated more highly with self/impulse control, home life/upbringing, risk taking, diligence, and emotional stability.

Validity. One theme that we have emphasized throughout the book is that validity of selection procedures is critical. This theme applies to integrity tests as well, but like all selection procedures, we need to ask: **Validity for what?** More specifically, what are we trying to predict with integrity tests? Determining the validity of integrity tests is difficult because of the problems of measuring a criterion variable with which to correlate integrity test scores. Theft and many other counterproductive work behaviors are not easily detected and recorded in individual workers' employment records. In some studies, polygraph results have served as a criterion, but polygraphs have questionable reliability and validity and, therefore, are a poor criterion. In addition, it is not known whether self-reported dishonesty is an accurate measure of actual dishonesty. Some validation studies have simultaneously collected and correlated self-reported dishonesty along with integrity test information but such a strategy can lead to highly inflated validity coefficients. Other validity studies of integrity tests have used theft, absenteeism, disciplinary action, termination, workers' compensation claims, and sabotage, among others as criteria. However, most of these behaviors likely have low frequencies of occurrence. The majority of workers would have a score of zero on these criteria. Therefore, the interpretability of such studies' results is unclear.[27]

In reviewing integrity test validity studies, Sackett and Wanek estimated the following population true validity coefficients: 0.13 for overt tests with *theft* as a criterion, 0.39 for overt tests with various *non-theft* criteria, and 0.29 for personality tests with *non-theft* criteria.[28] In general, they concluded that there is not enough data from meta-analytic studies to indicate that either overt or personality-oriented tests are superior to the other. Both types demonstrate validity across different criteria; depending on the criterion, one type will often yield higher validity than the other.

In related work, another meta-analysis looked at the relationships between both types of integrity tests and *voluntary absenteeism*. Results were corrected validity values of 0.33 and 0.09 for personality-oriented and overt tests, respectively. Differences between these validity coefficients indicated a considerable disparity in the predictive validity of the two types of tests, with personality-based tests more useful in the prediction of voluntary *absenteeism* than overt tests.[29]

A related study examined the validity of personality-oriented integrity scores with *maximal work performance* (individuals try to perform at their highest levels as opposed to typical or day-to-day performance) and found a correlation of 0.27.[30] Furthermore, integrity scores correlated 0.14 with *job knowledge*, and job knowledge had a 0.36 correlation with maximal work performance. Integrity seems to be related to maximal performance because it taps motivation of individuals, that is, a person exerting maximum effort and also because integrity is related to *job knowledge*. Both motivation and job knowledge are major components of individual differences in maximal performance. Based on these findings, it appears that integrity tests are valid for the prediction of *theft*, *general counterproductive behaviors*, and various types of *work performance*.

To understand these validity relationships better, Ones and her colleagues investigated the question of whether the relationship between integrity test scores and overall job performance is merely a function of the relationship between both of these variables and conscientiousness.[31] They did this by determining the correlation between integrity test scores and job performance while statistically controlling for conscientiousness. The conclusion is that although integrity tests overlap with various personality dimensions, they independently contribute to the prediction of job performance. Sackett and Wanek believed that this contribution occurs because integrity tests emphasize self-control and contain many items that measure this variable. Although self-control is generally considered part of the personality dimension of conscientiousness, relatively few items in most Big-Five inventories measure it. Therefore, integrity measures add to the prediction of job performance over conscientiousness measures because self-control is strongly related to job performance.[32]

We know that the preceding paragraphs are difficult to digest. The key is that integrity tests can be used to predict a variety of different criterion behaviors. So, once you get these relationships down, jump up in class and yell, "I got it." You will undoubtedly be the envy of all of your classmates, and your instructor will think that your knowledge is because of his/her teaching ability. This is a win–win situation if we ever saw one.

In addition to their use with different criteria, another issue that clouds the interpretation of integrity validity studies is the adequacy of the research studies investigating integrity tests. Many purported validity studies have been conducted by publishers of validity tests and often, while reporting results that support the validity of the tests, do not meet the highest standards of validation research design. Thus, some have questioned the results of such validation studies.[33]

In 1993, Deniz Ones and her associates published a massive, comprehensive meta-analysis of the integrity test literature. Their analyses included 665 criterion-related validity coefficients based on a sample size of 576,460 test takers. Among their findings, their analyses showed that the mean true validity coefficient for integrity tests given to job applicants and used to predict subsequent *supervisor-rated* job performance was 0.41.[34] Moreover, validity values were fairly similar for both overt and personality-based integrity tests in predicting *supervisory* ratings of job performance.[35] For all integrity tests (overt and personality-based) predicting *overall* job performance (that is, supervisory ratings, production records, commendations), the validity coefficient was 0.34. For all integrity tests (overt and personality-based) predicting counterproductive behaviors (that is, actual theft, admitted theft, dismissals for theft, illegal activities, absenteeism, tardiness, violence), the validity coefficient was 0.47.[36] Two possible explanations for these correlations are that (a) integrity tests reflect underlying personality dimensions (for example, conscientiousness), which are linked to productive work behaviors and (b) when supervisory ratings are used, supervisors use the occurrence of unproductive behaviors (to which integrity tests are related) in their judgments of job performance.

However, some researchers raised questions about Ones and her colleagues' findings regarding criterion-related integrity test validity because only 10 percent of their meta-analyzed studies were published in professional journals and, therefore, had not undergone rigorous peer review. Developers and publishers of the integrity tests authored the remaining studies.[37] Moreover, concerns also centered on the poor quality of some research methods used by test developers (for example, using self-report criterion measures of CWBs) and the vested interests that test publishers have in obtaining desired research outcomes, such as reporting only statistically significant validity coefficients and failing to report nonsignificant ones. The concern of those raising methodological questions regarding integrity test validity is that the methods used and potential biases present in the research could lead to inflated levels of estimated validity.

Some 15 years after Ones et al.'s meta-analysis, Chad Van Iddekinge and colleagues embarked on an updated meta-analysis focusing solely on the criterion-related validity of integrity tests. They employed a stringent set of screening criteria to identify those studies most likely to be methodologically sound and focusing solely on criterion-related validity. Initially, they located 324 integrity test studies. Then, they applied a number of criteria to identify those studies most relevant to their research purpose: To investigate "… the criterion-related validity of integrity-specific scales for predicting individual work behavior and whose conduct was consistent with professional standards for test validation."[38] The criteria used to select the studies were quite specific and extensive. Examples of the screening criteria included:

1. Both integrity test predictor and criterion data must be available on individual participants; studies using the polygraph as a criterion were excluded.

2. The predictor must be integrity tests (interviews and other tests were excluded) having integrity-specific scales whose content reflected overt or personality-based integrity tests.

3. Studies were excluded that focused on the integrity of current employees.

4. Integrity test scores must be examined for possible relationships with work-related criteria, including job performance, training performance, CWBs, or turnover.

5. Lab studies using students were excluded.

6. Validity studies must give complete details regarding study conduct; studies selectively reporting only significant validity coefficients and omitting nonsignificant validity coefficients were excluded.

From the 324 validity studies, 104 were found that met all study inclusion criteria.[39] Table 14.3 compares the two sets of meta-analyses integrity test results for the Ones et al. and Van Iddekinge et al. studies.[40] Results are shown for both job performance and counterproductive behavior criteria. The table shows the *overall* true validity

TABLE 14.3	Ones, et al. and Van Iddekinge et al.'s Meta-Analysis' Results of Integrity Test Validities in Predicting Job Performance and Counterproductive Behavior Criteria

Criterion/Test Type	Number of studies (K)	Number of participants (N)	True Validity Estimates (P)
Criteria—Job Performance			
Overt tests:			
Ones et al. meta-analysis	15	12,932	0.30
Van Iddekinge et al. meta-analysis	18	2,213	0.14
Personality-based tests:			
Ones et al. meta-analysis	102	27,081	0.37
Van Iddekinge et al. meta-analysis	18	12,017	0.18
Studies using applicants, predictive validity, and non-self-ratings of criterion			
Ones et al. meta-analysis	15	7,550	0.41
Van Iddekinge et al. meta-analysis	18	7,104	0.15
Criterion—Counterproductive behavior			
Overt tests:			
Ones et al. meta-analysis	305	349,623	0.55
Van Iddekinge et al. meta-analysis	43	11,751	0.38
Personality-based tests:			
Ones et al. meta-analysis	138	158,065	0.33
Van Iddekinge et al. meta-analysis	32	9,364	0.27
Studies using applicants, predictive validity, and non-self-ratings of criterion			
Ones et al. **overt** tests, non-theft meta-analysis	10	5,598	0.39
Ones et al. **personality-based,** non-theft meta-analysis	18	93,092	0.29
Van Iddekinge et al. both **overt** and **personality-based** tests, includes both theft and non-theft studies	10	5,056	0.11

Note: The table was adapted and based on Paul R. Sackett and Neal Schmitt, "On Reconciling Conflicting Meta-Analytic Findings Regarding Integrity Test Validity," *Journal of Applied Psychology* 97 (2012): 551. *K* = number of validity coefficients; *N* = number of participants; p = true validity estimates corrected for measurement error in the criterion.

estimates as well as validity findings for studies involving *operational* validity (that is, predictive validation studies using job applicants and non-self-ratings of employee job performance or counterproductive behaviors).

For job performance criteria, both overall and operational validity for overt and personality-based measures were higher in Ones et al.'s study than in Van Iddekinge et al.'s. For example, in operational validity, Ones et al.'s mean true validity of 0.41 is much higher than the 0.15 found by Iddekinge et al.'s. A similar pattern existed for both overt and personality-oriented tests in predicting counterproductive behavior criteria. Operational validities of overt and personality-based tests are more difficult to compare because the two meta-analyses differed in how they classified validation studies using theft versus non-theft as a criterion.

With regard to the two studies' (Ones et al. and Van Iddekinge et al.) reported validities, Sackett and Schmitt in a published perspective on Van Iddekinge et al.'s work posed the question: "Do we know why the conclusions (validities) differ" between the two studies? After considering several factors, such as sample sizes, criteria for including or excluding studies from the two meta-analyses, analytic problems, and corrections for statistical artifacts, they simply concluded, "No, we do not."[41] So, what, if anything, can we conclude from these two massive meta-analyses about the validity of integrity tests? We believe that Sackett and Schmitt answered this question best; they note "We think it best to conclude ... that integrity test scores are related to performance and counterproductive behavior outcomes but that the magnitude of the relationships is presently uncertain."[42] A second conclusion, based principally upon both Ones et al. and Van Iddekinge et al.'s research, we would add is that overt integrity tests appear to be a better predictor of counterproductive work behaviors than personality-oriented measures. In sum, both meta-analyses seem to agree that integrity tests are associated with important criteria. However, the precise reasons as to why the two meta-analyses found different estimates regarding the strength of these associations is unknown.

Usefulness of Integrity Tests

In Chapter 8, we discussed the concept of utility analysis derived from the use of valid predictors in pre-employment screening. William Harris and his colleagues sought to estimate, in dollar terms, the payoff of using integrity tests in pre-employment testing.[43] They assumed an average loss per employee due to theft of $1,905. They also assumed an applicant pass rate of 75 percent with an average test cost of $12.50 per applicant. Van Iddekinge et al.'s integrity test validity of 0.32 was also presumed. Next, they employed Brogden's test utility formula to determine basic utility derived from using an integrity test in hiring. Their calculations revealed that use of an integrity test in pre-employment decision making would lead, on average, to a savings of $201,470 per 1,000 job applicants for a typical organization.

False Positives.   The issue of false positives is identical to that discussed previously concerning polygraphs. A large percentage of applicants (estimated as 40 to 70 percent) commonly fail integrity tests, and a large number of those who fail may be incorrectly classified. Cutoff scores that cause these failure rates are usually set in one of two ways. The test publisher can set the score based on statistics gathered in test development. For the most part, it is in the best interest of the test publisher to set the cutoff score high enough to reduce the number of individuals who pass the test but are subsequently dishonest. In other words, it may be in the best interest of the test publisher to avoid false negatives, even at the cost of increased false positives. Cutoff scores can also be set by the organization using the integrity test. It is commonly in the best interest of the organization to minimize false negatives even at the cost of increased false positives. In such a case, the organization would set high cutoff scores. This would be especially true for those cases in which the applicant pool is large enough to absorb the rejection of high numbers of applicants and yet provide enough individuals to fill the open positions.

It is Sackett and Wanek's opinion that integrity test decision errors should be evaluated based on choosing among *multiple applicants*, rather than on a decision concerning a *single* individual.[44] That is, integrity tests are often used near the end of a selection program and given to applicants who have previously passed other WRCs' selection measures. If there are more applicants than open positions, and if the integrity test is valid, its use improves selection over the alternative, which is random selection among the remaining applicants or using some other selection procedure that is not job related.

Related to Sackett and Wanek's opinion is the fact that all selection tests have false positives. Selection specialists have not been very concerned with these decisions and have usually regarded having a valid test as beneficial for the results of selection. No special consideration of false positives is usually given. However, most selection tests do not have the social implications of an integrity test, in which a low score is as an indicant of dishonesty. For this reason, the use of personality-based integrity tests may be more socially acceptable than the use of overt measures. Although the rate of false positives *probably* does not differ between the two types, the implication of a low score is not as socially noticeable to test takers because they may view the test as a personality inventory rather than an integrity test.

Faking.   One concern of test users is that applicants may be able to fake their responses on integrity tests. Faking may be especially true for overt tests that directly ask about attitudes and previous instances of theft from employers. (That is, it simply does not make sense that many people would openly indicate instances of theft. However, various facets of integrity tests do not appear highly related to cognitive ability test scores.[45]) This concern is similar to the concern about faking on personality inventories, which we discussed in Chapter 12.

Research on faking on integrity tests generally comes to the same conclusion we drew about personality tests—faking does not seem to make a difference in the validity of the test.[46] One study instructed participants about how to distort their answers on an integrity test in several ways. The scores of these individuals were compared to those of other participants who were not instructed to distort and to those of job applicants who took the test as part of selection programs for various organizations. Participants instructed to distort scored higher on the integrity test than those not told to do so. However, they did not score as high as job applicants. The logical conclusions were that (a) individuals can distort their responses and score higher; (b) some applicants use such distortion in their responses, perhaps even to a great degree; (c) because validity coefficients were determined on samples of job applicants, such distortion does not make the test invalid; and (d) distortion by future job applicants will not be greater than it is for those for whom the test has been developed, and it will not affect the test's validity.[47] However, just as in the case of faking of personality inventories, this position may not indicate the full effect of distortion on selection decisions. We should remember that the validity of the test is a group-level statistic. Selection decisions are made based on individual-level data, and distortion may differentially affect applicants' scores. Therefore, those individuals who are selected when considering distortion may differ from those who would have been selected if no distortion had occurred. Other investigators have concluded that job applicants *can* fake integrity test responses; however, too little is known regarding the extent to which actual job applicants *do* fake.[48] Therefore, additional research involving actual job applicants has been called for to isolate more explicitly the extent and effects of faking on integrity tests used in selection decision-making applications.

Legal Issues in Integrity Testing

The Equal Employment Opportunity Commission (EEOC) has specifically commented that integrity tests, even personality-based ones, are not considered a medical examination because such tests assess only the propensity for dishonest behavior. Therefore, these tests can be used in selection programs before extending an employment offer. However, because the Americans with Disabilities Act (ADA) prohibits use of pre-employment medical exams, personality inventories designed to detect mental or physical health illnesses and those tests used to determine dishonesty are treated differently. Such tests are considered a medical examination and, therefore, prohibited. One personality inventory that would likely fall into this prohibited category is the Minnesota Multiphasic Personality Inventory (MMPI). In one legal case, a sheriff's office used a pre-employment psychological evaluation of job applicants applying to work in law enforcement. The court ruled that the psychological evaluation was a prohibited pre-employment medical examination as defined under the ADA.[49]

Two states have laws that restrict or limit the use of integrity tests in employment decision making. Massachusetts prohibits the use of a written "honesty" test administered to job applicants. Rhode Island does not expressly prohibit their use, but state law provides that such tests cannot serve as the "primary basis for an employment decision."[50]

Harris et al. observed that over the last 60 years, only about 30 formal complaints were filed against integrity tests. Of these, all were dismissed indicating that integrity tests do not elicit many legal complaints. Based on these data, we might add that in most cases where a legal complaint has arisen, it seems that complaints involving such tests are likely to be defensible.[51] For example, two studies examining adverse impact against protected groups due to integrity testing showed no adverse impact. In one meta-analysis study involving 724,806 job applicants, no adverse impact was found for several overt integrity tests with regard to gender, age, and ethnic group differences.[52] These results suggest that overt integrity tests are nondiscriminatory with respect to these protected group characteristics.

Finally, another important issue is whether a specific test includes any items that ask about previous drug or alcohol use. Such items cannot be used because the ADA prohibits inquiries about the extent of prior use of these substances.

Other Stuff. There have been recent attempts to develop integrity tests in formats other than the traditional true–false questionnaire. These formats include biodata questionnaires, forced-choice response formats, interviews, and situational judgment tests.[53] However, these new formats have not been used extensively; given the demonstrated validity of integrity tests, it is unclear as to what the potential advantage of some of these would be. For example, personal interviews would take much longer to administer than a paper-and-pencil or computerized integrity test and cost significantly more. Biodata forms have traditionally required large samples for validation, and some items may very closely resemble those of integrity tests.

There has been some research done on applicants' reactions to integrity testing; some of these studies find that individuals react more negatively to integrity tests than to many other forms of selection testing. However, most of these studies have used college students in the research projects. Others concluded that applicants saw integrity tests as an appropriate procedure management could use.[54] Very few studies have used actual job applicants or incumbent employees, samples that would be reflective of groups to whom the tests would normally be administered.

DRUG TESTING

Employees' use of drugs and alcohol has been of major concern to organizations since the 1960s. Drug testing has become increasingly common in work organizations, especially those that have safety sensitive jobs or receive government contracts. There are a number of reasons for testing job applicants for drug use or abuse; these include the following:

1. Deter employees from abusing alcohol and drugs

2. Prevent hiring individuals who use illegal drugs

3. Provide a safe workplace for employees

4. Protect the general public and instill consumer confidence that employees are working safely

5. Comply with state laws or federal regulations

6. Benefit from Workers' Compensation Premium Discount program

7. Reduce costs of health care claims, particularly short-term disability claims[55]

In addition, research has found that drug use is negatively associated with job performance, and positively correlated with accidents, injuries, absences, involuntary turnover, and job-withdrawal behaviors such as taking too many breaks and sleeping on the job.[56]

It is difficult to precisely know how many individuals or what percentage of the current workforce regularly uses drugs. The problem with measuring usage is that it relies on self-report data. That is, individuals must indicate in some way that, they have used drugs. Such an indication can be risky to individuals; so there is a general thought that any data gathered through self-report may be an underestimate of actual use. Measuring the deterioration in work performance attributable to drug use is, perhaps, even more difficult to do. The issue with this measurement is that there is not necessarily a linear relationship between the amount of a drug consumed and the decline of work performance. Individuals differ in their reactions to a specific amount of drugs; the same amount of a drug can produce different effects among individuals. Moreover, some people adapt to consistent use of drugs over time and develop the ability to absorb larger quantities of drugs due to a resistance to the effects of the drug.[57] It is not possible to estimate the effect of a given quantity of a drug on the work performance of an individual. The only sure way to measure deterioration in performance is to establish a standard of performance while an individual is free from drugs and then measure performance after drugs have been consumed. Obviously, such data are pretty much impossible to obtain.

Although dated (2006), one of the best estimates of drug use among United States workers and their drug impairment was obtained by Michael Frone.[58] He collected information from a carefully selected representative sample of 2,806 adults working in the 48 contiguous states and the District of Columbia. The data were gathered through a telephone survey that contained many questions about employee health and safety. Each respondent answered two questions about the use of six drugs: marijuana or hashish, cocaine or crack, sedatives, tranquilizers, stimulants, and analgesics. Questions were phrased to indicate use other than for prescribed medical purposes.

The first of the two questions asked how often each drug was used during the preceding 12 months. This question was designed to measure the percentage of the workforce who used drugs. The second question asked how often the respondent took each drug and got high or stoned. Responses to this question were interpreted as a measure of impairment. Keep in mind that there is a distinction between use and impairment. *Use* means that some amount of the drug has been consumed. *Impairment* means that the amount consumed was enough to cause deterioration in performance. Frone's research led to some of the following drug-use estimates:

1. Marijuana was used by 11.3 percent of the workforce (14.2 million workers).

2. Cocaine was used by 1.0 percent of the workforce (1.3 million workers).

3. At least one of four psychotherapeutic drugs was used by 4.9 percent of the workforce (6.2 million workers).

4. Marijuana use had caused 10.6 percent of the workforce (13.3 million workers) to become impaired.

5. Cocaine use had caused 0.9 percent of the workforce (1.2 million workers) to become impaired.

6. At least one of four psychotherapeutic drugs had caused 2.2 percent of the workforce (2.8 million workers) to become impaired.[59]

Illicit drug use was highest in the arts, entertainment, sports, media, and food preparation and serving occupations. Impairment was highest in legal, food preparation and serving, and building and grounds maintenance occupations. Men used and were impaired by drugs more frequently than women, and race was unrelated to use or impairment. Both age and education were negatively related to use and impairment—that is, older individuals and those who had completed more education used drugs less frequently and were impaired less frequently than younger or less-educated individuals. Among those who used a drug, 56 percent used it at least once a week and 41 percent were impaired at least one day a week. Frone concluded that although the absolute numbers for use and impairment are high, "they represent only 1.8 percent of the total workforce." Do note, however, his research was published in 2006 so the generalizability of his results to the current workforce is questionable.

Drug-Testing Methods

Paper-and-Pencil Tests. The simplest, and least controversial, drug test is the paper-and-pencil type. This test is identical in intent to the paper-and-pencil integrity tests discussed previously. Overt-type tests ask directly about drug usage with questions such as the following:

- Do you think that it is okay for workers to use "soft" drugs at work if this does not cause poor job performance?

- In the past 6 months, how often have you used marijuana at work?

- In the past 6 months, have you brought cocaine to work even though you did not use it at work?

General-purpose tests are adaptations of personality inventories, analogous to personality-based integrity measures developed to identify drug users. Unlike integrity tests, however, there is almost no public literature that evaluates the reliability or validity of this type of test. However, one court case ruled that pre-employment tests in which applicants were asked to indicate their use of legal and illegal drugs were unconstitutional, based on the Fifth Amendment's prohibition of involuntary self incrimination.[60] Therefore, it seems that a company would be limited in its ability to force an applicant to complete at least the overt-type test. For this reason, perhaps, organizations use paper-and-pencil tests infrequently to assess illegal drug use among job applicants.

Urine Tests.   A second type of test, the one used most often, is the urine test. First used in the 1960s, it was a way for hospital emergency room personnel to diagnose patients in a drug-induced coma for appropriate treatment. In the 1970s, demand for this type of testing increased with the need to monitor clients' compliance with treatment programs for methadone maintenance and other drug therapy programs. The desire of business organizations to control the problems associated with employee drug usage further increased the demand for these tests in the 1980s and that demand has continued to the present day.

Over the most recent two decades, positive workplace tests for cocaine and marijuana have fallen while abuse of prescription drugs (for example, amphetamines and pain killers) has risen.[61] Although these data show that drug testing indicates less marijuana use, national surveys show marijuana use is increasing. These contradictory findings might indicate that some applicants have used methods to "pass" the urine test, for example, using someone else's "clean" urine rather than their own to pass a pre-employment drug test. At the time we are writing this book, we reviewed many videos on YouTube giving viewers guidance on how to pass or "fake" a drug screening urine test.

Several reasons for the high usage of urine tests by employers are: (a) a basic urine test is relatively inexpensive, (b) results are returned quickly (usually within 24 hours), and (c) testing is usually very convenient for the applicant. For example, drug tests can be performed at a company job site using a drug-test technician from a drug-testing lab who comes to the site for testing. Alternatively, an applicant can be sent to the lab or an approved physician for the desired tests.

Many employers use drug-testing labs to perform a five-panel test of "street drugs," which includes cocaine, marijuana, phencyclidine (PCP-angel dust), opiates (heroin, codeine, morphine), and amphetamines (crystal meth). More complete but more expensive urine tests are the 10- or 12-panel tests, which include prescription drugs that are legal to have and use with an appropriate prescription. Drugs tested in these more complete panel tests include benzodiazepines (Xanax, Valium), barbiturates, methadone, propoxyphene, methaqualone (Quaaludes), hydrocodone, oxycodone, OxyContin, alcohol, and ecstasy.[62] Some employers are moving toward these more expensive testing panels because of new types of drugs becoming available and increased abuse of prescription drugs.

Commonly in employment testing, a drug is reported as present only if it has been detected in two separate tests using different analytic methods. In practice, this means two levels of testing: a *screening test* and a *confirmation test* (used only when the screening test indicates that a drug is present). If the screening test finds no drug presence or if the confirmatory test does not agree with the results of the screening test, the decision is that no drug is present. To conduct these tests, the urine sample is divided into two parts immediately after it is collected. Samples are usually identified by a number or code rather than by name of a person.

All urine tests assume that what enters the body through ingestion, injection, or inhalation must be excreted in some form. Most drugs are excreted, wholly or in part, into the urine via the liver, kidneys, and bladder. Although some drugs are excreted unchanged (for example, morphine), most drugs are broken down by the body; the products, or *metabolites*, can be found in the urine. The physical evidence of drug use differs from drug to drug. The testing procedures, then, must also differ for the different drug families, and new tests must be developed as new drugs come into use. To avoid error, standard thresholds (amount of drug present) of detection are set to determine the presence of a drug. If less than the threshold amount is detected, the decision is made that no drug is present. This theoretically reduces the possibility of drug presence being indicated by amounts of a legally permissible drug product.

Hair Analysis. A third drug-testing method is hair analysis, in which samples of hair including the root are taken from job applicants to be tested. Although more expensive than urine tests (currently, about twice as expensive), hair analysis is becoming more frequently used. The reason is that some job applicants have been able to fake urine tests (see our earlier comment regarding YouTube videos and urine tests). The basis of hair analysis is similar to that of urine analysis. That is, the use of drugs leaves chemical traces in human hair that remain after drug use. Hair analysis uses screening and confirmatory tests that are similar to those used for urine testing. Theoretically, because of the growth rate of scalp hair, hair analysis can detect drug use over a longer period of time than can urine testing. For example, an inch of hair is estimated to contain information relative to 90 days of potential drug use. To perform a hair analysis, the hair is divided into different samples and is washed multiple times to remove external contamination. The use of bleach or dye on the hair may lower drug levels slightly but not completely. If the purpose of a company's drug testing of job applicants is to identify any illegal drug use, hair testing would be preferable. Hair testing provides the longest period for detecting drug use, for example, for cannabis—1 to 3 months.

Oral Fluid Tests. For this test, the person being tested has an oral swab rubbed on the inside of the mouth. The swab is then sealed in a vial. Saliva on the swab is analyzed for the presence of drugs. Barring lab error, the test is always accurate. This test almost eliminates the risk of adulteration of a sample and makes it virtually impossible for donors to mask drugs in their systems or to use samples from others. A number of firms have expressed interest in the test because of ease of specimen collection and the difficulty job applicants would have in altering their results.

Accuracy of Chemical Tests

Because the physical properties of individual drugs are invariant, chemical tests should be completely accurate. False positives (individuals indicated as drug users who, in fact, are not users) may occur in an initial test. However, these errors should be eliminated by follow-up confirmation tests. Errors in confirmation tests occur only when the laboratory conducting the testing does not use appropriate, standardized procedures.

It is important to realize the limitations of the information obtained from these tests. A positive result means a presence of the drug above the threshold level set for detection. The result does not allow a determination of how much of the drug was used, how frequently it was used, how long ago it was used, the circumstances of its use, or the level of impairment in performance caused by the drug. Individuals differ in their absorption, metabolism, and tolerance of drugs. In addition, many drugs leave a metabolite trail long after any performance effects have faded; therefore, it is not accurate to assume automatically that a positive test is an infallible indicant of inability to perform. Finally, the threshold level obviously affects the results. Although commonly accepted threshold levels for detection do exist, some levels are so low that even passive inhalation of marijuana can yield a positive result.

Legal Issues in Pre-Employment Drug Testing

The most common form of drug testing takes place during pre-employment settings. In general, employers testing job applicants for drugs in the pre-employment phase are less legally exposed than organizations testing current employees. Considerably more legal risk is associated with testing current workers before making promotion decisions or with testing employees to detect drug users for disciplinary, safety, or counseling purposes. This is mainly because job applicants cannot take advantage of collective bargaining or challenge employment-at-will principles, as can employees who feel they have been wrongly treated.

The major questions about drug testing have centered on six legal arguments.[63] What is important to understand is that these arguments are most applicable to current *employees*; few apply directly to pre-employment testing of job *applicants*.

1. Testing represents an invasion of privacy.

2. Testing constitutes an unreasonable search and seizure.

3. Testing is a violation of due process.

4. Drug users are protected under the Americans with Disabilities Act.

5. Testing may violate the Civil Rights Act.

6. Testing may violate the National Labor Relations Act.

We briefly discuss these issues and, where applicable, comment on these issues relative to pre-employment drug testing.

By its very nature, the collection of urine, hair, or oral samples for testing is intrusive. Intrusion, physical or otherwise, on the private affairs of an individual has commonly been the basis for civil suits under the doctrine of *right of privacy*. However, this term offers protection only if the employer is a governmental institution or agency. Therefore, this defense is actually open only to a small number of job applicants. With regard to private companies, the courts have generally upheld the right of prospective employers to test job applicants for drug use as a precondition for employment. The right of privacy in nongovernmental firms *may* apply only to confidentiality in the collection and reporting of the drug test results. Collection practices should include guarantees of the privacy of the individual regarding the facilities provided as well as the procedures used in monitoring the specimen collection to ensure that it has not been altered. For certain jobs, it may be acceptable to require testing in the interests of public safety even at the cost of employee privacy. These are jobs in which employees could place themselves or others in substantial danger if they were under the effects of drug use. Examples of such jobs include airline pilot and other public transportation positions, chemical and nuclear power plant operators, and security officers.

The Fourth Amendment prohibits unreasonable search; the Fifth and Fourteenth Amendments guarantee the right of due process. Although they are frequently applied in public practices, these concepts have limited application to private industry. A central issue is the reason for the testing. It seems important that testing be linked to workplace problems such as accidents, theft, absenteeism, and sabotage. Data that indicate the existence of such problems before testing can serve as evidence the company was pursuing a legitimate self-interest. In the absence of such data, the company is at risk by seeming arbitrary in its actions and seeming to have little actual justification for its claims.

The question of due process, under which a person is innocent unless proven guilty, seems to deal with the validity of drug tests. Presumably, evidence provided by professionally conducted testing would constitute evidence of guilt.

The Americans with Disabilities Act (ADA) of 1990 prohibits discrimination against the disabled. The act clearly protects former drug users who are in rehabilitation but excludes individuals currently using drugs. In addition, drug tests are not treated as medical examinations under the ADA; however, tests given to determine an applicant's blood alcohol level would be treated as a medical examination and, therefore, would be covered by the ADA.[64] To avoid most liabilities under the ADA, employers conducting drug tests on job applicants often make a job offer before conducting a drug test. Since the ADA does not cover individuals applying for jobs who test positive for illegal drugs, a company can withdraw the job offer because of illegal drug use. If a positive drug test shows the presence of a legally prescribed drug, the positive result must be treated as confidential information.[65,66]

Title VII of the Civil Rights Act of 1964 could be a legal basis for discrimination if, as described previously, unequal treatment occurs. It is possible drug testing could also result in adverse impact, for example, if a greater percentage of minority than nonminority members are identified. The test would then have to be shown to be job related. Safety of others or demonstration of previous records of high rates of damage, accidents, or absenteeism could serve as evidence. The previously noted difficulty in linking positive results of a drug test with decrements in job performance could limit an organization's defense.

It is no surprise that drug testing has caused negative reactions among applicants as well as employees. Consequently, it is important for selection and HR specialists to understand how applicants and existing employees may react to a drug-testing program. In general, research has indicated that employees and applicants react more favorably to drug testing when (a) an advance warning of the testing is given, (b) the company uses rehabilitation of employees rather than termination when the presence of drugs is detected,[67] and (c) the drug testing adheres to fair detection procedures and explanation of results.

In addition, researchers have found that employees and applicants are more positive about drug testing when there is a perceived need for the test.[68] In this research, some of the acceptable reasons for testing included perceptions of danger, contact with the public, use of spatial ability in hazardous job tasks, and the performance of repetitive tasks. In addition, a company's restrictive confidentiality policy regarding access to results was associated with intention to apply for employment.[69]

Finally, when drug testing was required, individuals were more satisfied with either urinalysis or overt paper-and-pencil tests than with a personality inventory.[70] Not surprisingly, drug users had much more negative reactions to all forms of testing than did nonusers.[71] Most people do not regard the negative reactions of drug users to be a bad thing, however.

One current drug-testing issue facing companies is pre-employment drug testing of applicants for jobs located in states where marijuana has been legalized. We are not aware of any legal cases challenging an employer's refusal to hire someone who has tested positive for marijuana, and the applicant showed the employer a medical marijuana card. Some commentators have noted that nothing in the ADA requires an employer to hire someone who tests positive for marijuana but has a medical card for it.[72] The Department of Transportation has noted that medical marijuana is illegal for any safety-sensitive employee. Their guidelines clearly state that medical marijuana is not an acceptable explanation for a positive drug-test result.[73]

Guidelines for Drug-Testing Programs with Job Applicants

We conclude this section with a brief summary of important features of a drug-testing program used with job applicants. These features include the following:

1. A company is in the most legally defensible position when it limits testing to those positions that have major safety implications or a history of poor performance in specific areas that might be linked to drug usage. Failure to

conduct drug tests for some jobs in particular industries, such as transportation, can lead to penalties against an organization. For example, the Federal Airlines Administration levied a penalty of almost $600,000 against United Airlines for failure to perform pre-employment drug tests and receive negative results. United Airlines had transferred 13 people into safety-sensitive positions without testing for drugs and confirming negative results before their transfer. Such tests and results are required by the Department of Transportation prior to moving individuals into safety-sensitive positions.[74]

2. Private employers (versus public employers) have more latitude in conducting drug testing as they choose unless an employer is subject to federal regulations, such as those mandated by the Department of Transportation.

3. Private employers have more flexibility in their drug-testing programs with job applicants than with existing employees.

4. A combination of screening and confirmatory tests is necessary for valid drug testing. Such tests increase the cost of the program but are necessary given the seriousness of the matter.

5. A company should obtain written consent of the job applicant before testing and provide the individual with the test results afterward. Particular attention should be paid to those situations in which an individual is informed of positive results from the drug test. At a minimum, the person should be allowed to explain positive results in terms of legal drugs that he or she may have taken. A physician's verification may be required in such explanations. Some have also recommended that the individual who tested positive be offered the opportunity to submit part of the urine sample used in the testing to another laboratory for additional testing. This would be done at the individual's expense. If an individual were to refuse to be drug-tested, a private employer can reject the individual for employment.

6. Standardized procedures used in the testing program should be applied to *all* job applicants tested for drugs. Do not exempt some applicants from drug testing because it seems obvious that they are not taking drugs.

7. The program should be designed and reviewed periodically to ensure that privacy is afforded to individuals being tested. This means that urine collection procedures be standardized and attuned to the privacy of the individual. In addition, all results must be kept confidential, especially from supervisors of existing employees, unless there is a defined need to know.

GENETIC TESTING

In 2003, the Human Genome Project completed the mapping of roughly 25,000 genes that compose the human body.[75] Since then, scientists have discovered and continue to discover specific genes linked to certain diseases. For some diseases, the link between possession of a gene(s) and the development of a particular disease is strong; for other diseases, the link is far more tenuous. As additional links between gene possession and disease development discoveries are made (currently, tests for over 1,500 genetic diseases are available), these results will continue to have important implications for the delivery of health care in our society. Genetic testing and its associated results have important implications regarding employment issues as well.

For our purposes, we are concerned in this section with the implications of genetic testing for employers when selecting among job applicants. For instance, some employers have used applicants' genetic information to predict those most likely to miss work due to illness or develop devastating diseases that will drive up the company's health insurance costs. (Understand that although we focus on *job applicants*, the points in our discussion also apply to current and former employees, labor union members, apprentices, and trainees.)

What Is Genetic Testing?

Genetic testing is an analysis of human DNA, RNA, chromosomes, proteins, or metabolites that detects genotypes, mutations, or chromosomal changes. Such testing produces *genetic information* on (a) individuals (for our purposes, job applicants) who have been tested genetically, (b) family members of these individuals who have been tested genetically, or (c) the individuals' family members' health histories.[76] It is essential to emphasize that "family medical history" is included in the definition of genetic information.

Importantly, genetic information can be used by individuals to take pre-emptive action to mitigate various diseases that have a high probability of developing due to the presence of certain genetic markers linked to these diseases. For example, a woman who carries the BRCA1 and BRCA2 genes is almost twice as likely to develop breast cancer as those who do not.[77] Having genetic information, she can choose among a variety of options, such as having more frequent breast exams, using more sensitive diagnostic equipment than an x-ray, or taking action that is more aggressive by having her breasts removed. However, before the passage of certain laws, these impressive developments in genetic testing led to the misuse of genetic information by health insurers and employers. In some cases, insurers having access to genetic information denied coverage based on pre-existing conditions. In other cases, employers possessing knowledge of genetic information denied jobs to certain applicants or fired employees holding existing positions. The rationale behind these decisions is that applicants or employees having the wrong genetic profile might very well develop expensive diseases or become injured on the job thus increasing workers' compensation costs. By refusing to employ such applicants, employers could hold down rising health care and workers' compensation costs.

Legal Concerns

Before the passage of certain state and federal laws, employers could use genetic information to predict those job applicants most likely to develop costly diseases. By refusing to hire applicants possessing certain genes or having a history of certain diseases, even if those applicants were more qualified than applicants not having those genes, employers' medical costs could be reduced substantially. Health insurers also realized they could employ genetic information or family medical history to predict those applicants likely to develop diseases. Insurers used such information to deny those applicants health insurance or refused to pay for treatments because of pre-existing health conditions, resulting in substantial savings and enhanced profitability for insurance firms in the health insurance industry.

A key legal case raised the consciousness of the federal government regarding genetic testing and discrimination against certain racial minorities. In *Norman-Bloodsaw v. Lawrence Berkeley Laboratory*,[78] the Laboratory gave all job applicants a pre-employment medical exam. Without the individuals' knowledge or consent, among other tests run on the applicants, they tested for sickle-cell genetic markers that are linked to sickle-cell anemia. Sickle-cell anemia is a disease that affects African-Americans. Any applicant possessing that gene was refused employment.[79] The plaintiffs in the case won based on the Laboratory's invasion of applicants' privacy. Some might query if the Americans with Disability Act (ADA) would not also cover this case. Although plaintiffs in the case might have had the gene, and become disabled in the future, they were not disabled at the time of their employment application. Therefore, given the interpretation of the ADA, it did not offer the plaintiffs protection from discrimination because of their absence of a current disability at the time of their application.

The decision in favor of the plaintiffs in the *Lawrence Berkeley Laboratory* case led Congress to recognize that genetic discrimination could occur in the workplace through genetic testing. Genetic testing could produce adverse effects against gender, racial, and ethnic groups as well as applicant groups having certain diseases that were not related to the applicants' ability to perform their jobs.

The Genetic Information Nondiscrimination Act of 2008

To alleviate some of the discrimination problems Americans could experience through genetic testing, Congress passed a law prohibiting genetic discrimination. The intent of the law was to prohibit discriminatory actions arising from genetic testing that would prevent Americans from receiving health insurance or employment. In 2008, after 13 years of congressional debate, President George W. Bush signed the Genetic Information Nondiscrimination Act (GINA) into law. GINA consists of several parts or titles. Here, we focus only on Title II because it specifically addresses issues most relevant to employers. In general, Title II prohibits an employer, employment agency, labor organization, or joint labor-management committee from discriminating against employees (including job applicants and former employees), individuals, or members of these groups because of genetic information. The law specifically states, "*An employer may never use genetic information to make an employment decision because genetic information is not relevant to an individual's current ability to work.*"[80]

To date, relatively few legal cases have been tried in court involving genetic testing under the provisions of GINA. However, a number of formal genetic discrimination complaints have been filed with the Equal Employment Opportunity Commission (EEOC). Table 14.4 shows the total number of charges filed with the EEOC by complainants involving the use of genetic information for the period 2010–2013. Do note that data in the table include those charges filed under GINA along with concurrent charges under Title VII, the Age Discrimination in Employment Act, the Americans with Disability Act, and the Environmental Protection Act. Although the 4-year period is brief, the number of charges filed has steadily increased from 201 charges in 2010 to 333 charges in 2013.

Table 14.5 summarizes some of the job applicant protections and employer requirements of Title II in GINA. Employers should be aware of these requirements particularly

TABLE 14.4	Charges Filed by Employees and Job Applicants with the EEOC and Resolved Under the Genetic Information Nondiscrimination Act (GINA)			
	Fiscal Year 2010	Fiscal Year 2011	Fiscal Year 2012	Fiscal Year 2013
Number of Charges Filed	201	245	280	333
Monetary Awards to Complainants (millions)[a]	$0.08	$0.5	$2.1	$1.0

Note: Information reported in the table were adapted from www1.eeoc.gov//eeoc/statistics/enforcement/genetic.cfm.

[a]Does not include monetary benefits obtained through litigation.

TABLE 14.5	Employer Mandates and Job Applicant[a] Protection under Title II of the Genetic Information Nondiscrimination Act (GINA)

- Prohibits employers from using genetic information in any aspect of employment decision making, such as hiring and promoting
- Prohibits employers from requiring, requesting, or purchasing genetic information (including family medical history) about Job applicants or family members
- Exceptions to prohibitions against acquiring genetic information include:
  - Inadvertent collection of genetic information
  - Family medical history obtained as part of health or wellness programs offered by the employer on a voluntary basis
  - Family medical history acquired as part of the certification process for the Family Medical Leave Act (FMLA)
  - Genetic information collected through a genetic monitoring program that monitors the biological effects of toxic substances in the workplace where monitoring is required by law or voluntary on the employee's part
- Prohibits employers from disclosing genetic information about Job applicants
- Requires employers to keep genetic information confidential and in a separate medical file (information can be kept in the same file as other medical information as mandated under the Americans with Disabilities Act)
- State laws that provide more extensive protections to job applicants override GINA
- Applies to employers having 15 or more employees covered by the Americans with Disabilities Act and Title VII of the Civil Rights Act of 1964 where a complaint has been filed with the EEOC within 180 days of an incident

Note: Information in the table was obtained from http://www.eeoc.gov/laws/types/genetic.cfm and www.johnjohnson.info/wp-content/uploads/2013/05/gina.pdf. Retrieved on April 28, 2014.

[a]In addition to job applicants, GINA pertains to current and former employees, labor union members, apprentices, and trainees as well.

when conducting pre-employment medical exams. The applicant's personal physician should provide the medical record to the employer omitting all associated genetic information (see our earlier definition of genetic information). The purpose of the medical exam is to determine if the person has any medical issues that would prevent him or her from performing the job for which a conditional offer has been extended. The EEOC is responsible for enforcing Title II of GINA. Following the passage of GINA, the EEOC issued the final regulations in 2010 that clarify some of the specific details regarding GINA and its application.[81]

In general, the Act and associated regulations apply to covered organizations having 15 or more employees. Any charges against an employer must be filed with the EEOC within 180 days of the incident on which a complaint is based. Compensatory and punitive damages recoverable by a victim from an employer that was found to have violated GINA vary according to the size of the employer; a maximum penalty of $300,000 for employers having more than 500 employees can be assessed.[82]

From a professional practice perspective, we do not see a need for nor do we encourage an organization to engage in genetic testing or attempt to acquire genetic information on job applicants or employees. The exception to this guideline is if employers have jobs (for example, jobs in a carcinogen-rich environment, such as a uranium mine) that are part of a lawful medical surveillance program. In this case, employers might offer a voluntary genetic testing program where employees decide on their own whether to participate in the program. Only individual volunteers in the program would see their own results; the employer would not see individual results.[83]

WHAT'S NEXT? NEUROSCIENCE–BASED DISCRIMINATION

Given the number and variety of predictors that we have discussed so far, you must be thinking: "I've read about measures used in selection ranging from paper-and-pencil inventories to computer-administered tests to physical activities performed by job applicants. I've seen how the polygraph attempts to assess autonomic arousal of participants, how posing oral questions to interviewees might relate to important applicant attributes and even the analysis of bodily fluids to make inferences about job applicants' suitability for employment. I don't see how there could possibly be anything else that could be used to assess job applicants and predict their behavior. Could there?"

The short answer to your question is: *Possibly*, there might be; at least at some point in the future when enough scientific evidence is available and assuming the evidence as well as state/federal laws are supportive. Neuroscientists in studying the brain have begun to examine relationships between the neural circuits of the brain and the development of diseases, such as Alzheimer's as well as behaviors (such as racism, cooperativeness) and personality characteristics (such as extraversion, introversion).[84] Much of such work has been supported through the federally funded Human Connectome Project.[85]

Like genetic testing, neuroimaging of the pathways in the brain does not mean that perfect predictions can be made regarding the onset of disease or that certain behaviors will be manifested. Although significant progress has been made in the last 10 years, our current understanding of the brain's structures and their functioning are still developing. However, with current as well as future research involving the brain, it will be possible to describe in terms of probabilities the likelihood that certain neural wirings are linked to specific outcomes, such as disease and behavior. It is precisely these probabilities that worry scientists as well as attorneys concerned with the ethical impact of neural imaging and predicting outcomes, such as lying or certain job behaviors. Stephanie Kostiuk, an attorney in New York, notes that similar concerns arose during the 13 years of Congressional debate and negotiations taken to pass GINA into law. She suggests these same concerns should apply to neuroscience assessments in the context of human resource selection. In summarizing several key points in the Congressional deliberations regarding genetic information as it pertains to human resource selection, she writes

> As discussed in the congressional debate leading to the enactment of GINA, although predictive testing may only be probabilistic, it may still prove economically efficient from the perspective of an employer to rely on the information in making employment decisions. In pre-employment testing, an employer may not require certainty that an individual will manifest a disease or evidence a harmful trait. Merely probabilistic information is valuable in that it conveys the knowledge that the possession of a particular DNA sequence, or brain function or structure, places the applicant at a higher risk of doing so. When processing large numbers of applicants, an employer can significantly reduce costs by denying employment to those whose test results show them to be at a higher risk for a disease or other detrimental trait.[86]

Although some might argue that the difficulties in collecting neuro-information for selection purposes would be impractical, at least two companies (No Lie MRI, Inc.–www.noliemri.com and Cephos Corporation–www.cephosdna.com) offer functional magnetic response imaging (fMRI) brain scanning services to the public for employee screening (lying, deception, drug screening, resume validation), legal settings, and national security investigations. The fMRI is similar to an MRI, but it analyzes brain blood flow rather than structures. In general, the fMRI procedures detect activation in a region of the brain, designated by increases in the flow of blood in that region. The fMRI assesses the relative change in blood flow from one set of questions posed to a participant for which there is a known truthful answer to another set of questions about the topic of concern.[87] Some scientists have shown, at least in a low-stakes environment (such as a lab setting), the technology can detect lying. The two companies mentioned above state their methods yield approximately 90 percent accuracy.[88] However, to our knowledge, the techniques have not been admitted in court.[89] *If* additional scientific research shows that fMRI scans are accurate, and valid inferences can be made from these scans regarding CWBs, such as lying, or that individuals possess certain WRCs, such as conscientiousness, some firms will likely be interested in such services for employee screening. Particularly if the scans involve corporate executives, the expense for the service would likely be worth the investment. However, more research is needed to determine if such scans permit valid inferences of CWBs of importance to employers involved in human resource selection. From a legal perspective before such information can be introduced in court hearings, the information needed must

1. generally be accepted by the scientific community

2. have been tested under field conditions

3. have been subjected to peer review

4. have a known error rate

5. have standardized techniques for performing and analyzing scans.[90]

At present, there is not enough evidence available on these methods for human resource applications.

Stephanie Kostiuk has argued that just as in the case of genetic information, current technical shortcomings with the technology of neuroimaging will not stop companies from implementing the technology and using the information as a basis for selection decision making. Therefore, she has argued that a GINA-like federal statute be adopted entitled the Neuro Information Nondiscrimination Act (NINA) with Title I of the Act similar to Title II of GINA. That is, it would prohibit employers from "… requesting, acquiring, or disclosing neuro information and from discriminating on the basis of neuro information."[91]

REFERENCES

1. For an actual measure of counterproductive work behaviors, see Suzy Fox and Paul Spector, "Counterproductive Work Behavior Checklist." Retrieved on April 5, 2014 from http://shell .cas.usf.edu/~spector and Laurenz L. Meier and Paul E. Spector, "Reciprocal Effects of Work Stressors and Counterproductive Work Behavior: A Five-Wave Longitudinal Study," *Journal of Applied Psychology* 98 (2013): 529–539.

2. Chubb Corporation, "Taking Risks with Risk: Highlights from the Chubb 2010 Risk Survey." Retrieved on April 6, 2014 from http://www.chubb.com/businesses/csi/chubb4852.html.

3. R. C. Hollinger and A. Adams, "2009 National Retail Security Survey: Final Report," Gainesville, FL: University of Florida (2010).

4. J. Goodchild, "Retail Shrink, Theft Up in 2009: CSO Security and Risk Report." Retrieved on April 6, 2014 from http://www.csoonline.com/article/print/507263.

5. James C. Wimbush and Dan R. Dalton, "Base Rate for Employee Theft: Convergence of Multiple Methods," *Journal of Applied Psychology* 82 (1997): 756–763.

6. Employee Polygraph Protection Act of 1988, Public Law 100–347, 29 USC 2001.

7. David Z. Lykken, "Psychology and the Lie Detector Industry," *American Psychologist* 29 (1974): 725–739.

8. Ibid.

9. Gershon Ben-Shakhar and Karmela Dolev, "Psychophysical Detection through Guilty Knowledge Technique: Effect of Mental Countermeasures," *Journal of Applied Psychology* 81 (1996): 273–281.

10. John Jones and William Terris, "Selection Alternatives to the Preemployment Polygraph," in *Pre-employment Honesty Testing: Current Research and Future Directions,* ed. John W. Jones (Westport, CT: Quorum Books, 1991): 40.

11. Deniz S. Ones, Chockalingam Viswesvaran, and Frank L. Schmidt, "Integrity Tests Predict Counterproductive Work Behaviors and Job Performance Well: Comment on Van Iddekinge, Roth, Raymark, and Odle-Dusseau (2012)," *Journal of Applied Psychology* 97 (2012): 538.

12. William Terris and John Jones, "Psychological Factors Related to Employees' Theft in the Convenience Store Industry," *Psychological Reports* 51 (1982): 1219–1238.

13. Bureau of National Affairs, *Employee Testing: The Complete Resource Guide* (Washington, DC: Bureau of National Affairs, 1988).

14. Joyce Hogan and Robert Hogan, "How to Measure Employee Reliability," *Journal of Applied Psychology* 74 (1989): 273–279.

15. Nathan Luther, "Integrity Testing and Job Performance within High-Performance Work Teams: A Short Note," *Journal of Business and Psychology* 15 (2000): 19–25.

16. Christopher M. Berry, Paul R. Sackett, and Shelly Wiemann, "A Review of Recent Developments in Integrity Test Research," *Personnel Psychology* 60 (2007): 271–301.

17. Deniz S. Ones, Chockalingam Viswesvaran, and Frank L. Schmidt, "Comprehensive Meta-Analysis of Integrity Test Validities: Findings and Implications for Personnel Selection and Theories of Job Performance," *Journal of Applied Psychology Monograph* 78 (1993): 679–703. See also Deniz S. Ones, Chockalingam Viswesvaran, and Frank L. Schmidt, "Group Differences on Overt Integrity Tests and Related Personality Variables: Implications for Adverse Impact and Test Construction," *Conference of Society for Industrial and Organizational Psychology* (1996) and Deniz Ones, Frank L. Schmidt, and Chockalingam Viswesvaran, "Integrity and Ability: Implications for Incremental Validity and Adverse Impact," *Conference of Society for Industrial and Organizational Psychology* (1993).

18. Chad H. Van Iddekinge, Philip L. Roth, Patrick H. Raymark, and Heather N. Odle-Dusseau, "The Criterion-Related Validity of Integrity Tests: An Updated Meta-Analysis," *Journal of Applied Psychology* 97 (2012): 499–530.

19. Paul Sackett and Neal Schmitt, "On Reconciling Conflicting Meta-Analytic Findings Regarding Integrity Test Validity," *Journal of Applied Psychology* 97 (2012): 553.

20. Paul R. Sackett and C. J. Devore, "Counterproductive Behaviors at Work," in N. Anderson, Deniz S. Ones, H. K. Sinangil, and Chockalingam Viswesvaran, *Handbook of Industrial Work and Organizational Psychology,* (Sage: London, 2002): 145–164. See also Christopher M. Berry and Paul R. Sackett, "Interpersonal Deviance, Organizational Deviance, and Their Common Correlates," *Journal of Applied Psychology* 92 (2007): 410–424.

21. Berry, Sackett, and Wiemann, "A Review of Recent Developments in Integrity Test Research."

22. Paul R. Sackett and James E. Wanek, "New Developments in the Use of Measures of Honesty, Integrity, Conscientiousness, Dependability, Trustworthiness, and Reliability for Personnel Selection," *Personnel Psychology* 49 (1996): 787–829.

23. Bernd Marcus, Kibeom Lee, and Michael C. Ashton, "Personality Dimensions Explaining Relationships between Integrity Tests and Counterproductive Behavior, Big Five, or One in Addition," *Personnel Psychology* 60 (2007): 1–34.

24. Paul R. Sackett and James E. Wanek, "New Developments in the Use of Measures of Honesty, Integrity, Conscientiousness, Dependability, Trustworthiness, and Reliability for Personnel Selection," *Personnel Psychology* 49 (1996): 787–829.

25. Ibid.

26. James E. Wanek, Paul R. Sackett, and Deniz S. Ones, "Toward an Understanding of Integrity Test Similarities and Differences: An Item-Level Analysis of Seven Tests," *Personnel Psychology* 56 (2003): 873–894. See also Bernd Marcus, Stefan Hoft, and Michaela Riediger, "Integrity Tests and the Five-Factor Model of Personality: A Review and Empirical Tests of Two Alternative Positions," *International Journal of Selection and Assessment* 14 (2006): 113–130.

27. Paul R. Sackett, L. R. Burris, and C. Callahan, "Integrity Testing for Personnel Selection: An Update," *Personnel Psychology* 42 (1989): 491–529.

28. Sackett and Wanek, "New Developments in the Use of Measures of Honesty, Integrity, Conscientiousness, Dependability, Trustworthiness, and Reliability for Personnel Selection."

29. Deniz S. Ones, Chockalingam Viswesvaran, and Frank L. Schmidt, "Personality and Absenteeism: A Meta-Analysis of Integrity Tests," *European Journal of Personality* 17 (2003): 519–538.

30. Deniz S. Ones and Chockalingam Viswesvaran, "A Research Note on the Incremental Validity of Job Knowledge and Tests for Predicting Maximal Performance," *Human Performance* 20 (2007): 293–303.

31. Ibid.

32. Sackett and Wanek, "New Developments in the Use of Measures of Honesty, Integrity, Conscientiousness, Dependability, Trustworthiness, and Reliability for Personnel Selection."

33. Iddekinge, Roth, Raymark, Odle-Dusseau, "The Criterion-Related Validity of Integrity Tests: An Updated Meta-Analysis."

34. Ones, Viswesvaran, and Schmidt, "Comprehensive Meta-Analysis of Integrity Test Validities: Findings and Implications for Personnel Selection and Theories of Job Performance," 693.

35. Ibid., 694.

36. Ibid., 685.

37. Iddekinge, Roth, Raymark, and Odle-Dusseau, "The Criterion-Related Validity of Integrity Tests: An Updated Meta-Analysis," 500.

38. Ibid., 505.

39. Ibid.

40. The table was adapted from Paul R. Sackett and Neal Schmitt, "On Reconciling Conflicting Meta-Analytic Findings Regarding Integrity Test Validity," *Journal of Applied Psychology* 97 (2012): 551.

41. Ibid., 551.

42. Ibid., 552.

43. William G. Harris, John W. Jones, Reid Klion, David W. Arnold, Wayne Camara, and Michael R. Cunningham, "Test Publishers' Perspective on 'An Updated Meta-Analysis': Comment on Van Iddekinge, Roth, Raymark, and Odle-Dusseau (2012)," *Journal of Applied Psychology* 97 (2012): 535.

44. Sackett and Wanek, "New Developments in the Use of Measures of Honesty, Integrity, Conscientiousness, Dependability, Trustworthiness, and Reliability for Personnel Selection."

45. Christopher M. Berry, Paul R. Sackett, and Shelly Wiemann, "A Review of Recent Developments in Integrity Test Research," *Personnel Psychology* 60 (2007): 277.

46. Ones, Viswesvaran, and Schmidt, "Comprehensive Meta-Analysis of Integrity Test Validities: Findings and Implications for Personnel Selection and Theories of Job Performance."

47. Michael R. Cunningham, Dennis T. Wong, and Anita P. Barbee, "Self-Presentation Dynamics on Overt Integrity Tests: Experimental Studies of the Reid Report," *Journal of Applied Psychology* 79 (1994): 643–658.

48. Berry, Sackett, and Wiemann, "A Review of Recent Developments in Integrity Test Research," 284–285.

49. Susan J. Stabile, "The Use of Personality Tests as a Hiring Tool: Is the Benefit Worth the Cost?," *University of Pennsylvania Journal of Labor and Employment Law* 4 (2002): 287.

50. Ibid., 284.

51. Harris, Jones, Klion, Arnold, Camara, and Cunningham, "Test Publishers' Perspective on 'An Updated Meta-Analysis': Comment on Van Iddekinge, Roth, Raymark, and Odle-Dusseau (2012)," 535.

52. Deniz Ones and Chockalingam Viswesvaran, "Gender, Age, and Race Differences on Overt Integrity Tests: Results Across Four Large-Scale Job Applicant Data Sets," *Journal of Applied Psychology* 83 (1998): 35–42.

53. Berry, Sackett, and Wiemann, "A Review of Recent Developments in Integrity Test Research." See also Thomas E. Becker, "Information Exchange Article Development and Validation of a Situational Judgment Test of Employee Integrity," *International Journal of Selection and Assessment* 13 (2005): 225–232.

54. Ann M. Ryan and Paul R. Sackett, "Pre-employment Honesty Testing: Fakability, Reactions of Test Takers, and Company Image," *Journal of Business and Psychology* 1 (1987): 255.

55. www.dol.gov/elaws/asp/drugfree/drugs. Retrieved on April 15, 2014.

56. Matthew D. Paronto, Donald M. Truxillo, Talya N. Bauer, and Michael C. Leo, "Drug Testing, Drug Treatment, and Marijuana Use: A Fairness Perspective," *Journal of Applied Psychology* 87 (2002): 1159–1166.

57. Michael R. Frone, "Prevalence and Distribution of Illicit Drug Use in the Workforce and in the Workplace: Findings and Implications from a U.S. National Survey," *Journal of Applied Psychology* 91 (2006): 856–869.

58. Ibid.

59. Ibid.

60. *National Treasury Employees Union v. Von Raab*, 649 F. Supp 380 (1986).

61. Lauren Weber, *The Wall Street Journal Online*, Nov. 19, 2013.

62. www.dol.gov/elaws/asp/drugfree/drugs/dt.asp. Retrieved on April 17, 2014.

63. Deborah F. Crown and Joseph G. Rosse, "A Critical Review of Assumptions Underlying Drug Testing," in *Applying Psychology in Business: The Manager's Handbook*, ed. Douglas W. Bray, John W. Jones, and Brian D. Steffy (Lexington, MA: Lexington Books, 1991).

64. Linda C. Batiste, Accommodation and Compliance Series: Employees with Drug Addiction, www.askjan.org/media/drugadd; p. 3. Retrieved on April 15, 2014.

65. Ibid.

66. Dianna Stone and Debra Kotch, "Individuals' Attitudes Toward Organizational Drug Testing Policies and Practices," *Journal of Applied Psychology* 74 (1989): 518–521.

67. Bennett J. Tepper, "Investigation of General and Program-Specific Attitudes Toward Corporate Drug-Testing Policies," *Journal of Applied Psychology* 79 (1994): 392–401.

68. Stone and Kotch, "Individuals' Attitudes Toward Organizational Drug Testing Policies and Practices."

69. David A. Sujak, "The Effects of Drug-Testing Program Characteristics on Applicants' Attitudes toward Potential Employment," *Journal of Psychology* 129 (1995): 401–416.

70. Joseph G. Rosse, Richard C. Ringer, and Janice L. Miller, "Personality and Drug Testing: An Exploration of the Perceived Fairness of Alternatives to Urinalysis," *Journal of Business and Psychology* 10 (1996): 459–475.

71. Joseph G. Rosse, Janice L. Miller, and Richard C. Ringer, "The Deterrent Value of Drug and Integrity Testing," *Journal of Business and Psychology* 10 (1996): 477–485.

72. *Workers' Compensation Report,* 23 (May 1, 2012): 5.

73. www.dot.gov/odapc/medical-marijuana-notice. Retrieved on April 15, 2014.

74. Susan Carey, "FAA Proposes Fine Against United," *The Wall Street Journal Online* (June 17, 2011): 1.

75. www.genome.gov/10001772. Retrieved on April 27, 2014.

76. http://www.eeoc.gov/laws/statutes/gina.cfm and http://www.eeoc.gov/laws/types/genetic.cfm. Retrieved on April 28, 2014.

77. Lewis Maltby, "Brave New Workplace: Genetic Discrimination," *Illinois Public Employee Relations Report* 26 (2009): 1.

78. 135 F.3d 1260, 1269 (9th Cir. 1998).

79. Lewis Maltby, "Brave New Workplace: Genetic Discrimination," 26 (2009): 2.

80. http://www.eeoc.gov/laws/statutes/gina.cfm and http://www.eeoc.gov/laws/types/genetic.cfm. Retrieved on April 28, 2014.

81. https://www.federalregister.gov/articles/2010/11/09/2010-28011/regulations-under-the-genetic-information-nondiscrimination-act-of-2008.

82. http://www.eeoc.gov/employees/remedies.cfm. Retrieved on May 2, 2014.

83. Aaron Varner, "Title II of the Genetic Information Nondiscrimination Act and its Promulgating Regulations: Analyzing Employer Acquisition of Employee Genetic Information in the Context of Fairness and Privacy," *Labor Law Journal* 62 (2011): 211–212.

84. Stephanie A. Kostiuk, "After GINA, NINA? Neuroscience-Based Discrimination in the Workplace," *Vanderbilt Law Review,* 65 (2012): 958.

85. http://www.nytimes.com/2014/01/07/science/the-brain-in-exquisite-detail.html?_r=0. Retrieved on April 29, 2014.

86. Stephanie A. Kostiuk, "After GINA, NINA? Neuroscience-Based Discrimination in the Workplace." (2012): 960. Quoted with permission.

87. Joseph R. Simpson, "Functional MRI Lie Detection: Too Good to be True?" *The Journal of the American Academy of Psychiatry and the Law* 36 (2008): 491–492.

88. Ibid., 491.

89. http://www.washingtonpost.com/local/crime/debate-on-brain-scans-as-lie-detectors-highlighted-in-maryland-murder-trial/2012/08/26/aba3d7d8-ed84-11e1-9ddc-340d5efb1e9c_print.html. Retrieved on April 30, 2014.

90. *Daubert v. Merrell Dow Pharmaceuticals, Inc.*, 509 U.S. 579 (1993).

91. Stephanie A. Kostiuk, "After GINA, NINA? Neuroscience-Based Discrimination in the Workplace." (2012): 971.

USING SELECTION DATA

We can hear you now: "C'mon, guys! Hurry and finish this off. Enough is enough! I know that I'm supposed to do a job analysis and use reliable, job-related selection tests. But, how do I use all of this information to decide which applicants will receive job offers?"

The following, and incidentally only (whew!), chapter in Part 4 will help you take advantage of the job-related predictor information you collect. We believe that by applying the guidelines and suggestions that we offer, you will increase your chances of making the best personnel selection decisions. In this part, we use research to offer you practical advice on how you can use that information to interpret the scores that you have gathered. When you finish Part 4, we hope you will say something like, "Oh, I get it! Now, what did I do with those test and interview scores?"

Strategies for Selection Decision Making

Valentina selects about 100 employees each year for various positions at her company. She is proud of her skill in selection and boasts that she knows a good applicant when she sees one. However, an examination of employee records reveals a different story. Not all, but many of the employees Valentina hired turned out to be poor performers and were later terminated or left the company voluntarily; and one applicant whom Valentina rejected was hired by a competitor and is now their most productive manager. What is wrong with the selection process? Why is Valentina so overconfident about her hiring prowess?

The mystery is even more perplexing because Valentina's company has job-related selection procedures for use in its hiring process. In fact, the company hired consultants to help design its current selection system, which is considered state-of-the-art and capable of withstanding legal challenges. Applicant data are carefully collected and documented throughout each phase of the selection process.

In an interview with Valentina, flaws in her selection process became evident. Although Valentina collects information about each applicant using the company's selection procedures, she believes her job experience with the company and decision-making skill set have equipped her with what she really needs to make employment decisions. As she noted, "Give me 5 minutes of talking with a job applicant, and I can tell you who's going to be a winner and who's going to be a loser." Thus, she makes her final hire/no hire decisions by gut feelings, or intuition. She sizes up applicants using her collected data, incorporates that information with her self-perceived, decision-making skills, and then compares the applicant to her own mental image of an ideal employee. Those who make her "cut" are offered a position.

Two primary reasons explain the low quality of Valentina's selection decisions. First, although she has available applicant data collected from the company's selection procedures, she mentally combines the information from these procedures unsystematically and adds this information to her gut instincts. In fact, and unknown to her, Valentina is inconsistent in how she combines this information in many selection decisions. Second, Valentina is unaware of her true "hits" and "misses" as a decision maker because she does not keep records of her own decision-making outcomes, and the company does not audit her selection decisions periodically. Together, these practices lead to suboptimal selection decision making for both Valentina and her firm. It is important to realize that even when an organization collects reliable and valid selection procedure data, poor implementation of these procedures in selection decision making can undermine the entire selection system.

How can faulty selection decision making such as Valentina's be improved? To begin, we must focus on selection decision making as much as we do on developing and administering valid selection procedures. By following sound, systematic decision-making procedures and studying decision outcomes, managers can improve their effectiveness. In this chapter, we first focus on characteristics of selection decisions. Then, we outline and assess several methods for collecting and combining predictor information. Next, we list systematic decision-making strategies for using combined predictor information that can improve selection decision making. We conclude the chapter with practical advice for making selection decisions.

Selection decisions come in two basic varieties: simple and complex. Simple selection decisions involve one position opening with several applicants. Applicants are assessed on the work-related characteristics (WRCs) important to job success. The applicant who most closely approximates the requirements of the job is selected. Complex selection decisions are those involving a number of applicants and several position openings to fill. Here, the decision is not only whom to select, but which candidate is best for each job.

In either case, simple or complex, selection information can be overwhelming at times. In the current economic times where job openings are not plentiful, it is not unusual to receive at least several hundred applications for each job opening. At the university where one of your authors teaches, a recent academic advisor opening attracted more than 250 local applications. Imagine a situation that occurred in Duluth, Minnesota, a few years ago when 10,000 applicants applied for 300 operator positions at a paper mill. Or more recently, when an automobile manufacturer received more than 25,000 applications for several hundred openings. For professional job openings at well-respected organizations, application numbers can well be in the thousands. The data processing work alone must be staggering! These job application cases suggest that the information-processing demands placed on selection decision makers grow exponentially and can be represented by the following equation:

$$\text{Selection Information-Processing Demands} = \text{Number of Applicants} \times \text{Amount of Selection Data Collected}$$

Selection information-processing demands become even more amplified when there are many applicants, and many types of selection data are collected on each one. When time and other costs are factored into a decision, even simple selection decisions become costly.

Managers, supervisors, and others who hire employees have several decision options. They can decide to select (or promote or train) an applicant or to reject the applicant from further consideration. Another alternative is to defer the decision and gather more information. This may be done, for example, when all applicants for a position have been interviewed but no clear choice emerges. Additionally, a decision maker may choose to select an applicant and place him or her on probation. If the employee does not meet expectations during the probationary period, the relationship is terminated. Whatever option is chosen may result in either desirable or undesirable outcomes for the organization as well as the applicants.

Ideally, selection decisions result in desired outcomes; that is, employing those who will succeed and rejecting those who will not succeed in the job. However, even under the best circumstances, errors will be made in prediction. There are two types of selection decision errors: *false positives* (erroneous acceptances) and *false negatives* (erroneous rejections). False-positive errors occur when applicants successfully pass through all of the selection phases and are employed, but prove to be unsuccessful on the job. These errors are costly and sometimes disastrous depending on the nature of the job. Additionally, it may be difficult to terminate some false positives once they are hired, adding further to an organization's costs. Many organizations use a probationary period (for example, 6 weeks for nonexempt employees or 6 months for exempt employees) to reduce the long-term consequences of false-positive errors.

False-negative errors are equally problematic. These errors occur when applicants who would have been successful on the job are rejected. These applicants might have been rejected at any phase of the selection process. Although these errors are almost impossible to detect as compared to false-positive errors, they are equally damaging to the organization. For example, a design engineer applicant rejected at one organization will prove costly if she develops a new marketable product for a competitor. Likewise, an applicant from a legally protected group who was inappropriately rejected for a position may successfully challenge the incorrect decision in a costly lawsuit.

As decision makers, we obviously want to minimize our false-positive and false-negative errors. We are most interested in identifying *true positives* (applicants who successfully pass our selection measures *and* perform the job successfully) and *true negatives* (applicants who fail our selection measures *and* would not have performed the job successfully had they been hired). How do we do this? We begin by using standardized selection procedures that have the highest validity for our selection situation. (Recall from Chapter 6, *standardized* selection procedures are those in which the content, administration, and scoring are the same for all applicants.) Then, we employ proven decision-making strategies for combining and using scores obtained from these selection procedures as a basis for hiring job applicants. Answering the following three questions related to these points will enhance the quality of managers' employment decision making:

1. For a specific selection situation, what are the best methods for collecting predictor information on job applicants? For example, should we take a more holistic measurement of applicants using expert intuition or use procedures such as tests to take a more limited snapshot of an applicant?

2. Because we often collect applicant information using more than one predictor (for example, a test and a structured interview), how should we combine scores on the predictors to arrive at an overall score for selection decision-making purposes? For example, should experts use their professional judgment in deciding how to combine predictor score information or should they employ statistical tools for combining predictor score information in arriving at overall evaluation?

3. Once an overall or total score on two or more predictors is obtained, how should this overall score be used to make selection decisions? For example, what is the best way to use these overall scores (however they are derived) in deciding to whom to make an offer?

Decision makers cannot avoid selection errors entirely, but they can take precautions to minimize them. Correctly addressing the three questions raised here helps a decision maker take appropriate precautions and improve selection decision making. Systematic decision-making strategies such as those we discuss in this chapter can improve the chances of making correct decisions; intuition, gut instincts, premonitions, or other such subjective decision-making procedures are not so helpful.

Modes for Collecting Predictor Information

Although you may not have selected someone for employment, you probably have participated in other types of selection situations—choosing a roommate, deciding with whom you want to hang out, or voting on an individual's suitability for membership in a club. You may not have realized it at the time, but you collected "information" on these individuals, and you made some form of judgment. In some cases, your information came from something, perhaps, as formal as an application. In other cases, your information was collected informally while observing a person's physical traits (for example, physical attractiveness, height), style of dress, or conversation (for example, an accent). Once you obtained your selection information (and this may have occurred over a very brief period), you somehow combined your pieces of information to reach your selection decision.

When you think about it, many of us collect data about the people we meet. The data we collect and then how we mentally process and combine the data collected affect how we perceive or judge those people. Sometimes, the judgmental information we collect leads to accurate attributions about people, but in other cases, we make errors in our attributions based on the information collected and how we processed it. Maybe the way a person was dressed, his or her body shape, his or her mannerisms, or the way he or she spoke such as with a southern accent led you to infer an attribute about the person; then you later concluded that your initial assessments were "way off base." Well, if your answer is "no, I haven't made such mistakes," then congratulate yourself; you are one of the few. Most of us make these errors; some more frequently than others. For example, consider the following incident involving one of your authors:

> In January 1968, I met Achilles Armenakis (now a dear friend for over 40 years, current colleague, and professor at Auburn University) for the first time. When I first saw Achilles, he looked like Omar Sharif (a handsome actor at the time) in his prime (that is, dark olive complexion, dark eyes, and coal black hair). An associate director at a university bureau of business research where I had just taken a graduate research assistantship introduced Achilles to me. When I extended my hand, Achilles said nothing, slightly smiled, nodded toward me, and shook my hand. At the time, I reasoned, "He must be Greek, has just immigrated to the States, and doesn't understand English." So, while shaking Achilles' hand, I slowly uttered (in broken words), "My … name … is … Juuu … nnn … ior." ("Junior" is my nickname.) Achilles replied in a Louisiana drawl, "Nice to meet you." He was born and raised in Shreveport, Louisiana.

Since that embarrassing incident, recognition of the importance of "measurement error" in collecting and combining judgmental information on people, particularly that sort of information some use in personnel selection, has become particularly salient to the author. We will see how such judgmental errors can contribute to errors in collecting and combining information on job applicants.

In personnel selection, decision makers collect information from job applicants using predictors that generally reflect one of two different measurement philosophies. Table 15.1 summarizes these two viewpoints and examples of modes used to *collect* predictor information representing these philosophies.[1]

The first of these modes reflects the view that decisions concerning applicants' future job success are made with predictor modes that collect information on the whole

---

TABLE 15.1 Modes of *Collecting* Predictor Information from Job Applicants

	Mode of *Collecting* Predictor Information	
	Judgmental	**Mechanical**
Description	*Use* of human judgment by selection decision makers in collecting applicant information	*No use* of human judgment by selection decision makers in collecting applicant information
Example	Administration of an unstructured employment interview	Administration of a mental ability test

person. This mode has been categorized under a variety of labels such as "holistic," "clinical," or "judgmental" prediction. For our purposes, we use the term "judgmental." Judgmental modes used for collecting predictor information are based on the premise that intuitive expertise is the most effective means for collecting and understanding information regarding the whole person. Data are collected on applicants by individual assessors or group consensus assessments and then combined based on intuition or judgment.[2] It is this "whole person" information requiring integration by an expert(s) that is believed to yield accurate individual assessments. Thus, to understand the complicated attributes (motivations, behaviors, goals, etc.) collected on job applicants requires an assessment of applicants by an equally complicated individual, using tools such as psychological tests, unstructured/structured interviews, and observation.[3] Assessments can be tailored from one applicant to the next. Standardized methods of assessment, such as structured interviews or objective tests, are thought to provide only glimpses of the whole person.

The second mode for collecting predictor information has been labeled the "statistical," "actuarial," or "mechanical" method. We use the term "mechanical" to refer to modes for collecting applicant data without the use of human judgment. Objectively scored predictor data (such as that from a mental ability test) fall into this category. That is, every applicant completes the same predictor information, under the same conditions of administration, and there is a specific means for scoring applicant responses.

Modes for Combining Predictor Information

Once selection procedures' data have been collected, the diverse pieces of this information must somehow be combined to reach a selection decision. Table 15.2 summarizes two modes (*judgmental* and *mechanical*) for *combining* predictor information for selection decision-making purposes. When applicants' predictor data are combined using human intuition or "gut instincts" to reach an overall assessment, then predictor data have been combined *judgmentally*. For instance, a selection decision maker who looks at applicants' employment interview and ability test score results—and then forms a subjective, overall impression of the applicants—has combined predictor data judgmentally. There appears to be a preference for using expert intuition and judgment in employee selection.[4]

Predictor data that have been collected can also be combined using mechanical means. For example, predictor information combined by entering applicants' test and interview scores into a statistical equation developed to predict work performance involves use of a mechanical mode (for example, multiple regression, which we discussed in Chapter 8). This mode involves applying standard rules for combining predictor

TABLE 15.2	Modes of *Combining* Predictor Information from Job Applicants	
	Mode of *Combining* Predictor Information	
	Judgmental	**Mechanical**
Description	*Use* of human judgment by selection decision makers in combining applicant information	*No use* of human judgment by selection decision makers in combining applicant information
Example	Briefly reviewing applicants' test and interview scores, and from this information, forming a "gut impression" of applicant future work performance	Entering applicant's test and interviewscores in a statistically determined equation developed to predict future work performance

information, such as entering predictor scores into a multiple regression equation, multiplying the predictor scores × regression coefficients, and then summing the results to obtain a predicted work performance score for each job applicant.

Methods for Collecting and Combining Predictor Information

In this section, we describe six methods used for collecting and combining predictor information from job applicants. These methods describe how selection decision makers collect and combine predictor information mechanically, judgmentally, or both. Table 15.3 lists these methods and an example of each. As we will see, some methods are more effective than others.

Pure judgment is a method in which holistic or judgmental predictor data are collected and combined subjectively for selection decision making. No objective data (for example, test scores) are collected. For example, a decision maker subjectively collects information, after a cursory review of an applicant's resume, interviewing, or observing an applicant, and then forms an overall impression of the applicant's potential fit with the organization. The overall judgment may be based on some traits or standards in the mind of the decision maker (for example, general beliefs about what it takes to make a

TABLE 15.3 Methods of *Collecting* and *Combining* Predictor Information in Selection Decision-Making

Method of *Collecting* Predictor Information	Method of *Combining* Predictor Information	
	Judgmental	**Mechanical**
Judgmental	**Pure Judgment**	**Trait Ratings**
Example:	HR manager selects corporate recruiters based on a cursory review of applicants' resumes and his general impressions of applicants formed from his resume reviews.	Applicants for sales representative positions are interviewed by multiple interviewers; judgmental ratings are entered into a formula, and an overall interview score is calculated.
Mechanical	**Profile Interpretation**	*Pure Statistical*[a]
Example:	HR manager of telemarketing firm administers 3 objective tests to telemarketer job applicants. HR manager looks over the 3 test scores and forms an overall impression as to whom is best for the position.	Applicants for a sales manager position take a personality inventory and managerial skills test via computer. Predictor scores are combined by a formula calculated by the computer. Applicants' overall scores are rank-ordered from best to worst and given to the selection decision maker.
Judgmental + Mechanical	**Judgmental Composite** (Very Common Method Used)	*Mechanical Composite*[a]
Example:	Applicants for an automobile mechanic position take an objective mechanical ability test (mechanical) and have an unstructured interview (judgmental) with a shop manager. She looks at the test scores and thinks about the interviews to form overall impressions of the applicants.	Structured interview scores, general mental ability test scores, and conscientiousness personality inventory scores are calculated for applicants applying for middle management positions. Theses scores are combined using a formula, and applicants are ranked on the overall score from highest to lowest performer.

Note: **Judgmental**—involves collecting/combining predictor information using human judgment.
   Mechanical—involves collecting/combining predictor information without using human judgment.

[a]Methods in italics are generally superior methods for collecting and combining predictor information.

good employee), but these standards are not objective. The decision maker's role is to both collect and combine that information and make a decision about the applicant. However, no formal scoring of assessments of applicants is used. The hiring manager subjectively collects that information to form personal impressions; "gut feelings" or instincts regarding job applicants, and those assessments serve as the basis for employment decisions.

Trait ratings is a method in which judgmental data are collected and then combined mechanically. The decision maker judges and rates applicants based on interviews, application blanks, and so on. Ratings are then entered into a predetermined formula, added together, and an overall score is computed for each applicant. The decision maker's role is to collect information (that is, the ratings), but the decision is based on the results of the formula calculations. For example, applicants for a sales representative job are assessed in several interviews. The interviewers' judgmental ratings of applicants' interview performance are entered into a formula, and an overall score is computed across the interviewers' ratings. The highest-scoring applicant receives the job offer.

Profile interpretation is a method in which objective data are collected mechanically but combined judgmentally. The decision maker reviews all objectively collected data (from tests and other objective measures) and then makes an overall judgment of the applicant's suitability for the job. For example, a manager of a telemarketing firm who selects telemarketers by simply looking over three test scores and then forming an overall impression of whether the applicants would make successful operators, combines the test data judgmentally.

A *pure statistical* method involves collecting data mechanically and combining data mechanically. For example, an applicant applies for an administrative assistant position by responding to a clerical skills test and personality inventory via computer. The data collected are then scored and combined by a formula calculated by the computer. The selection supervisor receives a printout that lists applicants in the order of their overall combined scores.

A *judgmental composite* method is one in which both judgmental and mechanical data are collected and then combined judgmentally. This is one of the most commonly used methods, and the one used by Valentina in the example at the beginning of the chapter. The decision maker judgmentally combines all information about an applicant and makes an overall judgment about the applicant's likely success on the job. For example, mechanical ability test score (mechanical) information and unstructured interview (judgmental) information are collected on auto mechanic applicants. The selection manager looks at the information and makes overall judgments of whether to employ the applicants, but uses no formula or other formal means to calculate overall scores.

Mechanical composite is a method that collects both judgmental and mechanical data and then combines them mechanically. Test scores, structured interview ratings, or other predictor information is combined using a formula that predicts job success. For example, assessment centers used for managerial promotion decisions typically use a mechanical composite strategy for making decisions about whom to promote.

Which Method is Best?

In 1954, Paul Meehl released the most well-known and controversial publication on the role of clinical judgment in predicting human behavior.[5] Meehl concluded from his work that clinical experts' intuitive predictions of human behavior were significantly less accurate than predictions made using more formal, mechanical means (for example, using a statistical equation for combining predictor information). More than 30 years later,

Meehl reflected that no more than 5 percent of his findings in 1954 could be retracted. In fact, he noted that any retractions would give more support to what we have termed "mechanical" approaches.[6] Clearly, Meehl's work favored using mechanical approaches in collecting and combining information used to predict people's behavior.

A later review examined 45 studies in which 75 comparisons were made regarding the relative efficiency (superior, equal, or inferior in prediction) of various methods of collecting and combining predictor information just described.[7] Among the findings, *pure statistical* and *mechanical composite* methods for collecting and combining data were always either equal or superior to all other methods. These results have been replicated in numerous other studies.[8]

In a more recent review, Nathan Kuncel and his associates concluded from a review of the existing literature comparing mechanical versus judgmental methods in prediction that the major issue is *how* data are *combined* in making a prediction rather than how the data are collected.[9] They meta-analyzed 25 samples reported in 17 different studies to assess the relative predictive power of mechanical versus judgmental methods in predicting multiple work (job advancement, supervisory work performance ratings, and training performance) and academic achievement criteria for students. Our current interest is on their findings with regard to accuracy in predicting work performance. Specifically, they reported that mechanical methods of combining predictor data relative to clinical or judgmental combination methods improved the ability to predict work performance by more than 50 percent. (And, as an aside, mechanical methods exceeded clinical methods in predicting academic achievement as well.)

What was particularly impressive about their findings is that experts using the clinical combination method were knowledgeable of the job and the organization. Moreover, the experts had access to more extensive information on the job applicants than that covered by the mechanical methods. Kuncel et al. further concluded that the rate of identifying acceptable hires was *reduced* by more than 25 percent when judgmental data combination methods were used rather than mechanical means.[10]

Why does mechanical combination of predictor data yield better results than judgmental combination? Bernard Bass and Gerald Barrett[11] suggested several reasons for the superiority of mechanical over judgmental methods for making selection decisions. First, accuracy of prediction depends on the proper weighting of predictor scores to be combined, regardless of which approach is used. Because it is almost impossible to judge what weights are appropriate with any degree of precision, even mechanical approaches that use equal weightings of predictor scores are more likely to yield better decision outcomes than methods relying on human judgment.[12]

Second, decision makers relying on judgment can do as well as a statistical model only if they have been thorough, objective, and systematic in both collecting and combining the information. Previous research shows that such a possibility is very unlikely. Because many managers make selection decisions only sporadically, it is less likely they will be thorough, objective, and systematic in collecting and combining selection information. Moreover, individuals making assessments are often overwhelmed with subjective and objective information. Information overload is likely to lead to errors such as selective perception of information, imperfect information processing, limited capacity to process information, and biased reconstruction of events being observed.[13] Consequently, their decisions will not equal those of a statistical model.

Third, assessors are likely to add considerable error if they are allowed to "fine tune" predictions made mechanically.[14] Allowing assessors or decision makers to use their intuition or implicit theories (derived from past experience as well as other sources) of who is a good job applicant can bias their evaluations and ultimately decisions to select or reject an applicant. Inconsistency across decisions can have numerous causes: time pressure to make a decision, a bad day at home, or even comparisons and contrasts with the most recently considered job applicants.

Fourth, differences among assessors' abilities to make predictions based on assessor experience are likely to be rather small. Scott Highhouse notes that past research on assessors in assessment centers, employment interviewers, clinicians, social workers, and admission committees (among others working in assessor positions) has found that assessor experience has almost no effect on predictive accuracy.[15]

Finally, there is the problem of overconfidence of many selection decision makers. Overconfident decision makers tend to overestimate how much they know. Overconfidence contributes to decision makers' overweighting, or selectively identifying, only those applicant characteristics that confirm the decision makers' beliefs or hypotheses about those characteristics' association with some behavior. Disconfirming information that might not fit overconfident decision makers' hypotheses is largely ignored. Such decision makers do not learn from experience and therefore do not modify their methods.[16] In fact, assessor experience might actually enhance assessor biases and overconfidence.[17] Statistical models do not suffer from such errors and reduce the impact of individual biases on decision outcomes.

Implications for Selection Decision Makers

In summary, using standardized, more objective selection procedures in collecting applicant information, and then statistically combining the collected information, is better than using more subjective selection procedures and then subjectively judging how this information should be combined. Numerous studies in a wide variety of disciplines have generally confirmed this conclusion. Although subjective judgments resulting from gut feelings or intuition probably give selection decision makers both a feeling of control over the process and confidence in their judgments, use of subjective judgments is usually not warranted by the quality of decision outcomes.

In human resource selection, many of our most frequently used predictors (for example, the interview) involve some degree of judgment.[18] Judgment may play a role in how an applicant responds to a question or how the interviewer interprets the response to that question. When additional predictor information is collected from applicants, judgment can also play a role as selection decision makers combine the information to reach a decision. As we have seen, better selection decision making is more likely to occur when judgment plays less of a role in collecting and, in particular, combining selection procedure information. With this thought in mind, we recommend that selection decision makers consider the following:

1. Be particularly careful about relying too heavily on resumes and other initial information collected early in the selection process. Research has shown that even experts are prone to placing too much emphasis on preliminary information, even when such information is questionable.[19] For example, one experimental study involved actual human resource managers. Asking these managers to ignore preliminary information on job applicants, and even rewarding them for ignoring such information, failed to keep the managers from emphasizing preliminary information in their selection decision making.

2. Use standardized selection procedures (that is, procedures in which content, administration, and scoring are the same for all applicants) that are reliable, valid, and suitable for the specific selection purpose (for example, reducing absenteeism from work).

3. When feasible, use selection procedures that minimize the role of selection decision maker judgment in collecting information. For example, where appropriate—and assuming the selection procedures meet point #2 above—use structured employment interviews, weighted application blanks, objectively scored personality inventories, mental ability tests, work sample tests, physical ability tests, and computer-administered skill tests that have specific keys for scoring desirable and undesirable responses.

4. Avoid using judgment in *combining* data collected from two or more selection procedures used for determining applicants' overall scores. When combining selection procedure information that has been systematically derived and applied, applying a mechanical formula or a statistical equation (such as a multiple-regression equation) will generally enhance selection decision making. Even very simple formulas used for combining information obtained from different sources, when properly developed and applied, have been found to produce more accurate decisions than even the decisions of experts—when, that is, those expert decisions have been based on a subjective combining of predictor information.[20]

5. In some settings, managers having position authority might insist on interjecting their clinical intuition in combining their subjective judgments with other applicant information to arrive at some applicants' overall scores. However, a preponderance of the evidence is clear that when clinical judgments are used in combining data, there is a significant loss of information, and decision quality is substantially reduced. One strategy, although not optimal, that could be employed is to use mechanical methods to combine applicants' selection procedure scores to arrive at a final applicant pool.[21] Managers could be given the mechanically combined applicant results in the final pool and use that information as a decision anchor. Then, these managers could incorporate their (that is, ideally, limited "gut assessments" based on a consensus among participating managers) judgments regarding those applicants in the final decision pool. Alternatively, two lists of final applicants could be given to decision maker(s): one list showing the mechanically combined score results and the other showing clinically combined scores. That strategy makes the information public, and, possibly, encourages further deliberation before making final decisions.

Although ample evidence supports the use of mechanical approaches for making selection decisions, both managers and applicants continue to resist using them. Often managers resist change, and feel threatened when asked to use formulas for making selection decisions rather than their own "expert" judgments. Some managers object to their perceived loss of control of the selection process. Because the role of the manager shifts to providing input rather than making judgmental decisions, some selling may be necessary to convince managers that superior decisions will result from following such systematic procedures.[22]

Applicants are also likely to resist use of statistical models for making selection decisions. Research has shown that employers as well as applicants generally view standardized selection procedures as less effective than ones having less standardization.[23] This perception can be particularly true for rejected applicants. Robyn Dawes tells of an incident while visiting in Los Angeles. He overheard a woman recently rejected from a graduate program comment that "... it was 'horribly unfair' that she had been rejected by the Psychology Department at the University of California, Santa Barbara, on the basis of mere numbers, without even an interview."[24]

METHODS FOR COMBINING PREDICTOR SCORES

Andreas Graefe[25] describes an information-combining situation involving Benjamin Franklin more than 250 years ago that captures the essence of combining scores. Joseph Priestley, a friend of Franklin's, wrote to Franklin and asked for help in deciding if he should accept a job offer that would require him to move his family from one city to another in England. Franklin wrote a letter in response describing *how* Priestley should decide but not on what to decide. Franklin suggested that Priestley list the variables important to him, weight each variable by its importance to him, decide which city was favored by the variable, and then add up the variable scores to see which city is favored. Interestingly, more than 70 years later, Charles Darwin adopted Franklin's method to help him to decide whether or not to get married![26] (He chose to get married.)

Like Joseph Priestley, organizations are also faced with the problem of how to use predictor scores in selection decision making. For most jobs in many organizations, applicant information is obtained using more than one predictor. For instance, a company may collect application blank and reference check information, administer an ability test, and conduct an employment interview with all applicants for its position openings. Selection decision makers then face the problem of deciding whether predictor scores be combined and if so, how?

In the preceding section, we concluded that if an organization chooses to combine scores, mechanical strategies are better than judgmental ones for combining predictor scores. There are many different ways of mechanically combining predictor scores. In this section, we describe and give an example of two methods that conform to our prescription for using mechanical methods for *combining* predictor information. Each of these methods has a long history of use in a variety of disciplines including human resource selection. These methods are (a) multiple regression and (b) unit weighting. No assumptions are made by the methods about how the data are collected (either mechanically or judgmentally). Each focuses on systematic procedures for combining predictor information.

To make these methods easier to understand, let's look at an example that shows how decisions are made using each approach. Table 15.4 presents the data for the job of patient account representative. The job principally involves (a) error checking and processing patient records, (b) billing customers, (c) filing insurance forms, and (d) filing patient records. Four ability tests and a structured interview are used to obtain predictor information on applicants. The math test requires computing answers to problems involving addition, subtraction, multiplication, and division. Scores can range from 0 to 15. The filing test requires applicants to separate a deck of index cards into two decks (one by name and the other by number) and then sort them (alphabetically for the name stack and numerically for the number stack). Scores can range from 0 to 30. The spelling test requires applicants to circle the correctly spelled word in each pair of words provided. Scores can range from 0 to 65. The perceptual accuracy test requires applicants to compare simulated patient charts with simulated printouts of patient records and identify errors. Scores can range from 0 to 15. On each of the four tests, higher scores indicate better performance. The structured interview has five questions. It is scored numerically; a rating of 5 represents an excellent answer, 3 an average answer, and 1 a poor answer. Ratings of applicants' responses to the five interview questions are added; total scores can range from 5 to 25, with higher scores meaning better applicant interview performance. Now, how can we mechanically combine applicants' predictor scores to derive a predicted level of work performance that we can use in selection decision making?

TABLE 15.4	Patient Account Representative Selection Procedure and Applicant Score Data

Selection Procedure

Selection Procedure Characteristic	Math Test	Filing Test	Spelling Test	Perceptual Accuracy Test	Structured Interview
Maximum Possible Score	15	30	65	15	25
Regression Weights[a]	1	0.8	0.9	0.7	0.5
Cutoff Scores	7	22	50	6	10

Applicant Selection Procedure Scores

Applicant	Math Test	Filing Test	Spelling Test	Perceptual Accuracy Test	Structured Interview
Amanda Maale	6	30	55	15	25
Dave Mason	14	21	63	10	11
Carl Sagan	9	29	60	8	12
Rebecca Malpa	15	22	50	5	24
Cyndy O'Roarke	8	23	55	14	13

Note: The higher an applicant's score on a predictor, the better the applicant's performance on the predictor.

[a]The regression equation is $\hat{Y} = x_1 + 0.8x_2 + 0.9x_3 + 0.7x_4 + 0.5x_5$. The intercept value has been omitted.

Method One: Multiple Regression

We briefly discussed multiple regression in Chapter 6. As you recall, in this method each applicant is measured on each selection procedure. Multiple regression shows the maximum linear association between two or more selection procedures or predictors and a criterion for a sample of individuals. Assuming there is a significant relationship with a criterion and our regression equation has held up under cross-validation, applicants' predictor scores can be entered into an equation (called the prediction equation). Each predictor's relation with the criterion determines the regression weights in the equation. From the equation, a predicted criterion score (for example, predicted work performance) is obtained.

For example, suppose we give two tests that serve as predictors, X_1 and X_2, to all job applicants. Suppose further that we previously developed the following regression equation to predict work performance ($\hat{Y}$) using applicants' scores on the two tests (X_1 and X_2):

$$\hat{Y} = 5 + 2X_1 + 1X_2$$

where

$\hat{Y}$ = predicted work performance

5 = a constant or intercept value of the regression line

2, 1 = regression weights for test X_1 and test X_2

X_1, X_2 = applicants' scores on the tests

Now, assume we have three job applicants. Each takes both tests. Here are the applicants' scores on test 1 and test 2: Applicant A (50, 0); Applicant B (0, 100); and Applicant C (10, 80). To get their predicted work performance, we simply substitute each applicant's test scores in the preceding regression equation. In this particular case, our computations show all three applicants have the same predicted work performance, 105. Because it is possible to compensate for low scores on one predictor by high scores on another, multiple regression is sometimes referred to as a *compensatory* method. In contrast, there are noncompensatory strategies for using predictor scores, which require job applicants to score higher than a predetermined, specific score to be included in the final applicant pool. We will address some of these strategies in the next section of the chapter.

Multiple regression makes two basic assumptions: (a) the predictors are linearly related to the criterion, and (b) because the predicted criterion score is a function of the sum of the weighted predictor scores, the predictors are additive and can compensate for one another (that is, performing well on one of the predictors compensates for performing not so well on another predictor).

The multiple-regression strategy has several advantages. It minimizes errors in prediction and combines the predictors to yield the best estimate of applicants' future performance on a criterion such as work performance (at least for the sample on which the prediction equation is based). Furthermore, it is a very flexible method. It can be modified to handle nominal data, nonlinear relationships, and both linear and nonlinear interactions.[27] Regression equations can be constructed for each of a number of jobs using either the same predictors weighted differently or different predictors. The decision maker then has three options: (a) if selecting for a single job, then the person in the final applicant pool having the highest predicted criterion score is selected; if selecting for two or more jobs, the decision maker has the following additional options: (b) place each person on the job for which the predicted criterion score is highest, or (c) place each person on that job where his or her predicted score is farthest above the minimum criterion score necessary to be considered satisfactory.[28]

The multiple-regression approach has disadvantages as well. Besides making the assumption that scoring high on one predictor can compensate for scoring low on another, there are statistical issues that are sometimes difficult to resolve. For example, when a relatively small sample size is used to determine regression weights or the predictors are correlated with one another, the weights will not be stable from one sample to the next and standard errors of the weights increase.[29] For this reason, cross validation of the prediction equation is essential prior to application. If no preliminary screening of applicants is done, the multiple regression strategy requires assessing all applicants on all predictors, which can be costly with a large applicant pool.

The multiple-regression approach is most appropriate when a trade-off among predictor scores does not affect overall work performance. In addition, it is best used when the sample size for constructing the regression equation is large enough to minimize some of the statistical problems just noted. However, as the size of the applicant pool increases, costs of selection become much larger. The greater the number of predictors and criteria being studied, the larger the sample size required to properly use multiple regression, and the greater the costs involved in selection.

Table 15.4 provides the prediction equation that was developed hypothetically for the patient account representative job that we referred to earlier. We assume that the prediction equation has been cross-validated, as discussed in Chapter 8, and that our predictor battery is correlated with work performance. Note also that the prediction equation was developed on a large sample of, say, 300 job applicants, which compose the active applicant pool; we use only five job applicants taken from our applicant pool to illustrate use of the prediction equation for all members in the pool.

Overall composite predictor scores indicating predicted job success for each applicant are first calculated by entering the individual predictor scores into the prediction equation. Once overall scores have been calculated, then applicants can be rank-ordered based on their overall predicted work performance scores (from best to worst applicant). In our example in Table 15.4, rank ordering predicted criterion score results in the following order: **1** = Amanda Maale [predicted score = 102.5], **2** = Dave Mason [predicted score = 100], **3** = Carl Sagan [predicted score = 97.8], **4** = Rebecca Malpa [predicted score = 93.1], and **5** = Cyndy O'Roarke [predicted score = 92.2].

Method Two: Unit Weighting

Rather than using regression weights to determine a prediction equation, another option is to use unit weighting. Multiple-regression models are referred to as a *proper* linear model because the predictors are identified to maximize the relationship between the predictors and the criterion.[30] An *improper* linear model, which describes unit weighting as well as several other weighting schemes, is chosen by some nonoptimal means. For example, various predictor weights could be chosen based on a theory, job analysis results, subject matter experts' opinions, or in the case of unit weighting, given equal weights.[31] Unit weighting of predictors has been used successfully in a wide variety of disciplines and is particularly appropriate in certain human resource selection applications. For example, in a situation where only a small sample is available, multiple regression is not appropriate due to high sampling errors that affect the stability of regression weights. Some recommend that the ratio of observations to predictors be as high as 20:1 for multiple regression.[32] Previous research has shown that with sample sizes of up to 200, unit weights and regression weights perform about equally as well. However, when sample sizes are less than 75, unit weights perform better in prediction than regression weights.[33] There are several other guidelines that suggest when unit weighting will be most effective. These include (a) all predictor scores being combined are positively correlated with one another; (b) each predictor is correlated with the criterion; and (c) unit weighting performs well as the number of predictors being combined increases.[34]

Not only can unit weighting be used to predict a criterion, but suppose a suitable criterion were not available and regression weights cannot be developed; then what? Robyn Dawes[35] explains such a case where unit weighting of predictors might still be used. For example, he describes a situation where a university department is deciding on whom to admit to a graduate program. The department is interested in predicting long-term success, perhaps 20 years into the future, but such a criterion is not available. However, what is available is that the faculty has some ideas as to what predictors would successfully predict admitted students' long-term, academic career success. For example, they might reason that intelligence, persistence and success in past accomplishments, and certain life experiences are linked to career success. To measure these constructs, they might use GRE scores (an admissions test most graduate school applicants take) in applicants' files as a proxy for intelligence, undergraduate GPA from their transcripts to assess past persistence and accomplishments, and a biographical data form completed by applicants regarding their past life experiences and achievements as predictors. Because a standard regression analysis cannot be performed, unit weighting in combining applicant scores on these variables could serve as a composite predictor for evaluating the graduate program applicants.

An obvious question at this point is: How is unit weighting of predictors calculated? Robyn Dawes and Bernard Corrigan sum up the method pretty succinctly; they noted, "The whole trick is to decide what variables to look at and to know how to add."[36] To calculate unit weights, let's look at the example in Table 15.5. Recall from our earlier example with regression weights, we had five applicants who had completed four

| TABLE 15.5 | Combining Predictor Scores Through Multiple Regression and Composite z Scores[a] | | | | | |

Job Applicant	Math Test	z Score	... Structured Interview	z Score	Overall Predicted Work Success[a]	Composite z Score[b]	Applicant Rank[c]
Amanda Maale	6	−1.13	25	1.16	102.5	2.02	1
Dave Mason	14	0.92	11	−0.87	100.0	0.27	2
Carl Sagan	9	−0.36	12	−0.73	97.8	−0.03	3
Rebecca Malpa	15	1.18	... 24	1.02	93.1	−1.13	4
Cyndy O'Roarke	8	−0.61	13	−0.58	92.2	−1.14	5
Mean	10.4	0.0	17	0.0			
Standard Deviation	3.91	1.0	... 6.89	1.0			

Note: z Score $= \dfrac{\text{Selection Procedure Score} - \text{Mean of Selection Procedure Score}}{\text{Standard Deviation of Selection Procedure Score}}$

Due to space limitations, scores for only 2 of the 5 predictor scores obtained on the 5 job applicants are shown.

[a]The overall predicted job success score was obtained by entering the raw scores on the 5 predictors in the regression equation shown in Table 15.4. The higher the predicted score, the better the job performance of job applicants on the 5 predictors.

[b]The composite z score was obtained by summing the 5 z scores (only z scores for 2 predictors are shown) for each of the 5 job applicants. The higher a "+" composite z score, the better the performance of job applicants on the 5 predictors' composite z score. A + z score indicates the applicant scored above the mean. For example, the score of Amanda Maale indicates she scored over 2 standard deviations above the applicant pool composite mean z score. A − z score indicates the applicant scored below the mean z score of the applicant pool. For example, Cyndy O'Roarke scored over 1 standard deviation below the composite mean z score of the applicant pool.

[c]Lower ranked job applicants are the highest performing applicants on the selection procedures.

employment tests and a structured interview. Because of space concerns, we have shown in Table 15.5 just the Math Test scores and Structured Interview ratings for each of the five applicants. Notice that we have converted the raw math and interview scores into z scores. We would do that same conversion for all applicants' scores on the other three predictors before applying the unit weights. Then, we add all applicants' predictor z scores to obtain their composite z score. In this particular case, notice that the rank of the applicants from best to worst is the same for both the overall predicted score obtained through multiple regression and the composite z score obtained from unit weighting. Notice also too, this same process could be applied in deriving a composite criterion measure of supervisors' ratings of employee work performance if the components being added conform to the guidelines we mentioned earlier regarding unit weighting.

You might be wondering why we converted the predictor raw scores to z scores before adding them. The reason is that if we did not standardize the predictor scores, the predictors would have unequal variances, which will affect the weight of a predictor added into the composite score. The greater the variance in scores on a predictor, the greater the influence that predictor will have on the overall predicted score. Since we wanted the predictors to have equal weight, we standardized the predictor scores before adding them together. What a z score shows is the relative standing that an individual has on a predictor or composite predictor relative to others in the sample. For instance, a z score of +1.0 indicates that a job applicant is one standard deviation above the mean of all applicants' composite predictor z score. The higher the z score (and assuming a + score means better performance on the predictors associated with work performance), the better the applicant and the more likely he or she should receive a job offer.

Now, you might also be thinking: Suppose there was a justified reason for weighting one predictor more than other predictors. Is that possible? Yes, it is. Here, we run into a bit of a problem, however, when deciding how to weight predictors being combined. As we noted in our earlier example concerning one of your authors meeting a Greek colleague for the first time and the errors he made in combining his attributions' data, humans are subject to a number of influences that can affect how they process and combine information. Unit weighting helps avoid such issues. However, if there is a sound, theoretical reason or rational reason certain predictors should be weighted differently than others, then differential weights could be used. Again, standardize the predictor scores *before* assigning differential weights. Use caution with differential weighting; there should be a compelling reason for not using unit weights. As Robyn Dawes said, "… people—especially the experts in a field—are much better at selecting and coding information than they are at integrating it."[37]

STRATEGIES FOR MAKING EMPLOYMENT DECISIONS

After selection predictor data have been collected on job applicants and the predictors' scores calculated, employment decisions must be made as to which applicants in the final applicant pool will be extended offers of employment. If only one predictor is used, then decisions are made based on applicants' scores on this one predictor. Usually, however, more than one predictor is employed. When multiple predictors are used for selection, we can use one of the methods just discussed for combining predictor information.

At this point, let's assume that we have administered our selection measures and derived a final composite score for each applicant. We are now ready to make a hiring decision, but how should we evaluate applicants' composite selection procedure scores? For example, you saw in Table 15.4 that from the four tests and employment interview, we were able to derive a predicted work performance score using our prediction equation. Of the five applicants in our pool, which one(s) should receive offers? Numerous strategies concerned with selecting individuals for jobs have been reported in the human resource selection literature. We will devote our attention to describing several strategies including: (a) top-down selection, (b) cutoff scores, (c) multiple cutoff scores, (d) multiple hurdles, (e) a combination method, and (f) banding (including fixed and sliding bands).

Strategy One: Top-Down Selection

With the top-down selection approach, applicants' scores are rank-ordered from highest to lowest. Then, beginning with the applicant at the top of the list (the one who has the highest and best score on the selection procedure) and moving to the bottom, applicants are extended job offers until all positions are filled. If an applicant turns down a job offer, the next applicant on the list is offered the job.

Ranking applicants by their selection scores assumes that a person with a higher score will perform better on the job than a person with a lower score. If we assume that a valid predictor is linearly related to work performance (usually a safe assumption, particularly when the selection procedure is of a cognitive nature), then the higher applicants' scores are on a predictor, the better their work performance. The economic return of employing an applicant who scores at one standard deviation above the average score on a valid predictor can be as much as 40 percent more than employing an applicant scoring at the average on the valid predictor.[38] As far as work performance is concerned, maximum utility is gained from a predictor when top-down hiring is used (assuming those offered the job accept the offer).[39]

The importance of top-down selection is illustrated in one case involving U.S. Steel Corporation.[40] The plant changed from using top-down selection to using only employee seniority and minimum scores (equivalent to about the seventh grade) on a battery of valid cognitive ability tests. The tests were used for selecting entrants for the company's apprentice-training program. After using the new minimum selection criteria, U.S. Steel found that (a) performance on mastery tests given during training fell dramatically; (b) apprenticeship trainee failure and dropout rates rose significantly; (c) for those trainees completing the program, training time and training costs increased substantially; and (d) later work performance of program graduates fell.

The biggest problem with top-down selection, however, is that it will likely lead to adverse impact against legally protected racial/ethnic groups. This troublesome outcome is most likely when cognitively based predictors are used in selection such as mental ability tests. Because white applicants tend to score higher, on average, than black and Hispanic applicants on cognitive ability tests, adverse impact is likely to occur under top-down selection when the predictor is highly correlated with general mental ability. When adverse impact occurs, using cutoff scores in making employment decisions is one possible alternative.[41]

If we were to use our multiple-regression results as a basis for conducting top-down hiring, Amanda Maale (predicted job success score = 102.5) would be our top applicant; Cyndy O'Roarke (predicted job success score = 92.2) would be our poorest applicant.

Strategy Two: Cutoff Scores

In addition to top-down hiring, another strategy for using predictor scores in selection decision making is to use cutoff scores. A cutoff score represents a score on a predictor or combination of predictors below which job applicants are rejected. Before discussing several approaches to developing cutoff scores, we must address a few points. First, there is not just one cutoff score; a cutoff score can vary from one employment context to another. Judgment will necessarily play a role in choosing the method for setting the cutoff score and for determining the actual cutoff score value to be employed in selection. These decisions will be affected by any number of considerations—such as the number of applicants and percentage of those applicants who are extended a job offer and are actually hired for the positions in question, the costs associated with recruiting and employing qualified applicants, consequences of job failure (that is, error in predicting applicant work performance due to a cutoff score set too low), workforce diversity concerns, and so on.

Second, there is no single method of setting cutoff scores. A number of approaches can be used; their successful use depends on how appropriate the procedure chosen is for a particular situation and how effectively the specific procedures are applied. Finally, when a cutoff score is developed and used, the rationale and specific procedures for identifying that particular score should be carefully documented. Written documentation of cutoff score determination and justification is particularly valuable in an employer's defending against a claim of employment discrimination.

In setting cutoff scores, employers must maintain a delicate balance. That is, an employer can expose itself to legal consequences when cutoff scores are set too high, and many qualified applicants are rejected. Conversely, cutoff scores can lose utility if they are set so low that a selection procedure fails to screen out unqualified job applicants.[42]

Cutoff scores can be established in at least two general ways: (a) basing the cutoff score on how job applicants or other persons performed on a selection procedure (sometimes labeled *empirical* score setting procedures) and (b) using the judgments of knowledgeable experts (subject matter experts, SMEs) regarding the appropriateness of selection procedure content (such as items on a written test) to set the cutoff score. Now, let's take a brief look at some of these ways to determine cutoff scores.

Basing Cutoff Scores on Applicants' or Others' Performance

Empirical methods used to set cutoff scores are generally based on the relationship between scores on predictors and performance on the job as measured by a criterion.[43] Below, we briefly highlight several of these methods.

Local norms developed for an organization's own applicants can be helpful in some cutoff score setting methods. Thorndike's *"predicted yield" method*[44] requires obtaining the following information for establishing a cutoff score: (a) the number of positions available during some future time period, (b) the number of applicants expected during that time period, and (c) the expected distribution of applicants' predictor scores. The cutoff score is then determined based on the percentage of applicants needed to fill the positions. For example, if 20 machinists are needed and 250 people are expected to apply for the 20 position openings, then the selection ratio is 0.08 (20/250). Because 92 percent of the applicants will be rejected, the cutoff score should be set at the 92nd percentile on the local norms (norms based on the company's past experience with a selection procedure administered to the company's job applicants applying for similar positions) minus one standard error of measurement. (See our discussion of local norms in Chapter 6.)

In the *expectancy chart method*,[45] the same analytical procedure is used as in the Thorndike method to determine the expected selection ratio. Once the expected percentage of applicants that will be rejected is determined, the score associated with that percentile is identified minus one standard error of measurement. As mentioned earlier in our discussion of selection procedure norms, care must be taken to see that local norms are periodically updated because applicant pool members' abilities and other qualifications can change over time.

Cutoff scores can also be determined by administering the selection procedure to individuals (such as job incumbents) other than applicants and using that information as a basis for score development. In one study, undergraduate students were given tests that were to be used in selecting emergency telephone operators. The students' distribution of test performance scores (later verified by actual applicants' test scores) served as a basis for setting the cutoff scores. One note of caution: When a group of individuals other than applicants serves as a basis for deriving cutoff scores, care should be taken in determining that the group of individuals is comparable to the applicant pool for the job. When the groups are not comparable, legal questions concerning the fairness and meaningfulness of such scores can arise. For example, in hiring patrol police officers, physical tests of lung capacity have sometimes been used. In setting a minimum lung capacity cutoff score for patrol police officers, it would not be appropriate to determine a cutoff score based on how a group of university track athletes performed on the lung capacity measure. If discrimination is judged to have resulted from cutoff score use, legal concerns regarding the score are likely to involve the following question: Is the discriminatory cutoff score used in screening applicants measuring the *minimum* qualifications necessary for successful performance of the job?[46] In addition to validation information, an affected employer would also need to be able to demonstrate that the chosen cutoff score does, indeed, represent a useful, meaningful selection standard with regard to work performance, risks, costs, and so on.

Contrasting the two distributions of predictor scores made by successful and unsuccessful job incumbents is another empirical approach. Subject matter experts judge the overlay or overlap of the two score distributions and set the cutoff score where the two distributions intersect. This method is most useful when there is a (a) large enough number of incumbents in both groups to identify a distribution of scores and (b) strong relationship between scores on the predictor and work performance.

Finally, simple regression (one predictor) or multiple regression (two or more predictors), which we mentioned earlier, can also be used to set cutoff scores. Assuming that an adequate number of individuals' predictor and criterion scores are available, correlational methods permit cutoff scores to be set by *determining that specific predictor score associated with acceptable or successful work performance* as represented by the criterion. Of course, use of regression methods also assumes having an adequate relationship between the selection procedure and the criterion as well as a representative (of the applicant pool), large sample on which the statistical correlation is based. Thus, the assumptions that we described with regard to criterion-related validation strategies in our chapter on validity also apply to regression methods in setting cutoff scores.

Using Experts' Judgments

Cutoff scores are often set using judgmental or rational methods when empirical methods are not feasible. Under judgmental methods of cutoff score determination, the assessments of subject matter experts (for example, job incumbents and supervisors) serve as the basis for establishing the relationship between predictor scores and job success. These assessments, in turn, serve as a basis for cutoff score development. In most cases, these approaches are used with multiple-choice written tests (such as job knowledge tests); some judgmental approaches have been applied to other selection procedures as well. Next, let's review several of these judgmental methods and how they are used.

The *Ebel method*[47] is based on an analysis of the difficulty of test items. First, experts rate all test items on the following basis: (a) difficulty (hard, medium, and easy) and (b) relevance to work performance (essential, important, acceptable, and questionable). These ratings produce 12 categories of items. For each of the categories of items, judges are asked what percentage of the items a borderline test taker would be able to answer correctly; for example, "If a borderline test taker had to answer a large number of questions like these, what percentage would he or she answer correctly?" The cutoff score is calculated by multiplying the percentage of items correct times the number of questions in each category and then summing the products across all of the separate categories. Table 15.6 provides an example of this method.

In the *Angoff method*,[48] judges or subject matter experts, usually numbering 10 to 15, estimate the probability that a minimally qualified applicant could answer a specific test item correctly. These estimates are used to establish cutoff scores for the test. As William Angoff described it, "the judges would think of a number of minimally acceptable persons, instead of only one such person, and would estimate the proportion of minimally acceptable persons who would answer each item correctly. The sum of these probabilities, or proportions, would then represent the minimally acceptable score." Table 15.7 illustrates this procedure.

A variation of this procedure, described as the *modified Angoff method*, reduces the score calculated by the Angoff method by one, two, or three standard errors of measurement. This adjustment has been accepted in numerous court cases.[49]

For example, a modification of the Angoff procedure was accepted in *U.S. v. South Carolina* for use with written tests. The modification lowered the average Angoff estimate from one to three standard errors of measurement. The court based its acceptance on several considerations: the risk of error (that is, the risk that a truly qualified applicant might be excluded compared to the risk of including an unqualified applicant), the degree of agreement among subject matter experts in their evaluations of minimum

TABLE 15.6   The Ebel Method for Setting Cutoff Scores

| | Difficulty of Test Items | | | | | |
| | Easy | | Medium | | Hard | |
	Items	% Correct	Items	% Correct	Items	% Correct
Relevance to Job Performance						
Essential	22, 17, 10, 5, 2	90	12, 19	80	11, 15, 25	70
Important	1, 8, 23, 30	85	16, 26, 27, 29	70	4, 24	65
Acceptable	3, 6, 13	80	14, 21	65	18	55
Questionable	7	60	21, 32	50	none	—

Item Category	% Correct	Number of Items	Expected Score for Category
Essential			
easy	90	5	0.90 × 5 = 4.5
medium	80	2	0.80 × 2 = 1.6
hard	70	3	0.70 × 3 = 2.1
Important			
easy	85	4	0.85 × 4 = 3.4
medium	70	4	0.70 × 4 = 2.8
hard	65	2	0.65 × 2 = 1.3
Acceptable			
easy	80	3	0.80 × 3 = 2.4
medium	65	2	0.65 × 2 = 1.3
hard	55	1	0.55 × 1 = 0.55
Questionable			
easy	60	1	0.60 × 1 = 0.60
medium	50	2	0.50 × 2 = 1.0
hard	0	0	0
		Sum (Expected Cutoff Score) = 21.55	

competency, the workforce supply and demand for the job, race and gender composition of the jobs, and the standard error of measurement.[50]

Neal Schmitt and Richard Klimoski proposed a variation of the Angoff method.[51] Their variation was applied to a 25-item in-basket examination used as part of a promotional procedure in a governmental organization. Each of the 25 items was scored on a 4-point scale with 4 indicating a superior answer and 1 judged a clearly inferior response. Subject matter experts (job incumbents) were asked to review the in-basket items and provide responses to the following question for each item: "Consider a *minimally competent applicant* for a middle-level manager's position in state government. This is not an outstanding candidate or even an average applicant, but one who could perform on tests at a *minimally* satisfactory level. Now, look at each item and the scoring instructions for that item. What percentage of these *minimally competent* applicants would receive a score of 4 on these items? What percentage would receive a score of 3? Of 2? Of 1?" For example, one judge might rate an item as follows: 4 = 0 percent, 3 = 30 percent, 2 = 60 percent, and 1 = 10 percent. This judge indicates that most (60 percent) of

TABLE 15.7	The Angoff Method for Setting Cutoff Scores

Item Number	Proportion Answering Correctly
1	0.90
2	0.55
3	0.70
4	0.80
5	0.85
6	0.60
7	0.55
8	0.75
9	0.95
10	0.60
11	0.75
12	0.60
13	0.55
14	0.80
15	0.70
16	0.70
17	0.70
18	0.75
19	0.65
20	0.55
	Sum = 14.0
Unmodified Cutoff Score	14.0
Modified Cutoff Score (with 1 SEM = 2.1)[a]	11.9

[a]SEM = Standard Error of Measurement

the minimally competent applicants can write a response to this in-basket test item that would receive a score of 2. Average scores of judges for each item would be calculated. Then, these averages would be totaled across all items to determine the cutoff score. This method would also be useful for other selection procedures, such as for determining cutoff scores for structured interviews.

The Angoff procedure often produces higher cutoff scores than might be expected. To address this issue, the cutoff score is commonly lowered by one, two, or even three standard errors of measurement to limit the number of false negatives. However, these kinds of adjustments can produce unknown consequences for the employing organization.[52]

The *contrasting groups method* uses judgments of test takers rather than the test items as the basis for determining cutoff scores.[53] The first step is to divide test takers (usually job incumbents) into qualified and unqualified groups based on judgments of their knowledge and skills. The next step is to calculate the percentage of test takers who are qualified and unqualified at each test score. The cutoff score is chosen at that point where the proportion of qualified test takers is equal to the proportion of unqualified test takers. This score point assumes that rejecting unqualified candidates is as important as accepting qualified candidates. If it is desired to minimize either false-positive or false-negative errors, then the cutoff score is either raised or lowered.

When using judgments from subject matter experts to develop cutoff scores, a key concern of the courts is who served as an expert. For example, when physical ability tests are developed and validated, women and minority group members must be represented among the experts used. Ideally, their percentage representation among the subject matter experts would match their representation in the qualified applicant pool. Although it may be necessary to oversample women and minority group members to have adequate representation, random selection of full-time, nonprobationary job incumbents should generally be employed.[54]

Legal and Psychometric Issues

Some guidance on setting cutoff scores is given in two documents referred to for legal and psychometric selection standards. The *Uniform Guidelines on Employee Selection Procedures*[55] states the following about setting cutoff scores:

Where cutoff scores are used, they should normally be set so as to be reasonable and consistent with normal expectations of acceptable proficiency within the workforce. Where applicants are ranked on the basis of properly validated selection procedures and those applicants scoring below a higher cutoff score than appropriate in light of such expectations have little or no chance of being selected for employment, the higher cutoff score may be more appropriate, but the degree of adverse impact should be considered.

The *Principles for the Validation and Use of Personnel Selection Procedures* (*Principles*) states, "If based on valid predictors demonstrating linearity … throughout the range of prediction, cutoff scores may be set as high or as low as needed to meet the requirements of the organization."[56]

The *Principles* also note that some organizations choose to use a cutoff score rather than top-down selection. They may do this to enhance workforce diversity. However, use of minimum cutoff scores rather than top-down selection may result in a loss of work performance and consequent higher labor costs.[57] In summarizing earlier research by John Hunter in the 1970s, Frank Schmidt and John Hunter concluded that if the federal government as an employer had used top-down hiring with valid ability tests, one year's labor savings for hires would have been $15.6 billion. If a low cutoff score strategy had been adopted, one year's labor savings would have been $2.5 billion, a loss of 84 percent of labor costs that would have been achievable from using top-down selection.[58]

In reviews of the legal and psychometric literatures on cutoff scores, Wayne Cascio and his colleagues have offered a number of useful guidelines regarding score use. Any user seriously considering cutoff scores in selection should consider these guidelines. Several of these guidelines are listed in Table 15.8.

Strategy Three: Multiple Cutoff Scores

In this method, each applicant is assessed on each predictor. All predictors are scored on a pass–fail basis. Applicants are rejected if any one of their predictor scores falls below a minimum cutoff score. This method makes two important assumptions about work performance: (a) a nonlinear relationship exists among the predictors and the criterion—that is, a minimum amount of each important predictor attribute is necessary for successful performance of a job (the applicant must score above each minimum cutoff to be considered for the job), and (b) predictors are not compensatory. A lack of or deficiency in any one predictor attribute cannot be compensated for by having a high score on another (an applicant cannot have "0" on any single predictor).

TABLE 15.8	Selected Guidelines for Using Cutoff Scores in Selection Procedures

- Cutoff scores are not required by legal or professional guidelines; thus, first decide whether a cutoff score is necessary.
- There is not one best method of setting cutoff scores for all situations.
- If a cutoff score is to be used for setting a minimum score requirement, begin with a job analysis that identifies levels of proficiency on essential knowledge, skills, abilities, and other characteristics. (The Angoff method is one that can be used.)
- If judgmental methods are used (such as the Angoff method), include a 10 to 20 percent sample of subject matter experts (SMEs) representative of the race, gender, shift, and so on of the employee (or supervisor) group. Representative experience of SMEs on the job under study is a most critical consideration in choosing SMEs.
- If job incumbents are used to develop the cutoff score to be used with job applicants, consider setting the cutoff score one standard error of measurement below incumbents' average score on the selection procedure.
- Set cutoff scores high enough to ensure that at least minimum standards of work performance are achieved.

Note: The guidelines are based on Wayne F. Cascio and Herman Aguinis, "Test Development and Use: New Twists on Old Questions," *Human Resource Management* 44 (2005): 227; and Wayne F. Cascio, Ralph A. Alexander, and Gerald V. Barrett, "Setting Cutoff Scores: Legal, Psychometric, and Professional Issues and Guidelines," *Personnel Psychology* 41 (1989): 1–24.

The advantage of this method is that it narrows the applicant pool to a smaller subset of candidates who are all minimally qualified for the job. In addition, it is conceptually simple and easy to explain to managers.[59] This approach has two major disadvantages. First, like the multiple-regression approach, it requires assessing all applicants using all predictors. With a large applicant pool, the selection costs may be large. Second, the multiple-cutoff approach identifies only those applicants minimally qualified for the job. There is no clear-cut way to determine how to order those applicants who pass the cutoffs.

A multiple-cutoff approach is probably most useful when minimum levels of physical abilities are essential for work performance. For example, eyesight, color vision, and physical strength are required for such jobs as police, fire, and heavy manufacturing work.[60] Another appropriate use of multiple cutoff scores would be for jobs in which it is known that a minimum level of performance on a predictor is required in order to perform the job safely. If we were to use the multiple-cutoff procedure with our five applicants' selection procedure and cutoff scores shown in Table 15.4, Carl and Cyndy passed the cutoffs whereas Amanda, Dave, and Rebecca did not.

Strategy Four: Multiple Hurdles

In this strategy, each applicant must meet the minimum cutoff or hurdle for each predictor before going to the next predictor. That is, to remain a viable applicant, applicants must pass the predictors sequentially. Failure to pass a cutoff at any stage in the selection process results in the applicant being dropped from further consideration.

In a variation of the multiple-hurdle approach, called the *double-stage strategy*,[61] two cutoff scores are set, C1 and C2 (see Figure 15.1). Those whose scores fall above C2 are accepted unconditionally, and those whose scores fall below C1 are rejected terminally. Applicants whose scores fall between C1 and C2 are accepted provisionally, with a final decision made based on additional testing. This approach has been shown to be equal or superior to some of the other strategies at all degrees of selectivity.[62]

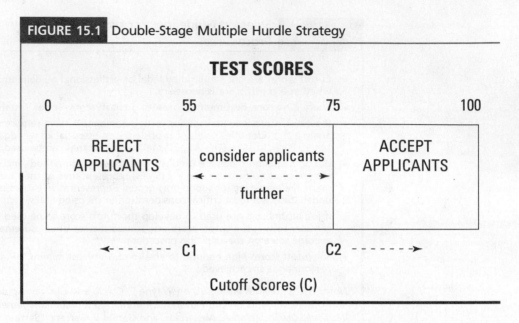

FIGURE 15.1 Double-Stage Multiple Hurdle Strategy

In the multiple-hurdle approach, like the multiple-cutoff strategy, it is assumed that a minimum level of each predictor attribute is necessary for successful job performance. It is not possible for a high level of one predictor attribute to compensate for a low level of another without negatively affecting work performance. Thus, the assumptions of the multiple-hurdle approach are identical to those of the multiple-cutoff strategy. The only distinction between the two is in the procedure for gathering predictor information. In the multiple-cutoff strategy, the procedure is nonsequential, whereas in the hurdle approach, the procedure is sequential. That is, applicants must achieve a minimum score on one selection procedure before they are assessed on another procedure. If they fail to achieve that minimum score, they are rejected.

The multiple-hurdle approach has the same advantages as the multiple-cutoff strategy. In addition, it is less costly than the multiple-cutoff strategy because the applicant pool becomes smaller at each stage of the selection process. More expensive selection devices can be used at later stages of the selection process on only those applicants likely to be hired. For example, we might use an inexpensive selection procedure, such as a weighted application blank, to prescreen large numbers of applicants before conducting any employment interviews (an expensive selection procedure). Interviews can then be conducted with the smaller number of applicants who pass the weighted application blank hurdle.

One major disadvantage of this approach relates to establishing empirical validity for each predictor. Because each stage in the selection process reduces the applicant pool to only those on the high end of the ability distribution, restriction of range is a likely problem. As in concurrent validation strategies, this means the obtained validity coefficients may be underestimated. An additional disadvantage is the increased time necessary to implement it. This time disadvantage is particularly important for those employment situations in which selection decisions must be made quickly. For example, in many computer software organizations, there may be a high demand for individuals with appropriate programming skills. Employment decisions have to be reached quickly, before competitors attract a viable applicant. In such a situation, a multiple-hurdle approach is likely not appropriate. Under this strategy, it takes time to administer a predictor, score it, and then decide whether to give the next predictor to the applicant. Good applicants may be lost before a final employment decision is reached.[63]

The multiple-hurdle approach is most appropriate in situations where subsequent training is long, complex, and expensive.[64] It is also a useful decision-making approach when an essential work-related characteristic (WRC) (that cannot be compensated for by the possession of higher levels of other WRCs) is necessary for work performance. For instance, typing is an essential skill for a clerical job. Better-than-average filing skills cannot compensate for the inability to type. An organization has no reason to further evaluate applicants who cannot pass the typing test. The multiple-hurdle approach is also appropriate when there is a large applicant pool and some of the selection procedures are expensive to administer. For example, when hiring for an information systems manager job, you may use a resume review as the first hurdle to narrow the applicant pool before administering more expensive assessment devices later to a smaller pool of applicants. Table 15.4 provides the cutoff scores for each predictor completed by our hypothetical job applicants. Assume the predictors are administered sequentially in the following order: math test, filing test, spelling test, perceptual accuracy test, and structured interview to the five job applicants. Amanda would be eliminated from the applicant pool after the math test. Dave would be eliminated after the filing test. Rebecca would be eliminated after the perceptual accuracy test. Carl and Cyndy would pass all hurdles and thus be equally acceptable for the job.

Strategy Five: Combination Method

In this strategy, each applicant is measured on each predictor. An applicant with any predictor score below a minimum cutoff is rejected. Thus, the combination method is identical to the multiple-cutoff procedure to this point. Next, multiple regression is used to calculate overall scores for all applicants who pass the cutoffs. Then, the applicants who remain can be rank-ordered based on their overall scores calculated by the regression equation. This part of the procedure is identical to the multiple-regression approach.

Consequently, the combination method is a hybrid of the multiple-cutoff and multiple-regression approaches. The combination method has two major assumptions. The more restrictive assumption is derived from the multiple-cutoff approach. That is, a minimal level of each predictor attribute is necessary to perform the job. After that level has been reached, more of one predictor attribute can compensate for less of another in predicting overall success of the applicants. This assumption is derived from the multiple-regression approach.

The combination method has the advantages of the multiple-cutoff strategy. But rather than merely identifying a pool of acceptable candidates, which is what happens when using the multiple-cutoff approach, the combination approach additionally provides a way to rank-order acceptable applicants. The major disadvantage of the combination method is that it is more costly than the multiple-hurdle approach, because all applicants are screened on all predictors. Consequently the cost savings are not afforded by the multiple-hurdle approach's reduction of the applicant pool. In addition, it is possible the multiple regression will suffer a lower correlation with the criteria due to using predictors in the multiple regression that are correlated with test scores on which preliminary screening decisions were made. Any shrinkage in the correlation will depend on the extent to which the predictors used to initially screen out applicants are correlated with predictors used in the multiple regression. A lower correlation would be due to range restriction (that is, reduced variance) in scores on the tests.

The combination method is most appropriate when the assumption of multiple cutoffs is reasonable and more of one predictor attribute can compensate for another above the minimum cutoffs. It is also more appropriate to use this approach when the size of the applicant pool is not too large and costs of administering selection procedures do not vary greatly among the procedures.

In the example in Table 15.4, Carl and Cyndy pass all of the cutoffs; Amanda, Dave, and Rebecca do not. Overall scores indicating the predicted success for each applicant who passes all cutoffs are then calculated by entering the remaining selection procedures scores into the regression equation for each applicant. Once the overall scores have been calculated, the applicants are rank-ordered based on their overall predicted scores. Ordering the applicants based on their overall predicted scores results in the following ranking: 1 = Carl [predicted score = 97.8] and 2 = Cyndy [predicted score = 92.2].

Strategy Six: Banding

As we mentioned earlier, one problem facing human resource selection decision makers is the fact that adverse impact frequently occurs against racial minorities with selection procedures such as mental ability tests. Race norming was one means developed for dealing with the problem of adverse impact arising from the use of selection procedures. However, the Civil Rights Act of 1991 prohibited race norming of selection procedure scores by employers.[65] In fact, the Act prohibits adjustment of scores, use of different cutoff scores, use of different norms derived for protected groups, or alteration of results of employment-related tests on the basis of ethnicity, religion, gender, or national origin.

An alternative in dealing with the problem of selection procedure adverse impact is the use of *banding* of selection procedure scores, which has received legal support.[66] Banding involves establishing ranges of selection procedure scores where applicants' scores within a range or band are treated the same. Within a band, any selection procedure score differences are seen as due to measurement error and thus equivalent. The rationale behind banding is that scores on selection procedures do not have perfect reliability and, therefore, these scores do not perfectly reflect individuals' true scores on the characteristic measured by the selection procedure. Because small differences among applicants' scores on a selection procedure are due to measurement errors (that is, selection procedure score unreliability), these differences are not considered meaningful.

We saw in our discussion of the standard error of measurement that small differences in predictor scores may not reflect true or real differences in the attributes measured by the predictor. As a result, several banding procedures have been developed to take into account selection procedure measurement error and incorporate that information in selection decisions. For those scores within a band, other means or attributes (for example, using random selection or applicant job experience) are used to choose among applicants from within a band.

Establishing Bands

Two forms of statistical methods have generally been used for determining whether selection procedure scores differ: (a) the standard error of measurement method and (b) the standard error of differences method. Both of these methods take into account two pieces of information: (a) the standard error of measurement (composed of the reliability and standard deviation of predictor scores), and (b) the level of confidence necessary for determining that predictor scores do or do not differ. These values affect the width of the band.[67] In the *standard error of measurement method*, the standard error of measurement is calculated for the selection procedure. Then, the standard error of measurement is multiplied by 1.96, and the product is subtracted from an applicant's selection procedure score. This calculation results in a range of scores that are basically equivalent 95 percent of the time. For example, assume that the standard error of measurement (SEM) is equal to 2.98. Multiplying 2.98 by 1.96 gives a product of 5.84. If the top applicant score on the predictor is 95, subtracting 5.84 results in a score of 89.16. Thus applicants' predictor scores between 89.16 and 95 are not significantly different and are considered equivalent.

In the *standard error of differences method* (the most frequently discussed method), the standard error of measurement is determined. Then 1 standard error of measurement is multiplied by the *square root* of $2\ (\sqrt{2} = 1.414)$. (*Technical Note:* The $\sqrt{2} \times$ SEM = the standard deviation of the *difference* between two independent predictor scores.)[68] This number is then multiplied by 1.96 to determine the range of scores where it is 95 percent certain that the difference is real and not due to error. For example, assume that the SEM = 2.98. The standard error of differences (SED) calculation is $1.96 \times 2.98 \times 1.414 = 8.26$. If the top selection procedure score is 95, subtracting 8.26 results in a score of 86.74. Applicants' scores between 86.74 and 95 are not significantly different.

Fixed and Sliding Bands

In *fixed bands* (also called *top-score referenced bands*), the range of the top band is determined from the highest selection procedure score achieved by an applicant. All applicants within the top band must be selected before applicants in lower bands can be chosen.

Fixed bands use the top applicant score attained as the starting point. The top score minus the band width (for example, 1.96×1 standard error of measurement $\times \sqrt{2}$) constitutes the band. Individuals within this band can be selected in any order because all scores within the band are considered equivalent. If more individuals must be selected than are in the first band, a second band is created. The highest remaining score is now the basis for determining the band of score values using the same procedure.

In Figure 15.2, we use the standard error of differences method to compute the relevant bands. For the fixed band example, three bands are shown. The first fixed band is created by taking the top applicant score (95) and subtracting the band width (8.26). This results in a band range from 86.74 to 95. One applicant is within the first band.

FIGURE 15.2 Illustration of Fixed and Sliding Bands for Comparing Test Scores

Example of Fixed Bands

Test Score Band	Applicant Test Scores
95.00 to 86.74	95
86.73 to 78.47	86 86 86 85 83 82 82 82 79
78.46 to 70.20	78 78 77 77 77 76 76 74 73 73 72 71

Example of Sliding Bands

Test Score Band	Applicant Test Scores
95.00 to 86.74	95
86.00 to 77.74	86 86 86 85 83 82 82 82 79 78 78
77.00 to 69.74	77 77 77 76 76 74 73 73 72 71

Note: Test scores *within* the same band are *not* considered to be significantly different; test scores in *different* bands are considered to be significantly different. Band widths were established by the standard error of differences method (SED), where SED = $1.96 \times 2.98 \times \sqrt{2} = 8.26$.

After that applicant has been selected, the second band is created by subtracting the band width (8.26) from 86.73 (the next highest score after selecting *all* applicants in the first band). This results in a band range from 78.47 to 86.73. Nine applicants are within the second band, and any one of them can be selected. These applicants are considered to have performed the same on the selection procedure. Any apparent differences are due to error. After all of the applicants in the second band have been selected, the third band is created by subtracting the band width from 78.46. This results in a band range from 70.20 to 78.46.

Sliding bands are also based on the top applicant's selection procedure score. However, once that applicant is selected, the band is recalculated using the next highest applicant score on the selection procedure. With sliding bands, each decision is based on those applicants still available for selection. This method recognizes that selection decision making is a sequential process. When one person is chosen, the next selected candidates are chosen relative to those candidates remaining in the applicant pool. To implement the procedure, the highest scorer determines the band range, as in the previous procedure. Once the top scorer is selected, the highest remaining scorer is used to establish the new band. Thus, the band slides down each time the top scorer in a band is chosen. The top scorer is the reference point used to identify those who are not reliably different. Use of sliding bands makes it possible to consider more applicants than would have been available under the fixed-band method.

In Figure 15.2, the first band is created by taking the top applicant score (95) and subtracting the band width (8.26). This results in a band range from 95 to 86.74. After the top scorer (95) has been selected, the second band is created by subtracting the band width from the next highest remaining score (86). This step results in a range from 86 to 77.74. Notice, as compared to our fixed-band example, we pick up two additional applicants—that is, the two individuals who scored 78. After the three applicants with the next highest scores have been selected, the band changes again. This time the band width is subtracted from 77, resulting in a band range of 77 to 69.74. Consequently, the band slides downward, including more applicants each time the high scorer is selected. (In this explanation, we described a situation in which selection decisions are made on the basis of the highest test score. Next, we describe other decision rules that have been used with banding.)

Selecting Within a Band

Once a band has been created, the next step is to choose a procedure for selecting individuals within a band. If selection decisions are based on a rank-ordering of raw test scores and top scorers are offered jobs first, white applicants generally receive a disproportionate number of job offers compared with minority group members because white applicants tend to score, on average, higher than some minority group members on some paper-and-pencil tests commonly used in personnel selection.[69] This result leads to disparate impact of the test on minority groups. Some selection researchers have advocated the banding of selection procedure scores as one remedy to the problem of disparate impact. However, banding does not correct for selection procedure score differences among protected groups; it does, however, provide some flexibility in selection decision making.[70]

Once bands have been created, other selection specifications are used in choosing individuals within the same band. For example, a number of public sector organizations have used WRCs such as the following:

- Interpersonal skills (ability to interact with people having diverse backgrounds)
- Job experience

- Work performance

- Training

- Work habits (attendance, punctuality, relationships with coworkers)

- Professional conduct (absence of citizen complaints, absence of disciplinary actions)[71]

To choose among those within the same band, race of applicants generally cannot be used.[72] Wayne Cascio and his colleagues raise an interesting question with regard to the use of various selection specifications for choosing among applicants within the same band. They wonder why, if a specification is reliable and valid, it is not used in the overall selection process along with other selection procedures.[73]

Advantages of Banding

Advocates of banding see a number of strengths that can result from incorporating banding procedures in hiring decisions. Sheldon Zedeck and his colleagues have noted several.[74] Among those mentioned are that an employer has more flexibility in making hiring decisions. For instance, if an employer were trying to comply with a legal mandate to diversify its workforce, it could identify women, minorities, or other underemployed applicant groups within a band. Preferences could be given to applicants falling within the same band, because all applicant scores within the band are considered equal. In addition to obtaining a more diverse workforce, an employer can emphasize secondary hiring factors that may be important, such as past attendance records, possession of special skills, types of training received, and so on. On the other hand, giving emphasis to a protected group characteristic when it is not legally mandated could legally jeopardize an organization.

Second, because performance on many selection measures explains only a relatively small percentage of the differences in criterion performance, use of secondary hiring factors helps an employer take into account those factors not measured by traditional selection methods. Finally, banding advocates have argued that simply basing the utility of a selection program on maximum economic gain resulting from top-down selection procedures views selection from a very narrow perspective. Utility calculations ignore the social and financial impacts that can accrue to an employer for not having a diverse workforce. Moreover, use of banding procedures does not necessarily result in substantial economic losses to an employer. As noted in the following section, others have questioned this conclusion.

Concerns Regarding Banding

Use of banding in giving job offers to protected group members can make it possible to choose a larger number of minorities than would be feasible under top-down hiring based on rank-ordering of applicants' test scores. However, there is debate as to whether using banding to identify equally qualified individuals and then choosing on the basis of minority status within the band will withstand legal challenge. Others have noted that utilizing banding involving a selection procedure that has high reliability but has disparate impact, will negatively affect the selection procedure's utility. In addition, it will lead to little reduction in adverse impact.[75]

Banding itself may not be illegal, but what occurs when selecting among applicants after the band has been created may be. Selecting applicants within a band on the basis of random selection, previous work performance, or some standard not associated with protected group status may be legal. However, using protected-group status (for example, race) as the sole basis for choosing among applicants may be illegal because of Section 106 of the 1991 Civil Rights Act. That section prohibits hiring on the basis of protected-group status (for example, race, sex, color, or national origin).[76] Of course, random selection within a band could be used, but that strategy seems to do little to increase minority employment.[77]

Research by Christine Henle has shed some light on the legal issues surrounding banding. She reviewed eight court cases involving the application of banding in public sector organizations. Among other findings, the courts did not support banding when applicant minority status was solely used to select from within the bands, even if it was done to remedy past discrimination in the organization. However, when minority preferences were coupled with other selection criteria (for example, job experience), the courts supported banding. Thus, from Henle's work, it appears the courts support the practice of banding with the caveat that minority status is used with other selection specifications in selecting from within bands.[78]

In addition to legal issues, there have been other concerns regarding banding as a selection practice. For one, any departure from top-down hiring based on applicants' ranked test scores leads to a loss of economic utility as reflected in work performance. Because test scores are, in most cases, linearly related to work performance,[79] any deviation from top-down hiring necessarily leads to a decrease in work performance of the group hired.[80]

Another concern with banding involves the value of banding in reducing adverse impact if preferential treatment cannot be given to minority group members. As we noted, preferential treatment of minorities within bands can lessen adverse impact. Without this treatment, however, banding would seem to have reduced effects on adverse impact and would decrease economic utility.[81] Wayne Cascio and his colleagues concluded that using banding has generally yielded modest reductions in adverse impact with little negative effects on selection procedure validity or utility. However, banding is not the final answer to the problem of adverse impact of selection procedures.[82]

Additionally, banding may involve an incomplete system for weighting factors other than test scores in selecting individuals within a band. Other than random selection, all banding systems involve ranking members within a band on some basis other than test scores (for example, education, training, or personal characteristics). These factors are assumed to be associated with work performance. However, the weights given these factors are rarely specified and may vary across bands and applicants. An explicit and consistent system for weighting these factors (for example, through multiple regression) would be a better approach.[83]

Another concern arises when bands are used that are perceived by some to be too wide. Several research studies have argued that current statistical procedures connected with banding produce bands that are inappropriately wide. The result is that too many applicants are judged as equal with respect to their scores on selection procedures. Moreover, many such scores within a band are statistically different and should be considered as such in selection decision making.[84]

In addition, bands that appear too wide make it difficult to explain how two scores appearing to be very different from one another are essentially equivalent. When this happens, it is a particular problem to describe to those negatively affected how a lower-scoring applicant is hired over a higher-scoring one.[85] Because it has been shown that reactions to banding are largely a function of the perceived relationship of banding with affirmative action,[86] this problem is probably magnified when affected individuals hold negative attitudes toward affirmative action programs.

Frank Schmidt has argued that a basic principle used in developing bands—that scores not significantly different from each other should not be treated differently—is not applied consistently in banding. Large score differences within a band are ignored, whereas small differences that may occur between scores in one band and scores in another are viewed as meaningful.[87] In response, Wayne Cascio and his associates have argued that Schmidt's viewpoint does not accurately describe banding, because the reference point is the highest remaining score in a band. This is because those individuals are the ones chosen in top-down hiring.[88]

A PRACTICAL APPROACH TO MAKING SELECTION DECISIONS

Several issues should be considered when choosing among selection decision-making procedures: (a) Should the procedure be sequential (for example, multiple hurdle) or nonsequential (for example, multiple regression or multiple cutoff)? (b) Should the decision be compensatory (for example, multiple regression) or noncompensatory (for example, multiple cutoff, multiple hurdle)? (c) Should the decision be based on ranking applicants, or should it be based on banding acceptable applicants?

In choosing among decision-making options, begin by assessing the job and nature of work performance. What determines success on the job? What factors contribute to success, and how are they related? After answering these questions, consider additional issues: (a) the number of applicants expected, (b) the cost of selection devices used, and (c) the amount of time you can devote to the selection decision.

Having decided on a selection decision-making strategy, implement the strategy systematically in order to reap the potential benefits. Results of numerous studies of decision making are clear: *If you can develop and use a mechanical selection decision-making strategy, such as we have described in this chapter, you can improve your personnel selection decision making.* Many selection decisions meet the criteria[89] necessary for building such a model: (a) the same decision is made repeatedly (normal turnover requires hiring for the same position numerous times), (b) data are available on the outcomes of past decisions (applicants are hired, and their performance can be tracked over time), and (c) you have good reason to expect the future will resemble the past (many jobs change very little, if at all, over time). When these decision-making strategies are built using sound validation strategies as discussed in this book, powerful decision aids become available to decision makers.

Because of the sporadic nature of selection and the small number of applicants employed, it is often not possible to build objective strategies. This is especially true for small businesses, where selection is but one of many important activities competing for the time of owners and managers. What can decision makers in this situation do to improve their selection decisions? Suppose a small business owner needs to employ an assistant.[90] First, she specifies what tasks this assistant will be asked to perform and the standards of performance that the assistant will be judged against. Next, she thinks of activities she could ask an applicant to do during the interview and selection process that are similar to, if not exactly, what the assistant would do on the job. After identifying some suitable job-related activities, the owner next thinks about what weights she should attach to each of the activities used for selection. Although these weights are subjective and not based on an empirical analysis of previous hires, they are at least made explicit before the selection process begins. By using some simplified rating process to assess each applicant on each selection activity, the owner has a systematic procedure for collecting data on applicants and ensuring that applicants are evaluated on the same work-related characteristics. Once the applicants have been processed in this manner, the final selection decision can be based on a "subjective linear model."[91] By multiplying the weights attached to each selection activity times the rating she gave each applicant, and then summing these products, an overall score can be calculated for each applicant that yields a systematically derived judgment of the applicant's probability for success on the job. Notice this process results in a systematic way of combining selection procedure data.

An even better subjective decision-making procedure than the one just described uses a technique called *bootstrapping*.[92] Bootstrapping is based on the assumption that even though people can often make sound judgments, they are not typically able to articulate how they made those judgments. Using this technique requires having the decision maker make judgments on a series of cases (for example, selection decision judgments based on a number of applicant files). Then, through regression analysis, it is possible to infer the weights used by the decision maker to arrive at a particular ranking. The regression analysis shows how much weight, on average, the decision maker puts on each of the underlying factors. As J. Edward Russo and Paul Schoemaker describe it, "In bootstrapping, you seek to build a model of an expert using his or her own intuitive predictions, and then use that model to *outperform* the expert on new cases."[93] This method works because when you ask a person to make a prediction, "you get wisdom mixed in with random noise." Judgments based on intuition suffer greatly from random noise caused by an array of factors ranging from fatigue and boredom to stress and anxiety. Bootstrapping produces a standard procedure for decision making that eliminates the random noise while retaining the "core wisdom." Consequently, by using bootstrapping, the decision will be made in the same way today, tomorrow, next week, and next year. Numerous studies support the finding that bootstrapped models consistently do better at prediction than simple intuitive judgments. This leads us to the fascinating conclusion that models of our own subjective decision-making processes can be built that outperform us! Nevertheless, when an objective strategy can be used, it still outperforms both bootstrapped models and simple intuition. It is always best to use an objective strategy whenever possible.

One last issue we must address when discussing a practical approach to selection decisions is procedural fairness. Whether you use a systematic objective strategy of decision making or a simple intuitive approach, it is critical that the procedures be perceived as fair. For selection procedures, we have used the term *face validity* to describe selection practices that applicants believe to be reasonable. In addition to selection instruments having face validity, decision-making procedures, too, must be seen as fair.

One factor that seems to affect whether decision-making procedures are viewed as fair is how well they are justified.[94] This seems especially important for dealing with applicants who are rejected during the selection process. Rejected applicants will accept their rejection better if they believe they were treated justly, they had a fair chance to obtain the job, and someone better qualified received the job. Objective decision-making models built on solid evidence should be easier to justify than intuitive models that cannot be clearly articulated. Regardless of the approach used, ensuring procedural fairness should be a major consideration when developing and applying selection procedures.

AUDITING SELECTION DECISIONS: LEARNING FROM YOUR SUCCESSES AND FAILURES

The only way you can improve your selection decision making is to learn from what you have done in the past. This dictum applies at both the organizational level and at the individual level. At the organizational level, validation studies can help improve overall organizational selection decision making by identifying scientifically those factors that predict job success and eliminating those factors that do not predict job success. Using validation strategies merely to comply with legal requirements is a gross underutilization of this powerful technology. Organizations that routinely validate their selection practices set the context in which good decisions can occur. Organizations that do not routinely validate their selection practices create a decision-making context that may or may not lead to desirable outcomes.

At the individual level, most managers do not think about their success and failure rate when it comes to making selection decisions. This is not surprising, when you consider the number of selection decisions that must be made over many years. Yet, it is surprising that managers are not held as accountable for their selection decisions as they are for other decisions such as capital equipment purchases. Are not a high number of bad selection decisions as damaging to an organization as the purchase of an unreliable piece of machinery? Several bad selection decisions can lead to lower productivity and high separation and replacement costs, as well as to potentially damaging litigation. How can managers be held accountable for their selection decisions and learn from their successes and failures?

The decision-making literature suggests that a simple box-score tally of successes and failures can improve decision making over time.[95] Decision makers learn from feedback that either supports or disconfirms their predictive models. Remember Valentina from the beginning of the chapter? This simple procedure may not have prevented her from making selection errors, but it would certainly have reduced her overconfidence about her decision-making ability! If these individual decision audits are made throughout the organization, both good and bad decision makers can be identified for either reinforcement or remedial training.

RECOMMENDATIONS FOR ENHANCING SELECTION DECISION MAKING

Even the best-designed selection systems will not produce sound selection decisions unless good selection decision-making procedures are used as well. To ensure that an organization maximizes the effectiveness of its selection system, we suggest the following prescriptions:

1. Use standardized, reliable, and valid selection procedures for collecting information on job applicants whenever possible.

2. Encourage managers and others making selection decisions to participate in the data-collection process (for example, rating an applicant's interview performance using valid, standardized methods), but discourage them from combining scores on selection instruments or from making decisions based on intuition or gut feelings.

3. When combining selection procedure scores, use a mechanical means for doing so, for example, multiple regression, unit weighting.

4. Train managers and others making selection decisions to make systematic decisions, preferably using one of the objective (mechanical) strategies described in the chapter.

5. Although it is difficult for small organizations to adopt some decision-making strategies, small businesses can specify, in advance, (a) the weight of standards to be used in evaluating candidates (for example, performance of activities

similar to those on the job), (b) the procedures used for judging whether applicants meet those standards (for example, a rating system for evaluating performance of these simulated activities), and then (c) the procedures for combining the standardized weights multiplied by the ratings given in order to arrive at an overall applicant score.

6. Decide whether a compensatory or noncompensatory method for selecting job applicants is going to be used. The relative value an organization places on minority hiring versus performance will likely affect the choice of selection method.

7. For organizations using cutoff scores, the modified Angoff procedure is acceptable.

8. Assuming that a selection procedure predicts work performance, and assuming that all applicants who are extended an offer of employment accept the offer, maximum work performance among the group hired will occur when top-down selection is used. However, disparate impact against racial minorities is likely to occur if the selection procedure on which employment decisions are based is highly correlated with general mental ability.

9. Banding of selection procedure scores has been supported in the courts. However, using minority status alone as a basis for selecting within bands is probably not legal in most employment settings. Overall, banding has had a minor but positive effect on reducing adverse impact.

10. For jobs in which selection has taken place, decide on a standard for defining a successful hire (for example, the selected person stayed on the job 6 months or more) and an unsuccessful hire (for example, the selected person's dollar sales fall below a minimum standard or his or her supervisory performance appraisal ratings fall below an acceptable level). Then, have managers keep track of their hits (correct selection decisions) and misses (incorrect selection decisions). Of course, it is generally infeasible to track the effects of false negatives that occur in selection decision making (that is, those individuals who were not hired because of their low scores on a selection procedure but who would have been successful on the job had they been employed).

11. Periodically audit selection decisions throughout the organization to identify areas or individuals needing improvement.

These prescriptions do not guarantee that you will always make correct decisions in selecting personnel for your organization. However, they are guaranteed to tilt the odds in your favor.

REFERENCES

1. Jack Sawyer, "Measurement *and* Prediction, Clinical *and* Statistical," *Psychological Bulletin* 66 (1966): 178–200.

2. Nathan R. Kuncel, Brian S. Connelly, David M. Kleiger, and Deniz Ones, "Mechanical Versus Clinical Data Combination in Selection and Admissions Decisions: A Meta-Analysis," *Journal of Applied Psychology* 98 (2013): 1060.

3. Scott Highhouse, "Stubborn Reliance on Intuition and Subjectivity in Employee Selection," *Industrial and Organizational Psychology* 1 (2008): 568.

4. Ibid.

5. Paul Meehl, *Clinical versus Statistical Prediction* (Minneapolis: University of Minnesota Press, 1954).

6. Paul Meehl, "Causes and Effects of My Disturbing Little Book," *Journal of Personality Assessment* 50 (1986): 370–375.

7. Sawyer, "Measurement *and* Prediction, Clinical *and* Statistical," 178–200.

8. For a review, see Benjamin Kleinmuntz, "Why We Still Use Our Heads Instead of Formulas: Toward an Integrative Approach," *Psychological Bulletin* 107 (1990): 296–310.

9. Kuncel, et al., "Mechanical Versus Clinical Data Combination in Selection and Admissions Decisions: A Meta-Analysis," 1060.

10. Ibid., 1064.

11. Bernard M. Bass and Gerald V. Barrett, *People, Work, and Organizations*, 2nd ed. (Boston: Allyn & Bacon, 1981), 397–398.

12. Philip Bobko, Philip Roth, and Maury Buser, "The Usefulness of Unit Weights in Creating Composite Scores: A Literature Review, Application to Content Validity, and Meta-Analysis," *Organizational Research Methods* 10 (2007): 689–709.

13. Scott Highhouse and John Kostek, "Holistic Assessment for Selection and Placement," in *APA Handbook of Testing and Assessment in Psychology: Vol. 1. Test Theory and Assessment in Industrial and Organizational Psychology*, ed. Kurt Geisinger (Washington, D.C.: American Psychological Association, 2013): 573.

14. Ibid., 572–573.

15. Scott Highhouse, "Stubborn Reliance on Intuition and Subjectivity in Employee Selection," *Industrial and Organizational Psychology* 1 (2008): 337.

16. Kleinmuntz, "Why We Still Use Our Heads Instead of Formulas: Toward an Integrative Approach," 298.

17. Winston R. Sieck and Hal R. Arkes, "The Recalcitrance of Overconfidence and Its Contribution to Decision Aid Neglect," *Journal of Behavioral Decision Making* 18 (2005): 29–53.

18. Drew Westen and Joel Weinberger, "When Clinical Description Becomes Statistical Prediction," *American Psychologist* 59 (2004): 608.

19. Talya Miron-Shatz and Gershon Ben-Shakhar, "Disregarding Preliminary Information When Rating Job Applicants' Performance: Mission Impossible?" *Journal of Applied Social Psychology* 38 (2008): 1271–1294.

20. Lewis Goldberg, "Diagnosticians vs. Diagnostic Signs: The Diagnosis of Psychosis vs. Neurosis from the MMPI," *Psychological Monographs* 79 (1965).

21. Kuncel, et al., "Mechanical Versus Clinical Data Combination in Selection and Admissions Decisions: A Meta-Analysis," 1070.

22. In the book by J. Edward Russo and Paul J. H. Schoemaker, *Decision Traps* (New York: Simon & Schuster, 1989), the authors provide several compelling strategies for convincing people to adopt mechanical approaches for combining predictive information.

23. Dalia L. Diab, Shuang-Yueh Pui, Maya Yankelevich, and Scott Highhouse, "Lay Perceptions of Selection Decision Aids in US and Non-US Samples," *International Journal of Selection and Assessment* 19 (2011): 210. Michael A. Lodato, Scott Highhouse, Margaret E. Brooks, "Predicting Professional Preferences for Intuition-Based Hiring," *Journal of Managerial Psychology* 26 (2011): 352–365.

24. Robyn M. Dawes, "The Robust Beauty of Improper Linear Models in Decision Making," *American Psychologist* 34 (1979): 580.

25. Andreas Graefe, "Improving Forecasts Using Equally Weighted Predictors," *Journal of Business Research* (in press).

26. Ibid.

27. Wayne F. Cascio, *Applied Psychology in Personnel Management*, 4th ed. (Englewood Cliffs, NJ: Prentice Hall, 1991), 286.

28. Milton L. Blum and James C. Naylor, *Industrial Psychology: Its Theoretical and Social Foundations* (New York: Harper & Row, 1969), 68–69.

29. See Wayne F. Cascio, E. R. Valenzi, and Val Silbey, "Validation and Statistical Power: Implications for Applied Research," *Journal of Applied Psychology* 63 (1978): 589–595; and Wayne F. Cascio, E. R. Valenzi, and Val Silbey, "More on Validation and Statistical Power," *Journal of Applied Psychology* 65 (1980): 135–138.

30. Dawes, "The Robust Beauty of Improper Linear Models in Decision Making," 571.

31. Ibid., 572.

32. Ibid., 574.

33. Philip Bobko, Philip Roth, and Maury Buster, "The Usefulness of Unit Weights in Creating Composite Scores: A Literature Review, Application to Content Validity, and Meta-Analysis," *Organizational Research Methods* 10 (2007): 693.

34. Ibid., 694.

35. Dawes, "The Robust Beauty of Improper Linear Models in Decision Making," 574.

36. Robyn M. Dawes and Bernard Corrigan, "Linear Models in Decision Making," *Psychological Bulletin* 81 (1974): 105.

37. Dawes, "The Robust Beauty of Improper Linear Models in Decision Making," 573.

38. Wesley A. Scroggins, Steven L. Thomas, and Jerry A. Morris, "Psychological Testing in Personnel Selection, Part II: The Refinement of Methods and Standards in Employee Selection," *Public Personnel Management* 37 (2008): 190.

39. Frank L. Schmidt, Mack J. Murray, and John E. Hunter, "Selection Utility in the Occupation of U.S. Park Ranger for Three Modes of Test Use," *Journal of Applied Psychology* 69 (1984): 490–497.

40. As described in John Hunter and Frank Schmidt, "Ability Tests: Economic Benefits versus the Issue of Fairness," *Industrial Relations* 21 (1982): 298.

41. Lorin Mueller, Dwayne Norris, and Scott Oppler, "Implementation Based on Alternate Validation Procedures: Ranking, Cut Scores, Banding, and Compensatory Models," in *Alternative Validation Strategies*, ed. S. Morton McPhail (New York, NY: John Wiley, 2007), 357.

42. Ibid., 365.

43. Ibid.

44. Robert L. Thorndike, *Personnel Selection: Test and Measurement Techniques* (New York: John Wiley, 1949).

45. Cascio, *Applied Psychology in Personnel Management*, 288.

46. *U.S. v. Delaware*, U.S. District LEXIS 4560 (2004). *Lanning v. SEPTA*, 308 F. 3d 286 (3rd Cir. 2002).

47. Robert L. Ebel, *Essentials of Educational Measurement* (Englewood Cliffs, NJ: Prentice Hall, 1972).

48. William H. Angoff, "Scales, Norms, and Equivalent Scores," in *Educational Measurement*, ed. Robert L. Thorndike (Washington, DC: American Council on Education, 1971), 508–600.

49. Richard E. Biddle, "How to Set Cutoffs for Knowledge Tests Used in Promotion, Training, Certification, and Licensing," *Public Personnel Management* 22 (1993): 63–80.

50. Dan Biddle and Nikki Sill, "Protective Service Physical Ability Tests: Establishing Pass/Fail, Ranking, and Banding Procedures," *Public Personnel Management* 28 (1999): 218–219.

51. Neal W. Schmitt and Richard J. Klimoski, *Research Methods in Human Resource Management* (Cincinnati: South-Western, 1991), 303.

52. Wayne F. Cascio, Rick Jacobs, and Jay Silva, "Validity, Utility, and Adverse Impact: Practical Implications from 30 Years of Data," in *Adverse Impact: Implications for Organizational Staffing and High Stakes Selection*, ed. James L. Outtz (New York, NY: Routledge, 2010), 271–322.

53. The contrasting groups method is described in detail in the discussion of setting cutoff scores for weighted application blanks. See George W. England, *Development and Use of Weighted Application Blanks* (Minneapolis: Industrial Relations Center, University of Minnesota, 1971).

54. Biddle and Sill, "Protective Service Physical Ability Tests: Establishing Pass/Fail, Ranking, and Banding Procedures," 218.

55. U.S. Equal Employment Opportunity Commission, Civil Service Commission, Department of Labor, and Department of Justice, *Adoption of Four Agencies of Uniform Guidelines on Employee Selection Procedures*, 43 Federal Register 38, 290–38, 315 (August 25, 1978).

56. Society of Industrial-Organizational Psychology, Inc., *Principles for the Validation and Use of Personnel Selection Procedures*, 4th ed. (Bowling Green, OH: Society of Industrial-Organizational Psychology, 2003), 46.

57. Ibid., 47.

58. Hunter and Schmidt, "Ability Tests: Economic Benefits versus the Issue of Fairness," 298.

59. Cynthia D. Fisher, Lyle F. Schoenfeldt, and James B. Shaw, *Human Resource Management* (Boston: Houghton Mifflin, 1990), 231.

60. Schmitt and Klimoski, *Research Methods in Human Resource Management*, 302.

61. Cascio, *Applied Psychology in Personnel Management*, 289.

62. Lee J. Cronbach and Goldine C. Gleser, *Psychological Tests and Personnel Decisions*, 2nd ed. (Urbana: University of Illinois Press, 1965).

63. Joann S. Lubin, "Speediest Companies Snaring Top Candidates," *Atlanta Journal-Constitution*, August 11, 1999, D1.

64. Richard R. Reilly and W. R. Manese, "The Validation of a Minicourse for Telephone Company Switching Technicians," *Personnel Psychology* 32 (1979): 83–90.

65. Lawrence Z. Lorber, "The Civil Rights Act of 1991," in *Legal Report* (Washington, DC: Society for Human Resource Management, Spring 1992), 1–4.

66. Herman Aguinis, ed., *Test-score Banding in Human Resource Selection: Legal, Technical, and Societal Issues* (Westport, CT: Quorum, 2004).

67. Scientific Affairs Committee, "An Evaluation of Banding Methods in Personnel Selection," *The Industrial-Organizational Psychologist* 32 (1994): 80.

68. Philip Bobko and Philip Roth, "Personnel Selection with Top-Score-Referenced Banding: On the Inappropriateness of Current Procedures," *International Journal of Selection and Assessment* 12 (2004): 293.

69. Frank L. Schmidt, "The Problem of Group Differences in Ability Test Scores in Employment Selection," *Journal of Vocational Behavior* 33 (1998): 272–292.

70. Cascio, Jacobs, and Silva, "Validity, Utility, and Adverse Impact: Practical Implications from 30 Years of Data," 271–322.

71. Christine A. Henle, "Case Review of the Legal Status of Banding," *Human Performance* 17 (2004): 428.

72. *Chicago Firefighters Local 2 v. City of Chicago*, 249 F. 3d 649 (7th Cir. 2001).

73. Cascio, Jacobs, and Silva, "Validity, Utility, and Adverse Impact: Practical Implications from 30 Years of Data," 281.

74. Sheldon Zedeck, Wayne F. Cascio, Irwin L. Goldstein, and James Outtz, "Sliding Bands: An Alternative to Top-Down Selection," in *Fair Employment Strategies in Human Resource Management*, ed. Richard S. Barrett (Westport, CT: Quorum Books, 1996), 228–230.

75. Gerald V. Barrett, Dennis Doyerspike, and Winfred Arthur, "The Current Status of the Judicial Review of Banding: A Clarification," *The Industrial-Organizational Psychologist* 33 (1995): 39–41. Herbert G. Heneman, Timothy A. Judge, and R. L. Heneman, *Staffing Organizations*, 3rd ed. (Burr Ridge, IL: Irwin McGraw-Hill, 2000).

76. Ibid.

77. Paul Sackett and L. Roth, "A Monte Carlo Examination of Banding and Rank Order Methods of Test Score Use in Personnel Selection," *Human Performance* 4 (1991): 279–295.

78. Henle, "Case Review of the Legal Status of Banding," 415–432.

79. W. M. Coward and Paul R. Sackett, "Linearity of Ability Performance Relationship: A Reconfirmation," *Journal of Applied Psychology* 75 (1990): 297–300.

80. Frank L. Schmidt, "Why All Banding Procedures in Personnel Selection Are Logically Flawed," *Human Performance* 8 (1995): 165–177.

81. Sackett and Roth, "A Monte Carlo Examination of Banding and Rank Order Methods of Test Score Use in Personnel Selection," 279–295.

82. Cascio, Jacobs, and Silva, "Validity, Utility, and Adverse Impact: Practical Implications from 30 Years of Data," 271–322.

83. Scientific Affairs Committee, "An Evaluation of Banding Methods in Personnel Selection."

84. Bobko and Roth, "Personnel Selection with Top-Score-Referenced Banding: On the Inappropriateness of Current Procedures" Philip Bobko, Philip Roth, and Alan Nicewander, "Banding Selection Scores in Human Resource Management Decisions: Current Inaccuracies and the Effect of Conditional Standard Scores," *Organizational Research Methods* 8 (2005): 259–273.

85. Zedeck, Cascio, Goldstein, and Outtz, "Sliding Bands: An Alternative to Top-Down Selection," 230.

86. Donald M. Truxillo and Talya N. Bauer, "Applicant Reactions to Test Store Banding in Entry-Level and Promotional Contexts," *Journal of Applied Psychology* 84 (1999): 322–339.

87. Schmidt, "Why All Banding Procedures in Personnel Selection Are Logically Flawed," 165–177.

88. Wayne F. Cascio, James Outtz, Sheldon Zedeck, and Irwin L. Goldstein, "Statistical Implications of Six Methods of Test Score Use in Personnel Selection," *Human Performance* 8 (1995): 133–164.

89. Russo and Schoemaker, *Decision Traps*, 138.

90. This procedure is similar to one described in Benjamin Schneider and Neal Schmitt, *Staffing Organizations* (Glenview, IL: Scott, Foresman, 1986), 416.

91. Russo and Schoemaker, *Decision Traps*, 131–134.

92. Ibid., 134–137.

93. Ibid., 135.

94. See, for example, R. J. Bies and D. L. Shapiro, "Voice and Justification: Their Influence on Procedural Fairness Judgments," *Academy of Management Journal* 31 (1988): 676–685.

95. Kleinmuntz, "Why We Still Use Our Heads Instead of Formulas: Toward an Integrative Approach," 296–310.

AUTHOR INDEX

A

Aamodt, Michael G., 395, 399, 428n147, 428n150, 430n174, 430n189, 430n191, 431n200

Acker, Stanley R., 345n20

Adams, A., 189n59, 639n3

Aguinis, Herman, 103n72, 237n4, 303, 330, 331, 347n56, 350n103, 427n142, 492n117, 497n179, 497n183, 497n187, 669, 683n66

Aiken, Lewis R., 237n3, 278n37, 532n4

Aiman-Smith, Lynda, 195n143

Albarracin, Dolores, 186n31, 186n32

Albright, Lewis E., 380, 423n80, 424n95

Alexander, Ralph A., 347n41, 347n48, 424n94, 669

Allen, David G., 190n76, 492n113, 496n169

Allen, Natalie J., 33

Alliger, George M., 500n238

Alvares, Kenneth M., 610n26

Anastasi, Anne, 277n18, 278n39, 532n3, 532n6

Anderson, Neil, 219, 465, 490n94, 491n110

Andler, Edward C., 407, 413, 423n75, 427n139, 430n186

Andrews, Kimberly D., 496n174

Angoff, William H., 665, 666, 667, 683n48

Anlauf, Manfred, 276n1, 276n5

Appel, Lawrence J., 276n2

Aquinis, Herman, 237n7, 238n19

Arad, Sharon, 35, 45n23, 45n24

Archer, Wayne B., 66

Arkes, Hal R., 681n17

Armenakis, Achilles A., 44n14, 193n121

Armon, Emma, 112

Arnold, David W., 572n87, 641n43, 642n51

Arthur, Winfred, 456, 601, 684n75

Arthur, Winfred., Jr., 487n53, 493n119, 533n28, 610n32, 611n41, 611n48, 612n60

Arvey, Richard D., 98, 103n74, 197n172, 340, 348n63, 348n65, 352n152, 352n155, 353n159, 427n134

Asch, Soloman E., 489n81, 499n211

Ash, Ronald A., 392, 424n102, 425n112, 425n116

Ash, Steven R., 193n112

Asher, James J., 362, 418n17, 608n3

Ashforth, Blake E., 190n77

Ashton, Michael C., 641n23

Ashworth, Steven, 509, 532n11, 571n77

Atwater, David, 418n19

Avery, Derek R., 156, 186n34, 188n56

Avolio, Bruce J., 426n128

B

Bachiochi, Peter D., 188n54

Bachrach, Daniel G., 43n10, 44n20

Baehr, Melany E., 100n30

Baker, Erica, 486n33, 491n104

Bakker, Arnold B., 484n15, 486n38, 500n227

Bakker, Paulien, 484n15, 486n38, 500n227

Balma, Michael J., 233, 238n23, 318, 348n76

Balsam, Tamar, 417n8

Bangert-Downs, R. L., 533n31

Banks, George C., 346n32, 348n67

Barbee, Anita P., 642n47

Barber, Alison E., 152, 173, 184n4, 184n6, 184n10, 185n17, 188n51, 191n83, 195n142, 437, 486n39

Baron, Helen, 492n112, 566n4, 569n46

Barratt, Clare L., 45n34

Barrett, Gerald V., 347n41, 347n48, 348n60, 421n58, 424n94, 562, 575n123, 654, 681n11, 684n75

Barrett, Richard S., 345n13

Barrick, Murray R., 195n146, 237n8, 344n2, 351n118, 372, 400, 418n14, 422n64, 424n96, 428n155, 429n161, 431n195, 447, 483n2, 486n34, 487n52, 487n54, 488n66, 489n76, 490n82, 490n83, 490n84, 490n89, 496n168, 496n172, 497n188, 497n191, 498n196, 498n200, 499n212, 499n216, 537, 544, 549, 550, 565n1, 566n8, 566n11, 566n12, 566n15, 566n16, 566n17, 567n18, 567n21, 568n31, 568n32, 568n34, 568n40, 569n41, 569n43, 570n60, 570n62, 570n66, 570n67, 571n76, 573n97, 575n115, 575n117, 575n121, 575n122, 575n124, 593

Bart, Barbara D., 424n99

Bartholomew, Craig B., 428n153, 429n163

Bartram, Dave, 574n106, 574n107, 574n111, 575n112

Bass, Bernard M., 654, 681n11

Bateman, Thomas S., 499n220, 568n39

Batiste, Linda C., 642n64

Bauer, Talya N., 195n143, 197n174, 198n186, 642n56, 684n86

Baxter, Gregory, 150n59

Bearden, Ronald M., 569n44

Beatty, Richard W., 26, 43n4, 149n53

Beaty, James, 533n26

Beaubien, Mathew, 101n41

Becker, William J., 190n80, 420n37

Beier, Margaret E., 612n57

Bell, Brad S., 422n68

Bennett, Winston., Jr., 500n238

Ben-Shakhar, Gershon, 640n9, 681n19

Benson, Michael J., 570n61

Bentson, Cynthia, 609n17

Berchtold, Matthias, 490n93

Bergeron, Diane M., 33, 44n19

Bergmann, Thomas J., 197n175

Bernardin, John, 26, 43n4, 101n45, 149n53

Bernerth, Jeremy B., 189n68

Bernstein, Ira, 278n33

Berry, Christopher M., 36, 44n21, 45n28, 45n29, 45n34, 485n31, 488n69, 493n124, 532n7, 533n21, 575n114, 619, 640n16, 640n21, 642n45, 642n48, 642n53

Bertolino, Marilena, 198n186

Betz, Nancy E., 348n61

Bevier, Craig A., 426n124, 532n17

Biddle, Daniel A., 74, 102n64, 148n32, 302, 337, 347n53, 347n54, 347n55, 352n140, 352n143, 683n50, 683n54

Biddle, Richard E., 683n49

Biderman, Michael D., 612n56

Bies, R. J., 685n94

Biesanz, Jeremy C., 499n218

Billsberry, Jon, 185n14

Binet, Alfred, 505

Bing, Mark N., 352n155

Blackman, Melinda C., 484n11, 484n13, 488n61, 570n57

Blair, Carrie A., 611n44

Blakley, Barry R., 534n45

Bland, Timothy S., 368, 420n40, 422n66

Blass, Fred R., 20n5

Bliesener, Thomas, 365, 418n22, 419n27

Blum, Milton L., 246, 277n9, 349n87, 682n28

Bobko, Philip, 101n48, 148n30, 149n57, 194n129, 350n102, 418n20, 419n30, 421n60, 427n132, 495n154, 515, 518, 532n17, 532n18, 533n25, 586, 587, 591, 606, 609n11, 609n12, 609n24, 612n55, 681n12, 682n33, 684n68, 684n84

Boehm, Virginia, 532n19

Bohner, Gerd, 186n28, 186n29, 186n30, 186n33

Bolino, Mark C., 144, 149n56

Bolster, B., 499n215

Bommer, William H., 43n7

Bono, Joyce E., 570n65, 571n73

Borman, Walter C., 45n24, 425n111, 569n44

Born, Marise P., 571n68, 612n52

Bosch, Flurin, 350n110

Boswell, Wendy R., 178, 186n25, 189n66, 190n74

Boudreau, John W., 189n66, 190n74

Bourasa, Pamila, 115

Bownas, David A., 101n45

Boyatzis, Richard E., 489n73

Boyd, Joseph L., 609n9

Bozeman, Dennis P., 429n160, 429n162

Braddy, Phillip W., 191n95

Bradley, Jill C., 612n51

Bragger, Jennifer DeNicolis, 463, 494n146, 494n150, 494n151

Brandli, Michael, 608n2

Bray, Douglas W., 609n15

Breaugh, James A., 152, 153, 155, 164, 184n3, 186n27, 186n37, 187n38, 187n39, 188n52, 191n93, 417n3, 417n6, 417n9

Brebels, Lieven, 44n13

Brecher, Ellyn, 494n146

Bretz, Robert D., Jr., 185n21, 189n69, 487n49

Bridges, Claudia M., 45n27

Brief, Arthur P., 43n9

Briggs, Katherine Cook, 545

Britt, M. F., 423n81

Brodie, W. M., 423n81

Brogden, Hubert E., 42, 46n38, 327, 349n93

Brown, Anna, 574n106, 574n107

Brown, Barbara K., 384, 385, 391, 424n101, 425n110, 495n162

Brown, Donald R., 278n28

Brown, Steven H., 346n36, 347n50

Brown, Victoria R., 198n184

Burger, Jerry M., 496n173

Burke, Eugene, 533n29

Burke, Michael J., 350n106

Burnett, Dawn D., 561, 575n119

Burnett, Jennifer R., 497n190

Buros, Oscar, 221

Burris, L. R., 641n27

Buster, Maury, 101n48, 395, 533n22, 587, 606, 609n12, 612n55, 681n12, 682n33

Butera, Hilary, 573n99

Button, Scott B., 102n57

Buyse, Tine, 612n58, 612n59

Bycio, Peter, 610n26

Byham, William C., 594, 609n16

C

Cable, Daniel M., 155, 185n15, 185n18, 186n26, 195n143

Caldwell, David F., 496n173

Caliguiri, Paula M., 197n167, 198n190, 491n109

Callahan, C., 641n27

Callender, John C., 495n160, 500n235

Camara, Wayne, 641n43, 642n51

Campbell, John P., 41, 45n36, 93, 102n68, 149n37, 324, 348n62, 348n70, 349n84, 418n13, 506, 532n10, 566n6, 570n61, 577, 578, 608n1

Campbell, Richard J., 609n15

Campion, James E., 484n9, 485n27, 490n90, 494n144, 581

Campion, Michael A., 53, 55, 100n16, 100n19, 197n174, 198n186, 384, 385, 391, 424n101, 425n110, 447, 448, 449, 450, 483n1, 483n3, 484n9, 485n27, 487n47, 487n51, 489n79, 490n86, 490n88, 490n90, 490n91, 490n96, 491n101, 491n108, 493n121, 493n123, 494n144, 494n147, 495n162, 496n175, 497n177, 497n181, 497n182, 498n206, 499n209, 499n221, 501n243, 501n244, 533n22, 534n39, 566n14, 608n5

Cappelli, Peter, 184n2, 189n64, 427n140

Carey, Susan, 643n74

Carless, Sally, 533n32

Carlson, Kevin D., 364, 365, 419n24, 422n63, 425n106

Carlson, Robert E., 499n217

Carpenter, Nichelle C., 44n21, 45n34

Carrier, Michael R., 294, 346n36

Carroll, Sarah A., 20n7, 487n46, 573n100

Carter, Min Z., 44n14

Cascio, Wayne F., 41, 42, 45n35, 46n37, 46n41, 101n40, 237n7, 238n19, 330, 349n95, 350n104, 350n107, 362, 427n142, 492n117, 497n179, 497n183, 497n187, 609n13, 609n14, 668,

669, 675, 676, 677, 682n27,
682n29, 682n45, 683n52,
683n61, 684n70, 684n73,
684n74, 684n82, 684n85,
685n88
Caspi, Avshalom, 566n7
Cattell, Raymond, 545
Cattin, Philippe, 317, 348n72
Ceci, Stephen J., 430n193
Cerdin, Jean-Luc, 198n190
Chan, Christopher CA, 492n114
Chan, David, 277n15, 611n49
Chao, Georgia T., 364, 399, 421n59,
423n77, 428n149
Chapman, Derek S., 20n7, 176,
198n187, 438, 446, 483n6,
484n14, 486n35, 486n36,
487n46, 489n77, 490n92,
491n105, 496n166, 500n240,
500n241
Chasteen, Christopher S., 610n30
Chen, Helen, 191n93
Cheung, Gordon W., 428n152,
428n154, 430n187
Chiaburu, Dan S., 566n11, 567n18,
568n31, 575n114, 575n117
Choudry, Niteesh K., 426n129
Christian, Michael S., 612n51
Christiansen, Neal D., 489n74,
573n102, 610n30, 610n31,
611n40
Chuang, Aichia, 187n41, 191n90,
486n41
Chung-Herrera, Beth G., 534n34
Cimander, Christin, 100n20
Clark, Kevin D., 20n6
Clark, Lee A., 569n49
Clark, Malissa A., 533n21
Clark, Mark A., 190n77, 196n166
Cohen, J. R., 351n119
Cohen, Jacob, 278n26, 278n27
Colakoglu, Saba, 198n190
Cole, Michael S., 424n100, 549,
570n59
Collins, Christopher J., 20n6, 155,
159, 165, 192n105
Collins, Judith M., 572n93, 610n29
Collins, Roger, 489n78
Combs, James G., 20n3
Conley, James J., 567n24
Connelly, Brian S., 489n72, 569n51,
571n75, 572n92, 680n2, 681n9,
681n21

Connolly, Terry, 190n80
Converse, Patrick D., 573n99
Conway, James M., 443, 485n26,
485n29, 485n30, 488n65,
488n67, 492n118, 493n122,
493n128, 497n185, 500n236,
569n52, 570n58
Cook, Mark, 336, 349n89
Cook, Russell T., 20n3
Cooper, L. A., 423n78
Cornel, Pater, 276n3
Cornelius, Edwin T., 278n25
Corrigan, Bernard, 660, 682n36
Cortina, Jose, 277n20, 483n4,
484n16, 485n19, 486n40
Costa, P. T., Jr., 544, 545, 567n29,
568n33
Courtright, Stephen H., 534n46
Coward, W. M., 684n79
Cranny, C. J., 300, 346n38
Crant, Michael J., 498n195, 568n38,
568n39
Crawford, Eean R., 567n30,
575n116
Crawford, Marnie Swerdlin, 534n45
Cremer, David De, 44n13
Crites, John O., 534n35
Cronbach, Lee J., 277n19, 327,
349n94, 683n62
Cronshaw, Steven F., 484n8, 485n24
Crook, Russell, 6
Cropanzano, Russell, 188n54
Crosby, Lawrence A., 45n27
Crown, Deborah F., 642n63
Cullen, Michael J., 574n103
Cunningham, Joseph W., 100n33
Cunningham, Michael R., 641n43,
642n47, 642n51

D

Dailey, John T., 424n91
Dalessio, Anthony T., 346n36
Dalton, Dan R., 639n5
Darnold, Todd C., 184n5, 344n2,
487n44, 487n45, 490n83,
496n172, 497n186, 499n212
Darwin, Charles, 657
Davis, Robert D., 45n30
Davison, H. Kristl, 352n155
Dawes, Robyn M., 656, 660, 662,
682n24, 682n30, 682n35,
682n36, 682n37
Day, David V., 422n67, 429n166

Day, Eric Anthony, 610n30, 610n32,
611n41
Deadrick, D. L., 347n49
Dean, Michelle A., 609n24
DeCorte, Wilfried, 533n23
DelVecchio, Devon, 193n112
Demaree, Robert G., 351n125
Demps, Julius, 486n33, 491n104
DeShon, Richard P., 498n193,
498n194
DeStefano, John, 140
Devlin, Steven E., 418n19
Devore, C. J., 640n19
Diab, Dalia L., 681n23
Dickel, Nina, 186n28, 186n29,
186n30, 186n33
Dickens, William T., 238n21
Dierdorff, Erich C., 44n20, 96,
103n70, 103n71, 103n76
Digman, John M., 567n26
Dilchert, Stephan, 45n30
Dineen, Brian R., 167, 168, 193n112,
193n116, 197n168, 486n42,
487n43
Dipboye, Robert, 444, 467, 469, 470,
473, 484n10, 484n12, 485n21,
485n23, 486n37, 488n59,
488n60, 488n70, 490n95,
491n102, 492n116, 494n148,
494n149, 495n152, 495n158,
495n159, 496n167, 497n178,
498n204, 499n213, 500n231,
566n14
Do, B. R., 533n27
Dolev, Karmela, 640n9
Doll, Sarah, 177
Donovan, John J., 573n95
Donovan, Michelle A., 35, 45n23,
573n101
Dorerspike, D., 347n48
Dorsey, David W., 45n24
Dougherty, Thomas W., 495n160,
500n235
Douglas, McDonnell, 121
Doyerspike, Dennis, 684n75
Drasgow, Fritz, 533n26, 533n27
Drazin, Hayagreeva, 189n65
Dreher, George F., 598, 609n25
DuBois, Philip, 532n2
Duehr, Emily E., 572n82, 572n83
Dugan, Beverly, 610n34
Duncan, Dale, 197n180
Dunford, Benjamin B., 189n66

Dunleavy, Eric M., 101n49
Dunn, Linda, 417n8
Dunn, Wendy, 566n16
Dunnette, Marvin D., 91n3, 361, 364, 526
Dunning, David, 574n104
Duran, Rochelle, 115
Dustin, Susan L., 233, 344n2, 490n83, 496n172, 499n212
Dwight, Stephen A., 573n95, 573n101
Dzieweczynski, Jessica L., 345n8, 346n37

E

Ebel, Robert L., 665, 666, 683n47
Ebert, Ronald J., 500n235
Eby, Lillian T., 425n118, 426n121, 426n125
Edens, Pamela S., 610n32, 611n41
Edwards, Bryan D., 612n51
Ehrhart, Karen H., 191n86, 534n34
Ehrhart, Mark G., 534n34, 611n47
Eidson, Carl E., Jr, 495n154, 569n56
Eisner, Susan, 424n98
Ellingson, Jill E., 572n92, 573n96
Ellis, Aleksander P. J., 498n193, 498n194
England, George W., 418n10, 418n11, 683n53
Englert, Paul, 611n39
Erdogan, Berrin, 198n186
Erwin, Frank W., 419n23, 419n24, 425n106
Evers, Arne, 219, 465

F

Facteau, Jeffrey D., 428n153, 429n163
Faley, Robert H., 302, 345n6, 345n10, 347n52, 348n65, 423n84, 427n134
Fan, Jinyan, 573n100
Farabee, A., 495n163
Farmer, William F., 569n44
Farr, James L., 533n33
Fay, Charles, 500n237
Feild, Hubert S., 44n14, 149n55, 189n68, 193n121, 424n100, 549, 570n59, 593
Feldman, Daniel C., 425n118, 426n121, 426n125
Ferris, Gerald R., 20n5, 498n198, 498n199
Fink, Laurence S., 487n48

Fiorito, Jack, 233
Firth, Patricia, 494n150, 494n151
Fisher, Cynthia D., 683n59
Flanagan, John C., 101n43
Fleenor, John W., 191n95
Fleisher, Matthew S., 611n42
Fleishman, Edwin A., 77, 102n52, 524, 525, 534n41, 534n42, 534n43
Fletcher, Robert H., 426n129
Flinders, Karl, 198n183
Flory, A., 425n109
Flynn, James R., 238n21, 277n8
Foldes, Hannah J., 572n82, 572n83
Foley, Richard T., 427n138, 430n181
Ford, J. Kevin, 425n117, 425n119, 427n135, 609n20
Ford, John J., 499n208
Forstner, Klaus, 276n1, 276n5
Foster, Mark S., 611n37, 611n38
Foster, Michael, 193n120
Fox, Suzy, 639n1
Fraefel, Laura, 608n2
Frank, Mark G., 489n78
Franklin, Benjamin, 657
Frederick, James T., 350n106
French, Nita R., 611n37
Frey, Deter, 487n58
Frierson, James G., 421n52
Frone, Michael R., 628, 642n57
Fugate, Mel, 190n77
Funder, David C., 484n11, 488n61, 569n50
Furnham, Adrian, 417n4
Furst, Stacie A., 44n19

G

Gael, Sidney, 100n26
Gao, Dingguo, 573n100
Gardiner, Helen P., 494n145
Gardner, Richard G., 575n114
Garrten, Annegret, 100n20
Gast-Rosenbery, Ilene, 510
Gatewood, Robert, 591, 593, 610n27, 611n37
Gaugler, Barbara B., 488n60, 609n17, 610n28, 610n33
Gebbia, Melissa I., 417n8
Gelfand, Michele J., 188n57
Gentry, William A., 611n38
Gerhardt, Megan W., 570n65, 571n73
Gerhart, Barry, 487n49

Ghiselli, Edwin E., 324, 332, 348n62, 348n70, 349n84, 350n113
Giacobbe, Ralph W., 45n27
Gialluca, Kathleen, 98, 103n74
Gibson, Wade M., 533n26
Gier, Joseph A., 450
Giles, William F., 189n68, 193n121, 424n100, 549, 570n59
Gilliland, Stephen W., 196n151, 345n7, 422n69
Glaze, Ryan M., 533n28, 611n48
Gleaves, David H., 572n93
Glennon, James R., 380, 423n80, 424n95
Gleser, Goldine C., 327, 349n94, 683n62
Goff, Maynard, 611n40
Goffin, Richard D., 399, 408, 410, 428n151, 431n194, 431n198, 573n102, 611n40
Goldberg, Lewis, 566n7, 567n27, 567n28, 681n20
Goldstein, Irwin L., 287, 345n14, 345n16, 345n17, 346n26, 346n35, 684n74, 684n85, 685n88
Gonzalez-Mule, Erik, 532n14
Goodchild, J., 639n4
Gooding, Richard Z., 346n40, 364
Goodman, Deborah, 485n26, 492n118, 493n128, 500n236
Goodstein, Leonard D., 571n78
Gordon, Leonard, 545
Gordon, Michael E., 197n172
Gordon, Raymond L., 500n234
Gordon, Thomas R., 426n131, 427n136, 501n242
Gosling, Samuel, 549
Gottier, Richard, 536, 537, 566n5, 566n13
Gough, Harrison, 545
Gowing, Marilyn K., 353n162
Graefe, Andreas, 657, 682n25
Grambow, Dana M., 188n52
Grant, Donald L., 609n15
Green, Samuel B., 102n58
Greenlaw, Paul S., 147n3, 147n5
Greer, Olen L., 350n107
Greising, Leslie A., 191n93
Griffeth, Rodger W., 484n17
Griffin, Barbara, 533n32
Gross, Jack, 142
Grossman, Paul, 148n29

Grote, Christopher L., 430n190, 431n201

Groth-Marnat, Gary, 277n11, 277n13, 278n32, 278n38

Grove, David, 476, 499n222

Guilford, J. P., 348n79, 545

Guion, Robert M., 20n9, 99, 101n34, 103n77, 228, 237n9, 238n18, 278n30, 300, 304, 346n34, 346n38, 347n59, 348n78, 353n156, 506, 532n8, 536, 537, 566n5, 566n13, 575n113, 608n4

Gulliksen, Harold, 264, 278n29

Gully, Stanley M., 199n194

Gunther, Katie M., 45n26

Gutman, Arthur, 101n49, 429n165, 429n170, 430n175

Guys, Melissa L., 532n7

H

Haaland, Stephanie, 610n31

Hackett, Rick D., 494n145

Hahn, Jeffrey, 591

Hahn, June, 610n26

Hanley, K., 495n163

Hansen, F., 184n9

Hanson, Mary Ann, 425n111, 509, 532n11, 571n77

Harold, Crystal M., 419n28, 556, 572n90

Harris, Michael M., 197n179, 335, 351n124, 487n48, 496n168, 498n196

Harris, William G., 625, 627, 641n43, 642n51

Harrison, Lisa, 117

Hartigan, J. A., 147n4, 351n133

Hartshorne, Hugh, 575n117

Hartwell, Chris J., 448, 489n79, 490n86, 490n88, 490n91, 491n108, 493n121, 493n123, 494n147, 496n175, 497n177, 499n221, 501n243, 501n244

Harvey, Robert J., 100n27, 102n69

Hass, Marcia E., 424n99

Hausdorf, Peter A., 197n180

Hause, Emily L., 184n11

Hausknecht, John P., 422n67, 429n166, 533n33

Haut, Allyson, 430n190, 431n201

Hayes, Theodore L., 488n60

Hazer, John T., 350n109, 431n196

Heath, Chip, 574n104

Hebl, Michelle R., 188n56

Hedge, Jerry W., 45n24

Hedges, Larry, 335, 351n126

Heetderks, Thomas D., 20n5

Heggestad, Eric D., 103n72

Heller, Daniel, 552, 571n71

Heller, Matthew, 565n3, 572n84

Henderson, Norman D., 534n40

Hendricks, Cynthia, 573n99

Heneman, Herbert G., 66, 379, 499n208

Henle, Christine A., 676, 684n71, 684n78

Hennessey, Harry W., Jr., 610n27

Henry, R. A., 347n47

Herbst, Dara, 407, 413, 423n75, 427n139, 430n186

Hernandez, Morela, 188n56

Higgins, Chad A., 410, 431n199, 498n198, 498n199, 567n21, 569n41

Highhouse, Scott, 160, 184n11, 190n73, 350n109, 655, 680n3, 681n13, 681n15, 681n23

Hill, Linda A., 189n67, 199n194

Hillery, Joseph M., 348n66

Hinton, Kimberly, 112

Hirsh, Hannah Rothstein, 510

Hoffman, Brian J., 601, 611n42, 611n44, 611n45

Hoffman, Calvin, 29, 43n8, 324, 337, 340, 349n85, 352n141, 352n149

Hofstede, Geert, 455, 492n111

Hogan, James B., 419n26

Hogan, Joyce, 524, 525, 526, 527, 534n44, 545, 550, 551, 570n63, 620, 640n14

Hogan, Robert, 545, 567n25, 620, 640n14

Holden, Lisa M., 29, 43n8, 340, 352n148

Holland, Brent, 550, 551, 570n63

Hollenbeck, John R., 353n158, 486n39, 566n14

Holley, William H., 149n55

Hollinger, R. C., 639n3

Holtom, Brooks C., 192n99

Holtz, Brian C., 417n5

Hom, Peter W., 484n17

Horovitz, Bruce, 197n170

Hough, Leatta M., 381, 418n15, 422n65, 509, 526, 532n11, 556,

567n19, 567n20, 569n45, 571n77, 572n91, 573n94, 573n96

Houston, Janis S., 569n44

Houston, Lawrence, 44n21

Hudson, Dayton, 556

Huett, D. L., 499n208

Huffcutt, Allen, 149n57, 442, 443, 456, 463, 468, 479, 480, 485n25, 485n29, 485n30, 488n65, 488n67, 488n68, 491n103, 493n119, 493n122, 495n153, 495n154, 495n155, 497n185, 500n226, 500n229, 500n233, 569n52, 569n56, 570n58

Hughes, Garry L., 425n108

Hulin, Charles, 301, 347n47

Hülsheger, Ute R., 490n94

Hunter, John E., 46n39, 46n40, 100n17, 100n18, 277n12, 277n22, 328, 330, 332, 333, 334, 335, 337, 347n51, 348n66, 349n88, 349n96, 349n97, 350n99, 350n101, 350n108, 351n114, 351n116, 351n121, 351n122, 351n132, 352n136, 364, 366, 392, 393, 399, 400, 418n21, 419n29, 419n31, 425n115, 426n120, 426n123, 426n126, 426n127, 427n137, 428n148, 429n164, 435, 485n28, 509, 510, 511, 512, 513, 514, 532n12, 532n15, 532n16, 533n20, 668, 682n39, 682n40, 683n58

Hunter, Rhonda F., 364, 399, 418n21, 419n31, 426n120, 428n148, 533n20

Huy, Le, 533n22

I

Ilies, Remus, 45n31, 570n65, 571n72, 571n73

Impara, James C., 237n11

Imus, Anna, 573n99

Inouye, Jillian, 567n26

In-Sue, Oh, 532n14, 533n22

Israelski, Edmond W., 581, 608n7

J

Jackson, Donald W., Jr., 45n27

Jackson, Doug, 545

Jackson, Duncan, 611n39

Jackson, Katherine, 78, 79, 81
Jackson, Susan J., 467, 497n178
Jacobs, Rick R., 126, 127, 148n31,
    393, 425n107, 426n122,
    491n109, 683n52, 684n70,
    684n73, 684n82
Jago, Ann I., 534n45
Jako, Robert A., 485n26, 492n118,
    493n128, 500n236
James, J., 431n196
James, Lawrence R., 335, 351n125,
    545
Janovics, Jay E., 489n74
Jansen, Anne, 608n2
Jansen, Paul G., 609n18
Janz, Tom, 451, 491n97, 491n98
Jarrett, Stephen M., 611n48
Jeanneret, P. Richard, 100n28,
    100n31, 103n75, 340,
    352n145
Jensen, Sanne S., 147n3, 147n5
Johnson, Erin, 45n31, 468,
    497n184
Johnson, James, 425n116
Johnson, Jonathan L., 43n7
Jolly, James P., 421n52
Jonas, Eva, 487n58
Jones, Daniel W., 276n2
Jones, David A., 20n7, 487n46
Jones, Edward, 155
Jones, John W., 572n87, 640n10,
    640n12, 641n43, 642n51
Jones, K. C., 490n85
Joseph, Dana L., 533n24
Judge, Timothy A., 185n18, 186n24,
    189n69, 379, 410, 431n199,
    488n66, 498n198, 498n199,
    540, 542, 550, 552, 561,
    565n1, 566n17, 567n21,
    567n30, 568n32, 568n35,
    569n41, 569n43, 570n62,
    570n65, 571n71, 571n72,
    571n73, 575n115, 575n116,
    575n121
Judice, T. Nichole, 499n218
Junco, Elliott, 194n128

K
Kacmar, Micki K., 495n161
Kahn, Steven C., 407
Kahneman, Daniel, 156, 186n36, 438,
    487n56, 491n99
Karl, Katherine, 496n165

Kataoka, Heloneida C., 499n207
Kausel, Edgar E., 187n46
Keeney, Michael J., 101n41
Kemp, C., 417n5
Kepes, Sven, 346n32, 348n67
Ketchen, David J., Jr, 20n3
Kethley, Bryan, 379, 395, 421n53,
    423n78, 425n114, 427n133,
    427n138, 430n181, 493n125,
    495n156
Kici, Guler, 101n44
Kilduff, Martin, 167
Kilian, Britta, 534n34
Kim, Mee Sook, 198n190
Kim, Sandra S., 188n57
Kim, Youngsang, 20n4
King, Nancy J., 430n188
King, Sandra, 407
Kinicki, Angelo J., 484n17
Kirsch, Michael, 346n40, 364
Klehe, Ute-Christine, 490n93,
    493n122
Kleiger, David M., 680n2, 681n9,
    681n21
Kleiman, Lawrence S., 302, 345n6,
    345n10, 347n52, 423n84
Kleinmann, Martin, 350n112,
    490n93, 608n2, 610n36,
    611n44
Kleinmuntz, Benjamin, 681n16,
    685n95
Klimoski, Richard J., 666, 683n51,
    683n60
Kline, Theresa J. B., 345n5
Klinger, Ryan L., 567n30, 575n116
Klion, Reid, 641n43, 642n51
Koc, Edwin, 177
Koch, Anna, 100n20, 101n44
Kohn, Laura, 491n102
Konig, Cornelius J., 350n110,
    350n112, 490n93, 608n2
Konz, Andrea, 97, 103n73
Kostek, John, 681n13
Kostiuk, Stephanie A., 638, 639,
    643n84, 643n86, 644n91
Kotch, Debra, 643n66, 643n68
Kramer, Maria L., 568n38
Kreiner, Glen E., 190n77
Kristof-Brown, Amy L., 467,
    496n176, 497n184
Kuder, George F., 255, 277n17
Kulik, C. C., 533n31
Kulik, J. A., 533n31

Kunce, Charles, 420n38, 420n42
Kuncel, Nathan R., 566n7, 601, 602,
    611n43, 654, 680n2, 681n9,
    681n21
Kutcher, Eugene, 463, 494n146,
    494n150, 494n151

L
Laczo, Roxanne M., 45n29, 225,
    238n15
Ladd, Robert T., 611n44
Lahy, Par, 503, 532n1
Lampierre, Laurent M., 494n145
Lance, Charles E., 611n37, 611n38
Landers, Ron N., 485n31, 488n69,
    493n124
Landy, Frank J., 77, 102n51, 300, 337,
    346n39, 352n139
Lanivich, Stephen E., 194n128
Lanyon, Richard L., 571n78
Latham, Gary P., 43n5, 43n6, 331,
    350n111, 449, 450, 470,
    488n71, 490n96, 499n207
Lautenschlager, Gary J., 419n32,
    419n33
Law, Kenneth S., 568n36
Lawler, Edward E., III, 20n10
Lawshe, Charles H., 233, 238n23,
    318, 345n4, 345n18, 348n76,
    457, 493n126
Le, H., 610n29
Leck, Joanne D., 188n55, 422n73
Lecznar, William B., 424n91
Ledvinka, James, 149n38
Lee, Kibeom, 33, 641n23
Lefkowitz, Joel, 417n8
Legree, Peter J., 612n61
Lenfant, Claude, 276n2
Leo, Michael C., 642n56
Leonard, Bill, 430n184
LePine, Marcie A., 186n25
Levashina, Julia, 448, 489n79,
    490n86, 490n88, 490n91,
    491n108, 493n121, 493n123,
    494n147, 496n175, 497n177,
    499n221, 501n243, 501n244
Levesque, Laurie L., 491n107
Levine, Edward L., 392, 395, 424n102,
    425n109, 425n112, 425n116,
    426n131, 427n136
Levine, Jonathan D., 424n102
Levishina, Julia, 483n3, 498n197
Lezotte, Daniel V., 574n105

Li, Ning, 540, 561, 566n11, 567n18, 568n31, 575n114, 575n117
Liden, Robert C., 487n50
Lievens, Filip, 75, 102n50, 102n53, 102n59, 197n179, 428n156, 428n157, 491n100, 498n202, 533n23, 533n29, 574n103, 606, 608n2, 610n30, 610n35, 612n50, 612n53, 612n58, 612n59
Lim, Choon-Hwa, 492n114
Limpaphayom, Wanthanee Lee, 427n138, 430n181
Lincoln, Robyn, 489n78
Ling, Juan, 193n112, 197n168
Lockwood, Chris A., 484n17
Loher, Brian T., 431n196
Lopez, Felix, 100n32, 573n100
Lorber, Lawrence Z., 683n65
Lorenzo, Robert V., 609n19
Lowe, Rosemary H., 379, 421n51
Lubin, Joann S., 683n63
Luchman, Joseph, 483n4, 484n16, 485n19, 486n40
Lüdtke, Oliver, 567n22
Luther, Nathan, 640n15
Lykken, David Z., 640n7
Lyon, Julie, 162

Lyons, Brian D., 101n41

M
Ma, Rong, 492n113
Maale, Amanda, 658, 660, 661, 663
Mabon, Hunter, 350n102
Macan, Therese H., 188n52, 470, 484n10, 485n21, 486n37, 490n95, 492n116, 494n149, 495n159, 495n163, 499n213, 500n230
Machwirth, L. I., 424n105
Mackenzie, Scott B., 43n7, 43n10, 44n12, 44n16
Madigan, R. M., 347n49
Mael, Fred A., 418n12, 423n83
Mahto, Raj V., 496n169
Malone, Michael P., 424n92
Malos, Stanley B., 494n144
Malpa, Rebecca, 658, 660, 661
Maltarich, Mark A., 532n13
Maltby, Lewis, 170, 643n77, 643n79
Manese, W. R., 683n64
Marcus, Bernd, 45n33, 641n23
Martin, Casey, 112

Mason, Dave, 658, 660, 661
Massengill, Douglas P., 197n172
Matiaske, Wenzel, 192n99
Matthew, Gerald, 568n37
Mattson, Joyce, 418n19
Maurer, Steven D., 500n237
Maurer, Todd J., 493n130, 496n174, 499n219
May, Mark, 575n118
Maye, Doris M., 426n131, 427n136
Mayfield, Eugene C., 499n217
Mazurkiewica, Mark D., 103n72
McCarthy, Julie M., 399, 408, 410, 428n151, 431n194, 431n198, 497n181
McClure, Tara K., 533n21
McCormick, Brian W., 534n46
McCormick, Ernest J., 66, 91n1, 100n28, 100n31, 101n38
McCrae, Robert R., 544, 545, 567n29, 568n33
McDaniel, Michael A., 150n58, 311, 346n32, 348n67, 392, 393, 425n115, 425n116, 426n127, 426n128, 473, 488n68, 499n219, 603, 610n29, 611n46, 612n54, 612n56, 612n61
McDonald, James, 180
McFarland, Lynn A., 419n28, 492n112, 566n4, 586, 587, 609n11, 609n12
McHenry, Jeffrey J., 41, 45n36, 509, 532n11, 571n77
McIntyre, Michael, 545
McKay, Patrick F., 150n58, 156, 186n34
McKenzie, Robert C., 46n39, 349n97, 350n101, 350n108
McNally, Rand, 361
McNelly, Theresa L., 610n32, 611n41
McPhail, S. Morton, 337, 340, 352n141, 352n147, 352n149
Meade, Adam W., 191n95, 611n45
Meehl, Paul, 653, 681n5, 681n6
Meier, Laurenz L., 45n32, 639n1
Melchers, Klaus, 608n2, 610n36, 611n44
Mellewigt, Thomas, 192n99
Meng, Hui, 573n100
Meriac, John P., 601, 611n42
Messick, Samuel, 345n3
Meyers, Isabel Briggs, 545
Michael, Joan J., 191n95

Michels, Kenneth M., 278n28
Miles, Jeffrey A., 491n107
Miller, Ernest C., 370, 420n45, 420n46
Miller, Janice L., 643n70, 643n71
Miller, Robert, 100n20
Miller, Rodney K., 408, 430n192
Mills, Amy E., 609n23
Miner, John, 554, 572n81
Miron-Shatz, Talya, 681n19
Mischel, Walter, 536, 566n10, 567n23, 569n54
Mitchell, James V., 278n40, 568n34
Mitchell, Jimmy L., 101n35
Mohamed, Amin A., 493n125, 495n156
Mol, Stefan T., 193n113
Mol, Stefen T., 571n68
Molinsky, Andrew, 492n115
Mook, Jonathan R., 572n85
Morgan, John, 494n150, 494n151
Morgeson, Frederick P., 53, 55, 96, 100n16, 100n19, 103n71, 103n76, 448, 483n1, 487n47, 487n51, 489n79, 490n86, 490n88, 490n91, 491n101, 491n108, 493n121, 493n123, 494n147, 496n175, 497n177, 497n182, 498n206, 499n209, 499n221, 501n243, 501n244, 537, 566n14
Morris, Jerry A., 682n38
Morris, Scott B., 148n32
Morrison, John D., 574n108
Morrison, Robert F., 382, 424n95
Morsh, Joseph E., 66
Moscoso, Silvia, 289, 345n21, 488n62, 493n127
Moser, K., 424n105
Mossholder, Kevin W., 44n14, 340, 352n152
Motowidlo, Stephen J., 43n9, 468, 497n190, 498n192, 612n57
Mount, Michael K., 45n31, 237n8, 351n118, 400, 424n96, 429n161, 488n66, 532n14, 534n46, 537, 544, 550, 552, 565n1, 566n8, 566n12, 566n15, 566n16, 566n17, 568n32, 568n40, 569n43, 570n62, 570n66, 570n67, 571n71, 573n97, 575n115, 575n121, 575n122, 575n124

Moynihan, Lisa M., 186n25
Muchinsky, Paul M., 534n37
Mueller, Lorin, 682n41
Mueller-Hanson, Rose A., 44n22
Mulaik, Stanley A., 351n125
Muldrow, Tressie W., 46n39, 349n97, 350n101, 350n108
Mumford, Michael D., 351n125, 381, 421n56, 421n58, 423n82, 534n41, 534n43
Murphy, Kevin R., 126, 127, 148n31, 294, 317, 345n8, 346n37, 348n71, 348n73, 351n115, 351n123, 537, 566n14
Murray, Mack J., 682n39
Mussio, Stephan J., 102n66, 197n172

N

Nagy, Gabriel, 567n22
Nagy, Mark S., 431n200
Nason, Earl, 487n57, 497n180
Nathan, Barry R., 29, 43n8
Naylor, James C., 246, 277n9, 327, 349n87, 349n92, 682n28
Nelson, Johnathon K., 44n22
Neuberg, Steven L., 499n218
Neubert, Mitch, 570n67
Newbolt, William H., 611n37
Newman, David, 162
Newmann, Daniel A., 533n24
Ng, Thomas W. H., 425n118, 426n121, 426n125
Nguyen, Nhung, 603, 611n46, 612n54, 612n56
Nickels, B. J., 417n7
Nicklin, Jessica A., 428n158
Nobile, Robert J., 407
Noe, Raymond A., 193n116, 346n40, 364
Noon, S. L., 347n47
Nooren, Patrick M., 302, 337, 347n53, 347n55, 352n140
Nordstrom, Cynthia R., 428n146
Norris, Dwayne, 682n41
Northrup, Lois, 510
Nunnally, Jum C., 278n33
Nyberg, Anthony J., 532n13

O

O'Boyle, Ernest, 237n4, 330, 331, 350n103
Ocasio, Benjamin P., 348n66
Odle-Dusseau, Heather N., 640n18, 641n33, 641n37

Offerman, Lynn R., 353n162
Oh, In-Sue, 575n114
Ones, Deniz S., 45n28, 45n30, 100n18, 277n23, 324, 347n42, 349n86, 351n132, 489n72, 537, 566n16, 569n51, 571n75, 572n82, 572n83, 619, 623, 624, 625, 640n11, 640n17, 641n26, 641n29, 641n30, 641n34, 642n46, 642n52, 680n2, 681n9, 681n21
Oostrom, Janneke K., 612n52
Oppler, Scott H., 425n111, 682n41
Organ, Dennis W., 43n11, 499n220
O'Roarke, Cyndy, 658, 660, 661, 663
Orr, John M., 335, 351n124
Ostroff, Cheri, 187n44, 196n166, 586, 609n10
Oswald, Frederick L., 367, 420n35, 420n36, 422n65, 567n19, 567n20, 569n45, 573n94, 573n98, 573n99
Otondo, Robert F., 190n76, 496n169
Outerbridge, A. N., 347n51
Outtz, James, 684n74, 684n85, 685n88
Owens, Lillian A., 423n81
Owens, William A., 361, 380, 381, 418n16, 419n23, 423n80, 423n82, 423n86, 423n88, 424n95, 424n97
Ozer, Muammer, 44n18

P

Paepe, Ananeleen De, 498n202
Page, Ronald C., 100n29, 492n112, 566n4
Paine, Julie Beth, 43n10
Pajo, Karl, 428n152, 428n154, 430n187
Palmer, David K., 484n9, 485n27, 490n90
Pan, Wei, 345n19
Parker, Debra, 488n60
Paronto, Matthew D., 642n56
Paronto, Matthew E., 197n174
Parsons, Charles K., 487n50
Pater, Irebe E. de, 568n35
Patterson, Fiona, 606, 612n53
Paullin, Cheryl, 418n15
Pearlman, Kenneth, 46n40, 100n17, 510, 533n26
Peck, Don, 20n12
Pedhazur, Elazur J., 237n2, 237n6, 278n31
Peluchette, Joy, 496n165

Perkins, Judy, 400
Perlson, Michael R., 345n20
Perrewe, Pamela L., 20n5
Perryman, Alexa A., 20n5
Peters, Douglas, 430n193
Peterson, Donald A., 499n217
Petkova, Antoaneta P., 185n21
Philbrick, Jane H., 424n99
Phillip, Niel, 609n13, 609n14
Phillips, James S., 347n41
Phillips, Jean M., 197n167, 199n194, 486n39
Piasentin, Kelly A., 20n7, 487n46
Plake, Barbara S., 237n11
Plamondon, Kevin E., 35, 45n23
Pleban, Robert J., 45n26
Ployhart, Robert E., 184n1, 197n178, 301, 347n43, 348n74, 348n80, 349n82, 417n5, 422n65, 422n70, 556, 572n90, 611n47
Plumlee, Lynnette B., 585, 609n8
Podsakoff, Philip M., 30, 43n7, 43n10, 44n12, 44n15, 44n16
Polyhart, Robert E., 20n4
Porter, W. R., 425n109
Posthuma, Richard A., 483n1, 487n47, 487n51, 491n101, 497n182, 498n206, 499n209
Postlethwaite, Bennett E., 534n46, 569n42
Potosky, Denise, 418n20, 419n30, 421n60, 515, 518, 532n18, 533n25
Premack, Steven L., 20n2
Preston, Jennifer, 194n127
Prien, Erich P., 43n2, 425n108
Priestley, Joseph, 657
Prieto, José M., 353n163
Prinz, Marion A., 610n36
Pryon, H. C., 407
Psotka, Joseph, 612n61
Pui, Shuang-Yueh, 681n23
Pulakos, Elaine D., 34, 35, 36, 44n22, 45n23, 45n24, 425n111, 487n57, 497n180
Pursell, Elliott D., 43n6, 449, 450, 490n96

Q

Quaintance, Marilyn K., 102n52
Quinoñes, Miguel A., 392, 393, 425n117, 425n119, 427n135, 430n177, 534n45

Quinoñes, Ralph L., 429n168
Quist, Joshua, 102n57

R

Raad, Boele De, 489n75
Rabinowitz, Peter A., 407
Rader, Mark, 486n32, 491n106
Ramos, Robert, 101n40, 349n95
Rao, Robert, 189n65
Ratcliffe, Shannon H., 495n161
Rau, Barbara L., 189n59
Raymark, Patrick H., 101n34,
    575n113, 640n18, 641n33,
    641n37
Ready, Douglas A., 189n67, 199n194
Reeve, Charlie L., 190n73
Reeves, Cody J., 534n46
Reilly, Greg, 532n13
Reilly, Richard R., 364, 399, 421n59,
    423n77, 428n149, 581, 608n7,
    683n64
Repa, Barbara Kate, 419n34
Reshef, Amir, 350n110
Rezell, Elizabeth J., 353n161
Ricci, Frank, 140
Rich, Gregory A., 43n7
Richardson, Marion W., 255, 277n17
Ricks, James H., 238n20
Rindova, Violina P., 185n21
Ringer, Richard C., 643n70, 643n71
Robbins, Steve B., 533n22
Roberson, Quineita M., 185n17
Roberts, Brent W., 566n7, 567n22
Roberts, Richard D., 568n37
Robiner, William N., 430n190,
    431n201
Robinson, David, 581, 608n6
Roccella, Edward J., 276n2
Roch, Sylvia G., 428n158
Rodell, Jessica B., 567n30, 575n116
Roehling, Mark V., 184n10, 186n25,
    191n83, 494n144
Rollins, Glen, 155
Ronan, William W., 43n2
Rosen, Benson, 44n19
Rosen, David, 407
Rosenthal, Douglas B., 609n17
Rosse, Joseph G., 556, 642n63,
    643n70, 643n71
Rosseau, Denise M., 20n11
Rostow, Cary D., 45n30
Roth, Philip L., 101n48, 148n30,
    149n57, 194n128, 194n129,

350n102, 418n20, 419n30,
    421n60, 426n124, 427n132,
    443, 463, 485n29, 485n30,
    488n65, 488n67, 488n68,
    493n122, 495n153, 495n154,
    495n155, 497n185, 514, 515,
    532n17, 532n18, 533n22,
    569n52, 569n56, 570n58, 586,
    587, 591, 606, 609n11, 609n12,
    609n24, 612n55, 640n18,
    641n33, 641n37, 681n12,
    682n33, 684n68, 684n77,
    684n81, 684n84
Rothstein, Hannah R., 351n117,
    351n120, 364, 365, 419n23,
    419n24, 422n62, 425n106,
    573n102
Rowe, Patricia, 499n214
Roy, Radha, 573n99
Rubin, Robert S., 44n20, 103n76
Rudolph, Amy S., 610n28
Russell, Craig J., 363, 418n18, 418n19
Russell, J. T., 184n7, 327, 349n91,
    356, 357, 417n1
Russo, J. Edward, 678, 681n22,
    685n89, 685n91
Ryan, Ann Marie, 197n178, 422n68,
    422n70, 455, 492n112,
    498n193, 498n194, 566n4,
    642n54
Ryan, Katherine, 43n11
Rybroek, George Van, 408
Rynes, Sara L., 20n8, 173, 184n5,
    195n142, 487n44, 487n45,
    487n49, 497n186

S

Saari, Lise, 449, 450, 490n96
Sackett, Paul R., 36, 45n28, 45n29,
    187n41, 191n90, 225, 238n15,
    324, 335, 346n24, 346n33,
    348n63, 351n124, 353n159,
    428n156, 429n159, 485n31,
    486n41, 488n69, 491n100,
    493n124, 532n7, 533n23,
    572n92, 573n96, 574n103, 598,
    601, 602, 609n25, 611n43,
    612n50, 612n58, 612n59, 619,
    624, 625, 626, 640n16, 640n19,
    640n21, 640n22, 641n24,
    641n26, 641n27, 641n28,
    641n32, 641n40, 642n44,
    642n45, 642n48, 642n53,

642n54, 684n77, 684n79,
    684n81
Sagan, Carl, 658, 660, 661
Saks, Alan M., 188n55, 422n73,
    496n170
Sala, Fabio, 489n73
Salas, Eduardo, 98, 103n74
Salgado, Jesus, 289, 345n21, 348n68,
    488n62, 490n94, 493n127,
    566n9, 571n69, 571n70
Sanchez, Juan, 75, 102n50, 102n53,
    102n59
Saucier, Gerard, 567n27, 567n28
Saunders, David M., 188n55, 422n73
Sawyer, Jack, 680n1, 681n7
Scarpello, Vida, 149n38
Schaefer, Arthur Gross, 429n168,
    430n177
Scherbaum, Charles, 341, 353n157
Schippmann, J. S., 426n124
Schlei, Barbara Lindemann, 148n29
Schmelkin, Liora Pedhazur, 237n2,
    237n6, 278n31
Schmidt, Frank L., 46n39, 46n40,
    100n17, 100n18, 277n12,
    277n22, 277n23, 290, 311, 328,
    330, 332, 333, 334, 335, 337,
    346n23, 346n25, 347n42,
    347n51, 348n66, 348n69,
    349n88, 349n96, 349n97,
    350n99, 350n101, 350n105,
    350n108, 351n114, 351n116,
    351n117, 351n121, 351n122,
    351n132, 352n136, 353n164,
    366, 392, 393, 400, 419n23,
    419n24, 419n29, 425n106,
    425n113, 425n115, 426n123,
    426n126, 426n127, 427n137,
    429n164, 435, 457, 478, 483n7,
    485n28, 486n32, 491n106,
    493n129, 499n219, 500n224,
    509, 510, 512, 513, 532n15,
    533n20, 610n29, 619, 640n11,
    640n17, 641n29, 641n34,
    642n46, 668, 676, 677, 682n39,
    682n40, 683n58, 684n69,
    684n80, 684n87
Schmit, Mark J., 101n34, 569n56,
    575n113
Schmitt, Neal, 45n24, 277n15, 284,
    336, 345n9, 346n40, 349n90,
    351n119, 351n127, 364, 367,
    420n35, 420n36, 420n38,

420n42, 485n22, 487n57, 497n180, 566n14, 573n98, 586, 609n10, 609n20, 609n23, 611n49, 624, 625, 641n40, 666, 683n51, 683n60, 685n90

Schneider, Benjamin, 97, 103n73, 284, 345n9, 345n14, 345n17, 346n26, 349n90, 685n90

Schneider, J. R., 351n119

Schoemaker, Paul J. H., 678, 681n22, 685n89, 685n91

Schoenfeldt, Barbara B., 345n20

Schoenfeldt, Lyle F., 345n20, 423n86, 423n88, 424n97, 683n59

Schuler, H., 45n33, 424n105

Schulte, M., 187n44

Schulz-Hardt, Stefen, 487n58

Schumsky, Donald A., 345n19

Schurig, Ira, 611n48

Schwab, Donald P., 499n208

Sciarrino, James, 608n3

Scott, John C., 574n105

Scroggins, Wesley A., 682n38

Scullen, Steven E., 425n106

Seashore, Harold G., 238n20

Segall, Daniel O., 533n26

Seibert, Scott E., 552, 568n38, 571n74

Selover, R. B., 534n38

Serlie, Alec, 612n52

Sever, Joy Marie, 185n21

Shaffer, Jonathan A., 569n42

Shahani-Denning, Comila, 484n10, 485n21, 486n37, 488n59, 490n95, 492n116, 494n149

Shaller, Elliot H., 111, 148n12

Shapiro, D. L., 685n94

Sharf, James C., 421n55

Shartle, Carol L., 424n90

Shaw, James B., 683n59

Shepherd, William, 533n26, 533n27

Sheps, Sheldon G., 276n2

Sherman, Mark, 569n47, 569n48, 572n80

Shimberg, Benjamin, 609n9

Shine, Lester C., 327, 349n92

Shiner, Rebecca, 566n7

Shipp, Abbie J., 44n19

Shos, Mindy K., 45n25

Shotland, Allison, 500n238

Sieck, Winston R., 681n17

Siers, Brian P., 489n74

Silbey, Val, 682n29

Sill, Nikki, 683n50, 683n54

Silva, Jay, 683n52, 684n70, 684n73, 684n82

Simola, Sheldene K., 484n18, 490n87

Simon, Lauren S., 567n30, 575n116

Simon, Theodore, 505

Simpson, Joseph R., 643n87

Skarlicki, Daniel P., 488n71

Slaughter, Jerel E., 157, 187n46, 188n54, 190n80

Small, Bruce, 479, 493n120, 499n223, 500n228

Smith, David E., 611n37

Smith, Dylan M., 499n218

Smith, Geoffrey W., 484n18

Smith, Marlene A., 303, 347n56, 490n87

Smith, Mary K., 102n66

Snell, Andrea F., 419n26

Sniezek, Janet A., 469, 498n201

Solamon, Jerry M., 493n130, 496n174, 534n34

Soltis, Scott M., 486n42, 487n43

Song, Lynda J., 568n36

Sorensen, Kerry L., 425n118, 426n121, 426n125

Soumerai, Stephen B., 426n129

Sparks, Paul C., 91n5, 419n23

Spector, Paul E., 45n32, 278n36, 639n1

Speer, Andrew B., 611n40

Springbett, B. M., 489n80, 499n210, 499n215

Stabile, Susan J., 642n49

Stalcup, Sue S., 368, 420n40, 422n66

Stanton, Jeffrey M., 190n73, 386, 424n104

Stead, William H., 424n90

Steiner, Dirk D., 196n151, 345n7, 422n69, 574n110

Stenquist, John, 521

Stetz, Thomas A., 101n41, 102n57

Stevens, Cynthia K., 165, 192n105, 495n157, 498n203

Stewart, Greg L., 344n2, 447, 483n2, 490n82, 490n83, 490n84, 496n172, 499n212, 562, 568n34, 570n66, 570n67, 575n120

Stillman, Jennifer A, 611n39

Stokes, Garnett S., 365, 419n26, 421n54, 423n78

Stone, Dianna L., 421n57, 643n66, 643n68

Stone, Eugene F., 421n57, 485n29, 485n30, 488n65, 488n67, 497n185

Stone, Nancy J., 443, 569n52, 570n58

Straus, Susan G., 491n107

Strauss, Judy Perkins, 429n161, 568n40

Stringfield, Paul, 428n152, 428n154, 430n187

Strobel, Anja, 100n20, 101n44

Strong, Mark H., 103n75, 340, 352n150

Stults, Daniel M., 609n20

Sturman, Michael C., 426n130

Stutzman, Thomas, 102n58

Sujak, David A., 643n69

Suls, Jerry M., 574n104

Super, Donald E., 534n35

Sutton, Karen, 112

Swider, Brian, 173, 195n146, 447, 483n2, 490n82, 496n168, 498n196

Switzer, F. S., 426n124, 532n17

Sylva, Hella, 193n113

T

Taggar, Simon, 484n18, 490n87

Taggart, James W., 191n93

Tannenbaum, Scott I., 500n238

Tarique, I., 491n109

Taylor, Erwin K., 42, 46n38

Taylor, H. C., 184n7, 327, 349n91, 356, 357, 417n1, 499n223, 500n228

Taylor, Jason E., 533n28, 611n48

Taylor, Paul J., 400, 428n152, 428n154, 430n187, 479, 493n120

Taylor, Susan M., 185n17, 197n175, 469, 498n201

Teachout, Mark S., 425n117, 425n119, 427n135

Telenson, Paul A., 424n94

Tepper, Bennett J., 643n67

Terpstra, David E., 353n159, 379, 395, 421n53, 423n78, 425n114, 427n133, 427n138, 430n181, 493n125, 495n156

Terris, William, 640n10, 640n12

Tesluk, Paul E., 393, 425n107, 426n122

Tett, Robert P., 561, 575n119

Thayer, Paul W., 499n217

Thissen, David, 278n40

Tholl, Ulrich, 276n1, 276n5

Thomas, Robert J., 189n67, 199n194

Thomas, Sanchez-Ku M., 610n29

Thomas, Scott C., 422n67, 429n166

Thomas, Steven L., 682n38

Thompson, Duane E., 51, 91n7, 91n14, 99, 101n37

Thompson, Naceema, 431n200

Thompson, Toni A., 51, 91n7, 91n14, 99, 101n37

Thoresen, Carl J., 567n21, 569n41

Thoresen, Joseph D., 611n38

Thorndike, Robert L., 238n17, 349n81, 664, 682n44

Thornton, George C., III, 589, 609n17, 610n27, 610n33

Tian, Siva T., 573n100

Tichy, Jan, 190n74

Tilton, Kendel, 431n196

Tippins, Nancy T., 455, 533n26

Todd, Samuel, 20n3

Tommasi, George W., 410, 428n146, 431n197

Toquam, Jody L., 509, 532n11, 571n77

Tower, Spencer L., 486n39

Trautwein, Ulrich, 567n22

Traver, Holly, 500n238

Trevor, Charlie O., 533n33

Triana, Mary, 400, 428n155, 431n195, 549, 570n60, 571n76

Troxtel, Deborah D., 493n130, 496n174

Trumbo, Don, 442, 488n64

Truxillo, Donald M., 197n174, 198n186, 422n69, 642n56, 684n86

Tsai, Amy, 431n196

Tsai, Wei-Chi, 185n20

Tucker, Jennifer S., 45n26, 198n186

Turban, Daniel B., 155, 185n15, 495n160

Tversky, Amos, 156, 186n36

Tye, Mary G., 379, 421n50, 422n71

Tyler, Peggy, 532n17

U

Uggerslev, Krista L., 20n7, 487n46

Ulm, Ronald A., 426n131, 427n136

Ulrich, Lynn, 442, 488n64

Urbina, Susana, 219, 237n1, 277n10, 277n16, 277n18

V

Valenzi, E. R., 682n29

Van der Molen, Henk T., 571n68, 612n52

Van der Zee, Karen I., 484n15, 486n38, 500n227

Van Dijke, Maius, 44n13

Van Iddekinge, Chad H., 20n5, 194n128, 194n129, 301, 324, 347n43, 348n74, 348n80, 349n82, 495n154, 497n181, 533n22, 569n56, 619, 623, 624, 625, 640n18, 641n33, 641n37

Van Rybroek, George J., 430n192

Van Scotter, James R., 190n76

Van Vianen, Annelies E. M., 568n35

Vargas, Patrick, 186n31, 186n32

Varner, Aaron, 643n83

Vaughn, Daly E., 198n184

Vecchio, Robert P., 184n8

Vera, Dusya, 45n25

Villado, Anton J., 487n53, 533n28

Villanueva, Aileen, 116

Vinkenburg, Claartje J., 609n18

Visweswaran, Chockalingam, 277n23, 324, 347n42, 349n86, 619, 640n11, 640n17, 641n29, 641n30, 641n34, 642n46, 642n52

Vodanovich, Stephen J., 371, 375, 379, 421n49, 421n50, 421n51, 421n61, 422n71, 422n72, 423n76

Voskuijil, Olga, 219, 465

W

Wainer, Howard, 278n40

Waldschmidt, David A., 426n128

Walker, H. Jack, 168, 189n68, 193n121

Wallace, J. Craig, 371, 375, 379, 421n49, 421n50, 421n61, 422n71, 422n72, 423n76

Walsh, W. Bruce, 348n61

Wanek, James E., 626, 640n22, 641n24, 641n26, 641n28, 641n32, 642n44

Wanous, John P., 20n2, 190n75

Watson, Clara, 138

Watson, David, 569n49

Wayne, Sandy J., 495n161

Weathers, Vaunne, 198n186

Webb, Sam C., 423n87, 424n93

Weber, Lauren, 642n61

Webster, Jane, 198n187

Wee, Serena, 516, 533n24

Weekley, Jeff A., 417n5, 419n28, 450, 556, 572n90, 612n61

Weichmann, Darrin, 422n68

Weinberger, Joel, 681n18

Weiner, John A., 574n108

Weller, Ingo, 165, 192n99

Werner, Jon M., 143, 144, 149n56

Wernimont, Paul F., 418n13, 577, 578, 608n1

Wesman, Alexander G., 275, 278n35

Wesson, Michael J., 185n17

West, Bradley J., 498n193, 498n194

West, Stephen G., 569n50

Westen, Drew, 681n18

Westoff, Karl, 100n20, 101n44

Wexley, Kenneth N., 43n5, 43n6

Whetzel, Deborah L., 612n54

White, Craig D., 611n48

White, Leonard A., 425n111

Whitener, Ellen M., 353n158

Whitney, David J., 487n57, 497n180

Whyte, Glen, 331, 350n111, 499n207

Wiemann, Shelly, 45n29, 619, 640n16, 640n21, 642n45, 642n48, 642n53

Wiesner, Willi H., 484n8, 485n24

Wigdor, A. K., 147n4, 351n133

Wiley, John, 213, 219

Wilk, Stephanie L., 427n140

Willemsen, Madde E., 571n68

Williams, Ella, 114

Williams, Felice, 399, 423n85, 428n147, 430n191

Williams, Karen B., 428n146, 431n197

Williamson, Ian O., 185n21

Williamson, Laura Gollub, 462, 494n144

Wilson, F. Robert, 288, 345n19

Wilson, Ian, 533n32

Wilson, Mark A., 102n69, 103n70

Wimbush, James C., 639n5

Winer, Benjamin J., 261, 278n28

Winkler, Silvan, 350n110, 350n112

Winter, Richard, 492n114

Wise, Lauress L., 41, 45n36

Witt, L. A., 45n25, 424n96

Witvliet, Carlijn, 491n110

Woehr, David J., 20n3, 479, 480, 500n226, 500n229, 500n233, 611n42
Wong, Chi-Sum, 568n36
Wong, Dennis T., 642n47

Y

Yang, Irene Wen-Fen, 185n20
Yankelevich, Maya, 681n23
Yerkes, Robert, 503
Yoder, Dale, 66
Yost, Amy Powell, 612n61
Youngcourt, Satoris S., 485n25, 491n103
Yu, Kang Yang Trevor, 186n26

Z

Zayas, Erick, 107
Zedeck, Sheldon, 287, 324, 345n14, 345n16, 345n17, 346n26, 346n35, 348n62, 348n70, 349n84, 675, 684n74, 684n85, 685n88
Zeidner, Moshe, 568n37
Zerga, Joseph, 47, 91n2
Zhang, Yang, 345n8, 346n37
Zhao, Hao, 552, 571n74
Zhou, Zhiging E., 45n32
Ziegert, Jonathan C., 191n86

Zimmerman, Ryan D., 195n146, 372, 400, 418n14, 422n64, 428n155, 431n195, 457, 467, 478, 483n7, 493n129, 497n184, 499n212, 500n224, 549, 566n11, 567n18, 568n31, 570n60, 571n76, 575n117
Zimmerman, Wayne, 545
Zink, Donald L., 429n165, 429n170, 430n175
Zweig, David, 446, 447, 483n6, 484n14, 486n35, 486n36, 489n77, 490n92, 496n166, 500n240, 500n241

SUBJECT INDEX

A

AAP. See Affirmative action programs (AAP)

Ability, 3, 83–84. *See also* Ability tests; Knowledge/skills/abilities (KSAs)
- general cognitive, 290

Ability tests, 216, 503–531. *See also* Cognitive ability tests
- clerical, 523–524
- coaching and, 520–521
- cognitive, 504–517
- definition of, 504
- history of, 503
- Internet and, 517–520
- mechanical, 521–523
- physical, 524
- practice and, 520–521
- recommendations for using, 528–531
- reliability of, 529–530
- validity of, 530–531

Absenteeism, 622

Absolute privilege, 402

Abstracted Business Information Database, 222

Achievement tests, 216, 504. *See also* Ability tests

Active candidates, 169

ADA. See Americans with Disabilities Act (ADA)

ADA Amendments Act of 2008, 113–115

Adaptive behavior, dimensions of, 35

Adaptive performance, 23, 34–36

Adarand Constructors, Inc. v. Pena, 133–134

Administrative errors, 480–481

Adverse impact, 514–517
- cognitive ability tests and, 514–517
- definition of, 119
- mental ability tests and, 514–517
- *Uniform Guidelines on Employee Selection Procedures,* 129

Affirmative action programs (AAP), 131–134
- consent decrees, 132–133
- court order, 132–133

federal contractors, 131–132
- voluntary, 133–134

After-acquired evidence, 367

Age, 376

Age Discrimination in Employment Act of 1967 (ADEA), 110, 142, 528

Agreeableness, 540, 550

Albemarle Paper Co. v. Moody, 51, 285

Alcohol, 630

Allesberry v. Commonwealth of Penn., 459, 462

Allstate Insurance Co, 406

Alternate forms, 251

Ambition, 540

American Banking Association, 223

American Civil Liberties Union, 118

American Foundation for the Blind, 223

American Psychological Association (APA), 223

American Society of Public Administration, 371

Americans with Disabilities Act (ADA), 85, 110–113, 158, 373
- drug testing and, 632–633
- genetic testing and, 635–636
- integrity testing and, 627
- personality tests and, 555
- workers' compensation records and, 413

Amphetamines, 630

Anchoring, 439

Angoff, William, 665

Angoff method, 665, 667

Antisocial behavior, 618

Applicants
- acceptability of, 401
- active candidates, 169
- attracting, 438–439
- attracting and generating interest of, 153–171
- cross-purposes with organizations, 13–14
- drug testing, 631–634
- information presented to, 163
- instructions for, 373–374
- limited information on, 13

maintaining interest of, 171–182
- measuring WRCs of, 441–445
- passive candidates, 169
- polygraph testing of, 616
- pool, 154
- population, 154
- predictability of number of, 163
- providing job information to, 437–438
- questions for, 374
- recruiting, 437–438
- selection measures, 11–12
- self-selection, 173–175

Application blanks, as predictor, 363–369

Application forms, 216
- appropriate and inappropriate questions asked on, 376–379
- biodata and, 360–363
- composition of, 373–374
- developing and revising, 375–383
- enhancing accuracy of, 367–369
- instructions for, 373–374
- legal implications of, 369–372
- for many types of jobs, 379
- nature and role of, 359–363
- questions for applicants, 374
- reference checks and, 396–416
- resumes and, 385–386
- selecting content for, 374–375
- as tool for gathering self-report data, 360
- training and experience evaluations and, 387–396
- using in HR selection, 386–387

Applied Psychological Measurement, 222

Aptitude tests, 216, 504. *See also* Ability tests

Army Alpha, 503

Arrest record, 378

Assessment centers, 578, 588–602.
- *See also* Simulation tests
- beginning of, 588
- behavioral dimensions and, 594
- categorizing participants' behavior in, 595–596
- definition of, 588

Assessment centers (*continued*)
　dimensions and, 589, 596–597
　observing participants' behavior in,
　　595
　overall evaluation ratings and,
　　596–597
　overview, 588
　simulation tests in, 590–592
　traditional assessment devices and,
　　589–590
　training of assessors, 592–596
　validity of, 597–602
Assisting, 30
Association of Conflict Resolution, 770
Association of Test Publishers (ATP),
　222, 223
AT&T, 435, 581, 588, 597–598
ATP. See Association of Test
　Publishers (ATP)
Attributes, 204
At-work personality test, 564
Australia, 620

B

Background information, 216
Background interview, 590
Bad behaviors. See Counterproductive
　work behaviors (CWBs)
*Bailey et al. v. Southeastern Area Joint
　Apprenticeship*, 459, 460–461
Banding, 672–677. *See also* Selection
　decisions
　advantages of, 675
　concerns regarding, 675–676
　establishing, 672–673
　fixed, 673–674
　overview of, 672
　selecting within, 674–675
　sliding, 673–674
　top-score referenced, 673–674
Bank of America, 435
Barbiturates, 630
Barrett, Gerald, 654
Barrick, Murray, 544
BARS. See Behaviorally Anchored
　Rating Scales (BARS)
Base rate, 327
Bass, Bernard, 654
Behavior description interview,
　451–452, 548
Behavioral dimensions, 443, 449
Behavioral Expectation Scales (BES),
　27–28
Behaviorally Anchored Rating Scales
　(BARS), 27–28
Belgium, 455, 559

Beliefs, 464–466
*Bennett Mechanical Comprehension
　Test*, 296, 522–523
Benzodiazepines, 630
Berry, Christopher, 619
Berry v. City of Omaha, 598
BES. See Behavioral Expectation
　Scales (BES)
Binet, Alfred, 505
Biodata. *See also* Application forms
　behavior-type, 362–363
　categories of, 361–363
　definition of, 360
　description of, 360–363
　developing questionnaire for,
　　379–380
　dimensions of, 382–383
　formatting into application form,
　　381
　pilot-testing items of, 381–382
　pool of, 380
　as predictor of job performance,
　　363–367
　prescreening items of, 381–382
　response-type, 361–362
　scoring firms of, 382–383
　validation studies, 364
Biographical data questionnaires, 216
Blacks, 463, 515–516
Bohach v. City of Reno et al., 386
Bona fide occupational qualifications
　(BFOQ) defense, 122
Books, 220–221
Boomerang effect, 178
Bootstrapping, 678
BRB Publications, 414
BRCA1 gene, 635
BRCA2 gene, 635
Bureau of National Affairs, 343
Burger King, 164
Buros Institute of Mental
　Measurements, 221, 274, 529
Byham, William, 594

C

California F Scale, 563
Campbell, John P., 508, 577
Campion, James, 581
Campus interviewing, 13
Canada, 620
Cardiovascular endurance, 525–526
CareerBuilder.com, 168, 169
Cascio, Wayne, 676
Case analysis, 592
CAT. See Computer adaptive testing
　(CAT)

Central Freight Lines, 110
Central tendency, 29
Cephos Corp., 638
Certification, 85
Characterization, 469–470
Cheating, 564
Checking references. See Reference
　checks
Child care, 377
Children, 377
　mental age of, 505
China, 455
Chinese, 6
Citizenship, 377
Civic virtue, 31
Civil Rights Acts of 1866, 116–117
Civil Rights Acts of 1871, 116–117
Civil Rights Acts of 1964, Title VII
　disparate treatment evidence and,
　　121
　drug testing and, 633
　Equal Employment Opportunity
　　Commission and, 106–108
　job analysis and, 50–51
　physical ability tests and, 527
　selection court cases, 141
　voluntary affirmative action
　　programs and, 133
Civil Rights Acts of 1991, 108–109, 672,
　676
Clerical ability tests, 523–524
Clubs, 378
Coaching, 520–521
Cocaine, 629, 630
Codeine, 630
Coefficient of determination, 312
Coefficient of equivalence and stability,
　249
Cognitive abilities, 36
Cognitive ability tests, 504–517, 520
　abilities measured by, 506
　adverse impact and, 514–517
　development of, 505
　implications for selection, 513–514
　importance in selection, 509
　internet and, 517–520
　measurement and, 505–506
　nature of, 507–508
　vs. other selection tests, 512–513
　Project A, 508
　validity generalization studies,
　　508–514
　validity of, 508–514
　Wonderlic Personnel Test, 506–507
Cohen's kappa, 260

Combination method, 671–672

Commerce Clearing House Employment Practice Guide, The, 374

Common measurement units, 234

Common Metric Questionnaire, 62

Compensatory damage, 108

Compensatory method, 659

Computer adaptive testing (CAT), 520

Concurrent validation, 294–298.
  See also Validation
  example of, 294–296
  vs. predictive validation, 300–301
  strengths and weaknesses of, 296–298

Confirmation bias, 439

Confirmation test, 630

Conscientiousness, 540, 550

Construct validation, 303–307

Constructs, 204, 303
  measured, 619–620

Consulting Psychologists Press, 221

Consumer Reporting Employment Clarification Act of 1998 (CRECA), 412

Consumer reports, 412

Content validation, 12, 282–294.
  See also Validation
  appropriateness of, 289–294
  vs. criterion-related validation, 293–294, 303
  examples of, 288–289
  face validity and, 284
  feasibility of, 304
  job analysis and, 284–285, 291–293
  overview, 282–284
  predictor fidelity and, 286–288
  selection procedures and, 286
  subject matter experts (SMEs), 285

Content Validation Form II (CVFII), 286

Content validity index (CVI), 457

Content validity ratio (CVR), 288

Contrasting groups method, 667

Conviction record, 378

Core self-evaluations (CSEs), 542

Correction for attenuation, 321

Correlation, 307–312

Corrigan, Bernard, 660

Cost per hire, 181

Costa, Paul, 544

Counterproductive work behaviors (CWBs), 23, 36–39, 613–639
  actions toward individuals, 38
  actions toward organizations, 38
  cognitive ability and, 512
  definition of, 613

drug testing, 628–634
  examples of, 37
  genetic testing, 634–637
  integrity testing, 617–628
  loss to theft and, 613
  neuroscience-based discrimination and, 638–639
  organizational citizenship behaviors and, 38–39
  overview of, 613–614
  polygraph testing, 614–617
  testing for, 613–639

Court cases
  Adarand Constructors, Inc. v. Pena, 133–134
  Albemarle Paper Co. v. Moody, 51, 285
  Allesberry v. Commonwealth of Penn., 459, 462
  Bailey et al. v. Southeastern Area Joint Apprenticeship, 459, 460–461
  Berry v. City of Omaha, 598
  Bohach v. City of Reno et al., 386
  David Taylor v. James River Corporation, 340
  E. E. Black, Ltd. v. Marshall, 528
  Equal Employment Opportunity Commission v. National Academy of Sciences, 401
  Frank Ricci et al. v. John DeStefano et al., 135, 140–141
  Gilbert v. City of Little Rock, Ark., 459, 460
  Griggs v. Duke Power Co, 51, 134–136
  Hall v. Buck, 402
  Harless v. Duck, 459, 461
  Jack Gross v. FBL Financial Services, 135, 141–142
  Jones v. Mississippi Dept. of Corrections, 459, 461
  Karraker v. Rent-A-Center, 555
  King v. TWA, 459, 460
  Lawrence Berkeley Laboratory case, 635–636
  Lilly v. City of Beckley, 133
  Maine Human Rights Commission v. Dept. of Corrections, 459, 461
  McDonnell Douglas v. Green, 120–121
  McKenna v. Nashville Banner Publishing Co., 367
  Minneapolis Commission on Civil Rights v. Minnesota Chemical Dependency, 459, 461

  Murphy v. United Parcel Service, 113
  Norman-Bloodsaw v. Lawrence Berkeley Laboratory, 635–636
  OFCCP v. Ozark Air Lines, 135, 141
  PGA Tour v. Martin, 112
  Robbins v. White-Wilson Medical Clinic, 459, 460
  Rudder v. District of Columbia, 135, 139–140
  Rutherford v. American Bank of Commerce, 401
  Soroka v. Dayton Hudson, 556
  Spurlock v. United Airlines, 135, 137
  Stamps v. Detroit Edison, 459, 460
  State v. Bonnell, 386
  Sutton v. United Air Lines, 113
  Toyota Motor Mfg., Ky., Inc. v. Williams, 114
  True v. Ladner, 402
  United States v. Georgia Power, 135, 136–137
  U.S. v. South Carolina, 665
  Watson v. Ft. Worth Bank & Trust, 135, 137–138, 458–459
  Weeks v. Southern Bell, 527
  Weiner v. County of Oakland, 459, 460

Creative Networks, LLC, 115

CRECA. See Consumer Reporting Employment Clarification Act of 1998 (CRECA)

Credit rating, 378

Credit Reporting Reform Act of 1996, 412

Criminal records, 413

Criteria, 205–206, 216–217

Criterion
  contamination of, 324–325
  reliability of, 321–322
  restriction of scores, 323
  unreliability of, 336
  validity coefficients and, 321–322

Criterion-related validation, 294–303.
  See also Validation
  concurrent, 294–298
  vs. content validation, 293–294, 303
  correlation and, 307–312
  courts and, 302–303
  empirical considerations in, 307–332
  feasibility of, 304
  over time, 301–302
  prediction and, 312–320
  predictive, 298–300
  requirements for, 301

Criterion-related validation (*continued*)
    sample sizes and, 307–310
    validity coefficients and, 307–310
Critical Incident Technique, 68–75
    advantages and disadvantages of, 70
    application of, 69–70
    collection of, 69
    description of, 68
    gathering, 69–70
    interview questions and, 72
    rating and classifying into job
        dimensions, 70
    situational interview and, 449
    task analysis inventory, integration
        with, 71–73
    work-elated characteristics and, 441
Cronbach's coefficient alpha (α)
    reliability estimates, 256–258
Cross-validation, 317–318
Crystal meth, 630
Culture, 540
Cutoff scores, 663–668. *See also*
    Selection decisions
    Angoff method, 665, 667
    basing on applicants' or others'
        performance, 664–665
    contrasting groups method, 667
    description of, 663–664
    Ebel method, 665–666
    expectancy chart method, 664
    expert judgments and, 665–668
    guidelines, 669
    legal issues in, 667
    modified Angoff method, 665–666
    multiple, 668–669
    predicted yield method, 664
    psychometric issues in, 667
CWBs. See Counterproductive work
    behaviors (CWBs)

D

Darwin, Charles, 657
Data, 16–17
    job sample, 217
    judgmental, 26–29, 217
    objective production, 217
    personnel, 217
    production, 24–26
    training proficiency, 217
Databases, 222
Datafrenzy.com, 169
*David Taylor v. James River
    Corporation*, 340
Dawes, Robyn, 660
Decisions and decision making.
    See Selection decisions

Defamation, 401–403
Demographic groups, 17–18
Department of Labor/Employment
    and Training Administration,
    23
Dictionary of Occupational Titles, 511
Differential validity, 515
Dimension ratings, 594
Dimensions, 589
Direct restriction, 323
Disability, 111
Discriminant validity, 598
Discrimination, 119–128
    avoiding, 166
    basis of, 143–146
    court cases, 458–462
    definition of, 119
    evidence, 120–122
    evidence of, 146–147
    Internet applicant, 127–128
    interviews and, 458–462
    neuroscience-based, 638–639
    research findings on, 462–463
    reverse, 133
    use of statistics, 122–127
Discriminatory impact, 401–403
Disparate impact, 129
    evidence, 122
    validity and, 564
Disparate treatment
    definition of, 119–120
    evidence, 120–122
Dollar criterion, 42
Domain sampling, 286
Double-stage strategy, 669
Dreher, George, 598
Driver's license, 379
Drug testing, 628–634. *See also* Tests
    accuracy, 631
    confirmation test, 630
    guidelines for job applicants,
        633–634
    hair analysis, 631
    legal issues in, 631–633
    methods, 629–631
    oral fluid tests, 631
    paper-and-pencil tests, 629–630
    reasons for, 628
    screening test, 630
    urine tests, 630–631
D-statistic, 515
Duke Power Co., 506
Dun's Business Rankings, 343
Dynamic flexibility, 525
Dynamic strength, 525

E

E. E. Black, Ltd. v. Marshall, 528
Ebel method, 665–666
Ecstasy (drug), 630
Education, 378
Education Resources Information
    Center (ERIC), 222
Educational records, 414
Edward Jones, 155
Edward's Personal Preference Schedule,
    563
EEO. See Equal Employment
    Opportunity (EEO)
EEOC. See Equal Employment
    Opportunity Commission
    (EEOC)
Effort, 3
Egyptians, 6
Electronic tests, 18–19, 518
E-mail reference checks, 406–407
Emergency contact, 379
Emotional intelligence, 444–445, 542
Emotional stability, 540
Empirical validation, 12
Employee Polygraph Protection Act of
    1988, 616
Employee referrals, 163, 166, 171
Employee Reliability Index, 620
Employee selection, federal guidelines
    on, 52–53
Employee specifications, 97–98
Employees
    polygraph testing of, 616–617
    theft, 613
Employment discrimination.
    See Discrimination
Employment interviews.
    See Interviews
Employment-at-will doctrine, 368
Enova International Inc., 177
Equal Employment Opportunity
    Commission (EEOC). *See also
    Uniform Guidelines on
    Employee Selection Procedures*
    ADA Amendments Act of 2008
        and, 115
    Americans with Disabilities Act
        (ADA) and, 158
    Genetic Information
        Nondiscrimination Act of 2008
        and, 636–637
    integrity testing and, 627
    personality tests and, 555
    Title VII Civil Rights Acts of 1964
        and, 106–108

*Equal Employment Opportunity
    Commission (EEOC) Guidelines
    on Employee Selection
    Procedures*, 51
*Equal Employment Opportunity
    Commission v. National
    Academy of Sciences*, 401
Equal Employment Opportunity (EEO)
    ADA Amendments Act of 2008
        and, 113–115
    affirmative action programs,
        131–134
    Age Discrimination in Employment
        Act of 1967 and, 110
    Americans with Disabilities Act of
        1990, 110–113
    Civil Rights Acts of 1866, 116–117
    Civil Rights Acts of 1871, 116–117
    Civil Rights Acts of 1991, 108–109
    discrimination and, 146–147
    Executive Order 11246, 109
    Executive Order 11478, 109
    Executive Order 13087, 110
    Executive Order 13672, 110
    Fifth Amendment, 116
    Fourteenth Amendment, 116
    Immigration Reform and Control
        Act of 1986 and, 115–116
    job performance measurement and,
        142–146
    laws, 6, 8, 106–119
    relevant labor market and, 123
    Title VII Civil Rights Acts of 1964
        and, 106–108
Equipment, 85
Equivalent forms reliability, 249–251
ERIC. See Education Resources
    Information Center (ERIC)
Error
    halo, 259
    score, 242–245
Errors of measurement, 241–245
    error score, 242–245
    standard, 272–274
    true score, 241–242
Ethnic restaurants, 118–119
Ethnicity, 376
Europe, 455
Evidence-based management, 15–16
Evidence-based selection (EBS), 16
Executive Order 11246, 109
Executive Order 11478, 109
Executive Order 13087, 110
Executive Order 13672, 110
Executive search firms, 169

Expectancy chart method, 664
Expectancy tables and charts, 312,
    318–320
Expectations, 464–466
Expert judgment, 42–43. *See also*
    Subject matter experts (SMEs)
Explosive strength, 525
Extent flexibility, 525
Extraversion, 540, 550

F
Face validity, 284, 678
Facebook, 168, 414, 447, 464
Factor analysis, 42
Fair Credit Reporting Act, 403, 412,
    413
Faking
    on integrity testing, 626–627
    in personality tests, 556–558
False negatives
    in polygraph testing, 615
    in selection decisions, 648–649
False positives
    in integrity testing, 625–626
    in polygraph testing, 615
    in selection decisions, 648
Family Educational Rights and Privacy
    Act, 403
Fast-food industry, 7, 164
FBL Financial Services, 141–142
Federal contractors, 131–132
Federal court records, 413–414
Federal regulation of business,
    106–119. *See also* Affirmative
    action programs (AAP);
    Discrimination; Equal
    Employment Opportunity
    Commission (EEOC); *Uniform
    Guidelines on Employee
    Selection Procedures*
Feedback,360-degree, 28
Fidelity, 579
Fifth Amendment, 116, 630, 632
Finish Line, Inc., 112
Fireman's Fund Insurance Co., 406
Fischer's Exact Test (FET), 127
Fisher & Phillips LLP, 180
Five-Factor Model, 537–538, 540,
    544–545, 556, 620–621
Fixed bands, 673–674
Fleishman, Edwin, 525–526
Flow statistics, 126–127
Forced-choice inventories, 545–546
Forecasting, 13
Former employers, 411–412
Four-fifths rule, 126–127

Fourteenth Amendment, 117, 632
Fourth Amendment, 632
France, 455
*Frank Ricci et al. v. John DeStefano et
    al.*, 135, 140–141
Franklin, Benjamin, 657
Frone, Michael, 628–629
Functional magnetic resonance
    imaging (fMRI), 638–639

G
GATB. See General Aptitude Test
    Battery (GATB)
Gender, 377
General Aptitude Test Battery (GATB),
    109, 340, 511
General cognitive ability (CGA), 290
General Mental Ability Test, 304
General Motors (GM), 16
Genetic Information
    Nondiscrimination Act of 2008
    (GINA), 636–637.
Genetic testing, 634–637 *See also* Tests
    definition of, 635
    Human Genome Project and, 634
    legal issues in, 635–638
Germany, 455
Gilbert v. City of Little Rock, Ark., 459,
    460
Glass Ceiling Commission, 108, 109
Glass Ceiling Effect, 109
Global recruiting, 181
Global trends
    interviews and, 454–455
    personality tests and, 558–559
Google, 16, 30
Gottier, Richard, 536, 537
Graefe, Andreas, 657
Great Recession, 7
Greece, 455
Greeks, 6
Griggs v. Duke Power Co, 51, 134–136
Gross body coordination, 525
Gross body equilibrium, 525
Guion, Robert, 536, 537

H
Habitual behaviors, questions of,
    476–477
Hair analysis, 631
Hall v. Buck, 402
Halo, 29
Halo error, 259
Hangover period, 160
Harless v. Duck, 459, 461
Hawaii Healthcare Professionals, Inc, 110

Head hunters, 169

Height, 376

Helping behavior, 30

Henle, Christine, 676

Heroin, 630

Heuristics, 470

Hewlett-Packard, 16

HEXACO model, 620

Hirediversity.com, 171

Hiring, 4

Hispanic Chamber of Commerce, 171

Hispanics, 463, 515–516

Hobbies, 378

Hogan, Joyce, 525–526, 550

Hogan Assessment Systems, Inc., 221

Hogan Personality Inventory (HPI), 618

Holdout group, 317

Holland, Brent, 550

Honeymoon period, 160

Human capital
    acquisition and development of, 6
    importance of, 6–7

Human Connectome Project, 638

Human Dynamics Laboratory, 17

Human Genome Project, 634

Human Performance, 222

Human resource management (HRM)
    courses, 16
    selection, 6

Human resource selection
    constraints, 5
    court cases, 134–142
    definition of, 3
    evidence of importance of, 6–7
    future interests, 5
    human resource systems and, 7–8
    information collection and
        evaluation in, 3–4
    for initial job, 4–5
    job analysis in, 47–99
    legal issues in, 105–147
    measurement in, 203–236
    objective of, 3
    overview, 1
    personality assessment for, 535–565
    for promotion, 5
    research vs, practice, 15–16

Human resource selection analyst
    abbreviated job tasks for, 88
    abbreviated WRCs for, 89
    selection plan for, 94–97
    selection procedures for, 91
    task performance for, 90

Human resource systems, 7–8

Hunter, John, 668

Hydrocodone, 630

I

IES. See Institute of Education
    Sciences (IES)

Illinois Supreme Court Rule 137, 756

Illusory correlations, 439

Immigration and Naturalization
    Service (INS), 116

Immigration Reform and Control Act
    of 1986 (IRCA), 115–116

Impairment, 629

Improper linear model, 660

In-basket test, 590–592

India, 455

Indirect restriction, 323

Individual charts, 319–320

Individual differences, 466–467

Individual initiative, 31

Individualization, 39–40

Individuals, measurement of, 14–15

Industrial electrician, 229

Information processing, 469–471

Initial job, selection for, 4–5

INS. See Immigration and
    Naturalization Service (INS)

Institute of Education Sciences (IES),
    222

Institutional charts, 320–321

Integrity testing, 617–628
    constructs measured, 619–620
    faking on, 626–627
    false positives in, 625–626
    legal issues in, 627–628
    overt integrity, 617–618, 621
    paper-and-pencil, 617
    personality-oriented, 618–619, 621
    usefulness of, 625–627
    validity of, 621–625
    variables, 620–621

Intel, 16

Intellect, 540

Intelligence, 507

Intentions, 464–466

Interclass correlation, 260

Interjudge reliability, 259

Internal consistency reliability
    estimates, 251–259

Internal selection, 177–178

Internal training, 7

International Academy of Collaborative
    Professionals, 770

*International Journal of Selection and
    Assessment*, 222

International Personnel Management
    Association (IPMA), 221, 223

Internet
    interview and, 464–466
    mental ability tests and, 517–520
    recruitment and, 167–170, 179–180
    reference checks, 406–407
    unproctored Internet testing,
        519–520

Internet applicant, 127–128

Internet-based selection, 18–19

Interns, 163, 177

Interrater agreement, 259–260

Interrater reliability estimates, 258–261,
    263

Interval scale, 210–212

Interviewers
    beliefs, 464–466
    decision making model for, 463–471
    evaluating information, 480–481
    expectations, 464–466
    individual differences, 466–467
    interviewing behavior, 482
    multiple independent, 478–479
    needs, 464–466
    receiving information, 480–481
    results of training of, 482
    scoring format, 479–480
    training, 480–481

Interviews, 216, 433–483
    anchoring and, 439
    appropriate use of, 548–549
    background, 590
    behavior description, 451–452, 548
    brief history, 435–436
    confirmation bias and, 439
    decision making in, 463–471
    designing, 452–454
    developing and designing, 436–439
    discrimination and, 458–462
    effect on attracting applicants,
        437–438
    evaluating as predictors, 455–458
    global trends and, 454–455
    illusory correlations and, 439
    intentions, 464–466
    limiting use of preinterview data in,
        473–483
    making selection decision and,
        439–452
    model of, 465
    overconfidence bias and, 439
    overview, 433–435
    in personality measurement,
        547–548

predictive validity of, 455–457
providing job information and,
    437–438
questions, 449–452, 474–478
recommendations for using, 471–483
reliability of, 457–458
restricting scope of, 472
screening vs. selection, 440–441
situational, 449–451, 476
social dynamics in, 482–483
social interaction during, 467–469
structured, 433, 445–449, 474
technology's role in, 454–455
unstructured, 433–434, 445–449
work related characteristics and,
    442–445
Interviews, job analysis, 54–62
    classification of content, 58–59
    considerations on applicability, 56
    description of, 55–56
    example of, 57–59
    guidelines for conducting, 61
    limitations of, 59–61
    reasons for, 55–56
    schedule for use with job
        incumbent, 56–57
Intraclass correlation, 260–261
Investigative agencies, 412
Investigative consumer reports, 412
IPMA. See International Personnel
    Management Association
    (IPMA)
I.Q., 507
IRCA. See Immigration Reform and
    Control Act of 1986 (IRCA)
Israelski, Edmond, 581
Italy, 455

J

Jack Gross v. FBL Financial Services,
    135, 141–142
Job adaptability inventory (JAI), 35
Job analysis, 9, 47–99
    collecting job information in, 53
    content validation and,
        284–285, 291–293
    critical incident technique, 68–75
    definition of, 47
    in development of selection
        measures, 225–226
    employee specifications, 97–98
    employment application questions
        and, 379–380
    growth in, 50
    interviews, 54–62
    key court cases, 51–52

legal issues in, 50–53
methods, 53–54
questionnaires, 62–68
role in human resource selection,
    48–50
screening interview and, 441
in selection procedures, 75
SME workshops, 73–75
strategic, 97
*Uniform Guidelines on Employee
    Selection Procedures* and,
    50, 52, 285
work-sample tests and, 582
Job component validity, 338–341.
    See also Validity
    accuracy of studies of, 340
    conducting studies of, 338–339
    criticisms of, 340
    overview, 338–339
Job content domain, 283, 284
Job experts, 441
Job information, providing, 437–438
Job knowledge, 444, 513–514
    integrity testing and, 622
Job performance
    adaptive performance, 23, 34–36
    counterproductive work behaviors,
        36–39
    organizational citizenship
        behaviors, 23
    Organizational citizenship
        behaviors, 29–34
    overview, 21–22
    prediction of, 23–24
    task performance, 23, 24–29
    viewing, 23
Job performance measures, 23–24
    characteristics of, 39–41
    court decisions addressing, 143–146
    equal employment opportunity and,
        142–146
    identification of, 10
    individualization, 39–40
    measurability of, 40
    organizational citizenship
        behaviors, 29
    organizational citizenship behaviors
        and, 32–33
    production data, 24–26
    relevance of, 40
    Uniform Guidelines and, 143
    variance, 40–41
Job tasks
    identifying, 582
    selecting, 583

Job-related questions, 474–475
Jobs
    measurement of, 14–15
    requirements, 11
    sample data, 217
Johnson & Johnson, 435
Jones v. Mississippi Dept. of Corrections,
    459, 461
Journal of Applied Psychology (JAP),
    222
Journal of Counseling Psychology, 222
Journal of Educational Measurement,
    222
*Journal of Occupational and
    Organizational Psychology*, 222
Journal of Personnel Psychology, 222
Journal of Vocational Behavior, 222
Journals, 222
Judgmental composite method, 653
Judgmental data, 26–29, 217
    BARS, 27–28
    BES, 27–28
    instruments, 26–28
    scales, 28–29
    simple behavioral scale, 26–27
    360-degree feedback, 28
    trait rating scales, 26
Judgmental instruments, 26–28

K

Karraker v. Rent-A-Center, 555
Kelley Drye & Warren, 110
King v. TWA, 459, 460
Klimoski, Richard, 666
Knack, 17
Knowledge, 83
Knowledge/skills/abilities (KSAs), 4,
    82–84, 648–649
Kostiuk, Stephanie, 638–639
KSAs. See Knowledge/skills/abilities
    (KSAs)
Kuder-Richardson reliability estimates,
    254, 263
Kuncel, Nathan, 654

L

Lahy, Par, 503
Lancaster mid-P (LMP) test, 127
Lawrence Berkeley Laboratory case, 636
Leaderless group discussion (LGD),
    591–592
Legal issues. *See also* Adverse impact;
    Discrimination; Disparate
    impact; Disparate treatment
    in cutoff scores, 667
    in drug testing, 631–633

Legal issues (*continued*)
  in genetic testing, 635–638
  in human resource selection,
    105–147
  in integrity testing, 627–628
  in job analysis, 50–53
  in personality tests, 554–558
  in physical ability tests, 526–528
  in reference checks, 401–406
Leniency, 29
Letters of recommendation, 408–411
Licensure, 85
Life Insurance and Market Research
    Association (LIMRA), 223
Lilly v. City of Beckley, 133
Linear regression, 313
LinkedIn, 167, 168, 414, 447

M
Macy's, 180
Mail reference checks, 407–408,
    409–410
*Maine Human Rights Commission v.
    Dept. of Corrections*, 459, 461
Maintenance supervisor, selection plan
    for job of, 473
Major bodily functions, 114
Major life activities, 114
Management Position Description
    Questionnaire29, 62
Management Progress Study, 588
Manager Profile Record, 364
Manager satisfaction, 181
Managerial and Professional Job
    Functions Inventory30, 62
Marijuana, 629, 630
Marital status, 377
Maximum possible validity, 281–282
McCrae, Robert, 544
McDaniel, Michael, 603
McDonald's, 180
McDonnell Douglas v. Green, 120–121
*McKenna v. Nashville Banner
    Publishing Co.*, 367
Measurement, 14–15, 203–236
  criteria and predictors, 205–206
  definition of, 204–205
  errors of, 241–245
  individual differences and, 206–207
  nature of, 203–207
  overview, 293
  role in selection, 203–212
  scales of, 207–212
  selection, 207–212
  standard error of, 272–274, 672–673
  standardization of, 212–231

Mechanical ability tests, 521–523
  Bennet Mechanical Comprehension
    Test, 522–523
Mechanical composite method,
    653–654
Meehl, Paul, 653
Mental ability tests, 504–517, 520
  abilities measured by, 506
  adverse impact and, 514–517
  development of, 505
  implications for selection, 513–514
  importance in selection, 509
  internet and, 517–520
  measurement and, 505–506
  nature of, 507–508
  vs. other selection tests, 512–513
  Project A, 508
  validity generalization studies,
    508–514
  validity of, 508–514
  Wonderlic Personnel Test, 506–507
Mental ability tests, internet and,
    517–520
Mental health, 377
Mental Measurements Database, 221
Mental Measurements Yearbook, 221,
    222, 274, 529, 543
Metabolites, 630
Methadone, 630
Methaqualone, 630
Military service, 377
Miner Sentence Completion (MSC)
    Test, 554
*Minneapolis Commission on Civil
    Rights v. Minnesota Chemical
    Dependency*, 459, 461
Minnesota Clerical Test, 523
Minnesota Mechanical Assembly Test,
    521
Minnesota Multiphasic Personality
    Inventory (MMPI)., 555, 627
Minorityjobs.net, 171
Missouri Rule 55.03(a), 756
MIT, 17
MMPI. See Minnesota Multiphasic
    Personality Inventory (MMPI).
Modified Angoff method, 665–666
Monster.com, 168, 169
Montana Rules of Civil Procedure 11,
    756
Morphine, 630
Motivation, 476
*Motor Performance Test for
    Maintenance Mechanics*, 581
Motor tests, 579

Motor vehicle department records, 413
Mount, Michael, 544
Mountain Gravel and Construction
    Company, 134
Movement quality, 525–526
Multiple hurdles, 669–671
Multiple regression, 315–316, 658–660
Murphy v. United Parcel Service, 113
Muscular strength, 525–526

N
Name, 376
National Association of Colleges and
    Employers (NACE), 177
National Criminal Information Center
    (NCIC), 413
National Instant Check System (NICS),
    413–414
National Research Council, 503
NCIC. See National Criminal
    Information Center (NCIC)
Needs, 464–466
Negligent hiring, 401, 403–406
*NEO Personality Inventory- Revised
    (NEO PI-R) Form S*, 296
NEO-Personality Inventory, 544
Netherlands, 620
Neuroscience-based discrimination,
    638–639
Neuroticism, 540
New employee
  cost per hire, 181
  failure rate, 181
  job performance, 181
  manager satisfaction with, 181
  training success, 181
  turnover, 181
New workers, teaching, 30
New Zealand, 535, 559
Nguyen, Nhung, 603
NICS. See National Instant Check
    System (NICS)
No Lie MRI, Inc., 638
Nominal scale, 209
*Norman-Bloodsaw v. Lawrence Berkeley
    Laboratory*, 635–636
Normative sample, 231
Norms, 231–233
North Carolina Department of
    Commerce, 23
Norway, 559

O
O*NET (Occupational Information
    Network), 23, 98, 340
Obesity, 117–118

Objective production data, 217
OCBs. See Organizational citizenship behaviors (OCBs)
Occupation Analysis Inventory, 62
Occupational health and safety (OH&S), 54–62
Occupational Information Network (O*NET), 23, 98, 340
OFCCP. See Office of Federal Contract Compliance Programs (OFCCP)
OFCCP v. Ozark Air Lines, 135, 141
Office of Federal Contract Compliance Programs (OFCCP), 52, 109, 128, 131–132
Office of Personnel Management, 52, 57
Office of Special Counsel for Unfair Immigration-Related Employment Practice, 116
Off-the-job conduct, 379
Ones, Deniz, 623
Online database, 222
On-site visits, 176–177
Openness to experience, 540, 550
Opiates, 630
Oral Directions Test, 342
Oral fluid tests, 631
Ordinal scale, 209–210, 234
Organization
    cross-purposes with applicants, 13–14
    resource-based theory of, 6
Organizational citizenship, 23, 29–34
Organizational citizenship behaviors (OCBs), 29–34
    cognitive ability and, 512
    counterproductive work behaviors and, 38–39
    examples of, 30
    measurement of, 33–34
    models, 30–31
    performance measures and, 32–33
    probable causes of, 31–32
Organizational compliance, 31
Organizational delinquency, 618
Organizational loyalty, 31
Orkin, 155
Otis Self-Administering Test of Mental Ability, 505
Overall Assessment Rating (OAR), 594, 597
Overconfidence bias, 439
Overt integrity tests, 617–618, 621
Oxycodone, 630

OxyContin, 630
Ozark Air lines, 141

P
Pain killers, 630
Paper-and-pencil tests
    drug testing, 629–630
    vs. electronic tests, 518
    integrity testing and, 617
PAQ. See Position Analysis Questionnaire (PAQ)
Parallel forms reliability, 249–251, 262
Paris Transportation Society, 503
Passive candidates, 169
Pearson Assessments, 221
Pearson product-moment correlation coefficient, 245, 246
PEDRs. See Post-exercise dimension ratings (PEDRs)
People analytics, 16
Percentiles, 233–234
Performance measures
    court decisions addressing, 143–146
    equal employment opportunity and, 142–146
    organizational citizenship behaviors and, 32–33
    Uniform Guidelines and, 143
Performance tests. See Simulation tests
Personal references, 412
Personality. *See also* Personality tests
    definition of, 536–538
    Five-Factor Model, 537–538
    observer ratings of, 546–547
    questions of, 476–477
    traits, 538–543
    use of, 536–538
Personality Characteristics Inventory (PCI), 544
Personality tests, 216. *See also* Tests
    faking in, 556–558
    Five-Factor Model, 544–545
    forced-choice inventories, 545–546
    global trends and, 558–559
    history, 536
    interviews, 547–548
    inventories, 543–544
    legal issues in, 554–558
    overview, 535
    projective techniques, 546
    ratings from other observers, 549
    recommendations for use of data from, 559–565
    self-report personality inventories, 545

self-report questionnaires, 544
    technology and, 558–559
    validity as predictor, 549–554
Personality traits, 83–84, 538–543
    job behaviors and, 560
Personality-oriented tests, 618–619, 621
Personality-Related Position Requirements Form (PPRF), 62, 560
Personnel analyst, 64
Personnel data, 217
Personnel Management Abstracts, 222
Personnel Psychology, 222
Personnel Selection Inventory, 617
PGA Tour v. Martin, 112
Phencyclidine, 630
Physical abilities analysis, 524–528
Physical ability tests, 524
    components of physical performance, 525–526
    legal issues in, 526–528
Physical attributes, 204
Physical characteristics, 376
Physical fidelity, 286–287
Physical health, 377
Physical performance, components of, 525–526
Physical requirements, 84–85
PJ fit, 172–173, 174, 180
Plato, 6
PO fit, 173, 174, 180
Poaching, 159
Police sergeant, work behavior and task statements for, 79, 81
Polygraph testing, 614–617
    of applicants, 616
    of employees, 616–617
    false negatives in, 615
    false positives in, 615
    limitations of, 615–617
    physiological data and, 614
    procedures, 614
Position Analysis Questionnaire (PAQ), 62, 339, 560
Post-exercise dimension ratings (PEDRs), 593, 600–601
Postoffer closure, 178–182
Potosky, Denise, 515
Practice, 520–521
Precision, 207
Predicted yield method, 664
Prediction, 13, 312–320
    realizing gains over time, 565
Prediction equation, 314, 658

Predictive validation, 298–300. *See also* Validation
  vs. concurrent validation, 300–301
  example of, 298–299
  strengths and weaknesses of, 299–300
  types of, 300
Predictive validity, 455–457
Predictors, 205–206, 216, 652–655
  collecting, 649–651
  combining, 651–652
  combining scores of, 657–662
  evaluating interviews as, 455–458
  fidelity of, 286–288
  reliability of, 321–322
  validity coefficients and, 321–322
Preemployment test publishers, 221
Prefabricated questionnaires, 62
Preinterview data, 473–483
Prescription drugs, 630
Present employee method, 294
Priestley, Joseph, 657
Principles for the Validation and Use of Personnel Selection Procedures, 223–224, 293
  content vs. criterion-related validation and, 303
  cutoff scores and, 668
  job analysis and, 50
  reliability of measures and, 268
  validity coefficients and, 324
Privacy, right of, 632
Proactive personality, 542–543
Procter & Gamble (P&G), 16, 476
Production data, 24–26
Pro-Ed, 221
Professional and Managerial Position Questionnaire, 62
Professional associations, 223–224
Profile interpretation, 653
Project A, 508, 536
Projective techniques, 546
  validity of, 553–554
Promotion, selection for, 5
Proper linear model, 660
Propoxyphene, 630
PsycARTICLES, 222
Psychological Abstracts, 222
Psychological Assessment Resources, 221
Psychological attributes, 204
Psychological fidelity, 286–287
Psychological Services, Inc., 221
PsycINFO, 222
Public assistance clerks, interview questions and scoring key for, 72

Public records, 412–414
  criminal records, 413
  educational records, 414
  federal court records, 413–414
  motor vehicle department records, 413
  workers' compensation records, 413
Punitive damage, 108
Purdue "Can You Read a Working Drawing?" Test., 296
Purdue Test for Electricians, 231, 296
Pure judgment, 652
Pure statistical method, 653–654

Q

Quaaludes, 630
Qualified privilege, 402
Questionnaires
  biographical data, 216
  common metric, 62
  position analysis, 62, 339, 560
  prefabricated, 62
  professional and managerial position, 62
  self-report, 544
  tailored, 62
Questionnaires, job analysis, 62–68
  description of, 62
  prefabricated questionnaires, 62
  tailored questionnaires, 62
  task analysis inventory, 62–69
Questions
  interview, 449–452
  job-related, 474–478
  multiple, 477–478
  of personality or habitual behaviors, 476–477
  of social interaction, 475–476
Quicktest (WPT-Q), 506

R

Race, 376, 463
Range restrictions, 322–324
Rater error, 29
Rating scale, 64–65
Ratio scale, 212
Realist job preview (RJP), 160
Recordkeeping, 130–131
Recruiters, characteristics of, 175–176
Recruitment, 151–183
  administration of, 179
  applicant self-selection in, 173–175
  attracting and generating interest, 153–171
  enhancing, 329
  global, 181

  internal selection, 177–178
  Internet and, 167–170, 179–180
  maintaining applicant interest in, 171–182
  message, 160–162
  methods, 162–171
  metrics, 181–182
  model of process, 153–182
  on-site visits, 176–177
  outcomes of, 438–439
  overview, 151
  postoffer closure, 178–182
  recommendations for enhancing, 182–183
  recruiter characteristics and, 175–176
  social networks and, 167–170
  sources, 164
  targeting strategies, 157–160
  technology's role in, 179–180
Refer-a-friend program, 166
Reference checks, 216, 396–416
  applicant acceptability and, 401
  consumer reports and, 412
  defamation of character and, 401–403
  discriminatory impact and, 401–403
  e-mail, 406–407
  former employers and, 411–412
  internet, 406–407
  investigative agencies and, 412
  investigative consumer reports and, 412
  legal issues in, 401–406
  letters of recommendation, 408–411
  mail, 407–408, 409–410
  methods of collecting information, 406–411
  nature and role of, 396–397
  negligent hiring and, 403–406
  overview, 396–397
  personal references and, 412
  public records and, 412–414
  reliability of data in, 398–401
  social media and, 414
  sources of, 411–414
  steps for using, 414–416
  telephone, 406–407
  types of data collected, 397–398
  validity of data in, 398–401
Reference sources, 220–221
Regression
  coefficient, 314
  equation, 314
  linear, 313

multiple, 315–316
simple, 313
weight, 314
Regression line, 313
Reily, Richard, 581
Relative Time Spent on Task Performance, 64
Relevant labor market (RLM), 123, 125, 126
Reliability
of ability tests, 529–530
administration and scoring of measure and, 271–272
Cronbach's coefficient alpha (A) estimates of, 256–258
definition of, 241
determining, 231
errors of measurement and, 241–245
homogeneity of measure's content and, 271
individual differences, 266–268
internal consistency estimates of, 251–259
interrater estimates of, 258–261, 263
of interviews, 457–458
Kuder-Richardson estimates of, 255, 263
length of measure and, 268–269
methods of estimating, 245–261, 266
overview of, 239–241
parallel or equivalent forms estimates of, 249–251
parallel or equivalent forms reliability, 262
of reference data, 398–401
response format and, 271
sample and, 268
of selection measures, 239–276
split-half estimates of, 252–255, 263
stability and, 268
standard error of measurement and, 272–274
test question difficulty and, 270–271
test-retest estimates of, 246–249, 262
of training and experience evaluations, 392
validity and, 281–282
Reliability coefficients, 245–246
description of, 261–264
evaluating, 274–275
factors influencing, 266–282
interpreting, 261–275
magnitude of, 264–266

Reliability scale, 618–619
Religion, 376
Republic, The (Plato), 6
Resource-based theory, 6
Resources for Human Development, Inc., 117
Resumes
indicators of fraud in, 384
items in, 385
online and internet-based screening of, 385–386
Retail industry, loss to theft in, 613
Reverse discrimination, 133
Revised EEO-1 Form, 123–124
Right of privacy, 632
RJP. See Realist job preview (RJP)
Robbins v. White-Wilson Medical Clinic, 459, 460
Robinson, David, 581
Romans, 6
Roth, Phil, 514
Royal Dutch Shell, 17
Rudder v. District of Columbia, 135, 139–140
Russo, J. Edward, 678
Rutherford v. American Bank of Commerce, 401

S
Sackett, Paul, 598, 619
Sample sizes, 341–343
Sampling design, 228
Saville & Holdsworth, Inc, 221
Scales of measurement, 207–212
characteristics of, 213
interval scale, 210–212
nominal scale, 209
ordinal scale, 209–210
ratio scale, 212
Schmidt, Frank, 668
Schmitt, Neal, 666
Schoemaker, Paul, 678
Scores
interpreting, 231–236
norms, 231–233
percentiles, 233–234
standard, 234–235
stanine, 234–235
T, 235
z, 235
Scoring procedures, 228
Scrambled Subcontractor Test, 581
Screening interview, 440–441
Screening test, 630
Second Life (online game), 180

Selection. See Human resource selection
Selection decisions, 647–680
auditing, 678–679
banding, 672–677
beliefs and, 464–466
combination method, 671–672
complex, 648
cutoff scores, 663–668
decision-making models, 463–471
expectations and, 464–466
false negatives in, 648–649
false positives in, 648
implications for makers of, 655–657
individual differences and, 466–467
information processing and, 469–471, 648
intentions and, 464–466
methods for collecting and combining predictor information, 652–655
methods for combining predictor scores, 657–662
modes for collecting predictor information, 649–651
modes for combining predictor information, 651–652
multiple cutoff scores, 668–669
multiple hurdles, 669–671
needs and, 464–466
outcomes of, 648
overview of, 647–648
practical approach to, 677–678
recommendations for enhancing, 679–680
simple, 648
strategies for, 647–680
top-down selection, 662–663
true negatives in, 649
true positives in, 649
Selection instrument, appropriateness of, 561–563
Selection interviews. See Interviews
Selection measurement, 207–212
administration of, 213
content of, 214, 230–231
criteria or measures of job success, 216–217
definition of, 212
implementing, 231
interpreting scores in, 231–236
measures used in HR selection, 215–217
predictors or selection procedures, 216

Selection measurement (*continued*)
    scoring of, 215
    selecting measuring method, 226
    source of, 563–564
Selection measures, 212–231
    choosing or developing, 218–219
    constructing, 224–231
    development of, 11–12
    information sources for, 220–224
    Internet-based, 18–19
    locating existing, 220–224
    personality tests and, 563–565
    planning and developing, 227–230
    reliability of, 239–276
    standards for evaluating, 217–218
    steps in developing, 225–231
Selection practice, 15–16
Selection procedures, 91–94
    content validation and, 286
    costing value of, 328–329
    job content and, 287
    validity of, 274–344
Selection programs
    constraints in developing, 13–19
    development of, 8–12
    job analysis, 9
    job performance measures, 10
    selection measures, 11–12
    validation procedures, 12
    work-related characteristics, 11
Selection ratio, 327
Selection research, 15–16
Selective staffing, 7
Self-development, 31
Self-report personality inventories, 545,
    550
Self-report questionnaires, 544
Self-selection, 173–175
Self-selection screens, 171
Severity, 29
Sexual harassment, 108
Signs, 577
Simon, Theodore, 505
Simple behavioral scale, 26–27
Simple regression, 313–315
Simulation tests, 577–608
    assessment centers, 588–602
    case analysis, 592
    consistency of behavior and,
        577–579
    definition of, 577–608
    in-basket, 590–591
    leaderless group discussion,
        591–592
    limitations of, 578–579

samples, 578
signs, 577
situational judgment tests, 602–608
types of, 579
work samples, 579–588
Situational interview, 449–451, 476
Situational judgment tests, 602–608.
    See also Simulation tests
Situational specificity hypothesis, 332
Skills, 83. *See also* Knowledge/skills/
    abilities (KSAs)
Skype, 454
Sliding bands, 673–674
SMEs. See Subject matter experts (SMEs)
Smoking, 118
Sociability, 540
Social dynamics, 482–483
Social intelligence, 444–445
Social interactions, 467–469, 475–476
Social media, 414
Social networking sites, 166–170
Society for Human Resource
    Management (SHRM), 223
Society for Industrial and
    Organizational Psychology, 324
Society of Industrial and
    Organizational Psychologists
    (SIOP), 223
Soroka v. Dayton Hudson, 556
*Sourcebook to Public Record
    Information, The*, 414
South Africa, 535, 559
Spain, 535, 559
Spearman-Brown formula, 254, 268–269
Split-half reliability estimates, 252–255,
    263
Split-sample method, 317
Sportsmanship, 30–31
Spurlock v. United Airlines, 135, 137
Stamina, 525
Stamps v. Detroit Edison, 459, 460
Standard deviation, 323
Standard error of differences method, 673
Standard error of estimate, 315
Standard error of measurement,
    272–274, 672–673
Standard Metropolitan Statistical Area
    (SMSA), 125
Standard scores, 234–235
Standardization group, 231
*Standards for Educational and
    Psychological Testing*, 223, 293
Stanford- Binet Intelligence Scale, 505
Stanine scores, 234–235
Stanton Survey, 617

State Farm Insurance, 16
State v. Bonnell, 386
Static strength, 525
Statistical procedure, 228
Stenquist, John, 521
Stenquist Mechanical Assembly Test, 521
Stock statistics, 123–125
Strategic job analysis, 97
Street drugs, 630
Structured interviews, 442–445, 474
    behavioral dimensions measured in,
        443
    dimensions of, 448
    overview, 433
    types of, 445–449
    vs. unstructured interviews, 445–449
Subject matter experts (SMEs), 55, 69
    in content validation studies, 285
    rating scales and screens, 76
    selecting and preparing, 73–74
    selection measures and, 228
    workshops, 73–75
Supervisory Profile Record, 364
Sutton v. United Air Lines, 113
Sweden, 535
Synthetic validity, 338–341, 342

T
T scores, 235
Taco Bell, 164
Tailored questionnaires, 62
Talent solutions, 169
Targeted recruiting, 157–160
Task
    characterization, 60
    identifying, 78–79
    identifying and rating, 74
    linking to work related
        characteristics, 86–87, 285
    rating, 79–80
    SME rating scales and screens, 76
    statement, 58–59
Task analysis inventory, 62–63
    advantages and disadvantages of,
        67–68
    application in selection, 65–67
    critical incidents, integration with,
        71–73
    for personnel analyst, 64
    steps and guidelines for developing,
        66
Task inventories
    categories of information in, 63
    characteristics, 63–65
    development of, 65
    nature of, 63–65

phrasing of tasks in, 64
rating scale, 64–65
Task performance, 23, 24–29
judgmental data, 26–29
production data, 24–26
Teamwork Orientation Inventory
(TOI), 304–306
Technology
interviews and, 454–455
personality tests and, 558–559
Telephone reference checks, 406–407
Test Collection database, 222
Test of Learning Ability, 518
Test publishers, 222–223
Test Reviews on Line, 221
Test-retest reliability coefficient,
246–249
Test-retest reliability estimates, 262
Tests, 216
Ability tests, 216
achievement, 504
Achievement tests, 216
aptitude, 504
Aptitude tests, 216
*Bennett Mechanical Comprehension
Test*, 296
clerical ability, 523–524
Drug testing, 628–634
electronic, 18–19, 518
Fischer's Exact Test (FET), 127
General Aptitude Test Battery,
109, 340
General Mental Ability Test, 304
Genetic testing, 634–637
in-basket, 590–592
integrity, 617–628
Lancaster mid-P (LMP) test, 127
mechanical ability, 521–523
Miner Sentence Completion (MSC)
Test, 554
Minnesota Clerical Test, 523
motor, 579
*Motor Performance Test for
Maintenance Mechanics*, 581
Oral Directions Test, 342
overt integrity, 617–618, 621
Personality tests, 216
personality-oriented, 618–619, 621
physical ability, 524
polygraph, 614–617
publishers, 222–223
*Purdue "Can You Read a Working
Drawing?" Test*, 296
Purdue Test for Electricians,
231, 296
Quicktest (WPT-Q), 506
Scrambled Subcontractor Test, 581
Simulation tests, 577–608
*Standards for Educational and
Psychological Testing*, 293
verbal, 579
Wonderlic Personnel Test,
231, 506–507
work-sample, 579–588
*Tests: A Comprehensive Reference for
Assessments in Psychology,
Education, and Business*, 221
Tests in Print (TIP) I–VIII, 221
Text sources, 220–221
*The Industrial-Organizational
Psychologist (TIP)*, 222
Theft, 613, 622
TheLadders.com, 161
TheMuse.com, 161
Thinking, Fast, and Slow (Kahneman),
439
360-degree feedback, 28
Threshold Traits Analysis System, 62
Thurstone Temperament Schedule, 563
Title VII Civil Rights Acts of 1964.
See Civil Rights Acts of 1964,
Title VII
Tools, 85
Top-down selection, 662–663
Top-score referenced bands, 673–674
*Toyota Motor Mfg., Ky., Inc. v.
Williams*, 114
Traditional assessment devices, 589–590
Trainability
measures, 217
measuring, 207–208
tests, 581
Training, 7
of asssssors in assessment centers,
592–596
of interviewers, 480–481
of judges in work-sample tests, 586
of new employees, 181
proficiency, 217
Training and experience (T&E)
evaluations, 387–396
education and, 390–392
examples of, 387–390
legal implications of, 395
nature and role of, 387–392
recommendations for using, 395–396
reliability of, 392
validity of, 392–394
work-related experience and,
390–392
Training proficiency data, 217
Trait rating scales, 26
Trait ratings, 653
Traits, 538–543
True score, 241–242
True v. Ladner, 402
Trunk strength, 525
Twitter, 168, 414
Typist-clerks, 290

U

Undercover Boss (television show), 155
Uniform Collaborative Law Act, 786
*Uniform Guidelines on Employee
Selection Procedures*
adverse impact, 129
cognitive ability tests and, 514
content validation and,
289–290, 293
discrimination and, 119
job analysis and, 50, 52, 285
performance measurement and, 143
recordkeeping and, 130–131
selection methods, 129
selection program, 129–130
selection requirements, 130
Unit weighing, 660–662
United Kingdom, 455, 559
United States v. Georgia Power, 135,
136–137
Unproctored Internet testing, 519–520
Unstructured interviews, 433–434,
445–449
Urine tests, 630–631
U.S. Employment Service, 511
U.S. Steel Corp., 663
U.S. v. South Carolina, 665
Utility analysis, 326–332
acceptance by practitioners,
331–332
applying to selection, 328–331
base rate and, 327
costing value of selection
procedures by, 328–329
definition of, 326
enhancing recruitment and, 329
preliminary work on, 326–328
selection ratio and, 327
using method with low validity and,
330–331
validity coefficient and, 312, 327

V

Validation, 634–637
concurrent, 294–298
construct, 303–307

Validation (*continued*)
  content, 282–294
  criterion-related, 294–303
  definition of, 280–281
  predictive, 298–300
  research, 343–344
  single *vs.* multiple criteria, 41
  for small sample sizes, 341–343
  when to use criteria in, 41–42
Validation procedures, 12
Validation study, 215, 282
Validity, 508–514
  of ability tests, 530–531
  of assessment centers, 597–602
  content validation, 282–294
  criterion-related validation, 294–303
  definition of, 279–281
  determining, 231
  differential, 515
  discriminant, 598
  disparate impact and, 564
  face, 678
  incremental, 564
  of integrity testing, 621–625
  job component, 338–341
  low, 330
  maximum possible, 281–282
  overview, 279
  predictive, 455–457
  of projective techniques, 553–554
  of reference data, 398–401
  reliability and, 281–282
  of self-report inventories, 550–553
  synthetic, 338–341, 342
  of training and experience
    evaluations, 392–394
  of work-sample tests, 586–588
Validity coefficients
  computing, 307–310
  criterion contamination and, 324–325
  definition of, 307
  interpreting, 312
  magnitude of, 321–325
  range restrictions and, 322–324
  sample sizes and, 310–312
  utility analysis and, 326–332
  violation of statistical assumptions
    and, 325
Validity generalization
  across jobs, 510–512
  cognitive ability tests and, 508–514
  conclusions from studies in, 334
  criticisms of, 334–337
  methods, 333–334

  overview, 332–333
  requirements, 337–338
  for same job, 509–510
Valium, 630
Valtera Corp., 221
Variance, 322
Ventura Corporation, 106–108
Verbal tests, 579
Videoconferencing, 454
Voluntary absenteeism, 622
Voluntary turnover, 512

W
Walk-in applicants, 163
Wall Street Journal, 180
Watson v. Ft. Worth Bank & Trust, 135,
    137–138, 458–459
Web sites, 167–170
Weeks v. Southern Bell, 527
Weight, 376
Weighting group, 317
Weiner v. County of Oakland, 459, 460
Welfare eligibility examiner, 60
Wernimont, Paul, 577
Wiemann, Shelly, 619
Wonderlic Personnel Test, 231, 506–507
Wonderlic Personnel Test, Inc., 221
Woodbine Health Care Center, 116
Word-of-mouth recruitment, 165–166
Work behaviors
  identifying, 78–79
  linking to work related
    characteristics, 86–87
  rating, 79–80, 81
Work context, relevance of, 561–563
Work effectiveness, 560–563
Work performance
  factors affecting, 15
  factors in, 3
  measurement of, 14–15
Work related characteristics (WRCs),
    4, 8
  adaptive performance and, 36
  assessment in interviews and, 472
  concurrent validation and, 295–296
  criteria, 205–206
  determining, 77–87
  determining relative importance of,
    92–93
  global, 455
  identification of, 11, 71
  identifying, 75–97
  identifying and rating, 74
  interview rating scales of, 480

  interviews and, 442–445
  knowledge, skills and abilities,
    82–84
  linking tasks to, 86–87, 285
  linking to job tasks and work
    behaviors, 86–87
  measuring, 441–445
  measuring and scoring, 227–228
  multiple questions for, 477–478
  multiple-hurdle approach and, 671
  panelists, 82
  physical fidelity and, 286–287
  predictors, 205–206
  preparing panelists, 82
  psychological fidelity and, 286–287
  rating, 85–86
  selecting rating panel, 80–82
  selection measures, 11–12
  selection procedures, 91–94
  SME rating scales and screens, 76
  soliciting from panelists, 82–85
Work requirements, 11
Work sample data, 217
Worker attributes, 11
Worker characteristics, 11
Work-sample tests, 579–588. *See also*
    Simulation tests
  contaminating factors, 584
  development of, 582–586
  examples of, 580
  independent test sections and,
    583–584
  job analysis and, 582
  job tasks and, 582
  rules for scoring, 585–586
  scoring procedures, 584
  standards, 585
  task selection and, 583
  test problems, 584
  testing procedures, 582–584
  validity of, 586–588
WRCs. See Work related
    characteristics (WRCs)

X
Xanax, 630
Xerox, 17

Y
Yerkes, Robert, 503
YouTube, 168

Z
z scores, 235